THE FACTS ON FILE
COMPANION TO THE

AMERICAN SHORT STORY

EDITED BY ABBY H. P. WERLOCK

Assistant Editor: James P. Werlock

Facts On File, Inc.

Dedicated to my father,
Thomas Kennedy Potter,
and my mother,
Abby Holmes Potter

In memory of
Henry Imada of Colorado
Teddy Miller of Minnesota
Paul Smith of Connecticut

Storytellers all, whose stories will never end. . . .

The Facts On File Companion to the American Short Story

Copyright © 2000 by Abby H. P. Werlock.

Facts On File, Inc.
132 West 31st Street
New York NY 10001

Library of Congress Cataloging-in-Publication Data
The Facts On File Companion to the American short story / edited by Abby H. P. Werlock.
p.   cm.
Includes bibliographical references and index.
ISBN 0-8160-3164-9 (alk. paper)
1. Short stories, American—Encyclopedias. I. Werlock, Abby H. P. II. Facts on File, Inc. III. Title: Companion to the American short story.
PS374.S5F33 2000
813'.0103—dc21   99-37703

Facts On File books are available at special discounts when purchased in bulk quantities for businesses, associations, institutions or sales promotions. Please call our Special Sales Department in New York at 212/967-8800 or 800/322-8755.

You can find Facts On File on the World Wide Web at http://www.factsonfile.com

Text design by Evelyn Horovicz
Cover design by Cathy Rincon

Printed in the United States of America

MP FOF 10 9 8 7 6 5 4 3 2

This book is printed on acid-free paper.

CONTENTS

ACKNOWLEDGMENTS

The Facts On File Companion to the American Short Story owes its genesis to several far-seeing people, chief among them James Warren, former acquisitions editor at Facts On File; Professor Alice Hall Petry, English Department Chair at Southern Illinois University; Dr. Mickey Pearlman, scholar, author, and editor; and Anne Dubuisson, former agent at the Ellen Levine Literary Agency. At St.Olaf College, President Melvin R. George and Dean Jon M. Moline offered encouragement and approved a year-long sabbatical, and Dean Kathie Fishbeck authorized a special leave as this book took shape.

A number of librarians shared with me their impressive resources and research skills: Robert Bruce, Betsy Busa, Professor Bryn Geffert, and Professor Mary Sue Lovett of the St. Olaf College Library answered a plethora of bibliographical inquiries; Jennifer Edwin of the Carleton College Library provided timely assistance with information on prize-winning stories; Professor Laurie Howell Hime of the Miami Dade Community College Library consistently contributed on- and off-line research skills; and Larry L. Nesbitt, Director, Mansfield State University Library, and Nancy Robinson of the Bradford County Library, Pennsylvania, provided invaluable help with interlibrary loan acquisitions. Moreover, I owe an immense debt to the many scholars and critics whose published work on the American short story

provided a significant foundation for my own research and writing. Their names appear in the bibliographies throughout the book.

The book has been greatly enhanced by the generous contributions of established scholars in diverse areas of American literature: Professors Alfred Bendixen, California State University at Los Angeles; Jacqueline Vaught Brogan, University of Notre Dame; Stephanie P. Browner, Berea College; J. Randolph Cox, St. Olaf College; Richard Deming, Columbus State Community College; Robert DeMott, Ohio University; Monika Elbert, Montclair State University; Christine Doyle Francis, Central Connecticut State University; Warren French, University of Swansea; Mimi Gladstein, University of Texas at El Paso; Harriet P. Gold, LaSalle College and Dawson College; Sandra Chrystal Hayes, Georgia Institute of Technology; Carol Hovanac, Ramapo College; Frances Kerr, Durham Technical Community College; Michael J. Kiskis, Elmira College; Denise D. Knight, State University of New York at Cortland; Paula Kot, Niagara University; Keith Lawrence, Brigham Young University; Caroline F. Levander, Trinity University; Saemi Ludwig, University of Berne; Suzanne Evertsen Lundquist, Brigham Young University; Robert M. Luscher, University of Nebraska at Kearny; Robert K. Martin, Université de Montréal; Michael J. Meyer, DePaul University; Fred Moramarco, San Diego

State University; Gwen M. Neary, Santa Rosa Junior College and Sonoma State University; Luz Elena Ramirez, State University of New York, College at Oneonta; Jeanne Campbell Reesman, University of Texas at San Antonio; Ralph E. Rodriguez, Pennsylvania State University; Jennifer L. Schulz, University of Washington; Wilfred D. Samuels, University of Utah; Carole M. Schaffer-Koros, Kean College of New Jersey; Ben Stoltzfus, University of California at Riverside; Darlene Harbour Unrue and John C. Unrue, University of Nevada at Las Vegas; Linda Wagner-Martin, University of North Carolina at Chapel Hill; Sylvia Watanabe, Oberlin College; Philip M. Weinstein, Swarthmore College; and Dr. Sarah Bird Wright, independent scholar and author.

For linking me with their talented graduate students who study the short story, I wish to thank Professors Suzette Henke, University of Louisville; Keneth Kinnamon, University of Texas at Austin; James Nagel, University of Georgia; Elaine Safer, University of Delaware; Alfred Bendixen; Robert DeMott; Mimi Gladstein; and Linda Wagner-Martin. I especially wish to acknowledge the expert contributions of these graduate students whose knowledge contributed so notably to the scope and accuracy of this book. Their names appear both in the list of contributors and after each of the entries they wrote. For technical help with the inevitable computer crises, I thank Paul Marino and Van Miller of Northfield, Minnesota, and Van Miller II, of Minneapolis, Minnesota.

I am most grateful to Diana Finch, my agent at the Ellen Levine Literary Agency, for monitoring this undertaking and making a number of helpful suggestions; Laurie Likoff, Editorial Director, Facts On File, for her long-term support of the entire project; and Michael G. Laraque, Chief Copy Editor, whose veteran editing skills helped make this a better book. Most of all, I thank Anne Savarese, my editor at Facts On File. She understood this book from the beginning, and without her intellect, insights, dedication, and sheer stamina, *The Facts On File Companion* would have been impossible to complete.

In writing and compiling the entries for this book, I was fortunate to have quiet writing retreats at the homes of Verna and John Cobb, in Tuxedo Park, New York; Jean and Marshall Case, in Troy, Pennsylvania; and Tom and Abby Potter, in Tallahassee, Florida. I wish to thank them along with the many lovers of short stories who discussed their favorites, particularly Marsha Case; Amy Gibson; Teddy, Van, Vannie, Andy, and Debby Miller; Dewey Potter; Meg and Matt Potter; Tony Wellman; and Jennifer and John Winton.

INTRODUCTION

"The Americans have handled the short story so wonderfully," said the Irish writer Frank O'Connor, that it constitutes "a national art form." Although by now it may seem an "old" form (since the first American short story was, arguably, published as early as 1789), it is still thriving: witness its sales, its apparent vogue among high school students, its increased use in college courses across the curriculum, the proliferation of public short story readings at bookstores, the explosion of book clubs, and the acclaimed National Public Radio series of short story readings "Selected Shorts." As the writer Shirley Ann Grau remarked in an interview, people are still reading the short story "like mad."

In response to readers' requests for more short fiction suggestions, an updated and revised edition of a reading group guide by Mickey Pearlman, *What to Read* (1999), includes a new chapter on short story collections. In fact, from Charles Brockden Brown and Washington Irving, through Mark Twain, Ernest Hemingway, Gertrude Stein, and William Faulkner, to Joyce Carol Oates, Raymond Carver, Sandra Cisneros, Louise Erdrich, John Edgar Wideman, and Amy Tan, short fiction—although it suffered a critical decline in the mid-20th century—has never really lost its popularity with the reading public.

To the contrary, short fiction has continued to appear in major magazines from the *New Yorker* and *Redbook* to *Esquire, Playboy,* and *Penthouse;* good story collections and anthologies are readily accessible through inexpensive paperback reprints; and, perhaps most important of all, short stories are *short*. In an era when even many novels seem noticeably shorter than they once were, the most obvious reason for the popularity of short stories may well lie in the response I have heard hundreds of times from readers of all types: "I like to keep them on my night table so I can read one or two before I fall asleep." Younger readers—particularly those who identify themselves as "Generation Xers"—say they feel drawn to the short story not only because of its length, but also because it seems less artificially wrapped up than the novel, and thus more like "real life." Remarking on the microcosmic relationship of the story to modern life, critic William Peden finds that the short story now appears as a "literary mirror" that reflects our postwar life in which change, obsolescence, and destruction have become the realities:

> Unlike the traditional novelists, the short story writer usually does not bring his powers to bear on the grand questions of where are we going, why are we here. Rather, he focuses his attention, swiftly and clearly, on one facet of man's experience; he illuminates briefly one dark corner or depicts one aspect of life.

Stories have existed in one form or another, of course, for as long as people have told them and listened to them. We can picture storytellers and their audiences as they probably existed thousands of years ago, huddling together near a fire, listening to someone's story both as a form of entertainment and as a means to ward off fear of the unknown lying outside the stone walls of their enclosure or the perimeter of the firelight. The oral telling of stories conjures up in modern readers a dual image of both community interaction and private individual response.

Most scholars agree that the first written stories can be traced to numerous sources—religious stories of the Greeks, the incomparable stories of Scheherezade, the instructive narratives of the European medieval times. Throughout the Renaissance, brief tales were popular, reaching a state of art in Italy and Spain with Giovanni Boccaccio's *Decameron* and Miguel de Cervantes's *Exemplary Novels*. Many critics believe, however, that the onset of the novel in the 18th century dampened the vogue of the story. Not until the 19th century did several factors unite to give rise to a new form of tale: the appearance of the periodical, or annual—apparently originating in Germany—as well as the new forms of romanticism whose moods and effects found expressive outlets in stories and poetry.

The history of the short story in the United States is a compelling story in itself. When the Englishman Sydney Smith in 1820 asked his withering question, "In the four quarters of the globe, who reads an American book?", American writers accepted the challenge. Although critics have argued over when, and according to which criteria, the first story actually appeared (two major contenders include the pseudonymous Ruricolla's "The Story of the Captain's Wife and an Aged Woman" in 1789 and the anonymous "The Child of Snow" in 1792), Washington Irving's *The Sketch Book*, published in 1819, is generally credited as the first American book of short stories. Rather neatly predating Smith's question by a year, *The Sketch Book* includes such classic stories as "Rip Van Winkle" and "The Legend of Sleepy Hollow," both surprisingly modern in their use of self-conscious narrators and ambiguous endings.

The definitions of the short story have modified since then and provide a source for much scholarly research today, but for more than a century, students have learned its basic tenets: most important, it is "short" when compared with the novel. Written in prose that may or may not be lyrical, it has a narrator, a plot, at least one developing character who grapples with problems, one or more themes, and a denouement. In the 20th century, writers have rebelled against some of these traditional elements, particularly those of plots and tidy conclusions.

The story has also evolved into a peculiarly American form. Although certainly writers of every nationality write excellent short fiction—indeed, the modern story would be unthinkable without the Russian Anton Chekhov and the French Guy de Maupassant, to name just two influential European practitioners—no country has embraced the form as enthusiastically and as prolifically as the United States has done. Early U.S. writers consciously included American settings and evoked distinctively American regions and speech patterns, as some contemporary writers continue to do. The short story has remained a peculiarly American artistic vehicle, however, not only for examining the myriad voices and philosophies of this large, diverse country, but also for viewing society's preoccupations with issues of race, gender, and class, national consciousness, and the spiritual and physical position of the individual in the sometimes overwhelming welter of American life. From Irving to the present, then, the American short story provides "an index of national consciousness" (Weaver xv).

After Irving came three writers of unquestionable talent who further refined the short story: Edgar Allan Poe, Nathaniel Hawthorne, and Herman Melville. Poe, a literary critic as well as a practitioner of the short story, sought to define the form. With the exception of poetry, which he believed to be the pinnacle of literary expression, he judged "the Tale" as the form that afforded "the best prose opportunity for display of the highest talent," finding it superior to the novel, the essay, and in some respects, even poetry. Poe, a superb craftsman himself, laid down guidelines for the taut, compressed, carefully considered and thoroughly unified story. His exacting standards concerned his friend Hawthorne, who believed his own tales somewhat pale and retiring in contrast. Yet Hawthorne, too, took a painstaking approach to his art, leaving written records of his short story approach. Both writers, according to Burton Raffel, were "important exemplars, inventive, imaginative, and above all sharply aware that the untethered, uncontrolled, unmastered pen simply could not accomplish" a first-rate short story (16). Melville, despite his admiration for both Poe and Hawthorne, voiced his frustration with a thinness of characterization, particularly in Hawthorne's stories. In Melville's tales we see a movement away from romanticism toward realism, especially in the characters of Benito Cerino and Billy Budd.

The shift toward realism, with its accompanying genre, the local color story, characterized much short fiction in the second half of the 19th century. Whereas romanticism concerns itself with an idealized conception of the way things should be, realism focuses on things as they seem to be. William Dean Howells, known as "the dean of American literature" and the closest thing to a czar that American literature has ever had (Raffel 20), in the mid-1880s sounded the call for verisimilitude, or realism, in all American writing, and many writers answered this call. In the end, however, these are but labels of convenience and, if readers look closely, they will find elements of both realism and romanticism after 1850 in such talented and differing authors as Melville, Mark Twain, and Sarah Orne Jewett. In fact, the mingling of romanticism and realism never really stopped: two so-called local colorists, Harriet Beecher Stowe and Hamlin Garland, despite their different concerns (Stowe with women and domestic life, Garland with men and war), write passages that appear almost identical in terms of both verisimilitude and idealism (Raffel 22–23).

Naturalism, another development of the literary realistic movement, called for a scientific objectivity when depicting "natural" human beings, yet its practitioners—Frank Norris and Stephen Crane, for instance—have also been called romantic and impressionistic. As Henry James pointed out, the

idea of the writer is paramount, not the debate over a realistic or a romantic formula; the only distinction James addressed was the difference between "good" and "bad" art. James believed strongly that the value of fiction lies in its greater or lesser ability to render a direct and intense "impression of life" (Raffel 24), and nearly every critic notes that he emphasizes the word *impression,* thereby pointing to the individual quality of the writer's vision.

A number of 19th-century short story writers continued to write into the 20th century. Along with others, Kate Chopin, Jewett, Edith Wharton, Jack London—and James, who died during World War I—wrote into the new era. In many ways the authors who did live into the new century and through World War I—not only Jewett, Wharton, and James, but also Twain, Theodore Dreiser, and Willa Cather—all implicitly or explicitly criticized the hypocrisy and conformity they saw across the United States and came to see themselves as aliens and outsiders at odds with the changing times. In any case, World War I, with its fragmentation of traditions and values, and the consequent rise of modernism, provides a sharp dividing line between the 19th and 20th centuries of American short fiction. Exactly 100 years after Irving published *The Sketch Book,* Sherwood Anderson is credited with enacting the modernist creed, "make it new," with the publication of his short story collection *Winesburg, Ohio,* in 1919.

"Never such innocence again," writes Paul Fussell of World War I in *The Great War and Modern Memory.* The effects of the war are evident even in those writers who did not write about it—Anderson or Dorothy Parker, for instance—and even in those who did not consider themselves modernists. Anderson's groundbreaking book of stories discarded realistic representations of behavior and things, replacing them with a more allusive, mystical, and poetic form more psychologically suggestive than anything previously written in American fiction. The modernist sense of fragmentation, of postwar loss and fragile instability, is evident in the short fiction that followed his lead, whether in work by the expatriate Americans in Europe or by those who stayed at home. In Paris, for instance, Ernest Hemingway and

Gertrude Stein sought radically new ways of expressing the upheaval, alienation, and disjunction they felt in the aftermath of the war, Hemingway in his terse, sharply pruned stories and Stein in her cinematic exploration of the further possibilities inherent in language and imagery. William Faulkner, in a style antithetical to Hemingway's, was every bit as experimental if not more so, stretching language as far as he could take it. Critics have observed that all the best short fiction writers of this period knew the terms from painting, from impressionism to cubism; perhaps Katherine Anne Porter's conscious use of images and symbols in her short story techniques best suggest the modernist writer's kinship with art.

Not all 20th-century writers were modernists, and many other popular practitioners of short fiction flourished—due in part, in an echo of the previous century, to American magazines. The so-called little magazines, such as the *Dial* and *Broom,* published the new and the experimental, and once again there was a call in post–World War 1 America for short stories to fill the widely circulated and successful magazines typified by the *Ladies' Home Journal* and *Saturday Evening Post. American Mercury* published numerous writers today considered classic—F. Scott Fitzgerald and Faulkner, for instance— and the *New Yorker,* debuting later, in 1925, also had a significant influence on the short story in following decades. O. Henry's stories continued to have enormous popular appeal, as did Ring Lardner's. Writers from the New South, from Eudora Welty and Jean Toomer to Porter and Flannery O'Connor, also were making their voices heard. The 1920s were called the Jazz Age, popularized, of course, by Fitzgerald, but they were also the heyday of the Harlem Renaissance, and they afforded significant outlets for regional writers. The 1920s left a legacy of experimentalism and diversity that future generations would, and still do, view with awe.

Historians and literary critics alike have noted the phenomenon of speaking of our eras in terms of decades; like literary labels, such coding oversimplifies the issues. Yet the advent of the stock market crash and the Great Depression ushered in a very different sort of literature in the 1930s. It is a fact that the years 1930 to 1945, through the end of World War II, saw the greatest outpouring of short fiction in American literary history. Although the financial hardships of the Great Depression resulted in the dramatic reduction of book publication (from 1929 to 1933, published books dropped from more than 200 million a year to a little more than 100 million), an enormous increase in magazines and the introduction of the Pocket Books paperback series stepped into the void (Watson 106). A public tired of the realities of the Depression and with unpaid free time on their hands craved entertainment and thus created a huge market for short fiction. One of the most significant innovations, called proletarian, or reform, literature, was not really new but had roots in the late 19th century. Its 1930s practitioners included James T. Farrell, Ruth Suckow, Langston Hughes, and Meridel LeSueur. In fact, most of the fiction written in the 1930s hearkened back to the era of Hawthorne and the tradition of American romanticism. Writers took on the old subjects—verities, Faulkner would say—of "young Americans, initiations, death and dying, fantasies" (Watson 105). Arguably, the literary characters descended from earlier ones such as Twain's Huck Finn appear in short stories rather than novels: Hemingway's Nick Adams, Porter's Miranda Rhea, Anderson's George Willard, Faulkner's Isaac McCaslin (Watson 110). R. W. B. Lewis identified both generations as variations on the American Adam, or the innocent in the New World. Versions of this Adamic protagonist occur in the short fiction of William Saroyan, Richard Wright, Farrell, Welty, and Kay Boyle. The hard times of the Depression may also have propelled certain authors back to the land itself, and to regionalism, as in the work of Midwesterners Suckow, Farrell, and Sinclair Lewis; Southerners Hughes, Toomer, Ellen Glasgow, and Erskine Caldwell; Pennsylvanians John O'Hara and John Updike; and Californian John Steinbeck.

The significance of the beat writers at mid-century, although they wrote little short fiction, lies in their desire to question the status quo. Their rebellious attitude appears in somewhat altered form in the concerns of some major contemporary writers who, distrustful of the American dream, become more and more attracted to the world of illusion as opposed to the "real" world of fact, and committed to a study of the act of writing itself. Such self-consciousness, or self-reflexivity as it has come to be called, is evident especially in the work of writers from Robert Coover and Donald Barthelme to Leslie Marmon Silko and Bernard Malamud. Their fiction, particularly that of the former two, became less about objective reality and more about its own creative processes; the artistic process became the subject of their stories.

Notwithstanding the beats and their similarly irreverent late 20th-century counterparts, general critical opinion seems to agree with short story theorist Charles E. May, who suggests that two different strands developed in the short story of the latter half of the century: the stark new realistic style made famous by Hemingway and the mythic romance style made equally famous by Faulkner. The two styles combined notably in the short fiction of Porter, Welty, Steinbeck, Wright, Carson McCullers, Truman Capote, Isaac Bashevis Singer, Malamud, and others writing past mid-century. The main characteristics of this modern blending include a pronounced use of the grotesque, the employment of the traditional structures and motifs of the folktale, a tangible aesthetic concern, a fascination with dreams, a firm commitment to the power of language, the use of surrealistic imagery, and a carefully developed style and unified poetic form (May, *The Short Story,* 19).

Because this combination continued into the second half of the 20th century, writers of the period between 1960 and 1990 fall roughly into two groups. On the one hand, the ultimate extreme of the mythic, romantic style is the fantastic stories—or anti-stories—of John Barth, Coover, Stanley Elkin, Richard Elman, and Barthelme, the postmodern writer who, more than any other, has specialized in the short story. On the other hand, the extreme of realism can be seen in the so-called minimalism of Raymond Carver, Ann Beattie, and Cynthia Ozick. The very fact that the mythic, romantic style is sometimes called magical realism, while the minimalist style is sometimes called hyperrealism, indicates that the twin streams of romance and realism are inextri-

cably blended in the works of contemporary short story writers, including those of Hispanic-American, Native American, Asian-American, and African-American cultures—Sandra Cisneros, Leslie Marmon Silko, Maxine Hong Kingston, and Toni Cade Bambara, for example. The mid- and late-20th century writers of urban or suburban fiction, too, sometimes blend magic and reality, as in the works of Singer, Malamud, Ozick, and John Cheever. The rise in the urban writers—Saul Bellow, for instance, writing of Chicago; Philip Roth, of New York and New Jersey; Ralph Ellison and James Baldwin, of New York, especially Harlem; Ann Petry, of New York and Connecticut—occurred simultaneously with the rise in New South writing and its more rural concerns. Robert Penn Warren writing of Tennessee and Kentucky, and Welty writing of Mississippi, inspired such younger writers as Peter Taylor of Tennessee, McCullers and O'Connor of Georgia, and Capote of Louisiana and Mississippi.

One of the most pronounced characteristics of post–World War II fiction has been a questioning of the traditional forms, even those of the experimental modernists. After the war, many of the "old" modernists continued to publish stories (Faulkner, Porter, and Wright, for example, lived into the 1960s). The lesson of these established writers seemed to be to write from one's own experience, and certainly many contemporary writers adhere to this principle, achieving thereby a new regionalism and a new ethnicity in short fiction. Alternatively, numerous American writers use the short story form to examine the postmodern condition, particularly by pushing that form to the edge of, or beyond, its limits. Thus such writers as Barthelme or William Gass abandon the neat sequential forms of narration in favor of fragmentation and distortion. Barth's story "Lost in the Funhouse" gives us probably the best-known postmodernist metaphor for the American condition: we cannot find our way in the distorted and illusory world that mockingly reflects our images. Characters might not—and certainly need not—develop or seem "real." Stories like these may teach us lessons about our own precarious positions in the world and about the possible inadequacy of the language we depend on for self-definition and self-realization (Weaver xv).

When examining contemporary short fiction, we need to know that for a time in the mid-20th century, the very survival of the short story sparked serious debate: was it time to ring its death knell, or was it destined to become the most significant vehicle for expressing the dissatisfied and fragmented existence in the postwar world? Numerous critics have noted that popular interest in the short story declined after World War II, for several reasons. The clearest and most persuasive is the disappearance or reorganization of the popular magazines—the *Saturday Evening Post,* for instance—that had brought such writers as Faulkner, Hemingway, and Welty into middle America. There no longer seemed a ready market for short fiction, although certainly the *New Yorker* provided an audience for what came to be known as the "New Yorker story" practiced by Jean Stafford, O'Hara, Cheever, Updike, and others. The late 20th century in the United States, fast paced and arguably obsessed with size and sales, has tended to value the novel over the short story: if it has fewer words, it must be less important, or so the theory goes. Nonetheless, several factors during recent decades have assured the continued relevance of and audience for the short story: the rise in the publication of anthologies and their required use in the high school, college, and university classroom; the increase in the number of creative writing courses that produce short stories; and the collection of prize-winning stories in annual publications such as *Best American Short Stories.*

Perhaps one of the clearest signs of the revival of interest in short stories occurs in the vigorous and scholarly examination of the form as an enormously important genre in its own right. Such academic scrutiny began in the 1960s with the publication of Charles E. May's *Short Story Theories* (1967) and continues today with such influential short fiction studies as Susan Lohafer's *Coming to Terms with the Short Story* (1983) and Lohafer's and Jo Ellyn Clarey's *Short Story Theory at a Crossroads* (1989), as well as with May's *The New Short Story Theories* (1994). Such valuable studies not only prove that

scholars take short stories seriously, but also ask theoretical questions about the special nature of the short form of fiction. The most general current debate, beginning in the 1980s, addresses the question of whether agreement on the definition and theory of such a varied form will ever occur. Students of short fiction disagree over such seemingly basic issues as length. No one has yet coined universally or even nationally satisfactory definitions that would allow clear distinctions among the short story (which can be less than a printed page in length), the short story proper, the long short story, the novella, and the short story cycle (volumes of interconnected stories). In fact, a number of critics deliberately find such definitions too restrictive. In the last few decades, these indistinct boundaries have extended still further to include novels comprised of chapters that were initially published as short stories in magazines.

The debate over the appeal of the story versus the novel will continue as well. Short stories tend to nudge us slightly off balance. We feel somewhat mystified about the nature of Roderick Usher's illness in Poe's "The Fall of the House of Usher," about why Bartleby "prefers not to" in Melville's "Bartleby the Scrivener," or why Goodman Brown abandons Faith to walk into the dark New England forest in Hawthorne's "Young Goodman Brown." Why do ordinary people stone a woman to death in Shirley Jackson's "The Lottery"? Why do the hills resemble white elephants in Hemingway's "Hills Like White Elephants"? Why would Laura eat from the Judas tree in Porter's "Flowering Judas" or Manley Pointer steal a wooden leg in O'Connor's "Good Country People"? Is the grandson of Phoenix Jackson really dead in Welty's "A Worn Path"? The short story tells a different story from the one a novel tells. By focusing on a single experience or sequence of thoughts, the entire story often becomes a metaphor for a familiar if unexamined part of our own lives. As such, in Gordon Weaver's view, the story not only presents a vision of life, but also points the way to a "moral revelation" and hence a springboard to action and change (Weaver xv). In her 1977 novel *Ceremony,* Silko tells stories of the Laguna Pueblo tribe and explains the centrality of stories in the lives of all people. They can literally bring us back to life, helping us to sharpen our awareness and our understanding of the seemingly mundane as well as the inexplicable and the spiritual. Rather than serving just as entertainment, they become essential to our moral and spiritual health: "You don't have anything if you don't have the stories."

❦   ❦   ❦

This book has been several years in the planning and implementation. Focusing on American short story authors from the early 19th century to the 1990s, *The Facts On File Companion to the American Short Story* has made special efforts to include all authors of merit, including previously ignored writers of both genders from all major cultural backgrounds. With few exceptions, these authors were either born in the United States or made or make their home there. Bringing together useful information on the "universe" of the short story, the *Companion* contains author entries that include dates, biographies, lists of stories and their critical reception, and selected bibliographies. The *Companion* also contains individual entries on literary terms, themes, historical events, locales, influential magazines and critics, and major short story prize awards. We found that certain short story characters are repeatedly cited by critics and teachers as notable representatives of American experience, and we therefore provide entries on these significant protagonists. Moreover, the book includes entries on the long short story, or novella—whose connection to and difference from the short story continues to be debated—and on such short story subgenres as regionalism, science fiction, and detective fiction.

Choosing writers and stories for this book was an arduous process. We tried to achieve a representative balance between 19th- and 20th-century writers and between so-called classic and contemporary writers. Naturally, we regret that we could not include even more writers and even more stories. In the event, we established some guidelines to facilitate the decision-making process: in the case of the older, more traditional writers, we chose stories that

appear frequently in the many anthologies available. In some cases in this book, significant writers, although closely identified with an era, do not appear simply because they primarily write novels rather than short fiction. In regard to contemporary writers, we tried to choose those who have published more than two collections, whose stories appear in popular anthologies, or who have won literary prizes and awards, as well as those who have gained a following among younger readers and scholars. In many of the story entries, we suggest alternative ways of reading that may not occur to a first-time reader. We have also included overviews of particular categories of short fiction to provide background and bibliography for further study: the book contains entries on Asian-American, African-American, Hispanic-American, and Native American literature. The book also contains entries on critical theory, with explanations of such frequently used terms as modernism and postmodernism. Appendices include winners of selected short story prizes, stories listed by subject and setting, and a selected bibliography of critical histories and theoretical approaches to the short story.

BIBLIOGRAPHY

Lohafer, Susan. *Coming to Terms with the Short Story.* Baton Rouge: Louisiana State University Press, 1983.

Lohafer, Susan, and Jo Ellyn Clarey, eds. *Short Story Theory at a Crossroads.* Baton Rouge: Louisiana State University Press, 1989.

May, Charles E., ed. *The New Short Story Theories.* Athens: Ohio University Press, 1994.

———. *The Short Story: The Reality of Artifice.* New York: Twayne, 1995.

Raffel, Burton. Introduction to *The Signet Classic Book of American Short Stories,* edited by Burton Raffel, 7–30. New York: New American Library, 1985.

Stevick, Philip. Introduction to *The American Short Story, 1900–1945: A Critical History,* edited by Philip Stevick, 1–31. Boston: Twayne, 1984.

Watson, James G. "The American Short Story: 1930–1945." In *The American Short Story, 1900–1945: A Critical History,* edited by Philip Stevick, 103–46. Boston: Twayne, 1984.

Weaver, Gordon. Introduction to *The American Short Story, 1945–1980: A Critical History,* edited by Gordon Weaver, xi–xix. Boston: Twayne, 1983.

A

"A & P" JOHN UPDIKE (1961) First published in the NEW YORKER and subsequently collected in *Pigeon Feathers* (1962), "A & P" presents a brisk retrospective first-person narration (see POINT OF VIEW) by Sammy, a brash cashier who recounts his unsuccessful attempt to impress Queenie, one of three teenage girls who comes shopping in the small seaside town grocery store where he works. Dressed only in bathing suits, Queenie and her friends immediately draw the attention of Sammy, his friend Stoksie, and the sheeplike shoppers for whom Sammy freely expresses his disdain. When Lengel, the unyielding manager, embarrasses the girls as Sammy rings up their purchase, Sammy quits, standing up for his principles and hoping to impress the girls. They have left the scene, however, and in the parking lot, he has an EPIPHANY: It reveals to him not only his present predicament but also the difficult life he will have thereafter.

With its fast-moving plot and seamless narrative, "A & P" is somewhat uncharacteristic of John UPDIKE's short fiction, which more often takes a lyrical form and employs a looser construction held together by a highly metaphoric style. Nonetheless, it is his most frequently anthologized story, perhaps because of its accessibility and relevance to students, its THEME of initiation, and its pronounced concluding epiphany. Much of the story's appeal derives from the narrative voice: Sammy's lively verbal performance displays a surprising elasticity of TONE, ranging from colloquial adolescent male slang to similes that may reveal an embryonic writer. While Sammy reveals sexist attitudes, his narration seeks approval for his individualistic gesture and casts him as an unsuspected hero, standing up for principles of decency toward others that Lengel fails to recognize when he chastises the girls for indecency. Initially Sammy joins Stoksie in leering at the girls; though his interest in Queenie's exposed flesh never wanes, he experiences a turning point when he observes the butcher sizing up the girls. Sammy also admires Queenie for her confident carriage—which, in quitting, perhaps he attempts to emulate—as well as her social status. Queenie embodies a socioeconomic realm to which Sammy, the son of working-class parents, desires access.

Sammy's quitting may be motivated by a combination of lust, admiration of Queenie's social status, and sentimental romanticism, but his gesture does not lack principle and quickly assumes more serious overtones. The link Sammy feels with Queenie vanishes as he crosses the supermarket's threshold for the last time and encounters not his dream girl but a premonition of the realities of married life: a young mother yelling at her children. While he has established a distance between himself and Lengel's narrow world, Sammy realizes the truth of the manager's warning that he will feel the impact of this

1

incident for the rest of his life. Indeed, Sammy refuses to stoop to self-pity and seems to savor the experience, even as he realizes it will have numerous unforeseen repercussions that will make life more difficult in the future.

BIBLIOGRAPHY

Dessner, Lawrence Jay. "Irony and Innocence in John Updike's 'A&P.'" *Studies in Short Fiction* 25 (1988): 315–17.

Detweiler, Robert. *John Updike.* Rev. ed. Boston: G. K. Hall, 1984.

Greiner, Donald. *The Other John Updike: Poems, Short Stories, Prose, Play.* Athens: Ohio University Press, 1981.

Luscher, Robert M. *John Updike: A Study of the Short Fiction.* New York: Twayne, 1993.

McFarland, Ronald E. "Updike and the Critics: Reflections on 'A & P.'" *Studies in Short Fiction* 20 (1983): 95–100.

Petry, Alice. "The Dress Code in Updike's 'A&P.'" *Notes on Contemporary Literature* 16.1 (1986): 8–10.

Porter, M. Gilbert. "John Updike's 'A&P': The Establishment and an Emersonian Cashier." *English Journal* 61 (1972): 1155–58.

Shaw, Patrick. "Checking Out Faith and Lust: Hawthorne's 'Young Goodman Brown' and Updike's 'A&P.'" *Studies in Short Fiction* 23 (1986): 321–23.

Wells, Walter. "John Updike's 'A&P': A Return Visit to Araby." *Studies in Short Fiction* 30 (1993): 127–33.

Robert Luscher
University of Nebraska at Kearney

ABNER SNOPES

Among the first in his rapacious clan to settle in YOKNAPATAWPHA COUNTY, and the father of the infamous Flem Snopes, Abner Snopes is best known as a barn burner and a mule thief who appears in a number of William FAULKNER's novels and who is the main character in the short story "BARN BURNING." In "Barn Burning," Abner is a hardened and embittered man who, resentful of his lot in life as a sharecropper, burns the barns of the planters from whom he leases land. In the novel THE UNVANQUISHED, Abner, after deserting from the Confederate army, steals mules from both the Union and Confederate forces, changes the brands, and resells them to both armies. See also SNOPES FAMILY.

BIBLIOGRAPHY

Beck, Warren, *Man in Motion.* Madison: University of Wisconsin Press, 1961.

H. Collin Messer
University of North Carolina

ABSTRACT EXPRESSIONISM

Twentieth-century artistic movement and literary style originating in Germany, particularly influenced by Swedish dramatist August Strindberg (1849–1912). Although mainly associated with theater, abstract expressionism also appears in literature, painting, and music. The hallmark of abstract expressionism is its radical revolt against REALISM. Instead of representing the world objectively, the author or artist attempts to express inner experience by representing the world as it appears to him or her personally, or to an emotionally distraught or abnormal character. Frequently this troubled mental condition represents the anxiety of the modern individual in an industrial and technological society moving away from order toward confusion or disaster. See also ABSURD and SURREALISM.

ABSURD

Dramatic and prose fiction works that portray the human condition as essentially and ineradicably ludicrous or farcical are termed "absurd." The style has its roots in the fiction of James Joyce and Franz Kafka. The major practitioners, however, emerged after WORLD WAR II in rebellion against the essential beliefs and values of traditional culture and its literature. The absurdists' fictional modern men and women—like their real-life counterparts—see their existence as meaningless and absurd. Notable practitioners in the theatrical world were Jean Genet, Eugene Ionesco, and Samuel Beckett, European writers loosely grouped under the rubric Theater of the Absurd, and Harold Pinter, the British playwright famous for the menace lurking beneath the surface of his deceptively ordinary domestic settings. Edward ALBEE is the best known American practitioner. Typically this mode is grotesquely comic as well as irrational. See also BLACK HUMOR and SURREALISM.

ADULTERY AND OTHER CHOICES

ANDRE DUBUS (1977)   Andre DUBUS's second collection of short stories (his first, *Separate Flights*, was published in 1975), *Adultery and Other Choices* focuses on themes of betrayal and acceptance; many of Dubus's characters are outsiders who desperately want in. The collection is divided into three sections: Part 1 involves stories of childhood and adolescence; Part 2 concerns stories of military life; Part 3 contains the long story "Adultery," the second installment in a three-part narrative that was later reprinted in *We Don't Live Here Anymore* (1984).

The opening three stories, "An Afternoon with the Old Man," "Contrition," and "The Bully"—as well as "Cadence," which appears later in the collection—concern the young Paul Clement (an ALTER EGO for the author) and his painful trek from childhood into manhood. Both "An Afternoon with the Old Man" and "Contrition" explore Paul's painful, deficient relationship with his father. Considered weak and inadequate by the "old man," Paul prefers to distance himself: "With his father he had lived a lie for as long as he could remember: he believed his father wanted him to be popular and athletic at school, so Paul never told him about his days" (*AOC*, 18). Paul's attempts to negotiate the codes of adolescence reveal his fear, cowardice, and cruelty. "The Bully" is framed by two disturbing scenes: As the story opens, Paul methodically kills a stray cat; as it concludes, he darkly envisions the recent drowning death of the boy who has bullied him. Like "The Bully," which involves Paul's cruel rejection of his friend Eddie, "Cadence" is also a story of betrayal: This time the victim is Hugh Munson, a fellow marine recruit whom Paul abandons following a forced training run. Despite such betrayals, Paul is often kind and sensitive, and we never fail to sense that he, too, is an outsider. Like Paul, Louise of "The Fat Girl" is a misfit; the story explores Louise's struggle for acceptance, contrasting her college friend Carrie's compassion with her husband Richard's cruel rejection.

The stories of military life in Part 2, such as "The Shooting," further the themes of betrayal and acceptance, but some are also tales of survival. In "Andromache," Ellen Forrest must piece together her life after the death of her husband. In "Corporal of Artillery," the 22-year-old Fitzgerald reenlists in the Marine Corps, out of his sense of duty to his wife, who is recovering from a nervous breakdown, and their three young children.

In "Adultery," the final story, Jack, Terry, Hank, and Edith are all unfaithful, but it is Edith's affair with the lapsed priest Joe Ritchie—a relationship founded on compassion and love—that complicates our reading of the meaning of "adultery." "All adultery is a symptom," thinks Edith, and we sense that she is right: The infidelities of *Adultery and Other Choices* merely hint at the larger, deeper erosions and betrayals that characterize many human relationships (*AOC*, 158).

BIBLIOGRAPHY
Kennedy, Thomas E. *Andre Dubus: A Study of the Short Fiction* Boston: Twayne, 1988.

Michael Hogan
University of North Carolina

AESOP'S FABLES

According to tradition, Aesop was a Greek slave who lived around 600 B.C. The FABLES are succinct tales, such as "The Tortoise and the Hare," in which talking animals illustrate human vices, follies, and virtues (see PERSONIFICATION).

AESTHETICISM

The Aesthetic movement developed in France and during the late 19th century became a European phenomenon among those adhering to the doctrine of "art for art's sake"—that is, the purpose of a work of art is simply to exist and to be beautiful. The roots of the Aesthetic movement lie in the German theory, proposed by the philosopher Immanuel Kant in 1790, that aesthetic contemplation is "disinterested," indifferent to both the reality and to the utility of the beautiful object; it was also influenced by the view of Edgar Allan POE (in "The Poetic Principle," 1850) that the supreme work is simply itself, "a poem written solely for the poem's sake." In other words, a work of art or literature need serve no moral, practical, or instructive purpose; it should, instead, appeal to viewers or readers solely on the basis of its beauty.

AESTHETICS   The general term for a sense of the beautiful. Although the term may be applied to art, music, or any work that appeals to the emotions rather than the intellect, an aesthete, one especially sensitive to beauty, responds strongly to lyrically and artistically appealing works of literature. Many of Katherine Ann PORTER's works, for example, have a strong aesthetic appeal.

AFFECTIVE FALLACY   An essay published in 1946 by W. K. Wimsatt, Jr., and Monroe C. Beardsley, some of the architects of NEW CRITICISM, defined affective fallacy as the error of evaluating a poem by its effects—especially its emotional effects—upon the reader. As a result of this fallacy, the literary work as "an object of specifically critical judgement, tends to disappear," so that criticism "ends in impressionism and relativism." This attempt to separate the appreciation and evaluation of fiction from its emotional and other effects on the reader has been severely criticized, on the grounds that a work of literature that leaves the reader unresponsive and impassive is not experienced as literature at all.

AFRICAN-AMERICAN SHORT FICTION
Despite the debt the African-American short story owes to the "national art form," as Frank O'CONNOR called the American short story, it, like the other genres of the African-American literary tradition, must be traced back to the site that in 1789 the freed slave Olaudah Equiano called his "nation of dancers, musicians and poets," in describing his traditional West African community of Essaka. Equiano recalled not only the integral role storytelling played in the daily life of the community but also its inextricable relationship to music and dance:

> Every great event, such as a triumphant return from battle, or other cause of public rejoicing, is celebrated in public dances, which are accompanied with songs and music suited to

the occasion . . . Each represents some interesting scene of real life. . . . And as the subject is generally founded on some recent event, it is therefore ever new (Equiano 14–15).

One may logically conclude, therefore, that the African-American short story begins with the oral lore African slaves brought with them from West Africa to the "New World" as early as the 15th century.

When, as American slaves, Africans gained access to literacy and language and began creating written texts, the results resounded with fictive elements—themes, characterization, and tropes—that drew, as John Henrik Clarke noted, "on the oral literature used in Africa to teach and preserve their group history" (Clarke xv), or the oral traditions Equiano so eloquently described. An excellent example is the paradigmatic African folk hero: the TRICKSTER. Although commonly found in the Anansesem (spider tales) of West Africa, the trickster was not, as Lawrence Levine points out, represented solely in animal tales, for "tricksters could, and did, assume divine and human forms as well" (Levine 103), as evident in such heroes as the Dahomey's Legba and the Yoruba's Esu and Orunmila. Often in these tales, one finds a confrontation in which the weak uses wit to overpower or evade the strong. The direct relationship between the African-American literary tradition and African culture is offered by Henry Louis Gates, who argues that the Signifying Monkey figure found in African-American profane discourse is Esu's "functional equivalent." Moreover, Gates maintains that "unlike his Pan-African Esu Cousins," the Signifying Monkey "exists not primarily as a character in a narrative but rather as a vehicle of narration itself. Like Esu, however, the Signifying Monkey stands as the figure of an oral writing within black vernacular language rituals" (Gates, *The Signifying Monkey*, 52).

In African-American literature this hero, theme, narrative mode, and linguistic ritual readily appear in the first written texts, from Equiano's *Interesting Narrative of Olaudah Equiano, or Gustavus Vassa, the*

African (1789) and Frederick DOUGLASS's now-classic 19th-century *Narrative of the Life of Frederick Douglass* (1845), to Ralph ELLISON's American masterpiece *Invisible Man* (1952) and Toni MORRISON's award-winning novel *Song of Solomon* (1977), in which the trickster role, aptly played by the heroine, Pilate, reaches magnificent heights.

These characteristics of the trickster are first found, however, in stories about the wily acts of Brer Rabbit, Brer Fox, and High John de Conquer/Fortuneteller, who as characters, are poised at all times to deceive their masters. As Darwin T. Turner notes, "These were folk tales which no individual proclaimed to be his unique creation. Certainly, individuals invented them, but later narrators felt free to modify them; for these stories about heroes—animal and human—whose character traits were well known to the listeners were the product of the race" (Turner 2). In sum, they served a communal function much in the way that stories, songs, and dance did in Equiano's "charming fruitful vale" (Equiano 2).

Not surprisingly, the same desire for freedom that fueled the first English written text by North American slaves (primarily through poetry and song), injected the black voice into the antislavery movement, and created the new autobiographical genre of the slave narrative, also form the impetus of the first narrative stories (in novel form) written by African Americans: *Clotel; or, the President's Daughter* (1853), by William Wells Brown, and *The Heroic Slave* (1853), by Douglass. Other works would follow during the same decade, which some scholars now identify as the first African-American literary renaissance, including Frank Webb's *The Garies and Their Friends* (1857), Martin R. Delany's *Blake; Or the Huts of America* (1859), and Harriet Wilson's *Our Nig; Or, Sketches from the Life of a Free Black* (1859), the first novel written by an African-American woman.

Debates about who published the first African-American short story or prose narrative abound. Contending that many first appeared in early magazines and newspapers, including the *African Methodists Episcopalian Review, Colored Home Journal,* and *Anglo-African Journal,* William R. Robinson traces the publication of the first short narrative stories to the well-known 19th-century poet George Moses Horton, who wrote religious stories for a Sunday school publication. Lemuel Haynes, author of *Mysterious Development; or Russell Colvin (Supposed to be Murdered), in Full Life and Stephen and Jesse Born, His convicted Murderers, Rescued from Ignominious Death by Wonderful Discoveries* (1820), is also given this honor, as is William Wells Brown. In 1859, Frances Ellen Watkins HARPER, abolitionist orator and author of *Iola Leroy; or Shadows of the Uplifted* (1892), published "The Two Offers," the first short story by an African-American woman.

There is no debate that Charles W. CHESNUTT was the first professional African-American short story writer, although Paul L. DUNBAR published the first collection of stories, *Folks From Dixie* (1898). A successful attorney who saw literature as a way of confronting racism and segregation, Chesnutt published "The Goophered Grapevine," his first short story, in the prestigious ATLANTIC MONTHLY in 1877. Steeped in folk material, his first collection of stories, *The Conjure Woman* (1899), was published by Houghton Mifflin Company, with the assistance and blessings of its editors, including Francis J. Garrison, the son of the abolitionist William Lloyd GARRISON. It was favorably reviewed by William Dean HOWELLS. Ironically, because Chesnutt used a white narrator, readers were not initially aware of the author's African-American identity.

In "The Goophered Grapevine," a story framed by the ostensibly superior white narrator, Chesnutt's black narrator of the inner story, Uncle Julius McAdoo, a shrewd former field-hand slave who enriches his recollection of slavery with CONJURE STORIES and voodoo tales and folk practices and beliefs, is patterned after the trickster hero. While playing the expected "darkie" role, well-masked Uncle Julius illuminates the darker side of the "peculiar institution," disrupting the romantic historical and literary conventions in which antebellum life had been enshrined by the plantation traditions of southern local colorists Thomas Nelson Page (author of *Marse Chan and Other Stories*) and

Thomas Dixon (author of *Leopard's Spots*). Chesnutt also published his second collection of stories, *The Wife of His Youth,* in 1899. By the turn of the century, Chesnutt had gained visibility and recognition for his work, although he was not considered a master of the short story during his lifetime.

By 1904, Dunbar, whose reputation for his folk poetry written in dialect had made him the most notable black poet in the United States at the turn of the century, published three more collections of stories, *The Strength of Gideon and Other Stories* (1900), *In Old Plantation Days* (1903), and *The Heart of Happy Hollow* (1904). Unlike Chesnutt, however, Dunbar embraced prevailing stereotypical images of blacks, despite what some critics also see as an element of protest in his work. His romantic portrayal of slavery (about which he learned from his parents and free blacks), with loyal slaves and benevolent masters in particular, resonates with Page's view of slavery as the "good ole days." A reviewer of *In Old Plantation Days* ranked his treatment of plantation life above that of Page: "Dr. Thomas Nelson Page himself does not make 'ole Marse' and 'ole Miss' more admirable nor exalt higher in the slave the qualities of faithfulness and good humor" (quoted in Laryea 119). Despite the fact that Dunbar is often considered more a follower than a trailblazer like Chesnutt, together they successfully initiated the African-American short story before the HARLEM REN-AISSANCE of the 1920s marked the true maturation of the African-American literary tradition.

Alain Locke and Langston HUGHES's declarations in their respective essays "The New Negro" and "The Negro Artists and the Racial Mountain" register the spectrum and dynamic energy of the African-American-inspired communal transformation and celebration, often called the Harlem Renaissance, that was witnessed by post–WORLD WAR I America. After proclaiming that "the Old Negro had become more myth than a man," Locke politely requested that "the Negro of today be seen through other than the dusty spectacles of past controversy" (Locke 3, 5). In contrast, Hughes pugnaciously pronounced: "We younger artists who create now intend to express our individual dark-skinned selves without

fear of shame. . . . We build our temples for tomorrow, strong as we know how, and we stand on top of the mountain, free within ourselves" (Hughes 1,271).

Hughes and his contemporaries, Jean TOOMER, Zora Neale HURSTON, Claude McKay, Rudolph Fisher, Eric Walrond, Dorothy WEST, and others, found a ready venue for their work in such black-owned journals and newspaper as *Crisis, Opportunity,* and *Negro World,* which sponsored annual contests to showcase talented new writers. In Harlem, the spiritual center of the "renaissance," the writers empowered their own voices by founding *Fire!,* a magazine edited by Wallace Thurman, Hurston, and Hughes, but they also sought mainstream publishers such as Boni and Liveright, the publisher of Toomer's CANE (1923). Toomer's complex landscape of southern black life transcends the debasing legacy of the plantation tradition, as seen through the penetrating eyes and heard in the haunting blues voices of the characters that people his lyrical stories, including "Karintha," "Fern," and "Blood Burning Moon."

Hurston gained attention when her story "Spunk" won *Opportunity*'s second-place prize for fiction in 1925. She added a new horizon to this landscape by looking at the black imagined self in such now-classic stories as "SWEAT" and "The GILDED SIX BITS," in which the black community (such as fictional Eatontown) surfaces as a major character, if not the very nucleus of its people's lives. In these stories, Hurston successfully demonstrates that in contrast to the way whites view "darkies," as expressed by the shopkeeper in "Gilded Six Bits"—"Laughin' all the time. Nothin' worries 'em" (GSB 98)—black life is ebullient and complex. Although Hughes uses his stories to celebrate and "sing" all aspects of African-American life, including the prevalence of the extended black family structure, as found in "Thank You, M'am," one critic notes that his first published collection, *The Ways of White Folks* (1934), "excoriates the guile and mendacity, self-deception and equivocation, insincerity and sanctimoniousness, sham, humbug, and sheer fakery of white America in all its dealings with the black minority" (Bone

253). In his best-known stories, those about the folk
~~an philosopher Jesse B. Simple (see SIMPLE
Hughes strips bare the facade of Harlem's
ones to show the interior lives of its resi-
~iving these "darker" brothers and sisters
voice and wisdom. The works of two other writers
of the renaissance, *Ginger Town* (1932) and *Banana
Bottom* (1933) by McKay and *Tropic Death* (1926) by
Walrond, feature stories set in their homelands, a
Caribbean island and a Latin American nation,
respectively. In the end, one may argue that stories
by Harlem Renaissance writers, as typified through
these authors, reveal a quest to unravel and provide
"a definition of the role of black people in the
world" (Litz i).

It would take the stories of the pen-wielding
"native son" and paradigmatic "black boy,"
Mississippi-born novelist Richard WRIGHT, however,
to win the attention of mainstream critics. With a
marxist emphasis on class rather than race in the
experience of the southern black sharecroppers (the
proletariat) in such stories as "Bright and Morning
Star" and "Down by the Riverside" from his first collection of short stories, *Uncle Tom's Children* (1938),
Wright confirmed the "universality" and legitimacy
of the African-American experience as the serious
fictional subject of American REALISM and NATURAL-
ISM. This collection won him a $500 prize in a *Story*
magazine contest. In "BIG BOY LEAVES HOME" and also
the stories in *Eight Men* (1960), particularly "THE
MAN WHO WAS ALMOST A MAN," the author of *Native
Son* (1940), who concerned himself as much with
art as with message, provided insights into the
oppression experienced by those whose lives in the
margin were overtly or covertly governed by the JIM
CROW laws. Clearly recognized for his craftsmanship, Wright, according to Clarke, "was given the
recognition that Chesnutt and Dunbar deserved but
did not receive . . . With the emergence of Richard
Wright the double standard for black writers no
longer existed" (Clarke xviii).

The most visible immediate beneficiary of
Wright's impact was Frank Yerby. Although better
known as the author of historical novels, such as
The Foxes of Harrow (1946), which do not treat the
African-American experience, Yerby won the 1944
O. HENRY MEMORIAL AWARD for his short story "Health
Card," in which discrimination is the central theme.
Equally significant were the other writers of the
Wrightian school of literary naturalism, Ann PETRY,
author of *The Street* (1946), and Chester Himes,
author of *If He Hollers Let Him Go* (1945). Himes's
first short story, "Crazy in the Stir," was published in
Esquire magazine in 1934. Petry's nationally
acclaimed "LIKE A WINDING SHEET" was first published
in *The Crisis* (1945) and later included in Martha
Foley's *Best Short Stories of 1946;* it gained Petry a
Houghton Mifflin Literary Fellowship. Her collection of stories *Miss Muriel and Other Stories* was published in 1971.

Modern and contemporary African-American
writers who gained recognition for their fiction during the last half of the 20th century, from Ralph W.
Ellison, James BALDWIN, and Paule Marshall to
Ernest J. GAINES, Alice WALKER, Toni Morrison, and
John Edgar WIDEMAN, have all employed the short
story form. In fact, to A. Walton Litz's general contention that "No important American writer of fiction has neglected the short story form, and in the
case of many writers . . . the short story represented their greatest achievement" (Clarke xviii), one
can readily include African-American writers. Three
anthologies of African-American short stories clearly confirm the significance of the contribution of
blacks Americans to the genre: *Black American Short
Stories: One Hundred Years of the Best,* edited by John
Henrik Clarke (Hill and Wang, 1963 and 1993),
*Calling the Wind: Twentieth Century African-American
Short Stories,* edited by Clarence Major (Harper-
Perennial, 1993), and *Children of the Night: The Best
Short Stories by Black Writers, 1967 to the Present,*
edited by Gloria Naylor (Little, Brown and
Company, 1995). These anthologies include works
by such well-known writers as Maya Angelou, Toni
Cade BAMBARA, Cyrus COLTER, Samuel Delaney,
Alexis DeVeaux, Rita Dove, Henry Dumas, Rosa
Guy, Gayl Jones, LeRoi Jones (Amiri Baraka),
Charles Johnson, William Melvin Kelley, Randall
Kenan, Jamaica KINCAID, John O. Killens, Terry
McMillan, James Alan McPherson, Clarence Major,

Albert Murray, Gloria Naylor, Ntozake Shange, John A. Williams, and Sherley Anne Williams. In addition, to name but a few, are the names of Don Belton, Larry Duplechan, Tina McElroy, Richard Perry, and Ann Allen Shockley.

As a genre, the short story will remain a favorite among well-established writers, as is illustrated by novelist Wideman, among whose collections are *Damballah* (1981), *Fever: Twelve Stories* (1989), *The Stories of John Edgar Wideman* (1992), and *All Stories Are True* (1993). Perhaps no other writer than Wideman so represents the distance African-American writers have traveled from Chesnutt and Dunbar to gain recognition and respectability for their stories. Not surprisingly, Wideman, who served as guest editor of *The Best American Short Stories 1996,* published by Houghton Mifflin, called attention to the best African-American short story writer of this generation, William Henry Lewis (*In the Arms of Our Elders,* 1994), by including his award-winning and widely anthologized story "Shades" in the collection.

BIBLIOGRAPHY

Baker, Houston A., Jr. *Singers of Daybreak: Studies in Black American Literature.* Washington, D.C.: Howard University Press, 1983.

Bell, Bernard. *The Afro-American Novel and Its Tradition.* Amherst: University of Massachusetts Press, 1987.

Bone, Robert. *Down Home: A History of Afro-American Short Fiction from Its Beginnings to the End of the Harlem Renaissance.* New York: G. P. Putnam's Sons, 1975.

Bruck, Peter, and Wolfgang Karrer, eds. *The Afro-American Novel Since 1960.* Amsterdam: B. R. Grüner, 1982.

Byerman, Keith, ed. *John Edgar Wideman: A Study of the Short Fiction.* New York: Twayne Publishers, 1998.

Clarke, John. Introduction to *Black American Short Stories: One Hundred Years of the Best.* Edited by John Clarke, xv–xxi. New York: Hill and Wang, 1993.

Equiano, Olaudah. *The Interesting Narrative of the Life of Olaudah Equiano, Written by Himself In Classic Slave Narratives.* Edited by Henry Louis Gates, Jr. New York: Mentor, 1987.

Gates, Henry Louis, Jr. *The Signifying Monkey: A Theory of Afro-American Literary Criticism.* New York: Oxford University Press, 1988.

Gates, Henry Louis, Jr., et al., eds. *The Norton Anthology of African American Literature.* New York: W. W. Norton, 1997.

Hill, Patricia Liggins, and Bernard Bell, et al., eds. *Call and Response: The Riverside Anthology of the African American Literary Tradition.* Boston: Houghton Mifflin, 1998.

Hughes, Langston. "The Negro Artist and the Racial Mountain." In *The Norton Anthology of African American Literature.* Edited by Henry L. Gates, Jr., 1,267–71. New York: W. W. Norton, 1997.

Hurston, Zora Neale. "The Guilded Six-Bits." In *The Complete Stories.* New York: HarperCollins, 1995, p. 98.

Laryea, Doris Lucas. "Paul Laurence Dunbar." In *Dictionary of Literary Biography.* Edited by Trudier Harris and Thadious Davis. Vol. 50, 106–22. Detroit, Mich.: Gale Research, 1986.

Lee, Robert A., ed. *Black Fiction: New Studies in the Afro-American Novel Since 1945.* London: Vision Press, 1980.

Levine, Lawrene W. *Black Culture and Black Consciousness.* New York: Oxford University Press, 1977.

Litz, Walton. Preface to *Major American Short Stories.* Edited by A. Walton Litz. New York: Oxford University Press, 1980.

Locke, Alain. "The New Negro." In *The New Negro.* Edited by Alain Locke, 3–16. New York: Johnson Reprint Corporation, 1968.

McMillan, Terry, ed. *Breaking Ice: An Anthology of Contemporary African American Fiction.* With a preface by John Edgar Wideman. New York: Penguin Books, 1990.

Major, Clarence, ed. *Calling the Wind: Twentieth Century African-American Short Stories.* New York: HarperPerennial, 1993.

Naylor, Gloria, ed. *Children of the Night: The Best Short Stories by Black Writers, 1967 to the Present.* New York: Little, Brown, 1995.

Robinson, William R., ed. *Early Black American Prose.* Dubuque, Iowa: William C. Brown Company, 1991.

Turner, Darwin T. Introduction to *Black American Literature: Fiction.* Edited by Darwin T. Turner, 1–6. Columbus, Ohio: Charles E. Merrill Publishing, 1969.

Young, Al, ed. *African American Literature: A Brief Introduction and Anthology.* Berkeley: University of California Press, 1996.

Wilfred D. Samuels
University of Utah

AGRARIANS, THE A group of Southern writers, including John Crowe Ransom, Allan Tate, Donald Davidson, Robert Penn Warren, Merrill

Moore, Laura Riding, and Cleanth Brooks, also called the Fugitives, from the title of a magazine of poetry and criticism championing agrarian REGIONALISM that they published from 1922 to 1925. In 1930 they issued a collective manifesto, "I'll Take My Stand: The South and the Agrarian Tradition by Twelve Southerners," which espoused an agrarian economy over an industrial one. This group was also important for developing the NEW CRITICISM, in which they considered a literary work as an autonomous composition, removed from social, philosophical, or ethical considerations. This group is often given credit for energizing a literary renaissance in the South.

AIKEN, CONRAD (POTTER) (1889–1973)

Born in Savannah, Georgia, on August 5, 1889, and educated at Harvard University, Aiken was a writer who also worked as editor, journalist, and consultant in poetry to the Library of Congress in Washington, D.C. Author of seven novels, three story collections, numerous collections of poetry and one of literary criticism, he won numerous literary prizes—including the Pulitzer (1930) and the National Book Award (1954). Surprisingly, however, his stories have been dropped from most anthologies.

His first collection of short fiction, *Bring! Bring! and Other Stories* (1925), contains at the very least two mesmerizing stories of adolescent awakening: "Strange Moonlight" depicts the effects of a young girl's death on the preadolescent HERO, and "The Last Visit" relates a boy's final visit to his grandmother. According to Edward Butscher, looming in the background of these stories, as well as of the classic "Silent Snow, Secret Snow," are Aiken's own traumatic memories of his father's suicide after murdering Aiken's mother.

Although Aiken's second collection, *Costumes by Eros,* enjoyed less critical success, his third collection, *Among the Lost People,* contains at least three finely wrought and memorable stories: "Mr. Arcularis," "Impulse," and "Silent Snow, Secret Snow," the most famous and, until recently, the most frequently anthologized. "Mr. Arcularis" evokes the "raging insecurity of a traumatized child now grown into a friendless old man" who, lies dying on an operating table (Butscher, "Conrad Aiken," 19). The main character in "Impulse," seems a younger version of Mr. Arcularis. "Impulse" addresses the prototypical American dilemma of immature men compelling mature women to assume the features of a monstrous mother. "Silent Snow, Secret Snow," a horror story in the manner of Edgar Allan POE, builds almost unbearable suspense in the reader as the young boy, Paul Hasleman, hears the soft and sibilant whispers of the falling snow creeping ever nearer until it will engulf his consciousness and likely his soul. Although critics, referring to Aiken's father's insanity as well as Aiken's fascination with psychology, commonly interpret the snow as a METAPHOR for the onset of mental disease (psychosis or schizophrenia), readers might also see the snow as the more traditional metaphor of death. The spellbinding quality, the inexorable use of the IMAGERY of coldness, and the realistic look inside Paul's mind guarantee the unforgettable effects of "Silent Snow, Secret Snow" on all readers.

BIBLIOGRAPHY

Aiken, Conrad. *Among the Lost People.* New York: Scribner, 1934.

——. *Bring! Bring! and Other Stories.* New York: Boni & Liveright, 1925.

——. *The Collected Short Stories.* Cleveland: World Publishing Co., 1960.

——. *Costumes by Eros.* New York: Scribner, 1928.

——. *The Short Stories of Conrad Aiken.* New York: Duell, Sloan and Pearce, 1950.

Butscher, Edward. *Aiken: Poet of White Horse Vale.* Athens: University of Georgia Press, 1988.

——. "Conrad Aiken." *Reference Guide to Short Fiction.* Edited by Noelle Watson. Detroit: Gale Press, 1994, pp. 18–19.

Denney, Reuel. *Aiken.* Minneapolis: University of Minnesota Press, 1964.

Hoffman, Frederick John. *Aiken.* New York: Twayne, 1962.

Lorenz, Clarissa M. *Lorelei Two: My Life with Aiken.* Athens: University of Georgia Press, 1983.

Marten, Harry. *The Art of Knowing: The Poetry and Prose of Aiken.* Columbia: University of Missouri Press, 1988.

Martin, Jay. *Aiken: A Life of His Art.* Princeton, N.J.: Princeton University Press, 1962.

Spivey, Ted Ray and Arthur Waterman, eds. *Aiken: A Priest of Consciousness*. New York: AMS Press, 1989.

Stevick, Philip. *The American Short Story, 1900–1945: A Critical History*. Boston: Twayne, 1984.

ALBEE, EDWARD (FRANKLIN) (1928–   )

Adopted grandson of Edward Franklin Albee, owner of the Keith-Albee vaudeville theaters, Albee in his youth lived the traveling life of his wealthy Westchester County adoptive parents. Although primarily known as a playwright, Albee helped popularize the theater of the absurd in numerous plays that adapted NOVELLAs and stories such as "The BALLAD OF THE SAD CAFE" by Carson MCCULLERS and "Bartleby the Scrivener," by Herman MELVILLE, as well as fiction by James Purdy, Giles Cooper, and Vladimir NABOKOV. From 1953, when Thornton Wilder encouraged him to try playwriting, Albee immersed himself in presentations of Theater of the Absurd plays by Europeans writing in this mode. With the production of the Broadway play *Who's Afraid of Virginia Woolf?* in 1962, Albee was hailed as a major new voice in the theater and excoriated as a writer of vulgar plays, but his vision dramatized American stories from both the 19th and 20th centuries.

ALCOTT, LOUISA MAY (1832–1888)

Although Louisa May Alcott was dubbed "The Children's Friend" by her first biographer, Ednah Dow Chaney, and her reputation rested on the particular strength of *Little Women* for nearly the next 100 years, the literary detective work of her modern biographer Madeleine Stern has resulted in an awareness of the breadth of Alcott's work. In addition to eight children's novels and an original collection of FAIRY TALES, Alcott also wrote three adult books and numerous short stories, many of which were published in "respectable" 19th-century periodicals such as *The Youth's Companion, Merry's Museum* (which Alcott also edited for a time), *The Commonwealth, The Independent, The Woman's Journal,* and *The Atlantic Monthly.* Alcott also published a number of other stories either anonymously or pseudonymously in the more torrid pages of Frank Leslie's *Illustrated Newspaper* and *The Flag of Our Union.* Whether children's fiction, adult fiction, or sensational fiction, two elements characterize Alcott's work: a professional writer's awareness of the conventions of the GENREs in which she wrote and a commitment to societal reform. Caught up in the fervor for reform in 19th-century America, Alcott was interested in education, abolition, women's rights, and temperance, among other issues; she used to sign her letters "Yours for reform of all kinds." She included radical themes within her work, often stretching the boundaries of the genres themselves.

Born in Germantown, Pennsylvania, Alcott spent most of her life in and around Concord and Boston, Massachusetts, drawn to that area by her father's opportunity to head a school in which he could put his reformist educational theories into practice. After his Temple School closed in 1840, Amos Bronson Alcott involved his wife and four daughters in a short-lived experiment in communal living at a farm called Fruitlands in 1843–44, which Louisa satirized nearly 30 years later in her short story, "TRANSCENDENTAL WILD OATS" (1873). Her father's Transcendentalist (see TRANSCENDENTALISM) inclinations brought to the family such friends as Ralph Waldo Emerson and Henry David Thoreau, but little income. When Alcott's mother, the more practical Abba May Alcott, founded an employment agency in Boston in order to provide for her family, Louisa and her sisters also sought whatever work was available to 19th-century women—household servant, teacher, governness, seamstress—but Louisa was also writing. Her brief experience as a CIVIL WAR nurse resulted in the novel *Hospital Sketches* (1863), which first brought her substantial public attention and encouraged her to publish *Moods* the following year.

Alcott, however, had also submitted a sensational short story, "Pauline's Passion and Punishment," to a contest sponsored by Frank Leslie's *Illustrated Newspaper,* and its publication in 1862, along with a $100 prize, encouraged a career in the papers that published short stories, a career that lasted through the 1860s and brought substantial income to the family, even though she never attached her name to these stories. The best of them are well-crafted tales of intrigue with complex female characters, such as "A Nurse's Story" (published in Frank Leslie's *Chimney Corner* in 1865–66) and "BEHIND A MASK" (published in *The Flag of Our Union* in several installments in 1866), whose republication beginning in 1975 launched the modern reconsideration of Alcott, especially her feminism. (See FEMINIST.) With the publication of *Little Women* in 1868, Alcott found herself suddenly wealthy and famous; "A March Christmas," an excerpt from the novel, has been reprinted so frequently that it has taken on a permanent life of its own as a Christmas story. She devoted herself increasingly to the demands of children's fiction the rest of her life, although she also was able to finish the long-abandoned manuscript of her adult novel, *Work,* which was published in 1873. Alcott died in 1888 from long-term effects of mercury poisoning, a result of the medication for the typhus she contracted during her stint as a Civil War nurse.

In all the genres in which she wrote, Alcott translated her life and reading experiences (particularly the work of Ralph Waldo Emerson, Nathaniel HAWTHORNE, Henry David Thoreau, Johann Wolfgang von Goethe, and Charlotte Brontë) into fiction that argued for the practical application of the ideals she valued. One attitude that cuts across all genres is her feminism. Alcott herself never married, and whether she is promoting individual career choices for her women in *Little Women* or in *Jo's Boys* (1886), depicting the struggles of women limited by society in *Moods* and *Work,* or raging against those limitations in darker works such as "Behind a Mask" (subtitled "A Woman's Power"), her commitment to choice is as clear as her understanding of how to present that THEME to each particular audience. Fascinating female characters, perceptive depictions of mother-daughter relationships, multithreaded PLOT structures, and realistic detail and dialogue in her work still bring 19th-century New England to life for modern readers.

BIBLIOGRAPHY
Alcott, Louisa May. *The Journals of Louisa May Alcott.* Athens: University of Georgia Press, 1989.
———. *Louisa May Alcott Unmasked: Collected Thrillers.* Boston: Northeastern University Press, 1995.
———. *The Selected Letters of Louisa May Alcott.* Boston: Little, Brown, 1987.
Bedell, Madelon. *The Alcotts: Biography of a Family.* New York: C. N. Potter, 1980.
Cheney, Ednah Dow. *Louisa May Alcott: Her Life, Letters, and Journals.* Boston: Roberts Brothers, 1889.
Elbert, Sarah. *A Hunger for Home: Louisa May Alcott and Little Women.* Philadelphia: Temple University Press, 1984.
Keyser, Elizabeth. *Whispers in the Dark: The Fiction of Louisa May Alcott.* Knoxville: University of Tennessee Press, 1993.
MacDonald, Ruth. *Louisa May Alcott.* Boston: Twayne, 1983.
Showalter, Elaine. "Introduction to Alternative Alcott." In *Louisa May Alcott, Alternative Alcott.* New Brunswick, N.J.: Rutgers University Press, 1988, p. xlviii.
———. *Sisters Choice.* New York: Oxford University Press, 1991.
Stern, Madeleine. *Critical Essay on Louisa May Alcott.* Boston: G.K. Hall, 1984.
———. *Louisa May Alcott.* Norman: University of Oklahoma Press, 1950.

Christine Doyle Francis
Central Connecticut State University

ALECK MAURY   A memorable character in Caroline GORDON's short stories tracing the life of an American sportsman, with detail comparable to those in the hunting and fishing tales of Ernest HEMINGWAY and William FAULKNER. The episodic novel *Aleck Maury, Sportsman* contains most of this material, as do the stories "Old Red," "The Presence," "One More Day," "To Thy Chamber Window, Sweet," and "The Last Day in the Field." Maury, a classics teacher known as "professor," is a Southern gentleman farmer, and his devotion to the outdoors constitutes a genuine philosophy, not a hobby. Constantly escaping his home and family, Aleck is compared to "Old Red," the fox; like the fox, Aleck is hunted, but through his wiliness he evades those who would end his freedom. In ill health and old age, Aleck's ritualistic farewell to the hunt, depicted in "The Last Day in the Field," is comparable to similar scenes in Faulkner's "THE BEAR" in GO DOWN, MOSES.

ALEXIE, SHERMAN (1966–) A Spokane/Coeur d'Alene Indian from Seattle, Washington, Sherman Alexie has earned high praise for his poetry and fiction, particularly for his short stories. Alexie's acclaimed *The Lone Ranger and Tonto Fistfight in Heaven,* first published in 1993, is a collection of 22 starkly lyrical and disturbing stories set in and around the Spokane Indian Reservation. His second SHORT STORY CYCLE, *Reservation Blues,* was published in 1996 and, following the same structure, features several characters from *The Lone Ranger and Tonto Fistfight in Heaven.*

In *The Lone Ranger and Tonto Fistfight in Heaven,* Alexie relates these linked stories through a powerful and direct first-person narrator (see POINT OF VIEW) who offers insights into the past as well as the present, alleviating suffering with occasional injections of wry humor, a traditional NATIVE AMERICAN antidote to pain. Thomas-Builds-the-Fire, the storyteller who has trouble finding an audience, can recall and describe, in magical realist (see MAGIC REALISM) and mythic fashion (see MYTH), events in which he participated in the distant past. Aunt Nezzy sews a traditional long beaded dress that turns out to be too heavy to wear, but she believes that the woman who can bear the weight of it will be the salvation of everyone. Jimmy Many Horses III is dying of cancer. The nine-year-old Victor snuggles next to his alcoholic parents, believing that the liquor fumes will help him sleep. Alexie transformed *The Lone Ranger and Tonto Fistfight in Heaven* into a screenplay for the film *Smoke Signals.*

Reservation Blues is again a blend of the direct and the magical, with its starting point in a long-dead blues singer, Robert Johnson, who, with his magic guitar, appears to Thomas Builds-the-Fire on the Spokane Reservation in eastern Washington. As a result, Thomas and his friends form Coyote Springs, an all-Indian Catholic rock band. The group tours the country, from Seattle to New York, in search of adventure and of their own identities.

Sherman Alexie is also the author of the recently published novel *Indian Killer* (1998) and three collections of poetry. In all his work, he depicts the distances between Indians and whites, reservation Indians and urban Indians, men and women, and modern Indians and the traditions of the past.

BIBLIOGRAPHY

Alexie, Sherman. *The Business of Fancydancing: Stories and Poems.* Brooklyn, N.Y.: Hanging Loose Press, 1992.

———. *First Indian on the Moon.* Brooklyn, N.Y.: Hanging Loose Press, 1993.

———. *Indian Killer.* New York: Warner Books, 1998.

———. *The Lone Ranger and Tonto Fistfight in Heaven.* New York: Atlantic Monthly Press, 1993.

———. *The Man Who Loves Salmon.* Boise, Idaho: Limberlost Press, 1998.

———. *Old Shirts & New Skins.* Elizabeth Woody, illust. Los Angeles: American Indian Studies Center, 1993.

———. *Reservation Blues.* New York: Warner Books, 1996.

———. *The Summer of Black Widows.* Brooklyn, N.Y.: Hanging Loose Press, 1996.

———. *Water Flowing Home: Poems by Sherman Alexie.* Boise, Idaho: Limberlost Press, 1995.

ALGER, HORATIO (1834–1899) A very popular author of boys' stories who wrote more than 100 books. His HEROES are newsboys, bootblacks, and similar characters who struggle against poverty and adversity, achieving success through hard work, self-reliance, and virtuous behavior. The Horatio Alger hero typically appears in such works as The Ragged Dick Series (1869), The Luck and Pluck Series (1869), and The Tattered Tom Series (1871). The theme of these stories expresses an American ideal; as a result, the true-life account of anyone who rises from "rags to riches" through personal virtue and industry may be referred to as a "true Horatio Alger story."

ALGONQUIN ROUND TABLE In the 1920s, a number of brilliant writers and others associated with the arts and literature began having lunch together regularly at the Algonquin Hotel in New York City. Among the earliest members of this group were Dorothy PARKER, Robert Benchley, and Robert Sherwood. Membership was by invitation only and

grew to include such luminaries as Alexander Woollcott, columnists Heywood Brown and Franklin Adams, playwrights George Kaufman and Marc Connelly, songwriter Irving Berlin, editor and founder of the *New Yorker* Harold Ross, and writers Edna FERBER and F. Scott FITZGERALD. They became famous for clever repartée distinguished by the barb, and blistering insults delivered cooly to friend and foe alike.

ALGREN, NELSON (1909–1981)

Born Nelson Algren Abraham, Algren wrote brutally realistic novels and stories about life in the Chicago slums. His first book, written in the depths of the GREAT DEPRESSION, was *Somebody in Boots* (1935), a proletarian or social protest novel. (See PROLETARIAN LITERATURE.) This was followed by *Never Come Morning* (1942), *The Man with the Golden Arm* (1949), and *A Walk on the Wild Side* (1956). Algren won the National Book Award for *The Man with the Golden Arm,* and *A Walk on the Wild Side* won high critical acclaim as perhaps the most influential comic novel to come out of the 1950s and as a precursor of the wild-sidedness of Ken Kesey's *One Flew Over the Cuckoo's Nest* and Joseph Heller's *Catch-22.* These novels, as well as his collection of stories, *The Neon Wilderness* (1947), depict the human casualties of a bleak urban landscape. Algren is often grouped with Richard WRIGHT and James T. Farrell, who wrote about similar themes in a Chicago setting.

Despite a reputation built largely on novels, however, Algren wrote more than 50 short stories that appeared in such disparate publications as *The Kenyon Review* and *Noble Savage, The Atlantic,* SATURDAY EVENING POST, ESQUIRE, *Playboy,* and *Dude.* Algren carefully chose his collection of 18 stories in *The Neon Wilderness* to include most of his best tales. He collected no others out of the dozens he wrote over the next nearly 40 years, although he included a few previously published stories, along with essays and poems, in *The Last Carousel.* Although no longer anthologized frequently, his two best stories are almost surely "A Bottle of Milk for Mother" and "How the Devil Came Down Division Street." Drug addiction, alcohol abuse, prostitution, gambling, prizefighting, and jail are the subjects of Algren's stories, both short and long. The characters are generally losers who frequent bars, brothels, and fleabag tenements or hotels. They live in a depressing, violent, naturalistic (see NATURALISM) world, but the depression is softened by Algren's sense of the gently comic and the ironic that pervades both the novels and the stories (see COMEDY and IRONY).

BIBLIOGRAPHY

Algren, Nelson. *The Last Carousel.* New York: Putnam, 1973.

———. *The Man With the Golden Arm.* Garden City, N.Y.: Doubleday, 1949.

———. *The Neon Wilderness.* Garden City, N.Y.: Doubleday, 1947.

———. *Never Come Morning.* New York: Harper & Brothers, 1942.

———. *A Walk on the Wild Side.* New York: Farrar, Straus & Cudahy, 1956.

———. *Somebody in Boots.* New York: Vanguard Press, 1935.

Cox, Martha Heasley and Wayne Chatterton. *Algren.* Boston: Twayne, 1975.

Drew, Bettina. *Algren: A Life on the Wild Side.* New York: Putnam, 1989.

Giles, James Richard. *Confronting the Horror: The Novels of Nelson Algren.* Kent, Ohio: Kent State University Press, 1989.

ALHAMBRA, THE (1832).

See IRVING, WASHINGTON.

ALIBI IKE

Appearing in Ring LARDNER's story "Alibi Ike," this character is a reincarnation of the hero of the FRONTIER HUMORIST tradition, carrying a bat and glove instead of a musket and powder. It does not matter to his fans that Alibi Ike, one of Lardner's best known creations, is semiilliterate. The fact that he is a baseball player is enough to cover him with glory. He displays the virtues of speed, agility, strength, endurance, along with the ethics of fair play and team play. He is crude and naive, with an excuse a minute, but he was a great favorite in the 1920s and became an American myth.

ALIDA SLADE

The ruddy complexioned, dark-browed friend of Grace Ansley in Edith WHAR-

TON'S "ROMAN FEVER." Wharton likely confused the two friends' portraits deliberately—all first-time readers have trouble distinguishing the two, despite Wharton's description of Grace as smaller and paler than Alida. The author emphasizes the similarity of their situations as women while simultaneously showing their lack of knowledge of each other. Readers generally tend to have less sympathy for Alida than for Grace, but careful reading reveals the pathetic emptiness of Alida's life as young woman, wife, and widow. Both she and Grace are mothers, and both have daughters, but Alida receives the ultimate surprise at the end of the story when she learns that Grace had a secret and that Alida's daughter Jenny has a stepsister.

ALLEGORY
A narrative in which agents and action, and sometimes setting as well, are contrived to signify a second, related order. There are two main types: historical and political allegory, in which the characters and action represent, or "allegorize," historical personages and events; and the allegory of ideas, in which the characters represent abstract concepts and the plot serves to communicate a doctrine or thesis. See, for example, Herman MELVILLE's BILLY BUDD, SAILOR, in which Billy appears as a Christ figure, or Joyce Carol OATES's WHERE ARE YOU GOING, WHERE HAVE YOU BEEN?" in which the teenage CONNIE represents Eve before the Fall on one hand and a decadent consumer society on the other.

ALLEN, PAULA GUNN (1939–   )
Paula Gunn Allen grew up in Cubero, New Mexico, a small town between the Laguna and Acoma Pueblo reservations. Of German, Laguna, Pueblo, Lebanese, Scottish, and Sioux descent, she points out that people of the Laguna Pueblo have long intermarried with others and often refers to herself as a "multicultural event." A creative writer, scholar, and teacher, she was a pivotal force in the Native American Renaissance of the early 1970s and has earned numerous accolades, including an American Book Award from the Before Columbus Foundation. Her work appears in more than 60 anthologies, ranging from mainstream publications to specialized collections that feature writings by literary theorists, women of color, and lesbians.

Allen's fiction, poetry, and scholarship reveal a range of cross-cultural sensibilities, bridging differences between such disparate perspectives as American Indian and European, reservation and urban, spiritual and academic, and traditional and mixed blood. At the same time, in all her stories she remains firmly grounded in her mother's Laguna Pueblo culture. In nearly every tale Allen demonstrates the central position of identity and culture, and thus she interweaves personal, family, and historical accounts with mythic stories from the Pueblo oral tradition. One such storytelling figure animates all of her writing: the Grandmother Spider from Cherokee and Laguna creation tales, who spins stories to ensure the survival of the people and whose intricate web sustains the relationships among the land, the communities that inhabit it, and the creative forces of the universe.

Even Allen's autobiographical novel, *The Woman Who Owned the Shadows* (1983), is actually a book about the importance of stories. Her PROTAGONIST, who feels at home neither in the Southwest nor San Francisco, recovers from a nervous breakdown, the death of her infant son, divorce, and near suicide by learning to understand her place in the old stories. With the aid of Grandmother Spider, she realizes that her life and the lives of her mother and grandmother parallel characters and incidents in ancient tribal narratives.

Allen is perhaps most recognized for *The Sacred Hoop: Recovering the Feminine in American Indian Traditions* (1986), a landmark collection of essays that asserts the resilience of Native women's spiritual traditions. Fusing personal, historical, and literary-critical perspectives, Allen explains the central concerns in her work, including the influence of story and ceremony on contemporary American Indian literature, the crucial role of Native American women in sustaining cultural traditions, the challenges faced by a mixed-blood writer, and the place of FEMINIST and lesbian perspectives in Native American studies.

In 1989 Allen edited *Spider Woman's Granddaughters,* the first collection of traditional and contemporary stories by Native American women. This volume distills materials from the written forms in which they had been previously published, such as "as-told-to" ethnologies or novels, and reorganizes them into sequences that reflect tribal oral traditions. Thus Delia Oshogay's rendition of the traditional Anishinabeg story "Oshkikwe's Baby" is connected to the retelling of Anishinabeg traditions in Louise ERDRICH's short story "American Horse"; an Okanogan COYOTE STORY is retold in "The Story of Green-Blanket Feet," excerpted from Humishima's novel *Cogewea, The Half-Blood;* and two versions of a Cochita Pueblo traditional Yellow Woman (the earth mother or corn mother figure) story appear next to modern retellings by Allen and her Laguna Pueblo cousin Leslie SILKO.

Allen further helped to usher Native American literature into the mainstream by editing two subsequent anthologies, *Grandmothers of the Light: A Medicine Woman's Source Book* (1991) and *Voice of the Turtle: American Indian Literature 1900–1970* (1994). In these collections, she identifies connections among multiple oral and written traditions.

As Allen's often-anthologized poem "Grandmother" suggests, reclaiming lost tribal practices, or "mending the tear with string," requires not only linking one's craft to traditional Pueblo arts, such as weaving and storytelling, but also creating new patterns and new stories. Occasionally Allen assumes the role of a TRICKSTER, using humor to disrupt academic or moral pieties. Her story "A Hot Time" (*Grandmothers of the Light*) features Grandmother Spider in a wry commentary on the "supposed infirmities of old age." In her work-in-progress *Raven's Road,* which she describes as a "medicine-dyke novel" (Coltelli, 33), the face of an old woman emerges in a test explosion of the atom bomb, suggesting a potent link between Yellow Woman and the uranium mined from Laguna lands. As Allen explains in an interview with Donna Perry, she remains committed to her role as a third-world woman writer who must challenge each of her multiple audiences.

BIBLIOGRAPHY

Allen, Paula Gunn. *The Woman Who Owned the Shadows.* San Francisco: Spinsters Ink, 1983.
———. *The Sacred Hoop: Recovering the Feminine in American Indian Traditions.* Boston: Beacon Press, 1986.
———. *Spider Woman's Granddaughters: Traditional Tales and Contemporary Writing by Native American Women.* Boston: Beacon Press, 1989.
———. *Grandmothers of the Light: A Medicine Woman's Source Book.* Boston: Beacon Press, 1992.
———. *Voice of the Turtle: American Indian Literature 1900–1970.* New York: Ballantine Books, 1994.
Bataille, Gretchen M., and Kathleen Mullen Sands. *American Indian Women: Telling Their Lives.* Lincoln: University of Nebraska Press, 1984.
Bruchac, Joseph. *Survival This Way: Interviews with American Indian Poets.* Tucson, Ariz.: Sun Tracks University of Arizona Press, 1987.
Coltelli, Laura. *Winged Words: American Indian Writers Speak.* Lincoln: University of Nebraska Press, 1990.
Eysturoy, Annie O. *This Is About Vision: Interviews with Southwestern Writers* Albuquerque: University of New Mexico Press, 1990.
Jahner, Elaine. "A Laddered, Rain-bearing Rug: Paula Gunn Allen's Poetry." In *Women and Western American Literature.* Edited by Helen Winter and Susan Rosowski. Troy, N.Y.: Whitson Publishing Co., 1982.
Lincoln, Kenneth. *Native American Renaissance.* Berkeley: University of California Press, 1983.
Perry, Donna. *Backtalk: Women Writers Speak Out: Interviews.* New Brunswick, N.J.: Rutgers University Press, 1993.
Ruoff, A. LaVonne Brown. *American Indian Literatures: An Introduction, Bibliographic Review, and Selected Bibliography.* New York: Modern Language Association of America, 1990.
Ruppert, Jim. "Paula Gunn Allen." In *Dictionary of Native American Literature.* Edited by Andrew Wiget. New York: Garland, 1994.
Smith, Lucinda Irwin. *Women Who Write,* Volume II. New York: J. Messner, 1994.
TallMountain, Mary. "You Can Go Home Again." In *I Tell You Now: Autobiographical Essays by Native American Writers.* Edited by Brian Swann and Arnold Krupat. Lincoln: University of Nebraska Press, 1987.

Lauren Stuart Miller
University of California at Berkeley

ALLISON, DOROTHY (1949–) Long
before her seemingly sudden rise to best-seller fame
with the novel *Bastard Out of Carolina,* Dorothy
Allison earned a devoted gay and lesbian following
with the publication of her poetry in *The Women
Who Hate Me* (1983) and her first collection of
short stories, *Trash* (1988). *Trash* garnered two
Lambda Literary Awards, for Best Small Press Book
and Best Lesbian Book. The stories in *Trash* offer up
the pain and passion of poor "white-trash" women
trying to assimilate in the world of lesbian middle-
class, college-educated life. In a recent interview,
Allison recalls living in a Tallahasse, Florida, les-
bian-FEMINIST collective in 1973, and the debt she
owes those women who stopped her from burning
her stories. Much material from the stories collected in *Trash* provided the basis for her first novel.
Bastard, which was a finalist for the 1992 National
Book Award, is a largely autobiographical story
focusing on the extended Boatwright family
through the eyes of Bone, the bastard daughter of
waitress Anney Boatwright. Bone's life is a harrowing tale of incest, abuse, and survival.

Following the success of *Bastard,* Allison published the nonfiction works *Skin: Talking About Sex,
Class & Literature* and *Two or Three Things I Know for
Sure,* the latter a memoir in which Allison weaves
together stories about her mother, aunts, sisters, and
cousins. If *Trash* reflects the conflicted confusion
from which emerged her desire to live, *Skin* provides
a valuable demonstration of Allison's growth
between *Trash* and *Two or Three Things.* In *Skin,* she
analyzes, measures, and draws conclusions not only
about her subject matter but also about her own
philosophy. By the time she wrote *Two or Three
Things,* then, Allison understood the central significance of stories to both her worldview and to her
art; indeed, the opening line is "Let me tell you a
story" (1). Her second novel, *Cavedweller,* appeared
in 1998.

In all of her work, Allison presents the lives of
poor white Americans, particularly women, without
romanticizing or flattening them. She draws heavily
from her own painful childhood in the South and

offers a prose style that is sharp-edged and riveting.
Allison's work adds another dimension to Southern
literature and its attendant themes of tormented sexuality, victimized women and children, and men
and women who cannot realize their dreams
because of their class.

The first in her family to graduate from high
school, Allison earned a bachelor's degree from
Florida Presbyterian College and a master's degree
from New York's New School of Social Research. In
the 1960s, she became a feminist activist and spent
the next 20 years editing and writing for lesbian and
feminist presses. She has taught at Florida State
University, Rutgers, Wesleyan, and the San
Francisco Art Institute. She now resides in
California with her partner and their son.

BIBLIOGRAPHY
Allison, Dorothy. *Bastard Out of Carolina.* New York: Dutton,
1992.
———. *Skin: Talking About Sex, Class & Literature.* Ithaca,
N.Y.: Firebrand Books, 1994.
———. *Trash.* Ithaca, N.Y.: Firebrand Books, 1988.
———. *Two or Three Things I Know for Sure.* New York:
Dutton, 1995.
———. *The Women Who Hate Me.* Brooklyn, N.Y.: Long
Haul Press, 1983.

Susan Thurston Hamerski
St. Olaf College

ALL STORIES ARE TRUE JOHN EDGAR
WIDEMAN (1992)   Originally a section of new
stories written especially for the larger collection *All
Stories Are True: The Stories of John Edgar Wideman*
(1992), *All Stories Are True* was published separately
in 1992. The title comes from a statement by the
Nigerian writer Chinua Achebe: "All stories are true,
the Igbo say." WIDEMAN uses this saying as a controlling METAPHOR for these stories of family, friends, and
community members dealing with the pain and
anguish of racism in contemporary America. The
stories in the collection comment on and support
one another through the power of memory and connection just as members of a family or a community sustain their own. Thus these stories do not
reflect a single narrative voice but, in typical post-

modern fashion (see POSTMODERNISM) many voices. Like a jazz piece, "Everybody Loves Bubba Riff" captures the orchestra of these multiple voices in a single, unpunctuated sentence as a community mourns the death of a young man. The title story, "All Stories Are True," continues stories of Wideman's mother and the fictional counterpart of his brother, Robby (here called Tommy), begun in his first short story collection, *Damballah* (1980). Other stories include "Casa Grande" and "Signs," a story about a young teacher receiving racist letters.

Tracie Guzzio
Ohio University

ALLUSION   An implied or indirect reference to a person, place, or event in history or previous literature. A terse allusion may be laden with relevant associations that amplify the emotions or ideas in a work of literature and connect them with the emotions or ideas of a previous work or historical event. In Joyce Carol Oates's "WHERE ARE YOU GOING, WHERE HAVE YOU BEEN?," for example, the reference to ARNOLD FRIEND's ill-fitting boots suggests an allusion to the cloven-hoofed devil, and intensifies Arnold's position as the PERSONIFICATION of evil that the young CONNIE faces in her valueless world.

ALTER EGO   Literally, a second self or an inseparable friend. In literature, critics sometimes view a fictional character as the author's alter ego: In Andre DUBUS's short story "Cadence," for example, the young Paul Clement appears to be an alter ego for Dubus, or in F. Scott Fitzgerald's "BABYLON REVISITED," CHARLIE WALES appears to be an alter ego for Fitzgerald. The term may also apply to two fictional characters to mean a double or DOPPELGANGER. For instance, In Henry JAMES's "THE JOLLY CORNER," the kindly Spencer is determined to meet his alter ego—the calculating businessman he might have become had he stayed in New York—in the house on the jolly corner.

AMBIGUITY   Commonly, "ambiguity" characterizes a statement that, intentionally or unintentionally, contains two or more incompatible or contradictory meanings. In literature, the term also refers to a word or idea that implies more than one meaning and usually leaves the reader feeling uncertain. Writers may use deliberate ambiguity to great effect, as when two or more diverse connotations have equal relevance. (See CONNOTATION AND DENOTATION.) See, for example, Herman MELVILLE's use of ambiguity in "BENITO CERINO."

AMERICAN ADAM   A term coined by R. W. B. Lewis in his book *The American Adam* (1955) to describe a literary theme and phenomenon in American literature, a theme he traces from the second quarter of the 19th century into the 20th: the American as an innocent abroad, a naïf subject to the cynical manipulations of worldly, conniving Europeans. The prototypes may encounter the evil closer to home, however, and may generally be viewed as innocents with unfulfilled potential, poised on the edge of a new life; they include such characters as Nathaniel HAWTHORNE's protagonist in "YOUNG GOODMAN BROWN," Herman MELVILLE's in "BILLY BUDD, SAILOR," Mark TWAIN's in *Huckleberry Finn* (1884), and Henry JAMES's Christopher Newman in *The American* (1877). James's tragic, innocent young woman in DAISY MILLER: A STUDY also exemplifies the theme. In the 20th century, Adamic protagonists who leave an EDEN-like setting to grapple with evil include Sherwood ANDERSON's GEORGE WILLARD, Ernest HEMINGWAY's NICK ADAMS, Katherine Anne PORTER's MIRANDA RHEA, and William FAULKNER's ISAAC (IKE) MCCASLIN. In contemporary literature, the Adamic figure appears frequently in stories featuring loners, outcasts, and misfits.

BIBLIOGRAPHY
Lewis, R. W. B. *The American Adam: Innocence, Tragedy, and Tradition in the Nineteenth Century.* Chicago: University of Chicago Press, 1955.

AMERICAN DREAM   A term originally used to define the aspiration peculiar to Americans in both life and fiction: to rise above one's situation at birth, to live self-sufficiently without financial worries, and to own land. Perhaps the best-known fictional articulation of the American dream occurs in John Steinbeck's *Of Mice and Men* (1937), in which the protagonist, George, repeatedly reminds his friend Lennie that one day they will stop working for another man, buy their own house, raise their own livestock, and "live off the fat of the land." Many writers, especially contemporary ones—Toni MORRISON, to cite just one example—demonstrate that the American dream has been accessible only to a privileged few. Others—Joyce Carol OATES, for example—suggest that even if attained, the dream is essentially hollow at its core. John BARTH has been credited with an updated metaphor for contemporary Americans and the dream in the title of his short story "LOST IN THE FUNHOUSE."

AMERICAN REVOLUTION (1775–1783)

Relations between Great Britain and its 13 colonies in North America had been deteriorating since the mid-1760s, when the British government passed a series of laws to increase its control over the colonies. Among these was the Proclamation of 1763 to halt the expansion of American colonies beyond the Appalachian Mountains; the Revenue Act of 1764 (the Sugar Act), which taxed molasses; the Quartering and Stamp Acts (1765), which made colonists pay part of the cost of stationing British troops in America and pay for tax stamps placed on newspapers, diplomas, and various legal documents; and the Townshend Acts of 1767, which placed duties on imported glass, lead, paper, and tea. Although the British Parliament canceled all Townshend duties except the one on tea in 1770, the basic issue of "taxation without representation" remained unresolved with many colonists who lived far from Britain and had become increasingly self-reliant. The passage in Britain of the Tea Act of 1773, which allowed the East India Company to sell its tea for less than smuggled Netherlands tea in the colonies, resulted in the Boston Tea Party later that year when patriots led by Samuel Adams disguised themselves as Indians, boarded British ships, and dumped their cargoes of tea into Boston Harbor. This revolt led to the Intolerable Acts of 1774, which closed Boston Harbor, restricted the Massachusetts legislature, and gave virtual dictatorial powers to the governor appointed by the king.

In response, the First Continental Congress met in Philadelphia in September 1774 and voted to cut off colonial trade with Britain unless the Intolerable Acts were repealed. They were not. In April 1775 fighting erupted between American patriots and British troops at Lexington and Concord, Massachusetts. The Second Continental Congress began meeting in Philadelphia in May 1775, established the Continental Army in June, and named George Washington the army's commander. In July 1775 the Congress approved the Olive Branch Petition, which declared that the colonies were loyal to the king and urged him to remedy their complaints. King George III ignored the petition and in August 1775 declared the colonies to be in rebellion; the British Parliament closed all American ports to overseas trade. Those actions convinced many delegates that a peaceful settlement of differences with Britain was impossible. Therefore, support for American independence continued to build. On July 4, 1776, the Congress adopted the Declaration of Independence and the United States of America was born.

Militarily, although the patriots won several victories in New England and the Southern colonies during the early months of the war, the British greatly outnumbered and outgunned the Continental Army. Daring leadership on the American side provided the edge. The defeat of General John Burgoyne's forces and the surrender of 6,000 British troops to General Horatio Gates at Saratoga, New York, in October 1777 was a turning point because it convinced the French that they could safely enter the war on the American side. This crucial development gave legitimacy to the revolution as well as foreign assistance in the form of money, troops, naval forces, and volunteers. The last major battle of the Revolutionary War was fought at Yorktown, Virginia, where combined French and American forces defeated those under the British General William Cornwallis. Almost a fourth of the British military force ship *America* (8,000 men) surrendered at Yorktown. Although this did not end the fighting, it brought to power early in 1782 a new group of ministers who began peace talks with the Americans, and a peace treaty was signed on September 3, 1783. This Treaty of Paris recognized the independence of the United States and established the nation's borders. U.S. territory extended west to the Mississippi River, north to Canada, and south approximately to Florida. The last British soldiers left New York City in November 1783.

ANALOGY
The comparison of two people or things, at least one of them familiar to the listener or reader, to demonstrate or emphasize similarity. Thus in "BILLY BUDD, SAILOR" and "BARTLEBY THE SCRIVENER," Herman MELVILLE uses the ship as an analogy for the world in general, or Bartleby as analogous to all people who resist conformity. Critics usually discuss analogies in more specific terms, SIMILE and METAPHOR.

ANDERSON, SHERWOOD (1876–1941)
A pioneer to aspiring modernist writers in the 1920s, Sherwood Anderson suffered a decline in his critical reputation before he died, and has now reclaimed a secure place as a significant influence in 20th-century American literature. In 1919, Anderson published WINESBURG, OHIO, the groundbreaking short story collection about his "GROTESQUE" characters in a small midwestern town. In 1921, along with T. S. Eliot, Anderson won the first literary award offered by the prestigious literary magazine *The Dial*. Influenced by James Joyce and Gertrude STEIN, whom he believed had revolutionized language, Anderson in turn influenced the younger writers Ernest HEMINGWAY and William FAULKNER. Although Faulkner and Hemingway eventually turned against him, they continued to acknowledge their debt; Faulkner, who viewed Mark TWAIN as the grandfather of American literature, called Anderson the father of Faulkner's entire generation of writers.

In addition to seven novels, the best of which are generally agreed to be *Poor White,* published in 1920, and *Dark Laughter,* published in 1925,

Anderson wrote three collections of short stories following *Winesburg—The Triumph of the Egg* (1921), *Horses and Men* (1923), *Death in the Woods and Other Stories* (1933)—and more were collected in the posthumous *The Sherwood Anderson Reader* (1947) and, recently, in *Certain Things Last* (1992). Anderson made his greatest contributions to the GENRE of the short story. Among the earliest American writers to respond to Freudian psychology (see FREUD), he rejected the traditional, carefully plotted chronologically told story in favor of emphasizing a forgotten or subconsciously submerged moment that has deeply affected a character's life. He also introduced the SHORT STORY CYCLE, a collection of interrelated stories that do not merely stand on their individual artistic merits, but extend artistic unity to the entire volume.

As illustrated in "THE EGG," "HANDS," and "I Want to Know Why," his characters, regardless of age, are not happy; most, having endured frustrated, lonely, and wasted lives, sound a bleak note that some critics speculate echoes Anderson's view of the post–WORLD WAR I situation in the United States. Anderson, a successful businessman for a while, disparagingly called himself "BABBITT," suffered hospitalization for a nervous collapse, gave up his job, and became a full-time writer. In 1913 he became part of the CHICAGO RENAISSANCE, an AVANT-GARDE group of writers that included poets Carl Sandburg, Vachel Lindsay, and Edgar Lee Masters, novelists Floyd Dell and Theodore DREISER, and LITTLE MAGAZINE editors Harriet Monroe and Margaret C. Anderson. The results of his efforts helped change the American short story. In his best fiction, Anderson managed to turn the speech of his boyhood in Clyde, Ohio (in part the model for Winesburg), into hauntingly sensory and lyrical prose that still manages to capture readers some 80 years after Anderson wrote the words.

BIBLIOGRAPHY
Anderson, Sherwood. *Alice, and the Lost Novel.* London: Elkin Mathews & Marrot, 1929.

———. *Anderson Reader.* Edited by Paul Rosenfeld. Boston: Houghton Mifflin, 1947.

———. *Certain Things Last: The Selected Short Stories of*

Sherwood Anderson, Edited by Charles E. Modlin, New York: Four Walls Eight Windows, 1992.

———. *Death in the Woods and Other Stories*. New York: Liveright, Inc., 1933.

———. *Horses and Men*. New York: B. W. Huebsch, Inc., 1923.

———. *The Portable Sherwood Anderson*.Edited by Horace Gregory. New York: Viking, 1949; revised edition, 1972.

———. *Short Stories*. Edited by Maxwell Geismar. New York: Hill and Wang, 1962.

———. *The Triumph of the Egg: A Book of Impressions from American Life in Tales and Poems*. New York: B. W. Huebsch, Inc., 1921.

———. *Winesburg, Ohio: A Group of Tales of Ohio Small Town Life*, 1919. Edited by Malcolm Cowley. New York: Viking, 1967.

Anderson, David D. *Sherwood Anderson: An Introduction and Interpretation*. New York: Holt, Rinehart and Winston, 1967.

———, ed. *Anderson: Dimensions of His Literary Art*. East Lansing: Michigan State University Press, 1976.

———, ed. *Critical Essays on Sherwood Anderson*. Boston: G. K. Hall, 1981.

Burbank, Rex. *Sherwood Anderson*. New York: Twayne, 1964.

Campbell, Hilbert H. and Charles E. Modlin. *Sherwood Anderson: Centennial Studies*. Troy, N.Y.: Whitson Publishing Company, 1976.

Crowly, John W. *New Essays on Winesburg, Ohio*. New York: Cambridge University Press, 1990.

Howe, Irving. *Sherwood Anderson*. Stanford, Calif.: Stanford University Press, 1951.

Rideout, Walter B. *Sherwood Anderson: A Collection of Critical Essays*. Englewood Cliffs, N.J.: Prentice-Hall, 1974.

Schevill, James. *Sherwood Anderson: His Life and Work*. Denver, Colo.: University of Denver Press, 1951.

Sutton, William A. *The Road to Winesburg: A Mosaic of the Imaginative Life of Sherwood Anderson*. Metuchen, N.J.: Scarecrow Press, 1972.

Taylor, Welford Dunaway. *Sherwood Anderson*. New York: Frederick Ungar Publishing Company, 1977.

Townsend, Kim. *Sherwood Anderson*. Boston: Houghton Mifflin, 1987.

Weber, Brom. *Sherwood Anderson*. Minneapolis: University of Minnesota Press, 1964.

White, Ray Lewis, ed. *The Achievement of Sherwood Anderson: Essays in Criticism*. Chapel Hill: University of North Carolina Press, 1966.

William, Kenny J. *A Storyteller and a City: Anderson's Chicago*. DeKalb: Northern Illinois University Press, 1988.

"ANGEL AT THE GRAVE, THE"

EDITH WHARTON (1901) "The Angel at the Grave," originally published in *Scribner's Magazine* (February 29, 1901) and in Edith WHARTON's short story collection *Crucial Instances* (1901), combines her interest in evolutionary theory and transcendental philosophy (see TRANSCENDENTALISM) with her awareness of the tensions inherent in a woman who chooses an intellectual life over a domestic one. The story illustrates both the sacrifices and joys that Paulina Anson experiences. The orphaned Paulina, granddaughter of the deceased Dr. Orestes Anson, returns to Anson's home, now a sacred site where her grandmother and aunts continue to pay homage to the memory of a man who was a well-respected colleague of the Transcendentalists. For a while the women cordially open the home to visitors who want to know Anson's domestic habits, but after a few years the public ceases to visit.

In the meantime, Paulina, the sole heir able to understand Dr. Anson's work, declines a marriage proposal in order to devote her life to cataloging his work and to writing his biography. Years later, when she finally presents her book to a publisher, she is devastated to learn that the public has lost interest in her grandfather's theories and that her life's work has been rejected. After this crushing disappointment, she discards her intellectual work, dons a black dress, and pursues domestic interests.

In an unexpected conclusion, a young scholar, George Corby, knocks at the family's door and asks for Paulina's assistance in tracing Dr. Anson's research on *amphioxus*. In a gesture reminiscent of a character in Edgar Allan POE's "THE PURLOINED LETTER" or Sigmund FREUD's study of Dora, Paulina "draw[s] a key from her old-fashioned reticule and unlock[s] a drawer" that holds Anson's documentation regarding this missing evolutionary link (CI 58). Anson's scientific journal, which Paulina has preserved, promises to reinstate the doctor in the scientific and philosophical registers, advance evolutionary studies, and revitalize Paulina through her intellectual collaboration with Corby. The story provides compelling evidence of Wharton's interest in evolutionary theory, her collaboration with Walter Berry, and her awareness of the cultural constructions of women's roles.

BIBLIOGRAPHY

Lewis, R. W. B. *Edith Wharton*. New York: Harper & Row, 1975.

Widdicomb, Toby. "Wharton's 'The Angel at the Grave' and the Glories of Transcendentalism: Deciduous or Evergreen?" *American Transcendental Quarterly* 6.1 (March 1992): 47–57.

Sandra Chrystal Hayes
Georgia Institute of Technology

"ANNUNCIATION" MERIDEL LESUEUR (1935)

Written during the 1920s and anthologized often, "Annunciation" is based on Meridel LESUEUR's own first pregnancy. The story begins during a bleak fall; everything around the pregnant female narrator is yellow, dead, and shriveled. The pregnant woman is poor and unnamed. On one hand, perhaps, her namelessness suggests her insignificance in her bleak world, yet on the other, it implies the universally female experience of pregnancy; she is Everywoman. (See EVERYMAN/EVERYWOMAN.) Her husband, Karl, is jobless and distant, yet she knows that the pregnancy is important and writes down her thoughts on scraps of paper she keeps in her pockets. She writes to record and explain the experience not only to herself but to others.

Just outside their small room in a boardinghouse stands a pear tree, and its importance to the woman increases daily. Through the tree's limbs, its promise of fruit, its curving leaves, she gathers strength. The tree itself speaks to her—the annunciation, an echo of the angel Gabriel's annunciation to Mary in the Bible—and she realizes she and the tree are on the same course in the "curve of creation." Through the pear tree the woman finds comfort and joy about the life growing within her.

As with so much of LeSueur's fiction, the structure of the story is circular, its rhythm repetitive. It is curved into itself, like the leaves on the pear tree or the curve of the pregnant woman's body. The woman does not venture far from her porch, her small room, yet she feels and understands her connection with life forces from the inner experience of gestation, of contemplating and listening to the pear tree. She watches the lives of the neighbors around her, and all she sees is life and "blossoming." Even the houses become "like an orchard blooming soundlessly."

At the end of the story, another woman—also nameless—offers sympathy upon news of the pregnancy. The husband, Karl, has not come home. The pregnant woman goes without supper. But she is changed. Instead of writing on small scraps of paper, she writes on a piece of wrapping paper. Symbolically, her poverty-ridden world is enlarged; she has unwrapped the gift of the future.

Susan Thurston Hamerski
St. Olaf College

ANTAGONIST

The fictional character in direct opposition to the PROTAGONIST. In Katherine Anne PORTER's "NOON WINE," for example, the protagonist, Mr. Thompson, kills Mr. Hatch, his antagonist. In William FAULKNER's "THE BEAR," the protagonist is Isaac McCaslin; the antagonist Isaac finally conquers is the bear itself.

ANTICLIMAX

Sometimes used as an equivalent for BATHOS. In a second usage, however, the term denotes a writer's intentional drop from the serious and elevated to the trivial and lowly, in order to achieve a comic or satiric effect. (See COMEDY.)

ANTITHESIS

A term used most frequently in poetry in reference to a parallel statement that demonstrates the polar differences between two people or things. The term also can be used in prose fiction, however, to describe two extremely different characters, values, and the like. Thus in Nathaniel HAWTHORNE's "RAPPACCINI'S DAUGHTER," the coldly scientific Dr. Rappaccini may be described as the antithesis of his innocent and beautiful daughter, Beatrice.

ANTIHERO

ANTIHERO The PROTAGONIST of a literary work who, instead of displaying the traditional attributes of a hero, such as dignity, courage, strength, vision, or ability, instead is graceless, petty, ineffectual, passive, and even stupid or dishonest. Contemporary usage applies the term to either male or female characters.

APHORISM

APHORISM A concise statement of a principle or the terse formulation of a truth or sentiment. The term was first used by the Greek physician Hippocrates, and the beginning sentence of his *Aphorisms* is a good example: "Life is short, art is long, opportunity fleeting, experience dangerous, reasoning difficult." Maxims, proverbs, and adages are all aphorisms.

APOLLONIAN AND DIONYSIAC

APOLLONIAN AND DIONYSIAC In *The Birth of Tragedy* (1872), Friedrich Nietzsche suggested that Greek tragedy resulted from the tension between the traits associated with two gods, Apollo, god of the sun, and Dionysius, god of wine. Whereas Apollo represents the classical emphasis on reason, structure, order, and restraint, Dionysus represents the opposite qualities of instinct, irrationality, emotion, chaos, and disorder. Hence the Apollonian is often associated with classicism, the Dionysian with romanticism. The clash of these two opposite tendencies can produce CATASTROPHE and TRAGEDY.

ARCHETYPE

ARCHETYPE A literary term derived from the work of Sir James Frazer and C. J. Jung. Frazer traced elemental or "archetypal" recurring myths common to many cultures, no matter how diverse. Jung used the term "archetype" to refer to repeated kinds of experiences occuring to both ancient ancestors and modern humans alike. Thus, unconsciously, all humans share memories of recurring figures or experiences. In literature, these may include the femme fatale or Lilith figure, the evil male, the descent to the underworld, the search for the father and mother, or the rebirth of the hero. Critics generally view the death-and-rebirth theme as the most basic of all archetypal themes. The term may also be used for the first in a pattern: for instance, Mark TWAIN's Huckleberry Finn is viewed as the archetype for such subsequent fictional American males as Ernest HEMINGWAY's NICK ADAMS or females such as Katherine Anne PORTER's, MIRANDA RHEA.

ARNOLD FRIEND

ARNOLD FRIEND Mephistophelan ANTIHERO (in Joyce Carol OATES's "WHERE ARE YOU GOING, WHERE HAVE YOU BEEN?") who singles out the adolescent CONNIE and hypnotizes her by pretending to be a young high school boy. His connections with the devil are implicit not only in his vulgar mannerisms and expressions but also in his ability to change shapes and, very likely, in the reason his feet don't fit his boots: His feet are probably cloven hooves, like those of the devil. A stunningly frightening figure, the PERSONIFICATION of evil, Arnold Friend abducts Connie, and one doubts that she will return alive.

"ARTIFICIAL NIGGER, THE"

"ARTIFICIAL NIGGER, THE" FLANNERY O'CONNOR "The Artificial Nigger" focuses on several themes that recur in Flannery O'CONNOR's fiction. It features tension between generations (an adult, Mr. Head, who is determined to prove his intellectual ability over a child); it discusses racial prejudice and overblown human egos; and, finally, its ending offers redemption and personal understanding about life to its PROTAGONISTS.

"The Artificial Nigger" begins with Mr. Head's decision to teach his grandson Nelson a lesson about the wicked city. The precocious child, almost his grandfather's mirror image, doubts whether Mr. Head actually knows much at all about the place on which he claims to be an expert. By defiant retorts and aggressive actions, Nelson suggests the fallibility of his grandfather and defies his adult authority. In return, the old man angrily asserts his higher intelligence (a character trait symbolized by his unusual name) by stressing the child's lack of experience—a fact heightened by Nelson's inability to recognize a Negro, whom Mr. Head considers not only lower class but part of the darkness and evil ways of Atlanta. Mr. Head also attempts to elicit

Nelson's approval and respect through his ability to keep them from getting lost during the visit.

During their train ride, Mr. Head deliberately takes out his hostility toward Nelson by demeaning the boy's abilities and by suggesting his total unpreparedness for the corruption that awaits them at their journey's end. When they confront a large black/mulatto man on the train, Mr. Head is quick to exploit the boy's naivete, his innocence regarding racial identity and the prejudice that accompanies it. Thus the boy is made to feel inferior, like the Negro, a parallel O'Connor develops in detail later in the story.

Other incidents on the train, however, indicate that it is Mr. Head as well as Nelson whose knowledge is limited. His constant talking and loud assertions are embarrassing as well as indicative of his bravado rather than his command of experiences. His prideful actions establish him as a know-it-all whose assertions of expertise are questionable at best. Nonetheless, Nelson seems convinced that he would be lost without the old man's help and guidance.

When the two finally arrive in Atlanta, Mr. Head nervously begins to act as tour guide, pointing out the enticements the place offers and the intricacies of his knowledge of the city. He authoritatively points out weight machines that predict human destiny ("Beware of dark women") as well as a sewer system with dark tunnels that he hopes will bewilder and scare Nelson properly. O'Connor uses characteristic religious symbolism in depicting Nelson's association of the city sewers with "the place where I came from," thus acknowledging that the source of his humanness is in the muck and refuse rather than in the pristine country. Such acknowledgment of one's original sin is reminiscent of such Nathaniel HAWTHORNE stories as "My Kinsman, Major Molineaux," in which a similar innocent is initiated into the ways of the world.

Unfortunately Mr. Head refuses to acknowledge his own association with this hell-like environment, labeling it instead a "nigger-heaven" where only those of inferior social status belong. Having lost his way and wandered into a totally black area of Atlanta, he begins to see his own shortcomings and hesitates to lower himself further by asking directions from a race of people whom he despises.

Even this small act of self-humiliation proves beyond him as he forces Nelson to fulfill this task, in the process encountering the dark woman of his fortune. Again Nelson is made to feel less than adequate, and he dismisses rather than follows the accurate advice. The two proceed to wander aimlessly, following streetcar tracks in hopes of finding the train that will take them home.

O'Connor is not finished, however, for although Nelson has grown considerably and experienced a rite of passage, Mr. Head has not undergone a similar transformation. After Mr. Head cruelly leaves Nelson asleep on a curb in a white neighborhood, in an attempt to teach the self-confident little boy a lesson, the child awakens suddenly and runs in terror, seeking the security of his grandfather's presence. The practical joke having backfired, Mr. Head races after him, but seconds later further alienates the child by denying he knows him.

This treachery or denial, of course, does not go unpunished, for Nelson returns the isolation and coldness and leaves Mr. Head feeling forlorn and guilty at his rejection of his own flesh and blood. As the sun begins to set, he is suddenly illuminated with a truth similar to the one Nelson has already acknowledged: "he is lost and cannot find his way." (See EPIPHANY.) Finally depicting Mr. Head's redemption from his prideful nature, the story closes with the "artificial nigger" of the title—a plaster statue that appears in a front yard. By emphasizing the statue's combination of a wry smile and an expression of misery, O'Connor suggests its appeal to both Nelson and Mr. Head: It allows them vicariously to see their own lowness and to understand that only through mercy and forgiveness can humankind cope with suffering.

Although the story begins in darkness and ends with a sunset, the author again affirms her belief that positives can overcome negatives. Surprisingly, in this story the penalty for attaining self-knowledge is not a character's death, as it normally is in O'Connor's fiction, but rather the symbolic death of an "old Adam," the foolish one who asserts personal superiority over others, whether black or white, young or old.

Michael J. Meyer
DePaul University

ASIAN-AMERICAN LITERATURE

In its broadest sense, Asian-American literature includes the literary production (from the late 1880s to the present) by American authors identified with those ethnic groups formerly designated as "Oriental." This shifting and rapidly expanding category currently includes writers of Chinese, Korean, Japanese, Filipino, Indian, Pakistani, Vietnamese, and Cambodian heritage.

Unlike African-American literature, which comes out of a more unified historical and cultural context dating back to the slave narratives of the Colonial era, Asian-American literature appears, at this emergent stage in its development, to be characterized as much, or more, by the diversity of the groups it represents and the tensions among them as by what pan-Asian critics view as a commonality of circumstance and experience. Nor are scholars agreed on the delineation of their discipline: The criteria for defining "common" experience, the role of cultural and generational difference, and the inclusion or exclusion of writing by immigrants are only a few of the issues dividing the field.

Prior to the 1960s there was writing by American authors of Asian descent, but nothing that could be called a tradition of Asian-American writing. For its first 80 years, from the appearance in 1887 of Yan Phou Lee's autobiographical account, *When I was a Boy in China,* the field that we now regard as Asian-American literature was characterized by relatively scant production and publication, the lack of a broad audience, and the isolation of writers within their ethnic communities. Novelists such as H. T. Tsiang and John Okada, writing during the years preceding and following WORLD WAR II, had difficulty reaching a reading public. Tsiang's six books were self-published by the author, then peddled at leftist political meetings around New York City, while the first run of Okada's *No-No Boy* sat undistributed in a Seattle warehouse for 20 years.

Writers of short fiction fared somewhat better, especially in Chinese and Japanese communities, which published first-language newspapers that provided a forum for their work. A few, like Edith Maude Eaton, the Canadian journalist of Eurasian descent who is acknowledged as the first Asian-American writer of short fiction, managed to reach a larger audience. Eaton, who wrote under the pen name of SUI SIN FAR, was publishing in such mainstream journals as *New England Magazine, Good Housekeeping,* and the *Boston Globe* between the late 1880s and the early 1900s. She is best known as the author of *Mrs. Spring Fragrance* (1912), her only book-length work, and "Leaves from the Mental Portfolio of a Eurasian," which appeared in the *Independent* in 1909. Her fiction is derived from personal experience and deals primarily with issues of culture contact. A couple of generations after Eaton, during the post–World War II era, Hisaye YAMAMOTO, a Japanese American journalist and short story writer, also succeeded in achieving national recognition, despite the widespread anti-Japanese sentiment of the time. In the 1950s her work was regularly selected by Martha Foley, then editor of the *Best American Short Stories* series, for inclusion in its annual lists of Distinguished Fiction. In 1955 "Yoneko's Earthquake" became the first story by an Asian American author to be included in the anthology.

The notion of a pan–Asian-American literary tradition emerged out of the ethnic studies movement of the late 1960s, when community organizers and writer-activists, such as Frank CHIN and the other young editors of the groundbreaking anthology *Aiiieeeee!* (1974), saw the political advantage of forming a national coalition of Asian communities under a common rubric and a common cause. This was, and continues to be, a challenging task, given the history of preemigration hostility among many of these groups. Early on, however, Chin and his associates realized the unifying power of a common literary tradition, and, having no such tradition to refer to—aside from the mainstream Eurocentric canon, set about constructing one. To this end they founded the Combined Asian Resources Project, dedicated to discovering and reissuing little-known works of Asian American literature, including Okada's *No-No Boy*. Then, in 1974, Frank Chin, Lawson Inada, Shawn WONG, and Jeffery Paul CHAN brought out the anthology in which they attempted to prescribe a politically based aesthetic, countering what they viewed as the Asian stereotypes perpetuated by mainstream-approved publications, such as *Fifth Chinese Daughter* by Jade Snow Wong. Many of the questions of exclusion and inclusion that continue to occupy Asian-American literary studies were raised by the editors of *Aiiieeeee!*

While providing a necessary counterpoint to the European-centered American tradition, Asian-American literature and literary studies has tended to emphasize the requirements of political activism on one hand and literary activity and analysis on the other. Much of the criticism within the field of Asian-American literary studies has, to this point, employed the perspective of social science and a narrow adherence to the sociological accuracy and instructive intent of the literary works. This might be read less as a permanent state of affairs, however, than a stage of development in an emerging field. Even now the status quo is being challenged as new work by Asian-American writers continues to be published at an unprecedented rate by mainstream presses, and a new generation of critics, such as Lisa Lowe, Wendy Motooka, and Joseph Won, who have a rigorous grounding in both literary analysis and cultural studies, begin to make themselves heard. Consistent with general trends, many more novels than short story collections are being published because of the present popularity of the long form, but exciting and accomplished work in short fiction has been produced by such writers as Bharati MUKHERJEE, Gish JEN, Fae Myenne NG, Chang Rae Lee, Jessica Hagedorn, Marianne Villanueva, David Wong LOUIE, and Peter Ho Davies.

BIBLIOGRAPHY

Chan, Jeffrey Paul, Frank Chin, Lawson Inada, and Shawn Wong, eds. *Aiiieeeee! An Anthology of Asian-American Writers*. Washington, D.C.: Howard University Press, 1974.

Hagedorn, Jessica, ed. *Charlie Chan Is Dead*. New York: Penguin, 1993.

Kim, Elaine H. *Asian American Literature: An Introduction to the Writings and Their Social Context*. Philadelphia: Temple University Press, 1982.

Lowe, Lisa. "Heterogeneity, Hybridity, Multiplicity: Marking Asian American Differences." *Diaspora* 1: 1 (Spring 1991): 21–44.

Motooka, Wendy. "Sentimentalism, Authenticity, and Hawai'i Literature." Paper presented at Pacific Writers Institute, July 6, 1977.

———. "Nothing Solid: Racial Identity and Identification in *Fifth Chinese Daughter* and 'Wilshire Bus.'" 1997. Forthcoming in *Racing and (E)rasing Language*. Edited by Safiya Henderson Holmes and Ellen Goldner.

Sui Sin Far. *Mrs. Spring Fragrance and Other Writings*. Urbana: University of Illinois Press, 1995.

Watanabe, Sylvia, and Carol Bruchac, eds. *Home to Stay*. Greenfield Center, N.Y.: Greenfield Review Press, 1989.

Won, Joseph. "The Joy Luck Club, the Woman Warrior, and the Problematics of the Exotic." Paper presented at the Association of Asian American Studies Conference, June 2, 1993.

Wong, Sau-ling Cynthia. *Reading Asian American Literature*. Princeton, NJ: Princeton University Press, 1993.

Sylvia Watanabe
Oberlin College

ATLANTIC MONTHLY   First published in Boston in 1857, the *Atlantic* has maintained its reputation as an attractive and informative political and literary magazine. The first editor was James Russell Lowell, and early contributors of essays, short stories, and poetry included such literary luminaries as Ralph Waldo Emerson, Oliver Wendell Holmes, Harriet Beecher Stowe, John Greenleaf Whittier, and Henry Wadsworth Longfellow. The tradition of publishing high-quality fiction has been a consistent characteristic of the magazine throughout its history, and its editors have proven adept at discovering and publishing significant work by unknown new authors as well as established ones. Twentieth-century writers published in the *Atlantic* have included Edith WHARTON, Mark TWAIN, Sarah Orne JEWETT, Dylan Thomas, Philip ROTH, Joyce Carol OATES,

Robert Graves, Albert Camus, Isaac Bashevis SINGER, Paul Theroux, and Ann BEATTIE.

ATOM BOMB   See COLD WAR.

"AT THE 'CADIAN BALL" KATE CHOPIN

(1892)   "At the 'Cadian Ball" is a compelling story in its own right, but it is most important as an illumination of the situation that Kate CHOPIN presents in her better-known story, "The STORM." Appearing in both stories is Calixta, a beautiful, sensuous young woman whose attraction to the wealthy planter Alcee Laballiere deeply disturbs Bobinot, the man she eventually marries. While the action of "At the 'Cadian Ball" predates that of "The Storm," the stories can be presented effectively in either sequence. "At the 'Cadian Ball" functions well as an introduction to the characters of the later story or as a means of looking back and discovering some explanation for the seemingly casual adultery of Calixta and Alcee. Either way, the stories are best read together, with a focus on how the choices Alcee and Calixta make in "At the 'Cadian Ball" lead to the incident that occurs in "The Storm."

"At the 'Cadian Ball" not only reveals many important details about the individual characters but also gives us a clear look at the social class structure of the characters' milieu, 19th-century Louisiana. Clearly, Alcee and Calixta are from two different worlds. Alcee is a young planter from a wealthy upper-class Creole family; Calixta is from the working-class "prairie people," the ordinary Cajuns (Acadians) of Louisiana. Calixta is shown to be set somewhat apart from her own people because of her openly sexual magnetism and flirtatious behavior, which gossip attributes rather condescendingly to her "Spanish blood." Although supposedly viewed "leniently" by her 'Cadian neighbors, Calixta is actually close to being considered not a "nice" girl. When she and Alcee Laballiere meet at the ball, held in the city of Assumption, it is not for the first time. Evidently they already have some sort of "past," for Bobinot decides to attend the ball out of nervous jealousy when he hears that Alcee may be there. Through Bobinot's thoughts, we discover that the main fuel for gossip about Calixta is an assumed scandalous liaison between her and Alcee the previous year in Assumption.

Chopin presents Alcee Laballiere as a misfit in his own society, just as she lets us see that Calixta does not entirely fit in with hers. Alcee is shown to be very different from the effete upper-class men, "with their ways and their manners," who visit his plantation in order to see his beautiful cousin, Clarisse. Alcee is hardworking, toiling long days at strenuous physical labor, impatient with social niceties, rash even in his business decisions. He is something of a gambler, choosing to risk a large amount of money and enormous personal effort on his 900 acres of rice, which a violent storm destroys in moments. Paradoxically, this destructive storm creates the emotions that drive Alcee to seek shelter with Calixta: Their passionate sexual encounter (either a distraction or, possibly, a comfort for Alcee) ultimately brings the previously cool and distant Clarisse to declare her love for him. Alcee leaves the warmth and sensuality of Calixta to follow the "aggravating[ly]" unattainable, beautiful, but physically cold Clarisse.

"AUTRES TEMPS . . ." EDITH WHARTON

(1911)   This story is a superb example of the tightly controlled and finely crafted narrative at which Edith WHARTON excelled in both long and short fictional forms. Clearly defined characters are placed in situations that offer dramatic social conflicts. While Wharton's resolution of these conflicts may offer surprises, it never leaves any loose ends.

Mrs. Lidcote, the protagonist of "Autres Temps . . . ," returns from Europe to New York after her daughter Leila's divorce and remarriage. Mrs. Lidcote, herself divorced long ago when such an action made her an outcast in wealthy "old New York" society, learns from her old friend Franklin Ide that Leila is happy, because times have changed in her social set and divorce is no longer a scandal. Mrs. Lidcote cannot believe that such change is possible, but after she visits Leila and her wealthy new husband in his magnificent family home in the Berkshires, she understands that Franklin is right.

Times have not changed for Mrs. Lidcote, however; her contemporaries, who remember her past, cut her socially. Even Leila seems afraid to include her mother with her other company at an important dinner party, and Mrs. Lidcote spends the first Berkshire weekend sequestered in her room until Leila's other guests leave. Back in a New York hotel, preparing to return to her apartment in Italy, Mrs. Lidcote is approached again by Franklin, who tells her that she is wrong to live like a recluse and that she should have joined the company at Leila's dinner party. Franklin says, "It looked as though you were afraid of them or as though you hadn't forgiven them. Either way, you put them in the wrong instead of waiting to let them put you in the right."

Deciding to test Franklin, Mrs. Lidcote asks him to go with her to meet her old acquaintance Margaret Wynn, whom she has seen earlier in the New York hotel. Franklin hangs back and then lies to her, saying that she will not find her old friend at the hotel, that her daughter's "young man was suggesting that they should all go out to a music-hall or something of the sort." Just as Leila had blushed when Mrs. Lidcote asked if her guests would "think it odd" if she joined the dinner party, so Franklin blushes when he explains why they should not look for Mrs. Wynn. Mrs. Lidcote understands what Wharton calls "the grim edges of reality" of her situation, and the story ends.

Mrs. Lidcote's strength of character is tested and found equal to the social ordeal she is forced to endure; of all the sympathetic characters in the story, she alone does not blush when forced to confront her situation. Margaret Wynn's daughter Charlotte blushes when her mother will not let her speak to Mrs. Lidcote at the hotel. The climax occurs in Wharton's description of Leila's blush at the end of the fifth section of the story: As Mrs. Lidcote watches her daughter's face, "the colour stole over her bare neck, swept up to her throat, and burst into flame in her cheeks. Thence it sent its devastating crimson up to her very temples, to the lobes of her ears, to the edges of her eye-lids, beating all over her in fiery waves, as if fanned by some imperceptible wind."

This closely observed blush exemplifies Wharton's technique of revealing her characters' inner psychological states through their outward manifestations. We know at once, as does Mrs. Lidcote, exactly what her daughter is thinking, although she is too embarrassed and not quite cruel enough to state those thoughts aloud. Times have changed for Leila, but Mrs. Lidcote lived in other times—"autres temps"—and society continues to condemn her according to the codes of that earlier era. The title of the story refers to the French idiom *autres temps, autres moeurs* (other times, other morals).

"AUTUMN HOLIDAY, AN" SARAH ORNE JEWETT (1880)

First published in HARPER'S magazine in October 1880, this early story by Sarah Orne JEWETT initially seems a pleasing if somewhat rambling account of the first-person narrator's walk through the Maine countryside. After evoking a detailed, realistic (see REALISM) picture of the narrator's pleasure in the flora and fauna she observes on this glorious sun-filled October day, Jewett describes her friendly, gossipy encounter with Miss Polly Marsh and her widowed sister Mrs. Snow, who is spending the day at Polly's house. Aunt Polly entertains the narrator and Mrs. Snow by recalling the antics of Captain Daniel Gunn, an apparently senile but harmless old man whom she met 50 years ago when visiting her cousin Statiry, Gunn's housekeeper. The story ends as the narrator departs with her father, the doctor, who has been seeing his patients and will take her home in his wagon.

On closer inspection, however, the story's tone—and undertone—implicitly raise issues of death, gender, and women's friendships. In her walk through the fields, the narrator conveys the combined loneliness and comfort she derives from the season and the outdoor sights: A solitary and nameless child's grave prompts a memory of a child's ruined boat she once saw, "a shipwreck of his small hopes" (AH 639), yet, paradoxically, she enjoys her contemplations in the warm sun. When the narrator approaches Aunt Polly's house, her thoughts have been on aging and autumn, but as she sees the two cheerful old bodies" (640) at their twin spinning wheels, they convey a sense of good spirits, wisdom, and purpose. Aunt Polly then begins her storytelling, focusing on Daniel Gunn, who, in his old age, believed he was his dead sister Patience. When he insisted on wearing her clothing, imitating the way she knitted, and attending church services and the Female Missionary Society meetings, "folks used to call him Mrs. Daniel Gunn" (643).

Underlying the kindly humor and compassion with which Aunt Polly relates the story and the community's good natured tolerance of Daniel's behavior, however, is a more somber question. Aunt Polly wonders whether Daniel Gunn's friends and relatives would have been so tolerant had he been "a flighty old woman" (646) instead of a valued and respected man suffering the mental vagaries of old age. Only when the doctor arrives to fetch his daughter does Mrs. Snow confide to the narrator the information that Aunt Polly has omitted from her story: During her visit, Daniel Gunn's nephew Jacob had proposed to Polly, but she turned him down. The story invites unanswered questions: Why does Aunt Polly tell the story of the community's broad-minded view of this cross-dressing man? Why does she omit references to Jacob's offer of marriage?

Why does the narrator value the company of the two aging sisters? And how do we account for the bleakly abrupt ending? We know only that the narrator describes Polly, "a famous nurse," as "one of the most useful women in the world" (641); that after the narrator's short "holiday," the ride home with her father took "much longer" than her walk through the country; and that when she reached home, the fine autumn day had declined into one of darkness and cold.

BIBLIOGRAPHY

Jewett, Sarah, Orne. "An Autumn Holiday." In *Major Writers of Short Fiction: Stories and Commentaries."* Edited by Ann Charters. Boston: Bedford–St. Martin's, 1993, pp. 637–647.

AVANT-GARDE A French phrase meaning "advanced guard" or "vanguard," usually applied to art or literature that is new, original, or experimental in ideas and techniques. Such art is sometimes bizarre and often attacks established conventions. In the early 20th century, for instance, Gertrude STEIN's linguistic experiments were considered avant-garde, as were John BARTH's later experiments focusing on fiction as a subject of fiction.

B

BABBITT George Follansbee Babbitt is the protagonist in Sinclair Lewis's novel *Babbitt* (1922). A conceited, arrogant, complacent businessman, he tries for a time to escape his comfortable and successful but dull and middle-class existence, but learns that he fears for his reputation and thus returns to the status quo. The name has become synonymous with the stereotype of the American businessman, whose raison d'être is to make money and avoid making waves by following conventions.

"BABYLON REVISITED" F. SCOTT FITZGERALD (1931) F. Scott FITZGERALD's most anthologized story, "Babylon Revisited," develops its THEME of guilt, alienation, and reparation through the PROTAGONIST CHARLIE WALES, an American expatriate who has returned to Paris from his new home in Prague in the hope that he can regain custody of his young daughter, Honoria, who has been in the care of relatives. Charlie apparently has reformed after a long period of dissipation, which the narrative suggests may have contributed to his wife's death. He is now a successful businessman and his wife's sister, Marion Peters, has agreed to return Honoria to his care. During the reclamation visit, however, two of Charlie's alcoholic friends from the past arrive and make a scene, causing Marion to change her mind about his suitability as a guardian. The story closes as Charlie disconsolately ponders the six more months of waiting to which Marion has consigned him. There are strong symbolic suggestions that his past indulgences will permanently prevent reunion with his daughter.

Originally published in 1931 in the SATURDAY EVENING POST, the story was revised for Fitzgerald's fourth story collection, *Taps at Reveille,* in 1935. Fitzgerald shortened the second version and made a number of stylistic changes, but otherwise the two versions are essentially the same. The revised version did not eliminate a few inconsistencies in logic and chronology: It is unclear how long Charlie has been away from Paris or how long his period of dissipation lasted, because he mentions differing lengths of time.

Among the story's psychological complexities is the question of Charlie's conflict. Some readers see him as a man tormented by his past mistakes, attempting to atone for them in the present but still haunted by their lingering repercussions. Other readers suggest that Charlie's problem is not the conflict between his past actions and present desires but an internal division in himself. These close readers of the story find evidence that Charlie has a subconscious desire to sabotage the reformed, upstanding image he has created: successful businessman, devoted father, humble relative. The degree to which his self-destructive tendency is a healthy resistance to social coercion rather than an imp-of-the-perverse impulse is one of the story's ambiguities.

In part, "Babylon Revisited" is a fictionalized version of Fitzgerald's own confrontation with past indulgences. In 1924 he arrived with his wife Zelda in Paris, where they made the acquaintance of other expatriate Americans. During a two-year stay in France, Fitzgerald's relationships with the rich and famous provided opportunities for socializing that challenged his discipline and focus. His excessive drinking led to obnoxious public displays, quarrels with friends, and marital problems. As the 1920s drew to a close, his alcoholism had become a serious health problem and Zelda had her first mental breakdown. Fitzgerald placed their daughter Scottie in boarding school.

While "Babylon Revisited" reflects Fitzgerald's own difficulties, many readers also see in Charlie Wales the symbolic representation of Europe's transition from the Roaring Twenties to the more somber 1930s. Americans went to Paris after World War I in search of escape or novelty, but the stock market crash in 1929 (see GREAT DEPRESSION) brought the gay times to an end. Charlie's alcoholic friends Duncan and Lorraine represent the hangers-on who refuse to admit that the world has changed.

Charlie Wales's personal suffering is at least partially created in and conditioned by a society in which appearance rather than character is the dominant value. Marion Peters judges her brother-in-law only by his friends' improper behavior. She does not understand Charlie's longing for his daughter, nor does she acknowledge the guilt he carries for his past. The strength of character that has enabled him to reconstruct his life is invisible to her. Her middle-class propriety is as shallow as Duncan and Lorraine's bohemian pleasure-seeking. As a study of the historical moment or of modern society, the story emphasizes the unsatisfactory choices Charlie faces. He can enter the rigid confines of the smug middle class; embrace the rootless, self-indulgent existence of Lorraine and Duncan; or choose loneliness. Modern life as alienation is a common Fitzgerald theme.

In its ghostly evocation of the way one's past can occupy the present, "Babylon Revisited" also suggests a universal human problem: For some actions committed, there may be no complete atonement. One must live forever with the results of irreparable damage. In the last scene, when Charlie asks the bartender what he owes him, the reader perceives the IRONY: long after the present transaction, Charlie will still be paying for all the drinks of his past.

BIBLIOGRAPHY

Baker, Carlos. "When the Story Ends: 'Babylon Revisited,'" in *The Short Stories of F. Scott Fitzgerald: New Approaches in Criticism*. Edited by Jackson R. Bryer. Madison: University of Wisconsin Press, 1982.

Gross, Seymour L. "Fitzgerald's 'Babylon Revisited.'" *College English* 25 (1963).

Hostetler, Norman H. "From Mayday to Babylon: Disaster, Violence, and Identity in Fitzgerald's Portrait of the 1920s," in *Dancing Fools and Weary Blues: The Great Escape of the Twenties*. Edited by Lawrence R. Broer and John D. Walther. Bowling Green, Ohio: Bowling Green State University Popular Press, 1990.

Male, Roy. R. "'Babylon Revisited': A Story of the Exile's Return." *Studies in Short Fiction* 2 (1965).

Toor, David. "Guilt and Retribution in 'Babylon Revisited.'" *Fitzgerald/Hemingway Annual* (1973).

Frances Kerr
Durham Technical Community College

"BABYSITTER, THE" ROBERT COOVER (1969)

One of the most gripping stories of recent times, "The Babysitter" reveals the sometimes violent and obscene fantasies of various CHARACTERS as they recall—or seem to recall—the events of a babysitter's evening with the children of an average suburban couple. Was the babysitter raped? Was she seductive? Did anything at all happen to her? In addition to creating suspense, Robert COOVER's technique—resembling William FAULKNER's in its multiple perspectives of the same event—is brilliantly conceived, laying bare the raw chauvinism of the various male narrators and leaving the reader to determine what actually happened.

BALDWIN, JAMES (1924–1987)

James Baldwin was born in Harlem on August 2, 1924, the illegitimate son of Emma Berdis Jones. In 1927 his mother married David Baldwin, a clergyman, and subsequently had eight additional children, for whom the young Jimmy helped provide care. Greatly affected by his stepfather's growing bitterness, mocking cruelty, and rejection in an environment of racism, homophobia, and theological anguish, Baldwin, a black homosexual, suffered a crisis of identity that shaped his life and work.

His talent was recognized early by teachers and artist friends, among them Orilla Miller and HARLEM RENAISSANCE poet Countee Cullen, who introduced him to the theater, music, film, and a wider world of books. Cullen also suggested he apply to the prestigious De Witt Clinton High School in the Bronx, to which Baldwin was accepted in the fall of 1938. Struggling with his repressed homosexuality during his high school days, he sought refuge in the church and became a boy preacher for a short time but left disillusioned. After graduation, unsuccessful jobs, and the death of his stepfather, he moved to Greenwich Village. There he met Richard WRIGHT, who used his influence to get Baldwin a Eugene F. Saxton Memorial Trust Fellowship in 1945. Baldwin left the United States for Paris in 1948 and remained abroad, living in France, Switzerland, and Turkey for most of the remainder of his life.

In 1947 and 1948, prior to leaving for Paris, Baldwin wrote book reviews for *The Nation* and *New Leader* and gained considerable recognition for his essay "The Harlem Ghetto" in *Commentary* (February 1948). His career was launched by his early essays, which helped him develop his own aesthetic and gain the attention of a larger audience. In particular, "Everybody's Protest Novel" (1949) and "Many Thousands Gone" (1951), which attacks Harriet Beecher Stowe's *Uncle Tom's Cabin* and Wright's *Native Son*, revealed Baldwin's lifelong concern about defined roles and racial categories and permanently alienated Richard Wright.

Assisted by numerous fellowships and grants, including a Guggenheim Fellowship (1954), a National Institute of Arts and Letters grant (1956), and a Ford Foundation grant-in-aid (1959), Baldwin produced a large body of work including six novels; a volume of short stories, *Going to Meet the Man* (1965); a children's story, *Little Man, Little Man: A Story of Childhood;* three collections of essays; individually published essays and dialogues; three volumes of plays and scenarios; and two volumes of poetry.

Some have suggested that much of Baldwin's writing career is a long attempt to exorcise "the demons within" and a quest for personal identity. Others regard him primarily as an essayist whose stories and novels are highly autobiographical. Baldwin preferred to identify himself as a "witness" whose responsibility was "to write it all down." There is a strong link between Baldwin's nonfiction and his fiction, and in his novels he attempts to translate into art social issues discussed in his essays (racism, dehumanization, categorization, and the efficacy and redemptive power of love). During the struggle in the United States for civil rights in the 1960s Baldwin's work became more political, especially after the death of Malcolm X; nevertheless, despite his deep and passionate commitment to the movement, occasionally he found himself at odds with those who he believed were leaning too heavily on ideology and seeking answers in separatism. For a time he was estranged from much of the black American community after Eldridge Cleaver's attack on his homosexuality and accusation that Baldwin had rejected his blackness.

Baldwin's literary reputation has benefited from the passing of time. The distance from the turbulent 1960s and early 1970s has enabled readers and critics to view his work in a clearer light. Few writers have been more in conflict with themselves and with the world around them, and few worked more diligently to maintain their artistic integrity in the face of enormous challenges. In 1986 French President François Mitterrand presented Baldwin with the Legion of Honor. James Baldwin died in St. Paul de Vence, France, on December 1, 1987.

BIBLIOGRAPHY

Baldwin, James. *The Amen Corner: A Drama in Three Acts.* New York: French, 1968.

———. *Another Country.* New York: Dell Publishing, 1962.

———. *Blues for Mr. Charlie.* New York: Dell Publishing, 1964.

———. *The Devil Finds Work: An Essay*. New York: Dial, 1976.

———. *A Dialogue*. Philadelphia: Lippincott, 1973.

———. *Evidence of Things Not Seen*. Cutchogue, N.Y.: Buccaneer, 1985.

———. *The Fire Next Time*. New York: Dell, 1963.

———. *Giovanni's Room*. New York: Dial Press, 1956.

———. *Go Tell It on the Mountain*. New York: Knopf, 1953.

———. *Gypsy and Other Poems*. Searsmont, Maine: Gehenna Press, 1989.

———. *If Beale Street Could Talk*. New York: Dell Publishing, 1974.

———. *Jimmy's Blues*. New York: St. Martin's Press, 1985.

———. *Just Above My Head*. New York: Dial Press, 1979.

———. *No Name in the Street*. New York: Dial Press, 1972.

———. *Nobody Knows My Name: More Notes of a Native Son*. New York: Dial Press, 1961.

———. *Notes of a Native Son*. Boston: Beacon Press, 1955.

———. *Nothing Personal*. New York: Dell Publishing, 1964.

———. *One Day When I Was Lost: A Scenario Based on Alex Hayley's "The Autobiography of Malcolm X."* New York: Dial Press, 1972.

———. *The Price of the Ticket: Collected Nonfiction, 1948–1985*. New York: St. Martin's/Marek, 1985.

———. *A Rap on Race: Margaret Mead and James Baldwin*. Philadelphia: Lippincott, 1971.

———. *Tell Me How Long the Train's Been Gone*. New York: Dell Publishing, 1968.

Bloom, Harold. *James Baldwin*. New York: Chelsea House Publishers, 1986.

Campbell, James. *Talking at the Gates: A Life of James Baldwin*. New York: Viking, 1991.

Eckman, Fern Marja. *The Furious Passage of James Baldwin*. Philadelphia: Lippincott, 1966.

Kinnamon, Keneth. *James Baldwin: A Collection of Critical Essays*. Englewood Cliffs, N.J.: Prentice-Hall, 1974.

Leeming, James. *James Baldwin: A Biography*. New York: Knopf, 1994.

O'Daniel, Therman B. ed., *James Baldwin: A Critical Evaluation*. Washington, D.C.: Howard University Press, 1977.

Porter, Harold A. *Stealing the Fire: The Art and Protest of James Baldwin*. Middletown, Conn.: Wesleyan University Press, 1989.

Standley, Fred L. and Nancy V. Burt, eds. *Critical Essays on James Baldwin*. Boston: G. K. Hall, 1988.

Standley, Fred L. and Louis Pratt, eds., *Conversations With James Baldwin*. Jackson: University Press of Mississippi, 1989.

Weatherby, William J. *James Baldwin: Artist on Fire*. New York: Dell Publishing, 1989.

John Unrue
University of Nevada at Reno

BALLAD   The traditional or popular ballad is a poem or narrative song that has been passed down orally, appearing in various forms because each poet or singer likely introduced changes. Many folk ballads came to the United States from Great Britain, with the traditional THEMES of love, murder, or the supernatural, but native American forms developed as well, with subjects such as frontiersmen, cowboys, and railroadmen, as in the ballads of Casey Jones and JOHN HENRY. One of the most memorable prose uses of the term is Carson MCCULLERS's THE BALLAD OF THE SAD CAFE, a NOVELLA fascinating for the way the author uses musical ALLUSIONS and LEITMOTIFS to highlight the title's significance.

BALLAD OF THE SAD CAFE, THE CARSON MCCULLERS (1951)

A NOVELLA that, like a BALLAD, tells the ultimately tragic tale of MISS AMELIA EVANS, daughter of one of the most important men in this nameless, rural Georgia town. Miss Amelia falls in love with a hunchback, dwarflike stranger who convinces her that he is her COUSIN LYMON. Ultimately Miss Amelia's buoyant mood and the cafe she runs become "sad" and begin to wither away after Lymon falls in love with Marvin Macy, Miss Amelia's estranged husband. Together the two men conspire to defeat this powerful, sensitive, eccentric woman in this GROTESQUE yet empathetic story, described by various critics in terms of FAIRY TALE, MYTH, FABLE, or PARABLE. Above all, it is a love story, a variation of the ageless love triangle.

The story opens in the present with the image of Miss Amelia in self-imprisoned exile in her gray and rotting house. Gradually the story moves backward, revealing Miss Amelia's past, along with her accomplishments: The six-foot-tall Miss Amelia is a shrewd businesswoman who fills the roles of town doctor and bootlegger. Briefly married to Marvin Macy, the local roué, she feels an aversion to sex, cannot bear his demonstrations of love, and kicks him out of her large house. Miss Amelia has numerous so-called masculine characteristics—indeed, the only topic that embarrasses her is that of "female problems"—and one way to interpret her CHARACTER is that she is androgynous or bisexual. (Carson MCCULLERS and her husband, Reeve McCullers, were both bisexual.)

Whatever her feelings about love, she falls for Cousin Lymon, the hunchback, a TRICKSTER figure who appears in town and charms Miss Amelia, who invites him to stay in her house. Lymon, the archetypical mysterious stranger (see ARCHETYPE), seems to know everything, and the smitten Miss Amelia will do anything he asks. As their relationship grows, Miss Amelia opens the cafe that draws the entire community together in harmony and happiness. But the moment Marvin Macy reenters the scene, Cousin Lymon falls ecstatically in love with him. Some critics point to evidence that perhaps Lymon and Macy knew each other in the penitentiary in Atlanta. Others, however, believe their uniting against Miss Amelia merely demonstrates the capricious nature of love. In an epic battle scene, Miss Amelia beats Marvin Macy in the fight for Lymon but is destroyed when Lymon jumps on her back in a successful effort to help his lover. The two destroy the cafe and run off together, leaving the town a sad and desolate place and Miss Amelia in the self-imprisonment with which the story opened. The only relief—if indeed it is relief—in the tragedy is a final brief description of 12 men on a chain gang outside of town: They sing a song both mournful and joyful, perhaps suggesting the inescapable nature of the human condition.

BIBLIOGRAPHY

Carr, Virginia Spencer. *The Lonely Hunter: A Biography of Carson McCullers*. Garden City, N.Y.: Doubleday, 1975.
McCullers, Carson. *The Ballad of the Sad Cafe: Collected Stories of Carson McCullers*. Boston: Houghton Mifflin, 1987, pp. 195–254.

BAMBARA, TONI CADE (1939–1995)

Born and raised in New York City, Toni Cade adopted the name Bambara from the signature on a sketchbook she found in her great-grandmother's trunk. She was a linguist who believed that language determined how one perceived the world, but could just as often be used to misinform, to misdirect, and to intimidate as to actually inform. The era in which she matured and wrote, the 1960s and 1970s, was the time of the struggle for civil rights in America by African Americans and many of Bambara's observations and concerns are politically motivated, but her understanding of racial and interracial, gender, and generational conflicts are often tempered with humor. She uses African-American diction and syntax to give rhythm to her stories about ordinary people in situations described without condescension or sentimentality. According to critic Eleanor W. Traylor, her importance as a writer was as much the consequence of Bambara's significant role among African-American writers who came to prominence in the 1960s—known as the Black Arts Movement—as it was the consequence of her own style (Traylor 2703). Cade published two story collections, *Gorilla, My Love* (1972) and *The Seabirds Are Still Alive* (1977).

BIBLIOGRAPHY

Bambara, Toni Cade, ed. *The Black Woman: Anthology.* New York: New American Library, 1970.
Bambara, Toni Cade. *Gorilla, My Love.* New York: Random House, 1972.
———. *Raymond's Run.* Mankato, Minn.: Creative Education, 1990.
———. *The Salt Eaters.* New York: Random House, 1980.
———. *The Seabirds Are Still Alive: Collected Stories.* New York: Random House, 1977.
———, ed., with Leah Wise. *Southern Black Utterances Today.* Chapel Hill N.C.: Institute of Southern Studies, 1975.
———. *State of the Art.* Minneapolis: Minnesota Center for Book Arts/Tournesol Press, 1987.
———, ed. *Tales and Stories for Black Folks.* Garden City, N.Y.: Zenith Books, 1971.
Burks, Ruth Elizabeth. "From Baptism to Resurrection: Bambara and the Incongruity of Language." *Black Women Writers (1950–1980): A Critical Perspective.* Edited by Mari Evans. Garden City, N.Y.: Anchor Books, 1984.
Hargrove, Nancy D. "Youth in Bambara's *Gorilla, My Love.*"
Hull, Gloria. "'What It Is I Think She's Doing Anyhow:' A

Reading of Bambara's *The Salt Eaters.*" *Conjuring Black Women, Fiction, and Literary Tradition.* Edited by Marjorie Pryse and Hortense J. Spillers. Bloomington: Indiana University Press, 1985.

Prenshaw, Peggy Whitman, ed. *Women Writers of the Contemporary South.* Southern Quarterly Series. Jackson: University Press of Mississippi, 1984.

Traylor, Eleanor W. "Toni Cade Bambara." In *The Heath Anthology of American Literature.* Vol. 2, 3rd ed. New York: Houghton Mifflin, 1998, pp. 2702–03.

Vertreace, Martha M. "The Dance of Characters and Community," in *American Women Writing Fiction: Memory, Identity, Family, Space.* Edited by Mickey Pearlman. Lexington: University Press of Kentucky, 1989.

Willis, Susan. "Problematizing the Individual: Bambara's Stories for the Revolution," in *Specifying Black Women Writing the American Experience.* Edited by Susan Willis. Madison: University of Wisconsin Press, 1987.

BANKS FAMILY The Banks family is one of many that dwell in the heavenly valley where John STEINBECK'S *The Pastures of Heaven* (1932) is set: "Of all the farms in the Pastures of Heaven the one most admired was that of Raymond Banks" (PH 131). Raymond owns the most beautiful land in the valley and has covered it with chickens and ducks. People admire not only the farm but also Raymond and the parties he throws.

Raymond loves children, who often come to watch him kill his chickens. Instead of killing them quickly by breaking their necks, Raymond prefers to stab them with a knife. Although the hearts are still beating when Raymond spills their entrails, he explains to the children that the chickens really are already dead.

Only Bert Munroe, Raymond's old schoolmate, discovers Raymond's most disturbing hobby: A couple of times a year, Raymond witnesses hangings at the San Quentin Penitentiary, where Bert is a warden. These are Raymond's only vacations, and he finds them enjoyable and invigorating. After Raymond invites Bert to an execution, Bert spends a great deal of time thinking about it and decides not to go. He knows that, if he goes, he will be unable to sleep another night in his life. When Bert tells Raymond how sick his hobby is, he not only hurts Raymond's feelings but also ruins whatever pleasure Raymond derived from his little escapades.

Throughout the work, the Munroe family continues in the pattern illustrated by this episode between Bert and Raymond: They consistently yet inadvertently ruin the dreams, aspirations, and often twisted but happy lives of the other members of the community. This is a common theme that runs throughout many of Steinbeck's other works: Dreams are just delusions that can never be realized.

BIBLIOGRAPHY
Mann, Susan Garland. *The Short Story Cycle: A Genre Companion and Reference Guide.* New York: Greenwood Press, 1989.

Steinbeck, John. *The Pastures of Heaven.* New York: Penguin Books, 1995.

Kathleen M. Hicks
University of Texas at El Paso

"BARN BURNING" WILLIAM FAULKNER (1938) William FAULKNER's complex father-son story details the emotional effects of combined poverty, exclusion, and revenge, made poignant and painful because the POINT OF VIEW is that of a nine-year-old boy, Colonel Sartoris (Sarty) Snopes (see SNOPES FAMILY). Set in the 1890s, the story exudes the depression and poverty in Faulkner's mythical YOKNAPATAWPHA COUNTY in the post–CIVIL WAR years. The main characters are ABNER SNOPES, Civil War veteran (who partakes in Miss Rosa Millard's mule-stealing business with the Yankees during the Civil War in the connected short story collection THE UNVANQUISHED). Ab Snopes, Sarty's father, is both an unpleasant and sympathetic CHARACTER. The title may at some level allude (see ALLUSION) to one of Faulkner's favorite activities in the teens and '20s, barnstorming in his private plane. More significantly, however, the burning and the fires clearly suggest the unabated rage Snopes feels in this complicated tale of class hierarchy. Although in the 1930s many writers published proletarian fiction (see PROLETARIAN LITERATURE), "Barn Burning" rises above the genre and still speaks to readers across class and family lines, remaining remarkably contemporary.

The story opens in a country store with Ab Snopes facing the local and informal jury that has charged him with arson. He is guilty, and Sarty's interior thoughts show a boy conflicted between loyalty to his father and humiliation over his behavior. Snopes is aggrieved at his life as an itinerant farmer who never owns his own land but works for monied plantation owners. After he burns their barns, he moves on to still another job, remaining only briefly until he burns again. Faulkner takes pains to delineate the social structure in this story: Because Ab Snopes is "white trash," at the bottom of the social scale and, to his mind, even worse off than the black butler who works for the wealthy Major de Spain, he strictly enforces his own hierarchy within his family, as illustrated through his treatment of them as well as the clearly metaphorical sleeping arrangements (see METAPHOR). Ab, his wife, and his eldest son (the infamous Flem Snopes of the Snopes Trilogy), have beds, while Sarty, his daughters, and his unmarried and nameless sister-in-law sleep on pallets. Indeed, this powerless spinster figure appears in numerous Faulkner works.

Few readers can help sympathizing with Ab, the man without a future, the man who teaches his sons that blood is more important than any abstract value. Yet somehow Sarty (named for Colonel Sartoris of *Flags in the Dust* and several Faulkner short stories) has imbibed such values as truthfulness, decency, and respect for others. When Ab and Sarty visit the de Spain house with its big white columns and Ab deliberately smears his dung-covered boots on Mrs. de Spain's French rug, then nearly destroys the rug with his vicious scrubbing, Sarty still tries to defend his father. Only when he sets fire to the barn does Sarty break free to warn Major de Spain. In the ambiguous ending (see AMBIGUITY), we hear the gunshots, but we are not sure whether Ab has been killed. He is dead to Sarty, however, who still demonstrates his desire to believe in his father's bravery but sets out alone in the opposite direction. Similar to James in Ernest GAINES's "THE SKY IS GRAY," Sarty's overriding values are those of his mother. His journey away from his father's moral deficiencies resembles that of NICK ADAMS in Ernest HEMINGWAY's "INDIAN CAMP."

BIBLIOGRAPHY

Blotner, Joseph. *Faulkner: A Biography.* New York: Random House, 1984.

Carothers, James. *Faulkner's Short Stories.* Ann Arbor: University of Michigan Research Press, 1985.

Faulkner, William. "Barn Burning." In *American Short Stories.* 6th ed. Edited by Eugene Current-García and Bert Hitchcock. New York: Longman, 1997, pp. 377–390.

Ferguson, James. *Faulkner's Short Fiction.* Knoxville: University of Tennessee Press, 1991.

BARNES, DJUNA   (1892–1982)

Djuna Barnes was born in rural New York and was educated by her grandmother, the journalist and author Zadel Barnes. Barnes spent the 1910s in Greenwich Village, where she established a reputation as a brilliant and daring journalist. She also published short fiction, poetry, and plays in a number of periodicals and illustrated many of her writings. In the early 1920s, Barnes went to Paris, where she became a dashing figure in the expatriate literary scene of the Left Bank. Her novel *Nightwood* (1936) is notable for its experimental style and earned Barnes her greatest literary fame. T. S. Eliot edited *Nightwood* and wrote an introduction for it. Barnes returned to America in the late 1930s and lived in New York until her death in 1982.

Most of Barnes's short stories were written before she went to Europe in the 1920s and depict the immigrant population of New York. An atmosphere of NATURALISM pervades many of the stories in that the narrator is detached from, yet observant of, the forces at work in shaping CHARACTERS' destinies and records the often-sordid details of their lives. Barnes tempers naturalism with richly elaborate description, her strength in these stories. Her dense METAPHORS and witty EPIGRAMS combine incongruous elements; for example, a balding man's head sheds its hair as instinctively as a beautiful woman's clothes fall from her body. Barnes's THEMES include sin and death and the seemingly hopeless human desire for transcendence or redemption. "A Night Among the Horses" (1918) and "Beyond the End"

(1919, later retitled "Spillway"), both first published in the *Little Review,* are among Barnes's finest stories. "Aller et Retour" (1924), in which a strong and sophisticated woman futilely encourages her estranged daughter to acquire worldly knowledge, is also highly acclaimed.

BIBLIOGRAPHY

Barnes, Djuna. *Collected Stories of Djuna Barnes.* Edited by Philip Herring. Los Angeles: Sun & Moon Press,1995.

Kannenstine, Louis F. *The Art of Djuna Barnes: Duality and Damnation.* New York: New York University Press, 1977.

Karen Fearing
University of North Carolina

"BARON OF PATRONIA, THE" GERALD VIZENOR (1988)

One of the stories in *The Trickster of Liberty: Tribal Heirs to a Wild Baronage,* "The Baron of Patronia" is an introduction to Gerald VIZENOR's comical patriarch, Luster Browne and his family, who live on a reservation in northern Minnesota. Luster inherits a mysterious and uninhabited plot of land on the reservation, thought by the government to be worthless. The estate turns out to be lucrative and magical, a place where mallards remain in winter and mysterious "panic holes" provide outlets for man and beast to unload stress. Luster finds a wife in Novena Mae, and the two create a large family that prospers on the land. The nontraditional education the children receive from their parents is incorporated into their daily lives: Luster tells creation and TRICKSTER stories as he works, jumps, and walks; Novena Mae teaches the children to read by writing on leaves and the hard snow.

As in much NATIVE AMERICAN fiction, humor goes hand in hand with adversity. An undercurrent in this comic tale (see COMEDY) is a lesson in how to deal with the harsh realities of life. Luster gives his children names like Shadow Box, Mouse Proof, and China to enable them to "endure the ruthless brokers of a tragic civilization." Vizenor writes in dense trickster fashion as he pokes fun at everyone from somber government officials to highbrow audiences at colleges, who earnestly consume ludicrous "wild shoe" stories, to lowbrow audiences, who purchase instruction manuals entitled "How to Be Sad and Downcast and Still Live in Better Health than People Who Pretend to be So Happy."

Calvin Hussman
St. Olaf College

BARRY, LYNDA (1956–)

Lynda Barry is a contemporary artist and writer best known for her creative and effective use of the comic strip, combining art and storytelling in her narrative. A product of divorce and an unstable childhood, Barry draws on her background in much of her work and chronicles the challenges, frustrations, and delights of childhood.

She is best known for her serial *Ernie Pook's Comeek* (found in weekly city newspapers), which chronicles the lives of Maybonne, Marlys, and Freddy, the not-quite-wanted young children of a lower socioeconomic background. Barry captures the essence of childhood in a form that is distinctly youthful—her playful drawings and characters' syntax are awkward and childlike. Not popular in school, the children are often troubled, yet earnest, loyal, and honest. The stories are reminiscent of J. D. SALINGER's *Catcher in the Rye* in that children on the fringes witness and articulate the "phoniness" of adults' actions. Barry takes this concept further by showing from a child's eye (see POINT OF VIEW) the frustration of their inability to rectify problems brought on by adults, including molestation, rape, running away from home, and racial and homophobic prejudice. Although often troubled, unlike Salinger's Holden Caulfield, Barry's characters are optimistic. Her stories and other work range from the gut-wrenching, to the teen angst world of dating, to the hilarious and whimsical. Also an essayist, Barry has written for national magazines and newspapers, focusing mainly on the special perspectives of children and the challenges that face them.

BIBLIOGRAPHY

Barry, Lynda. *Big Ideas.* Seattle: Real Comet Press, 1983.

———. *Cartoon Collections Girls + Boys.* Real Comet Press, 1981.

———. *Come Over Come Over.* New York: HarperPerennial, 1990.

———. *Cruddy.* New York: Simon & Schuster, 1999.

———. *Down the Street.* New York: Perennial Library, 1989.

———. *Everything in the World.* New York: Perennial Library, 1986.

———. *The Freddie Stories.* Seattle: Sasquatch Books, 1999.

———. *The Fun House.* New York: Perennial Library, 1987.

———. *Girls and Boys.* Seattle: Real Comet Press, 1981.

———. *The Good Times Are Killing Me.* Seattle: Real Comet Press, 1988.

———. *It's So Magic.* New York: Harperperennial, 1994.

———. *My Perfect Life.* New York: Harperperennial, 1992.

———. *Naked Ladies, Naked Ladies, Naked Ladies.* Seattle: Real Comet Press, 1984.

———. *Shake, Shake, Shake a Tail Feather.* New York: Harper & Row, 1989.

Calvin Hussman
St. Olaf College

BARTH, JOHN (SIMMONS) (1930–)

John Barth has been described as a master of contemporary fiction. Born in Cambridge, Maryland, he briefly studied jazz at the Juilliard School of Music before he entered Johns Hopkins University as a journalism major. He received his B.A. in creative writing from Johns Hopkins University in 1951 and his M.A. degree one year later. Barth has combined his long writing career with teaching at Pennsylvania State University, the State University of New York at Buffalo, and his alma mater, where he was Alumni Centennial Professor of English and Creative Writing from 1973 to 1990. In his retirement, Barth continues to publish fiction.

Although he is best known for his novels, Barth's stories "Night-Sea Journey," "LOST IN THE FUNHOUSE," "Title," and "Life-Story" from his collection of short fiction, *Lost in the Funhouse: Fiction for Print, Tape, Live Voice,* are widely anthologized. The book consists of 14 stories operating in a cycle that begins with the anonymity of origins and ends with the anonymity of a death and, withal, the narrator's exhaustion of his art. Three stories, "Ambrose His Mark," "Water Message," and "Lost in the Funhouse," reveal turning points in the life of Ambrose, a developing character throughout the collection. The three stories depict his naming as an infant; his first consciousness of fact, both in conflict and alliance with a romanticized truth; and a larger apprehension of life suffused with his first sexual consciousness. Barth's characters, or voices, are all natural storytellers compelled to make sense of their observations and experiences; they become METAPHORS for states of love, art and civilization. As they quest, the author joins them so that Barth's consciousness of his artistic technique often conforms with his consciousness of his characters and his subject matter.

In 1968 *Lost in the Funhouse* was nominated for the National Book Award, but *Chimera* won it in 1973. *Chimera* (1972) contains three NOVELLAS, each of which retells a MYTH. Like Barth, the HEROes of the three myths—Scheherazade, Perseus, and Bellerophon—are in the process of reorientation to discern their future. Although many reviewers see *Lost in the Funhouse* and *Chimera* as proof that Barth has been swallowed up by his own self-conscious obsession, others maintain that subsequent books demonstrate Barth's ability to invent new work by recycling both traditional literature and his own.

His most recent work, *On with the Story,* published in 1996, is a collection of short stories ostensibly told by one spouse to another while they are vacationing. Many of the stories involve middle-age academics and writers. This book has been described as an ambitious work that gives full scope to Barth's talent.

BIBLIOGRAPHY
Lindsay, Alan. *Death in the Funhouse: John Barth and Poststructural Aesthetics.* New York: Peter Lang, 1995.

Shulz, Max F. *The Muses of John Barth: Tradition and Metafiction from "Lost in the Funhouse" to "The Tidewater Tales."* Baltimore: Johns Hopkins University Press, 1980.

Harriet P. Gold
LaSalle College
Dawson College

BARTHELME, DONALD (1931–1989)

Although born in Philadelphia and raised in Texas, Barthelme moved to New York in 1962 and essentially became a New York writer who focused on the complexities, confusions, violence and apathy of urban life, but from an absurdist's viewpoint (see ABSURD). Often using disjointed prose and employing collage-like clichés, television ads, items from popular journalism, and media jargon, his short stories have been called "verbal objects," the written equivalent of pop art, reflecting his belief that contemporary reality can be described only in fragments. He was one of the most celebrated of the experimental writers to emerge in the 1960s, and his distinctive style is often imitated. One of the few POSTMODERNIST writers to focus almost exclusively on short fiction, Barthelme published most of his best work in the NEW YORKER prior to book publication.

Barthelme's characteristic themes and methods appear as early as his first story collection, *Come Back, Dr. Caligari* (1964), and are clearly in evidence in such stories as "BASIL FROM HER GARDEN." Barthelme's penchant for witty SATIRE and PARODY, as well as an imaginative, irreverent sense of the comedy of contemporary life, helps make him one of the most significant of the AVANT-GARDE writers of the late 20th century. In addition to the humor, however, Barthelme demonstrated an increasing interest in MYTH, building on his readers' familiarity with heroic stories and characters and reinventing them in contemporary ways. *Sixty Stories* (1981) collects many of his best short fictions to that date.

BIBLIOGRAPHY

Barthelme, Donald. *Amateurs.* New York: Farrar, Straus & Giroux, 1976.
———. *City Life.* New York: Farrar, Straus & Giroux, 1970.
———. *Come Back, Dr. Caligari.* Boston: Little, Brown, 1964.
———. *The Dead Father.* New York: Farrar, Straus & Giroux, 1975.
———. *The Emerald.* Los Angeles: Sylvester & Orphanos, 1980.
———. *Forty Stories.* New York: Putnam, 1987.
———. *Great Days.* New York: Farrar, Straus & Giroux, 1979.
———. *Guilty Pleasures.* New York: Farrar, Straus & Giroux, 1974.
———. *The King.* New York: Harper & Row, 1990.
———. *Overnight to Many Distant Cities.* New York: Putnam, 1983.
———. *Paradise.* New York: Putnam, 1986.
———. *Presents.* Dallas, Tex.: Pressworks, 1980.
———. *Sadness.* New York: Farrar, Straus & Giroux, 1972.
———. *Sam's Bar.* Garden City, N.Y.: Doubleday, 1987.
———. *Sixty Stories.* New York: Putnam, 1981.
———. *The Slightly Irregular Fire Engine; or The Thinking, Dithering Djinn.* New York: Farrar, Straus & Giroux, 1971.
———. *Snow White.* New York: Atheneum, 1967.
———. *The Teachings of Don B: The Satires, Parodies, Fables, Illustrated Stories, and Plays of Donald Barthelme.* Edited by Kim Herzinger. New York: Turtle Bay Books, 1992.
———. *Unspeakable Practices, Unnatural Acts.* New York: Farrar, Straus & Giroux, 1968.
"Barthelme Issue" of *Critique* vol 16, no. 3, 1975.
Couturier, Maurice and Regis Durand. *Donald Barthelme.* New York: Methuen, 1982.
Gordon, Lois. *Donald Barthelme.* Boston: Twayne, 1981.
Klinkowitz, Jerome. *Barthelme: An Exhibition.* Durham, N.C.: Duke University Press, 1991.
McCaffery, Larry. *The Metafictional Muse: The Works of Robert Coover, Barthelme, and William H. Gass.* Pittsburgh, Penn.: University of Pittsburgh Press, 1982.
Molesworth, Charles. *Donald Barthelme's Fiction: The Ironist Saved From Drowning.* Columbia: University of Missouri Press, 1982.
Roe, Barbara L. *Donald Barthelme: A Study of the Short Fiction.* New York: Twayne, 1992.
Stengel, Wayne B. *The Shape of Art in the Stories of Barthelme.* Baton Rouge: Louisiana State University Press, 1985.
Trachtenberg, Stanley. *Understanding Barthelme.* Columbia: University of South Carolina Press, 1990.

BARTHES, ROLAND (1915–1980) It is difficult to overestimate Roland Barthes's impact on current trends in contemporary literary theory (see POSTMODERNISM). His influence has profoundly reshaped literary theory not only in Europe, but also throughout the English-speaking world, particularly the United States. Born and raised in Bayonne, France, Barthes went on to become a professor, France's highest academic position, at the Collège de France, where he taught literature and semiotics until his accidental death in 1980. If for no other reason, Barthes's career is intriguing in that he recurrently revised and renewed his thinking, constantly broadening the range of his inquiries while embracing further developments in literary theory. His wide-ranging intellectual capacity and interests led him, throughout his career, to adopt and subsequently reject several schools of literary criticism. The deepening philosophical inquiries that motivate literary theory can be traced in the movement of Barthes's own essays, from STRUCTURALISM to popular culture studies and POSTSTRUCTURALISM with its investigations into new models of understanding the act of reading.

Barthes's highly idiosyncratic thinking is marked by two relatively consistent concerns. The first is the reader's participation in the authorship of the literary text. In one highly influential essay, Barthes proclaims the death of the author, by which he means that the reader has supplanted the author as the creator of meaning. A text has meaning, he suggests, only in relation to the mind of the reader, whom Barthes encourages to be as playful and creative as possible.

Barthes's second major concern is intellectual honesty. "I advance indicating my mask" was his mantra as a literary critic. In Barthes's view, all acts of interpretation come loaded with assumptions or, more precisely, with ideologies. This does not mean, however, that interpretation is a hopeless task; instead, it suggests that the interpreter must acknowledge and subsequently understand the way his or her own ideology affects the reading of a text. Failure to understand this amounts to intellectual bad faith. Therefore criticism, for Barthes, "is not an homage to the truth . . . [but] a construction of the intelligibility of our own times."

With his first book, *Writing Degree Zero* (1953), an extended response to Jean Paul Sartre's *What Is Literature?* (see EXISTENTIALISM), Barthes established himself as a high structuralist, employing the ideas of form and structure of grammar suggested by linguistic pioneers Ferdinand de Sausseur and Roman Jakobson to interpret the poetry of the French symbolists. Barthes argued that the French symbolists believed in the act of writing as an end unto itself, not merely as a means of expressing information. With his *Mythologies* (1957), Barthes broadened his

field of inquiry from French literature to the "grammar" or codes that inform European cultural ideas: in short, the "functions" at work not only in literature but in other social and cultural mores as diverse as advertising and the striptease. Barthes applied the methodologies of sociolinguistics and structural anthropology to various cultural manifestations in order to bring an empirical and scientific rigor, if not objectivity, to the act of interpretation.

Language was Barthes's primary theme throughout his career, whether the literary language of Balzac's NOVELLA *Sarrasine,* the cinematic language of Sergei Eisenstein's *Rasputin,* or even the social language of the fashion industry. The premise that meaning is a process, not a static, qualitative essence lies at the heart of Barthes's work. Arguably Barthes's most exciting work deals with ideas of textuality, or what constitutes a text, as distinct from a work of literature, and the eroticism of the act of reading and writing. In his later work, Barthes saw all reading as an act of rewriting a text, a way of actively engaging and producing meaning within the limits of a text's language. The text is a field of possibilities and ambiguities, Barthes argued, which a reader does not so much consume as participate in. A text, because of its many meanings, asks the reader to become an active collaborator in interpreting it. Because of this new model of literary writing and the shift of emphasis from literature as product to the newly foregrounded process of reading, Barthes declared in such essays as "From Work to Text" and "The Death of the Author" that the traditional practice of defining a work in terms of the author and the author's oeuvre was no longer relevant.

Over the years, Barthes's own writing shifted from the lively but densely academic style of his early career to an essay form that blended criticism with the type of style that characterized the literature he wrote about: fragmentary, nonlinear, and often self-reflexive, or self-absorbed. Clearly, Barthes, as he matured, illustrated by example his belief that criticism was a way of actively participating with a text, criticism was itself a process, and he strove to blur the boundaries between art and criticism. Indeed, in Barthes's last work he focused on the eroticism inherent in the process of reading, that union of reader and text, and turned from philosophical insights on literature to himself, in *Roland Barthes on Roland Barthes* and *Camera Lucida*. Barthes's influence on contemporary theories remains formidable and can be seen in the work of Susan Sontag, Paul de Man, and countless others.

BIBLIOGRAPHY

Barthes, Roland. *A Barthes Reader.* New York: Hill and Wong, 1982.

———. *The Grain of the Voice: Interviews, 1962–1980.* New York: Hill and Wong, 1985.

———. *Roland Barthes.* Trans. Richard Howard. Berkeley: University of California Press, 1994.

———. "What Is Criticism?" In *Critical Essays.* Chicago: Northwestern University Press, 1978.

Brown, Andrew. *Roland Barthes: The Figures of Writing.* New York: Oxford University Press, 1992.

Knight, Diana. *Barthes and Utopia: Space, Travel, Writing.* New York: Oxford University Press, 1997.

Martinsson, Yvonne. *Eroticism, Ethics and Reading.* Stockholm: Almquist & Wiksell International, 1996.

Miller, D. A. *Bringing Out Roland Barthes.* Berkeley: University of California Press, 1992.

Richard Deming
Columbus State Community College

Shannon Zimmerman
University of Georgia

"BARTLEBY THE SCRIVENER" HERMAN MELVILLE (1856)

Originally appearing in *Putnam's Monthly* in 1853 and later published as part of the 1856 collection entitled *The Piazza Tales*, "Bartleby" is arguably Herman MELVILLE's strongest work of short fiction and is often placed alongside his novel *Moby-Dick* as representative of the author's rich, complex genius. The story, with its subtitle "A Story of Wall Street," is narrated by an elderly Wall Street lawyer who specializes in bonds, mortgages, and title deeds, eschewing juries and trial law. He is, as he himself says, an "eminently safe man," one who has come to know all that he cares to about the world beyond his office and practice. The narrator employs two law copyists, Turkey and Nippers, who, because of their idiosyncratic temperaments, are both effective for only half of any given workday. To increase the office's productivity, the narrator hires Bartleby as a new copyist.

Bartleby begins his tenure strongly, voraciously throwing himself into the work, but soon his behavior begins to change. By the third day, when asked to help out on a tedious bit of proofreading, Bartleby declines, saying "I would prefer not to." As the weeks progress, Bartleby meets more and more requests from his employer and coworkers with his stock response, until finally he does no work at all and yet seems to have taken up residence at the office. Throughout the story Bartleby's behavior and response change not at all, even as the circumstances around him do. Bartleby's staunch passivity forces the employer finally to move his office. He leaves Bartleby, who would not leave the premises even after being fired, behind. The new tenants have the scrivener tossed into debtor's prison, where he later dies.

Clearly, the story is less about Bartleby than it is about the narrator, who when initially introduced is entirely passive and complacent. Indeed, the narrator discovers very little about Bartleby other than a rumor that he had once worked in the dead letter office. In response to Bartleby's fate, however, the narrator becomes capable of feeling pity and compassion. In this way, the scrivener acts as a FOIL, allowing the reader to learn about the narrator and to see the way he develops throughout the story. As the narrator changes, so does the tone of the story he relates. At first Bartleby's behavior seems comical, as does the narrator's emotional inability to force Bartleby to comply with his requests. When Bartleby's response fails to change even as his situation becomes more dire, however, Bartleby himself seems locked into his fate, unable to be anything but passively resistant. The tone turns bleaker as Bartleby draws further into an impenetrable wall of unresponsiveness, and the narrator's outlook becomes more and more existential (see EXISTENTIALISM).

There is no shortage of varied readings of "Bartleby." Some argue that the scrivener represents Melville himself, whose fame diminished the more he moved away from writing the South Sea romances on which he had begun his literary career and toward the more challenging experiments in narrative modes found in *Pierre* and *Moby-Dick*. Other readings emphasize the story's intrinsic existentialism. Jorge Luis Borges even has argued that Melville's story prefigures the KAFKAESQUE use of psychological tensions in fiction. At the very least, "Bartleby" is Melville's most cohesive and ultimately most moving work, perhaps because it focuses not on grand epic or social tragedy, as is found in BENITO CERENO or *BILLY BUDD, SAILOR*, but instead on the personal and tragic plight of an individual and the narrator's inability to truly understand him. As always, Melville's characteristic use of SYMBOLISM and resonant IMAGERY make this text particularly open to various critical and theoretical approaches.

BIBLIOGRAPHY
Bloom, Harold. *Modern Critical Interpretations: Billy Budd, "Benito Cereno," "Bartleby the Scrivener," and Other Tales.* New York: Chelsea House, 1987.
Inge, M. Thomas. *Bartleby the Inscrutable: A Collection of Commentary on Herman Melville's Tale, "Bartleby the Scrivener."* Hamden, Conn.: Archon Books, 1979.
McCall, Dan. *The Silence of Bartleby.* Ithaca, N.Y.: Cornell University Press, 1989.
Melville, Herman. *Great Short Works of Herman Melville.* New York: Perennial Library, 1969.

Richard Deming
Columbus State Community College

BASIL AND JOSEPHINE STORIES, THE
F. SCOTT FITZGERALD (1973)   Between 1928 and 1931, when F. Scott FITZGERALD had trouble making progress on his novel *Tender Is the Night,* he returned to memories of his adolescence and young manhood to compose two story sequences for the SATURDAY EVENING POST. For several years during and after their composition, Fitzgerald considered publishing the stories as a book. His hesitation was the result of the dilemma that more than any other defined his career: If he published successful stories in popular magazines he could support himself financially, but he risked being typecast as a popular entertainer instead of a serious artist. He decided

not to rework the stories for a book in part because he wanted his novel to make its debut unencumbered by associations with his lighter fiction.

In his fourth story collection, *Taps at Reveille* (1935), he published five of the Basil stories and three stories from the Josephine (see JOSEPHINE PERRY) sequence. In 1973 Jackson R. Bryer and John Kuehl collected all 14 of the stories in one volume as *The Basil and Josephine Stories.*

BASIL DUKE LEE is modeled closely on Fitzgerald himself, and Josephine Perry is a fictionalized version of Geneva King, the wealthy debutante from Chicago with whom Fitzgerald had a brief, disappointing romance during his Princeton years. Both story sequences are romantic (see ROMANTICISM) in TONE and style, as Fitzgerald contrasts the urgent, narcissistic desires of young people with the harsh limitations of reality they encounter. Fitzgerald describes the humiliations and disillusionments that accompany the maturation process with the same emotional precision he brought to his early fiction, such as "BERNICE BOBS HER HAIR" and the novel *This Side of Paradise.*

The Basil stories begin in 1909 with Basil at age 11 and follow him as he attends boarding school in the East, ending with his departure for Yale. Although the stories reflect comfortable middle-class life in the conservative Midwest, Basil's yearnings and his foolish mistakes in managing them make him at moments a sympathetic and universally recognizable adolescent on the brink of manhood. Only eight of the nine stories were published in the *Post.* "That Kind of Party," which describes kissing games played by 10- and 11-year-old children, was apparently considered inappropriate for publication by the editors, according to Arthur Mizener. In other stories, Basil learns the difference between romantic illusions and reality in his relationships with both women and men and in his literary accomplishments. Basil is a character divided between romantic exuberance and a moral honesty that allows him, by slow degrees, to develop a saving pragmatism. As a study of the effect of American middle-class mores on a romantic, artistic boy as he grows up, the Basil stories identify the rebellions and concessions necessary for the preservation of an individuality that avoids egotism.

Josephine, of the five Josephine Perry stories, is the spoiled and snobbish daughter of a wealthy, established family. The stories, which begin when she is 16, and end just before she turns 18, reveal the sexual politics of the time: A woman considered "speedy" was popular; once she became "fast," however, her reputation was ruined. Josephine narrowly avoids acquiring the latter term in "A Woman with a Past," and in other stories she deftly makes her way through a succession of men whom she regards as objects for acquisition and display. Once she has kissed them, all the excitement of the chase subsides immediately as she looks to the next conquest.

In the last story in the sequence, "Emotional Bankruptcy," Josephine experiences her only moment of insight into her reckless pursuit of self-satisfaction as she realizes, in the company of a man she ought to love, that she is incapable of feeling anything anymore. This is the first story in which Fitzgerald developed the concept he would return to later in fiction and in his three autobiographical pieces for ESQUIRE collectively referred to as "The Crack-Up" essays. People have limited emotional capital, he believed; spending it recklessly all at once leaves one depleted for later experiences.

BIBLIOGRAPHY

Bryer, Jackson R., and John Kuehl, eds. "Introduction," F. Scott Fitzgerald, *The Basil and Josephine Stories*. New York: Collier Books, 1973.

Eble, Kenneth. *F. Scott Fitzgerald*. Rev. ed. Boston: Twayne Publishers, 1977.

Nagel, James. "Initiation and Intertextuality in The Basil and Josephine Stories." In *New Essays on F. Scott Fitzgerald's Neglected Stories*. Edited by Jackson R. Bryer. Columbia: University of Missouri Press, 1996.

Piper, Henry Dan. *F. Scott Fitzgerald: A Critical Portrait*. New York: Holt, Rinehart and Winston, 1965.

Frances Kerr
Durham Technical Community College

BASIL DUKE LEE   Basil Duke Lee is the PROTAGONIST of F. Scott FITZGERALD's short story sequence about a boy growing up in the conservative Midwest at the turn of the 20th century. Over the course of the nine stories, Basil develops the multidimensional quality of a CHARACTER in a novel. Basil demonstrates "negative capability"—John Keats's terms for the ability to hold in one's mind two opposing ideas at the same time. Basil can experience his romantic exuberance while perceiving it objectively, which teaches him to separate illusion from reality. This learning process occurs in all nine stories as he experiences disillusionment in romances with girls, in social competition among the boys at his boarding school, and in his literary pursuits and love of fantasy. His ability to perceive the moral consequences of his urgent desires brings him to the realization that "life for everybody is a struggle"—a discovery necessary for maturation. (See "BASIL AND JOSEPHINE STORIES, THE".)

BIBLIOGRAPHY

Eble, Kenneth. *F. Scott Fitzgerald*. New York: Macmillian, 1977.

Frances Kerr
Durham Technical Community College

"BASIL FROM HER GARDEN" DONALD BARTHELME (1985)   "Basil from Her Garden," first published in the NEW YORKER on October 21, 1985, and reprinted in *The Best American Short Stories 1986* (see Appendix I), is a postmodernist tale (see POSTMODERNISM) using METAFICTIONAL, minimalist techniques. (See MINIMALISM.) Barthelme's presentation of a disconnected dialogue between two PROTAGONISTS, identified only as Q and A, raises unresolved ethical issues. This dialogue simultaneously suggests a question-and-answer—a Q and A—interview and a therapy session. Oddly, however, A always seems to raise the ideas essential to the story's meaning, whereas Q seems to be the respondent: Although A literally appears in the role of patient or client, Q appears to question his own sense of depression in a world whose values no longer seem certain. Thus A provides the answers to Q's questions about his— and, the text implies, the modern reader's—dilemma. Another possibility is that A and Q are merely two sides of one personality, DOPPELGANGERS.

Together, A and Q consider such human foibles as adultery and guilt. A tells Q about his eclectic interests, including bowhunting, environmentalism, adultery, and the CIA. Their discussion, at times both comic (see COMEDY) and ABSURD, ranges across philosophical and moral fields, and when Q observes that the Bible's Seventh Commandment forbids adultery, A defends his extramarital activities, which, he explains, are in fact confined to one woman, Al Thea. Indeed, to make his point about various human connections, A refers to several women: Al Thea, with whom he is having an affair; his wife, Grete, who, he says, does not deserve his philandering; his hair cutter, Ruth, a "good" person; and his unnamed neighbor for whom he feels the sort of friendship that consists in neighborly good deeds: he fixes her dead car batteries, and she, in return, offers him her fresh garden-grown basil. Although for Q many questions remain (he reveals his fantasy solution of working in Pest Control), the story's final note of qualified optimism and possibility recalls the ending of Edward ALBEE's play *Who's Afraid of Virginia Woolf?* Critic Barbara L. Roe suggests that "Basil From Her Garden" be read in conjunction with Barthelme's story, "Kierkegaard Unfair to Schlegel" (Roe 62).

BIBLIOGRAPHY

Barthelme, Donald. "Basil From Her Garden," in *The Best American Short Stories 1986*. Edited by Raymond Carver and Shannon Ravenel. Boston: Houghton Mifflin, 1986, pp. 1–9.

Klinkowitz, Jerome, with Asa Pictatt and Robert Murray Davis. *Donald Barthelme: A Comprehensive Bibliography and Annotated Secondary Checklist*. Hamden, Conn.: Shoestring Press, 1977.

Roe, Barbara L. *Donald Barthelme: A Study of the Short Fiction*. New York: Twayne, 1992.

"BATTLE ROYAL" RALPH ELLISON (1948)

Ralph ELLISON's "Battle Royal," also published as the first chapter of *Invisible Man* (1952), previews the major THEMES that arise in much 20th-century African-American fiction (See AFRICAN-AMERICAN SHORT FICTION.) The story uses first-person narration, but Ellison chooses to leave the narrator nameless, suggesting his invisibility to white culture and his ongoing attempt to construct an identity.

The first-person narrator (see POINT OF VIEW) is the adult man recalling a scene from his youth from a perspective of 20 years. Referring twice in one paragraph to a time "eighty-five years ago," he simultaneously alludes to the Emancipation Proclamation (see CIVIL WAR) and belatedly honors his grandparents, particularly his grandfather, who came of age during both the war and RECONSTRUCTION. On his deathbed, his grandfather revealed that he had been a "traitor" and a "spy": He might have seemed an "Uncle Tom," but in fact he had fought a covert "war" and hoped that his son, the narrator's father, would continue to fight (BR 1519). Establishing the battle IMAGERY, then, the narrator describes the horrors of his "battle royal" before he delivers his high school graduation speech.

As a youth, the narrator had believed that his grandfather was crazy, that his words were a "curse" (1520), and that a young black man could achieve success only by pleasing the town's white leaders. When these "big shots" invite him to deliver his graduation speech at the best hotel in town, he naively agrees, but when he arrives, he is plunged into a version of hell. Like Nathaniel Hawthorne's YOUNG GOODMAN BROWN, he sees a gathering of the town's most prominent white men—educators, merchants, pastors, judges—all of whom participate in the liquor-ridden, smoke-filled rite called the "battle royal." Through his description, Ellison succinctly demonstrates the way the white men use women and African Americans to remind them of their "place." A young blonde woman with a tattoo of the American flag on her belly dances nude for the pleasure of the men. The tattoo makes her the PERSONIFICATION of the AMERICAN DREAM—a dream that the narrator and nine other black youths are forced to look at, but must never touch. In another sense, of course, the woman represents the symbol of sacred white womanhood whom blacks gaze upon only at their peril, evoking the white male fears of black sexuality that resulted in the lynching of so many black men. Near the end of the performance, as the men obscenely prod and probe this "circus kewpie doll," tossing her into the air like a toy, the narrator notes the "terror and disgust" in her eyes that mirror his own, thereby implicitly equating the subjugation of American women with that of African Americans.

In the actual battle, the white men force these "boys" to fight among themselves. Yelling racial slurs, the white men enjoy pitting black against black, casually betting on them as they would bet on racehorses or other animals. With the narrator's realization that he must fight Tatlock, the biggest "boy" of all, comes the first subtle hint that he has inherited his grandfather's subversive tendencies: He suggests that they only pretend to fight. Tatlock, however, fails to understand that by fighting the narrator he is only pleasing the white men, and he naively takes pride in his victory, transferring to the narrator the hostility that should be directed at the white men. In the final stage of the battle, the youths are forced to fight each other for coins scattered on an electrified rug so that they suffer shocks each time they try to acquire the money. At the conclusion of this episode, the white men toss one of the black boys in the air just as they had the white woman, demonstrating their power. As Bernard Bell has explained, the bizarre scenes dramatize "a pattern of behavior designed by whites to emasculate and humiliate black men: reinforcing the taboo against sexual contact between black men and white women, duping young blacks into fighting each other rather than their primary oppressors, and encouraging them to sacrifice moral values for material gain" (Bell 197).

When the bloodied narrator delivers his Booker T. Washington–inspired speech, it is anticlimactic; no one cares what he has to say, although when he inadvertently uses the phrase "social equality," the white men force him to retract the words. Although at this point he hastily acquiesces, his use of the words foreshadow more subversive activities to come. First, however, as he says at the end, he must acquire a college education, and thus he accepts the scholarship to the black state college. Nonetheless, his dream of his resisting grandfather stays with

him, and will ultimately help him not only to use the system but also to understand that his grandfather was correct: Subservience will not bring African Americans out of slavery, 20th-century style.

BIBLIOGRAPHY

Bell, Bernard. *The Afro-American Novel and Its Tradition.* Amherst: University of Massachusetts Press, 1989.

Ellison, Ralph. "Battle Royal." In *The American Tradition of Literature.* Edited by George Perkins and Barbara Perkins. Boston: McGraw Hill, 1999, pp. 1519–1528.

Amy Strong
University of North Carolina at Chapel Hill

BATHOS　Originating with the Greek critic Longinus, the word, meaning "depth," was parodied by Alexander Pope in 1727 in his essay "On Bathos, or Of the Art of Sinking in Poesy." Ever since, the word has been used for an unintentional descent in literature when, straining to be pathetic or passionate or elevated, the writer overshoots the mark and drops into the trivial or the ridiculous. ANTICLIMAX is sometimes used as an equivalent for bathos.

BAYARD SARTORIS　A young boy in the first of the interconnected stories in William FAULKNER'S THE UNVANQUISHED, "Ambuscade," Bayard grows from boyhood to young manhood. He is the son of Colonel John Sartoris, who is away fighting in the CIVIL WAR during many of the stories. Bayard enacts a coming-of-age ritual when he seeks to avenge Miss Rosa Millard's death and then another when he refuses to avenge his father's death, firmly ignoring the code of vengeance demanded of him by the traditions of the Old South. He also becomes one of Faulkner's sensitive men who feel drawn to but refuse the attentions of attractive women. (See also GAVIN STEVENS.) In "An Odor of Verbena," Bayard refuses the attentions of the young DRUSILLA HAWKE, a young widow now married to his father. After the Civil War Bayard becomes president of the bank in Jefferson and survives until, in Faulkner's novel *Flags in the Dust,* his grandson and namesake, a WORLD WAR I veteran, drives him in a fast car and old Bayard suffers a heart attack.

"BEAR, THE" WILLIAM FAULKNER (1942)

The most frequently anthologized story from the interconnected stories in GO DOWN, MOSES, "The Bear" details the profoundly moving relations among the young white boy Ike McCaslin, the Chickasaw Indian Sam Fathers, and several other black and white characters, including Ash, the black cook, and Major de Spain, the prominant white landowner who also appears in Faulkner's story "BARN BURNING." The story concerns Ike's coming-of-age hunt for the bear, which he finally kills. Considered one of Faulkner's greatest stories, "The Bear" contains passages of lyrically haunting intensity as civilization and nature metaphorically clash in the encounters between humans and woods, and between humans and animals. As critics belatedly realized, however, "The Bear" can be better understood not as an isolated story, but as one significant story interrelated with six others. Only in this context does the reader understand why Ike, although he successfully kills Old Ben, the bear, can fulfill the roles of neither savior nor hero: As the other stories amply attest, Ike cannot rid himself of his heritage of racism.

Trained for years by Sam Fathers, Ike is at his peak when he enters the woods, his skills second only to those of the Chickasaw. By the time we see him in "The Bear," he confidently decides that he needs none of the accoutrements of civilization and, as he enters the woods, discards his gun, his watch, his compass. While tracking Old Ben Ike displays courage and, through some of the finest language in the 20th century short story, experiences a spiritual union with nature. Before Ben dies, the unarmed Ike has moved close enough to see a tick on Ben's leg, and to breathe in the odor of his hide. This day will live forever in Ike's memory, but by the end of the story its potential has already diminished: Sam Fathers dies shortly after Old Ben, and loggers move ever more swiftly to destroy the woods.

Although Ike understands the Indians and nature and has respect for both, his weaknesses have to do with women and with blacks, as revealed in his final appearance in the story, "Delta Autumn." In this story the 80-year-old Ike—who as a boy in "The Bear" showed such promise for respecting all races as well as the environment—displays racism and sexism when he rejects the loving overtures of a nameless black woman who reveals her kinship to him. Significantly, old Ike's action occurs during WORLD WAR II: the world is in chaos, and he cannot relinquish the ways of the Old South. The ideal union with nature and his fellow creatures that Ike so passionately sought in "The Bear" is, to use one of the story's most recurring words, doomed.

"BEAST IN THE JUNGLE, THE" HENRY JAMES (1903)

Henry JAMES's "The Beast in the Jungle" (1903) is unusual in its concentration of focus. Although the story is relatively long (about 50 pages), it contains only two characters. The narrative is not continuous, but rather a series of dramatic scenes, always limited to meetings of the two characters. Their names, *May* Bartram and John *March*er, suggest the sustained motif of the seasons, rendered as the passage from late youth to old age and death. Marcher believes that he is "being kept for something rare and strange, possibly prodigious and terrible," a fate that is figured by the "beast" of the title. May waits in vain for some response from Marcher. After May's death, Marcher concludes, "The escape would have been to love her; then, then he would have lived." Instead, "no passion had ever touched him."

Marcher is part of a tradition of passive aesthetes in American literature, from Coverdale in Nathaniel HAWTHORNE's *The Blithedale Romance* to Prufrock in T. S. Eliot's "The Love Song of J. Alfred Prufrock." Many traditional readings of this late tale link its THEMES to the famous passage in James's novel, *The Ambassadors,* where Strether exclaims, "Live! live all you can! It's a mistake not to!" In these interpretations Marcher, who is apparently indifferent to May's desire, does not live, or at least does not live well, or self-interrogatively. Leon Edel, a biographer of James, claims that the tale has a biographical basis in James's indifference to the writer Constance Fenimore WOOLSON. According to Edel, James had "taken her friendship, and never allowed himself to know her feelings" ("Introduction" 10).

In a famous essay, Eve Kosofsky Sedgwick argues against such a romanticized reading as Edel's—which she terms homophobic because it imagines heterosexuality as the exclusive solution to the absence of love. Sedgwick situates Marcher in the tradition of the Victorian bachelor, the unmarried man of leisure and, frequently, the aesthete. She sees in these figures an example of what would soon be created as the homosexual, for the moment just on the cusp of coming into being. Sedgwick argues that we should look not for homosexual acts or consciousness in the text but rather for the unsaid, for the gaps of language that avoid precision. In this sense, to readers interested in the history of sexuality, homosexuality is present through its panicked absence in "The Beast in the Jungle."

BIBLIOGRAPHY
Edel, Leon, ed. *The Complete Tales of Henry James.* Vol. 11, 1900–1903. Philadelphia: Lippincott, 1964.
Sedgwick, Eve Kosofsky. "The Beast in the Closet: James and the Writing of Homosexual Panic." In *Sex, Politics, and Science in the Nineteenth-Century Novel.* Edited by Ruth Bernard Yeazell. Baltimore: Johns Hopkins University Press, 1986, pp. 148–186.

Robert K. Martin
Université de Montréal

BEAT GENERATION

The writers celebrated as the creators of a "beat generation" never thought of themselves as establishing or perpetuating an organized movement. As Gary Snyder observed after receiving the PULITZER PRIZE for poetry in 1974, the term properly applies only to a small circle of friends, particularly Neal Cassaday, Allen Ginsberg, John Clellon Holmes, and Jack KEROUAC, who gathered around William Burroughs in New York City in 1948. Burroughs remained a close friend of the group, but his own experimental work is greatly different in style and purpose from that of the beats. Holmes introduced the term "beat generation" in his little-noticed first novel *Go* (1952). Earlier that year Kerouac had already published his first novel, *The Town and the City,* a conventional romantic BILDUNGSROMAN influenced by Thomas Wolfe that gave

no hint of Kerouac's later work. He completed the third version of ON THE ROAD in 1951, but publishers quickly rejected it.

The "movement" became news after a public poetry reading at the Six Gallery in San Francisco on October 13, 1955, by Philip Whalen, Philip LaMantia, Gary Snyder, Michael McClure, and Allen Ginsberg, who crowned the evening by reading the just completed first part of his poem *Howl.* He scored a howling success, and Lawrence Ferlinghetti, proprietor of the local City Lights bookshop, immediately offered to publish the finished poem in his new pocket poets series of paperbacks. The first edition, printed in London, where production costs were lower then, attracted enough attention to sell out locally. When a second printing arrived on March 25, 1957, it was held up by U.S. Customs as obscene. Although Customs released the pamphlet in May, city police stepped in to institute condemnation proceedings against Ferlinghetti as the publisher. A nationally publicized trial ensued, at which distinguished poets and academics came to the defense of Ferlinghetti and Ginsberg. The testimony of University of California professor Mark Schorer particularly influenced Municipal Court Judge Clayton Horn's decision on October 3, clearing the poem of not possessing, as the prosecution charged, "the slightest redeeming social importance."

This verdict was followed up by two articles by poet Kenneth Rexroth, leader of the long-established San Francisco Renaissance group: "San Francisco Letter" in the second issue of New York City's *Evergreen Review,* which also contained the text of the poem, and "Disengagement: The Art of the Beat Generation," in the Arabel Porter's influential *New World Writing,* a semiannual publication in the New American Library. *On the Road* was then published at last in October 1957 and received a tremendous and sales-promoting controversial reception.

Ginsberg's and Kerouac's writings attracted hordes of dissatisfied young people from all over the country to San Francisco's North Beach, where poetry readings flourished in coffeehouses and Rexroth and Ferlinghetti hosted poetry-jazz sessions that they believed gave the movement its greatest importance in a merging of the arts at popular nightclubs.

The city, and especially the police, who still smarted from losing the "Howl" case, however, grew increasingly aggravated by the presence on the streets of a motley crew of camp followers that popular columnist Herb Caen labeled "beatniks," especially since drugs had become a significant part of communal rituals. Poet and University of California professor Thomas Parkinson, who championed the beat movement, prepared in 1961 *A Casebook on the Beat,* a popular book providing materials for college research papers on the subject. In it he expressed great annoyance at the poets being lumped together with sensation-seekers and drew a useful distinction between the beats as serious, dedicated, hardworking artists and the beatniks as untalented loafers for whom life was one long party. Finally complaints from tourists about panhandlers and local pressure groups drove the police to begin a series of raids that drove many of the serious beats, led by Pierre DeLattre, poet and novelist proprietor of the popular Bread and Wine Mission, to Mexico, especially San Miguel Allende, where Neal Cassady later died. The beat scene shifted back to New York City, dominated by Leroi Jones (who later changed his name to Amiri Baraka) and Diane di Prima, who later abandoned the movement for greater involvement in 1960s activism that the original beats eschewed.

During the high years on North Beach, the movement that denied being a movement engendered only one publication suggesting a central focus, *Beatitude* (pronounced *beat*-i-tude), a mimeographed poetry journal that produced 15 issues at irregular intervals in 1959 and early 1960, supported by Lawrence Ferlinghetti. He selected from them a *Beatitude Anthology,* which contained only 25 poems and few prose pieces (mainly letters, no short stories), warning that even all of these were not "on the beat frequency."

There certainly was no beat "movement" if one thinks of "movements" in terms of groups organized around programs for collective action. The originators' concept of the high-minded but elusive aim of their writing was best summarized in 1982 by Allen Ginsberg at a small convocation that celebrated the 25th anniversary of the publication of *On the Road.* Ginsberg took exception to some remarks by dynamic activist Abbie Hoffman: "I think there was one slight shade of error in describing the Beat movement as primarily a protest movement. . . . That was the thing that Kerouac was always complaining about; he felt that the literary aspect or the spiritual aspect or the emotional aspect was not so much protest at all but a declaration of unconditioned mind beyond protest, beyond resentment, beyond loser, beyond *winner—way* beyond winner. . . ." This was the "disengagement" from conventionally received ideas that Kenneth Rexroth had first noted characterized the beat generation.

If this movement did constitute any kind of youthful rebellion, it was the last one so far to have its origins in a literary tradition. Ginsberg and Kerouac were well read in both CLASSIC and AVANT-GARDE literature. Their works were contemplative not action-provoking. Subsequently passingly fashionable groups such as the hippies and Yippies derived their impetus from rock music and activist paintings. The beats were the last defenders of the Word, seeking uncompromised language to transcend the propaganda of the brainwashers.

Movement or not, the beat remains a living force at Naropa Institute, founded in 1975 in Boulder, Colorado. There the 1982 convocation was one of many events sponsored by the Jack Kerouac School of Disembodied Poetics, long lovingly administered by Allen Ginsberg and Anne Waldman. It seeks to keep alive the tradition of mystical transcendence rather than activitist triumph as the aim of human striving.

Warren French
University of Swansea

BEAT LITERATURE If indeed there was a beat movement that left a landmark legacy of American writings of the mid-20th century, short stories constituted no part of it. The beats produced hardly any short stories at all. John Clellon Holmes, one of the original beat contingent in New York City in the early 1950s, published a few short stories in AVANT-GARDE magazines that have become virtually unobtainable; but these have never been collected, and Holmes considered himself not so much as a beat writer as the historian of his circle.

The three major retrospective anthologies of beat writing contain two very short stories by William S. Burroughs ("What Washington? What Orders?" [*The Beat Book,* 186–88] and "My Face" [*The Beat Book,* 188–94]) and one by Ed Sanders from *Tales of Beatnik Glory* ("A Book of Verse" [*The Portable Beat Reader,* 511–16]). The only writer known principally for his short stories included in Ann Charters's two-volume contribution to the *Dictionary of Literary Biography, The Beats,* subtitled *Literary Bohemians in Postwar America* (1983), is Michael Rumaker; and he is primarily associated with the Black Mountain School, a group whose often-downbeat writings testified to its affinities with the beats but which lacked the emphasis on mystic transcendence, "the unconditioned mind" that Allen Ginsberg stressed.

Charters's later *Portable Beat Reader* (1992) contains nothing that can be considered a short story; the prose pieces scattered throughout the text are excerpts from novels or autobiographies, personal letters, and confessions. Brenda Knight's *Women of the Beat Generation* (1996) similarly contains representative works from this long-neglected and important group, also primarily excerpts from autobiographies. The only short story is Hettie Jones's previously unpublished "Sisters, Right!" the touching account of strangers' perception of a white mother's relationship to her black daughter; Jones was married to the black beat poet Leroi Jones before he changed his name to Amiri Baraka. Like Jack Kerouac's novel, *On the Road,* the three-page story is thinly disguised autobiography, similar in style and content to Leroi Jones's poetry.

The lack of the beats' interest in the short story form may be explained by the similarity of their novels and confessional autobiographies to their poetry, which is generally intensely personal and free in form, influenced principally by the enormously influential 19th and 20th century poets Walt Whitman and William Carlos Williams.

Short story writing in the United States in the 1950s was dominated by tight construction, tersely clipped wording, and an impersonal, ironic story line (see IRONY) fostered by Whit Burnett's STORY magazine and the NEW YORKER, widely emulated by avant-garde little magazines and academic reviews. Part of the "disengagement" that the beats sought was from the editors and readers of these publications, who prized values that the beats distrusted. Rather than the ironic impersonality of the stories of William FAULKNER, Robert Penn Warren, and other influential members of the Southern-based New Critical school (see NEW CRITICISM), the beats sought inspiration in the loquacious, sometimes embarrassingly confessional outpourings of Whitman and Hart Crane. Principal beat works were marked by torrents of words, pointing a finger of guilt at a money-worshiping society and seeking self-absolution. Since WORLD WAR I, beginning with Sherwood ANDERSON, Ernest HEMINGWAY, and F. Scott FITZGERALD, in the United States the short story form had become the most disciplined form of American creative writing, especially under the tutelage of the developing university creative writing programs.

Allen Ginsberg in *Howl* saw Moloch, an ancient biblical god to whom children were sacrificed, not only in "endless oil and stone" but also as the evil force that frightened the poet out of his "natural ecstasy," which the beats sought through their disengagement from the "academies" that expelled "the best minds" of the generation for "publishing obscene odes on the windows of the skull." At the time when curiosity about the beats was at its peak, the possibilities of the short story form held no attraction for them.

Ironically, it is in two unprecedently long short stories published in the *New Yorker* that the beat concepts of "disengagement" and "unconditioned mind" were most strikingly projected. Even though J. D. SALINGER dismissed the "Dharma Bums" condescendingly in the second of these two stories, in both "Zooey" and "Seymour: An Introduction," climactic episodes (see CLIMAX) in his Glass family saga, he shared through them the beats' central concepts of "the unconditioned mind, beyond protest, beyond resentment, beyond loser, . . . *way* beyond winner." Fictional fantasies sometimes inspire unrecognized companions.

BIBLIOGRAPHY

Ann Charters, ed. *The Beats: Literary Bohemians in Postwar America.* Vol. 16, Parts 1 and 2 of *Dictionary of Literary Biography.* Detroit: Gale Research Co., 1983.

———, ed. *The Portable Beat Reader.* New York: Penguin Books, 1992.

Cherkovski, Neeli. *Ferlinghetti: A Biography.* Garden City, N.Y.: Doubleday, 1979.

French, Warren. *The San Francisco Poetry Renaissance, 1955–1960.* Boston: Twayne, 1991.

Holmes, John Clellon. *Passionate Opinions.* Fayetteville: University of Arkansas Press, 1988.

Jones, Leroi. *The Moderns: An Anthology of New Writing in America.* New York: Corinth Books, 1963.

Knight, Arthur and Kit. *The Unspeakable Visions of the Individual.* Vols. 5–14. California, Penn.: A.W. Knight, 1977–1984.

Knight, Brenda, ed. *Women of the Beat Generation: The Writers, Artists, and Muses at the Heart of Revolution.* Berkeley, Calif.: Conari Press, 1996.

Parkinson, Thomas, ed. *A Casebook on the Beat.* New York: Thomas Y. Crowell Co., 1961.

Tytell, John. *Naked Angels: The Lives and Literature of the Beat Generation.* New York: McGraw Hill, 1976.

Waldman, Anne, ed. *The Beat Book: Poems and Fiction of the Beat Generation.* Boston: Shambhala Publications, 1995.

Warren French
University of Swansea

BEATTIE, ANN (1947–)

Establishing herself as a talented chronicler of the generation reared in the 1960s, Ann Beattie has earned praise for both novels and short fiction, particularly for her ability to reproduce the ambience of contemporary life. Born in Washington, D.C., she graduated from American University in 1969, earned an M.A. from the University of Connecticut the following year, began publishing stories in the NEW YORKER, and, in 1979, published her first collection of stories, *Distortions,* and her first novel, *Chilly Scenes of Winter.* Since then she has published six additional short fiction collections and four novels.

The hallmarks of Beattie's fiction include emphatically realistic dialogue and the physical details as well as the specter of spiritual emptiness in contemporary life. Headlines, current soap operas, popular music, and even accurate depictions of weather contribute to the realism of her fiction, and she acknowledges a debt to Ernest HEMINGWAY for the laconic exchanges between and among her characters. Often compared to Raymond CARVER for her minimalist style (see MINIMALISM), Beattie portrays middle-aged children of the 1960s who attempt to discover meaning behind the vacant facade of their lives.

Beattie's work is not completely bleak, however. She has a wry, satiric sense of humor, although often so subtle that the reader may miss it altogether. Beattie's fictional people do not suggest NIHILISM, but appear to value the bonds of friendship, and, through their genuine attempts to communicate with others, they attempt to invest their lives with meaning.

BIBLIOGRAPHY

Beattie, Ann. *Backlighting.* Worcester, Mass.: Metacom Press, 1981.

———. *The Burning House.* New York: Random House, 1982.

———. *Chilly Scenes of Winter.* Garden City, N.Y.: Doubleday, 1976.

———. *Distortions.* Garden City, N.Y., Doubleday, 1976.

———. *Falling in Place.* New York: Random House, 1980.

———. *Love Always.* New York: Random House, 1985.

———. *Park City: New and Selected Stories.* New York: Alfred A. Knopf, 1998.

———. *Picturing Will.* New York: Vintage, 1991.

———. *My Life, Starring Dara Falcon.* New York: Alfred A. Knopf, 1997.

———. *Secrets and Surprises.* New York: Random House, 1978.

———. *What Was Mine: Stories.* New York: Random House, 1991.

———. *Where You'll Find Me and Other Stories.* New York: Linden Press/Simon & Schuster, 1986.

Gelfant, Blanche H. "Beattie's Magic Slate or The End of the Sixties." *New England Review* I, 1979.

Gerlach, John. "Through 'The Octoscope': A View of Beattie." *Studies in Short Fiction* 17, Fall 1980.

Montresor, Jaye Berman. *The Critical Response to Ann Beattie.* Westport, Conn.: Greenwood Press, 1993.

Murphy, Christina. *Ann Beattie.* Boston: Twayne, 1986.

Rainwater, Catherine and William J. Scheick, eds. *Contemporary American Women Writers: Narrative Strategies.* Lexington: University Press of Kentucky, 1985.

Samway, Patrick H. "An Interview with Ann Beattie." In *America.* Vol. 162: 18, May 12, 1990, pp. 469–471.

"BEHIND A MASK" LOUISA MAY ALCOTT (1866)

"Behind a Mask: or, A Woman's Power," perhaps more than any other work, stimulated the reconsideration of Louisa May ALCOTT's career that has taken place since 1975. The tale, originally published anonymously in *The Flag of Our Union* in four installments (October-November 1866), was the title piece of Madeleine Stern's first collection of recovered Alcott sensation tales in 1975. The dark, GOTHIC tone, the complex nature of its HEROINE, and the barely suppressed rage against the condition of 19th-century women made it an ideal piece with which critics could begin to explore other dimensions of Louisa May Alcott, "The Children's Friend."

"Behind a Mask" owes much to Alcott's reading of Charlotte Brontë's *Jane Eyre* and perhaps also of William Thackeray's *Vanity Fair,* while lodging a distinctly American protest against the British class system and celebrating America as the land of opportunity, or at least opportunism. It follows the exploits of Jean Muir, who, as the tale opens, meekly enters the Coventry mansion to report for employment as governess to 16-year-old Bella. Jean is received by the Coventrys with typical condescension. When Jean retires to her room for the evening, however, the reader learns she is not the 19-year-old waif she claims to be but a 30-year-old, divorced former actress with false teeth, a wig, and a drinking problem. Jean's acting skills are tested and found equal to the task as she works her way into and through the hearts of the younger Coventry son, Ned (Edward), and the elder son, Gerald, finally marrying their uncle, the elderly Lord Coventry. Tension builds as Jean seeks to secure her future before her former lovers can expose her. The power of this story rests largely on Alcott's characterization

of her complex heroine. On one hand, Jean is undoubtedly deceitful and manipulative. She already has brought one family to the brink of ruin, but they discover her sordid past just in time to prevent her marriage to their young son. The IMAGERY in the tale casts her at least as a calculating actress (when the family enacts a number of tableaux for entertainment, Jean is the only one of the women not worn out by the experience, which suggests how accustomed she is to acting), and often as a witch. Alcott also allows us to see another side of Jean, however: a young woman who longs for family and security, who tried the life of governess and companion before turning to acting in an attempt to support herself and who is desperate as often as she is powerful. Further, Jean brings life, laughter, and conversation to the dull Coventry household. She encourages Gerald to gain a commission for Ned in order to give him something to do (only partly to get him out of the way), and she inspires Gerald himself to take charge of his lands. Significantly, both the servants (who see through Jean more readily than the upper-class characters) and the Coventrys themselves grow to appreciate her lively presence.

While the unsavory nature of her heroine kept Alcott from claiming the story as her own when it was first published, Jean's activeness and determination make her a heroine who could be if not a sister to *Little Women's* Jo March or *Work's* Christie Devon, at least a distant relative. In other ways, too, this tale contains familiar Alcott THEMES. A belief in hard work and a disdain for class consciousness (although Alcott herself was not totally immune to such attitudes) permeate much of Alcott's work. The story also highlights Alcott's longtime interest in the theater. She acted in community groups, wrote plays for such groups, and attended as many performances in Boston as she could. Her visions of actresses and acting in this tale and others ("V.V.: or, Plots and Counterplots" [1865], "A Double Tragedy: An Actor's Story" [1865], *Work* [1873], and *Jo's Boys* [1886]) are nearly always sympathetic and frequently positive, unlike those in most fiction of the time. Real performances in Alcott's work, like the tableaux in "Behind a Mask," frequently reveal rather than conceal. This tightly plotted tale with its memorable heroine is one of the best of the short stories Alcott dared not put her name to during her lifetime, and one that has helped readers and critics know her better a century later.

BIBLIOGRAPHY

Elliott, Mary. "Outperforming Femininity: Public Conduct and Private Enterprise in Louisa May Alcott's 'Behind a Mask,'" *American Transcendental Quarterly* 8 no. 4 (December 1994): 299–310.

Fetterley, Judith. "Impersonating 'Little Women': The Radicalism of Alcott's 'Behind a Mask'," *Women's Studies* 10 no. 1 (1983).

Keyser, Elizabeth. *Whispers in the Dark: The Fiction of Louisa May Alcott.* Knoxville: University of Tennessee Press, 1993.

Smith, Gail K. "Who Was That Masked Woman? Gender and Form in Louisa May Alcott's Confidence Stories." In *American Women Short Story Writers: A Collection of Critical Essays.* Edited by Julie Brown. New York: Garland Publishing, 1995.

Stern, Madeleine. Introduction to *Behind a Mask: The Unknown Thrillers of Louisa May Alcott.* New York: William Morrow, 1975.

Christine Doyle Francis
Central Connecticut State University

BELLOW, SAUL (1915–)

Born in Lachine, Quebec, Canada, Saul Bellow is the son of Russian Jewish immigrants. He learned Yiddish, Hebrew, English, and French as he grew up in Montreal. In 1924, Bellow moved with his family to Chicago; after earning a B.A. at Northwestern University in 1937 and serving in the merchant marine during World War II, he lived in Paris and taught English at Princeton and New York University before returning to live in Chicago. A distinguished professor at the University of Chicago for many years, Bellow is one of the most respected contemporary writers in the United States. His numerous awards culminated in the Nobel Prize for Literature and the Pulitzer Prize in 1976. Although primarily known as a novelist, Bellow has written two collections of short stories, *Mosby's Memoirs and Other Stories* (1968), and *Him with His Foot in His Mouth and Other Stories* (1989), as well as several NOVELLAS and plays.

Along with other post–World War II American writers, Bellow has focused on the problems of the modern urban man in search of his identity. His early rootless heroes are convinced of the need for freedom, yet in their searches they frequently find loneliness and despair. As many critics have pointed out, however, after his pessimistic characters of the 1940s, Bellow became disillusioned with modernist angst (see MODERNISM), and Bellow's subsequent characters in both novels and short fiction appear more affirmative, more cheerful, able to confront the vicissitudes of modern life by asserting the worth and dignity of the individual human spirit.

In "Mosby's Memoirs," for example, the title story of the collection, Dr. Willis Mosby is in Mexico, trying to write his memoirs. After brooding over his past, he realizes that he needs to inject some humor into the manuscript, and so writes the story-within-a-story, about Lustgarden, a New Jersey shoe salesman, lately turned capitalist. His luck as an entrepreneur, however, is no better than it was as a marxist. At first the Lustgarden story serves as COMIC RELIEF, but then becomes serious as we realize that Lustgarden is a sort of psychic double, or DOPPELGANGER, for Mosby. Other stories in the collection—"A Father-to-be," for instance, in which the father projects a nightmarish future for his relationship with his son-in-law, serves the same alter-ego function.

Him with His Foot in His Mouth, a collection of five stories, evokes the vitality and humor of characters who survive and endure partly by engaging in conversations with willing listeners. In one of the most striking, "What Kind of a Day Did You Have?", Bellow presents a moving portrait of the intellectual—although readers may find, as have feminist critics, that this, and other, male protagonists are better delineated than female ones. Victor Wulpy, ill and knowing that death is imminent, can still engage in the excitement of intellectual thought and thus, in essence, cheat death a little longer. By continuing to confront the major human issues and conflicts—artistic, philosophic, sexual, and mortal—about art and morality, sex and death, he lives on, and in this role Wulpy is emblematic of Bellow's main characters in these two collections of short stories. Unlike some of his contemporaries, Bellow shows in his short fiction, as well as in his celebrated longer work, that the antidote to modern ills is to assume responsibility for them and to celebrate one's humanity.

BIBLIOGRAPHY

Bellow, Saul. *The Adventures of Augie March.* New York: Viking, 1953.

———. *Dangling Man.* New York: New American Library, 1944.

———. *The Dean's December.* New York: Harper & Row, 1982.

———. *Henderson the Rain King.* New York: Viking, 1959.

———. *Herzog.* New York: Viking, 1964.

———. *Him with His Foot in His Mouth and Other Stories.* New York, Harper & Row, 1984.

———. *Humboldt's Gift.* New York: Viking, 1975.

———. *More Die of Heartbreak.* New York: William Morrow, 1987.

———. *Mosby's Memoirs and Other Stories.* New York: Viking, 1968.

———. *Mr. Sammler's Planet.* New York: Viking, 1970.

———. *Seize the Day, with Three Short Stones and a One-Act Play.* New York: Viking, 1956.

———. *A Theft.* New York: Penguin, 1989.

———. *The Victim.* New York: New American Library, 1947.

Bradbury, Malcolm. *Saul Bellow.* London: Methuen, 1982.

Braham, Jeanne. *A Sort of Columbus: The American Voyages of Saul Bellow's Fiction.* Athens: University of Georgia Press, 1984.

Clayton, John Jacob. *Saul Bellow: In Defense of Man.* Bloomington: Indiana University Press, 1968; revised edition, 1979.

Cohen, Sarah Blacher. *Saul Bellow's Enigmatic Laughter.* Urbana: University of Illinois Press, 1974.

Detweiler, Robert. *Saul Bellow: A Critical Essay.* Grand Rapids, Mich.: Eerdmans, 1967.

Dutton, Robert R. *Saul Bellow.* New York: Twayne 1971; revised edition, 1982.

Fuchs, Daniel. *Saul Bellow: Vision and Revision.* Durham, N.C.: Duke University Press, 1984.

Goldman, L. H. *Saul Bellow's Moral Vision: A Critical Study of the Jewish Experience.* New York: Irvington, 1983.

Kulshrestha, Chirantan. *Saul Bellow: The Problem of Affirmation.* Atlantic Highlands, N.J.: Humanities Press, 1979.

Malin, Irving, ed. *Saul Bellow and the Critics.* New York: New York University Press, 1967.

Malin, Irving. *Saul Bellow's Fiction.* Carbondale: Southern Illinois University Press, 1969.

Newman, Judie. *Saul Bellow and History.* New York: St. Martin's, 1984.

Porter, M. Gilbert. *Whence the Power? The Artistry and Humanity of Saul Bellow.* Columbia: University of Missouri Press, 1974.

Rodrigues, Eusebio L. *Quest for the Human: An Exploration of Saul Bellow's Fiction.* Lewisburg, Penn.: Bucknell University Press, 1981.

Rovit, Earl. *Saul Bellow.* Minneapolis: University of Minnesota Press, 1967.

———. ed. *Saul Bellow: A Collection of Critical Essays.* Englewood Cliffs, N.J.: Prentice Hall, 1975.

Scheer-Schazler, Brigitte. *Saul Bellow.* New York: Ungar, 1973.

Tanner, Tony. *Saul Bellow.* New York: Barnes & Noble, 1967.

Trachtenberg, Stanley, ed. *Critical Essays on Saul Bellow.* Boston: G. K. Hall, 1979.

BENÉT, STEPHEN VINCENT (1898–1943)

Born in Bethlehem, Pennsylvania, Benét lived in Paris from 1926 to 1929, and during the 1930s and early 1940s was an active lecturer and radio propagandist for democracy. Recipient of poetry prizes, he also was awarded the Pulitzer Prize in 1929 and 1944; the O. Henry award in 1932, 1937, and 1940; and an American Academy Gold Medal the year of his death. One of America's most famous poets during his lifetime and a prolific writer of numerous books, plays, movie scripts, and opera libretti, Benét is best known for *John Brown's Body,* his epic narrative poem of the CIVIL WAR, and "THE DEVIL AND DANIEL WEBSTER," a short story. His work is characterized by his interest in FANTASY and American themes, including stories of American history, stories celebrating the country's ethnic and cultural diversity, and contemporary narratives. The patriotic and romantic themes of Benét's work (see ROMANTICISM) became less fashionable after his death and led some critics to label him an old-fashioned, quaint, and chauvinistic writer who wrote "formula stories" designed to appeal to mainstream readers. However, his use of fantasy, American historical and folk events, and his idealized, lyrical style created a subgenre of writing known as "the Benét short story" that continues to attract readers in the late 20th century.

BIBLIOGRAPHY

Benét, Stephen Vincent. *The Barefoot Saint.* Garden City, N.Y.: Doubleday, Doran & Company, Inc., 1929.

———. *The Devil and Daniel Webster.* New York: Readers' League of America, 1937.

———. *The Last Circle: Stories and Poems.* New York: Farrar, Straus, 1946.

———. *The Litter of Rose Leaves.* New York: Random House, 1930.

———. *O'Halloran's Luck and Other Short Stories.* New York: Penguin Books, 1944.

———. *Selected Poetry and Prose,* edited by Basil Davenport. New York: Holt, Rinehart and Winston, 1960.

———. *Short Stories: A Selection.* New York: Council on Books in Wartime, 1942.

———. *Tales Before Midnight.* New York: Farrar & Rinehart, Inc., 1939.

———. *Thirteen O'Clock: Stories of Several Worlds.* New York: Farrar & Rinehart, Inc., 1937.

Benét, William Rose. *Stephen Vincent Benét: My Brother Steve.* New York: The Saturday Review of Literature and Farrar & Rinehart, 1943.

Fenton, Charles A. *Benét: The Life and Times of an American Man of Letters.* New Haven, Conn.: Yale University Press, 1958.

Holditch, W. Kenneth. "Stephen Vincent Benét." In *Reference Guide to Short Fiction.* Edited by Noelle Watson. Detroit: St. James Press, 1994, pp. 66–68.

Stroud, Parry Edmund. *Benét.* New York: Twayne, 1962.

"BENITO CERENO" HERMAN MELVILLE (1856)

First appearing in *Putnam's Monthly Magazine* and later published as one of the stories collected in *The Piazza Tales,* Herman MELVILLE'S "Benito Cereno" stands as one of the author's strongest and darkest works. Melville uses elements of suspense and mystery to tell the story of the *San Dominick* and its captain, Don Benito Cereno. As is often the case with Melville's fiction, the title character is not so much the story's main PROTAGONIST but instead serves as the FOIL for the narrative's true focus. In this case the protagonist is Captain Amasa Delano, American commander of *The Bachelor's Delight,* a large trader ship off the coast of South America who comes across the *San Dominick,* a Spanish merchant ship carrying slaves and apparently lost and adrift. After boarding the ship, Delano quickly discerns that all is not as it appears, as he is greeted by Don Benito Cereno, an inebriated captain who can barely stand and seems not at all fit to command, and Babo, Cereno's personal slave, whose fawning over Cereno seems to mask his control of the captain. As the story unfolds, it becomes increasingly clear to Delano that Babo is really the one in command and that the slaves have taken over the ship. In the years right before the CIVIL WAR, such a slave uprising embodied a powerful political and personal threat to Melville's American audience. The volatile racial, moral, and cultural tensions on board the ship create a claustrophobic setting in which the story's events unfold.

As morally complex as any of Melville's other work, this story juxtaposes the worldly and broken Don Cereno, who seems complicit in his own fallen state, and Captain Delano, who in his relative trust and innocence is blind to the portent of Cereno's fate. The circle of deception arising in the exchanges of Babo, Cereno, and Delano forces the reader to doubt even the possibility of any objective truth. Melville's taut prose is punctuated here, as elsewhere, with a resonant SYMBOLISM culminating in the hauntingly poignant IMAGERY of the *San Dominick* and its figurehead, a skeleton wrapped in canvas with "Follow the Leader" scrawled on the hull beneath it.

As he does in such longer works as *Pierre, Moby-Dick,* and *The Confidence Man,* Melville brings together many different GENRES and modes in "Benito Cereno" in order to subvert the reader's expectations. With this story he combines elements of the South Sea adventure tale, by which he established his career with *Typee* and *Omoo,* and the suspense and psychological tension of the mystery. He further complicates the story by including in the DENOUEMENT extracts from a legal deposition that tells the "facts" in a light very different from the preceding narrative. By doing this Melville calls into question the authority of history, which is itself, at least in his story, as much an artifice as any fiction.

The blurring of genres and types of discourse that occurs in "Benito Cereno," together with its moral ambiguity, makes this a particularly rich story that invites interpretation by contemporary literary theorists, particularly those in POSTSTRUCTURALISM and postcolonial studies. Although not well received by his contemporaries, Melville's "Benito Cereno," like the rest of the author's work, continues to become more relevant to modern readers.

BIBLIOGRAPHY
Bloom, Harold. *Modern Critical Interpretations: Billy Budd, "Benito Cereno," "Bartleby the Scrivener," and Other Tales.* New York: Chelsea House, 1987.
Burkholder, Robert E., ed. *Critical Essays on Herman Melville's "Benito Cerino."* New York: G. K. Hall, 1992.
Melville, Herman. *Great Short Works of Herman Melville.* New York: Perennial Library, 1969.
Nnolim, Charles E. *Melville's "Benito Cerino": A Study in Name Symbolism.* New York: New Voices Publishing Co., 1974.

Richard Deming
Columbus State Community College

"BERNICE BOBS HER HAIR" F. SCOTT FITZGERALD (1920)

"Bernice Bobs Her Hair" is one of F. Scott FITZGERALD's signature pieces about the savage underside of the privileged classes. First published in the SATURDAY EVENING POST, Fitzgerald included it in his first story collection, *Flappers and Philosophers* (1920). The story's style is light, charming, and precise in its evocation of a world of car rides and country club dances where girls compete with each other for the flattering attention of bland young men. When Bernice comes to visit her cousin Marjorie, her social awkwardness makes her the object of gossip and pity. After instruction from Marjorie in how to appear charming and sincere while engaging in empty banter, Bernice becomes so accomplished a social actress that she threatens to surpass her cousin in popularity. When Marjorie retaliates, her viciousness concealed under charm, Bernice loses her popularity at once. Bernice has the final word, however, with a retaliatory act in which she forgoes all pretense of social grace.

That the shy and awkward Bernice could suddenly become a master of repartee is part of the story's visible machinery. Fitzgerald, however, worked within the magazine fiction formula to present a scathing portrayal of upper-class society. The story sometimes is described as an anatomy of young women's social competition, but its scope is much larger. The narrative opens with a panoramic scene of the country club at night under a black sky and then moves in to the "largely feminine" balcony where "a great babel of middle-aged ladies with sharp eyes and icy hearts" oversees the flirtations of the young couples below. No fathers are visible in the story. Bernice's Aunt Josephine dispenses old-fashioned advice just before she falls asleep, suggesting the exhausted state of her narrow view of the world. Like other modernist writers of the early 20th century, Fitzgerald mockingly feminized the conservative middle class. When Bernice bobs her hair, she becomes a symbol of a new masculine vigor and independence. Her hair is associated throughout the story with feminine charm and beauty. By cutting it she symbolically rejects and escapes the small-minded world of her social class. The story is an example of Fitzgerald's modernist vision and his skill at using popular magazine fiction for serious social analysis.

BIBLIOGRAPHY
Beegel, Susan F. "'Bernice Bobs Her Hair': Fitzgerald's Jazz Elegy for Little Women." In *New Essays on F. Scott Fitzgerald's Neglected Short Stories.* Edited by Jackson R. Bryer. Columbia: University of Missouri Press, 1996.
Matthew Bruccoli, "On F. Scott Fitzgerald and 'Bernice Bobs Her Hair.'" In *The American Short Story.* Edited by Calvin Skaggs. New York: Dell, 1977.

Frances Kerr
Durham Technical Community College

BESTIARIES

A popular form during the medieval period in England, these stories made allegorical (see ALLEGORY) use of the traits of beasts, birds, and reptiles, often assigning human attributes to animals who talk and act like the human types they actually represent. (See PERSONIFICATION.) Most of these animal FABLES were didactic as well as entertaining, clearly including moral and religious lessons. AESOP'S FABLES provide a classic example of the medieval bestiary. In the United States, African American writers have long used the bestiary, early examples of which appear in the UNCLE REMUS tales published by Joel Chandler HARRIS. Although in Euro-American literature a more common form for children, they exist in numerous other writings for adults, as in, for example, Don Marquis's stories and verses about a cockroach and a cat, *archie and mehitabel*. NATIVE AMERICAN writers have a long history of using a form of bestiary, from early tales in the oral tradition through Mourning Dove's coyote stories to Sherman ALEXIE'S story collection, the LONE RANGER AND TONTO FISTFIGHT IN HEAVEN. (See COYOTE STORY.)

BEST OF SIMPLE, THE   See SIMPLE STORIES.

BETTS, DORIS (1932–)   A native of Statesville, North Carolina, Doris June (Waugh) Betts attended the Women's College of the University of North Carolina (now UNC-Greensboro; 1950–53) and the University of North Carolina at Chapel Hill (1954). She began a journalism career at 18, writing and eventually editing for several North Carolina newspapers between 1950 and 1975. She married Lowry Matthews Betts in 1952 and, while rearing three children, continued to work as a journalist and fiction writer. Betts began teaching creative writing at UNC–Chapel Hill in 1966. She has written essays, served on several university commissions and writing panels, and is Alumni Distinguished Professor of English at the University of North Carolina at Chapel Hill.

Betts's first collection of short stories, *The Gentle Insurrection* (1954), won the G. P. Putnam-University of North Carolina Fiction Award. Her fiction writing career spans over four decades and includes five novels (including *The River to Pickle Beach* [1972] and *Heading West* [1981]) and two other story collections (*The Astronomer and Other Stories* [1966] and *Beasts of the Southern Wild and Other Stories* [1973]). She received a Guggenheim fellowship in fiction in 1958 and was a National Book Award Finalist in 1974 for her surrealistic collection *Beasts*. (See SURREALISM.) Betts's fiction is set predominantly in small Southern towns and concerns local, unexceptional people struggling between a search for personal identity and a commitment to family. Her allusive writing (see ALLUSION) contains elements of southern GOTHIC and GROTESQUE and has been compared to that of Walker Percy, Flannery O'CONNOR, Wallace Stevens, and Eudora WELTY. More than a regional Southern writer (see REGIONALISM), Betts explores such universal THEMES as racial prejudice, love, aging, mortality, and time. Critics praise her rich talent for CHARACTERIZATION, her feel for time and place, and her gift for depicting the treasures of the commonplace with humor, simplicity, and tough objectivity. Betts is a master of the short story; "The Astronomer," "The Mother-in-Law," and "The Hitchhiker" are considered three of her best. In recent years she has challenged herself to master the novel form. Each of Betts's succeeding novels has received greater scholarly acclaim. Her novel, *Souls Raised from the Dead* (1994), affirms human courage as a child succumbs to a fatal disease and the members of her fractured, far-from-perfect family find some compassion for one another. Her most recent novel is *The Sharp Teeth of Love* (1997).

BIBLIOGRAPHY

Evans, Elizabeth. "Another Mule in the Yard: Doris Betts' Durable Humor." *Notes on Contemporary Literature* (March 1981).

Holman, David M. "Faith and the Unanswerable Questions: The Fiction of Doris Betts." *Southern Literary Journal* (Fall 1982).

Inge, Tonette Bond, ed., *Southern Women Writers: The New Generation.* Tuscaloosa: University of Alabama Press, 1990.

Brenda M. Palo
University of North Carolina at Chapel Hill

BIERCE, AMBROSE (GWINNET) (1842–1914?)   At the age of 19, Bierce joined the Ninth Indiana Infantry and fought through the entire CIVIL

WAR, serving with distinction despite suffering severe wounds at the Battle of Kenesaw Mountain. He never lost the overwhelming memories of those years, and his story collections, *In the Midst of Life* (first titled *Tales of Soldiers and Civilians;* 1893), and *Can Such Things Be?* include his finest war tales with their descriptions of the misery, ghastliness, and shocking brutality of war. The 15 stories in *Tales of Soldiers* combine violent and contrived naturalism with realistic and factual descriptions of combat life, each story concerning the death of the good and the brave. Bierce was a clear master of the short story, and war, with its own framework of irony, fore-shortening of time, and rapid transitions and con-frontations, provided the setting and structure in an appropriate form. The war stories—a major contri-bution to fiction—show Bierce as one of the best military short story writers in American literary his-tory. Post–WORLD WAR I writers such as Erich Maria Remarque and Ernest HEMINGWAY later emulated the tone of disillusionment embodied in Bierce's work. Bierce was also a scathing satirist (see SATIRE), and many of his most witty and sardonic observations of the American scene appeared as a collection of aphorisms in *The Devil's Dictionary* (1911), first published as *The Cynic's Word Book* (1906). He also wrote ghost and horror stories in which he used local color as background and darkly disturbing analysis of the human psyche in his plots. Bierce had a notable ability to establish an atmosphere of horror through realistic, suggestive detail, but few of these are as successful as the war stories with their realistic ironies. Bierce traveled to Mexico in 1913, served with Pancho Villa's forces, and is presumed to have been killed in battle in 1914.

BIBLIOGRAPHY

Bierce, Ambrose. *Can Such Things Be?* New York: Cassell, 1893.

———. *Cobwebs from an Empty Skull.* New York: Routledge, 1874.

———. *Collected Works,* 12 Vols. New York: Walter Neale, 1909–1912.

———. *Complete Short Stories.* Edited by and with intro by Ernest Jerome Hopkins. New York: Ballantine, 1970.

———. *The Devil's Advocate: A Reader.* Edited by Brian St. Pierre. San Francisco: Chronicle Books, 1987.

———. *Fantastic Fables.* New York: Putnam, 1899.

———. *Nuggets and Dust Panned Out in California.* London: Chatto and Windus, 1873.

———. *The Stories and Fables.* Edited by and with intro by Edward Wagenknecht. Owings Mills, Md.: Stemmer House, 1977

———. *Tales of Soldiers and Civilians.* San Francisco: Steele, 1891; as *In the Midst of Life,* London: Chatto and Windus, 1892; revised edition, New York: Putnam, 1898.

Davidson, Cathy N., ed. *Critical Essays on Bierce.* Boston: G. K. Hall, 1982.

———. *The Experimental Fictions of Bierce: Structuring the Ineffable.* Lincoln: University of Nebraska Press, 1984.

Fatout, Paul. *Bierce, The Devil's Lexicographer,* Norman: University of Oklahoma Press, 1951.

———. *Bierce and the Black Hills,* Norman: University of Oklahoma Press, 1956.

McWilliams, Carey. *Bierce: A Biography.* Boston: Little, Brown, 1929.

O'Connor, Richard. *Bierce: A Biography.* Boston: Little, Brown, 1967.

Saunders, Richard. *Bierce: The Making of a Misanthrope.* San Francisco: Chronicle Books, 1985.

Wiggins, Robert A. *Bierce.* Minneapolis: University of Minnesota Press, 1964.

Woodruff, Stuart C. *The Short Stories of Bierce: A Study in Polarity.* Pittsburgh: University of Pittsburgh Press, 1964.

"BIG BLACK GOOD MAN" RICHARD WRIGHT (1957)

Initially published in ESQUIRE in November 1957, this frequently anthologized story—the last one Richard WRIGHT wrote—reappeared in his 1960 collection, *Eight Men.* As Ann Charters has noted, the story, set in Copenhagen, reflects Wright's expatriate experience (Charters 1374). For American readers especially, the geographical dis-tance from the American South initially gives the story an emotional distance, too, as does the Danish PROTAGONIST Olaf Jenson who speaks eight lan-guages. Yet Wright makes Olaf—who spent 10 years living in New York City—a symbol for white igno-rance and bias. By the end of the story, Wright has not only illustrated the THEME of racism—of white prejudice toward African Americans—but also driven home the point that racism has no national bound-aries. Further, by employing Lena, a Danish prostitute, as a foil to Olaf, Wright implies intriguing gender differences vis-à-vis racism: white women lack the sexual fears that contribute to white men's biases toward black men. Jim, the American black man, embodies white male fears of the African-American male threat.

Olaf personifies whiteness in notably unpleasant ways (see PERSONIFICATION). Significantly, his "watery grey" eyes cannot see clearly, despite his thick glasses, and the third-person narrator (see POINT OF VIEW) describes him as "pasty-white" and harmlessly idiotic (1375, 1381). Olaf, an ex-sailor who is now the night porter in a waterfront hotel, clearly views himself as a man's man who understands and aids the students and sailors in their need for whisky and women. Yet when the black stranger appears and asks for a room, a bottle of whiskey, and a woman, Olaf recoils in fear and disgust: hypocritically thinking that he views all people equally, he singles out this black man as inhuman. Jim, whom Olaf views as a black giant, a black mountain, a black beast, makes Olaf feel "puny" and worthless. Nor can Olaf resist asking Lena about the first of numerous nights she will spend with Jim. Lena, however, who truly views Jim as simply "a man" without Olaf's adjectives denoting his size and color, turns to Olaf furiously: "What the hell's that to you!" she snaps (1380).

Wright injects some humor into the scene when Jim puts his hands around Olaf's throat, so terrifying the little white man that he loses control of his sphincter muscles. The next year when Jim returns, his action becomes clear: He was measuring Olaf's throat to establish his neck size. He now presents to Olaf six perfectly fitting white nylon shirts in thanks for Olaf's introducing Jim to Lena. Yet when Jim calls Olaf a good man, Olaf cannot return the compliment without adding the adjectives big and black—and on his way out, Jim grinningly tells him to "drop dead." Cognizant of Olaf's seemingly incurable prejudice, Jim is on his way to see Lena, who, we learn, has left her profession and has been waiting for Jim to return. The ironic twist is that Olaf is correct in fearing Jim's attractiveness to the white woman, not because he embodies sex or animalism, but because Jim is a good man, an adjective we cannot apply to Olaf.

BIBLIOGRAPHY
Charters, Ann. "Richard Wright." In *Major Writers of Short Fiction: Stories and Commentary.* Edited by Ann Charters, Boston: St. Martin's, 1993, pp. 1372–75.
Wright, Richard. "Big Black Good Man." In *Major Writers of Short Fiction: Stories and Commentary.* Edited by Ann Charters, Boston: St. Martin's, 1993, pp. 1375–85.

"BIG BLONDE" See PARKER, DOROTHY.

"BIG BOY LEAVES HOME" RICHARD WRIGHT (1936) "Big Boy Leaves Home" was first published in the 1936 anthology *The New Caravan,* the first of Richard WRIGHT's stories to receive critical attention in the mainstream press. Reviews in the *New York Times,* the *Saturday Review of Literature,* and the *New Republic* agreed that it was the best piece in the anthology. With THEMES, characters, and a plot that would come to typify Wright's protest fiction, this graphically violent, naturalistic story (see NATURALISM) follows a young black boy whose trouble with the law forces him to grow up too quickly.

In a scene reminiscent of Mark TWAIN's *Huckleberry Finn,* the story begins as four truant black boys in a sunny Southern countryside "play the dozens" (trade rhyming insults), sing songs, wrestle, and discuss trains, the North, and racism. The group's leader, Big Boy, incites the others to go swimming in a creek forbidden to blacks. Their idyll is disrupted when a white woman stumbles upon the naked boys; her screams bring her husband, Jim, who shoots two of the four. Big Boy wrestles with Jim for the gun, shooting him in the struggle. In this scene, Wright draws up an African American literary STEREOTYPE, one that reverses the JIM CROW–era stereotype of the black male rapist: the white woman as a sexual predator, life-threatening to black men because her cry of rape (or in this case, her mere presence) inevitably results in their deaths.

Upon Big Boy's arrival home, his family summons the church elders, who quickly arrange for the boys to hide in a kiln until morning when Elder Peters's son will drive them to Chicago. Concealed in the kiln, Big Boy must witness the whites' extended, brutal torture and murder of his friend Bobo, who becomes the third of the four boys to die. By the time the truck arrives, Big Boy has grown numb and detached; Wright uses terse, simplistic sentences reminiscent of those of Ernest HEMINGWAY to indicate Big Boy's transition from naive boy to wanted criminal, a change next experienced by Wright's well-known PROTAGONIST Bigger Thomas in the novel *Native Son*.

BIBLIOGRAPHY

Fabre, Michel. *The Unfinished Quest of Richard Wright.* New York: Morrow, 1973.

Joyce, Joyce Ann. *Richard Wright's Art of Tragedy.* Iowa City: University of Iowa Press, 1986.

Kinnamon, Keneth. *The Emergence of Richard Wright: A Study in Literature and Society.* Ann Arbor, Mich.: UMI Books on Demand, 1972.

Margolies, Edward. "The Short Stories: Uncle Tom's Children, Eight Men," in *Critical Essays on Richard Wright* Edited by Yoshinobu Hakutani. Boston: G. K. Hall, 1982.

Kimberly Drake
Virginia Wesleyan College

"BIG TWO-HEARTED RIVER" ERNEST HEMINGWAY (1925)

"Big Two-Hearted River" is a story without dialogue, yet most readers admire Ernest HEMINGWAY's often praised CHARACTERIZATION of his protagonist, NICK ADAMS, and the way Nick seeks and faces experience. One of Hemingway's best-known characters, Nick appears in many of the stories in IN OUR TIME (published as a brief series of vignettes in 1924 as *in our time,* and published the following year in an expanded version as *In Our Time*). After Hemingway's death, "Big Two-Hearted River" was republished along with those selected by editor Philip Young for *The Nick Adams Stories* (1972). In one of his letters to his publisher, Hemingway hinted at the creative impulse within him that worked to produce his fiction: he admired people who know they must eventually die, but behave very well along the way (see HEMINGWAY CODE). As numerous critics have pointed out, "Big Two-Hearted River" contains all the elements that make it a quintessential Hemingway tale. According to short story critic Ann Charters, these include the focus on the woods, its creatures, and fishing, the carefully honed sentences, the characteristic understatement, the meticulous attention Nick devotes to the rituals of camping and fishing, "the repetitions of key words (*good, satisfactory, fine, pleasant, tighten, alive*)," and the mysterious sense of unease that threatens to unbalance the protagonist (Charters 74).

The story opens as Nick, recently returned from the Italian battlefields of WORLD WAR I—although, as Hemingway pointed out, the word *war* never appears—steps off the train at the town of Seney, Michigan. The town's life-filled river contrasts sharply with the desiccated landscape (an apparently deliberate evocation of a WASTE LAND motif) through which Nick has passed on his train ride, and he is immediately drawn to the exquisitely described trout steadying themselves in the current of the river. The two "hearts" of the river are, on one level, the two "parts" of the story; on another level they are the two "hearts" of Nick, who according to some critics suffers from a divided conscience. Nick's fishing trip is really a flight from his past rather than a journey toward his future. We sense that Nick, who admires the trout's ability to steady itself in the current, emulates this activity in his own ritualistic enactment of the rites of camping and fishing—from his mastery of location by reading natural signs, to his methodical camp making, coffee brewing and cooking, and his elaborate preparations for fishing. Nick derives satisfaction from predictability and control rather than good fortune or surprise. He apparently thinks of every detail to which the camper or fisherman might attend, demonstrating a keen awareness that grows from experience.

Problems arise for Nick when he ceases his activities. Even as Nick conceives of his newly pitched tent as his home, a good place, he becomes almost panic-stricken. He regains mastery of his feelings by preparing dinner in the same ritualistic way and with the same careful attention to detail he engages in when fishing: Nick feels content as long as he believes he can control the details of his life. Part I ends tranquilly with a quiet night that gives no hint of the confusion that will arise on the following day's fishing expedition. A single mosquito slips through the netting Nick has affixed to the tent's entrance, but he immediately takes a match to the insect, extinguishing the problem (Charters 74). He will not so easily solve the larger problems that will enter his life.

Hemingway's use of sexual innuendo and METAPHOR to describe Nick's encounter with the trout and the river becomes another Hemingway trademark (as in "The Last Good Country," for example). Fishing allows Nick to penetrate a completely different world. As the trout bites the bait and pumps against the current, Nick's rod becomes a living thing, bending in "jerks" against the pull of the trout and then tightening into "sudden hardness" as the trout leaps upward (BTHR 551, 552). The excitement of hooking the fish leaves him shaken, slightly nauseous, and unprepared for the feeling of dread that overcomes him when he stops to rest near where the river narrows into swamp. The tangled fauna there would confound any methodical attempts at traversal. He wishes he had brought something to read to occupy his mind, and feels a sharp aversion to wading into the murky water. The threat of loss of control—and perhaps of the dark thoughts intruding on his activity—so frightens Nick that he abruptly stops fishing to return to the safe haven of his camp. He reassures himself that he has many more days when he can fish in the swamp, but at this stage of his development he appears unwilling to accept that challenge. While some critics see the DENOUEMENT in a positive light that suggests Nick's recovery, the swamp metaphorically implies, at the very least, a future frought with danger and difficulty.

"Big Two-Hearted River," with its deliberate dearth of explanation for Nick's sense of unease and dread, provides a near-perfect example of Hemingway's oft-cited "iceberg" technique (like an iceberg, only one-eighth of the story's meaning is visible on the surface) and continues to tantalize readers and critics alike. Equally plausible interpretations include Nick as wounded war veteran, as the author contemplating his own suicide, as a modern frontier hero, and as a Waste Land figure. Readers may also gain further understanding by reading "A Way You'll Never Be," the story that precedes "Big Two-Hearted River" in *The Nick Adams Stories*.

BIBLIOGRAPHY

Benson, Jackson J., ed. *New Critical Approaches to the Short Stories of Ernest Hemingway.* Durham, N.C.: Duke University Press, 1990.

Benson, Jackson. *The Short Stories of Ernest Hemingway: Critical Essays.* Durham, N.C.: Duke University Press, 1975.

Brenner, Gerry, and Earl Rovit. *Ernest Hemingway, Revised Edition.* Boston: Twayne, 1990.

Flora, Joseph M. *Ernest Hemingway: A Study of the Short Fiction.* Boston: Twayne, 1989.

Hemingway, Ernest. *In Our Time.* New York: Scribner's, 1925.

———. *The Nick Adams Stories.* Edited by Philip Young. New York: Scribner's, 1972.

Lynn, Kenneth S. *Hemingway.* New York: Simon & Schuster, 1988, 102–108.

Reynolds, Michael S., ed. *Critical Essays on Ernest Hemingway's "In Our Time,"* Boston: G. K. Hall, 1983.

BILDUNGSROMAN A term used to classify a novel that takes as its main subject the moral, intellectual, and psychological development of a PROTAGONIST. Usually such novels trace the maturation of a youthful protagonist into adulthood. Contemporary examples of bildungsroman range from Ralph ELLISON's *Invisible Man* and Tillie OLSEN's *Yonnondio* to Paul Auster's *Mr. Vertigo*. For examples of short stories as bildungsroman, see, for instance, Carson MCCULLERS's "Wunderkind," Katherine Anne PORTER's "The Grave," Tillie Olsen's "O, YES," and Zelda Fitzgerald's "Miss Ella."

Richard Deming
Columbus State Community College

BILLY BUDD, SAILOR HERMAN MELVILLE (1924) *Billy Budd, Sailor* is Herman MELVILLE's final piece of writing. It is a NOVELLA left unpublished at the time of Melville's death in 1891. The narrative relates the story of Billy Budd, a 21-year-old sailor serving aboard the British merchant vessel *Rights-of-*

Man. Billy is forced aboard the H.M.S. *Bellipotent,* whose name means "war power," to fight in the king's service against the French in 1797. Billy is one of several Melville characters portrayed as "handsome sailors." He is a good seaman and well liked by the officers and crew of the *Bellipotent*—except by the master-at-arms, John Claggart, who bears an ill-defined malice toward Billy. Strangely, Claggart is both attracted to and repulsed by Billy's youth and beauty, and his animosity toward the young sailor seems to stem from an inherent source of evil. As Merton Sealts aptly points out, Billy and Claggart "stand in sharp contrast as types of innocence and worldly experience" (*"Billy Budd, Sailor,"* in John Bryant, ed., *A Companion to Melville Studies* [1986], 408).

Seeking to entrap Billy, Claggart has one of his men attempt to bribe him into participating in a mutiny, but Billy refuses. Claggart responds by going to Captain Vere and formally accusing Billy of mutiny. Billy, who stutters, is called to the captain's cabin, and when he is confronted by the charges facing him, he is unable to answer them because of his stammer. Powerless to voice his indignation, Billy turns to his accuser and strikes Claggart a deadly blow to the head. A battlefield court-martial court ensues, and, against his nobler feelings but in accord with military law, Captain Vere condemns Billy to hang for striking and killing a superior officer. The crew is assembled and, neck in the noose and just moments before he is hoisted to the yardarm, Billy calls out, "God Bless Captain Vere" (*BBS,* 123). Christlike, "Billy ascended; and, ascending, took the full rose of the dawn" (*BBS,* 124). We learn at the end of the narrative that Captain Vere, mortally wounded in battle, called out with his final breath, "Billy Budd, Billy Budd" (*BBS,* 129).

Melville's work was left, unpublished, in 351 manuscript leaves written in both pencil and pen and heavily corrected and revised. The author left no directions for its publication, and, as far as we know, he never mentioned the work. *Billy Budd* was not published until 1924, when Raymond Weaver included it in the *Complete Works of Melville.* In 1928 Weaver produced an altered version, and F. Barron Freeman followed in 1948 with yet another rendering of the text. The text edited by Harrison Hayford and Merton M. Sealts, Jr., for the University of Chicago Press entitled *Billy Budd, Sailor (An Inside Narrative)* (1962) is now generally accepted as the standard. Critical reception of *Billy Budd* reflects the problematic nature of the text itself, and the novella has been variously interpreted. Some have read it as Melville's final testament, accepting the inevitability of evil; in the 1950s the prevailing readings of *Billy Budd* foregrounded irony as Melville's dominant concern. Current work focuses more on religious, social, political, and historical readings of *Billy Budd.* That the text is susceptible to so many readings points to its complexity as a work of art. One point is clear: Melville lived through an age that saw sailing ships replaced by steam-powered vessels and that saw an array of technological improvements, particularly in implements of warfare. That Melville, as witness to these changes, should temper his ROMANTICISM in *Billy Budd,* the only prose he wrote after 1857, seems inevitable. To claim that the work demonstrates Melville's acceptance of change fails to acknowledge the complexity of his views, for at the end of his life Melville apparently concluded that a future mediated by his earlier romantic perception was severely flawed, perhaps impossible. After viewing the carnage of the American CIVIL WAR, Melville likely found it impossible to portray the earthly superiority of an innocent figure like Billy Budd. Nevertheless, in the final pages of the novella, Billy's spirit does indeed survive long after his death in the lore of his fellow sailors.

BIBLIOGRAPHY

Bryant, John. *A Companion to Melville Studies.* Westport, Conn.: Greenwood, 1986.

Hayford, Harrison, and Merton M. Sealts, Jr. *Billy Budd, Sailor (An Inside Narrative).* Chicago: University of Chicago Press, 1962.

Parker, Hershel. *Reading Billy Budd.* Evanston, Ill.: Northwestern University Press, 1990.

Cornelius W. Browne
Ohio University

"BINGO VAN" LOUISE ERDRICH First published in the NEW YORKER and later anthologized in *Talking Leaves: Contemporary Native American Short Stories* (1991), "Bingo Van" is the seventh chapter in *Bingo Palace,* the fourth book in Louise ERDRICH's series of novels. In the story Erdrich plays with the concept of luck, questioning the fundamental meaning of fortune, and hints at the tensions between reservation residents and surrounding nonreservation communities. Narrator Lipsha Morrisey, a well-meaning and lackluster "healer," uses his power to win a van at the Bingo Palace. The van enables Lipsha to become involved with an attractive young single mother and brings him into contact—and subsequently into conflict—with the non-Indian world off the reservation. As the story plays out, the van turns out to be far from a lucky prize, and Lipsha is better off without it.

Calvin Hussman
St. Olaf College

BIRTHA, BECKY (1948–) Born in Hampton, Virginia, in 1948, Becky Birtha graduated from the State University of New York at Buffalo in 1973 and taught preschool children for ten years. Her first collection of short stories, *For Nights Like This One: Stories of Loving Women,* was published in 1983. After receiving an M.A. in fine arts from Vermont College in 1984, she was awarded a fellowship from the Pennsylvania Council of the Arts. She completed a second volume of short stories, *Lovers Choice,* in 1987. Central to her fiction is the lesbian experience, in which relationships between women are depicted as part of a "normal, familiar, and comfortable reality."

"BIRTHMARK, THE" NATHANIEL HAW-THORNE (1843) Similar to Nathaniel HAW-THORNE's "RAPPACCINI'S DAUGHTER" in its presentation of a beautiful woman who lives with a scientist obsessed with perfection, "The Birthmark" features Aylmer, who, aspiring to perfection and divinity, falls in love with and marries Georgiana, whose beauty he increasingly believes is marred by a tiny birthmark. Under her husband's influence, Georgiana loses her belief in her own beauty, normalcy, and self-worth, making this story as relevant—and as depressing—today as it was in Hawthorne's time. Indeed, the narrator's statement about Aylmer's journals could easily be Hawthorne's self-reflexive comment about the story itself: "as melancholy a record as mortal hand had ever penned" (10:49). Despite the protests of Aminadab, his laboratory assistant (who, as FOIL to the spiritually superior Aylmer, clearly represents earthiness), Aylmer believes not only that the birthmark is a flaw in his wife's perfection but also that his removal of it—his ability to control nature—will provide him proof of his absolute power. By the time the operation begins, Georgiana acquiesces: She has moved from anger at her husband for having married her in the first place, to a total identification with his views of her flaw, her humanity. Although Aylmer successfully removes the birthmark, Georgiana will die, but not before she absolves him of all guilt, submitting to his higher spiritual and scientific power.

"The Birthmark" yields intriguing results from both religious and FEMINIST perspectives. Critics have long noted the Christian implications of human fallibility in this story and see Aylmer as mistakenly playing God, failing to understand that God created the flaws as well as the beauty of nature and humanity. Georgiana, sacrificed for her husband's spiritual transcendence, may be seen as a Christ figure. From a feminist viewpoint, however, her increasing reliance on her husband and her view of him as superior makes her a perfect symbol of woman—in this case, wife—as victim of male arrogance and power. Numerous narrative intrusions suggest clearly the author's agreement with this interpretation.

BIBLIOGRAPHY

Bunge, Nancy. *Nathaniel Hawthorne: Studies in the Short Fiction.* New York: Twayne, 1993.

Hawthorne, Nathaniel. "The Birthmark." In *Mosses From an Old Manse: The Centenary Edition of the Works of Nathaniel Hawthorne,* vol. 10. Edited by William Charvatt, Roy Harvey Pierce, et al. Columbus: Ohio State University Press, 1962–1968, pp. 38–56.

"BLACK CAT, THE" EDGAR ALLAN POE

(1843) While living in Philadelphia, Edgar Allan POE published "The Black Cat" shortly after "THE TELL-TALE HEART" (1843). Both are psychological studies using first-person POINT OF VIEW to explore mental instability, obsession, murder, and the inability of characters to conceal feelings and actions. Although the narrator is reflecting on past events through writing, the sentence structure and rhythm of "The Black Cat," as in many of Poe's tales, replicate speech, and the inverted syntax—or untraditional word placement in sentences—represents the confused and illogical mental state of the alcoholic narrator. This tale is also linked with Poe's "The Imp of the Perverse" (1845), as both are examinations of condemned men who do evil simply because they know they should not.

The tale begins with the obsessed and/or UNRELIABLE NARRATOR, a familiar device in Poe's stories, who assures readers that he will relate a common tale of ordinary events. Furthermore, he insists that he has no interest in cause and effect. Yet the events he describes are far from ordinary: Becoming obsessed with his cat, he first gouges out its eye and later hangs it. When the narrator's house burns down, the GOTHIC image of the cat with the noose around its neck remains imprinted on a bedroom wall. Shortly thereafter another cat appears that resembles the first. The man's affection for the new cat soon turns to disgust. When the man's wife stops him from killing the cat, he turns the ax on her instead. He then conceals her corpse behind a brick cellar wall. Shortly afterward, feeling absolutely no guilt over the brutal murder of his wife, the man brags to police investigators about the solid structure of his house, taps the cellar wall, and hears the cat's spine-tingling howling from behind it. In this use of IRONY, the murderer's confidence and jubilation, along with the mysterious cat, are his undoing. Or, to use Charles E. May's words, "it is not guilt that undoes him, but glee, as he raps on the very wall behind which his wife's body rots upright" (May 75).

"The Black Cat" is one of Poe's sharpest psychological profiles, starkest statements about human motivation, and most unified tale. Indeed, in the very explication of the narrator's motive—his paradoxical obsession with both the exultation and agony of damnation—lies the impressively rendered unity of the story. It was included in a new edition of his tales in 1845 and has since been reprinted in subsequent collections, anthologies, and school readers.

BIBLIOGRAPHY

Hammond, J. R. *An Edgar Allan Poe Companion: A Guide to the Short Stories, Romances and Essays.* Totowa, N.J.: Barnes & Noble Books, 1981.

May, Charles O. *Edgar Allan Poe: A Study of the Short Fiction.* Boston: Twayne, 1991.

Poe, Edgar Allan. "The Black Cat." In *Collected Works of Edgar Allan Poe,* vol. 3. Edited by Thomas O. Mabbott, Cambridge, Mass.: Harvard University Press/Belknap Press, 1978, pp. 849–859.

Anna Leahy
Ohio University

BLACK HUMOR

A 20th-century technique that achieves morbidly humorous effects through the use of sardonic wit and morbid or GROTESQUE situations. The narrator's tone often evokes resignation, anger, or bitterness. Similar to the literature of the ABSURD, black humor frequently depicts a farcical, fantastic world—either dreamlike or nightmarish—featuring naive characters who play out their roles in a world in which the events are simultaneously comic, brutal, horrifying, or absurd. Short stories using black humor include John BARTH's "LOST IN THE FUNHOUSE" and Flannery O'CONNOR's "A GOOD MAN IS HARD TO FIND." Novels frequently used to exemplify black humor include Kurt VONNEGUT's *Slaughterhouse-Five* and Joseph Heller's *Catch-22*. Edward ALBEE's play *Who's Afraid of Virginia Woolf* provides an example of black humor in modern drama.

BLACK MASK

The first HARD-BOILED FICTION magazine in the DETECTIVE SHORT FICTION vein. Founded in 1919 by editor Joseph T. Shaw, *Black*

Mask published such now-CLASSIC detective fiction writers as Raymond CHANDLER and Dashiell HAMMETT, and established the hard-boiled formula that many critics trace to the early work of Ernest HEMINGWAY. Characterized by crime, sordid environments, and a clipped, terse, often crude dialogue, *Black Mask* stories enjoyed immense popularity in the 1920s and 1930s. In 1946 Shaw collected many of them in *The Hard-Boiled Omnibus: Early Stories from Black Mask.*

"BLUE HOTEL, THE" STEPHEN CRANE (1898)

"The Blue Hotel" is justifiably one of Stephen CRANE's most famous and most frequently anthologized stories. The brilliantly blue color of the hotel, standing prominently in the prairie town of Fort Romper, Nebraska, creeps into the imagination as more than merely the bizarre backdrop for the action. Its very color suggests something out of place in the middle of the prairie. The blue hotel itself is a METAPHOR for the inexplicable but violent human emotions enacted both within and without its walls, where the fury of the snowstorm echoes the anger that erupts among the men who remain sheltered at the hotel.

Early in the story, a train interrupts the quiet of the town and the peaceful social order represented by the hotel. Disembarking is a nervous-looking Swede whose head is filled with dime-novel accounts of the Wild West. On entering the hotel he meets the other characters: Pat Scully, owner of the hotel; Mr. Blanc, a diminutive Easterner; a nameless cowboy; and Johnnie, Scully's excitable son. From the beginning, the Swede announces that he expects to be killed; of course, by the end of the story his prophecy comes true. Either entirely or half crazy and hysterical throughout most of the action, the Swede refuses to be calmed by Scully or the others, eventually making them feel somewhat hysterical as well. The story dramatizes the reasons for and the results of uncontrolled human behavior. Part of Crane's considerable achievement here, according to Chester L. Wolford, lies in the complex misperceptions the characters exhibit in relation to one another, misleading the readers as well as themselves

(Wolford 30). Does Scully realize the effect of his liberal pouring of liquor for the paranoid Swede? Does Mr. Blanc understand the ramifications of not telling the others that Johnnie is cheating in the card game? Does the cowboy realize his role in inciting the Swede's violence? When the Swede kills Johnnie and survives, only to be killed himself when he attacks another hotel customer for cheating, has he brought on his own death, or were all of the others complicit? The Easterner believes that they all collaborated in the two murders. Crane leaves the reader to ponder the connection between order and chaos, free will and DETERMINISM, the individual versus the group—and the blue of the hotel compared with the white of the snowstorm.

BIBLIOGRAPHY
Crane, Stephen. "The Blue Hotel." *University of Virginia Edition of the Works of Stephen Crane,* vol. 5. Edited by Fredson Bowers. Charlottesville: University of Virginia Press, pp. 142–170.

Kazin, Alfred. "On Stephen Crane and 'The Blue Hotel.'" In *The American Short Story,* vol. 1. Edited by Calvin Skaggs. New York: Dell, 1977, pp. 77–81.

Wolford, Chester L. *Stephen Crane: A Study of the Short Fiction.* Boston: Twayne, 1989.

BONNER, SHERWOOD (KATHERINE SHERWOOD BONNER MCDOWELL) (1849–1883)

Katherine Sherwood Bonner McDowell grew up in Holly Springs, Mississippi, the daughter of a sometime physician whose first responsibility was managing the family plantation. After a brief marriage she moved to Boston in 1873, where she wrote for HARPER'S, *Harper's Weekly,* and *Lippincott's.* Befriended by Henry Wadsworth Longfellow, she worked for a time as his secretary. Much of her writing is of high quality, demonstrating a fine ear for DIALECT. Had she not died of cancer at age 34, her promising career might have led her to greater fame.

Her work includes *Like Unto Like* (1878), a novel of CIVIL WAR and RECONSTRUCTION days, and two collections of short stories, *Dialect Tales* (1883) and *Suwanee River Tales* (1884). Although a number of her sketches of blacks seem the tales of a novice rather than of a fully developed and self-confident writer, Bonner's stories of Tennessee moonshiners and her tales of rural folk on the Illinois prairie reveal a notable talent for grimly realistic portrayals of both characters and action. Ironically, one of her most powerful stories, "A Volcanic Interlude" (1880), was published in *Lippincott's* but never in either of her collected volumes.

BIBLIOGRAPHY

Bonner, Sherwood. *Like Unto Like.* New York: Harper, 1878. As *Blythe Herndon,* bound with *Janetta* by Julia Chandler. London: Ward, Lock, 1882.

———. *Dialect Tales.* New York: Harper, 1883.

———. *Suwanee River Tales.* Boston: Roberts, 1884.

———. *Gran'mammy. Little Classics of the South: Mississippi.* New York: Purdy, 1927.

Frank, William L. *Sherwood Bonner.* Boston: Twayne, 1976.

McAlexander, Hubert H. *The Prodigal Daughter: A Biography of Sherwood Bonner.* Baton Rouge: Louisiana State University Press, 1981.

BONNIN, GERTRUDE SIMMONS   See ZITKALA SA

BOWLES, PAUL (FREDERIK) (1910–1999)

Born in New York City, Paul Bowles lived in Tangier, Morocco, since 1947. Since the publication of his first novel, *The Sheltering Sky* (1949), Bowles has been viewed as undeniably talented, because of his style, but controversial, due to his subject matter. Some readers regard him as a cult figure, noting his ties to and influence on writers of the BEAT GENERATION; others find his work difficult to read, focused as it often is on the horror, violence, and NIHILISM of 20th-century life. The appeal of his work lies chiefly in Bowles's adroit manipulation of language, and in his determination to explore—as did Edgar Allan POE, the American writer whom he most admired—the depths of the human soul. Bowles is also frequently linked with European EXISTENTIALIST writers like Jean-Paul Sartre, whose *No Exit* Bowles translated in 1946.

Bowles wrote a number of tales based on FOLKLORE and rendered in images and techniques of SURREALISM or MAGICAL REALISM, as in "The Scorpion," in which a cave-dwelling woman's divided attraction to both independence and a man of the outer world is ultimately depicted in a dream in which she swallows the scorpion, suggesting in this instance either sex or death or both. In addition to these sorts of stories, and to those of brutality and perversion—"A Distant Episode" and "The Delicate Prey," for example—Bowles wrote "The Garden," one of his most admired stories. An impressive and artistically wrought PARABLE about social intolerance and individual human difference, it demonstrates the way a man's neighbors and even his wife turn on him because, unlike them, he finds genuine pleasure in tending his garden.

BIBLIOGRAPHY

Bertens, Hans. *The Fiction of Paul Bowles: The Soul Is the Weariest Part of the Body.* Atlantic Highlands, N.J.: Humanities Press, 1979.

Bowles, Paul. *Collected Stories 1939–1976.* Santa Barbara, Calif.: Black Sparrow Press, 1979.

———. *The Delicate Prey and Other Stories.* New York: Random House, 1950.

———. *The Hours after Noon.* London: Heinemann, 1959.

———. *A Hundred Camels in the Courtyard.* San Francisco: City Lights, 1962.

———. *In the Red Room.* Los Angeles: Sylvester and Orphanos, 1981.

———. *Let It Come Down.* New York: New Directions, 1949.

———. *A Little Stone.* London: Lehmann, 1950.

———. *Midnight Mass.* Santa Barbara, Calif.: Black Sparrow Press, 1981.

———. *Pages from Cold Point and Other Stones.* London, Owen, 1968.

———. *The Sheltering Sky.* New York: New Directions, 1949.

———. *The Spider's House.* New York: Random House, 1955.

———. *Things Gone and Things Still Here.* Santa Barbara, Calif.: Black Sparrow Press, 1977.

———. *Three Tales.* New York: Hallman, 1975.

———. *The Time of Friendship.* New York: Holt Rinehart, 1967.

———. *Up Above the World.* New York: Simon & Schuster, 1966.

———. *Without Stopping: An Autobiography.* New York: Putnam, 1972.

Caponi, Gena Dagel. *Paul Bowles,* Twayne's United States Authors 706. New York: Twayne; Prentice Hall International, 1998.

Dillon, Millicent. *You Are Not I: A Portrait of Paul Bowles.* Berkeley: University of California Press, 1998.

Evans, Oliver. "Paul Bowles and the Natural Man." In *Recent American Fiction.* Boston: Houghton Mifflin, 1963.

Mottram, Eric. *Paul Bowles: Staticity and Terror.* London: Aloes, 1976.

"Paul Bowles Issue." *Review of Contemporary Fiction* 2.3 (1982).

Pounds, Wayne. *Paul Bowles: The Inner Geography.* Bern, Switzerland: Peter Lang, 1985.

Sawyer-Lauçanno, Christopher. *An Invisible Spectator: A Biography of Paul Bowles.* New York: Grove Press, 1989.

Stewart, Lawrence D. *Paul Bowles: The Illumination of North Africa.* Carbondale: Southern Illinois University Press, 1974.

BOYLE, KAY (1902–1992)

Born in Ohio, but a resident of Europe for 30 years, Kay Boyle was an expatriate writer of the 1930s who won the O. Henry Memorial Award for the short story in 1935 and 1941. Although she wrote novels, poetry, essays, and memoirs, she is known chiefly as a writer of short fiction. Many of her stories appeared in the NEW YORKER before World War II, and were subsequently published as *Wedding Day and Other Stories* (1930), *First Lover and Other Stories* (1933), and *The White Horses of Vienna and Other Stories* (1936). The best of these prewar tales, collected in *Thirty Stories* (1946), treat such subjects as love, marriage, and death. Boyle is well known, too, as a writer who drew on war and political confrontation for subject matter. Critically acclaimed are the stories of postwar Germany in *The Smoking Mountain: Stories of Germany During the Occupation* (1951).

Boyle's prose has a lyric intensity that vividly depicts specific scenes and images: Whether she is describing scenes of natural beauty, the atrocities of war, or individual suffering, her powerful evocations remain with the reader.

As an expatriate living in Europe and writing about the Americans she observed there, Boyle has been compared with such writers as Henry JAMES and Edith WHARTON, and in fact she shares with them the thematic motifs of innocents abroad. Indeed, as critic James G. Watson has observed, undergirding a great deal of Boyle's short fiction is the AMERICAN ADAM, the idealist from EDEN poised to fall from innocence. Illustrative of this theme is Boyle's "Kroy Wen," a story originally appearing in the *New Yorker:* the title (*New York* spelled backwards) provides the clue to the reversal of roles as well as of myth in the story, in which the Europeans are the innocents, the American the world-weary cynic. Unlike either James or Wharton, moreover, Boyle additionally infused her writing with political concerns and issues with which she was actively and personally concerned. She unflinchingly addresses American racism, for instance, just as she addresses the racism of Hitler.

"The White Horses of Vienna" is likely Boyle's most frequently anthologized story. Set in Austria in the mid-1930s, the Austrian doctor and his wife live in a white house on a hill above the tensions and political disarray that infects Europe. When the doctor is injured, however, he and his wife have no choice but to let the newly arrived physician—Dr. Heine, a Jew—tend to him. The patient relates a tale of a crippled Lippizaner stallion at the Spanish Riding School of Vienna, clearly symbolic of the destruction of Austrian ideals, and clearly equated with the now crippled Austrian doctor. He has fallen just as all Europe will fall—as will Dr. Heine, who endures anti-Semitic insults of the Austrian doctor's wife. At the end of the story, she serves Heine pork and actually sets him on fire. All three characters will pay a terrible price for their sins—whether of commission or omission—against the individual, the community and country, and the human spirit.

BIBLIOGRAPHY

Bell, Elizabeth S. *Kay Boyle: A Study of the Short Fiction.* New York: Twayne, 1992.

Boyle, Kay. *Avalanche.* New York: Simon & Schuster, 1944.

———. *The First Lover and Other Stories.* New York: Smith and Haas, 1933.

———. *The Crazy Hunter: Three Short Novels.* New York: Harcourt Brace, 1940.

———. *Death of a Man.* New York: Harcourt Brace, 1936.

———. *Fifty Stories*. New York: Doubleday, 1980.

———. *The First Lover and Other Stories*. New York: Cape and Smith, 1933.

———. *A Frenchman Must Die*. New York: Simon & Schuster, 1946.

———. *Generation Without Farewell*. New York: Knopf, 1960.

———. *Gentlemen, I Address You Privately*. New York: Smith, 1933.

———. *His Human Majesty*. New York: McGraw Hill, 1949.

———. *Life Being the Best and Other Stories*. Edited by Sandra Whipple Spanier, New York: New Directions,1988.

———. *Monday Night*. New York: Harcourt Brace, 1938.

———. *My Next Bride*. New York: Harcourt Brace, 1934.

———. *1939*. New York: Simon & Schuster, 1948.

———. *Nothing Ever Breaks Except the Heart*. New York: Doubleday, 1966.

———. *Plagued by the Nightingale*. New York: Cape and Smith, 1931.

———. *Primer for Combat*. New York: Simon & Schuster, 1938.

———. *The Seagull on the Step*. New York: Knopf, 1955.

———. *Short Stories*. Paris: Black Sun Press, 1929.

———. *The Smoking Mountain: Stories of Post War Germany*. New York: McGraw Hill. 1951.

———. *Thirty Stories*. New York: Simon & Schuster, 1946.

———. *The Underground Woman*. Garden City, N.Y.: Doubleday, 1975.

———. *Wedding Day and Other Stories*. New York. Cape and Smith, 1930.

———. *Three Short Novels*. Boston: Beacon Press, 1958.

———. *The White Horses of Vienna and Other Stories*. New York: Harcourt Brace, 1936.

———. *Year Before Last*. New York: Smith, 1932.

Boyle, Kay, with Robert McAlmon. *Being Geniuses Together.* New York: Doubleday, 1968.

Elkins, Marilyn. *Metamorphosing the Novel: Kay Boyle's Narrative Inventions*. New York: Peter Lang, 1993.

Elkins, Marilyn, ed. *Critical Essays on Kay Boyle*. New York: G. K. Hall, 1997.

Spanier, Sandra Whipple. *Boyle: Artist and Activist.* Carbondale: Southern Illinois University Press, 1986.

Watson, James G. "The American Short Story, 1900–1945: A Critical History." In *The American Short Story, 1900–1945*. Edited by Philip Stevick. Boston: Twayne, 1984, pp. 103–146, p. 116.

BOYLE, T. CORAGHESSAN (1948–   )

T. Coraghessan Boyle was born in Peekskill, New York, in 1948. Although he came to literature relatively late (Boyle claims he did not read serious fiction until he was 18), he quickly established himself as a literary star once he began writing. After earning a Ph.D. from the Iowa Writer's Workshop and after serving, for a time, as the fiction editor at the *Iowa Review,* Boyle received a series of prestigious awards. In 1977 his stories earned the writer a Coordinating Council of Literary Magazines Award for Fiction as well as a National Endowment for the Arts Fellowship. *Descent of Man* (1977), a collection of Boyle's early short stories, won the St. Lawrence Award for Short Fiction, while sections of his first novel, *Water Music* (1981), received the Aga Kahn Award. *Greasy Lake and Other Stories* (1985), Boyle's second collection of short fiction, was generally well received by critics, and in 1988 Boyle won the prestigious Pen/Faulkner Award for Fiction for his novel *World's End* (1987). *The Road to Wellville* (1993) was published to enthusiastic reviews and was subsequently made into a feature film.

Frequently compared to such writers as Thomas Pynchon and Donald BARTHELME, Boyle's energetic, erudite, and highly self-conscious fiction is marked by an irreverent style of narration, a style befitting the writer's frequently ABSURDist inclinations. "Descent of Man," for instance, reports the experience of a man whose girlfriend casts him aside in favor of an especially intelligent chimpanzee who translates Nietzsche at the primate research center where she works. Boyle presents a similarly skewed character in "GREASY LAKE." Attempting to explain his unlikely participation in a near rape, the unnamed narrator of this widely anthologized coming-of-age tale compares his would-be victim to "the toad emerging from the loaf in [Bergman's film] *Virgin Spring,* lipstick smeared on a child: she was already tainted."

Prominent thematic concerns (see THEME) in Boyle's fiction include the impact of history on the present (*World's End*), the misplaced priorities of contemporary society ("Bloodfall," "Greasy Lake") and the triumph of nature over civilization ("Descent"). Religion, politics and popular culture are frequent targets of the writer's satire.

BIBLIOGRAPHY

Boyle, T. Coraghessan. *Budding Prospects: A Pastoral*. New York: Viking, 1984.

———. *The Collected Stories of T. Coraghessan Boyle*. New York: Granta Books, 1993.

———. *If the River was Whiskey: Stories*. New York: Viking, 1989.

———. *Without a Hero*. New York: Viking, 1994.

Shannon Zimmerman
University of Georgia

BRADBURY, RAY(MOND DOUGLAS)

(1920–   )   Born in Waukegan, Illinois (an idealized version of which appears in some of his fiction as Green Town, Illinois), Bradbury established an early reputation as a writer of short fiction with sinister and sensational plots dealing with the freaks, magicians and exotic creatures of carnivals and circuses and the fiends and monsters of the movies, incorporating themes of FANTASY, horror, and the macabre.

With the publication of *The Martian Chronicles* in 1950, Bradbury also established himself as a premier writer of SCIENCE FICTION, although as previous and later works show, space fantasies are only one of the vehicles he uses for an allegorical expression of humankind's hopes and fears. Space fantasy in which technology plays a major role also allows Bradbury to address one of his major social concerns, that of human's relationship to machine and to each other in the modern world. In much of his work, Bradbury shows his compassion for people struggling against tragic ironies, often successfully, in the belief that there is a vital, spiritual dimension to the banal world of daily existence. A prolific writer, Bradbury has also published novels, children's stories, and poetry, and written plays, screenplays, and television plays.

BIBLIOGRAPHY

Bradbury, Ray. *The Autumn People*. New York: Ballantine, 1965.

———. *The Best of Bradbury*. New York: Bantam, 1976.

———. *Dandelion Wine*. New York: Doubleday, 1957.

———. *Dark Carnival*. Sauk City, Wisc.: Arkham House, 1947.

———. *The Day It Rained Forever*. London: Hart Davis, 1959.

———. *Death Is a Lonely Business*. New York: Knopf, 1985.

———. *Dinosaur Tales*. New York: Bantam, 1983.

———. *Fahrenheit 451*. New York: Ballantine, 1953.

———. *The Golden Apples of the Sun*. New York: Doubleday, 1953.

———. *I Sing the Body Electric!* New York: Knopf, 1969.

———. *The Illustrated Man*. New York: Doubleday, 1951.

———. *The Last Circus, and The Electrocution*. Northridge, Calif.: Lord John Press, 1980.

———. *Long after Midnight*. New York: Knopf, 1976.

———. *The Machineries of Joy*. New York: Simon and Schuster, 1964.

———. *The Martian Chronicles*. New York: Doubleday, 1950.

———. *A Medicine for Melancholy*. New York: Doubleday, 1959.

———. *A Memory for Murder*. New York: Dell, 1984.

———. *The October Country*. New York: Ballantine, 1955.

———. *Selected Stories*. Edited by Anthony Adams. London: Harrap, 1975.

———. *Silver Locusts*. London: Hart Davis, 1951.

———. *The Stories of Ray Bradbury*. New York: Knopf, 1980.

———. *To Sing Strange Songs*. Exeter, Devon: Wheaton, 1979.

———. *Something Wicked This Way Comes*. New York: Simon & Schuster, 1962.

———. *Tomorrow Midnight*. New York: Ballantine, 1966.

———. *Twice Twenty-Two: The Golden Apples of the Sun. A Medicine for Melancholy*. Garden City, New York: Doubleday, 1966.

———. *The Vintage Bradbury*. New York: Random House, 1965.

———, with Robert Bloch. *Bloch and Bradbury*. New York: Tower, 1969.

Indick, Benjamin P. *The Drama of Ray Bradbury*. Baltimore: T-K Graphics, 1977.

Johnson, Wayne L. *Ray Bradbury*. New York: Ungar, 1980.

Mengeling, Marvin E. "Ray Bradbury's *Dandelion Wine*: Themes, Sources, and Style." *English Journal* (October 1971).

Nolan, William F. *The Ray Bradbury Companion*. Detroit: Gale, 1975.

Olander, Joseph D., and Martin H. Greenberg, eds. *Ray Bradbury*. New York: Taplinger, 1980.

Slusser, George Edgar. *The Bradbury Chronicles*. San Bernardino, Calif.: Borgo Press, 1977.

Toupence, William F. *Ray Bradbury and the Poetics of Reverie: Fantasy, Science Fiction, and the Reader.* Ann Arbor, Mich.: UMI Research Press, 1984.

BRAUTIGAN, RICHARD GARY (1935–1984)

Richard Brautigan began writing as a teenager in his home town of Tacoma, Washington. He spent the first two decades of his life in the Pacific Northwest—primarily in Washington and Oregon—a region featured in much of his fiction. His adult years were divided among Montana's Paradise Valley, Tokyo (his work contains a special affection for Japan and the Japanese), and California. While still in his 20s, he was estranged from his mother and sisters, and his absent father first heard of his existence after Brautigan committed suicide in a secluded house in Bolinas, California, north of San Francisco. He was married for a short time and had one daughter.

Brautigan began publishing poetry in San Francisco in 1955, during the heyday of the BEAT GENERATION. Over a 25-year period, he produced one collection of short stories, *Revenge of the Lawn: Stories 1962–1970* (1971), eight collections of poetry and several single poems, and ten novels. Genre distinctions often blur in his work, and some of his novels can be read structurally as SHORT STORY CYCLES. Brautigan's greatest critical and popular success came in the 1960s, when his first three novels, *A Confederate General from Big Sur* (1964), *Trout Fishing in America* (1967), and *In Watermelon Sugar* (1968), made him a literary hero and a prominent counterculture voice. Brautigan fell from critical favor in the 1970s and 1980s, although he was more popular in Japan, France, and Germany. He has been compared to the French writers Appolinaire, Baudelaire, and Rimbaud, and to Americans Ernest HEMINGWAY, Kurt VONNEGUT and John BARTH. Brautigan's writing is part of "New Fiction" and features a first-person, self-reflexive narrator who examines cultural myths with wry humor and irreverence and determines finally that America is located only in the imagination. His METAFICTIONal texts are comprised of startling, extreme METAPHORS, and are concerned with death, childhood, loneliness, heterosexual imagery, lost time, identity, and memory. His narrator often takes a naive, whimsical, or surrealistic (see SURREALISM) view of life's small details. Recently scholarly attention to Brautigan's fiction has increased, as his writing is reexamined within its postmodern context.

BIBLIOGRAPHY

Chenetier, Marc C. *Richard Brautigan.* New York: Methuen, 1983.
Foster, Edward Halsey. *Richard Brautigan.* Boston: Twayne, 1983.

Brenda M. Palo
University of North Carolina at Chapel Hill

"BRIDE COMES TO YELLOW SKY, THE" STEPHEN CRANE (1898)

Critics generally agree that, along with "THE BLUE HOTEL," "The Bride Comes to Yellow Sky" marks a new maturity in Stephen CRANE in which history plays a significant role in the story's meaning. A long-held view is that in this story Crane provides a PARODY, a mock epic treatment of the demise of the Wild West, invaded and tamed by Easterners. As parody, it mocks the Wild West expectations of readers, and, as mock epic, it reverses presumptions about Western heroes. Samuel I. Bellman goes one step further and sees the story as a BURLESQUE, a vaudeville scene enacted by clowns (Bellman 656). The plot is deceptively simple: Marshall JACK POTTER, riding into town not on a stallion but in a train, has told none of the townsfolk, including Scratchy Wilson, his deputy, that he aims to become domesticated and therefore has married the woman who accompanies him home to Yellow Sky. A married marshall is, of course, unthinkable in the CLASSIC western tale: Like Leatherstocking, the Lone Ranger, and their DETECTIVE FICTION descendants, SAM SPADE and PHILIP MARLOWE, heroes should ride off into the sunset after a gunbattle—and ride off single. This comic tale upsets every component of the Western formula: Not only does the HERO marry, but he marries a rather plain and dutiful middle-age woman. Both newlyweds seem awkward and out of their element on the train.

Once in town, the narrator describes Scratchy Wilson to a newcomer—and to the reader: Scratchy is drunk, wielding his pistol and ready for a shoot-up. But Crane clearly has no intention of allowing a classic gun duel. When Scratchy and Jack have their confrontation, we find no blazing guns, no clipped, witty dialogue. To the contrary, Scratchy is so drunk that he drops his pistol; Jack tells him he's no longer carrying one and intends to settle down peaceably with his wife. Scratchy shuffles off down the sandy road. If Scratchy represents the old West and Jack the new, the old has lost its glamour and the new seems regrettably tame. In the words of Chester L. Wolford, implicitly alluding to T. S. Eliot, the Wild West dies not "with a bang, but with a whimper" (Wolford 30).

BIBLIOGRAPHY

Bellman, Samuel I. "Stephen Crane." In *Reference Guide to Short Fiction*. Edited by Noelle Watson. Detroit: St. James Press, 1994, pp. 655–656.

Crane, Stephen. "The Bridge Comes to Yellow Sky." In *University of Virginia Edition of the Works of Stephen Crane*, vol. 5. Edited by Fredson Bowers. Charlottesville, Va.: University of Virginia Press, pp. 109–120.

Wolford, Chester L. *Stephen Crane: A Study of the Short Fiction*. Boston: Twayne, 1989.

BROTHER Main CHARACTER of James BALDWIN'S "Sonny's Blues," whose life is imperfectly perceived by his older brother, who is also the first person-narrator. Brother gets into trouble because of hard times at home; eventually he is caught with drugs and completes a jail sentence. The narrator, who has had his own problems and has worked hard to carve out his own career as a teacher, realizes he has not listened to his brother. Ironically, Brother becomes teacher to the narrator when he invites him to a nightclub to listen to him play blues music. The narrator finally understands not only the racism that has shaped both their lives but the brotherly love that can strengthen both of them.

BROWN, CHARLES BROCKDEN (1771–1810)

Born in Philadelphia to a prosperous Quaker Family, Brown attended Friend's Latin School and then studied law from 1787 to 1793, although he abandoned the profession without ever practicing. Brown fled Philadelphia in 1793 during the yellow fever epidemic. The fifth installment of his serial fiction, "The Man at Home," recounts the experience of a family suffering during the epidemic. In the same year Brown encountered in New York members of the Friendly Club, who were committed to furthering a distinctly American literature and who included William Dunlop, Brown's biographer. In 1798 Brown began publishing short essays and fragments in a number of periodicals, including the Philadelphia *Weekly Magazine*.

Traditional critical wisdom holds Brown to be the first American author to attempt to make a living from his writing, and critical appraisals of his art vary widely, although none denies his historical importance. He is known primarily for his novels, gothic romances that show an obvious debt to Samuel Richardson, William Godwin, and Anne Radcliffe. Critics have gone so far as to insist that all his work aside from his novels is outside the domain of serious students of American literature.

But such a critical stance unnecessarily hinders a full evaluation of Brown's work. The shorter pieces and essays demand attention in their own right, in particular "Somnambulism," a proto-detective story with a sleepwalking protagonist; "Lesson on Concealment"; and "The Man at Home." Some of his stories—"Thessalonica," for example—are characterized by didactic historical writing that tends to put off the modern reader and that too often obscures a deeper, underlying sociological awareness. Scott and Keats both gladly read Brown, and Shelley lauded him, but at times Brown's work seems overwhelmed by a sense of longing and despair that he attempts to transpose onto an American landscape. An unhappy tension often exists between the European forms and the American setting. Although Brown advocated high critical standards for American fiction, his own work seems overly indebted to European influences, and his language sometimes seems artificially or hastily conceived. These problems aside, his work is psychologically probing and gives loose rein to a deep curiosity about the forces that prompt human action, especially those pathologies that tend to provoke evil or mitigate human happiness.

Brown produced most of his fiction over five years and then turned his interest toward publishing journals, among them the *Literary Magazine and American Register* and *The American Register, or General Repository of History Politics, and Science.* He also edited *The Monthly Magazine and American Review.* Brown's work, flawed though it is, shows concern for the emerging state of American letters, and his fascination with the darker corners of the human psyche open the way for later American writers like Nathaniel HAWTHORNE and Edgar Allan POE.

BIBLIOGRAPHY

Ringe, Donald A. *Charles Brockden Brown.* New York: Macmillan, 1991.

Rosenthal, Bernard, ed. *Critical Essays on Charles Brockden Brown.* Boston: G. K. Hall, 1981.

Warfel, Harry R., ed. *The Rhapsodist and Other Uncollected Writings by Charles Brockden Brown.* New York: Scholars' Facsimiles & Reprints, 1943.

Weber, Alfred, ed. *Somnambulism and Other Stories.* New York: Peter Lang, 1987.

Cornelius W. Browne
Ohio University

BROWNE, CHARLES FARRAR   See WARD, ARTEMUS.

BUCK, PEARL S. (1892–1973)   Pearl
Sydenstricker Buck, the daughter of American missionaries to China, was born in West Virginia and educated in Shanghai, China, until she returned to the United States at age 17 to attend Randolph-Macon Woman's College. Widely known as a prolific novelist who wrote fiction based on her experiences while living in China, Buck wrote her best-known novel, *The Good Earth,* in 1931. She received the Pulitzer Prize in 1932, the William Dean Howells Medal for Distinguished Fiction in 1935, and the Nobel Prize for Literature in 1938. Despite her fame as a novelist, with over 60 books to her credit, Pearl

Buck was a prolific writer of short stories and NOVELLAS. Indeed, one could argue that her first impulse was to write shorter rather than novel-length works, for evidence exists that she—like numerous other writers of her time—was under pressure from publishers to produce longer work: Her first story, "A Chinese Woman Speaks," published in *Asia* magazine in 1925, became her first book, *East Wind: West Wind* (1930), when combined with another short story. It told the tale of a Chinese husband who wishes his wife to unbind her feet and become his equal, and of the wife's brother, who shocks the family by marrying an American woman who in due course gives birth to a mixed race child. Even her next novel, *The Good Earth,* began as a short story, published in *Asia* magazine in 1928 and entitled "The Revolutionist."

Buck published numerous short story collections in her lifetime, always preferring CHARACTER and PLOT—the simple lines of a story she believed her reader wanted—to the literary techniques of MODERNISM. In her fiction as well as her numerous nonfiction essays and articles, she wrote passionately about East-West issues as well as about black-white relations in the United States. She significantly influenced the work of such writers as Tillie OLSEN. In 1949, with her husband, Richard Walsh, Buck established Friendship House for orphans from various Asian countries. During the VIETNAM WAR, the house grew to include mixed race or Amerasian children. After her death it became the Pearl Buck Foundation.

BIBLIOGRAPHY

Buck, Pearl. *American Argument.* New York: John Day Co., 1949.

———. *American Triptych: Three "John Sedges" Novels.* New York: John Day Co., 1958.

———. *The Angry Wife.* New York: John Day Co., 1947.

———. *A Bridge for Passing.* New York: John Day Co., 1962.

———. *Bright Procession.* New York: John Day Co., 1952.

———. *China Flight.* Philadelphia: Triangle Books/Blakiston Company, 1945.

———. *China Sky.* Philadelphia: Blakiston, 1942.

———. *The Chinese Novel.* New York: John Day, 1939.

————. *Come, My Beloved.* New York: John Day Co., 1953.

————. *Command the Morning: A Novel.* New York: John Day Co., 1959.

————. *East Wind: West Wind.* New York: John Day, 1930.

————. *The Exile.* New York: John Day, 1936.

————. *Far and Near: Stories of Japan, China and America.* New York: John Day Co., 1947.

————. *Fighting Angel: Portrait of a Soul.* New York: P. F. Collier, 1936.

————. *The First Wife and Other Stories.* New York: John Day Co., 1933.

————. *Fourteen Stories.* New York: John Day Co., 1961.

————. *God's Men.* New York: John Day Co., 1951.

————. *The Good Earth.* New York: John Day Co., 1931.

————. *Hearts Come Home and Other Stories.* New York: Pocket Books, 1962.

————. *The Hidden Flower.* New York: John Day Co., 1952.

————. *A House Divided.* New York: John Day Co., 1935.

————. *House of the Earth.* New York: John Day Co., 1935.

————. *Imperial Woman.* New York: John Day Co., 1956.

————. *The Joy of Children.* New York: John Day Co., 1964.

————. *Kinfolk.* New York: John Day Co., 1949.

————. *Letter From Peking.* New York: John Day Co., 1957.

————. *The Living Reed.* New York: John Day Co., 1963.

————. *The Long Love.* New York: John Day Co., 1949.

————. *The Mother.* New York: John Day Co., 1934.

————. *My Several Worlds: A Personal Memoir.* New York: John Day Co., 1954.

————. *Of Men and Women.* New York: John Day Co., 1941.

————. *Other Gods: An American Legend.* New York: John Day Co., 1940.

————. *The Patriot.* New York: John Day Co., 1939.

————. *Pavilion of Women.* New York: John Day Co., 1946.

————. *Peony.* New York: John Day Co., 1948.

————. *Portrait of a Marriage.* New York: John Day Co., 1945.

————. *The Promise.* New York: John Day Co., 1943.

————. *The Proud Heart.* New York: John Day Co., 1938.

————. *Satan Never Sleeps.* New York: Pocket Books, 1962.

————. *Sons.* New York: John Day Co., 1932.

————. *The Spirit and the Flesh.* New York: John Day Co., 1944.

————. *Stories of China.* New York: John Day Co., 1964.

————. *The Story of Dragon Seed: Twenty-Seven Stories.* New York: John Day Co., 1944.

————. *Tell the People.* New York: John Day Co., 1945.

————. *Today and Forever: Stories of China.* New York: John Day Co., 1941.

————. *The Townsman.* New York: John Day Co., 1945.

————. *Voices in the House.* New York: John Day Co., 1953.

————. *The Young Revolutionist.* New York: Friendship Press, 1932.

BUKOWSKI, CHARLES (1920–1994)

A counterculture writer of novels and short stories, Bukowski depicts the "lower end" of America in his work. His prose style is simple and straightforward, although he experiments with third- and first-person POINTS OF VIEW and a varying use of capital letters: in some stories no proper nouns are capitalized and in others every letter of dialogue is in capital letters. The language he uses is blunt and often crude, and much of his work is infused with dark humor.

Bukowski's work was published primarily by small, underground presses and LITTLE MAGAZINES. He wrote a weekly column, "Notes of a Dirty Old Man," for the underground newspaper *Open City,* a collection of which was published in 1973. His first collection of short stories entitled *Erections, Ejaculations, Exhibitionists and General Tales of Ordinary Madness* was published in 1972.

BIBLIOGRAPHY

Bukowski, Charles. *Bring Me Your Love.* Santa Barbara, Calif.: Black Sparrow Press, 1983.

————. *Erections, Ejaculations, Exhibitions and General Tales of Ordinary Madness.* San Francisco: City Lights, 1972: abridged edition, as *Life and Death in the Charity Ward,* London: London Magazine Editions, 1974; selections, edited by Gail Chiarello, as *Tales of Ordinary Madness* and *The Most Beautiful Woman in Town and Other Stories.* San Francisco: City Lights, 2 vols., 1983.

————. *Hot Water Music.* Santa Barbara, Calif.: Black Sparrow Press, 1983.

————. *Notes of a Dirty Old Man.* North Hollywood, Calif.: Essex House, 1969.

————. *South of No North.* Los Angeles: Black Sparrow Press, 1973.

————. *There's No Business.* Santa Barbara, Calif.: Black Sparrow Press, 1984.

"Charles Bukowski Issue." *Review of Contemporary Fiction* (Fall 1985).

Fox, Hugh. *Charles Bukowski: A Biographical Study.* Somerville, Mass.: Abyss, 1968.

Sherman, Jory. *Bukowski: Friendship, Fame, and Bestial Myth.* Augusta, Ga.: Blue Horse Press, 1982.

BULOSAN, CARLOS (1911–1956)

Carlos Bulosan was born in Binanlon, the Philippines, to poor and illiterate parents. His father was a farmer; his mother sold dried fish in the local market. At the age of 17 he left the Philippines permanently for the United States, although he never became a U.S. citizen.

Bulosan's most popular work remains his autobiographical memoir, *America Is in the Heart* (1946). Short stories published during his lifetime, however, appeared in the NEW YORKER, *Harper's Bazaar*, SATURDAY EVENING POST, *Town and Country, The Arizona Quarterly,* and *New Masses.* His short story collection, *The Laughter of My Father* (1944), which he wrote in 12 days, was also a best-seller during the year it appeared and contributed significantly to his international reputation. Three posthumous works collected additional stories: *On Becoming Filipino* (1975), *The Philippines Is in the Heart* (1978), and *The Power of Money and Other Stories* (1990). Bulosan also wrote the novel *The Cry and the Dedication* (published posthumously in 1995), three books of poetry, and numerous essays.

At least three THEMES are crucial to Bulosan's fiction: first, the immigrant's unattainable longing to find acceptance in America as an American; second, the grievous plight of the poor and disenfranchised around the world and in America itself; and third, the necessity of learning from all life experiences, especially tragic, violent, and horrifying ones. Bulosan's writing is characterized by a compelling sense of intimacy and immediacy, so that all he wrote feels autobiographical even when it is not.

Bulosan's first 14 years in the United States were, in his own words, "violent years of unemployment, prolonged illnesses and heart-rending labor union work on the farms of California" (Kunitz). And although he nearly died of tuberculosis at the age of 31, he gradually recovered to become a famous writer and editor. Most of his writing was squeezed into what he called "two restless years" between 1944 and 1946; the final ten years of his life constituted "a decline into poverty, alcohol, loneliness, and obscurity" (Kim)—at least in part because of changing political winds that left Filipino Americans somewhat out of favor following World War II. Bulosan died in Seattle of pneumonia (likely resulting in part from his earlier struggles against tuberculosis and cancer) at the age of 42.

BIBLIOGRAPHY

Bulosan, Carlos. *The Laughter of My Father.* London: Michael Joseph, 1945.

———. *On Becoming Filipino: Selected Writings of Carlos Bulosan.* Philadelphia: Temple University Press, 1995.

———. *The Philippines Is in the Heart: A Collection of Stories.* Quezon City: New Day Publishers, 1978.

———. *The Power of Money and Other Stories.* Manila: Kalikasan Press, 1990.

Kim, Elaine. *Asian American Literature: An Introduction to the Writings and their Social Context.* Philadelphia: Temple University Press, 1982.

Kunitz, Stanley, ed. *Twentieth Century Authors.* New York: Wilson, 1955.

San Juan, E., Jr. Introduction. *On Becoming Filipino: Selected Writings of Carlos Bulosan.* Philadelphia: Temple University Press, 1995.

University of Singapore Society. *The Filipino Short Story.* Singapore: 1980.

Keith Lawrence
Brigham Young University

BURLESQUE

A form of COMEDY that contrives to arouse amusement rather than contempt by the use of distortion, e.2xaggeration, and imitation. The essence of burlesque is the apparent discrepancy between the subject matter and the manner of presentation, in that a style ordinarily serious may be used for a nonserious subject or vice versa.

BUSCH, FREDERICK (1941–)

Frederick Busch is a humanist with an unwavering focus on the family. He is not alone in this late 20th-century emphasis on the most consistent source of consolation many people know: His THEME has been pursued by such contemporaries as Raymond CARVER, Grace PALEY, Peter TAYLOR, and John UPDIKE. Busch celebrates the tenaciousness with which his characters grapple with and relate to blood kin as a bulwark against the anxiety and fear of death that pervade nearly all his stories, collected in *Breathing Trouble* (1973), *Domestic Particulars* (1976), *Hardwater Country* (1979), and *Too Late American Boyhood Blues* (1984).

Few writers attempt to narrate from as many POINTS OF VIEW—male as well as female, adult as well as a child's. Busch's imagistic and carefully detailed depictions are equally catholic, whether of countryside or city. Natural SETTINGS can provide salvation, as in "Trail of Possible Bones" (*Domestic Particulars*), or evoke fear, as in "What You Might as Well Call Love" (*Hardwater Country*). Busch conveys his characters' actions in meticulous detail, from hooking up a television to performing pediatric duties.

Domestic Particulars contains 13 linked stories that follow the life of one New York City family from 1919 to 1976, with Clair Miller and her son, Harry, as focal characters. Busch describes Brooklyn, the Upper West Side, and Greenwich Village with extraordinary clarity in these stories that attempt to define the essence of family both literally and figuratively.

BIBLIOGRAPHY

Busch, Frederick. *Breathing Trouble and Other Stories.* London: Calder and Boyars, 1974.

———. *Domestic Particulars: A Family Chronicle.* New York: New Directions, 1976.

———. *Hardwater Country.* New York: Knopf, 1979.

———. *I Wanted a Year Without Fall.* London: Calder and Boyars, 1971.

———. *Invisible Mending.* Boston: Godine, 1984.

———. *Manual Labor.* New York: New Directions, 1974.

———. *The Mutual Friend.* New York: Harper & Row, 1978.

———. *Take This Man.* New York: Farrar, Straus & Giroux, 1981.

———. *Too Late American Boyhood Blues.* Boston: Godine, 1984.

———. *Sometimes I Live in the Country.* Boston: Godine, 1986.

C

C. AUGUSTE DUPIN One of the earliest detectives in American fiction, Dupin's appearance in Edgar Allan POE's tales of "ratiocination" established the formula, still imitated today, of the intellectual detective using meticulous detail and his powers of deduction to solve the crime. His amateur status (not affiliated with the police) and cold logic have become familiar characteristics of the literary detectives modeled on him, from Agatha Christie's Hercule Poirot and Sir Arthur Conan Doyle's Sherlock Holmes to Raymond CHANDLER's Philip Marlowe and Dashiell HAMMETT's SAM SPADE. Dupin's bewildered, nameless friend and narrator—to whom he explains his brilliant deductions—also started the trend of the FOILS to these detectives, most celebrated in the relationship between Holmes and his puzzled sidekick, Dr. Watson.

CABLE, GEORGE WASHINGTON (1844–1925) American novelist and short story writer who probably gave Americans their most memorable view of 19th-century Louisiana life in all its multiculturalism and diversity, particularly New Orleans Creole life. Born in New Orleans of New England Puritan background on his mother's side and of a Virginia slaveholding family of German descent on his father's side, Cable had to leave school at age 14 when his father died. He worked in the custom-house, fought with the 4th Mississippi cavalry during the CIVIL WAR, contracted malaria, and began his writing career as a columnist for the *New Orleans Picayune*. Cable achieved national attention with his publication of "'Sieur George" in SCRIBNER'S *Monthly* in 1873. Within the next three years *Scribner's* published the stories that would gain Cable a national reputation as a LOCAL COLOR realist (see REALISM).

Those stories—"Belles Demoiselles Plantation," "'Tite Poulette," "Madame Delicieuse," "Jean-ah Poquelin," and others—were collected in *Old Creole Days* in 1879. Cable was adept at conveying the language, speech patterns, and character of the region. Particularly notable was "Jean-ah Poquelin," composed during the final period of RECONSTRUCTION in the South: Cable set the story in the period after the Louisiana Purchase in 1803, dramatizing the conflict between the old French colonial civilization, represented by Poquelin, and the new American order in New Orleans. A parallel could be seen then, and may be seen now, between the older French and the current Yankee intrusion. Soon afterward Cable wrote two novels, *The Grandissimes* in 1880 and *Madame Delphine* in 1881. They examine pre–Civil War New Orleans life, with particular attention to black-white relations and the unfair treatment of African Americans.

Successful enough to become a full-time writer, Cable wrote essays and novels more and more sympathetic to the exploitation of blacks and to reform of the prison system. Indeed, the growing resentment of his treatment of these issues led to his decision to move to Northampton, Massachusetts, in 1885, where he became friendly with Mark TWAIN and continued to urge reform both in his writing and his speeches. Today he is viewed as a thoughtful writer who depicted the moral dimensions of interethnic relations, imaginatively understood the impact of the past on the present, and displayed an imaginative sensitivity to the exotic aspects of his region. Cable helped prepare the ground for William FAULKNER, Eudora WELTY, Flannery O'CONNOR, and other modern southern writers.

BIBLIOGRAPHY

Bikle, Lucy Leffingwell C(able). *George W. Cable: His Life and Letters.* New York: Scribner's, 1928.

Butcher, Philip. *George W. Cable.* New York: Twayne, 1962.

Cable, George Washington. *Dr. Sevier.* Boston: Ticknor and Company, 1884. Reprint. New York: Scribner's, 1974.

———. *The Grandissimes.* New York: Charles Scribner's Sons, 1880. Rev. ed. 1883. Reprint. Athens, Ga.: University of Georgia Press, 1988.

———. *John March, Southerner.* New York: Scribner's, 1894. Reprint. New York: Garrett Press, 1970.

———. *Madame Delphine.* New York: C. Scribner's, 1881. Reprint. St. Claire's Shores, Mich.: Scholarly Press, 1970.

———. *The Negro Question.* Edited by Arlin Turner. New York: Norton, 1968.

———. *Old Creole Days.* New York: Scribner's, 1879. *Old Creole Days: Stories of Creole Life.* Gretna, La.: Pelican Pub. Co., 1991.

Payne, James Robert. "George Washington Cable's 'My Politics': Context and Reivision of a Southern Memoir." In *Multicultural Autobiography: American Lives.* Edited by James Robert Payne. Knoxville: University of Tennessee Press, 1992.

Petry, Alice Hall. *A Genius in His Way: The Art of Cable's "Old Creole Days."* Rutherford, N.J.: Fairleigh Dickinson University Press, 1988.

Turner, Arlin. *George W. Cable: A Biography.* Baton Rouge: Louisiana State University Press, 1956.

Turner, Arlin, ed. *Critical Essays on George W. Cable.* Boston: G.K. Hall, 1980.

CAIN, JAMES M(ALLAHAN) (1892–1977)

Born in Annapolis, Maryland, James M. Cain received B.A. and M.A. degrees from Washington College; served with the American Expeditionary Force in France during WORLD WAR I; worked as a reporter for the *Baltimore American,* the *Baltimore Sun,* and the *New York World;* and wrote pieces for the *American Mercury* and the NEW YORKER. During the GREAT DEPRESSION Cain moved to California, where he worked briefly for Paramount movie studios before becoming the author of popular murder mysteries and "tough-guy" novels, including *The Postman Always Rings Twice* (1934) and *Double Indemnity* (1943), both of which were made into successful films. Cain also wrote scores of short stories, 17 of which were published in such magazines as the *American Mercury, Redbook,* ESQUIRE, and LADIES' HOME JOURNAL, nine of which are collected, along with essays and sketches, in *The Baby in the Icebox,* published in 1981.

Two of Cain's stories, "Pastorale" (1928) and "The Baby in the Icebox," attracted considerable critical and popular attention. Both use a HARD-BOILED FICTION–style first-person narrator; Cain was an admirer of Ring LARDNER and consciously imitated his narrative style when writing "Icebox." H. L. Mencken, editor of the *American Mercury,* praised the story and published it in 1933, and in that same year it was made into a film entitled *She Made Her Bed.*

Like Raymond CHANDLER and Dashiell HAMMETT, Cain belongs to the "tough-guy" tradition, and like them, Cain writes about the working classes of California and the seamier side of life, which is the other side of the mythic "golden land." A number of critics have pointed out the value of these writers—popular entertainers all—who not only depict the violence always close to the surface in American life, but also shed light on the urgent problems of social history. In short, they demonstrate one way to understand society.

Like the naturalists (see NATURALISM), Cain made full use of his familiarity with specific areas of knowledge such as the law and even of the intricacies of the restaurant business, as in "Postman" and "Icebox," among others. Along with Hammett and Chandler, Cain used California to his advantage: while Chandler focused on Los Angeles and Hammett on San Francisco, Cain set his stories in Glendale, a Los Angeles suburb. "The Baby in the

Icebox" realistically describes the garish stretches of highway dotted with gas stations that have become endemic to the entire country.

Like his peers, Cain writes out of the tradition of PROLETARIAN LITERATURE. He is less interested in social criticism, however, than in an examination of his characters themselves, who, as David Madden notes, "add up to an impressive gallery of American public types" (Madden 164). The genre's concern with violence, love, and money not only produces a perspective of the 1930s and 1940s, but also "provides insights into the AMERICAN DREAM–turned–nightmare and into the all-American boy–turned–tough guy" (Madden 165).

BIBLIOGRAPHY

Cain, James M. *The Baby in the Icebox and Other Short Fiction.* Edited by Roy Hoopes. New York: Holt, Rinehart and Winston, 1981.

———. *The Butterfly.* New York: Alfred A. Knopf, 1947.

———. *Cain × 3: Three Novels.* Alfred A. Knopf, 1969.

———. *Career in C Major.* New York: Alfred A. Knopf, 1943.

———. *Double Indemnity.* New York: Alfred A. Knopf, 1943.

———. *The Embezzler.* New York: Alfred A. Knopf, 1943.

———. *Galatea.* New York: Knopf, 1953.

———. *The Government.* New York: Knopf, 1930.

———. *Jealous Woman.* New York: Avon Book Co., 1950.

———. *Love's Lovely Counterfeit.* New York: Knopf, 1942.

———. *The Magician's Wife.* New York: Dial Press, 1965.

———. *Mignon.* New York: Dial Press, 1965.

———. *Mildred Pierce.* New York: Knopf, 1941.

———. *The Moth.* New York: Knopf, 1948.

———. *Past All Dishonor.* New York: Knopf, 1946.

———. *The Postman Always Rings Twice.* New York: Knopf, 1934.

———. *The Root of His Evil.* New York: Avon Book Co., 1951.

———. *Serenade.* New York: Knopf, 1937.

———. *Sinful Woman.* New York: Avon Editions, Inc., 1947.

———. *Three of a Kind.* New York: Knopf, 1943.

Madden, David. *James M. Cain.* New York: Twayne, 1970.

CALDWELL, ERSKINE (PRESTON)
(1903–1987)   After a series of menial jobs and a stint as a professional football player, Caldwell began his writing career around 1930. Judging by the many millions of copies of his novels and short story collections sold in paperback editions in several countries, within 20 years, Caldwell was probably the most popular writer of fiction in the world. The books and stories that established his reputation deal primarily with life among sharecroppers and blacks in his native Georgia. His earthy and starkly tragic representations (see TRAGEDY) of Southern depravity and racial injustice initially earned him acclaim as a social critic. The novels *Tobacco Road* (1932) and *God's Little Acre* (1933), incorporating a mix of violence, deformed characters, subhuman lack of compassion, and an almost mystical interpretation of human potential, became phenomenally successful, as did his short story collection *Jackpot,* published in 1940 with 75 stories from the previous decade. With Caldwell's remarkable success came a growing critical belief that he was not so much exposing the bleak actualities of life in the South among characters who were often helpless, spiritually castrated, and sadistic, as he was exploiting them for publicity and financial gain. Caldwell was a master teller of TALL TALES who wrote in a direct style. His impeccable ear for DIALECT is evident in the bulk of his stories, as is the lilt of BLACK HUMOR and the stab of black melodrama.

BIBLIOGRAPHY

Arnold, Edwin T., ed. *Caldwell Reconsidered.* Jackson: University Press of Mississippi, 1990.

Caldwell, Erskine. *American Earth.* New York: Scribner's, 1931; as *A Swell-Looking Girl,* New York: New American Library, 1951.

———. *The Black and White Stories of Caldwell.* Edited by Ray McIver. Atlanta: Peachtree, 1984.

———. *The Caldwell Caravan: Novels and Stories.* New York: World Publishing Co., 1946.

———. *Certain Women.* Boston: Little, Brown, 1957.

———. *The Complete Stories of Erskine Caldwell.* Boston: Little, Brown, 1953.

———. *The Courting of Susie Brown.* Boston: Little, Brown, 1952.

———. *A Day's Wooing and Other Stories.* New York: Grossett & Dunlap, 1944.

———. *Georgia Boy.* New York: Duell, Sloan & Pearce, 1943.

―――. *Gulf Coast Stories.* Boston: Little, Brown, 1956.

―――. *The Humorous Side of Caldwell.* Edited by Robert Cantwell. New York: Duell, Sloan & Pearce, 1951; as *Where the Girls Were Different and Other Stories,* 1962.

―――. *Jackpot: The Short Stories.* New York: Duell, Sloan & Pearce, 1940; abridged ed., as *Midsummer Passion,* 1948.

―――. *Kneel to the Rising Sun and Other Stories.* New York: Viking, 1935.

―――. *Mama's Little Girl: A Brief History.* Portland, Me.: The Bradford Press, 1932.

―――. *Men and Women: 22 Stories.* Boston: Little, Brown, 1961.

―――. *A Message for Genevieve.* Portland, Me.: The Old Colony Press, 1933.

―――. *Midsummer Passion and Other Tales of Maine Cussedness.* Edited by Charles G. Waugh and Martin H. Greenberg. Boston: Yankee Books, 1990.

―――. *The Sacrilege of Alan Kent.* Portland, Me.: Falmouth, 1936.

―――. *Southways: Stories.* New York, Viking, 1938.

―――. *The Pocket Book of Erskine Caldwell Stories,* New York: Pocket Books, Inc., 1947.

―――. *Stories.* Edited by and with intro by Henry Seidel Canby. Duell, Sloan & Pearce, 1944; as *The Pocket Book of Stories of Life: North and South.* New York: Pocket Books, 1983.

―――. *We Are the Living: Brief Stories.* New York: Viking, 1933.

―――. *When You Think of Me.* Boston: Little, Brown, 1959.

―――. *Where the Girls Were Different and Other Stories.* Edited by Donald A. Wollheim. New York: Avon, 1948.

―――. *A Woman in the House.* New York: Signet Books, 1949.

Cassill, R. V. "Erksine Caldwell." In *Reference Guide to Short Fiction.* Edited by Noelle Watson. Detroit: St. James Press, 1994, pp. 96–98.

Devlin, James E. *Caldwell.* Boston: Twayne, 1984.

Korges, James. *Caldwell.* Minneapolis: University of Minnesota Press, 1969.

MacDonald, Scott, ed. *Critical Essays on Caldwell.* Boston: G. K. Hall, 1981.

Mcllwaine, Shields. *The Southern Poor-White from Lubberland to Tobacco Road.* Norman: University of Oklahoma Press, 1939.

Sutton, William A. *Black Like It Is/Was: Caldwell's Treatment of Racial Themes.* Metuchen, N.J.: Scarecrow Press, 1974.

CALISHER, HORTENSE (1911–)

Although she writes novels as well as short stories, Calisher is perhaps best known for her anthologized stories, such as "In Greenwich There are Many Gravelled Walks." She typically develops a story by hints and subtleties and information that the characters themselves reveal. Calisher, a master of style and language, uses precise, powerful verbs to give scenes life and immediacy. Although her stories are not primarily stories of character, but of complex situation, Calisher nonetheless offers intricately drawn insights into her fictional people. The full range of her short fiction is contained in *Collected Stories* (1975).

BIBLIOGRAPHY

Brophy, Brigid. *Don't Never Forget: Collected Views and Reviews.* London: J. Cape, 1966.

Brown, Kathy. "Hortense Calisher." *Current Biography* (November 1973).

Calisher, Hortense. *In the Absence of Angels: Stories.* Boston: Little, Brown, 1964.

―――. *Tale for the Mirror: A Novella and Other Stories.* Boston: Little, Brown, 1962.

―――. *Extreme Magic: A Novella and Other Stories.* Boston: Little, Brown, 1964.

―――. *The Railway Police, and The Last Trolley Ride.* Boston: Little, Brown, 1966.

―――. *The Collected Stories of Hortense Calisher.* New York: Arbor House, 1975.

―――. *Saratoga, Hot.* Garden City, N.Y.: Doubleday, 1985.

"Interview with Hortense Calisher." *Paris Review* (Winter 1987).

CANE JEAN TOOMER (1923)

Considered a highly influential work in the formative stages of the HARLEM RENAISSANCE, Jean TOOMER's *Cane,* a montage of short stories, prose vignettes, folk songs, poetry, and drama, looks at the ways erotic relationships, racism, and class stratification prevent black men and women from achieving either social acceptance or a positive connection with their Southern folk heritage. Along with other prominent Harlem Renaissance writers of the 1920s and 1930s, such as Langston HUGHES, Countee Cullen, Claude McKay, Zora Neale HURSTON, and Arna Bontemps, Toomer also examines black history in America, Africa as an important part of black cultural identity, and the role of folk culture in African-American society. Stylistically, *Cane's* fragmentary and experimental structure, as well as its STREAM-OF-CONSCIOUSNESS narration, places it in the context of such modernist works as Sherwood ANDERSON's WINESBURG, OHIO, Ernest HEMINGWAY's IN OUR TIME, and William FAULKNER's GO DOWN, MOSES. (See MODERNISM.)

Cane has a three-part structure. The first part, set in the fictional town of Sempter, Georgia, focuses on women characters who struggle against social limitations. The male narrators of "Karintha" and "Fern," for example, see these women as sexual objects, and, throughout much of Cane, women are objectified and victimized by the men who desire to possess them. At the same time, physical beauty empowers these women: "Men had always wanted her, this Karintha, even as a child, Karintha carrying beauty, perfect as dusk when the sun goes down". On the other hand, "Blood-Burning Moon" overtly explores issues of racism and the ramifications of MISCEGENATION (interracial marriage) in the South. Louisa, caught between two men battling for her affections, watches both Bob Stone, who is white, and Tom Burwell, who is black, destroy each other. After Tom kills Bob in a fight, the white community executes him. As the flames engulf Tom and the portentous folk singing dies away in the community, Toomer presents a terrifying and somewhat mythical image of racism in the early 20th century.

The second part, primarily set in Washington, D.C., depicts the ineffectual relationships between black men and women resulting from the harmful impact of urban materialism. In "Rhobert," for example, Toomer shows how the PROTAGONIST suffers under the burdens and financial pressures of urban life: "Rhobert wears a house, like a monstrous diver's helmet, on his head" (40). Burdened by the weight of the unaccustomed ways of white city life, these rural black men nonetheless affirm their masculine sensibilities. The cost to black women, however, is enormous. In the story "Avey," men have ostracized the female protagonist by relegating her identity to that of a prostitute, and like Karintha and Fern, Avey does not have the opportunity to tell her own story. In "Box Seat" Dan Moore, like so many of the male narrators and characters in Cane, admires and seeks some connection with the past. He feels alienated from the black heritage of the South. Dan also perceives Muriel (like the character of Dorris in "Theater") as trapped by her desire for acceptance in a higher social class. Even though he thinks he can potentially save her from the influence of class, he does not change anything. As Susan Blake suggests, "Dan can dream, but he cannot act" (205).

In the third part, the drama "Kabnis" brings the reader back to Georgia. Ralph Kabnis, a Northern-educated black man, has moved South to teach. Frustrated with the meaninglessness he perceives in religion, the educational system, and black American history, Kabnis seeks meaning in his relationships with both men and women. In his search for some connection with his cultural heritage, Kabnis, having lost his job as a teacher, tries to fit into the unaccustomed Southern blue-collar world of Halsey's shop, only to realize that he is still an outsider. A "completely artificial man," Kabnis cannot respond to the glory of his heritage. Unlike Kabnis, Father John Lewis is the visionary who appeals to Carrie Kate, the young woman character; she sees in Father John the redemptive vision of the African American heritage. At the end of the play, however, when Father John speaks and Kabnis falls to his knees before Carrie Kate, Toomer suggests that spiritual redemption is possible for Kabnis: "Light streaks through the iron-barred cellar window . . . Outside, the sun arises from its cradle in the tree-tops of the forest" (116).

BIBLIOGRAPHY

Baker, Houston, Jr. Singers of Daybreak: Studies in Black American Literature. Washington, D.C.: Howard University Press, 1974.

Blake, Susan. "The Spectatorial Artist and the Structure of Cane." In Therman B. O'Daniel, ed., Jean Toomer: A Critical Evaluation. Washington, D.C.: Howard University Press, 1988.

Byrd, Rudolph P. Jean Toomer's Years with Gurdjieff: Portrait of an Artist 1923–1936. Athens: University of Georgia Press, 1991.

Toomer, Jean. Cane. New York: Liveright, 1975.

Thomas Fahy
University of North Carolina at Chapel Hill

CANIN, ETHAN (1961–)

Canin has been praised for the clean, classic tone and shape of his stories, which have appeared in such magazines as ESQUIRE and the ATLANTIC MONTHLY. In 1985 and 1986, two were reprinted in *Best American Short Stories*. His first story collection, *Emperor of the Air,* contains nine carefully crafted tales that demonstrate the mystery and knowledge awaiting those who try to illuminate the meaning of their everyday existence. The characters range from children— "Star Food," for instance, depicts a young boy whose curiosity protects a thief—to adults—for example, the man in "The Year of Getting to Know Us" who confronts his father's infidelity, or the retired couple in "We Are the Nightime Travelers" who fall in love with each other for the second time. Canin's recent book, *The Palace Thief: Stories,* published in 1995, contains four long short stories, or NOVELLAS, in which Canin presents characters who muse on the past, often focusing on humiliating moments and trying, with varying degrees of success, to understand why they seemed helpless as their lives took them in unforeseen directions.

BIBLIOGRAPHY

Canin, Ethan. *Blue River.* New York: Warner Books, 1992.
———. *Emperor of the Air: Stories.* New York: HarperCollins, 1989.
———. *For Kings and Planets.* New York: Random House, 1998.
———. *The Palace Thief: Stories.* New York: Picador USA, 1995.
Canin, Ethan, and Diane Sterling, eds. *Writers Harvest 2.* New York: Harcourt Brace, 1996.

CAPITALISM

An economic system characterized by private ownership of property and the means of production, and embodying the concepts of individual initiative, competition, supply and demand, and the profit motive. The importance and impact of capitalism grew with the Industrial Revolution, which began in Great Britain in the mid-18th century and gained impetus in the United States after the CIVIL WAR. By the early 20th century, unbridled capitalism had created vast credit, manufacturing, and distributing institutions, and the social and economic aspects of the system had transformed much of the world. The attendant abuses, however, particularly the exploitation of labor, social dislocation, and monopolistic practices, caused pure capitalism to be circumscribed in the early part of this century by the growth of labor unions and by laws enacted to break up and prevent monopolies and to address social and labor concerns, environmental problems, and product and worker safety.

CAPOTE, TRUMAN (1924–1984)

The acclaimed author of *A Tree of Night and Other Stories* (1949), *Breakfast at Tiffany's: A Short Novel and Three Stories* (1958), and a variety of works in other genres, including *In Cold Blood* (1966), Truman Capote set all his fiction either in his native Alabama or his adopted home, New York City. Capote is most revered, however, for his dark themes and his lonely characters whose subtly and intricately depicted psychology reverberate with readers. Despite his relatively sparse output as a short fiction writer, therefore, Capote— winner of three O. HENRY MEMORIAL AWARDS (1946, 1948, 1951), among numerous others—seems assured an established place among important 20th-century American short story writers.

A Tree of Night contains many of Capote's best stories. Somewhat reminiscent of Katherine Anne PORTER's work in tone, Capote's stories reveal the internal realities of his protagonists as the author uses lyrical symbolism to blend identity issues, dreams, illusions, and disillusion. Also characteristic of Capote's technique is the use of SURREALISM and fantasy and Southern GOTHIC to evoke the presence of evil. In the title story, "A Tree of Night," a young woman named Kay takes a train in which the eerie old couple seated next to her alarm her by their attentions, particularly the old man, who touches her on the cheek. In a stunning DENOUEMENT, in which the old man becomes the wizard of Kay's childhood, the old woman takes Kay's purse and draws Kay's raincoat over her head. The story leaves many unanswered questions as Kay ponders her childhood and identity. Other bleak tales in the collection include "Master Misery," in which the young protagonist, Sylvia, leaves her Ohio home to live in New York. When Sylvia discovers that she can sell her dreams to a man who specializes in collecting those of others, her lonely lot is given temporary meaning. Master Misery, however, finally strips Sylvia of all her dreams, leaving her about to be violated by a literally dirty old man. The bizarre story reaches mythic proportions as it narrates a depressing romance for modern times. In this same vein is "Miriam," whose middle-aged protagonist, Mrs. Miller, is haunted by Miriam, a strange child dressed all in white who ultimately moves into Mrs. Miller's apartment and appropriates her most personal belongings.

BIBLIOGRAPHY

Brinnin, John Malcolm. *Truman Capote: Dear Hearty, Old Buddy.* New York: Lawrence/Delacorte, 1986.

Capote, Truman. *Answered Prayers: The Unfinished Novel.* Edited by Joseph M. Fox. New York: Random House, 1987.

———. *Breakfast At Tiffany's: A Short Novel and Three Stories.* New York: Random House, 1958.

———. *A Christmas Memory.* New York: Random House, 1966.

———. *The Dogs Bark: Public People and Private Places.* New York: Random House, 1973.

———. *The Grass Harp.* New York: Random House, 1951.

———. *In Cold Blood: The True Account of a Multiple Murder and Its Consequences.* New York: Random House, 1965.

———. *Jug of Silver.* Mankato, Minn.: Creative Education, 1986.

———. *A Christmas Memory.* New York: Random House, 1966.

———. *Other Voices, Other Rooms.* New York: Random House, 1948.

———. *Local Color.* New York: Random House, 1950.

———. *The Muses Are Heard.* New York: Random House, 1956.

———. *Music for Chameleons.* New York: Random House, 1980.

———. *Observations.* New York: Simon & Schuster, 1959.

———. *One Christmas.* New York: Random House, 1983.

———. *The Thanksgiving Visitor.* New York: Random House, 1968.

———. *A Tree of Night and Other Stories.* New York: Random House, 1949.

———. *Trilogy: An Experiment in Multimedia,* with Eleanor and Frank Perry. New York: Macmillan, 1969.

———. *The White Rose.* Newton, Iowa: Tamazunchale, 1987.

Clarke, Gerald. *Capote: A Biography.* New York: Simon & Schuster, 1988.

Creeger, George R. *Animals in Exile: Imagery and Theme in Capote's "In Cold Blood."* Middletown, Conn: Wesleyan University Center for Advanced Studies, 1967.

Dunphy, Jack. *"Dear Genius . . .": A Memoir of My Life with Truman Capote.* New York: McGraw-Hill, 1987.

Garson, Helen S. *Truman Capote.* New York: Ungar, 1980.

Nance, William L. *The Worlds of Truman Capote.* New York: Stein & Day, 1970.

Reed, Kenneth T. *Truman Capote.* Boston: Twayne, 1981.

Rudisill, Marbie, and James Simmons. *Truman Capote: The Story of his Bizarre and Exotic Boyhood.* New York: Morrow, 1983.

Walker, Jeffrey. "1945–1956: Post–World War II Manners and Mores," in *The American Short Story, 1945–1980: A Critical History.* Edited by Weaver. Boston: Twayne, 1983, pp. 22–24.

Windham, Donald. *Lost Friendships: A Memoir of Truman Capote, Tennessee Williams, and Others.* New York: Morrow, 1987.

CARICATURE   Any fictional representation of a person or fictional character that exaggerates, distorts and aims to amuse. The term may also be used pejoratively, as when a critic finds an author's CHARACTERIZATION flat, thin, or clichéed. See also CHARACTER.

CARVER, RAYMOND (1938–1988)   Raymond Carver's untimely death in August 1988 at the age of 50 cut short the career of one of the most influential and talented short story writers in contemporary America. At the time of his death, Carver had published four collections of short fiction: *Will You Please Be Quiet Please* (1976), *Furious Seasons* (1977), *What We Talk About When We Talk About Love* (1981), and *Cathedral* (1983). Most of the stories in these collections as well as some new material were gathered for the posthumously published *Where I'm Calling From* (1988), which contains virtually all of his major fiction. Carver also wrote five collections of poetry, although his reputation as a poet has lagged behind the view of him as the major short story craftsman of his generation.

Born in 1938 to Clevie and Ella Beatrice Carver in Clatskanie, Oregon, Carver's childhood was anything but serene. His father's alcoholism and the scenes that it provoked remained etched in his mind all his life, and provided material for several of his stories, told from a boy's perspective. In "Nobody Said Anything," for example, after the child narrator hears his mother and father arguing, he plays hooky from school and goes fishing to get his troubled family life out of his mind. He encounters another boy along the river, and together they catch a fairly large fish. They divide the fish in half and when the boy, proud of his catch, takes his portion home to show to his father, the father screams, "Take that goddamn thing out of here! . . . Take it the hell out of the kitchen and throw it in the goddamn garbage!" The story contrasts the child's innocence and sense of wonder about the world with the discordant, dysfunctional adult world in which the child is forced to live.

Characters loosely based on Carver's father or mother appear in "The Third Thing That Killed My Father Off," "Boxes," "So Much Water So Close to Home," and especially "Elephant," one of his best stories, in which the narrator considers his father nostalgically from the perspective of a middle-age divorced man who is being badgered for money by his ex-wife, his two children, his mother, and his brother. In a dream the narrator sees his father, pretending to be an elephant, carrying his son on his shoulders. He remembers this as a carefree time in contrast to the reality of his present as a recovering alcoholic, whose own family sees him only as a source of money. He plays the roles of father, son, husband, and brother with only the burdens of those roles and none of the pleasures. In the end, however, the narrator embraces his life for what it is rather than continuing to complain about it.

In 1957 Carver married Maryann Burk, his teenage sweetheart—he was 19 and she was 16 at the time of the wedding—and their tumultuous marriage lasted for 20 years. They were separated in 1977, and shortly thereafter Carver began a long relationship with the poet Tess Gallagher that culminated in their marriage in 1988, the year of Carver's death. The period of his marriage to Maryann provided material for his best and most characteristic stories.

Carver had a watershed year in 1977. Although he had already published his first collection of stories and established a reputation as a "minimalist" writer (see MINIMALISM), he was drinking heavily and had been hospitalized a number of times for alcohol toxicity. When a doctor told him that he would die if he continued drinking, Carver faced his alcoholism squarely, gave up drinking, and began going to Alcoholics Anonymous meetings. Alcohol became a prominent "character" in his fiction and figures centrally in such stories as "Chef's House," "A Serious Talk," "What We Talk About When We Talk About Love," "Careful," "Vitamins," "Where I'm Calling From," "Menudo," and "Elephant," among others.

Although Carver's consciousness of alcohol's impact on individual lives is an important feature of much of his fiction, it is not alcohol but human relationships, particularly those between heterosexual couples, that is his abiding theme.

Carver wrote a significant number of "multiple couple" stories, where two or more heterosexual couples spend some time together socializing, usually drinking, often flirting, and almost always miscommunicating. Stories of this type include "Feathers," "Neighbors," "Put Yourself in My Shoes," "What's in Alaska," "Tell the Women We're Going," and "After the Denim," to name the most prominent.

"What We Talk About When We Talk About Love," one of his most often anthologized, carefully structured and engaging stories, combines the alcohol motif with the dual couple THEME. Two couples, Mel and Terri and Nick and Laura, sit around a kitchen table drinking gin and talking about love. Mel and Terri's tumultuous and volatile history is explicitly contrasted with that of Nick and Laura, who are also in a second marriage but have known one another for just a year and are still in the flush of a new love. The couples are further contrasted with their previous partners as well as with a long-married elderly couple who have been in a serious automobile accident: Their van was broadsided by a drunk driver. Mel, who is a heart surgeon, tells the story of the old couple, who clearly symbolize enduring monogamous love, and finds it hard to comprehend such devotion.

The world he lives in and represents consists of "serial" replaceable relationships, and even though the two couples are supposedly "in love," the story raises the question of what love means in a world that no longer regards it with the sanctity of previous generations. As Mel's long quasi-monologue continues, the couples consume two bottles of gin and the kitchen gets darker and darker. The story, which had begun in a brightly lit kitchen with four sober individuals trying to dissect the ways of the heart, ends in total darkness, with four drunks totally in the dark when it comes to knowing just what it is that we do talk about when we talk about love.

A few of Carver's masterpieces don't quite fit into this pattern of multiple (often alcoholic) couple stories. "A Small Good Thing" deals with a couple's grief over the accidental death of their eight-year-old son; in "Cathedral," a socially withdrawn, resentful narrator who views the world stereotypically awakens to the possibility of connections with other human beings through a lesson he learns from a blind man. And in his last story, "Errand"—one of Carver's least characteristic but most memorable— the death of Anton Chekhov becomes a meditation on the narrator's own impending death.

In all, Carver's influence on the American short story in the late 20th century has been nearly as large as Ernest HEMINGWAY's influence on an earlier generation. Carver disliked the term "minimalist," and it is surely a misleading way to characterize his work. That work brings great clarity and precision to how we live in the fragmented world of late 20th century America and deals with those most enduring of subjects: relationships between men and women, loss, love, and death. He wrote about these things not minimalistically but with economy, grace, craft, and insight.

BIBLIOGRAPHY
Campbell, Ewing. *Raymond Carver: A Study of the Short Fiction*. Twayne; Maxwell Macmillan Canada; Maxwell Macmillan International, 1992.
Carver, Raymond. *Put Yourself in My Shoes*. Santa Barbara, Calif.: Capra, 1974.
———. *Cathedral*. New York: Knopf, 1983.
———. *Elephant*. Fairfax, Calif.: Jungle Garden, 1988.
———. *Fires*. Santa Barbara, Calif.: Capra, 1983.
———. *Furious Seasons and Other Stories*. Santa Barbara, Calif.: Capra, 1977.
———. *If It Please You*. Northridge, Calif.: Lord John, 1984.
———. *The Pheasant*. Worchester, Mass.: Metacom, 1982.
———. *The Stories of Raymond Carver*. London: Picador/Pan, 1985. Reprint. Ridgwood, N.J.: Babcock & Koontz, 1986.
———. *Those Days: Early Writings*. Edited by William L. Stull. Elmwood, Conn.: Raven, 1987.
———. *What We Talk About When We Talk About Love*. New York: Knopf, 1981.
———. *Where I'm Calling From*. New York: Atlantic Monthly, 1988.
———. *Will You Please Be Quiet, Please?* New York: McGraw-Hill, 1976.
Helpert, Sam. *Raymond Carver: An Oral Biography*. Iowa City: University of Iowa Press, 1985.
Meyer, Adam. *Raymond Carver*. New York: Twayne, 1995.
Nesset, Kirk. *The Stories of Raymond Carver: A Critical Study*. Athens: Ohio University Press, 1995.
Runyon, Randolph. *Reading Raymond Carver*. Syracuse, N.Y.: Syracuse University Press, 1992.
Saltzman, Arthur. *Understanding Raymond Carver*. Columbia, S.C.: University of South Carolina Press, 1988.

Fred Moramarco
San Diego State University

CASH   A wonderfully memorable young black man (in Eudora Welty's story "LIVVIE") who dresses in the colors of the rainbow and falls in love with the young Livvie, whose life is drab and constrained while married to old Solomon. Cash, who proclaims to Livvie, "I been to Nashville—I ready for Easter!" represents all the possibilities ahead of them when, fortuitously, Solomon dies. Cash's name (suggestive of his willingness to spend money, unlike the cautious Solomon), together with his joyful approach to life and disregard of time (he breaks Solomon's watch), provides clues to Livvie's bright future with him.

"CASK OF AMONTILLADO, THE"   EDGAR ALLAN POE (1846)   First published in *Godey's Lady's Book* in November 1846, Edgar Allan POE's well-known short story, "The Cask of Amontillado," is a carefully crafted tale of revenge and retribution. The story contains one of Poe's most common motifs, that of being buried alive. Borne down by the weight of the "thousand injuries" of the ironically named Fortunato, MONTRESOR carefully concocts the ultimate scheme for revenge (*Complete Tales* 666). In the Italian season of Carnival, Montresor wittingly lures Fortunato, his detested enemy, the intoxicated connoisseur of wines, down into his family's ancient, GOTHIC vaults, supposedly to sample a cask of Amontillado. Fortunato is led deep into the nitre-encrusted catacombs, where Montresor unexpectedly chains him in a deep recess and quickly walls him in. The horror of the situation is ironically juxtaposed with the pathetic jingling of the bells on Fortunato's jester's cap. Montresor's remorselessness in the face of his terrible deed is astonishing. One should expect this, however, from a member of a family whose motto is "Nemo me impune lacessit," or "No one provokes me with impunity" (*Complete Tales* 667). The tale is an apt demonstration of Poe's ability to capture the terror of confinement and being buried alive. Poe explored this THEME further in other stories, most notably in the NOVELLA *THE FALL OF THE HOUSE OF USHER* (1839).

A. N. Stevens suggests that Poe first heard the anecdote upon which he might have based this story when he was a private in the army in 1827. While stationed at Fort Independence in Boston Harbor, Poe saw a gravestone erected to the memory of a Lieutenant Massie, who had been unfairly killed in a duel by a bully named Captain Green. According to the story, Captain Green had been so detested by his fellow officers that they decided to take a terrible revenge on him for Massie's death. They pretended to be friendly and plied him with wine until he was helplessly intoxicated. Then, carrying the captain, the officers forced his body through a tiny opening that led into the subterranean dungeons. His captors shackled him to the floor, then, using bricks and mortar, sealed him up alive inside. Captain Green undoubtedly died a horrible death within a few days.

BIBLIOGRAPHY

Hammond, J.R. *An Edgar Allan Poe Companion.* Totowa, N.J.: Barnes & Noble Books, 1981.

Poe, Edgar Allan. "The Cask of Amontillado," in *The Complete Tales and Poems of Edgar Allan Poe.* New York: Barnes & Noble, 1992.

Stevens, Austin N., ed. *Mysterious New England.* Dublin, N.H.: Yankee, Inc., 1971.

Kathleen M. Hicks
University of Texas at El Paso

CASSILL, R(ONALD) V(ERLIN) (b. 1913)

Born in Cedar Falls, Iowa, Cassill began his artistic career as a painter and teacher of art. The most noteworthy literary quality of his prose fiction is its "visual" nature: the use of color, the precise visual detail, and sensitivity to proportion. Although primarily a novelist, Cassill's, most sustained work is often in short fiction, such as stories in *The Father* (1965) and *The Happy Marriage* (1965) about the family and the provincial qualities of the Midwest, Iowa in particular.

BIBLIOGRAPHY

Cassill, R. V. *The Father and Other Stories.* New York: Simon & Schuster, 1965.

———. *The Happy Marriage and Other Stories.* West Lafayette, In.: Purdue University Press, 1967.

———. *Three Stories.* Oakland, Calif.: Hermes House, 1982.

"R. V. Cassill Issue." *December* 23 nos. 1–2 (1981).

Walkiewicz, E. P. "1957–1968: Toward Diversity of Form." In *The American Short Story,* 1945–1980. Edited by Gordon Weaver. Boston: Twayne, 1983, pp. 35–76.

CATASTROPHE

Corresponding to the more common modern word DENOUEMENT, catastrophe is the Greek word for the unwinding of the plot at the end of a play. Because it frequently involved the death of the HERO, it usually implied a dramatically unhappy or tragic ending. The word may be applied to any sort of literature, including short stories in which the ending involves a horrific upset of balance and order.

"CATBIRD SEAT, THE" JAMES THURBER (1945)

Based on a famous METAPHOR used by the sports radio announcer Walter (Red) Barber, the title refers to an advantaged position in human relationships. Red Barber, the well-known baseball commentator and "Voice of the Dodgers" during the

1940s, often used his native South Florida expressions, such as "He's in the catbird seat," meaning one has ideally positioned oneself for victory. THURBER'S story involves Mr. Martin, a "Walter Mitty" type of man (See "SECRET LIFE OF WALTER MITTY, THE") who confronts Mrs. Ulgine Barrows, a large, overbearing woman, the story's source for Barber's expressions such as "catbird seat" and "tearing up the pea patch." Because Mrs. Barrows threatens Mr. Martin's position and plans to reorganize his department, the story offers a humorous and immensely satisfying if vicarious solution to harrassment in the workplace.

The major difference between Mr. Martin and Walter Mitty is that Martin actually copes with his problem through action, whereas Mitty merely escapes his domineering wife by entering heroic daydreams. Conducting a mental trial of Mrs. Barrows, the mild-mannered Martin pronounces her guilty and demands the death penalty. Even better than the murder he initially plans, however, is the "strange and wonderful" idea to blow up her department: It literally explodes, catapulting Mrs. Barrows through the door and effectively eliminating her as a threat. The story entertainingly dramatizes the difficulties individuals face in the modern business world, and champions the individual who in the end outwits the system.

"CATHEDRAL" RAYMOND CARVER (1982)
Appearing first in ATLANTIC MONTHLY and reprinted in *Best American Short Stories, 1982,* Raymond CARVER'S "Cathedral" exemplifies his departure from the minimalist style (see MINIMALISM) of his earlier three collections. It is also acclaimed as one of the finest efforts from one of our greatest short story writers. Carver himself seemingly sensed as much; in an interview with Mona Simpson, he remarked: "When I wrote 'Cathedral' I experienced this rush and I felt, 'This is what it's all about, this is the reason we do this'" (quoted in Mona Simpson interview, "The Art of Fiction" 76 *Paris Review* [1983]: 207).

The story opens with the agitated narrator awaiting the visit of Robert, an old friend of the narrator's wife. Robert, who is blind, has recently suffered the death of his wife. The narrator resents Robert's visit, in part because the blind man represents a connection to his wife's past: She worked for Robert as a reader in Seattle, during her relationship with a childhood sweetheart that ended badly. Because his wife and Robert communicate (via audiotape), the blind man also represents a part of his wife's current life from which the narrator is excluded. The narrator's unwillingness to welcome Robert into his home "exposes his own rather repellent insularity and lack of compassion" (Saltzman 152).

Yet Robert's arrival initiates the narrator's transformation. After a hearty meal, the wife falls asleep; Robert and the narrator—"Bub," as Robert calls him—turn their attention to a television show about cathedrals. The narrator asks Robert if he knows what a cathedral looks like, and after Robert answers that he does not, the host attempts to describe one. The narrator feels that he cannot adequately help Robert envision a cathedral, but at Robert's suggestion, he gathers a pen and some heavy paper. With Robert's hand on top of his own, the narrator begins to draw an intricate cathedral.

A brief comparison with "Fat," the opening story of *Will You Please Be Quiet, Please?* Carver's first collection, illuminates why critics heralded "Cathedral" as a turning point in Carver's writing. Both stories involve unnamed first-person narrators (see POINT OF VIEW) who encounter an "other": in "Fat," it is a grotesquely fat diner; in "Cathedral," it is Robert. Furthermore, both narrators seek to identify with that person. Yet while "Fat" concerns the failure of the imagination (the narrator's lover Rudy and her friend Rita fail to comprehend the significance of the narrator's encounter), "Cathedral" suggests the capacity of the imagination. As the blind man encourages the narrator to close his eyes but to keep drawing, the narrator comes to a greater understanding not only of Robert but of himself as well. In the midst of this shared, epiphanic (see EPIPHANY) experience, the narrator confesses: "It was like nothing else in my life up to now" (228).

BIBLIOGRAPHY
Campbell, Ewing. *Raymond Carver: A Study of the Short Fiction.* New York: Twayne, 1992.

Gentry, Marshall Bruce, and William L. Stull, eds.
    Conversations with Raymond Carver. Ann Arbor: University
    of Michigan Press, 1990.
Meyer, Adam. *Raymond Carver.* New York: Macmillan, 1995.
Saltzman, Arthur M. *Understanding Raymond Carver.*
    Columbia, S.C.: University of South Carolina Press, 1988.

Michael Hogan
University of North Carolina at Chapel Hill

CATHER, WILLA (SIBERT) (1873–1947)

Willela (Willa) Sibert Cather was born in Back
Creek Valley, Virginia, in 1873. At the age of nine,
she moved with her family to a homestead on the
Nebraska plains. The dramatic change of lifestyle
and landscape provided the adult Cather with many
of the THEMES that recur in her fiction: the soul-searing
nature of life on the land, the confluence of cultures
in the settlement of the Midwest, and the power of
memory. As an adult, Cather lived in Pittsburgh and
New York City. Ironic or tragic contrasts between
rural and urban culture frequently drive the conflicts in her stories; many of her characters are
artists, especially composers or singers, who find
both opportunity and exploitation in big cities.
Although Cather's stature as a major American
writer rests primarily on her 12 novels, she produced short fiction for 20 years before attempting
her first long work. At her death in 1947, she had
published over 60 stories in "LITTLE" MAGAZINES as
well as the most popular periodicals of the day,
including SCRIBNER'S, *Smart Set,* and MCCLURE'S.

Cather's distinctive stylistic trait is a precision with
evocative details, both physical and psychological;
consequently, her work has been placed in the
American realist (see REALISM) and romantic traditions. Like her mentor Sarah Orne JEWETT, Cather is
frequently described as a regional writer (see REGION-
ALISM). She also has been compared to modernists
like Fitzgerald and Hemingway (see MODERNISM) for
her laconic indirection and her lament for the loss of
shared values and traditions in the modern world.
Irony and ambiguity are regular features in her fiction. Cather's gallery of complex women characters,
many of whom display an androgynous transcen-

dence of traditional women's roles, makes her a
major contributor to women's literary traditions.
Recent studies have examined Cather's life and work
in the context of a closeted lesbian identity.

Cather's writing career began when she was a student at the University of Nebraska (1890–95) with
the publication of the short story "Peter" in 1892, the
first of four early stories about Nebraska notable for
their grim naturalistic vision (see NATURALISM). By
1896 she had published nine stories while attending
college and working for the *Nebraska State Journal* as
a feature columnist and theater critic. From 1896 to
1900 Cather established an arduous lifestyle as a
serious short fiction writer who earned her living as
a part-time journalist and full-time editor first at
Home Monthly and then at the Pittsburgh *Leader.* In
the stories of this period, she began to explore her
interest in both exceptionally gifted individuals and
ordinary people whose dignity and perseverance she
admired. "Nanette, An Aside" (1897) examines a
performing artist who lives intensely in and for her
music, sacrificing human relationships for art. "The
Sentimentality of William Tavener" (1900) is Cather's
first realistic portrait of a strong-willed Nebraska
farm woman. In a romantic vein, "Eric Hermannson's
Soul" (1900) presents the primitive nature of sexual,
aesthetic (see AESTHETICISM), and religious impulses
as both dangerous and redemptive.

In 1899, when Cather met Isabelle McClung, the
daughter of a Pittsburgh judge, she was invited to
live in the McClung mansion, where she was given
a quiet study in which to write. During the next six
years, Cather became a high school teacher of Latin
and English. She continued to publish stories, produced a book of poetry (*April Twilights,* 1903), and
brought out her first story collection, *The Troll
Garden* (1905). The seven stories in the latter volume concern the demands of creativity and commitment in both art and human relationships. Her
most anthologized story, "PAUL'S CASE," clarifies art's
potential to corrupt as well as enrich when used to
escape reality. "The Sculptor's Funeral" and "A
Wagner Matinee" are generally ranked with her best
work. Commentators have noted that most of the
marriages in this volume are unhappy because of

one partner's dominance over the other. Cather neither married nor formed romantic attachments to men. Her strong commitments were to art and three women: Louise Pound, Isabelle McClung, and her domestic partner, Edith Lewis, with whom she lived for nearly 40 years.

From 1906 to 1912 Cather held an editor's position at *McClure's magazine* and continued to mature as an artist. In "The Enchanted Bluff" (1909) she established the complex attitude toward the past she would later develop in novels about Nebraska. "Behind the Singer Tower" (1912) is overt social criticism: It challenges the American corporate mentality and its potential to nourish individual ambition at the expense of compassion and honesty. In "The Bohemian Girl" (1912) she created archetypal Nebraska characters whose conflicts she later incorporated into two novels, *O Pioneers!* and *My Ántonia.*

The year 1912 was a turning point in Cather's life: She published her first novel, *Alexander's Bridge,* and she left *McClure's* to become a full-time writer. With her success as a novelist, Cather's story production declined but never ceased entirely. From 1913 to 1920 she published three stories about urban business professionals, a psychological GHOST STORY, and her second collection, *Youth and the Bright Medusa* (1920), which contained four stories, revised, from *The Troll Garden* and four recently published in magazines. Three of the latter stories concern singers whose talent is easily exploited by family and friends in a society that commodifies art. The strongest work in the collection is "COMING, APHRODITE!" (originally bowdlerized and published as "Coming, Eden Bower!"), a bold representation of sexual attraction between two artists who confront the temptations of fame.

From 1922 to 1932 most of Cather's creative effort went to producing six novels, but she also wrote the story "Uncle Valentine" (1925), a tragic tribute to a family of gifted, eccentric individuals who endure loneliness rather than accept conformity. The story also presents industrialization as a destructive force on the American scene. In "DOUBLE BIRTHDAY" (1929) two men look back with insight on the atypical choices that have made them true individuals. In 1932 Cather published her third collec-

tion, *Obscure Destinies,* which consists of three stories about death, loss, and intergenerational legacies: "OLD MRS. HARRIS," "NEIGHBOR ROSICKY," and "TWO FRIENDS." From the Library Edition of her collected works (1937–41) she excluded most of her early stories, judging them not worth preserving. Three stories composed near the end of her life were collected and published posthumously in 1948 as *The Old Beauty and Others.*

BIBLIOGRAPHY
Arnold, Marilyn. *Willa Cather's Short Fiction.* Athens: Ohio University Press, 1984.

Cather, Willa. *Uncle Valentine and Other Stories: Willa Cather's Uncollected Short Fiction, 1915–1929.* Edited by Bernice Slote. Lincoln: University of Nebraska Press, 1973.

———. *Willa Cather's Collected Short Fiction, 1892–1912.* Edited by Virginia Faulkner. Lincoln: University of Nebraska Press, 1965.

Gerber, Philip. *Willa Cather.* New York: Twayne, rev. ed. 1995.

O'Brien, Sharon. *Willa Cather: The Emerging Voice.* New York: Oxford University Press, 1987.

Wasserman, Loretta. *Willa Cather: A Study of the Short Fiction.* Boston: Twayne, 1991.

Woodress, James. *Willa Cather: A Literary Life.* Lincoln: University of Nebraska Press, 1987.

Frances Kerr
Durham Technical Community College

"CAT IN THE RAIN" ERNEST HEMINGWAY (1924)

In a rare moment in "Cat in the Rain," first published in the Paris edition of *in our time,* Ernest HEMINGWAY seems to show concern for the unfulfilled female. Like many of his other works of fiction, the story is about Americans abroad. An unnamed American woman and her husband are cooped up in their hotel room as the rain beats down outside the window. Looking down, the woman sees a cat crouched under an outdoor table, trying not to get wet. She decides she wants to have that cat. When she goes down to rescue it, however, the cat has disappeared. The woman returns unsatisfied and unhappy. She thinks about all the changes she wishes to make in her life. When she begins to tell her husband about her aspirations, all he tells her is: "Oh, shut up and get something to read"

(CITR 170). At that moment the Padrone, or innkeeper she so admires sends up the maid with the cat. Hemingway suggests the woman now realizes that she will have to look outside of her marriage to find fulfillment.

BIBLIOGRAPHY
Flora, Joseph. *Ernest Hemingway: A Study of Short Fiction.* Boston: Twayne, 1989.
Hemingway, Ernest. "Cat in the Rain." In *The Short Stories of Ernest Hemingway.* New York: Collier Books, 1986.

Kathleen M. Hicks
University of Texas at El Paso

CHAN, JEFFERY PAUL (1942–) Jeffery
Paul Chan was born and raised in Stockton, California. Although he is known primarily as a critic and literary historian, his short stories are increasingly influential, particularly within the Asian American community. He has published in the *Yardbird Reader,* the *Amerasia Journal,* and a number of regional periodicals. Currently a professor of Asian American Studies at San Francisco State University, Chan lives with his wife and two children in Marin County north of San Francisco. In terms of the politics of ASIAN AMERICAN LITERATURE, he is closely aligned with Frank CHIN.

Chan's best-known story is "The Chinese in Haifa" (1974), whose blintz-eating Chinese American PROTAGONIST initiates an affair with his Jewish neighbor's blond wife after his own marriage goes awry. Using somewhat exaggerated depictions of sexual prowess, the story seeks to undercut STEREOTYPES of Asian American males as effeminate and impotent—as nonmale and non-American—while simultaneously suggesting the alienation of Asian American males in a society that refuses to fully acknowledge them.

BIBLIOGRAPHY
Chan, Jeffery Paul, et al., eds. *The Big Aiiieeeee! An Anthology of Chinese American and Japanese American Literature.* New York: Meridian, 1991.
Kim, Elaine. *Asian American Literature: An Introduction to The Writings and Their Social Context.* Philadelphia: Temple University Press, 1982.

Keith Lawrence
Brigham Young University

CHANDLER, RAYMOND (THORNTON)
(1888–1959) DETECTIVE FICTION writer fully considered the equal of Dashiel HAMMETT and James M. CAIN. Born in Chicago and educated in Great Britain, Chandler put the city of Los Angeles on the literary map (and the geographical map for Europeans) with his realistic depictions of the mean and dirty along with the rich and famous. Known for his CLASSIC novels such as *The Big Sleep* (1939) and *Farewell My Lovely* (1940), Chandler also wrote short stories; in fact, *The Big Sleep* is comprised of two short stories, "Killer in the Rain" and "The Curtain," he had first published in the BLACK MASK, the leading pulp magazine of the 1930s, which also published Cain, Hammett, and others now viewed as classic writers of detective stories and novels.

Chandler's stories are collected in two volumes, *The Simple Art of Murder* (1950) and *Killer in the Rain* (1964). *The Big Sleep* became a film hit, with William FAULKNER as one of the scriptwriters and Humphrey Bogart and Lauren Bacall playing the leads. Chandler's HERO, PHILIP MARLOWE, had his genesis in numerous stories wherein Chandler invented a detective less interested in solving murders than in righting social wrongs. Like Edgar Allan POE, Chandler also laid down guidelines for the murder mystery and the detective hero in his classic essay, "The Simple Art of Murder." His dictates influenced not only his own fiction, but also that of countless others after him.

BIBLIOGRAPHY
Chandler, Raymond. *The Big Sleep.* New York: Knopf, 1939.
———. *Farewell My Lovely.* New York: Knopf, 1940.
———. *The High Window.* New York: Knopf, 1940.
———. *Killer in the Rain.* New York: Ballantine, 1964.
———. *The Lady in the Lake.* New York: Knopf, 1943.
———. *Little Sister.* New York: Ballantine Books, 1949.
———. *The Long Goodbye.* Boston: Houghton Mifflin, 1954.
———. *Playback.* New York: Ballantine, 1958.
———. *The Simple Art of Murder.* Boston: Houghton Mifflin, 1950.
Durham, Philip. *Down These Mean Streets A Man Must Go: Raymond Chandler's Knight.* Chapel Hill: University of North Carolina Press, 1963.

CHAPPELL, FRED (1936–) Born in Canton, North Carolina, and currently writer-in-residence at the University of North Carolina at Greensboro, Chappell has published 14 volumes of poetry (the best known of which is *Midquest,* 1981); he received the Bollingen Prize in Poetry in 1985. His short stories, five of which have been included in *Best American Short Stories,* often fuse the LYRIC language of his award-winning poetry with the vernacular tradition and BURLESQUE elements of oral storytelling. While most often credited with only two collections of short stories—*Moments of Light* (1980) and *More Shapes Than One* (1991)—Chappell has also published three unified collections of short fiction that his publisher labels as novels.

All three of these SHORT STORY CYCLES contain related stories unified by Chappell's narrative PERSONA, Jess Kirkman, and by the North Carolina mountain setting; while most stories in these collections can be read independently, they are clearly enriched by the context the others provide. *I Am One of You Forever* (1985) is a BILDUNGSROMAN loosely structured around a series of visits by Jess's strange uncles and his close relationship with Johnson Gibbs, who lives with the family. In the process of telling these stories, Jess chronicles his own emergence as a storyteller who discovers his niche in the family and the region as well as the importance of both on his art. *Brighten the Corner Where You Are* (1989) episodically traces a day of misadventure in the life of Jess's father, who must testify before the local school board concerning charges that he has been teaching evolution—but not until he has chased a devil-possum, encountered a talking goat on the school roof, and held a Socratic dialogue on the theory of evolution with his class. *Farewell, I'm Bound to Leave You* (1996) complements the previous works by focusing on female strategies for survival in stories that Jess relates in his mother's and grandmother's voices. Like the other works in this trilogy, this latest volume comprises an artistic rescue and celebration of a vanishing mountain realm, transcending LOCAL COLOR in its exploration of the ordinary world's mystery.

More Shapes Than One begins with a cluster of stories concerning historical characters and the epiphanies (see EPIPHANY) that revitalize their vision. In the remainder of the volume, Chappell experiments with a variety of voices and genres, ranging from SCIENCE FICTION to horror to the TALL TALE, most often verging into SURREALISM and burlesque. Chappell's poetic talents animate his best short fiction, which explores the nature of the imagination and the connection to one's place of origin. METAPHOR informs his vision of the world, transforming the facts of everyday existence into a lyrical and often magical realm in such stories as "The Beard," "The Storytellers," "Bacchus," and "Linneaus Forgets." The lyric prose of his stories blends erudition, epiphany, and an elegant style with the earthiness of Appalachian DIALECT and the burlesque of the tall tale.

BIBLIOGRAPHY

Campbell, Hilbert. "Fred Chappell's Urn of Memory: *I Am One of You Forever.*" *Southern Literary Journal* 25.2 (1993): 103–11.

Chappell, Fred. *Brighten the Corner Where You Are.* New York: St. Martin's Press, 1989.

———. *Farewell, I'm Bound to Leave You.* New York: Picador USA, 1996.

———. *I Am One of You Forever: A Novel.* Baton Rouge: Louisiana State University Press, 1985.

———. *Moments of Light.* New York: New South Co., 1980.

———. *More Shapes Than One.* New York: St. Martin's Press, 1991.

Edgerton, Clyde, et al. "Tributes to Fred Chappell." *Pembroke Magazine* 23 (1991): 77–92.

Garrett, George. "A Few Things about Fred Chappell." *Mississippi Quarterly* 37.1 (1983–84): 3–8.

Gray, Amy Tipton. "Fred Chappell's *I Am One of You Forever:* The Oneiros of Childhood Transformed." *The Poetics of Appalachian Space.* Edited by Parks Lanier. Knoxville: University of Tennessee Press, 1991.

Hobson, Fred. *The Southern Writer in the Postmodern World.* Athens: University of Georgia Press, 1991.

Powell, Dannye Romine. *Parting the Curtains: Voices of the Great Southern Writers.* Winston-Salem, N.C.: John F. Blair, 1994.

Stuart, Dabney. "'What's Artichokes?': An Introduction to the Work of Fred Chappell." *The Fred Chappell Reader.* New York: St. Martin's Press, 1987. xi–xx.

Robert M. Luscher
University of Nebraska at Kearney

CHARACTER   A fictional person in literature or drama. In *Aspects of the Novel* (1927), E. M. Forster introduced the now widely accepted distinction between two-dimensional or "flat" characters, who have little individualizing detail, and "round" characters, whose complexity echoes that of real-life human beings. Although flat characters may perform an important function in the work (as METAPHOR or FOIL, for instance), the reader does not view them as realistic. In Nathaniel HAWTHORNE's story "YOUNG GOODMAN BROWN," for example, Brown appears as a central figure in an ALLEGORY. In his growing disillusion with his beliefs and with the townspeople, Brown remains clearly indispensable to the tale, yet he is flat, not round. Round characters possess a complexity of temperament, motivation, thought, and dialogue that reminds readers of real people. Eudora WELTY's narrator in "WHY I LIVE AT THE P.O.," Ernest HEMINGWAY's NICK ADAMS and Raymond CARVER's myriad short story characters, for example, convincingly replicate the foibles, the yearnings, and the recognizable responses of modern people.

CHARACTERIZATION   The methods authors use to depict the characters they create. An author's major approaches to characterization include showing and telling. In showing, or the dramatic method, characters—seemingly independent of the author—may behave in such a way that they speak and act as believeable, or "round" (see CHARACTER). In telling, the author presents characters, usually intervening with some commentary or evaluation, illustrating with action from time to time; or allows characters to tell their own stories.

CHARLES (CHICK) MALLISON   Young boy and man who appears in William FAULKNER's novels and stories. In addition to playing key roles in such novels as *Intruder in the Dust* and *The Mansion,* Chick appears in stories with his uncle GAVIN STEVENS, the majority of which are in the collection *KNIGHT'S GAMBIT.* In addition to the humor Chick's behavior provides, his POINT OF VIEW sustains the perspective of an amusing and only partially informed narrator and commentator. Chick thus becomes one of Faulkner's UNRELIABLE NARRATORS. In a sense, as successor to Gavin, he is the last of the narrators, including ISAAC (IKE) MCCASLIN and Horace Benbow, but without their tortured sensibilities. He is morally sound, however, and performs some heroic acts as he aligns himself with blacks and women to correct wrongs and to illuminate bigotry. Chick is thus aligned with the modern South.

CHARLIE WALES   In F. Scott FITZGERALD's "BABYLON REVISITED," Charlie Wales enters the story as a reformed alcoholic PROTAGONIST. A third-person narrator provides us with information on his background when he lived the profligate expatriate life in Paris, the "Babylon" of the story. He desperately wishes to reclaim his honor—as signified in the name of his daughter, Honoria, who is being withheld from him by a disapproving sister-in-law, Marion, until he proves himself a fit father. There are at least two ways to view Charlie: first, as a sympathetic character who has truly repented of his formerly wicked ways and is now being unfairly judged by Marion; second, as a man who is not being honest with himself and still has not come to terms with his own responsibility for Helen's death. Many critics also view him as an alter ego for Fitzgerald, who lived a similarly dissolute life in the Paris of the 1920s and who suffered similar reversals after the 1929 stock market crash and the GREAT DEPRESSION that ensued. This biographical viewpoint is not without problems, however, as the real Fitzgerald had to cope not with his wife's death but instead with her collapse into madness. (Zelda Fitzgerald outlived her husband by seven years.) As the ambiguous DENOUEMENT implies, the careful reader must consider this character in all his complexity: Will he stop drinking altogether? Will he regain his daughter—and his honor? Critics have reached no consensus on these issues.

CHEEVER, JOHN (WILLIAM) (1912–1982)   Born in Quincy, Massachusetts, in 1912, John Cheever published more than 200 stories before his death in 1982. His remarkable writing career began at age 18 with the publication of his first story, "Expelled," in the *New Republic*, based upon his expulsion from Thayer Academy in South Braintree, Massachusetts. Determined to fulfill a long-held ambition to make his living as a writer, Cheever lived a bohemian life in New York City during the 1930s, publishing stories in the NEW YORKER, the ATLANTIC MONTHLY, COLLIER'S and STORY. While serving four years in the Army during World War II, he maintained his remarkable output, publishing his first collection of stories, *The Way Some People Live,* in 1942. After the appearance of five more story collections, four novels, and numerous *New Yorker* stories, he published the retrospective *The Stories of John Cheever* in 1978, the first short story collection ever to appear on the *New York Times* best-seller list: It won the Pulitzer Prize for fiction, the National Book Critics Circle Award, and an American Book Award.

Cheever's second book, *The Enormous Radio and Other Stories* (1953), earned him a reputation, reaffirmed over the decades, as one of the most talented American short story writers of the second half of the 20th century. *The Housebreaker of Shady Hill and Other Stories* (1958) focuses on the personal problems of wealthy but troubled American suburbanites. The settings of *Some People, Places, and Things That Will Not Appear in My Next Novel* (1961), *The Brigadier and the Golf Widow* (1964), and *The World of Apples* (1973), range from contemporary America to Italy.

Because he wrote deceptively simple stories, critics and readers alike have found Cheever's literary techniques difficult to classify. Over the course of hundreds of stories, Cheever clearly became less concerned with the restrictions of GENRE and increasingly experimental in terms of literary technique. He experimented in various and complex ways, and, although not a postmodernist (see POSTMODERNISM), he developed a notably lyrical style and infused his stories with SATIRE, REALISM, MAGICAL REALISM, FANTASY, and even modern GOTHIC qualities. "THE ENORMOUS RADIO," for example, one of his best-known stories, seems conventional and realistic as it introduces a complacently successful New York couple, but with the intrusion of the fantastic radio into the lives of Jim and Irene Wescott, their middle-class existence shatters to reveal deep wounds and insecurities beneath their patina of respectability.

Cheever has also demonstrated a keen eye and a clear penchant for examining the fabric that holds together or destroys relationships between characters who, at first glance, seem respectable and unremarkable. Another of his most frequently anthologized stories, "THE FIVE FORTY-EIGHT" displays his sympathetic sensitivity to women and family members who are used and abused by powerful men—and his obvious, though subtly expressed, delight in describing Miss Dent's revenge on Blake, her abuser. Moral retribution awaits a number of his other characters—Neddy Merrill, in "The Swimmer," Cash Bentley, in "O Youth and Beauty," Charlie Pastern in "The Brigadier and the Golf Widow" and various expatriate Americans in his Italian stories.

Cheever also invented the mythical setting of SHADY HILL, an affluent suburb that frequently seems to be EDEN gone awry. Since his death, Cheever, a writer whose talents critics have compared to those of Edgar Allan POE, Nathaniel HAWTHORNE, Stephen CRANE, and Ernest HEMINGWAY, has held his own as one of the most talented chroniclers of 20th-century American life.

BIBLIOGRAPHY

Avedon, Richard. "John Cheever, 1981." *The New Yorker,* Feb. 20–27, 1995: 202.

Baumgartner, M. P. *The Moral Order of a Suburb.* New York: Oxford University Press, 1988.

Cheever, John. *The Brigadier and the Gold Widow.* New York: Harper & Row, 1964.

———. *The Enormous Radio and Other Stories.* New York: Funk & Wagnalls, 1953.

———. *The Housebreaker of Shady Hill and Other Stories.* New York: Harper, 1958.

———. *The Journals of John Cheever.* New York: Knopf, 1991.

———. *Some People, Places, and Things That Will Not Appear in My Next Novel.* New York: Harper. 1961.

CHESNUTT, CHARLES WADDELL 91

———. *The Stories of John Cheever.* New York: Knopf, 1978.

———. *Thirteen Uncollected Stories.* Chicago: Academy Chicago Publishers, 1994.

———. *Uncollected Stories.* Chicago: Academy Chicago Publishers, 1988.

———. *The Way Some People Live: A Book of Stories.* New York: Random, 1943.

———. *The World of Apples.* New York: Alfred A. Knopf, 1973.

Cheever, Susan. *Home Before Dark.* Boston, Houghton, 1984.

———. *John Cheever.* New York: Ungar, 1977.

Coale, Samuel. "Cheever and Hawthorne: The American Romancer's Art." In *Critical Essays on John Cheever,* edited by R. G. Collins. Boston: G. K. Hall, 1982.

Collins, Robert G., ed. *Critical Essays on John Cheever.* Boston: G. K. Hall, 1982.

Donaldson, Scott. *John Cheever: A Biography.* New York: Delta, 1988.

Greenberg, Clement. "Avant-Garde and Kitsch." In *Perceptions and Judgements, 1939–1944,* edited by John O'Brian. Chicago: Chicago University Press, 1986.

Hausdorff, Don. "Politics and Economics: The Emergence of the *New Yorker* Tone." In *Studies in American Humor* 3.1 (1984): 74–82.

Hunt, George W. *John Cheever: The Hobgoblin Company of Love.* Grand Rapids, Mich.: Eerdmans, 1983.

Hutcheon, Linda. *A Theory of Parody.* New York: Methuen. 1985.

Irvin, Rea. *Good Morning, Sir: The Sixth New Yorker Album.* New York: Harper and Brothers, 1933.

MacDonald, Dwight, ed. *Parodies: An Anthology from Chaucer to Beerbohm—and After.* New York: Random House, 1960.

Morace, Robert A. "John Cheever" *Reference Guide to Short Fiction.* Edited by Noelle Watson. Detroit: Gale Press, 1994, pp. 118–119.

O'Hara, James Eugene. *John Cheever: Study of the Short Fiction.* Boston: Twayne, 1989.

Rovit, Earl. "Modernism and Three Magazines: An Editorial Revolution." *The Sewanee Review* 18.4 (1985):541–553.

Waldeland, Lynne. *John Cheever.* Boston: Twayne, 1979.

Warren, Austin. *The New England Conscience.* Ann Arbor: Michigan University Press, 1966.

Whyte, William. *The Organization Man.* New York: Simon & Schuster, 1956.

CHESNUTT, CHARLES WADDELL

(1858–1932) Charles Waddell Chesnutt was born in Cleveland, Ohio, the son of free blacks who returned to their home of Fayetteville, North Carolina, after the CIVIL WAR. Chesnutt became a teacher but by 1883 moved back to Cleveland, where he passed the bar exam and began his own court reporting business. Despite his social and economic success, Chesnutt still desired to make a living by the pen, and devoted much of his time to writing. He concentrated on what he knew best: the history and African American folklore that he had heard as a child. He found an audience in 1887 when the prestigious ATLANTIC MONTHLY published his story, "The Goophered Grapevine." It marked the first time that an African-American writer's fiction had appeared in the magazine. In 1899 two collections of his short stories were published, *The Conjure Woman* and *The Wife of His Youth and Other Stories of the Color Line.* Following the success of these two books, Chesnutt closed his business to focus on writing full time.

The DIALECT stories of *The Conjure Woman* placed it in early criticism as a representative work of REGIONALISM and REALISM popular in the late 19th century. Chesnutt used the stories to subvert the romantic vision of plantation literature (which extolled the lost plantation society and longed for the antebellum era) written by Joel Chandler HARRIS and Thomas Nelson Page, and as social commentary on the problems of the Reconstructionist South. (See RECONSTRUCTION.) The stories are told by the ex-slave Uncle Julius McAdoo, an ironic counterpart of Harris's UNCLE REMUS. Each story (with the exception of "Dave's Neckliss") is a conjure tale designed to illustrate Uncle Julius's cleverness and wit at the expense of the narrator, John, a Northern businessman. CONJURE STORIES drew on the superstitions of folk characters and used blacks in often witty ways against "white folks" as a means of amusement on the surface but as a means of survival at a far more serious level. The tales share another characteristic. Set in the days of slavery, they illustrate the tragic lives of slaves and the imagination and faith that they had to possess in order to preserve themselves and their community. Stories such as "The Goophered Grapevine," "The Conjurer's Revenge,"

"Po Sandy," and others showed slaves turned into trees, plants, and animals through conjuring. Chesnutt's bitterly ironic implication is that African Americans were not considered "human" before slavery was abolished and that because of racist laws and attitudes, nothing had changed for them in the late 19th century.

Also published in 1899, the stories in *The Wife of His Youth and Other Stories of the Color Line* focus primarily on the psychological and social problems facing mixed race people, those living on "the color line." Countering the stereotypical (see STEREOTYPE) picture of the tragic mulatto, Chesnutt analyzed the results of MISCEGENATION and mob violence in such works as "The Sheriff's Children." Chesnutt's realistic portrayal of class and color prejudice within the African-American community can be found in stories such as "The Wife of His Youth" and "The Matter of Principle." One of the most well-received stories in the collection is "The Passing of Grandison." The story reveals the true nature beneath a seemingly docile slave who dupes his master, Dick Owens, and helps his family escape to the North.

Chesnutt published his last piece of short fiction, "Baxter's Procrustes," in 1904. He was largely overlooked by critics in the early 20th century in favor of the writers of the HARLEM RENAISSANCE but has since gained respect for illustrating the broad and diverse range of African American experience and for drawing attention to the nation's continuing problems of racism.

He published his first novel, *The House Behind the Cedars,* in 1900. His novel *The Marrow of Tradition* appeared in 1901. Its social realism and plea for racial tolerance garnered high praise from the critic William Dean HOWELLS, but it angered many other reviewers. Chesnutt's last novel, *The Colonel's Dream,* was published in 1905 to little fanfare. No longer able to support his family entirely from his writing, he reopened his business. Recently Chesnutt has received recognition for his outstanding contribution to the development of African American fiction, particularly in the short story. (See also AFRICAN-AMERICAN SHORT FICTION.)

BIBLIOGRAPHY
Andrews, William. *The Literary Career of Charles W. Chesnutt.* Baton Rouge: Louisiana State University Press, 1980.
Render, Sylvia Lyons. *Charles Chesnutt.* Boston: Twayne, 1980.
Sundquist, Eric J. *To Wake the Nations.* Cambridge, Mass.: Belknap Press of Harvard University Press, 1993.

Tracie Guzzio
Ohio University

CHICAGO RENAISSANCE (A.K.A. "LITTLE RENAISSANCE")

The term *Chicago Renaissance* describes the artistic and literary renewal associated with two distinct groups of principally midwestern writers and artists. The first was an avant-garde group of writers in the 1910s that included novelists and short fiction writers Sherwood ANDERSON, Floyd Dell, Theodore DREISER, and James T. Farrell; poets Carl Sandburg, Vachel Lindsay, and Edgar Lee Masters; and LITTLE MAGAZINE editors Harriet Monroe (of the Chicago-based *Poetry*) and Margaret C. Anderson (*The Little Review*). These writers and others, whom outsiders considered rebels and bohemians, openly criticized the provincialism and materialism they perceived in American society and culture.

This group existed more or less separately from the African-American exponents of the Chicago Renaissance, flourishing from the end of the HARLEM RENAISSANCE in about 1935 to the civil rights era of the early 1950s. This group contributed significantly toward increased recognition of black women writers, particularly Gwendolyn Brooks, Lorraine Hansberry, Margaret Walker, and Dorothy WEST. Interaction between the black and the white Chicago Renaissance did occur, particularly among younger African-American writers and Dreiser, Farrell, Masters, and Sandburg, and under the editorship of Monroe, *Poetry* magazine advanced the careers of Langston HUGHES and Gwendolyn Brooks.

"CHILDREN ARE BORED ON SUNDAY" JEAN STAFFORD (1948)

Jean STAFFORD's first *NEW YORKER* story and one of only two (along with "An Influx of Poets") emerging from her marriage to the poet Robert Lowell, this story is not anthologized as frequently as one would expect. Judged as a brilliant tale by virtually all Stafford critics, it has contemporary resonances with all who have experienced a sense of loneliness or marginalization and its destructive aspects. Ironically, as Mary Ann Wilson notes, the story's reception replicates the very subject of the story itself: Stafford's literary acquaintances derided her for appearing in a middle-brow publication such as the *New Yorker,* just as her young woman in the story is "excoriated" by the literati (Wilson 63).

Biographical parallels aside, however, Stafford's story, a "PARABLE of a lost soul," movingly depicts Emma, the young woman, judged by the same people whose standards she rejects. Emma, the third-person narrator and controlling consciousness in the story, by chance encounters at the Metropolitan Museum of Art a man named Alfred Eisenstein, whom she recalls as an artist who had made her feel inferior at a recent cocktail party. The story is divided into three sections: a flashback to the superficial New York artists' party; Emma's current observations of young boys in the museum and her connection of them with Alfred as a first-generation immigrant who, like herself, is an outsider driven to alcoholism and nervous collapse; and finally, Emma and Alfred's meeting outside the museum, greeting each other like long-lost friends. Together they enter a Lexington Avenue bar, clinging to each other like children, and order martinis. The LYRICally romantic ending may be viewed literally or cynically, depending on how seriously the reader takes the final ALLUSION to a Van Eyck painting of souls in hell.

BIBLIOGRAPHY

Stafford, Jean. *Children Are Bored on Sunday.* New York: Harcourt Brace, 1953.

Wilson, Mary Ann. *Jean Stafford: A Study of the Short Fiction.* New York: Twayne, 1996.

CHILDREN OF LONELINESS ANZIA YEZIERSKA (1923)

In *Children of Loneliness,* Anzia Yezierska presents nine poignant stories about Jewish immigrants living on the East Side of New York City: "Children of Loneliness," "Brothers," "To the Stars," "An Immigrant Among the Editors," "America and I," "A Bed for the Night," "Dreams and Dollars," "The Song Triumphant," and "The Lord Giveth." She introduces these works of fiction with "Mostly About Myself," a nonfiction chapter about her writing, in which she claims, "My one story is hunger. Hunger driven by loneliness" (CL 12).

Yezierska's style is simple and emotional (some say sentimental). DIALECT and autobiographical material permeate the stories, giving them the raw, realistic edge that typifies the author's work. Characters such as Hanneh Breineh, the gritty boardinghouse manager, appear in multiple stories, unifying the collection. What seem at first to be straightforward, even simplistic THEMES become, in Yezierska's hands, revelations of the paradoxes inherent in the immigrant experience. In the title story, for example, the PROTAGONIST, Rachel Ravinsky, a newly Americanized teacher, abandons her self-sacrificing mother and otherworldly rabbi father for an American-bred college beau, Frank Baker, who, she believes, will scorn their old country ways. She soon discovers, however, that she feels uncomfortable with Frank, a social worker who sees her people as "picturesque" and romanticizes their poverty (CL 51). Rachel fits nowhere, and that is the irony of the book.

The author examines the immigrants' conflicts, pitting economic and spiritual needs, communal and individual expectations, and the yearning for both assimilation and ethnic identity one against the other; she provides no easy middle ground for her characters. The conflicts of the artist reflect the conflicts of the immigrant in such stories as "The Song Triumphant," whose subtitle, "The Story of Berel Pinsky, Poet of the People, Who Sold his Soul for Wealth," introduces two of Yezierska's recurring themes: the necessity of artistic integrity and the fact that inspiration comes from one's own people. The struggle to maintain a pure aesthetic while attaining a public voice is conflated with the effort to retain one's own identity in an alien world (themes also seen in "To the Stars" and "An Immigrant Among the Editors").

Other stories that deal with selling one's soul for money emphasize the crass materialism that surfaces as a reaction to years of deprivation. Yezierska claims in her introductory chapter that "the dollar fight that grew up like a plague in times of poverty, killing the souls of men, still goes on in times of plenty" (CL 22). In "Dreams and Dollars" the card table and the "King of Clothing," Moe Mirsky, represent the ugly competition of the consumer culture that often replaces the "hunger driven by loneliness."

Yezierska seeks a third option, the compromise finally reached by Pinsky in "The Song Triumphant." Pinsky rejects Broadway and returns to the East Side, where he works at a machine for his living and writes honest poetry about his fellow workers. Pinsky thus alleviates his loneliness while satisfying both his physical and artistic hunger.

BIBLIOGRAPHY

Henriksen, Louise Levitas. *Anzia Yezierska: A Writer's Life.* New Brunswick, N.J.: Rutgers University Press, 1988.

Shapiro, Ann R. "The Ultimate Shaygets and the Fiction of Anna Yezierska." *MELUS* 21.2 (Summer 96): 79–88.

Yezierska, Anzia. *Red Ribbon on a White Horse.* New York. Scribner's, 1950.

Gwen M. Neary
Santa Rosa Junior College
Sonoma State University

"CHILD WHO FAVORED DAUGHTER, THE" ALICE WALKER (1973)

First published in 1973 in the collection *In Love & Trouble: Stories of Black Women,* this story offers a GOTHIC tale of love, lust, and dismemberment in three parts, told in a lyric prose style interspersed with bits of poetry. "The Child Who Favored Daughter" begins in the same way that it concludes: An unnamed black man with a shotgun waits on his porch for a school bus. In the first section, he awaits his own daughter's return from school in order to confront her about an intercepted love letter written to a white lover who has spurned her to marry a white woman.

The second section sketches the psychological makeup of the father, which includes an incestuous desire for his sister (ironically and confusingly named "Daughter"), virulent racism, a fear of sexually liberated women, and a history of physical abuse in his own childhood home. The events surrounding his sister's life and death form the character of the young brother who presumes that everyone will disappoint and betray him and therefore must be punished accordingly. This young man grows into the older abusive husband (he beats his wife into a cripple who eventually deserts her family) and father of a daughter who, unfortunately for her, is "a replica in every way" of his dead sister, Daughter.

The father's sadism toward women culminates on the day that he finds his daughter's letter. She will not deny that she loves a white man, even after her father beats her with a belt (a fairly regular occurrence). In the face of his daughter's refusal to deny her love for the white man, the father suddenly hacks off her breasts with his pocket knife and "flings what he finds in his hands to the yelping dogs." The story's elliptical final paragraph concludes with the father back on his porch once again waiting for the school bus with his shotgun, only now he waits in vain. All the daughters are dead. In the beginning of the story Walker hints that the father-daughter bond implicitly involves violence when daughters come of age and prefer other men to their own fathers. The conclusion of her story suggests an ironic twist on the OEDIPAL MYTH, in which the Greek Oedipus killed his father and married his mother, lighting a tragic fuse that burns until his wife Jocasta and, later, his daughter Antigone commit suicide. In Walker's story, the father has slain his own Antigone.

BIBLIOGRAPHY

Boose, Lynda E., and Betty S. Flowers, eds. *Fathers and Daughters.* Baltimore: Johns Hopkins University Press, 1989.

S. L. Yentzer
University of Georgia

CHIN, FRANK (1940–)

Frank Chin was born in Berkeley, California, and grew up in the Chinatowns of Oakland and San Francisco. He earned his B.A. from the University of California at Santa Barbara and his M.F.A. from the Writer's Workshop at Iowa State University, where he attended on a Writer's Workshop fellowship. His stories have appeared in *Panache,* the *Carolina Quarterly, City Lights Journal,* and the *Chouteau Review;* eight of them are collected in *The Chinaman Pacific & Frisco R.R. Co.* (1988). He is also the author of personal essays; literary criticism; several award-winning plays, including *The Chickencoop Chinaman* (1981); and a novel, *Donald Duk* (1991). He lives in the Los Angeles area.

In his stories, Chin argues that, as a group, Chinese American males are dressed in a fake identity created by white Americans and by illusory memories of what it is to be "Chinese." Chin's PROTAGONISTs struggle for a unique identity that is self-created and that is neither Chinese nor American but Chinese American. Contrary to Asian American paradigms established by Toshio MORI and others, Chin believes the Asian American community is claustrophobic and self-destructive. As Elaine Kim has observed, Chin's notion of valid identity is "built around the Asian American man's being accepted as American," and to be accepted, the Asian American male finds it necessary "to challenge the STEREOTYPE of quaint foreigners, to reject the notion of the passive, quiet Asian American, and to move away from the stultifying limitations of the glittering Chinatown ghetto." Thus Chin's protagonists are at odds with those of many other Asian American writers, who value the strong ethnic identity that provides security, stability, and a strong sense of community.

As with the fiction of Jeffery Paul CHAN, the writings of Frank Chin often employ an exaggerated sexuality. Chin's male protagonists METAPHORically establish their identities—sometimes ironically, sometimes not—through sexual conquests, often of white women. This, together with Chin's mean-spirited dismissal of Asian American women writers in his literary criticism and in the afterword to *The Chinaman Pacific & Frisco R.R. Co.,* has persuaded some readers that Chin is misogynistic and even racist.

Writers and scholars who embrace his politics of ASIAN AMERICAN LITERATURE believe that Chin, in distancing himself from writers like Maxine Hong KINGSTON, Amy TAN, Gish JEN, and David Henry Hwang by labeling them "fake" writers who distort or destroy Asian culture and perpetuate white stereotypes of Asians and Asian Americans, is courageously staking out a moral high ground that "real" Asian Americans eventually may occupy. The more cynical of his detractors believe such a position is both arbitrary and illogical, especially in its naive or false understanding of basic principles of folklore, oral narratives, and cross-cultural discourse, and that it unsuccessfully masks a profound jealousy of writers who have been far more influential than he.

BIBLIOGRAPHY
Chin, Frank. "Come All Ye Asian American Writers of the Real and the Fake." In Jeffery Paul Chan et al., eds., *The Big Aiiieeeee! An Anthology of Chinese American and Japanese American Literature.* New York: Meridian, 1991.
Kim, Elaine. *Asian American Literature.* Philadelphia: Temple University Press, 1982.
Li, David Leiwei. "The Formation of Frank Chin and Formations of Chinese American Literature." In *Asian Americans,* edited by Shirley Hune et al. Comparative Global Perspectives. Pullman: Washington State University Press, 1991.

Keith Lawrence
Brigham Young University

CHOPIN, KATE (1850–1904)

Although Kate Chopin is known primarily for her 1899 novel *The Awakening,* in her lifetime she was celebrated as the author of LOCAL COLOR stories set in Louisiana. Born in St. Louis in 1850 to an Irish father and French Creole mother, Chopin experienced two tragedies in her early childhood: the death of her father in 1855 and the loss of her half brother, a Confederate soldier, to typhoid in the CIVIL WAR. She married Oscar Chopin, a French Creole from Louisiana, in 1870, and they lived in New Orleans until 1879, when business losses forced them to relocate to a family farm near Natchitoches, Louisiana. The Chopins had six children. When her husband died of yellow fever in 1883, Kate Chopin managed his businesses until she moved to St. Louis to reside with her mother. Following the death of her mother in 1885, Chopin began to write, encouraged by her physician friend Dr. Kohlenbeyer. In 1890 she published her first novel, *At Fault,* at her own expense. Her first literary successes were children's stories, published in *Youth's Companion* and *Harper's Young People.*

The 1894 publication of *Bayou Folk,* a collection of 23 tales and sketches, by Houghton Mifflin & Co., earned Chopin national fame as a master of REGIONALISM. Set exclusively in Louisiana, primarily Natchitoches and New Orleans, the stories centered on the lives of Creoles and Cajuns. Reviewers praised her keen ear for DIALECT and the picturesque evocations of rural life. William Marion Reedy (*Sunday Mirror,* April 15, 1894) judged her Louisiana stories superior to those of George Washington CABLE and declared the volume "the best literary work that has come out of the Southland in a long time."

In 1897 Chopin's second volume of short stories, *A Night in Acadie,* was published by Way and Williams. *Acadie* is, in some ways, a continuation of *Bayou Folk;* the second volume shares the same Louisiana locales and even some of the same characters featured in first collection. However, as Barbara Ewell notes, in *Acadie* "Chopin's bayou world persists, but its romance and charm seem diminished, its happy endings muted" (KC, 94). The influence of the French realists (see REALISM), most notably Guy de Maupassant, whose work Chopin translated, sets these stories apart from conventional local color stories such as those by Joel Chandler HARRIS.

Although Chopin received several enthusiastic reviews for *Acadie,* critics objected to the "unnecessary coarseness" of some of the material (*Critic,* April 16, 1898), a charge that would be leveled at her masterpiece, *The Awakening,* the following year. According to one reviewer, "Like most of her work . . . *The Awakening* is too strong drink [*sic*] for moral babes and should be labelled 'poison'" (*St. Louis Post-Dispatch,* May 21, 1899). Although it is widely claimed that the novel was banned, Emily Toth refutes those charges (KC, 422–425).

Chopin published little in the final years of her life. Her last volume of stories, entitled *A Vocation*

and a Voice, was slated for publication, but the manuscript was returned. On August 20, 1904, after a strenuous day at the St. Louis World's Fair, Chopin collapsed. She died two days later, apparently of a brain hemorrhage.

The past few decades have witnessed a revival of interest in Chopin, in part initiated by the publication in 1969 of Per Seyersted's *Kate Chopin: A Critical Biography* and *The Complete Works* and by the burgeoning FEMINIST movement. In addition to examining gender issues in Chopin's works, scholars are investigating her treatment of race, the cultural contexts of her fiction, and her position in the literary canon. Chopin has been associated with a variety of late-19th-century literary groups or movements: impressionism, realism, regionalism, AESTHETICISM, and NATURALISM. Her fiction also anticipates MODERNISM and MINIMALISM.

BIBLIOGRAPHY

Boren, Lynda S., and Sara de Saussure Davis, eds. *Kate Chopin Reconsidered: Beyond the Bayou.* Baton Rouge: Louisiana State University Press, 1992.

Chopin, Kate. *The Complete Works of Kate Chopin.* Baton Rouge: Louisiana State University Press, 1969.

Ewell, Barbara. *Kate Chopin.* New York: Ungar Publishing Co., 1986.

Koloski, Bernard. *Kate Chopin: A Study of The Short Fiction.* New York: Twayne, 1996.

Seyersted, Per. *Kate Chopin: A Critical Biography.* Baton Rouge: Louisiana State University Press, 1969.

Toth, Emily. *Kate Chopin.* New York: Morrow, 1990.

Mary Anne O'Neal
University of Georgia

"CHRYSANTHEMUMS, THE" JOHN STEINBECK (1938)

Although critical attention now focuses on numerous stories by John STEINBECK as his reputation as a short story writer continues to grow, "The Chrysanthemums" is generally considered not only his best but among the very best in 20th-century American literature. This remarkable work, first published in *The Long Valley,* presents a complex, sensitive portrait of 35-year-old Elisa Allen, the repressed wife of a SALINAS VALLEY rancher.

Set during the years of the GREAT DEPRESSION, the story takes place on a Saturday, the last weekday of the last month of the year, and focuses on a woman in middle life who can coax blooms from chrysanthemums, the last flowers of the year. A wealth of critical commentary has examined every aspect of this tale, noting the bleak fog that enshrouds the valley, the constricting fence that surrounds Elisa's tidy house, and Steinbeck's artful use of SYMBOLISM and IMAGERY to evoke Elisa's situation.

At the opening of the story, the narrator juxtaposes Elisa, who is tending to her chrysanthemums, to the mechanistic world outside her fenced garden: It is a man's world, peopled by her husband and his male clients associated with cars and tractors. This metallic imagery prepares us for the arrival of the itinerant tinker who travels the country fixing such household items as knives, scissors, and pots. At first Elisa firmly resists his request for repair work, but this unkempt and pronouncedly grimy man—apparently a perversion of the archetypal romantic dark stranger (see ARCHETYPE)—slyly compliments her chrysanthemums, causing Elisa to believe he shares her interest in her creative talents, and she invites him into her enclosed yard. Her explanation of the needs of the chrysanthemums becomes sexually charged as Elisa's breast swells with passion, and she makes METAPHORS of the nighttime stars that drive their points into one's body, producing a "hot and sharp and—lovely" sensation ("Chrysanthemums" 400). The tinker deflates this figuratively sexual crescendo by reminding her that nothing is pleasurable if "you don't have no dinner," shaming Elisa into bringing him some saucepans to mend. He leaves with an obviously false promise to deliver Elisa's pot of chrysanthemums to a "lady" down the road.

From a Freudian perspective, Steinbeck's use of sexual innuendo seems fairly obvious: Both the valley and the pots suggest female sex, whereas the knives and scissors suggest the male. Mere hours later, on her way out to dinner with Henry, the emotionally and sexually recharged Elisa understands almost immediately that the dark spot on the road is the chrysanthemums: The tinker has thrown away the symbols of female creative potential and kept the pot with its generic female shape. Just as he has no use for the late-blooming chrysanthemums, he has no use for her, the 35-year-old individual woman. Critics continue to debate Elisa's future: whether she has been defeated or whether, like the chrysanthemums, she will bloom again.

BIBLIOGRAPHY

Steinbeck, John. "The Chrysanthemums." In *American Short Stories.* 6th ed. Edited by Eugene Current-García and Bert Hickock. New York: Longman, 1997, pp. 396–403.

"CHURCH MOUSE, A" MARY E. WILKINS FREEMAN (1891) Published in *A New England Nun and Other Stories,* "A Church Mouse" portrays a poor but rebellious New England spinster, Hetty Fifield, who loses her home and moves into the church meetinghouse, appointing herself sexton, a position typically held by a male. After the male officials try unsuccessfully to evict her, Mr. Gale, a church deacon and town selectman, solicits his wife's help. Mrs. Gale, recognizing Hetty's desperation and determination to stay, puts a stop to the uncharitable attempt to oust her and offers her Christmas dinner the next day. Hetty rings the church bells to celebrate the holiday that finally has brought her peace and independence after a lifetime of caring for and depending on others. The bells, then, symbolize New World "liberty" bells as well as the echo of Old World traditions long forgotten in the pinch-penny Puritan village.

Mrs. Gale, too, declares her independence from narrow-minded bigotry when she tells Hetty, "Of course, you can stay in the meetin'-house" (CM 416). The narrator describes her as follows: "Mrs. Gale stood majestically, and looked defiantly around; tears were in her eyes" (CM 416). She also finds other women sympathetic to Hetty; together, these women overwhelm the "masculine clamor" (CM 415) and "the last of the besiegers" (SF 417) to bring a bit of Christmas peace to their tiny corner of the earth.

Critics often group this story with other Freeman stories that examine the "strong but healthy will" of the New England woman (Westbrook 50), who, as a feminist critic reminds us, is a descendant of non-conformist Anne Hutchinson (M. Pryse, "Afterword," in M. Pryse, ed., *Selected Stories of Mary Wilkins Freeman* [1983], 340). Other critics view "A Church Mouse" as a comment on the effects of poverty, a FEMINIST THEME, since "the poorest of the poor in the Freeman village are women" (Reichardt 53).

BIBLIOGRAPHY

Jewett, Sarah Orne. *Short Fiction of Sarah Orne Jewett and Mary Wilkins Freeman.* Edited by Barbara H. Solomon. New York: New American Library, 1979.

Reichardt, Mary R. *Mary Wilkins Freeman: A Study of the Short Fiction.* New York: Twayne, 1997.

Tutwiler, Julia. "Two New England Writers in Relation to Their Art and to Each Other." In *Critical Essays on Mary Wilkins Freeman.* Edited by Shirley Marchalonis. Boston: G. K. Hall, 1991.

Westbrook, Perry. *Mary Wilkins Freeman.* Boston: Twayne, 1988.

Gwen M. Neary
Santa Rosa Junior College
Sonoma State University

"CIRCUMSTANCE" HARRIET PRESCOTT SPOFFORD (1860, 1863)

First published in the ATLANTIC MONTHLY in May 1860, this story was included in Harriet Prescott SPOFFORD's first collection of short stories, *The Amber Gods and Other Stories* (1863). The unnamed female PROTAGONIST's captivity by an "Indian Devil" panther is supposedly based on the experience of Spofford's maternal great-grandmother, but the story, a symbolic romance, can be read on several levels.

The woman's nightmarish experience in the forest depicts a test of faith, a journey into a psychic wilderness, and a confrontation with sexuality and death. The sexual violence represented by the panther's "savage caresses" both suggests the woman artist's sense of vulnerability and exposure and provides a female counterpart to initiation tales such as Nathaniel HAWTHORNE's "YOUNG GOODMAN BROWN." The protagonist, a SCHEHERAZADE-like figure whose song saves her life but who ultimately must please the beast, represents the trials of the 19th-century

woman artist, whose voice was necessary for survival but also was controlled by a potentially hostile reading public. In addition to portraying the protagonist as EVERYWOMAN, Spofford also particularizes her experience as American. Through the frontier setting and depiction of the "Indian Devil" as well as the protagonist's fear of violation and cannibalism and search for providential meaning—all of which echo Indian captivity narratives—Spofford explores the importance of myth in the creation of national identity. Concluding with a reference to the last lines of John Milton's *Paradise Lost,* in which Adam and Eve depart from the garden, the story recasts the newly liberated protagonist as a New World Eve who has endured the initiation through which Americans gained imaginative possession of the landscape.

BIBLIOGRAPHY

Dalke, Anne. "'Circumstance' and the Creative Woman: Harriet Prescott Spofford." *Arizona Quarterly* 41.1 (Spring 1985): 71–85.

Fetterley, Judith. *Provisions: A Reader from 19th-Century American Women.* Bloomington: Indiana University Press, 1985.

Paula Kot
Niagara University

CISNEROS, SANDRA (1954–)

Perhaps one of the best known Chicana writers (see HISPANIC-AMERICAN SHORT FICTION), Sandra Cisneros gained national recognition when, in 1989, Random House published a revised version of her 1984 novella *The House on Mango Street.* In addition, *Bad Boys* (1980), *My Wicked, Wicked Ways* (1987), and most recently *Loose Woman* (1995) attest to Cisneros's talent as a poet. In 1995 she was awarded a MacArthur "Genius" Fellowship, and she is currently working on a novel. The publication of *Woman Hollering Creek and Other Stories* (1991) marked Cisneros's entry into the short story genre, and it was, indeed, a celebrated entry: The collection received both the Lannan Foundation 1991 Literary Award for Fiction and the PEN Center West Award for best fiction of 1991.

Divided into three sections—"My Lucy Friend Who Smells Like Corn," "One Holy Night," and "There Was a Man, There Was a Woman"—*Woman Hollering Creek* charts, through a number of characters, the development from youth to womanhood, making it a BILDUNGSROMAN of sorts. *The House on Mango Street* uses both the narrative voice and vignette form in the opening section, as Cisneros gives us a child's account of growing up Chicana. One of the more frequently anthologized selections, "Barbie-Q," for instance, humorously delves into the race, class, and gender anxieties of growing up with the Mattel Barbie doll and the role it has played in constructing beauty norms and gender roles. The second section, comprised of two stories—"One Holy Night" and "My *Tocaya*"—examines sexual awakening from the perspective of two adolescent girls and critiques the way in which adults and schools tend to mystify and circumnavigate sex education discussions, often at the children's own peril. It is in the final section that the title story appears; among other things, it contests the representation of women in the popular media (namely in the *telenovela*) and in cultural myths like the story of La Llorona, the woman who allegedly killed her children and now spends her evenings crying and searching for them.

These representational conflicts come to the fore in the abusive marriage of the principal female character, Cleófilas, and in her meeting with Felice, her independent, self-determined female savior. The conflict between man and woman in this story represents an overarching THEME for this final section, in which Cisneros explores the relationship struggles between men and women, including a tour-de-force story of the Mexican revolutionary leader Emiliano Zapata and his wife and lovers.

Cisneros's narrative experimentation deserves note, for her formal theatrics transcend rigid classifications of the short story. While many of her stories conform to more traditional definitions of the genre, Cisneros also includes, for instance, a five-page dialogue between two women over the Marlboro man's sexuality, with absolutely no narrative exposition: that is, we read only the conversational exchange between these women. Also, the distribution of the names of Tejanas and Tejanos, who sacrificed their lives in the battle of the Alamo, throughout "Remember the Alamo" disrupts its narrative flow and rewrites the historical record, which has effaced their names and misrepresented the battle as an Anglo versus Mexican event. Finally, the collection of *milagritos,* or prayers, to a number of saints that comprises "Little Miracles, Kept Promises" demonstrates the formal range of the story form and Cisneros's uncanny ear for dialogue.

BIBLIOGRAPHY

Eysturoy, Annie O. *Daughters of Self-Creation: The Contemporary Chicana Novel.* Albuquerque: University of New Mexico Press, 1996.

Kanellos, Nicolás, ed. *The Hispanic Literary Companion.* New York: Visible Ink Press, 1997.

———. *Hispanic American Literature: A Brief Introduction and Anthology.* New York: HarperCollins College Publishers, 1995.

López, Tiffany Ana, ed. *Growing Up Chicana/o.* New York: William Morrow, 1993.

Moraga, Cherríe, and Gloria Anzaldúa, eds. *This Bridge Called My Back: Writings by Radical Women of Color.* Watertown, Mass.: Persphone Press, 1981.

Quintana, Alvina E. *Home Girls: Chicana Literary Voices.* Philadelphia: Temple University Press, 1996.

Rodríguez Aranda, Pilar E. "On the Solitary Fate of Being Mexican, Female, Wicked and Thirty-three: An Interview with Writer Sandra Cisneros." *The Americas Review* 18 1 (1991): 64–80.

Simmen, Edward, ed. *North of the Rio Grande: The Mexican American Experience in Short Fiction.* New York: Mentor, 1992.

Ralph E. Rodriguez
Pennsylvania State University

CIVIL WAR (1861–1865)   Also known as the War of Rebellion, the War of Secession, and the War Between the States, the Civil War broke out between the Northern United States (the Union) and 11 Southern states that seceded to form the Confederate States of America (the Confederacy). The war resulted from deep-seated differences over economic and social issues, particularly those of tariff regulations and the extension of slavery. The principal objective of the North was to maintain the Union, but after 1862 the emancipation of slaves became a secondary objective.

In reaction to Abraham Lincoln's election to the presidency in 1860, South Carolina seceded, followed by ten other Southern states that formed the Confederacy and elected Jefferson Davis as its president in 1861. Although the Union suffered a setback when routed by the Confederates at the Battle of Bull Run, and although the most brilliant generals led the confederate troops, the superior forces of the North ultimately prevailed. Despite the best efforts of Robert E. LEE and Thomas (Stonewall) Jackson, the South was eventually defeated at the BATTLE OF GETTYSBURG, Pennsylvania, and at Vicksburg, Mississippi, in 1863. In 1864 Union General Ulysses S. Grant laid siege to Richmond, Virginia, and General William Tecumseh Sherman destroyed the Confederates in his famous and controversial march to the sea through Georgia. General Lee surrendered to General Grant at Appomattox Courthouse, Virginia, on April 9, 1865.

With the possible exception of the Napoleonic Wars, the Civil War has produced the most writing and the greatest number of books of any conflict in history. Among the most famous novellas and novels are Stephen CRANE's *The Red Badge of Courage,* William FAULKNER's *Absalom, Absalom!* and Margaret Mitchell's *Gone with the Wind.* Various aspects of the conflict are depicted in numerous short stories by Ambrose BIERCE, Sherwood BONNER, George Washington CABLE, William FAULKNER, F. Scott FITZGERALD, Ellen GLASGOW, Barry Hannah, Joel Chandler HARRIS, William Dean HOWELLS, Thomas Nelson Page, and Mark TWAIN.

CLASSIC

CLASSIC   Originally used to describe artistic works of the Greeks and Romans, in the 20th century the term is customarily applied to any work that has achieved recognition for its superior quality or for its place in an established tradition. In American literature, for instance, Nathaniel HAWTHORNE's *The Scarlet Letter* is commonly recognized as a "classic" American novel and Washington IRVING's "THE LEGEND OF SLEEPY HOLLOW" as a classic

American story. The term may also be applied to works in terms of literary genre; thus, Henry JAMES's *THE TURN OF THE SCREW* is a classic American GHOST STORY, Flannery O'CONNOR's "A GOOD MAN IS HARD TO FIND" is a classic tale in the genre of American Southern GOTHIC. "Classic" also may be applied to authors.

Although the obvious meaning is generally accepted outside of academia, much recent criticism questions not only the components—what constitutes a "classic" work?—but also the people who make the decisions. Scholars and critics help make or break a work by publishing reviews and commentary, but sometimes the public acclaim of and demand for a work is so great that, despite the disapproval of intellectuals, a work continues to be read. Publishers, too, play a significant role: If a book is allowed to go out of print, it cannot be bought and read. Until the past two decades, this has been the case with much women's literature. It is also the case with literature by so-called minorities, who until relatively recently had difficulty finding publishers. In terms of short fiction, yet another major issue is the academic tendency to prefer longer works, such as novels, over short fiction. Thus the term "classic" is in a constant state of evaluation.

"CLEAN, WELL-LIGHTED PLACE, A"

"CLEAN, WELL-LIGHTED PLACE, A"
ERNEST HEMINGWAY (1933)   Two waiters, one young and one older, discuss an old man who sits, late at night, drinking brandy in the cafe. We learn from their dialogue that he attempted suicide the week before. A soldier and a girl pass by in the street. The younger waiter is impatient, eager to go home to his wife. The older waiter speaks his understanding of the old man's needs and despair. After closing the cafe, the older waiter thinks of the nothingness of life that creates the need for some light and cleanliness. He goes to a bodega and then home, where, sleepless till daylight, he thinks about the need for a clean, well-lighted place. He discounts his insomnia, which he is sure many others must suffer from as well.

Commonplace reading of the story sees the older waiter as sympathetic, empathizing with the old man. The younger waiter, who is married, is more callous and wants only to go home. He spills the old man's drink; he says an old man is a "nasty thing." Critics have long disagreed, however, about the consistency of each waiter's perspective, a confusion created by Ernest HEMINGWAY's technique of using dialogue without always identifying his speakers precisely.

Spare and short, "A Clean, Well-Lighted Place" develops almost entirely by dialogue. The narrative depends on the reader's ability to provide the framework of existential despair (see EXISTENTIALISM) and NIHILISM, the encounter with the cultural wasteland, and loss of faith. For many it is the seminal story in Hemingway's short story catalog, the quintessential illustration of his theory of omission. It is one of his most anthologized short stories. A. E. Hotchner quotes the author as saying it "may be my favorite story."

It was first published in *Scribner's Monthly* in 1933 and then in Hemingway's short story collection *Winner Take Nothing*. Since that time it has been widely anthologized, as it is a quintessential example of Hemingway's spare and dramatic style and nihilistic vision. This is distilled in the older waiter's PARODY of the Lord's Prayer, as he substitutes the Spanish word "nada" (nothing) for all the key terms: "Our nada who art in nada, nada be thy name. . . . Give us this nada our daily nada. . . ." The effect is powerful: the loss of faith, the despair, the lonely encounter with the nothingness of existence. The term "a clean, well-lighted place" has become a code for whatever refuge modern beings choose to help them make it through the night and withstand the enveloping darkness.

BIBLIOGRAPHY

Bennett, Warren. "The Manuscript and the Dialogue of 'A Clean, Well-Lighted Place.'" *American Literature* (1979): 613–624.

Flora, Joseph M. *Ernest Hemingway: A Study of the Short Fiction.* Boston: Twayne, 1989.

Gabriel, Joseph F. "The Logic of Confusion in Hemingway's 'A Clean, Well-Lighted Place.'" *College English* (May 1961): 539–546.

Hoffman, Steven K. "Nada and Clean Well-Lighted Place: The Unity of Hemingway's Short Fiction." *Essays in Literature* (1979): 91–110.

Johnston, Kenneth G. *The Tip of the Iceberg: Hemingway and the Short Story.* Greenwood, Fla.: Penkevill Publishing Co., 1987.

Kerner, David. "The Ambiguity of 'A Clean, Well-Lighted Place.'" *Studies in Fiction* (1992): 561–573.

———. "The Foundation of the True Text of 'A Clean, Well-Lighted Place.'" *Fitzgerald-Hemingway Annual* (1979): 279–300.

Mimi Reisel Gladstein
University of Texas at El Paso

CLIMAX The rising action that leads to the culmination of the HERO's or HEROINE's fortunes. (See PLOT.)

CLOSE READING The cornerstone of NEW CRITICISM, which advocated the explication of a text through close attention to its literary techniques, particularly image, symbol, and IRONY. Despite the demise of New Criticism among scholars and critics, many still believe that New Criticism's legacy of close reading remains the key to understanding a novel or story.

CLOSURE A term that has been adopted relatively recently to indicate an ending to a literary work that may or may not "end" in a definitive way; thus a short story may or may not achieve closure by the end of the tale. For instance, F. Scott FITZGERALD's "BABYLON REVISITED" ends on an ambiguous note as CHARLIE WALES ponders his future. Fitzgerald withholds closure: We never learn whether Charlie's sister-in-law allows his daughter to return to him or whether Charlie truly acknowledges his reprehensible past behavior.

COFER, JUDITH ORTIZ (1952–) Judith Ortiz Cofer was born in Hormigueros, Puerto Rico, and grew up there and in Paterson, New Jersey, until her family moved to Augusta, Georgia, in 1968. When her father went on tours of duty in the navy, Ortiz Cofer, her mother, and her brother lived in

Puerto Rico with her maternal grandmother. Moving between the urban, English-speaking Paterson and the rural, Spanish-speaking Hormigueros gave Ortiz Cofer the major THEMES that inform her novel, short stories, creative nonfiction, and poetry. Ortiz Cofer uses this variety of genres to examine what she knows intimately: the lives of Puerto Rican women on the island and on the mainland, the resulting bicultural conflicts and strengths, and the role of storytelling in both Spanish-speaking and English-speaking cultures.

Her first publications were books of poetry, beginning with *Latin Women Pray* (1980). Her first novel, *The Line of the Sun* (1989), was nominated for a Pulitzer Prize. In 1990 she published *Silent Dancing: A Partial Remembrance of a Puerto Rican Childhood,* an autobiographical work of creative nonfiction and poetry. Ortiz Cofer called the prose pieces *"ensayos"*—Spanish for "essay" and "rehearsal"—to define her own attempts to blend the essay with her slightly fictionalized reconstructions of memory (12). In *The Latin Deli* (1993), the creative nonfiction, poetry, and short stories illustrate the lives of Puerto Ricans living in a New Jersey barrio, a residential area comprising one ethnic group. Finally, *An Island Like You: Stories from the Barrio* (1996) is a collection of short stories written about young adults living in a Puerto Rican barrio. She is currently working on her second novel.

BIBLIOGRAPHY

Bruce-Novoa, Juan. "Judith Ortiz Cofer's Rituals of Movement." *The Americas Review* 19 (Winter 1991): 88–99.
Cofer, Judith Ortiz. *An Island Like You: Stories of the Bario.* New York: Puffin Books, 1995.
———. *The Latin Deli: Prose and Poetry.* Athens: University of Georgia Press, 1993.
———. *Latin Woman Pray.* Fort Lauderdale, Fla.: Florida Arts Gazette Press, 1980.
———. *The Line of the Sun.* Athens: University of Georgia Press, 1989.
———. *The Native Dancer.* Bourbonnais, Ill.: Lieb/Schott Publications, 1981.
———. *Peregrina.* Golden, Colo.: Riverstone Press, 1986.
———. *Silent Dancing: A Partial Remembrance of A Puerto Rican Childhood.* Houston, Tex.: Arte Público Press, 1990.
———. *The Year of Our Revolution: New and Selected Stories and Poems.* Houston: Tex.: Piñata Books, 1998.

Nancy L. Chick
University of Georgia

COLD WAR   The name given to the political and economic competition and military confrontation between the United States and other democratic capitalist countries and the Soviet Union and other communist countries from the end of WORLD WAR II to the disintegration of the Soviet Union and its empire in the 1980s. Most of this period was marked by strained diplomatic relations, nuclear terror, unparalleled espionage and intrigue, and the "exporting of revolution." The period of greatest tensions and danger was from the late 1940s to the late 1960s; at this time disputes between the Soviet Union and the Allies over the occupation policies and reunification plans of Germany caused the Soviets to tighten military, political, and economic control over the occupied countries (Poland, Czechoslovakia, Hungary, Romania, Bulgaria, and East Germany) of eastern Europe, virtually annexing them to the Soviet Union. That portion of the Cold War included the Berlin Airlift (1948–49); the beginning of the arms race after the Soviets exploded an atomic bomb in 1949 and a hydrogen bomb in 1952; the communist takeover of China (1949); the KOREAN WAR (1950–53); the construction of the Berlin Wall (1961), which divided Germany into a communist East and noncommunist West until 1989, the Cuban Missile Crisis (1962); and the VIETNAM WAR (1954–75). By the late 1960s, relations had become less strained in a period of detente and the signing of various nuclear nonproliferation and strategic arms limitation treaties.

COLLIER'S   From 1888 to 1957, *Collier's* was one of the leading mass-circulated, illustrated magazines in the country. In the early 20th century, *Collier's* followed the lead of MCCLURE'S magazine and took up campaigns against various social ills, such as child labor, and in favor of rights such as women's suffrage. Throughout its history, the magazine was known for superb illustrations and the strength of the fiction it published. Fiction writers of consequence included Edith WHARTON, P. G. Wodehouse, Frank Norris, Henry JAMES, Jack LONDON, H. G. Wells, Bret HARTE, Conan Doyle, O. HENRY, Kathleen Norris, Pearl BUCK, and John STEINBECK. *Collier's* remained popular in the 1950s but suffered continuing financial losses and ceased publication in 1957.

COLTER, CYRUS (1910–)   Born in Noblesville, Indiana, Colter published his first collection of short stories, *The Beach Umbrella,* in 1970. He writes in the style of modern REALISM and keeps his authorial self unobtrusive while using colloquial dialogue and developing the story by entering briefly into the minds of characters. The subject of each story is often an apparently small event, as in "Rescue," which tells of a woman who agrees to marry a man she does not love. Colter's style is masterly and his imagination for situation is fertile.

BIBLIOGRAPHY
Colter, Cyrus. *The Amoralists and Other Tales: Collected Stories.* New York & St. Paul, Minn.: Thunder's Mouth Press, 1988.
———. *The Beach Umbrella and Other Stories.* Iowa City: University of Iowa Press, 1970.
———. *A Chocolate Soldier.* New York & St. Paul, Minn.: Thunder's Mouth Press, 1988.
———. *City of Light: A Novel.* New York & St. Paul, Minn.: Thunder's Mouth Press, 1993.
———. *The Hippodrome.* Chicago: Swallow Press, 1973.
———. *Night Studies: A Novel.* Chicago: Swallow Press, 1997.
Colter, Cyrus, and Michael Anania, eds. *The Rivers of Eros.* Chicago: Swallow Press, 1972.
Reilly, John M. "Cyrus Colter." *Contemporary Literature* (1986).

COMEDY   A term originally applied only to drama, and then in medieval times to nondramatic prose fiction, today any prose fiction that entertains, delights, or amuses the reader through its wit, humor, or ridicule may be recognized as comedy. Unlike TRAGEDY, comedy nearly always provides a happy ending for characters and readers. Comedy also may take the form of farce or BURLESQUE, and as COMIC RELIEF in stories with ultimately serious themes. The comic form is variously employed in such stories as Mark TWAIN's "The Jumping Frog of Calaveras County," James THURBER's, "THE SECRET LIFE OF WALTER MITTY," William FAULKNER's, "Mule in the Yard," Dorothy PARKER's "The Waltz," and Phillip ROTH's "THE CONVERSION OF THE JEWS." See also BLACK HUMOR.

COMIC RELIEF   A device used to lighten the tragic effect or to alleviate the tension in a somber or tragic work. Although sometimes merely intrusive and amusing, in the best stories humorous characters, dialogues, or situations actually function to illuminate and deepen the ultimately serious meaning of the work. Although classic examples occur in Shakespeare (the gravediggers' scene in *Hamlet* [V.i], the drunken porter scene in *Macbeth* [II, iii], the speeches of the Fool in *King Lear*), the use of comic relief continues in American fiction. A primary example of comic relief occurs in Flannery O'CONNOR's "GOOD COUNTRY PEOPLE."

"COMING, APHRODITE!"   WILLA CATHER (1920)   First published in the magazine *Smart Set* (August 1920) as "Coming, Eden Bower!" and included in the collection *Youth and the Bright Medusa* (1920), the story relates the brief, passionate love affair between a painter and an opera singer in Washington Square, a bohemian section of New York City during the early 20th century. The story is Cather's most explicit treatment of sexual passion, but it is equally concerned with two different kinds of artistic success. The painter, Don Hedger, is willing to forgo friends, fame, and material comfort to pursue groundbreaking originality in his art. The singer, Eden Bower, wants a large, appreciative audience for her stunning but standard portrayal of heroic characters. Many years after their affair, both artists have found success on their own terms. The story pursues one of Cather's persistent ironic THEMES: The production of art, whether for human enrichment or entertainment, necessitates isolation.

A good example of Cather's craftsmanship, the story uses references to Greek myth along the archetypal images of birds, light, and darkness to create a dense visual and symbolic tapestry, with AMBIGUITY a dominant effect. Is Don Hedger, whose name implies the trimming of natural growth, an artist whose disciplined labor produces works of excellence, or is he meant to suggest that romantic love prunes too much of the artistic soul? Some commentators have described Eden Bower as an exquisite representation of the eternal feminine principle, but others see her as an Eve-like temptress who threatens to seduce Hedger away from his high aesthetic ideals. She also can be seen as one of Cather's many strong, androgynous women who defy traditional gender expectations.

The magazine version of the story, published first, was altered to avoid offending censorship crusaders at a time when more than one publisher had been taken to court. Besides the title change, in this bowdlerized version Eden Bower's nudity was deleted from one scene, as were a number of descriptions with sexual overtones.

BIBLIOGRAPHY
Arnold, Marilyn. *Willa Cather's Short Fiction*. Lincoln: University of Nebraska Press, 1984.
Cather, Willa. *Uncle Valentine and Other Stories: Willa Cather's Uncollected Short Fiction, 1915–1929*. Edited by Bernice Slote. Lincoln: University of Nebraska Press, 1973.

Frances Kerr
Durham Technical Community College

"CONFESSION" EDITH WHARTON (1936)

"The Confession," adapted from Edith WHARTON's incomplete and unpublished play, *Kate Spain,* and published in *The World Over,* alludes to the notorious case of Lizzie Borden. It recounts the romance of two American travelers, Mr. Severance and Kate Ingram, who meet in an European hotel. Severance, a convalescing American banker, and Ingram, a quiet, pale woman with "unquiet" hands, an unknown past, and the power to monopolize Severance's heart and mind, must negotiate with Ingram's companion, Cassie Wilpert, a heavy, unrefined Irish woman who attempts to prevent the couple's growing affection. Severance successfully woos Ingram but is disconcerted when she becomes agitated by the appearance of an American journalist.

Later this journalist, whom Severance had known in New York, tells him that Ingram is really Kate Spain, who was acquitted of a murder charge in a much-publicized trial three years earlier. Severance denies this possibility, although he recalls receiving strange looks from the hotel staff whenever he has been with her. He discounts the journalist's comments and eagerly plans to propose marriage. When he learns that Kate and Cassie have unexpectedly fled, he traces them to a small pension in Italy and declares his love to Kate. She confesses that she is Kate Spain and sadly rejects his offer because she knows that they would be hounded by people curious about her role in the murder and because Cassie would never permit her to marry.

The story thus implies that Kate Spain has left the prison of her tyrant father's house for that of her present captivity with her companion Cassie. The next morning Cassie comes to Severance's room and angrily insists that he leave Kate. When he refuses, she warns him that she is going to tell him details that will kill him. The moment she reaches for a document in her purse, she collapses from a stroke. She never regains consciousness, and within a month, she is dead. Severance reassures Kate that Cassie told him nothing and suggests that she remove any papers in Cassie's purse that might embarrass her. Later she insists that he read the document which Cassie had meant to show him and repeats that she cannot marry him. To ease her concern, he refuses to read the document but agrees to take it with him.

The last section of the tale is narrated by Severance seven years later. He reports that he and Kate were married for five years of uncommon happiness. Now that she is dead, he plans to burn Cassie's unopened document. He argues that Kate's insistence that he read it marks her an honest woman.

Barbara White, who has written extensively on Wharton's short fiction, notes the emphasis on a secret, hidden past in the period in which Wharton wrote this story. White finds evidence of incest in Wharton's life and suggests that the author tried to exorcise it in stories such as "Confession." Particularly in this story, written in her last decade,

Wharton appears to have survived and, perhaps, triumphed: Kate has killed her father, and although she feels divided into two selves, one half can marry the man whose name suggests her severed life and who exonerates her from her past (BW 104).

BIBLIOGRAPHY
Lewis, R. W. B., and Nancy Lewis, *The Letters of Edith Wharton*. New York: Macmillan, 1988.
White, Barbara. *Edith Wharton: A Study of the Short Fiction*. New York: Macmillan, 1991.

Sandra Chrystal Hayes
Georgia Institute of Technology

"THE CONFESSIONAL" EDITH WHARTON

(1901) First published in a volume entitled *Crucial Instances* (1901), "The Confessional" weaves together Italian political intrigue, religious questions, and domestic relationships in a manner similar to Edith WHARTON's novel *The Valley of Decision*. Its four shifts of confessors and confessants could serve as a study of punishment, silence, and power and can be listed among Wharton's stories of voiceless women and loveless marriages. It is told by an American narrator, an accountant who listens to the confession of the dying priest, Don Egidio.

Egidio relates his ties to the aristocratic Da Milano family, who adopted and reared him as a brother to the scholarly Count Roberto Siviano Da Milano, a man committed to improving the conditions of peasants and to promoting the cause of Italian liberty. The count had married a young woman he had observed at mass whom he saw as the embodiment of his beleaguered country, now degraded by Austrian invaders. His much-younger bride, exchanged by her family for appropriate compensation, finds entertainment with the count's half brother and sister-in-law and with their cousin, a handsome Austrian officer.

Crucial personal and political battles converge as ambitions divide the family. On the eve of the count's departure to the revolution, his half brother and wife "confess" that they know the countess has had an adulterous relationship with the Austrian soldier. Assuming that the count will discredit his wife and

that he will then name his nieces and nephews successors to the family fortune, the two propose that the count disguise himself as Egidio in order to hear the countess's confession. After quarreling with the priest, the count impersonates him and hears his wife's confession. The next morning he meets with the family to announce her innocence. He leaves for Milan, heroically engages in battles for several months, and then disappears. Meanwhile his wife gives birth to a daughter, but her "marble breast" gives no milk. Don Egidio, who had permitted the deceitful confession, confesses his own guilt in so doing to his bishop and is sent to New York as penance.

Four years later, when the priest is called to tend to an ailing professor, he realizes that the man is Count Roberto. The count teaches Italian and shares his meager income with other Italian expatriates. The two agree never to discuss the past and live as close friends for another eight years. Don Egidio concludes his tale with the justification for his own sin: "[The Count's] just life and holy death intercede for me, who sinned for his sake alone."

The many Wharton readers who find evidence and implications of incest in her fiction point to this early story, with its apt title, as a primary example. This THEME of past secrets continues and intensifies in Wharton's later works. Notably, the count (clearly a father figure) has under false pretenses listened to the confession of his young wife (clearly a daughter figure) when in fact a man, not she, has sinned. The transference of guilt to another man at least suggest that Wharton may have been "confessing" and also reassigning the blame to a male figure.

BIBLIOGRAPHY
Lewis, R. W. B. *Edith Wharton*. New York: Scribner's, 1975.
Singley, Carol. *Edith Wharton: Matters of Mind and Spirit*. New York: Cambridge University Press, 1995.
White, Barbara. *Edith Wharton: A Study of the Short Fiction*. New York: Macmillan, 1991.

Sandra Chrystal Hayes
Georgia Institute of Technology

CONFLICT

In a work of fiction, the struggle between the main character and opposing forces.

External conflict occurs between the protagonist and another character or force. Internal conflict occurs within the character himself or herself.

CONJURE STORIES

Conjure is a blend of religion and magic with roots in Africa and was brought to the New World by those who were forceably removed from Africa and enslaved. Since their Christian oppressors did not allow the practice of traditional African religions, conjure was practiced secretly by slaves without the knowledge of masters and overseers. In North America, South America, and the Caribbean, conjure was rooted in African views on magic and spirituality and based on the belief that forces and spirits beyond the visible world influence events. In practice, the person performing conjure was usually a woman, and it was believed that her skills allowed her to cast a spell upon a chosen victim. The items used by the conjurer to create a spell varied widely, from hair to roots to grave dust. Carol S. Taylor Johnson has noted the origins of conjure visible in Olaudah Equiano's 1789 narrative *The Life of Olaudah Equiano, or Gustavus Vassa, the African*. In this slave narrative, the multiple roles held by priests as religious figures, healers, and magicians in African culture are readily visible. For Africans thrust into an antagonistic culture in America, conjure persisted as a social link to African beliefs and offered a means of binding slave communities outside the religious systems of European American culture.

In American short fiction, perhaps the most successful and well-known conjure writer is Charles W. CHESNUTT. In his popular *The Conjure Woman* (1899), Chesnutt provides a glimpse into the beliefs and practice of conjure while also recognizing its subversive potential. In the stories of this collection, Uncle Julius is an old black caretaker of a North Carolina plantation who relays vivid tales of conjure from his days as a slave. In "The Goophered Grapevine," for example, Uncle Julius attempts to convince John, a white Northerner, not to purchase an abandoned vineyard. Julius tells John that the vineyard had been conjured by local conjure woman Aunt Peggy so that anyone who eats the grapes will die within a year. John buys the vineyard nonetheless and discovers Julius's ulterior motive for the story—his own sale of the grapes, which provided a "respectable revenue." The remaining stories in *The Conjure Woman* follow a similar pattern—portraying both the power of conjure in the black oral tradition and white disregard for and misunderstanding of its practice. Conjure fiction has not been limited to African American writers, however. In his 1929 story "THAT EVENING SUN," for example, William FAULKNER also explores conjure, but instead focuses on the power that conjuring holds in the African American imagination. In this story Nancy, a black woman, appears to have been conjured by Jesus, a male conjurer or "badman" who is preparing to kill her. While Nancy is nearly paralyzed with fear, the white Compson family does not understand the situation she is confronting. They simply dismiss her behavior as erratic and urge her to continue her work as housekeeper. Both examples here illustrate the gap in white and black attitudes toward conjure and its lingering 20th-century cultural presence, particularly in the American South.

BIBLIOGRAPHY

Brodhead, Richard H. "Introduction." In Charles Waddell Chesnutt, *The Conjure Woman and Other Tales*. Edited by Richard H. Brodhead. Durham, N.C.: Duke University Press, 1993, 1–21.

Chesnutt, Charles Waddell. *The Conjure Woman and Other Tales*. Edited by Richard H. Brodhead. Durham, N.C.: Duke University Press, 1993.

Faulkner, William. "That Evening Sun." In *Collected Stories of William Faulkner*. New York: Random House, 1950.

Taylor, Carol S. "Conjuring." In *The Oxford Companion to African American Literature*. Edited by William L. Andrews et al. New York: Oxford University Press, 1997.

Chris McBride
California State University at Los Angeles

CONNELL, EVAN S(HELBY), JR. (1924–)

As a writer of short fiction, Connell's reputation rests mainly on the characters of Mr. and Mrs. Bridge, who appeared first in several sketches collected in *The Anatomy Lesson* (1957). The Bridges are affluent upper-middle-class suburbanites who live near Kansas City, Missouri, and are "vaguely baffled" by life. To Connell, they represent a kind of person found in a sterile, provincial culture, such as the Midwest, who have achieved wealth but lack the sophistication to enjoy their lives.

BIBLIOGRAPHY
Blaisdell, Gus. "After Ground Zero." *New Mexico Quarterly* (Albuquerque) (Summer 1966).
Connell, Evan S. *The Anatomy Lesson and Other Stories.* New York: Viking, 1957.
———. *At the Crossroads: Stories.* New York: Simon & Schuster, 1965.
———. *St. Augustine's Pigeon: The Selected Stories.* Edited by Gus Blaisdell. Berkeley: North Point Press, 1980.

CONNIE

Adolescent girl in Joyce Carol OATES's "WHERE ARE YOU GOING, WHERE HAVE YOU BEEN?" who, with some valid reasons, deplores and ignores her parents. The results for her are horrific: From the evil personified in ARNOLD FRIEND, who has correctly chosen her as someone incapable of resisting his power, she learns that she has nothing to depend on, nothing to protect her. Particularly notable are Oates's depiction of the realistic details of Connie's life, her teenage interests, her small, quiet signs of rebellion—and finally her appalled realization that she is utterly powerless to defend herself.

CONNOTATION AND DENOTATION

In literature, "denotation" refers to the concrete meaning or dictionary definition of a word or words, while "connotation" refers to the emotional implications and associations that words may suggest. A standard example involves the difference between "house" and "home": "House" denotes the place where one lives, but "home"—in addition to denoting one's residence—connotes coziness, intimacy, familial values, and privacy. The distinction between the two words achieved widespread recognition with the publication of I. A. Richards's *Principles of Literary Criticism* (1924).

CONSPICUOUS CONSUMPTION

Term coined by American economist Thorstein Veblen (1857–1929) in his influential book *The Theory of the Leisure Class* (1899) to describe the human tendency—particularly of the monied class—to purchase and own goods that set them apart from their peers. Numerous American short stories have fruitfully explored the theme: for example, Willa CATHER's "PAUL'S CASE: A STUDY IN TEMPERAMENT," Joyce Carol OATES's "Shopping," and F. Scott FITZGERALD's "THE DIAMOND AS BIG AS THE RITZ" and "BABYLON REVISITED."

"CONVERSATION WITH MY FATHER, A" GRACE PALEY (1974)

Grace PALEY has stated that this story is autobiographical and, although she never wrote a story for her father about a neighbor, as the narrator does in this story, Paley's father once asked her: "Why can't you write a regular story, for God's sake?" (qtd. in Charters 1158). The first-person narrator in "Conversation with My Father," faced with her 86-year-old father's approaching death, visits him in the hospital. Although neither speaks of the short time that remains for him, most readers are aware of the undercurrents lying just beneath the surface of the banter and joking between father and daughter.

In response to her father's request to write a story for him in the manner of Chekhov or de Maupassant, the narrator, who is also a writer, brings him the skeleton of a story she wishes to tell about her neighbor across the street. The unadorned bare bones state merely that in an attempt to join her son in his drug addiction, the mother becomes a junkie as well—but when her son cures himself, she remains at home, alone and still addicted.

When the narrator's father tells her that she cannot compose a real story as the Russian and French writers can, she returns with a second draft, this time adding touches of COMEDY and REALISM. We realize that Paley is writing not in the 19th-century mode of Chekhov and de Maupassant but in the 20th-century mode of POSTMODERNISM. On one level, the narrator, like SCHEHEREZADE, attempts to entertain her father through her storytelling, putting off not her death but his. On another, self-reflexive level, Paley the author is telling a story about telling a story. The difference between her way and her father's way signals a generational difference that separates the two as well as his Russian birth as opposed to her American birth. Experientially, too, father and daughter see different endings to this story: The father sees tragedy, whereas the daughter-writer sees hope and possibility. There is also an intriguing element of control in this American-born daughter's role as writer: She can make the story end in whatever way she chooses. In her love for her father, however, after speaking her mind, she keeps her promise to her family and lets him have the last word: He believes she will never see tragedy head on. Although some critics view this ending as evidence of the daughter's inability to face her father's imminent death, an alternative view is that the daughter, despite her recognition of misfortune around her, has lived a life so different from her father's that she can truthfully put her faith in a more optimistic outcome.

BIBLIOGRAPHY

Charters, Ann. "Grace Paley, A Conversation with Ann Charters." In *Major Writers of Short Fiction: Stories and Commentary*. Edited by Ann Charters. Boston: Bedford Books/St. Martin's Press, 1993, 1156–1160.

Paley, Grace. "A Conversation with My Father." In *Enormous Changes at the Last Minute*. New York: Farrar, Straus & Giroux, 1974.

"CONVERSION OF THE JEWS, THE" PHILIP ROTH (1959)

Although Philip ROTH's *Goodbye, Columbus and Five Short Stories,* published in 1959, received the Jewish Book Council's Daroff Award in that year and the National Book Award in 1960, the Jewish community vehemently accused Philip Roth of, among other things, condemning his own people. In *Reading Myself and Others,* Roth's attempt to defend himself against such attacks, he asserts that "the STEREOTYPE as often arises from ignorance as from malice; deliberately keeping Jews out of the imagination of Gentiles, for fear of the bigots and their stereotyping minds, is really to invite the invention of stereotypical ideas" (166).

Throughout *Goodbye, Columbus,* Roth, like Ernest HEMINGWAY in IN OUR TIME, wrote from his experiences. For Roth, growing up in a Jewish neighborhood, attending Hebrew school, and joining the army, for example, provided a colorful landscape for exploring the struggles and conflicts of assimilated Jews in a predominantly Christian, American society. In "The Conversion of the Jews," a FABLE about religious hypocrisy and abuse, Ozzie Freedman, a young boy in Hebrew school, questions the teachings and authority of Rabbi Binder. The names "Freedman" and "Binder" have a humorously allegorical resonance (see ALLEGORY) in that neither realizes he is bound and restricted by the rigid blinders of orthodox religion.

If God could create the world in six days, Ozzie muses, "He [could] let a woman have a baby without intercourse" (GC 141). As Ozzie continues to question some of the tenets of Judaism, the tension escalates until Rabbi Binder hits him. With memories of his mother, who had struck him the previous night for the first time, Ozzie locks himself on the school's rooftop and threatens to jump. In an ironic inversion of the religious and, more specifically, adult oppression imposed on Ozzie, he forces his peers, the firemen trying to save him, Rabbi Binder, and his mother to kneel and proclaim a belief in Jesus Christ.

Although Ozzie begins by questioning Jewish dogma, his story tries to give us a larger understanding that religion should be about love, not coercion: "Don't you see . . . you should never hit anybody about God" (GC 158). Like many of Roth's characters who struggle against coercion, from religion, women, families, or government, Ozzie feels both the strength and the limitations of his cultural heritage. As he jumps into the firemen's net, he reenters a world of moral AMBIGUITY—one where struggles with his identity as a Jew are just beginning.

BIBLIOGRAPHY

Baumgarten, Murray and Barbara Gottfried. *Understanding Philip Roth.* Columbia, S.C.: University of South Carolina Press, 1990.

Cooper, Alan. *Philip Roth and the Jews.* Albany, N.Y.: State University of New York, 1996.

Halio, Jay L. *Philip Roth Revisited.* New York: Twayne, 1992.

Roth, Philip. *Goodbye Columbus and Five Short Stories.* Boston: Houghton Mifflin, 1959.

———. *Reading Myself and Others.* New York: Farrar, Straus & Giroux, 1961.

Thomas Fahy
University of North Carolina

COOVER, ROBERT (LOWELL) (1932–)

Born in Charles City, Iowa, Coover was reared in several midwestern states. He attended Southern Illinois University and Indiana University, and later spent a three-year tour in Europe as a naval officer. On his return, he attended the University of Chicago and became intrigued with the work of Samuel Beckett and Alain Robbe-Grillet, among others. Coover's first stories were published in the *Evergeen Review,* the LITTLE MAGAZINE in the forefront of publishing metafictional experimental tales by such writers as John Hawkes, Joseph Heller, Thomas Pynchon, Donald BARTHELME, and John BARTH. Like many of his generation, Coover was also strongly influenced by the experimental fiction of such South American writers as Jorge Louis Borges and Julio Cortázar, evident in his use of MAGICAL REALISM, the ABSURD, and the self-conscious attention to the devices of storytelling.

In 1969 Coover published his first short story collection, *Pricksongs and Descants,* which bears comparison with other experimental writing of the period—Barth's LOST IN THE FUNHOUSE, for instance. As author and critic Jerome Klinkowitz points out, both seem indebted to the way Borges exploits the fictive components of what one normally views as reality (138). In his most frequently anthologized story, "THE BABYSITTER," Coover appears to describe in realistic terms (see REALISM) a familiar middle-class evening: the parents leave their children in the charge of a baby-sitter. Coover's introduction of multiple perspectives into the story, however, calls reality into question, for he clearly demonstrates the chasms between one person's reality and another's. This story aptly demonstrates Coover's ability to ground the reader in reality, then removing most of its recognizable aspects through his use of FABLE and METAFICTION, MAGICAL REALISM, and ABSURDITY.

BIBLIOGRAPHY

Coover, Robert. *Aesop's Forest.* Santa Barbara, Calif.: Capra Press, 1986.
———. *Charlie in the House of Rue.* Lincoln, Mass.: Penmaen Press, 1980.
———. *The Convention.* Northridge, Calif.: Lord John Press, 1982.
———. *Gerald's Party: A Novel.* New York: Linden Press/Simon & Schuster, 1986.
———. *In Bed One Night and Other Brief Encounters.* Providence, R.I.: Burning Deck, 1983.
———. *A Night at the Movies; or, You Must Remember This.* New York: Linden Press/Simon & Schuster, 1987.
———. *The Origin of the Brunits: A Novel.* New York: Putnam, 1966.
———. *Pinocchio in Venice.* New York: Linden Press/Simon & Schuster, 1991.
———. *The Public Burning.* New York: Viking, 1977.
———. *A Political Fable.* New York: Viking, 1980.
———. *Pricksongs and Descants.* New York: Dutton, 1969.
———. *Spanking the Maid.* New York: Grove Press, 1982.
———. *The Universal Baseball Association, Inc., J. Henry Waugh, Prop.* New York: Random House, 1968.
———. *Whatever Happened to Gloomy Gus of the Chicago Bears?* New York: Linden Press/Simons & Schuster, 1987.
Cope, Jackson I. *Coover's Fictions.* Baltimore: Johns Hopkins University Press, 1986.
Gass, William H. *Fiction and the Figures of Life.* New York: Harper & Row, 1970.
Gordon, Lois. *Coover: The Universal Fictionmaking Process.* Carbondale, Ill.: Southern Illinois University Press, 1983.
Gunn, Jessie. "Structure as Revelation: Coover's *Pricksongs and Descants.*" *Linguistics in Literature* 2.1 (1977).
Hansen, Arlen J. "The Dice of God: Einstein, Heisenberg, and Coover." *Novel* 10 (1976).
Heckard, Margaret. "Coover, Metafictions, and Freedom." *Twentieth Century Literature* 22 (1976).
Klinkowitz, Jerome. "Robert Coover." In *Reference Guide to Short Fiction.* Edited by Noelle Watson. Detroit: St. James Press, 1994, pp. 138–139.
McCaffery, Larry. *The Metafictional Muse: The Works of Coover, Donald Barthelme, and William H. Gass.* Pittsburgh, Penn.: University of Pittsburgh Press, 1982.
Schmitz, Neil. "Coover and the Hazards of Metafiction." *Novel* 7 (1974).
Schulz, Max. *Black Humor Fiction of the Sixties.* Athens: Ohio University Press, 1973.
Shelton, Frank W. "Humor and Balance in Coover's *The Universal Baseball Association, Inc.*" *Critique* 17 (1975).

COUNTRY OF THE POINTED FIRS, THE SARAH ORNE JEWETT (1896)

Initially serialized in the ATLANTIC MONTHLY—the leading literary periodical when Sarah Orne JEWETT was most prolific—*The Country of the Pointed Firs* is, according to many critics (as well as authors such as Willa CATHER), her strongest and most representative work. Critics praised the NOVELLA, her 17th book, for having an exquisite writing style, for capturing New England life, land, and language, and for using REGIONALISM, the picturesque, and NATURALISM.

The Country of the Pointed Firs consists of semirelated sketches of people and place, interconnected by an outsider narrator who enters a pastoral, preindustrial region from an industrialized city. Jewett had been concerned with people and place since she began publishing in 1868; in *Country*, perhaps her most masterful attempt at this sort of writing, small cross-sections of the lives of an insular, stereotypically (see STEREOTYPE) New England community based in the fictional town of Dunnet Landing, Maine, intersect and comment on one another. Some of the residents of Dunnet Landing, notably Almira Todd, later appeared in Jewett's short stories, such as "The Foreigner" (1900).

The residents of Dunnet Landing are long-term Maine residents. Jewett tells their stories in a style most often described as weblike, or artistically connected in a complex pattern. These characters have a very close community, and, not surprisingly, their closeness has a somber as well as a communal quality: They frequently exclude those who are not of Dunnet Landing and of European (generally French) descent. Like any small town, Dunnet Landing has characters (in all senses of the word) who refuse to conform to town standards; William Blackett, Captain Littlepage, and Joanna Todd, for instance, attain almost mythic status for their deviance. Those who, like Marie Harris, do not blend in racially, also refuse to adhere to community morals and thus appear coarse and uncivilized.

The narrative pointedly deviates from a traditional, patriarchal way of storytelling, instead almost always weaving outward from Almira Todd's home. (The female METAPHOR of weaving appears apt here.)

Dunnet Landing also focuses on women's friendships: Mrs. Todd and Mrs. Fosdick, lifelong friends, discuss each other's families as if they were their own; Mrs. Todd and Mrs. Blacket share an emotional trip to Green Island; and, in a pivotal scene, Mrs. Todd and the narrator gather pennyroyal, a medicinal herb, for Mrs. Todd's homemade medicine. The land is pastoral, industry is absent, and the trees—firs and spruces—are mentioned as frequently as town locales, like the Bowden farm and Elijah Tilley's fish house. The town, cast as fiercely regional, lies notably distant from the urban landscape where the female narrator used to live.

Many conversations and storytelling moments occur, such as long semidivergent anecdotes by Captain Littlepage and Elijah Tilley, but other stories explicitly address the significance of tradition. Mrs. Todd and Mrs. Fosdick relate the tale of Joanna Todd, who disappeared into self-imposed exile. The narrator—as participant, observer, and the reader's way into the story—travels to Shellheap Island, stands at Joanna's grave, and, as the character frequently does, philosophizes about life inside and outside the world of Dunnet Landing. Ultimately, although the stories of *Country* feature moments of suffering, particularly of women under the subtly present arm of patriarchy, the majority of the tales connect through Jewett's meticulously artistic examinations—often expressed through scenes of EPIPHANY—of love, community, understanding, discovery, and individual fulfillment (Heller xxii).

BIBLIOGRAPHY

Heller, Terry. Introduction. In Sarah Orne Jewett, *The Country of the Pointed Firs and Other Fiction*. New York: Oxford University Press, 1996, vii–xxv.

Howard, June, ed. *New Essays on "The Country of the Pointed Firs."* New York: Cambridge University Press, 1994.

Jewett, Sara Orne. *The Country of the Pointed Firs and Other Fiction*. New York: Oxford University Press, 1996.

Anne N. Thalheimer
University of Delaware

COUSIN LYMON

The hunchbacked dwarf in Carson MCCULLER's *THE BALLAD OF THE SAD CAFE* with whom Miss AMELIA EVANS becomes utterly and irretrievably smitten. In terms of his appearance, we learn how misshapen and physically unappealing he is; in terms of his character, we learn how self-centered, selfish, and lazy he is. Thus his purpose, as a grotesque character, is to personify the beloved, which McCullers famously describes in her classic passage on the characteristics of and differences between the lover and the recipient of that love. Cousin Lymon uses Miss Amelia, of course and, in the end, is himself smitten by Marvin Macy, who cares nothing for Lymon but uses him to defeat Miss Amelia—who has wounded him indelibly by throwing him out of the house. The NOVELLA introduces the possibility that Lymon and Macy first met each other in prison. Whether literally true or not—and there is evidence both for and against a previous acquaintance—McCullers unquestionably demonstrates through the personalities of both men that they recognize the evil thoughts in one another.

COYOTE STORY

Coyote is a character in numerous Native American TRICKSTER tales (see also NATIVE AMERICAN STORYTELLING). A complex figure, Coyote has been described as more ANTI-HERO than HERO, a Native American version of the European EVERYMAN, a flawed character whose greatest weaknesses are vanity and pride. Coyote stories vary from tribe to tribe, but in general Coyote is credited with shaping the past—especially in creation stories—and with embodying hope for the future. Jay Miller notes that the best Coyote stories are heard at wakes, "helping to relieve the grief and keep everyone awake" (Miller ix). Simultaneously edifying and entertaining, Coyote stories have a kinship with traditional European beast FABLES and with the African-American tales told by UNCLE REMUS. Examples of Coyote stories occur in Peter Blue Cloud's 1990 collection *The Other Side of Nowhere: Contemporary Coyote Tales* and in Mourning Dove's *Coyote Stories*, first published in 1933.

BIBLIOGRAPHY

Blue Cloud, Peter. *The Other Side of Nowhere: Contemporary Coyote Tales*. Fredonia, N.Y.: White Pine Press, 1990.

Miller, Jay. "Introduction to the Bison Book Edition." In *Coyote Stories,* by Mourning Dove and edited by Heister Dean Guie, v–xvii. Lincoln: University of Nebraska Press, 1990.

Mourning Dove. *Coyote Stories*. Edited by Heister Dean Guie. Lincoln: University of Nebraska Press, 1990.

CRANE, STEPHEN (1871–1900)

Stephen Crane was born on November 1, 1871, the 14th and youngest child of Methodist minister Jonathan Townley Crane and his wife, Mary Helen Peck Crane. Young Stephen attended various colleges, but he did not take his higher education very seriously. His talent for writing appeared at an early age, and his first article, on the explorer Henry M. Stanley, was published in the February 1890 issue of *Villette*. In 1891 and 1892 he assisted an older brother on stories for the New York *Tribune* to gain further experience in journalistic writing. The writing style Crane developed while working for the newspaper remained with him throughout his career.

Although Stephen Crane is perhaps most remembered for his NOVELLA of the CIVIL WAR, *THE RED BADGE OF COURAGE* (1895), his short stories also show his flair for narrative and description. One of his notable stories is "THE OPEN BOAT," which first appeared in the June 1897 issue of *Scribner's*. This short story grew from the author's personal involvement in the sinking of the *Commodore*, a tugboat that was bringing weapons to Cuba. In this story of four men striving toward shore in a dinghy after their ship has gone down, Crane combines his talent as a journalist with his fiction-writing skill. The resulting tale draws together the "personal and [the] universal" (Davis 191), allowing Crane to tell his own story of that horrific event while also illuminating the struggle of man against the forces of nature.

Other short stories by Crane reveal his strong background in newspaper writing and his ability to combine fact and fiction. His urge toward REALISM in his creation of characters and their situations led him to stand in a breadline without a winter coat when working on "The Men in the Storm" (1894), so that he could accurately describe what it felt like to be cold. Crane also voluntarily slept in a flophouse while he was writing "An Experiment in Misery" (1894) in order to gain a sense of his characters' sufferings in that environment. While some have criticized this element of Crane's writing, claiming that its realism is overly harsh, his ability to write of other people's trials and emotions in such a direct way is one of the characteristics that draws readers to his work. Besides writing of societal ills, Crane also had a passion for history, specifically war history. Although he did not witness the Civil War firsthand, with "Red Badge" Crane proved he could write accurately and poignantly about the experience of battle.

Considered one of his best works on this THEME, "The Upturned Face" (1900) captures the scene of a small group of soldiers and their commanding officer burying a fallen comrade in the midst of combat. In just a handful of pages Crane creates the sounds and emotions of the battle raging both around and within the men as they hesitate to cover their dead friend's cold blue face with dirt. Crane makes the scene immediate for the reader by describing the "windy sound of bullets," the "button . . . brick-red with drying blood," and the "plop" the earth makes as it covers the body of the dead man. This characteristic use of sensory details also operates powerfully in Crane's "Death and the Child" (1898), "The Price of the Harness" (1898), and "An Episode of War" (1899), which are counted among the best of his later war stories.

Crane wrote *Whilomville Stories* (1900), his last major collection of short fiction, while he was battling tuberculosis near the end of his life. These fourteen stories center on scenes of small town life, and many of them have children and childhood as their central theme. Crane's ability to write of human struggles and their accompanying emotions is shown as masterfully in these vignettes of the agonies and ecstasies of childhood as in the war stories that made him famous. For example, "His New Mittens," gives the reader a glimpse inside the mind of a young boy caught between his mother's order not to ruin his red mittens and the taunts of a group of boys playing in the snow. Crane raises the conflicts suffered by this child and the children in the other tales in this collection to the level of the conflict of the men in "The Open Boat" or "The Upturned Face," and he shows the same desire for realism as he does in "An Experiment in Misery." Perhaps Crane's desire to show realistically the significance of childhood events stemmed from his knowledge of his own impending death.

Stephen Crane died in Badenweiler in the Black Forest on June 5, 1900, after a long illness and multiple hemorrhages; he was only 28. During his brief life, Crane's writing had a great impact not only on the general public but also on other writers. In October 1897 Crane had met and befriended novelist Joseph Conrad. Conrad greatly respected and admired Crane's work, and he realized his new friend's incredible talent for capturing events and places he had not actually experienced. The two authors shared their work with each other and remained close friends until Crane's death. Although Crane died at 28, he produced a fairly large body of work. In the four years before his death, he wrote five novels, two collections of poetry, two volumes of war stories, three other story collections, and a variety of journalistic pieces. Stephen Crane's place in the canon of American literature is firmly established, and his short stories remain of interest in studies of such issues as realism and the effects of journalism on fiction writing.

BIBLIOGRAPHY

Adams, Richard P. "Naturalistic Fiction: 'The Open Boat.'" *Tulane Studies in English* 4 (1954): 137–46.

Bais, H.S.S. *Stephen Crane: A Pioneer in Technique.* New Delhi: Crown, 1988.

Beer, Thomas. *Crane: A Study in American Letters.* New York: Knopf, 1923.

Benfey, Christopher E.G. *The Double Life of Crane.* New York: Knopf,1992.

Bergon, Frank. *Stephen Crane's Artistry.* New York: Columbia University Press, 1975.

Berryman, John. *Crane.* New York: Sloane, 1950.

———. *Stephen Crane: The Red Badge of Courage.* Portree, Isle of Skye, Scotland: Aquila, 1981.

Bloom, Harold, ed. *Stephen Crane.* New York: Chelsea House, 1987.

Cady, Edwin H. *Stephen Crane.* New York: Twayne, 1962; revised edition, 1980.

Colvert, James B. *Crane.* San Diego: Harcourt Brace, 1984.

Crane, Stephen. *The Complete Short Stories & Sketches of Stephen Crane.* Edited by Thomas A. Gullason. Garden City, N.Y.: Doubleday, 1963.

———. *The Little Regiment and Other Episodes of the American Civil War.* New York: Appleton, 1896.

———. *The Monster and Other Stories.* New York: Harper, 1899; augmented ed. New York: Harper, 1901.

———. *The Open Boat and Other Tales of Adventure.* New York: Doubleday and McClure, 1898.

———. *The Portable Crane.* Edited by Joseph Katz. New York: Viking, 1969.

———. *Prose and Poetry* (Library of America). Edited by J. C. Levenson. New York: Library of America, 1984.

———. *The Sullivan County Sketches.* Edited by Melvin Schoberlin, Syracuse, N.Y.: Syracuse University Press, 1949; revised ed. published as *Sullivan County Tales and Sketches.* Edited by R. W. Stallman. Ames: Iowa State University Press, 1968.

———. *Whilomville Stories.* New York: Harper, 1900.

———. *Wounds in the Rain: War Stories.* New York: Stokes, 1900.

———. *The Works of Stephen Crane,* 10 vols. Edited by Fredson Bowers. Charlottesville: University of Virginia Press, 1969–76.

Davis, Linda H. *Badge of Courage: The Life of Stephen Crane.* Boston: Houghton Mifflin, 1988.

Gibson, Donald B. *The Fiction of Crane.* Carbondale: Southern Illinois University Press, 1968.

———. *The Red Badge of Courage: Redefining the Hero.* Boston: Houghton Mifflin, 1988.

Haliburton, David. *The Color of the Sky: A Study of Crane.* Cambridge: Cambridge University Press, 1989.

Hoffman, Daniel. *The Poetry of Crane.* New York: Columbia University Press, 1957.

Holton, Milne. *Cylinder of Vision: The Fiction and Journalistic Writing of Crane.* Baton Rouge: Louisiana State University Press, 1972.

Kissane, Leedice. "Interpretation Through Language: A Study of the Metaphors in Crane's 'The Open Boat.'" *Rendezvous* 1 (1966).

Knapp, Bettina L. *Stephen Crane.* New York: Ungar, 1987.

LaFrance, Marston. *A Reading of Crane.* Oxford, England: Clarendon, 1971.

Mariani, Giorgio. *Spectacular Narratives: Representations of Class and War in Stephen Crane and the American 1890s.* New York: Peter Lang, 1992.

Metzger, Charles R. "Realistic Devices in Crane's 'The Open Boat.'" *Midwest Quarterly* 4 (1962).

Mitchell, Lee Clerk, ed. *New Essays on The Red Badge of Courage.* New York: Cambridge University Press, 1986.

Nagel, James. *Crane and Literary Impressionism.* University Park: Pennsylvania State University Press, 1980.

Pizer, Donald, ed. *Critical Essays on Stephen Crane.* Boston: G. K. Hall, 1990.

Robertson, Michael. *Stephen Crane, Journalism, and the Making of Modern American Literature.* New York: Columbia University Press, 1997.

Solomon, Eric. *Stephen Crane in England: A Portrait of the Artist.* Columbus: Ohio State University Press, 1964.

———. *Crane: From Parody to Realism.* Cambridge, Mass.: Harvard University Press.

Stallman, R. W. *Stephen Crane: A Biography.* New York: George Braziller, 1968.

Tibbets, A. M. "Crane's 'The Bridge Comes to Yellow Sky.'" *English Journal* 54 (1965).

Weatherford, Richard, ed. *Stephen Crane: The Critical Heritage.* Boston: Routledge, 1973.

Wolford, Chester L. *The Anger of Crane: Fiction and the Epic Tradition.* Lincoln: University of Nebraska Press, 1983.

———. *Stephen Crane: A Study of the Short Fiction.* San Diego, Calif.: Greenhaven Press, 1989.

Sara J. Triller
University of Delaware

CYBERPUNK A popular GENRE named for its computer cowboy heroes and related to SCIENCE FICTION. Cyberpunk stories are set in a futuristic, dystopic environment—the opposite of utopian—in which computer technology plays an important role. Although the cyberpunk world can be described as postmodern, the genre is distinguished from literary POSTMODERNISM by a more traditionally realistic style. The PROTAGONISTS of cyberpunk stories are technologically proficient, lonely adventurers struggling with issues of identity and forced to use computer skills to fight menacing forces of domination. William GIBSON, whose collection of short stories, *Burning Chrome,* is exemplary of cyberpunk, is the genre's best-known author.

Karen Fearing
University of North Carolina at Chapel Hill

D

DADA Originating from the French word for hobby horse, the term was chosen randomly from the dictionary for the literary and artistic movement founded in 1916 in Zurich by Tristan Tzara, artist Hans Arp, poet Hugo Ball, and medical student Richard Huelsenbeck. The movement intentionally rejected all traditional philosophical and artistic values. Its leaders intended dadaism as a protest against WORLD WAR I and its awesome destruction of civilization. The *Dada Review* proclaimed its intention to replace logic and reason with deliberate madness and to substitute intentionally discordant chaos for established notions of beauty or harmony in the arts. Dadaists mocked conventional behavior; some dada meetings turned into riots; art exhibits were mocking hoaxes. The artist and writer André Breton and his followers became interested in the subconscious, breaking with Tzara in 1921 and officially founding SURREALISM in 1924. Gertrude STEIN's radical experiments with language have roots in dadaism. Revived in the 1930s in parts of England and the United States, certain aspects of dadaism survive in the "theater of the ABSURD." In retrospect critics recognize much of dadaism's shock value in certain forms of POSTMODERNISM, and, although the term is normally applied to art and poetry, it can usefully describe radical experiments in short fiction in both the early and late 20th century.

"DAEMON LOVER, THE" SHIRLEY JACKSON (1949) In "The Daemon Lover," James (Jamie) Harris, a handsome author, deserts his dowdy, 34-year old fiancée. The plot of this short story may be indebted to "The Demon Lover" by Elizabeth Bowen, whom Jackson ranked with Katherine Anne PORTER as one of the best contemporary short story writers. When Jamie Harris disappears, he shatters his bride's dreams of living in a "golden house in-the-country" (DL 12). Her shock of recognition that she will never trade her lonely city apartment for a loving home mirrors the final scenes of "THE LOTTERY" and "The Pillar of Salt" as well as many other stories in which a besieged woman suffers a final and often fatal blow.

In "The Daemon Lover," the second story in *The Lottery and Other Stories,* Jackson's collection of 25 tales, the reader sees James Harris only through his fiancée's eyes as a tall man wearing a blue suit. Neither the reader nor anyone in the story can actually claim to have seen him. Nonetheless, this piece foreshadows the appearance of Harris in such other stories in the collection as "Like Mother Used to Make," "The Village," "Of Course," "Seven Types of Ambiguities," and "The Tooth." As James Harris wanders through the book, he sheds the veneer of the ordinary that covers his satanic nature.

The IRONY in "The Daemon Lover" is that the female PROTAGONIST becomes suspect as she hunts for the mysterious young man "who promised to marry her" (DL 23). Everywhere she searches, she encounters couples who mock her with the not-so-subtle insinuations that she is crazy. Indeed, at the end of the story she may well have gone insane; the narrative is ambiguous on this point. Significantly, however, if the nameless woman has indeed lost her mind, it is James who is responsible. Although some critics speculate that the disruptive male figure—both in this story and the others in the collection—are hallucinations of a sexually repressed character, the epilogue to *The Lottery,* a ballad entitled "James Harris, The Daemon Lover," suggests otherwise: He is, in fact, the devil himself.

For Jackson, *The Lottery* is more than a GHOST STORY; "The Daemon Lover" in particular and the collection in general critique a society that fails to protect women from becoming victims of strangers or neighbors. As in "The Lottery," Jackson's shocking account of a housewife's ritualistic stoning, or in "The Pillar of Salt," which traces a wife's horror and growing hysteria when she has lost her way, the threatened characters are women. Although many of Jackson's stories are modern versions of the folk tale of a young wife's abduction by the devil, and although her characters are involved in terrifying circumstances, the point is that these tales seem true: They are rooted in reality. Thus, Jackson exposes the threat to women's lives in a society that condones the daemon lover.

BIBLIOGRAPHY

Oppenheimer, Judy. *Private Demons: The Life of Shirley Jackson.* New York: Putnam, 1988.

Wylie, Joan. *Shirley Jackson: A Study of the Short Fiction.* New York: Twayne, 1994.

Harriet P. Gold
LaSalle College
Dawson College

DAHLBERG, EDWARD (1900–1977)

Dahlberg's early life hardly portended his emergence as a novelist, essayist, poet, and critic. Born to an unmarried woman, he spent much of his childhood in orphanages and at age 17 was on the road as a hobo. His first novels, *Bottom Dogs* (1929) and *From Flushing to Calvary* (1932), drew on personal experience and were examples of PROLETARIAN LITERATURE, which included novels and short stories sympathetic to the struggles and plights of the working class. Both of Dahlberg's novels received critical attention and a significant readership. Although Dahlburg wrote these novels in the style of NATURALISM, however, the style of his later work became more allusive and epigrammatic. (See ALLUSION and EPIGRAM.) His POINT OF VIEW was intensely personal and moral, and his criticism considered incisive. His critical works, which include *Do These Bones Live?* (1941; rev. as *Can These Bones Live?,* 1960), *The Flea of Sodom* (1950), and *The Sorrows of Priapus* (1957), attacked modern culture and criticized such American literary icons as William FAULKNER, Ernest HEMINGWAY, and F. Scott FITZGERALD. Among the few writers whom he praised were Henry David Thoreau, Sherwood ANDERSON, and Theodore DREISER. Dahlberg's views are echoed in such stories as those in Anderson's WINESBURG, OHIO, Hamlin GARLAND's "Under the Lion's Paw," Richard WRIGHT's "THE MAN WHO WAS ALMOST A MAN," and—somewhat ironically given his lack of admiration for Faulkner—Faulkner's "BARN BURNING."

DAISY MILLER: A STUDY HENRY JAMES (1878, 1879)

Henry JAMES's NOVELLA—or *nouvelle,* as he called it—literally took the reading public by storm when it appeared in serial form in the British magazine *Cornhill* in 1878. It features an unsophisticated, strikingly lovely young woman from Schenectady, New York, who travels to Europe and defies the conventions of a group of Europeanized Americans who enforce the rules of the older European community with unthinking severity. Published in book form in 1879 and as a play in 1883, *Daisy Miller* aroused a good deal of controversy, some reviewers calling it a libel on American manners, but it later became one of the most popular of James's writings. William Dean HOWELLS reportedly said that members of society divided themselves into "Daisy Millerites" or "Anti-Daisy

Millerites," and Daisy Miller hats appeared everywhere (Hocks 32). Today the story still appears as a standard in American literature anthologies and continues to arouse readers' interest.

The story is told through a nominal first-person narrator, but all the information is filtered through the central consciousness of Frederick Winterbourne, a young expatriate American who has lived in Europe since age 12. On meeting Daisy, her mother, Mrs. Miller, and her brother, Randolph, at a hotel in Vevey, Switzerland, he finds himself fascinated with Daisy but somewhat shocked at her disregard of European customs regarding the proper behavior for a young unmarried woman. Throughout the story he seeks to discover whether Daisy is essentially "innocent," but in the process he—and the reader—learns a good deal about his own prejudices and motivations. Winterbourne learns the answer at the end of the story, but too late: Daisy dies, and he must share some of the responsibility for her death.

Winterbourne's name suggests his coldness, and, indeed, he lives most of the year in Geneva, Switzerland, characterized in the novella as a dark, grim, brooding locus of Protestantism. James uses locale to point up differences in temperament, and Rome—the site of Daisy's death—is in some senses Geneva's opposite, suffused in sunshine and color, attractive with its cathedrals but also implicitly dangerous with its pre-Christian sites of antiquity. Winterbourne never comes to terms with his rather hypocritical view of sex: He pays lip service to the proprieties espoused by his aunt, Mrs. Costello, and her coterie, yet the narrator reminds us more than once that he constantly "studies" in Geneva, an apparent euphemism for his affair with a safely married foreign woman. Winterbourne ignores or fails to recognize his sexual response to Daisy; her obstreperous 12-year-old brother (the same age as Winterbourne when he moved to Europe) provides an intriguing male counterpart to Winterbourne with his Freudian brandishing of his "alpenstock," a hiking stick, as they discuss American girls.

Most critics find Daisy Miller perplexing, difficult to pin down. Many see her as frivolous, as indeed in some sense she is. But she is natural, good, and, as we learn with Winterbourne (whose viewpoint we find difficult to shake) at the end, completely innocent. The very fact that her innocence is an issue makes Daisy a sympathetic figure: Roman fever, or malaria, is the ostensible cause of her death, but it becomes a METAPHOR for the attitude toward and preoccupation with her innocence, her virtue. Daisy dies precisely because the concept means so much to Winterbourne and his wealthy social group. A FEMINIST perspective helps to illuminate this story's complexity and to decipher the reprehensible nature of the men like Winterbourne—and the women like his aunt who help them perpetuate the standards of behavior for young women. Daisy Miller's fate provides a fascinating contrast to the women in Edith WHARTON's "ROMAN FEVER," almost surely a woman writer's response to James's novella.

BIBLIOGRAPHY
Hocks, Richard A. *Henry James: A Study of the Short Fiction.* Boston: Twayne, 1990.
James, Henry. *Daisy Miller: A Study. The Complete Tales of Henry James.* Edited by Leon Edel. Philadelphia: Lippincott, 1961–64, vol. 18.

"DARING YOUNG MAN ON THE FLYING TRAPEZE, THE"   See SAROYAN, WILLIAM.

DARWIN, CHARLES ROBERT (1809–1882)
An English naturalist, Charles Darwin published *On the Origin of Species* (1859), which sets forth his theory of natural selection, to angry reactions and bitterly controversial reviews. Darwin's observations of animals led to his now famous statement that only the "fittest" of any species survive; the process is nature's way of weeding out the weakest of any species so that only the strongest remain to propagate their kind. This theory, known as Darwinism, has had a profound influence on human concepts of life, and the book is considered one of the most important works ever in the field of natural philosophy. His ideas were generated on the H.M.S. *Beagle* on an expedition (1831–36) to southern Pacific islands, South American coasts, and Australia. Darwin's theories have influenced stories by such writers as Jack LONDON and Tennessee Williams.

DAVIS, REBECCA (BLAINE) HARDING
(1831–1910) Rebecca Davis is considered one of the first American realist writers. (See REALISM.) Although Davis was reared in a well-to-do household in industrial Wheeling, West Virginia, her first published story, "Life in the Iron Mills," which appeared in ATLANTIC MONTHLY in April 1861, grimly portrayed the sordid lives of iron-mill workers, who were depicted doing brutally hard work and living in a world devoid of emotional or spiritual uplift, hope, or justice. This work was a precursor to the "muckraking" literature (see MUCKRAKERS) that would be published at the turn of the century. This story, which introduced new elements of NATURALISM and realism to American literature, brought Davis fame and the acquaintance of other professional authors, including Nathaniel HAWTHORNE. She continued to write, addressing such problems as racial bias and political corruption, but none of these efforts equaled her first work in imaginative power. "Life in the Iron Mills" influenced Tillie OLSEN to such a degree that she introduced and republished the story in 1972. Davis was also an associate editor of the *New York Tribune,* and some critics have reassessed her as a more talented and more important writer than her renowned son, Richard Harding DAVIS.

BIBLIOGRAPHY
Davis, Rebecca Harding. *Life in The Iron Mills and Other Stories.* Edited by with an afterword by Tillie Olsen. New York: Feminist Press, 1972.
Rose, Jane Atteridge. "Reading 'Life in the Iron Mills' Contextually: A Key to Rebecca Harding Davis's Fiction." In *Conversations: Contemporary Critical Theory and the Teaching of Literature.* Edited by Charles Moran and Elizabeth F. Penfield. Urbana, Il.: National Council of Teachers of English, 1990.

DAVIS, RICHARD HARDING (1864–1916)
The son of Rebecca Harding DAVIS, Richard Davis was a journalist who covered wars all over the world and was among the leading reporters of his time. He is typically associated with the MAUVE DECADE of the 1890s, and although his fiction is largely viewed as superficial, he was a talented storyteller; indeed, he was one of the highest-paid and most popular short story writers of his era. Davis wrote novels, plays, and stories in which he created such notable characters as Gallegher, the enterprising office boy, and the good-deed-doer Cortland Van Bibber. Davis's fiction often depicted the superficial nature of turn-of-the-century society, of which he was a prominent member.

DAY, CLARENCE (SHEPHARD), JR.
(1874–1935) Clarence Day primarily wrote humorous stories. His best-known works were based on reminiscences of his parents. One of these, "Life with Father" (1937), was made into a long-running Broadway play in 1939 by Russel Crouse and Howard Lindsay. With a gentle humor, Day recalls his rather domineering father and his soft-spoken mother, whose will nearly always prevailed.

BIBLIOGRAPHY
Day, Clarence, Jr. *God and My Father.* New York: Knopf, 1932.
———. *Life with Father.* New York: Knopf, 1935.
———. *Life with Mother.* New York: Knopf, 1937.

"DEATH OF A BEAUTIFUL WOMAN"
Edgar Allan POE's famous (or infamous, according to many FEMINIST critics) dictum first set out in his essay "The Philosophy of Composition," originally published in *Graham's Magazine* in April 1846. Poe contends that beauty is the province of poetry and death the most melancholy of poetical topics; hence, when the poet combines the two concepts, "the death of a beautiful woman" is the world's most poetical topic. Further, the best person to tell the story of her death is the grieving lover. The THEME occurs in many Poe stories, such as "LIGEIA" and "THE FALL OF THE HOUSE OF USHER," but as critics have pointed out, it also occurs in much literature of both the 19th and 20th centuries. See, for example, Nathaniel HAWTHORNE's "RAPPACCINI'S DAUGHTER" and "THE BIRTHMARK," Henry JAMES's *DAISY MILLER,* Kate CHOPIN's "DESIREE'S BABY," and Dorothy PARKER's "Big Blonde."

DECADENCE A term used in both literary and art history for the decline that marks the end of a great artistic period. The term is relative to the particular period it identifies, and the general characteristics of decadence are often self-consciousness, artificiality, overrefinement, and perversity. (See MAUVE DECADE.)

"DEER IN THE WORKS" KURT VONNEGUT (1955)

In this story family man David Potter contemplates giving up his own weekly small-town newspaper in favor of taking a public relations job at the Ilium Works of the Federal Apparatus Corporation. The Works is a sprawling maze of clanking machinery and pollution. Potter fears that his newspaper income may not continue to support his growing family, so he tries to convince himself that he'll be better off as a company man, with the life insurance, health care, and future pension that accompany a long-term commitment to the Works.

After learning that a deer is loose on the grounds, his new supervisor sends Potter off to cover the story. The plan is to snap some photos, write up a press release, then serve the venison at the company's Quarter-Century Club, where 25-year veterans dine and smoke cigars.

Along the way, David becomes hopelessly lost. By the time he stumbles upon the scene, the overwhelming environment has numbed his spirit and sickened his body. Potter finds himself between the deer—its antlers broken and its coat smeared with soot and grease—and a gate leading to lush, green pine woods. With little hesitation he opens the gate, releasing the deer into the woods. As the deer's white tail disappears into the trees, David follows it, leaving the Ilium Works behind without looking back.

What is most interesting about this story beyond its message of following one's heart and the familiar THEME of the dehumanizing effect of the Big Corporation is that it is largely an autobiographical FANTASY. Before making a living as a writer, Vonnegut had a public relations job with General Electric, which he openly loathed. It is entirely possible that Vonnegut's experience at GE was a major contributing factor to his pursuit of short stories as a means to write his way out of his day job. While his stories later financed the writing of his novels, they first provided him an escape from the corporate world. One has to wonder whether most (or any) of Vonnegut's short stories would have come to be had he instead owned a small-town weekly newspaper.

David Larry Anderson

"DELTA AUTUMN" WILLIAM FAULKNER (1942)

The sixth chapter of William FAULKNER's GO DOWN, MOSES, "Delta Autumn" tells the story of Ike McCaslin's last hunting trip into the Mississippi Delta. While earlier chapters record young Isaac's rite of passage in the big woods, in this chapter we are presented with an older Uncle Ike, who "no longer told anyone how near eighty he actually was because he knew as well as they did that he no longer had any business making such expeditions" (GDM 336). Ike's age, however, is not so much at issue here as is his heritage when he discovers that his nephew Roth fathered a child by a mulatto woman in the Delta during their hunting trip the year before. While the hunting party jokes with Roth about his interest in hunting does instead of bucks, Uncle Ike is filled with "amazement, pity, and outrage" (GDM 361). For Ike discovers that he knows the mother of the child: She is the granddaughter of James Beauchamp, or Tennie's Jim, a black descendant of Ike's grandfather, Lucius Quintus Carothers McCaslin, whose sins Ike discovers in "THE BEAR." Thus, says Faulkner critic Cleanth Brooks, "Isaac knows that once more a descendant of old Carother's McCaslin's slave Eunice has been injured by a descendant of old Carothers" (Brooks 272).

The confrontation between Ike and this young woman, which is the most important exchange in the story, provides Faulkner with the dramatic setting within which to explore further Ike's repudiation of his land and of his heritage because of the sins of Carothers. Ultimately, Faulkner seems to call into question Ike's decision to repudiate the young woman and her baby, characterizing it as one born more out of irresponsibility than honor.

BIBLIOGRAPHY
Brooks, Cleanth, *William Faulkner: The Yoknapatawpha Country.* New Haven, Conn.: Yale University Press, 1963.
Faulkner, William. *Go Down, Moses.* New York: Random House, 1942.

H. Collin Messer
University of North Carolina at Chapel Hill

DE MAN, PAUL (1919–   )

One of the foremost architects of the school of literary criticism known as deconstruction, de Man was born in Antwerp in 1919. He received a Ph.D. from Harvard University in 1960 and subsequently became a professor of English at Yale University, where he, Geoffrey Hartman and J. Hillis Miller became known as the Yale School Critics. Although De Man's reputation has been tarnished by the discovery of early articles written for the pro-Nazi newspaper *Le Soir,* he articulated the practice of deconstruction with passion and intelligence.

De Man once provocatively told an interviewer that he never had an idea on his own. His ideas, he claimed, always came from a text. In this way, De Man meant to draw attention to his own rigorous form of close reading. Unlike the close readings of the NEW CRITICISM, which were to be conducted with certain predetermined issues in mind, De Man's characteristic practice is to expose the "aporia" (ambivalence) of literary texts by following the logic (or, more precisely, the antilogic) of the text in question without recourse to extratextual resources. In a famous example, De Man criticizes literary scholars who have always read the last lines of William Butler Yeats's "Among School Children" ("How can we know the dancer from the dance?") as a rhetorical question. What textual evidence do critics have for such a view, De Man asks, and what happens if we read these lines as a question about which the poet is genuinely curious? Such a view is demonstrably more faithful to the text in question. Moreover, as De Man goes on to show, it significantly alters any interpretation of the poem by pointing to the ways in which a text's "official" meaning is undermined by the rhetorical (i.e., figural) properties of language—the unstable and alien symbol system in which that meaning is constituted.

BIBLIOGRAPHY
De Man, Paul. *Blindness and Insight: Essays in the Rhetoric of Contemporary Criticism,* 2nd ed. Minneapolis: University of Minnesota Press, 1983.
———. *The Resistance to Theory.* Minneapolis: University of Minnesota Press, 1986.
Graef, Ortwin de. *Titanic Light: Paul de Man's Post-Romanticism, 1960–1969.* Lincoln: University of Nebraska Press, 1995.
Lehman, David. *Signs of the Times: Deconstruction and the Fall of Paul De Man.* New York: Poseidon Press, 1991.
Norris, Christopher. *Paul de Man, Deconstruction and the Critique of Aesthetic Ideology.* New York: Routledge, 1988.

Shannon Zimmerman
University of Georgia

DENOUEMENT

From the French word for "untying," in fiction and drama, *denouement* refers to the final unwinding of the tangled elements of the plot that ends the suspense; it follows the CLIMAX. The word is also applied to the resolution of complicated sets of actions in life. See CATASTROPHE and SURPRISE ENDING.

DESANI, G(OVINDAS) V(ISHNOODAS) (1909–   )

G. V. Desani's published fiction consists of one novel, *All about H. Hatten,* and a small number of short stories, collected as *Hali and Collected Stories.* In *Hali,* Desani, born in Kenya, educated in India, and currently professor emeritus at the University of Texas at Austin, offers 23 stories and FABLES, along with a dramatic prose poem, "Hali," that range from bleakness to ironic COMEDY and from supernatural tales to highly mannered satires. The prose poem—which tells the story of Hali, who loves Rooh, whose death plunges Hali into grief and a mystical journey—is most noteworthy as an example of private mythology turned into accessible invocation. The supernatural element in many of the other fictions is strong: "The Valley of Lions," for example, is short and visionary; "Mephisto's Daughter" concerns a narrator who has access to "Old Ugly's daughter"; and "The Lama Arupa" follows the holy man of the title through "several states of consciousness" after his death, until he returns as a chicken. "The Merchant of Kisingarh" is told by a deceased merchant speaking through his son, a sometime medium. These pieces manage to be both wry and penetrating by turns. "A Border Incident," more traditional, tells of a man punished for deserting his post to save a boy's life. Desani also offers a mock lecture ("Rudyard Kipling's Evaluation of His Own Mother") on one of Kipling's more ludicrous compositions, and he closes with the phantasmagoric "The Mandatory Interview of the Dean," a hilarious satire of bureaucracy and officiousness. Desani's varied collection is impressive in its use of religious and personal mythology—and lushly descriptive of a sensibility and a culture that is part English, part Indian, and uniquely Desani's own.

"The Last Long Letter" records the ecstatic visions of a young man, a suicide who casts his soul back into the opaque void of the universe, where it had been a light, as he has previously cast his jeweled ring into the depths of the sea to symbolize his belief that from time to time spirit illuminates matter but then withdraws, leaving all in chaos and darkness until its next coming. Taken together, these stories, mainly satires and fantasies, further exemplify the talent that made *All about H. Hatten* one of our century's major contributions to the literature of the ABSURD.

Desani immigrated to the United States and became a U.S. citizen in 1979.

BIBLIOGRAPHY

Desani, G. V. *All about H. Hatten: A Novel.* New Paltz, N.Y.: McPherson, 1986.

———. *Hali & Collected Stories.* New York: McPherson, 1991.

"DESIRE AND THE BLACK MASSEUR"
TENNESSEE WILLIAMS (1946) This Tennessee Williams short story, written in 1946, was first published in the 1948 volume *One Arm and Other Stories.* The tale is at once a sadomasochistic fantasy and a homosexual ALLEGORY of religious atonement. Anthony Burns is a 30-year-old clerk in an unnamed city that seems to be New Orleans; he is

an "incomplete" and timid creature about to achieve and atone for his previously unrealized masochistic desire. When his coworker recommends a massage to help cure his backache, Burns encounters a huge "Negro" masseur who senses in Burns "an unusual something" and assaults Burns's body with blows of increasing violence that eventually bring Burns to orgasm. For Burns, suffering is intrinsically tied to sexual release, and with his first massage, Burns fulfills his desires. The story moves swiftly to its inevitable conclusion as his massages escalate in their level of violence. Burns and the masseur are evicted from the bathhouse after the masseur breaks Burns's leg, so they continue at the masseur's home. The CLIMAX of the story takes place during the week of Lent (this celebration of "human atonement"), when the Negro masseur slowly beats Burns to death with the latter's full consent, and then, in a symbolic act of cannibalistic communion, takes "twenty-four hours to eat the splintered bones clean." In the tale's DENOUEMENT the masseur obtains another job in a massage parlor and is "serenely conscious of fate bringing toward him another, to suffer atonement as it had been suffered by Burns."

Atonement in "Desire and the Black Masseur" is defined as the "surrender of self to violent treatment by others." The ceremonial violence of Burns's destruction and the fact that his death coincides with Easter seem to point to a concept of Christ as an anonymous EVERYMAN with unconscious erotic desires who is crucified for our sins while "the earth's whole population twisted and writhed beneath the manipulation of the night's black fingers and the white ones of day with skeletons splintered and flesh reduced to pulp, as out of this unlikely problem, the answer, perfection, was slowly evolved through torture." Exactly what the sins of the world are remain ambiguous: Is it "incompletion," whether sexual or spiritual, or is it desire in itself? Spirituality, desire, and even death are inseparable in the GOTHIC love story of Anthony Burns and his black giant, and so, too, Williams seems to say, is our own redemption through the death of this masochistic Christ figure.

BIBLIOGRAPHY

Vannatta, Dennis. *Tennessee Williams: A Study of the Short Fiction*, New York: Macmillan, 1988.

S. L. Yentzer
University of Georgia

"DESIREE'S BABY" KATE CHOPIN (1892)

Kate CHOPIN's brief but mesmerizing story opens in medias res, with Madame Valmonde preparing to visit her adopted daughter Desiree, recently married to the wealthy Louisiana plantation owner Armand d'Aubigny and even more recently delivered of a baby girl. Then, in a series of FLASHBACKS, the narrator reveals Desiree's uncertain origins as a foundling, her beauty as she grew to womanhood, and Armand's passionate proposal of marriage. The narrator then returns to the present and, using briefly effective images, sketches the hierarchical plantation system of whites, quadroons, and blacks. Using Mme. Valmonde's perspective, the narrator reveals that the baby does not look white—and so the tragedy of this story moves rapidly to its completion.

According to critic Ann Charters, few readers would not be horrified and disgusted by the results of the racism and sexism that permeate this story. No one could believe that Armand Aubigny's inhuman cruelty to his wife Desiree and his child is warranted. The only real uncertainty for the reader concerns Armand's foreknowledge of his own parentage: Did he know that his mother had Negro blood before he married Desiree, or did he discover her revealing letter later on? If he *did* know beforehand (and it is difficult to believe that he did not), his courtship of and marriage to Desiree were highly calculated actions, with Desiree chosen because she was the perfect woman to be used in an "experimental" reproduction. If their child(ren) "passed" as white, Armand would be pleased and would keep the marriage intact. If not, Desiree, the foundling, would be the perfect victim to take the blame.

This may seem to be judging Armand too harshly, because the narrator does describe his great passion for Desiree, so suddenly and furiously ignited.

Certainly Armand behaves like a man in love. But Chopin inserts a few subtle remarks that allow us to question this, at least in hindsight: "The wonder was that he had not loved her before; for he had known her since his father brought him home from Paris, a boy of eight, after his mother died there." It does seem unlikely that a man of Armand's temperament would conceive this sudden intense desire for "the girl next door," a sweet, naive young woman whom he has known for most of his life. Right from the beginning, Chopin also reveals details about his character that are unsettling, even to the innocent and loving Desiree. The basic cruelty of Armand's nature is hinted at throughout the story, particularly regarding his severe treatment of "his negroes."

Armand's reputation as a harsh slavemaster supports the presumption that he has known about his own part-Negro ancestry all along. He did not learn this behavior from his father, who was "easy-going and indulgent" in his dealings with the slaves. The knowledge that some of his own ancestors spring from the same "race of slavery" would surely be unbearable to the proud, "imperious" Armand, and the rage and shame that this knowledge brings would easily be turned against the blacks around him. In much the same way, when Armand realizes that his baby is visibly racially mixed, he vents his fury viciously on his slaves, the "very spirit of Satan [taking] hold of him."

Modern readers will find many disturbing aspects to this story. The seemingly casual racism is horrifying. Feminists are likely to take exception (as they sometimes do to Chopin's *The Awakening*) to Desiree's passive acceptance of Armand's rejection of her and his child and her apparently deliberate walk into the bayou. Suicide is not the strong woman's answer to the situation, but Desiree is definitely not a strong woman. What she does have is wealthy parents who love her and are willing to take care of her and the baby. Why does she feel that she has to end her life? Gender and class roles and structures were so rigid in this period that it was impossible for a woman to cross those lines very far; the racial barrier was the most rigid of all. No mixing of black and white blood would ever be condoned in that society, so Desiree's baby would never find acceptance anywhere. The only hope in the tale is the portrait of Mme. Valmonde, but she is powerless to prevent the tragedy the brutal system has both set in motion and perpetuated.

BIBLIOGRAPHY

Charters, Ann. *Resources for Teaching Major Writers of Short Fiction.* Boston: Bedford-St. Martin's, 1993, pp. 43–44.

Chopin, Kate. *The Complete Works of Kate Chopin.* Edited by Per Seyersted. Baton Rouge: Louisiana State University Press, 1969.

Koloski, Bernard. *Kate Chopin: A Study of the Short Fiction.* New York: Twayne, 1996.

DE SPAIN   Always signifying a "man's man" in William FAULKNER's stories, Manfred de Spain appears in Faulkner's *The Town* and *The Mansion* as the true love of the earth goddess Eula Varner. He also appears in numerous short stories, such as "BARN BURNING," in which he displays a degree of sympathy and a sense of justice to such benighted characters as the hapless ABNER SNOPES. He is Faulkner's only SPANISH-AMERICAN WAR hero.

DETECTIVE SHORT FICTION   The detective story is often defined narrowly to prevent confusing it with the crime story or the puzzle story. Frederic Dannay, writing as his alter ego Ellery Queen in 1942, summed it up most succinctly when he called it "a tale of ratiocination, complete with crime and/or mystery, suspects, investigation, clues, deduction, and solution; in its purest form the chief character should be a detective, amateur or professional, who devotes most of his (or her) time to the problems of detection" (Queen, The Detective Short Story: A Bibliography, v).

The pure detective story begins with the crime (murder, robbery, or blackmail, for instance) during which the criminal makes mistakes and inadvertently leaves clues that the detective must be clever enough to recognize. The detective fits together the evidence and identifies the perpetrator of the crime. This formula differs from that of the crime story in which the criminal may be the central figure and the story concerns his motive for committing the crime. He may or may not escape the law. The puzzle story involves the solution to a mystery or quandary; a crime may not even have occurred. (Edgar Allan POE's "The Gold Bug," 1843, is an example of a puzzle story.) The suspense story, meanwhile, has no central detective to solve the mystery but may have a protagonist who becomes involved in events and situations that must be resolved by the end of the story. There are also variants of the detective story, such as the police procedural in which the police solve the mystery by the use of official police methods. Many readers refer to all of these stories as murder mysteries, even when there is no murder and little mystery. The pure detective story resembles a crossword puzzle and involves the reader in attempting to discover the solution to the mystery along with the detective.

The earliest example of a detective story appears in "The History of Bel" in the apocryphal scriptures: Daniel spreads ashes on the floor of the temple and, by identifying the footprints left behind, reveals who has been stealing the offerings from the altar. Other early literary examples featuring crime solvers are Boccaccio's *Decameron,* Chaucer's *The Canterbury Tales, The Arabian Nights,* and Voltaire's *Zadig; or, The Book of Fate.*

The detective story as we have come to recognize it owes its creation to Poe, whose influence may be one reason for considering the short form preferable to the long form. Indeed, probably because of Poe's major role in defining the form, early writer-critics such as Howard Haycraft, Ronald Knox, Dorothy L. Sayers, Vincent Starrett, H. Douglas Thomson, Charles Honce, G. K. Chesterton, Charles Bragin, and E. C. Bentley argued for the short story as the proper form for detective fiction. The short detective story centers on one intensive idea (the crime committed and the detective's solution) where the situation must be resolved quickly to maintain the desired effect. There is little room for depth of characterization or a change of setting as in the novel.

In three short stories—"THE MURDERS IN THE RUE MORGUE" (1841), "The Mystery of Marie Roget"

(1842), and "THE PURLOINED LETTER" (1844)—Poe set down most of the elements now considered necessary for the true detective story. These include the omniscient private citizen–detective; his less-than-astute assistant, who sometimes serves as narrator; and an official police representative, who may offer a theory that the detective proves wrong. Other elements include the discovery of false clues or "red herrings," and the gradual unraveling of the solution to the mystery that culminates in a dramatic scene in which the explanation is provided. Robert A. W. Lowndes has actually identified 32 of these elements central to the detective story in Poe's three tales about C. AUGUSTE DUPIN, the first fictional detective to appear in a series of stories.

Fifty years later, Sir Arthur Conan Doyle in the Sherlock Holmes stories for the *Strand* magazine (beginning in 1891) adapted Poe's elements and created a more realistic relationship between Holmes, the detective, and Dr. Watson, the narrator. Doyle also created the trademark element of the enigmatic phrase by which the detective hints at the solution, toying with both the narrator and the reader, without making the solution explicit. The most famous is the passage about the "dog in the night time" in Doyle's "Silver Blaze" (collected in *The Memoirs of Sherlock Holmes*, 1982) in which the dog's failure to bark or attack in the night time suggests that the criminal was someone with whom the dog was familiar.

The success of the Sherlock Holmes short stories in particular, and the popularity of detective fiction in general, inspired the editors of general fiction magazines to add series about detectives to their schedules. A succession of stories with a continuing central character brought readers back for each succeeding issue and sold magazines. Each editor wanted his own Sherlock Holmes who could entice the customers. Few of these fictional detectives are remembered today, but there was a time when *Cosmopolitan*, the SATURDAY EVENING POST, COLLIER'S, LADIES' HOME JOURNAL, and other publications included detective stories in their pages on a regular basis. Among these were the scientific detective stories featuring Craig Kennedy (e.g., "The Silent Bullet,"

[1912]), by Arthur B. Reeve (1880–1936); the Thinking Machine stories (e.g., "The Problem of Cell 13" [1907]), by Jacques Futrelle (1875–1912); stories of Average Jones, fraudulent advertising investigator (e.g., "The Man Who Spoke Latin" [1911]), by Samuel Hopkins Adams (1871–1958); of Uncle Abner, Virginia squire (e.g., "Doomdorf Mystery" [1918]), by Melville Davisson Post (1871–1930); of Jim Hanvey (e.g., "Common Stock" [1923]), by Octavus Roy Cohen (1891–1959); and of Professor Poggioli (e.g., "A Passage to Benares" [1929]), by Pulitzer Prize–winning author T. S. Stribling (1881–1965). These stories appeared in addition to serialized detective novels in the same periodicals.

The most significant change in the development of the genre came in the 1920s in the pages of the American pulp magazine BLACK MASK. The first important author in the pages of *Black Mask* was Dashiell HAMMETT, the father of the hard-boiled detective story (see HARD-BOILED FICTION). Hammett spun fairy tales inhabited by real people. In the words of his most significant successor, Raymond CHANDLER, in "The Simple Art of Murder" (1944), Hammett "gave murder back to the people who commit it for reasons, not just to provide a corpse" and didn't use fancy poisons or weapons either (Chandler, 234). The two of them, working independently, revitalized the genre with stories of detectives SAM SPADE, the Continental Op, Hammet's earliest series detective, a nameless operative for the Continental Detective Agency, and PHILIP MARLOWE, Chandler's private eye. Other writers followed, and emulated, but never duplicated the achievements of Hammett and Chandler. Eventually the two (along with Ross MacDonald) became a triumvirate representing the hard-boiled school. Other pulp magazines such as *Dime Detective* and *Detective Fiction Weekly* imitated the format and content of *Black Mask*.

The hard-boiled detective story is the urban equivalent of the Western in American fiction. Like other stories of REALISM, the detective story deals with human problems but in a world in which the problems can be solved. The situations are often fantastic; their authors render them realistic through their writing styles, especially the believable dialogue and the detailed descriptions of actual places.

During his lifetime Hammett published only five novels but dozens of short stories. In spite of the popularity of these stories in both the pulp and slick magazines, the recognition of Hammett's contribution to the short story did not really come until various presses began to collect and publish his short stories in the 1940s, making them as available as his novels to a wider public.

Chandler's first story, "Blackmailers Don't Shoot," appeared in *Black Mask* in December 1933. Other stories were published in *Dime Detective* and *Detective Story*. His first short story collection, *Five Murderers*, was published in 1944 by Avon Murder Mystery Monthly (which released in trade paperback format a monthly collection featuring a different author, either a novel or a collection of short stories). Chandler's stories were also collected belatedly in both hardcover and paperback editions, and eventually two volumes that included all of his stories were published in England. Some writers of the genre— James M. CAIN, for instance—were never published in the pulp magazines and are better known for their novels than their short stories, although recently Cain's stories have been collected and republished.

Ellery Queen's contribution to the genre was twofold: as writer of the detective stories about Ellery Queen (with the famous Challenge to the Reader—to solve the crime just before the denouement) and as editor of what became the premiere specialist publication after *Black Mask*, *Ellery Queen's Mystery Magazine* (*EQMM*), which began in 1914. Countering the not-quite-"respectable" reputation of most detective magazines, Queen intended *EQMM* to be the equivalent of a high-brow literary magazine for readers of popular fiction. The editor set out to publish the best of the old stories as well as to encourage new writers. To this end he celebrated the "first" story by a new writer in each issue and ran contests for the best new detective and crime fiction. Editor Queen was a stern and objective judge. In 1946 William FAULKNER submitted "An Error in Chemistry," a story in his sequence about

GAVIN STEVENS (the short stories were collected in 1949 as *KNIGHT'S GAMBIT*) and received second prize.

The editor boasted of having launched several significant writers on a career of crime. Stanley Ellin's famous "The Specialty of the House" first appeared in its pages in 1948; so did Robert L. Fish's Holmesian pun-filled parodies about detective Schlock Homes; individual issues published stories by international authors. In 1948, Argentinean writer Jorge Luis Borges's (1899–1986) "The Garden of Forking Paths" was published in a translation by mystery writer and critic Anthony Boucher.

Book collections of detective stories from these and other periodicals preserved the works of many writers. Collections of stories by a single author often represented an interesting quirk in publishing. Publishers found that short stories in book form did not sell as well as novels, so the collections were sometimes disguised as novels by breaking the individual episodes up into chapters and numbering them sequentially throughout the entire book. Examples of these include Jack Boyle's *Boston Blackie* (1919), Richard Harding Davis's *In the Fog* (1901), T. W. Henshaw's *Cleek: The Man of the Forty Faces* (1910), and Frank L. Packard's *The Adventures of Jimmie Dale* (1917).

Anthologies of stories by many writers have made unique contributions to the detective short story not only by preserving some of the best examples of the form, but by providing the editors with a forum, in the introductions, for examining the history and development of the genre. Some of the more significant ones include *The Omnibus of Crime* (1929), edited by Dorothy L. Sayers; *The World's Great Detective Stories* (1927), edited by Willard Huntington Wright (better known as the author of the Philo Vance detective novels, signed S. S. Van Dine); and Ellery Queen's centennial volume *101 Years' Entertainment: The Great Detective Stories 1841–1941* (1941). Queen enjoyed editing "theme" anthologies with contents following a common motif, stories marking a first appearance in the United States or stories by writers not known for writing detective fiction (such as Sinclair Lewis's "The Post-Mortem Murder" [1921] and Ring LARD-

NER's "Haircut" [1926]; Ernest HEMINGWAY's "The Killers" [1926] is often cited as well).

Recent anthologies edited by other authorities include the annual collection sponsored by the Mystery Writers of America and the annual collection of the best stories of the year drawn from several periodicals. *The Best Detective Stories of the Year* began in 1946 with 15 volumes edited by David E. Cooke, followed by two more volumes edited by mystery writer Brett Halliday, then six edited by Anthony Boucher, and six edited by Allen J. Hubin. In 1976 Edward D. Hoch assumed the editorship of the series, which in 1982 changed its title and focus to *The Year's Best Mystery & Suspense Stories.*

Ellery Queen became a critic, as well as a writer of fiction, with a number of essays on different aspects of the genre in *EQMM* and two significant bibliographies: *The Detective Short Story: A Bibliography* (1942) and *Queen's Quorum: The 101 Most Important Books of Detective-Crime Short Stories* (1948; revised and expanded, 1969). The latter contains a running commentary and history of the genre. It has also influenced collectors to acquire first editions of the volumes Queen recommends.

Perhaps ironically, then, a form that began in the mass media has now become a very specialized and almost elite genre. The market for such periodical fiction has shrunk appreciably, and many writers lack the incentive to write for the minimal fees offered for short stories as opposed to full-length novels. The only newsstand magazines to publish detective fiction are the two specialist publications *Alfred Hitchcock's Mystery Magazine* and *Ellery Queen's Mystery Magazine,* and *Playboy.* In the place of the once voluminous periodicals, only a few publishers include anthologies of detective fiction on their regular lists or specialize in collections of detective short stories. Since September 1994, the firm of Crippen and Landru has issued a collection of short works by contemporary writers at the rate of four volumes a year. Among the authors have been Edward D. Hoch, Margaret Maron, Marcia Muller, Bill Pronzini, and James Yaffe.

Indeed, perhaps the key to the detective short fiction market lies in the scores of recent minority and women writers who in the last two decades, especially, have reshaped the classic hard-boiled detective into a different breed. Acclaimed Chicana/o writers include Rolando Hinojosa, featuring his detective Rafe Buenrostro; Michael Nava and his gay amateur sleuth Henry Rios; Manuel Ramos and his hard-boiled Luis Montez; Lucha Corpi and her activist crime solver Gloria Damasco; and Rudolfo Anaya and his private investigator Sonny Baca. Cuban American Carolina Garcia-Aguilera, with her detective Lupe Solano, has been compared favorably with Patricia Cornwell and Sara Paretsky. Among the most acclaimed African-American mystery writers are Walter Mosley, with his hard-boiled Los Angeles private detective Easy Rawlins, and Valerie Wilson Wesley, who features a liberated private investigator, Tamara Hayle. Notable, too, are Gar Anthony Haywood and his sleuth Aaron Gunner, Grace F. Edwards (Mali Anderson), Eleanor Taylor Bland (Marti MacAlister), Barbara Neely (Blanche White), and Hugh Holton (Larry Cole). To date, however, these writers have not written short stories. Leading the field are the *Sisters in Crime* anthologies, publishing since 1989 award-winning detective stories by women.

The number and popularity of women writers in the genre has grown dramatically, with notable portraits of such female private investigators as Sue Grafton's Kinsey Milhone and Diane Mott Davidson's Goldy Bear. The most recently published anthology, *The Best of Sisters in Crime* (1997), includes stories by aforementioned Grafton, Davidson, Maron, and Muller, as well as Mary Higgins Clark, Joan Hess, Sharyn McCrumb, Joyce Carol OATES, Nancy Pickard, Sara Paretsky, and Julie Smith. In a recently published study of women detective fiction writers, *Busybodies, Meddlers, and Snoops* (1998), Kimberly J. Dilley notes the changing view of fictional women detectives: no longer seen as stereotypic and passive and certainly no longer overlooked by critics, women mystery writers and their women characters over the last two decades have begun creating a new type of hero— the modern female detective, an independent, intelligent, witty, and compassionate woman who can take care of herself. Dilley analyzes the new female serial detectives and explores their struggles with issues of gender and FEMINISM in their day-to-day lives and the ways they have profoundly altered the genre's standard plotlines and protagonists.

BIBLIOGRAPHY
Bakerman, Jane. *Then There Were Nine: More Women of Mystery.* Bowling Green, Ohio: Bowling Green State University Popular Press, 1985.

Bargainnie, Earl F. *Ten Women of Mystery.* Bowling Green, Ohio: Bowling Green State University Popular Press, 1981.

Barzun, Jacques, and Wendell Hertig Taylor. *A Catalogue of Crime.* Rev. ed. New York: Harper & Row, 1989.

Chandler, Raymond. "The Simple Art of Murder." In *The Art of the Mystery Story.* Edited by Howard Haycraft. New York: Simon & Schuster, 1946.

Cox, J. Randolph. *Masters of Mystery and Detective Fiction: An Annotated Bibliography.* Englewood Cliffs, N.J.: Salem Press, 1989.

Dilley, Kimberly J. *Busybodies, Meddlers, and Snoops.* Greenwich, Conn.: Greenwood Publishing, 1998.

Haycraft, Howard. *Murder for Pleasure: The Life and Times of the Detective Story.* New York: D. Appleton-Century, 1941.

Haycraft, Howard, ed. *The Art of the Mystery Story.* New York: Simon & Schuster, 1946.

Lowndes, Robert A. W. "The Contributions of Edgar Allan Poe." In *The Mystery Writer's Art.* Edited by Francis M. Nevins, Jr. Bowling Green, Ohio: Popular Press, 1970.

Mundell, E. H., Jr., and G. Jay Rausch. *The Detective Short Story: A Bibliography* and Index. Manhattan: Kansas State University Library, 1974.

Pronzini, Bill, and Marcia Muller. *1001 Midnights: The Aficionado's Guide to Mystery and Detective Fiction.* New York: Arbor House, 1986.

Queen, Ellery, ed. *The Detective Short Story: A Bibliography.* Boston: Little, Brown, 1942; reprint with new introduction by editor. New York: Biblo & Tannen, 1969.

———. *101 Years' Entertainment: The Great Detective Stories 1841–1941.* Boston: Little, Brown, 1941.

———. *Queen's Quorum: A History of the Detective-Crime Short Story as Revealed in the 106 Most Important Books Published in this Field Since 1845; Supplements Through 1967.* New York: Biblo & Tannen, 1969.

Shaw, Joseph Thompson. *The Hardboiled Omnibus: Early Stories From "Black Mask."* New York: Simon & Schuster, 1946.

Wallace, Marilyn, ed. *The Best of Sisters in Crime.* New York: Berkeley Prime Crime, 1997.

J. Randolph Cox
St. Olaf College

DETERMINISM   The word is a shortened version of the scientific term "biological determinism," which describes the belief that one's destiny is "determined" by heredity and environment, not good deeds, faith, God's "grace," or adherence to the precepts of organized religions, such as Christianity, Judaism, or Islam. Determinism emerged as a result of the scientific discoveries by Charles Darwin and others in biology, geology, and astronomy in the mid-19th century. Another major influence was rapid industrialization, especially of the United States. These developments shattered the previously held concept that the individual was the center of the universe and instead posited the idea that human beings are insignificant players in a cruel, ironic world where there are no longer any heroes or villains, only unfeeling nature. This deeply pessimistic philosophy is present in such turn-of-the-20th-century authors as Ambrose BIERCE, Stephen CRANE, and O. HENRY. It remains a THEME throughout 20th-century American literature, reflected in the works of Sherwood ANDERSON, Ernest HEMINGWAY, Saul BELLOW, John CHEEVER, John BARTH, and others. It is often discussed as an aspect of literary NATURALISM.

BIBLIOGRAPHY
Conron, John. *The American Landscape.* New York: Oxford University Press, 1964.

Cowley, Malcom. "A Natural History of American Naturalism." In *Documents of Modern Literary Realism.* Edited by George J. Becker. Princeton, N.J.: Princeton University Press, 1967.

Hofstadter, Richard. *Social Darwinism in American Thought.* Boston: Allyn & Bacon, 1964.

Horton, Rod W., and Herbert W. Edwards. *Backgrounds of American Literary Thought,* 3rd ed. Englewood Cliffs, N.J.: Prentice-Hall, 1974.

Howard, June. *Form and History in American Naturalism.* Chapel Hill: University of North Carolina Press, 1985.

Michaels, Walter Berm. *The Gold Standard and the Logic of Naturalism: American Literature at the Turn of the Century.* Berkeley: University of California Press, 1987.

Pizer, Donald. *Realism and Naturalism in Nineteenth-Century American Literature,* revised ed. Carbondale: Southern Illinois University Press, 1984.

Pizer, Donald, ed. *Cambridge Companion to American Realism and Naturalism.* Cambridge, Eng.: Cambridge University Press, 1995.

Carol Hovanac
Ramapo College

DEUS EX MACHINA

From the Latin meaning "god from a machine." In Greek tragedy this practice involved a god literally appearing at the last moment to provide the solution to the tangled problems of the main characters. The god is let down from the sky on a sort of crane. The phrase has come to have a pejorative ring, particularly in short fiction, where it is criticized as the writer's inability to resolve problems without resorting to the crutch of a sometimes hastily introduced character.

"DEVIL AND DANIEL WEBSTER, THE" STEPHEN VINCENT BENÉT (1937)

A popular short story first published in the SATURDAY EVENING POST and then in the collection *Thirteen O'Clock,* it was adapted as an opera (1938) with music by Douglas S. Moore and later as a play (1931) and a film (1941, under the title *All That Money Can Buy*). The story involves Jabez Stone, a New England farmer, who sells his soul to the Devil in exchange for riches. The eloquent Daniel Webster argues Stone's case before a devilish and prejudiced jury and saves him from having to pay his debt.

DEVOTO, BERNARD A(UGUSTINE) (1897–1955)

American historian and critic who first gained recognition for his *Mark Twain's America* (1932), a rebuttal of Van Wyck Brooks's *The Ordeal of Mark Twain* (1920). De Voto taught at Northwestern University and Harvard University and wrote for HARPER'S magazine (1935–55). His most respected work is his historical study of the American West in three volumes, one of which (*Across the Wide Missouri*) won the Pulitzer Prize in 1947. His view of the frontier as a richly diverse source of FOLKTALE, MYTH, and song helped popularize the concept of the West and helped encourage writers whose stories focused on the West.

DEVRIES, PETER (b. 1910)

After working at *Poetry* magazine from 1938 to 1944, DeVries began a long association with the NEW YORKER, in which most of his short fiction was published. A comic writer in the *New Yorker* tradition of James THURBER and S. J. Perelman, DeVries is funny, witty, and unfailingly clear. He is a satirist (see SATIRE) who applies his antic humor to the foibles and excesses of affluent middle-class exurbanites.

DEXTER GREEN

Dexter Green, in F. Scott FITZGERALD's "Winter Dreams," is an important figure in modern literature, representing the effect on the individual of the American dream of unlimited opportunity. He is a caddie for the wealthy patrons of a country club, and his winter dreams are off-season fantasies about the "glittering things" in life. Like Fitzgerald's character BASIL DUKE LEE, Dexter Green appears to be both a romantic and a realist (see ROMANTICISM and REALISM): His imagination and hard work together enable him to leave his humble beginnings to become a successful Wall Street financier by the time he reaches his mid-30s. Like other young men in Fitzgerald's fiction, Dexter Green falls in love forever with Judy Jones, a beautiful woman who appears indifferent to her many admirers; for years, however, she remains his fertile image of ideal love and the possibility of life's promises. When he learns by chance that she has become a matronly housewife married to an abusive philanderer, he collapses in tears, understanding that with the loss of his idea of her, he has lost his youthful belief in the freshness of life's possibilities—and the motive for acquiring his "glittering things." Recent interpretations have described Dexter Green as a pitiful rather than a tragic romantic figure. He cannot accept the unexciting fact that Judy Jones is average; instead, he idealizes her physical beauty to emotionally finance his materialism.

BIBLIOGRAPHY
Burhans, Clinton S., Jr., "'Magnificently Attuned to Life': The

Value of 'Winter Dreams'" in *Studies in Short Fiction* 6 (1968–69).

McCay, Mary A. "Fitzgerald's Women: Beyond 'Winter Dreams.'" In *American Novelists Revisited: Essays in Feminist Criticism.* Edited by Fritz Fleischmann, 1982.

Frances Kerr
Durham Technical Community College

DIAL, THE A magazine founded in Concord, Massachusetts, in 1840, by Theodore Fuller and Ralph Waldo Emerson as the organ of the New England TRANSCENDENTALISM movement. Fuller served as its editor from 1840 to 1842, and Emerson, with Henry David Thoreau's help, took over until 1844, when the magazine ceased publication. During its short history, it wielded a great deal of influence in literary, philosophic, and religious thought. Since 1844 other magazines have taken the same name. In 1880 a conservative group founded the third *Dial* in Chicago. When the magazine moved to New York in 1918, it became the outstanding literary review of its time. Until 1920, with the aid of Conrad AIKEN, Randolph Bourne, and Van Wyck Brooks, it published articles by leading radical thinkers, including John Dewey and Thorsten Veblen. After 1920 the magazine was devoted to the encouragement of AVANT-GARDE authors. The poet Marianne Moore became editor in 1925. The magazine ceased publication four years later. A fourth *Dial,* first a literary quarterly edited by James Silberman, then an annual, ran from 1959 to 1962.

DIALECT According to the Oxford English Dictionary, the word "dialect" entered the English language in 1577 and is etymologically related to the Greek *dialektos.* The Greek term means conversation or discourse, but it connotes (see CONNOTATION AND DENOTATION) a regional variety of a particular language. This, of course, is the most familiar meaning of "dialect," but the word also can refer to a specialized discourse based on factors other than geography. Thus, one may speak of a scholarly dialect or the dialect of a certain scientific community. In the most general sense, then, a dialect is merely one variant of a standardized language system.

Some scholars, however, have been troubled by the notion of a "standard" language. In his widely cited *Keywords,* for instance, Raymond Williams points out that languages exist only in dialect form, and he thus dismisses the belief in a standard language from which all variants derive as a "metaphysical notion." A dialect, then, is perhaps best thought of as one language strand among many which, taken together, constitute the language itself.

Ever since Mark TWAIN famously used the dialects of both white and black Americans in *The Adventures of Huckleberry Finn,* writers have been employing dialects to establish a further sense of realism in their characters' speech. Such writers include Dorothy ALLISON, William FAULKNER, Joel Chandler HARRIS, Zora Neale HURSTON, and Richard WRIGHT, to name only a few of the many writers who employ this technique.

Shannon Zimmerman
University of Georgia

"DIAMOND AS BIG AS THE RITZ, THE"
F. SCOTT FITZGERALD (1922) This story's unusual mixture of FANTASY and REALISM made it hard for F. Scott FITZGERALD to find a publisher, and this blending of genres bewildered or disturbed its first readers. The story appeared originally in *The Smart Set* in 1922 under the title "The Diamond in the Sky" and in a shorter version in Fitzgerald's story collection *Tales of the Jazz Age.* Some commentators have called it a modern FAIRY TALE about the moral education of John Unger, who visits the Washington Braddock family on their fantastic underground estate in Montana. The Braddocks hoard a monstrous diamond and kill all visitors to keep them from revealing its presence. Some critics have described the story as a satire on American materialism that also incorporates the traditional boy-girl romance PLOT. In its unusual mixture of genres, the story holds a unique position in Fitzgerald's canon and confirms the range of his fictional interests.

BIBLIOGRAPHY
Buell, Lawrence, "The Significance of Fantasy in Fitzgerald's Short Fiction." In *The Short Stories of F. Scott Fitzgerald:*

New Approaches in Criticism. Edited by Jackson R. Bryer. Madison: University of Wisconsin Press, 1982.

Frances Kerr
Durham Technical Community College

DIASPORA Exile or dispersion, used in the past almost invariably with reference to the exile of the Jewish people from the land of Israel. Diaspora can refer not only to the state of being in exile but also to the place of exile—any place outside of Israel where Jews are living—to the communities in exile, and the state of mind that results from living in exile. Inherent in the term is usually the Jew's feeling of living as a member of a relatively defenseless minority, subject to injustice if not to outright persecution, of an unfulfilled life and destiny as a Jew, and of living in an unredeemed—although not unredeemable—world.

In the last decade the term "diaspora" has been applied with increasing frequency to members of the African community, with nearly identical connotations. (See CONNOTATION AND DENOTATION.) Thus, for example, the term can refer to stories by Cynthia OZICK, on one hand, as well as to those by Ralph ELLISON, John Edgar WIDEMAN, and Richard WRIGHT, on the other.

DIDION, JOAN (1934–) Born in Sacramento, California, Joan Didion has worked as a columnist for *Vogue, SATURDAY EVENING POST, ESQUIRE,* and the *National Review,* among others. Her nonfiction views on American life have been taken up by many contemporary fiction writers. Didion's insight into the culture of the 1960s focuses on her native California as a METAPHOR for the lost AMERICAN DREAM. Her novels, too, depict the disorder, loss, anxiety, and human and cultural disintegration of modern life. In Didion's books, the pioneering American spirit is replaced by a lack of belief, a creed of "me-ism," and eternal motion without direction. These same observations can be seen in the fiction of such writers as Joyce Carol OATES, Bobbie Ann MASON, John BARTH, and others.

Although much of her writing focuses on California, Joan Didion is not provincial. She uses her immediate milieu to envision, simultaneously, the last stand of America's frontier values pushed to their limits and the manifestations of craziness and malaise that have initiated their finale. Thus her THEMES in both short fiction and nonfiction appear in her novel *Play It As It Lays,* set in Los Angeles: Her characters—whose pasts have been completely obliterated—have problems with failed marriages, abortion, mental instability, and freeway phobias.

BIBLIOGRAPHY
Didion, Joan. "California Blue." *Harper's* (October 1976).
———. "The Welfare Island Ferry." *Harper's Bazaar* (June 1965).
———. "When Did the Music Come This Way? Children Dear, Was It Yesterday?" *Denver Quarterly* (Winter 1967).
Henderson, Katherine Usher. *Joan Didion.* New York: Ungar, 1981.

DIES IRAE From the Latin for "day of wrath." A famous medieval hymn about the Last Judgment, it is used in the Roman Catholic Mass for the Dead and on All Soul's Day, religious occasions liberally employed by such writers as Edward ALBEE, Tennessee Williams, Ann Rice, and others, to suggest the threatening cloud hanging over modern characters doomed by their superficial obsessions and lack of spiritual beliefs.

DIONYSIAC See APOLLONIAN AND DIONYSIAC.

DISCOURSE Used as a word for discussion, or to describe a form of conversational expression, discourse traditionally has been separated into direct (She said, "I feel sad") or indirect (She said that she was sad). A more explicit theoretical use of the term has occurred in the last few decades, however, in reference to the heavily weighted way that each of us communicates with one another. The French linguist Emile Benveniste divided the terms "language" and "discourse," with language referring to speech or writing used objectively and discourse emphasizing the implications of the understanding—or lack thereof—between speaker or writer, on one hand, and listener or reader, on the other. Thus in fiction, for example, although the text may seem to describe a person, a situation, or an idea—and may in fact do so—its most important function is "performative" (Eagleton 118), that is, to achieve certain effects on the reader.

BIBLIOGRAPHY

Eagleton, Terry. *Literary Theory: An Introduction.* Minneapolis: University of Minnesota Press, 1983.

"DISPLACED PERSON, THE" FLANNERY O'CONNOR (1954)

Generally agreed to be one of Flannery O'CONNOR's best stories as well as an excellent entree to her work, "The Displaced Person" offers all the major hallmarks of the first-rate story. It first appeared in *Sewanee Review* in 1954. Echoing throughout the story is the phrase "displaced person": Although the term initially refers to Mr. Guizac, the literal so-called D.P., a refugee from Poland, by the end of the story we realize that everyone—including the reader—is a displaced person at some point, severed by race, class, or gender prejudice from the mainstream community. Other major O'Connor THEMES support the story, as well: the South, the Catholic faith, and her use of the grotesque.

"The Displaced Person" begins as Mr. Guizac, the displaced foreigner, appears in a Southern rural area where class and color lines are already in place. He finds work with Mrs. McIntyre who, as owner of the farm, considers herself superior to Mr. and Mrs. Shortley, the poor whites, and to the "Negroes," Sulk and Astor, all four of whom work for her. The Shortleys dislike and distrust the industrious Mr. Guizac, who, they fear, will take their place on the farm. As Ann Charters notes, their suspicious, fear-driven attitude is the American version of those in Europe who would put people like Mr. Guizac in concentration camps. Mrs. Shortley thus forms an unlikely alliance across color lines with Sulk and Astor in an attempt to shore up the position of herself and her husband.

Mrs. Shortley's fears prove well grounded. Mrs. McIntyre, impressed with Mr. Guizac's willing devotion to farm work, decides to fire the Shortleys and replace them permanently with Mr. Guizac. Initially the two women seem to be FOILS; O'Connor gradually reveals to us, however, that despite their different social positions, Mrs. McIntyre (ironically, "entire" only in her complete self-interest) and Mrs. Shortley (short on compassion) are linked through their egotism and selfishness (Paulson 64). Mrs. Shortley, on the verge of escaping the farm before she is literally replaced, dies a violent death that recalls the concentration camp pictures she has seen in a newsreel. In her displacement and violent death, she begins to understand suffering.

With Mrs. Shortley's death, Mrs. McIntyre's problems would appear to have ended: Mr. Guizac is helping her to modernize the farm into a model of efficiency. However, she learns that, to save his niece from the concentration camp, he plans to bring her over to marry Sulk. Since Mrs. McIntyre cannot abide the thought of interracial marriage (racism temporarily overrides self-interest here), she forms another unlikely alliance, this time with Mr. Shortley, on whom devolves the responsibility to devise a way to kill Mr. Guizac. As we hear the sounds of the dying Mr. Guizac, crushed under the tractor wheel, we see Mrs. McIntyre and Mr. Shortley joined in their responsibility for Guizac's death. Their collaboration is short-lived, though, and Mrs. McIntyre ultimately is left with no one to help her but Astor and his wife, and the priest. Forced to sell off all the farm equipment, she is literally left with nothing but a place.

Many critics view the priest as the central consciousness of this tale. He, along with the revelatory images of the peacock, always associated with Christ in O'Connor's stories, provides some sense of the redemptive meaning of Christianity. Seeing Shortley as a Devil figure and Guizac as a Christ figure might seem an easy way out, but O'Connor's stories are too complex for easy ALLEGORY, in which the characters represent pure good or pure evil. Indeed, even Mrs. Shortley, in death, finally has her vision in which the meaning of the peacock is revealed to her. And O'Connor extends the possibility that Mrs. McIntyre, alone on her farm with a black couple and a priest, may learn true equality and humility. In addition to a Christian and humanitarian message is a historical or sociological one. Mr. Guizac, the displaced person, was the truest American of all: Having emigrated from his own country, he arrived in America determined to succeed and was too busy working and helping others to succumb to either class or race prejudice. In this sense, as nearly always occurs in O'Connor's stories, Georgia—or the South—becomes a microcosm for the United States, in all its horror and all its possibility.

BIBLIOGRAPHY

O'Connor, Flannery. "The Displaced Person." *Flannery O'Connor: The Complete Stories.* New York: Farrar, Straus & Giroux, 196–235.
———. "The Displaced Person." *The Sewanee Review,* v. 62 n. 4 (October–December 1954): 634–635.
Paulson, Suzanne Morrow. *Flannery O'Connor: A Study in the Short Fiction.* Boston: Twayne Publishers, 1988.

DIVAKARUNI, CHITRA (1956–)

Chitra Banerjee Divakaruni was born in Calcutta, India, and lived in several cities in India before immigrating to America at the age of 19 to pursue graduate studies in English. She earned her M.A. degree from Wright State University in Dayton and her Ph.D. from the University of California at Berkeley. Divakaruni's first collection of short stories, *Arranged Marriage* (1995), won a 1996 American Book Award as well as two regional awards given to authors from the Bay Area. An accomplished poet who has written several volumes of poetry, Divakaruni is also the author of an acclaimed first novel, *The Mistress of Spices* (1997). Involved in a variety of women's causes, since 1991 Divakaruni has been president of MAITRI, a support service for South Asian Women in the San Francisco area. Divakaruni lives near San Francisco with her husband and two sons; she teaches creative writing at Foothill College.

The title of Divakaruni's story collection becomes a METAPHOR for the immigrant experience in contemporary America, particularly the experience of women from South Asia. But while the collection insists on the powerless subservience of immigrant women in their "arranged marriage" with American culture, it also affirms their capacity for renewal and rebirth, suggesting that subservience may be transcended through self-knowledge and compassion.

BIBLIOGRAPHY

Mehta, Julie. "Arranging One's Life: Sunnyvale Author Chitra Divakaruni Talks About Marriages and Stereotypes." *Metro: Santa Clara Valley's Weekly Newspaper,* October 3, 1996. (http://www.metroactive.com/papers/metro/10.03.96/books-9640html)

Keith Lawrence
Brigham Young University

DIXIE

The name for the pre–CIVIL WAR American South and for the name of the popular song entitled "I Wish I Was in Dixie's Land," composed by Daniel Decatur Emmett in 1859. A great favorite in the South, the song was taken up by the soldiers in the Confederate army during the Civil War. Fanny Crosby wrote a Union version of the text in 1861, known as "Dixie for the Union."

The origin of the word "Dixie" is obscure. It has been suggested that it is related to the Mason-Dixon line separating the North and the South during the Civil War; others believe that a Louisiana bank, printing its pre–Civil War bills in French with the word DIX (French for ten) in the middle of the ten-dollar notes, made the South the land of "dixies." A further, ironic derivation is from the name of a slaveholder on Manhattan Island in the late 18th century; so benevolent was he that when his slaves were moved down south, they pined for "Dixie's land" up north.

DIXON, STEPHEN (1936–)

Born in New York City, Stephen Dixon is a prolific, often humorous writer who has attracted a large and loyal readership. Although it was his novel *Frog* (1991) that was nominated for both the National Book Award and the PEN/FAULKNER AWARD, Stephen Dixon is even better known as one of the finest experimental modern American short story writers. While stopping short of the antirealistic experiments of authors such as Robert COOVER, Dixon nevertheless writes strikingly innovative fiction. In books like *Fourteen*

Stories, Movies, No Relief, and *Long Made Short,* to name only a few, he portrays with great humor and insight the peculiar anxieties of contemporary urban life as well as the precarious conduct of our modern relationships.

Dixon's reputation is built on his short stories, and, in addition to his collections of short fiction, in 1994 he published *The Stories of Stephen Dixon,* which contains the stories Dixon himself considers to be his best over the past 30 years, from 1963 to 1993. All his major themes are contained in this work, including his concern with the tenuous stability of human relationships and characters who feel trapped, cheated, or terrified by the urban scene in which so many of them must live. As a result, many of his characters speak either in incomplete, coded exchanges or nonsequiturs.

His stories are both fabulous and rooted in the specific detail of everyday existence, written in a style both experimental and realistic (see REALISM) that has prompted comparisons to such early AVANT-GARDE 20th-century writers as novelist Franz Kafka and dramatist Samuel Beckett—and even to the imaginative writer Lewis Carroll, author of *Alice in Wonderland.* His is a prolific talent that often produces varied perceptions of Dixon as a stylist who experiments with such techniques as BLACK HUMOR, FANTASY, MAGICAL REALISM, and SURREALISM, yet who remains accessible and, to numerous readers, addictive. He has been praised for his "unpredictable" and "disturbing" qualities, his surrealism, yet also for his gifts for dialogue and narrative technique that convincingly portrays the absurdities of complex, contemporary urban life, and the melancholy realities of human relationships.

BIBLIOGRAPHY

Dixon, Stephen. *Fourteen Stories.* Baltimore, Johns Hopkins University Press. 1980.
———. *Falls and Rise: A Novel.* San Francisco: North Point Press, 1985.
———. *Frog.* Latham, N.Y.: British American Pub., 1991.
———. *Gould: A Novel in Two Novels.* New York: Holt, 1997.
———. *Long Made Short.* Baltimore: Johns Hopkins University Press, 1994.
———. *Man on Stage: Play Stories.* Davis, Calif.: Hi Jinx, 1996.
———. *Movies.* Berkeley, California: North Point Press, 1983.
———. *No Relief* Ann Arbor, Michigan, Street Fiction Press. 1976.
———. *Quite Contrary: The Mary and Newt Story.* New York: Harper, 1979.
———. *The Stories of Stephen Dixon.* New York: Holt, 1994
———. *30: Pieces of a Novel.* New York: Holt, 1999.
———. *Time to Go.* Baltimore: Johns Hopkins University Press, 1984.
Klinkowitz, Jerome. *The Self-Apparent Word,* Carbondale: Southern Illinois University Press, 1984.
———. "Stephen Dixon: Experimental Realism," in *North American Review,* March 1981.
"Stephen Dixon Issue" of *Ohio Journal,* (Fall-Winter) 1983–84.
Stephens, Michael. *The Dramaturgy of Style.* Carbondale: Southern Illinois University Press, 1985.

"DOCTOR AND THE DOCTOR'S WIFE, THE" ERNEST HEMINGWAY (1924, 1925)

As with so many of Ernest HEMINGWAY's short stories, "The Doctor and the Doctor's Wife" (first published in the *Transatlantic Review* and later in his collection IN OUR TIME [1925]) offers certain highly autobiographical details from Hemingway's life. In particular, the story reflects his early life growing up in the Michigan woods, as Hemingway explains in a letter to his father: "I put Dick Boulton and Billy Tabeshaw as real people with their real names because it was pretty sure they would never read the *Transatlantic Review.* I've written a number of stories about the Michigan country—the country is always true—what happens in the stories is fiction" (*Letters,* March 20, 1925, 153). Despite the apparent disclaimer, many biographers have found autobiographical parallels between the depiction of Dr. Adams and his wife and Hemingway's own father and mother.

The opening scene of the story sets the stage for the conflict between Dr. Adams and the Indian men he has hired to cut up logs for him. Dick Boulton, Billy Tabeshaw, and Eddy come out of the wilderness heavily armed, Eddy with the long crosscut saw, Billy Tabeshaw with two large cant hooks, and Dick with three axes, and they enter a gated area that marks off Dr. Adams's territory. The ensuing conflict over who is the rightful owner of the "driftwood" logs can be seen as one more incident in the ongoing struggle for land between whites and Indians. Dr. Adams eventually backs down from the threat of violence posed by Dick Boulton and goes inside his own home, only to have his authority challenged again—this time by his wife, a practicing Christian Scientist whose faith denies the importance of his medical profession. The strain of their marriage is further symbolized by the sexual impotence underlying Dr. Adams's gesture with his gun: "He was sitting on his bed now, cleaning a shotgun. He pushed the magazine full of the heavy yellow shells and pumped them out again. They were scattered on the bed."

Nick Adams enters this story only in the final scene, after his mother asks Dr. Adams to send Nick to see her. Both father and son reject her request in favor of heading into the wilderness together. What they leave behind (the woman) and what they embrace (the wilderness) fulfills a pattern that will be replayed many times in Hemingway's later works.

BIBLIOGRAPHY

Baker, Carlos, ed. *Ernest Hemingway: Selected Letters, 1917–1961.* New York: Scribner's, 1981.
Smith, Paul. *A Reader's Guide to the Short Stories of Ernest Hemingway.* Boston: G. K. Hall & Co., 1989.

Amy Strong
University of North Carolina at Chapel Hill

DOCTOROW, E(DGAR) L(AWRENCE) (1931–)

E. L. Doctorow cannot be readily assigned to any single school of contemporary fiction; rather, his works synthesize various important strains in postmodernist writing. (See POSTMODERNISM.) Doctorow's formal inventiveness, wit, and covertly apocalyptic philosophy link him with such practitioners of METAFICTION as Thomas Pynchon, Donald BARTHELME, and John BARTH; his fascination with "facts"—invented or real—links him with New Journalists and "nonfiction novelists." The New Journalists, who reported on news stories using a first-person narrative voice (see POINT OF VIEW) as well as writerly observation, insight, and wit, included such practitioners as Truman CAPOTE, Norman MAILER, and Tom Wolfe; nonfiction novelists used all the tools of fiction to write about an actual event, as exemplified in Capote's *In Cold Blood* (1966). But Doctorow decries the self-reflexivity of much contemporary fiction.

Although best known as a novelist, particularly for *Ragtime* (1975), a historical work set in the 1920s, and *The Book of Daniel* (1971), based on the execution of Julius and Ethel Rosenberg, Doctorow has also written "The Songs of Billy Bathgate" (1968) and *Lives of the Poets* (1984), a story collection focusing on the characters' inner tensions between past and present, memory and reality. The concluding novella, containing a writer whose life resembles Doctorow's, unifies the entire collection with its suggestion that contemporary literature lacks purpose and that the writer exists on the fringes as a marginal entity.

Born in New York City, Doctorow is a recipient of the National Book Critics Circle award and an American Academy award, both in 1976.

BIBLIOGRAPHY

Doctorow, E. L. *Lives of the Poets: Six Stones and a Novella.* New York: Random House, 1984.
———. "The Songs of Billy Bathgate." In *New American Review*, Vol. 2. Edited by Theodore Solotaroff. New York: New American Library, 1968.
Levine, Paul. *E. L. Doctorow.* London: Methuen, 1985.
Trenner, Richard, ed. *E. L. Doctorow: Essays and Conversations.* Princeton, N.J.: Ontario Review Press, 1983.

DOERR, HARRIET (1910–)

The acclaimed author of *Stones for Ibarra,* a widely praised collection of interlocking short stories that won the American Book Award in 1984, Harriet Doerr has also written a well-reviewed novel entitled *Consider This, Senora* and, in 1996, *The Tiger in the Grass,* a collection of 15 stories and "inventions," as Doerr calls them. A California resident, Doerr composes the majority of her stories by drawing on her memories of her many years in Mexico.

Stones for Ibarra is comprised of the stories that result when Richard and Sara Everton move from San Francisco to an old family home and abandoned mine in Mexico. The mood of the entire collection is established in the opening story, in which Richard and Sara lose their way. The tales involve a sense of rootlessness and also an intimacy with death: The narrator reveals that Richard is dying of cancer and segues into a LYRICAL but realistic (see REALISM) comparison of the American and Mexican attitudes toward death. Related to the THEMES of death and loss is the Evertons' desire to connect the present with the past. Although at first they have trouble understanding the Mexicans' very different attitudes toward these issues, the stories gradually reveal the way the Evertons learn life-changing lessons from their neighbors.

One of the most memorable images—in a work renowned for its lyrical, imagistic style—is of the window into Sara and Richard's house. Doerr invites the reader, along with the Mexican neighbors, to peer into the windows of the foreigners, the Evertons, and watch them gradually reveal themselves. The timelessness of the stones of the landscape, too, and their association with death and eternity provide another central METAPHOR that links these stories. Doerr is adept at humor as well, presenting all her characters, Mexican and American, in both their ignorance and their wisdom.

Critics have observed that the story of Richard, Sarah, and their Mexican friends is set on a landscape that remains both constant and surprising, described in a narrative tone of affectionate and patient wisdom. Perhaps the cumulative effect results from the author's long germination period: Harriet Doerr received her B.A. at age 67 and published this (her first) book a year later. *The Tiger in the Grass,* her most recent story collection, again uses memory as a LEITMOTIF. This collection reveals the same startling sensitivity and sculpted prose with which Doerr habitually conjures the light, smells, and sounds of Mexico with enrapturing clarity, creating characters both amusing and tragic. Reviewers note that the precision of Doerr's style is likely the felicitous result of her having kept her stories to herself for so long, polishing every image, every story, with striking and unforgettable gemlike clarity.

BIBLIOGRAPHY
Doerr, Harriet, *Consider This, Senora.* New York: Penguin, 1993.
———. *Stones for Ibarra.* New York: Penguin, 1984.
———. *The Tiger in the Grass: Stories and Other Inventions.* New York: Penguin, 1996.

DON JUAN   The archetype of the romantic lover, the "Don Juan type" has evolved and appeared in many forms, but his most enduring is that of his first appearance in Tirso de Molina's *El Burlador de Sevilla,* which gave the HERO the identity that he has retained ever since: Don Juan, a nobleman of Seville. The internal complications of his nature have endlessly fascinated writers and composers, and the name of Tirso's hero quickly became a synonym for an obsessive and unscrupulous pursuer of women. The most famous of all forms of the story is undoubtedly Mozart's great opera *Don Giovanni* (1787), written to a libretto by Lorenzo da Ponte. Another noteworthy musical work is Richard Strauss's tone poem *Don Juan* (1888). In literature, Byron immortalized him in the poem *Don Juan,* begun in 1819 and unfinished at his death. Many short fiction writers allude (see ALLUSION) directly or indirectly to Don Juan–like characters, as in Zora Neale HURSTON's "The Gilded Six-Bits," or use such contemporary ironic inversions as ARNOLD FRIEND in Joyce Carol OATES's "WHERE ARE YOU GOING, WHERE HAVE YOU BEEN?," Manley Pointer in Flannery O'CONNOR's "GOOD COUNTRY PEOPLE," or COUSIN LYMAN in Carson MCCULLERS's THE BALLAD OF THE SAD CAFE.

DON QUIXOTE MIGUEL DE CERVANTES (1605, 1615)   A novel by Miguel de Cervantes credited by many as the first Western novel. Alonso Quijano is a country gentleman, kindly and dignified, who lives in the province of La Mancha. His mind is so crazed by reading chivalric romances that he believes himself called on to redress the wrongs of the whole world. Changing his name to Don Quixote de la Mancha, he asks Sancho Panza, an ignorant rustic, to be his squire, with whom he enjoys various adventures. Although it is generally agreed that Cervantes meant his novel to be a SATIRE on the exaggerated chivalric romances of his time, some critics have interpreted it as an ironic story of an idealist frustrated and mocked in a materialistic world, while others see it more specifically as a commentary on the Catholic Church, contemporary Spain, or the Spanish character. Many American writers have used the story, both humorously and satirically, from Washington IRVING's Ichabod Crane in "THE LEGEND OF SLEEPY HOLLOW" to William FAULKNER's GAVIN STEVENS in *KNIGHT'S GAMBIT* to James Thurber's "THE SECRET LIFE OF WALTER MITTY."

DOPPELGANGER

From the German "double" and "walker," an apparition that generally represents another side of a CHARACTER's personality. The doppelganger can personify one's demonic counterpart (as in E. T. A. Hoffman's *The Devil's Elixirs,* 1816), or an alter ego, as in Edgar Allan POE's "William Wilson" (1839). Frequently the appearance of the apparition presages imminent death. For suggestive modern variations on the doppelganger THEME, see also William FAULKNER's "Elly," Peter TAYLOR's "First Confession," and M. Evelina Gulang's "Talk to Me, Milagros" in *Her Wild American Self.*

"DOUBLE BIRTHDAY" WILLA CATHER (1929)

First published in *Forum,* "Double Birthday" is one of many stories by Willa CATHER that celebrate idiosyncrasy while contemplating its costs. Two Albert Engelhardts, an uncle and his nephew born on the same day 25 years apart, value art, beauty, and intense emotional experiences over the disciplined life that brings social approval and material security. Pitied needlessly by their old friends in prestigious circles, the two bachelors share unusual priorities and the top floor of a shabby house in a working-class district. At 80, Dr. Engelhardt's life is animated by memories of a young German singer he discovered and in whom he invested money and faith, believing her destined for brilliance until her death from cancer at age 26. The loss left him desolate but deeply gratified to have experienced the extremity of passion that leads to

sacrifice. One of the ironies in the story's romantic vision (see ROMANTICISM) is that what one loses can become a permanent treasure. The younger Albert, now 55, spent his share of the family fortune on art and travel, enjoying every moment completely but never planning financially for the future. On their shared birthday, they toast their past devotions, not without a sense of loneliness. In their company is Margaret Parmenter, a wealthy friend from the past that Cather uses to register the men's odd sincerity, which moves her to renew their lapsed friendship despite her vastly different social class.

Told in dialogue and third-person description (see POINT OF VIEW), the story includes FLASHBACKS that unite the characters' past and present lives. Rather than nostalgic, the story's mood is vigorous, almost insistent, in its romanticism, suggesting that Cather's purpose is not to evoke the charm of old memories but to assert the simultaneous and vigorous appearance of both past and present in these characters' recollections.

BIBLIOGRAPHY

Arnold, Marilyn. *Willa Cather's Short Fiction.* Athens: Ohio University Press, 1984.

Cather, Willa. *Uncle Valentine and Other Stories: Willa Cather's Uncollected Short Fiction, 1915–1929.* Edited by Bernice Slote. Lincoln: University of Nebraska Press, 1973.

Frances Kerr
Durham Technical Community College

DOUGLASS, FREDERICK (1817?–1895)

American abolitionist, orator, and journalist. The son of a slave and a white man, Douglass escaped to the North in 1838. A speech he delivered at an antislavery convention in Nantucket in 1841 made such an impression that he was soon in great demand as a speaker. Mobbed and beaten because of his views, he described his experiences in an outspoken *Narrative of the Life of Frederick Douglass* (1845). He also founded and for 17 years published *The North Star,* a newspaper that advocated the use of black troops during the CIVIL WAR and civil rights for freedmen. Douglass was the first African American to speak publicly and to write about his experiences.

DREISER, THEODORE (1871–1945)

Born in Terre Haute, Indiana, Theodore Dreiser grew up in a poor family that was forced to move often and, as Dreiser later told his friend and literary adviser, H. L. Mencken, could not always afford shoes for all ten children. Dreiser's siblings had a reputation for being tough, wild, and flirtatious. His father, although briefly successful as a wool manufacturer, was destitute after his factory burned down and he could not repay the debt for fleece and machinery bought on credit. Dreiser's fiction draws on this background: It breaks with conventional literary gentility, and it chronicles with accuracy and compassion the economic struggles and intimate lives of men and women.

Dreiser is primarily known as a novelist, but his best short stories show a sophisticated understanding of the short story form, perhaps because Dreiser worked in journalism throughout his life. After a string of odd jobs in Chicago, Dreiser finally escaped his family's poverty by working as a reporter. As a free-lancer, he wrote popular pieces, including portraits of famous people and places. For several years he edited *The Delineator,* a popular women's magazine published by Butterick, the sewing pattern company.

Dreiser's experience in journalism did not, however, guarantee success for his stories. HARPER'S and ATLANTIC MONTHLY published some of his nonfiction work, but they repeatedly rejected his stories. "The Last Phoebe" (1914), a sad tale of an old man searching vainly for his dead wife, was rejected by more than ten magazines, even though Dreiser reduced his asking price from $600 to less than $200. Editors judged that Dreiser's stories were not what the public wanted. After publishing "Free" (1918), a story about an unhappily married man, the SATURDAY EVENING POST received many complaints from readers who thought the story promoted divorce. In 1918 *Redbook* rejected a story because the characters were German.

Dreiser's best short fiction explores THEMES similar to those in his novels—the allure of big cities, the power of sexual desire, the appeal of money, and the erosion of traditional mores. Dreiser's first novel, *Sister Carrie,* portrays the rise of a poor girl to stardom in Broadway musicals and the decline of a well-to-do businessman into homelessness. The novel is based, in part, on the life of his sister Emma, and Dreiser describes without judgment the sexual liasons of his unmarried HEROINE. The sexuality of young women is also the subject of Dreiser's second novel, *Jennie Gerhardt,* and of the short story "OLD ROGAUM AND HIS THERESA."

Dreiser was often accused of immorality in his life as well as his work. He was married twice, had several affairs, and was charged with adultery while in Kentucky reporting on a coal miners' strike. Dreiser insisted that sexual desire should not be judged by conventional mores, and although the publishing house of Doubleday effectively suppressed *Sister Carrie,* publishing it but never advertising it, Dreiser continued to write honestly, although never crudely, about sexuality.

Dreiser's training as a journalist is evident in much of his work. In "NIGGER JEFF," a disturbing tale of a cub reporter sent to cover a lynching, Dreiser suggests that good journalism requires a strong aesthetic sense (see AESTHETICISM). His most acclaimed novel, *An American Tragedy* (1925), is a fictional reworking of a much-publicized trial of a young man who murdered his pregnant working-class girlfriend. Dreiser's style is often reportorial, thick with details and facts.

Many of Dreiser's best short stories are collected in *Free and Other Stories* (1918), and many of his best CHARACTER sketches are in *Twelve Men* (1919). Other collections include *Chains: Lesser Novels and Stories* (1927) and *A Gallery of Women* (1929).

Dreiser was deeply influenced by the social philosophers of the day, in particular Herbert Spenser, and his work is often considered part of American literary NATURALISM. Dreiser's fiction does not, however, describe only determined lives. He also portrays with great compassion the inchoate yearnings of characters who are pushed and pulled by the forces of desire, nature, and society. Dreiser's style and philosophy have, at times, been maligned as clumsy and unsophisticated. Nevertheless, he was a major influence on young writers, and his fiction offers astute, realistic (see REALISM), and moving representations of the desires and lives of ordinary people.

BIBLIOGRAPHY
Dreiser, Theodore. *An American Tragedy.* New York: Boni & Liveright, 1925.
———. *Free and Other Stories.* New York: Boni & Liveright, 1918.
———. *Chains: Lesser Novels and Stories.* New York: Boni & Liveright, 1927.
———. *A Gallery of Women.* New York: Horace Liveright, 1929.
———. *Jennie Gerhardt.* New York: Boni & Liveright, 1911.
———. *Sister Carrie.* New York: Doubleday, Page & Copy, 1900.
———. *Twelve Men.* New York: Boni & Liveright, 1919.
Gerber, Philip L. *Theodore Dreiser.* New York: Twayne, 1964.
Griffin, Joseph. *The Small Canvas: An Introduction to Dreiser's Short Stories.* Rutherford, N.J.: Fairleigh Dickinson University Press, 1985.
Lingeman, Richard. *Theodore Dreiser.* 2 vols. New York: Putnam, 1986.
Menken, H. L. "Theodore Dreiser," in *A Book of Prefaces.* H. L. Mencken. Edited by Garden City, New York: Doubleday 1917.
Swanberg, W. A. *Dreiser.* New York: Scribner, 1965.

Stephanie Browner
Berea College

DRUSILLA HAWKE

One of William FAULKNER's finest and most sympathetic, if enigmatic, characters, Drusilla appears in several stories in THE UNVANQUISHED. On one level it is possible to view her, with her tragic destiny, as metaphoric of the American South during and after the CIVIL WAR; on another she becomes emblematic of Faulkner's many heroic women who, although technically defeated by outside (male) forces, remain defiantly "unvanquished." She is the prototypical young woman who runs races faster and rides horses better than any man, and who actually joins the Confederate army disguised as a man, yet is beaten by "those skirts" she is forced to wear. Her name, vaguely reminiscent of Druids and pre-Christian rituals combined with the warlike bird, makes her an astonishingly strong and unique character in the Faulkner canon of short stories and novels alike.

DUBOIS, W(ILLIAM) E(DWARD) B(URGHARDT) (1868–1963)

American civil rights leader and writer. The descendant of a French Huguenot and an African slave, DuBois received his B.A., M.A., and Ph.D. degrees from Harvard. Among the first important leaders to advocate complete economic, political, and social equality for blacks, DuBois cofounded the National Negro committee (later the NAACP) in 1909. He taught history and economics at Atlanta University from 1897 to 1910 and from 1932 to 1944. In the intervening years, he served as editor of the NAACP magazine, *Crisis.* He lived the last two years of his life in Ghana, joined the Communist Party, and edited the *African Encyclopedia for Africans.* Among his many influential writings are *The Souls of Black Folk* (1903), *John Brown* (1909), and *The Black Flame* (1957). His *Autobiography* appeared posthumously in 1968. Often called the intellectual father of black Americans, DuBois was a significant factor in shaping the aims of the writers connected with the HARLEM RENAISSANCE. His influence also can be seen in the work of Langston HUGHES and Zora Neale HURSTON.

DUBUS, ANDRÉ (1936–1999)

Although he began writing in the early 1960s, Dubus shares little with the magical realists (see MAGIC REALISM) or even the postmodernists (see POSTMODERNISM)—writers such as John BARTH and Robert COOVER—whose fiction manipulates language, logic, and reality, flouting the boundaries of writing. Dubus's fiction, instead, concerns itself with ordinary people enduring, sometimes suffering through, ordinary lives. His characters are largely blue-collar people: construction workers, bartenders, waitresses, and mechanics. They inhabit the Merrimack Valley, a cluster of dying mill towns and old farms located north of Boston.

André Dubus, the son of André Jules and Katherine (Burke) Dubus, was born August 11, 1936 in Lake Charles, Louisiana. After graduating from Christian Brothers High School, Lafayette (1954) and McNeese State College, Lake Charles

(1958), he was commissioned a second lieutenant in the U.S. Marine Corps. In 1963 Captain Dubus resigned his commission and enrolled in the University of Iowa's Writers' Workshop program. After completing both his M.F.A. (1965) and a brief teaching assignment in Louisiana, Dubus began teaching at Bradford College in Massachusetts, where he remained until retiring to write full time in 1984. Over a half-dozen story collections, two novels, and an essay collection later, Dubus was one of the most highly regarded American short story writers of the late 20th century. His awards include two National Endowment for the Arts Grants (1978 and 1985), two Guggenheim Grants (1977 and 1986), and the MacArthur Fellowship (1988).

Dubus's stories are emotionally bruising accounts of shattered marriages, fractured families, and daily struggles with faith. While there is much of the HEM-INGWAY tradition in Dubus's language, his female characters are fellow sufferers. And although his fiction is often compared to that of Raymond CARVER, Dubus's fictional landscape is more spiritually lush, his humanism more forgiving. In "A Father's Story," for example, a father chooses to protect his daughter by covering up her crime, an accidental vehicular homicide. Both Dubus's Catholicism and his Marine Corps experience seem to infuse his stories: His characters often either struggle for structure or hunger for spirituality as they grapple with the messiness of their lives.

In July 1986, while coming to the aid of a stranded motorist, Dubus was struck by a car and lost his left leg in the accident. Many of the essays in *Broken Vessels* (1991) concern the implications of his accident. They are without self-pity but can be as wrenching as his fiction: In one Dubus relates how he watches helplessly as his baby daughter crawls away from his wheelchair toward an exerciseycle bicycle and, disregarding his shouts of warning, inserts her finger into the cycle's sprocket, severing her finger.

But Dubus was primarily a short story writer, and in *Broken Vessels* he explained his affection for the genre in which he excelled: "I love short stories because I believe they are the way we live. They are what our friends tell us, in their pain and joy, their passion and rage, their yearning and their cry against injustice" (104).

BIBLIOGRAPHY

Dubus, André. *Adultery and Other Choices*. Boston: Godine, 1977.
———. *Broken Vessels*. Boston: Godine, 1991.
———. *Dancing After Hours*. New York: Knopf, 1996.
———. *Finding a Girl in America: Ten Stories and a Novella*. Boston: Godine, 1980.
———. *The Last Worthless Evening: Four Novellas and Two Stories*. Boston: Godine, 1986.
———. *The Lieutenant*. New York: Dial Press, 1967.
———. *Separate Flights*. Boston: Godine, 1975.
———. *The Times are Never So Bad: A Novella and Eight Short Stories*. Boston: Godine, 1983.
———. *Voices From the Moon*. Boston: Godine, 1984.
———. *We Don't Live Here Anymore*. New York: Crown, 1984.
Kennedy, Thomas E. *André Dubus: A Study of the Short Fiction*. Boston: Twayne, 1988.

Michael Hogan
University of North Carolina at Chapel Hill

DUNBAR, PAUL LAWRENCE (1872–1906)

Poet and short story writer noted for his use of African THEMES and DIALECT, Dunbar wrote during the time REGIONALISM was in vogue and was almost unquestionably influenced by Thomas Nelson Page (see AFRICAN-AMERICAN SHORT FICTION). The son of former Kentucky slaves, Dunbar was fascinated to hear his mother's stories and his father's tales of his experiences as a Union soldier during the CIVIL WAR. This love of stories translated into the publication of his first story and, shortly afterward, with the financial help of former schoolmates Orville and Wilbur Wright, the collection *Oak and Ivy* in 1893. Dunbar's poetry lacks the bitterness of the work of later black writers. He also wrote novels, including *The Uncalled* (1898) and *The Sport of the Gods* (1902).

Dunbar's best story collection is probably *The Strength of Gideon and Other Stories*, published in 1900. Its 20 narratives cover a broad range. Some treat the imagined loyalty of ex-slaves both tenderly and sarcastically; others examine the hostility of the Northern environment and the shortcomings of urban life. The tales of RECONSTRUCTION, set in a time when blacks were attempting to become part of the body politic, remain pertinent today. Perhaps nowhere is the indifference of the white political structure more poignantly presented than in "Mr. Cornelius Johnson, Office Seeker." Johnson is both a believing fool and a sad figure of a man who is not only a victim but also a victimizer. His hope for a political future in payment for his support of white politicians understanding of the political process are told with an admirable economy of language—as in the ironic use of "Mr." in the title.

BIBLIOGRAPHY

Brawley, Benjamin. *Paul Laurence Dunbar: Poet of His People.* Chapel Hill, N.C.: University of North Carolina Press, 1936.

Cunningham, Virginia. *Paul Laurence Dunbar and His Song.* New York: Dodd, Mead, 1947.

Dunbar, Paul Laurence. *The Fanatics.* New York: Dodd, Mead, 1901. Reprint. Salem, N.H.: Ayer Co., 1991.

———. *Folks From Dixie.* New York: Dodd, Mead, 1898. Reprint. City Freeport, N.Y.: Books for Libraries, 1971.

———. *The Heart of Happy Hollow.* New York: Dodd, Mead, 1904. Reprint. Freeport, N.Y.: Books for Libraries Press, 1970

———. *In Old Plantation Days.* New York: Dodd, Mead, 1903, 1967.

———. *The Love of Landry.* New York: Dodd, Mead, 1900. Reprint. Upper Saddle River, N.J.: Gregg Press, 1969.

———. *Lyrics of the Hearthside.* New York: Dodd, Mead, 1899. Reprint. New York: AMS Press, 1972.

———. *Lyrics of Love and Laughter.* New York: Dodd, Mead, 1903, 1979.

———. *Lyrics of Lowly Life.* New York: Dodd, Mead, 1896.

———. *Lyrics of Sunshine and Shadow.* New York: Dodd, Mead, 1905. Reprint. Salem, N.H.: Ayer Company, 1991.

———. *Majors and Minors: Poems.* Toledo, Ohio: P.L. Dunbar, Hadley & Hadley, 1895.

———. *Oak and Ivy.* Ohio: A.W. McGraw, 1893, 1997.

———. *The Sport of the Gods.* New York: Dodd, Mead, 1902. Reprint. Salem, N.H.: Ayer Company, 1990.

———. *The Strength of Gideon and Other Stories.* New York: Dodd, Mead, 1900. Reprint. Salem, N.H.: Ayer, 1990.

———. *The Uncalled.* New York: Dodd, Mead, 1898. Reprint. New York: AMS Press, 1972.

Dunbar-Nelson, Alice Moore. *Paul Laurence Dunbar: Poet Laureate of the Negro Race.* Philadelphia: Reverdy C. Ransom, 1914.

Gayle, Addison, Jr. *Oak and Ivy: A Biography of Paul Laurence Dunbar.* Garden City, N.Y.: Doubleday, 1971.

Gould, Jean. *That Dunbar Boy: The Story of America's Famous Negro Poet.* New York: Dodd, Mead, 1958.

Lawson, Victor. *Dunbar Critically Examined.* Washington, D.C.: The Associated Publishers, 1941.

Martin, Jay, ed. *A Singer in the Dawn: Reinterpretations of Paul Laurence Dunbar.* New York: Dodd, Mead, 1975.

Revell, Peter. *Paul Laurence Dunbar.* Boston: Twayne, 1979.

Wiggins, Lida Keck. *The Life and Works of Paul Laurence Dunbar: Containing his Complete Poetical Works, his Best Short Stories, Numerous Anecdotes and a Complete Biography of the Famous Poet.* Naperville, Ill.: L. Nichols & Company, 1907.

DUNBAR-NELSON, ALICE MOORE (1875–1935)

Born of mixed black, NATIVE AMERICAN, and white ancestry into upper-class creole society in New Orleans, Alice Nelson attended Straight College (later named Dilliard University). In 1898 she married the poet and short story writer Paul Laurence DUNBAR. She was a teacher of English, an activist for racial causes, and a FEMINIST. Her first novel, *Violets and Other Tales,* was published when she was 20. Dunbar-Nelson was a prolific writer of short stories, plays, poems, newspaper columns, speeches, and essays in black journals and anthologies. She was a presence in the HARLEM RENAISSANCE. In her stories, she developed her fictional characters in pointed contrast to the traditional STEREOTYPES of blacks in the minstrel roles and plantation stories prevalent in turn-of-the-century literature and thus helped establish the short story form in African American literature. (see also AFRICAN AMERICAN SHORT FICTION.)

BIBLIOGRAPHY

Dunbar-Nelson, Alice Moore. *The Goodness of St. Rocque and Other Stories* New York: Dodd, Mead, 1899.

———. *Violets, and Other Tales* Boston: *Monthly Review,* 1895.

DUPIN, C. AUGUSTE   See C. AUGUSTE DUPIN.

E

EASTER In Christianity, Easter is the spring season when Jesus is said to have risen from the grave after His crucifixion. It follows a much older tradition of fertility, renewal, and rebirth as the earth returns to life. Following MODERNISM's lead, T. S. Eliot's THE WASTE LAND featured a post–WORLD WAR I perverse spring in which April is "cruel" and corpses "bloom." Numerous writers make METAPHORical use of the springtime to indicate a renewal for their characters. Eudora WELTY, for instance, uses the death of an old man to make way for the new and younger lover of the title character in "LIVVIE." Other writers use Easter symbolism inversely to show an ironic malaise in their characters; as in for example, Sherwood ANDERSON's "THE EGG" and John UPDIKE's "SEPARATING."

EASTLAKE, WILLIAM (DERRY) (1917–)

William Eastlake appears initially to be a writer of utmost paradox. Although he was born in New York City and grew up in New Jersey, and although after WORLD WAR II he traveled in Europe and lived for a time in Los Angeles, he purchased land and lived for some years as a rancher and writer in a remote area of New Mexico. Eastlake developed into an ardent regionalist (see REGIONALISM) and a shrewd observer of contemporary Native American life, interests apparent in his artistically wrought fiction. His stories have been reprinted in *The O. Henry Awards:* *Prize Stories* and *Best American Short Stories* (see APPENDIX).

The subjects of his art are Native Americans, tourists, and cattlemen, the settings the glitzy towns and the sagebrush. Beneath this carefully detailed, naturalistic surface (see NATURALISM), the themes include the values implicit in the behavior and moral attitudes of the protagonists, yet these are frequently treated with irony, humor, and compassion, suggesting Eastlake's niche in the American literary tradition. His move to the west, his stints as war correspondent in Vietnam, and his concern with cultural and political issues identify him with such 19th-century writers as Stephen CRANE and Jack LONDON. Ernest HEMINGWAY, however, seems the dominant influence on Eastlake's use of terse dialogue and understatement as well as the protagonists' search for value in times of both war and peace. Eastlake has received favorable critical attention for his short fiction; of the stories in his collection, *Jack Armstrong in Tangier* (1984), at least four have been included in major anthologies. These works demonstrate Eastlake's penchant for vividly detailed description and a genuine if pessimistic perspective on contemporary life.

BIBLIOGRAPHY

Bamberger, W. C. *The Work of William Eastlake: An Annotated Bibliography & Guide.* San Bernardino, Calif.: Borgo Press, 1993.

Eastlake, William. *The Bamboo Bed*. New York: Simon & Schuster, 1969.

———. *The Bronc People*. New York: Harcourt Brace, 1958.

———. *Castle Keep*. New York: Simon & Schuster, 1966.

———. *A Child's Garden of Verses for the Revolution*. New York: Viking, 1970.

———. *Dancers in the Scalp House*. New York: Viking, 1975.

———. *Go in Beauty*. New York: Harper & Row, 1956.

———. *Jack Armstrong in Tangier*. Flint, Mich.: Bamberger, 1984.

———. *The Long, Naked Descent into Boston: A Tricentennial Novel*. New York: Viking, 1977.

———. *Lyric of the Circle Heart: The Bowman Family Trilogy* (American Literature Series). Normal, Ill.: Dalkey Archive Press, 1996.

———. *Portrait of an Artist With Twenty-Six Horses*. New York: Simon & Schuster, 1963.

———. *Prettyfields: A Work in Progress*. Santa Barbara, Calif.: Capra Press, 1987.

———. "Three Heroes and a Clown." In *Man in the Fictional Mode*. Evanston, Ill.: McDougal, Littell, 1970, pp. 52–65.

Haslam, Gerald W. *William Eastlake*. Austin, Tex.: Steck-Vaughn Co., 1970.

ECCLESIASTES A book of the Old Testament, once believed to have been written by Solomon because of the opening textual reference to "the words of the preacher, the son of David, king in Jerusalem" but since generally assigned to an unknown author in the third century B.C. The book has a somewhat despairing tone, with an emphasis on the evil in man and the universality of death. In a world of despotism and oppression, the one good reserved for man is to "rejoice in his labor, for this is the gift of God." Ecclesiastes appealed to many writers of the 1920s, notably T. S. Eliot and Ernest HEMINGWAY, who alluded (see ALLUSION) to its passages in such works as *The Waste Land* and *The Sun Also Rises,* respectively. Many modernists, (see MODERNISM) took their cue from these definitive fictions and adopted in their works the gloomy mood and the inevitability of death.

EDEN In the Old Testament Book of Genesis, Eden is the garden in which Adam and Eve lived before the Fall of Man. In Eden, the first couple lived a carefree life until, in disobedience to God's command, they ate the forbidden fruit from the tree of knowledge. God expelled Adam and Eve from the garden, and since that time man has had to live "by the sweat of his brow." In the book of Genesis, however, the Bible makes clear that the garden was not destroyed after their expulsion but only barred to them by an angel with a flaming sword. It was widely believed in the Middle Ages that the Earthy Paradise, sometimes identified with the Garden of Eden, a place of beauty, peace and immortality, existed on earth in some undiscovered land. The word "eden" often is used to describe an idyllically beautiful place. Subtle and not-so-subtle ALLUSIONS to gardens exist in many American short stories from Nathaniel HAWTHORNE's "RAPPACCINI'S DAUGHTER" to Sandra CISNEROS's *THE HOUSE ON MANGO STREET.*

"EGG, THE" SHERWOOD ANDERSON (1921) Sherwood ANDERSON published his third short story collection, *The Triumph of the Egg,* containing this title story, in 1921. Narrated retrospectively by the nameless son, now an adult, the story of his father contains in its first paragraph the seeds of the unhappy tale that follows: His father, says the narrator, was perfectly happy with his life as a farmhand until he learned ambition. Quite logically, the son suggests that the father probably learned this American trait when he married, late in life, the taciturn schoolteacher who induced her new husband to start a chicken farm. From this point on, the narrator uses eggs and chickens to chronicle the unhappy and downward-spiraling movement of his family's life in and near Bidwell, Ohio.

Anderson's narrative strategy in this story is to reverse the traditional, life-affirming symbol of the egg in parallel with his reversal of the traditional American myth that hard work brings success, a rise in fortunes, and happiness. Eggs, traditionally a symbol of new life, are associated in Christian cultures with EASTER and the resurrection of Christ; in other cultures they have the same meaning, associated with spring and rebirth. Yet the narrator seems not to see that his own birth—from an egg—also plays a role in the failure of his parents' farm and, after the move to town, of their restaurant. He tells us that his mother wanted nothing for herself, but, once her son was born, had great ambition for her husband and son. The narrator surmises that she probably had read of Abraham LINCOLN's and James Garfield's mythic rise from impoverishment to president and may have wished the same success for her own son. Indeed, in later life he knows that she had hoped he could leave the farm and the small town and rise in the world.

In any event, in his recollection of his youth on the chicken farm, the offspring of the eggs bring nothing but worry, disease, and death; the young son has brooding and somber memories of his childhood and at one point speaks directly to the readers, warning that whatever we do, we should never put our trust in chickens. Any alternative is better: prospecting for gold in Alaska, trusting a politician, or believing that good will eradicates evil.

For a time, because they work hard, the mother and father's business realizes a small profit. Foolishly, however, the father decides that he will achieve even more success if he can entertain his customers. He tries to force a customer to look at the grotesque freak chickens—those born with two heads or five legs—that he keeps in a jar of alcohol behind the restaurant counter. The man is, predictably, sickened by the sight. When this endeavor fails, the nervous but determined father attempts two silly egg tricks in front of the reluctant customer, who tries to ignore him. When the tricks fail, the final blow occurs, literally, when the frustrated father throws an egg at the customer, who barely makes his escape. The pathetic father breaks down completely; the narrator son still remembers joining his father in an outpouring of wailing and grief. Apparently the sadness continues into the narrator's adulthood, for, as he contemplates the reason for the cycle of chicken-egg-chicken, he notes that, even all these long years later, he is his father's son. The pessimism of those early years, along with its sense of defeat, remains in the narrator's tone: The AMERICAN DREAM remains unattainable for those who are not Lincoln or Garfield.

BIBLIOGRAPHY
Anderson, Sherwood. *The Triumph of the Egg: A Book of Impressions of American Life in Tales and Poems.* New York: B.W. Huebsch, Inc., 1921.
Crowley, John W., ed. *New Essays on Winesburg, Ohio.* New York: Cambridge University Press, 1990.

"ELI, THE FANATIC" PHILIP ROTH (1959) With "Eli, the Fanatic," the last and longest short story in *Goodbye Columbus* (1959), Philip ROTH became one of the first Jewish American writers to explore "the repressed shame and guilt Western Jews felt about the HOLOCAUST" (Baumgarten and Gottfried 54). Because of their disassociation with European Jews and their lack of involvement in World War II, the assimilated Jews of Woodenton have turned to a sheltered community life to avoid facing both their guilt and the atrocities of the war. As Leo Tzuref—the head of a nearby Orthodox community comprised of 18 refugee children and one Hasidic Jew—explains to Eli during their second meeting: "What you call law, I call shame. . . . They hide their shame" (266).

Like the PROTAGONISTS in "THE CONVERSION OF THE JEWS" and "Defender of the Faith," Eli Peck struggles with his religious and cultural identity. As a lawyer, he unwittingly becomes a liaison between the yeshivah (a traditional school of Judaism) and Woodenton, whose Jews want to oust the Orthodox group for violating a zoning code. Torn by his sympathies for both communities, he proposes a solution that will allow the yeshivah to remain on Woodenton property so long as the Hasidic Jew wears secular, "American" clothing. Essentially, this stipulation asks the Hasid to surrender his religious and cultural identity: "The suit the gentleman wears is all he's got . . . Tzuref, father to eighteen, had smacked out what lay under his coat, but deeper, under the ribs" (GC 263, 265).

When the Hasid and Eli exchange clothing, Eli, by putting on this black outfit, must literally and symbolically confront his own religious identity: "Eli looked at what he wore. And then he had a strange notion that he was two people. Or that he was one person wearing two suits" (GC 289). Even though he tries to embrace the spiritual component of his Jewish identity, his attempts are extreme and superficial. Finally, while looking at his newborn son through a glass window at the hospital, Eli experiences his second breakdown and must be carried away by the attendants. Even though he wears the Hasid's clothing, he is trying to fit into a tradition he is not part of and doesn't understand. Like many of Roth's other works, this story raises many questions about "Jewish" identity in America without posing any answers.

BIBLIOGRAPHY
Baumgarten, Murray, and Barbara Gottfried, *Understanding Philip Roth*. Columbia, S.C.: University of South Carolina Press, 1990.

Brent, Jonathan, "'The job,' says Roth, 'was to give pain its due,'" In *Conversations with Philip Roth*. Edited by George J. Searles. Jackson: University of Mississippi Press, 1992.

Cooper, Alan. *Philip Roth and the Jews*. Albany, N.Y.: State University of New York Press, 1996.

Halio, Jay L. *Philip Roth Revisited*. New York: Twayne, 1992.

Roth, Philip. *Goodbye, Columbus and Five Short Stories*. New York: Vintage Books, 1993.

———. *Reading Myself and Others*. New York: Farrar, Straus & Giroux, 1961.

Thomas Fahy
University of North Carolina at Chapel Hill

"ELIZABETH STOCK'S ONE STORY" KATE CHOPIN (1894)

This story begins with the announcement that Elizabeth Stock, an unmarried postmistress of Stonelift, died of consumption (tuberculosis) at St. Louis City Hospital. The narrator, a visitor in the village, was permitted to examine the contents of Elizabeth's desk and found a manuscript. The bulk of the story is that manuscript, Elizabeth Stock's one story, an account of how she lost her position as postmistress. As she was sorting mail one day, she read an urgent post card addressed to a businessman. She admits she often read postcards, reasoning that it is human nature to be inquisitive and that anyone writing anything personal would use a sealed envelope. Recognizing the importance of the message, she walked in the rain to deliver the mail personally, contracting in the process the illness that led to her eventual death. Although she went to great lengths to perform her duties, she was promptly dismissed from her position, ostensibly because of her negligence. The real reason she was fired, however, was that an official in St. Louis wanted to give the job to his son.

Barbara Ewell describes Elizabeth Stock as "one of CHOPIN's strongest, most self-possessed females" (168) and argues that the story "conceals a high degree of technical contrivance and sophistication in its artlessness" (KC 168). Emily Toth regards this tale as "one of [Chopin's] most bitter and hopeless stories," a "somber version" of Bret HARTE's popular "Postmistress of Laurel Run" (315). An example of literary REALISM, "Elizabeth Stock's One Story" also resembles the fiction of Mary E. Wilkins FREEMAN in its unsentimental depiction of village life.

BIBLIOGRAPHY
Chopin, Kate. *The Complete Works of Kate Chopin*. Baton Rouge: University of Louisiana Press, 1969.

Ewell, Barbara. *Kate Chopin*. New York: Ungar, 1986.

Toth, Emily. *Kate Chopin*. New York: Morrow, 1990.

Mary Anne O'Neal
University of Georgia

ELKIN, STANLEY (LAWRENCE) (1930–1995)

Born in Brooklyn, New York, Elkin has won acclaim for his three NOVELLAS in *Searches and Seizures*, and his stories in *Criers and Kibitzers, Kibitzers and Criers* have appeared in numerous anthologies. In *The Living End*, a triad of long stories about heaven and hell, Elkins creates a whole cosmos, laced and grained with detail. The most widely read of Elkin's books, *The Living End* ranges from the life of a Minneapolis-St. Paul liquor salesman to the secrets God held back from man: PROTAGONISTS question, for example, why dentistry holds a higher place in the sciences than astronomy, or why biography is more admired than dance. These stories encompass the banalities of conventional wisdom and the profundities of larger issues. Elkin's gifts are primarily, however, those of the novelist. Shorter forms do not allow Elkin room for the accretion of CHARACTER that marks the novels, so situations and people in the stories—with the significant exceptions just noted—can seem simply eccentric. In the novels, repetition of image and action, rhetorical intensity, even digressions and included tales have a cumulative effect difficult to achieve in the stories.

BIBLIOGRAPHY

Bailey, Peter J. *Reading Stanley Elkin*. Boston: Houghton Mifflin, 1985.

Bargen, Doris G. *The Fiction of Stanley Elkin*. Bern, Switzerland: Peter Lang, 1980.

Elkin, Stanley. *Criers and Kibitzers, Kibitzers and Criers*. New York: Random House, 1966.

———. *Early Elkin*. Flint, Mich.: Bamberger, 1985.

———. *Eligible Men*, London: Gollancz, 1974; as *Alex and the Gypsy*, London: Penguin, 1977.

———. *The Living End*. New York: Dutton, 1979.

———. *The Making of Ashenden*. London: Covent Garden Press, 1972.

———. *Searches and Seizures*. New York: Random House, 1973.

Guttman, Allen. *The Jewish Writer in America*. New York: Oxford University Press, 1971.

Lebowitz, Naomi. *Humanism and the Absurd*. Evanston, Ill.: Northwestern University Press, 1971.

Olderman, Raymond. *Beyond the Wasteland*. New Haven, Conn.: Yale University Press, 1972.

Tanner, Tony. *City of Words*. New York: Harper & Row, 1971.

ELLISON, HARLAN (1934–)

Harlan Ellison, often labeled a SCIENCE FICTION writer, rejects that term and prefers to regard his work as "MAGIC REALISM." Joseph McLellan of the *Washington Post* has called him a "lyric poet, satirist, explorer of odd psychological concerns, moralist, one-line comedian, purveyor of pure horror and of black comedy." He writes in a highly personal literary language, infused with his own interpretations of myth and moral ALLEGORY. Critic Ben Bova has said that Ellison has an "electromagnetic aura that strikes sparks" but that "underneath all his charisma, behind all the shouting and fury, is one simple fact: he can write circles around most of the people working in this business" (Swigart 8).

A native of Cleveland, Ohio, Ellison is the son of Louis Laverne Ellison, a dentist and jeweler, and Serita Rosenthal Ellison. He published his first story at the age of 13 and, when he was 16, founded a science fiction society. In 1953 he began publishing the *Science Fantasy Bulletin,* which later became *Dimensions.* He attended Ohio State University for two years, then took on miscellaneous jobs while establishing his writing career. He served in the U.S. Army and has had several marriages.

Ellison edited *Roque Magazine,* was the founder and editor of Regency Books, and has lectured at various colleges and universities. He worked in television in the 1960s, writing scripts for *The Alfred Hitchcock Hour, Star Trek, The Outer Limits,* and other programs. His biographer George Edgar Slusser has stated that his own PERSONA serves "as the means of binding and unifying collections" (Dillingham 162) and humanizing his short fiction by means of autobiographical comments. Known as a critic of mass culture, he edited the anthologies *Dangerous Visions: 33 Original Stories* (Doubleday, 1967) and *Again, Dangerous Visions* (Doubleday, 1972). His film criticism has been compiled in *Angry Candy* (Houghton Mifflin, 1988). His other books include *I Have No Mouth and I Must Scream* (Pyramid, 1967), *Paingod and Other Delusions* (Pyramid, 1975); *Phoenix Without Ashes* (Fawcett, 1975); *Deathbird Stories: A Pantheon of Modern Gods* (Harper & Row, 1975); *The Illustrated Harlan Ellison* (Baronet, 1978); *Strange Wine: Fifteen New Stories from the Nightside of the World* (Harper, 1978); *Shatterday* (Houghton Mifflin, 1980); *The Deadly Streets* (Ace Books, 1983); *Harlan Ellison's Watching* (Underwood-Miller, 1989), and *Mefisto in Onyx* (Mark V. Ziesing Books, 1993). He has won HUGO and NEBULA AWARDS and special achievement awards of the World Science Fiction Convention.

Ellison also writes under various pseudonyms, including Lee Archer, Robert Courtney, E. K. Jarvis, and Clyde Mitchell (magazine pseudonyms); Phil ("Cheech") Beldone, C. Bird, Cordwainer Bird, Jay Charby, Price Curtis, Wallace Edmondson, Landon Ellis, Sley Harson, Ellis Hart, Al[lan] Maddern, Paul Merchant, Nabrah Nosille, Bert Parker, Jay Solo, and Derry Tiger.

Slusser has called Ellison a "tireless experimenter with forms and techniques," and believes he has produced "some of the finest, most provocative fantasy in America today" (CR 170). Ellison's characters are often Americans living at the psychological edge of civilization, turning to attack the status quo, the accepted order of the universe. An example is "Shatterday"; in the introduction to this story, Ellison states bleakly that each person must assume responsibility for both past and future. In this story, he refers to such Jungian archetypes as "shadow," "persona," "anima" and "animus." In much of his fiction, Ellison makes use of CLASSIC myths. For example, "The Face of Helene Bournow" reflects the LEGEND of Persephone, queen of the underworld and goddess of reviving crops. "I have No Mouth and I Must Scream" may be traced to the Prometheus myth, and some of the tales in *Deathbird Stories* echo Norse myths.

One of his more famous stories, widely reprinted, is "'Repent, Harlequin,' Said the Ticktockman," which reveals the futility of protest in effecting social change. Ellison uses as an epigraph a passage from Thoreau's essay "Civil Disobedience," beginning

> The mass of men serve the state thus, not as men mainly, but as machines, with their bodies. . . . A very few, as heroes, patriots, martyrs, reformers in the great sense, and men, serve the state with their consciences also, and so necessarily resist it for the most part; and they are commonly treated as enemies by it (1754).

The Ticktockman is the Master Timekeeper, guardian of the state-as-machine. The HERO, Harlequin (whose real name is Everett C. Marm), tries to instigate reforms but is ultimately subdued and brainwashed. His name recalls the commedia dell'arte, the improvisatory Italian street theater in which Harlequin, dressed in motley, is the stock figure of pathos and COMEDY, the satirist who is much loved by others but is unlucky in love. The critic Thomas Dillingham has remarked that such a figure "may well be diverse enough to encompass the complexities of Ellison's presentation of himself." The sense of identity is a strong component of much of Ellison's work; often, as in "'Repent, Harlequin!'" a person with a weak sense of self awakens and tries to oppose the evils about him, often caused by invidious exterior forces.

Critic J. G. Ballard has described Ellison as "an aggressive and restless extrovert who conducts his life at a shout and his fiction at a scream" (169). This assessment seems particularly apt in view of Harlequin's unattainable Utopia. It is also relevant to the story "I Have No Mouth, and I Must Scream," a modern FABLE about AM, a computer system made up of the remnants of the computerized weapon systems of World War III. It decides to destroy all life; "one day AM woke up and knew who he was, and he linked himself, and he began feeding all the killing data, until everyone was dead." It spares five humans, playing with them like balls in a pinball machine. One of them, Ted, kills his companions to release them from AM, but then, like Everett Marm, hero of "'Repent, Harlequin!'" becomes imprisoned inside himself. He realizes that he is human but is powerless to express it and is doomed to suffer indefinitely. Darren Harris-Fain suggests that, although the machine is portrayed as anthropomorphic and also divine, it is really only Ted who is "both fully human and fully godlike in the story." (144) "Delusion for a Dragon Slayer" shows the effects of a flawed subconscious, when a man is not equal to his dreams and is unable to correct his errors. One of Ellison's later stories, "The Whimper of Whipped Dogs," was based on the Kitty Genovese story (a young woman who was murdered in New York City while onlookers failed to help her). Ellison writes from the POINT OF VIEW of one of the witnesses, who later must face the possibility of violence in her own life and discards the sentimentality she once possessed.

Beginning as early as the 1960s, Ellison expressed his concern about society's readiness to grapple with the implications of our technological future. Today, in light of the World Wide Web, the Internet, mammoth electronic databases, and the burgeoning use of personal computers, his remarkable insights seem more relevant, perhaps, than at any time in the past four decades.

BIBLIOGRAPHY

Ballard, J. G. *Contemporary Reviews,* New Revision Series, vol. 5, 169.

Bova, Ben. "Electromagnetic Aura": "Fagin, & Other Harlan Ellisons," in Swigart, *A Bibliographical Checklist,* 8.

Crow, John, and Richard Erlich. "Mythic Patterns in Ellison's A Boy and His Dog." *Extrapolation* 18 (1977): 162–166.

Dillingham, Thomas F. "Harlan Ellison." *Dictionary of Literary Biography* 8, pp. 162, 8.

Ellison, Harlan. *Again, Dangerous Visions.* New York: Doubleday, 1972.

———. *Angry Candy.* New York: Houghton Mifflin, 1988.

———. *Dangerous Visions: 33 Original Stories.* New York: Doubleday, 1967.

———. *The Deadly Streets.* New York: Ace Books, 1983.

———. *Deathbird Stories: A Pantheon of Modern Gods.* New York: Harper & Row, 1975.

———. *Harlan Ellison's Watching.* Los Angeles, Calif: Underwood-Miller, 1989.

———. *I Have No Mouth and I Must Scream.* New York: Pyramid, 1967.

———. *The Illustrated Harlan Ellison.* New York: Baronet, 1978.

———. "Magic Realism": *Contemporary Reviews,* New Revision Series, vol. 5: 169.

———. "Memoir: I Have No Mouth, and I Must Scream." *Starship: The Magazine About Science Fiction* 17:3: 6–13.

———. *Mefisto in Onyx.* Shingletown, Calif.: Mark V. Ziesing Books, 1993.

———. *Paingod and other Delusions.* New York: Pyramid, 1975.

———. *Phoenix Without Ashes.* New York: Fawcett, 1975.

———. *Strange Wine: Fifteen New Stories from the Nightside of the World.* New York: Harper & Row, 1978.

———. *Shatterday.* Boston: Houghton Mifflin, 1980.

Harris-Fain, Ted. "Created in the Image of God: The Narrator and the Computer in Harlan Ellison's 'I Have No Mouth, and I Must Scream,'" 144.

Malekin, Peter. "The Fractured Whole: The Fictional World of Harlan Ellison." *Journal-of-the-Fantastic-in-the-Arts,* 1:3: 21–26.

McLellan, *Washington Post: Contemporary Reviews,* New Revision Series, Vol. 5, 169.

Rubens, Philip M. "Descents into Private Hells: Harlan Ellison's 'Psy-Fi.'" *Extrapolation* 20 (1979): 378–85.

Slusser, George Edgar. *Contemporary Reviews,* New Revision Series, vol. 5, 170.

Thoran, Henry David. "Resistance to Civil Government." [Reprinted in 1866 as "Civil Disobedience."] In *The Norton Anthology of American Literature,* 5th Ed., Vol. 1. Edited by Nina Baym. New York: W. W. Norton & Company, 1998, pp. 1752–1767.

White, Michael D. "Ellison's Harlequin: Irrational Moral Action in Static Time." *Science Fiction Studies* 4 (1977): 161–65.

Sarah Bird Wright

ELLISON, RALPH (WALDO) (1914–1994)

Born in Oklahoma City, Oklahoma, and recipient of diverse honors, Ellison won the National Book Award for his novel *Invisible Man* (1952). In a poll conducted in 1965 by *Book Week,* a group of critics selected *Invisible Man* as the most distinguished work of fiction to appear in the post–WORLD WAR II period. In the opinion of scholars George and Barbara Perkins, "That poll may be taken as a tribute not only to the power of the novel but also to the continuing literary reputation of a man who, although past 50, had published only one other volume, a collection of essays called *Shadow and Act* (1964)," (69). In addition to *Invisible Man,* Ellison's skill in fiction is apparent in a number of short stories that remained uncollected until after his death, but were published as *Flying Home and Other Stories* in 1996.

From the time of his earliest published writing Ellison was interested in the universal THEME of identity, but he always conceived the theme in the context of black culture. "Slick Gonna Learn," for instance, which tells of an aborted beating of a black working man, describes experiences typical of the special circumstances of African American life. Several stories ("Afternoon," "That I Had the Wings," "Mister Toussan," "A Coupla Scalped Indians"), which represent young black boys contending with fear and guilt, learning of sex, and fantasizing retaliation on whites who despise them, might describe the nameless HERO of *Invisible Man* in adolescence, while "Flying Home," in which Todd, a young black aviator, discovers his kinship to a black peasant, employs race and culture as the basic terms for self-discovery. Todd, one of the black eagles from the Negro air school at Tuskeegee, is a descendent of Icarus, of the Greek myth, and of James Joyce's Stephen Daedalus. When he falls to earth in rural Alabama, Todd is saved by an old black peasant who uses folk tales to help the young man understand his identity.

"A Party Down at the Square," unpublished in Ellison's lifetime, is a tour de force. By narrating a lynching in the voice of a Cincinnati white boy visiting his uncle in Alabama, Ellison compels the reader to experience the worst of human situations. The white boy's most telling response comes from his insides when, to his shame, he vomits.

BIBLIOGRAPHY

Bloom, Harold, ed. *Ralph Ellison*. New York: Chelsea House, 1986.

Bluestein, Gene. *The Blues as a Literary Theme*. Indianapolis: Bobbs-Merrill, 1967.

Dietze, Rudolf F. *Ralph Ellison: The Genesis of an Artist*. Nuremberg: Carl, 1982.

Ellison, Ralph. *The Collected Essays of Ralph Ellison*. Edited by John F. Callahan. New York: Random House, 1995.

———. *Conversations with Ralph Ellison*. New York: Modern Library, 1995.

———. *Flying Home and Other Stories*. New York: Random House, 1996.

———. *Going to the Territory*. New York: Random House, 1986.

———. *Invisible Man*. New York: Random House, 1952.

———. *Juneteenth*. New York: Random House, 1999.

———. *Shadow and Act*. New York: Random House, 1954.

Fischer-Hornung, Dorothea. *Folklore and Myth in Ralph Ellison's Early Works*. Stuttgart: Hochschul, 1979.

Frank, Joseph. "Ralph Ellison and Dostoevsky." *New Centerion* (September 1983).

Gibson, Donald B. *Five Black Writers: Essays*. New York: New York University Press, 1970.

Hersey, John, ed. *Ralph Ellison: A Collection of Critical Essays*. Englewood Cliffs, N.J.: Prentice-Hall, 1973.

"Interview with Ralph Ellison. *Atlantic* (December 1970).

O'Meally, Robert G. *The Craft of Ralph Ellison*. Cambridge: Harvard University Press, 1980.

———. "The Rules of Magic: Hemingway as Ellison's 'Ancestor.'" *Southern Review* (Summer 1985).

Perkins, George, and Barbara Perkins, eds. *Contemporary American Literature*. New York: Random House, 1968, pp. 69–70.

"Ralph Ellison Issue." *CLA Journal* (March 1970).

"ENORMOUS RADIO, THE" JOHN CHEEVER (1953)

Opening with a description of a New York City couple, Jim and Irene Wescott, who aspire someday to move to Westchester, "The Enormous Radio"—first published in the NEW YORKER before reappearing in the 1953 collection *The Enormous Radio and Other Stories*—begins as a realistic story (see REALISM) about people who, a few decades later, would be called "yuppies." Irene and Jim, the uninvolved, third-person narrator tells us, fit the profile of successful couples with reasonably good incomes, a reasonably fashionable address, and the prescribed total of two children. They differ from their neighbors only in their serious interest in classical music.

Almost immediately, however, in a move that today we call MAGIC REALISM, CHEEVER introduces a new radio into their lives, a radio described as powerful, uncontrollable, and more than faintly disturbing. (See PERSONIFICATION.) Unlike nonmagic radios, this one tunes in to neighbors' private conversations. Irene identifies these people because she can recognize their voices. She becomes mesmerized by the way the radio transmits the marital arguments, conversations of drunken revelers, angry words spoken to children, disclosures of dishonest behavior, and secret liaisons she never would have imagined. In Irene's reactions to the worry, hypocrisy, and even violence among her neighbors, the story portrays her desperately clinging to a belief in Jim and herself as different from all the others with their sordid secrets.

Voyeuristically, the reader sees into Irene's and Jim's lives just as Irene eavesdrops, through the radio, on the lives of their neighbors. Despite Irene's pleas for reassurance that they are different from the others, Jim finally snaps and angrily contradicts her rosy and complacent view of their relationship. He yells furiously at her—and Jim's words and tone sound exactly like those of other men shouting at their wives, those angry voices Irene has listened to through the radio. Like the other men, he complains to her that he is tired and overworked, feeling already old at age 37. He then criticizes Irene's extravagance and inability to manage finances, accusing her of stealing jewelry from her dead mother, cheating her sister, and hypocritically forgetting her visit to an abortionist, an act he now discloses he has always thought of as out-and-out murder.

Irene feels humiliated and ill after Jim's outburst but, significantly, makes no move to contradict him. Our final view of her shows her standing by the radio, childishly hoping for loving, kind words, obviously still in denial about the reality of Jim's accusations. Jim continues to yell at her through the door. Because we know that Irene fears that the malevolent radio might transmit their voices just as it has transmitted those of her neighbors, we cannot be sure that the radio is not doing exactly that. In any case, the radio has done its work, and a return to innocence is impossible. The story itself, like an enormous radio, has transmitted to readers the ugly facts that, like Irene, we would prefer not to confront. Instead, we may just listen to the calm voice of the radio announcer in the final lines of the story, hearing impersonally the headlines about good deeds and ill and an hourly report on the weather.

BIBLIOGRAPHY

Cheever, John. *The Enormous Radio and Other Stories.* New York: Harper & Row, 1953.

O'Hara, James Eugene. *John Cheever: A Study of the Short Fiction.* Boston: Twayne, 1989.

EPIGRAM   In Greek, epigram means "inscription," but its meaning has been extended to include any very short poem that is polished, condensed, and pointed. Often an epigram ends with a surprising or witty turn of thought. The epigram was especially popular as a literary form in classic Latin literature after Martial, the Roman epigrammist, established the enduring model for the caustically satiric epigram. It was also used by European and English writers of the Renaissance and neoclassical periods. Samuel Coleridge wrote of it:

What is an epigram? A dwarfish whole,
Its body brevity, and wit its soul.

EPILOGUE   *Epilogue,* from the Greek meaning "to say in addition," is the final part that completes and rounds off the design of a work of literature. An epilogue is the opposite of a prologue, the author's brief remarks to the reader that appear before the beginning of a work of fiction.

EPIPHANY   In Christian theology, an epiphany is the manifestation or appearance of Jesus Christ in the world. The Feast of the Epiphany celebrates the coming of the Magi as Christ's first manifestation to the Gentiles. The Irish writer James Joyce adapted the term to secular experience to mean a sudden revelation of the essential nature of a person, object, or scene. This moment of sudden recognition is an epiphany. Thus, a fictional character may experience a revelation—or an epiphanic moment—when all becomes radiantly clear.

ERDRICH, LOUISE (1954–)   Louise Erdrich, the eldest of seven children, grew up in Wahpeton, North Dakota, where her parents Ralph Louis Erdrich (a German American) and Rita Joanne Gourneau (a Chippewa) taught at the Bureau of Indian Affairs school on the Turtle Mountain reservation. She received a B.A. from Dartmouth College in 1976 and an M.A. in Creative Writing from Johns Hopkins University in 1979. While she was a student at Dartmouth, she began her writing career with poetry when *Ms.* magazine published one of her poems, which later won the 1975 American Academy of Poets Prize. Her first major publication was a collection of poems entitled *Jacklight* (1984). She had also begun the stories that later became *Tracks* (1988), one of which she published under the title "Fleur."

After receiving her master's degree, Erdrich returned to Dartmouth as the Native American writer in residence. There she met writer and professor Michael Dorris, the head of Dartmouth's Native American Studies Program. They married in

1981 and began a writing partnership that involved conceptualizing, revising, and editing each other's work. Using the pseudonym Milou North, they first published a series of stories that gained recognition for the authors. One story, "The World's Greatest Fisherman," later became the opening for Erdrich's first novel, *Love Medicine* (1984). The immediate and overwhelming success of this book, which won the National Book Critics Circle Award for Fiction, earned Erdrich a Guggenheim Grant to write *The Beet Queen* (1986).

In these two works plus *Tracks* (1988) and *The Bingo Palace* (1993), covering the years 1860 to 1864, Erdrich presents an epic story of a group of interrelated families that reflected her own heritage. In and around the fictional town of Argus, North Dakota, live the Pillagers, Nanapushes, Kashpaws, and Puyats of the Chippewa tribe; the Lazarres and the Morriseys, half-breeds; and the Adares and Jameses, the whites of Argus. Erdrich's stories revolve around the tangled lives of her characters on the reservation, in Argus, and beyond. Both internal and external forces threaten the Chippewa tribe with extinction, yet certain tribal members promise that their culture will survive, even if they cannot remain on their homeland. These works are multiple-narrator novels, or SHORT STORY CYCLES. They contain chapters (some of which may appear independently as short stories) narrated by different characters, and they often disrupt the traditional chronological sequence of novels with cyclical or nonlinear narrative time.

Erdrich and Dorris also coauthored *The Crown of Columbus* (1991), a novel that reexamines the anniversary of Christopher Columbus's voyage to the New World told from the modern perspectives of a Native American woman named Violet Twostar and a New England Protestant poet named Roger Williams. Since then Erdrich has published another novel in the short story cycle mode, entitled *Tales of Burning Love* (1996), a departure from her focus on the Native American tribal community; and *The Antelope Wife* (1998). Her short stories have appeared in the ATLANTIC MONTHLY, *Ms., Mother Jones, Chicago,* and the *Paris Review.* She had separated from Michael Dorris shortly before he committed suicide in 1997.

BIBLIOGRAPHY

Chavkin, Allan, and Nancy Feyl Chavkin. *Conversations with Louise Erdrich and Michael Dorris.* Jackson: University of Mississippi Press, 1994.

Dorris, Michael, and Louise Erdrich. *The Crown of Columbus.* New York: HarperCollins, 1991.

Erdrich, Louise. *The Antelope Wife.* New York: HarperCollins, 1998.

———. *The Beet Queen: A Novel.* New York: Henry Holt, 1986.

———. *The Bingo Palace.* New York: HarperCollins, 1993.

———. *The Blue Jay's Dance: A Birth Year.* New York: HarperCollins, 1995.

———. *Love Medicine: A Novel.* New York: H. Holt and Co., 1984.

———. *Love Medicine: New and Expanded Version.* New York: H. Holt, 1993.

———. *A Reader's Guide To The Fiction Of Louise Erdrich: "Love Medicine," "The Best Queen," "Tracks," "The Bingo Palace."* New York: HarperPerennial, 1994.

———. *Tales of Burning Love.* Rockland, Mass.: Wheeler, 1996.

———. *Tracks.* 1988.

———. "Whatever Is Really Yours: An Interview with Louise Erdrich." In *Survival This Way: Interviews With Native American Poets.* Edited by Joseph Bruchac. Tucson: Sun Tracks-University of Arizona Press, 1987.

Wong, Hertha D. "Adoptive Mothers and Thrown-Away Children in the Novels of Louise Erdrich." In *Narrating Mothers: Theorizing Maternal Subjectivities.* Edited by Brenda O. Daly and Maureen T. Reddy, 1991.

Nancy L. Chick
University of Georgia

ESQUIRE   An instant success when introduced in 1933, *Esquire* magazine was directed at a previously neglected audience, males—specifically college-educated, professional men aged 25 to 45. With full-page cartoons, articles on business, sports, and fashion, and features on a wide range of issues as well as fiction, *Esquire* in its heyday was slick, informative, and humorous. The tone was one of quality in all respects, from clothing to fiction. Its first issue, which included contributions by Ernest HEMINGWAY, John Dos Passos, Ring LARDNER, Erskine

CALDWELL, George Ade, and Dashiell HAMMETT, set the tone for its writing. Subsequently the magazine published many, if not most, well-known and noted American authors.

"EUROPE" HENRY JAMES (1900)

"Europe," originally published in the story collection *The Soft Side,* is a useful encapsulation in short story form of the symbolic use of Europe that Henry James had employed so successfully in the novella *DAISY MILLER* and later in a number of his novels. The tale opens with a nameless and now expatriate American male character who, during his visits to his family in Boston, followed with amused interest the lives of the three Rimmle sisters and their mother, Mrs. Rimmle. Introduced to the Rimmles by his sister-in-law, the narrator confesses that in the long hall of his memory, their collective story is worthy of an anecdote. Any reader the least bit familiar with James immediately grows alert: If the tale of these women merits nothing more in his memory than an anecdote, a parenthesis, will this narrator be trustworthy, or will we ultimately find him unreliable? (See UNRELIABLE NARRATOR.)

The narrator says that he enjoyed his visits to Brookbridge, a thinly veiled renaming of Cambridge. There, in a square white house with a neat brick walk, live the Rimmle family of women, Mr. Rimmle having passed on before the narrator entered the scene (although the narrator somewhat wittily places Mr. Rimmle's birth around the time of the Battle of Waterloo). Having established his own youth at the time of meeting—and having established the Rimmles as the acme of New England culture and Puritanism—he begins the chronologically sequenced story of Rebecca (Becky), Maria, and Jane.

From the earliest time anyone can recall, Mrs. Rimmle has been telling her daughters that as soon as her health permits, she shall accompany them to Europe, where she had once traveled with her eminent husband. The promise of Europe dangles in front of these girls for decades, for Mrs. Rimmle's health is never quite good enough. All three of the daughters have familiarized themselves with the idea of Europe, Becky, the literary sister, most of all. The scholar of the family, she has edited and translated all the letters from associates who praised her father's many professional achievements. On first meeting the sisters, the narrator learns that since Mrs. Rimmle cannot be left alone, their idea is that Becky and Jane, the pretty sister, should be the first to go. The narrator, obliquely attracted to Jane, senses her submerged and restless passion. When he receives a letter from his sister-in-law telling him that the trip never materialized, he feels sympathy for them and acknowledges his genuine feeling for the young women.

The years wear on, the narrator travels to Europe several times and continues to visit the Rimmles whenever he is in Boston. He refers to himself and his sister-in-law as "students" of the "case," recalling the subtitle "A Study" in Winterbourne's narrative about Daisy Miller. Although he jokes with his sister-in-law that the sisters should hasten their mother's death, he privately admits that if only two could go, he would choose Maria as the one to stay, and if only one could go, he would choose Jane, whom he thinks should burst free and go on her own. Then, without warning, he learns that Jane has gone and stubbornly refuses to leave Florence, Italy. Indeed, she intends to travel to Asia and has become a flirt. Moreover, says the sister-in-law, Becky is sending her money.

When the narrator travels to Boston, an unrecognizable Becky comes to visit him—unrecognizable because she has so aged that she looks exactly like her mother. She surprises him with the news that Jane will never leave Europe, and Mrs. Rimmle, although alive, is dead. He finds Mrs. Rimmle looking like a mummy; she tells him Jane is dead and now Becky is going. To Europe? the narrator asks. But for Becky, Europe seems to have become a private METAPHOR for death. Only the thought of it had kept her alive, and the implication is that with the realization that she will never see Europe, Becky has no reason to continue living. When he next visits, Becky is dead, but the shrunken mother remains seated in the midst of the shrinelike tributes to her husband. Maria looks even older than Becky had.

The mother repeats to him that Jane will never come back, and he imagines Jane in the flush of a second youth. The mother, now called a witch, says that Becky has gone to Europe. Clearly, then, the differing equations of Europe—with death by the mother and with sex and passion by the daughters, two of whom, failing to experience either, succumb to death literally or figuratively—reflect a discrepancy that the narrator reports but fails to understand. The mother has a terrible tale to tell, for after returning from Europe with her husband, she lived a death-in-life existence and tries to prevent her daughters from sharing her fate. But the exact nature of that fate—and being married to the man whose presence still rules the house—can be surmised only by the reader, for the narrator, who classifies the women as so many museum specimens, can never fathom that even he has missed the point.

BIBLIOGRAPHY

James, Henry. "Europe." In *American Short Stories*, 4th ed.Edited by Eugene Current-Garcia and Walton R. Patrick. Glenview, Ill.: Scott, Foresman, 1982, 189–206.

"EVENING SUN, THAT"   See "THAT EVENING SUN."

"EVERYDAY USE" ALICE WALKER (1973)

Probably Alice WALKER's most frequently anthologized story, "Everyday Use" first appeared in Walker's collection, *In Love and Trouble: Stories by Black Women*. Walker explores in this story a divisive issue for African Americans, one that has concerned a number of writers, Lorraine Hansberry, for instance, in her play, *Raisin in the Sun* (1959). The issue is generational as well as cultural: In leaving home and embracing their African heritage, must adults turn their backs on their African-American background and their more traditional family members? The issue, while specifically African-American, can also be viewed as a universal one in terms of modern youth who fail to understand the values of their ancestry and of their immediate family. Walker also raises the question of naming, a complicated one for African Americans whose ancestors were named by slaveholders.

The first-person narrator of the story is Mrs. Johnson, mother of two daughters, Maggie and Dicie, nicknamed Dee. Addressing the readers as "you," she brings us directly into the story while she and Maggie await a visit from Dee. With deft strokes, Walker has Mrs. Johnson reveal essential information about herself and her daughters. She realistically describes herself as a big-boned, slow-tongued woman with no education and a talent for hard work and outdoor chores. When their house burned down some 12 years previous, Maggie was severely burned. Comparing Maggie to a wounded animal, her mother explains that she thinks of herself as unattractive and slow-witted; yet she is good-natured, too, and preparing to marry John Thomas, an honest local man. Dee, on the other hand, attractive, educated, and self-confident, has left her home (of which she was ashamed) to forge a new and successful life.

When she appears, garbed in African attire, along with her long-haired friend, Asalamalakim, Dee informs her family that her new name is Wangero Leewanika Kemanio. When she explains that she can no longer bear to use the name given to her by the whites who oppressed her, her mother tries to explain that she was named for her aunt, and that the name Dicie harkens back to pre–Civil War days. Dee's failure to honor her own family history continues in her gentrified appropriation of her mother's butter dish and churn, both of which have a history, but both of which Dee views as quaint artifacts that she can display in her home. When Dee asks for her grandmother's quilts, however, Mrs. Johnson speaks up: Although Maggie is willing to let Dee have them because, with her goodness and fine memory, she needs no quilts to help her remember Grandma Dee, her mother announces firmly that she intends them as a wedding gift for Maggie. Mrs. Johnson approvingly tells Dee that Maggie will put them to "everyday use" rather than hanging them on a wall.

Dee leaves in a huff, telling Maggie she ought to make something of herself. With her departure, peace returns to the house, and Mrs. Johnson and Maggie sit comfortably together, enjoying each other's company. Although readers can sympathize with Dee's desire to improve her own situation and to feel pride in her African heritage, Walker also makes clear that in rejecting the African-American part of her heritage, she loses a great deal. Her mother and sister, despite the lack of the success that Dee enjoys, understand the significance of family. One hopes that the next child will not feel the need to choose one side or the other, but will confidently embrace both.

BIBLIOGRAPHY

Walker, Alice. "Everyday Use." In *Major Writers of Short Fiction: Stories and Commentary*. Edited by Ann Charters. Boston: St. Martin's, 1993, pp. 1282-99.

EVERYMAN/EVERYWOMAN

EVERYMAN/EVERYWOMAN This term comes from the medieval morality play entitled *Everyman* (c. 1500), in which the protagonist, Everyman, receives a summons from Death and attempts to persuade his friends—named for various items and virtues such as Worldly Goods, Kindred, Fellowship, and Beauty—to accompany him on his journey. Various life-changing experiences occur along the way, with the help of other wayfarers such as Knowledge and Confession. In modern fiction, Everyman and Everywoman apply to any character who represents us in their recognition and employment of their weaknesses and strengths along life's pathway. Harriet Prescott SPOFFORD's "CIRCUMSTANCE," for instance, features an Everywoman character, and Nathaniel HAWTHORNE's "YOUNG GOODMAN BROWN," an Everyman.

"EVERYTHING THAT RISES MUST CONVERGE" FLANNERY O'CONNOR (1965)

"EVERYTHING THAT RISES MUST CONVERGE" FLANNERY O'CONNOR (1965) As with many of Flannery O'CONNOR's short stories, "Everything That Rises Must Converge" deals with the Christian concepts of sin and repentance. The specific sin O'Connor focuses on in this story is pride. As a Catholic, O'Connor considered this offense against God a venial sin, an attempt to place human power and ability above God's. O'Connor's portrayal is set in the South, centering on two white characters: an elderly woman living in the past glories of her racial heritage and her college-educated son Julian, who considers himself liberated from such stereotypical (see STEREOTYPE) racist views of life. The story begins with the two embarking on a bus journey to an exercise class for the mother. As they travel, each character reveals not only racial prejudice but also severe antagonism toward each other.

Julian Godhigh, as part of a "new" generation, prides himself on the fact that he is unlike his mother in applying racial stereotypes: Such actions are obsolete echoes of a distant past, and he considers himself above them. Embarrassed constantly by his mother's egotistical attitude (a fact emphasized by her overweight condition), Julian decides he will use the bus trip to "cut her down to size." By attempting to make his mother see her own flaws instead of those of an "inferior" race, he will force her to come face to face with "who she really is." Such self-discovery in spite of self-deception then becomes the major thematic (see THEME) emphasis of this tale. Ironically, however, both Julian and his mother progress from inaccurate self-images to the stark realization that the character traits they so prize are in fact petty and worthless.

Julian's way of forcing self-discovery in his mother includes fraternizing with black people on the bus, an act his mother considers outrageous but that Julian perceives as evidence of his tolerance and lack of racial bias. He feels his mind is obviously superior to hers, and thus he alone can see her flagrant mistakes. Mother, on the other hand, emphasizes the value of the heart over the head and insists that human feelings and emotions are more important than intelligence. Since she "feels" superior, she must be so, and Julian's actions are therefore both insensitive and inconsiderate.

O'Connor reveals the flaws of both Godhighs through repeated imagery and through the use of DOPPELGANGERs or doubles. Using the phrase "Rome wasn't built in a day," O'Connor suggests the tottering world of Julian and his mother: their existence is truly not the "Julian" age of Rome's expansion and success but rather an indication of its ultimate fall. In addition, through the use of doppelgangers,

O'Connor points out the similarities of the seeming disparate races by introducing a black woman who boards the bus wearing the same purple hat that Julian's mother has picked out earlier in the day. Carrying a small boy, the woman is the mirror image of her white counterpart. Julian, duly noting only part of the parallel, sees this as a delicious put-down of his mother's arrogance, but fails to note the parallels to himself in the little boy, who is also cowed and dominated by a fiercely aggressive parent.

Mother, fascinated by the young boy's cuteness, is pleased when he sits down next to her, and symbolically O'Connor suggests that the mothers have exchanged sons. As the bus ride continues, Julian must watch as his mother continues to try to attract the young black boy's attention, all the while fostering the condescending attitude to another race that Julian so despises. Eventually, when both parent/child pairs depart the bus at the same stop, Julian's mother offers the child a shiny new penny, an indication of her insensitivity and her feelings of superiority. Julian exults when his mother receives a fierce blow from the black mother's purse that knocks her to the ground. With prideful lack of pity and forgiveness, Julian believes his mother has received only the punishment she deserves. When, however, he notes that the blow has resulted in a heart attack or stroke that threatens his mother's life, Julian finally understands that sin must be met with mercy and that his own self-centered attitude has prohibited him from ministry until it is too late.

O'Connor's intriguing title for the story seems to suggest that all of life (classes, races, and religions) eventually will have to intersect, just as pure laws of physics would predict that everything on earth that rises eventually will converge somewhere in space. Whether this action causes a disastrous collision or a peaceful merging of equals is left to the characters and to the reader.

Michael J. Meyer
DePaul University

EXISTENTIALISM
A philosophical theory that gained a great deal of attention during and after WORLD WAR II, especially in Europe. Based on the premise that one simply exists in a meaningless world before one can acquire a defined character, existentialism asserts the twin concepts of free will and responsibility. Because we are born into a value-less world in which no God exists, each individual must bear the responsibility for making meaning out of an ABSURD, lonely, anxiety-producing existence. In the process, one must often overcome feelings of anguish and despair. Existentialism, particularly as expressed and made popular by the French writer-philosopher Jean-Paul Sartre, was persuasively used in the novels of such European writers as Albert Camus, Simone de Beauvoir, Fyodor Dostoyevski, and Franz Kafka (see KAFKAESQUE), and aroused the interest of numerous American writers. Ernest HEMINGWAY, for instance, thematically incorporates existentialism into his celebrated story, "A CLEAN, WELL-LIGHTED PLACE."

EXODUS
In the Old Testament of the Bible, the story of the liberation of the people of Israel from slavery in Egypt in the 15th century B.C. and their safe passage through the Red Sea, led by Moses, to Mount Sinai. Direct and indirect ALLUSIONS to Exodus occur in such stories as Ralph ELLISON's "King of the Bingo Game" and William FAULKNER's GO DOWN, MOSES.

"EYES, THE" EDITH WHARTON (1910)
One of Edith WHARTON's most respected ghost stories (see GHOST STORY), "The Eyes" is a modern GOTHIC tale that illustrates a haunted inner consciousness. The external horror of the tale is a reflection of internal evil, much as it is in Henry JAMES's "THE TURN OF THE SCREW." Like James, Wharton uses ghostly encounters as a setting for psychological study and personal discovery.

The story begins after a gathering at Andrew Culwin's home, where friends have been telling ghost stories. The narrator describes Culwin as a rationalist who does not believe in ghosts. Culwin sees himself as mentor to young male artists. After everyone else leaves, Phillip Frenham, a young intellectual, asks his host to tell a ghost story of his own. Culwin reveals to the narrator and Frenham the tale of ghostly eyes that have haunted him on several occasions. The framing narrative of "The Eyes" allows the reader to understand the source of these visitations, while revealing Culwin's misogynistic, detached, and cruel character.

Culwin is first visited by the eyes following his marriage proposal to his cousin, Alice. He has pursued her out of scientific curiosity, to "find out the secret of her content." Culwin is awakened that evening by the glowing eyes. He is so frightened that he leaves for Europe without a word to Alice. Months later Alice asks Culwin to befriend her cousin, Gilbert, a young man who wants to be a writer. Culwin lies to Gilbert about his talent in order to satisfy his own selfish desire to impress the young man. Afterward Culwin is again haunted by the eyes. Once Gilbert learns how Culwin has used him, the eyes disappear. After Culwin finishes his story, Frenham realizes that he is the next victim of Culwin's manipulation, and Culwin finally sees that he himself is the source of the hideous eyes.

BIBLIOGRAPHY

Fedorko, Kathy A. *Gender and the Gothic in the Fiction of Edith Wharton.* Tuscaloosa: University of Alabama Press, 1995.

Wharton Edith. *Collected Short Stories.* 2 vols., edited by R. W. B. Lewis. New York: Scribner's, 1968.

White, Barbara. *Edith Wharton: A Study of the Short Fiction.* New York: Twayne, 1991.

Tracie Guzzio
Ohio University

F

FABLE A short story or tale, usually epigrammatic (see EPIGRAM), exemplifying a moral thesis or demonstrating correct or "good" behavior. A fable's characters can include gods, people, animals, or even inanimate objects, and the fable itself illustrates a moral, usually stated at the end in the form of an epigram by either the narrator or one of the characters. Most common is the beast fable, in which animals talk and act like the human types they represent. (See PERSONIFICATION.) In the fable of the race between the hare and the tortoise, for example, the hare runs quickly but has no stamina; the tortoise finishes the race ahead of the hare, illustrating the moral "Slow and steady wins the day." An early set of beast fables was attributed to Aesop, a Greek slave of the sixth century B.C.; in the 17th century the Frenchman Jean Fontaine wrote a set of witty fables in verse. In *Animal Farm* (1945), the British writer George Orwell expanded the beast fable into a sustained satire on the political and social conditions of the age. See also Chaucer, for example, "The Nun's Priest's Tale," and James Thurber's *Fables for Our Time* (1940). A form of beast fable occurs in NATIVE AMERICAN stories; Mourning Dove, for instance, writes coyote stories that include many tales in which animals demonstrate human characteristics. (See also AESOP'S FABLES, COYOTE STORY.)

FAIRY TALE The fairy is a mythical being with a diminutive human form, a mischievous temperament, and magical powers. The description of these tiny creatures varies from the graceful, delicate English pixie to the gnarled, old Irish leprechaun. Other types of fairies are Arabian genies, Scandanavian trolls, and German elves. The fairy tale is a simple narrative that usually includes fairies but might also include giants, ogres, and other supernatural beings in magical or fantastic settings written for the amusement of children. The Danish writer Hans Christian Andersen wrote many original fairy tales, and the German Brothers Grimm published a well-known collection.

"FALL OF THE HOUSE OF USHER, THE" EDGAR ALLAN POE (1839) Long considered Edgar Allan POE's masterpiece, "The Fall of the House of Usher" continues to intrigue new generations of readers. The story has a tantalizingly horrific appeal, and since its publication in *Burton's Gentleman's Magazine* scholars, critics, and general readers continue to grapple with the myriad possible reasons for the story's hold on the human psyche. These explanations range from the pre-FREUDian to the pre-WASTE LAND and pre-Kafka-cum-nihilist (see KAFKAESQUE and NIHILISM) to the biographical and the cultural. Indeed, despite Poe's distaste for ALLEGORY, some critics view the house as a METAPHOR for

155

the human psyche (Strandberg 705). Whatever conclusion a reader reaches, none finds the story an easy one to forget.

Poe's narrative technique draws us immediately into the tale. On a stormy autumn (with an implied pun on the word "fall"?) evening, a traveler—an outsider, like the reader—rides up to the Usher mansion. This traveler, also the first-person narrator and boyhood friend of Roderick Usher, the owner of the house, has come in response to a summons from Usher. We share the narrator's responses to the gloomy mood and the menacing facade of the House of Usher, noticing, with him, the dank lake that reflects the house (effectively doubling it, like the Usher twins we will soon meet) and apprehensively viewing the fissure, or crack, in the wall. Very soon we understand that, whatever else it may mean, the house is a metaphor for the Usher family itself and that if the house is seriously flawed, so are its occupants.

With this foreboding introduction, we enter the interior through a GOTHIC portal with the narrator. With him we encounter Roderick Usher, who has changed drastically since last the narrator saw him. His cadaverous appearance, his nervousness, his mood swings, his almost extrahuman sensitivity to touch, sound, taste, smell, and light, along with the narrator's report that he seems lacking in moral sense, portrays a deeply troubled soul. We learn, too, that his twin sister Madeline, a neurasthenic woman like her brother, is subject to catatonic trances. These two characters, like the house, are woefully, irretrievably flawed. The suspense continues to climb as we go deeper into the dark house and, with the narrator, attempt to fathom Roderick's malady.

Roderick, a poet and an artist, and Madeline represent the last of the Usher line. They live alone, never venturing outside. The sympathetic narrator does all he can to ease Roderick's hours, recounting a ballad by Roderick, which, entitled "The Haunted House," speaks figuratively of the House of Usher: Evil and discord possess the house, echoing the decay the narrator has noticed on the outside. During his stay Roderick tells the narrator that

Madeline has died, and together they place her in a vault; she looks deceptively lifelike. Thereafter Roderick's altered behavior causes the narrator to wonder whether he hides a dark secret or has fallen into madness. A week or so later, as a storm rages outside, the narrator seeks to calm his host by reading to him a romance entitled "The Mad Trist." The title could be evidence that both the narrator's diagnoses are correct: Roderick has a secret (perhaps he has trysted with his own sister?) and is now utterly mad. The tale unfolds parallel to the action in the Usher house: as Ethelred, the hero of the romance, breaks through the door and slays the hermit, Madeline, not dead after all, breaks though her coffin. Just before she appears at the door, Roderick admits that they have buried her alive and that she now stands at the door. Roderick's admission comes too late. Just as Ethelred now slays the dragon, causing the family shield to fall at his feet, Madeline falls on her brother (the hermit who never leaves the house), killing them both and bringing down the last symbol of the House of Usher. As the twins collapse in death together, the entire house disintegrates into the lake, destroying the double image noted at the opening of the story.

The story raises many questions tied to gender issues: Is Madeline Roderick's female double, or DOPPELGANGER? If, as many critics suggest, Roderick is Poe's self-portrait, then do Madeline and Roderick represent the feminine and masculine sides of the author? Is incest at the core of Roderick's relationship with Madeline? Is he (like his creator, some would suggest) a misogynist? FEMINISTS have for some time now pointed to Poe's theory that the most poetic subject in the world is the "DEATH OF A BEAUTIFUL WOMAN." Is Madeline's return from the tomb a feminist revenge story? Does she, like the Ethelred of the romance, adopt the male role of the hero as she slays the evil hermit and the evil dragon, who together symbolize Roderick's character? Has the mad Roderick made the narrator complicit in his crime (saying "we" rather than "I" buried her alive)? If so, to what extent must we view him as the UNRELIABLE NARRATOR? Is the narrator himself merely reporting a dream—or the after-effects of opium, as he vaguely intimates at points in the story? Or, as critic and scholar Eugene Current-Garcia suggests, can we generally agree that Poe, like Nathaniel HAWTHORNE, was haunted by the presence of evil? If so, "perhaps most of his tales should be read as allegories of nightmarish, neurotic states of mind" (Current-Garcia 81). We may never completely plumb the psychological complexities of this story, but it implies deeply troubling questions and nearly endless avenues for interpretation.

BIBLIOGRAPHY

Current-Garcia, Eugene. *The American Short Story Before 1850.* Boston: Twayne, 1985.

May, Charles E. *Edgar Allan Poe: Studies in the Short Fiction.* Boston: Twayne, 1991.

Poe, Edgar Allan. "The Fall of the House of Usher." In *The Heath Anthology of American Literature,* 3rd ed. Edited by Paul Lauter. Boston: Houghton Mifflin, Vol. 1, 1461–1474.

Strandberg, Victor. *"The Fall of the House of Usher."* *Reference Guide to Short Fiction.* Edited by Noelle Watson. Detroit: Gale Press, 1994, 704–05.

FALSE DAWN EDITH WHARTON (1924)

One of Edith Wharton's many stories of New York, *False Dawn* was published with the subtitle *The 'Forties* in 1924 as the first of four volumes in a set entitled *Old New York.* This NOVELLA recounts the experiences of Lewis Raycie, son of an old New York family. As a young man departing on his European grand tour, he is given $5,000 by his father to spend on artwork for the family collection. Instead of buying what is popular at the time, however—such as works by Carlo Dolce, Salvator Rosa, and, ideally, Raphael—Lewis becomes aware of a "revolution in taste" in Europe through meeting the English writer and critic John Ruskin. Following Ruskin's pre-Raphaelite tastes, Lewis instead purchases works by Primitive artists Giotto de Bondone, Carpaccio, Mantegna, and Piero della Francesca. His father, furious with his choices, disowns him and dies within a year. Lewis marries his childhood sweetheart, Beatrice Kent, and in order to make a living, they attempt to charge admission to see the collection but are unsuccessful.

In the conclusion of the novella, set several years later, a young narrator learns of how the Raycies, shamed, went off to live alone in the country and died at an early age, along with their daughter Louisa. The collection was passed on and finally found, 50 years later, in the attic of the elderly Miss Alethea Raycie's house. It was now priceless, "one of the most beautiful collections of Italian Primitives in the world" (FD 367), but the inheritor of the collection, Netta Cosby, sold the works to various museums in order to buy jewels, Rolls-Royces, and a house on Fifth Avenue.

The novella exhibits Wharton's masterful use of IRONY, a pervasive characteristic of her work, in treating the division between crass new-money values, which Wharton often identified with Americans, and aesthetic taste and connoisseurship, traits Wharton herself valued and often associated with Europeans. The novella also illustrates REALISM in its careful detailing of life in New York of the 1840s. R. W. B. Lewis notes a connection to Wharton's own life in the novella; she "wove an account of her parents' courtship" (458) into the work when she described Lewis Raycie, in the face of family disapproval, sailing an improvised boat down Long Island Sound in the early morning to meet his sweetheart, as Wharton's father George Frederic Jones had done in order to meet her mother, Lucretia Rhinelander.

BIBLIOGRAPHY

Brooks, Van Wyck. *The Dream of Arcadia: American Artists and Writers in Italy 1760–1915.* New York: Dutton, 1958.

Lewis, R. W. B. *Edith Wharton: A Biography.* New York: Scribner's, 1975.

Rae, Catherine M. *Edith Wharton's New York Quartet.* Lanham, Md.: University Press of America, 1984.

Wharton, Edith. *False Dawn (The 'Forties).* In *Wharton: Novellas and Other Writings.* New York: Literary Classics of the United States, 1990.

Charlotte Rich
University of North Carolina at Chapel Hill

FANTASY

A narrative or situation in fiction with no basis in the real world. Authors may use fantasy for pure entertainment, or for serious commentary, direct or implied, on real-world issues and situations. Much SCIENCE FICTION and UTOPIAN fiction employs fantasy, as in the stories of Isaac Asimov or Ray BRADBURY, for instance. Fantasy is a major component of the fairy tale or the FABLE. It may also be an element of MAGICAL REALISM in contemporary American fiction, as in the stories of John BARTH, for example, and in numerous stories by African-American, Hispanic-American, and Native American writers.

FARRELL, JAMES T.　See STUDS LONIGAN.

FASCISM　A political philosophy that exalts nation and race at the expense of the individual. Major concepts include dictatorial leadership, a one-party system, an aggressive military policy, control at all levels of individual and economic activity, and the use of special police forces to instill fear and suppress opposition. The modern term derives from the party led by Benito Mussolini, who ruled Italy from 1922 until the Italian defeat in WORLD WAR II, and was later applied to include Adolf HITLER's regime in Germany and Francisco Franco's government in Spain, among others.

FAULKNER, WILLIAM (CUTHBERT) (1897–1962)　For many critics and readers, William Faulkner remains the most significant writer of the 20th century: He invented a unique voice, a highly charged, rhetorical, compelling one of urgent intensity. Known as one of the greatest and most genuinely innovative modernists (see MODERNISM), Faulkner published 19 novels and more than 75 short stories between 1926 and 1962. Like other CLASSIC American authors, Nathaniel HAWTHORNE or Henry JAMES, for instance, Faulkner is best known for his ground-breaking novels: The Sound and the Fury; As I Lay Dying; Light in August; Absalom, Absalom!; and GO DOWN, MOSES. His short stories, however, have been regularly anthologized and have attracted an enormous amount of critical attention. Indeed, contemporary readers are likely as familiar with "A ROSE FOR EMILY" or "THE BEAR" as they are with the novels. Like the novels, a majority

of Faulkner's stories are set in the South, particularly in YOKNAPATAWPHA COUNTY, which Faulkner invented and peopled with fictional black and white residents. In both novels and stories, moreover, many of the same individuals and families appear. Some of Faulkner's major fictional families include the Sartoris, SNOPES, DE SPAIN, Compson, Sutpen, McCaslin, and Carothers families. Throughout Faulkner's canon, these characters appear and reappear, carefully delineated, their family histories often spanning several generations.

Faulkner was born in Oxford, Mississippi, and lived there for most of his life, except for brief trips until he moved to Charlottesville, Virginia, where he was writer-in-residence at the University of Virginia. Thus the Deep South is the locus of most of his stories: By setting them in Yoknapatawpha County, reintroducing characters, filling in gaps of MYTH, LEGEND, THEME, situation, and CHARACTER, and continually experimenting with these and other techniques, Faulkner extended the world of the short story. Faulkner, Katherine Anne PORTER, Ernest HEMINGWAY, Eudora WELTY, and F. Scott FITZGERALD in his later years formed the core of the modernist short story writers. Faulkner wrote some stories that rank among the best in the world: "A Rose for Emily," "Dry September," and "BARN BURNING," to name just three.

"A Rose for Emily" is one of the most frequently anthologized, along with "THAT EVENING SUN," and "Barn Burning." A number of the stories from Go Down, Moses have been published separately ("The Bear" being the most famous), and stories collected in THE UNVANQUISHED are important CIVIL WAR stories that also give the background of the major families. Faulkner's short story collections published during his lifetime include These 13: Stories (1931), Doctor Martino and Other Stories (1934), Go Down Moses, and Other Stories (1942) KNIGHT'S GAMBIT (1949), Collected Stories (1950), Big Woods (1955), Jealousy and Episode: Two Stories (1955), Uncle Willy and Other Stories (1958), and Selected Short Stories (1961). Posthumously published are Barn Burning and Other Stories (1977) and Uncollected Stories (1979). Two individual stories, "Barn Burning" and

"A Courtship," won the O. Henry Prizes for 1939 and 1949, respectively, and *Collected Stories* won the National Book Award for Fiction in 1950.

Critic James G. Watson makes a key point when he says that although Faulkner was first and foremost a writer of novels which range over and define an entire locale, it is also true that the short stories play a critical role in explaining and in amplifying that world; indeed, in some cases the novels are indebted to the stories (Watson 126). For instance, "Wash" and "Evangeline," although published after the novel, contain the seeds of *Absalom, Absalom!* (1936), whereas *The Hamlet* (1940) actually incorporates a number of revisions of five previously published stories. Both *The Unvanquished* (1938) and *Go Down, Moses* (1942) are novels consisting entirely of short stories as chapters, the majority of them previously published.

The range of Faulkner's stories extends in many directions, featuring NATIVE AMERICANS, blacks, and whites, with attention to the larger issues with which the United States continues to grapple. Some of his most memorable stories about Native Americans include "Red Leaves," concerned with two Indians in pursuit of a slave who does not wish to die with his master, a tribal chief, and "A Justice," which depicts two interracial love affairs, the Indian Pappy's with a slave woman and Ikkemotubbe's with a Creole woman. The "yellow" child of Ikkemotubbe and the slave woman is named "Had-Two-Fathers," but as critics have pointed out, it should be "Had-Three-Fathers," since Pappy does not know that the slave woman's child is actually Ikkemotubbe's. The child reappears as the adult Sam Fathers in "The Bear." Faulkner wrote an entire SHORT STORY CYCLE about Yoknapatawpha blacks, published as *Go Down, Moses.* His stories about blacks are counterpointed by those about poor whites, most famously exemplified in "Barn Burning." And his stories about women are legion, ranging from background stories to women in novels (for example, "There Was a Queen" provides insight into Narcissa Benbow, featured in *Flags in the Dust* and *Sanctuary*), to those that examine gender restrictions and the way they can warp one's human-ity ("A Rose for Emily," for instance, and "Dry September"). This theme reappears in Faulkner's tribute to DRUSILLA HAWKE in the stories of *The Unvanquished.*

One significant fact about Faulkner's story collections is that he envisioned them contrapuntally—that is, he arranged them in an order that, far from being random, evoked a special kind of unity. This unity is easier to see in the short story cycles such as *Go Down, Moses, The Unvanquished,* and even *Knight's Gambit,* in which the same characters reappear in stories that are more or less sequential. This order is less easy to discern in larger collections, such as *These Thirteen,* and even less so in *Collected Stories.* Faulkner, however, insisted that the order was there, and critics continue to study the connections among the stories. In *Dr. Martino and Other Stories,* the author even divided the book into six subsections that juxtapose past and present, Yoknapatawpha and the world outside. For *Big Woods,* five years later, he gathered together his hunting stories.

In many ways the unity of Faulkner's stories complements the unity of his novels; in fact, they are indispensable in assessing the unity of his entire oeuvre. Like the novels, the stories stand alone—and, like the novels, when viewed as part of the entire Yoknapatawpha saga, they contribute to our understanding of the people, the history, the region, the changing eras, and, ultimately, Faulkner's artistic rendering not only of a microcosm of the United States but also of humanity at large.

BIBLIOGRAPHY

Faulkner, William. *Absalom, Absalom!* New York: Random House, 1936.

———. *As I Lay Dying.* New York: Random House, 1930.

———. *Big Woods.* New York: Random House, 1955.

———. *Collected Stories.* New York: Random House, 1950.

———. *Doctor Martino and Other Stories.* New York: Smith and Haas, 1934.

———. *A Fable.* New York: Random House, 1954.

———. *Father Abraham.* Edited by James B. Meriwether. New York: Random House, 1984.

———. *The Faulkner Reader.* Edited by Saxe Commins. New York: Random House, 1954.

————. *Go Down, Moses, and other Stories.* New York: Random House, 1942.

————. *The Hamlet.* New York: Random House, 1940; excerpt, as *The Long Hot Summer.* New York: New American Library, 1958.

————. *Intruder in the Dust.* New York: Random House, 1948.

————. *Jealousy an Episode: Two Stories.* Minneapolis, Minn: Faulkner Stories, 1955.

————. *Knight's Gambit.* New York: Random House, 1949.

————. *Light in August.* New York: Smith and Haas, 1932.

————. *The Mansion.* New York: Random House, 1959.

————. *Miss Zilphia Gant.* Dallas, Tex.: The Book Club of Texas, 1932.

————. *Mosquitoes.* New York: Boni and Liveright, 1927.

————. *Notes on a Horsethief.* Greenville, Miss.: Levee Press, 1950.

————. *Novels 1930–1935.* Library of America. Edited by Joseph Blotner and Noel Polk. New York: Literary Classics of the United States. 1985.

————. *Novels 1936–1940.* Edited by Joseph Blotner. New York: Library of America, 1990.

————. *The Portable Faulkner.* Edited by Malcolm Cowley. New York: The Viking Press, 1967.

————. *Pylon.* New York: Smith and Haas, 1935.

————. *Requiem for a Nun.* New York: Random House, 1951.

————. *The Reivers: A Reminiscence.* New York: Random House, 1962.

————. *Sanctuary.* New York: Cape and Smith, 1931.

————. *Sartoris.* New York: Harcourt Brace, 1929. *As Flags in the Dust.* Edited by Douglas Day. New York: Random House, 1973.

————. *Selected Short Stories.* New York: The Modern Library, 1961.

————. *Soldiers' Pay.* New York: Boni & Liveright, 1926.

————. *The Sound and the Fury.* New York: Cape and Smith, 1929.

————. *The Town.* New York: Random House, 1957.

————. *These Thirteen: Stories.* New York: Cape and Smith, 1931.

————. *Uncle Willy and Other Stories.* London: Chatto and Windus, 1958.

————. *Uncollected Stories.* Eited by Joseph Blotner. New York: Random House, 1979.

————. *The Unvanquished.* New York: Random House, 1938.

————. *The Wild Palms.* New York: Random House, 1939.

Watson, James G. "The American Short Story: 1930–1945." In *The American Short Story 1900–1945.* Edited by Philip Stevick. Boston: Twayne, 1984, pp. 103–46.

FAUSTIAN   Pertaining to either the historical Georg Faust, a 15-century German magician and astrologer, or to the various subsequent literary works by Christopher Marlowe, Goethe, Thomas Mann, and others loosely based on his life. According to legend, Faust sold his soul to the devil in exchange for youth and all personal and worldly experience. In modern usage, striking a "Faustian bargain" implies using any means, including unsavory ones, to attain one's goal.

FEMINISM/FEMINIST CRITICISM   Often used synonomously with the term *women's movement*, feminism in its largest sense is concerned with political and social equality for women. Historically, the women's, or feminist, movement in the United States is divided into roughly three eras: the antebellum period (1830–60), the progressive era (1900–WORLD WAR I), and the 1960s and 1970s, when the study of women became a major focus. Today, most critics generally agree that there is no one kind of feminism; the study of women recognizes individual differences but has attempted to find common subjects of agreement: for instance, that patriarchal society oppresses women and minorities, among whom a close link exists; that women have been marginalized; and that texts by women must be recovered, reissued, publicized, studied, and interpreted.

Growing out of the post–WORLD WAR II women's movement—three of whose founding works, Simone de Beauvoir's *The Second Sex* (1949), Betty Friedan's *The Feminine Mystique* (1963), and Kate Millett's *Sexual Politics* (1969), included sustained analyses of the representation of women in literature—feminist criticism has pursued what Elaine Showalter calls "feminist critique" (analysis of the works of male authors, especially in the depiction of women and their relation to women readers) on the one hand and "gynocriticism" (the study of women's writing) on the other. Feminist critiques provide new and illuminating ways to interpret male authors' work. In William FAULKNER'S "A ROSE FOR EMILY," for instance, a traditional interpretation views Emily, the protagonist, as a grotesque metaphor for the decaying southern aristocracy. A feminist critique, however, reveals Emily as a casualty of patriarchy and literally of her own father and lover; her unconventional way of fighting back reveals her sense of identity and makes her portrait much more sympathetic. Relatedly, gynocriticism has been responsible for resurrecting numerous "lost" women writers—Kate CHOPIN, Edith WHARTON, and Zora Neale HURSTON. Feminist critics who worked to rediscover and recover women writers' works include Patricia Meyers Spacks (*The Female Imagination,* 1975), Ellen Moers (*Literary Women,* 1976), Elaine Showalter (*A Literature of Their Own,* 1978), and Nina Baym (*Women's Fiction,* 1978).

In addition to recovering neglected works by women authors through the ages and creating a canon of women's writing, feminist criticism has become a wide-ranging exploration of the construction of gender and identity, the role of women in culture and society, and the possibilities of women's creative expression. The 1970s spawned a wealth of ways to approach both images of women in literature by men and books written by women. Some of the most influential texts that call into question the old male-oriented literary criticism include Adrienne Rich's essay "When We Dead Awaken: Writing as Re-vision" (1971) and Carolyn Heilbrun's "Feminist Studies: Bringing the Spirit Back to English Studies" (1979). Near the end of the decade, feminist critics began to focus less on patriarchy and more on issues of gender differences, suggesting that women's reading, writing, and criticism differ from men's. Significant voices in this recent phase of feminist criticism include Rich (*Of Woman Born,* 1976), Nancy Chodorow (*The Reproduction of Mothering,* 1979), Judith Fetterly (*The Resisting Reader,* 1978), Janice Radway (*Reading the Romance,* 1984), Annette Kolodny (*The Lay of the Land,* 1976, and *The Land Before Her,* 1984), and Jane Tomkins (*Sensational Designs,* 1985).

One strongly debated issue in current feminist criticism is the difference between the American school and the French school, as argued in Toril Moi's influential book *Sexual/Textual Politics: Feminist Literary Theory* (1985). Moi opposes such American feminist critics as Showalter and coauthors Sandra Gilbert and Susan Gubar of *The Madwoman in the Attic* (1979) for what she perceives as a naive treatment of texts and for participating in the liberal humanist—and patriarchal—tradition. On the other hand, Moi praises such French feminists as Julia Kristeva, Hélène Cixous, and Luce Irigaray, who view texts from a psychoanalytic perspective and interpret women and the feminine through close examination of the problems of language.

Although in the 1970s an increasing number of women of all colors perceived the cultural and academic marginalization of women, white women paid little attention to the differences among women. Much of the important work in researching differences, recovering texts, and staking new literary ground in the 1980s was being performed by women of color, including Alice Walker (*In Search of Our Mothers' Gardens: Womanist Prose,* 1983), Gloria Anzaldua (*Borderlands/La Frontera: The New Mestiza,* 1987, and *Making Face, Making Soul—Haciendo Caras,* 1990), Cherrie Moraga (*This Bridge Called My Back: Writings by Radical Women of Color,* with Gloria Anzaldua, 1981), Paula Gunn Allen (*The Sacred Hoop,* 1986, and *Spider Woman's Granddaughters,* 1989), and numerous others. From the 1980s, women of all color began focusing on differences among women, resulting in the current views of a much more diverse and individualized femininism and feminist criticism.

BIBLIOGRAPHY

Davidson, Cathy N., and Linda Wagner-Martin. *The Oxford Companion to Women's Writing in the United States.* New York: Oxford University Press, 1995.

Gilbert, Sandra M., and Susan Gubar. *The Madwoman in the Attic.* New Haven, Conn.: Yale University Press, 1979.

Gilbert, Sandra M., and Susan Gubar, eds. *The Norton Anthology of Literature by Women: The Tradition in English.* New York: Norton, 1985.

Moers, Ellen. *Literary Women.* New York: Oxford University Press, 1976.

Moi, Toril. *Sexual/Textual Politics: Feminist Literary Theory.* New York: Routledge, 1985.

Showalter, Elaine. *A Literature of Their Own.* Princeton, N.J.: Princeton University Press, 1977.

Showalter, Elaine, ed. *The New Feminist Criticism: Essays on Women, Literature, and Theory.* New York: Pantheon, 1985.

Vandell, Kathy Scales. "Literary Criticism." In *The Oxford Companion to Women's Writing in the United States.* Edited by Cathy N. Davidson and Linda Wagner-Martin, 524–27. New York: Oxford University Press, 1995.

Warhol, Robyn R. "Feminism." In *The Oxford Companion to Women's Writing in the United States.* Edited by Cathy N. Davidson and Linda Wagner-Martin, 307–14. New York: Oxford University Press, 1995.

FERBER, EDNA (1887–1968)

A prolific writer of novels, plays, and stories, Edna Ferber actually launched her long career as a popular and highly successful writer of fiction with several collections of short stories. Her story "No Room at the Inn" was issued as a GIFT BOOK in 1941 and was included in the 1947 collection of Ferber stories entitled *One Basket.* In 1925 she won the PULITZER PRIZE for her novel *So Big* (1924), and a classic musical play was created from her novel *Showboat* (1926). Many of Ferber's works were also made into movies.

BIBLIOGRAPHY

Ferber, Edna. *Buttered Side Down.* New York: Frederick A. Stokes, 1912.

———. *Cheerful, By Request.* Garden City, N.Y.: Doubleday, Page & Company, 1918.

———. *Emma McChesney & Co.* New York: Frederick A. Stokes, 1915.

———. *Gigolo.* Garden City, N.Y.: Doubleday, Page & Company, 1922.

———. *Half Portions.* Garden City, N.Y.: Doubleday, Page & Company, 1920.

———. *Mother Knows Best: A Fiction Book.* Garden City, N.Y.: Doubleday, Page & Company, 1927.

———. *No Room at the Inn.* Garden City, N.Y.: Doubleday, Doran and Company, Inc. 1941.

———. *Old Man Minick: A Short Story.* Garden City, N.Y.: Doubleday, Page, 1924.

———. *One Basket: Thirty-One Short Stories.* New York: Simon & Schuster, 1947.

———. *Personality Plus: Some Experiences of Emma McChesney and Her Son, Jock.* New York: Frederick A. Stokes Company, 1914.

———. *Roast, Beef, Medium: The Business Adventures of Emma McChesney.* New York: Frederick A. Stokes Company, 1913.

———. *So Big.* Cleveland, Ohio: World Publishing Company, 1924.

———. *They Brought Their Women: A Book of Short Stories.* Garden City, N.Y.: Doubleday, Doran and Company, 1933.

———. *Your Town.* Cleveland, Ohio: World Publishing Co., 1948.

FEVER JOHN EDGAR WIDEMAN (1989)

Fever, John Edgar WIDEMAN's second short story collection, contains some of his most anthologized and respected work. The title reverberates through many of the stories as a symbol of the disease of racism in America, past and present. The stories are also characterized by a distinctive postmodern style. (See POSTMODERNISM.) Included in the collection are "Surfiction," "Little Brother," "Doc's Story," and "Valaida," a story inspired by the life of jazz trumpeter Valaida Snow (c. 1900–1956) that illustrates the connections between victims of hate and oppression across time and the world. The hallmark of the collection is the title story "Fever." Based on historical accounts of the yellow fever epidemic in Philadelphia in 1798, the story traces the exploits of Richard Allen, an African American minister, and Dr. Benjamin Rush, a local physician credited with halting the epidemic. Allen and members of his congregation helped to aid the sick and bury the dead. City leaders questioned the motives of the sacrifices made by Allen and his followers, and accused them and others of African descent of causing and carrying the disease. This event is also the source of Wideman's novel *The Cattle Killing* (1996). "Fever" and other stories in the collection question the ways that traditional history has silenced the lives and achievements of marginalized people, thus continuing racist attitudes and perceptions.

Tracie Guzzio
Ohio University

"FIRE AND CLOUD" RICHARD WRIGHT (1938)

"Fire and Cloud" was among the first of Richard WRIGHT's literary efforts to bring him critical attention and praise. In 1938 it won first prize of $500 among 600 entries in a *Story Magazine* contest; that same year it won an O. HENRY MEMORIAL AWARD ($200) and was included in Wright's *Uncle Tom's Children: Four Novellas* (1938). Wright explained that he wrote this story out of a "desire on my part to depict in dramatic fashion the relationship between leaders of both races." Wright's Communist affiliation is visible in his portrayal of a successful interracial protest march, although his PROTAGONIST is ultimately more of a Christian black nationalist than a Communist.

Set in the rural South of Wright's childhood, "Fire and Cloud" is influenced by both proletarian REALISM and NATURALISM; its protagonist, the Reverend Dan Taylor, is poor, uneducated, and controlled by the white leadership, but in order to defend the lives of his oppressed people, he forges an alliance with local Communists and develops a proletarian consciousness. The story depicts a small town in a depression-era crisis: Landowning whites have refused to let impoverished blacks farm their property, and town leaders won't provide food relief, leaving the black community hungry and desperate enough to join a Communist protest march. At the beginning of the story, Wright builds dramatic tension by placing members of each of the factions pressuring Taylor in different rooms of his house: In one room are the mayor, chief of police, and head of the anti-Communist Red Squad; in another are the Communists Hadley and Green; in another are a group of starving parishioners begging Taylor to help them; in the basement is the deacon board, including Deacon Smith, who wants to run Taylor out of the church so that he can take his place. Unable to take a stand, Taylor frantically placates each group, trying to defuse the potentially explosive conflict among the whites, the blacks, and the Communists. Wright accurately depicts the nuances of racial tensions in these scenes: the mayor and the Communists both use a form of psychological blackmail on Taylor, holding him accountable for the lives of the black community threatened by hunger on one side and by lynching on the other.

After being whipped into unconsciousness by a group of whites who also beat other parishioners, Taylor realizes that his attempts to keep the various factions at bay have resulted in his isolation and vulnerability. Telling his son that God is in the people, he incites his congregation to march, and when the protest is a success, he renews his faith both in God and in the power of the people. Critics have viewed this ending as too ideological and the characters as unrealistic STEREOTYPES. (Wright's awkward use of DIALECT contributes to this impression.) Others argue that Wright finds a nice balance between ideology and story. Either way, "Fire and Cloud" is one of the rare Wright stories with a happy ending.

BIBLIOGRAPHY

Fabre, Michel. *The Unfinished Quest of Richard Wright.* New York: Morrow, 1973.

Gibson, Donald. *The Politics of Literary Expression: Essays of Major Black Writers.* Westport: Conn.: Greenwood Press, 1981.

Joyce, Joyce Ann. *Richard Wright's Art of Tragedy.* Iowa City: A University of Iowa Press, 1986.

Kinnamon, Keneth. *The Emergence of Richard Wright: A Study in Literature and Society.* Urbana: University of Illinois Press, 1972.

Margolies, Edward. "The Short Stories: *Uncle Tom's Children, Eight Men.*" In *Critical Essays on Richard Wright.* Edited by Yoshinobu Hakutani. Boston: G. K. Hall, 1982.

Writer's Club Bulletin (Columbia University) 1 (1938).

Young, James O. *Black Writers of the Thirties.* Baton Rouge: University of Louisiana Press, 1973.

Kimberly Drake
Virginia Wesleyan College

FISHER, DOROTHY CANFIELD (1879–1959)

Unlike many American writers with turbulent lives and tumultuous relationships, Dorothy Fisher was born to loving, responsible parents who encouraged her literary ambitions. After enjoying a happy and productive childhood, she married John Fisher, a man with whom she was in love and in whose company she was able to be productive: Between 1907 and 1958 she published 40 books.

Her husband shared her commitments to education, peace, feeding the hungry, healing the hurt, and ending prejudice, concerns Fisher incorporated into her fiction. Dorothy Fisher introduced Americans to the type of education practiced by Maria Montessori, now known as "Montessori schools."

FITZGERALD, F(RANCIS) SCOTT (KEY) (1896–1940)

Born into the upper middle class in 1896 in St. Paul, Minnesota, F. Scott Fitzgerald was fascinated by the paradoxes of the American class system. In stories and novels, he fictionalized his own experiences as an outsider attempting to enter the privileged world of the wealthy. He was among the expatriate writers in Paris in the 1920s whose fiction reflected the cultural transformations in Europe and America in the early 20th century. As a realist (see REALISM), he is sometimes called a social historian in fiction, but his work incorporates romantic THEMES (see ROMANTICISM) as well, such as the distance between imagination and reality and the impossibility of recreating the past.

Fitzgerald enjoyed extraordinary popularity in the first decade of his career, beginning with the novel *This Side of Paradise* (1920), which he followed immediately with a collection of stories, *Flappers and Philosophers*. His depiction of glamorous young people in pursuit of excitement, love, or a dream of the moment captured a mood that, for many readers, epitomized the Jazz Age. In addition to four novels, he published over 150 short stories in popular magazines, such as *Redbook* and MCCALL'S. As a regular contributor to the SATURDAY EVENING POST, he received $4,000 per story at the height of his career. Fitzgerald published four collections of stories, each of which was timed to appear in conjunction with a novel. In 1922 *The Beautiful and Damned* was followed by *Tales of the Jazz Age*. After *The Great Gatsby* came *All the Sad Young Men* in 1926, and *Tender is the Night* followed the collection *Taps at Reveille* in 1935.

In the 1930s Fitzgerald's reputation began to fade dramatically as troubles in his personal life interfered with his productivity. His wife, Zelda, was hospitalized permanently, suffering from schizophrenia; his own alcoholism became life-threatening. In the 1920s the couple had lived an extravagant life of international travel, expensive homes, and lavish parties; the subsequent decade brought illness and debt. After 1935 ESQUIRE was the only magazine that published his stories consistently—at about 10 percent of the price he had commanded in his prime. Nonetheless, Fitzgerald continued to write, although he feared he had became a relic consigned to the past. In 1937 he was under contract as a script writer for M-G-M, but he also began work on a fifth novel, *The Last Tycoon,* while continuing to produce stories. In 1940 he died suddenly of a heart attack at age 44.

In the years since his death, reassessments of Fitzgerald's life and work have returned him to his former stature as an important American author. The critic Malcolm Cowley inspired new interest in the stories in 1951 when he collected 28 of them in *The Stories of F. Scott Fitzgerald.* At that time, most of Fitzgerald's short fiction was uncollected and without published commentary. Since Cowley's volume, several new collections have appeared, followed by a slow but steady stream of critical reappraisal.

Fitzgerald made a number of disparaging remarks about his magazine stories, but he also expressed pride in their craftsmanship. Their quality is uneven because he produced many surprisingly quickly, in order to earn money. Others deserve the serious critical attention they have begun to receive.

The stories display Fitzgerald's versatility. Like the novels, they often combine social realism with a romantic theme of loss or disillusionment; however, Fitzgerald also used his stories to experiment with fantasy and humor, including farce and BURLESQUE. In "The Curious Case of Benjamin Button" (1922), he created a character who was born an old man instead of an infant. "Head and Shoulders" (1920) resembles a burlesque COMEDY routine as the husband and wife—a philosopher and acrobat, respectively—switch professions as well as traditional gender roles in marriage. Fitzgerald's stories are sometimes hard to classify because he often mixed techniques from different genres in the same story. In "Gretchen's Forty

Winks" (1924), stage comedy devices combine with serious social criticism when a husband drugs his wife in order to pursue the advertising accounts that will bring them financial comfort.

Many of Fitzgerald's stories achieve a complex irony with this combination of opposing tones. Sometimes Fitzgerald used his stories to develop themes he did not explore in the novels, such as differences between the American North and South. In "The Ice Palace" (1920) a Georgia woman discovers that her personality has been permanently shaped by Southern culture: Life in the North with her future husband is impossible. "The Baby Party" (1924) and "The Adjuster" (1924) describe the trials of domestic life with young children, a theme that receives no extended attention in the novels.

Biographical criticism is the most common approach to the stories as readers continue to find in the fiction correlations with Fitzgerald's personal life. Bibliographical approaches include the examination of story-and-novel clusters to track the way a theme or character from a short story ends up in a novel. The short story "Winter Dreams" (1922), for example, has been described—along with several others—as the basis for *The Great Gatsby*: The midwestern PROTAGONIST of the story bears a striking resemblance to Jay Gatsby, who, despite his move to New York City and his fabulous business success, never marries the woman he has idealized all his life.

Fitzgerald wrote three long stories sometimes called NOVELLAS or novelettes: "The Rich Boy" (1926), "THE DIAMOND AS BIG AS THE RITZ" (1922), and "May Day" (1920). Along with "BABYLON REVISITED" (1931), these three stories are usually considered his best work in the genre. In "The Rich Boy" Fitzgerald developed his trademark theme of the effect of wealth on character. He used fantasy and satire in "The Diamond as Big as the Ritz" to explore the same theme. "May Day" sometimes is described as Fitzgerald's foray into NATURALISM; others see Marxist overtones in its anatomy of the American class structure. "Babylon Revisited," Fitzgerald's most anthologized story, has been described as an autobiographical atonement for his extravagance in the 1920s and a reflection on expatriate life in Paris. A number of stories have an international theme that recalls the work of Henry JAMES, including "The Swimmers" (1929) and "One Trip Abroad" (1930).

Fitzgerald published three successful story sequences. From 1928 to 1931 the *Saturday Evening Post* published the BASIL DUKE LEE stories, featuring a fictionalized version of Fitzgerald in his youth, and the JOSEPHINE PERRY stories, which were based on the author's memories of Genevra King, a wealthy socialite he fell in love with during his Princeton years. At the time of his death, *Esquire* was publishing his light, satirical story sequence about a Hollywood hack writer named PAT HOBBY. The 17 stories were collected posthumously in 1962 as the PAT HOBBY STORIES.

BIBLIOGRAPHY

Bryer, Jackson R., ed. *New Essays on F. Scott Fitzgerald's Neglected Short Stories*. Columbia: University of Missouri Press, 1996.

———, ed. *The Short Stories of F. Scott Fitzgerald: New Approaches in Criticism*. Madison, Wisc.: University of Wisconsin Press, 1982.

Fitzgerald, F. Scott. *All the Sad Young Men*. New York: Scribner's, 1926.

———. *Flappers and Philosophers*. New York: Scribner's, 1920.

———. *The Stories of F. Scott Fitzgerald*. Edited by Malcolm Cowley. New York: Scribner's, 1951.

———. *Tales of the Jazz Age*. New York: Scribner's, 1922.

———. *Taps at Reveille*. New York: Scribner's, 1935.

Kuehl, John, ed. *F. Scott Fitzgerald: A Study of the Short Fiction*. Boston: Twayne, 1991.

Mellow, James R. *Invented Lives: F. Scott and Zelda Fitzgerald*. Boston: Houghton Mifflin, 1984.

Petry, Alice Hall. *Fitzgerald's Craft of Short Fiction: The Collected Stories, 1920–1935*. Tuscaloosa: University of Alabama Press, 1989.

Piper, Henry Dan. *F. Scott Fitzgerald: A Critical Portrait*. New York: Holt, Rinehart and Winston, 1965.

Frances Kerr
Durham Technical Community College

"FIVE-FORTY-EIGHT, THE" JOHN CHEEVER (1954) John CHEEVER's story, first published as part of the collection *The Housebreaker of Shady Hill*

(1958), is notable for the way it presents, through an apparently uninvolved, objective third-person narrator, a man's callous and reprehensible treatment of a female employee. The story's powerful impact is due in part to the narrator's nonjudgmental tone but also to the details this narrator presents by limiting the POINT OF VIEW so that the action unfolds through Mr. Blake's thoughts, allowing the reader to decipher the meaning of his behavior and to applaud Miss Dent when, at the end of the story, she bests him. In brief, Cheever has given us a tale of sexual harassment, 1950s style.

The story opens with Blake's startled recognition of Miss Dent as he steps out of the elevator in his office building. At first he cannot recall her name, and we follow him along the street, momentarily wondering if she is a stalker, wondering if we should sympathize with him. Through a series of FLASHBACKS the story provides the information we need: Miss Dent, a shy and timid temporary employee, falls in love with Blake when she comes to work for him. After he engages in sex with her, he feels distaste for her powerlessness and her poverty. Clearly, Blake is a powerful businessman, accustomed to using people to achieve his goals.

He thinks he has eluded her as he boards the commuter train home to SHADY HILL. He recognizes two of his neighbors seated in the same car, but neither greets him with friendliness. We learn that the woman neighbor knows about Blake's shameful treatment of his wife, Louise, who has turned to her for sympathy. The other neighbor offends Blake because of his casual way of dressing and because Blake's son spends nearly all his time with this man's kind and amiable family. Apparently neither Louise nor Blake's son has the power to speak out against him and he has punished them both, ceasing to sleep with or speak to his wife and forbidding his neighbors to entertain his son. Blake feels angry at these personal betrayals by both his wife and his son; ironically, of course, he fails to reckon with his own betrayal of them.

His superiority and power wielding are about to end, however, as Miss Dent boards the train, shoves a concealed pistol into his side, and tells him why and how he has wrecked her life. Although she has been institutionalized for emotional problems and has been unemployed since Blake fired her six months earlier, she demonstrates a newfound strength and a self-confident voice as she castigates him for his arrogance, his superficiality, his self-centeredness. Not only does she know more about love than he, she says, but she knows she is a better person than he. The story ends in an act that is more self-affirmation than punishment of Blake: Miss Dent forces him to kneel at her feet and put his face in the dirt, thereby avenging herself and attaining self-respect (Charters 35). Timid no longer, Miss Dent understands the phallic power of the gun and the authority of a self-confident voice: Cheever has artfully constructed the story so that readers feel justified in approving Blake's humiliation and applauding Miss Dent's newfound confidence.

BIBLIOGRAPHY

Charters, Ann. *Resources for Teaching: Major Writers of Short Fiction.* Boston: St. Martin's Press: 1993, 34–36

Cheever, John. *The Stories of John Cheever.* New York: Knopf, 1978.

O'Hara, James E. *John Cheever: A Study of the Short Fiction.* Boston: Twayne, 1989.

FLASHBACK The interruption of the chronological sequence in a literary, theatrical, or cinematic work by the interjection of events that occurred earlier. The technique may be a memory, a reverie, or a confession by a character.

"FLEUR" LOUISE ERDRICH (1986) Originally published in ESQUIRE in August 1986, "Fleur" later appeared as the first chapter of *Tracks*, published in 1988. It exemplifies Louise ERDRICH's blend of REALISM and magic (see MAGICAL REALISM). Narrated in the first person by Pauline (see POINT OF VIEW), a character in her own right who appears in Erdrich's *Love Medicine*, the story focuses on Fleur Pillager, a Chippewa Indian of the Ojibway tribe (see NATIVE AMERICAN SHORT FICTION) who lives in various locales on and around the Chippewa reservation in North Dakota. Fleur has powers that even her own community find upsetting. Indeed, Pauline frequently talks with the voice of the reservation, using "we" in a way reminiscent of William FAULKNER's narrator in "A ROSE FOR EMILY." Pauline tells us that Fleur has drowned twice, can turn into a bear at night, and kills any man who tries to interfere in her life.

To illustrate this last trait, Pauline—who views herself as unattractive and invisible—relates the unforgettable story of Fleur in Argus, North Dakota, in the summer of 1920. While working for a butcher, Fleur proves adept at playing poker with three unpleasant white men (the character named Lily, for instance, is pasty white, with cold flat eyes like those of a snake), and they cannot bear the thought of losing to this "squaw" who plays and wins steadily throughout the summer. One particular steamy midwestern night Fleur captures the jackpot from the men who, in a nightmarish scene filtered through Pauline's confused memory, retaliate by raping Fleur. According to Pauline, Fleur avenges herself by conjuring up a tornado, and the girl, feeling guilty for failing to prevent Fleur's rape, locks the men in the ice house. The tornado destroys the men while miraculously avoiding the possessions of the innocent.

Fleur and Pauline eventually return to the reservation, where stories swirl around Fleur in mythic fashion. Whether or not she really does "mess with evil (657)," as Pauline and the community believe, Fleur earns our admiration and respect: Still connected to the old, traditional tribal medicines and ways, Fleur lives a proudly independent life and answers to no one, especially to men.

BIBLIOGRAPHY
Erdrich, Louise. "Fleur." In *American Short Stories*. 6th edition. Edited by Eugene Current-García and Bert Hitchcock. New York: Longman, 1997, pp. 655–663.

"FLIGHT" JOHN STEINBECK (1938)

John STEINBECK's "Flight" first appeared in his collection of short stories *The Long Valley* in 1938. It is a carefully constructed coming-of-age tale that chronicles a 19-year-old boy's ascent to manhood, quick regression to hunted animal, and thence to his "manly" and untimely death. The PROTAGONIST in the story is Pepe, whom his mother refers to as nothing more than a "lazy peanut." Apparently Pepe has spent his entire life in indolent ease, basking in the warm sunshine on his mother's small farm in California. One beautiful day Mama decides to send Pepe to Monterey to fetch medicine for the family. Pepe, excited that his mother is allowing him to make such a journey alone, takes her decision as a sign that he will finally become a man and assume the responsibilities of his deceased father. Mama even lets Pepe wear his father's hat and green silk scarf tied around his neck. Pepe promises Mama that he will be careful, for he is a man now. Mama merely scoffs and reminds him that he is a young boy. The third-person narrator indicates, however, that Mama realizes and fears that Pepe will become a man too soon, although she does not realize how soon.

When Pepe returns that night, he has killed a man with his father's beautiful knife. Mama, devastated and fearing for her son's life, sends him away. As the narrator describes Pepe's flight into the hills, the depiction becomes increasingly animalistic—a pattern of imagery Steinbeck frequently returns to in many of his works—as, like the snake and wild cat, he crawls and slithers among the rocks and brush to flee his pursuers. Not until the very end of the story, however, does Pepe enact his one truly manly deed. No longer able to run, he stands high on top of a rock and faces his pursuers' bullets head on. Thus, according to the precepts of his family and his culture, Pepe dies a "man."

The artistry of the story undercuts Pepe's naive view. It invites us to question the meaning of manhood, to regret that Pepe learns nothing of the irony of his view of manhood, to mourn the loss of a youth with such bright potential, and to reevaluate these devastating social codes. "Flight" is not the only story in which Steinbeck ridicules society's conventions and beliefs about the meaning of manhood. Disgust with society's absurd rituals and conventions as well as the callousness of such institutions as banking and business, runs throughout most of his work.

BIBLIOGRAPHY

Steinbeck, John. "Flight." *The Long Valley.* New York: Book-of-the-Month Club, 1995.

Timmerman, John. *The Dramatic Landscape of Steinbeck's Short Stories.* Norman: University of Oklahoma Press, 1990.

———. "Introduction." In *The Long Valley.* New York: Book-of-the-Month Club, 1995.

Kathleen M. Hicks
University of Texas at El Paso

"FLOWERING JUDAS" KATHERINE ANNE PORTER (1930)

In this NOVELLA from her first collection, *Flowering Judas and Other Stories,* published in 1930, Katherine Anne PORTER creates a totally rootless character, an American expatriate in Mexico with ties to neither the past nor the future. Laura finds no reason to recall her previous life or to think back to her former country. In the opinion of many critics, Laura herself is the Judas of the title— a title that takes its symbolism from the ALLUSION to the biblical Judas, betrayer of Christ. Others see the tale as a PARABLE of the effects of revolution and renunciation, with several contenders for the role of betrayer. The dreamlike aura of the story adds to the difficulty of interpreting its meaning. Critic Charles E. May points out that Laura is named for the lovely and unattainable—and thus idealistic—HEROINE of Petrarch's sonnets (710).

The story opens with Laura paying polite attention to Braggacio, revolutionary hero and the other main character in the story. The disgusting physical description of Braggacio, a coarse, gross, lustful man who embodies the sexist qualities of machismo, contrast with Laura's more ethereal qualities. Laura, by refusing to flee, and Braggacio, by revoking his formerly ascetic behavior, have already betrayed the ideals of the revolution. Laura rejects her three suitors, finding none of them attractive; she seems zombielike, unable to act and unable to say yes to anyone who needs her. Indeed, the narrator makes clear that the one word that characterizes Laura is "no." The conflicts within Laura are readily apparent: She hides her voluptuous body beneath a shapeless and nunlike dress, she pays lip service to the revolution but sneaks into the Catholic chapel, and she facilitates the suicide of Eugenio, the imprisoned revolutionary to whom she brings poison. In critic James G. Watson's summation, Laura is "lovely without love, Catholic without faith, a socialist without ideals" (141).

At the end of the story, Laura dreams of the dead Eugenio, who offers her the fruit of the flowering Judas tree, also known as the redbud-tree into which Judas is supposed to have metamorphosed (Charters 154). In the end, in her refusal to participate in the literal and figurative communion of life, and in her passive participation in death, Laura becomes the quintessential modern woman, the counterpart of T. S. Eliot's WASTE LAND characters. Porter takes her title from Eliot's poem "Gerontion," and clearly, in creating Laura, Porter had his paralyzed ANTI-HEROes in mind.

BIBLIOGRAPHY

Charters, Ann. *Resources for Teaching Major Writers of Short Fiction.* Boston: St. Martin's Press, 1993.

May, Charles E. "Flowering Judas." In *Reference Guide to Short Fiction.* Edited by Noelle Watson. Detroit: St. James Press. 1994, 710.

Porter, Katherine Anne. "Flowering Judas." In *The Collected Stories of Katherine Anne Porter.* New York: Harcourt, Brace and World, 1965.

Watson, James G. "The American Short Story: 1930–1945." In *The American Short Story, 1900–1945.* Edited by Philip Stevick. Boston: Twayne, 1984, 103–146.

FOIL

Any fictional character who, through appearance or behavior, contrasts with and thereby underscores the distinctive characteristics or actions of another. A foil is often (but not always) a minor character who sets off the opposite traits of a major character.

FOLKLORE

Since the mid-19th century, the term "folklore" has been the general word applied to traditional stories, myths, and rituals handed down primarily by example and through oral rather than written form. Folklore can include LEGENDS, superstitions, songs, tales, spells, riddles, proverbs, nursery rhymes; pseudoscientific lore about the weather, plants, and animals; customary activities at births, marriages, and funerals; and traditional dances and forms of drama performed on holidays or at communal gatherings.

FORESHADOWING

The inclusion of material in a work to hint, suggest, or prepare for later action and events. The technique sometimes may also produce in the reader a feeling of anxiety or suspense. For example, in Edgar Allan POE's THE FALL OF THE HOUSE OF USHER, the crack or fissure in the wall of the house noted near the beginning of the tale foreshadows the splitting and ultimate demise of the entire Usher family. After reading any story that uses foreshadowing, readers may recall or look back to see when they first anticipated the outcome.

"FRANNY" AND "ZOOEY" J. D. SALINGER (1955, 1957)

"Franny" (first published in the NEW YORKER on January 29, 1955) and its companion short story "Zooey" (also published in The New Yorker, on May 4, 1957) detail the lives of two members of J. D. SALINGER's epic Glass family. The stories of Francesca (Franny) Glass and her older brother, Zachary (Zooey) Martin Glass, were published together in book form in September 1961 as Franny and Zooey, which reached the top of the New York Times best-seller list in the year it was published.

Each sibling is troubled by religion. Franny finds too much ego and phoniness (two things Salinger was transfixed with, ascribing the same characteristics to Catcher in the Rye's Holden Caulfield) in herself and those around her. Zooey tries to assist her by way of a telephone call in which he disguises his voice and leads her to a sort of inner peace. Franny is often seen as a hopeless romantic searching for faith, while Zooey is cast as the realistic intruder on this fantasy land. Zooey is all intellect and sharp wit, while Franny is the fragile character—her dialogue is reminiscent of Holden Caulfield—who seemingly suffers at the hands of the world. Franny and Zooey, like many of Salinger's characters, are unhappy with

how the world is. Franny's personal discontent is most manifest in her predilection for self-absorption and fakery, which she sees in everyone around her. Zooey sees mental problems in his associates and considers quitting his job.

"Franny" begins with Franny meeting her boyfriend at a coffeehouse. They talk, eventually digressing into a tangent about religion and philosophy, in which Franny reveals her hypersensitivity and withdrawal from her daily activities. Her only joy and source of relief is found in her "Jesus Prayer," which distracts her from the egocentric people in her life, including her professors and her boyfriend. She eventually faints and is taken home.

Zooey, in his section, explains his sister's breakdown, his own ulcer, and their shared religious preoccupation as a result of their torturous childhood. Their education came via two older siblings: Seymour (whose suicide was described in Salinger's 1948 story "A Perfect Day for Bananafish") and Buddy (a self-described neurotic). Before the educational basics began, Franny and Zooey were deeply steeped in religion and philosophy in all its various forms.

The joint moral of each story seems to be tolerance and understanding, but at a certain price. These stories explore religion, psychology, familial relationships, and the ever-present human quest not only for a sense of purpose but also for a unique understanding of life, the world, and one's own place. In this way Franny and Zooey both seem typical Salinger characters in that they question the world and their place in it, while turning as equally critical eye to those surrounding them. Religion, however, seems more central an issue here than in other Salinger short stories, although family connections—and connections to other people—remain constant THEMES in Salinger's work.

Anne N. Thalheimer
University of Delaware

FREEMAN, MARY E(LEANOR) WILKINS (1852–1930)

An impressively prolific author, Massachusetts-born Mary E. Wilkins Freeman published 14 novels and 15 collections of short fiction during her 50-year career as an author. Writing of her native New England and its folk, she excelled at the short story form and was a popular success in her own time. Although praised for her use of atmosphere, setting, and mood, Freeman herself focused on people and CHARACTER. Indeed, recent critics have resisted the traditional classification of Freeman as a LOCAL COLOR writer and find this classification far too narrow for "her profound insights into human nature and social relationships" (Westbrook, "Mary E. Wilkins Freeman," 290). Recognized as a realist (see REALISM) by such critics and writers as William Dean HOWELLS and Hamlin GARLAND, Freeman chronicled the changing New England of her era, including Brattleboro, Vermont, where she lived from ages 15 to 31, and Randolph, Massachusetts, where she spent the subsequent two decades before marrying Charles Freeman and moving with him to Metuchen, New Jersey.

Freeman began selling stories to such magazines as *Harper's Bazaar* and established herself as a significant voice with the publication of *A Humble Romance* (1887), set in rural Vermont, and *A New England Nun and Other Stories* (1891), containing some of her best stories; these stories continue to be widely anthologized. She wrote plays, poetry, and novels as well, but with the possible exceptions of two novels—*Pembroke* (1894) and *The Shoulders of Atlas* (1908)—her talent lies in her short fiction, much of which displays impressive psychological depth.

Because Freeman wrote a large number of stories that feature strong and determined women, recently she has become the object of a good deal of attention from FEMINIST scholars. Like Edith WHARTON, together with whom in 1926 Freeman was elected to the National Institute of Arts and Letters, Freeman did not consider herself a feminist—but again, as with Wharton, much of that attitude mirrored those of other women of her time. Leah Glasser positions Freeman's voice between the bold protesting voice of Charlotte Perkins GILMAN and the softer, calmer voice of Sarah Orne JEWETT: In Glasser's words, Freeman's stories "offer women

strategies of subterfuge, methods of coping and surviving through seeming compromise" (xx), yet some of her strongest stories, such as "Sister Liddy," demonstrate the confining, conflicted choices women still face today.

"Sister Liddy" focuses on Polly, who has been locked away in an asylum for the insane. In this image of the imprisoned woman who has resisted conformity, the trope of the MADWOMAN IN THE ATTIC comes to mind. The asylum's female inmates, all women or children, spend hopeless and meaningless lives against the backdrop of random and chaotic noise. Glasser compares Polly to Charlotte Perkins Gilman's narrator in the "YELLOW WALLPAPER," because Polly creates a double, or DOPPELGANGER— but Polly's double is Sister Liddy, a conventional and successful young woman for whom life seems perfectly balanced and blissful. Yet one can see a second sister to Polly in Sally, the screaming, violent madwoman, possibly a METAPHOR for all the women who rebel against society's insistence that they shape themselves after the ideal married woman symbolized in Sister Liddy (Glasser 230–231).

More successfully rebellious women appear in such stories as "Louisa." Louisa is a young woman who has lost her job as a schoolteacher. Refusing her widowed mother's wish that she marry a rich suitor whom she does not love, she works as a fieldhand on neighboring farms and independently farms the family land, thereby supporting herself, her mother, and her senile grandfather. Likewise, in the more widely known "THE REVOLT OF MOTHER," the wife rebels against her husband in order to acquire a better home and better living conditions than he had managed to provide. A similarly strong woman is celebrated in "A CHURCH MOUSE."

BIBLIOGRAPHY

Foster, Edward. *Mary E. Wilkins Freeman.* New York: Hendricks House, 1956.

Freeman, Mary E. Wilkins. *The Best Stories,* Edited by Henry Wysham Lanier. New York: Harper, 1927.

———. *The Copy-Cat and Other Stories.* New York: Harper, 1914.

———. *Edgewater People.* New York: Harper, 1918.

———. *The Fair Lavinia and Others.* New York: Harper, 1907.

———. *The Givers: Short Stories.* New York: Harper, 1904.

———. *A Humble Romance and Other Stories.* New York: Harper, 1887. As *A FarAway Melody and Other Stories.* Edinburgh: D. Douglas, 1892.

———. *The Love of Parson Lord and Other Stories.* New York: Harper, 1900.

———. *A New England Nun and Other Stories.* New York: Harper, 1891.

———. *Selected Short Stories of Mary E. Wilkins Freeman.* Edited by Marjorie Pryse. New York: Norton, 1983.

———. *Silence and Other Stories.* New York: Harper, 1898.

———. *Six Trees: Short Stories.* New York: Harper, 1903.

———. *Understudies: Short Stories.* New York: Harper, 1901.

———. *The Wind in the Rose-Bush and Other Stories of the Supernatural.* New York: Doubleday, Page & Company, 1903.

———. *The Winning Lady and Others.* New York: Harper, 1909.

Glasser, Leah. *In A Closet Hidden: The Life and Work of Mary E. Wilkins Freeman.* Amherst, Mass.: University of Massachusetts Press, 1996.

Westbrook, Perry D. *Mary Wilkins Freeman.* New York: Twayne, 1967. Revised edition. Boston: Twayne, 1988.

Westbrook, Perry D. "Mary E. Wilkins Freeman." In *Reference Guide to Short Fiction.* Edited by Noelle Watson. Detroit: Gale Press, 1994, pp. 189–90.

FREUD, SIGMUND (1856–1939)

Austrian psychiatrist, founder of psychoanalysis. He devised the technique of free association in which patients under the guidance of an analyst allowed material, such as emotional episodes in their past that had been repressed in the unconscious, to emerge to conscious recognition. He also used dream interpretation, in which he analyzed patients' dreams for their symbolic content, because he believed dreams were a person's means of expressing repressed emotions, and repression was the cause of neurotic behavior. His most controversial work dealt with his theories about the sexual instinct, or the libido: Freud maintained that a primary motivating factor in human behavior, including that of children, was sexual in nature, and ascribed most neuroses to the repressive influence of social and individual inhibitions about sex. Freud's ideas had a great impact on the thinking of the 20th century, influencing anthropology, education, and especially the fine arts and literature.

FRONTIER HUMORISTS

For several decades before the CIVIL WAR these early humorists were keen-eyed observers of the human scene. For the most part they were not professional writers, and they probably thought of themselves as recording rather than imaginatively creating the tales they wrote. Although they play a minor part in the development of the short story because their metier was generally the sketch or anecdote, collections like A. B. Longstreet's *Georgia Scenes* (1835), W. T. Thompson's *Major Jones's Courtship* (1843), J. J. Hooper's *Some Adventures of Captain Simon Suggs* (1845), and G. W. Harris's SUT LOVINGOOD (1867) contain selections that show a drift toward plotted narrative.

The humorous anecdote or TALL TALE was essentially an oral genre, and when transferred to print it usually retained the voice and verbal mannerisms of the teller. Sut Lovingood, for instance, tells of his scrape and his practical jokes in a vernacular that identifies him as a Tennessee hill-country boy, a "nat'ral born durn'd fool." If the language is comic, the DIALECT is reasonably accurate and gives the story an immediacy much greater than if it had been told in literary language.

BIBLIOGRAPHY

Harris, George Washington. "Sut Lovingood: Yarns Spun by a 'Nat'ral Born Durn Fool.'" In *The Harper American Literature,* vol. I. Ed. Donald McQuade. New York: Harper & Row, 1987, p. 2209.

FUGITIVES, THE   See AGRARIANS, THE.

G

GAINES, ERNEST (1933–) Born on River Lake Plantation near New Roads, Louisiana, Ernest Gaines moved from the locale that would become the animating force behind his fiction to Vallejo, California, with his parents when he was 15. Before graduating from San Francisco State College in 1957, he published his first short story. After completing a year of graduate work at Stanford on a creative writing fellowship, Gaines began writing novels—a critic advised him that they were more marketable than short stories. In addition to his 1968 collection of stories, *Bloodline,* Gaines has written six novels: *Catherine Carmier* (1964); *Of Love and Dust* (1967); *The Autobiography of Miss Jane Pittman* (1971); *In My Father's House* (1978); *A Gathering of Old Men* (1983); and *A Lesson Before Dying* (1993), which won the National Book Critics Circle Award.

Gaines's works all share a common setting—Bayonne, Louisiana—a locale comparable to William FAULKNER's fictional YOKNAPATAWPHA COUNTY, although, unlike Faulkner, Gaines has not created characters that appear in more than one work. Influenced by Ernest HEMINGWAY, Faulkner, and the Russian novelist Ivan Turgenev, Gaines depicts the African American experience in the changing South; his fiction is thoroughly grounded in region and community.

Bloodline collects five stories concerning young black male PROTAGONISTS struggling to transcend the limitations imposed by their environment and their past. Beyond physical setting, this SHORT STORY CYCLE is unified by various THEMES that develop concurrently as the stories progress: the definition of black manhood through conflict with white social institutions; the role of women and the community in relation to social progress; the failure of traditional religion; and the importance of visionary characters in defining the nature of change. Arranged chronologically according to the age of the protagonists, these stories depict a progressive awareness of the nature of racial oppression and its individual and communal implications. "A Long Day in November" (revised and published separately as a children's book in 1971) chronicles the separation and reconciliation of six-year-old Sonny's parents through the child's viewpoint. (See POINT OF VIEW.) "THE SKY IS GRAY" (filmed for public television in 1980) presents the trials posed by segregation from the viewpoint of a nine-year-old whose mother brings him to town for a dental appointment. Both stories portray the black male's struggle to achieve manhood in the context of a female-dominated community and within the barriers erected by the dominant white society.

"Three Men" depicts the spiritual and ethical growth of Proctor Lewis, whose encounter with two other men and a young boy in prison spurs his decision to break the cycle of powerless dependence and misdirected anger by enduring suffering in prison instead of allowing the paternalistic plantation owner to bail him out. In "Bloodline," Copper, a mulatto veteran, returns home to the plantation on which he was born to claim his legacy from the white uncle who owns it. While Copper's adamant militancy is not presented as the ultimate solution, Copper does obtain recognition of kinship from his uncle, who suffers a similar lack of compassion and vision. "Just Like a Tree" concludes the collection on a hopeful note when Emmanuel, a young civil rights activist engaged in nonviolent resistance, moves away. He is not motivated by hatred or by the community's more conservative feminine elements but instead by his Aunt Fe, who preserves the memory of historical oppression. A composite of ten different narrative voices—black and white—this final story mirrors the unresolved tension of the collection's other voices. Read as a short story cycle, Gaines's collection depicts a community in the process of dissolution, struggling to preserve a communal past (that is, its bloodline) as individuals move toward self-realization that threatens to erase it.

BIBLIOGRAPHY

Babb, Valerie Melissa. *Ernest Gaines*. Boston: Twayne, 1991.

Bryant, Jerry H. "Ernest J. Gaines: Change, Growth, and History." *Southern Review* 10 (1974): 851–64.

Byerman, Keith E. *Fingering the Jagged Grain: Tradition and Form in Recent Black Fiction*. Athens: University of Georgia Press, 1985.

Callahan, John F. "Hearing Is Believing: The Landscape of Voice in Ernest Gaines's *Bloodline*." *Callaloo* 7 (1984): 86–112.

Doyle, Mary Ellen. "Ernest J. Gaines: An Annotated Bibliography, 1956–1988." *Black American Literature Forum* 24 (1990): 125–50.

Duncan, Todd. "Scene and Life Cycle in Ernest Gaines's *Bloodline*." *Callaloo* 1 (1978): 85–101.

Estes, David C. *Critical Reflections on the Fiction of Ernest J. Gaines*. Athens: University of Georgia Press, 1994.

Gaines, Ernest. *Bloodline*. New York: Dial, 1968.

Gaudet, Marcia, and Carl Wooton. *Porch Talk with Ernest Gaines: Conversations on the Writer's Craft*. Baton Rouge: University of Louisiana Press, 1990.

Hicks, Jack. "To Make These Bones Live: History and Community in Ernest Gaines's Fiction." *Black American Literature Forum* 11 (1977): 9–19.

Lowe, John. *Conversations with Ernest Gaines*. Jackson, Miss.: University Press of Mississippi, 1995.

Rowell, Charles. "The Quarters: Ernest Gaines and the Sense of Place." *Southern Review* 21 (1985): 733–50.

Werner, Craig Hansen. *Paradoxical Resolutions: American Fiction since Joyce*. Urbana: University of Illinois Press, 1982.

Robert M. Luscher
University of Nebraska at Kearney

GALE, ZONA (1874–1938)

Stark REALISM characterizes the writing of Zona Gale in her novels and stories. A native of Wisconsin, Gale primarily wrote about small-town life in the Midwest. Her four-volume collection of short stories, *Friendship Village* (1908), focuses on the citizens of a small town based on her hometown of Portage, Wisconsin.

GARDNER, ERLE STANLEY (1889–1970)

A practicing lawyer for many years, Gardner initially wrote stories published in pulp magazines under several pseudonyms, including A. A. Fair. He proceeded to write over 100 books and became one of the most successful writers of DETECTIVE SHORT FICTION in American publishing history. Most of his stories employed either Perry Mason, perhaps the most famous lawyer in American fiction, or the district attorney Douglas Selby. Gardner's stories are noted for their fast action, clever legal devices, and ingenious plotting.

BIBLIOGRAPHY

Gardner, Erle Stanley. *Ellery Queen Presents Erle Stanley Gardner's The Amazing Adventures of Lester Leith*. New York: Davis Pub., 1981.

———. *The Case of the Murderer's Bride and Other Stories*. New York: Davis Publications, 1969.

———. *The Human Zero, The Science Fiction Stories of ESG*. New York: Morrow, 1981.

———. *Whispering Sands: Stories of Gold Fever and the Western Desert*. New York: Morrow, 1981.

———. *Pay Dirt and Other Whispering Sand Stories of Gold Fever and the Western Desert*. New York: Morrow, 1983.

GARLAND, (HANNIBAL) HAMLIN
(1860–1940) Born in rural poverty in Wisconsin and reared on a succession of farms in Iowa and South Dakota, Garland went to Boston on 1884. Despite loneliness and poverty, he educated himself at the public library, found a teaching position, and met William Dean HOWELLS and others in the Boston literary circle. Influenced by the realistic techniques of Howells, who encouraged him in his literary efforts, and by a return visit to his family in South Dakota, where he observed the loneliness and drudgery of farm life from a new perspective, Garland found his subject. He published his first story in HARPER'S *Weekly* in 1888, and published a collection of stories about rural prairie life entitled *Main-Travelled Roads: Six Mississippi Valley Stories* in 1891. These stories about the poverty and heroic, silent endurance of ordinary folk in the "Middle Border" states (Wisconsin, Minnesota, Nebraska, and the Dakotas) launched his career as a full-time writer. The collection was one of the first to contain the stories linked by a common theme and location, a link later honed by such writers as Sarah Orne JEWETT in THE COUNTRY OF THE POINTED FIRS and Sherwood ANDERSON in WINESBURG, OHIO.

Although today critics view Garland's writings as early contributions to NATURALISM, as well as talented illustrations of REGIONALISM and LOCAL COLOR, in 1894 he published *Crumbling Idols*, in which he explains his own literary theory. Garland uses the term "veritism" to describe his particular version of realism: He based his observation about the actual lives of the midwestern characters in a knowledge of sociology and a use of local color firmly rooted in a sense of place. His technique is evidenced in two other story collections, *Prairie Folks* (1893) and *Wayside Courtships* (1897), both later edited to form the collection *Other Main-Travelled Roads*, published in 1910.

Of the many fine stories in *Main-Travelled Roads*, Garland's frequently anthologized "Under the Lion's Paw" exemplifies the author's reformist beliefs that the lives of the rural poor are needlessly exploited by profit-seeking absentee landlords who give the lie to the AMERICAN DREAM. Tim Haskins and his wife,

Nettie, driven out of Iowa in the depression of the 1880s, seek a better life in Kansas. The Haskinses are befriended by Steven Council and his wife, Sarah, who demonstrate to the newcomers the feasibility of owning and successfully farming their own land. Tim and Nettie and their children do find a farm, but when Tim—after spending three years on improvements—is finally ready to purchase it, he and his family suffer the exploitations of the capitalist (see CAPITALISM) land speculator Jim Butler, who raises the price. When Tim, enraged almost to the point of committing murder, nearly impales Butler on his pitchfork, some critics see Tim as the lion trapping Butler under his paw. Nonetheless, when Tim eventually consents to Butler's increased price, Tim clearly falls under the "paw" of Butler.

Other notable stories include "Among the Corn Rows," a rural romance, and "A Branch Road," both of which employ rescue plots inspired by Garland's sympathy for his mother's life of hopeless drudgery (and hence his active support of FEMINIST causes). "Up the Coulee," another often-published story, in which a son returns from the city to find his mother and younger brother living in rural poverty, provides still another example of Garland's concern with his mother's lot and his impulse to re-create it, illustrate her plight, and give her a better life. "The Return of a Private" explores the homecoming of a Union CIVIL WAR veteran who, having fought for an ideal, must now contend with poverty and the harshness of nature on his Wisconsin farm, along with the injustice of his fellow humans.

In an almost metaphorically American way, Garland found himself drawn to both the comfortable existence and literary establishment of the East, and then to the hope and possibilities of the West. From his eastern perspective, he created the stories illuminating the hard lives of rural midwestern farm folk, and, as critic Robert Franklin Gish notes, from his western perspective, writing his Klondike and Dakota gold rush adventures, Garland "more or less discovered, and certainly advanced, the Western novel" with its faith in the AMERICAN DREAM (Gish 203). Besides the short stories on which his reputation firmly rests, Garland wrote a number of novels and autobiographical narratives. In 1922 he received the Pulitzer Prize in biography for *A Daughter of the Middle Border*, which, together with the frontier story of his wife, traces his family's progress from early pioneer times until WORLD WAR I.

BIBLIOGRAPHY

Bryer, Jackson R., and Eugene Harding. *Hamlin Garland and the Critics: An Annotated Bibliography.* Troy, N.Y., Whitston Publishing Co., 1973.

Garland, Hamlin. *The Book of the American Indian.* New York: Harper, 1923.

————. *Crumbling Idols.* Chicago: Stone and Kimball, 1894.

————. *Hamlin Garland's Diaries.* Edited by Donald Pizer. San Marino, Calif.: Huntington Library, 1968.

————. *Jason Edwards: An Average Man.* Boston: Arena Publishing Co., 1892.

————. *Main-Travelled Roads: Six Stories of the Mississippi Valley.* Boston: Arena, 1891.

————. *Other Main-Travelled Roads.* New York: Harper, 1910.

————. *Prairie Folks.* Chicago: F. J. Schulte & Company, 1893; revised edition: New York: Macmillan, 1899.

————. *Rose of Dutcher's Coolly.* Chicago: Stone and Kimball, 1895.

————. *A Son of the Middle Border.* New York: Macmillan, 1917.

————. *They of the High Trails.* New York: Harper & Brothers, 1916.

————. *Wayside Courtships.* New York: D. Appleton and Company 1897.

Gish, Robert Franklin. *Garland: The Far West.* Boise, Idaho: Boise State University, 1976.

————. "Hamlin Garlin." In *Reference Guide to Short Fiction.* Edited by Noelle Watson. Detroit: St. James Press, 1994, pp. 202–03.

Holloway, Jean. *Garland: A Biography.* Austin: University of Texas Press, 1960.

McCullough, Joseph B. *Garland.* Boston: Twayne Publishers, 1978.

Nagel, James, ed. *Critical Essays on Garland.* Boston: G.K. Hall, 1982.

Pizer, Donald. *Garland's Early Work and Career.* Berkeley: University of California Press, 1960.

Silet, Charles L.P., Robert E. Welch and Richard Boudreau, eds. *The Critical Reception of Garland 1891–1978.* Troy, N.Y.: Whitston Publishing Co., 1985.

GARRISON, WILLIAM LLOYD (1805–1879)   A prominent abolitionist from Massachusetts who in 1831 founded *The Liberator,* a weekly newspaper in which he campaigned for the immediate and complete abolition of slavery. Garrison advocated Northern succession from the Union, because the Constitution permitted slavery, and he opposed the CIVIL WAR until LINCOLN issued the Emancipation Proclamation in 1862. *The Liberator* ceased publication in 1865 after slavery was abolished with passage of the Thirteenth Amendment to the Constitution. Garrison's sharing the lecture platform with African-American abolitionists and writers Frederick DOUGLASS and Frances HARPER showed his indirect support of their literary endeavors. The abolitionists' consciously active role in promoting literature, however, did not occur until they recruited such intellectuals as William Ellery Channing, fellow Transcendentalist Ralph Waldo Emerson (see TRANSCENDENTALISM), and poets Henry Wadsworth Longfellow and James Russell Lowell. In 1899, Garrison's son, Francis J. Garrison, in his role as editor at Houghton Mifflin Company, encouraged Charles W. CHESNUTT and helped publish his first collection of stories, *Conjure Woman and Other Stories.*

GAVIN STEVENS   Gavin Stevens has been variously described as William FAULKNER's "Favorite," his "Good Man," and his "Footloose Knight." Truly an admirable, albeit quixotic, figure, Stevens is arguably one of Faulkner's most important characters: He plays an active role in more of the author's works than any other character. In six novels and nearly a dozen short stories, Faulkner uses Gavin Stevens, a YOKNAPATAWPHA COUNTY attorney, to explore many of his chief concerns as a writer.

Nearly all of the Gavin Stevens stories can be grouped into one of three categories. The short stories and NOVELLA that comprise *Knight's Gambit* (1949) consistently focus on the vital role that language plays in Stevens's life as well as his earnest efforts as county attorney to discover and execute humane truth and justice. The second grouping, which consists primarily of *Light in August* (1932), *GO DOWN, MOSES* (1941), *Intruder in the Dust* (1948), and *Requiem for a Nun* (1951), present Gavin's (and Faulkner's) increasingly honest confrontation with the issue of race in the South. These are arguably the most important of the Gavin Stevens stories because they reflect, through Gavin, the development of Faulkner's increasingly liberal and sympathetic view of "the race problem in the South." Consisting of "By the People" (1955), *The Town* (1957), and *The Mansion* (1959), the final grouping could be appropriately titled "Stevens v. SNOPES," as they tell about the noble attorney's decades-long struggle against Faulkner's most notorious family of characters, who symbolize the unscrupulous rapacity of the post-RECONSTRUCTION South.

BIBLIOGRAPHY

Faulkner, William. *Faulkner in the University.* Edited by Joseph L. Blotner and Frederick L. Gwynn. Charlottesville: University of Virginia Press, 1959.

Watson, Jay. *Forensic Fictions: The Lawyer Figure in Faulkner.* Athens: University of Georgia Press, 1993.

H. Collin Messer
University of North Carolina at Chapel Hill

GAY MALE SHORT FICTION

Just as fiction can be about anything, so too is gay male fiction not necessarily just about gay men; rather, as David Leavitt explains, a gay male short story can be one "that illuminates the experience of love between men, explores the nature of homosexual identity, or investigates the kinds of relationships gay men have with each other, with their friends, and with their families" (*The Penguin Book of Gay Short Stories,* xxiii). That is, gay male short fiction is not just fiction that is written by gay men but actually encompasses all of the relationships gay men have—relationships that include all readers, regardless of sexual identity.

While relationships between women can be found in American short fiction during the 19th century, relationships between men are harder to come by, even though the short story as a genre was blossoming at this time. One reason for the lack of gay male representation could be the societal prohibition against such relationships: Male-male relationships verging on the homoerotic were vehemently discouraged and outlawed by the sodomy laws of the time. Examples of homosexual/homosocial bonding can be found in novels and poetry from the 19th century, such as in Herman MELVILLE's sea novels and Walt Whitman's *Calamus* poems, but these relationships are almost always placed in settings and institutions dominated by men, such as the military, the sea, or boarding schools, or in imaginary/utopian spaces. In these settings, the gay male relationship could be read simply as a close friendship, while at the same time, codes and symbols also could point to an underlying homosexual THEME.

Not surprisingly, then—since the concept of homosexuality as identity rather than behavior is relatively contemporary—gay male presence in the American short story does not really emerge until the turn of the 20th century. One example can be found in Henry JAMES's short story "The Great Good Place." James presents a bachelor who falls asleep amid all the pressures of his business and social engagements and dreams of a halcyonic place of harmony and happiness. In this place he finds only men, and he attaches himself to one man in particular, who is identified only as "Brother." They determine that this special place will always be perfect, because "not everyone will find it, there would never be too many." Rather than assigning a traditional name to the place, the men call it "The Great Good Place" as well as "The Great Want Met." When the PROTAGONIST awakes, he finds his sleep has lasted only a few hours, although it seemed like weeks. The story ends with the protagonist affirming that what he felt and experienced in the dream "*was all right*"; it is perhaps James's most open affirmation of homosexuality in all of his works.

Even after some short story writers ventured to present gay male relationships away from the ship or the barracks, they still placed their characters in faraway places, perhaps in order to distance the threat of the homosexual relationship from the reality of American culture: Gay males could be represented more openly in these spaces but was still not allowed to be a part of American culture. Therefore in the 1950s, Paul BOWLES, in "Pages from Cold Point," and Gore Vidal, in "Pages from an Abandoned Journal," are able to tell stories detailing homosexual relationships, which are allowed to flourish only in the Caribbean and Europe. These stories also point to a common theme for stories of gay men prior to the 1960s and '70s: In both stories the gay male lives a tortured existence, ultimately leading to death or persecution. As in films and popular fiction of the time, gay men were shown to be troubled by their sexuality and to live unhappy, unfulfilled lives. Although perhaps this was the only way gay men could be represented in a culture that outwardly condemned them—that is, homosexuality could exist in fiction only as long as it was ultimately shown to be wrong—these works nonetheless demonstrate the struggles gay men encountered on their way to achieving happiness and acceptance.

In the summer of 1969 New York City police raided the Stonewall Inn, a gay bar in Greenwich Village, because of an alleged liquor license violation. People from the bar and the surrounding neighborhood fought back against the police for two days. In the weeks and months following what soon became known as the Stonewall riots (or even just "Stonewall"), gays and lesbians across the nation and the world began to organize a more cohesive and effective effort against the kind of abuse and oppression typified by Stonewall. The Stonewall riots and the subsequent gay rights movement provided writers with the opportunity to change the negative image of the gay man. As gay males began to find more acceptance in mainstream American society, and as representations of their lives increased, outlets for these new stories proliferated as well. In the 1970s, still lacking mainstream publication sources, magazines, journals, and newspapers devoted to gay and lesbian issues and culture sprouted in major American cities: Such publications as *Gay Sunshine, Mouth of the Dragon,* and *Christopher Street* provided outlets for gay and lesbian fiction as well as information for gays and lesbians. Related small presses, such as the Gay Sunshine Press, the Sea Horse Press, and Calamus Press, emerged, providing another opportunity for fiction related to gay and lesbian issues to be printed and read.

One of the most popular themes to emerge in these forums was the "coming-out" story, where the gay male protagonist comes "out of the closet" into a homosexual identity. Edmund White has argued that gay and lesbian identity requires the construction of a coming-out narrative. To this day gay male short stories focus heavily on the process of coming out and the resulting effects on the gay male and those around him.

Once the gay male was able to "come out" in short fiction, the opportunities for an expansion of the roles available to him increased. Before Stonewall, gay men were represented in fiction as either effeminate or macho, nymphomaniacal or frigid, in denial or suicidal. After Stonewall, gay men in short stories could have more than just one-night stands; they could have lasting relationships with other men and could even survive happily until the end of the story. Gay male fiction showed that gay men are everywhere in American society: They are uncles, fathers, nephews, and sons (as in Christopher Coe's story "Gentlemen Can Wash Their Hands in the Gents'") and fellow coworkers (as in Daniel Curzon's "Victor," a story as much about the struggles of being a teacher as the struggles of being a gay man).

For years artists masked references to gay sexual acts by using codes or subtexts. For example, physical affection between men often has been hidden under the guise of hypermasculine activity, as in the intense wrestling scene in D. H. Lawrence's *Women in Love* or on film in the Roman war epics of *Ben Hur* and *Spartacus*. Gay male short story writers began to describe sex in sometimes shockingly explicit ways. Just as authors of postmodern fiction (see POSTMODERNISM) were pushing the boundaries of sexual propriety in fiction, so, too, were authors of gay fiction using their newfound but still limited acceptance to explore sexuality in their works.

As AIDS entered the lives of gay men in the 1980s, this harrowing disease become a major theme in gay male short fiction. Indeed, it can be argued that literature devoted to the impact of AIDS on American gay male society developed into its own subgenre as authors attempted to respond to this crisis. Most stories dealing with acquired immune deficiency syndrome (AIDS) have centered on the impact of the illness on relationships—those between lovers, as in Michael Cunningham's story "Ignorant Armies," where a man deals with his lover's death and then his own, or between friends, as in David Leavitt's story "A Place I've Never Been," told through the eyes of a woman coming to terms with her friend's impending death. As AIDS has persisted as a disease that knows no boundaries, however, so have authors expanded their view past the sorrowful stories of urban gay men: Sam Rudy, in his story "Sheet Music," chronicles the story of a married man caring for another man dying of AIDS in a small town, while David Feinberg looks at AIDS through a comic lens in his story "Despair."

Although the stories of white gay men predominate, the stories of gay men of color recently have begun to come to the fore with their own anthologies, such as Essex Hemphill's Brother to Brother: New Writings by Black Gay Men (1991). In addition, stories of other groups of gay men, whose voices have been silenced or ignored by both heterosexuals and homosexuals, such as stories about sadomasochistic relationships or of gay men with disabilities, also have begun to appear in both gay publications and mainstream media.

While the history of anthologies of gay male short fiction is relatively short, the number and diversity of anthologies are impressive. The anthologizing of gay male short fiction began with The Other Persuasion (1977) and Ian Young's On The Line: New Gay Fiction (1981) and was continued by the highly successful Men on Men series, begun in 1986 by George Stambolian. Major publishers soon joined this trend, with anthologies by Penguin and Faber and the annual Best American Gay Fiction by Little, Brown.

BIBLIOGRAPHY

Bouldrey, Brian, ed. Best American Gay Fiction. Boston: Little, Brown, 1996.

Bowles, Paul. "Pages from Cold Point." The Delicate Prey and Other Stories. New York: Random House, 1950.

Coe, Christopher. "Gentlemen Can Wash Their Hands in the Gents'." The Penguin Book of Gay Short Stories. Edited by David Leavitt and Mark Mitchell. New York: Penguin, 1994.

Cunningham, Michael. "Ignorant Armies." The Penguin Book of Gay Short Stories, edited by David Leavitt and Mark Mitchell. New York: Penguin, 1994.

Curzon, Daniel. "Victor." Human Warmth and Other Stories. San Francisco: Grey Fox Press, 1981.

Feinberg, David B. "Despair." Spontaneous Combustion. New York: Viking, 1991.

Fuss, Diana ed., Inside/Out: Lesbian Theories, Gay Theories. New York: Routledge, 1991.

Hemphill, Essex. Brother to Brother: New Writings by Black Gay Men. Boston: Alyson Publications, 1991.

James, Henry. "The Great Good Place." Scribner's Magazine 27 (January–June 1900).

Kleinberg, Seymour. The Other Persuasion: Short Fiction about Gay Men and Women. New York: Vintage, 1977.

Leavitt, David. "A Place I've Never Been." In A Place I've Never Been. New York: Viking, 1990.

Leavitt, David and Mark Mitchell, eds. The Penguin Book of Gay Short Stories. New York: Penguin, 1994.

Malinowski, Sharon, ed. Gay & Lesbian Literature. Detroit: St. James Press, 1994.

Malinowski, Sharon, Christa Brelin, and Malcolm Boyd, eds. The Gay and Lesbian Literary Companion. Detroit: Visible Ink Press, 1995.

Mars-Jones, Adam, ed. Mae West is Dead: Recent Lesbian and Gay Fiction. Boston: Faber & Faber 1983.

Rudy, Sam. "Sheet Music." In The Gay Nineties: An Anthology of Contemporary Gay Fiction. Edited by Phil Willkie and Greg Baysans. Freedom, Calif.: Crossing Press, 1991.

Sedgwick, Eve Kosofsky. Epistemology of the Closet. London: Harvester Wheatsheaf, 1991.

Summers, Claude J. Gay Fictions: Wilde to Stonewall: Studies in a Male Homosexual Literary Tradition. New York: Continuum, 1990.

Summers, Claude J. ed. The Gay and Lesbian Literary Heritage: A Reader's Companion to the Writers and Their Works, From Antiquity to the Present. New York: H. Holt, 1995.

Vidal, Gore. "Pages from an Abandoned Journal." A Thirsty Evil: Seven Short Stories. New York: The Zero Press, 1952.

White, Edmund, ed., The Faber Book of Gay Short Fiction. Boston: Faber & Faber, 1991.

Willkie, Phil and Greg Baysans, eds. The Gay Nineties: An Anthology of Contemporary Gay Fiction. Freedom, Calif.: Crossing Press, 1991.

Young, Ian, ed. On The Line: New Gay Fiction. Trumansburg, New York: Crossing Press, 1981.

Gregory M. Weight
University of Delaware

GENRE Stemming from the French word meaning "kind" or "type," *genre* traditionally has been used to describe the separate sorts of fiction: comedy, epic, lyric, pastoral, and tragedy. It is also the word used to designate distinct categories of literature: short story, novel, play, poem, or essay. Television play and film scenario are also considered genres, as are DETECTIVE FICTION and SCIENCE FICTION. In the 20th century, particularly, the concept of genre has stimulated controversy as numerous writers deliberately blur the distinctions and tend to use several genres in one work.

GEORGE WILLARD The reporter in Sherwood ANDERSON's SHORT STORY CYCLE *WINESBURG, OHIO,* who becomes involved with the chief characters in various stories but often fails to understand the import of the human lessons contained therein. A character in his own right, George also may be viewed as the PROTAGONIST of a BILDUNGSROMAN, for the linked stories demonstrate his gradual coming of age. Appearing in the first short story cycle in American literature in 1919, George presages such other protagonists as Ernest HEMINGWAY's NICK ADAMS, William FAULKNER's ISAAC (IKE) MCCASLIN (see "THE BEAR" and *GO DOWN, MOSES*), and Katherine Anne PORTER's MIRANDA RHEA.

GERONIMO (1829?–1909) Born in what is now the state of Arizona, Geronimo became a leader of the Chirichua Apache Indian tribe. After the Chirichua Reservation was abolished in 1876, Geronimo led repeated raids against United States government forces. He and his followers finally surrendered in 1886 and were transported to Florida, where they were incarcerated as prisoners of war. Later sent to Fort Sill, Oklahoma, Geronimo eventually converted to Christianity and lived as a prosperous farmer. He is featured in Leslie SILKO's "A Geronimo Story" in *The Man to Send Rain Clouds,* edited by Kenneth Rosen (New York: Viking Press, 1974).

GETTYSBURG, BATTLE OF Fought from July 1 to 3, 1863, this battle was a major turning point in the American CIVIL WAR and is considered the high-water mark for the Confederacy in its war with the Union. In late June General Robert E. LEE led the Army of Northern Virginia across the Rappahannock River and invaded the North. Union forces at first believed his intended aim was to attack Washington, D.C. When they belatedly learned Lee's army was continuing to move north toward Pennsylvania, they sent units of the Army of the Potomac in pursuit. Representatives of the two armies met by accident on July 1 near the small town of Gettysburg, and both commanders decided to fight there. By the end of the first day, Union forces under General George G. Meade had taken a strong defensive position on a ridge to the south of the town. Lee attacked the left flank of these defenses on July 2, but after initial successes his forces were thrown back. On the following day Lee sent his forces against the Union center in an attack that ended with the famous charge by General George E. Pickett, whose troops briefly penetrated the Union lines before being thrown back. The battle was over and Lee withdrew his battered army back to Virginia. Of 75,000 men, his army suffered nearly 23,000 casualties (killed, wounded, missing, or captured). The Northern army of 90,000 had an almost equal number of casualties.

Considered a major victory for the North, this battle also generated the most controversy for the remainder of the war and years afterward. For Southerners, the debate centered on Lee's decision to stand and fight in a place not of his choosing against a well-entrenched Northern army, and, especially, the role of Lee's cavalry under General J. E. B. Stuart, who left the Confederate army without "eyes" for several maddening days while he was raiding Union facilities near Harrisburg, Pennsylvania. For Northerners, the debate centered on General Meade's decision not to pursue and perhaps annihilate the battered Army of Northern Virginia, which may have needlessly prolonged the war. On November 19, 1863, Abraham LINCOLN dedicated the cemetery on the battlefield and delivered his brief but famous speech known as the Gettysburg Address.

Numerous references to this battle and to these controversial generals occur in stories by Ambrose BIERCE and William FAULKNER.

GHOST STORY

The ghost story, which flowered in America, from 1870 to 1930, arises from a long oral tradition grounded in folk beliefs and quasi-religious teachings (or speculations). In these contexts, ghosts often have been presented as arbiters or recipients of a crude form of social justice in a world in which such justice seems lacking. For example, a ghost will identify a murderer or provide a reason for a slave to evade a master's demands. A bully will be forced to wander the earth in chains in the afterlife. The oral tradition has established certain ghostly conventions: Ghosts are pale, for example; they leave no footprints; they seldom speak; and only chosen, sensitive mortals can perceive their presence.

British authors of the late 18th and early 19th century popularized ghosts in GOTHIC fiction. Horace Walpole and Anne Radcliffe wrote novels that strongly influenced the short supernatural fiction that followed. Some of the novels are episodic in form, with many subplots. Each episode (such as the story of Emily and the bandits in *Mysteries of the Castle Udolpho*) can be viewed as a kind of short story, woven into the main plot.

German romantics (see ROMANTICISM) also contributed to the development of the American ghost story. Tales by E.T.A. Hoffman, Ludwig Tieck, Friedrich Novalis, and others painted eerie, supernatural landscapes and haunted medieval castles, explored psychological and theological concepts, and presented the spirit guide and the DOPPELGANGER as significant figures. Sigmund FREUD's essay "The Uncanny" analyzes "The Sandman" by E. T. A. Hoffmann and attributes its power to disturb to repressed desires and family secrets. The German influence can be seen in later stories by Edgar Allan POE and Nathaniel HAWTHORNE.

Modern readers associate ghost stories with Halloween. However, ghost stories were, until recently, closely allied with Christmas traditions. They were read around the fire on long winter nights during the holiday season. In addition, wandering spirits were believed to be a part of the misrule or disorder said to occur during the Christmas season. Spirits, benign or malignant, embodied all the forces mortals could not control.

Victorian writers capitalized on this idea, often questioning the established social order in their ghost stories. Almost everyone knows the plot of Dickens's "A Christmas Carol," which portrays the transformation of Scrooge from greedy businessman into a man full of Christmas spirit. Other Dickens ghost stories, such as "The Body Snatchers," also warn readers against the single-minded pursuit of wealth and progress. Dickens and publishers such as Mary Braddon made the Victorian ghost story available to large numbers of subscribers, who avidly read the Christmas issues of *Household Words, Belgravia Temple Bar,* and other periodicals.

The December and January issues of *Scribner's,* HARPER'S, and ATLANTIC MONTHLY also contained ghost stories. Several factors contributed to their development.

The first of these was the Spiritualist movement, the belief that humans can communicate with the parted souls, which began in 1848. This movement became associated with other progressive causes, including feminism (see FEMINIST), nonauthoritarian religion, and abolition. Prominent Americans such as William Lloyd GARRISON, William James, and Lydia Maria Child were attracted to Spiritualist circles. By the 1870s, however, many Spiritualists were discredited—some discovered to be outright frauds. The public imagination turned to fiction for its accounts of spirits. A strong reform element permeates the fiction as it did the religion. Ghosts provide justice to women, children, and the poor in stories by Mary Wilkins FREEMAN, Georgia Wood Pangborn, and Edith WHARTON.

REGIONALISM and its spirit of place also contributed to the American ghost story. Hawthorne set the stage early with his tales of New England Puritan life. His characters in "YOUNG GOODMAN BROWN" are reflected in Freeman's "The Little Maid at the Door";

both are based on regional, historical THEMES. Ellen GLASGOW's ghost stories are similarly steeped in history, that of a defeated and haunted South (see her "Dare's Gift" and "Whispering Leaves"). Western TALL TALES seem to have influenced stories by Western writers; the folk tale is never far beneath the surface, no matter how sophisticated the author may be.

The new psychology also influenced the ghost story. Alienists (physicians who treat mental disorders) hold central roles in many stories, including the feminist work of Freeman, Glasgow, and Charlotte Perkins GILMAN. Some of the tales respond to ideas promulgated by Oliver Wendell Holmes and S. Weir Mitchell, prominent doctors who also wrote fiction (not ghost fiction, however) based on their practices. Many writers sought to find a relationship between science and theology. William James, for instance, sought to substantiate the presence of spirits through his American Society for Psychic Research and established psychology as an economic discipline. His brother Henry JAMES, on the other hand, explored the individual psyche through stories such as "THE JOLLY CORNER" and "THE TURN OF THE SCREW" and left science to others. In so doing, he wrote some of the best 19th-century ghost stories. Psychological themes continued to be popular during the 20th century in stories by Joyce Carol OATES, Shirley JACKSON, and Lester del Rey.

Feminist critic Nina Auerbach argues that social change and its accompanying instability led to the evocation of ghosts in 19th-century fiction (in *Private Theatricals: The Lives of the Victorians* [1990], 53–83). The late 20th century saw a renewed interest in tales of the supernatural. Stories published today often are influenced by modern technology, space exploration, and Einstein's theories of time and energy. Many contemporary ghost stories (such as those by Harlan ELLISON, Lisa Tuttle, and Phyllis Eisenstein) merge the ghost story with SCIENCE FICTION.

With all their technological trappings, however, ghost stories still serve an age-old purpose. Our environment alienates us, our machines intimidate us, and our social systems fail to deliver the justice we feel we deserve. Therefore, our imaginations suspend reality as we know it and explore the liminal regions in which spirits confront and sometimes transcend the terrors of this world and those beyond.

BIBLIOGRAPHY
Carpenter, Lynette and Wendy K. Kolmar, ed., *Haunting the House of Fiction: Feminist Perspectives on Gost Stories by American Women*. Knoxville: University of Tennessee Press, 1991.

Kerr, Howard, John W. Crowley, and Charles L. Crow, eds., *The Haunted Dusk: American Supernatural Fiction, 1820–1920*. Athens: University of Georgia Press, 1983.

Lundie, Catherine A., ed. *Restless Spirits: Ghost Stories by American Women, 1872–1926*. Amherst: University of Massachusetts Press, 1996.

McSherry, Frank D., Jr., Charles G. Waugh, and Martin Greenberg, eds., *Great American Ghost Stories*, vol. 1. Nashville, Tenn.: Rutledge Hill Press, 1991.

Robillard, Douglas, ed., *American Supernatural Fiction: From Edith Wharton to the Weird Tales Writers*. New York: Garland, 1996.

Salmonson, Jessica Amanda, ed. *What Did Miss Darrington See? An Anthology of Feminist Supernatural Fiction*. New York: Feminist Press, 1989.

Gwen Neary
Santa Rosa Community College/Sonoma State University

GIBBSVILLE, PENNSYLVANIA

Based on Pottsville, Pennsylvania, the town where John O'HARA was reared, Gibbsville provides the backdrop for O'Hara's numerous so-called Pennsylvania novels, and for a large number of his more than 400 short stories. O'Hara uses Gibbsville to present his often satiric contempt for the shallow values of his suburbanite characters. Gibbsville, once the heart of the anthracite fields, suffered from the coal miners' strike in 1925 and never completely recovered: by the 1930s, mired in the GREAT DEPRESSION, Gibbsville is also the source of psychological depression in its rootless, dissatisfied characters who seek release in alcohol, adultery, and sometimes suicide. Often compared with William FAULKNER's YOKNAPATAWPHA COUNTY, Gibbsville provides the literary map for O'Hara's depiction of the realities of suburban life and becomes the symbol of the failure of the AMERI-CAN DREAM.

GIBSON, WILLIAM (1944–)

Gibson, who is often called the founder of the CYBERPUNK genre, became famous for his first novel, *Neuromancer* (1985), for which he was awarded the HUGO, NEBULA, and Philip K. Dick awards. Gibson wrote the short stories collected in *Burning Chrome* (1986) before *Neuromancer*, and they are classic examples of cyberpunk. Although they share some features with DETECTIVE FICTION and western film, Gibson's stories are futuristic and, in some respects, postmodernist. (See POSTMODERNISM.) The future according to Gibson is a world of technological domination, corporate and syndicated crime, stark economic contrasts, and fierce struggles for survival. Another, virtual world, that of the "matrix" or "cyberspace" formed by the connections between the world's computers, exists alongside the actual world in *Burning Chrome,* and cyberpunk HEROes adeptly navigate it. Many of the characters' bodies have been technologically altered so that they have computerized eyes, enhanced muscular or neural capabilities, or weapons implanted in their fingers. Plastic surgery and drug use abound. Bonds of family and community have been fractured or destroyed, and the hero, although cautious and sus-picious, sometimes makes human contacts and bonds as he tries to buck the system. The hostile environment complicates the establishment of a sta-ble identity, an implicit goal of Gibson's heroes. Most of the stories are narrated in first person (see POINT OF VIEW), and the dialogue is gritty and realis-tic, exhibiting the slang of the fictional world. There are frequent references to late-20th-century popular culture. The first story in *Burning Chrome,* "Johnny Mnemonic," in which the title character makes a liv-ing by storing and transporting computerized infor-mation in his brain, was made into a feature film in 1994.

Karen Fearing
University of North Carolina at Chapel Hill

GIBSON GIRL

The slim-waisted American beauty with a pompadour hairstyle created by the illustrator Charles Dana Gibson (1867–1944) came to portray the Gay Nineties' looks and manners of the ideal woman. Although Dana was a successful illustrator for various magazines, including HARPER'S and SCRIBNER'S, and many books, he is best known for this creation, for which his wife, Irene Langhorne, was the model.

GIFT BOOK

Popular in both the United States and England in the 19th century, these annually published collections contained stories, poems, and essays on sale as gifts around Christmastime. Of genuine significance in American literary history, gift books were the single best market for short fic-tion in the United States during the first half of the 19th century.

"GIFT OF THE MAGI, THE" O. HENRY (1906)

Although many critics do not view O. HENRY's stories as first rate literature, some of his many hundreds of tales have become CLASSIC. "The Gift of the Magi," touching as it does a common human chord, is one of those stories. Not tragic, perhaps sentimental or a little didactic, it combines the THEMEs of married love and selflessness with the techniques of suspense and the O. Henry SURPRISE ENDING.

Della Dillingham Young and her husband, Jim, on the edge of poverty but deeply in love, wish to purchase Christmas gifts that will surprise and please the other. The narrator focuses on Della as she tries to figure a way to find enough money to buy her husband a fine gift. Each of them has a prize possession: Jim's is a gold watch that belonged to his father and his grandfather, and Della's is her long, thick, luxurious hair. Suddenly Della realizes that she could sell her hair for enough money to buy Jim a gold chain for his watch. The touches of realistic detail (see REALISM) add to the poignancy of her sac-rifice: She had only $1.87 but, with the sale of her hair, she receives the $20 to buy the watch chain.

At home, feeling shorn and sheepish, Della greets Jim with her schoolboyish haircut. Because the narrator has focused on Della's thoughts rather than Jim's, readers feel suspense in waiting for his response. Not only does he tell her that he will love her no matter what she does with her hair, but he gives her two beautiful jeweled, tortoiseshell combs that she had admired. When Della gives him the watch chain, he suggests putting their fine presents away for a while: He has sold his watch so that he could buy Della the combs for her hair. The narrator points out that the two may have unwisely sacrificed their valuable possessions, but they are the wisest gift givers of all. Despite the moral and the sentiment—or perhaps because of them—"The Gift of the Magi" in its very simplicity appeals to a love and loyalty for which many modern readers, no matter how sophisticated, may still yearn.

BIBLIOGRAPHY
Blansfield, Karen Charmaine. *Cheap Rooms and Restless Hearts: A Study of the Formula in the Urban Tales of Porter.* Bowling Green: Bowling Green State University Press, 1988.
Henry, O. "The Gift of the Magi." In *Stories* Edited by Harry Hansen. New York: Heritage Press, 1965.

GILDED AGE

A name given to the post–CIVIL WAR era of economic expansion, greed, and gaudy wealth typified by the Vanderbilts, Morgans, Goulds, and other "captains of industry," financiers, and tycoons. The term came from the book *The Gilded Age* (1873) by Charles Dudley Warner in collaboration with Mark TWAIN. Stephen CRANE and Edith WHARTON, for instance, wrote of the effects of this wealth on the individual.

"GILDED SIX-BITS, THE" ZORA NEALE HURSTON (1933)

Appearing in STORY magazine and traditionally considered Zora Neale HURSTON's most accomplished story, favorable reception of "The Gilded Six-Bits" helped bring Hurston to the attention of critics and publishers and resulted in the publication of her first novel, *Jonah's Gourd Vine* (1934). Whether readers and critics have actually plumbed the story to it's full extent, however, is called into question with the recent rise in popularity of her earlier story "SWEAT" and its sympathetic portrayal of a wife's situation. Although "The Gilded Six-Bits" clearly addresses the themes of hypocrisy, money, infidelity, and marital love, a reading of Hurston's themes in earlier stories, along with a feminist critical perspective (see FEMINIST CRITICISM), suggests that the third-person narrator implicitly criticizes marriage and depicts it as a subtle form of prostitution. Readers who interpret the story this way can connect Hurston with the social and gender concerns of such other contemporaries as Edith WHARTON.

Hurston depicts Missie May and Joe, a young married couple, as sharing a happy and loving relationship. Beneath the surface of their Edenic bliss, however, the alert reader notes that Hurston portrays Missie May as childlike (even her name sounds babyish), and pointedly illustrates Joe's superior attitude toward her. Each Saturday he returns home from work and hurls, throws, and chunks silver dollars at the door, having trained Missie May to pick them up and pile them next to her plate at dinner. Like a father, he "indulgently" allows his wife to search his pockets for hidden treats (568), contradicts her when she says she's hungry, because only men, he implies, work hard enough to have an appetite, and insists that he "parade" his pretty wife in front of Otis, the big spender from Chicago. Missie May resists the trip, protesting that Joe is all the man she needs, but he unwittingly sets her up for adultery by praising Otis, whom he tries to emulate, and extolling his pieces of gold and envying all his "pretty womens" (567). The equation of money, sex, and maleness cannot but filter dimly into Missy May's consciousness.

When Joe arrives home early one night and surprises Missy May in bed with Otis, she confesses that Otis promised the gold in return for sex. Missie May is grateful that, rather than leaving her, Joe allows her to continue to cook for and wait on him, and perform the services of a masseuse. Moreover, he gives her the gold piece he had ripped from Otis's vest when he struck him, and Missie May, feeling like a prostitute, returns the money—which in any case turns out to be only a gilded half-dollar. When, months later, Missie May gives birth to a baby boy that looks exactly like Joe, she has redeemed herself: He uses the gilded coin to buy candy for her and the baby.

As with many Hurston stories and novels, the African-American characters are sympathetically treated, especially when they interact with whites. When Joe buys the candy from the clerk and pridefully tells him that Otis never fooled him, the clerk's reaction is like the white sheriff's in William FAULKNER's "PANTALOON IN BLACK": the clerk insensitively and erroneously remarks that "these darkies" never have problems, they just laugh "all the time" (574). Yet when Hurston refocuses on the couple, her narrator remains implicitly critical of the unequal nature of the relationship: Joe returns home and chunks 15 silver dollars at the door. Still weak from childbirth and unable to run, but clearly grateful for her reinstatement in Joe's good graces, Missie May "crept there as quickly as she could" (574). The complexity of the story and the ways readers continue to interpret it assures it a long-lasting place in 20th-century literature.

BIBLIOGRAPHY
Hurston, Zora Neale. "The Gilded Six-Bits." In *Major Writers of Short Fiction: Stories and Commentary*. Edited by Ann Charters. Boston: St. Martin's, 1993, pp. 566–74.

GILMAN, CHARLOTTE (ANNA) PERKINS (STETSON) (1860–1935)

The great-niece of author and abolitionist advocate Harriet Beecher Stowe, Charlotte Perkins Gilman was born in Hartford, Connecticut, and is best remembered today for her autobiographically inspired short story, "THE YELLOW WALL-PAPER" (1892), which chronicles the nervous breakdown of a young wife and mother. Gilman was able to write with authority about the terrifying consequences of chronic depression because, from early adulthood, she struggled with episodes of severe melancholia. After her engagement and subsequent marriage in 1884 to her first husband, Charles Walter Stetson, her depression deepened. Following the birth of her daughter Katharine in 1885, Gilman underwent a rest cure for neurasthenia—a term used to describe

a condition of depression accompanied by feelings of helplessness and uselessness—and subsequently suffered a nervous breakdown. She gradually recovered her health after separating from Stetson in 1888 and divorcing him six years later.

Gilman moved to Pasadena, California, in 1888; she began writing short fiction in 1890. By the end of her long career, she had published nearly 200 short stories. Regrettably, although she remained remarkably prolific, she would never again write a story that rivaled the power and poignancy of "The Yellow Wall-Paper," which is superior to her other literary works in artistry and execution. With the notable exception of this story, in fact, critics generally have not been enthusiastic about Gilman's fiction, citing as deficiencies its heavy didacticism, its uneven quality, and its tendency to resist easy classification.

Owing to the constant pressure of deadlines, Gilman wrote hastily and without revision. Always on the brink of poverty, she frequently subordinated quality to quantity, turning work out quickly in an effort to secure a much-needed income. Early in her career, she experimented with tales in the popular GOTHIC tradition. In addition to "The Yellow Wall-Paper," published in *New England Magazine* and originally characterized as a horror story, other stories by Gilman in the gothic tradition include "The Giant Wistaria" (1891), "The Rocking Chair" (1893), and "The Unwatched Door" (1894). After her conversion in the early 1890s to nationalism, a movement promoting an end to capitalism and advancing the peaceful, progressive, ethical, and democratic improvement of the human race, Gilman's literary style changed, and she began to emphasize THEMES of social reform. Both the Nationalist movement and her support of reform Darwinism—a philosophy advocating conscious intervention in the evolutionary process for the purpose of controlling human destiny—profoundly shaped her fictional landscape. In most of her works published after 1895, Gilman re-created the world according to her vision of the ideal. Through her fiction, she attempted to illustrate tangible solutions to problems arising from a patriarchal society in which women often were expected to assume obsequious roles.

Among the themes that emerge in Gilman's reform fiction are the need for women to become economically self-sufficient (as in "Making a Change," 1911; "Mrs. Beazley's Deeds," 1911; and "Mrs. Elder's Idea," 1912); the importance of sisterhood (as in "Turned," 1911; "Being Reasonable," 1915; and "Dr. Clair's Place," 1915); the promotion of human rights issues (as in "The Boys and the Butter," 1910, and "Joan's Defender," 1916); and the value of utopian communities (as in "Maidstone Comfort," 1912, and "Bee Wise," 1913). Gilman constructed stories around such provocative topics as sexual harassment, blackmail, bribery, venereal disease, streetcar safety, tainted milk, social motherhood, and yellow journalism—subjects that she also addressed in her poetry and essays.

Gilman experimented briefly with other fictional styles in 1894 and 1895, when she served as editor of *The Impress,* a literary weekly published by the Pacific Coast Women's Press Association. Sixteen of her stories appeared in "Studies in Style," a series that featured works written in imitation of such well-known authors as Louisa May ALCOTT, Hamlin GARLAND, Nathaniel HAWTHORNE, Henry JAMES, Edgar Allan POE, Mark TWAIN, and Mary E. Wilkins FREEMAN. The experiment, however, was little more than a gimmick used to promote the ailing newspaper, and Gilman quickly abandoned the practice once *The Impress* folded.

In the first decade of the 20th-century, Gilman turned her attention to book-length theoretical treatises; during this time she published only a handful of stories. When she returned to fiction writing, however, in the years prior to WORLD WAR I, she found that editors did not share her enthusiasm for reform fiction and her work became increasingly difficult to place. She decided, therefore, to single-handedly write, edit, and publish her own monthly magazine, the *Forerunner.* In circulation from 1909 until 1916, the *Forerunner* was the most ambitious project of Gilman's long career and the forum in which the majority of her fiction appeared.

Although Gilman's goal of publishing a separate volume of her stories was never realized, dozens of her works have been collected and reprinted in recent years. In addition to her fiction, Gilman also produced close to 500 poems, a handful of plays, nine novels, hundreds of essays, and a posthumously published autobiography. By 1925, however, her writings no longer appealed to the postwar generation, and she virtually disappeared from the public eye.

In 1934 her second husband and first cousin, George Houghton Gilman, whom she married in 1900, died suddenly from a cerebral hemorrhage. In 1935, after battling inoperable breast cancer for three years, Gilman—an advocate of euthanasia—ended her life by inhaling chloroform. Gilman's death, like her life, was meant to be instructive.

Although Gilman feared that she would be forgotten by later generations, her legacy has been ensured as a result of her 1994 induction into the National Women's Hall of Fame in Seneca Falls, New York. A critical reevaluation of her fiction continues as her work becomes increasingly available.

BIBLIOGRAPHY

Gilman, Charlotte Perkins. *The Yellow Wall-Paper and Selected Stories of Charlotte Perkins Gilman.* Edited by Denise D. Knight. Newark: University of Delaware Press, 1994.

Hill, Mary A. *Charlotte Perkins Gilman: The Making of a Radical Feminist, 1860–1896.* Philadelphia: Temple University Press, 1980.

Knight, Denise D. *Charlotte Perkins Gilman: A Study of the Short Fiction.* Boston: Twayne, 1997.

Lane, Ann J., ed. *The Charlotte Perkins Gilman Reader.* New York: Pantheon Books, 1980.

Scharnhorst, Gary. *Charlotte Perkins Gilman.* Boston: Twayne, 1985.

Denise D. Knight
SUNY Cortland

"GIRL" JAMAICA KINCAID (1978)

Jamaica KINCAID's "Girl" is a SHORT-SHORT STORY; it is only one paragraph in length, and that paragraph is actually punctuated as one long sentence, a series of dependent and independent clauses separated by semicolons. The story's details provide insight into a young girl's relationship with her judgmental and domineering mother. The story's POINT OF VIEW is unusual and effective: The tale consists of a catalog of advice given to the daughter by the mother. The cumulative effect of this listing is to show the way the mother attempts to shape every area of the daughter's life ("Wash the white clothes on Monday . . . soak salt fish overnight before you cook it . . . you mustn't speak to wharf-rat boys . . . this is how to sew on a button . . . this is how you grow okra. . . ."). In this list Kincaid uses a technique similar to STREAM OF CONSCIOUSNESS, presenting the mother's litany filtered through the daughter's consciousness. More disturbing than the mother's advice, though, is her judgment; ostensibly she intends her advice to keep her daughter from being "the slut you are so bent on becoming." Twice the daughter interrupts the mother's listing, but the mother's catalog of the daughter's "faults" continues.

This story addresses many of the THEMES of *At the Bottom of the River* (1983), Kincaid's first short story collection: disconnection between mothers and daughters, role conflicts, lack of communication, and isolation in the midst of community. Its fragmented style is also typical of the experimental narratives and dreamlike imagery of other stories in this collection.

Karen Weekes
University of Georgia

GLASGOW, ELLEN (ANDERSON GHOLSON) (1873–1945)

Ellen Glasgow was born in Richmond, Virginia, the eighth in a family of ten children. Too sickly to attend school, she was educated at home, where she read science and philosophy voraciously. In her autobiography, *The Woman Within,* published in 1954 long after her death, she describes an isolated and unhappy childhood that was partly exacerbated by growing deafness. She identified with her frail mother and resented her overbearing father; much of her later work deals with women who suffer in unequal relationships with men.

Glasgow's first publication, a short story titled "A Woman of Tomorrow" (1895), describes a woman's choice of her career over love. In the end, although she briefly regrets never having children, the HEROINE is happy with her life's decision.

Glasgow is best known for her novels, most of which are set in Queensborough, Virginia, the fictional Richmond, and deal with the uneasy relationship between the Old South and the New South and the troubled relationships between men and women. At the beginning of her career, critics viewed Glasgow as a rebel because she portrayed the South as it really was instead of idealizing and romanticizing it as most other Southern writers of her time did. (See REALISM.) By the end of her career, however, more revolutionary writers such as Thomas Wolfe and William FAULKNER had taken her place and the literary public saw her as staid and conservative. She wrote 20 novels and was awarded the PULITZER PRIZE for the last one published during her lifetime, *In This Our Life* (1941), partly in recognition of her past achievements.

Glasgow's decision to focus on the novel rather than the short story was a conscious one made after a publisher and friend, Walter Hines Page, told her she would be more successful as a novelist. But she did publish 13 stories in various magazines, seven of which were collected into a volume entitled *The Shadowy Third and Other Stories* (1923). Most of these stories were written between 1916 and 1924 during a period when she needed money but did not have the emotional energy for a longer work.

Like her contemporary Edith WHARTON, Glasgow wrote two main types of stories: those that deal with marriage and those that focus on the supernatural. The marriage stories reflect many of the same THEMES that appear in her novels. For instance, in "JORDAN'S END" (1923) an aristocratic but worn-out Southern family slowly decays as their mansion decays around them, and a Southern lady gets away with murder. Similar situations occur in the later novels *Barren Ground* and *In This Our Life.*

The supernatural stories often reflect the author's unhappy childhood. In the title story of her collection, "THE SHADOWY THIRD" is the ghost of the wife's recently dead child, offspring of a previous marriage, who can be seen only by sensitive characters. The overbearing husband cannot see the child, but the frail and mournful mother can. Assuming that his wife is insane, the husband commits her to an asylum where she soon dies, but the ghost child gets her revenge by tripping her stepfather on the stairs and causing him to fall to his death. Although Glasgow's reputation does not rest on these stories, many are excellent examples of her work and offer insights into her novels' themes and into her own life.

Two of her most famous novels, *Virginia* (1913) and *Barren Ground* (1925), present opposite ways that women cope with trying relationships. Virginia, the heroine of the novel that bears her name, represents the traditional lady of the Old South. After being abandoned by a philandering husband, she becomes a pathetic shell. Dorinda Oakley, the heroine of *Barren Ground,* is abandoned by the father of her baby; after losing the baby, she becomes a stronger woman who successfully runs her own farm and vows to live without love.

BIBLIOGRAPHY

Inge, M. Thomas, ed. *Ellen Glasgow: Centennial Essays.* Charlottesville: University Press of Virginia, 1976.

Meeker, Richard K. "Introduction." In *The Collected Stories of Ellen Glasgow.* Baton Rouge: Louisiana State University Press, 1963.

Thiebaux, Marcelle. *Ellen Glasgow.* New York: F. Ungar Publishing Co., 1982.

Betina I. Entzminger
University of North Carolina at Chapel Hill

GLASPELL, SUSAN (1882–1948)   Born in

Davenport, Iowa, Susan Glaspell was reared with traditional midwestern values and graduated from Drake University in 1899. As a reporter for the *Des Moines Daily News,* she began writing stories in the LOCAL COLOR tradition, seeking, like her contemporaries Zona GALE and Mary French, to preserve those special qualities of place, speech, and thought that made her region unique. Unlike Glaspell, her husband, George Cram Cook, whom she married in 1913, resisted what he saw as the provinciality of Davenport and the ROMANTICISM he perceived in his wife's works.

She and her husband moved to Provincetown, Massachusetts, and, in 1915, with a small group of other Greenwich Villagers, established the Provincetown Players, an experimental theater designed to present new drama and combat the commercialism of Broadway. Among playwrights whose work was first introduced by this theater was Eugene O'Neill. Although Glaspell went on to become a professional playwright herself and won the Pulitzer Prize for *Alison's House* (1930), based on the life of Emily Dickinson, she also wrote novels, the best known of which is *Judd Rankin's Daughter* (1945) and short stories, including "A JURY OF HER PEERS" (1917), a story based on her play *Trifles* (1916).

BIBLIOGRAPHY

Glaspell, Susan. *Alison's House: A Play in Three Acts.* New York: S. French, 1930.

———. *Ambrose Holt and Family.* New York: Stokes, 1931.

———. *Inheritors: A Play in Three Acts.* New York: Dodd, 1921.

———. *Judd Rankin's Daughter.* New York: Grosset & Dunlap, 1945.

———. *Plays.* New York: Dodd, Mead, 1920.

———. *The Verge: A Play in Three Acts.* Boston: Small, Maynard & Co., 1922.

Waterman, Arthur E. *Susan Glaspell.* New York: Twayne, 1966.

———. "Susan Glaspell." *American Literary Realism* 4 (Spring 1971): 183–191.

GLOSS   A brief explanation of a difficult or

obscure word or expression in the margin or between the lines of a text. Glosses can provide a running commentary and explanation of a difficult text or can be an interlinear (between-the-lines) translation. A glossary is a collection or list of textual glosses.

GO DOWN, MOSES   WILLIAM FAULKNER

(1942)   *Go Down, Moses,* William FAULKNER's twelfth novel, is generally ranked as one of his greatest—not least because it doubles as a unique collection of short stories. Most of these stories had been published separately between 1935 and 1942, in such popular magazines as HARPER'S, COLLIER'S, and the SATURDAY EVENING POST. Their middlebrow magazine audience differed greatly from the tiny highbrow public interested in Faulkner's novels. Thus, the genesis of this text—the transformation of what Faulkner at first derisively called "stories about niggers" (Grimwood 228) into tragic tales of racial torment, each an unexpected prism on the others—is virtually a story in its own right. Delayed recognitions that vividly recast all that has gone before are a signature event in Faulkner's work. In like manner, the making of *Go Down, Moses* is premised on his discovery (with almost all the individual pieces already done) that he has on his hands the sage of a single seven-generational black and white family. Their interlocking lives—humorous, abusive, guilt-driven, above all inextricable—convey his version of the haunted South itself.

Although the formal structure of *Go Down, Moses* is unique, Sherwood ANDERSON's WINESBURG, OHIO (1919) and James Joyce's *Dubliners* (1914) may well have served as models. Anderson was Faulkner's first mentor, and Joyce was his great modernist (see MODERNISM) precursor. Both of them deploy the multiple stories of stymied individual lives to suggest the contours of a larger shared malaise. For Anderson and Joyce the community in distress is a town. For Faulkner it is both less and more: a family but also a culture and a history. The seven stories of individual lives come together to produce a novel of Faulkner's entire race-tormented region.

The opening story, "Was," is whimsical in tone (its narrator is a nine-year-old boy), and it revolves around a series of hunts. Two white brothers (Uncle Buck and Uncle Buddy) are chasing their escaped "nigger" (Tomey's Turl), another white man (Hubert) is trying to marry off his sister (Sophonsiba) to Uncle Buck, the black man (Tomey's Turl) is escaping his owners in order to court his sweetheart (Tennie, one of Hubert's slaves), and the unmarried white woman (Sophonsiba) is trying to snare Buck for a husband. These hunts merrily echo each other, CLIMAXing in a game of poker between Hubert and Buck that will determine who pairs off with whom and (literally) at what price. Only later will the read-

er recognize that Turl is Buck and Buddy's half brother (concealed MISCEGENATION is at the heart of this text) and that the year of these shenanigans is 1859—just before the outbreak of the CIVIL WAR and the end of innocence.

In the next story, "The Fire and the Hearth," set in the 1940s, Faulkner painstakingly explores the perspective of the black characters. Lucas Beauchamp (offspring of Turl and Tennie) ceases to be a stereotypical (see STEREOTYPE) "nigger." Faulkner devotes page after page to Lucas's memories, ordeals, and desires. These poetic passages reveal the fineness of Lucas's mind, and although he remains a black man caught up in the racist South, he is agile enough to outwit the various whites who would exploit him. Despite his restless schemes, Lucas manages to preserve his marriage with Molly. The title of this story points to a domestic warmth outside the reach of any white family in Faulkner's work. Lucas heroically accommodates all the pressures—racial, domestic, gendered—that surround him. In this he is the counterpart for Faulkner's other heroic figure (yet to appear): ISAAC (IKE) MCCASLIN, a dreamer, idealist, and hunter who finds sustenance in the unspoiled wilderness.

"Pantaloon in Black," the next story, may be the most moving story about race that Faulkner ever wrote. He positions us inside the mind of Rider, the grief stricken black man whose young wife has just died. (See POINT OF VIEW.) Inconsolable, inarticulate, suffocating, Rider moves through the woods at an almost epic pace, desperately seeking release in liquor or violence. Our bond with this character is so intimate that we watch, hypnotized, as Rider finally seals his fate by killing with a razor the white man who has just cheated him with crooked dice. Then, suddenly, after this moment-by-moment intensity, the story switches from Rider's mind to that of the deputy who has tried unsuccessfully to jail him and has seen his body once the white man's family has taken its revenge. The deputy understands nothing of what he has witnessed, for Faulkner has rendered a distress no white person in Rider's world can understand when it rages inside a black body.

The next pair of stories—"The Old People" and "THE BEAR"—build on each other, as they gradually introduce the boy Ike McCaslin to his twin heritage: the guilt-saturated inheritance of McCaslin property and the liberating ritual of the wilderness hunt. Ike's childhood is structured on the promise, and then the reality, of participating in the autumnal hunt in the big woods. For this development a further cast is needed: Sam Fathers, part Indian and part black, Ike's guide in both the art of the hunt and the communal sharing with the wild that it permits; Old Ben, the legendary bear; Lion, the wild dog that is alone capable of bringing the bear down; and Boon Hogganbeck, part Indian, wholly untamed. In a climactic encounter that is both embrace and murder, celebration and farewell, Boon and Lion and Old Ben merge in an act of pure beauty and violence. Ike watches as Boon bestrides the beleaguered bear, "working and probing the buried blade," finally bringing them all down together.

Four of the five sections of "The Bear" rise to and descend from this climactic moment in which the figures of the wilderness—Old Ben, Lion, Sam Fathers—embrace, deal out their death, and die themselves. The wilderness enters its autumnal phase, yet Ike McCaslin will be shaped by this scene forever. Five years later, at age 21, he renounces his McCaslin property and heritage, telling his cousin quietly that "Sam Fathers set me free" (286). Indeed, this narrative of renunciation fills the experimental fourth section of "The Bear," in which Faulkner explores the widest cultural ramifications of the hunt. Ike discovers, in the ledgers of the McCaslin commissary, the race-tormented history of his family, sees that Tomey's Turl is actually his grandfather's son by a black woman and realizes that the old man evaded this bond by giving money instead: "*I reckon that was cheaper than saying My son to a nigger* he thought" (258). Brooding on his family's refusal to acknowledge their own black offspring, Ike rejects his blood heritage, becoming "uncle to half a county and father to no one" in his lifelong retreat to the woods.

Faulkner treats Ike's withdrawal with compassion, yet he shows, in the next story, "DELTA AUTUMN," that the family's racist history continues unabated. In this last hunt (dated 1940s) Ike encounters a mysterious woman with a child; she is looking for Ike's great-nephew Roth. As in a dream, it turns out that, although her skin does not reveal it, she is black (is in fact the great-granddaughter of Tomey's Turl) and that her fleeing lover is Roth. Miscegenation upon miscegenation, the 1940s nonacknowledgment echoing that of the 1830s, Ike sees the futility of his attempt to escape, as he gazes on the woods ruined by loggers and their machinery.

Futility is likewise the THEME of the last story, "Go Down, Moses," which centers on a ceremonial returning of the corpse of the black Samuel Worsham Beauchamp to his grieving Southern family. Roth had earlier "exiled" Samuel from the plantation for theft. The young man had moved to the urban North, turned criminal, and been caught and executed. Samuel's family awaits the return of his body, singing of Roth's casting out of Samuel as betraying him to Pharaoh—"'Sold him in Egypt and now he dead.' 'Oh yes, Lord. Sold him in Egypt.'" (363). If this 150-year history is powerless to envision black life freed from white Pharaoh's grasp, it at least acknowledges the pathos of black death, the community (white and black) bringing one of their own home to be laid to rest. On this note of ceremonial grief, Faulkner concludes *Go Down, Moses.*

BIBLIOGRAPHY

Faulkner, William, *Go Down, Moses*. New York: Random House, 1942.

Grimwood, Michael. *Heart in Conflict: Faulkner's Struggles with Vocation*. Athens: University of Georgia Press, 1987.

Harrington, Evans, and Ann J. Abadie, eds. *Faulkner and the Short Story*. Jackson: University of Mississippi Press, 1992.

Matthews, John T. *The Play of Faulkner's Language*. Ithaca, N.Y.: Cornell University Press, 1982.

Snead, James. *Figures of Division: William Faulkner's Major Novels*. New York: Methuen, 1986.

Sundquist, Eric. *Faulkner: The House Divided*. Baltimore: Johns Hopkins University Press, 1983.

Wagner-Martin, Linda, ed. *New Essays on Faulkner's Go Down, Moses*. New York: Cambridge University Press, 1996.

Weinstein, Philip M., ed. *The Cambridge Companion to William Faulkner.* New York: Cambridge University Press, 1995.

Philip M. Weinstein
Swarthmore College

GOLDEN APPLES, THE EUDORA WELTY
(1949)   When Eudora WELTY published *The Golden Apples* in 1949, critics did not know whether to treat it as an experimental novel or as a collection of interconnected short stories. But Welty included the separate pieces from *The Golden Apples* in her *Collected Stories of Eudora Welty* (1980), making it clear that she intended them as stories. This seven-piece cycle (see SHORT STORY CYCLE) covers 40 years in the life of the small community in MORGANA, MISSISSIPPI. Each story focuses on different central characters, who also appear on the periphery in other stories at different stages of their lives. In the first story, Katie Rainey, mother of the rebellious Virgie Rainey, introduces the reader to Morgana's residents, especially the promiscuous and wandering King McLain. In the final story, "The Wanderers," Katie's funeral takes place and Virgie, who at the funeral recognizes a kinship with the now aged King McLain, finally gets her chance to escape Morgana, completing the cycle.

In depicting the residents of Morgana, Welty alludes to Greek, Roman, Celtic, and Germanic MYTHS and LEGENDS, thematically demonstrating the relatedness of all human communities, regardless of time and place (see THEME). Like all people, mythic or mundane, ancient or modern, the characters in *The Golden Apples* seek beauty, love, contentment, and passion, each in his or her own way. The title of the cycle is found in William Butler Yeats's poem "The Song of the Wandering Aengus," which describes the Celtic hero Aengus's quest for eternal happiness in the form of a beautiful girl. And the Golden Apples also refer to the Greek legend in which the apples, as symbols of perfect beauty and passion, were awarded by Paris to Aphrodite, causing jealousy among the goddesses who became partially responsible for beginning the Trojan War. We also find counterparts for many of Welty's characters in myth. King McLain, who has many love affairs and children throughout Mississippi, and who first appears to us in "A Shower of Gold," is a Zeus fig-

ure. Loch Morrison, the heroic boy who saves a drowning orphan in "Moon Lake," is a youthful Perseus. Cassie Morrison, Loch's older sister, comes to deep understandings of the other characters that she is unable to express in "June Recital" and is, as her name indicates, a Cassandra figure.

In "June Recital" we also meet Virgie Rainey, the rebellious but talented young girl, and Mrs. Eckhart, the misunderstood artist and piano teacher. These characters, while seemingly opposite, have much in common as they learn to understand themselves in relation to the world, and both are linked to a portrait of Perseus slaying the Medusa that hangs above Mrs. Eckhart's piano. As Virgie Rainey reflects in "The Wanderers," in order for there to be heroes, there also must be victims, and she and her piano teacher contain qualities of both figures.

Although all these characters have mythic counterparts, *The Golden Apples* is not merely an ALLEGORY. The characters are also real, 20th-century Southerners, described in vivid detail, making the reader feel that even the most ordinary of us has a connection to myth.

BIBLIOGRAPHY
Evans, Elizabeth. *Eudora Welty*. New York: Ungar, 1981.
Vande Kieft, Ruth M. *Eudora Welty*. Boston: Twayne, 1987.

Betina I. Entzminger
University of North Carolina at Chapel Hill

GONZALEZ, N. V. M. **(1915–)**   N. V. M. Gonzalez was born in Mindoro, the Philippines. He began writing as soon as he finished high school, but it would be more than 10 years before the publication of his first book of short stories, *Seven Hills Away* (1947). This collection was deeply admired in the Philippines and attracted enough international attention that two years later Gonzalez was offered a writing fellowship at Stanford University, where he studied under Wallace Stegner. Gonzalez is a professor emeritus of English literature at California State University at Hayward; he is also the international writer-in-residence at the University of the Philippines, Manila.

Although Gonzalez has lived in the United States since 1949, most of his story collections—including *Children of the Ash-Covered Loam* (1954), *Look, Stranger, on this Island Now* (1963), and *Mindoro and Beyond* (1979)—and the majority of his separately published stories have appeared exclusively in the Philippines. Most American readers know Gonzalez only through *The Bread of Salt and Other Stories* (1993), which brings together 19 representative stories spanning the length of Gonzalez's writing career. Gonzalez also has written several novels and numerous essays.

A postcolonial writer in perspective and THEMES, Gonzalez uses a compassionate TONE and gentle IRONY to explore the subjugation of the Filipinos by the West and especially by America, grieving over Filipinos' loss of myth and of traditional connections to the land and the utter absence of any kind of replacement culture.

BIBLIOGRAPHY
Campomanes, Oscar V. "Filipinos in the United States and Their Literature of Exile." In *Reading the Literatures of Asian America.* Edited by Shirley Geok-lin Lim and Amy Ling. 1992.
Gonzalez, N. V. M. *The Bread of Salt and Other Stories.* Seattle: University of Washington Press, 1993.
———. *Children of the Ash-Covered Loam, and Other Stories.* Manila, P.I.: Benipayo Press, 1954.
———. *Look, Stranger, on this Island Now.* Manila, P.I.: Benipayo Press, 1963.
———. *Mindoro and Beyond: Twenty-One Stories.* Quezon City, P.I.: University of Philippines Press, 1979.
———. *Seven Hills Away.* Denver, Colo.: A. Swallow, 1947.

Keith Lawrence
Brigham Young University

"GOOD ANNA, THE" GERTRUDE STEIN (1909)

Throughout *Three Lives,* in which "The Good Anna" appears, Gertrude STEIN explores the heterosexual and lesbian relationships of three common women, Anna, Melanctha, and Lena. In her attempts to capture the thoughts and consciousness of these women, Stein uses a number of stylistic innovations that contributed significantly to the development of MODERNISM, influencing such writers as Ernest HEMINGWAY. In "The Good Anna," for example, Stein employs inverted grammatical patterns, repetition, and simple language to characterize Anna, the PROTAGONIST, as a stubborn, matter-of-fact, hardworking German immigrant. At the same time, the ironic and understated narration, which creates a humor that is often incongruous with the story's events, suggests some of Stein's larger social criticisms.

The good Anna works for numerous men and women who seemingly take advantage of her kindness. As she tries to enforce her own moral code of "good" and "bad" on the world (including her dogs Peter, Baby, and Rags), Anna struggles with her own lesbian desires for Mrs. Lehntman: "The widow Mrs. Lehntman was the romance in Anna's life" (30). Ironically, Anna's attempts for moral and emotional control over others prevent the fulfillment of her own emotional needs, leaving her "bitter with the world . . . for its sadness and wicked ways of doing" (65, 69). Unable to change those around her, she loses her money, friends, and health. Having defined herself by her work ethic, she eventually works herself to death running a boardinghouse. Stein subtly uses the story of Anna to make a powerful critique of the destructiveness of a society that locks women into restrictive, "feminine" roles even as it represses homosexuality.

BIBLIOGRAPHY
DeKoven, Marianne. *A Different Language: Gertrude Stein's Experimental Writing.* Madison: University of Wisconsin Press, 1983.
Fahy, Thomas. "Iteration and Narrative Control in Gertrude Stein's 'The Good Anna,'" *Style* 34:1 (2000).
Wagner-Martin, Linda. *"Favored Strangers": Gertrude Stein and Her Family.* New Brunswick, N.J.: Rutgers University Press, 1995.

Thomas Fahy
University of North Carolina at Chapel Hill

"GOOD COUNTRY PEOPLE" FLANNERY O'CONNOR (1955)

In a memorable contribution to her stories that use the GROTESQUE, Flannery O'CONNOR's "Good Country People" ironically reverses the old saying that country people are good and its corollary, simple. Set in Georgia, the story features three women and a Bible salesman.

Like most of O'Connor's stories, the unselfconscious third-person narrator injects comic (see COMEDY) overtones or, more accurately, those of BLACK HUMOR, to entertain readers as they become acquainted with these markedly peculiar characters. Mrs. Hopewell, the initiator of the "good country people" idea, speaks in clichés equivalent to "have a good day." Her FOIL is her maid, Mrs. Freeman, who, in her fascination with all forms of sickness, disease, and abnormality, tells revolting tales about her daughters (Glynese and Carramae) and exhibits a perverse fascination with Mrs. Hopewell's large, hulking, 32-year-old daughter, Joy. Joy had lost her leg at age 10; she lumbers and stumps around on a wooden one and has changed her name to Hulga. JOY-HULGA brags to the two older women about her doctorate in philosophy, boasting that she believes in nothing at all.

When MANLEY POINTER arrives on the scene with his Bibles and his humorously phallic name, the reader expects that Hulga will exert her strong will on him and seduce him. But he has only been playing the part of a simple, good country person, and his briefcase contains a false bottom under which he keeps liquor, condoms, and items he steals from women with deformities. He has, he informs Hulga as he runs off with her wooden leg, believed in nothing since birth. Hulga, for all her degrees and pride in her intellectual power, has been played for a fool, losing not her virginity but her carefully cultivated outward sense of superiority to others less educated. As Ann Charters points out, "However dastardly Pointer's actions, he forces Hulga to feel and acknowledge her emotions for the first time," and our final impression is that Hulga may learn from this humbling experience, becoming "less presumptuous and closer to psychic wholeness" (136). Hulga and her mother must correct and surmount their complacency and naïveté, for the story suggests that without a strong philosophy and spiritual beliefs, they remain at the mercy of the Manley Pointers and Mrs. Freemans, significantly connected

through their similar names, who also believe in nothing but have less difficulty surviving.

BIBLIOGRAPHY

Charters, Ann. *Resources for Teaching: Major Writers of Short Fiction*. Boston: Bedford Books/St. Martin's, 1993.

O'Connor, Flannery. "Good Country People." In *Contemporary American Literature*. Edited by George Perkins and Barbara Perkins. New York: Random House, 1988, 168–181.

GOOD HOUSEKEEPING   A monthly magazine directed primarily at women and homemakers that has offered household advice, recipes, articles, and fiction since 1885. Among writers published in the magazine have been W. Somerset Maugham, James Hilton, Mary Roberts Rinehart, Sinclair Lewis, Daphne du Maurier, and John P. Marquand.

GOODMAN BROWN   See "YOUNG GOODMAN BROWN."

"GOOD MAN IS HARD TO FIND, A" FLANNERY O'CONNOR (1952)   Frequently anthologized, "A Good Man Is Hard to Find" exemplifies Flannery O'CONNOR's Southern religious grounding. The story depicts the impact of Christ on the lives of two seemingly disparate characters. One is a grandmother joining her son's family on a trip to Florida. Accompanied by a silent daughter-in-law, a baby, two unpleasant children, and her smuggled cat, she wheedles the son into making a detour to see a plantation that she remembers from an earlier time.

Moments of recognition and connection multiply as the seemingly foreordained meeting of the grandmother and the killer she has read about in the paper takes place. She upsets the basket in which she has hidden her cat; the cat lands on her son's neck, which causes an accident. Soon three men appear on the dirt road, and the grandmother recognizes one of them as the notorious killer the Misfit.

O'Connor weaves the notion of punishment and Christian love into the conversation between the Misfit and the grandmother while, at the same time, the grandmother's family is being murdered. Referring to the similarity that he shares with Christ, the Misfit declares that "Jesus thrown everything off balance" (27), but he admits that unlike Christ, he must have committed a crime because there were papers to prove it. When the grandmother touches his shoulder because she sees him as one of her own children, she demonstrates a Christian love that causes him to shoot her.

This story typifies O'Connor's mingling of COMEDY, goodness, banality, and violence in her vision of a world that, however imperfect, most readers inevitably recognize as part of their own. O'Connor views the world as a place where benevolence and good intentions conflict with perversity and evil, and her PROTAGONISTs frequently learn too late that their lives can crumble in an instant when confronted by the very real powers of darkness.

BIBLIOGRAPHY

Kessler, Edward. *Flannery O'Connor and the Language of Apocalypse.* Princeton, N.J.: Princeton University Press, 1986.

Orvell, Miles. *Flannery O'Connor: an Introduction.* Jackson: University Press of Mississippi, 1991.

Sandra Chrystal Hayes
Georgia Institute of Technology

GORDON, CAROLINE (1895–1981)

A talented novelist and short story writer, Caroline Gordon both celebrates the stability of the past and details the complex social, psychological, and political transition from the Old South to the New. Although she has a distinctive voice and vision, her studies of middle-class Southerners and the passing of the old cultured agrarian way of life link her with writers like Eudora WELTY or Peter TAYLOR. Her stories take place in Kentucky and Tennessee, and include "The Captivity," a well-known Native-American captivity story, as well as several Civil War tales about the Union army's invasion of the rural South (for instance, "Hear the Nightingale Sing," "The Forest of the South," and "The Ice House"). Gordon is probably best known, however, for her insightful and meticulously crafted stories about ALECK MAURY, Southern sportsman, that have prompted comparison to the hunting and fishing tales of Ernest HEMINGWAY and William FAULKNER (Schaefer 214). The episodic novel, *Aleck Maury, Sportsman,* contains most of the Maury material, as do numerous stories from *The Forest of the South* (1945), including the acclaimed "Old Red."

These related stories feature Aleck, a.k.a. Professor Maury, classics teacher, gentleman farmer, and above all else, avid sportsman. Gordon makes Maury into a central consciousness similar to that used by Henry JAMES. He understands that he devotes himself to fishing because, as with Hemingway's NICK ADAMS, it provides a way for confronting and coming to terms with his own identity. Essentially at war with his family and others who represent a constricted and socialized life, Maury understands that they are like hunters engaged in the sport of capturing him as he, like Old Red, the fox, desperately seeks his freedom. With "The Presence," "One More Day," "To Thy Chamber Window, Sweet," and "The Last Day in the Field," Gordon completes the saga of the Professor; in "The Last Day in the Field," she depicts an aging Aleck whose failing health instigates his ritual farewell to the hunt.

BIBLIOGRAPHY

Fraistat, Rose Ann C. *Gordon as Novelist and Woman of Letters.* Baton Rouge: Louisiana State University Press, 1984.

Gordon, Caroline. *Aleck Maury, Sportsman.* New York: Charles Scribner's Sons, 1934. As *The Pastimes of Aleck Maury: The Life of a True Sportsman.* London: Dickson & Thompson, 1935.

———. *Collected Stories.* New York: Farrar, Straus & Giroux, 1981.

———. *The Forest of the South.* New York: C. Scribner's Sons, 1945.

———. *The Garden of Adonis.* New York: C. Scribner's Sons, 1937.

———. *The Glory of Hera.* Garden City, N.Y.: Doubleday, 1972.

———. *Green Centuries.* New York: Scribner's, 1941.

———. *The Malefactors.* New York: Harcourt Brace, 1956.

———. *None Shall Look Back.* New York: Charles Scribner's, 1937.

————. *Old Red and Other Stories.* New York: Scribner's, 1963.

————. *Penhally.* New York: Scribner's, 1931.

————. *The Strange Children.* New York: Scribner's, 1951.

————. *The Women on the Porch.* New York: Scribner's, 1944.

Gordon, Caroline, and Allen Tate, eds. *The House of Fiction: An Anthology of the Short Story.* New York: Scribner's, 1950; revised edition, 1960.

Landess, Thomas H., ed. *The Short Fiction of Gordon: A Critical Symposium.* Irving, Tex.: University of Dallas Press, 1972.

Makowsky, Veronica A. *Gordon. A Biography.* New York: Oxford University Press, 1989.

McDowell, Frederick P. W. *Gordon.* Minneapolis: University of Minnesota Press, 1966.

Schaefer, William J. "Caroline Gordon." In *Reference Guide to Short Fiction.* Edited by Noelle Watson. Detroit: St. James Press, 1994, pp. 214–15.

Stuckey, W. J. *Gordon.* New York: Twayne Publishers, 1972.

Waldron, Ann. *Close Connections: Gordon and the Southern Renaissance.* New York: Putnam, 1987.

GOTHIC A term used to describe fiction whose major characteristics include magic, chivalry, mystery, terror, the irrational, and the perverse—and often a villain pursuing a helpless virgin. The word *gothic* originally referred to the Goths, a Germanic tribe, and later came to signify "Germanic," and then "medieval." The British writer Horace Walpole is credited with writing the first gothic novel (*The Castle of Otranto,* 1764). Set in a medieval castle, it features elements we have come to associate with the fictional gothic: trap doors, winding underground tunnels, dark staircases, and mysteriously slamming doors. Mary Shelley's *Frankenstein* (1818), with its monster and its dark horrors, provides another example of the typical gothic novel. The popular form—a subgenre of romanticism—spread throughout Europe, particularly Germany, and reached the United States, where its earliest practitioner was Charles Brockden BROWN. In the short story, Edgar Allen POE practiced gothic horror; an excellent example is "THE CASK OF AMONTILLADO," in which the vengeful MONTRESOR leads his victim down a long tunnel under a castle and then walls him up alive, the bet-

ter to enjoy his revenge.

In the 20th century, the term *gothic* is often applied to stories that, although lacking the medieval atmosphere, achieve the effect of dark mystery and terror. William FAULKNER's "A ROSE FOR EMILY" is frequently referred to as "Southern gothic," as is much of the work of Flannery O'CONNOR and Carson MCCULLERS. In modern literature, the term *gothic*—including Southern gothic—is frequently associated with the grotesque, or a focus on the weird, bizarre, or fantastic. To some writers, both the gothic and the grotesque—as in Sherwood ANDERSON's *WINESBURG, OHIO* or Erskine CALDWELL's "A Mid-Summer Passion"—appear an appropriate metaphor for the modern human condition. The 20th-century movement of SURREALISM also claims the gothic mode as a forerunner.

BIBLIOGRAPHY
Eisenger, Chester E. "The Gothic Spirit in the Forties." In *Fiction of the Forties.* Edited by Chester E. Eisenger. Chicago: University of Chicago Press, 1963.

Harmon, William, and C. Hugh Holman. *A Handbook to Literature.* 7th ed., 237–38, 239–40. Upper Saddle River, N.J.: Prentice Hall, 1995.

"GREASY LAKE" T. CORAGHESSAN BOYLE (1987) T. Coraghessan BOYLE's widely anthologized coming-of-age tale initially published in *Greasy Lake and Other Stories,* tells the story of three young men—Digby, Jeff, and an unnamed narrator—who are abruptly ushered into adulthood through a painful experience at the lake of the story's title on the third night of summer vacation. The story is set in an era that no longer values manners and polite behavior, the narrator tells us. Consequently, the characters strike "elaborate poses" designed to demonstrate how dangerous they are. "Poses" is the operative term here, though, for we quickly learn that these three young men are actually innocent, suburban upper-middle-class college boys whose fascination with an idealized form of DECADENCE demonstrates how far removed they are from the real thing. These boys favor Hollywood movies and the novels of André Gide, while their wildest exploits typically involve drinking excessively and hurling raw eggs at random mail boxes. At Greasy Lake, however, the boys participate in real evil for the first time and are profoundly altered by the experience. In short, they are ushered from the world of innocence to that of experience.

After mistakenly identifying a car parked at Greasy Lake as that of their friend Tony Lovett, Digby, Jeff, and the narrator decide to play a practical joke and harass Lovett, whom they suspect is having an intimate moment with his girlfriend. As they begin to flash the lights and honk the horn of the narrator's mother's station wagon, however, it dawns on the narrator that this car is not Lovett's. Indeed, it is the car of a "bad greasy character" with whom the boys soon fight. During the fight, which Boyle depicts as a ritual, the narrator hits the man with a tire iron and assumes he has killed him. The boys then turn to the man's girlfriend. As they are about to attack her, however, another car pulls into the lot and the boys disperse. The narrator dives into the lake, where he encounters a dead body and recoils in horror.

As the narrator and his friends hide in the woods, the "bad greasy character" regains consciousness; he and the boys from the second car then demolish the station wagon. Just after the vandals leave, another car drives into the lot. Two young, drug-addled women step out of the car, one of them saying to the boys, "You guys look like some pretty bad characters" (71). One woman offers the boys drugs, but the narrator, indicating his revulsion at the decadence that had once seemed so appealing, declines the offer, thinking that he "was going to cry" (71). The story concludes as he puts the wrecked and barely driveable car in gear and "creep[s] back toward the highway," (71) back toward a world of innocence that is now, we are led to believe, largely inaccessible to him.

BIBLIOGRAPHY

Boyle, T. Coraghessan. "Greasy Lake." In *An Introduction to Fiction.* Edited by X. J. Kennedy. Boston: Little, Brown & Co., 4th ed., 1987, pp. 64–71.

Shannon Zimmerman
University of Georgia

GREAT DEPRESSION, THE   The Great Depression began in the United States with the stock market crash of October 1929. Thousands of stockholders, including banks, lost large sums of money, and within a short time many banks, factories, and businesses closed, causing millions of Americans to become jobless. The national unemployment rate, which was 3 percent in 1925, reached 25 percent in 1933. Americans were not the only ones affected; a worldwide business slump in the 1930s made this depression the worst and longest period of high unemployment and low business activity in modern times. It also caused a sharp decrease in world trade as each country tried to protect its own industries by raising tariffs on imports. The conditions brought on by the depression were a factor in Adolf Hitler's consolidation of power in Germany and Japan's decision to invade China.

In the United States, farmers were severely affected. The farm depression of the 1920s caused by low prices for farm products became even worse in the 1930s. From 1929 to 1933 prices fell about 50 percent, partly because farmers produced a surplus of crops and partly because high tariffs made exports unprofitable. Severe droughts and dust storms in parts of the Midwest and Southwest created what became known as the Dust Bowl, which destroyed thousands of farms. Many farmers migrated west to seek work in the fertile agricultural areas of California.

Shortly after being sworn in as president in 1933, Franklin D. Roosevelt called Congress into a special session, known as the Hundred Days, to pass a massive legislative package to relieve the depression. This program, called the New Deal, established relief programs such as the Civilian Conservation Corps (CCC) and Works Progress Administration (WPA) and recovery programs including the National Recovery Administration (NRA) and the Public Works Administration (PWA). It also created agencies to supervise banking and labor reforms: the Federal Deposit Insurance Corporation (FDIC) to insure bank deposits, the National Labor Relations Board (NLRB) to prevent unfair labor practices and monitor union elections, and the

Securities and Exchange Commission (SEC) to protect investors from buying unsafe stocks and bonds. The Social Security Act (1935) provided money to retired and unemployed persons.

Although the New Deal programs may have increased the confidence of many Americans in their government, the depression continued and about 15 percent of the workforce was still unemployed in 1940. The Great Depression did not end in the United States until 1942, with the nation's entry into World War II.

The depression gave rise to such groups as the American Writers' Congress of 1935, many of whose members advocated PROLETARIAN LITERATURE, and to magazines such as *Partisan Review, New Masses,* and *The Anvil.* The era provides a powerful backdrop for numerous stories by such writers as Saul BELLOW, James BALDWIN, F. Scott FITZGERALD, Ernest HEMINGWAY, Langston HUGHES, Zora Neale HURSTON, Meridel LESUEUR, Tillie OLSEN, Dorothy PARKER, and John STEINBECK.

"GREENLEAF" FLANNERY O'CONNOR (1956)

By emphasizing intense archetypal imagery, Flannery O'CONNOR raises her short story, "Greenleaf," to a complex level. O'Connor's choice of symbolic names, her suggestion of mythological fertility cults, and her use of light and dark images all serve to raise the reader's consciousness regarding class prejudice, and to paint an accurate picture of the new South, where individuals of little heritage have begun a systematic takeover from those landowners once identified as aristocrats.

O'Connor uses a third-person limited omniscient POINT OF VIEW to tell the story of Mrs. May (a questionable aristocrat with limited potential) and her two sons, Wesley and Scofield. These sons are contrasted with the earthy Greenleaf, a lower-class hired man whom Mrs. May has employed to look after her property, and to Greenleaf's twin boys, O.T. and E.T. Mrs. Greenleaf also serves as a FOIL to Mrs. May as the hopeless widow who, forced to undergo a self-evaluation, tries at the same time to come to terms with the changing conditions of her environment. Her former feelings of power in her household have

shifted strangely, and the rise of individuals like the Greenleaf family (whose name suggests progress and growth) suggests to her that the control she so values is gradually being subsumed by "white trash" people whose social heritage is questionable at best.

O'Connor uses a scrub bull ordinary and lacking in pedigree, belonging to O.T. and E.T. as a symbol for the encroaching aggression of this "lower" class. The archetypal bull (indicative of mythical sexuality, as in the Minoan culture in general and the Greek myth of Europa in particular), having escaped from the Greenleaf boys' pasture, first appears outside Mrs. Greenleaf's house, devouring her foliage. Mrs. May views its escape as a threat to her own herd of cattle, indeed to her very existence. If the bull, with its inferior genes, is allowed to breed with her herd, the offspring will no doubt be inferior as well. The bull's desire to mate and its less-than-satisfactory breeding quality suggest a parallel to the Greenleafs, who also pose a threat to the "superior" May family. While her two sons dissipate their lives with disappointing occupations (Scofield sells "nigger" insurance and Wesley teaches at a second-rate university), Mrs. May observes that the Greenleaf boys have had distinguished military careers, married French wives, and produced offspring as well as developed a state-of-the-art milk farm. Automated and advanced by its owners' persistence and determination, the Greenleaf farm is shown to be productive, as opposed to the sterility represented by the Mays. The narrator implies the takeover of a lazy, unconcerned society by a tough (although genealogically less impressive) new working class.

Once again O'Connor centers on the sin of pride. As Mrs. May egotistically bewails her fate at the hands of inferiors, it becomes obvious that despite her so-called iron hand, her farm has withered and her own offspring have lost respect for her. Their sarcastic and mocking back talk suggests their own awareness of their mother's flaws, while their apathy toward their own situations implies that there are real reasons behind their failure to obtain the success attained by their doubles.

Mrs. May shows her determination to regain control and assert her power in her attempt to force Mr.

Greenleaf into killing the scrub bull and eliminating its potential to "romance" her. Combining light and dark imagery (Mrs. May's growing insight is suggested through recurring sun images), O'Connor asks a PROTAGONIST to confront who she really is as opposed as to whom she mistakenly identifies with and whom she desires to be. Unfortunately, Mrs. May persists in her delusions, seeing herself as her own God and dismissing the primitive religiosity of Mrs. Greenleaf as meaningless ritual rather than a true trust in a higher power.

Mr. Greenleaf is expected to perform his god's/employer's every demand, and, as he reluctantly contemplates the task of tracking down and shooting the bull, Mrs. May is ironically led to confront her tormentor and nemesis face to face. O'Connor again employs light imagery as Mrs. May appears deliberately to close her eyes to the truth despite the brightness that encompasses her. Instead she envisions Mr. Greenleaf being gored to death by the bull and thus removed as a potential threat. Because of her impatience with Greenleaf's hesitancy, she attempts to summon him by honking a truck horn, an act that infuriates the bull, which not only charges Mrs. May but inflicts an ironic reversal on her by goring her to death, burying its horns in her lap. This act completes the sexual merger that O'Connor's imagery has implied throughout the story and reiterates a frequent O'Connor THEME: Only in death does understanding of self become complete. O'Connor closes by describing Mrs. May

as one who has regained her sight but who cannot bear looking at the brilliant light. As her life expires, her final discovery is shown to be in vain: Human pride is revealed as the most destructive element in the effort to discover one's true self.

Michael J. Meyer
DePaul Univeersity

GROTESQUE   Originally used to describe ancient paintings and decorations found in the *grotte,* or underground chambers, of Roman ruins, the term grotesque in fiction applies to fantastic (see FANTASY), bizarre, often ugly or unnatural presentations of characters, themes, and moods. It is widely perceived as an American genre, dating back to Edgar Allan POE's 19th-century *Tales of the Grotesque and Arabesque,* continuing into the 20th century in Sherwood Anderson's *WINESBURG, OHIO* [*A Book of the Grotesque]* and in stories by such writers as Erskine CALDWELL, William FAULKNER, Flannery O'CONNOR, and Eudora WELTY.

GUGGENHEIM GRANT (JOHN SIMON GUGGENHEIM MEMORIAL FOUNDATION FELLOWSHIP)   Established by U.S. Senator and Mrs. Simon Guggenheim as a memorial to their son, who died on April 26, 1922, the Guggenheim grant recognizes men and women of high intellectual and personal qualifications who have already demonstrated a capacity for productive scholarship or exceptional creative ability in the arts.

H

HAMMETT, (SAMUEL) DASHIELL
(1894–1961) A leading exponent of the "hard-boiled" school of detective writing, Hammett used his eight years of experience as a Pinkerton detective to give his stories authenticity. (See HARD-BOILED FICTION.) His stories are fast-paced and intricately plotted, frequently violent and realistic (see REALISM), although his style is spare. Many critics credit him with elevating the detective story to the level of literature in terms of sophisticated plot and original characterization. Most of his more than 75 stories first appeared in the popular magazine BLACK MASK, and his most famous work, *The Maltese Falcon,* was first published in that magazine as a five-part serial. In that novel he introduced the classic tough, realistic, hard-boiled detective, SAM SPADE. Virtually all of Hammett's published writing was done between 1922 and 1934, but in that time he transformed the genre of DETECTIVE FICTION and strongly influenced later writers in the field such as Raymond CHANDLER, Horace McCoy, and Erle Stanley GARDNER.

BIBLIOGRAPHY

Edenbaum, Robert I. "The Poetics of the Private Eye: The Novels of Hammett." In *Tough Guy Writers of the Thirties.* Edited by David Madden. Carbondale, Southern Illinois University Press, 1968.

Durham, Philip. "The Black Mask School." In *Tough Guy Writers of the Thirties.* Edited by David Madden. Carbondale: Southern Illinois University Press, 1968.

Gregory, Sinda. *Private Investigations: The Novels of Hammett.* Carbondale: Southern Illinois University Press, 1984.

Hammett, Dashiell. *The Adventures of Sam Spade and Other Stories.* Edited by Ellery Queen. New York: Dell Publishing Company, 1944. As *They Can Only Hang You Once,* 1949; selection, as *A Man Called Spade,* 1945.

———. *The Big Knockover: Selected Stories and Short Novels.* New York: Random House, 1966. As *The Hammett Story Omnibus.* Edited by Lillian Hellman. London: Cassell, 1966.

———. *The Continental Op.* New York: Dell Publishing Company, 1945.

———. *The Continental Op: More Stories From the Big Knockover.* New York: Dell Publishing, 1925.

———. *The Creeping Siamese.* New York: Dell, 1950.

———. *Dashiell Hammett Omnibus.* New York: Grosset & Dunlap, 1930.

———. *Dead Yellow Women.* New York: Dell, 1947.

———. *Hammett Homicides.* New York: Dell, 1946.

———. *The Maltese Falcon.* New York: Knopf, 1930.

———. *A Man Named Thin, and Other Stories.* New York: Ferman, 1962.

———. *Nightmare Town.* New York: Dell, 1948.

———. *Red Harvest.* New York: Knopf, 1929.

———. *The Return of the Continental Op.* New York: Dell, 1945.

———. *Woman in the Dark.* New York: Lawrence E. Spivak, Publisher, 1951.

Hellman, Lillian. *An Unfinished Woman.* Boston: Little, Brown, 1969.

———. *Pentimento.* Boston: Little, Brown, 1973.

———. *Scoundrel Time.* Boston: Little, Brown, 1976.

Johnson, Diane. *The Life of Dashiell Hammett.* London: Chatto and Windus, 1983. As *Dashiell Hammett: A Life.* New York: Fawcett Columbine, 1985.

Layman, Richard. *Shadow Man: The Life of Hammett.* New York: Harcourt Brace, 1981.

Marling, William. *Dashiell Hammett.* Boston: Twayne, 1983.

Nolan, William F. *Hammett: A Casebook.* Santa Barbara, Calif.: McNally & Loftin, 1969.

———. *Hammett: A Life at the Edge.* New York: Congdon and Weed, 1983.

Symons, Julian. *Hammett.* San Diego: Harcourt Brace, 1985.

Wolfe, Peter. *Beams Falling: The Art of Hammett.* Bowling Green, Ohio: Bowling Green University Popular Press, 1980.

"HANDS" SHERWOOD ANDERSON   Sherwood ANDERSON's story "Hands" might be called a portrait. Like a formal painted portrait, it not only depicts Wing Biddlebaum, the central figure, as he exists but also uses background props to reveal his past and define his circumstances. Wing's hands are the focal image of the portrait. The story also depends for effect on a series of painterly tableaux, from the sunset landscape with berry pickers with which it begins to the silhouette of Wing as a holy hermit, praying over and over the rosary of his lonely years of penance for a sin he did not commit. The use of synecdoche in which a part becomes representative of the whole, in the title keeps the tale of the unfortunate Wing in the reader's memory; we recall his hands far longer than we do his name.

Part of Anderson's SHORT STORY CYCLE, WINESBURG, OHIO (1919), "Hands" also features GEORGE WILLARD, the reporter in the tales who, as a character in his own right, may be viewed as the progenitor of Ernest HEMINGWAY's NICK ADAMS. George is one of the few people in Winesburg who feels sympathetic to the peculiar Wing, and Wing will speak to no one but George. Wing had arrived in Winesburg two decades previously under unexplained circumstances. Gradually the unnamed third-person narrator reveals Wing's background: He had been a teacher in Pennsylvania, popular and well liked by the boys who attended his school. Wing treated them gently, touching their shoulders or tousling their hair. Through a series of misunderstandings, a half-witted boy accuses Wing of making sexual advances on him, and Wing barely escapes the boys' outraged fathers. Neither Wing nor George Willard experiences any clear revelation or makes any climactic decision. Wing never understands why he was driven out of Pennsylvania—he realizes only dimly that his hands were somehow to blame—and George is afraid to ask the questions that might lead them both to a liberating understanding of Wing's experience.

The reader, however, is not permitted to remain in the dark. With the clear understanding of the way the crudity and narrow-minded suspicion of his neighbors have perverted Wing's selfless and innocent love for his students into a source of fear and shame comes a poignant sorrow for the waste of a good man's life. Wing's hands may be the pride of Winesburg for their agility at picking strawberries, but the nurturing love that they betoken is feared by everyone, including George and even Wing himself, whose loneliness is as great as his capacity to love, and from which, by a cruel irony, it arises.

HARA, MARIE (1943–   )   Born and raised in Honolulu, where she currently lives. Marie Hara is a writer, teacher, journalist, and publicist. Her stories have been published in *Bamboo Ridge, Chaminade Literary Review,* and *Honolulu Magazine;* they appear with increasing frequency in anthologies of adolescent and ASIAN AMERICAN LITERATURE, and were published as a collection entitled *Bananaheart* in 1994. Hara has been active in promoting literature and the arts in Hawaii, working for the Hawaii Literary Arts Council and codirecting the first Talk Story Conference in 1978.

Her stories, like those of fellow Hawaiian Darrell H. Y. LUM, often employ Hawaiian Creole English; Hara is especially gifted in hearing how people of all ages talk and, largely through dialogue, creating sharply delineated and convincing CHARACTERs in her stories. An important THEME is that despite Hawaii's multicultural society, not all cultures are equally valued or respected.

BIBLIOGRAPHY
Hara, Marie. *Bananaheart and Other Stories: A Collection of Short Stories.* Honolulu: Bamboo Ridge Press, 1994.

Keith Lawrence
Brigham Young University

HARA, MAVIS (1949–) Mavis Hara was born and raised in Honolulu. She received her B.A. from the University of Hawaii and her M.A. in education from the University of California, Santa Barbara. In addition to working as a freelance and professional writer, she has taught English in Japan. Her fiction has appeared in *Bamboo Ridge* and in several anthologies.

Because many of her stories have teenage PROTAGONISTs, she has acquired a reputation and following as an author of adolescent literature. Her characters are vivid, funny, and absolutely convincing. Beneath the casual tone, however, Hara's fiction is invariably concerned with significant ethnic THEMES: America's cultural colonization of much of the world, racial and gender inequity, the perpetuation of Eurocentric ideals in Asian American communities, the plight of contemporary Hawaiians, and the continuing dilution of Hawaiian culture.

Keith Lawrence
Brigham Young University

HARD-BOILED FICTION A type of American crime story, closely associated with the magazine BLACK MASK (founded 1919), this genre is characterized by a strong sense of REALISM generated by laconic, often crude dialogue, the depiction of cruelty and bloodshed at close range, and the use of sordid environments. Dashiell HAMMETT, who wrote his stories for *Black Mask,* is the acknowledged founder and chief proponent of this type of writing, which subsequently was used by others including Raymond CHANDLER and Erle Stanley GARDNER. Early works in this genre were critically acclaimed as serious literature, and Hammett was frequently compared to Ernest HEMINGWAY, but later novels of this type, by such writers as Mickey Spillane, degenerated into sensationalism and gratuitous violence.

HARLEM RENAISSANCE This historical period, also known as the New Negro Renaissance, refers to the proliferation of literature, music, visual arts, and political essays by African American and African Caribbean writers and artists living or working in the Harlem neighborhood of New York City in the 1920s. Most cultural historians designate 1925 as the inaugural year of the Harlem Renaissance. In March of 1924, Charles Johnson, editor of *Opportunity* magazine, hosted a dinner at the racially integrated Civic Club. Known as the "dress rehearsal" of the Harlem Renaissance, the dinner gathered together black writers and white editors and publishers to recognize a number of emerging black writers, such as Zora Neale HURSTON and Jean TOOMER. Their work was the first to receive serious critical attention since James Weldon Johnson's *Autobiography of an Ex-Coloured Man* (1916) and W. E. B. DUBOIS's *Darkwater* (1920). Among the white guests was Paul Kellogg, editor of the *Survey Graphic,* who offered to devote an entire issue of his magazine to black arts and letters. Kellogg's special edition "Harlem: Mecca of the New Negro" appeared in March 1925 and included articles on race prejudice, jazz, and Harlem as well as poetry and short stories such as Du Bois's "The Black Man Brings His Gifts" and Rudolph Fisher's "The South Lingers On." The *Oppportunity* dinner (and its subsequent literary contest) as well as the *Survey Graphic* issue inspired Alain Locke to edit *The New Negro,* an anthology of drawings, essays, poetry, and short stories, which was published at the end of 1925. Most of the black fiction writers whose names have become nearly synonymous with the Harlem Renaissance contributed short stories to *The New Negro.* The anthology includes Rudolph Fisher's "The City of Refuge" and "Vestiges;" two sections of Jean Toomer's lengthy prose poem *CANE;* and Zora Neale Hurston's "Spunk."

Editor Alain Locke was known, along with Charles Johnson, as one of the "midwives" of the Harlem Renaissance. In his introduction to *The New Negro* he rallied black and white intellectuals, artists, and writers to recognize that "for the present, more immediate hope [for alleviating race prejudice] rests in the reevaluation by white and black alike of the Negro in terms of his artistic endowments and cultural contributions, past and prospective" (15). Locke's statement marks the spirit of optimism and the focus on artistic production associated with Harlem in the 1920s. However, it also points to several disputes within the Harlem community. First, Harvard-educated Locke and other "midwives" were criticized for being elitist, for ignoring and silencing the working class by granting black intellectuals alone the responsibility for uplifting the race. Second, W. E. B. DuBois voiced the concern that the kind of interracial collaboration Locke called for would result in black writers pandering to the desires of a white publishing industry that continued to market less-than-uplifting representations of blacks. (The most extreme criticism of interracial relations during this period came from Marcus Garvey, whose back-to-Africa campaign attracted thousands of mostly working-class Harlemites.) Although DuBois shared Locke's goal of using artistic production to uplift the race, he was concerned that black writers would strip their work of any overtly political content in order to make it more palatable to white audiences and critics.

DuBois represented the older generation of intellectuals who, from the turn of the century through the 1920s, helped to set the stage for the Harlem Renaissance. Locke, Hurston, Langston HUGHES, and Claude McKay were part of the younger generation whose writing reflected a departure from didactic conventions devoted to conservative or "middle-class" representations of the black community. *Fire!!* a journal "Devoted to the Younger Artists," which, because of lack of funding, saw only one printing, promised a more AVANT-GARDE forum than the literary department of DuBois's *Crisis.* Younger-generation writers often included in their fiction representations of the working class through rural South folk THEMES or gritty urban settings, thinly veiled sexual references, and the speakeasy/cabaret life in Harlem. *Fire!* gave writer Richard Bruce Nugent his Harlem Renaissance debut with his short story "Smoke, Lilies, and Jade," which further fueled DuBois's fear that the new writers would "turn the Negro renaissance into decadence." Other short story contributions to *Fire!!* included Hurston's "SWEAT," Wallace Thurman's "Cordelia the Crude," and Gwendolyn Bennet's "Wedding Day."

Many cultural histories and criticism of the period associate the beginning of the GREAT DEPRESSION in 1929 with the end (and the "failure") of the Harlem Renaissance. Some critics judge the movement a failure because of writers' and artists' inability to ameliorate race prejudice, and for their economic dependence on white patrons and publishers. This criticism tends to overlook the important alliances that the period fostered between black writers and publishers such as Alfred Knopf, Albert Boni, and Horace Liveright as well as the mutual cultural and intellectual borrowing between black and white writers and the movement's social, economic, political, and geographic context. The 1920s was marked not only by the excesses and optimism of the Jazz Age but also by an influx of European immigrants as well as urban migration from the rural South; by a spirit of nativism (manifested in immigration restriction acts and a resurgence of the KU KLUX KLAN, even in Northern cities); and by massive industrial development, which brought individuals within the city into closer contact. Although Harlem itself bore the imprint of racial violence and systematic segregation, the Harlem Renaissance marks an extraordinary effort toward racial tolerance and revolutionary cultural forms that extended even beyond the geographic boundaries of New York—to Paris, Chicago, and the West Coast—and that resonates through the later works of such writers as Richard WRIGHT, Ralph ELLISON, Toni MORRISON, and Ann PETRY.

Other Harlem Renaissance short stories include Nella Larsen's "The Wrong Man" (1926), "Freedom" (1926), and "Sanctuary" (1930); Eric Walrond's GOTHIC collection *Tropic Death* (1926); Claude McKay's *Gingertown* (1932); and Langston Hughes's *The Ways of White Folk* (1934).

BIBLIOGRAPHY

Anderson, Jervis. *This was Harlem: A Cultural Portrait, 1900–1950.* New York: Farrar, Straus & Giroux, 1982.

Douglass, Ann. *Terrible Honesty: Mongrel Manhattan in the 1920s.* New York: Farrar, Straus & Giroux, 1995.

Huggins, Nathan. *Harlem Renaissance.* New York: Oxford University Press, 1971.

———. *Voices From the Harlem Renaissance.* New York: Oxford University Press, 1994.

Hurston, Zora Neale. *The Complete Stories.* New York: HarperCollins, 1995.

Hutchinson, George. *The Harlem Renaissance in Black and White.* Cambridge, Mass.: Belknap Press of Harvard University Press, 1995.

Larsen, Nella. *An Intimation of Things Distant: the Collected Fiction of Nella Larsen.* New York: Anchor Books, 1992.

Lewis, David Levering. *When Harlem Was in Vogue.* New York: Oxford University Press, 1981.

Lewis, David Levering, ed. *The Portable Harlem Renaissance Reader.* New York: Viking, 1994.

Locke, Alain. *The New Negro: Voices of the Harlem Renaissance.* New York: Atheneum, 1992.

Wall, Cheryl. *Women of the Harlem Renaissance.* Bloomington: Indiana University Press, 1995.

Jennifer L. Schulz
University of Washington

HARPER, FRANCES ELLEN WATKINS

(1825–1911)   Poet, novelist, short story writer, abolitionist lecturer, agent on Underground Railroad, leader in the women's and temperance movements, and magazine columnist, Frances E. W. Harper was born free in Baltimore, Maryland. Her short story "The Two Offers," now recognized as the first story published by an African-American woman, appeared in *The Anglo-African Magazine* in 1859. The two protagonists—the conservative, traditional Laura and the activist writer Janette—represent the choices open to women: following convention and marrying, or following personal interests and not marrying. Laura feels the disappointing loss of her failed marriage, having followed Society's conventions, while Janette, like Harper, embodies the feminist perspective of a woman committed to her political beliefs and her art.

Orphaned by the age of three, Harper was raised by an uncle who operated a school for free blacks. Her talents in writing and elocution surfaced early, as did her interest in radical politics and religion. At approximately age 25 she became the first female teacher at the Union Seminary, established by the African Methodist Episcopal Church in Columbus, Ohio. Interactions with fugitive slaves, along with her own tenuous status, led Harper to abandon the classroom for the abolitionist platform, which she often shared with Frederick DOUGLASS and William Lloyd GARRISON, and was well known for her fiery

lectures and such poignant poems as "The Slave Mother" and "Bury Me in a Free Land." In 1854 Harper published her first collection of poems, *Poems on Miscellaneous Subjects,* a book that many critics argue pioneered a tradition of African-American protest poetry. Her best-known novel, *Iola Leroy; or, Shadows Uplifted,* was published in 1892.

BIBLIOGRAPHY

Ammons, Elizabeth. "Legacy Profile: Frances Ellen Watkins Harper (1825–1911)." *Legacy: A Journal of American Women Writers* 2, no. 2 (Fall 1985): 61–66.

Harper, Frances Ellen Watkins. *A Brighter Coming Day: A Frances Ellen Watkins Harper Reader.* Edited by Frances Smith Foster. New York: Feminist Press, 1990.

———. *Iola Leroy, or, Shadows Uplifted.* Philadelphia: Garrigues, 1892.

———. *Minnie's Sacrifice; Sowing and Reapin; Trial and Triumph: Three Rediscovered Novels.* Edited by Frances Smith Foster. Boston: Beacon Press, 1994.

———. *Moses: A Story of the Nile.* Philadelphia: Merrihew & Son, Printers, 1869.

———. *Sketches of Southern Life.* Philadelphia: Merrihew & Son, Printers, 1872.

Riggins, Linda N. " The Works of Frances E. W. Harper: An 18th-Century Writer." *Black World.* 22. no. 2 (1972): 30–36.

Rosenthal, Debra J. "Deracialized Discourse: Temperance and Racial Ambiguity in Harper's 'The Two Offers' and *Sowing and Reaping.*" In *The Serpent in the Cup: Temperance in American Literature.* Edited by David S. Reynolds. Amherst: University of Massachusetts Press. 1997, pp. 153–64.

Scheick, William J. "Strategic Ellipses in Harper's 'The Two Offers.'" *Southern Literary Journal* 23, no. 2 (Spring 1991): 14–18.

Wilfred D. Samuels
University of Utah

HARPER'S

First published in 1850 as *Harper's New Monthly Magazine,* it became *Harper's Monthly Magazine* after 1900 and *Harper's Magazine* in 1925. Until the 1920s it was an illustrated literary magazine devoted to the publication of essays, poetry, and fiction, including the serialization of novels by popular English and American authors. A column called "The Easy Chair," in which important and influential articles on contemporary fiction appeared, was written by a series of distinguished editors, including William Dean HOWELLS and G. W. Curtis. After WORLD WAR I, *Harper's* abandoned the illustrated format and increased its economic, political, and social analysis, although it retained an emphasis on poetry, fiction, and reviews.

HARRIS, JOEL CHANDLER (1848–1909)

Born near Eatonton, Georgia, in 1848, Joel Chandler Harris is most famous for his humorous adaptations of African-American folk LEGENDs in the UNCLE REMUS stories. Many of these 220 tales first appeared in the *Atlanta Constitution* before being published as collections in *Uncle Remus, His Songs and His Sayings* and *Nights with Uncle Remus*. Although the tales were about animals, Harris also used them as vehicles for his conciliatory THEME, having the kindly ex-slave, Uncle Remus, electing to remain on the plantation of his former mistress and her Yankee husband after the CIVIL WAR and relating these tales to their young son.

Perhaps more significantly, these stories depict the efforts of African Americans to preserve their humanity through these often allegorical animal tales (see ALLEGORY), many of which describe the triumph of the seemingly powerless, through intelligence and wit, over superior and often brutal force. These tales had been transmitted orally by slaves for several generations before Harris preserved them in written form. One of the most famous is the CLASSIC story of the Tar Baby; other characters who have entered American MYTH include B'rer Rabbit and B'rer Fox. In these and many other stories, Harris tried to preserve the best of the Old South as well as promote reconciliation during the post–Civil War RECONSTRUCTION period. Reconciliation between the North and the South, between whites and ex-slaves, and even between Southern social classes was a common theme in Harris's writing.

BIBLIOGRAPHY

Bickley, R. Bruce. *Joel Chandler Harris*. Boston: Twayne, 1978.

———, ed. *Critical Essays on Joel Chandler Harris*. Boston: G. K. Hall, 1981.

Cousins, Paul M. *Joel Chandler Harris: A Biography*. Baton Rouge: Louisiana State University Press, 1968.

Harlow, Alvin F. *Joel Chandler Harris: Plantation Storyteller*. New York: J. Messner, Inc. 1941.

Harris, Joel Chandler. *Aaron in the Wildwoods*. Boston: Houghton Mifflin, 1897.

———. *Balaam and His Master: And Other Sketches and Stories*. Boston: Houghton Mifflin, 1891.

———. *The Bishop and the Boogerman*. New York: Doubleday, Page & Company, 1909. As *The Bishop and the Bogie-Man*. London: Murray, 1909.

———. *The Chronicles of Aunt Minervy Ann*. New York: Scribner's, 1899.

———. *The Complete Tales of Uncle Remus*. Edited by Richard Chase. Boston: Houghton, Mifflin, 1955.

———. *Daddy Jake and the Runaway and Short Stories Told after Dark*. New York: Century 1889.

———. *Free Joe and Other Georgian Sketches*. New York: Scribner's, 1887.

———. *Little Mr. Thimblefinger and His Queer Country: What the Children Saw and Heard There*. Boston: Houghton Mifflin, 1894.

———. *Mr. Rabbit at Home*. Boston: Houghton Mifflin, 1895.

———. *A Little Union Scout: A Tale of Tennessee During the Civil War*. New York: McClure, Phillips, 1904.

———. *The Making of a Statesman and Other Stories*. New York: McClure, Phillips, 1902.

———. *Mingo and Other Sketches in Black and White*. Boston: Osgood, 1884.

———. *Nights With Uncle Remus: Myths and Legends of the Old Plantation*. Boston: Houghton Mifflin, 1883.

———. *A Plantation Printer: The Adventures Of A Georgia Boy During The War*. New York: Appleton, 1892. As *On The Plantation*. Boston: Houghton Mifflin, 1892.

———. *Old Plantation*, 1880; as *Uncle Remus and His Legends of the Old Plantation*. New York: Appleton, 1881. As *Uncle Remus: or, Mr. Fox, Mr. Rabbit, and Mr. Terrapin*. New York: Routledge, 1881. Rev. ed., 1895.

———. *Stories of Georgia*. New York: American Book Co., 1896, Rev. ed., 1896.

———. *On the Wing of Occasions*. New York: Doubleday, Page, 1900.

———. *Plantation Pageants*. Boston: Houghton Mifflin, 1899.

———. *Tales of the Home Folks in Peace and War*. Boston: Houghton Mifflin, 1898.

———. *Told by Uncle Remus: New Stories of the Old Plantation*. New York: McClure, Phillips, 1905.

———. *Uncle Remus and Brer Rabbit*. New York: F. A. Stokes, 1907.

————. *Uncle Remus and His Friends: Old Plantation Stories, Songs, and Ballads, with Sketches of Negro Character.* Boston: Houghton Mifflin, 1892.

————. *Uncle Remus and the Little Boy.* Boston: Small, Maynard, 1910.

————. *Uncle Remus: His Songs and His Sayings: The Folklore of the Old Plantation.* New York: Appleton, 1880.

————. *Uncle Remus Returns.* Boston: Houghton Mifflin, 1918.

————. *Wally Wanderoon and His Story-Telling Machine.* New York: McClure, Phillips, 1903.

————. *The Witch Wolf: An Uncle Remus Story.* Cambridge, Mass.: Bacon & Brown, 1921.

Harris, Julia Collier. *The Life and Letters of Joel Chandler Harris.* Boston: Houghton Mifflin, 1918.

HARRISON, JAMES THOMAS (JIM) (1937–)

Fiction writer, poet, and essayist Jim Harrison was born on December 11, 1937, in Grayling, Michigan, the second of five children. He received B.A. and M.A. degrees from Michigan State University and taught briefly at the State University of New York at Stony Brook. In 1960 he married and worked for the next several years as a carpenter, a well-digger, and a block mason to support his family. Harrison and his family later moved to a farm in Lake Leelanau, Michigan.

Much of Harrison's fiction is recognizably autobiographical: In 1945, during his first sexual experience, Harrison was blinded in his left eye; in 1962 his father and younger sister were killed in a car accident. The THEMES of blindness and alienation, loss and relationships, as well as a preoccupation with food and the outdoors, figure prominently in his narratives. He is closely associated with fiction writer Thomas MCGUANE, writer/painter Russell Chatham, and adventurer Guy de la Valdene, all of whom are world-class gourmands and sportsmen. Harrison has published short fiction and essays in *Sports Illustrated* and *ESQUIRE* (including a long-running column titled "The Raw and the Cooked"), and he is perhaps the most prolific American NOVELLA writer. He has published nine novellas in three collections: *LEGENDS OF THE FALL* (1979), *THE WOMAN LIT BY FIREFLIES* (1990), and *JULIP* (1994). The novellas have gained critical attention for their sketches of uniquely American

characters and the range of PROTAGONISTs and landscapes they describe: from the estranged wife Clare in *The Woman Lit by Fireflies,* to the contemporary American rogue Brown Dog, who is featured in both *Brown Dog* (from *The Woman Lit by Fireflies*) and *The Seven-Ounce Man* (from *Julip*); from the wilderness of Upper Peninsula Michigan to the desert of the American Southwest.

Harrison's narratives are grounded in the deepest traditions of American and European literature: Mark TWAIN, William FAULKNER, Gerald VIZENOR, Rainer Maria Rilke, and Loren Eiseley, among others, have influenced his writing. While Harrison's fiction is often darkly humorous and ironic, the novellas seriously detail the encroachment of a complex society on a decreasing physical and psychic wilderness.

BIBLIOGRAPHY

Harrison, Jim. *Legends of the Fall.* New York: Delacorte Press, 1979.

————. *Julip.* Boston: Houghton Mifflin, 1994.

————. *The Woman Lit by Fireflies.* Boston: Houghton Mifflin, 1990.

Reilly, Edward C. *Jim Harrison.* New York: Twayne, 1996.

Patrick A. Smith
Ohio University

"HARRISON BERGERON" KURT VONNEGUT (1961)

If one were to read "Harrison Bergeron" today without knowing when the story was written, one might assume it to be a criticism of the "political correctness" that hit its peak in late 1980s America. But the story was written in 1961—long before anyone was accused of being "un-PC"—when the civil rights movement was in full swing, a fact that easily can alter one's perception of this curiously prophetic cautionary tale.

"The year was 2081, and everybody was finally equal," the story begins. Thanks to the office of the Handicapper General, no one is smarter or stronger or prettier than anybody else. The strong are weighted down with "sashweights and bags of birdshot." Those of above-average intelligence wear devices that blast loud noises in their ears, preventing them from "taking unfair advantage of their brains."

The title character is a 14-year-old genius, athlete, and giant. Seven feet tall, carrying enough handicaps to look "like a walking junkyard," Harrison escapes from prison where he is held on suspicion of plotting to overthrow the government. He breaks into a television studio during a live broadcast and strips off all his handicaps, declaring that he will now fulfill his human potential. Soon after this outburst, he is shot dead by the Handicapper General of the United States.

While the story is cloaked in humor, at its core there are many profound questions about egalitarianism. At a time when American blacks were struggling to achieve basic civil liberties, it is fascinating that Vonnegut would choose to caution readers that the quest for equality can go too far.

David Larry Anderson

HARTE, (FRANCIS) BRET(T) (1836–1902)

Although born and reared in New York, Bret Harte's best work is associated with California. He arrived there in 1855 at age 19 and mined for gold before becoming a school teacher and, later, a journalist. During the 1860s Harte wrote most of his most durable fiction, including the stories "M'Liss," "The Luck of Roaring Camp," and "The Outcasts of Poker Flat," and the poem "Plain Language from Truthful James." His collection of poetry, *The Last Galleon and Other Tales,* and a satirical work, *Condensed Novels,* were published in 1868. Harte gained a national reputation with these stories of the West that combined humor and sentimentality, vivid characterization, and colorful dialogue. He returned east in 1871 and continued to write extensively, but his work was deemed to lack originality and his reputation declined sharply. His best work is still anthologized, however, and Harte is credited as a pioneer in Western LOCAL COLOR writing.

BIBLIOGRAPHY

Duckett, Margaret. *Mark Twain and Harte.* Norman: University of Oklahoma Press, 1964.

Harte, Bret. *The Ancestors of Peter Atherly and Other Tales.* Leipzig: B. Tauchnitz, 1897.

————. *Barker's Luck and Other Stories.* Boston: Houghton Mifflin, 1896.

————. *The Bell-Ringer of Angels and Other Stories.* Boston: Houghton Mifflin, 1894.

————. *The Best Short Stories of Bret Harte.* Edited by Robert N. Linscott. New York: The Modern Library, 1967.

————. *California Stories.* Franklin Center, Pa.: Franklin Library, 1984.

————. *Drift From Two Shores.* Boston: Houghton, Osgood, 1878. As *The Hoodlum Bard and Other Stories.* London: Ward, Lock and Co., 1878.

————. *An Episode of Fiddletown and Other Sketches.* London: Routledge, 1873.

————. *Flip and Other Stories.* London: Chatto & Windus, 1882.

————. *An Heiress of Red Dog and Other Sketches.* Leipzig: B. Tauchnitz, 1879.

————. *The Heritage of Dedlow Marsh and Other Tales.* New York: Macmillan, 1889.

————. *Jeff Briggs's Love Story and Other Sketches.* Leipzig: B. Tauchnitz, 1880.

————. *Jinny.* New York: Routledge, 1878.

————. *The Lost Galleon and Other Tales.* San Francisco, Calif: Towne & Bacon, 1867.

————. *The Luck of Roaring Camp and Other Sketches.* 1870. Boston: Fields, Osgood. Rev. ed., 1871.

————. *The Man on the Beach.* London: Routledge, 1878.

————. *My Friend, The Tramp.* New York: Routledge1877.

————. *On the Frontier.* New York: Routledge, 1884.

————. *Mr. Jack Hamlin's Mediation and Other Stories.* Boston: Houghton Mifflin, 1899.

————. *Mrs. Skaggs's Husbands and Other Sketches.* Boston: Osgood, 1873.

————. *A Protegeé of Jack Hamlin's and Other Stories.* Boston: Houghton Mifflin, 1894.

————. *Representative Selections.* Edited by Joseph B. Harrison. New York: American Book Co., 1941.

————. *Sally Dows, and Other Stories.* Boston: Houghton Mifflin, 1893.

————. *A Sappho of Green Springs and Other Tales.* Boston: Houghton Mifflin, 1891.

————. *Stories in Light and Shadow.* Boston: Houghton Mifflin, 1898.

————. *Stories of the Sierras and Other Sketches.* London: J. C. Hotten 1872.

————. *Tales of the Argonauts and Other Sketches.* Boston: Houghton Mifflin, 1875.

————. *Tales of Trail and Town.* Boston: Houghton Mifflin, 1898.

————. *Trent's Trust and Other Stories.* Boston: Houghton Mifflin, 1903.

————. *The Twins of Table Mountain*. Boston: Houghton Osgood, 1879.

————. *Wan Lee, The Pagan and Other Sketches*. London: Routledge, 1876.

————. *The Writings of Bret Harte*. 20 vols. Boston, Houghton Mifflin, 1914.

Morrow, Patrick D. *Bret Harte*. Boise, Idaho: Boise State College, 1972.

————. *Harte, Literary Critic*. Bowling Green, Ohio: Bowling Green State University Popular Press, 1979.

O'Connor, Richard. *Harte: A Biography*. Boston: Little, Brown 1966.

Stewart, George Rippey. *Harte, Argonaut and Exile*. Boston: Houghton Mifflin, 1931.

HAWTHORNE, NATHANIEL (1804–1864)

Nathaniel Hawthorne, perhaps best known—at least to the general American public—as the author of *The Scarlet Letter* (1850), was, in fact, a prodigious author of short stories before ever writing a novel. Hawthorne began his career by anonymously writing the GIFT BOOKS popular in the early half of the 19th century, at the urging of a friend, he collected his short stories into a book. He published this first collection, *Twice-Told Tales,* in 1837. By the time of its reprinting five years later, with additional material, Edgar Allan POE and Henry Wadsworth Longfellow had written glowing reviews of his work, and Herman MELVILLE had firmly backed Hawthorne as a major talent.

Twice-Told Tales included stories of varying length, such as "The Gray Champion" (originally published in the *New-England Magazine,* 1835) and "The Prophetic Pictures" (in *Token,* 1837), both of which feature Hawthorne's fascination with religion, sin, and issues of redemption combined with his historically accurate, realistic depiction of New England Puritanism. (See REALISM.) The most widely known story from this collection, "The Minister's Black Veil" (*Token,* 1836), prefigures the connected issues of identity, hypocrisy, and sin so central to *The Scarlet Letter;* members of a New England congregation find themselves transfixed with their minister who refuses to remove the black veil that hides his face. Because they cannot see beneath the veil, the congregation believes that evil lurks under it,

while the minister believes that evil walks among everyone: Their spiritual devoutness, however, may vary widely beneath the METAPHORical veil that masks their true nature. The minister wears a physical manifestation of the moral AMBIGUITY inherent in all human beings regardless of their perceived public piety or religious fervor. His congregation wants him to lift the veil to prove he is neither evil nor disfigured, but the minister refuses to do so. This tension between the actual and the perceived—between reality and hypocrisy—drives the story.

The unknown, whether a physical object, scientific conjecture, or moral ambiguity, constitutes a major factor in all of Hawthorne's works, and the author presents it through ALLEGORY and symbolism. Hawthorne's works frequently address the human condition and the capacity of mortal man to sin. Hawthorne felt deep concern with the human capacity for self-isolation and a prideful, distorted sense of superiority; his characters, both in his novels and short stories, fall prey to this disturbing state.

Hawthorne's three most widely anthologized stories, "YOUNG GOODMAN BROWN" (initially published in the *New-England Magazine* in 1835), "THE BIRTHMARK" (in *Pioneer,* 1843) and "RAPPACCINI'S DAUGHTER" (in *Democratic Review,* 1844), eventually reappeared in *Mosses from an Old Manse* (1846), his best-known collection of short stories. "The Birthmark" is the story of a man, a woman, and one fatal flaw, the latter represented by a heavily symbolic birthmark. Ironically, the fatal flaw lies not in the so-called physical deformity of the birthmark but in those who overlook true beauty (both spiritual and physical) as they pridefully attempt to imitate God, or even usurp His power, in their effort to attain perfection, whether through the technological or the spiritual.

In "The Birthmark," a scientist strives to improve his wife, Georgiana—a devout woman whose great beauty he finds marred only by her birthmark—to the point of perfection. However, his attempt to improve on God's work, the human form, ultimately proves disastrous: The scientist ultimately destroys and loses exactly what he has tried unnecessarily to improve. In "Rappaccini's Daughter," Hawthorne uses the same plot with only slight variation. Again, a beautiful woman dies because, despite—or because of—her great beauty, the men in the tale believe that she harbors a fatal flaw. Dr. Rappaccini attempts to keep his daughter Beatrice to himself by slowly feeding her plant poison; eventually she becomes as lethal as the plants her famous father cultivates to boil down into medicines. Because she becomes poisonous, Beatrice can have no more suitors, and thus her father preserves her purity and innocence for himself alone.

Both Georgiana, in "The Birthmark," and Beatrice, the title character of "Rappaccini's Daughter," die at the hands of men of science: Georgiana from her husband's attempt to remove the birthmark, and Beatrice from consuming an antidote to the poison coursing through her veins. In these stories Hawthorne implicitly indicts technological advancement and science, along with the masculine attitudes of superiority and knowledge that literally give men the power of life and death over women. Clearly, Georgiana and Beatrice die because they are women and therefore, from the male perspective, associated with danger. Beatrice's crisis and eventual death directly result from her awakening desire and the entrance of her first (and only) suitor, while Georgiana's results from her innocent but misplaced trust in her husband, whose feverish attempt to remove the "stain" from her face eventually kills her. Both women also share an inexorable link to nature, a popular 19th-century metaphor for femininity; Georgiana's successful testing of her fatal drink on a plant leads her to believe it will also succeed with her, while Beatrice, in essence, becomes nature through the plant toxins that conquer her body.

"Young Goodman Brown" presents these same problematic questions regarding gender roles and purity, although the ostensible emphasis lies on a spiritual rather than a physical plane. Feminism has long cast a skeptical eye on Hawthorne's representations of women as evil temptresses or innocent victims; while a FEMINIST reading of Hawthorne's works has a wealth of material to draw from, readers should also consider the era in which Hawthorne wrote and note that he often presents ethically and morally suspect male characters as well. These men pay heavily

for their sins, as does Young Goodman Brown, who follows his wife, the aptly named Faith, into the New England woods one dark night. As he walks, joined by a character astute readers may recognize as the Devil, he sees—or thinks he sees—that the numerous pious, pure townspeople actually engage in witchcraft. Brown's disillusionment heightens as he believes he has misjudged not only town elders, teachers, and men and women of the church but, finally, Faith herself. Brown's sin is not that he doubts God but, instead, that he becomes morally superior and isolationist; he ruins his life not because of religion but because he believes so unflinchingly in his own moral and ethical rightness.

In the opinion of most critics, later stories and sketches, collected in *The Snow Image and Other Thrice-Told Tales* (1852) and *Tanglewood Tales* (1853), lack the compelling force of Hawthorne's earlier work, although his signature preoccupations infiltrate stories such as "Alice Doane's Appeal" (*Token,* 1835) and "The Antique Ring" (*Sargent's New Monthly Magazine,* 1843). Hawthorne himself never intended to include these works in collections, but his editor did so after Hawthorne's death.

BIBLIOGRAPHY

Arvin, Newton. *Hawthorne.* Boston: Little, Brown, 1929.

Bell, Millicent. *New Essays on Hawthorne's Major Tales.* New York: Cambridge University Press, 1993.

Bunge, Nancy L. *Hawthorne: A Study of the Short Fiction.* New York: Twayne, 1993.

von Frank, Albert J., ed. *Critical Essays on Harthorne's Short Stories,* Boston: G. K. Hall, 1991.

Hawthorne, Julian. *Nathaniel Hawthorne and His Wife.* Boston: Osgood, 1884.

Hawthorne, Nathaniel. *The Complete Works of Nathaniel Hawthorne.* 12 vols. Boston: Houghton Mifflin 1883. Vol. XIII added about 1891.

———. *The Complete Writings of Nathaniel Hawthorne.* 22 vols. Boston & New York: Houghton Mifflin, 1900.

———. *The Complete Writings of Nathaniel Hawthorne.* 22 vols. Boston & New York: Houghton Mifflin, 1903.

———. *The Centenary Edition of the Works of Nathaniel Hawthorne.* Edited by William Charvat, et al.

———. *Hawthorne's Short Stories.* Edited by Newton Arvin. New York: Knopf, 1946. Reprint. Columbus: Ohio State University Press: 1963.

James, Henry. *Hawthorne*. London: Macmillan, 1879.

Mellow, James R. *Nathaniel Hawthornd and His Times*. Boston: Houghton Mifflin, 1980.

Newman, Lea Bertani Vozar. *A Reader's Guide to the Short Stories of Nathaniel Hawthorne*. Boston: G. K. Hall, 1979.

Payne, Tom, ed. *Encyclopedia of Great Writers*. New York: Barnes & Noble, 1997.

Wagenknecht, Edward. *Nathaniel Hawthorne: Man and Writer*. New York: Oxford University Press, 1961.

————. *Nathaniel Hawthorne: The Man, His Tales and Romances*. New York: Continuum, 1989.

Waggoner, Hyatt. *Hawthorne: A Critical Study*. Rev. ed. Cambridge: Harvard University Press, 1963.

Young, Philip. *Hawthorne's Secret: An Untold Tale*. Boston: Godine, 1984.

Anne N. Thalheimer
University of Delaware

HEMINGWAY, ERNEST (1899–1961)

Born in Oak Park, Illinois, Ernest Hemingway grew up in comfortable circumstances as the oldest son and second of the six children of Grace Hall, an accomplished singing teacher, and Dr. Clarence Hemingway, a well-loved physician. He began writing early, publishing in his high school newspaper and literary magazine. Rather than go to college, Ernest took a job with the *Kansas City Star,* where, it is argued, he honed his skills by developing the recommended journalistic virtues of writing in short, declarative sentences, avoiding adjectives, and telling interesting stories. Readers of his fiction, however, have come to understand that this writing style, while it may make his works disarmingly accessible, is also, as the title of one study of his short fiction informs us, only "the tip of the iceberg": that is, seven-eighths of the story's meaning lies submerged while only one-eighth is visible on the surface.

In WORLD WAR I Hemingway enlisted in the Red Cross Ambulance Corps and was badly wounded while distributing chocolate and cigarettes to troops on the Italian front. During his hospital recuperation, he fell in love with Agnes von Kurowsky, a nurse. She was the first mature romance of his life, and her subsequent rejection of him was a great blow. He recovered, however, to marry four times.

Literary recognition came early, and Hemingway benefited from the sponsorship and support of significant literary figures such as Sherwood ANDERSON, F. Scott FITZGERALD, Ezra Pound and Gertrude STEIN. With his first wife, Hadley Richardson, he lived in Paris and traveled through Europe, working as a correspondent for the *Toronto Star.* Living in the center of the artistic ferment that was at the heart of the Modernist movement (see MODERNISM), Hemingway explored narrative strategies and thematic concerns (see THEME) in his early fiction that put him in its vanguard. His was a style so distinctive that it is credited with informing 20th-century prose; it is, in the words used to present him the Nobel Prize for literature, a "powerful, style-making mastery of the art of modern narration."

Early critical recognition came first with the limited edition of *Three Stories and Ten Poems* (1923) and then the commercial publication of IN OUR TIME (1925), an unusual juxtaposition of stories and vignettes in the form of a literary collage, or of fragments that achieve a sort of ironic unity. *In Our Time* contains a number of stories featuring NICK ADAMS, the character some critics view as Hemingway's alter ego. Once Hemingway achieved some fame, his writing, both fiction and nonfiction, garnered a wider audience from initial publication in mass-audience magazines such as ESQUIRE, *Cosmopolitan,* and ATLANTIC MONTHLY. *The Old Man and the Sea* was first serialized in *Life.* Other important story collections include *Men Without Women* (1927), *Winner Take Nothing* (1933), and *The Fifth Column and The First Forty-nine Stories* (1938). His most famous novels are *The Sun Also Rises* (1926), *A Farewell to Arms* (1929), *For Whom the Bell Tolls* (1940), and *The Old Man and the Sea* (1952). Several posthumous works have also gained wide readership, including *A Moveable Feast* (1964), *Islands in the Stream* (1970), and *The Garden of Eden* (1986).

The short story was Hemingway's natural milieu and the genre most unequivocally admired by his readers. Carlos Baker, his first biographer, calls it his early and hardest kind of discipline, one that taught him his craft. Whatever else about Hemingway that has come under attack—his personality, his problematic sexuality, his "macho" perspective, his self-glorification—he wrote short stories that are many critics and readers acclaim among the best of the 20th century. Late in his career he wrote an essay, originally meant as the introduction to an anthology for students of his most popular stories, called "The Art of the Short Story." In it he rearticulated his credo that "if you leave out important things or events that you know about, the story will be strengthened" (quoted in Lynn). His caveat, of course, was that you can leave out only what you know, not what you don't know.

As Fitzgerald was called the chronicler of the Jazz Age, so Hemingway was the historian for the Lost Generation. Living with a loss of faith, in a world of insecurities, and dealing with disillusionment, his characters try to create coping mechanisms to get them through, trying to divert their attention from the pain and—in the words of a nameless character in "A CLEAN, WELL LIGHTED PLACE"—from the "nada." Jake Barnes, the main character in *The Sun Also Rises,* voices the basic existential concern of most of Hemingway's PROTAGONISTs in both the long and the short fiction: "I did not care what it was all about. All I wanted to know was how to live in it. Maybe if you found out how to live in it you learned from that what it was all about."

Hemingway lived life at a high pitch, traveling the world and hobnobbing with the rich and famous. After his first divorce, he married Pauline Pfeiffer, whose wealth made possible their adventurous life together. One of his books, *The Green Hills of Africa,* is about their African safari with friends. Word of these and similar adventures were trumpeted in the world press, and as Hemingway grew older and more celebrated, his grizzled countenance, instantly recognizable, was known by many who had never read a word he wrote. He was the writer as superstar, a world celebrity, who achieved a mythic status in which he was confused with the characters he created. This biographical reading of his works extended till well after his death. Still, his star quality was such that he created tourist attractions of the places he celebrated in his writing, be they towns such as Pamplona or restaurants such as Botins in Madrid.

In his public PERSONA, Hemingway fed the myth. It has been suggested that he came to believe his own publicity, a situation that proved deleterious for his writing. Although he remained loyal to many old friends, many others who helped him rise became casualties of his cruelty and competitiveness.

The complexity and controversy of Hemingway's life has inspired an inordinate number of biographies and memoirs, from the authorized and meticulously researched *Ernest Hemingway: A Life Story* by Carlos Baker to the controversial psychological reading of his struggle with an ambiguous sexual identity in Kenneth S. Lynn's *Hemingway.* Friends, siblings, and sons also have written their remembrances of what it was like to know Ernest Hemingway. He attracted; he repelled. In 1954, after two successive plane crashes in Africa, he was reported dead but in fact had survived. In the same year he won the Nobel Prize for Literature. His later years were plagued by health problems and accidents, made worse by his heavy drinking. After a series of physical and mental problems, he killed himself in Ketchum, Idaho, in 1961.

BIBLIOGRAPHY

Baker, Carlos. *Hemingway: The Writer as Artist.* Princeton, N.J.: Princeton University Press, 1980.

Beegel, Susan F., ed. *Hemingway's Neglected Short Fiction: New Perspectives.* Ann Arbor, Mich.: UMI Research Press, 1989.

Benson, Jackson J., ed. *New Critical Approaches to the Short Stories of Ernest Hemingway.* Durham, N.C.: Duke University Press, 1990.

Donaldson, Scott. *The Cambridge Companion to Hemingway.* Cambridge, England: Cambridge University Press, 1996.

Flora, Joseph M. *Ernest Hemingway: A Study of the Short Fiction.* Boston: Twayne, 1989.

Johnston, Kenneth G. *The Tip of the Iceberg: Hemingway and the Short Story,* Greenwood, Fla.: Penkevill Publishing Company, 1987.

Lynn, Kenneth S. *Hemingway.* New York: Simon & Schuster, 1987.

Mellow, James R. *Hemingway: A Life Without Consequences.* Reading Mass.: Addison-Wesley, 1992.

Mimi Reisel Gladstein
University of Texas at El Paso

HEMINGWAY CODE   Ernest HEMINGWAY advocated a particular code of behavior through various characters in his novels and short stories. The Hemingway hero tries to show loyalty to his friends, to behave well in difficult situations (with "grace under pressure"), to behave with courage and stoicism, to lose well, and to avoid loquacity. The character Robert Wilson, the hunting guide in "THE SHORT HAPPY LIFE OF FRANCIS MACOMBER," for example, acts according to this code.

HENRY, O. (WILLIAM SYDNEY PORTER)
(1862–1910)   William Sydney Porter's career as the legendary O. Henry spanned the mere eight years between his arrival in New York in 1902 and his death there in 1910. During that time he published more than 300 stories in such popular magazines such as *Everybody's,* MCCLURES, *Munsey's, Smart Set,* and the New York *Sunday World,* for which he wrote a story per week for several years. His stories have been collected in nearly 20 volumes, 13 of them published within his lifetime. The enormous impact of O. Henry's work—despite changing tastes and trends in critical opinion—remains pervasive and indisputable. Admired by millions of Americans and translated into a welter of foreign languages, O. Henry and his "all-American" short stories inspired the debut, in 1919, of the O. HENRY MEMORIAL AWARDS, an honor still coveted by contemporary writers, whose winning stories are published annually in a single volume. Over the years, O. Henry stories have been used in or adapted to radio, television, film, and stage, and today the World Wide Web boasts numerous sites and scores of pages devoted to the author, his work, and his critical reception.

As scholar and critic Eugene Current-García has demonstrated, the central question for contemporary readers is the one that has excited critical debate since the decade after O. Henry died: "Was he a genuine literary artist or a literary mountebank, a creative innovator of narrative prose fiction or an artful dodger and con man?" (Current-García xi). Critical opinion has ranged from the adulatory, comparing him with the likes of Joseph Conrad, Thomas Hardy, Henry JAMES, Guy de Maupassant,

and Edith WHARTON, to the virtual dismissal by critics and scholars from 1930 to the present. Despite his pronounced absence from the indices of all major university literary anthologies, however, bookstores and public libraries attest to the continued enthusiasm for the O. Henry story with its characteristic SURPRISE ENDING.

Although O. Henry gained much of his fame by writing about the lives of the "four million" inhabitants of the New York City of his era, his American qualities inhere also in his Post-RECONSTRUCTION southern roots and in his western sojourn: His life and work spanned much of the vast country. Some 30 of Porter's stories are set in and deal directly with the South, 80 with the West, and 26 with Central America, where he lived for some months. Among his best southern stories are "Vareton Villa: A Tale of the South," which LAMPOONS the excessive biases of both northerners and southerners and emanates from the tall tale tradition of FRONTIER HUMOR; "The Rose of Dixie," a satiric treatment of southern journalism, replete with the characteristic surprise ending; the hilarious "The Ransom of Red Chief," another example of O. Henry's use of the tall tale; and "The Municipal Report," one of his most critically acclaimed stories demonstrating his use of LOCAL COLOR description and DIALECT.

The southwestern stories are based on his experiences while living in Texas and in prison, where he served three years of a five-year sentence on conviction of embezzlement, an indisputably traumatic force in O. Henry's life. In a number of these stories one sees his belief in DETERMINISM, his characters as mere pawns in a large, indifferent world, encounters between criminals and law enforcement officials, and the theme of "reformation or rehabilitation" (Current-García 41). The most famous of these is "A Retrieved Reformation," the story of Jimmy Valentine, a burglar whose safe-cracking wizardry was later dramatized in both play and film. Another of his finest tales is "Caballero's Way," a perennially popular story involving the Cisco Kid and a Texas Ranger. With this tale, O. Henry's talents have been compared to those of Stephen CRANE, and versions of "the Kid's" exploits continue as part of American mythology.

After his release from prison and his move to New York, O. Henry wrote more than 140 stories about the people he daily observed on subways, in restaurants, on park benches. He liked to choose a few who captured his attention and then create stories about them. Current-García has noted the irony of O. Henry's move to Irving Place and his respectful pilgrimage to the home of Washington IRVING, the first American writer to capture the New York scene. Notable similarities exist between these two city-life chroniclers, not least their lack of interest in moralizing or politicizing the circumstances and characters they portrayed. Both writers, moreover, favored SATIRE, humor, romance, BURLESQUE, and both made innovative contributions to the short story form (see COMEDY and ROMANTICISM) (Current-García 58). Of the many memorable New York stories, O. Henry is almost surely best remembered for "THE GIFT OF THE MAGI" and "THE LAST LEAF," tales of human love and generosity that have attained classic status and can move even most postmodern readers, despite some critics' charges of sentimentalism. "Let Me Feel Your Pulse," the last story he ever wrote as he wasted away from an incurable disease, continues to receive praise as one of his finest.

Although numerous critics have accused O. Henry of romanticizing such issues as poverty—in "The Cop and the Anthem," "A Madison Square Arabian Night," "The Unfinished Story," "The Unfurnished Room," for example—others view him as a writer who believes in a common human bond that unites us all: Far from thinking as an idealist, then, he is a man who believes in ideals. In this sense, the unresolved controversy over O. Henry's talents is one of philosophy rather than literary criticism. Whatever perspective the critical reader holds, O. Henry has made an indelible mark on the American short story, and his tales promise to reach into the next century.

See "THE GIFT OF THE MAGI," "THE LAST LEAF."

BIBLIOGRAPHY

Arnett, Ethel Stephens. O. Henry from Polecat Creek. Greensboro, N.C.: Piedmont Press, 1962.

Blansfield, Charmaine. Cheap Rooms and Restless Hearts: A Study of Formula in the Urban Tales of Porter. Bowling Green, Ohio: Bowling Green State University Popular Press, 1988.

Current-García, Eugene. O. Henry. New York: Twayne, 1965.

———. O. Henry: A Study of the Short Fiction. New York: Twayne, 1993.

Davis, Robert H. and Arthur B. Maurice. The Caliph of Bagdad. New York: Appleton, 1931.

Ejxenbaum, Boris Mikhailovich. O. Henry and the Theory of the Short Story. Translated by I.R. Titunik. Ann Arbor: University of Michigan Press, 1968.

Gallegly, Joseph. From Alamo Plaza to Jack Harris's Saloon: O. Henry and the Southwest He Knew. The Hague: Mouton, 1970.

Henry, O. The Best of O. Henry: One Hundred of His Stories. London: Hodder and Stoughton, 1929.

———. The Best Short Stories of O. Henry. Edited by Bennett Cerf and Van H. Cartmell. New York: The Modern Library, 1945.

———. Cabbages and Kings. New York: A.L. Burt, 1904.

———. Complete Works. New York: Doubleday, Page & Company for Funk & Wagnalls, 1926.

———. Complete Writings. 14 vols. Garden City, N.Y.: Doubleday, Page and Co., 1917.

———. Cops and Robbers: O. Henry's Best Detective and Crime Stories. New York: L. E. Spivak, 1948.

———. The Four Million. New York: A.L. Burt, 1906.

———. The Gentle Grafter. Garden City, N.Y.: Doubleday, Doran, 1908.

———. Heart of the West. New York: The McClure Company, 1907.

———. Let Me Feel Your Pulse. New York: Doubleday, Page & Company, 1910.

———. More O. Henry: One Hundred More of the Master's Stories. London: Hodder and Stoughton, 1933.

———. O. Henry Westerns. Edited by Patrick Thornhill. London: Methuen, 1961.

———. O. Henryana: Seven Odds and Ends: Poetry and Short Stories. Garden City, N.Y.: Doubleday, Page & Company, 1920.

———. Options. New York: Grosset & Dunlap, 1909.

———. The Pocket Book of O. Henry Stories. Edited by Harry Hansen. New York: Pocket Books, 1948.

———. Roads of Destiny. New York: Doubleday, Page & Company, 1909.

———. Rolling Stones. New York: Collier, 1912.

———. Selected Stories of O. Henry. Edited by C. Alphonse Smith. Garden City, N.Y.: Doubleday, Page & Company, 1922.

———. Sixes and Sevens. Garden City, N.Y.: Doubleday, Page & Company, 1911.

————. The *Stories of O. Henry.* Edited by Harry Hansen. New York: Heritage Press, 1965.

————. *Strictly Business: More Stories of the Four Million.* New York: Collier, 1910.

————. *The Trimmed Lamp and Other Stories of the Four Million.* New York: A.L. Burt Co., 1907.

————. *The Two Women.* Boston: Small, Maynard, 1910.

————. *The Voice of the City: Further Stories of the Four Million.* Garden City, N.Y.: Doubleday, Doran, 1908.

————. *Waifs and Strays: Twelve Stories.* Garden City, N.Y.: Doubleday, 1917.

————. *Whirligigs.* New York: Collier, 1910.

Kramer, Dale. *The Heart of O. Henry.* New York: Rinehart, 1954.

Langford, Gerald. *Alias O. Henry: A Biography of William Sidney Porter.* New York: Macmillan, 1957.

Long, Eugene Hudson. *O Henry: American Regionalist.* Austin, Texas: Steck-Vaughn, 1969.

————. *O. Henry: The Man and His Work.* New York: Russell & Russell, 1949.

O'Connor, Richard. *O. Henry: The Legendary Life of William S. Porter.* Garden City, N.Y.: Doubleday, 1970.

Smith, C. Alphonse. *O. Henry Biography.* Garden City, N.Y.: Doubleday, Page & Company, 1916.

HERO/HEROINE   In a literary or dramatic work, the main character on whom one's interest is focused. Many FEMINIST critics now eschew the term "heroine": all central figures in fiction, female or male, are called heroes. Also called the PROTAGONIST.

"HILLS LIKE WHITE ELEPHANTS"
ERNEST HEMINGWAY (1927)   The frequently anthologized "Hills Like White Elephants" first printed in *transition* magazine in 1927 is often read and taught as a perfect illustration of Ernest HEMINGWAY's minimalist (see MINIMALISM), self-proclaimed "iceberg" style of writing: In much of Hemingway's fiction what is said in the story often is less important than what has not been said. Like the iceberg—only one-eighth of which is visible above the surface— Hemingway's fiction is much richer than its spare language suggests. Hemingway has great faith in his readers and leaves them to discern what is truly happening from the scant facts he presents on the surface of his story. On a superficial level, *Hills* is merely about a man, a woman, and an "awfully sim-ple operation" (HLWE 275). What the narrator never actually tells the reader, however, is that "awfully simple operation" is an abortion, a taboo subject in 1925. Underneath the surface of this story are THEMES and motifs that are characteristic of many of Hemingway's other works as well. Like many of those works, *Hills* tells the story of an American abroad and depicts the strained relationships between men and women that clearly intrigued the author. Like many of the relationships Hemingway portrays, this man and woman apparently have nothing in common but sex and the heavy consumption of alcoholic beverages.

Hills is also a story of avoidance. Instead of having a significant, rational conversation about the issue at hand, the "girl," Jig, says only that the hills of Spain look like white elephants. "Wasn't that clever?" she asks the unnamed man (HLWE 274). This rather inconsiderate male companion agrees, but he actually wants to talk about the procedure. Jig would rather not discuss it. When he pressures her, she replies, "Then I'll do it. Because I don't care about me." Jig is the typical Hemingway female, selfless and sacrificial. She is prepared to have the abortion, but the reader is left with the distinct impression that any previous magic between the couple is gone. "It isn't ours anymore," Jig tells the American (HLWE 276). The unfortunate accident of pregnancy has ruined the relationship; it will never be the same. Hemingway explores many of the same themes in his important war novel *A Farewell to Arms* and in *The Sun Also Rises.*

BIBLIOGRAPHY

Hemingway, Ernest. "Hills Like White Elephants." 1927. Reprinted in *The Complete Short Stories of Ernest Hemingway: The Finca Vigia Edition.* New York: Scribner's, 1987.

Johnston, Kenneth. "'Hills Like White Elephants': Lean, Vintage Hemingway." *Studies in American Fiction* (1982).

Renner, Stanley. "Moving to the Girl's Side of Hills." *The Hemingway Review* (1995).

Kathleen M. Hicks
University of Texas at El Paso

HISPANIC-AMERICAN SHORT FICTION

Hispanic-American writers, also known as Latinos, come from a rich variety of historical situations, ethnicities, classes, and backgrounds. Though not sharing one specific cultural experience, Hispanic-American authors often dialogue with one another as they "document" their past, their present, and their vexed relationship to the United States and Latin America. This documentation through fiction reveals a continuing debate about Hispanic-American literature—whether it articulates a *search for identity* or whether it *affirms identity* through first-person narration (Horno-Delgado 3). In either case, one can assess the short story by considering the audience, language, and technique of Latino writers and by familiarizing oneself with the politics shaping Hispanic-American cultures, especially those of Mexican Americans, Puerto Ricans, and Cuban Americans.

Hispanic literature has grown from publication in 19th-century newspapers to 1980s literary journals such as *Revista Chicano-Riqueña* and *Americas Review* and 1990s academic presses and the mainstream publication of anthologies. Arte Publico Press is perhaps the largest publisher of Hispanic-American fiction, coordinating with the Recovering the U.S. Hispanic Literary Project at the University of Houston. Most recently, the World Wide Web avails itself as a literary space in a number of languages; the short story is especially suited for Internet viewing and is likely to be popular among students and independent writers (Ramirez).

As in other kinds of ethnic writing, the issue of language is an important one. Depending on the degree of assimilation or on ideologies associated with language, Hispanic-American writers express themselves in English, Spanish, or a combination of the two. Texan novelist Tomás Rivera, one of the foundational figures of contemporary Hispanic-American letters, wrote . . . *y no se lo tragó la tierra* [*And the Earth Did Not Devour Him*] (1971) in Spanish. Yet Spanish continues to be a problematic means of asserting Latino identity because, like English, it is a colonial inheritance. With increasing frequency, instead, Latino authors inject Spanish into English prose which underscores divided allegiances. In addition, writers such as Helena María VIRAMONTES and Nicholasa Mohr sometimes employ slang or ghetto speech, echoing African-American rhythms and articulating subcultural affiliation. Language, in turn, shapes the authorial techniques and themes of Hispanic-American fiction.

Hispanic-American writers explore changes in their communities through daily routines, or travel through "the visitor," a device that uses an outsider's perspective. Often biographical and autobiographical, Hispanic-American short stories provide memorable images of neighborhoods of Miami, the bustling tenements of New York City, migrant workers, and working-class families. Generally speaking, though, Hispanic-American literature has shifted its settings (and its politics) from agricultural reform to personal adjustment in cities and suburbs.

A common technique is to use a moment in the present as a trigger to review the past or anticipate the future. This allows readers to examine opposing values between a conservative, patriarchal Spanish-American society and a Westernized, commercialized, and potentially liberating one. In Marisella Veiga's "Fresh Fruit" (1992), the housewife-narrator spies on her young, single neighbor, Susana (Poey and Suarez 349). From the narrator's perspective, Susana has learned troubling "American ways" at school; she lives alone, drives alone, works alone, and eats alone, buying ready-made food. The reader learns through the narrator's criticism—and perhaps through her envy—that Susana is not interested in saving money or in "forming a home with a husband." For the traditional Latino, Susana's life seems socially empty, but when the housewife-narrator admits her own restlessness and her husband's infidelities, one sees a validation of those "American ways," ways that liberate women from the confines of their homes. Hispanic-American fiction, therefore, has much to contribute to larger discourses of women's roles in a patriarchal but transformative society. A survey of the three largest Hispanic-American groups—Mexican Americans, Puerto Ricans, and Cuban Americans—becomes useful as we address specific authors and texts.

MEXICAN AMERICAN

The Treaty of Guadalupe-Hidalgo of 1848 converted Mexican land into U.S. territory—now the American Southwest—and demanded new approaches and eventually new languages in literary production. According to critic Raymund A. Paredes, 19th-century memoirists and novelists responded to their U.S. citizenry through criticism, introspection, or nostalgia. By the mid-20th century, key writers such as Josephina Niggli and José Villarreal articulated assimilationist concerns in, respectively, *Mexican Village* (1945) and *Pocho* (1959), both of which are widely excerpted and anthologized (Paredes in Gutierrez and Padilla, 40–41).

At the other end of the cultural spectrum lie the realist, perhaps anti-assimilationist, oral traditions that continue to influence Mexican-American literature, particularly poetry (Limón). For members of Mexican-American culture lacking education, the *corrido,* or ballad, has been a staple. Enduring, widely accessible, and malleable to the artist's purpose, the *corrido* has allowed cultural artists to question Anglo authority, especially in matters of land and labor. The corrido, the poem, and later the short story also expressed the hopes and frustrations of the farm workers' movement, led by César Chávez.

Since the farm workers' movement, and after civil rights activism, many writers have identified themselves as "Chicano" or "Chicana." Chicano authors self-consciously participate through their writing in an ongoing struggle for fair labor practices, access to education, and the right to speak Spanish and to preserve Mexican-American traditions and ways of being. Short stories writers such as Denise Chavez, Viramontes, and Sandra CISNEROS draw on these traditions and revive the past through their narrative details, which include prayers, *remedios* (cures, both natural and supernatural), culinary arts, and horticulture. Even in, or perhaps especially in, urban settings the routines of the past are important. Viramontes's "The Moths" (1985) demonstrates this through the dying grandmother figure, Abuelita, and the 14-year-old narrator (Augenbraum and Olmos 433). Together, the women—one old and sage, the other young and rebellious—save old coffee cans, puncture them, and garden with the newly made pots. This pastoral activity contrasts sharply with the narrator's insulting and violent family. Abuelita provides an alternative to her granddaughter's dysfunctional home life and its compulsory Catholicism. Although the grandmother dies, the narrator takes careful measures to preserve the past. The narrator gathers clean linen, gently washes Abuelita, and cradles her frail torso. The story ends in adolescent self-revelation, a coming-of-age theme common to other works, such as Cisneros's collection of short stories *Woman Hollering Creek* (1991).

PUERTO RICAN

Puerto Ricans form the second major group of Hispanic-American writers. Living on the island or on the mainland, their views on American culture will differ accordingly. Indeed, when Puerto Rico became a U.S. commonwealth in 1898, its writers regarded this new imperial presence with interest and trepidation, as evidenced in Ana Roqué's epistolary novel *Luz y sombra* (1903), which explores two women's lives as they attempt to deal with European influences and U.S. policies. In a similar vein is Manuel Zeno Gandía's *La Charca* (1894), which focuses on the land as it will be of interest to U.S. development (Flores, quoted in Gutierrez 67). Yet Puerto Rico's distance from the United States and its Spanish influences tended to make its literature somewhat inaccessible to American readers until recently, when translations have become more common.

Like Mexican-American literature, Puerto Rican writing gained momentum after the civil rights movement and continues today with novelists such as Piri Thomas and Magali Garcia Ramis, and poets such as Julia Burgos. Short story writers include Abraham Rodriguez, Jr., Judith Ortiz COFER, and Nicholasa Mohr, all of whom live in the United States and all of whom cross cultures in their depiction of Puerto Rican life.

In "Mr. Mendelsohn," Mohr captures the essence of the Bronx barrio as a cross section between the young and old, the Latino and Jewish (Augenbraum and Stavans 131). A sharp contrast is the drug-based, gang murder of a young pregnant woman in Abraham Rodriguez, Jr.'s "Roaches" (Poey and Suarez 267). The premise of this story is that watching real life is more dramatic than watching television. Rodriguez reveals his range as a writer in his quieter, though no less hopeful, story of teenage sex, pregnancy, and high school attrition in "The Lotto" (1992) (Gonzalez 36). Both stories show the tough, merciless side of Puerto Rican life in the Bronx and reveal a gritty bankruptcy of morals, a postmodern disconnection with society. Thus Puerto Rican short stories span the humanitarian, nostalgic outlook to a perhaps more troubling postmodern passivity.

CUBAN AMERICAN

Cuban American writers represent the third major Hispanic-American group and perhaps the most willing to assimilate. Their literary tradition began, in part, with revolutionary José Martí, one of the first Cuban exiles to publish in the United States. His essay "Nuestra America" (1891) helped his compatriots, and indeed Latin Americans more broadly, to define *mestizo* (mixed-race) cultures, cultures threatened by the effects of European colonialism and U.S. intervention. Fidel Castro's assumption of military power in 1959 took up Martí's rallying cry to make Cuba resistant to U.S. domination. But this came at the price of Cubans who sought repatriation to the United States. This first wave of exiles has been able to maintain its island connections. For writers such as Cristina Garcia and her short story protagonists, relationships to the island are vexed. We see in Garcia's *Dreaming in Cuban* (1992) a range of cultural accommodations and sacrifices from Celia's pre–Castro regime romance and Felicia's fear and intrigue with forbidden island spaces, to Lourdes's winning, though sometimes painful, adaptation to American life in New York City.

The fast pace of the American city and changes to the family structure are equally important to Virgil Suarez's "Miami During the Reagan Years" (1994). In Suarez's story, the narrator's mother intends to remarry, and the narrator's father has no major objections, for he is living with someone else himself (Gonzalez 384). This collapse of generational behavior is paralleled by divisions of education and class in other works. Cecilia Rodríguez-Milanés's "Abuelita Marieleta" (1992) exposes the pretensions of middle-class Cuban Americans living in Miami and recent "marieletas" who hide their "boat people" status (Poey and Suarez 287).

Meanwhile, Marisella Veiga shows a preoccupation with women's roles in the Caribbean (Gonzalez 173). An island narrative, Veiga's "The Graduation" traces the positive effects of academic and technical education on women. The narrator takes stock of her duties as a housewife while her female relations obtain manicurist certification and secretarial training. Thus even in the islands, Latino literature reveals the U.S. challenges to Spanish-American culture and the inevitable, if not necessary, disruption of gender roles.

In addition to these three groups, the immigration of Latin Americans contributes an important political and historical dimension to Hispanic-American fiction. Dominican Republicans, Guatemalans, and Chileans, who fled the U.S.-backed military regimes in their own countries, write about their experiences growing up or adapting to life in the United States. Julia Alvarez's novels (*How the Garcia Girls Lost their Accents, ¡Yo!,* and *In the Time of the Butterflies*) deal, to varying degrees, with the effects of Rafael Trujillo's regime on women—the ones who were oppressed or killed and the ones, like Alvarez and her narrators, who fled the Dominican Republic to the United States. Alvarez's chapters, sometimes anthologized as short stories, illustrate the successful integration of the historical and the uniquely personal imaginings of Hispanic-American writers.

One final consideration in Hispanic-American fiction is its scholarly reception. Most criticism of Hispanic-American literature focuses on novels and poetry, but such critics as Ray Gonzalez and Nicolás Kanellos are now shifting attention to the short story form. Gonzalez and Kanellos provide useful introductions in their respective anthologies, *Currents from the Dancing River: Contemporary Latino*

Fiction, Nonfiction and Poetry, and *Short Fiction by Hispanic American Writers of the United States* (1994). In addition, broader criticism relevant to the short story can be found in Ramón Gutierrez and Genero Padilla's *Recovering the U.S. Hispanic Literary Project* (1993) and in Asunción Horno-Delgado's *Breaking Boundaries: Latina Writing and Critical Readings* (1989).

BIBLIOGRAPHY

Augenbraum, Harold, and Margarite Fernández Olmos, eds. *Latino Reader: An American Literary Tradition from 1542 to the Present.* Boston: Houghton Mifflin, 1997.

Augenbraum, Harold, and Ilan Stavans, eds. *Growing Up Latino: Memoirs and Stories.* Boston: Houghton Mifflin, 1993.

Cisneros, Sandra. *Woman Hollering Creek and Other Stories.* New York: Vintage Books, 1991.

Garcia, Cristina. *Dreaming in Cuban.* New York: Ballantine Books, 1992.

Gonzales, Ray, ed. *Currents in the Dancing River: Contemporary Latino Fiction, Nonfiction, and Poetry.* New York: Harcourt Brace, 1993.

Gutierrez, Ramón, and Genero Padilla, eds. *Recovering the U.S. Hispanic Literary Heritage.* Houston: Arte Publico Press, 1993.

Horno-Delgado, Asunción, and Eliana Ortega, et al., eds. *Breaking Boundaries: Latina Writing and Critical Readings.* Amherst: University of Massachusetts Press, 1989.

Kanellos, Nicolás. *Short Fiction by Hispanic Writers of the United States.* Houston: Arte Publico Press, 1993.

Limón, José. *Mexican Ballads, Chicano Poems: History and Influence in Mexican American Social Poetry.* Berkeley: University of California Press, 1992.

Martí, José. *Nuestra America.* Havana: Casa de las Americas, 1974.

Poey, Delia, and Virgil Suarez. *Iguana Dreams: New Latino Fiction.* New York: HarperCollins, 1992.

Ramirez, Luz Elena. "E 314: Chicano and Latino Literature—Family Narratives," Department of English, University of Texas at Austin. [On-line] URL: http://www.cwrl.utexas.edu/~ramirez/assignments/narrative.html. Fall 1996–Spring 1997.

Rivera, Tomás. *. . . y se no lo trago la tierra. / . . . And the Earth Did Not Devour Him.* Translated by Evangelina Vigil-Pinón. Houston: Arte Publico Press, 1971.

Luz Elena Ramirez
State University of New York, College at Oneonta

HITLER, ADOLF (1889–1945)   Adolf Hitler was born in Austria and served in the Bavarian Army in WORLD WAR I. He blamed Germany's defeat in that war on Jews and Marxists, and with others founded the National Socialist (Nazi) Party in 1920. In 1923 the Nazis unsuccessfully attempted to overthrow the Bavarian government, and Hitler was imprisoned. While in jail, he wrote *Mein Kampf* (My Struggle), a book filled with anti-Semitism, power worship, disdain for morality, and his strategy for world domination. The GREAT DEPRESSION brought his Nazi movement mass support after 1929. A spellbinding orator, Hitler understood mass psychology and proved himself a master of deceitful strategy. He manipulated virulent anti-Semitism and anticommunism to gain support of workers as well as bankers and industrialists. He became chancellor in 1933, and soon afterward the Reichstag (legislature) gave him dictatorial powers.

Hitler's aggressive and ruthless foreign policy was appeased by Western nations until he invaded Poland in 1939 and war was declared. Hitler's equally brutal internal policies included the "Final Solution," which aimed to eliminate targeted minorities, primarily Jews, in the infamous concentration camps. Millions were killed in what is known as the HOLOCAUST. WORLD WAR II ended in 1945 with Germany defeated and the country in ruins. Hitler committed suicide before being captured, leaving as a legacy the memory of the most dreadful and evil tyranny of modern times. ALLUSIONS to Hitler occur directly or indirectly in such stories as Cynthia OZICK's "The Shawl" and William FAULKNER's GO DOWN, MOSES.

HOLMES, OLIVER WENDELL (1809–1894)   A physician and a professor at the Harvard Medical School, Holmes also wrote important medical papers, essays, and novels. He is best remembered for the series of sketches he wrote for the *ATLANTIC MONTHLY* under the title *The Autocrat of the Breakfast Table.* The stories in this series, notable for their wit and originality, combined fiction, essay, conversation, drama, and verse, and were collected in book form (*The Autocrat of the Breakfast Table,*

1858). Other essays were published as *The Professor at the Breakfast Table* (1859) and *The Poet at the Breakfast Table* (1872).

HOLOCAUST

Soon after Adolf HITLER was named chancellor of Nazi Germany in 1933, anti-Semitism was enacted into law and ceased only with the crushing defeat of Germany at the end of WORLD WAR II in Europe in 1945. Most Jews who did not flee Germany were sent to concentration camps and, after World War II began in 1939, the Nazis implemented Hitler's "final solution of the Jewish question," which called for the extermination of all Jews in any country conquered by the Germans. By the war's end, more than 6 million Jews had been systemically murdered in what became known as the Holocaust.

HOMOSEXUALITY IN LITERATURE

With the increasing impact of the gay rights movement and acceptance of gays in mainstream society, gay studies and gay literature are emerging as respected fields. Defining "gay literature" is sometimes difficult, given the frequent vague and subtle references to gay characters or THEMES found in works. Not all gay literature deals specifically with sex; most focuses on emotion. Writer Christopher Isherwood said it best when he explained that being gay does not involve the act of sex; instead, it is the proclivity or the ability to fall in love with another member of the same gender.

In general, however, fiction is termed gay when it incorporates a gay theme or gay character into its narrative. Thus, not all gay literature is written by gay authors; nor do all gay authors write gay fiction. No single piece of gay fiction can claim to be emblematic of the "gay experience," for as the growing numbers of gay short stories shows, this "experience" is different in each story. Further, gay literature also can share traits of other thematic clusters of literature, such as FEMINIST, NATIVE AMERICAN, AFRICAN AMERICAN, and such genres as DETECTIVE FICTION, ghost stories (see GHOST STORY), and comedies (see COMEDY).

From the early days of civilization, there have always been gay thinkers and writers. Among them is Greek philosopher Plato, who has been among the most influential historically in the fields of philosophy and literature. Despite the much-heated debate over William Shakespeare's sexuality, many critics believe his work—littered with cross-dressing characters and same-sex affectionate themes—strikes a definite gay or bisexual chord. In premodern America, Walt Whitman and Herman MELVILLE were reputed to have been gay. In general, their better-known works do not contain overt sexual references, but their sexuality has been the subject of much biographic and bibliographic research and scholarly debate, and has led to new interpretations of their works in recent years.

Historically, literary greats have been a driving force of the modern gay movement, which began in the late 1800s. As the example of Oscar Wilde shows, the road for these writers was far from easy. In his infamous 1895 trial for homosexuality, the British courts found the prolific and prize-winning Wilde guilty and sentenced him to a two-year jail term of hard labor. In both his writings and in the notoriety of his personal life, Wilde brought the issue into international focus.

For the first part of the 1900s, gays were more or less "invisible," living underground lives in the United States. Gay men and women organized a vast network through friends, businesses, and bars. Numerous laws targeted homosexuals. Gays lived with the constant threat of the police raids on gay establishments, which brought with them brutality, arrests, and public embarrassment.

The gay lives of literary giants Virginia Woolf and Gertrude STEIN were widely known in literary circles, yet until recently scholarship about their sexuality or any subtle themes in their work has been minimal. Stories such as Henry JAMES's "The Pupil" (1891) are so subtle that the unsuspecting reader would not realize the underlying gay theme. In other stories, such as Willa CATHER's widely anthologized "Paul's Case" (1905), the homoeroticism and sexuality of the characters are elusive yet present. Given the public intolerance of homosexuality, much of Stein's writing that was overtly lesbian in theme was withheld from publication until later in the century.

At midcentury psychological associations told Americans that homosexuality was abnormal behavior, thereby contradicting the *Kinsey Report,* which indicated that nearly 10 percent of Americans were homosexual. At this point the literary world began to note and accept more direct gay references in fiction. The African American writer James BALDWIN introduced gay themes in his novel *Go Tell It on the Mountain* (1953) and later—more boldly—in *Giovanni's Room* (1956). Central to the beat movement and preceding the "free love" years of the 1960s, Allen Ginsberg brought an "in-your-face" homoerotic sexuality to his poetry. Other gay American authors writing early to midcentury include the poet H. D. (Hilda Doolittle), playwrights Tennessee Williams and Edward ALBEE, Christopher Isherwood, and fiction writers Gore Vidal and John CHEEVER.

The birth of the contemporary gay rights movement was heralded in 1969 at a small gay bar in the Greenwich Village section of New York City (see GAY MALE SHORT FICTION). Although it did not gain the momentum of the civil rights and women's rights movements of the time, this marked the beginning of an age when gays stopped hiding underground and became advocates for their rights. Later that year the National Institute of Mental Health recommended that the United States repeal laws against homosexual sex between consenting adults.

With the onslaught of acquired immune deficiency syndrome (AIDS) in the early 1980s, the gay community became one of the hardest-hit groups. During the early years of AIDS, a panic swept through the gay community since doctors and researchers did not know exactly how the disease was contracted. As AIDS became more prevalent, its threat acted as a mobilizing force for the community. The specter of AIDS is present in most recent literature, whether directly or lurking in the shadows.

Gay literature has made a significant impact in the literary landscape in the 1980s and '90s. Universities offer courses in gay and lesbian literature and culture, and the number of gay-themed books being published has increased considerably in recent years. Numerous anthologies of short gay

fiction include *The Faber Book of Gay Short Fiction* (1991), *Penguin Book of Gay Short Stories* (1994), *Penguin Book of Lesbian Short Stories* (1994), the series *Men on Men* (beginning in 1988) series, *Women on Women* (beginning in 1990) and even an anthology of gay and lesbian science fiction, *Kindred Spirits* (1984). In addition, many nonfiction compilations of stories about being gay have been published, including coming-out stories and reflections on definitions of families and hometowns. Most bookstores now have sections devoted to gay, lesbian, and bisexual literature; indeed, some are devoted almost entirely to the topic.

Bisexual literature often is included in this gay category yet it has a foot in both sexual camps. ALLUSIONS to the complex sexuality of bisexuals can be found in writings by Carson MCCULLERS, especially in her "BALLAD OF THE SAD CAFE" (1951), or Louise ERDRICH's *The Beet Queen* (1986).

See also LESBIAN THEMES IN SHORT STORIES.

BIBLIOGRAPHY

Malinowski, Sharon, and Christa Brelin, eds. *The Gay and Lesbian Literary Companion.* Visible Ink Press, 1995.

Nestle, Joan, and Naomi Holoch, eds. *Women on Women: An Anthology of American Lesbian Short Fiction.* New York: NAL Dutton, 1990.

Stambolian, George, ed. *Men on Men: Best New Gay Fiction.* New York: Plume, 1986.

White, Edmund, ed. *The Faber Book of Gay Short Fiction.* Boston: Faber and Faber, 1991.

Calvin Hussman
St. Olaf College

HOOD, MARY (1946–)

Georgia native and resident Mary Hood established herself as an important new Southern writer with her first short story collection, *How Far She Went* (1984), which won the Flannery O'Connor Award for short fiction and several other prestigious awards.

Often compared in subject and style to other Southerners Flannery O'CONNOR, Carson MCCULLERS, and Eudora WELTY, Hood writes stories usually set in rural Georgia and peopled with conflicted, struggling, and often isolated local residents. She has a direct, unstinting approach to her subject and, like

O'Connor and William FAULKNER, does not flinch from depicting the violence and confusion inherent in modern life. Hood presents dialogue as storytelling Southerners truly speak it: rich with colloquialisms, full of humor and detail. "How Far She Went," the often-anthologized title story of her first collection, tells of a woman raising her granddaughter and trying to protect her from a brutal encounter. The granddaughter learns the surprising depth of her grandmother's strength and courage; when a pistol-wielding tough tells the old woman to go to hell, "'Probably will,' her granny told him. 'I'll save you a seat by the fire.'"

Hood is a prolific writer, frequently contributing fiction and nonfiction to periodicals including the *Georgia Review*, HARPER'S, and the KENYON REVIEW. She has published a second collection of short stories, *And Venus Is Blue* (1986), and a novel, *Familiar Heat* (1995).

BIBLIOGRAPHY

Hood, Mary. *And Venus Is Blue*. New York: Ticknor & Fields, 1986.

——. "A Stubborn Sense of Place." *Harper's* (August 1986): 35–45.

——. *How Far She Went*. Athens: University of Georgia Press, 1984.

Pope, Dan. "The Post-Minimalist American Story; or, What Comes After Carver?" *The Gettysburg Review* 1 (Spring 1988): 331–342.

Karen Weekes
University of Georgia, Athens

HOPKINSON, FRANCIS (1737–1791)

Francis Hopkinson was born and reared in Philadelphia, the son of a prominent lawyer. Professionally, Hopkinson followed in his father's footsteps upon receiving the first diploma from the Academy of Philadelphia (now the University of Pennsylvania) in 1757. Although his work was to remain in politics, law, and trade, Hopkinson became known in the 1760s through his poetry, musical works, and, more important, essays on politics. A staunch supporter of American independence, Hopkinson scathingly satired Loyalist politicians and supporters in pamphlets and in popular periodicals, such as the *Pennsylvania Magazine*, often embroiling himself in public battles that resulted in a somewhat tarnished reputation. At the same time, Hopkinson's writings enjoyed popular acclaim and notice, particularly "A PRETTY STORY," an allegorical (see ALLEGORY) rendering of the tense state of British-American relations. Hopkinson's stature in Colonial American literary and political culture was such that he was elected to represent New Jersey at the Continental Congress, where he signed the Declaration of Independence.

During and following the AMERICAN REVOLUTION, Hopkinson continued his support of the American side by using his scathing wit against the British cause. He purportedly also used his artistic flair to design the American flag. Following the war, Hopkinson continued to write social and political satire and commentary for popular magazines and was also appointed a district court judge in Pennsylvania. The news of his sudden death from a stroke was largely ignored by the press, who both loved and hated this talented and patriotic, although often bombastic, man of letters.

BIBLIOGRAPHY

Hastings, George Everett. "Francis Hopkinson." In *Dictionary of American Biography*. Edited by Allen Johnson, Dumas Malone, et al. New York: Charles Scribner's Sons, 1932.

——. *The Life and Works of Francis Hopkinson*. Chicago: University of Chicago Press,1926.

Levernier, James A. "Francis Hopkinson." In *Reference Guide to American Literature*. Edited by Jim Kamp. 1994.

Marshall, George N. *Patriot with a Pen: The Wit, Wisdom, and Life of Francis Hopkinson, 1737–1791, Gadfly of the Revolution*. West Bridgewater, Mass.: C. H. Marshall, 1993.

Zall, Paul M. *Comical Spirit of Seventy-six: The Humor of Francis Hopkinson*. San Marino, Calif: Huntington Library, 1976.

Gregory M. Weight
University of Delaware

HOUSE ON MANGO STREET, THE

SANDRA CISNEROS (1984) Categorized by critics as a NOVELLA, SHORT STORY CYCLE, or collection of prose poems, *The House on Mango Street* (1984) employs a unique, cross-genre form that characterizes the work as postmodern. (See POSTMODERNISM.) In it Sandra

CISNEROS captures the diverse voices and stories that she has encountered in the Chicano/Chicana community.

The House on Mango Street is unified by the voice of its narrator, a young Latina named Esperanza. The work is in many ways a typical BILDUNGSROMAN. It centers on the development of Esperanza's artistic voice as she experiences the confusing and often harsh world around her. Many vignettes focus on the problems facing young Latina women in the community and the forces that keep them from finding creative and personal fulfillment. The work concludes as most bildungsroman do, with the artist's withdrawal from the community. Esperanza, however, unlike most other artist/HEROes, promises to return for those in her neighborhood who do not have the opportunities that she has had—those whose voice cannot be heard except through her art.

BIBLIOGRAPHY

Cahill, Susan. *Writing Women's Lives.* New York: HarperPerennial, 1994.

Cisneros, Sandra. *The House on Mango Street.* Houston, Tex.: Arte Publico Press, 1984.

McCracken, Ellen. "Sandra Cisneros' *The House on Mango Street:* Community-Oriented Introspection and the Demystification of Patriarchal Violence." In *Breaking Boundaries: Latina Writing and Critical Readings.* Edited by Asuncion Horno-Delgado, Eliana Ortega, Nina M. Scott, Nancy Saporta Sternbach, Elaine N. Miller. Amherst: University of Massachusetts Press, 1989, pp. 62–71.

Olivares, Julian. "Sandra Cisneros' *The House on Mango Street,* and the Poetics of Space." In *Chicana Creativity and Criticism: New Frontiers in American Literature.* Edited by Maria Herrera-Sobeck and Helena Maria Viramontes. Albuquerque: University of New Mexico Press, 1996, pp. 233–44.

TuSmith, Bonnie. *All of My Relatives: Community in Contemporary Ethnic American Literatures.* Ann Arbor: University of Michigan Press, 1993.

Tracie Guzzio
Ohio University

HOWELLS, WILLIAM DEAN (1837–1920)

An editor and prodigious writer of novels, short stories, drama, poetry, essays, criticism, reviews, biographies, autobiography, and travel books, William Dean Howells was likely the most influential person in American literature during his lifetime. Howells's vast output was widely read and appreciated by a large audience; he promoted prominent and emerging American writers; and he promulgated seminal international arts and their concepts in America. Thus, Howells was known to his admirers as the "dean" of American letters.

Born in March 1837 in a still mostly rustic Ohio, Howells was the second of eight children in a close-knit, economically humble but proud, respectable, and culturally aware family. Particularly close to his mother, Howells was also shaped by his father, whose politics and religion made him an abolitionist and a follower of the Swedish philosopher-theologian, Emmanuel Swedenborg (1688–1772), whose mystical visions influenced numerous writers. Howells's initiation to letters came early by setting type for his father, who owned newspapers in several Ohio locations. In part because those papers did not succeed, the family moved often.

Lacking extensive formal education, the autodidactic Howells was nevertheless well read and deeply ambitious as a writer. Howells published a poem when he was only 15 and a story the following year, but his first significant writing was as a journalist. In 1860 this work took Howells to New England, where he met many giants of American literature, including James Russell Lowell, Oliver Wendell HOLMES, Ralph Waldo Emerson, Henry David Thoreau, Walt Whitman, and Nathaniel HAWTHORNE.

Journalism also led to his first important book, an 1860 biography of Abraham LINCOLN. In turn, the Lincoln book earned Howells the American consulship at Venice in 1861, where he remained during the CIVIL WAR. Upon his return to the United States, Howells began work as an editor, eventually serving in that capacity at some of the finest magazines of his day: ATLANTIC MONTHLY, HARPER'S *Monthly,* and *The Nation.* Howells relished this role, because it allowed him to encounter and further the careers of other writers.

The many many writers whom Howells supported or celebrated were diverse both in background and in emphasis, and included controversial writers, women writers, and writers of color. Most were younger than Howells, including Abraham Cahan, Charles CHES-

NUTT, Stephen CRANE, Emily Dickinson, Paul Laurence DUNBAR, Mary Wilkins FREEMAN, Hamlin GARLAND, Charlotte Perkins GILMAN, Frank Norris, and Edith WHARTON. As for his contemporaries, Howells was very close to both Henry JAMES and Mark TWAIN.

As advocate and practitioner of literary REALISM, or the accurate portrayal of everyday life of ordinary people, Howells was opposed to popular sentimental and romantic fiction. He was convinced that literature should do more than just entertain; it also should instruct and uplift, but gracefully and not by means of didacticism. His concerns included many of the major phenomena of the time: urbanization, industrialization, and social and economic inequality and injustice. Over time Howells came to espouse socialism.

His commitment to an accurate account of the human condition did not completely extend to sexuality as a motivating force; Howells largely dealt with it indirectly in his fiction. This restraint, along with other of his more conservative propensities, contributed to the derision and dismissal of Howells's work late in his career. Among others, Frank Norris, Ambrose BIERCE, H. L. Mencken, Sinclair Lewis, and Van Wyck Brooks complained that his fiction was too optimistic and wanting in vitality and insight.

In the 1930s, however, his reputation underwent revision and revival, which has continued to the present. Howells is once again recognized for his impact on American literature. He is best known as a novelist, and his finest contributions in this genre are usually seen as *A Modern Instance* (1882), *The Rise of Silas Lapham* (1885), *A Hazard of New Fortunes* (1890), and *The Landlord at Lion's Head* (1897). These works reveal his skill and scope in subject, treatment, and technique.

His 36 works of drama are in *The Complete Plays of W. D. Howells* (1960), while some of Howells's observations on literature can be found in *Criticism and Fiction* (1891) and the three-volume *Selected Criticism* (1992). *My Mark Twain* (1910) is probably his most distinguished biography, and his travel books include *Venetian Life* (1866). As for autobiography, *Years of My Youth* (1916) stands out. Much of his correspondence is collected, in *Life in Letters of William Dean Howells* (1928).

Often overlooked if not unknown, the short stories are an important reflection on Howells' biography. In *Selected Short Stories of William Dean Howells* (1997), Ruth Bardon points out that Howells's 46 works in this genre span his career and reflect both his biography and the development of his literary theories and practice; they include popular romance, realism, psychological realism, and psychic romance. The most often anthologized of Howells's short fiction is "Editha" (1905).

Those of Howells's collections that contain at least one short story are *Suburban Sketches* (1871); *A Day's Pleasure and Other Sketches* (1881); *A Fearful Responsibility and Other Stories* (1881); *Christmas Every Day and Other Stories Told for Children* (1893); *A Pair of Patient Lovers* (1901); *Questionable Shapes* (1903); *Between the Dark and the Daylight* (1907); *The Daughter of the Storage and Other Things in Prose and Verse* (1916).

BIBLIOGRAPHY

Cady, Edwin. *The Realist at War: The Mature Years, 1885–1920.* Westport, Conn.: Greenwood, 1986.

———. *The Road to Realism: The Early Years, 1837–1885.* Syracuse: Syracuse University Press, 1956.

Carrington, George, Jr. *The Immense Complex Drama: The World and Art of the Howells Novel.* Columbus: Ohio State University Press, 1966.

Crowley, John. *The Mask of Fiction: Essays on W. D. Howells.* Amherst: University of Massachusetts Press, 1989.

Eble, Kenneth. *William Dean Howells,* 2nd ed. Boston: Twayne, 1982.

Prioleau, Elizabeth. *The Circle of Eros: Sexuality in the Work of William Dean Howells.* Durham, N.C.: Duke University Press, 1983.

Geoffrey C. Middlebrook
California State University at Los Angeles

"HOW THE GRINCH STOLE CHRISTMAS" DR. SEUSS (1957)

Having gone through 53 printings, translations into more than 20 languages, sales of more than 200 million copies, and transformation into a much-loved 1966 television Christmas classic, Dr. Seuss's justly revered 1957 story "How the Grinch Stole Christmas" shares the moral framework of that other famous Christmas story, Charles Dickens's "A Christmas Carol." Seuss's plot focuses on the emotional growth of one solitary creature, the Grinch, who has a heart "two sizes too small" and lives in a cave just north of Who-ville, friendless save for his much-abused dog, Max. Loathing the feasting and singing and sheer happiness of Christmas, the Grinch garbs himself as St. Nick with poor Max in tow as a reindeer and steals every present, every decoration, and every tree in Who-ville on Christmas Eve. Poised to drop the Christmas goodies off a cliff, the Grinch waits for the sounds of Whos wailing; instead, he hears singing. Amazed by the possibility that perhaps Christmas will come to Whos even without decorations and presents, the Grinch experiences an EPIPHANY during which his "small heart / Grew three sizes that day!" He returns all the treats and trimmings to the Whos and participates in the holiday revelry.

Told in 52 brief pages with the simple patterns and repetitions of nursery school rhymes and wonderfully invented words (the word "grinch" has irrevocably entered the commonplace vernacular to describe any stingy or crabby person), the story is deceptively simple. Like the rest of Dr. Seuss's tales, it is as much for adults as for children. Where Seuss's "The Lorax" warns against the destruction of the environment and *The Butter Battle Book* warns against the danger of weapons proliferation, this story teaches us that Christmas is a feeling, not a sale. Long before the era of malls in which Christmas displays go up in August, "Grinch" speaks without didacticism against the commodification of the holiday spirit and for the genuine sentiment of love and togetherness.

BIBLIOGRAPHY
MacDonald, Ruth K. *Dr. Seuss.* New York: Twayne, 1988.

S. L. Yentzer
University of Georgia

HUBRIS   In Greek tragedies, hubris (from the Greek *hybris,* meaning pride or insolence) was the character flaw of pride or overweening self-confidence that led a person to disregard a divine warning or to violate a moral law, resulting in the hero's downfall. In general use, the term has come to mean wanton arrogance. Instances of hubris abound in short fiction, from Joel Chandler HARRIS's UNCLE REMUS tales to Jack LONDON's "TO BUILD A FIRE."

HUGHES, (JAMES) LANGSTON (1902–1967)   Perhaps best known today as the major poet of the HARLEM RENAISSANCE and as one of the major American poets of the 20th century, Langston Hughes nonetheless produced impressive work in a wide variety of genres, including essays, dramas, autobiography, and newspaper columns. Less well known is that Hughes wrote stories for such mainstream publications as ESQUIRE and SCRIBNER'S and published eight collections of short stories between 1934 and 1965. Hans Ostrom points out that one reason Hughes's stories are not better known lies in the critical tendency to associate AFRICAN-AMERICAN SHORT FICTION with novels (ix). (Witness the attention paid to novels by Claude McKay, Richard WRIGHT, Ralph ELLISON, James BALDWIN, Toni MORRISON, Alice WALKER.)

Hughes's first collection, *The Ways of White Folks (1934),* implicitly announced his effort to examine the gap between the white and African American views of life in general and the hypocrisy of white Americans in race relations in general. Using an ironic, unsentimental TONE he overturns, in Phillip A. Snyder's words, "the traditional white/black power structure," managing not to gloss over the human weaknesses of his African American characters and their own cultural foibles, and using "blues" humor (257). Showing a Marxist influence (Hughes wrote some of the tales while in the Soviet Union), the stories dramatize such issues as lynching, white promiscuity, and slavery. The essentially political nature of his stories sets them apart from those of such other practitioners as James Joyce, Katherine Mansfield, and Ernest HEMINGWAY (Ostrom 18).

Laughing to Keep from Crying (1952), Hughes's second short fiction collection, contains stories that originally appeared in such magazines as the NEW YORKER, *Esquire,* and STORY. Although they continue to illuminate such realities as "passing," segregation, particularly in hotels and restaurants, and the racism and hypocrisy that still so pointedly exists in American society, these stories are more optimistic in tone than most of the earlier stories, ultimately suggesting that African Americans have a richer future ahead.

Perhaps related to the lightening in tone from the first to the second collection, Hughes had already published the first of SIMPLE STORIES; a total of four collections featuring the popular JESSE B. SIMPLE would subsequently appear. In his use of blues cynicism, weariness, and humor, in his devotion to African-American FOLKLORE, and in his clear devotion to the working class in his stories, Hughes made a lasting contribution to American short fiction.

BIBLIOGRAPHY

Berry, Faith. *Hughes: Before and Beyond Harlem.* Westport, Conn.: Lawrence Hill, 1983.

Emmanuel, James A. *Langston Hughes.* New York: Twayne, 1967.

Hughes, Langston. *The Best of Simple.* New York: Hill & Wang, 1961.

———. *Laughing to Keep from Crying.* New York: Holt, 1952.

———. *Simple Speaks His Mind.* New York: Simon & Schuster, 1950.

———. *Simple Stakes a Claim.* New York: Rinehart, 1957.

———. *Simple's Uncle Sam.* New York: Hill & Wang, 1965.

———. *Simple Takes a Wife.* New York: Simon & Schuster, 1953.

———. *Something Uncommon and Other Stories.* New York: Hill & Wang, 1963.

———. *The Ways of White Folk.* New York: Knopf, 1934.

Hughes, Steven C. *Langston Hughes and the Blues.* Normal: University of Illinois Press, 1988.

Meltzer, Milton. *Hughes: A Biography.* New York: Harper & Row, 1968.

Miller, R. Baxter. *The Art and Imagination of Hughes.* Lexington: University Press of Kentucky, 1991.

O'Daniel, Therman B., ed. *Langston Hughes, Black Genius: A Critical Evaluation.* New York: Morrow, 1971.

Ostrom, Hans. *Langston Hughes: A Study of the Short Fiction.* New York: Twayne, 1993.

Rampersad, Arnold. *The Life of Langston Hughes: I, Too, Sing America (1902–41),* vol. 1. New York: Oxford University Press, 1986.

———. *The Life of Hughes: I Dream a World (1941–1967),* vol. 2. New York: Oxford University Press, 1988.

Rummel, Jack. *Langston Hughes.* New York: Chelsea House, 1988.

Snyder, Phillip A. "Langston Hughes." In *Reference Guide to Short Fiction.* Edited by Noelle Watson. Detroit: Gale Press, 1994, 256–58.

HUGO AWARD

The Science Fiction Achievement Award given annually since 1955 in honor of Hugo Gernsback (therefore referred to almost exclusively as the Hugo). It is an "amateur" award: Recipients are chosen by SCIENCE FICTION readers and fans, as opposed to other science fiction awards, such as the NEBULA, which are given at the recommendation of professional panels or readers.

HURSTON, ZORA NEALE (1891?–1960)

Born in Eatonville, Florida, Zora Neale Hurston—although she died in poverty and obscurity—is recognized today as the best African-American woman writer before World War II. Despite her abusive father, who often mistreated his wife and eight children, Hurston had a mother who encouraged achievement and success, and grew up in a town devoid of racism: Eatonville was an all-black town. Hurston's successes were remarkable. She studied at Howard University with Alain Locke, whose anthology, *The New Negro,* published in 1925, was to revolutionize the black arts, and at Barnard College with Franz Boas, a prominent anthropologist who encouraged Hurston's interest in African and African-American FOLKLORE. With Langston Hughes and Wallace Thurman, Hurston established *Fire!!,* a magazine devoted to black literature; the magazine also published "SWEAT," one of Hurston's best stories.

With the publication of some of her earlier stories, Hurston embarked on a career of folklorist and fiction writer, merging both interests in her stories and novels, most of which are characterized by realistic details of African-American culture and DIALECT (see REALISM). Her two most frequently anthologized stories are "THE GILDED SIX-BITS" and "Sweat," tales that present a complex portrait of African-American characters and culture. Indeed, Hurston was criticized by a number of men with whom she was associated in the HARLEM RENAISSANCE: both Langston Hughes and Richard WRIGHT deplored her refusal of allegiance to racial and political causes and, in return, the resolutely nonideological Hurston called the major intellectuals and artists in Harlem culture "the niggerati."

Her iconoclastic vision produced an admirable body of work, including eight short stories. Three of the most notable appeared in *Opportunity*: "Drenched in Light" depicts a young girl similar to Hurston; "Muttsy" portrays a marriage that seems doomed to fail, and "Spunk," in which Hurston deploys MAGICAL REALISM, is actually a GHOST STORY relating the haunting of a husband who has just murdered his wife's lover. Hurston wrote four novels (*Jonah's Gourd Vine*, published in 1934; *Moses, Man of the Mountain,* in 1935; the acclaimed *Their Eyes Were Watching God*, in 1937; and *Seraph on the Suwanee*, in 1948), and numerous essays, articles, and literary reviews for newspapers and magazines. Her two folklore collections are *Mules and Men* (1935) and *Tell My Horse* (1938), and she published her much admired autobiography, *Dust Tracks on a Road*, in 1942, for which Hurston's picture appeared on the cover of the *Saturday Review of Literature*. After the 1930s, however, and with the GREAT DEPRESSION effectively ending the Harlem Renaissance, Hurston, whose seemingly conservative views alienated her from the black community and the black press, supported herself by working as a maid. She died in the poorhouse in Saint Lucie County, Florida, and was buried in a grave that remained unmarked until the writer Alice WALKER discovered it and placed a gravestone on it. As Hurston's biographer Robert Hemenway points out, more of her work is in print today than at any point during Hurston's lifetime (Hemenway, "ZNH" 1537).

BIBLIOGRAPHY

Awkward, Michael, ed. *New Essays on Their Eyes Were Watching God*. New York: Cambridge University Press, 1990.

Bloom, Harold, ed. *Zora Neale Hurston*. New York: Chelsea House, 1986.

Curry, Renee R. "Zora Neale Hurston." In *Reader's Guide to Short Fiction*. Edited by Noelle Watson. Detroit: St. James Press, 1993, p. 259–59.

Hemenway, Robert E. *Zora Neale Hurston: A Literary Biography*. Normal: University of Illinois Press, 1977.

———. "Zora Neale Hurston." In *The Heath Anthology of American Literature*. Vol. 2 Edited by Paul Lauter. Lexington, Mass: D. C. Heath and Company, pp. 1535–37.

Hurston, Zora Neale. *Dust Tracks on a Road: An Autobiography*. Philadelphia: Lippincott, 1942.

———. *Jonah's Gourd Vine*. Philadelphia: Lippincott, 1934.

———. *I Love Myself When I am Laughing . . . and Then Again When I am Looking Mean and Impressive: A Hurston Reader*. Edited by Alice Walker. Old Westbury, N.Y.: Feminist Press, 1979.

———. *Moses, Man of the Mountain*. Philadelphia: Lippincott,1939.

———. *Mules and Men*. Philadelphia: Lippincott, 1935.

———. *Seraph on the Sewanee*. New York: Scribner's, 1948.

———. *Spunk: The Selected Stories*. Berkeley, Calif.: Turtle Island, 1985.

———. *Tell My Horse*. Philadelphia: Lippincott, Berkeley, Cal., Turtle Island, 1938; as *Voodoo Gods: An Inquiry into Native Myths and Magic in Jamaica and Haiti*. London: Dent, 1939.

———. *Their Eyes Were Watching God*. Philadelphia: Lippincott, 1937.

Hurston, Zora Neale, ed. *Caribbean Melodies for Chorus of Mixed Voices and Soloists*. Philadelphia: Ditson, 1947.

Nathiri, N. Y., ed. *Zora! A Woman and Her Community*. Orlando, Fl.: Sentinel Communications, 1991.

Turner, Darwin T. *In a Minor Chord: Three Afro-American Writers and Their Search for Identity*. Carbondale: Southern Illinois University Press, 1971.

HYPERBOLE

HYPERBOLE   This figure of speech, which in Greek means "overshooting," is bold overstatement, or extravagant exaggeration of fact, used either for serious or comic effect. Understatement is the opposite of hyperbole.

I

"I'M A FOOL" SHERWOOD ANDERSON
(1923) The myth about Sherwood ANDERSON—
that in the middle of a successful advertising career
he repudiated the moneymaking ethics and the reg-
imentation of business in order to realize himself as
a writer—has become part of our literary tradition,
an ironic reversal of the Horatio ALGER myth. After
working in advertising for 12 years, he realized that
he was being dishonest with words and dishonest
with himself. He wanted to uproot himself, to walk
out the door and out of that baleful phase of his life.
Thus he walked away from his desk and out of
town. The central concern of the stories for which
Anderson is celebrated today is that of young boys
growing into manhood. This THEME links his CLASSIC
cycle of related stories about Winesburg, Ohio, and
the subject of *Horses and Men* (1923) and its three
famous monologues that recapture his summers at
the race tracks: "I Want to Know Why," "The Man
Who Became a Woman," and "I'm a Fool."

In these oral narratives, the racetrack setting and
the sounds and earthy smells of the stables, the
closeness of horses and men, represent the easy, intimate, and idyllic relationship that Anderson was
convinced existed between human beings and the
natural world before the onslaught of the machine.
Like the raft and the river in Mark TWAIN's
Huckleberry Finn, the stables and the racetrack are
places of contentment and escape, EDENIC oases for
the adamic adolescent. Horses in this context
embody the noble fulfillment of purposeful nature;
they are dependable, honest, and fine, while adults
are ambiguous, devious, and phony. Each of these
three monologues is a tale of resistance to the loss of
boyhood innocence and of reluctant initiation into
the complexities of manhood, especially the shadowy complexities of adult sexuality.

The emotional tone of these tales, on which so
much of their lasting appeal is based, mixes boyish
bewilderment, frustration, and vulnerability. The
boy-man in each suffers from feelings of inferiority
(social and sexual), and he speaks from the depths
of his being, confessing his burden of guilt and confusion in order to come to terms with it and to sub-
due it forever. His pitiful search for the meaning of
the experience, for understanding, is his reason for
telling the story, for taking us into his confidence.

Although the main incident in "I'm a Fool" has
occurred some time before the telling of the tale, the
big lumbering fellow who confesses it still fails to
understand why it happened. He had told a lie to
impress the young woman with whom he is in love,
but he blames his foolishness on "the dude in the
Windsor tie" and on being slightly drunk, not on the
unresolved conflict of values that is tearing him up
inside, the conflict between life in the stables and
life in the grandstand. He is in mild revolt against
the dude's false air and against the false respectability of his middle-class mother and his schoolteacher

sister—respectability imposed by a binding morality and a restrictive society where money and position are at stake. Yet even he capitulates to the social importance of appearances when he meets the girl in the soft blue dress. And when he must, he, too, can put up a good front; deceiving comes easily when he is at the mercy of economic and social forces beyond his control. It is only afterward, on the beach, against the background of a clump of roots sticking up like arms, that he realizes that his denial of his origins, of his identity, will hold him back from the fulfillment of the tenderness and love that he feels. But he never understands why.

Anderson's main techniques in dramatizing the story are to convert the oral monologue into a dialogue and a series of incremental dramatic scenes, and to rearrange time in an orderly manner. The unskilled speaker in the story, unable to control his responses, rambles and runs on, in and out of time, relating events that occured in the past, events that occured on the day of the races (which was some time ago, before PROHIBITION), and disclosing his present, compulsive desire to make himself look cheap. That the story should adapt to a dramatic form as faithfully as it does attests to Anderson's painstaking, original craftsmanship and to his finesse in making colloquial conversation—essentially, an ancient way of storytelling—serve the needs of modern fiction and drama. In Anderson's dramatic monologue, the artless rambling of the boy-man, not only continuously reveals his CHARACTER in ways he does not even suspect but also artfully pushes the action forward.

Anderson sold "I'm a Fool" to the literary magazine the DIAL for less than $100 because he could not successfully sell it to the mass market, where editors found it unfinished and vague. But so was life, Anderson argued, and he continued to write stories that an admiring Virginia Woolf was later to call "shell-less"—stories that exposed the vulnerable areas and the secrets of thwarted lives and that illuminated the obscure realm of personal relationships.

By the example of the crisis in his own life, Sherwood Anderson is said to have liberated man from timetable servitude to business; by the example of his art, he is said to have liberated the short story from its previous dependence on slick plots and trick endings. Generations of writers have followed and will continue to follow his example in both areas. Almost all good modern fiction writers, including Ernest HEMINGWAY and William FAULKNER, whom Anderson so generously helped at the beginning of their literary careers, are beholden to him. Although Sherwood Anderson was a provincial in his choice of subject matter, in his concentration on the limited lives of limited human beings, he was a pioneer in his narrative techniques. (See POINT OF VIEW.)

BIBLIOGRAPHY

Anderson, Sherwood. *The Portable Sherwood Anderson.* Edited by Horace Gregory. New York: Viking, 1949.

———. *Sherwood Anderson: Short Stories.* Edited by Maxwell Geismar. New York: Hill & Wang, 1962.

———. *Winesburg, Ohio.* Edited by Malcolm Cowley. New York: Viking, 1960.

Papinchak, Robert Allen. *Sherwood Anderson: A Study of the Short Fiction.* New York: Twayne, 1992.

Small, Judy Jo. *A Reader's Guide to the Short Stories of Sherwod Anderson.* New York: G. K. Hall, 1994.

IMAGERY The term refers to the collection or pattern of images, the representations of the sensory details in a literary work. Images typically employ one or more of the five senses (sight, sound, touch, taste, smell). For example, Nathaniel Hawthorne's "RAPPACCINI'S DAUGHTER" relies heavily on visual and olfactory (evoking the sense of smell) imagery to evoke the alluring but poisonous beauty of Dr. Rappaccini's garden.

"INDIAN CAMP" ERNEST HEMINGWAY (1924) Originally printed in the April 1924 *Transatlantic Review* as "Work in Progress," and published the following year as part of IN OUR TIME, "Indian Camp" is Ernest HEMINGWAY's earliest NICK ADAMS story. It focuses primarily on the relationship between father and son, and on its attendant rites of initiation into the world of adult experience: childbirth, suicide, loss of innocence.

The boy, Nick Adams, accompanies his doctor father to the Indian camp where a pregnant woman has serious complications as she labors to give birth. Dr. Adams ultimately saves her life and that of the baby by performing a Cesarean operation, but, shortly afterward, the woman's husband commits suicide. A number of specific questions have puzzled critics for decades: Why does the Indian husband kill himself? What is Uncle George's role, and why does he disappear by the end of the story? How are we supposed to feel toward Dr. Adams? Though the story is consistently read as a father-son initiation tale, these sorts of questions encourage readers to look beyond the simple and benevolent fact that Dr. Adams almost surely saved the life of the Indian woman and her baby, and focus attention on some of the more disturbing aspects of the story. First, the Indian woman's screams have been going on for a long time, so long that the men of the village have purposely moved out of earshot; but Dr. Adams tells Nick that the screams "are not important" (IC 68) and chooses not to hear them. As a doctor, he may adopt this attitude as a professional necessity in order to accomplish the difficult task of performing the operation without anesthetic. Conversely, it may indicate his callousness to the woman's evident pain.

Readers' views of Dr. Adams may then influence the way they interpret the Indian husband's suicide: Why does he slit his throat moments after Dr. Adams has operated and the baby is successfully delivered? Do readers see a connection between the presence of Uncle George and the husband's decision to kill himself? Is Uncle George the father of the baby, as some critics suggest? Readers must also decide whether Uncle George's remark to Dr. Adams, "Oh, you're a great man, all right" (IC 69), is meant seriously or sarcastically. Hemingway's oblique and sparse writing style encourages such open-ended questions, and his ending to the story refuses to settle on a single, clear resolution. A short burst of questions from Nick to his father on the significance of life and death leave him with this final thought: "he felt quite sure he would never die" (IC 70). Nick's reflections on immortality, here in the protective warmth of his father's arms, may represent his last moments of youthful innocence before he falls into such adult experiences as romance and war in the later chapters of *In Our Time.*

BIBLIOGRAPHY
Hemingway, Ernest. "Indian Camp." In *The Complete Short Stories of Ernest Hemingway.* New York: Scribner's, 1987, pp. 65–70.
Smith, Paul. *A Reader's Guide to the Short Stories of Ernest Hemingway.* Boston: G.K. Hall, 1989.

Amy Strong
University of North Carolina at Chapel Hill

IN OUR TIME ERNEST HEMINGWAY (1925, 1930)

The publishing dates, the authoritative text, even the genre of the text all prove intensely problematic for Ernest Hemingway's early stories and arguably his best sustained work. Published in Paris in 1924 as *in our time,* a series of vignettes, it was published in New York in 1925 in an expanded version entitled *In Our Time.* When either literary scholars or the popular audience refers to the "Hemingway style," it is the style of *in our time* (and of *The Sun Also Rises,* published one year later) that people have in mind. Among the best-known stories in the collection are "BIG TWO-HEARTED RIVER" and "Indian Camp," featuring NICK ADAMS, their modernist PROTAGONIST. (See MODERNISM.)

Sometimes regarded as a mere collection of short stories, sometimes seen as a SHORT STORY CYCLE in the vein of James Joyce's *Dubliners,* sometimes heralded as the literary descendent of Sherwood ANDERSON's WINESBURG, OHIO, Hemingway's *in our time* has more in common with Jean TOOMER's *CANE*—another textually and generically complicated work—than with any other well-known work. In fact, the "pretty good unity" (to cite Hemingway's own words about *in our time;* Baker 26) that characterizes both *in our time* and *Cane* might accurately be described as an ironically fragmentary unity, in which dissonance is an integral part of both structure and THEME. In other words, the fragments themselves contribute to a peculiar sort of unity.

The best discussion of the complicated publishing of the works that finally constitute *in our time* is

Michael J. Reynolds's "Hemingway's *In Our Time:* The Biography of a Book." Beginning with "My Old Man" and "Out of Season" (the first of which is clearly indebted to Anderson), portions of what would finally make *in our time* were published as *Three Stories & Ten Poems* in 1923. The same year, six of the vignettes or "interchapters" that would finally be interlaced between the nominal 14 stories of the 1925 publication were published in *little review,* one of the most influential of the LITTLE MAGAZINES. The following year 18 sketches (two of which would be retitled as short stories in the 1925 version) were published as a small chapbook entitled *in our time* (Paris: Three Mountains Press). Over 1924 and the first half of 1925, numerous individual short stories that would be collected in *in our time* also appeared in a variety of journals. However, in 1925 the first major version of *In Our Time* as we know it was published by Boni & Liveright, including 16 sketches (called "chapters" but unlisted on the contents page) and 14 short stories. In 1930 a new piece (similar in tone to the vignettes or chapters) prefaced the work and was called "An Introduction by the Author"; it would later be retitled as "In the Quai at Smyrna" (first in *The First Forty-Nine Stories*) and later in the republication of *In Our Time* by Scribner's in 1955.

It is little wonder that Hemingway's highly influential and earliest sustained artistic work has proven so critically elusive. Of the individual short stories comprising *in our time,* possibly "Indian Camp" and the two-part "Big Two-Hearted River" are the best known. As these two short stories might suggest, many of the nominal short stories in *In Our Time* roughly tell the story of Nick Adams (sometimes considered to be a surrogate for Hemingway himself), first growing up in Michigan (with a doctor for a father), rejecting early relationships with women, exploring Europe, then facing both WORLD WAR I and its aftermath. These stories—as well as others, such as "Mr. and Mrs. Elliot," "Soldier's Home," or "Cat in the Rain"—have much in common with Hemingway's subsequent work, *The Sun Also Rises* (SAR)—the work that became known as the hallmark of the "Lost Generation" (a phrase Gertrude STEIN used dis-

missively and which Hemingway reproduced as the epigraph to *Sun*). At least superficially, the stories seem to record a certain ennui, a loss of faith in traditional ideals and values, and a certain resignation to an emasculated and impoverished modern world. Taken with the interchapters, a series of vignettes appearing between longer stories, (at least one of which, "Chapter VI," includes Nick), however, the collected stories and volume *In Our Time* make a heavy indictment against the war, violence, even misogyny that the stories alone appear partially to record, if not condone. In fact, the brutal violence of bullfighting and war depicted in the interchapters seems the logical extension of the accounts of fishing or boxing found in the stories. Read as a collective work, *In Our Time* ironically dismantles the patriarchal, if not sexist, assumptions that past scholarship wrongly attributed to the author as the "HEMINGWAY CODE," and strongly suggests that the supposedly innocent age preceding World War I was not so innocent after all.

Despite the controversies and complications of *in our time,* stylistically this work changed modern American prose. The rigorous, terse, realistic style that Hemingway created in this work (albeit with notable and unusual uses of repetition—all stylistic strategies he may have learned from Gertrude Stein) has been imitated frequently but rarely matched. How Hemingway accomplished this artistic feat is at least partially recorded in his posthumously published *A Moveable Feast,* an autobiographical narrative (and partial fiction) that records his life during the writing of *in our time.*

BIBLIOGRAPHY

Frye, Northrup. *Anatomy of Criticism.* Princeton, N.J.: Princeton University Press, 1957, 365.

Hemingway, Ernest. *In Our Time.* New York: Boni & Liveright. 1925, 1930; Reprint, New York: Scribner's 1958, 1970.

———. Letter to E. Wilson, October 18, 1924, p. 26 in Carlos Baker. *Ernest Hemingway: A Life Story.* New York: Scribner's, 1967.

Moddlemog, Deborah. "The Unifying Consciousness of a Divided Conscience: Nick Adams as Author of *In Our Time.*" *American Literature* (1988): 591–610.

Reynolds, Michael. *Critical Essays on Hemingway's In Our Time.* 1983.
———. "Hemingway's *In Our Time:* The Biography of a Book." In *Modern American Short Story Sequences.* Edited by Gerald Kennedy. New York: Cambridge University Press, 1995.
Smith, Paul. *A Reader's Guide to the Short Stories of Ernest Hemingway.* 1989.
Wagner-Martin, Linda. "Toomer's *Cane* as Narrative Sequence." In *Modern American Short Story Sequences.* Edited by Gerald Kennedy. New York: Cambridge University Press, 1995.
Winn, H. "Hemingway's *In Our Time:* 'Pretty Good Unity'" *Hemingway Review* (1990): 124–40.

Jacqueline Vaught Brogan
University of Notre Dame

INTENTIONAL FALLACY

A critical term that means the author's stated or implied intentions may well be fallacious, misleading, or even useless for the reader who interprets the author's work, because the author's design or plan in writing the work may not correspond to what was actually produced. In other words, a reader's reliance on an author's intention when writing the piece may lead the reader to an erroneous interpretation. Intentional fallacy suggests that the true meaning of a work should be found only by analyzing the actual text without any reference to the author's avowed or supposed purpose, which may introduce factors personal to the author, such as state of mind, that could be irrelevant to the actual work.

IRONY

An author's use of a reality different from the one that the fictional characters apprehend. Irony is normally divided into two types: verbal irony, in which the tone of the narrator or speaker contradicts the spoken words, and dramatic irony, in which the reader understands a state of affairs more fully than the character or characters do; it is usually the reverse of the reality the characters perceive.

IRVING, WASHINGTON (1783–1859)

Born in New York City and named after the Revolutionary War hero and first president of the United States, Washington Irving is considered the first American author and short story writer. His life roughly spanned the period between the REVOLUTIONARY WAR and the CIVIL WAR. Although he was trained for a profession in law and worked in business for a time, Irving's real interest was writing. In 1808–09, he wrote much of *Salamagundi*, a satirical magazine, in collaboration with his brother William and brother-in-law James Kirke Paulding, demonstrating his talent and potential. *Diedrich Knickerbocker's History of New York*, published in 1809, a BURLESQUE account of Dutch colonists in New York, earned him literary recognition. The work solidified the term for the KNICKERBOCKER school, a literary circle influenced by the wits associated with *Salamagundi*; it included William Cullen Bryant, James Fenimore Cooper, and Clement Clark Moore.

It was Irving's *The Sketch Book*, however, published serially in both England and the United States from 1819 to 1820, that became the first American book to win international recognition. Cooper, considered the first significant American novelist, provided Irving's only competition, and Irving remains secure in his position as the first significant short story writer. Moreover, his belief that the new country provided a unique opportunity for a national literature, and his recognition of the story as a distinct form of fiction, helped pave the way for such great writers as Nathaniel HAWTHORNE and Herman MELVILLE in the generation that succeeded him. Groups such as the southwestern humorists, tellers of TALL TALES, learned from Irving to use details from American country life to achieve noteworthy effect in their writings.

The Sketch Book, also narrated by Diedrich Knickerbocker but set in rural New York, is a collection of the short tales, essays, and occasional pieces, including "THE LEGEND OF SLEEPY HOLLOW" and "RIP VAN WINKLE," the two stories that have entered the realm of American MYTH. In both tales Irving employs the supernatural in a comic way to achieve the resolution of the action, and uses these techniques again in "The Specter Bridegroom," another well-known tale from *The Sketch Book*.

When a bridegroom dies on the way to his wedding, a friend impersonates him. The bride's family subsequently learns that the bridegroom has died, but they believe simply that they have seen his ghost. Ultimately, the "specter" returns and elopes with the bride.

The Sketch Book was written during the 17 years that Irving lived abroad, finding an international audience. During these expatriate years, Irving wrote *Bracebridge Hall*, a series of sketches about British country life and characters, published in 1822, and the less successful *Tales of a Traveller*, published in 1824. Its best known story is "The Adventure of a German Student," a bizarre GHOST STORY set in Paris during the French Revolution. Irving used the pseudonym of GEOFFREY CRAYON when writing these three books of stories. Though some are more successful than others, taken together they illustrate his comprehensive vision of the components of the American tale: clear, engaging prose, sharp visual images, and a conscious use of native material. Moreover, he understood the significance of the role of the imagination and the relative insignificance of the artist in a materialistic society, the vacuum created in a culture that looked only to the present, and the need for American fiction to identify a specific historical context (McQuade 788). By creating Sleepy Hollow, Irving became the first of numerous American writers to invent a mythic locus for his stories, just as William FAULKNER later invented in his YOKNAPATAWPHA COUNTY, John STEINBECK his SALINAS VALLEY, or Eudora WELTY her MORGANA, MISSISSIPPI.

During his years in Spain, Irving published *The Alhambra*, another collection of tales published in 1931 and commonly known as "the Spanish Sketch Book." Irving actually lived in the Alhambra, in Granada, while writing these tales, and they were very well received, particularly "The Legend of the Rose of Alhambra" and "The Legend of the Moors." This collection marked the end of Irving's career as a fiction writer, however. While in Spain he had also written a biography of Christopher Columbus, and with his return to the United States—cloaked with him an international reputation and an honorary

degree from Oxford University—he channeled his talents into history and biography.

Although he was first and foremost a writer, over the years Irving served in many positions, including magazine editor, New York State militia colonel, businessman, and diplomat. During the final years of his life, while living at Sunnyside, the house he had purchased in Tarrytown, New York, this quintessential American writer wrote a five-volume biography of George Washington. Irving died shortly after publishing the first volume.

BIBLIOGRAPHY

Alderman, Ralph, ed. *Washington Irving Reconsidered: A Symposium.* Hartford: Transcendental Books, 1969.

Antelyes, Peter. *Tales of Adventurous Enterprise: Irving and the Poetics of Western Expansion.* New York: Columbia University Press, 1990.

Bowden, Mary Weatherspoon. *Washington Irving.* Boston: Twayne, 1981.

Brooks, Van Wyck. *The World of Washington Irving.* New York: E.P. Dutton, 1944.

Dorsky, Jeffrey Rubin. *Adrift in the Old World: The Psychological Pilgrimage of Irving.* 1988.

Hedges, William L. *Irving: An American Study 1802–1835.* Baltimore: Johns Hopkins Press, 1965.

Irving, Pierre M. *Life and Letters of Irving.* 4 vols. New York: Putnam, 1862–64.

Irving, Washington. *Complete Works.* Richard Dilworth, Rust et al., eds. Boston: Twayne; Madison: University of Wisconsin Press, 1969–1989.

———. *The Complete Tales* of Washington Irving. Edited by Charles Neider. Garden City, N.Y.: Doubleday, 1975.

———. *The Sketchbook of Geoffrey Crayon, Gent.* Edited by Haskell Springer. Boston: Twayne, 1978.

———. *Washington Irving: History, Tales and Sketches.* Edited by James W. Tuttleton. New York: Library of America, 1983.

Kime, Wayne R. *Pierre M. Irving and Washington Irving: A Collaboration in Life and Letters.* Waterloo, Ont.: Wilfred Laurier University Press, 1977.

Leary, Lewis. *Irving.* Minneapolis: University of Minnesota Press, 1963.

McQuade, Donald, ed. "Washington Irving." In *The Harper American Literature.* Vol 1. New York: Harper & Row, 1987, pp. 785–90.

Myers, Andrew B., ed. *A Century of Commentary on the Works of Irving.* Tarrytown N.Y.: Sleepy Hollow Restorations, 1976.

————. *The Worlds of Irving.* Tarrytown N.Y.: Sleepy Hollow Restorations, 1974.

Reichart, Walter A. *Irving and Germany.* Ann Arbor: University of Michigan Press, 1957.

Roth, Martin. *Comedy and America: The Lost World of Irving.* Port Washington, N.Y.: Kennikat, 1976.

Rubin-Dorsky, Jeffrey. *Adrift in the Old World: The Psychological Pilgrimage of Irving.* Chicago: University of Chicago Press, 1988.

Wagenknecht, Edward. *Irving: Moderation Displayed.* New York: Oxford University Press, 1962.

Williams, Stanley T. *The Life of Irving.* 2 Vols. New York: Oxford University Press,1935.

Woodress, James. "Washington Irving." In *Reader's Guide to Short Fiction.* Edited by Noelle Watson. Detroit: St. James Press, 1993, pp. 262–65.

ISAAC (IKE) MCCASLIN

The chief character of William FAULKNER's *GO DOWN, MOSES,* Isaac McCaslin matures from boyhood to manhood in this SHORT STORY CYCLE. A curious figure in the BILDUNGSROMAN, Ike easily captures our sympathy as he tests and ultimately proves his manhood in a series of hunts for Old Ben, the bear in the story "THE BEAR." Therein Ike learns that ownership of property (nature) is analogous to owning slaves, and therefore wrong; he firmly rejects both courses. Ike also forfeits his wife and all possibility of children, however. As he grows older, his limitations become increasingly noticeable until, in "Delta Autumn," his rejection of the nameless black woman and distant relative ultimately displays his inability to surmount racial prejudice, and, feminist critics would argue, a latent misogyny.

"I STAND HERE IRONING" TILLIE OLSEN (1956)

"I Stand Here Ironing," first published in *Prairie Schooner* as "Help Her to Believe," became the opening story of Tillie OLSEN's collection *Tell Me a Riddle* (1961). It is a mother's monologue, instigated by a school counselor's request that she come in to discuss her daughter Emily. She recalls the obstacles she faced as a single mother during the GREAT DEPRESSION and their inevitable consequences on her first born. She was forced to send Emily to live with her in-laws on two different occasions when she could not find work. When she was working and they were able to be together, she had to leave her daughter in inadequate day care with indifferent caretakers. She regrets the effect of her worries on Emily, especially when she compares Emily's good behavior to the stubborn demands of the younger children in the family. Even after her second marriage, when circumstances improved, mother and daughter were again separated when she was convinced to send Emily, who was not recovering well from the measles, away to convalesce. But the convalescent home's rules, which restricted parental contact and discouraged close attachments, only taught Emily isolation.

Thin and awkward as a young girl, labeled "slow" at school, Emily faced difficulties and disappointments in her peer world that were exacerbated by her family's frequent moves. She resented her younger, more attractive, and more outgoing sister, Susan. She had to help care for her four younger siblings, whose needs often took precedence, leaving little time for her to attend to her schoolwork or for her mother to attend to her. Forced to become self-sufficient at an early age, she learned not to need attention and came to shun her mother's efforts to nurture her.

Her talent as an actor brought her attention and success: audiences loved her humor and charisma. But her mother lacked the means to support her daughter's talent with acting lessons, and Emily was left to develop her gift on her own. The mother knows Emily probably will never realize her full potential. Emily's happiness when she bounds in at the end of the story reassures her mother, but the fatalism of her daughter's final remark—that she is not going to take her midterm examinations because "in a couple of years when we'll all be atom-dead they won't matter a bit" (ISHI 11)—depresses her. Within her realistic resignation to the circumstances of her daughter's life lies her decision to "Let her be" and her hope: "Help her to know," she asks, "that she is more than this dress on the ironing board, helpless before the iron" (ISHI 12).

BIBLIOGRAPHY

Bauer, Helen Pike. "A Child of anxious, not proud, love': Mother and Daughter in Tillie Olsen's 'I Stand Here Ironing.'" In *Mother Puzzles: Daughters and Mothers in Contemporary American Literature*. Edited by Mickey Pearlman. Westport, Conn.: Greenwood, 1989.

Coiner, Constance. *Better Red: The Writing and Resistance of Tillie Olsen and Meridel Le Sueur*. New York: Oxford University Press, 1995.

Faulkner, Mara. *Protest and Possibility in the Writing of Tillie Olsen*. Charlottesville: University Press of Virginia, 1994.

Frye, Joanne S. "'I Stand Here Ironing': Motherhood as Experience and Metaphor." In *The Critical Response to Tillie Olsen*. Edited by Kay Hoyle Nelson and Nancy Huse. Westport, Conn.: Greenwood, 1994.

———. *Tillie Olsen: A Study of the Short Fiction*. New York: Macmillan, 1995.

Olsen, Tillie. *Tell Me a Riddle* Chicago: Lippincott, 1961.

Orr, Elaine Neil. *Tillie Olsen and a Feminist Spiritual Vision*. Jackson: University Press of Mississippi, 1987.

Pearlman, Mickey, and Abby H. P. Werlock. *Tillie Olsen*. New York: Twayne, 1991.

Kelley Reames
University of North Carolina at Chapel Hill

J

JACK POTTER The town marshal of Yellow Sky, Texas, (in Stephen Crane's "THE BRIDE COMES TO YELLOW SKY.") Without disclosing his intentions, Potter has traveled to San Antonio, taken a bride, and is returning to Yellow Sky feeling he has betrayed his neighbors by marrying. As he sneaks back to his house from the train station with his bride, he accidentally encounters his nemesis, Scratchy Wilson, a gunslinger, the last of a gang who lived in Yellow Sky. In a comical exchange, Potter subdues the dumbfounded Wilson. The encounter represents the domestication of the town, the end of lawlessness, and the promise of civic order.

JACKSON, SHIRLEY (HARDIE) (1919–1965) Although Shirley Jackson wrote six novels and approximately 100 short stories, she is identified almost exclusively with one story, "THE LOTTERY" (1949), which describes the ritualistic murder of a housewife in a small American town. The THEME of this story is a terrifying one, memorable for the way it sweeps aside romantic notions of rural folk, but Jackson's stories covered the spectrum from the fantastic to the realistic to the humorous. Her early fiction often dealt with socially sensitive topics such as racism ("After You, My Dear Alphonse" and "Flower Garden"), and mental retardation ("Behold the Child Among His Newborn Blisses"). The stories included in the collection *The Lottery, or, the Adventures of James Harris* often combine REALISM with the fantastic, and typically portray a significant threat to at least one character's well-being, usually a woman's. Jackson's later work included stories that explored unbalanced minds and bizarre situations, as well as humorous sketches about family life, many based on personal experience. Her stories appeared in magazines as disparate as the NEW YORKER, LADIES' HOME JOURNAL, *Playboy*, and HARPER'S. Jackson was recipient of the Mystery Writers of American Edgar Allan Poe Award in 1961.

BIBLIOGRAPHY

Byall, Joan Wylie. *Shirley Jackson: A Study of the Short Fiction.* New York: Twayne Publishers, 1993.

Hyman, Stanley Edgar, ed. *Come Along with Me.* New York: Viking Press, 1968.

Jackson, Shirley. *Hangsaman.* New York; Farrar, Straus and Young, 1951.

———. *Life Among the Savages.* New York; Farrar, Straus and Young, 1953.

———. *The Lottery; or, The Adventures of James Harris.* New York; Farrar, Straus, 1949.

———. *The Magic of Shirley Jackson.* 1966.

———. *Raising Demons.* New York; Farrar, Straus and Cudahy, 1957.

———. *The Sundial.* New York; Farrar, Straus and Cudahy, 1958.

———. *We Have Always Lived in the Castle.* New York: Viking Press, 1962.

JACKSON, THOMAS JONATHAN ("STONEWALL") (1824–1863)

A Confederate general in the U.S. CIVIL WAR, Jackson won his sobriquet at the first battle of Bull Run, when he and his brigade "stood like a stone wall" against union attacks. He was General Robert E. LEE's most able and trusted lieutenant and played a major role in the Confederate victory at the second battle of Bull Run, the standoff at Antietam, and the victories at Fredricksburg and Chancellorsville. While returning from a reconnaisance during this latter battle, Jackson was mortally wounded by gunfire from his own troops. Stonewall Jackson is alluded to in stories of the Civil War as well as in more modern war stories such as Barry Hannah's "Midnight and I'm Not Famous Yet."

JAMES, HENRY (1843–1916)

Along with Edgar Allan POE, one of the foremost practitioners of the short story. An American expatriate who had been reared in both New York and Europe, James the writer considered the American scene from afar, most often from Lamb House, his residence in Rye, England. Known today—at least in scholarly circles—as much for his theories of literature as for his writing, James's contributions to the modern story can hardly be overstated. Although he did in fact write more about the novel than about the short story, his theories apply to all fiction. James was an ardent practitioner of the short story and the NOVELLA—*nouvelle* was his preferred term—publishing 112 stories and novellas between 1864 and 1910. Never known for their fast pace, compression, or dramatic action, James's stories are remarkable for their meticulous psychological shadings and for their use of the author's "central intelligence" device, the gradual revealing of facts, emotion, or action through the thoughts of a character, usually a pivotal one.

Although James has been compared with Nathaniel HAWTHORNE as an important American writer of short fiction, Hawthorne in no sense developed or evolved in the notable ways that James progressed. Because his work was published over so many decades, James's fiction is customarily divided into three phases or periods: early, middle, and late. In terms of short fiction, DAISY MILLER represents work of the early period, "THE REAL THING" and *THE TURN OF THE SCREW* the middle, and "THE BEAST IN THE JUNGLE" the late. The stories also may be grouped under several well-established THEMES. Among the most prominent are the international theme, exemplified in such early stories as *Daisy Miller,* "A Passionate Pilgrim," " A Bundle of Letters," or "An International Episode," and in such late and admired stories as "The Marriages," "The Bench of Desolation," and "The Beast in the Jungle." Another significant theme involves artists and writers, exemplified in, for instance, "The Lesson of the Master," "The Real Thing," and "The Figure in the Carpet." Still other important themes include supernatural or ghostly ones—but always overlaid with the psychological, as in "The Turn of the Screw," "The Altar of the Dead," "The Great Good Place," and "THE JOLLY CORNER," which also uses the motif of the double or DOPPELGANGER. Further, James wrote tales that evoke social COMEDY or TRAGEDY. Some of the previously mentioned stories fall under the rubric of comedy ("An International Episode"); others include "The Point of View," "The Liar," "Lady Barbarina," and "The Birthplace." "EUROPE" and "The Beast in the Jungle" espouse tragic themes, as do such stories as "The Pupil," "Julia Bride," and "A Round of Visits" (Hocks 4–6).

The early James was a proponent of REALISM, or psychological realism, along with such writers as William Dean HOWELLS, Sarah Orne JEWETT, Mary E. Wilkins FREEMAN, Hamlin GARLAND, Kate CHOPIN, and others. As he moved beyond realism, or attempted to transcend it, he became less interested in action and increasingly interested in subtlety and nuance, psychology and perception. James became a British subject late in life, largely in reaction to his irritation with the reluctance of the United States to enter WORLD WAR I. He died at his home a year later.

BIBLIOGRAPHY

Anderson, Quentin. *The American Henry James.* New Brunswick, N.J.: Rutger's University Press, 1957.

Auchincloss, Louis. *Reading Henry James.* Minneapolis: University of Minnesota Press, 1975.

Dupee, F. W. *Henry James.* New York: Sloane, 1956.

Edel, Leon. *Henry James: A Life.* New York: Harper & Row, 1985.

Fogel, Daniel Mark. *Daisy Miller: A Dark Comedy of Manners.* Boston: Twayne, 1990.

Habegger, Alfred. *Henry James and the "Woman Business."* New York: Cambidge University Press, 1989.

Hall, Richard. "The Sexuality of Henry James," *New Republic,* April 28 and May 5, 1979.

Hocks, Richard A. *Henry James: A Study of the Short Fiction.* Boston: Twayne, 1990.

James, Henry. *The Complete Notebooks of Henry James,* ed. Leon Edel and Lyall Harris Powers. New York: Oxford University Press, 1987.

————. *Literary Criticism,* 2 vols. Edited by Leon Edel and Lyall H. Powers. Cambridge, England: Cambridge University Press, 1984.

————. *The Novels and Tales of Henry James.* New York Edition. 26 vols. New York: Scribner's 1907–1917.

————. *The Tales of Henry James.* 8 vols. (projected). Edited by Magbool Aziz. Oxford, Eng.: Oxford University Press, 1973– .

Jones, Vivian. *James the Critic.* New York: St. Martin's, 1985.

Poole, Adrian. *Henry James.* New York: St. Martin's, 1991.

Springer, Mary Doyle. *A Rhetoric of Literary Character: Some Women of Henry James.* Chicago: University of Chicago Press, 1978.

Tanner, Tony. *Henry James: The Writer and His Work.* Amherst: University of Massachusetts Press, 1985.

Weinstein, Philip M. *Henry James and the Requirements of the Imagination.* Cambridge, Mass.: Harvard University Press, 1971.

JEN, GISH (1955–)

Gish Jen grew up in Scarsdale, New York; her parents had immigrated to the United States from Shanghai during the 1940s. Jen graduated from Harvard with a B.A. in creative writing; she earned her M.F.A. degree from the Writers' Workshop at the University of Iowa in 1983. Before devoting herself to a writing career, she taught English in China and attended business school at Stanford. Her stories have appeared in the *Iowa Review, Yale Review, Southern Review,* NEW YORK-ER, ATLANTIC MONTHLY, and *Boston Globe Magazine.*

Her two novels and most of her semiautobiographical short stories (including the frequently anthologized "In the American Society" and "What Means Switch") explore the lives of the Chang family. Jen insists that while she is concerned with the phenomenon of outsiderness in American culture, particularly as it characterizes the Asian immigrant condition, her writing is most truly centered on an earnest fascination with America (*Heath* 10).

Her first novel, *Typical American* (1991), incorporated several of her early short stories; it was nominated for the National Book Critics Circle Award. Jen has received writing grants from a number of bodies including the NEA, the Guggenheim Foundation (see GUGGENHEIM GRANT), and the Massachusetts Artists Foundation.

BIBLIOGRAPHY

"Profile of Gish Jen." *Heath Anthology of American Literature Newsletter.* 1992. [http://www.georgetown.edu/tamlit/newsletter/numb8tex.html]

Satz, Martha. "Writing about Things that Are Dangerous: A Conversation with Gish Jen." *Southwest Review* (1993).

Keith Lawrence
Brigham Young University

JEREMIAD

In modern times a jeremiad may refer to any work that foretells destruction because of the evil of a group. Originally a severe expression of grief, a prolonged lamentation, or a complaint, the word derives from the biblical prophet Jeremiah, after whom the Old Testament book was named. The book of Jeremiah contains many autobiographical sections as well as descriptions of Jerusalem during the time of the fall of that city to the Babylonians in 586 B.C. In "Jeremiah's Lamentations," occuring in the midst of havoc and destruction, the prophet expresses his profound sorrow over the capture of Jerusalem and realizes that true religion lies in the heart rather than in the temple.

JESSE B. SIMPLE

Although early on in Langston HUGHES's so-called SIMPLE STORIES Jesse is referred to as Jesse B. Semple, in the bulk of the tales he is called Jesse B. Simple, the name by which he is commonly known and discussed today. Simple has been characterized as Harlem folk hero, African

American EVERYMAN, TRICKSTER, and the black counterpart of Mark TWAIN's Huck Finn. Simple offers his garrulous and comic but wise and perceptive insights into African American culture in conversations with Boyd, his friend and FOIL who narrates the tales. Boyd has been variously described as playing Boswell to Simple's Dr. Johnson and Watson to his Holmes. Simple, who uses street talk (see DIALECT), has both wives and girlfriends. Essentially a loner like Hughes himself, Simple, born out of Hughes's imagination during WORLD WAR II, "lived" into the era of civil rights. Through Simple, Hughes helped destroy the false STEREOTYPE of the African American male created by white society.

JEWETT, SARAH ORNE (1849–1909)

Now known mainly as a New England regional writer, Sarah Orne Jewett produced a substantial body of work between 1868 and 1900. Jewett was born in 1849 in South Berwick, Maine, which was to remain her home her entire life. The daughter of a well-to-do physician, for a time she considered a career in medicine, but she was too frail to take on the demands of medical school. Jewett began her writing career at the age of 18.

Her first short story, "Jenny Garrow's Lovers," was published in the magazine *Flag of Our Union* in 1867, and her second, "Mr. Bruce," was accepted by the *ATLANTIC MONTHLY*, whose assistant editor at the time was William Dean HOWELLS. Howells may have sensed some awkwardness in the love stories and is reputed to have asked: "Sarah, was thee ever in love?" To which Jewett replied, "No sir, whatever made you think that?"

Jewett's first novel, *Deephaven*, was published in 1877, after several of the chapters had appeared separately in the *Atlantic Monthly*. Deephaven was a city girl–meets–country girl story about two young women who spend a summer on the seacoast of Maine. Jewett's knowledge of her home state shines through this novel, and many of her colorful characters are stereotypical (see STEREOTYPE) Downeasters. The urban-meets-rural THEME would recur in later stories and novels, namely *Marsh Island*, in which a country girl chooses between two suitors, one from the city and one from the farm. Jewett's sentimental attachment to country life is evident; in each of these stories the farm life or rural setting emerges as superior to city or urban dwelling.

Jewett's best-known short story appeared in her second collection, *A White Heron and Other Stories*, which can be considered Jewett's best collection. It contains the two types of stories that are her hallmarks: stories that emphasize the natural environment and those in which Jewett's characters are impecunious old women. "A WHITE HERON" is the tale of an ornithologist who comes to the countryside from the big city in order to find a rare bird specimen for his museum. On his trek through the woods he meets Sylvia, a girl of nine, and asks for her help in locating the nesting place of the white heron. Sylvia has explored the woods and forests near her home and knows that, from a certain treetop, the nest can be seen. The young ornithologist also has offered the princely sum of $10 to Sylvia if she leads him to the nest. She realizes that to share the knowledge of the heron's nesting place would lead to the death of the beautiful bird. Discovering that she is attracted to the young man, Sylvia is torn between pleasing him by revealing the heron's nest and remaining true to herself by preserving a part of her beloved New England natural heritage. This simple story, which contains a moral worthy of today's environmental movement, is Jewett's most popular and has been anthologized often.

Sarah Orne Jewett's most widely read published work was her third, the NOVELLA entitled *THE COUNTRY OF THE POINTED FIRS*, published in 1896. It is the tale of a declining New England town, Dunnet Landing, and of its inhabitants. In *Country*, Jewett's maturity as a writer comes into focus. The CHARACTERS are well drawn, especially the women, and she depicts a place and a time that reflect her view of New England and its unique character. Jewett came of age during the American CIVIL WAR and, as a young woman, experienced the expansion of the Industrial Revolution throughout her home region, which was to change New England and its way of life forever. Dunnet Landing was a town that was experiencing the gradual changes from a rural to an urban lifestyle, and Jewett depicts the profound changes in people's lives wrought by the change from farm life to factory life.

The second style of story for which Jewett is known concerns elderly ladies in somewhat reduced circumstances. Although neither elderly nor poor, Jewett was able to depict the lives of these women in stories and sketches. Two in particular stand out: "Miss Tempy's Watchers" and "The Flight of Betsey Lane." Jewett is reported to have said to Willa CATHER, "When an old house and an old woman come together in my brain with a click, I know a story is under way."

"Miss Tempy's Watchers" is one such sketch, in which not one but two old ladies and an old house come together. Two old friends are reunited at the wake of a third friend, Miss Tempy Dent. As was customary, they sit up throughout the night watching over her coffin. They begin to reminisce about the life of their late friend, whose presence is made to seem very real to her watchers. In describing the departed Miss Dent, Jewett creates the impression that she is in the room with her mourners. Perhaps because of this supernatural presence, the two ladies engage in a spirited discussion of the virtues of Miss Dent and resolve to be better friends to one another—the kind of friend that Tempy had been to them.

This sketch, as Sarah Orne Jewett called many of her stories, is so called because it lacks a dramatic plot. This is not to say the story goes nowhere, rather that it is character-driven, not an action story. It is simply a portrait of three characters, two women finely drawn and a third brought to life through their reminiscenses.

A second story in which Jewett portrays the lives of elderly women is "The Flight of Betsey Lane." Here Jewett deftly portrays three old friends who are residents of the Byfleet Poor House, being cared for by the many village residents rather than a few relatives. Betsey Lane, at 69 the youngest of the trio, spent most of her life in the employ of a well-to-do family who left her with a retirement pension. A woman of a generous nature, Betsey Lane soon uses up her pension on lavish gifts for friends and rela-

tives. She is forced by circumstances to take up residence in the town poorhouse, where she quickly befriends Miss Peggy Bond and Mrs. Lavinia Dow.

These three ladies share work at the poorhouse, which consists of planting corn in the adjacent fields. Betsey Lane, bored with work and reduced circumstances, dreams of attending the Philadelphia Centennial Exposition. Her friends tell her this is impossible, until she receives a visit from the daughter of her former employer. The young woman still has a sentimental attachment to Betsey and leaves her with $100 to spend as she pleases. Betsey makes secret plans to go to Philadelphia. Early one morning she slips away to the train station, where she offers to mend the train conductor's jacket in exchange for a ride to Philadelphia on the freight train. This is how Betsey Lane arrives, unobserved, at the Centennial Exposition. She spends three wonderful days there, staying in a rooming house and enjoying the carnival atmosphere. She does not forget her friends, and buys them each a gift with her new wealth.

In Byfleet, no one knows what has become of Betsey Lane, and the speculation is that she wandered off and drowned in the great pond on the poorhouse property. Mrs. Dow and Miss Bond are determined to find their missing friend. On the ninth day of her disappearance, they go down to the pond to see whether they can find some trace of her. Just as they arrive at the pond, they spy the figure of their old friend approaching. She has returned home to relate her adventures at the Philadelphia Centennial Exposition and to share her generous gifts with her friends.

Unlike her fictional characters, Sarah Orne Jewett did not lead a restricted life. Although she never married, she maintained a 30-year relationship with Annie Fields, the widow of the editor George Ticknor Fields. The two women made four trips to Europe, where Jewett befriended many of the literary figures of the 19th century, including Rudyard Kipling, Alfred Tennyson, and Christina Rosetti. In the United States, she was on friendly terms with many literary figures of her day, notably Julia Ward Howe, Harriet Beecher Stowe, Willa CATHER,

William Dean Howells, John Greenleaf Whittier, and Henry Wadsworth Longfellow.

Jewett's last novel, *The Tory Lover,* was published in 1901. It is a sentimental love story set in the time of the AMERICAN REVOLUTION. Some of Miss Jewett's trademarks, notably her description of the physical beauties of New England, are present in this book, but it lacks the substance of *The Country of the Pointed Firs.* In 1902 Jewett was thrown from a horse-drawn carriage, and the resulting injuries put an end to her literary career. In 1909 she suffered a stroke and died at her childhood home in South Berwick, Maine.

BIBLIOGRAPHY

Auchincloss, Louis. *Pioneers and Caretakers: A Study of Nine American Women Novelists.* Minneapolis: University of Minnesota Press, 1961.

Cary, Richard. *Sarah Orne Jewett.* New York: Twayne, 1962.

Jewett, Sarah Orne. *The Best Stories of Sarah Orne Jewett.* Gloucester, Mass.: Houghton Mifflin, 1965.

Matthiessen, Francis Otto. *Sarah Orne Jewett.* Gloucester, Mass.: Houghton Mifflin, 1965

Nagel, Gwen L. "Sarah Orne Jewett." In B. E. Kimbel and W. E. Grant, *Dictionary of Literary Biography: American Short Story Writers Before 1880,* vol. 74. Detroit: Gale, 1988, 208–232.

"Sarah Orne Jewett." In D. Poupard, *Twentieth Century Literary Criticism,* vol. 22. Detroit: Gale, 1987, 114–151.

"(Theodora) Sarah Orne Jewett." In D. Pizer and E. Herbert, *Dictionary of Literary Biography: American Realists and Naturalists,* vol. 12. Detroit: Gale, 1987, 326–338.

Laurie Howell Hime
Miami Dade Community College

JHABVALA, RUTH PRAWER (1927–   )

Ruth Prawer Jhabvala was born in Cologne, Germany. Hers was one of the last Jewish families permitted to leave Nazi Germany; the family emigrated to Britain in 1939. Her father committed suicide in 1948 after learning that his entire family, with the exception of his wife and children, had died in the HOLOCAUST.

Jhabvala earned her M.A. in English literature from Queen Mary College in 1951; that same year she married Cyrus Jhabvala, an architect, and the couple moved to Delhi, India. By 1953 Jhabvala had published her first novel, considering herself a full-time writer despite the demands of raising three daughters. She is the author of more than 15 books, including five short story collections: *Like Birds, Like Fishes* (1963), *A Stronger Climate* (1968), *An Experience of India* (1972), *How I Became a Holy Mother* (1976), and *Out of India* (1986). A crucial member of the Merchant-Ivory film team, she has written more than a dozen screenplays; she received an Academy Award for her adaptation of E. M. Forster's *A Room with a View* (1987). Her collection *Out of India* was chosen by the *New York Times Review of Books* as one of the Best Books of 1986.

In her most recent story collection, *East into Upper East: Plain Tales from New York and New Delhi* (1998), the "East" of Ruth Prawer Jhabvala's East into Upper East refers to India's sprawling metropolis, New Delhi, while the "Upper East" refers to that other big city, New York. In this work, Jhabvala explores the nature of love on two continents. These stories, written over the last 20 years, reaffirm her as a spellbinding urban fabulist. (See FABLE.) The subtitle of the collection is *Plain Tales from New York and New Delhi,* and, indeed, Jhabvala tells her complicated stories in a straightforward, elegant, economic manner, yet her multifaceted CHARACTERS find themselves in complex situations. The first tales take place in New Delhi. The characters are mostly educated and affluent Indians grappling with changes wrought by the former colony's independence. Sumitra, in the story "Independence," becomes a kind of guide and hostess for men who have newly come into power. In "Expiation," the narrator, an affluent cloth broker, must deal with a much-beloved but mentally unstable younger brother. Many years of closing his eyes to the evidence of his brother's delinquency eventually puts the entire family at risk. Sunil, in "Farid and Farida," is a new kind of businessman, marketing "Indianness" abroad. A marriage that had soured when transported from India to London comes to life again in an unconventional way when the estranged spouses meet again years later under a banyan tree in India.

Jhabvala moves from the six stories set in India to New York with "The Temptress," a transitional story in which an Indian holy woman is literally imported to the United States by a wealthy American. From there the author delves into the lives of Manhattanites. In "Fidelity," for example, Dave, his wife, Sophie, and his sister, Betsy, live in a symbiotic relationship stronger than betrayal, disappointment, and even death. All but the last of the remaining stories are firmly grounded in the United States, and in these stories Jhabvala's keen insights into the complexities of human relationships become even more evident, showing that human love and need take many different forms. These engrossing domestic tales depict the emotional lives and complex psychologies of intense lovers, quarreling married couples, weary elders, and their restless adult children.

Because Jhabvala divides her time between Delhi and New York City, because she writes about India rather than Europe of her Jewish heritage, and because her perspectives and ideals are decidedly multinational rather than exclusively Indian, she is sometimes claimed as an Asian American author.

While the style and structure of Jhabvala's fiction has been compared to those of 19th-century European novels, the comparison is rendered inaccurate by her postcolonial stance, her insistent irony, and what might be called her shorthand manner of moving through scenes. While her fiction reveals India and her cultures to the world, it also reveals the profound (and sometimes profoundly tragic) extent to which the world, especially the colonizing influences of Europe and America, is evident in—and represented by—India.

BIBLIOGRAPHY
Bawer, Bruce. "Passage to India: The Career of Ruth Prawer Jhabvala." *The New Criterion* 6:4 (December 1987): 5–19.

Dahr, T. N. "Jhabvala's 'An Experience in India': How True and Right?" *Panjab University Bulletin* (Arts): 21:2 (October 1990): 21–27.

Dudt, Charmazal. "Jhabvala's Fiction: The Passage from India." In *Faith of a Woman Writer*. Edited by Alice Kessler-Harris. Westport, Conn.: Greenwood, 1988, pp. 159–64.

Gooneratne, Yasmine. "Film Into Fiction: The Influence of Ruth Prawer Jhabvala's Early Cinema Work Upon Her Fiction." In *Still the Frame Holds: Essays on Women Poets and Writers*. Edited by Roberts, Shelia, and Yvonne Pacheco Tevis. San Bernardino, Calif.: Borgo, 1993.

Jhabvala, Ruth Prawer. *A Backward Place*. London: John Murry, 1965.

———. *Amrita: Or To Whom She Will*. New York: Norton, 1955.

———. "Disinheritance," *Blackwoods* (April 1979): 4–14.

———. *Esmond in India*. London: Allen & Unwin, 1958.

———. *An Experience of India*. New York: Norton, 1972.

———. *Get Ready for Battle*. London: John Murray, 1962.

———. *Heat and Dust*. London: John Murray, 1975.

———. *The Householder*. London: John Murray, 1960.

———. *In Search of Love and Beauty*. London: John Murray, 1983.

———. *Like Birds, Like Fishes*. London: John Murray, 1963.

———. *The Nature of Passion*. London: Allen & Unwin, 1956.

———. *A New Dominion*. London: John Murray, 1972.

———. *Poet and Dancer*. London: John Murray, 1993.

———. *Three Continents*. London: John Murray, 1987.

———. *To Whom She Will*. London: Allen & Unwin, 1955.

———. *Travellers*. New York: Simon & Schuster, 1987.

McDonough, Michael. "An Interview with Ruth Prawer Jhabvala." *San Francisco Review of Books* 11, no. 4 (Spring 1987): 5–6..

Newman, Judie. The *Ballistic Bard: Postcolonial Fictions*. Chapter 3. London: Edward Arnold, 1995, pp. 29–50.

Rubin, David. "Ruth Jhabvala in India." *Modern Fiction Studies* 30, no. 4 (Winter 1984): 669–683.

Sucher, Laurie. *The Fiction of Ruth Prawer Jhabvala: The Politics of Passion*. London: Macmillan, 1989.

Keith Lawrence
Brigham Young University

JIM CROW A term, possibly derived from the title of an early black minstrel song, that refers to the segregation of blacks and whites and the policies and laws enforcing it. Although practiced in the South during RECONSTRUCTION with the establishment of "Black Codes" that restricted the civil rights of freed slaves, Jim Crow became formalized in laws following the U.S. Supreme Court ruling in *Plessy v. Ferguson* (1896). According to this ruling, the 14th Amendment to the Constitution mandated political but not social equality, and therefore racially segregated "separate but equal" facilities were constitutional. Even though the Supreme Court overturned *Plessy v. Ferguson* in *Brown v. Board of Education* (1954), widespread segregation—and Jim Crow—continued in the South until the civil rights movement in the early 1960s. This movement, led by Martin Luther King, Jr., and others, resulted in such legislation as the Civil Rights Acts of 1964 and 1968 and the Voting Rights Act of 1965, prohibiting discrimination on the basis of color, race, religion, or national origin in public accommodations, schools, employment, and voting.

JOHN HENRY   The legendary black hero John Henry is the subject of BALLADS, TALL TALES, a novel, and a song. He was a man of prodigious strength who worked as a roustabout on river steamboats or was employed in the building of railroads. In one notable tale, Henry dies of overexertion after winning a contest with a steam drill. The basis for the tales and the man may well have been the exploits of a giant black man who worked on the Chesapeake & Ohio Big Bend Tunnel in the 1870s. Although not mentioned specifically, he may be the inspiration for Richard WRIGHT's "BIG BLACK GOOD MAN."

JOHNSON, DOROTHY M. (1923)   Born in Iowa, Dorothy Johnson moved to Montana with her family at age eight. Educated at Montana State University, she moved to New York City in 1935, where she spent the next 15 years as a magazine editor. Upon returning to Montana, Johnson embarked on a journalism career for local newspapers and subsequently joined the journalism faculty at the University of Montana. Drawing on the stories told to her by her grandparents, she became a prolific writer about the West of the 1800s. Her works include short stories, novels, nonfiction, and juvenile literature.

Johnson seems to have enjoyed popularity at both ends of the literary spectrum: Many of her works received critical praise, and adaptations of several of her short stories became Hollywood film CLASSICS. She received literary awards from the Western

Writers of America and the Western Heritage Association. Critics in the *New York Times Book Review* and *Best Sellers* characterize her writing as "historically accurate," "sensitive in avoiding the sensationalized and stereotypical image of the American Indian," and "vivid in her portrayal of Indian customs and practices."

Three of her works were made into films. *The Hanging Tree* (1959) was followed by *The Man Who Shot Liberty Valance* (1962), which was directed by John Ford with John Wayne, Jimmy Stewart, and Lee Marvin as leads. Told as a FLASHBACK, it traces a complex relationship between a U.S. Senator (Stewart), an obscure rancher (Wayne), and their dealings with a gunfighter (Marvin).

Also in the Indian tradition, "A Man Called Horse" was made into a movie starring Richard Harris. Harris plays an English aristocrat captured by the Sioux and forced to endure painful and humiliating rituals to acquire acceptance. A highlight of both the film and the story is the realistic depiction of the Sun Vow ceremony.

A recurring THEME in many of Johnson's stories is the capture of white children by hostile Indians and their subsequent integration into tribal life, stories no doubt passed on to her by her grandparents. Unlike most interpretations of her era, which focused on atrocities, Johnson's stories portray the NATIVE AMERICAN lifestyle as appealing, and she takes special care in presenting details of daily life and ceremonial occasions. The tone of her work is reminiscent of the widely successful film *Dances With Wolves*, yet in her time, this portrayal of Indian culture was uncommon. Her sensitivity in this area resulted in her being named an honorary member of the Blackfeet tribe.

BIBLIOGRAPHY

Johnson, Dorothy M. *All the Buffalo Returning*. Lincoln: University of Nebraska Press, 1996, 1979.

Johnson, Dorothy M., and Robert Townley Turner. *The Bedside Book of Bastards*. New York: McGraw-Hill, 1973.

Johnson, Dorothy M. *The Bloody Bozeman: The Perilous Trail to Montana's Gold*. New York: McGraw-Hill, 1971.

———. *Buffalo Woman*. Thorndike, Me.: G. K. Hall, 1997, 1977.

————. *Famous Lawmen of the Old West*. New York: Dodd, Mead, 1963.

————. *Farewell to Troy*. Boston: Houghton Mifflin, 1964.

————. *Flame on the Frontier; Short Stories of Pioneer Women*. New York: Dodd, Mead, 1967.

————. *Giuliano the Innocent*. London: A. Dakers, 1946.

————. *The Hanging Tree*. New York: Ballantine, 1957.

————. *Indian Country*. New York: Ballantine Books, 1953. Published as *A Man Called Horse*. New York: Ballantine, 1970.

————. *Lost Sister*. New York: Ballantine, 1956.

————. *Some Went West*. New York: Dodd, Mead & Co., 1965.

————. *Warrior for a Lost Nation: A Biography of Sitting Bull*. Philadelphia: Westminister Press, 1969.

————. *When You and I Were Young, Whitefish*. Missoula, Mont.: Mountain Press Pub. Co., 1982.

————. *Witch Princess*. Boston: Houghton Mifflin, 1967.

Lawrence Czudak
St. Joseph's Academy

"JOLLY CORNER, THE" HENRY JAMES (1908)

First published in the *English Review*, this story, frequently interpreted in conjunction with "THE BEAST IN THE JUNGLE" and *THE TURN OF THE SCREW*, begins in medias res. Spencer Brydon, age 56, who has just returned to New York from Europe after a 23-year absence, is speaking to Alice Staverton, an old friend whom, we quickly learn, he visits as often as possible. Spencer has returned to oversee two inherited city houses, one a rental property he is renovating, the other, on the "jolly corner," filled with memories of his boyhood and adolescence. Since then he has been a wanderer, a free man who has enjoyed pleasures, frivolities, and infidelities Alice only dimly comprehends. He views Alice as lovely, flowerlike, one who shares memories of their youthful days in a New York far less chaotic than it appears now. They enter the house on the jolly corner that Spencer has decided to keep, having already hired Mrs. Muldoon, a housekeeper, who is pleased with the arrangements as long as she need not enter the premises after dark.

In their conversation, Spencer confesses to Alice that he is drawn to the house as he is drawn to the question of an alter ego, the self he might have become had he not left for Europe. Together they conclude he would have become a billionaire living on the proceeds of the construction of the skyscrapers that now punctuate the city skyline. Spencer is determined to meet his alter ego, or DOPPELGANGER, in the house on the jolly corner, and Alice confesses to him that she has seen that other Spencer twice in her dreams. She refuses, however, to discuss him further.

The rest of the tale is a suspenseful GHOST STORY, one in which Spencer, alone at night in the house, summons the courage to stalk his double and to draw him out. Indeed, the uncharacteristic hunting METAPHORS have prompted at least one critic to note a resemblance to a motif more commonly associated with Ernest HEMINGWAY. Other critics have noted that Spencer seems a double for the author himself, as James wrote the story after returning to New York following a two-decade-long absence. After so many years in Europe, James might well have wondered what sort of man he might have been had he stayed in the New York of his youth.

After some spine-tingling near encounters with his alter ego, including one scene in which he briefly appears to consider suicide by jumping from the window, Spencer faces the monstrous, hideous apparition, an utter stranger who looms larger than he, and falls into unconsciousness. Hours later Spencer looks up into the faces of Mrs. Muldoon and Alice. He believes he has died and that Alice has resurrected him. She reassures him that he never became the dreadful beast he would have been had he not left New York and that by having faced his double, Spencer can understand his true self as it has developed. The depth of Alice's love is measured in her admission that she would have loved him in either form. As critic Richard A. Hocks points out, Spencer is "saved by the regenerative power of love; in more psychoanalytic terms, his divided self is regenerated with her help" (80). A homosexual interpretation is possible as well, especially if "The Jolly Corner" is compared with recent studies, such as Eve Kosofsky Segwick's on "The Beast in the Jungle." Spencer's numerous ALLUSIONS to "Europe" and to the pleasures he had engaged in as a wandering bachelor at the very least suggest that we should look more closely into the autobiographical connections between James and his PROTAGONIST.

BIBLIOGRAPHY

Hocks, Richard A. *Henry James: A Study of the Short Fiction*. Boston: Twayne, 1990.

James, Henry. "The Jolly Corner." In *Major Writers of Short Fiction*. Edited by Ann Charters. Boston: St. Martin's Press, 1993, 591–616.

Sedgwick, Eve Kosofsky. "The Beast in the Closet: James and the Writing of Homosexual Panic." In *Sex, Politics, and Science in the Nineteenth-Century Novel*. Edited by Ruth Bernard Yeazell. Baltimore: Johns Hopkins University Press, 1986, 148–186.

"JORDAN'S END" ELLEN GLASGOW (1923)

"Jordan's End," which first appeared in Ellen GLASGOW's collection *The Shadowy Third* (1923), shows the influence of Edgar Allan POE's story "THE FALL OF THE HOUSE OF USHER," a kinship that Glasgow acknowledged. In Glasgow's story, the ill-fated Jordan family resides in their eerily GOTHIC family estate, Jordan's End, which is similar to the House of Usher. The declining families in both Jordan's End and Usher suffer from mysterious mental and physical ailments, believed to be the result of inbreeding. But in Glasgow's story the main representatives of the Jordan family are husband and wife rather than brother and sister, Mr. Jordan having married a woman from a neighboring town to strengthen the family's failing bloodline.

Recognizing in the development of her husband's incurable madness the fate of his father, grandfather, and uncles, Mrs. Jordan administers an overdose of a narcotic left by the doctor. Unlike Poe's story and contrary to the title's implications, however, the Jordan line does not end at the story's close. Mrs. Jordan, having been brought in from the outside, does not suffer the same fate as her husband, and the couple have a young son whom the mother plans to send away to school, in hope that the family name will survive to begin a new, although less patrician, line. The doctor in "Jordan's End" serves a similar function to the narrator in Usher, an objective outsider who describes the haunting family situation to the reader.

"Jordan's End" also introduces THEMES that are found in Glasgow's later novels. The decaying Southern aristocracy appears in other works such as *Barren Ground* (1925), *The Sheltered Life* (1932), and *In This Our Life* (1941). The latter two also present the concept of a Southern womanhood that is above the law. Although technically Mrs. Jordan murders her husband, she appears otherworldly and untouchable to the doctor, and her crime goes unreported.

BIBLIOGRAPHY

"Introduction." Ellen Glasgow, *The Collected Stories of Ellen Glasgow*. Edited by Richard Kilburn Meeker. Baton Rouge: Louisiana State University, Press, 1963.

Thiebaux, Marcelle. *Ellen Glasgow*. New York: Ungar, 1982.

Betina I. Entzminger
University of North Carolina at Chapel Hill

JOSEPHINE PERRY

Josephine Perry is the PROTAGONIST of F. Scott FITZGERALD's five-story sequence (see THE BASIL AND JOSEPHINE STORIES) about a beautiful, wealthy socialite. More like the finely drawn sketch of a social type than a fully developed CHARACTER, Josephine has been described as a femme fatale and a vampiric product of upper-class wealth—a beautiful girl without moral conscience, whose sole motive in life is satisfaction of egoistic desires. Josephine also represents the social changes in the 1920s, when young women abandoned the demure femininity of their mothers. She embodies the element of defiant independence that came to be associated in the popular imagination with the New Woman. She is the first of Fitzgerald's characters to be associated with his concept of "emotional bankruptcy": living from conquest to conquest in a fever of excitement, she exhausts her emotional capacity. On her 18th birthday, she discovers she is no longer capable of feeling anything at all.

BIBLIOGRAPHY

Bryer, Jackson R. and John Kuehl, eds. "Introduction." *The Basil and Josephine Stories*. New York: Scribner's, 1973.

Eble, Kenneth. *F. Scott Fitzgerald.* New York: Twayne, 1963. Rev. ed., 1977.

Frances Kerr
Durham Technical Community College

JOY-HULGA   The central figure in Flannery O'CONNOR's story "GOOD COUNTRY PEOPLE" with whom readers easily identify, despite her grotesque characteristics. Wounded as a child, she has a weak heart and an artificial leg, and as a doctor of philosophy, she believes herself superior to those around her. Her lack of spiritual beliefs renders her powerless in her bizarre seduction by an uneducated but street-smart country boy named MANLEY POINTER.

JULIP JIM HARRISON (1994)   The three stories in Jim HARRISON's third NOVELLA collection—*Julip, The Seven-Ounce Man,* and *The Beige Dolorosa*—describe diverse characters and landscapes from three different POINTS OF VIEW. The PROTAGONISTS here, as in Harrison's other novella collections, THE WOMAN LIT BY FIREFLIES (1990) and LEGENDS OF THE FALL (1979), are intimately associated with their surroundings, which range from Florida and the Midwest to Upper Peninsula Michigan to the American Southwest.

Bobby, Julip's brother, is serving seven to ten years in prison for wounding three best friends who had at one time all been Julip's lovers. Julip, a young dog trainer, travels from the Midwest to Florida to have her brother moved from Raiford State Prison to a mental hospital, where he is more likely to obtain early release. Julip's relationship with the three older men is complex and awkward, and they await Julip's return with some trepidation. She finds them and convinces them that they should testify on Bobby's behalf. Julip's burgeoning sexuality and her relationships with her mother, her father, the lovers, and her friend Marcia form a subtext for her journey, which ends as she walks to her own car and heads north, eager to get back to the dogs (82). The story is written in the third-person omniscient POINT OF VIEW and is the most traditional of the three narratives.

In *The Seven-Ounce Man,* Brown Dog, Harrison's American picaro, or adventurer, who appears earlier in *The Woman Lit by Fireflies,* continues to eat, drink, and womanize his way through the Upper Peninsula wilderness. Brown Dog, still on the run from the law, protests the excavation of Indian burial mounds, the site of which Brown Dog has divulged to his former lover Shelley Thurman (in *Fireflies,* that is; in *Brown Dog,* she is called Shelley Newkirk). The novella's 97 pages are divided into three sections, which alternate from third-person omniscient to Brown Dog's own distinctive voice. The protagonist's journey parallels Huckleberry Finn's as, like Huck, Brown Dog heads west (182).

In *The Beige Dolorosa,* the English professor Phillip Caulkins moves to the desert to escape the politics of academia, after he is falsely accused of sexual harassment, and to stave off what he believes are the early effects of Alzheimer's disease. In the desert, Caulkins awakens to a nature he has never known. He catalogs the wildlife and plants he finds on his journeys in the Arizona landscape in an attempt to regain control of his life: "When I first began closely observing nature a month ago I found the experience a bit unbalancing, though the concepts weren't new. Notions such as otherness and the thinginess of reality are scarcely new to a literary scholar. What is new is the vividness of the experience" (243). The novella is written in the first person and convincingly portrays the fragmentation Caulkins feels as he fights for clarity.

The protagonists of these three novellas all work within their particular landscapes to remember their pasts and to order their futures. While Harrison's fiction is often comical, his characterization is poignant, his characters human in their shortcomings.

BIBLIOGRAPHY
Harrison, Jim. *Julip.* Boston: Houghton Mifflin, 1994.
Reilly, Edward C. *Jim Harrison.* New York: Twayne, 1996.

Patrick A. Smith
Ohio University

"JURY OF HER PEERS, A" SUSAN GLASPELL (1917)   Originally written and performed in 1916 as a play called *Trifles,* "A Jury of Her Peers" appeared in *Everyweek* on March 5, 1917, and became Susan GLASPELL's best-known story. On one level, readers may see it as an evocative LOCAL COLOR tale of the Midwest, but its fame and popularity rest largely on its original PLOT and strongly feminist theme. Indeed, the story anticipates the feature-length film "The Burning Bed" and the legal issues debated in the 1970s and beyond: When is a wife justified in murdering her husband?

When the story opens, Minnie Foster Wright has been taken to jail for the possible murder of her husband, John Wright, names suggesting the diminutive and powerless wife and the confident husband. The PROTAGONISTS of the story are Martha Hale, friend to Minnie since childhood, and Mrs. Peters—whose first name we never learn, married to Sheriff Peters, a blustery overpowering man who seems a double for John Wright. The men—including the sheriff, the county attorney, and Martha's domineering husband, Mr. Hale—comb the house for evidence to convict Minnie for murder. So confident are they in their methods, however, that they fail to search the kitchen, the province of women, whose work they repeatedly criticize and belittle.

Martha and Mrs. Peters, the female sleuths in this story (which actually may be viewed as a form of DETECTIVE FICTION), examine the kitchen and, through such evidence as jam jars, quilts, an empty bird cage and, finally, a dead bird, deduce the loneliness, poverty, and emotional devastation of Minnie Foster's marriage. The loud, heavy footsteps of the men punctuate the two women's gradual understanding that Minnie Foster murdered her husband in the same way that he had cruelly killed her canary. Although Martha Hale has been sympathetic all along, the little bird corpse is the deciding factor for Mrs. Peters, who recalls a similar incident in her youth: She easily could have killed the boy who destroyed her cat. More important, however, is Mrs. Peter's awakening to the similarities between Minnie's husband and her own. She joins Martha in conspiring to hide the dead bird, thus destroying the only physical evidence of Minnie's motivation to murder. Minnie has been judged by a jury of her peers, and they have found her innocent.

BIBLIOGRAPHY

Glaspell, Susan. "A Jury of Her Peers." In *American Short Stories*. 6th edition. Edited by Eugene Current-García and Bert Hitchcock. New York, Longman, 1997, pp. 285–99.

K

KADOHATA, CYNTHIA (1956–)

Cynthia Kadohata was born in Chicago. Her short stories have been published in the NEW YORKER, the *Pennsylvania Review,* and *Grand Street;* they also have been widely anthologized. She is also the author of three novels, *This Floating World* (1989), *In the Heart of the Valley of Love* (1992), and *Dragon Road* (1994), which incorporate previously published stories. Kadohata currently lives in Los Angeles.

Kadohata's fiction features complex and often surprising characters, evocative details, and warm humor. Her PROTAGONISTS are generally female, but her male characters also are developed in rich and sympathetic ways. While her fiction carefully delineates representative segments of Japanese American culture, Kadohata's central interest is always the universal quality of human experience.

Keith Lawrence
Brigham Young University

KAFKAESQUE

The stories and novels of the Austrian writer Franz Kafka (1883–1924) often depict a nightmarish world of ABSURDity and paradox, of aimlessness and futility, of ethical, philosophic, and religious uncertainty, in which his protagonist is tormented by an unrelieved and unexplained anxiety. Kafka dramatized the alienation of the individual in a fathomless world. The adjective "Kafkaesque" describes a situation in which the goal is difficult or impossible to attain, usually because of the "red tape" of a faceless bureaucracy.

KAZIN, ALFRED (1915–1998)

Alfred Kazin was a literary critic whose first book, *On Native Grounds* (1942), traced the development of American prose from the time of William Dean HOWELLS. Subsequent critical works included *The Inmost Leaf* (1955), *Contemporaries* (1962), and *Bright Book of Life* (1973), which traced the development of prose from Ernest HEMINGWAY to Norman MAILER. In *An American Procession* (1984), Kazin presented a critical appraisal of the literary greats of American literature from Henry David Thoreau to William FAULKNER and Hemingway.

BIBLIOGRAPHY

Kazin, Alfred. *An American Procession.* New York: Knopf, 1984.
———. *Bright Book of Life.* New York: Dell, 1973.
———. *Contemporaries, From the Nineteenth Century to the Present.* Boston: Little, Brown, 1962.
———. *The Inmost Leaf.* New York: Harcourt, Brace, 1955.
———. *On Native Grounds.* New York: Harcourt, 1942.

KENYON, REVIEW, THE (1939–1970, 1979–)

Founded in 1939 at Kenyon College in Gambier, Ohio, the *Kenyon Review* quickly became a preeminent scholarly journal of poetry, short stories, and NEW CRITICISM that consistently sought out unpublished and innovative writers. The review was an influential force in literary taste and criticism during its years under John Crowe Ransom, a Southern poet and political conservative, who went on to edit the review for 21 years. Through his involvement teaching at Vanderbilt University and in the Fugitive and Agrarian movement (see AGRARIANS), Ransom formed lifelong friendships with Allen Tate and Robert Penn Warren. The two were consistent contributors to the journal, as were many other distinguished writers such as W. H. Auden, Cleanth Brooks, Lawrence Ferlinghetti, Northrop Frye, and Marianne Moore. While the *Kenyon Review* began primarily as a poetry outlet (in its first four years, the journal published only four short stories), after the *Southern Review* expired in 1947, the amount of space devote to fiction increased seven times over. Thus the *Kenyon* came to be one of the American Big Four of scholarly periodicals along with the PARTISAN REVIEW, the *Sewanee Review*, and the *Hudson Review*. Peter TAYLOR was a regular contributor, and the *Kenyon's* first Fellow in Fiction was Flannery O'CONNOR; her stories "The Life You Save May Be Your Own" and "THE ARTIFICIAL NIGGER" were first published in the spring issues in 1953 and 1955, respectively. While the *Kenyon's* influence waned during the late 1950s when the market for scholarly journals became saturated, it still serves as a hallmark of high-quality poetry, fiction, and criticism.

BIBLIOGRAPHY

Crump, Galbraith M., ed. *The Kenyon Poets: Celebrating the Fiftieth Anniversary of the Founding of The Kenyon Review.* Gambier, Ohio: Kenyon College, 1989.

Janssen, Marian. *The Kenyon Review 1939–1970: A Critical History.* Baton Rouge: Louisiana State University Press, 1989.

S. L. Yentzer
University of Georgia

KEROUAC, JACK (LOUIS) (1922–1969)

Jack Kerouac was born of French-Canadian parents in the textile mill town of Lowell, Massachusetts. Offered football scholarships, he attended Horace Mann School in New York City for his senior year (1939–40) and Columbia College the next. At the outbreak of World War II, however, he enlisted in the navy, was discharged for resisting military discipline, and spent the rest of the war in the merchant marine and writing a novel. After the war he briefly studied writing and literature at the New School for Social Research in New York City, but then dropped out: He had in effect begun his career as the wandering chronicler of the BEAT GENERATION, along with Allen Ginsberg, William S. Burroughs, and other literary friends with whom he evolved the concept of beat life and its artistic aims and methods.

Although Kerouac published no short fiction during his lifetime, among his papers exist a number of sketches, short stories, and NOVELLAS, including manuscripts entitled "Book of Sketches," written in 1952 and 1953; "Short Stories, Shorts," written from 1940 to 1953; "Hartford Stories," written in 1941; as well as two novella-length works written in French (Brinkley 63). The Kerouac estate has authorized historian Douglas Brinkley to edit and publish many of these pieces, along with a new biography of Kerouac (Brinkley 49).

Among the many books Kerouac published in the 1950s, it was ON THE ROAD (1957) that brought him fame. This book, widely accepted as the quintessential beat novel (see BEAT LITERATURE), recorded Kerouac's travels throughout the United States and Mexico with his friend Neal Cassady and others. By the time he had published *On the Road*, Kerouac was convinced his art could succeed only if it emanated directly from experience, a technique he called "spontaneous prose," similar to jazz, writing "without consciousness" in a pure flow of expression. He consistently maintained that at the heart of the Beat experience was a religious quest. Indeed, Kerouac's book, *The Dharma Bums*, featuring poet Gary Snyder, has been credited with setting off the "rucksack revolution"—young people traveling widely and inexpensively, and, suspicious of Western technology and philosophy, feeling drawn to the religions of the East (Waldman 16). Kerouac died in St. Petersburg, Florida, of complications related to alcoholism.

BIBLIOGRAPHY

Brinkley, Douglas. "In the Kerouac Archive." *The Atlantic Monthly* 282: 5 (November 1998): 49–76.

Challis, Chris. *Quest for Kerouac.* London: Faber & Faber, 1984.

Charters, Ann. *Kerouac: A Biography.* San Francisco: Straight Arrow, 1973.

Clark, Tom. *Jack Kerouac.* San Diego, Calif.: Harcourt Brace, 1985.

Gifford, Barry, and Lawrence Lee. *Jack's Book: An Oral Biography.* New York: St. Martin's, 1978.

Hipkiss, Robert A. *Jack Kerouac, Prophet of the New Romanticism.* Lawrence: Regents Press of Kansas, 1976.

Hunt, Tim. *Kerouac's Crooked Road.* Hamden, Conn.: Archon, 1981.

Nicosia, Gerald. *Memory Babe: A Critical Biography of Jack Kerouac.* New York: Grove, 1983.

Waldman, Anne, *The Beat Book: Poems and Fiction of the Beat Generation.* Boston: Shambhala, 1966.

Weinrich, Regina. *The Spontaneous Poetry of Jack Kerouac.* Carbondale: Southern Illinois University Press, 1986.

KINCAID, JAMAICA (1949–)

Jamaica Kincaid was born Elaine Potter Richardson in St. John's, Antigua, in 1949; she left Antigua in 1965 to become an *au pair* in New York City. After enrolling in the New School for Social Research, where she studied photography, and Franconia College in New Hampshire, Kincaid became a staff member of the NEW YORKER in 1976, and since then has often published both fiction and nonfiction in that periodical and others. Her Caribbean background figures prominently in her first three books, *At the Bottom of the River* (1983), *Annie John* (1985), and *A Small Place* (1988). *At the Bottom of the River* is a short story collection that presents the day-to-day life of island dwellers in Antigua, often given in a cataloging of tasks; her story "GIRL" is an example of this style and subject. Both *At the Bottom of the River* and *Annie John,* however, have as their thematic core (see THEME) the resistance and conflict that arise between mothers and daughters and the inevitable imposition of the domestic on females in that culture. *A Small Place* is a collection of essays about the exploitation of the Caribbean islands by tourism.

Both *Annie John* and *Lucy* (1990) are novels that also can be considered SHORT STORY CYCLES. Their chapters present narratives complete in themselves that, taken together, trace the development of their titular PROTAGONISTS. *Annie John's* exotic locale and details are striking: bleached white shirts drying on stones in the yard, breadfruit dishes, a fabulously grimy "red girl" whom Annie adores, monsoon rains; but while these images are fascinating and memorable on a literal level, they also add figurative resonance to the stories. *Lucy* is the tale of an *au pair* who left the Caribbean in her teens; her resentment toward her mother and her alienation from home are themes that unite *Lucy* with the earlier *Annie John* and to many of the stories in *At the Bottom of the River.*

Kincaid has been overwhelmingly well received by critics, and she continues to be a major figure in New York literary circles. *Autobiography of My Mother* was published in 1995 and *My Brother: A Memoir* in 1997. She also has written the introduction to *Generations of Women* (1998) and edited *My Favorite Plant: Writers and Gardeners on the Plants They Love* (1998).

BIBLIOGRAPHY

Cudjoe, Selwyn R. "Jamaica Kincaid and the Modernist Project: An Interview." *Callaloo* 12 (Spring 1989): 396–411.

Edwards, Audrey. "Jamaica Kincaid: Writes of Passage." *Essence* (May 1991): 86–90.

Ferguson, Moira. "A Lot of Memory: An Interview with Jamaica Kincaid." *Kenyon Review* 16 (Winter 1994): 163–188.

Garis, Leslie. "Through West Indian Eyes." *New York Times Magazine,* October 7, 1990, 6.

Kincaid, Jamaica. "Putting Myself Together." *New Yorker,* February 20, 1995, 93–101.

Kreilkamp, Ivan. "Jamaica Kincaid: Daring to Discomfort." *Publishers Weekly,* January 1, 1996, 54–55.

Mendelsohn, Jane. "Leaving Home: Jamaica's Voyage Round Her Mother." *Village Voice Literary Supplement* (October 1990): 21, 89.

Karen Weekes
University of Georgia

KING, STEPHEN (1947–) A late-20th-century phenomenon in the genres of GOTHIC horror, fantasy, and SCIENCE FICTION literature, Stephen King has been called the heir to Edgar Allan POE and has been compared with the likes of Ray BRADBURY and H. P. Lovecraft. His fame rests on his novels, yet as all King aficionados know, he has written four collections of short fiction, several of which contain works that have been made into feature films. King has published stories in magazines since the early 1970s and continues to do so in periodicals ranging from *Cavalier, Whispers, Twilight Zone Magazine,* and *The Magazine of Fantasy and Science Fiction,* to such mainstream publications as *Cosmopolitan,* LADIES' HOME JOURNAL, *Penthouse, Playboy, Redbook,* and the NEW YORKER. *Night Shift* (1978), *Skeleton Crew* (1985), and *Nightmares and Dreamscapes* (1993) combine previously published stories with those written especially for the collections, and *Different Seasons* (1982) contains four NOVELLAS.

One of King's most critically acclaimed stories is "The Mist," a Faustian tale first published in *Dark Forces* in 1980 and revised for *The Skeleton Crew* five years later. The characters in the story become engulfed in a terrifyingly opaque mist apparently caused by a malfunction from scientific experiments at a nearby government facility. Conjuring a number of moral dilemmas for his characters as each reacts differently, King subtly injects into the horror story questions about religion, science, and materialism. Set in and around Bridgton, Maine, the tale features the protagonist, David Drayton, who makes his living creating artificial representations of human life. Ultimately pitted against Drayton's attempts to view the mist from a rational, scientific perspective are members of the Flat Earth Society (which includes a New York City attorney), who refuse to believe in the mist at all, and members of a religiously oriented group, who interpret the mist as God's punishment.

Other notable stories include the four novellas from the collection *Different Seasons. Rita Hayworth and Shawshank Redemption,* one of these novellas, is set in the Shawshank penitentiary in Maine. Told from the point of view of Red, the first-person narrator, the tale examines the theme of innocence. It was later made into a feature film, *The Shawshank Redemption. The Body,* an autobiographical story told from the first-person viewpoint of Gordon Lachance—an ALTER EGO for Stephen King (Winter 120)—is set in Castle Rock, Maine, a fictional locale that King frequently uses. Based on a childhood memory, King's story opens with young Gordon finding a corpse in the woods. This novella, too, was made into a feature film entitled *Stand By Me.* Still another novella, made into a feature film, in the collection, *The Apt Pupil,* describes a young Todd Bowden's fascination with and final corruption by the HOLOCAUST memories of an aged Nazi war criminal.

King's most recent story collection (which includes a nonfiction piece, a teleplay, and some poetry) is *Nightmares & Dreamscapes* (1993). The subjects include vampires, zombies, an evil toy, man-eating frogs, the burial of a mafioso in a Cadillac, a disembodied finger, and an evil stepfather. The style ranges from King's well-honed horror to a Ray Bradbury–like fantasy voice to an ambitious pastiche of Raymond CHANDLER and Ross MacDonald. Perhaps both despite and because of the popularity of his work—and thus the traditional hostility from "literary" academics—King's work has received attention from a number of scholars who have written serious studies of his work, particularly during the last decade.

BIBLIOGRAPHY
Beahm, George, ed. *The Stephen King Companion.* Kansas City, Mo.: Andrews & McMeel, 1989.
Winter, Douglas E. *Stephen King: The Art of Darkness.* New York: New American Library, 1984.

KINGSTON, MAXINE HONG (1940–)

Maxine Hong Kingston was born and raised in Stockton, California. She graduated from the University of California at Berkeley in 1962 with a B.A. in English. Although portions of what Kingston eventually published as the nonfiction *The Woman Warrior* (1976) and *China Men* (1980) appeared earlier in *Viva, Bamboo Ridge, Hawaii Review, The* NEW YORKER, *The New York Times,* and the *Seattle Weekly,* Kingston did not become famous until after her first book appeared, hit the best-seller lists, and was awarded the National Book Critics Circle Award.

China Men also sold well and received the National Book Award the year it was published. Kingston is also the author of a novel, *Tripmaster Monkey: His Fake Book* (1989), and *Hawai'i One Summer* (1998), a collection of personal reminiscences. Kingston has taught English in both Hawaii and California, living for extended periods in each and claiming both states as her home.

Kingston's importance to the Asian-American short story is twofold. First—as Kingston apparently intended when she wrote them—the frequently anthologized short narratives comprising *The Woman Warrior* and *China Men* are neither fiction nor nonfiction. Kingston herself resists labels, asking that she not be classed as an autobiographical, ethnic, or FEMINIST writer but simply a human writer. While Kingston's first two books grew out of real experience, the narratives themselves are shaped as short stories, with plot development, carefully moderated structures, tension between PROTAGONIST and ANTAGONIST, and symbolism. Due to this aesthetic shaping, Kingston's narratives must be considered in any discussion of the Asian American short story.

Second and more important is Kingston's legacy to other Asian American authors and to authors in general. Her narrative style, her manipulation and personalization of Asian mythology and culture, her focus on female relationships, and her calculated assessment of a multiracial American audience have had an enormous influence on authors of the 1980s and 1990s, especially such Asian American authors as Amy TAN, David Henry Hwang, Gish JEN, Fae Myenne NG, Chitra DIVAKARUNI, Gus Lee, and Sigrid NUNEZ. In *Woman Warrior,* in particular, Kingston's concepts of "talk-story," GHOST STORY, FABLE, and acquiring a voice have had significant impact on understanding the "double binds" around the feet and psyches of the daughters of Chinese American immigrants.

BIBLIOGRAPHY

Kingston, Maxine Hong. *China Men*. New York: Vintage Press, 1989.
———. *Hawai'i One Summer.* Honolulu: University of Hawaii Press, 1998.
———. *Tripmaster Monkey: His Fake Book.* New York: Vintage Press, 1990.
———. *The Woman Warrior: Memoirs of a Childhood Among Ghosts.* New York: Vintage Books, 1989.
Kim, Elaine H. *Asian-American Literature.* Philadelphia: Temple University Press, 1982.
Ling, Amy. "Maxine Hong Kingston and the Dialogic Dilemma of Asian American Writers." *Bucknell Review* (1995).
Perry, Donna. "Maxine Hong Kingston." In *Backtalk: Women Writers Speak Out.* New Brunswick, N.J.: Rutgers University Press, 1993.
Seshachari, Neila C. "An Interview with Maxine Hong Kingston." *Weber Studies* (1995).

Keith Lawrence
Brigham Young University

KNICKERBOCKER GROUP Diedrich Knickerbocker was a fictional Dutch character created by Washington IRVING. The name—associated with New York because of its numerous Dutch residents—was used to describe a group of writers, including Irving, James Fenimore Cooper, and William Cullen Bryant among others, who lived in or near New York City. Although the group's association was due to proximity and friendship rather than commonly held literary principles, it was significant because it marked the emergence of New York over Boston as a literary and cultural center in the early 19th century.

***KNIGHT'S GAMBIT* WILLIAM FAULKNER (1949)** Consisting of five short stories and a NOVELLA, William FAULKNER's *Knight's Gambit* was published in 1949. Called "the GAVIN STEVENS volume" by Faulkner, *Knight's Gambit* is essentially a collection of murder mysteries in which Stevens, YOKNAPATAWPHA COUNTY attorney and the quixotic knight-errant of the title, plays the role of the clever and winsome country lawyer who successfully solves each case, at times bravely confronting killers and other notorious rascals; in the more intense scenes, often he is threatened; he is even shot once. Beyond the surface concerns of the murders themselves, however, Stevens struggles with some deeper philosophical matters in these stories, particularly regarding the puzzling incompatibility of justice and truth. In one story, "An Error in Chemistry," Stevens and the sheriff discuss this paradox:

> "I'm interested in truth," the sheriff said. "So am I," Uncle Gavin said. "It's so rare. But I am more interested in justice and human beings."
> "Ain't truth and justice the same thing?" the sheriff said.
> "Since when?" Uncle Gavin said.

Gavin proceeds to discuss the inconsistent relationship between, and sometimes the corruption of, these two virtues.

All five stories and the title novella, "Knight's Gambit," appear in chronological order, covering the years 1936 to 1941 in Yoknapatawpha history, and they highlight Steven's efforts to confront the tension created by unjust truth and unscrupulous justice. They also reflect Stevens's necessary, if painful, maturation during a time when the world around him is growing increasingly complex and incompatible with his noble and chilvaric ideals. Ultimately, Stevens is shown to be a man suspended between two worlds—a status symbolized by his Phi Beta Kappa key (received at Harvard and followed by a Ph.D. at Heidelberg University in Germany) and a family heritage that hearkens back to the 18th-century foundations of Yoknapatawpha County. Equal to the tension he feels regarding truth and justice and human beings is his ambivalence— one that Faulkner surely shared—toward his heritage as a Southerner and his role in his community.

BIBLIOGRAPHY

Faulkner, William. *Knight's Gambit*. New York: Random House, 1949.

Gresset, Michael, and Patrick Samway, eds. *Faulkner and Idealism: Perspectives from Paris*. Jackson: University of Mississippi Press, 1983.

H. Collin Messer
University of North Carolina at Chapel Hill

KOBER, ARTHUR (1900–1975) Noted for his DIALECT stories set in the Bronx, New York, or Hollywood, Kober's "Bella Stories" and others were first published in the NEW YORKER magazine between 1926 and 1958 before being reissued in collected form as *My Dear Bella* (1941) and *Bella, Bella Kissed a Fella* (1951).

KOREAN WAR (1950–53) The first major armed confrontation of the COLD WAR occurred when Soviet- and Chinese-backed North Korea invaded U.S.-backed South Korea in 1950. Fighting between the North Korean and Communist Chinese forces and the South Korean U.S. and U.N. forces ended with an armistice in 1953, with the armies facing each other at the 38th Parallel, as they had before the war began. Perhaps because the Korean War came so soon after the cataclysmic events of WORLD WAR II and ended not long before the prolonged and divisive VIETNAM WAR began, it is sometimes referred to as the Forgotten War.

KRISTEVA, JULIA (1941–) A French literary theorist of Bulgarian origin, Kristeva is also a psychoanalyst, professor of linguistics, and novelist. Under the tutelage of Roland BARTHES, her early research defined language as a complex signifying process and culminated in her revolutionary concept, semiotics—a literary theory involving preoedipal processes that subvert and call into question the traditional meaning of language. Kristeva emphasizes the power of poetic language to subvert traditional (male) writing and challenge prevailing social, political, and historical systems. Associated with poststructuralist feminism, Kristeva questions notions of sexual difference, rejects the idea of feminine writing, and proposes a concept of femininity that includes diverse perspectives. (See FEMINISM, POSTSTRUCTURALISM.

Brenda M. Palo
University of North Carolina at Chapel Hill

KRUTCH, JOSEPH WOOD (1893–1970) Joseph Wood Krutch was a critic, essayist, and English professor at Columbia University and elsewhere. His critical works include *Edgar Allan Poe: A*

Study of Genius (1926), *Five Masters: A Study in the Mutations of the Novel* (1929), and *The American Drama Since 1918* (1939; revised ed. 1957). His essays are collected in *The Modern Temper* (1929), *The Measure of Man* (1954), and *Human Nature and the Human Condition* (1959). His interest in the environment and in psychoanalytical interpretations of literature as well as his pleas for humanistic values in an industrialized, technological society influenced both readers and writers of his day.

KU KLUX KLAN A white-supremacist secret society that was formed originally in 1866, after the CIVIL WAR, by ex-Confederates in Pulaski, Tennessee, to intimidate newly enfranchised blacks and prevent them from voting. It was formally disbanded in 1871 after Congress passed acts to suppress it. In 1915 the KKK was revived in Georgia, advocating white supremacy and the maintaining of "pure Americanism." Membership was confined to American-born Protestant whites. The group attacked blacks, Catholics, and Jews as well as ideas such as Darwinism. (See DARWIN.) By the early 1920s there were an estimated 20 million clansmen throughout the United States, and the movement was politically significant, especially in some Southern states. The Klan's power and size declined precipitously after 1923 following press exposés of its terrorist activities. Attempts to revive the society in the 1940s, '60s, and '70s failed, but it remains a small, fringe, racist organization. The name derives from the Greek word *kuklos,* which means band or circle.

KUNSTLERROMAN A German term that means "artist novel," the *Kunstlerroman* is an important subtype of the BILDUNGSROMAN ("novel of education"). The *Kunstlerroman* is a novel that depicts the development of novelists or other artists into the stage of maturity in which they recognize their artistic destiny and achieve mastery of their artistic craft. Examples of this type of novel are James Joyce's *A Portrait of the Artist as a Young Man* and Marcel Proust's *Remembrance of Things Past.* Despite the term's connection to the novel, it can be used with regard to artist figures in short fiction as well.

L

LADIES' HOME JOURNAL   Owing its start to a column in the weekly newspaper *Tribune and Farmer* in the 1880s, the *Ladies' Home Journal* now enjoys an autonomous existence as one of the most widely circulated magazines in the United States.

By November 1889 the *Journal* had reached a circulation of 1 million. Its popularity was due to the short stories and serialized novels it published, written by some of the most popular writers of the day, including Ella S. Wheeler and Margaret S. Harvey. It quickly became a woman's survival manual, featuring departments that offered practical advice on child rearing, useful household hints, instructions for crafts, and inspirational essays on a variety of topics. The magazine had a traditional bias and never editorially endorsed woman suffrage. In 1935 its husband-and-wife editorial team of Beatrice and Bruce Gould fashioned it as the conservative voice to America's women, in the belief that women were wives and mothers first. According to Beatrice, it was "a woman's job to be as truly womanly as possible. I mean to nourish her family, and to rest them, to guide them, and to encourage them."

Despite this editorial creed, not all women were included. Women of color, for instance, generally were overlooked, despite occasional columns by the wife of civil rights leader Medgar Evers. Second-wave FEMINISTS went so far as to storm the office of the *Journal* in March 1970, demanding a chance to put out a "liberated" issue of the magazine and also calling for an end to "exploitative" advertising. The editors heeded the protest and, in the August issue, included an eight-page supplement written by supporters of the feminist/women's movement. Editorial course has shifted as a result, and today, although articles on beauty, fashion, food, child rearing, and home care still predominate, editorials on travel, business, and national and international affairs are prevalent.

Laura S. Behling
Gustavus Adolphus College

"LADY, OR THE TIGER?, THE" FRANK R. STOCKTON (1882)   Frank R. Stockton (1834–1902) originally entitled this story "The King's Arena," and after its appearance in 1882, it became the most famous story ever published in *Century Magazine*. Related by a caustic first-person narrator (SEE POINT OF VIEW) who clearly disagrees with the feudal nature of kings and courtiers who set themselves above commoners, the story takes place in an unnamed barbaric country. The king discovers that a handsome young man, a commoner, whose low social rank prohibits his marrying royalty, has fallen in love with the king's daughter—a crime that, the author remarks wryly, became common enough in later years. The trial of the young man takes place in the king's arena. He must choose

to open one of two doors. Behind one waits a ferocious beast who will tear him to pieces; behind the other, is a beautiful maiden who will marry him immediately. If he chooses the beast, he is automatically guilty; if he chooses the maiden, he proves his innocence.

Of all those in the arena—including the king—only the clever princess has discovered the secret of what lies behind each door. She has made her decision to send a signal to the young man, and she does so, indicating the door on the right. In reaching her decision, the princess has agonized between the dreadful images of the savage and bloody death, and of the young man married to the beautiful maiden of whom the princess is intensely jealous. The young man moves immediately to the door the princess has indicated, and the story ends with the narrator's question to the reader: "Which came out of the door,—the lady, or the tiger?" (Stockton 10). Although similar to a SURPRISE ENDING, the final sentence differs in that it leaves the reader without a DENOUEMENT. Five years later, Stockton followed with "The Discourager of Hesitancy" (1887), which promises to solve the puzzle, but in fact this story, too, leaves the question unanswered.

BIBLIOGRAPHY

Stockton, Frank R. "The Lady, or the Tiger?" In *The Lady, or the Tiger? And Other Stories.* New York: Scribner's, 1914.

"LADY OF LITTLE FISHING, THE" CONSTANCE FENIMORE WOOLSON (1875)

Appearing in *Castle Nowhere: Lake Country Sketches,* "The Lady of Little Fishing" exemplifies Constance Fenimore WOOLSON's strengths as a writer of both LOCAL COLOR and REALISM. The grandniece of James Fenimore Cooper and friend and possible intimate of Henry JAMES, Woolson produced short stories of Great Lakes and Florida coast life that led literary scholar & critic Fred Lewis Pattee to call her "the most unconventional feminine writer" to appear in America in the second half of the 19th century (250).

"The Lady of Little Fishing" explores the influence of an itinerant woman preacher on a small Lake Superior logging community in the summer of 1850. Told from the perspective of a former resident, the narrative illustrates how a woman's public speech produces order and temperance in a hitherto lawless male community. On one hand, the lady's irreproachable purity and the desire that it produces in her male listeners cause them to reorganize their previously ill-mannered and uncouth community so that they distinguish between public and private behavior; on the other, the lady's awakening love for one unregenerate logger finally destroys the community. Published a few years before Henry James wrote *The Bostonians,* Woolson's account of the nature of the female orator's public power may have inspired James's satirical portrayal of Olive Chancellor, the strong-willed Boston FEMINIST of that novel.

BIBLIOGRAPHY

Levander, Caroline. *Voices of the Nation: The Politics of the Female Voice and Women's Public Speech in Nineteenth-Century Literature and Culture.* New York: Cambridge University Press, 1997.

Pattee, Fred Lewis. *The Development of the American Short Story: An Historical Survey.* New York: Harper & Brothers, 1923.

Torsney, Cheryl. *Constance Fenimore Woolson: The Grief of Artistry.* Athens: University of Georgia Press, 1989.

Torsney, Cheryl, ed. *Critical Essays on Constance Fenimore Woolson.* New York: G.K. Hall, 1992.

Woolson, Constance Fenimore. "The Lady of Little Fishing." In *Castle Nowhere: Lake-County Sketches.* New York: Harper, 1875.

Caroline F. Levander
Trinity University

LAFARGE, OLIVER (HAZZARD PERRY) (1901–1963)

An anthropologist and writer, Oliver LaFarge was known as a leading authority on NATIVE AMERICANS, particularly the Navajo. He won the PULITZER PRIZE for the novel *Laughing Boy* (1929), which dealt with life among the Navajo. Many of his other novels and stories also concern Native Americans, as was the nonfiction history, *As Long as the Grass Shall Grow* (1940). Recent reevaluations, however, particularly by Native Americans such as

Louis Owens, see Lafarge's work in the tradition of white "literary colonization" of the Vanishing Indian: thus Lafarge joins the ranks of Herman MELVILLE (Queequeg), Mark TWAIN (Injun Joe), and William FAULKNER (Chief Doom), all of whom, according to Owens, appropriated the "Indian as the quintessential naturalistic [see NATURALISM] victim" and entered him into "the Vanishing American Hall of Fame" (Owens 23).

BIBLIOGRAPHY

Lafarge, Oliver. *As Long as the Grass Shall Grow.* New York: Alliance Book Corp.; Toronto: Longmans, Green & Co., 1940.

———. *The Enemy Gods.* Boston: Houghton Mifflin, 1939.

———. *Laughing Boy.* Cambridge, Mass.: Houghton Mifflin, 1929.

———. *Raw Material.* Boston: Houghton Mifflin, 1945.

Owens, Louis. *Other Destinies: Understanding the American Indian Novel.* Norman & London: University of Oklahoma Press, 1992.

LAMPOON From the refrain *lampons* ("let's drink") in 17th-century French satirical drinking songs, a lampoon is a malicious, often scurrilous satirical piece of writing that attacks an individual's character or appearance. The lampoon flourished in 17th- and 18th-century England and sometimes took the form of extended satire, as with Alexander Pope's attack on Joseph Addison—a fellow writer whom Pope depicts as a jealous Atticus—in "An Epistle to Dr. Arbuthnot" (1735). The form fell into disuse as a result of public disapproval and the rise of modern libel laws. The term still is used to describe a verbal or written piece of pointed mockery directed at a person or institution, as loosely demonstrated in the *Harvard Lampoon* and the *National Lampoon.*

LARDNER, RING (GOLD WILMER) (1885–1933) Ring Lardner was a newspaper humorist, sportswriter, and short story writer known for his satirical stories and sketches about life in early 20th-century America. Lardner had an infallible ear for vernacular (see DIALECT) and an exceptional gift for PARODY. His stories were told in the language of the subject, whether athlete, songwriter, secretary, or chorus girl. He also created a gallery of fictional boobs who commented perceptively on the social scene and the emergence of an avaricious, pretentious, and largely ignorant middle class. A small number of Lardner's 128 short stories have been anthologized regularly.

Lardner's years as a newspaperman—and his famous baseball column, "In the Wake of the News"—taught him how to hold readers' interest. He understood the importance of a tight narrative; of pace, tone, and voice; and of appeal to eye and ear. Humor and satire were central to his vision. To the 1920s, Lardner brought a new kind of short story that emphasized the masculine personality, the world of sports, the wise boob as hero, particularly ALIBI IKE, the crude but endearing baseball player who became an American myth.

Significantly, Lardner brought to the American literary tradition a new interest in colloquial dialect, colorful and vibrant, if filled with grammatical lapses, malapropisms, and redundancies. Lardner also was especially adept at using the technique of the letter, as he does in his famous novel, *You Know Me, Al* (1916) and, especially, the monologue. Two of his most famous stories, "The Golden Honeymoon," and "Haircut," use the monologue in extremely revealing ways. In "The Golden Honeymoon," Lardner uses both dialogue and monologue to develop the story of a couple on a trip to celebrate their 50th wedding anniversary. They are tedious, short-tempered, quarrelsome, and silly; the husband's interior monologue reveals his jealousy when they run into his wife's old beau. Nonetheless, beneath these qualities Lardner reveals the decreasing size of the couple's world, their aging faculties, and their somewhat pathetic attempts to hold onto their love as well as their lives, for they know they have little time remaining.

"Haircut" is told by a barber, the first-person narrator, and the result, as numerous critics have wryly observed, is a story, with a sharp, cutting edge. The barber exposes both the mentality of the small town as well as his own limited reasoning abilities, his insensitivity, and his primitive, shallow PERSONA.

This story influenced such writers as Ernest HEM-INGWAY and William FAULKNER, who used POINT OF VIEW in a similar way in a number of their stories.

BIBLIOGRAPHY

DeMuth, James. *Small Town Chicago: The Comic Perspective of Peter Dunne, George Ade, and Lardner.* Port Washington, N.Y.: Kennikat Press, 1980.

Elder, Donald. *Lardner: A Biography.* Garden City, N.Y.: Doubleday, 1956.

Evans, Elizabeth. *Lardner.* New York: Ungar, 1979.

Friedrich, Otto A. *Lardner.* Minneapolis: University of Minnesota Press, 1965.

Geismar, Maxwell. *Lardner and the Portrait of Folly.* New York: Crowell, 1972.

Lardner, Ring. *The Big Town.* Indianapolis: Bobbs-Merrill, 1921.

———. *First and Last.* New York: Scribner's, 1934.

———. *How to Write Short Stories.* New York: Scribner's, 1924.

———. *Lose With a Smile.* New York: Scribner's, 1933.

———. *The Love Nest and Other Stories.* New York: Scribner's, 1926.

———. *Own Your Own Home.* Indianapolis: Bobbs-Merrill, 1919.

———. *The Portable Ring Lardner.* New York: Viking Press, 1946.

———. *The Real Dope.* Indianapolis: Bobbs-Merrill, 1919.

———. *The Ring Lardner Reader.* New York: Scribner's, 1963.

———. *Round Up.* New York: Scribner's, 1929.

———. *Shut Up, He Explained.* New York: Scribner's, 1962.

———. *Some Champions.* New York: Scribner's, 1976.

———. *What of It?* New York: Scribner's, 1925.

———. *You Know Me Al.* New York: George Doran, 1916.

Lardner, Ring Jr. *The Lardners: My Family Remembered.* New York: Harper & Row, 1976.

Patrick, Walton R. *Lardner.* New York: Twayne, 1963.

Yardley, Jonathan. *Ring: A Biography of Lardner.* New York: Random House, 1977.

LASCH, CHRISTOPHER (1932–)

A professor of history, Christopher Lasch is a social critic and cultural historian known for his analyses of contemporary American cultural and political phenomena. *The New Radicalism in America, 1889–1963: The Intellectual as a Social Type* (1965) is a collection of essays dealing with the psychological motivations of 20th-century social activism. *The Culture of Narcissism* (1979) deals with an increasingly self-centered view of the world and its effect on the family and the community. *The Minimal Self* (1984) examines individual freedom and privacy issues. Lasch consistently challenges contemporary Americans' reliance on experts to determine standards of behavior and thought. His criticism leads, sometimes explicitly, sometimes implicitly, to a questioning of the self-reflexive stance taken by many novelists and short story writers whose work falls under the rubric of POSTMODERNISM.

"LAST LEAF, THE" O. HENRY (1907)

One of the most famous of the O. HENRY tales, "The Last Leaf" (1907) not only concludes with the usual O. Henry SURPRISE ENDING, but, like "A Service of Love," also is conveyed with a narrative tone of sadness and even despair. Two young women artists, Sue and Joanna (Johnsy), share a brownstone in New York. In a cold and wintry November, Johnsy catches pneumonia (personified as an icy ravager who smites his victims as he strides through Greenwich Village) and has resigned herself to dying; the doctor gives her one chance in 10 unless she can find a reason to live. Johnsy tells the distraught Sue that with the fall of the last leaf on the ivy vine that clings to the wall outside her window, she will die. Sue reveals the situation to their failed artist friend Mr. Behrman; he poses for the sketch of an old hermit miner that Sue must finish for her editor; then Sue lies down to sleep for an hour. When she awakens, she and Johnsy look out the window to see that one leaf has survived the nighttime rains and gusty winds, encouraging Johnsy to disregard her previous "foolish" belief that she is near death. As she recovers, however, the doctor informs them that Mr. Behrman has died of pneumonia. He had been found soaking wet, his body lying next to a ladder, a lantern, and some paint brushes. The clear implication is that Behrman braved the cold and rain while printing the last leaf (which actually had fallen) on the wall so that Johnsy would not die.

This story, like many of O. Henry's, has been called implausible and sentimental. It nevertheless appeals to readers in the generosity of the selfless Mr. Behrman and in the uniqueness of the plot. The irony of Mr. Behrman's losing his life to save Johnsy's emanates from the same selflessness exhibited in the husband and wife in the well-known O. Henry story "THE GIFT OF THE MAGI."

"The Last Leaf" may be interpreted from feminist and lesbian perspectives, too, to produce some intriguing readings (see FEMINISM and LESBIAN THEMES IN SHORT STORIES). From a feminist viewpoint, the skeptical doctor and the male-personified illness try to undermine the women's aspirations. The doctor asks Sue if Johnsy has anything worth thinking about to keep her alive, either a man or an interest in women's fashions. Johnsy's longings lie not in sex or clothing styles, but, Sue responds, in art: she hopes someday to travel to Italy to paint the Bay of Naples. From this perspective, the women emerge victorious: helped by the old European artist, they defy the illness and the doctor and survive to continue their work as independent women artists. From the lesbian viewpoint, however, the story has a more somber message. Clearly Johnsy and Sue may be viewed as lesbians: Johnsy's name is a masculinized version of Joanna; Sue alternately swaggers and whistles, and talks baby talk to Johnsy, calling herself Johnsy's "Sudie." Moreover, the story centers on Johnsy in bed, with Sue leaning her face on the pillow or putting her arm around her. Not only do the male doctor and Mr. Pneumonia attempt to break up the pair, but in the very survival of these women, a man, Mr. Behrman, must die—a plot suggesting a hostility toward lesbian women at the core of the story.

BIBLIOGRAPHY
Henry, O. "The Last Leaf." In *The Collected Works of O. Henry.* Vol. 2, 1,455–1,459. Garden City, N.Y.: Doubleday, 1953.

LEE, ROBERT E(DWARD) (1807–1870) At the outset of the CIVIL WAR, Lee was offered command of the U.S. forces, but he declined and returned to his native Virginia after the state seceded from the Union. He took command of the Army of Northern Virginia and, shortly before the war ended, was given command of all Confederate forces. Considered by most historians to be the greatest general of the Civil War, his outnumbered, outgunned army won several major battles with the North before losing the BATTLE OF GETTYSBURG. Lee was a master strategist and an inspirational leader of men. Idolized by his troops and admired in both the North and South, he exhibited the best qualities of a gentleman of the Old South: chivalry, courage, and loyalty to his state and people.

LEGEND A traditional, unverifiable, usually fabulous (see FABLE) narrative in prose, song, verse, or ballad passed down (often orally) in a community, often conveying the lore of the culture and widely accepted as in some sense true. A legend is distinguished from myth by its closer relation to historical fact than to the supernatural.

"LEGEND OF MISS SASAGAWARA, THE" HISAYE YAMAMOTO (1950) Originally published in the KENYON REVIEW (December 1, 1950), this story depicts CONFLICTs among cultures, genders, and generations. Miss Mari Sasagawara, the 33-year-old unmarried daughter of a Buddhist priest, is a famous Nisei ballerina who suffers the indignities of living with six families in Block 33 of a WORLD WAR II Arizona internment camp. Sensitive and reticent by nature, she must live with little privacy among 15,000 other Japanese Americans. When Miss Sasagawara displays her outrage through several acts of unconventional behavior, she is sent to a Phoenix sanitarium for several months. When she returns, she talks to others in a more relaxed manner and offers a ballet class to the children in the camp. Her previous unorthodox behavior resumes, however, and when a nocturnal wandering frightens a family in her compound, she is sent to a California institution.

The "LEGEND" is constructed by Kiku, a woman writer able to escape the camp by attending college in Philadelphia but unable to escape the haunting image of Sasagarawa, the imprisoned woman artist.

Kiku's tale dismantles notions of American justice, artistic freedom, and gender equity. It indicts Sasagarawa's physical and patriarchal imprisonment when it argues that her father's dedication to meditation supersedes his ability to relate to his daughter. The narrative culls impressions received from a variety of sources: Kiku's friend Elsie, hospital workers, and, finally, a poetry journal in which Kiku reads a poem by the displaced ballerina. Concluding the story, Miss Sasagarawa's poem contrasts gender and generational responses to imprisonment. It juxtaposes an Issei man (first generation Japanese-American) who gains freedom to seek Nirvana when he is released from the constraints of providing for his family against a Nisei woman (second generation Japanese-American) who, unable to express her passions and frustrations, endures a painful existence that she attributes to the man's madness.

BIBLIOGRAPHY

Cheung, King-Kok. "Double-Telling: Intertextual Silence in Hisaye Yamamoto's Fiction." *American Literary History* 3.2 (1991): 96–113.

———. "Thrice Muted Tale: Interplay of Art and Politics in Hisaye Yamamoto's 'The Legend of Miss Sasagawara.'" *MELUS* 173 (1991–92): 109–25.

McDonald, Dorothy Ritsuko, and Katherine Newman: "Relocation and Dislocation: The Writings of Hisaye Yamamoto and Wakako Yamauchi." *MELUS* 63 (1980): 21–38.

Yamamoto, Hisaye. "The Legend of Miss Sasagawara" (1950). In *Seventeen Syllables and Other Stories*. Latham, N.Y.: Kitchen Table: Women of Color Press, 1988.

Sandra Chrystal Hayes
Georgia Institute of Technology

"LEGEND OF SLEEPY HOLLOW, THE" WASHINGTON IRVING (1820)

Washington IRVING's famous opening to this story, which first appeared in *The Sketch Book* in 1820, evokes the dreamlike, almost mystical quality of the Hudson River Valley. It also brings the reader to Sleepy Hollow, where almost anything might have happened in 1790—the approximate date of the story, now become LEGEND, of Ichabod Crane and the Headless Horseman. Ichabod, we learn, was an awkward, homely, gangling schoolteacher with too great an imagination: he fears that one night on his way home from gossiping and telling ghost stories with the Dutch wives, he might meet a ghost himself.

Ichabod is also smitten with Katrina Van Tassel, the pretty daughter of a well-to-do farmer. Ichabod is not solely interested in her charms: the narrative makes clear that his imagination surveys the munificent crops and livestock on the family farm and covets them as well. Unfortunately for Ichabod, he has a rival in Brom Van Brunt, often called Brom Bones because of his great physical strength. A FOIL to Ichabod as well as his rival for Katrina's hand, Brom Bones is also fun-loving, clever, and skillful on a horse. After a particularly rousing evening at the home of Mynheer Van Tassel, when Ichabod has spent the entire evening dancing with Katrina, he thinks he may have won her affections. We never know the exact nature of his talk with Katrina, but he leaves the party in low spirits. On his way home, Ichabod's nightmares come true: The Headless Horseman pursues him, throws his head at him, and knocks him to the ground. Although the next day the villagers find his horse, his saddle, and a smashed pumpkin, Ichabod is never again seen in Sleepy Hollow. Brom Bones marries Katrina and laughs at the mention of smashed pumpkins.

In addition to providing fine entertainment, the story seems particularly American. One reading is that Ichabod, with his awkwardness and overstimulated imagination, could not fit into the mold of the American male; lacking in the "right" qualities, he is bested by Brom Bones and fails to capture the woman of his dreams. We should remember, however, that although the Dutch women believe Ichabod has been spirited away by ghosts or phantoms, a traveler says that he has seen Ichabod in New York, where he has become a successful lawyer and judge. If one believes this traveler, Ichabod performs yet another American feat, leaving home for the big city and snatching a victory from defeat. Sleepy Hollow might just have been too small for a man of Ichabod's imagination. One also might infer a humorous if wistful comment on the position of male teachers, a historic one in the United States, and one that reappears in William FAULKNER's ALLUSION to Ichabod Crane when describing his schoolmaster character in *The Hamlet* (1949).

BIBLIOGRAPHY
Irving, Washington. "The Legend of Sleepy Hollow." In *The Complete Tales of Washington Irving.* Edited by Charles Neider. Garden City, N.Y.: Doubleday, 1975.
Myers, Andrew B. *A Century of Commentary on the Works of Washington Irving.* Tarrytown, N.Y.: Sleepy Hollow Restorations, 1976.

LEGENDS OF THE FALL JIM HARRISON
(1979)   *Legends of the Fall* is the first of Jim HARRISON's three NOVELLA collections and, like the other two, it contains narratives: *Legends of the Fall, Revenge,* and *The Man Who Gave Up His Name.* Harrison recalled, "I always loved the work of Isak Dinesen, and Knut Hampson [sic], who wrote three or four short novels, so I thought I would have a try at it" (Bonetti 65). He said his agent told him no one would publish the stories; the collection became the author's first commercial success.

The title story in *Legends of the Fall* details almost a century in the history of the Ludlow family. The narrative focuses on Tristan, whom Harrison has suggested is an American Cain, against the backdrop of WORLD WAR I. Tristan Ludlow becomes an odd sort of HERO, having avenged his brother's death in the war by scalping Germans, going temporarily mad, and marrying Susannah so she can give him a son to take the place of his dead brother. Tristan then goes to sea and leaves his brother Albert to remarry Susannah. Throughout the narrative Tristan is a loner, "much like a LEGENDary western outlaw hero" (Reilly 82). His isolation is made complete by the death of his wife Isabel Two when she is struck by a ricochet from the gun of a federal agent. Critics "have been divided about whether *Legends of the Fall* is an epic or a saga" (Reilly 78) despite its brevity. Certainly the novella is epic in its scope and in the depth of the TRAGEDY and redemption of Tristan's life.

Revenge is similar in scope to *Legends of the Fall,* and the outcome is no less tragic: Cochran, a retired fighter pilot, has had an affair with the beautiful wife of his friend, a wealthy Mexican drug lord whose nickname is Tibey (from the Spanish *tiburon,* shark). Cochran is beaten nearly to death, and Miryea, Tibey's wife, is forced to take heroin, raped, cut, and sent to a brothel. Tibey later moves Miryea to an asylum, where she dies. Cochran is left to sort out the motives and means for revenge on his old friend.

Harrison told Kay Bonetti in an interview that he wrote *The Man Who Gave up His Name* "in a time of extreme duress. I envisioned a man getting out of the life he had created for himself with the same intricate carefulness that he'd got into it in the first place. I suppose I was pointing out that if you're ethical you can't disappear" (65–66). The story line is simple enough, although the underlying THEME of the search for order and meaning goes much deeper: Nordstrom meets his wife at college, marries her, becomes vice president of Standard Oil, and amicably divorces her after they grow apart. In his early middle age, Nordstrom has taken to dancing, as he does at the beginning of the narrative. He searches for an answer to the disintegration of his life, and like Harrison's other PROTAGONISTS who return to the land and their roots to restore order and purpose in their lives, Nordstrom returns home after the death of his father (Reilly 75). Finally, Nordstrom makes peace with himself by working as a cook in Islamorada, Florida, and dancing with the waitresses.

Critics tend to compare the styles of Harrison and Ernest HEMINGWAY. While this novella collection contains, as do many Hemingway works, a certain amount of macho posturing, the compression of the rich details of life and death, the diversity of the characters, the originality of the voice, and the intricate analyses of human nature resemble Hemingway's artistic strengths and point up the strengths of Harrison's short fiction.

BIBLIOGRAPHY
Bonetti, Kay. An Interview with Jim Harrison. *The Missouri Review* 8.3 (1985): 65–86.
Harrison, Jim. *Legends of the Fall.* New York: Delacorte, 1979.
Reilly, Edward C. *Jim Harrison.* New York: Twayne, 1996.

Patrick A. Smith
Ohio University

LE GUIN, URSULA K. (1929–)

Ursula K. Le Guin, one of the most distinguished and prolific contemporary SCIENCE FICTION writers working today, grew up in Berkeley, California; she holds an A.B. from Radcliffe College and an A.M. from Columbia University. Her father, Aldred Kroeber, was an anthropologist and her mother, Theodora Kroeber, a psychologist and writer. The wife of historian Charles Le Guin, she has three children. Early in her career Le Guin combined writing with teaching French at Mercer University in Macon, Georgia, and at the University of Idaho. She later served as visiting lecturer and writer in residence at several universities, including the University of Reading, England; Tulane University; Portland State University; and the University of California at San Diego.

Le Guin has suggested that her interest in what has been called "world-building," the creation of imaginative parallel universes, derived from her parents' interest in studying diverse cultures; both wrote, for example, on NATIVE AMERICANS and taught her to be willing to "get outside of your own culture" and to understand how "culture affects personality." She has received NEBULA, HUGO, and Newbery Silver Medal awards, a Fulbright fellowship, and many other honors. She has also written juvenile tales, poetry, and critical essays.

Le Guin brings a special interpretation to the genre of science fiction. She has insisted that its function is not simply the invention and portrayal of distant galaxies or worlds alien to us. Rather, it has a serious narrative mission to raise and examine the larger ethical issues and questions of the Age of Science. Such concerns, for example, might be the potential misuse of computer technology by the federal government to overregulate and oppress citizens, the THEME of the NOVELLA *The New Atlantis.*

Another well-known story is "Those Who Walk Away from Omelas," which was published in *The Wind's Twelve Quarters* (1975) and won a Hugo award. This story depicts a pastoral utopia, almost within the realm of possibility today, a society with few laws but not "fantastic" in the sense of extraterrestrial. There is only one problem: the society considers happiness stupid and banal; only pain is

intellectual and interesting. Yet the society has no guilt, even over an innocent, wretched child, malnourished and living in a dark closet, condemned to eternal emotional and physical torture. The child is the scapegoat, and the behavior of the citizens exhibits man's inhumanity to man. Le Guin explains in a headnote that the central idea for "this psychomyth, the scapegoat," came from an essay by William James, "The Moral Philosopher and the Moral Life." She began the story, however, not by focusing on James's "lost soul" but with one word, "Omelas" (Salem, Oregon, spelled backward).

The title of "Vaster Than Empires and More Slow," also published in *The Wind's Twelve Quarters,* is taken from Andrew Marvell's poem "To His Coy Mistress": "Our vegetable love should grow/Vaster than empires, and more slow." In a headnote, Le Guin states that every individual gets lost, every night, in his or her own forest; we all have "forests in our minds." The phrase "vegetable love" refers to the way in which Osden, the PROTAGONIST, is absorbed into the forest world of the planet he is investigating.

John UPDIKE has stated that the social sciences inform Le Guin's fantasies "with far more earthy substance than the usual imaginary space-flight." Le Guin refuses to consider evil banal or pain irrelevant; our perception of them determines the moral quality of life itself. Science fiction may, therefore, be called a "literature of ideas." In contrast, what is often called realistic (see REALISM) fiction is more likely to explore individual psyches and personal relationships than the structure and principles of society as a whole.

An important theme in Le Guin's work is the journey, one of the CLASSIC and enduring archetypes of fiction and poetry from the time of Homer and earlier (also known as the *Bildungsreise,* or educational journey into nature and back home again). The process of literal travel reflects man's inner search for self-knowledge and answers to the meaning of life. "True journey is return," Le Guin writes in one of her journey novels, *The Dispossessed* (1974). The landscape of the journey results in learning that, as Peter Brigg observes, it stands as a "paradigm of all human experience" for both traveler and reader. The journey theme also occurs in many of her short stories, including "Things," published in *The Wind's Twelve Quarters* (originally published in *Orbit* as "The End"). The title signifies the end of the world, but the ending has been called enigmatic; the characters go beyond mere things to board sailboats that will supposedly take them to the islands.

Le Guin received the annual Nebula award for "The Day Before the Revolution," published in *The Dispossessed* (1974). It is the story of Odo, the woman founder of an anarchistic society, depicted in old age on the eve of the revolution she has inspired. Le Guin has called Odo's rejection of the totalitarian state and reliance on mutual aid "the most idealistic . . . of all political theories." After her death, her theories lead to the colonization of the moon.

Critic James Bittner observes that Le Guin's heroes frequently make circular journeys to fulfill needs they have themselves determined, adding an ethical or moral dimension. In their quests for "home, freedom, and wholeness" the characters learn to disregard "self-regarding individualism" in favor of "cooperative partnership" and to value their roots (33).

Serious science fiction writers, including Le Guin, do not rely simply on evoking an unregulated and fanciful realm of the supernatural but take pride in making plausible deductions from current scientific knowledge, in carrying out research, and in checking facts. The imaginary worlds created by Le Guin include Earthsea, Hainish, Orsinia, and the West Coast. Her mystic visions have caused her to be regarded as a literary successor to J. R. R. Tolkien. Le Guin's fiction "may be filled with wizards, aliens, and clones," write Joseph Olander and Martin Greenberg, but "the vision contained in her stories and novels is, above all, what is most permanent about the human condition (13)."

BIBLIOGRAPHY

Arbur, Rosemarie. "Le Guin's 'Song' of Inmost Feminism," *Science Fiction Studies* 2.5 (1978): 143–55.

Bittner, James W. *Approaches to the Fiction of Ursula K. Le Guin.* Ann Arbor, Mich.: UMI Research Press, 1984, 33.

Brigg, Peter. "The Archetype of the Journey in Ursula K. Le Guin's Fiction." In *Ursula K. Le Guin.* Edited by J. D. Olander and M. H. Greenberg. New York: Toplinger Publishing Co., 1979, 36.

Bucknall, Barbara J. *Ursula K. Le Guin.* New York: Frederick Ungar, 1981.

Clareson, Thomas D., ed. Special Ursula K. Le Guin Issue. *Extrapolation* 21 (Fall 1980).

Cummins, Elizabeth. *Understanding Ursula K. Le Guin.* Columbia: University of South Carolina Press, 1990.

De Bolt, Joe, ed. *Ursula K. Le Guin: Voyager to Inner Lands and to Outer Space.* Port Washington, N.Y.: Kennikat Press, 1979.

Le Guin, Ursula K. *Always Coming Home.* New York: Harper & Row, 1986.

———. *The Beginning Place.* New York: Harper & Row, 1980.

———. *Blue Moon over Thurman Street.* Portland, Or.: NewSage Press, 1993.

———. *City of Illusions.* New York: Ace Books, 1967.

———. *The Compass Rose.* New York: Harper & Row, 1982.

———. *The Dispossessed: An Ambiguous Utopia.* New York: Harper & Row, 1974.

———. *The Eye of the Heron and Other Stories.* New York: Harper & Row, 1980, 1983.

———. *The Farthest Shore.* New York: Atheneum, 1972.

———, ed. "Introduction" *The Norton Book of Science Fiction.* New York: Norton, 1993.

———. *The Left Hand of Darkness.* New York: Ace Books, 1969.

———. *Orsinian Tales.* New York: Harper & Row, 1976.

———. *Planet of Exile.* New York: Ace Books, 1966.

———. *Rocannon's World.* New York: Ace Books, 1966; Harper & Row, 1977.

———. *Tehanu: The Last Book of Earthsea.* New York: Atheneum, 1990.

———. *The Tombs of Atuan.* New York: Atheneum, 1971.

———. *Unlocking the Air and Other Stories.* New York: HarperCollins, 1996.

———. *The Wind's Twelve Quarters* New York: Harper & Row, 1975.

———. *The Word for World Is Forest.* New York: Putnam, 1976.

———. *A Wizard of Earthsea.* Berkeley: Parnassus Press, 1968.

Lewis, Naomi. "Earthsea Revisited," *Times Literary Supplement* 28 (April 1972): 284.

Mullen, R. D., and Darko Suivin, eds. *Science Fiction Studies: Selected Articles on Science Fiction 1973–1975* Boston: Gregg, 1976.

Olander, Joseph D., and Martin Harry Greenberg, eds. *Ursula K. Le Guin.* New York: Taplinger Publishing Co., 1979, 13.

Selinger, Bernard. *Le Guin and Identity in Contemporary Fiction.* Ann Arbor, Mich.: UMI Research Press, 1988.

Shippey, T. A. "The Magic Art and the Evolution of Works: Ursula Le Guin's *Earthsea Trilogy,*" *Mosaic* 10 (Winter 1970): 147–63.

Slusser, George E. *The Farthest Shores of Ursula K. Le Guin.* San Bernadino, Calif.: Borgo Press, 1976.

Spivack, Charlotte. *Ursula K. Le Guin.* Boston: Twayne, 1984, 85.

Updike, John. "Imagining Things," *The New Yorker,* June 23, 1980, 94.

Sarah Bird Wright

LEITMOTIF

LEITMOTIF   A German word meaning a leading or guiding pattern. In operas, such as those of Richard Wagner, a recurrent musical theme that coincides with each appearance of a given character, problem, emotion, or thought serves as a leitmotif. The term also is applied to a similar device when used in literature and has been notably employed by such authors as Thomas Mann, Virginia Woolf, William FAULKNER, and James Joyce.

LESBIAN THEMES IN SHORT STORIES

The historical record of lesbianism in the American short story has not received the same amount and depth of attention from historians and literary critics as has male homosexuality. Moreover, critics still disagree about what constitutes lesbian writing. Is the author a known lesbian? Is there evidence of a lesbian relationship within the text? If lesbianism is in disguise and relies on repetitive word play and double entendre, as does Gertrude STEIN's "MISS FURR AND MISS SKEENE" (1923), can that text be read as "lesbian" if only a limited number of people understand it? These difficulties are complicated by the imprecision of defining lesbian relationships through history. Terms such as "female friendships" and "Boston marriages," both commonly used in the 19th century to describe intimacy between women, were quickly discarded in the early decades of the 20th century when sexological theories about the "female invert" reduced woman-to-woman intimacies, emotional or physical, to aberrant sexuality. Today the difficulties remain, although they have changed in focus. No longer is sexual intimacy at issue; rather, many lesbian-feminists, disagreeing with writers of previous generations, argue that no form of sexual expression should be a forbidden subject in lesbian literature.

Perhaps the most inclusive, although by no means uncontroversial, standard by which to identify the lesbian in the American short story is to apply the idea in Adrienne Rich's essay "Compulsory Heterosexuality and Lesbian Existence" that woman-to-woman intimacies can be plotted along a "lesbian continuum." If all attachments between women (emotional, physical, or both) are read as some degree of "lesbianism," then contemporary readers can consider 19th-century stories that only vaguely suggest intimacy as "lesbian texts."

Mary E. Wilkins FREEMAN's "Two Friends" (1887) is one of her many short stories that focus on New England "spinsters" who, despite opportunity to marry, preferred to remain with each other in a "Boston marriage." Abby and Sarah, two friends in their 50s, have lived together happily for their entire adult lives in a small New England town. Thirty years previously, however, Abby's aunt had given Abby permission to marry John Marshall, a message Sarah was supposed to relay to Abby but never did. When Sarah finally confesses, Abby laughingly tells her, "I wouldn't have had John Marshall if he'd come on his knees after me all the way from Mexico!"

Sarah Orne JEWETT's "Martha's Lady" (1897) details the relationship between a wealthy woman and her maid that is as intimate and permanent as Freeman's portrayal. In "Tommy, the Unsentimental" (1899), Willa CATHER presents a tomboyish woman whose gender ambiguity prompts her community to judge that "it was a bad sign when a rebellious girl like Tommy took to being sweet and gentle to one of her own sex, the worst sign in the world." Yet Cather keeps Tommy within acceptable sexual behavior; she is even allowed to express some amused affection for men.

Yet as the 20th century approached, "suspicion" and outright rejection of lesbian relationships occurred as psychological and medical theories from men such as Havelock Ellis and Richard von Krafft-Ebing became more thoroughly disseminated and believed in American society. The lesbian in short fiction began to assume some of the "inverted" or "abnormal" qualities that science ascribed to her. Constance Fenimore WOOLSON's "Felipa" (1876) focuses on an androgynous, "dark-skinned" Felipa and her intense emotional attachment to the "tall, lissome" Christine. When Christine accepts a marriage proposal from Edward Bowne, however, Felipa's love turns self-destructive; in her jealous rage, she stabs Edward. Felipa's grandfather, unable to dismiss the passion as "nothing," knowingly closes the story by judging that Felipa was in love with both Christine and Edward, but her violence against Edward shows the danger of lesbian attachments: "the stronger [love] thrust the knife." Mary E. Wilkins Freeman, who less than ten years before provided a loving portrayal of Sarah and Abby, presents in 1895 "The Long Arm," a DETECTIVE STORY, in which the murderer is discovered to be a mannish woman, desperate and even demonically possessed. Phoebe Dole kills Martin Fairbanks in an attempt to maintain possession of Maria Woods, to whom Fairbanks was about to propose.

Characterization of the lesbian as an evil obstacle to heterosexual unions continued throughout the early decades of the 20th century. Catherine Wells's "The Beautiful House" (1912) begins with a positive portrayal of a romantic attachment between Mary and Sylvia. But when the handsome Evan Hardie enters the story, the women's relationship is torn apart for the more socially affirming heterosexual relationship between Evan and Sylvia, and Mary is left a heartbroken spinster. Helen Hull's "The Fire" (1917) follows a similar plot. Cynthia is an art student of Miss Egert; it is clear that mutual emotional attraction, if not physical intimacy, exists between them. When Cynthia's mother forbids her to see Miss Egert again for unspoken but easily inferred reasons, the literal bonfire that closes the story also METAPHORically consumes the suggested lesbianism.

Although O. HENRY's "THE LAST LEAF" (1907) does not portray lesbianism as a hindrance or precursor to heterosexuality, the characterization of one of the two women friends as deathly ill and determined to die as soon as the last leaf falls from the ivy outside her window signals the unhealthiness of woman-to-woman intimacies, which was proposed as scientific fact in O. Henry's time. Yet John Held, Jr.'s "Ride of the Valkyries" (1930), collected in *Grim Youth*, presents a stereotypical young woman who casually announces to the man seated next to her at her parents' dinner party that she is a lesbian. Sherwood ANDERSON's "That Sophistication" (1933) also provides a glimpse of lesbians as they interact among guests of all kinds at a party in Paris. Such nonchalant remarks would seem to suggest that by 1930 lesbianism, even if presented as the sexual novelty of the expatriate moment, was socially acceptable and even sophisticated. But "The Knife of the Times" (1932) by William Carlos Williams removes any pretense of acceptability; lesbianism is the violent "knife" that cuts through social decorum.

During the last decades of the 19th and early decades of the 20th centuries, a particular type of fiction arose that took as its setting, and often its subject, the activities unique to women's colleges, which had only recently been founded. Often the plot focused on one of the seemingly innumerable "crushes" or "smashes" or "spoons" that developed between two female students, usually of different ages. The alternative sexual relationships between schoolgirls in these stories supports Havelock Ellis's 1902 contention that women's colleges were "the great breeding ground" of lesbianism. In "The School-Friendships of Girls," Ellis suggests that lesbianism is an "abnormality" that affected any woman who had a "crush"; according to "authorities," this entailed more than 60 percent of students at women's colleges. Josephine Dodge Daskam's collection of *Smith College Stories* (1900) contains ten episodes of life at a women's college, including "A Case of Interference," which provide intimate glimpses into the excitement, embarrassment, and despair that accompanied female friendships.

Two stories published in popular periodicals examine liaisons within the girls' school: "The Lass of the Silver Sword" by Mary Constance Dubois (published serially in ST. NICHOLAS in 1908–9) and Jeanette Lee's "The Cat and the King" (published in the LADIES' HOME JOURNAL in 1919). Dubois's story initially focuses on the boarding school adventures of two women, Carol Armstrong, 18 years old, and the younger Jean Lennox, who has fallen madly in love with Carol "at first sight." But soon after Carol and Jean's pledge of friendship, the story shifts to a summer camp where the girls spend their time plotting playful jokes against the neighboring boys' camp and striking up socially acceptable friendships with the boys. By the end of the story, Carol and Jean still are friends, but the interest of each has shifted to a relationship that is heterosexual. "The Cat and the King" does not end with the same affirmation of heterosexuality, but it is clear that Flora Bailey's crush on the older Annette Osler has been rightfully displaced by her even more passionate interest in science.

In the middle decades of the 20th century, the lesbian in American literature all but disappeared. When she did resurface in American fiction, it was in the pulp novels of the 1950s and '60s. Relying on the heterosexually modeled gender dichotomies of masculine and feminine, the lesbian was relegated to either a butch or femme role, a time Joan Nestle remembers in "Esther's Story" (1987). If a lesbian character were able to escape such portrayals, she was most often turned into a sexual predator of vampiric proportions. During the 1970s, however, in the hands of women who were involved in the awakening politics of feminism, civil rights, and gay liberation, the lesbian in the American short story began to enjoy a more liberated existence; through the rise of feminist bookstores, journals, and publishing houses, she was given a space in which to thrive.

In 1970 the New York group Radicalesbians distributed a pamphlet that began with the question: "What is a lesbian?" As answer they wrote, in part: "A lesbian is the rage of all women condensed to the point of explosion. . . . She may not be fully conscious of the political implications of what for her began as personal necessity, but on the same level she has not been able to accept the limitations and oppression laid on her by the most basic role of her society—the female role." In their short stories, writers began to dismantle the confusion of sex and gender and allow their characters the full range of gendered expression in their intimate relationships. Moreover, the lesbian in the American short story was offered roles that were traditionally portrayed by heterosexual women: mother, grieving lover, and emotionally and sexually fulfilled woman. Textually, positive images of love between women appeared in relationships that were open and unhidden. In addition, many of these fictional lesbians were the creations of women who proudly identified themselves as women-loving women.

The "romantic friendships" between women at the turn of the 20th century were seemingly benign compared to the defiant expressions of Radicalesbian love. The short stories of the last three decades occupied a far different place on Rich's continuum as authors depicted not only the emotional attraction between women but also, often explicitly, the physical desire. Dorothy Allison's "A Lesbian Appetite" (1988) and Sapphire's "Eat" (1988) together link sexual satiation with the physical contentment that food brings. Allison's PROTAGONIST dreams of throwing a dinner party and inviting all the women in her life: "Everybody is feeding each other, exclaiming over recipes and gravies, introducing themselves and telling stories about great meals they've eaten"; for the first time in her life, the narrator concludes, she is not hungry.

Joan Nestle's "Liberties Not Taken" (1987) suggests that Jean, even though married and mother of three young children, enjoys intimacy with women. Told from the POINT OF VIEW of an adolescent girl who works as nanny for the children one summer, Nestle explores the girl's awakening lesbian sexuality and her physical infatuation with Jean. The sexual awakenings of adolescents receive fictional attention by authors intent on exploring this pivotal time when sexual orientation is ofen ill-defined. Emma Perez in "Gulf Dreams" (1991) relates the story of a

15-year-old girl whose sexual passions are awakened by an older friend of her sister's. A girls' boarding school provides the setting for Rebecca Brown's story "Bread" (1984), of a strong but unreciprocated adolescent love, told from the first-person point of view. When the narrator unintentionally usurps the authority of her beloved, her love turns ugly and distasteful.

Adolescent coming-of-age stories introduce the numerous accounts of adult women who struggle to maintain the pretense of heterosexuality or marriage despite their lesbian longings. Beth Nugent's "City of Boys" (1992) tells of the passionless acts of heterosexual sex by the woman who dreams of passion with her woman lover. Jane Rule's "His Nor Hers" (1985) examines the successful pretense of one woman who maintains the shell of a marriage so that she may continue her intimacies with women. When her husband requests a divorce, Gillian's sexual appetites suddenly disappear as she realizes that since heterosexual cover no longer exists, "the illusion of freedom that he had given her" also has disappeared.

Confronted with a society that still often denies the lesbian's very existence, authors have been careful to plot the REALISM of love and loss in the lesbian short story. The grieving process after the loss of a lover, either through a breakup, as in Leslie Lawrence's "My Lesbian Imagination" (1987), or death, is poignantly explored in numerous short stories. Pearl, in Becky BIRTHA's "In the Life" (1987), mourns her lover's death and lives her remaining days remembering and longing for a reunion. In "A Life Speckled with Children" (1987), Sherri Paris poignantly details the double loss Sabra feels—unlucky in love but also unlucky because of the relationships with her lovers' children she also loses as a result of the breakups. Interweaving a NATIVE AMERICAN past with the narrator's present, Beth Brant explores the loss of children by force in "A Long Story" (1985). Likening the removal of Native American children from their families by the American government to the modern-day reality that sees children stripped from their lesbian mothers, Brant links cultures and generations within the lesbian present.

Some authors, however, prefer to imagine a future where the relationships between women are not only of primary importance but also exist in a world without men. SCIENCE FICTION writer Joanna Russ, in "When it Changed" (1972), imagines the community of Whileaway where women pairs have children by merging ova and share child rearing and social governance. When "real Earth men" come to Whileaway, it is clear to the women that they will lose their way of life; they fear they will be relegated to the ancient inequalities that once existed between men and women—inequalities that are, of course, based on contemporary society. Sarah Schulman envisions a different change in women's relationships; in "The Penis Story" (1986), Ann awakes one morning to find that she has become a "lesbian with a penis." Assumption of the phallus provides Ann with a power she has never felt before as well as awe from women who now want to sleep with her. Eventually, however, Ann desires "to be a whole woman again" by having her penis surgically removed, since, she reflects, "she never wanted to be mutilated again by being cut off from herself." Russ's and Schulman's stories clearly challenge the heterosexual status quo. The visions they articulate, like the controversial sodomasochistic world of Pat Califia's "The Finishing School" (in *Macho Sluts* 1988) and "The Vampire" (1988), broaden the range of the lesbian short story in the late 20th century, transgressing fictional boundaries in order to suggest a more fully articulated and inclusive, albeit conflicting, lesbian world.

BIBLIOGRAPHY

Castle, Terry. *The Apparitional Lesbian: Female Homosexuality and Modern Culture.* New York: Columbia University Press, 1993.

Faderman, Lillian, ed. *Chloe Plus Olivia: An Anthology of Lesbian Literature from the Seventeenth Century to the Present.* New York: Viking, 1994.

Faderman, Lillian. *Surpassing the Love of Men.* New York: Morrow, 1981.

Farwell, Marilyn. "Toward a Lesbian Literary Imagination." *Signs* 14.1 (1988): 100–118.

Nestle, Joan, and Naomi Holoch, eds. *Women on Women.* New York: NAL-Dutton, 1990.

Radicalesbians. "The Woman Identified Woman." 1970. In *For Lesbians Only: A Separatist Anthology*. Edited by Sarah Lucia-Hoagland and Julia Penelope. London: Onlywomen Press, 1988.

Reynolds, Margaret, ed. *The Penguin Book of Lesbian Short Stories*. New York: Viking Penguin, 1993.

Rich, Adrienne. "Compulsory Heterosexuality and Lesbian Existence." In *Blood, Bread, and Poetry*. New York: Norton, 1980, 23–75.

Trujillo, Carla. ed. *Chicana Lesbians: The Girls Our Mother Warned Us Against*. London: Third Woman Press, 1991.

Zahava, Irene, ed. *Lavender Mansions: 40 Contemporary Lesbian and Gay Short Stories*. Boulder, Colo.: Westview Press, 1994.

Zimmerman, Bonnie. *The Safe Sea of Women: Lesbian Fiction, 1969–1989*. Boston: Beacon Press, 1990.

Laura L. Behling
Gustavus Adolphus College

LESUEUR, MERIDEL (1900–1996)

Meridel LeSueur wrote about the harsher realities of life, and particularly women's lives, such as pregnancy, abortion, prostitution, sterilization, and physical abuse by men—areas of life ignored or trivialized by the popular writers of her day. She also wrote about immigrants, Native Americans, and ecology decades before such subjects entered literary popularity. Born in February 1900 in Murray, Iowa, LeSueur's radical literature and views took root early through the influence of activist socialist parents. By 1916 LeSueur had quit school and had worked in a variety of jobs including dancer, silent screen actress extra, stunt woman, and factory worker. She was always writing.

Many of her short stories were published during the 1920s and '30s, including "Persephone" (*Dial* 82 [1927]); "Laundress" (*American Mercury* [1927]); "Spring Story" (reprinted from *Scribner's Magazine* in O'Brien, *Best Short Stories of the Year 1931*); "The Horse" (*Story magazine* [1935]), and "ANNUNCIATION" (*Best Short Stories of the Year 1936*). In 1940 the short story collection *Salute to Spring* was published; on the jacket were quotes of praise by Sinclair Lewis, Zona GALE, Carl Sandburg, and Nelson ALGREN. It seemed LeSueur's place in literature was assured. But soon after she became yet another victim of MCCARTHYISM in the COLD WAR following WORLD WAR II. Her stories were deemed too radical and she was blacklisted. Mainstream publishers refused her work; at one point only Alfred Knopf would publish her children's fiction.

For decades, LeSueur pieced together a living and continued to write short stories, poetry, novels, and journalistic pieces, all in a lyrical style, blending stories of common people with images drawn from nature and myth. With the resurgence of feminism (see FEMINIST) in the 1970s, her work received renewed attention and acclaim. Her work was reprinted and previously unpublished work was collected and published for the first time. She continued to write in the midst of a schedule filled with speaking engagements and readings. Even in the last year of her life, an experimental novel *The Dread Road* was published. LeSueur always remained true to her belief that the writer could and should serve as activist and revolutionary.

BIBLIOGRAPHY

LeSueur, Meridel. *Chanticleer of Wilderness Road: A Story of Davy Crockett*. Duluth, Minn.: Holy Cow! Press, 1990, 1981.

———. *Crusaders*. New York: Blue Heron Press, 1955.

———. *The Dread Road*. Albuquerque: West End Press, 1991.

———. *The Girl: A Novel*. Minneapolis: West End Press, 1985.

———. *Harvest: Collected Stories*. Cambridge, Mass.: West End Press, 1977.

———. *Harvest Song: Collected Essays and Stories*. Albuquerque: West End Press, 1990.

———. *I Hear Men Talking and Other Stories*. Minneapolis: West End Press, 1984.

———. *I Speak from the Shuck*. Browerville, Minn.: Ox Head Press, 1992.

———. *Nancy Hanks of Wilderness Road: A Story of Abraham Lincoln's Mother*. New York: Knopf, 1949.

———. *North Star Country*. New York: Duell, Sloan & Pearce, 1945.

———. *Ripening: Selected Work*. 2d ed. Edited by Elaine Hedges. New York: Feminist Press, 1990.

———. *Salute to Spring*. New York: International Publishers, 1940.

———. *Worker Writers.* Minneapolis: Blue Heron Press, 1982.

———. *Winter Prairie Woman: A Short Story.* Minneapolis: Minnesota Center for Book Arts, 1990.

Schleuning, Neala. *America, Song We Sang Without Knowing: The Life and Ideas of Meridel Lesueur.* Mankato, Minn. & Minneapolis: Little Red Hen Press, 1983.

Susan Thurston Hamerski
St. Olaf College

"LIGEIA" EDGAR ALLAN POE (1838)

Suffused with a gloom reminiscent of that of "THE FALL OF THE HOUSE OF USHER," "Ligeia" remains one of Edgar Allan POE's best-known stories. It achieves Poe's goal of the "single effect" through the narrator's focus on Ligeia, his deceased wife. In a tightly knit plot that relies on sensational incidents, the narrator's sharp focus on Ligeia leads to the stunning and ambiguous DENOUEMENT. In the tale Poe also makes use of the UNRELIABLE NARRATOR whom the reader must constantly distrust.

This powerful tale about Ligeia, a strong-willed woman who wills herself back to life in the body of Rowena, the narrator's second wife, may be read, as critic Gordon Weaver observes, as a story of either madness or the occult (Current-García 67). Clearly the narrator is obsessed with Ligeia. Having remarried, he treats his second wife abominably as he recalls for the readers the history of his relationship with Ligeia. We notice Poe's careful references to the narrator's opium habit and the overly rich, sensuous gloom in the castle apartment in which he and Rowena live, but feel mesmerized by the narrator's description of Ligeia. The suspense builds incrementally, and only when we see that Ligeia has entered Rowena's body do we realize the many questions the narrative raises.

Poe leaves many of the details of the story mysterious and unresolved. The narrator cannot remember Ligeia's surname, for example, nor can he recall the name of the city where they met; these lapses seem distinctly odd in the narrative of an undying love. He may indeed be mad, he may indeed be suffering the extreme effects of opium, and most readers can accept the ghost of Ligeia and her reappearance in another's body. With those interpretations, the story remains a masterpiece of suspense, of horror, of obsessive men. Yet another interpretation is possible, however, from a FEMINIST viewpoint: if one understands the narrator's tone in much the way one understands the tone of the Duke in Robert Browning's later poem, "My Last Duchess," Ligeia's character becomes the reason for the narrator's anger as well as madness. Her erudition, her brilliance, her voluptuousness as well as her forceful personality may well have plagued her husband until he had no choice but to kill her. Moreover, many critics have pointed to the poem-within-the-story as performing a function similar to that same device in "The Fall of the House of Usher." Indeed, the "Conqueror Worm" of the husband's poem in "Ligeia" has both phallic and murderous connotations. Having killed the strong wife so odious to him, the narrator may then have used Ligeia's fortune to buy the castle and marry her FOIL. Viewed in this way, Ligeia, like MADELINE USHER, becomes the avenging woman who refuses to allow the narrator a peaceful moment, underscored with his hysterical, desperate calling of her name at the end of the story.

Whatever interpretation the reader chooses, Poe, once again, demonstrates his genius in continuing to puzzle, to terrify, above all to intrigue his readers even a century and a half removed from him. With Poe we always feel that he has more to tell us, could we but fathom the psychological depths of his artistry.

BIBLIOGRAPHY

Current-García, Eugene. *The American Short Story Before 1850.* Boston: Twayne, 1985.

May, Charles E. *Edgar Allan Poe: Studies in the Short Fiction.* Boston: Twayne, 1991.

Poe, Edgar Allan. "Ligeia." In *Heath Anthology of American Literature,* 3rd ed. Edited by Paul Lauter. Boston: Houghton Mifflin, 1450–1461.

"LIKE A WINDING SHEET" ANN PETRY (1945)

Representative of Ann PETRY's naturalist (see NATURALISM) fiction, "Like a Winding Sheet" portrays the daily experience of racism as a cause of domestic violence. Throughout his degrading workday, the PROTAGONIST Johnson suppresses the urge to strike the faces of the white women who insult him, reiterating his vow never to hit a woman. FORESHADOWING the story's violent end, however, Johnson observes that his hands have developed a separate life of their own. Upon his arrival home, his hands escape his control and release his rage onto his beloved wife, Mae. This frequently anthologized story appears in *Best American Short Stories 1946*, a volume dedicated to Petry, as well as in Petry's *Miss Muriel and Other Stories*.

BIBLIOGRAPHY
Andrews, William L., et al. *The Oxford Companion to African-American Literature*. New York: Oxford University Press, 1997.

Barksdale, Richard, and Kenneth Kinnamon, eds. *Black Writers of America: A Comprehensive Anthology*. Englewood Cliffs, N.J.: Prentice Hall, 1972.

Davis, Arthur P., J. Saunders Redding, and Joyce Ann Joyce, eds. *New Calvacade: African-American Writing from 1760 to Present*. Washington D.C.: Howard University Press, 1991.

Ervin, Hazel Arnett. *Ann Petry: A Bio-Bibliography*. 1993.

Holliday, Hilary. *Ann Petry*. New York: G.K. Hall, 1996.

Washington, Gladys J. "A World Made Cunningly: A Closer Look at Ann Petry's Short Fiction." *CLA Journal* 30.1 (September 1986): 14–29.

Kimberly Drake
Virginia Wesleyan College

"LILACS" KATE CHOPIN (1896)   Originally published in the *New Orleans Times-Democrat* (December 20, 1896), "Lilacs" centers on the annual visit of an opera singer, Adrienne Farival, to the Sacré-Coeur convent school she attended in her youth. In the beginning of the story, Adrienne makes a dramatic entrance wearing fashionable clothes and bearing expensive gifts. Despite a cold reception from the Mother Superior, Adrienne remains in the convent, sharing a room with her childhood friend, now Sister Agathe, and participating in the daily rites. After two weeks of dutiful service, Adrienne returns to her sumptuous apartment in Paris and resumes her life of DECADENCE. She mistreats her servants, pelting one with hothouse roses, and treats her suitors callously. She keeps her yearly retreat a secret, allowing others to believe she is idling at a spa. The next spring when she again smells the lilacs blooming, she makes another pilgrimage to "the haven of peace, where her soul was wont to refresh itself," but this time, she is refused admittance ("Lilacs," 365). The Mother Superior returns the expensive gifts Adrienne has given through the years, causing Adrienne to weep at the rejection. The story ends with Sister Agathe crying in her room as the lilacs that Adrienne has left on the convent steps are swept away.

"Lilacs" has interesting biographical relevance, for CHOPIN herself was educated at the Sacred Heart Academy in St. Louis, and her best childhood friend later became a nun. Although critics such as Edmund Wilson have detected a "serene amoralism" in her works (PG 592), Chopin was deeply influenced by her religious upbringing and returned to the church near the end of her life (Seyersted 185). While "Lilacs" may be interpreted as an indictment of Roman Catholicism, the central focus, as Elmo Howell points out, is not the church but "an individual soul at odds with itself" (106). Adrienne's tragic dilemma is that she cannot reconcile her worldly existence with her spiritual longing.

BIBLIOGRAPHY
Chopin, Kate. *The Complete Works of Kate Chopin*. Baton Rouge: Louisiana State University Press, 1969.

Howell, Elmo. "Kate Chopin and the Pull of Faith: A Note on "Lilacs." *Southern Studies* (Spring 1979): 103–109.

Seyersted, Per. *Kate Chopin: A Critical Biography*. Baton Rouge: Louisiana State University Press, 1969.

Toth, Emily. *Kate Chopin*. New York: Morrow, 1990.

Wilson, Edmund. *Patriotic Gore*. New York: Oxford University Press, 1966.

Mary Anne O'Neal
University of Georgia

LIM, SHIRLEY GEOK-LIN (1944–   )
Shirley Geok-lin Lim was born in Malaysia of Chinese Malaysian heritage. She moved to America at age 24, beginning a new life as a student and then as a teacher and writer in California.

Lim is the author of three short story collections, *Another Country and Other Stories* (1982), *Life's*

Mysteries (1995), and *Two Dreams: New and Selected Stories* (1997). She also has published two volumes of poetry and an autobiography, *Among the White Moon Faces* (1996), edited two anthologies of ASIAN AMERICAN LITERATURE, and written or edited five volumes of literary criticism.

"Mr. Tang's Girls," one of the stories in the collection in *Another Country,* won the *Asiaweek* short story competition in 1982. The stories are concerned primarily with the domains of women in Chinese Malaysian society. But for American readers inclined to read Asian stories either from a sense of smugness or to satisfy tastes for the exotic, Lim has a surprise. The weaknesses in the characters of her ANTAGONISTS (often Chinese Malaysian males) subtly echo telling attributes of western—and particularly American—society, so that the sensitive reader is made to feel the universality of crucial social flaws, especially those relevant to gender inequity, to sexual arrogance and abuse, to the objectification of girls and women. In "A Pot of Rice," for instance, the PROTAGONIST Su Yu rebels against her husband, Mark, who arrives home from work to find that Su Yu, rather than fixing his dinner, has covered the dining table with food offerings to her recently deceased father. Mark retreats angrily into the bedroom and turns on the television. "'This is the first time,' he said loudly, hoping she would hear in the kitchen, 'you haven't served me first'" (291).

BIBLIOGRAPHY

Edelson, Phyllis. Review of Lim's works. In *The Forbidden Stitch: An Asian American Women's Anthology.* Edited by Shirley Geok-lin Lim et al. Corvallis, Oreg.: Calyx Books, 1989.

Lim, Shirley Geok-lin. *Among the White Moon Faces.* New York: Feminist Press, 1996.

———. *Another Country and Other Stories.* Singapore: Times Books International, 1982.

———. "A Pot of Rice." In *Home to Stay: Asian American Women's Fiction.* Edited by Sylvia Watanabe and Carol Bruchac. Greenfield Center, N.Y.: Greenfield Review Press, 1990.

———. *Life's Mysteries.* Singapore: Times Books International, 1995.

———. *Monsoon History.* London: Skoob, 1994.

———. *Two Dreams: New and Selected Stories.* New York: Feminist Press, 1997.

Lim, Shirley Geok-lin, and Amy Ling. *Reading the Literatures of Asian America.* Philadelphia: Temple University Press, 1992.

Keith Lawrence
Brigham Young University

LIMINALITY   A term originating from anthropological and cultural research on ceremony and ritual, liminality indicates that persons, objects, places, events, or times are between one state and another. This ambiguous position of being at a threshold or border, neither completely here nor there, implies suspension and paradox. For example, a mixed-race teenager leaning in a doorway, on New Year's Eve, while riding in a mobile home from the United States to Canada, is a multiply liminal figure. Scholars have studied liminality in such short fiction writers as Willa CATHER, Nathaniel HAWTHORNE, Washington IRVING, Henry JAMES, Herman MELVILLE, and Edgar Allan POE.

Brenda M. Palo
University of North Carolina at Chapel Hill

LINCOLN, ABRAHAM (1809–1865)   The 16th president of the United States (1861–65), Lincoln presided over the most divisive period of American history. His eloquence, steadfastness of purpose, and considerable political skills contributed greatly to defeating the South in the CIVIL WAR, preserving the Union, and abolishing slavery. He was assassinated within a week after General Robert E. LEE surrendered to General Ulysses S. Grant at Appomattox to end the war. Considered with George Washington to be one of the truly great presidents, Lincoln attained the status of LEGEND and folk hero soon after his death.

LITTLE MAGAZINES   Initially appearing in the first two decades of the 20th century and becoming major forces in publishing by about 1920, the little magazines provided a remarkable opportunity for innovative modernist writers (see

MODERNISM). Their unofficial role was an adversarial one against official culture. Small, significant, and elite (in that they published the AVANT-GARDE writings of a coterie of new writers), the least successful of these magazines published little that we remember today, but the most successful—even those that lasted only briefly—published stories still considered extraordinary.

Among the most significant of the hundreds of little magazines that sprang up are *Poetry: A Magazine of Verse,* begun in 1912; the *Little Review,* in 1914; *Seven Arts,* in 1916; the *Dial,* in 1917; the *Frontier,* in 1920; *Reviewer* and *Broom,* in 1921; *Fugitive,* in 1922; *This Quarter,* in 1925; *Transition* and *Hound and Horn,* in 1927. Although *Broom,* published in the early 1920s in Rome, Berlin, and New York, ran for less than three years, it featured short stories by Sherwood ANDERSON and James Stephens, and criticism by short story writers Conrad AIKEN and Jean TOOMER. *The Little Review* published James Joyce's *Ulysses* (1922) in serial form, and the *Dial* was the first to publish T. S. Eliot's THE WASTE LAND (1922). On the pages of the *Double Dealer,* published for three and a half years in New Orleans, appeared short fiction by William FAULKNER, Carl Van Vechten, and Thornton Wilder. Stories by Katherine Anne PORTER, Kay BOYLE, and Erskine CALDWELL ran in *Hound and Horn,* and nearly every significant modernist short fiction writer published in *Story,* which appeared from 1931 through 1948. Although the little magazines paid nothing to contributors and reached a tiny market, they recognized talent and innovation and assured their writers a thoughtful and committed readership.

Several little magazines with left-wing political orientations also appeared during this era, including the *New Masses* (1911–17), the *Liberator* (1918–26), and the *New Masses* (1926–48), publishing works by Philip Gold and Tillie OLSEN, for example. Combining poetry, short stories, essays, and reviews, quarterlies also arose during this period: the *Prairie Schooner* began in 1927, the *Partisan Review* in 1934, the *Quarterly Review of Literature* in 1943, and the *Hudson Review* in 1948, along with

the *Southern Review* (1935–42), the *Kenyon Review* (1939–70), and *Accent* (1940–60). In the 1950s and 1960s appeared little magazines reacting against the quarterlies, most of which had lost their avant-garde status. The most significant include the *Black Mountain Review* (1954–57), the *Evergreen Review* (1957–73), *Yugen* (1958–62), associated with the BEAT MOVEMENT, and *Kulchur* (1960–65). The most successful of this period— the *Paris Review,* begun in 1953, and *Tri Quarterly,* begun in 1958—continue to influence critical and literary opinion. In the last three decades of the 20th century, little magazines have proliferated, numbering well over a thousand. They have provided an especially important outlet for so-called ethnic writers and for writers of experimental short fiction.

"LIVVIE" EUDORA WELTY (1942) One of Eudora Welty's frequently anthologized stories, "Livvie" focuses on the title character, a 24-year-old African-American woman whose old and ill husband Solomon lies dying in their home. Solomon had married Livvie when she was 16 and, although the narrator points out that he has given her everything he thought she wanted, he has kept her a virtual prisoner in the house that he has perfected over his years as a respected farmer. Wise like his Old Testament namesake in terms of owning and operating a cotton farm complete with his own field hands, Solomon echoes him as well in terms of the patriarchal biblical tradition with which he is associated. Contrary to the SYMBOLISM suggested in her name, the protected and naive Livvie has led a static existence lacking experience, vividness, and passion. Because she is trapped at the end of the Natchez Trace that no one visits either on foot or by car, Livvie has never lived for herself, but performs the role of caretaker, first for the white baby she tended before she married, and now for Solomon, whom she increasingly thinks of in terms of a baby himself. Livvie keeps the house spotless and prepares meals for herself (which she devours hungrily) and for Solomon (who loses his appetite as he draws nearer to death). She feels proud of her ability to maintain silence so as never to disturb her husband.

Livvie is associated not only with images of hunger and silence, but also with those of roundness and fertility, in contrast to Solomon, associated with images of rigidity and stasis. Whereas Livvie eats eggs, symbolic of life, Solomon rejects them. Significantly, the story takes place just before EASTER and, in yet another ironic twist to a biblical story, just before Livvie arises from her deadened state, she is visited by a white woman, Miss Baby Marie. Miss Baby Marie, her name a variation of Mary, mother of Christ, and a reminder of the childish state of both Solomon and Livvie, literally opens Livvie's door and causes her to examine herself in the mirror. Livvie, wearing the bright lipstick the white women wishes to sell her, suddenly understands—though she does not articulate the thought—that Solomon is dying and that a potentially bright future awaits her.

In an admirably crafted, tightly knit story replete with FORESHADOWING, Welty has prepared the reader for Livvie's metaphorical ascension. When the young woman meets Cash McCord, one of Solomon's field hands, the passion between them is natural, mutual, and instantaneous. Cash seems destined to cut the umbilical cord between Livvie and her husband who is at once childish and old enough to be her father. The ANTITHESIS of Solomon, always associated with darkness, Cash has spent money on brightly colored clothing and tells Livvie that he is "ready for Easter." Yet this story contains no villains: Cash resists the impulse to strike Solomon down, and the old man dies naturally, realizing on his deathbed his error in taking Livvie from her home and preventing her from meeting others her own age. The story ends in utter joy as Cash and Livvie embrace under a spring-flowering peach tree: The sun shines, a redbird sings, and Livvie drops the heavy silver watch Solomon has bequeathed her. She is joyously reborn, her life just beginning and she youthfully ignores the constraints of time.

LOCAL COLOR The speech, DIALECT, customs, and other features characteristic of a certain region provide the local color in a work of fiction. In the late 19th century, a number of American writers consciously incorporated local color to enhance the REALISM of their work. They included Bret HARTE and Joaquim Miller (the West); Mark TWAIN (the Mississippi); Joel Chandler HARRIS and George Washington CABLE (the South); Hamlin GARLAND (the Midwest); and Sarah Orne JEWETT (New England). O. HENRY and Damon Runyon are further examples of local color writers. The term "local color writing" denotes works that use local color primarily for entertainment by emphasizing or dwelling on the particular and peculiar characteristics of a region or people. It lacks the basic seriousness of realism in that, generally, it does not use locale as a vehicle to explore larger and more universal issues. The term is called into question by some contemporary critics, FEMINISTS in particular, because it sometimes is used in a condescending or pejorative manner. Much local color writing was in the form of the sketch or short story and was published in mass-circulation magazines.

LONDON, JACK (JOHN GRIFFITH LONDON) (1876–1916) Jack London's unique philosophy of life, the work he performed to express it, and his artistic sincerity find their greatest fulfillment in his short fiction. Notwithstanding the merits of his nonfiction and his novels, such as *The Call of the Wild* (1903), which made him America's leading international author; as well as compelling sociological studies such as *The People of the Abyss* (1903), his autobiographical novel, *Martin Eden* (1909); and the haunting visionary fantasy, *The Star Rover,* it is in London's nearly 200 short stories, published from 1899 to his death in 1916, that one finds his finest treasures as a writer. His career reflected the major intellectual currents of his day: socialism and individualism, Darwinism (see DARWIN) and Nietzsche, materialism and spiritual yearning. These conflicting stances found expression in the often startling combinations of NATURALISM and ROMANTICISM in his diverse body of fiction.

London, one of the inventors of the modern American short story, is viewed by many critics as second in importance only to Edgar Allan POE, and his body of work presents an astonishing range of narrative experimentations, diverse characters, and international settings that prepared America's reading public for the advent of literary MODERNISM. Through the existentialism exemplified by the HERO of "TO BUILD A FIRE" (1908), the ragged aesthetic that consumes the heart of the child laborer in "The Apostate" (1911), the awful power of the feminine in "The Night-Born" (1913), and the religious and racial alterity of the old Hawaiian fisherman in "The Water Baby" (1919), London's short stories imagine for us the outlooks and voices of hundreds of characters, from the Indians of the Klondike as they confront the gold-seeking "Sunlanders" to the native peoples of the Pacific Rim encountering their rapacious colonizers, as in "The Red One." London's call for the writer to encompass the world from "magnet to Godhead" was a fitting one; he best embodies Ralph Waldo Emerson's description of the American scholar as one who would learn from nature, learn from books, be a man of action, and, finally, act as a consummate observer. London's famed eclecticism and seemingly inexhaustible energy found their discipline as well as their release in the carefully crafted form of the short story.

London's career may be divided into four roughly chronological concentrations: the Northland tales, which present characters' engagement with nature and each other within the code of brotherhood of the North, as in "To Build A Fire"; the middle socialist period, in which the streets of Oakland and San Francisco, California, are the setting for characters' communal conflicts, as in "South of the Slot"; an experimental phase that saw London breaking out of the "Jack London" formula of adventure and social protest and adventure to work with new subject matter and narrative structures, especially involving racial and sexual others, as in "The Mexican"; and finally the late South Seas stories written during his last few months, as in "The Red One."

Too often in the past, critics have allowed London's adventurous life to obscure the central activity within that life: writing. Living in the great age of the magazine in America, and faithfully writing his 1,000 words per day, Jack London spent a majority of his time and thought on crafting the short story. His was an unusual apprenticeship, combining as it did the rigor of library and typewriter with another kind of rigor as he struggled to come to terms with his boyhood illegitimacy and poverty in Oakland. His early life as a child laborer, oyster pirate, hobo, sailor, gold prospector, and even (briefly) college student made way for his true calling, after he found his medium in his first successful short story, "An Odyssey of the North," published in the ATLANTIC MONTHLY in 1900. His was a representative voice of his time, with economic uncertainties at home, imperialistic excursions abroad, and emergent movements such as feminism (see FEMINIST) and socialism. Fin-de-siècle America had grown impatient with the warmed-over romanticism proffered in the nation's periodicals. In John Barleycorn (1913), London said of his entry into the successful magazine market that "Some are born to fortune, and some have fortune thrust upon them. But in my case I was clubbed into fortune, and bitter necessity was the club"—a statement about his own personal sense of REALISM and how that realism was mirrored by the new desires of his audience. London made no secret of his writing for cash, and this fact is connected to the new American realism—literary naturalism—he helped invent. He never lost sight of his own self-described cardinal virtue, his sincerity, and neither did his audience.

Alongside William Dean HOWELLS, Mark TWAIN, Stephen CRANE, Frank Norris, Theodore DREISER, and others, London developed literary naturalism into new and diverse forms, finally reconciling in his late South Seas fiction the DETERMINISM it generated with an inner sense of a world beyond the material, particularly after his reading of the works of psychologist Carl Jung. Despite his frequent characterization as merely a "red-blooded" naturalist writer for men and boys, his stories reveal that his abiding interest was not in a clichéd notion of "man vs. nature" but in human nature—rather like William FAULKNER's notion of the "human heart in conflict with itself." Like Faulkner, London places that conflict within both domestic and alien social constructions and contextualizes it within race and gender.

Throughout his career London attempts to enter community after community and to show them from the inside, as if his own need to belong, which drove him as a youth, was at last transmuted into a dynamic new art for a new century, particularly in its emphasis on reshaping tradition through his radical social critique.

Many readers are surprised by London's frequent use of strong female characters—as shown, for example, in "The Red One"—and even more by his evident feminist views. In part his thinking about women evolved because of the women in his own life, beginning with his rejection by his own mother and father and his consequent lifelong search for belonging, accompanied by his inner quest for identity as a writer, which caused him to seek the androgynous self of artistic freedom. Fortunately he enjoyed loving relationships with his stepsister Eliza London Shepard and his childhood nurse, Virginia Prentiss; but the most important woman in his life was his second wife, Charmian Kittredge London, who, following his divorce from Bess Maddern London (with whom he had two daughters, Joan and Becky London), became his beloved "mate woman." With Charmian he built and ran the Beauty Ranch in Sonoma Valley, California, and undertook his famed adventuring and writing careers.

BIBLIOGRAPHY

Kingman, Russ. *A Pictorial Life of Jack London.* New York: Crown, 1979.

Labor, Earle, and Jeanne Campbell Reesman. *Jack London,* revised ed. New York: Twayne, 1994.

London, Jack. *The Complete Stories of Jack London.* 3 vols. Edited by Earle Labor, Robert C. Leitz III, and I. Milo Shepard. Stanford, Calif.: Stanford University Press, 1993.

———. *The Letters of Jack London.* 3 vols. Edited by Earle Labor, Robert C. Leitz III, and I. Milo Shepard. Stanford, Calif.: Stanford University Press, 1988.

Jeanne Campbell Reesman
University of Texas at San Antonio

LONE RANGER AND TONTO FISTFIGHT IN HEAVEN, THE   See ALEXIE, SHERMAN.

LOST GENERATION SHORT STORIES

As part of the modernist (see MODERNISM) imperative to "Make it new," writers of the 1920s and '30s consistently wreaked havoc with existing genre conventions. "Poems" no longer rhymed and scanned predictably; essays and reviews had a subjective, even idiosyncratic, slant; plays were anything but three long acts; and the well-made moralizing short story had given way to the "sketch," the prose poem improvisation, some innovative grouping of pages that offended editors and readers alike. Because the short story has become so intrinsically an American province, readers have difficulty appreciating how bold short story writers of the Lost Generation were. Damned (and seldom published) by commercial editors, they persisted in writing in this form—and changed the world's understanding of what a short story might be.

This AVANT-GARDE current was tempered and influenced by the fact that some short story writers of the time were making large sums of money by publishing more conventional stories in slick American magazines. It might be said that the visibly experimental stories of Djuna BARNES, Jean TOOMER, Ernest HEMINGWAY, Kay BOYLE, Katherine Anne PORTER, and others were prompted into being by the possibility of earning good money. The near notoriety of F. Scott FITZGERALD's financial success from 1920 on dominated most young writers' imaginations; indeed, during the 1930s, when William FAULKNER's novels had been monetary disasters, he set himself the task of writing simple, or at least easily accessible, short fiction to try to recoup his losses on the publication of his first half-dozen novels. His careful records of which stories had been sent to which magazines showed the power of the financial imperative.

The tug-of-war between aesthetic merit and moneymaking potential made the struggle for the modern short story form a truly American activity. It also generated a literal flood of short fiction that helped effect the change from the notion that only Guy de Maupassant or Edgar Allan POE could craft a story to a willingness to recognize even the brief prose poem segments of Ernest Hemingway's *in our time* (1924) (and the later *IN OUR TIME;* 1925) as stories. The short story was fast becoming one of the most interesting of literary forms.

F. Scott Fitzgerald's 1920 short story collection, *Flappers and Philosophers,* may have planted the seed of a romanticized disillusion that made the phrase "Lost Generation" appealing to the post—WORLD WAR I generation. Hemingway, in one epigraph to his 1926 novel *The Sun Also Rises,* wryly quoted Gertrude STEIN as having used the phrase (when in reality it was Stein's garage mechanic, speaking of a French prewar generation). The phrase struck many war survivors, especially those living abroad, as a kind of defiant rallying cry. The realists (see REALISM) who had known war were often those who demanded the new in art; just as history could not be repeated, neither could earlier aesthetics (see AESTHETICISM) be effective for modern times.

The best of Fitzgerald's stories blended realism with illusion, and the influence of his first works—"Benediction," "The Ice Palace," even "Bernice Bobs Her Hair"—grew to be as important as those of Sherwood ANDERSON's 1919 WINESBURG, OHIO. The grotesque, as Anderson described his lost characters, were less picturesque and more real in Fitzgerald and Glenway Wescott (as they had been, somewhat earlier, in Ambrose BIERCE, Jack LONDON, and Stephen CRANE). The first half of the 1920s saw remarkable stories—and collections—peaking in books that were central to readers' views of both the literary form and of gender relations in the United States. Fitzgerald's 1926 collection of stories (his third) was *All the Sad Young Men;* Hemingway's 1927 collection of stories (his second) was *Men Without Women.* The stories in each drew from the patterns that already existed in both *Winesburg* and Jean Toomer's CANE (1923), where women were featured as objects of men's desire rather than as subjects. Similary, in these collections of some of the greatest stories of the century ("THE RICH BOY," "The Undefeated"), male characters sorted through their lives—analyzing, assessing, dissecting—and placed sexual satisfaction, or romance, low on their list of priorities. In many of these stories men, struggling to find dignity and belief, abandoned any hope of finding love.

Perhaps that paradigm helped to explain the difficulty some other American writers of the time had in finding publication, much less fame. Katherine Anne Porter's stories, like those of Djuna Barnes, Zora Neale HURSTON, Tillie OLSEN, and Willa CATHER, seemed enigmatic: For readers who understood Fitzgerald and Hemingway, women protagonists led lives that seemed either frustrating or bizarre. By the early 1930s stories by William Faulkner, Thomas Wolfe, William Carlos Williams, Nathanael West, and, somewhat later, John STEINBECK, Albert Maltz, Richard WRIGHT, and other male writers were also finding acceptance. Until assessments that began during the 1980s, the bravura performance of short story writers of the Lost Generation was marked as gendered: crucial to the development of the short story as the world knew it, fascinating in its variation and vitality, and almost exclusively male-oriented in its CHARACTERS and THEMES.

BIBLIOGRAPHY

Clark, Suzanne. *Sentimetal Modernism.* Bloomington: University of Indiana Press, 1991.

Dolan, Marc. *Modern Lives, A Cultural Re-reading of "The Lost Generation."* West Lafayette, Ind.: Purdue University Press, 1996.

Faulkner, Peter, ed. *The English Modernist Reader, 1910–1930.* Iowa City: University of Iowa Press, 1986.

Gilbert, Sandra M., and Susan Gubar. *No Man's Land: The Place of the Woman Writer in the Twentieth Century.* 2 Vols. New Haven: Yale University Press, 1989.

Ingram, Forrest. *Representative Short Story Cycles of the Twentieth Century: Studies in a Literary Genre.* The Hague: Mouton, 1971.

Kennedy, J. Gerald, ed. *Modern American Short Story Sequences.* New York: Cambridge University Press, 1995.

Kenner, Hugh. *The Proud Era.* Berkeley: University of California Press, 1971.

Koppelman, Susan. "Short Story." In *Oxford Companion to Women's Writing in the United States.* Edited by Cathy N. Davidson and Linda Wagner-Martin. New York: Oxford University Press, 1995, pp. 798–803.

Lohaffer, Susan, and Jo Ellyn Clarey, ed. *Short Story Theory at a Crossroads.* Baton Rouge: Louisiana State University Press, 1989.

Linda Wagner-Martin
University of North Carolina at Chapel Hill

"LOST IN THE FUNHOUSE" JOHN BARTH (1968)

"Lost in the Funhouse" begins with young Ambrose, who was possibly conceived in "Night-Sea Journey," now an adolescent, traveling to Ocean City, Maryland, to celebrate Independence Day. Accompanying him through his eventual initiation are his parents, his uncle Karl, his older brother Peter, and Magda, a 13-year-old neighbor who is well developed for her age. Ambrose is "at the awkward age" (LF 89) when his voice and everything else is unpredictable. Magda becomes the object of his sexual awakening, and he feels the need to do something about it, if only barely to touch her. The story moves from Ambrose's innocence to his stunned realization of the pain of self-knowledge. BARTH uses printed devices—italics, dashes, and so on—to draw attention to the storytelling technique throughout the presentation of conventional material: a sensitive boy's first encounters with the world, the mysterious "funhouse" of sexuality, illusion, and consciously realized pain.

As the story develops, Barth incorporates comments about the art of fiction into the narrative: "Should she have sat back at that instant, his hand would have been caught under her. . . . The function of the *beginning* of a story is to introduce the principal characters, establish their initial relationship, set the scene for the main action . . . and initiate the first complication or whatever of the rising action" (LF 92). These moments, when the voice seems to shift outside Ambrose's consciousness, actually unite the teller with the tale, Barth with his PROTAGONIST, and life with art. As the developing artist, Ambrose cannot forget the least detail of his life, and he tries to piece everything together. Most of all, he needs to know himself, to experience his inner being, before he will have material to translate into art.

When Ambrose is lost in the carnival funhouse, he develops this knowledge. Straying into an old, forgotten part of the funhouse, he becomes separated from the mainstream—the funhouse represents the world for lovers—and has fantasies of death and suicide, recalling the "negative resolve" of the sperm cell from "Night-Sea Journey." Ambrose also finds himself reliving past incidents with Magda and imagining alternative futures.

These experiences lead to Ambrose's fantasy that he is reciting stories in the dark until he dies, while a young girl behind the plyboard panel he leans against takes down his every word but does not speak, for she knows his genius can bloom only in isolation. This fantasy is the artistic parallel to the sperm's union with "Her" in "Night-Sea Journey." Barth thus suggests that the artist's creative force is a product of a rechanneled sexual drive. Although Ambrose prefers to be among the lovers in the funhouse, he is constructing his own funhouse in the world of art.

Harriet P. Gold
LaSalle College
Dawson College

LOST LADY, A WILLA CATHER (1923)

Like Willa CATHER's novels *O Pioneers!* (1913) and *My Antonia* (1918), *A Lost Lady*, a NOVELLA-length work, is linked with the landscape of the western American plains. *A Lost Lady* is set in the Colorado prairie town of Sweet Water, where the history of Marian Forrester unfolds, as seen primarily through the eyes of her youthful admirer Niel Herbert.

As in much of Cather's work, the driving tension in *A Lost Lady* grows out of shifting values as the stewardship of the American West passes from pioneers to speculators and developers. From the outset, we learn that there were two distinct social strata in the prairie states: the homesteaders and hand-workers who were there to make a living, and the bankers and gentlemen ranchers who came from the Atlantic seaboard to invest money and to develop the great West (9–10). Nineteen-year-old Marian Ormsby becomes Captain Forrester's bride after he rescues her from a near-fatal fall in the Sierras. He is honorable and compassionate, 25 years her senior, and a member of the first small band of whites to enter the West. He prepared the way for the railroad, and influential members of the western upper class regularly visit the Forrester home, which, although a bit gaudy, is the finest in town. Financial crisis strikes Captain Forrester when he personally covers deposits made by poor working folk when a bank on whose board he served fails, and his bankruptcy, incurred through honesty and compassion, marks the beginning of his decline. As he physically declines, first falling from his horse, then suffering a stroke, and finally dying, he signifies the passing of his era.

To Niel Herbert, himself part of the new generation of Westerners, it is Marian who most effectively mirrors the decline of the West. Physically beautiful and passionate, she seems to him the perfect consort for a past ideal he has not yet perceived as lost. He imagines her the epitome of loyalty until he discovers her in a passionate extramarital affair with Captain Forrester's young bachelor friend, Frank Ellinger. Ivy Peters, pictured at the beginning of the narrative as a cruel adolescent slitting the eyes of a woodpecker, exemplifies the worst of the new West. Peters gradually gains control of the Forrester land, and after Captain Forrester dies, he enters into a crass liaison with Marian Forrester, solidifying her decline in Herbert's eyes.

Men like Ivy Peters see the land primarily as a resource from which to derive material wealth, and degradation of the land also marks the passing era. On the Forrester place, the captain and Marian have always kept a pristine marsh in its natural state. Peters, upon assuming control of the property, drains the wetlands and plants it in wheat, but we learn that he emptied the land of its beauty not because he could grow crops on it but because by doing so he could obliterate a few acres of something he hated, although he could not name it, and could assert his power over the people who had loved those unproductive meadows for their idleness and silvery beauty (106). The West becomes a world in which men like Captain Forrester and land like Sweet Water Marsh cannot survive.

Marian Forrester survives, however, and she returns to her childhood home in California after Peters marries and moves into the Forrester house. She meets a wealthy Englishman living in Buenos Aires, remarries, and moves to South America, where she prospers. Herbert takes years to reconcile his conflicting feelings for Marian Forrester; he can-not forgive her for not passing away with the era she so clearly represented to him. Recently much insightful critical attention has focused on the short-falls of Herbert's selective telling of history and on Cather's FEMINIST perception. Although this criticism is valuable, it seems clear that Cather, at least in *A Lost Lady,* remains most deeply concerned with the demise of the western prairie that helped form her life and usher her into art.

BIBLIOGRAPHY

Cather, Willa. *A Lost Lady.* New York: Knopf, 1923.
———. *On Writing: Critical Studies on Writing as Art.* New York: Knopf, 1920.
Murphy, John J., ed. *Critical Essays on Willa Cather.* Boston: G.K. Hall, 1984.
Roskowski, Susan J. "*Willa Cather and the Fatality of Place: O Pioneers!, My Antonia, and A Lost Lady.*" In *Geography and Literature: A Meeting of the Disciplines.* Edited by William E. Mallory and Paul Simpson-Housely. Syracuse, N.Y.: Syracuse University Press, 1987.
———. "Willa Cather's *A Lost Lady:* The Paradoxes of Change." *Novel* 11.1 (1977).
Urgo, Joseph R. "How Context Determines Fact: Historicism in Willa Cather's *A Lost Lady.*" *Studies in American Fiction* 17.2 (1989).

Cornelius W. Browne
Ohio University

"LOTTERY, THE" SHIRLEY JACKSON (1949)

Like so many of Shirley JACKSON's stories, "The Lottery" was first published in the NEW YORKER and, subsequently, as the title story of *The Lottery: or, The Adventures of James Harris* in 1949. It may well be the world's most frequently anthologized short story. A modern horror story, it derives its effect from a reversal of the readers' expectations, already established by the ordinary setting of a warm June day in a rural community. Readers, lulled into this false summer complacency, begin to feel horror, their moods changing with the narrator's careful use of evidence and suspense, until the full realization of the appalling ritual murder bursts almost unbearably on them.

The story opens innocently enough, as the townspeople gather for an unidentified annual event connected to the harvest. The use of names initially seems to bolster the friendliness of the gathering; we feel we know these people as, one by one, their names are called in alphabetical order. In retrospect, however, the names of the male lottery organizers—"Summer" and "Graves"—provide us with clues to the transition from life to death. Tessie, the soon-to-be-victim housewife, may allude (see ALLUSION) to another bucolic Tess (in Thomas Hardy's novel *Tess of the D'Urbervilles*), whose promising beginnings transformed into gore and death at the hands of men.

Scholar and critic Linda Wagner-Martin observes that only recently have readers noticed the import of the sacrificial victim's gender: In the traditional patriarchal system that values men and children, mothers are devalued once they have fulfilled their childbearing roles. Tessie, late to the gathering because her arms were plunged to the elbow in dishwater, seems inconsequential, even irritating at first. Only as everyone in the town turns against her—children, men, other women invested in the system that sustains them—does the reader become aware that this is a ritual stoning of a scapegoat who can depend on no one: not her daughter, not her husband, not even her little boy Davy, who picks up an extraordinarily large rock to throw at her.

No reader can finish this story without contemplating the violence and inhumanity that Jackson intended it to portray. In the irony of its depiction lies the horror of this CLASSIC tale and, one hopes, a careful reevaluation of social codes and meaningless rituals.

BIBLIOGRAPHY

Jackson, Shirley. *The Lottery: or, The Adventures of James Harris*. New York: Farrar, Straus, 1949.

Wagner-Martin, Linda. "The Lottery." In *Reference Guide to Short Fiction*. Edited by Noelle Watson. Detroit: St. James Press, 1994, 783–784.

"LOUDEST VOICE, THE" GRACE PALEY (1956)

Grace PALEY's autobiographical story is a humorous account of events that transpired when she was a New York City grammar school student chosen to narrate the Christmas play because she had the loudest voice of any child in the school. In the story, she fictionalizes herself as Rose Abramovitch, Rose's immigrant Jewish mother who is upset at what she thinks is the way the school is indoctrinating the children with Christian traditions. Her father is more tolerant, telling her mother that she's now in America and reminding her that she wanted to emigrate because anywhere else—Palestine, Europe, Argentina—would have been fraught with danger. In humorous understatement, he chides her for fearing Christmas in the United States.

In the second half of the story, the reader realizes that the narrator is cast in the speaking role of Jesus Christ himself. Rose speaks of Christ's childhood as lonely, utters his famous words of the Garden of Gethsemane: "My God, my God, why has thou forsaken me?" and ends by proclaiming to the largely Jewish audience of parents who have come to see their children in the school play, "as everyone in this room, in this city—in this world—now knows, I shall have life eternal" (LV 1155).

Any shock these words might have held for her parents is defused when they return home after the play. When Mr. Abramovitch kids the Jewish neighbor Mrs. Kornbluh, whose daughter played the Virgin Mary, Mrs. Kornbluh refuses to take the bait and asks instead why the Christian children in the school had such small roles. Mrs. Abramovitch understands why: "You think it's so important they should get in the play? Christmas . . . the whole piece of goods . . . they own it."

In the final paragraphs of the story, as Rose remembers how she fell asleep happily listening to her parents and remembering her success in the play, the hold of her Jewish traditions certainly has not been shaken; indeed, she prays for "all the lonesome Christians." She confidently expects the Jewish God to whom she directs her prayers with the traditional Hebrew salutation, "Hear, O Israel . . ." to hear her. After all, whether speaking Yiddish or English, she knows she has the loudest voice.

BIBLIOGRAPHY

Isaacs, Neil David. *Grace Paley: A Study of the Short Fiction*. Boston: Twayne, 1990.

Paley, Grace. "The Loudest Voice." In *Major Writers of Short Fiction*. Edited by Ann Charters. New York: St. Martin's, 1993, 1,151–1,156.

LOUIE, DAVID WONG (1954–) David Wong Louie was born in Rockville Center, New York. He received his B.A. from Vassar College and his M.F.A. from the University of Iowa, where he attended the Writers' Workshop. His stories have appeared in the *Iowa Review, Ploughshares, Chicago Review,* and *Best American Short Stories* (1989). His first short story collection, *Pangs of Love* (1991), received the Ploughshares First Book Award and the Los Angeles Times Award for First Fiction in 1991. Louie has also received fellowships from the National Endowment for the Arts, the California Arts Council, the McDowell Colony, and Yaddo. He currently lives in the Los Angeles area and teaches in the English Department and the Asian American Studies Center at the University of California at Los Angeles.

Reminiscent of and comparing favorably to the stories of Amy TAN and Maxine Hong KINGSTON, those in Louie's *Pangs of Love* explore the lives of Asian immigrants and of their American-born children. Many of Louie's stories tend to focus on the alienation of the American male in general and the Asian American male in particular; METAPHORS for this alienation range from forced sacrifice to denied paternity. Louie also deflates STEREOTYPES of the Asian male as the well-behaved and mild-mannered intellectual by purposely exaggerating the libidos and rebellious natures of certain male characters; these characterizations have garnered praise from Frank CHIN and Jefferey Paul CHAN. In "Disturbing the Universe," Louie uses the device of the FABLE in a scene near the Great Wall as peasants, criminals, and scholars at a labor camp participate in the invention of baseball. As in other of Louie's stories, his characters try to Americanize each other with names like Edsel and Bagel. His stories and characters are often quirky and amusing as Louie dramatizes their often surreal (see SURREALISM) attempts to adapt to a new culture without forgetting the old ways.

Other Louie stories featuring very different male PROTAGONISTs and complex, sensitively portrayed female characters also have won plaudits from critics. "Displacement," reprinted in *Best American Short Stories 1989* concerns Mrs. Chow, 35, who immigrates to the United States with her husband. Mr. and Mrs. Chow find employment in the home of a widow who has suffered a stroke and who treats the Chows abominably. In a moment of poignant clarity, Mrs. Chow sees a billboard with a rendering of a glamorous American woman and realizes that she must learn to cope with the new country, for she will never return to the old. Similarly, the title piece, about a son and his mother who speaks no English, takes the two in a rented car to another son's house, where the narrator and his mother watch wrestling on television. In another moment of clarity, the mother realizes that the world has changed for good and that she must relearn its shape. Louie uses another female POINT OF VIEW in "Inheritance," where the narrator comes of age after appearing on a television news program in support of a protest against a bombing of an abortion clinic.

BIBLIOGRAPHY
Wong, David Louie. *The Barbarians Are Coming.* New York: Putnam, 2000.
———. *Pangs of Love: Stories.* New York: Knopf, 1991.
Wong, Sau-ling Cynthia. "Chinese/Asian American Men in the 1990s: Displacement, Impersonation, Paternity and Extinction in David Wong Louie's *Pangs of Love.*" In *Privileging Positions: The Sites of Asian American Studies.* Edited by Gary Y. Okihiro et al. Pullman, Wash.: Washington State University Press, 1995.

Keith Lawrence
Brigham Young University

LOVE MEDICINE LOUISE ERDRICH (1984)
Winner of the National Book Critics Circle award in 1984, *Love Medicine* began as a short story. Author Louise ERDRICH, in close collaboration with her husband, Michael Dorris, planned it as a novel, yet many readers view it as a series of interconnected stories with reappearing characters, themes, and settings; indeed, many of the individual chapters have

been anthologized as short stories. *Love Medicine* forms part of a SHORT STORY CYCLE; although published before the others, it chronologically takes place after *Tracks* (1988) and *Tales of Burning Love* (1996). Erdrich's style has been highly praised for its lyricism on the one hand, and for its crisp, direct clarity on the other.

The stories in *Love Medicine*, told from different characters' points of view, begin in 1981, move back to 1934, and then conclude in 1948, a fragmentation that obliquely underscores the fragmentation of the Native Americans themselves. Several times the narrators relate the same scene from several different perspectives. Set on the Chippewa reservation in North Dakota, the stories focus on the Kashpaw, the Lamartine/Nanpush, and the Morrisey families. The first and one of the most memorable stories is that of June Kashpaw, who meets her death in a blizzard on Easter Sunday. The story is told from the perspective of her niece, a college student, who struggles to understand the meaning of June's death. As Louis Owens observes, however, June is something of a TRICKSTER figure, and after her death, she constantly reappears, like Christ, in the subsequent stories, thereby conflating her Native American and Christian background (Owens 195). In the subsequent stories appear such unique characters as Lulu Lamartine, a passionately intense woman, also a trickster figure; Marie Lazarre, a strong-willed woman who passes on that strength to her children; Nector Kashpaw, who loves Lulu but married Marie and fathered their child, June; and Sister Leopolda, whose confusion over her identity and her place in the world of the reservation sent her into the convent. (In *Tracks*, we learn that Leopolda, or Pauline, is actually Marie's mother.)

Critics have pointed out that part of Erdrich's success in the stories of *Love Medicine* lies in her refraining from pointing the finger of blame at her white readers, with whom the book has been both a popular and critical success (Owens 205). Beneath the warmly human tales, some told with a comic voice, some with a deeply tragic one, however, Erdrich provides a complex and compassionate portrait of a dispossessed people.

BIBLIOGRAPHY

Owens, Louis. *Other Destinies: Understanding the American Indian Novel.* Norman: University of Oklahoma Press, 1992.

Wiget, Andrew O. "Louise Erdrich." In *The Heath Anthology of American Literature*, 3rd ed. Edited by Paul Lauter. Boston: Houghton Mifflin, 1997, 3,133–34.

LUM, DARRELL H. Y. (1950–)

Darrell H. Y. Lum was born and reared in Hawaii. He is the author of two collections of short stories, *Sun* (1980) and *Pass On, No Pass Back!* (1990); a children's book, *The Golden Slipper: A Vietnamese Legend* (1994); and *Pake: Writings by Chinese in Hawaii*, with Erick Chock, winner of the 1997 Hawaii Award for Literature. Lum is cofounder of Bamboo Ridge Press, a nonprofit literary and scholarly press established in 1978 to encourage the publication of works by and about the peoples of Hawaii. Lum has also written several plays.

Lum's stories have been widely anthologized; they also have appeared in *Manoa, Bamboo Ridge, Seattle Review, Chaminade Literary Review*, and *Hawaii Review*. Lum is the recipient of a National Endowment for the Arts (NEA) Fellowship; in 1992, *Pass On, No Pass Back!* won the National Book Award from the Association for Asian American Studies.

Although Lum writes more traditional stories as well, many of his stories are written entirely in Hawaiian Creole English, intimately capturing the emotions, energy, and consciousness of his Hawaiian characters. Particularly notable for Lum's use of Hawaiian pidgin DIALECT are "No Pass Back" and "Toads" from *Pake* and "Beer Can Hat" and "Primo Doesn't Take Back Bottles Anymore" from *Sun*. His most commonly anthologized stories are humorous, some of them darkly so, and are typified by an bold defensiveness toward judgmental or condescending non-Hawaiians. Other stories, such as "Streams in the Night," are quietly yet deeply tragic. Through his writing Lum aims to help preserve Asian Hawaiian culture as well as to depict racial and cultural inequities within the larger contexts of Hawaiian and American society.

BIBLIOGRAPHY

Fujita-Sato, Gayle K. "The Island Influence on Chinese American Writers." *Amerasia Journal* (1990).

Lum, Darrell H. Y. "On Pidgin and Children in Literature." In *Infant Tongues: The Voice of the Child in Literature.* Edited by Elizabeth Goodenough et al. Detroit: Wayne State University Press, 1994.

Lum, Darrell, ed. *Best of Bamboo Ridge.* Honolulu: Bamboo Ridge Press, 1987.

Lum, Darrell. *The Golden Slipper: A Vietnamese Legend.* Mahwah, N.J.: Troll Association, 1994.

———. *Hot-Pepper-Kid And Iron-Mouth-Chicken Capture Fire and Wind.* New York: Macmillan/McGraw-Hill, 1997

———. *A Little Bit Like You.* Honolulu: Kumu Kahua, 1991.

Lum, Darrell, and Eric Chock, eds. *Pake: Writings by Chinese in Hawaii.* Honolulu: Bamboo Ridge Press, 1997.

———. *Pass On, No Pass Back!* Honolulu: Bamboo Ridge Press, 1990.

———. *Sun: Short Stories and Drama.* Honolulu: Bamboo Ridge Press, 1980.

Keith Lawrence
Brigham Young University

"LUST" SUSAN MINOT (1989)

The initial story in Susan MINOT's 1989 collection, *Lust and Other Stories,* this short tale sets the stage in both THEME and subject for the stories that will follow. The 12 stories portray different types of estrangement in heterosexual relationships: shifts in passion and fidelity, the longing for and frustration of true intimacy. Lust rather than love seems to be the chief (or only) possible link, tenuous though it is, between men and women.

"Lust" exemplifies this bleak theme. The story catalogs an unnamed young girl's sexual experiences in a series of isolated scenes, all told in first-person POINT OF VIEW from the perspective of the girl involved. Each experience is related in a short paragraph, separated by a blank line from the next; there is no transition between events. The cumulative effect of this barrage of brief paragraphs is to reinforce the fragmented nature of the girl's sexual encounters; each is short, without any intersection with other areas of her life. A subtle shift in perspective traces her metamorphosis from innocence to cynicism. In her initial encounters, her love interest "had a halo from the campus light behind him. I flipped," but only a few paragraphs later she has become "a body waiting on the rug." In spite of her sometimes gentle lovemaking, tender moments where her lover "rocked her like a seashell," she eventually feels "diluted, like watered-down stew," filled with "an overwhelming sadness." Minot's language is invariably frank and direct, and the story is filled with striking images and details that depict the scenes as well as the isolation of the characters in them.

Karen Weekes
University of Georgia

LYRIC

A term used originally to describe a poem sung to music played on a lyre. Now used to describe a subjective, melodic poem that expresses the author's personal emotion or sentiment rather than the straightforward narration of a tale. In prose, the term "lyric" or "lyrical" is applied to a writer whose style expresses emotion with imagination and poetic phrasing.

M

MCCALL'S From its inception in 1876, this magazine has aimed primarily at a female audience with a varying focus at different times on home-making, style and fashion, and beauty features, but also including fiction and essays on contemporary issues. The earliest contributors of fiction included Rudyard Kipling and Willa CATHER, and regular contributors in the 1920s and 1930s included Heywood Broun, F. Scott FITZGERALD, and J. P. Marquand. The magazine has published book exerpts and other works from numerous authors such as John STEINBECK, Herman Wouk, Rachel Carson, MacKinlay Kantor, Ray BRADBURY, Simone de Beauvoir, Shirley JACKSON, Joyce Carol OATES, Nora Ephron, Germaine Greer, and John Fowles.

MCCARTHYISM The term "McCarthyism" has become synonymous with "witch hunts," black-lists, and the use of rumor, innuendo, and unsubstantiated charges to destroy reputations. It describes the techniques used in the early 1950s by Senator Joseph R. McCarthy (1908–57), Republican from Wisconsin, as chairman of the Senate Permanent Investigations subcommittee: The committee conducted public hearings on the supposed infiltration by communists of the United States government, especially the State Department, and the entertainment industry. McCarthy's sensational methods and irresponsible charges aroused great controversy, and after a series of hearings (1953–54) on alleged communist subversion of the U.S. Army, the Senate formally censured McCarthy. The McCarthy hearings were one of the most publicized outgrowths of the COLD WAR, the nonshooting war between western democracies and the communist Soviet Union, which began in the aftermath of WORLD WAR II and ended with the tearing down of the Berlin Wall in 1989. McCarthy's legacy was the ruination of many careers and reputations and the opprobrious term that bears his name. The atmosphere evoked by the McCarthy hearings had negative effects on the careers of authors ranging from playwright Arthur Miller to DETECTIVE FICTION writer Dashiell HAMMETT to short story writer Tillie OLSEN, to name only a few.

MCCLURE'S A magazine founded by S. S. McClure in 1893 with a solid reputation for informative features on science, exploration, personalities, and other matters of interest, and for fiction by writers of note, including Rudyard Kipling, Thomas Hardy, Robert Louis Stevenson, Joel Chandler HARRIS, and Stephen CRANE. McClure used his magazine to spearhead the "muckraking" movement in the first decade of the 20th century (see MUCKRAKERS). By 1906 *McClure's* was the most widely read mass-circulation magazine in the country. That same year, however, most of his writers and staff left because of differences with McClure, and the magazine declined steadily in influence and popularity. Publication ceased in 1929.

MCCULLERS, CARSON (1917–1967)
Born in Columbus, Georgia, Lula Carson Smith, as she was known then, moved to New York City in 1934, then permanently to Nyack, New York, in 1944, returning to Georgia only for brief visits. Like other Southern writers working at a distance from their birthplaces, such as Katherine Anne PORTER, McCullers consistently set her stories in the South. Although critics have described McCullers's writing as grotesque, freakish, morbid, and GOTHIC, she insisted that her intent was to portray the poignancy of lonely people seeking love and community. She wrote two NOVELLAS—*Member of the Wedding,* in 1946, and *BALLAD OF THE SAD CAFE,* in 1951—and 20 short stories, collected under various titles, as well three novels, plays, and two books of verse.

The lonely and inexplicable nature of love is one of McCullers's constant THEMES. McCullers and her husband, Reeve McCullers, each had both female and male lovers, the complexities of which suggest themselves in McCullers's novel *Reflections in a Golden Eye* (1941) and her novella *Ballad of the Sad Cafe.* McCullers's exploration of androgyny in much of her work is shown not only in her depiction of MISS AMELIA EVANS in *Ballad of the Sad Cafe* but also in such ambiguously named young girls as Mick in *The Heart is a Lonely Hunter* (1940) and Frankie in *The Member of the Wedding.* Throughout the wedding preparations and celebrations, Frankie and the cook, Berenice, speculate on and struggle with the need for independence as opposed to the need for freedom, ending with Berenice's decision to stay with her secure but unexciting current husband and Frankie's unsatisfied need to connect with both the bride and the groom.

Judged her best story by most critics, "Madame Zilensky and the King of Finland" portrays two musicians, the somewhat colorless Mr. Brook and the fiery, passionate Madame Zilensky. Madame Zilensky shocks Mr. Brook with her wild tales about the various fathers of her children, none of whom was married to her, and then shocks him still fur-ther by informing him that he can believe nothing she says. Gradually the narrator unveils the secret lives of both characters, suggesting the divided inner self common to all McCullers's major characters. The story displays the author's ability to portray individual complexity while using touches of the comic to humanize her characters. (See COMEDY.) Other stories include "The Jockey," a tragicomic tale of racehorse owners and the jockey they exploit; two marriage tales, "The Sojourner" and "Domestic Dilemma," an examination of a husband's still-vibrant love, despite the intermingled feelings of hatred, for his alcoholic wife; and "Wunderkind," the finest of McCullers's coming-of-age stories.

McCullers's successes were characterized by an impressive determination and tenacity despite debilitating illnesses from adolescence, including crippling strokes, paralysis, and cancer. Finally, in 1967, she suffered a massive brain hemorrhage followed by a coma from which she never emerged. When she died on September 29, Carson McCullers left behind a distinguished body of work that continues to intrigue her large audience.

BIBLIOGRAPHY
McCullers, Carson. *The Ballad of the Sad Cafe.* Boston: Houghton Mifflin, 1951.
———. *Clock Without Hands.* Boston: Houghton Mifflin, 1961.
———. *The Heart Is a Lonely Hunter.* Boston: Houghton Mifflin, 1940.
———. *The Member of the Wedding.* Boston: Houghton Mifflin, 1946.
———. *The Mortgaged Heart.* Edited by Margarita G. Smith. Boston: Houghton Mifflin, 1971.
———. *Reflections in a Golden Eye.* Boston: Houghton Mifflin, 1941.
———. *The Square Root of Wonderful.* Boston: Houghton Mifflin, 1958.
———. *Sweet as a Pickle, Clean as a Pig.* Boston: Houghton Mifflin, 1964.

MCGUANE, THOMAS (1939–   )
Although Thomas McGuane is best known for his seven novels and a collection of essays on sport, *An Outside Chance,* he has published one collection of short stories, *To Skin a Cat* (1986). Stylistically, these stories seem to

distill McGuane's already spare novels into powerful and focused vignettes and concrete images. The characters in the stories range from contemporary Western archetypes (McGuane often shows concern for the decline of the 19th-century West [Westrum 100]), to a naive widower and his nymphomaniacal neighbor, to a middle-age insurance salesman who steals dogs in a rebellion against society.

McGuane was born on December 11, 1939, in Wyandotte, Michigan, the oldest of three children. He attended Michigan State University, the Yale School of Drama, and Stanford University. McGuane grew up in a family of avid readers—both his parents were English majors in college, and he was exposed to the works of Ernest HEMINGWAY and F. Scott FITZGERALD from an early age.

McGuane is a close friend of fiction writer, essayist, and poet Jim HARRISON, whom he met while they were both students at Michigan State. Harrison helped him publish his first novel, *The Sporting Club,* when McGuane's writing career stalled after a bittersweet year at Stanford as a Wallace Stegner Fellow. The two, along with painter/writer Russell Chatham and professional adventurer and photographer Count Guy de la Valdene, are known for their gastronomic exploits and their love of hunting and fishing. Although his use of dialogue has been compared to Hemingway's, McGuane's "interest in hunting and fishing has led reviewers and critics to a perhaps-too-facile comparison with FAULKNER and Hemingway" (Westrum 3). McGuane's use of BLACK HUMOR to mock the excesses of American life and his use of ABSURD situations and crazed HEROes demand examination on their individual merits.

BIBLIOGRAPHY

McGuane, Thomas. *To Skin a Cat.* New York: Dutton/Seymour Lawrence, 1986.

Westrum, Dexter. *Thomas McGuane.* Boston: Twayne, 1991.

Patrick A. Smith
Ohio University

MADAME DE TREYMES EDITH WHARTON

(1907) Published in the August 1907 issue of *SCRIBNER'S* magazine and in book form the following February, this NOVELLA exhibits Edith WHARTON's subtle REALISM and is one of her works depicting Americans in France. It tells of Fanny de Malrive, née Frisbee, a once free-spirited New Yorker now married to a French marquis. Like several of Wharton's female PROTAGONISTS, Fanny is trapped in an unhappy marriage and constricted by the "sacred institutions" of the Parisian Faubourg St-Germain aristocracy (*MDT* 229). Estranged from her dissolute husband, she has fallen in love with John Durham, a friend from her New York youth. She hopes to marry Durham and return to America, but she fears that her Catholic husband will refuse a divorce and that he may claim custody of their son, the heir to the family title.

Durham meets the marquis's sister, Madame de Treymes, a mysterious, keenly intelligent woman who herself is guilty of adultery, and he seeks her help in getting the family to consent to a divorce. He cannot decide if she is well intentioned or deceitful like her brother, but ultimately she confesses that the Malrives are agreeing to the divorce in order to claim custody of the boy and raise him according to their values: "'We abhor divorce—we go against our religion in consenting to it—and nothing short of recovering the boy could possibly justify us'" (*MDT* 280). Therefore, Fanny essentially will be forced to choose between the man she loves and her son; the story concludes with Durham's saddened resolution to tell Fanny of the choice she must make.

Cynthia Griffin Wolff notes that the "mannered complexities" of the French aristocracy are "captured in the perverse and elusive nature of the lady whose name gives the story its title" (Wolff 134), while R. W. B. Lewis asserts that Fanny de Malrive "enacts another, Paris-based version of Edith Wharton's dominant THEME. She has escaped New York only to be imprisoned within a disastrous marriage—an entrapment more complete than anything Wharton had contrived for the women in her American tales" (Lewis 166). Shari Benstock believes that the novella "reveals the dark underside of old Faubourg life and satirizes the naïveté of Americans hoping to break through its class prejudices and papal customs" (Benstock 158). In this respect, the novella uncharacteristically denounces a culture that Wharton was drawn to and usually praised.

BIBLIOGRAPHY

Benstock, Shari. *No Gifts from Chance: A Biography of Edith Wharton*. New York: Scribner's, 1994.

Lewis, R. W. B. *Edith Wharton: A Biography*. New York: Harper & Row, 1975.

Wharton, Edith. *Madame de Treymes*. In *Wharton: Novellas and Other Writings*. New York: Library of America, 1990.

Wolff, Cynthia Griffin. *A Feast of Words: The Triumph of Edith Wharton*. New York: Oxford University Press, 1977; 2nd ed. New York: Addison Wesley,

Charlotte Rich
University of Georgia

MADELINE USHER The voiceless and cataleptic twin sister of RODERICK USHER in Edgar Allan POE's "THE FALL OF THE HOUSE OF USHER" whose existence Poe depicts literally as life in death. Although Roderick and the nameless male narrator bury her alive, Madeline bursts through her coffin and falls on her brother, bringing death to both of them and an end to the House of Usher. An example of Poe's DEATH OF A BEAUTIFUL WOMAN idea, Madeline also may be the victim of incest and, by killing her brother, an avenger of the evil he has brought into the family. She is equated with the male avenger in the story within a story that the narrator reads.

MADWOMAN IN THE ATTIC, THE SANDRA M. GILBERT AND SUSAN GUBAR (1981) *The Madwoman in the Attic,* a landmark text in FEMINIST literary criticism, examines the ways the social circumstances of 19th-century women authors influenced their literary production. More specifically, Sandra M. Gilbert and Susan Gubar argue that women authors had to overcome two primary obstacles: first, the woman author had few female literary precursors and therefore turned to a male-dominated literary tradition that could not adequately encompass the woman's quest for self-definition. Second, 19th-century male writers seldom depicted fully realized female CHARACTERS but instead relied on two polarized, reductive characterizations of women: the angel and the monster.

Gilbert and Gubar reveal the ways that such canonical women authors as Jane Austen, Mary Shelley, the Brontës, George Eliot, and Emily Dickinson combated the social and cultural constraints on their writing. As Gilbert and Gubar demonstrate, each author creates a "madwoman" in her fiction or poetry to dramatize the self-division she feels as a woman writing within a literary tradition that excludes her own reality and history. The madwoman acts as a counterpart to the HEROINE, but she also functions as "in some sense the author's double, an image of her own anxiety and rage" (78). (See DOPPELGANGER.)

The most influential chapter in *Madwoman in the Attic* focuses on Charlotte Brontë's novel *Jane Eyre,* a text that—with its presentation of the quintessential madwoman, Bertha Mason Rochester—forms the centerpiece of Gilbert and Gubar's argument. Bertha acts out Jane Eyre's secret, long-repressed desires for destruction, rebellion, confrontation, and rage, emotions that can be traced back to Jane's frustrated desire for equality with her future husband, Edward Rochester. In order for Jane to attain a measure of independence and equality, Rochester must be stripped of his mastery, and, through Bertha's violent death, an important transformation takes place. Bertha's decision to burn down Thornfield Hall leaves Rochester blind, maimed, and unmarried, opening the possibility for Jane to join him as an equal. The happy ending is dampened by the fact that Jane and Rochester go to live in Ferndean, a geographically and spiritually isolated area that testifies to the rarity, and perhaps the unreality, of such an egalitarian union between a man and woman in 19th-century society. In fact, Gilbert and Gubar point out that "Charlotte Brontë was never again to indulge in quite such an optimistic imagining" (371). Their argument can be applied to many stories about women, including, for example, Charlotte Perkins GILMAN's "THE YELLOW WALL-PAPER."

Amy Strong
University of North Carolina

MAGICAL REALISM A term introduced by Cuban novelist Alejo Carpentier in his prologue to

El reino de este mundo (1949; tr. *The Kingdom of the World,* 1957) to describe his concept that both the events of everyday life and the fabulous could be conflated. (See FABLE.) Influenced by French SURREALISM, Carpentier saw in magic realism the capacity to enrich the idea of the "real" by incorporating all dimensions of the imagination, including magic, myth, and religion. Magic (or magical) realism characterizes the work of numerous Latin American writers, such as Gabriel García Márquez. Recent American writers who have experimented with the technique include Toni MORRISON, particularly in her novels *Beloved* and *Song of Solomon,* and Louise ERDRICH and Sandra CISNEROS.

"MAGIC BARREL, THE" BERNARD MALAMUD (1958)

Bernard MALAMUD has been reckoned a magician himself in that, as one of the most significant Jewish American writers of the 20th century, he helped acquaint readers with Jewish culture as he simultaneously placed Jewish fiction into the mainstream of American literature. *The Magic Barrel* won the National Book Award in 1959 and is generally regarded as his best short story collection. "The Magic Barrel" features Leo Finkel, a young man studying at New York University to become a rabbi, and Salzman, the marriage broker to whom Leo turns because his studies have prevented him from having a social life. Salzman is part salesman, part fantasy figure as he speaks of having an office somewhere in the air and a barrel full of beautiful potential marriage partners from whom Leo may choose. As in many of Malamud's stories, Leo suddenly awakens from his preoccupation with his studies to the painful realization that he lacks love in his life, both human and spiritual.

A good deal of the story's appeal revolves around its down-to-earth COMEDY (Salzman's DIALECT, his humorous, exaggerated merchandizing of the women, his lunching on strong-smelling whitefish, his request that Leo come for a "glass tea") as well as on the various intepretations of the ending. In general, it contains the Malamud THEME of love reaching those who suffer; in particular, on other levels, various interpretations seem possible.

After Leo rejects the women that Salzman describes to him (they are too old, or "used goods," or too homely, too intellectual, and so on), he finally sees Stella, the one woman he is destined to spend his life loving. Is the irony that she seems, to some critics, to be "as much more as virgin" (Weaver 59), thus ensuring Leo a rocky marriage? Or does she, like Leo, symbolize the newer generation of Americans who, unlike their parents, marry for love rather than according to the dictates of the marriage brokers? Or had Salzman intended all along to unite Leo with this woman—who turns out to be Salzman's daughter? In any interpretation, Malamud's story is a 20th-century love story that could have occurred only in America.

BIBLIOGRAPHY

Malamud, Bernard. "The Magic Barrel." In *American Short Story Masterpieces.* Edited by Raymond Carver and Tom Jenkls. New York: Delacorte Press, 1987, 295–310.

Weaver, Gordon. *The American Short Story, 1945–1980.* Boston: Twayne, 1983.

MAILER, NORMAN (1923–)

Although Norman Mailer has written few short stories, most of which appear in *Advertisements for Myself* (1959), a collection of stories, essays, and parts of novels, his influence on contemporary writing has been significant. Mailer's short story "The Time of Her Time" features Sergius O'Shaughnessy, a character who also appears in Mailer's 1997 novel *The Deer Park,* and has received critical acclaim. His first book, *The Naked and the Dead* (1948), was widely acclaimed as the best novel to come out of WORLD WAR II, and its author was seen by many as the finest writer of his time. Two years in the army in the Pacific during the war had given him the material for *The Naked and the Dead,* and the G.I. Bill provided him with the means for study at the Sorbonne while he awaited its publication. He seemed eminently prepared for a major literary career.

For years he appeared to most critics to have failed in fulfilling his early promise: His books, fiction and nonfiction, lacked the firm sense of a reality, based on accurate and objective observation, that contributed greatly to the success of *The Naked and the Dead.* (See REALISM.) In the meantime, Mailer's energies seemed more and more concentrated in other directions. Increasingly, he seems to have moved away from the traditional realistic novel in favor of expressing the difficulties of a personality at odds with the current social and political absurdities. With other writers of the 1960s, particularly Tom Wolfe and Truman CAPOTE, he became a practitioner of the new journalism that combined authorial involvement with the traditional role of objective reporter, and his success in this genre began to win back the critics. He was an editor of *Dissent* (publishing there the influential essay "The White Negro" in 1957) and cofounder of the *Village Voice.* He wrote columns for ESQUIRE, was a participant in the 1967 anti–VIETNAM WAR march on the Pentagon, became a filmmaker, and ran for mayor of New York City.

Like HEMINGWAY, with whom he is often compared, Mailer is a writer whose works provide a controversial chronicle of post–World War II America and thus demonstrate the continuing importance of his voice.

BIBLIOGRAPHY

Mailer, Norman. *Advertisements for Myself.* New York: Putnam, 1959. Reprint. Cambridge, Mass.: Harvard University Press, 1992.

———. *The Naked and the Dead.* New York: Rhinehart, 1948.

———. *The Short Fiction of Norman Mailer.* New York: Tor Books, 1981.

Manso, Peter. *Mailer: His Life and Time.* New York: Simon & Schuster, 1985.

Mills, Hilar. *Mailer: A Biography.* New York: Empire, 1982.

MALAMUD, BERNARD (1914–1986)

Born in Brooklyn, New York, only a few months before WORLD WAR I, Bernard Malamud grew up during the GREAT DEPRESSION, earned an M.A. in English from Columbia University in 1942, published his first novel in 1952 and first story collection in 1958, and had a long teaching career at Oregon State University, Bennington College, and Harvard University. Known primarily as a novelist, Malamud published three collections of short stories: *The Magic Barrel* (1958), *Idiots First* (1963), and *Rembrandt's Hat* (1973). *The Magic Barrel* won the National Book Award in 1959. A number of the stories are set in Italy, and some but by no means all involve Jewish characters. The title story, "THE MAGIC BARREL," is generally considered the finest and is the most anthologized of his stories.

The full range of human suffering in both its tragic and COMIC elements characterizes Bernard Malamud's writing from his first novel, *The Natural* (1952) to *God's Grace* (1982) and in the short stories collected in *The Stories of Bernard Malamud* (1983). Although the central figure of the "wandering Jew" can be found in the tales, many of which take place in New York, most critics agree that Malamud transcends the label of ethnic or LOCAL COLOR writer. His stories evoke place, New York especially, and American Jewish experience, but as many critics note, his characters are human first, Jewish second. Ultimately, his stories have widespread universal appeal, particularly through Malamud's evocation of spiritual longing and crisis, terror and loneliness, failure and success, and the need for companionship and spiritual growth.

A moving example is contained in "The Jewbird," also from *The Magic Barrel.* The Cohen family suddenly find themselves giving shelter and food to a skinny, starving, ragged crow that flies in through their apartment window one day. The crow is a magic crow, however, and speaks in Yiddish. Mrs. Cohen and her little son Maurie like the bird, whose name is Schwartz, and who helps Maurie with his homework. Mr. Cohen, however, is suspicious and dislikes Schwartz from the outset. Despite the pleading of his wife and son, he treats the bird abominably and eventually kills him. As with most of Malamud's stories, it may be read, on one level, as a sad tale of anti-Semitism; on another, as a story of those anywhere who bear malice toward their fellow human beings.

Malamud's second novel, *The Assistant* (1957), is an acknowledged masterpiece and has been made into a feature film, as have been *The Natural* and *The Fixer* (1962). Enough of Malamud's stories are anthologized, however, to ensure that he will be known among the significant 20th-century writers of short fiction.

BIBLIOGRAPHY

Astro, Richard, and Jackson Benson, eds. *The Fiction of Bernard Malamud.* Corvallis: Oregon State University Press, 1977.

Cohen, Sandy. *Bernard Malamud and the Trial by Love.* Amsterdam: Rodopi, 1974.

Field, Leslie, and Joyce Field, eds. *Bernard Malamud: A Collection of Critical Essays.* Englewood Cliffs, N.J.: Prentice-Hall, 1975.

―――. *Bernard Malamud and the Critics.* New York: New York University Press, 1970.

Helterman, Jeffrey. *Understanding Bernard Malamud.* Columbia: University of South Carolina Press, 1985.

Malamud, Bernard. *The Assistant.* New York: Farrar, Straus & Cudahy, 1957.

―――. *The Fixer.* New York: Farrar, Straus & Giroux, 1962.

―――. *God's Grace.* New York: Farrar, Straus & Giroux, 1982.

―――. *Idiots First.* New York: Farrar, Straus, 1963.

―――. *The Magic Barrel.* New York: Farrar, Straus & Cudahy, 1958.

―――. *A Malamud Reader.* Edited by Philip Rahv. New York: Farrar, Straus & Giroux, 1967.

―――. *The Natural.* New York: Harcourt Brace, 1952.

―――. *Rembrandt's Hat.* New York: Farrar, Straus & Giroux, 1973.

―――. *The Stories of Bernard Malamud.* New York: Farrar, Straus & Giroux, 1983.

―――. *Two Fables.* Pawlet, Vt.: Banyan 1978.

Richman, Sidney. *Bernard Malamud.* New York: Twayne, 1967.

"MALE AND FEMALE" FRANCES (JOSEPHA) GREGG (1925?, 1991)

"Male and Female" presents Frances Gregg's fictional version of the triangular relationship she shared with H. D. (Hilda Doolittle) and Ezra Pound around 1910. H. D.'s troubled alliance with Pound was mingled with her love of Gregg (1884–1941), a student at the Pennsylvania Academy of Fine Arts and recipient of some of her earliest poems. Gregg and her mother accompanied H. D. on a trip to London in 1911. While H. D., in her novels *Asphodel* and *HERmione,* characterizes Gregg as mocking and insensitive, Gregg, in her own story "Male and Female," creates Jennie, a fictional alter ego who is sincere and naive. In "Male and Female," Sheila, the H. D. character, is cold and sophisticated and manipulates Jennie, Gregg's fictional counterpart. Jennie struggles against Hezekiah's (or Pound's) misogyny and with her sense of herself as a woman. She finally asserts herself by planning to marry, an act that comes across as a betrayal in H. D.'s novels.

BIBLIOGRAPHY

Gregg, Frances. "Male and Female." In *That Kind of Woman.* Edited by Bronte Adams and Trudi Tale. New York: Carroll and Graf Publishers, Inc., 1993.

―――. *The Mystic Leeway.* Ottawa: Carleton University Press, 1995.

Karen Fearing
University of North Carolina at Chapel Hill

MANIFEST DESTINY

A theory, popular in the 19th century, that the United States had both the right and the duty to expand its territory and influence in North America. At a time of growing national confidence and population growth, this idea provided a rationale for the harsh and unfair treatment of NATIVE AMERICANS in the country's westward expansion and helped justify the SPANISH-AMERICAN WAR (1898).

MANITOU

The NATIVE AMERICAN, specifically, Algonquian, word for the supernatural force that pervades the natural world. Manitou can represent either the great good spirit (Gitche-Manito) or the great evil spirit (Matche-Manito). The good spirit is symbolized by an egg and the evil one by a serpent. The belief in and the power of the spiritual concept of Manitou recurs repeatedly in Native American stories.

MANLEY POINTER

In Flannery O'CONNOR'S "GOOD COUNTRY PEOPLE," a grotesque figure who plays the role of a simple country Bible salesman when, in reality, he shares with another character, Mrs. Freeman, a sick fascination with people's deformities. The phallic implications of his name ("man," "pointer") are somewhat misleading in that his perverse form of seduction is to steal women's glass eyes and artificial legs instead of their virginity. He runs off scot free at the end of the story, having fooled both Mrs. Hopewell and her daughter, JOY-HULGA.

MAN TO SEND RAIN CLOUDS, THE: CONTEMPORARY STORIES BY AMERICAN INDIANS (1974)

First published in 1974, in the height of the NATIVE AMERICAN renaissance, *The Man to Send Rain Clouds,* edited by Ken Rosen, is the first collection of contemporary stories by Native Americans. It features 14 well-integrated stories by southwestern writers R. C. Gorman (Navajo), Joseph Little (Mescalero Apache), Larry Littlebird (Laguna/Santo Domingo Pueblo), Simon Ortiz (Acoma Pueblo), Opal Lee Popkes (Choctaw), Leslie Marmon SILKO (Laguna Pueblo), and Anna Lee Walters (Pawnee/Otoe). Like much Native American literature, the stories are grounded in place: the landscape itself takes on the forcefulness of a character. Although they articulate grief, bitterness, and displacement, they also celebrate the resilience and resourcefulness of Native American cultures. They replicate oral traditions in which the same story is told by several storytellers, or take on different nuances in different contexts. (See CONNOTATION AND DENOTATION) For example, Ortiz's "The Killing of a State Cop" and Silko's "Tony's Story" offer varying accounts of an actual event that occurred in New Mexico. The title piece, Silko's "Man to Send Rain Clouds," demonstrates a mix of cultural traditions in its understated celebration of the burial of a beloved grandfather.

BIBLIOGRAPHY

Rosen, Kenneth, ed. *The Man to Send Rain Clouds: Contemporary Stories by American Indians.* New York: Viking Press, 1974.

Lauren Stuart Muller
University of California at Berkeley

"MAN WHO WAS ALMOST A MAN, THE" RICHARD WRIGHT (1939)

Adapted by an editor from the last two chapters of Richard WRIGHT's novel *Tarbaby's Dawn,* this story appeared under the name "Almos' a Man" in *Harper's Bazaar* in 1939, and then in the *O. Henry Award Prize Stories of 1940.* Perhaps because he had not adapted the story himself, Wright claimed that he had not wanted it to be published. In 1944 Wright conceived of a collection called *Seven Men,* in which he intended to resurrect work that had been cut or rejected by publishers, including a revised version of "Almos' a Man." By 1959 this collection had become *Ten Men,* a title borrowed from Theodore DREISER; however, Wright's agent, Paul Reynolds, advised him to cut two of the stories. Wright agreed, and *Eight Men* had been accepted for publication at the time of Wright's death in 1960.

Turning the previously published and adapted story "Almos' a Man" into "The Man Who Was Almost a Man," Wright made the PROTAGONIST younger and unmarried, which makes his escape in the final scenes unambiguous. (In the original, the protagonist abandons his wife and child.) In the revised version, the 17-year-old Dave believes that owning and firing a gun will earn him respect and make him a man. When his first shot accidentally kills his employer's mule, however, he faces two years of wage slavery to compensate his employer, a prospect he can't stomach. After sneaking out of his home and firing the gun in the woods, he hitches a ride on a train bound for somewhere where he could be a man. This plot, a boy's painful yet liberating transition to adulthood after an unplanned or accidental killing, is a favorite of Wright's; Dave is similar to Wright's protagonists Big Boy and Bigger Thomas, although he is less intelligent and reflective, and thus a more strictly naturalist character, than either. (See NATURALISM.)

BIBLIOGRAPHY

Fabre, Michel. *The Unfinished Quest of Richard Wright.* New York: Morrow, 1973.

Margolies, Edward. "The Short Stories: *Uncle Tom's Children, Eight Men.*" In *Critical Essays on Richard Wright.* Edited by Yoshinobu Hakutani. Boston: G.K. Hall, 1974.

Wright, Richard. *Eight Men.* New York: World, 1961.

Kimberly Drake
Virginia Wesleyan College

MAPLES Joan and Richard Maple are the couple featured in John UPDIKE's *Too Far to Go* (1979), considered by many critics Updike's finest collection of stories. In "Wife-wooing," after a day of cataloguing his wife's flaws, Richard surprises himself by his feelings of love and wonderment for Joan. In the stories, the two keep pulling apart and coming back together, alternately feeling passionate love and engaging in infidelities. In "Separating," Richard displays reluctance (if not cowardice) in telling his children he has decided to leave Joan. "Gesturing" focuses on Joan, who decides that she wants Richard out of the house. Yet at the end of the book, they have learned that the arguments and the adultery are less real than their children and their promise to grow old together.

MARX, KARL (1818–1883) The German socialist who wrote some of the most influential economic and political books of his century and who therefore affected the thinking of many 20th-century people, ordinary workers and intellectuals alike. Together with Friedrich Engels, Marx wrote *The Communist Manifesto* (1848), in which he issued the call: "workers of the world, unite: you have nothing to lose but your chains." He believed that class struggle was inevitable, as was a revolution of the workers, whom he dubbed "proletariat," against the capitalists, the "bourgeoisie." (See CAPITALISM.) His ultimate goal was a classless society that would permit no individual to own personal property. Marx and his theories had a notable effect on writers, particularly during the 1930s, ranging from those who joined the Communist party (Philip Gold and Tillie OLSEN, for instance) to those who, like John Steinbeck, had sympathy for the ordinary workers whom marxism aimed to help. (See also MCCARTHYISM.) Marxism has also influenced literary theory. (See MARXIST CRITICISM.)

MARXIST CRITICISM Named for Karl MARX (and based on his work with Friedrich Engels and others), marxism assumes the independent reality of matter and its priority over mind (dialectical materialism). Valuing labor, the socialization of institutions, the class struggle, and the ultimate seizure of power through revolution, it seeks—through the victorious proletariat—to establish a classless society. Like Charles DARWIN and Sigmund FREUD, Marx greatly influenced much 20th-century thought, even that of those who disagreed with his theories. Marxism particularly inspired American writing in the 1930s, most notably fiction with "radical sociological leanings" and the sociologically based literary criticism that responded to such fiction and developed in later decades under the name marxist criticism (Harmon and Holman 307). Assuming the credibility of economic DETERMINISM, marxist critics judge fiction from an economic perspective, addressing questions about the economic status of the characters and its influence on their social and political position, their actions, and their fate. Indeed, from a marxist critical perspective, the extent to which the writer includes these economic details and their ramifications helps determine the success or failure of the work.

BIBLIOGRAPHY

Harmon, William, and C. Hugh Holman. *A Handbook to Literature,* 7th ed. Upper Saddle River, N.J.: Prentice Hall, 1996.

MASON, BOBBIE ANN (1940–) Raised on a farm in western Kentucky, Bobbie Ann Mason graduated from the University of Kentucky in 1962, earned an M.A. from the State University of New York at Binghamton in 1966, and finished her Ph.D. at the University of Connecticut in 1972. Before turning to fiction, Mason wrote an academic book on Vladimir NABOKOV and a study of the Nancy Drew books for children. She demonstrated notable artistry in her first book of fiction, *Shiloh and Other Stories,* published in 1982, which won the PEN/Faulkner Award and the Ernest Hemingway Foundation Award. In 1985 Mason published a moving novel, *In Country,* that considered the effects of the VIETNAM WAR on survivors and relatives.

The title story of Mason's first collection exemplifies her understated and highly effective literary techniques, particularly ALLUSION and narrative voice (see POINT OF VIEW). More frequently anthologized than any of her other stories, "Shiloh" seems, on first reading, a simply told story of a marriage in trouble. Mason's use of present tense, however, rather than evoking simplicity, suggests that the couple has deliberately shut out the past trauma of their child's death. Set in the contemporary South, the story introduces Norma Jean as "Leroy Moffitt's wife," yet in the opening scene, she is exercising her pectoral muscles; we learn that she is taking college courses. The opening phrase suggests the traditional gender roles underlying the marital problems, and the resonances of the name, Norma Jean, recall a more famous Norma Jean, a.k.a. Marilyn Monroe, the American mid-century film star and quintessential sex goddess. The couple embarks on a second honeymoon, ironically, to Shiloh, scene of one of the bloodiest battles of the CIVIL WAR. Although Norma Jean is clearly trying to change her physical and intellectual situation, Leroy, suspicious of "women's lib," is less open to change (see FEMINISM). Critics differ on their views on the fate of the marriage, but Linda Wagner-Martin, for one, is optimistic, suggesting that Leroy, too, begins to "understand" (Wagner-Martin 2116).

Mason's stories share some important connections with those of Raymond CARVER and Ann BEATTIE. Although Mason focuses on rural Kentucky folk while Beattie writes of sophisticates, and although Mason's stories are far less bleak than Carver's, all three writers address the contemporary feeling of alienation that permeates late-20th-century life. Mason has distinguished herself, however, with her seriocomic cataloging of the signs and signifiers of late-20th-century culture, including McDonald's, Burger King, and a wealth of brand-name items. She mentions current events, from Betty Ford's mastectomy to recent television commercials, interspersed with discussions of such timeless staples of Southern life as country-fried ham and peas (Perkins 638).

BIBLIOGRAPHY
Mason, Bobbie Ann. *Clear Springs: A Memoir.* New York: Random House, 1999.
———. *Feather Crowns: A Novel.* New York: HarperCollins, 1993.
———. *The Girl Sleuth.* Athens: University of Georgia Press, 1995.
———. *In Country.* New York: Harper & Row, 1985.
———. *Love Life: Stories.* New York: Harper & Row, 1988.
———. *Midnight Magic: Selected Stories of Bobbie Ann Mason.* Hopewell, N.J.: Ecco Press, 1998.
———. *Nabokov's Garden: A Study of Ada.* Ann Arbor, Mich.: Ardis, 1974.
———. *Shiloh and Other Stories.* New York: Harper & Row, 1982.
———. *Spence + Lila.* New York, Harper & Row, 1998.
Perkins, George, and Barbara Perkins. "Bobbie Ann Mason." In *Contemporary American Literature.* Edited by George Perkins and Barbara Perkins. New York: Random House, 1988, pp. 637–38.
Wagner-Martin, Linda. "Bobbie Ann Mason." In *The Heath Anthology of American Literature.* Vol. 2. Edited by Paul Lauter. Boston: D. C. Heath and Company, 1990, pp. 2115-116.

MASON AND DIXON'S LINE Between 1763 and 1767, the English surveyors Charles Mason and Jeremiah Dixon laid the boundary line that divided Maryland and Pennsylvania. During the CIVIL WAR, the name was used to designate the line separating the free states (north of the line) from the slave states (south of the line). In common usage, the Mason-Dixon line denotes the boundary between the Old South and the North.

MASSES, THE One of the "LITTLE" MAGAZINES, it published left-wing articles, stories and poems between its founding in 1911 and its abrupt demise in 1917, when federal authorities closed its doors. Its editors included Floyd Dell, Max Eastman, John Reed, and Louis Untermeyer. The *Masses* was succeeded by the *Liberator* (1918–26) and the *New Masses* (1926–48), in whose pages appeared such writers as Tillie OLSEN, and then *Masses & Mainstream* (1948–   ), among whose editors were W. E. B. DUBOIS and Paul Robeson.

MATTHIESSEN, PETER (1927–   ) Peter Matthiessen was born in New York City, the son of

an architect who was also a trustee of the Audubon Society, and from whom Matthiessen inherited a vivid interest in the natural world. After serving two years in the U.S. Navy, Matthiessen attended Yale University, receiving his B.A. in 1950 and spending his junior year at the Sorbonne. Matthiessen's short story "Sadie," written during his senior year, won the Atlantic Prize in 1950. Matthiessen remained at Yale, teaching creative writing for one year, after which he returned to Paris and founded, along with Harold L. Humes, the prestigious journal the *Paris Review*.

Matthiessen's short stories and essays have appeared in the ATLANTIC MONTHLY, HARPER'S, the NEW YORKER, the SATURDAY EVENING POST, and many other periodicals. His short fiction is collected in a chapbook, *Midnight Turning Gray* (1984), and in a collection entitled *On the River Styx and Other Stories* (1988), which reprints six of the seven stories from *Midnight Turning Gray*. Like his novels and nonfiction, Matthiessen's short fiction is informed by his acute observation of the natural world. Accompanying his vision is a profound sense of loss at the escalating disappearance of environments and traditional cultures. Matthiessen is rightly considered one of this century's foremost writers on wilderness and the natural world.

Indeed, Matthiessen has traveled extensively and written widely on disappearing cultures and environments. Although he says he is happier writing fiction, Matthiessen is highly respected for his nonfiction, the finest example of which is his 1978 record of his trek through Nepal, *The Snow Leopard,* which won both the National Book Award and the American Book Award. He also has written an examination of the treatment of NATIVE AMERICANS in South Dakota (*In the Spirit of Crazy Horse*, 1983).

BIBLIOGRAPHY

Dowie, William. *Peter Matthiessen.* New York: Macmillan, 1991.

Matthiessen, Peter. *At Play in the Fields of the Lord.* New York: Random House, 1965.

————. *Blue Meridian.* New York: Random House, 1971.

————. *The Cloud Forest.* New York: Viking, 1961.

————. *Far Tortuga.* New York: Random House, 1975.

————. *In the Spirit of Crazy Horse.* New York: Viking, 1983.

————. *Men's Lives.* New York: Random House, 1986.

————. *Midnight Turning Gray.* Bristol, R.I.: Roger Williams, 1984.

————. *On the River Styx and Other Stories.* New York: Random House, 1988.

————. *The Snow Leopard.* New York: Viking, 1978.

————. *The Tree Where Man Was Born.* New York: Dutton, 1972.

————. *Under the Mountain Wall.* New York: Viking, 1962.

————. *Wildlife in America.* New York: Viking, 1959. Rev. ed. 1987.

Cornelius W. Browne
Ohio University

MAUVE DECADE A term used to describe the literary and social scene of the 1890s. The term comes from the title of a book written in 1926 by Thomas Beer (1889–1940), who, in trying to capture the essence of that decade in America, chose mauve as the significant tone, "pink turning to purple." Mauve contrasted with the color yellow, already used to describe the similar era in England.

"MAY DAY" F. SCOTT FITZGERALD (1920) "May Day" is one of F. Scott FITZGERALD's three long stories sometimes called NOVELLAS or novelettes. The title has three CONNOTATIONS: the maritime distress call "mayday," a spring rite, and the socialist labor holiday. As the mixed connotations suggest, Fitzgerald purposefully mingles satire, ROMANTICISM, REALISM, and whimsy to render the post–WORLD WAR I mood of the country on May 1, 1919, which historians have described as a mixture of exhilaration and moral depletion. On that day in history, servicemen in several American cities organized to attack groups of people who had gathered to observe the socialist holiday.

Fitzgerald's story takes place in New York City, where one of these violent episodes occurred. His story documents not only a historical occasion but also the fragmentation of the social structure. The characters include a cross-section of New Yorkers: wealthy socialites, socialist idealists, military men, waitresses and shop girls, a woman of lower-class origin desperate to improve her circumstances—and Gordon Sterrett, a struggling artist who eventually kills himself.

Events in Fitzgerald's own life probably became the basis for the character Sterrett, the artist who struggles against poverty. Fitzgerald wrote "May Day" after a one-year writing frenzy in which he produced his first novel while turning out advertising copy to support himself. Zelda Sayre had turned down his marriage proposal because of his limited financial prospects. His determination to change her mind, break into the fiction market, and escape the ad work that cheapened his talent are fictionalized in Sterrett, whose suicide has been described by some readers as the result of his own weakness and by others as the abuse of artists in a philistine society.

The story's content and structure reflect Fitzgerald's interests at the time in socialism and in the naturalistic fiction of Frank Norris. His compression of the action into a single day and the cameralike device of zooming in on an individual and then opening out to the larger scene are devices used in NATURALISM and MODERNISM.

BIBLIOGRAPHY

Martin, Robert K. "Sexual and Group Relationships in 'May Day.'" *Studies in Short Fiction* 15 (1978).

Mazzella, Anthony J. "The Tension of Opposites in Fitzgerald's 'May Day.'" *Studies in Short Fiction* 14 (1977).

Tuttleton, James W. "Seeing Slightly Red: Fitzgerald's 'May Day.'" In *Short Stories of F. Scott Fitzgerald: New Approaches in Criticism.* Edited by Jackson R. Bryer. Madison: University of Wisconsin Press, 1982.

Frances Kerr
Durham Technical Community College

MELODRAMA

A literary term that originally and literally described a play accompanied by music, it has come to mean any literary work that makes a blatant appeal to the emotions of the audience. Melodrama is based on a romantic PLOT and rarely includes well-developed CHARACTERS. Although most often applied to plays, the adjective "melodramatic" also can describe—usually pejoratively—plots or characters in short stories, novels, and films. The old film series *The Perils of Pauline,* for example, usually featured an improbably gifted HERO who at the last possible minute saves the helpless HEROINE from death or ruin at the hands of the stereotypical villain. (See STEREOTYPE.)

MELVILLE, HERMAN (1819–1891)

Author of one of America's acknowledged masterpieces, the epic novel *Moby-Dick,* during his lifetime Herman Melville never knew that his works, which ranged from novels and short fiction to poetry, would have such widespread and lasting influence in the 20th century. Critically berated and publicly ignored during his own time, Melville's work was rediscovered in the 1920s, and such texts as *Moby-Dick,* BILLY BUDD, "BENITO CERENO," and "BARTLEBY THE SCRIVENER" have gained prominent positions in the American canon.

Born in New York City in 1819, Melville, a contemporary of Walt Whitman, was the son of Allan Melvill (the *e* was added in the 1830s), an affluent importer and merchant, and Maria Gansvoort Melvill, the daughter of an AMERICAN REVOLUTIONary War hero. Melville's family lived comfortably until 1830, when his father's business failed. Not long after they relocated to Albany, Allan Melvill died in bankruptcy in 1832 and Melville had to withdraw from his studies to take various jobs to help support the family. After working numerous jobs over the next few years, including teaching school, Melville eventually signed aboard the whaler *Acushnet* in 1841, beginning the adventures on which he based the first few novels of his literary career. At that time, desertion was common among sailors, and Melville deserted the *Acushnet* in the Marquesas and lived briefly in the Taipi Valley. He then shipped aboard an Australian whaler, which he also deserted. He was imprisoned briefly in Tahiti but soon escaped, then served on the American frigate *United States* before finally returning to America in 1845. His first two books, *Typee* (1846) and *Omoo* (1847), both of which were enormously popular at the time, fictionalize his adventures at sea as well as his life among the cannibals in the Taipi Valley in the form of a high-sea romance.

In 1847 Melville married Elizabeth Knapp Shaw, daughter of Lemuel Shaw, Chief Justice of the Massachusetts Supreme Court, and moved back to New York. With *RedBurn* (1849) and *White-Jacket* (1850), he continued to write fictionalized accounts of his adventures as a sailor, but Melville was reaching a pivotal point in his career. In *Mardi* (1849) he began experimenting with the generic formulas he had employed in his other novels, taking aesthetic and formal risks. *Mardi* provided the first evidence of this new ambition: It is a densely symbolic and philosophical work, quite different from the fiction Melville's legion of readers had come to expect. The novel, a financial failure, marked the beginning of the end of Melville's popularity during his lifetime.

In 1850 Melville moved his family to Pittsfield, Massachusetts, in the shadow of Mount Greylock and a few miles from the home of Nathaniel HAWTHORNE, who had become a close friend as well as a profound influence. Melville was drawn to the darkness and moral AMBIGUITY that he felt defined *Mosses from an Old Manse* and Hawthorne's other work. It is clear now that the attributes Melville so admired in the older author's work were the very qualities he was developing in *Moby-Dick*, the novel on which he himself was hard at work.

Published in 1851, *Moby-Dick* signaled the beginning of the "new" Herman Melville, as ambitious an author as America has ever seen. In his epic novel, Melville conflates Shakespearean rhetoric with a sailor's vernacular, weaving together fiction, exposition, narrative, dramatic stage directions, and even art criticism in his story of Ishmael, Captain Ahab, and the fate of the *Pequod*. The novel is informed by the spiritual, philosophical, and intellectual tensions between faith and EXISTENTIALISM that Melville would continue to explore for the rest of his career. Hawthorne once remarked in his journals that Melville had "pretty much made up his mind to be annihilated and that he could neither believe, nor be comfortable in his unbelief." This movement between faith and doubt put him in stark contrast with fellow New Englanders Ralph Waldo Emerson, Walt Whitman, and Henry David Thoreau.

Moby-Dick sold poorly, as did his next novel, *Pierre* (1852), which dealt with a young writer who abandons his home in order to live with his half sister. With this novel Melville attempted to subvert the conventions of the popular sentimental romance GENRE, but the work's unremitting darkness, violence, and suggestions of incest alienated the public. Strangely, Melville had intended to write a novel that would be a popular success, but his obsessions with indeterminacy and the collision between cultural conventions and individual will took control of his narrative. In several of the stories that were to be collected in *The Piazza Tales* in 1856, Melville attempted to explore reality as an artifice of history, culture, and identity. In the same year he finished work on his last novel, *The Confidence Man,* whose main character assumes so many identities that the reader questions whether there is any central, essential self at all.

With his career as a professional writer at an end and failing in several attempts at obtaining consular positions abroad, Melville finally was appointed a customs inspector in New York City in 1866. Melville's later life was fraught with tragedy and failure, including the suicide of one son in 1867 and the death of another son in 1876. However, Melville continued writing and published several collections of poetry, including *Battle Pieces and Aspects of War* (1866), his meditations on the CIVIL WAR, which had profoundly affected him.

It is clear that Melville's obsessions are more suited to the 20th century than they were to his own. The elements that kept his work from earning serious critical appreciation in the 19th century—the ambiguity, fragmentation, inscrutable symbolism, and lack of closure—are the very characteristics that draw modern readers and scholars alike to his work.

BIBLIOGRAPHY
Arvin, Newton. *Herman Melville.* New York: Sloane, 1950.
Bloom, Harold, ed. *Herman Melville.* New York: Chelsea House, 1986.
Melville, Herman. *The Complete Works of Herman Melville.* Edited by H. Hayford et al. Evanston and Chicago, Ill.: Northwestern University Press and the Newberry Library, 1968–1990.

Olson, Charles. *Call Me Ishmael.* New York: Reynal and
  Hitchcock, 1947.
Parker, Hershel. *Herman Melville: A Biography, Vol. 1,
  1819–1851.* Baltimore: Johns Hopkins University Press,
  1996.
Renker, Elizabeth. *Strike through the Mask: Herman Melville
  and the Scene of Writing.* Baltimore: Johns Hopkins
  University Press, 1996.

Richard Deming
Columbus State Community College

METAFICTION   Metafiction comes into play
whenever a writer calls attention to the difference
between the reality of an event and the reality of
language. The baseball player who hits a home run,
for example, is real enough, but the narrative that
describes the home run is not the event itself. In
metafiction, conventional writing—the kind of writing that emphasizes the telling of a story (the home
run)—is replaced by its opposite, the story of
telling—that is, how description works. When this
happens, language becomes the main character in a
process that evolves according to norms that are different—different, that is, from those of classic REAL-
ISM. Words, whatever the prior event may be, take
on a life of their own and generate permutations,
associations, and contradictory meanings. All
metafiction calls attention to the fact that language
is man made. Instead of imitating reality, it rivals it.
Words, associations, and images develop an autonomy that once were reserved for flesh-and-blood
characters in novels and short stories.

Art's self-consciousness, however, is not a new
phenomenon. In the *1001 Nights,* for example,
SCHEHEREZADE's stories contribute to the idea of art
as stories within stories. What is new is the proliferation of metafiction since the 1950s. In the
United States, the fiction of John BARTH, Donald
BARTHELME, and Robert COOVER, among others, have
contested traditional forms by emphasizing the
machinery of writing and the ideologies encoded in
language. Metafiction mocks and exaggerates cultural codes in order to present the creative process
as a reflexive, self-contained, and, in large measure,
nonreferential artifact.

BIBLIOGRAPHY
Federman, Raymond, ed. *Surfiction: Fiction Now and
  Tomorrow,* 2nd ed. Chicago: Swallow, 1981.
Stoltzfus, Ben. *Postmodern Poetics: Nouveau Roman and
  Innovative Fiction. Occasional Papers in Language, Literature
  and Linguistics.* Edited by Orrin Frink. Series A, no. 35
  (March 1987).
Waugh, Patricia. *Metafiction: The Theory and Practice of Self-
  Conscious Fiction.* New York: Methuen, 1984.

Ben Stoltzfus
University of California at Riverside

METAPHOR   Long accepted as one of the most
useful and widely adapted literary techniques, a
metaphor is an implied comparison between any
two things, characters, situations, or concepts.
Metaphor is related to but different from SIMILE, in
that simile suggests the comparison, while
metaphor states it directly: Thus "her teeth are like
pearls" is a simile, and "her teeth are pearls" is a
metaphor. Authors may use metaphors briefly—for
the purpose of description, for instance—or they
may extend metaphor in a complicated way.
Throughout William FAULKNER's short story collection, *The Unvanquished,* DRUSILLA HAWKE becomes an
extended metaphor for the American South; in
Chitra DIVAKARUNI's collection, *The Mistress of Spices,*
the title becomes an extended metaphor for the
immigrant experience in contemporary America,
particularly the experience of women from
Southeast Asia.

METONYMY   A Greek word meaning "a
change of name." In writing, the term denotes the
application of one thing to another with which it
has become closely related in experience. For example, "the crown" can stand for a king or queen. An
integral part of the structuralist school of literary
criticism, it fell into disfavor during the poststructuralist era and is now enjoying an increased attention as post-poststructuralists rediscover its value in
determining the meaning of a literary work. (See
POSTSTRUCTURALISM.) Thus in Zora Neale HURSTON's
"SWEAT," for instance, the use of the word "sweat"

may be profitably examined as a metonomy for the word "work," which defines Delia's entire life: She works seven days a week to acquire a house, some land, a mule, and a cart.

MINIMALISM A modern literary style subscribing to the idea that "less is more," minimalism is characterized by economy and brevity, providing the reader with the bare amount of information necessary to understand the story. Although often applied to works by such contemporary writers as Bobbie Anne MASON and Susan MINOT, the term also can be used to describe works by Ernest HEMINGWAY, who famously described his technique as similar to an iceberg, and Edith WHARTON, who said she counted on her readers to "fill in the gaps."

MINOT, SUSAN (1956–) Born into a north Boston suburb on December 7, 1956, Susan Minot was raised a Roman Catholic. She attended Boston University and earned a B.A. from Brown University (1978) as well as an M.F.A. from Columbia University (1983). Minot worked as an editorial assistant for the *New York Review of Books* in 1981 and as assistant editor of *Grand Street* from 1982 to 1986. During this time she was publishing the first of the short stories that would establish her in the New York literary world. Her stories have appeared in periodicals including the NEW YORKER, ATLANTIC MONTHLY, and *Paris Review*, and she has received awards including the Prix Femina and the O. Henry Memorial Award.

Many of the early stories published in these periodicals reappear in *Monkeys* (1986). Although promoted as a novel, this work also can be considered a SHORT STORY CYCLE; its discrete chapters follow an upper-middle-class Boston family through changes that include adjusting to one of the parents' deaths and the movement from childhood through adolescence and early adulthood of most of the seven children. Several of the key events in the work happen between chapters, a stylistic peculiarity that contributes both to the categorization of the book as a collection of short stories rather than a novel and to the emphasis in Minot's work, like that of Ernest HEMINGWAY, on what is unstated and inferred.

Minot's collection *Lust and Other Stories* appeared in 1989. The emphasis in this work is on sexual relationships rather than familial ones, but the book's THEMES, including despair, lack of intimacy, and frustrated desires, echo those of her first book. The first and last selections in *Lust and Other Stories,* "LUST" and "The Man Who Would Not Go Away" are both surreal, successful experiments in POINT OF VIEW that exemplify Minot's deft narrative touch and her unsparing approach to her subjects. (See SURREALISM.) Minot's recent work includes the novels *Folly* (1992) and *Evening* (1998).

BIBLIOGRAPHY

Maynard, Joyce. "Inside: Why Susan Minot Isn't Tama Janowitz." *Mademoiselle* (July 1989): 56–60.

Minot, Susan. *Evening: A Novel.* New York: Alfred A. Knopf, 1998.

———. *Lust and Other Stories.* New York: Houghton Mifflin, 1989.

———. *Monkeys.* New York: Dutton, 1986.

Minot, Susan, and Bernardo Bertolucci, eds. *Stealing Beauty.* New York: Grove/Atlantic, 1996.

Minot, Susan, and Jane Rosenman, eds. *Folly.* New York: Houghton Mifflin, 1992.

Pryor, Kelli. "The Story of Her Life." *New York,* June 12, 1989, 52–55.

Thiebaux, Marcelle. "Susan Minot." *Publisher's Weekly,* November 16, 1992, 42–43.

Tyler, Anne. "The Art of Omission." *New Republic,* June 23, 1986, 34–36.

Wilson, Robley. "Interview with Susan Minot." *Short Story* 2 (Spring 1994): 112–18.

Karen Weekes
University of Georgia

MIRANDA RHEA Appearing in Katherine Anne PORTER's stories (two in *Pale Horse, Pale Rider,* 1939; six in *The Leaning Tower and Other Stories,* 1944; and two more in *The Collected Stories of Katherine Anne Porter,* 1965, to form the section subtitled "The Old Order"), Miranda Rhea is to some extent an autobiographical protagonist. When taken together, her stories constitute a BILDUNGSROMAN that chronicles Miranda's developing sense of self through childhood and into young adulthood. Miranda moves from a confused and angry sense that ancestors and adults enjoy a more definite identity than she ("Old Mortality") and the brink of nightmare ("Pale Horse, Pale Rider"), to a discovery and appreciation of her own "source" symbolized in her grandmother, who helps her fuse past and present ("The Source," "The Journey," and "The Grave"). At the end, Miranda understands the bittersweetness of life and death, past and present, and their contributions to her own unique sense of self.

MISCEGENATION
A mixture of races, especially marriage or cohabitation between a white person and a member of another race. Because of its association with the "antimiscegenation laws" in the United States in the 19th century, laws that prevented marriage and sexual relations between whites and any persons of color, the term has declined in use. Many people use the more neutral term "mixed race" when describing marriages or children born of a union between those of different ethnic or racial backgrounds.

MISS AMELIA EVANS
Androgynous HERO-INE in Carson MCCULLERS's BALLAD OF THE SAD CAFE who loves Cousin Lymon, the hunchback, who in turn loves Miss Amelia's former husband, Marvin Macy. Miss Amelia has money, prestige, and talent (in "doctoring," moonshining, and litigation), but demonstrates a decided discomfort with her femininity until she falls in love with Lymon. When Marvin, aided by Lymon, defeats Miss Amelia in a boxing match, she closes her cafe and her heart, boarding up her house and retiring to a form of self-imprisonment.

"MISS FURR AND MISS SKEENE" GERTRUDE STEIN (1922)
Originally published in the collection *Geography and Plays* (1922), "Miss Furr and Miss Skeene" has received critical attention for two reasons. First, much has been made of Gertrude STEIN's experimentations with language and their consequent challenges to and elaborations on the modernist tradition. (See MODERNISM.) "Miss Furr and Miss Skeene" relies on repetitious word play to complicate the relatively straightforward tale of Helen Furr and Georgine Skeene, two women who choose to live together. Second, because of its use of double entendre, particularly with the word "gay," the story suggests a subversive and positive rendition of a lesbian relationship. (See LESBIAN THEMES IN SHORT STORIES, GAY MALE SHORT FICTION, and HOMOSEXUALITY IN LITERATURE.)

Helen Furr escapes her boredom and moves in with the exciting Georgine Skeene. In the text, although Helen and Georgine are seen in the company of "dark and heavy" men, it is implied that they enjoyed their sexual pleasures with each other, not with the opposite sex. At the end of the story, Georgine leaves Helen to live with her brother for two months, but Helen does not return home to her parents. Rather, Helen "did go on being gay," and, in fact, was "gay longer every day than they had been being gay when they were together being gay." She also becomes a teacher, "telling some about being gay" and "taught very many then little ways they could use in being gay."

The text itself remains impervious to an easy reading because it never allows secure judgments about characters and action. Much of the reader's inability to decide absolutes is due to Stein's at times exasperating style. Constructing her story from a deliberately limited lexicon, Stein repeats certain words, such as "gay," "regularly," and "cultivating," changing the meaning of the word each time it is used. First introduced in the seventh sentence of the story—"She [Helen Furr] did not find it gay living in the same place where she had always been living"—the word "gay" initially seems to mean no more than that Helen is somehow bored at home. Not until "gay" begins to undergo its series of permutations does its other meaning come into prominence, leading readers to question the heterosexual status quo in which Stein was writing. In October 1923 *Vanity Fair* reprinted the story, thereby increasing the audience of those who knew the underground meaning of Stein's playful "gayness."

BIBLIOGRAPHY

Behling, Laura. "'more regularly gay and in a wholly new way': Marketing a Heterosexual Cure to Gertrude Stein in *Vanity Fair.*" *Journal of Modern Literature* 21.1 (1997): 151– .

Stein, Gertrude. *Selected Writings of Gertrude Stein.* Edited by F. W. Dupee and Carl Van Vechten. New York: Vintage, 1990.

Wineapple, Brenda. "Gertrude Stein: Woman Is a Woman Is." *The American Scholar* 67.1 (1998).

Laura L. Behling
Gustavus Adolphus College

MISS MURIEL AND OTHER STORIES
See PETRY, Ann.

MODERNISM
The modernism movement has many credos: Ezra Pound's exhortation to "make it new" and Virginia Woolf's assertion that sometime around December 1910 "human character changed" are but two of the most famous. It is important to remember that modernism is not a monolithic movement. There are, in fact, many modernisms, ranging from the "high" or canonical modernism of a few AVANT-GARDE authors like T. S. Eliot and James Joyce to the African American modernism embodied in the writers of the HARLEM RENAISSANCE. Modernism was a global phenomenon, but it had different impacts in Europe, Britain, and the United States, and it was reflected differently in writing and in the plastic arts (especially painting, sculpture, and architecture). Further, no consensus exists concerning the period that modernism is said to cover. Sometimes it is said to have begun at the turn of the 20th century with Joseph Conrad and W. B. Yeats; other times it said to have begun with WORLD WAR I. It could perhaps end in the 1930s or at the end of WORLD WAR II or it might continue today, for the theorist Frederic Jameson has claimed that so-called POSTMODERNISM is actually just another form of modernism. Such writers as Raymond CARVER or Toni MORRISON might be considered to write in a kind of modernist style. Despite the divergent opinions, most critics likely would agree that modernist expression is epitomized in James Joyce's *Ulysses* and Eliot's THE WASTE LAND, both published in 1922, and that modernism is the name put to the new paradigm for presenting the diverse facets of 20th-century culture.

Some of the shared characteristics of modernism can be identified. In the aftermath of postenlightenment culture, there was a call for a distinct gesture that could describe the quality of living. In other words, modernism inscribed a particular sense of radical rupture with the past and a perception of cultural crisis. Modernity, as Jurgen Habermas says, "revolts against the normalizing functions of tradition: modernity lives in the experience of rebelling against all that is normative." The normative changes associated with modernity include a sense of cultural crisis brought on by World War I and the sense that the new 20th century brought the world closer to the apocalypse; Western notions of progress and superiority were breaking down. Karl MARX, Charles DARWIN, and Sigmund FREUD all offered so-called master narratives that helped to explain history and to produce a new historical self-consciousness. Well-held precepts and norms for religion, sexuality, gender, and the family of the past Victorian world were also collapsing. Conflicts over racial, gender, class, religious, and colonial systems of oppression were coming to the fore. Large-scale migrations from rural areas into overcrowded urban centers and technological change also were causing cultural dislocation, and a preeminent modernist figure became the alienated and nihilistic self in a usually urban world. (See NIHILISM.) The numb and dislocated PROTAGONISTS of Ernest HEMINGWAY's fiction provide good examples.

These very real historical and cultural exigencies resulted in aesthetic crises and compensatory strategies. This radically new modern world could be reflected adequately only in a new order of art, and writers reacted with various formal innovations. This search for order was also a response to what many artists perceived as a lack of coherence in ROMANTICISM, the "movement" that preceded modernism. Romanticism's "soft" or emotional expression and its valuing of sensibility and imagination over reason and the actual, of nature over culture and art, was inadequate to express a rhetoric of loss and new beginning. The search for order in the modern world can be seen in the private mythologies of T. S. Eliot, which in turn hearken back to a classical world and in Joyce's reworking of the tale of Ulysses; this kind of self-conscious use of myth to organize the details of a work reflected a new literary self-consciousness. William FAULKNER's fictional YOKNAPATAWPHA COUNTY in Mississippi also might be a kind of private modernist landscape populated with Faulkner-invented mythical families of the Sartorises and the Snopeses; even Hemingway's macho heroic codes of behavior are modernist versions of ancient paradigms of honorable behavior.

In a kind of aesthetic attempt to purify culture by purifying language, modernist writers emphasize the role of language and form as, for instance, in much of Hemingway's spare prose and Gertrude STEIN's poetry or her famous assertion that "a rose is a rose is a rose." Other times, instead of seeming simplicity, artists relied on elitist, purposefully dense, and almost impenetrable prose and poetry; many would point to Faulkner's novels, Ezra Pound's cantos, and Joyce's *Finnegans Wake* as examples. Literary PERSONAe and masks in literature became very self-aware and self-reflexive; the characters of F. Scott FITZGERALD and Hemingway, for instance, clearly contain many of their creators' traits as well as their biographical details, and Eliot's speaker in the poem "The Love Song of J. Alfred Prufrock" shares many similarities with the writer himself. In addition to self-referentiality, the search for luminous epiphanies and moments of insight and intersection with the transcendent are omnipresent in modernist fiction. (See EPIPHANY.)

Perhaps it is useful also to consider modernism in terms of both content and form. Thus a short story such as Fitzgerald's "BABYLON REVISITED" may not seem so obviously new and innovative in its language and form as a Hemingway story, but its reflection of postwar spiritual and moral crisis gives it a distinctly modernist content and tone. Modernism also might be accused of less innovation than its proponents pretended: After all, Eliot's formalism was neoclassical; Faulkner's natural world was very romantic in its own way. Modernism was thus double-voiced,

double-visioned: It stepped free of the past and announced the new aesthetic era, yet simultaneously it failed to encompass or adequately survey the past, which perhaps accounts for the involvement of many modernists with political FASCISM and intellectual elitism. Attempts at impersonality and formality emerged from a modernist belief that superior, more realistic art comes from knowledge born of reasoned discrimination and rationality. In a self-conscious enactment of nihilism and artistic self-possession, the modernist seems to say that there is a transcendent order out there, and he or she can write it.

BIBLIOGRAPHY

Eysteinsson, Astradur. *The Concept of Modernism.* Ithaca, N.Y.: Cornell University Press, 1990.
Habermas, Jurgen. *The Philosophical Discourse of Modernity: Twelve Lectures.* Cambridge, Mass.: Polity, in association with Basil Blackwell, 1987. Reprint: Cambridge, Mass.: Massachussetts Institute of Technology Press, 1990.
Kenner, Hugh. *A Homemade World: The American Modernist Writers.* New York: Alfred A. Knopf, 1975.

S. L. Yentzer
University of Georgia, Athens

MONTAGE   Derived from the French word *monter* (to mount), the filmic device refers to the assembly of "cuts" or shots of scenes into a coherent whole. In fiction, the montage technique can establish a scene or an atmosphere through brief pictures or impressions following one another in seemingly random fashion. John UPDIKE, for instance, is well known for his literary deployment of the montage, sometimes used in interior monologue.

MONTRESOR   Montresor, the first-person narrator of the story, in Edgar Allan POE's "THE CASK OF AMONTILLADO," is surely one of the most vengeful and obsessed characters in American literature. Because of a series of mysterious old insults dealt him by Fortunato, Montresor plots Fortunato's death and succeeds by enticing him into the catacombs and then walling him up alive. His tale continues to fascinate readers for several reasons. One is that the reader never knows the nature of Montresor's grievance against Fortunato, so the reader may never evaluate whether his murder of the unfortunate man is justifiable. Another is that Montresor tells the story a half-century after the fact. Although some readers see the story as a confession and therefore a belated victory for Fortunato, most agree that five decades have passed and Montresor still delights in revealing the specific details of his crime.

MOOD The atmosphere the author creates through specific details and word choice in fiction. Edgar Allan POE evokes a bleak and somber mood in "THE FALL OF THE HOUSE OF USHER," whereas Eudora WELTY creates a light-hearted mood in the very different story, "WHY I LIVE AT THE P.O." Mood is subtly different from TONE in that mood conveys the attitude of the author toward the subject, and tone conveys the attitude of the author toward the reader.

MOORE, LORRIE (1957–) A native of Glen Falls, New York, Marie Lorena Moore was graduated from St. Lawrence University summa cum laude and earned an M.F.A. from Cornell University in 1978. She began accruing her numerous awards during her college career, winning first prize in *Seventeen* magazine's short story contest in 1976. Besides prizes at St. Lawrence and Cornell, Moore has received fellowships from the National Endowment for the Arts and the GUGGENHEIM GRANT, and was named a finalist in fiction by the Associated Writing Programs in 1983.

Moore has written in a variety of genres; she has published two novels, *Anagrams* (1986) and *Who Will Run the Frog Hospital?* (1994); a book for young readers, *The Forgotten Helper* (1987); and three collections of short stories, *Self-Help* (1985), *Like Life* (1990), and *Birds of America* (1998). *Self-Help* is a collection of nine short stories, six of which are told in the imperative voice, a PARODY of the modern "self-help" mania. Readers learn "How to Be an Other Woman," "How to Become a Writer," and "How"; all of these stories are explorations of how to survive as a woman in a complexity of relationships and demands. Written with a more traditional narrative voice, *Like Life* features stories that explore

some of the same THEMES of *Self-Help,* and all of Moore's stories also resonate with understated humor. In *Birds of America,* her third story collection, Moore continues to evoke both magic and desolation, both humor and bleakness, finding in everyday moments the stuff of reality and of sharply realized CHARACTERS. In "Willing," for example, a depressed Hollywood starlet discovers in her heart "small dark pits of annihilation" into which she throws herself. Death is present in other stories in the collection too, as is grief for its victims, from the housecat in "Four Calling Birds, Three French Hens" to the failed marriage in "Which Is More Than I Can Say About That."

Anagrams, Moore's first novel, could be considered a SHORT STORY CYCLE because of its presentation of various facets of the PROTAGONIST in discrete chapters that are complete in themselves. Moore's writing is fresh and direct, full of accurate dialogue and surprising insights about our peculiar modern world and the relationships we try to create and maintain within it.

BIBLIOGRAPHY

Giles, Jeff. "Books: Lorrie Moore." *Interview* (June 1990): 171.

Kakutani, Michiko. "Books of The Times." Review of *Self-Help, New York Times,* March 6, 1985, C21.

Moore, Lorrie. *Anagrams.* New York: Warner Books, 1997.

———. *Birds of America.* New York: Knopf, 1998.

———. *Like Life.* New York: Plume, 1991.

———. *Self-Help.* New York: Warner Books, 1995.

———. *Who Will Run the Frog Hospital?* New York: Knopf, 1994.

Moore, Lorrie, ed. *I Know Some Things: Stories About Childhood by Contemporary Writers.* Boston: Faber and Faber, 1994.

Sassone, Ralph. "This Side of Parody: Lorrie Moore Gets Serious." *Village Voice,* June 12, 1990, S15.

Karen Weekes
University of Georgia

MORGANA, MISSISSIPPI Eudora WELTY's fictional town of Morgana is the setting for the short story collection *The Golden Apples* (1949). Throughout the stories, various characters search for meaning in their lives; some leave Morgana temporarily, but eventually all return in an attempt to understand their ties to Morgana, their relationships with one another, and their own sense of self. Morgana has been compared to William FAULKNER's YOKNAPATAWPHA COUNTY, John O'HARA's GIBBSVILLE, PENNSYLVANIA, and John UPDIKE's OLINGER, PENNSYLVANIA.

MORI, TOSHIO (1910–1980)

Toshio Mori was born in Oakland, California, and grew up in nearby San Leandro, then an agricultural community but now swallowed up in Oakland itself. His parents were first-generation Japanese Americans, and Japanese was Mori's first language. His mother, although illiterate, taught him to love storytelling through her vibrant and moving oral narratives; she above all others encouraged him to become a writer. His first collection of stories, *Yokohama, California* (1949), was dedicated to her. During WORLD WAR II Mori was interned with other family members at the Topaz Relocation Center near Delta, Utah, where he was camp historian and one of the editors of the camp magazine, *Trek*. His stories were published in a variety of regional periodicals and in several anthologies, including *New Directions* and *Best American Short Stories of 1943*. A second collection, *The Chauvinist and Other Stories* (1979), together with a novel based on his mother's life, *The Woman from Hiroshima* (1978), were published shortly before Mori's death in San Leandro in 1980. Four unpublished novels and dozens of unpublished or uncollected short stories were discovered among his papers following his death.

Yokohama, California, reissued by the University of Washington Press in 1985, remains the best-known and most critically acclaimed of Mori's works, and it is generally recognized as the first short story collection published by a Japanese American author. Its 22 short stories and sketches depict the tightly knit Japanese American community in and around Oakland during the mid-1900s. Mori suggests, through a multiplicity of PROTAGONISTs and viewpoints (see POINT OF VIEW), that strong ethnic identity provides Japanese Americans with personal security and communal stability, together with appropriate appreciation for (or protection from) surrounding white American influences. As with the bulk of Mori's work, this collection portrays *Issei*—first-generation Japanese Americans—as larger-than-life characters of enormous fortitude and capacity; as Elaine Kim has noted, Mori's portraits of *Issei* women are especially sensitive and complex (163–164).

BIBLIOGRAPHY
Kim, Elaine. *Asian American Literature.* Philadelphia: Temple University Press, 1982.

Mori, Toshio. *The Chauvinist and Other Stories.* Los Angeles: Asian American Studies Center, University of California, 1979.

———. *The Woman from Hiroshima.* San Francisco: Isthmus Press, 1978.

———. *Yokohama, California.* Caldwell, Idaho: Caxton Printers, 1949.

Keith Lawrence
Brigham Young University

MORRISON, TONI (1931–)

Born Chloe Anthony Wofford on February 18, 1931, in Lorain, Ohio, Toni Morrison is the daughter of George Wofford and Ramah Willis Wofford, Southerners who migrated North looking for better opportunities. She was raised in the insular black community of Lorain until she left for college at Howard University, where she changed her name to Toni because of her classmates' difficulty in pronouncing her given name. Chloe Anthony Wofford finally became Toni Morrison when she married Harold Morrison. She subsequently earned a B.A. from Howard and an M.A. from Cornell University. She began a teaching career in English and creative writing at various colleges, had two sons, and divorced her husband in 1964 when she moved to New York to work in editing.

Morrison began her writing career with *The Bluest Eye* in 1970. This novel traces the effects of white standards of beauty in a black community as these impossible ideals destroy a young black girl named Pecola Breedlove. She is consumed by the desire for the blue eyes of Shirley Temple and little white dolls, assuming that the world would look much better and much more full of love than through her own "ugly" eyes. The effect of these impossible standards is a THEME in Morrison's other works as well.

Morrison also explores the individual's search for self. Her second novel, *Sula* (1973), centers on the title character, a free spirit who becomes the town pariah for recognizing no boundaries in her self-fulfilling sexuality. In a community based on boundaries—it is named "the Bottom" as a joke by the white community, which segregated the blacks in the undesirable land atop a hill—a woman who does not honor borders cannot survive. In her 1977 novel *Song of Solomon,* which won the National Book Critics Circle Award, Morrison turns to the black male self. Guided from a selfish life to the discovery of his familial roots, Milkman Dead journeys through the powerful puzzle of a child's song and his grandfather's death to learn to fly.

Morrison's only short story, "Recitatif," first published in Imamu Amiri and Amina Baraka's 1983 anthology of black women's writing, *Confirmation,* traces the development of a cross-racial friendship from two girls' first meeting in an orphanage through their joyful and painful meetings as adults. By using ambiguous STEREOTYPES that could refer to either blacks or whites, Morrison avoids assigning a race to either character. This produces confusion in readers, who find it difficult to imagine characters without racial identities and may be tempted to read class differences as indicators of race.

Placed in St. Bonaventure because their mothers cannot care for them—Twyla's parties too much, and Roberta's is ill—Twyla and Roberta already distrust members of a different race when they are forced to be roommates. Nevertheless, otherwise alone in difficult circumstances, they become friends. Twyla, embarrassed by her mother, especially on the day both their mothers visit, appreciates that Roberta knows not to ask too many questions—and that she shares her food.

They meet years later when Roberta and two male friends eat at a Howard Johnson's where Twyla works. Twyla responds to Roberta's condescension by asking about Roberta's mother, thus violating their former trust. But by the next time they meet, at a grocery store, both women are married, and talking restores their former bond, despite the class differences that Twyla's concern about grocery prices and Roberta's chauffeur-driven limousine make apparent. Class loyalties later divide them, however: Their subsequent meeting finds them on opposite sides of the argument over busing, Twyla for and Roberta against it. Their arguments become personal, and Roberta accuses Twyla of participating in an incident at the orphanage that she had wanted to forget—the knocking down and kicking of the mute kitchen worker Maggie, who also is of indeterminate race. On their final meeting, Roberta tells Twyla that they did not attack Maggie, they just watched. But she admits that she wanted to, as Twyla has admitted to herself, and it is this shared desire that still haunts them and, like the memories of their love for each other that helped them survive a painful past, unites them.

Morrison's haunting novel of MAGICAL REALISM, *Beloved* (1987), won the PULITZER PRIZE FOR FICTION. *Beloved* reaches back to the CIVIL WAR, confronting the unspeakable effects of slavery on black women.

In addition to her seven novels, Morrison became, in 1993, the first African American woman to win Nobel Prize for Literature. Hailed for her thematically powerful, artistically rendered novels of African American experiences, she has also won the National Book Critics Circle Award for *Song of Solomon* and the Pulitzer Prize for *Beloved.* Currently Robert F. Goheen Professor at Princeton University, she also has published a critical work, *Playing in the Dark: Whiteness and the Literary Imagination* (1992), in which she calls for critics to analyze the ways in which white American authors have used Africanist characters to define blackness, whiteness, and what it means to be an American.

BIBLIOGRAPHY

Abel, Elizabeth. "Black Writing, White Reading: Race and the Politics of Feminist Interpretation." *Critical Inquiry* 19 (1993).

Bloom, Harold. *Modern Critical Views: Toni Morrison.* New York: Chelsea House, 1990.

McKay, Nellie Y. *Critical Essays on Toni Morrison.* Boston: G.K. Hall, 1988.

Morrison, Toni. "The Art of Fiction 134," Interview with Elissa Schappell, *Paris Review* 35 (1993).

———. "Recitatif." In *Confirmation.* Edited by Imamu Amiri Baraka (LeRoi Jones) and Amina Baraka. New York: Morrow, 1983.

Nancy L. Chick
University of Georgia

Kelley Reames
University of North Carolina at Chapel Hill

MRS. SPRING FRAGRANCE SUI SIN FAR

(1912)   The title of a seminal short story collection by SUI SIN FAR (Edith Maud Easton); it is believed to be the first published collection of short stories by an Asian American author.

As a group, the stories in the collection poignantly display the hypocrisy and otherwise unchristian attitude of white American society; they lament Western obsessions with race, money, and position; and they anticipate the writings of Jade Snow Wong, Maxine Hong KINGSTON, and Amy TAN in their warmly humorous portraits of women who slyly manipulate their positions to acquire freedom of movement, thought, and influence.

In addition to the title story of the collection, which gently mocks the shallowness of American culture and the questionable aim of new immigrants to become Americanized, commonly anthologized stories from *Mrs. Spring Fragrance* include "The Land of the Free," an ironic consideration of American freedom from the immigrant's perspective; "What About the Cat?" a children's story doubling as a masterful poetically written work; and "Pat and Pan," a simple but heartwrenching depiction of learned racism.

BIBLIOGRAPHY
Sui Sin Far. *Mrs. Spring Fragrance and Other Writings.* Edited by Amy Ling and Annette White-Parks. Urbana: University of Illinois Press, 1995.

Keith Lawrence
Brigham Young University

MUCKRAKERS   Reformers, including journalists and writers, who drew attention to or exposed corruption in politics, abuses in business and industry, and other social problems in the first decade of the 20th century. The term "muckraker" was first used by President Theodore Roosevelt in a 1906 speech to describe their efforts. Roosevelt was not being entirely complimentary, for, although he agreed with the reformers' aims, he considered their methods sensational and, at times, irresponsible. MCCLURE'S magazine provided a major forum for many reformers and, as a result, became one of the most influential mass-circulation periodicals of its era. Ida M. Tarbell and Lincoln Steffens both wrote for *McClure's* and published two of the best-known "muckraking" books: Tarbell's *The History of Standard Oil* (1904) and Steffens's *Shame of the Cities* (1904). Upton Sinclair's *The Jungle* (1906), concerning the meat-packing industry, is a notable example of a "muckraking" novel.

MUKHERJEE, BHARATI (1940–)   Bharati Mukherjee was raised in Calcutta, attending the universities of Calcutta and Baroda and receiving her master's degree in English and ancient Indian culture. She emigrated to America in 1961 to attend the Iowa Writer's Workshop, eventually earning M.F.A. and Ph.D. degrees from the University of Iowa. From 1968 to 1972 she lived in Canada; after returning to the United States she began writing in earnest. She became an American citizen in 1988, commenting that she feels she belongs in the United States, a country that offers hope to everyone. Mukherjee has written two volumes of short stories, *Darkness* (1985) and *The Middleman* (1987); five novels, the most recent of which is *Leave It to Me* (1997); and several nonfiction works, two of which were coauthored by her husband, writer Clark Blaise. Mukherjee received the National Book Critics Circle Award in 1987 for *The Middleman;* she is also the recipient of GUGGENHEIM, National Endowment for the Arts, and Woodrow Wilson fellowships.

A story anthologized with increasing frequency is "A Wife's Story" (1988), a carefully crafted narrative with an intriguing twist. The wife, Panna, travels to the United States to study, and some time later the husband comes to visit her. The story opens in the United States with Panna watching a play that insults Indian men and women. On the surface, it seems to have little or no effect on her: She continues to play tourist guide to her visiting husband and, on the day he is to return to India, she prepares to make love to him to make up for her years of absence. Panna glories in her beautiful, perfumed body yet at the same time exults in her freedom. The reader must decide whether she has forgotten the insults, deflected them to her husband—or a deeply buried part of herself— or decides that American insults are part of the American way of accepting the alien, urging her to forget past ethnic and cultural ties.

Some critics describe Mukherjee's stories as clinical and detached, perhaps because the depiction of emotion or motivation often seems secondary to the precise delineation of appearance, action, and place. Although most of her PROTAGONISTS are Indian American, her thematic concerns are universal: the possibility of human intimacy, the tension between individualism and community, the opportunities and responsibilities associated with race and gender, the challenges and blessings of living in contemporary multiethnic societies, the nature and consequences of guilt, the power of goodness in the face of pervasive evil. (See THEME.) Mukherjee has said that her writing was profoundly affected by her ceasing to view herself as an expatriate longing for a lost homeland and by her determining instead to find her own place in an adopted country made up largely of other immigrants.

BIBLIOGRAPHY

Alam, Fakrul. *Bharati Mukherjee*. New York: Twayne, 1996.
Dhawan, R. K. *The Fiction of Bharati Mukherjee: A Critical Symposium*. New Delhi: Prestige, 1996.
Mukherjee, Bharati. *Darkness*. Markham, Ont.: Penguin, 1985.
———. *Jasmine*. New York: Grove Weidenfeld, 1989.
———. *Holder of the World*. New York: Knopf, 1993.
———. *The Middleman and Other Stories*. New York: Grove, 1988.
———. *The Sorrow and the Terror: The Haunting Legacy of the Air India Tragedy,* New York: Viking, 1987.
———. *The Tiger's Daughter*. Boston: Houghton Mifflin, 1971.
———. *Wife*. Boston: Houghton Mifflin, 1975.
Mukherjee, Bharati, and Clark Blaise. *Days and Nights in Calcutta*. Garden City, N.Y.: Doubleday, 1977.

Keith Lawrence
Brigham Young University

MUNROE FAMILY The Munroe family in John STEINBECK's SHORT STORY CYCLE *PASTURES OF HEAVEN* move to Las Pasturas del Cielo, the Pastures of Heaven—a California valley—in 1928. Associated through gossip with a curse—the unifying mythical device of the stories—the family members seem to bring bad luck or worse to every valley resident with whom they interact: for example, Bert Munroe prospers to the detriment of the man from whom he purchases a farm; a comment by Mrs. Munroe causes a man to leave the valley for the city. Critics debate whether the fault lies within the Munroes themselves or within the other characters of the valley.

BIBLIOGRAPHY

Fontenrose, Joseph. *John Steinbeck: An Introduction and Interpretation*. New York: Holt, Rinehart & Winston, 1963.

"MURDERS IN THE RUE MORGUE, THE" EDGAR ALLAN POE (1841) Edgar Allan POE's "The Murders in the Rue Morgue" is an extension of his GOTHIC tales as well as the first DETECTIVE FICTION, although the word "detective" had not been coined yet. This story, along with "The Mystery of Marie Roget" (1843) and "THE PURLOINED LETTER" (1845), feature amateur detective C. AUGUSTE DUPIN, whose careful perception often seems intuitive and who serves as the model for Arthur Conan Doyle's Sherlock Holmes, Agatha Christie's Hercule Poirot, and other detectives. At a time when the public was becoming concerned with crime and when police were developing strategies for criminal investigation, "The Murders in the Rue Morgue" establishes a particularly urban narrative that imposes itself on the detective's private quarters. The story depends on narrative unity and also establishes such conventions as the crime committed in a locked room, the detective's reliance on keen observation, and the use of a first-person POINT OF VIEW that is not the detective's.

This story begins in the style of an essay but becomes a narrative about the mysterious and gruesome murders of a woman and her daughter. Dupin succeeds in solving the mystery and determining that the murderer is a sailor's orangutan because Dupin, unlike the police, looks at the crime as extraordinary, sees the murders in relation to larger events and from different angles, and discovers the hidden pattern. More specifically, he notes peculiarities in witnesses' accounts, recognizes the brutality and disorder of the crime as inhuman, and pieces together clues such as the extraordinarily large span of the bruises on the victim's throat as well as nonhuman hair found in the victim's hand. The orangutan makes literal the METAPHOR of murder as a bestial act and, as in many of Poe's tales including "THE BLACK CAT" (1843) and "THE TELL-TALE HEART" (1843), presents a motiveless murderer.

BIBLIOGRAPHY

Eco, Umberto, and Thomas A. Sebeok, eds. *The Sign of Three: Dupin, Holmes, Peirce.* Bloomington: Indiana University Press, 1983.

Levine, Stuart, and Susan Levine, eds. *The Short Fiction of Edgar Allan Poe.* Indianapolis: Bobbs-Merrill, 1990.

Anna Leahy
Ohio University

MYTH   In its broadest usage, myth is any idea, true or false, in which people believe. By presenting supernatural episodes, myth explains and interprets natural events. All literatures incorporate mythology; the myths most familiar to English-speaking readers include Greek, Roman, and Norse, and American literature, in its diversity, includes myths from numerous other cultures as well. Myth often arises from folktale (see FOLKLORE): Sandra CISNEROS's "Woman Hollering Creek," for example, relates the Hispanic myth of La Llorona. Paula Gunn ALLEN and Leslie Marmon SILKO incorporate the Native-American mythic personae of Spider Woman and COYOTE in their stories, and Charles Waddell CHESNUTT uses African-American CONJURE STORIES in his tales. Myth may apply to characters, stories, and places. William FAULKNER, for instance, frequently names his characters after those in myths—Jason in "THAT EVENING SUN" is from Roman myth; Isaac in *GO DOWN, MOSES,* from biblical—and he invented an entire mythical county called YOKNAPATAWPHA in which to place the many characters in his short stories and novels.

N

NABOKOV, VLADIMIR (1899–1977) Born in Russia as Vladimirovich Nabokov, he published his first novel in Russian under the name of Vladimir Sirin, which he continued to use until 1938. Nabokov achieved widespread fame, and notoriety, in the late 1950s after the publication of *Lolita* (Paris, 1955; New York, 1958), his fourth novel written in English and the one for which he is most widely known. Charged with sensationalism at the time of publication, Nabokov's erotic novel may be credited with loosening up the acceptable sexual content of contemporary fiction. Nabokov challenged the prevailing fictional assumptions of the past and, while at Cornell University, taught a course called Masterpieces in European Fiction: Among his students in this stunningly popular class was Thomas Pynchon. Nabokov's influence on late-20th-century writers extends from Pynchon (*V., Gravity's Rainbow*) to Robert COOVER to Edward ALBEE, who produced a stage adaptation of *Lolita* in 1981.

Much of his story up until his emigration to the United States is told in the remarkable autobiography *Speak, Memory* (1952; revised 1966; previously titled *Conclusive Evidence*, 1951). Nabokov was born in St. Petersburg, Russia, into a wealthy aristocratic family. Forced to emigrate in 1919 as a result of the Russian Revolution, he attended Cambridge University and lived in both Berlin and Paris before moving in 1940 to the United States, where he supported himself by holding a variety of academic positions, culminating in his 11 years as professor of Russian literature at Cornell (1948–59). He became a U.S. citizen in 1945. After 1959 he moved to Switzerland, where he continued to write until his death.

NANCY MANNIGOE Nancy Mannigoe, laundress and occasional cook for the Compson family, is the focus of Quentin's memories in William FAULKNER's "THAT EVENING SUN" (1931). Suspected of drunkenness and cocaine use, Nancy is arrested for prostitution and becomes pregnant, presumably by one of her white male visitors. Her husband, Jesus, leaves town in anger, but Nancy comes to fear he has returned. The Compsons provide temporary protection, but at the end of the story Nancy sits alone in her cabin, rocking and moaning, sure that Jesus will kill her that night. Nancy also appears in Faulkner's 1951 novel *Requiem for a Nun*.

BIBLIOGRAPHY

Faulkner, William. *Collected Stories of William Faulkner.* New York: Random House, 1950.

Johnston, Kenneth G. "The Year of Jubilee: Faulkner's 'That Evening Sun.'" *American Literature* 46 (1974).

Kuyk, Dirk, Jr., Betty M. Kuyk, and James A. Miller. "Black Culture in William Faulkner's 'That Evening Sun.'" *Journal of American Studies* 20 (1986).

Slabey, Robert M. "Faulkner's Nancy as 'Tragic Mulatto.'" *Studies in Short Fiction* 27 (1990).

Kelley Reames
University of North Carolina, Chapel Hill

NARRATOR   See POINT OF VIEW.

NATIVE AMERICAN SHORT FICTION

Led by renowned authors Leslie Marmon SILKO, Louise ERDRICH, Michael Dorris, and Simon Ortiz, Native American fiction is enjoying a surge in popularity and acclaim by the public and scholars. N. Scott Momaday's winning of the PULITZER PRIZE IN FICTION in 1969 for *House Made of Dawn* marked the first time a Native American was honored in this way for contributing to American literature. In the 1990s, perhaps in response to the recent shift in focus and increased scholarly and popular attention regarding the plight of Native Americans in American history (the films *Dances With Wolves* and *Pocahontas*, for example), works by Native Americans are numerous; the genre now has a prominent place in the classroom and in the bookstore, with many titles of biography, fiction, history, and poetry published, purchased, and taught. Some Native Americans believe strongly in using "Native American," a term they find more accurately describes their culture and race, whereas others use the term "American Indian." There is no consensus either among tribes or among writers.

Many Americans are increasingly aware of the complex history of the tribes of Native Americans. It is difficult to point to a specific "Native American experience," since the numerous tribes have a multitude of diverse traits; peaceful, nomadic, and warring tribes lived in all regions of North America and spoke between 1,000 and 2,000 different languages. But Native Americans do have some similar qualities and an eventual shared history. Most tribes did not espouse or comprehend the concept of land ownership—to them land, like air, existed for all creatures to share. Their cultures were integrated closely with nature and spirits of their ancestors. Tribes had a strong sense of community, great respect for nature, and a dazzling array of ceremonies that integrated and celebrated communal living in the natural world.

The coming of the Europeans in the 1500s heralded a drastic change in Native American cultures. Once Francisco Vázquez de Coronado's conquistadors clashed with the Zuñi warriors in 1540, the American Indian people of the North American continent were in a perpetual state of war until almost the 20th century. In addition, the indigenous people faced the problems of famine and the lack of immunity to European diseases. Such viral diseases as influenza and the mumps worked like a plague on many Indian tribes. Due to a combination of war, disease, and famine, the population of Native American peoples diminished from the 2,500,000 of pre-Columbus years, to 250,000 at the end of the 1800s. (The population has since grown back to 1.3 million.)

Several tribes signed treaties they did not fully understand, forfeiting their rights to land, and moved to reservations on poor-quality land; other tribes, not wanting to concede their land rights, fought wars against the new American government. With the concept of MANIFEST DESTINY and the western expansion of the United States, the U.S. Congress passed the Indian Removal Act in 1830, moving many Indians to Oklahoma and setting the precedent for future removals. After gold was discovered on Cherokee land in 1838, the Indian inhabitants were forcibly moved in what is called the Trail of Tears. Many wars between U.S. government and tribes ensued, climaxing with the Sioux War in 1876 and the Barrock War, which returned the Barrock Indians to the reservation in Idaho in 1877. The final battle was the Wounded Knee Massacre of 1890, with the killing of Chiefs Sitting Bull and Big Foot, in addition to more than 200 others, including women and children. In 1924 Native Americans were given the right to vote. Slowly over the years the U.S. government has sought to redress some of its errors in its treatment of them. Still, reservations residents confront pervasive poverty, violence, and alcoholism. Many Native Americans continue to be disgruntled with their plight, and as recently as 1973 members of a protest group seized the village of Wounded Knee and challenged federal authorities to repeat the 1890 massacre. After 72 days, two deaths, and many injuries, the group surrendered, having brought national attention to the Sioux grievances.

Many THEMES and narratives in literature are driven by the conflict between PROTAGONIST and environment, and Native American literature is hardly an exception. In addition to taking on the themes just addressed, Native American writers often incorporate their individualistic tribal "touch" to their writing or introduce their tribe's TRICKSTER figure, an often mischievous, humorous, and changing character who transforms its gender and form between animal and human. Further, many Native American writers use narrative styles that are more oral in nature and less constrained by traditional Western notions of structure and time (for example, introduction, beginning, body, conclusion). In other words, since time does not stop and since it works to continue that which has occurred since the beginning of time, many Native American writers approach their writing as only a part of the continuum, simply a snapshot of time; thus, their stories often conclude at a moment contrary to most readers' expectations.

Historically, a central characteristic or theme in Native American literature is "orality." For thousands of years, tribal stories were passed on verbally from generation to generation; as the story passed, it changed from storyteller to storyteller. This oral quality might explain in part the reason for the long delay in the inclusion of Native American writers in the American literary canon. Storytelling, often used to explain why phenomena appear as they do (how landmarks came to be or how mountains formed) or to entertain, is prominent in Native American literature and provides a more "spoken" feel to the writing style.

Many contemporary stories chronicle the way Native American people have struggled to survive in the face of the modern world, with its harsh realities of poverty, racism, and alcoholism. In stories written today, for example, Leslie Marmon Silko writes about Yellow Woman and the dangers of adultery, whereas Louise Erdrich incorporates a shiftless healer and themes of love in a reservation setting replete with poverty, alcoholism, and gambling. Much contemporary fiction focuses on the status of the community and family, preservation of the earth, tradition and ceremony, the context of and in conflict with the increasingly technological and violent world. Writers such as Joy Harjo, Linda Hogan, Mary Tallmountain, James Welch, and Gerald VIZENOR are distinctively Native American in the way they incorporate both the noble themes and harsh current realities in their stories that form part of the continuum from "time immemorial."

BIBLIOGRAPHY
Lesley, Craig, ed. *Talking Leaves: Contemporary Native American Short Stories.* New York: Dell, 1991.

Calvin Hussman
St. Olaf College

NATIVE AMERICAN STORYTELLING
Storytelling is as essential to human survival as food and water. Without stories we cannot remember the past, understand the present, or look forward to a future. Without stories we cannot share our experiences with others or describe our sometimes intimate relationship with the earth, our kindred, or the power of creation. By telling a story, we give meaning to experience. Sacred narratives are simply those stories about ancestors who have provided significant and respected examples of how best to live in a complex world full of wonder.

Most Native American authors believe these assertions about the power of narrative. Despite the vast range of cultural differences existing among the 310 Native American tribes in the United States, writers from these varied communities acknowledge the relationship between orally transmitted narratives and single-authored works of short fiction. In fact, myths, rituals, LEGENDS, TRICKSTER stories, and FOLKLORE formulate the worldview against which Native American writers often measure their characters' experiences. Both traditional storytellers and creative writers use language to maintain, transform, or heal their environment—an environment created to sustain all life-forms in harmonious cooperation. In communal settings, storytellers are often intimate friends of the listeners. Individual authors try, through print, to extend such intimacy to unknown readers. For example, Gerald VIZENOR (Chippewa) calls printed texts "dead voice"; Greg Lesley names them "talking leaves"; and Clifford E. Trafzer (Wyndot) designates pieces of short fiction "paper spirits." Such designations focus on discourse as a "saying" (continuing conversations or dialogues) rather than a "said" (something finished and therefore preempted).

In 1991 Joseph Bruchac (Abenaki) helped organize a festival of Native writers from North America. More than 200 published authors participated. Bruchac told this audience that their ability to write was given by the creator, and, therefore, writers have an "obligation to return that gift, to make use of it in a way that serves the people and the generations to come" (Bruchac xix). Pulitzer Prize winner N. Scott Momaday (Kiowa) also suggests that humans achieve their "fullest realization" of their "humanity in such an art and product of the imagination as literature—and here I use the term *literature* in its broadest sense. This is admittedly a moral view of the question, but literature is itself a moral view, and it is a view of morality" (Momaday 105). Both these well-known authors treat writers as morally obligated to help readers relate with gratitude and respect to all that exists in the complex web of life.

Many Native American writers relate to each other as if they were members of a transtribal community. Most are familiar with the grandfathers of short fiction by Native writers: Ralph Salisbury (Cherokee; b. 1926), Maurice Kenny (Mohawk; b. 1929), Carter Revard (Osage; b. 1931), Gerald Vizenor (Minnesota Chippewa; b. 1934), Duane Niatum (Klallam; b. 1938), and Simon Ortiz (Aroma Pueblo; b. 1941). Literary production is not male-dominated among Native peoples; Native women have equal stature. The grandmothers of short fictions are Mary Tall Mountain (Koyukon Athabascan; b. 1918), Elizabeth Cook-Lynn (Crow-Creek-Sioux; b. 1930), Diane Glancy (Cherokee; b. 1941), Linda Hogan (Chickasaw; b. 1947), Leslie Marmon SILKO (Laguna Pueblo; b. 1948), and Karen

Louise ERDRICH (Chippewa; b. 1954). These award-winning authors are the best-known short story writers; however, numerous other gifted writers, including Sherman ALEXIE (Spokane and Coeur d'Alene) Beth Brandt (Mohawk), are quickly gaining equal stature.

Several THEMES are central to the concerns of Indian writers; storytelling as survival; trickster discourse as radical, comic, and fractious; the loss and importance of land and culture; the problems of assimilation—mixed blood conflicts, lost identity, alcoholism, domestic violence, poverty; kinship disillusion and reunion; the interdependence between the physical and spiritual environments; and the possibility of the reenchantment of the world. Historically, colonization and government policies pushed many tribes to near extinction. Readers, therefore, might expect Native literature to constitute victims' tragic tales. This is not the case, however. While most writers do describe the horrors Native peoples have experienced, their overall thrust is toward survival and reclamation. In many ways contemporary Indian writers have become autoethnographers. That is, these authors recontextualize their ethnic inheritance through imaginative works.

Leslie Silko's *Storyteller* (1981) exemplifies this autoethnographic effort. *Storyteller* is a collection of Laguna creation narratives, ancestral stories, tribal folklore, and imaginative fiction woven together to show the synchronic or intertextual nature of these expressions. For Silko, time is like an ocean. Events occurring 500 years ago impact life as much as those occurring five minutes ago. And events occurring in time are often variations or reenactments of mythic events. Female characters in this text, for example, often resemble the mythic Yellow Woman whose adventures bring her suffering yet fulfill the pressing needs of her community. For Silko, these immemorial stories convey the endurance of the *feminine* (the grandmothers—birth, death, and rebirth).

Louise Erdrich's collection of stories in *Love Medicine* explores the impact of the death of June Morrisey, an estranged tribal member, on various members of the Chippewa community in North Dakota. Few contemporary writers of any ethnic group have so clearly and empathetically communicated the tangle of genealogical ties in mixed blood, postassimilationist communities as skillfully as Erdrich. Euroamerican and Native American characters people her narratives as co-inhabitants in each others' stories.

Two Cherokee writers—Robert J. Conley and Diane Glancy—do for the Cherokee Nation what Silko and Erdrich have done for the Laguna and Chippewa. Conley's *The Witch of Goingsnake and Other Stories* (1988) communicates the values of the Cherokee people as they have been passed down through generations. Diane Glancy's *Firesticks* tells the stories of individuals who have been unable to share in such passed on narratives: "There was the darkness of a dream again. And in that darkness, the burning firesticks the men used to carry from the holy Keetowah fire to light the smaller fires in the cabins. Light of darkness. New life from ashes. . . . But now we had lost our ceremonies" (Glancy 125). Glancy's characters stumble toward forgiveness, remembrance, and the recognition of place. Their firesticks either pass down fragments of memory out of the ashes of ineffectual lives or are unconscious attempts to reconnect to what is holy.

MAGICAL REALISM plays a huge role in contemporary Native fiction. The thread linking the stories in Clifford E. Trafzer's collection *Blue Dawn, Red Earth* is that these "almost hallowed" stories contain "something good and magical . . . that might be given to others" (18). Witches, shamans, spirits, and spells impact the lives of the characters in many of the 30 stories by "not well known" authors in this collection. Characters witness "unspeakable" things that testify to the ongoing connection between the dead, the living, and the not-yet-born. If nothing else, these 30 authors demonstrate that a spiritual landscape coexists with the physical, one that is accessible in times of loneliness, need, misfortune, and misbehavior.

Humor makes so many collections of short fiction by Native Americans so unsentimental yet ultimately affirming. Trickster discourse erupts in many tales. Carter Revard, Gerald Vizenor, and Peter Blue Cloud (Mohawk) are noted for their contemporary uses of trickster patterns. Revard's "Report to the Nation: Claiming Europe" is a very ironic, humorous tale turning the table on "discovery" narratives in America. "It may be impossible to civilize the Europeans. When I claimed England for the Osage Nation, last month, some of the English chiefs objected," the story begins (Revard). Vizenor's collections of short stories are primarily trickster narratives—comic tales and metaphors that challenge the truth claims of Natives and Anglos alike. Blue Cloud's short story collections contain trickster tales on topics from the creation to elitist poets. An example of Blue Cloud's wit is "The First Missiles," a story about Coyote's "full-stomach-greedy-for-more syndrome" (Blue Cloud 11). Coyote, a great thinker (and forgetter of the meaning of sweat baths), tries to horde the water in all the desert springs by surrounding them with arrows triggered to explode if anyone tries to drink from them. When his task is completed, Coyote travels to another desert to claim the springs there. To his amazement, Coyote himself becomes the object of many arrows. He has forgotten that his twin brother, in the eastern valley, was a thinker like himself. He also has forgotten that bows and arrows are tools, not weapons, and such forgetfulness leads to Coyote's death.

The Native Americans continue to publish short fiction at an unprecedented pace; it will be subject to continuous interpretation and changing literary and critical opinion. What is written about this topic today will need to be revised tomorrow. What will probably not change, however, is that the gifts—the stories—continue to be given.

BIBLIOGRAPHY

Bruchac, Joseph. "Foreword." In *Smoke Rising: The Native North American Literary Companion*. Edited by Janet Witalcc. Detroit: Visible Ink Press, 1995.

Blue Cloud, Peter. *The Other Side of Nowhere: Contemporary Coyote Tales*. Fredonia, N.Y.: White Pine Press, 1990.

Conley, Robert J. *The Witch of Goingsnake*. Norman: University of Oklahoma Press, 1988.

Erdrich, Louise. *Love Medicine*. New York: HarperCollins, 1984.

Glancy, Diane. *Firesticks*. Norman: University of Oklahoma Press, 1993.

Lesley, Craig, ed. "Introduction." *Talking Leaves: Contemporary Native American Short Stories*. New York: Dell, 1991.

Momaday, N. Scott. "Man Made of Words." In *Literature of the American Indians: Views and Interpretations*. Edited by Abraham Chapman, New York: Meridian, 1977.

Revard, Carter. "Report to the Nation: Claiming Europe." In *Earth Power Coming*. Edited by Simon Ortiz. Tsaile, Ariz.: Navajo Community College Press, 1983.

Silko, Leslie Marmon. *Storyteller*. New York: Seaver Books, 1981.

Trafzer, Cliffors E. "Introduction." *Blue Dawn, Red Earth*. New York: Anchor Books, 1996.

Vizenor, Gerald. *Dead Voices*. Norman: University of Oklahoma Press, 1992.

Suzanne Lundquist
Brigham Young University

NATURALISM

The term "literary naturalism" is used to describe a body of literature that emerged in the late 19th and early 20th centuries. The central concerns of naturalism are the forces that shape and move humanity and our inability to control them. Naturalism has its origins in the work of French writer Emile Zola, who saw the naturalist as a scientist describing human behavior as a product of the forces that conditioned it, and of Charles Darwin, whose *On the Origin of Species* (1859) postulated that humans evolved from lower animals and were therefore controlled by the same basic instincts. Darwin's theories led to the survival-of-the-fittest concept of human social evolution.

In a literary sense, Donald Pizer has argued that American naturalism is informed by the "ideological core" that "man is more circumscribed than conventionally acknowledged"(20). In particular, naturalism believes that the powerful dominate the weak, "few can overcome the handicaps imposed upon them by inadequacies of body and mind, and that many men have instinctive needs that are not amenable to moral suasion or rational argument"(20). American naturalism began in the 1890s, led by Stephen CRANE, Frank Norris, Theodore DREISER, and Jack LONDON. These writers chose to work with a prose that was more sparse and THEMES that were more deterministic than the realists who preceded them. (See DETERMINISM.) In contrast to REALISM, which attempted to capture ordinary American life as it unfolded in cities and rural areas in the middle and late-19th century, naturalism employed harsher outdoor settings and placed characters in trying situations where they often confronted natural forces. For example, while Henry JAMES's novella *DAISY MILLER: A STUDY* opens: "At the little town of Vevey, in Switzerland, there is a particularly comfortable hotel," Stephen Crane begins "A Mystery of Heroism": "The dark uniforms of the men were so coated with dust from the incessant wrestling of the two armies that the regiment almost seemed a part of the clay bank which shielded them from the shells." Images of dust and battle do not find their way into American realism, just as Swiss retreats and "comfortable" hotels are not the stuff of American naturalism. In this break from the tradition of realism, naturalism questioned moral and situational certainties and drew attention to the forces of fate, determinism, and environment that shape individuals.

Environment is key to the fiction of Jack London, and this connection to setting is apparent in his Klondike fiction, which he began publishing in 1899. In stories such as "TO BUILD A FIRE," London explored the harsh Alaskan wilderness and its effect on men seeking their fortunes during the Yukon gold rush. In that story the harsh arctic environment confronts a single traveler who foolishly believes that he can endure the chilling wilderness alone. This man is typical of the PROTAGONISTs of naturalism, who fail to heed warnings because of their own egotism and their disregard for nature's power and its indifference to human suffering. Even though "[I]t had been days since he had seen the sun" and the temperature was 50 degrees below zero, the man receives "no impression" from his surroundings. The reason, we are told, is that "he was without imagination." Warned by an old prospector not to travel alone after the temperature drops below 50 degrees below, the man thinks that he will survive on his own and calls the old man "rather womanish." Later, however, the man freezes to death because his numb hands will not allow him to hold a match and start a life-saving fire. In contrast to the man's disregard for nature, his traveling companion—a large native husky—is fully aware of the dangers of the temperature. The narrator explains: "The animal was depressed by the tremendous cold. It knew that it was not time for traveling. Its instinct told it a truer tale than was told to the man by the man's judgement." Attuned to the dangers of this climate, the dog survives its master. Human egotism, the story suggests, is the weakness of humanity, and the price for disregarding the ascendancy of nature in this and many other naturalistic stories is death.

Perhaps the most skilled naturalist, both in THEME and use of language, is Stephen Crane. In his novels and short fiction, central naturalistic themes of humanity against nature are investigated. His story "THE OPEN BOAT" stands as a model of what American naturalism sought to explore and evoke in its methods. In this story of four men adrift in a lifeboat off the coast of Florida after a shipwreck, Crane's attention to impressionistic language links theme and technique. He begins: "None of them knew the color of the sky," and says of the treacherous ocean facing the men: "There was a terrible grace in the move of the waves, and they came in silence, save for the snarling of the crests." This concise attention to language helps Crane to address the relationship between humanity and the universe. The men first feel anger at "this old ninny-woman, Fate" who brings them close to land while still threatening to drown them. Later, however, the men are reduced to resignation over their insignificant position in the universe. The narrator explains: "When it occurs to a man that nature does not regard him as important, and she feels that she would not maim the universe by disposing of him, he at first wishes to throw bricks at the temple, and he hates deeply the fact that there are no bricks and no temples." Three of the men survive as the boat is swamped by waves near shore, but one is drowned. Only after this traumatic event on the lifeboat can the three survivors interpret the "great sea's voice." Herein lies a central tenet of naturalism: Humanity, like London's prospector, is subject to the same natural laws as all animals. As such, humans are subject to the same limitations, and it is a painful realization that humankind holds no special place in the universe. As humans are governed by the same laws as all of nature, literary naturalism suggests that those who attempt to question, combat, or suppress nature will find only failure.

BIBLIOGRAPHY

Crane, Stephen. "The Open Boat." In *The Great Short Works of Stephen Crane*. Edited by James B. Colvert. New York: Harper Perennial, 1994, 277–302.

Lauter, Paul, ed. *The Heath Anthology of American Literature*, vol. 2, 2nd ed. Lexington, Mass.: D.C. Heath, 1994.

London, Jack. "To Build a Fire." In *To Build a Fire and Other Stories*. New York: Bantam, 1988, 164–182.

Pizer, Donald. *The Theory and Practice of American Literary Naturalism*. Carbondale: Southern Illinois University Press, 1993.

Chris McBride
California State University at Los Angeles

NEBULA AWARDS   The Nebula Awards were established in 1966 by the Science Fiction Writers of America to recognize excellence in SCIENCE FICTION writing by honoring the best novel, NOVELLA, novelette, and short story published during the previous calendar year. In addition, the Grand Master Award is presented to recognize lifetime contributions to the field of science fiction.

"NEIGHBOUR ROSICKY" WILLA CATHER (1930, 1932)   First published in *Woman's Home Companion* (April/May, 1930) and included as one of three stories in *Obscure Destinies* (1932), "Neighbour Rosicky" dramatizes an old Bohemian farmer's final days. The story is a CHARACTER study of Anton Rosicky but also a portrait of a happy, productive family; a philosophical reflection on the place of death in the cycle of life; and a subtle social commentary on the American drive for success at the expense of a full life in the present. The story has affinities with both American REALISM and ROMANTICISM. Willa CATHER uses FLASHBACKS to contrast

Rosicky's past life as a tailor in London and New York with his life as husband and father on a Nebraska farm. His naturally generous spirit and capacity for hard work have matured under the duress of farming life; city life had provided excitement and cultural stimulation but left him restless and unfulfilled.

The story echoes others in the Cather canon that contrast rural and urban life. Knowing his heart is in poor condition, Rosicky spends his final winter clarifying for his children the legacy he has left them: not just the farm property but also the spiritual strength to build a satisfying life on it. He delivers his last gifts through grim stories of city life, the respect he displays for his family, and acts of kindness to his new daughter-in-law who has trouble adjusting to farm life. His death comes not as a tragedy but as the peaceful end to a long life in which he created—not by force of will but by acceptance and perseverance—personal fulfillment and family happiness. The story is considered one of Cather's best, notable for its realistic dialogue and description and its successful balance of character development with social analysis. The story also contains one of her few portraits of a mutually sustaining marriage.

BIBLIOGRAPHY

Arnold, Marilyn. *Willa Cather's Short Fiction*. Athens: Ohio University Press, 1984.

Cather, Willa. *Uncle Valentine and Other Stories: Willa Cather's Uncollected Short Fiction, 1915–1929*. Edited by Bernice Slote. Lincoln: University of Nebraska Press, 1973.

Rosowski, Susan J. *The Voyage Perilous: Willa Cather's Romanticism*. Lincoln: University of Nebraska Press, 1986.

Frances Kerr
Durham Technical Community College

NEW CRITICISM

New Criticism is a movement in 20th-century literary criticism that arose in reaction to those traditional "extrinsic" approaches that saw a text as making a moral or philosophical statement or as an outcome of social, economic, political, historical, or biographical phenomena. New Criticism holds that a text must be evaluated apart from its context; failure to do so causes the AFFECTIVE FALLACY, which confuses a text with the emotional or psychological response of its readers, or the INTENTIONAL FALLACY, which conflates textual impact and the objectives of the author.

New Criticism assumes that a text is an isolated entity that can be understood through the tools and techniques of CLOSE READING, maintains that each text has unique texture, and asserts that what a text says and how it says it are inseparable. The task of the New Critic is to show the way a reader can take the myriad and apparently discordant elements of a text and reconcile or resolve them into a harmonious, thematic whole. (See THEME.) In sum, the objective is to unify the text or rather to recognize the inherent but obscured unity therein. The reader's awareness of and attention to elements of the form of the work means that a text eventually will yield to the analytical scrutiny and interpretive pressure that close reading provides. Simply put, close reading is the hallmark of New Criticism.

The genesis of New Criticism can be found in the early years of the 20th century in the work of the British philosopher I. A. Richards and his student William Empson. Another important figure in the beginnings of New Criticism was the American writer and critic T. S. Eliot. Later practitioners and proponents include John Crowe Ransom, Cleanth Brooks, Allen Tate, Robert Penn Warren, René Wellek, and William Wimsatt. In many ways New Criticism runs in temporal parallel to the American modern period.

From the 1930s to the 1960s in the United States, New Criticism was the accepted approach to literary study and criticism in scholarly journals and in college and university English departments. Among the lasting legacies of New Criticism is the conviction that surface reading of literature is insufficient; a critic, to arrive at and make sense of the latent potency of a text, must explore very carefully its inner sanctum by noting the presence and the patterns of literary devices within the text. Only this, New Criticism asserts, enables one to decode completely.

New Criticism brought discipline and depth to literary scholarship through emphasis on the text and a close reading thereof. However, the analytic and interpretive moves made in the practice of New Criticism tend to be most effective in LYRIC and complex intellectual poetry. The inability to deal adequately with other kinds of texts proved to be a significant liability in this approach. Furthermore, the exclusion of writer, reader, and context from scholarly inquiry has made New Criticism vulnerable to serious objections.

Despite its radical origins, New Criticism was fundamentally a conservative enterprise. By the 1960s, its dominance began to erode, and eventually it ceded primacy to critical approaches that demanded examination of the realities of production and reception. Today, although New Criticism has few champions, in many respects it remains an approach to literature from which other critical modes depart or against which they militate.

BIBLIOGRAPHY

Brooks, Cleanth. *The Well Wrought Urn: Studies in the Structure of Poetry.* New York: Reynal and Hitchcock, 1947.

Guerin, Wilfred, et al. *A Handbook of Critical Approaches to Literature,* 4th ed. New York: Oxford University Press, 1999.

Jancovich, Mark. *The Cultural Politics of the New Criticism.* Cambridge, England: Cambridge University Press, 1992.

Lentricchia, Frank. *After the New Criticism.* Chicago: University of Chicago Press, 1980.

Ransom, John. *The New Criticism.* New York: New Directions, 1941.

Spurland, William, and Michael Fischer, eds. *The New Criticism and Contemporary Literary Theory: Connections and Continuities.* New York: Garland, 1995.

Willingham, John. "The New Criticism: Then and Now." In *Contemporary Literary Theory.* Edited by Douglas Atkins and Janice Morrow. Amherst: University of Massachusetts Press, 1989, 24–41.

Geoffrey C. Middlebrook
California State University at Los Angeles

"NEW ENGLAND NUN, A" MARY E. WILKINS FREEMAN (1891)

Originally published in *Harper's Bazaar* in 1887 and in 1891 as the title story in *A New England Nun and Other Stories,* the story opens onto a scene of pastoral rural New England calm. In complete harmony with this scene is the PROTAGONIST, Louisa Ellis, as the third-person narrator takes the reader into her painstakingly—if not obsessively—ordered house. Louisa, who lives alone in the house now that her mother and brother have died, owns two animals: a canary that she keeps in a cage and a dog, Caesar, that she keeps on a chain in her yard. For 15 years she has faithfully waited for the return of Joe Daggett, her fiancé, who went to Australia to make his fortune.

The narrator depicts Joe's return as a coarse, masculine intrusion into Louisa's feminine and well-appointed house and life. His hearty sexuality echoes that of Caesar, doomed to be forever chained because he once bit a passerby. Louisa herself seems like the canary, comfortable within the boundaries of her enclosure. Clearly, the maleness and femaleness that Joe and Louisa represent cannot adapt to each other. Because both have become set in their gendered ways, and because both are decent and honorable people determined to keep their long-ago engagement promises, Louisa feels relief when, without their awareness, she stumbles across Joe and Lily Dyer, the pretty girl who takes care of his mother. Louisa overhears them confessing their love for one another. The next day, to their mutual relief, Louisa and Joe release each other from their engagement.

This much of the story is clearly told. In the ambivalence of the ending, however, Freeman challenges the reader to evaluate Louisa's situation. By giving up marriage and, in those days, her only possible sexual outlet, has she sacrificed too much? Why must women make such choices? Will she actually feel happier living alone, owning her house, keeping her passions chained along with Caesar? Is she a version of Freeman herself, especially in her love of extracting essences from the herbs she gathers (seen by some critics as a METAPHOR for the writing process)? Freeman's story and the ramifications of Louisa's decision resonate with the reader long after the story actually ends.

BIBLIOGRAPHY

Freeman, Mary E. Wilkins. "A New England Nun." In *Selected Short Stories*. Edited by Marjorie Pryse. New York: Norton, 1983.

Glasser, Leah Blatt. *In a Closet Hidden: The Life and Works of Mary E. Wilkins Freeman*. Amherst: University of Massachusetts Press, 1996.

NEW YEAR'S DAY EDITH WHARTON (1924)

One of Edith WHARTON's many stories of New York, it was published with the subtitle *The 'Seventies* in 1924 as the last of four volumes in a set entitled *Old New York*. This NOVELLA depicts with subtle REALISM the reactions within Old New York society to the scandalous affair of Mrs. Lizzie Hazeldean. The tale opens in the residence of the Parrett family as they watch a fire in the Fifth Avenue Hotel. The blaze forces the hotel's occupants outside the building, and the family is shocked to see Mrs. Hazeldean exit with a well-to-do bachelor, Henry Prest. Most of the story, however, recounts Lizzie's past and the causes leading to her affair.

The narrator, a young boy during the New Year's Day fire and now a young man, recounts how as a young woman Lizzie had been left to depend on others after her father, a rector, was professionally ruined by rumors of illicit relations with female parishioners. Taken in by an unwilling aunt, she soon escaped by marrying a respectable lawyer, Charles Hazeldean. The narrator reflects on the limited options of the young Lizzie and others like her, a common THEME in Wharton's work: "Among the young women now growing up about me I find none with enough imagination to picture the helpless incapacity of the pretty girl of the 'seventies, the girl without money or vocation, seemingly put into the world only to please, and unlearned in any way of maintaining herself there by her own efforts" (547).

Six years after their marriage, Charles Hazeldean fell deeply ill and had to give up his work. Unfit for any other means of earning money, Lizzie entered into the affair with Prest for purely economic reasons, investing the money he gave her to support herself and Charles. She finally reveals this fact to Prest, who is appalled to learn that she formed the liaison out of financial need and love for her husband. After Charles's death, Prest proposes marriage to Lizzie, but she refuses in candid terms that are themselves "banned" in their world: "'You thought I was a lovelorn mistress; and I was only an expensive prostitute'" (532).

Ignoring New York society's gossip about her, Lizzie continues to live alone and befriend intellectual young men, in an existence similar to Ellen Olenska's in Paris in *The Age of Innocence*. The cold responses of other society women toward her are conveyed with irony. The narrator becomes temporarily infatuated with her but soon realizes his foolishness; however, he has formed an enduring respect for her: "She had done one great—or abominable—thing; rank it as you please, it had been done heroically" (546). The novella closes with the narrator's learning of Lizzie's death, which seems to him her reunion with her beloved dead husband. Cynthia Griffin Wolff notes that this tale "recapitulated familiar themes of Edith Wharton's writing and interweaved versions of her family and friends," including Wharton herself as the young narrator (367).

BIBLIOGRAPHY

Rae, Catherine M. *Edith Wharton's New York Quartet*. Lanham, Md.: University Press of America, 1984.

Saunders, Judith P. "A New Look at the Oldest Profession in Wharton's *New Year's Day*." *Studies in Short Fiction* 17 (1980): 121–26.

Wharton, Edith. *New Year's Day (The 'Seventies)*. In *Wharton: Novellas and Other Writings*. Edited by Cynthia Griffin Wolff. New York: Library of America, 1990.

Wolff, Cynthia Griffin. *A Feast of Words: The Triumph of Edith Wharton*. New York: Oxford University Press, 1995.

Charlotte Rich
University of Georgia, Athens

NEW YORKER, THE

Perhaps the premier general magazine in America for those with wide interests and an appreciation of intellectual good humor and style. Usually an issue contains one or two stories (many by prize-winning authors); profiles; movie, play, and book reviews; as well as poetry and notable cartoons. The *New Yorker* was established in 1925 by Harold Ross, who brought to its pages such short story writers as Robert Benchley, John O'HARA, Dorothy PARKER, S. J. Perelman, J. D. SALINGER, James THURBER, and Rebecca West, among others. After Ross died in 1951, William Shawn succeeded him as editor; under Shawn's guidance, the editorial commentary and public involvement increased while the format and tone remained unchanged. In 1987 Robert Gottlieb became the editor, followed by Tina Brown (1992–98) and David Remnick. Contemporary short story writers published in the *New Yorker* range from Hortense CALISHER, to Ward Just, to Jamaica KINCAID, to Bobbie Ann MASON.

NG, FAE MYENNE (1956–)

Fae Myenne Ng was born and reared in San Francisco. Her stories have been published in HARPER'S, the *American Voice, Bostonia,* and other magazines; they have also appeared in such anthologies as the *Pushcart Prize VII.* Several of Ng's most prominent short stories were integrated into her first novel, *Bone* (1993), which, set in San Francisco's Chinatown, explores the sometimes grim lives of the Leong family as they grapple with the realities of Chinese American culture. One such story, "The Red Sweater," features a young Chinese American woman narrator trying to understand the way stories connect her to her parents and the past while she comes to terms with her own sense of the present: "You have to be heartless" (116), she concludes. Ng currently lives in New York City.

BIBLIOGRAPHY

Ng, Fae Myenne. *Bone.* New York: Hyperion, 1993.
———. "A Red Sweater." In *Home to Stay: Asian American Women's Fiction.* Edited by Sylvia Watanabe and Carol Bruchac. Greenfield Center, N.Y.: Greenfield Review Press, 1990.
Ueki, Teruo. "A Reading of Fae Myenne Ng's *Bone.*" *Asian American Literature Association Journal* (1995).

Keith Lawrence
Brigham Young University

NICK ADAMS

A recurring character in many of Ernest HEMINGWAY's short stories, Nick Adams offers a highly autobiographical figure, and *The Nick Adams Stories* represents the closest thing we can find to a BILDUNGSROMAN in Hemingway's writing. Although Nick Adams stories were originally published in three separate short story collections, IN OUR TIME (1925), *Men Without Women* (1927), and *Winner Take Nothing* (1933), they have since been collected in chronological order and published as *The Nick Adams Stories* (1969). Nick's life can be traced from the earliest years growing up in northern Michigan struggling with admiration and shame before his doctor-father and his devout, withdrawn mother, to his chaotic years serving in WORLD WAR I and on to adulthood, marriage, and his establishment as a writer. The stories, as a whole, illustrate THEMES typically associated with Hemingway's writing: male bonding, loss of wilderness, loss of ideals, initiation into adulthood. With its trim language and sparse characterizations, the Nick Adams stories also provide CLASSIC examples of Hemingway's "iceberg theory": "If a writer of prose knows enough about what he is writing about, he may omit things that he knows and the reader, if the writer is writing truly enough, will have a feeling of those things as strongly as though the writer had stated them. The dignity of movement of an ice-berg is due to only one-eighth of it being above water" (Hemingway, *Death in the Afternoon,* 192).

Leaving so much below the surface opens the stories to many diverse approaches; for example, playing with the name itself—Adams—Nick's loss of innocence parallels that of his biblical namesake. Or, if we read the stories as peculiarly American, we may situate the loss of wilderness theme in a long tradition of such lamentations beginning with Mark TWAIN's *Huckleberry Finn* and moving up to F. Scott FITZGERALD's *The Great Gatsby* and William FAULKNER's GO DOWN, MOSES. The stories do not readily welcome a FEMINIST approach, except insofar as they show the failure of communication between men and women. Hemingway's deservedly famous "BIG TWO-HEARTED RIVER" encapsulates the most memorable motifs of the Nick Adams stories. It is here that Nick indulges in his simple yet nearly spiritual pastimes of hunting, fishing, camping, and while he delicately tiptoes around the specters that threaten to haunt his mind, the reader can recall precisely what Nick wishes to avoid thinking of: his writing, his father, his wound, the war, the land. All have been themes throughout the Nick Adams stories, and the recurring rebirth imagery throughout "Big Two-Hearted River" adds power and resonance to its final line: "There were plenty of days coming when he could fish the swamp (556)." By fusing the physical and psychological landscapes, Hemingway uses this story as a kind of resting place for Nick Adams, a place that allows his most autobiographical character to glance backward at the same time that he foreshadows the many stories yet to come. (See FORESHADOWING.)

BIBLIOGRAPHY
Hemingway, Ernest. *Death in the Afternoon.* New York: Scribner's, 1932.
———. "Big Two-Hearted River." In *Major Writers of Short Fiction: Stories and Commentaries.* Edited by Ann Charters. Boston: Bedford Books of St. Martin's, 1993, pp. 543–556.
Smith, Paul. *A Reader's Guide to the Short Stories of Ernest Hemingway.* Boston: G.K. Hall & Co., 1989.

Amy Strong
University of North Carolina, Chapel Hill

"NIGGER JEFF" THEODORE DREISER (1901, 1918)

"Nigger Jeff" is an early story in Theodore DREISER's career, but like his mature fiction it offers stark, detailed descriptions of powerful emotions that drive men and women into tragic situations. The story is a compelling and disturbing one about a lynching. The story portrays a weak-willed mob turned away by a resolute sheriff, the shattered and fearful accused black man, the grieving mother of the hanged man, the vengeful father of the violated white woman, and the mob that finally seizes and hangs the accused. Here, as in other Dreiser fiction, no character is HEROic but all are sympathetically portrayed. The characters are driven by powerful emotions they do not understand and cannot control. Even the law, in the guise of the sheriff, cannot prevent the lynching.

"Nigger Jeff" is also an initiation story of a young reporter who is sent to cover the event. Eugene Davies is at first eager and naive, then horrified, and finally committed to getting the whole story down on paper. For Davies, and for Dreiser, the story includes not only the lynching but also the beauty of the spring day as the body dangles at the end of the rope and the scene later at the black man's house where the body is laid out and the mother sits sobbing in the corner.

The story was written in 1899, a year before Dreiser's first novel, *Sister Carrie,* and is probably based on a lynching Dreiser witnessed in 1893 as a reporter for a St. Louis newspaper. In the last two decades of the 19th century there were more than 100 *recorded* lynchings each year. By the 1890s lynchings were sometimes well-publicized, festive events, with newspapers carrying advance notices and railroad agents selling excursion tickets. At the same time, many spoke out against lynchings in newspapers, magazines, and public speeches.

Although Dreiser makes no explicit political statement about lynchings in "Nigger Jeff," the story is in keeping with his lifelong political activism. Dreiser's political commitment sprang from a childhood of poverty, and is extended to covering a coal miners' strike in Appalachia and to joining the Communist party late in his life.

The subject and Dreiser's treatment of it are bold. Not surprisingly, he published the story in the small monthly *Ainslee;* he was friendly with one of the editors of this traditional, far from radical magazine. Later the story was included in the collection *Free and Other Stories* (1918).

BIBLIOGRAPHY
Dreiser, Theodore. "Introduction." In *Harlan Miners Speak: Report on Terrorism in the Kentucky Coal Fields.* New York: Harcourt, Brace, 1932, pp. i–xii.
Pizer, Donald. "Theodore Dreiser's 'Nigger Jeff': The Development of an Aesthetic." *American Literature* 41 (November 1969): 331–341.
Schapiro, Charles. *Theodore Dreiser: Our Bitter Patriot.* Carbondale: Southern Illinois University Press, 1962.

Stephanie P. Browner
Berea College

NIHILISM From the Latin *nihil*, which means "nothing," the word "nihilism" generally means to have no belief in God and to eschew adherence to all traditional institutions. The term specifically refers to an extreme form of revolutionism that developed in Russia in the 1850s and gained strength from 1870 onward. The movement aimed at anarchy and the complete overthrow of the state, law, order, and all institutions, and advocated the use of terrorism and assassination to achieve these goals. The code of the Nihilists was to annihilate the ideas of God, civilization, marriage, property, morality, and justice while pursuing only the freedom found in individual happiness. Ivan Turgenev gave this movement its name in his novel *Fathers and Sons*.

NIN, ANAÏS (1903–1977) Although Anaïs Nin published various drafts of her short stories in small literary journals such as *Dyn, The Booster,* and *Circle,* and also published two collections of short stories entitled *Under a Glass Bell and Other Stories* and *Waste of Timelessness and Other Early Stories,* critical interest in her short stories has revived only recently. The delay may be attributed to her fame as diarist rather than as novelist and story writer as well as to her controversial status as a FEMINIST who did not believe in alienating men.

Her most famous short story, "Birth," was first published in the collection *Twice a Year* (1938), edited by Nin and containing stories by such writers as Theodore DREISER and e. e. cummings. "Birth" exemplifies a number of influences Nin felt as an artist. Although it incorporates surrealist imagery (see SURREALISM), the story remains rooted in woman's unique physical and psychological experience, a taboo subject for women writers of her time. The story also demonstrates Nin's craft as a writer who distilled autobiographical accounts from her diaries in order to create fictional works. She also published three NOVELLAS—*Stella, Winter of Artifice,* and *The Voice*—in a collection entitled *Winter of Artifice: Three Novelettes* (1948).

Nin was born in Neuilly, France, to Joaquin Nin, a Cuban pianist-composer, and Rosa Culmell Nin, a French Danish singer. Shortly after her parents' separation, Nin emigrated to the United States with her mother and brothers. The record of this trip serves as the beginning of Nin's diary, which she continued throughout her life. The family lived in Richmond Hill, New York, where Anaïs met her husband, banker Hugh Guiler, and the couple lived in New York City until they moved to Paris in 1924. In Paris Nin began slowly to abandon her solitary efforts at writing and to associate with other artists and movements. She is as well known for her long-term affair with Henry Miller as for her two volumes of erotica, a *roman fleuve,* or STREAM-OF-CONSCIOUSNESS novel, entitled *Cities of the Interior* and her expurgated and unexpurgated diaries.

BIBLIOGRAPHY

Bair, Deirdre. *Anaïs Nin.* 1995.
Jason, Philip K., ed. *The Critical Response to Anaïs Nin.* New York: Putnum, 1996.
Nin, Anaïs. *Anaïs Nin Reader.* Edited by Philip K. Jason. Chicago: Swallow, 1973. Reprint. New York: Avon, 1974.
———. *Little Birds.* London: W. H. Allen, 1979.
———. *A Model and Other Stories.* London: Penguin, 1995 (taken from *Little Birds*). Originally published: London: W. H. Allen, 1979.
———. *The Mystic of Sex: A First Look at D. H. Lawrence and Other Writings, 1931–1974.* Santa Barbara, Calif.: Capra Press, 1995.
———. *Stories of Love.* Ringwood, Vic.: Penguin, 1996.
———. *Under a Glass Bell and Other Stories.* London: Penguin Books, 1978. Originally published: London: Poetry Society, 1947, 1948.
———. *Waste of Timelessness: and Other Early Stories.* Weston, Conn.: Magic Circle Press, 1977.
———. *The White Blackbird and Other Writings.* Edited by Kanoko Okamoto. Santa Barbara, Calif.: Capra Press, 1985.
———. *Winter of Artifice: Three Novelettes.* Chicago: Swallow Press, 1948.
Spencer, Sharon. *Collage of Dreams: The Writings of Anaïs Nin.* Chicago: Swallow Press, 1977, 1981.

Kerri Horrine
University of Louisville

"NOON WINE" KATHERINE ANNE PORTER (1936) Katherine Anne PORTER's story is subtitled "1896–1905," but she wrote it in 1936, and the story has the unmistakable atmosphere of the GREAT DEPRESSION. Characters of ordinary background seem helplessly entangled in a web of DETERMINISM in "Noon Wine": the lazy if well-meaning dairy farmer Mr. Thompson; the physically debilitated if kind Mrs. Thompson; their two scruffy, mischievous little boys; and their silent Swedish handyman Mr. Olaf Helton, who brings prosperity to the farm with his conscientious care of the property. As Edward Butscher notes, Porter manages to "plumb the dark, modernist undercurrents (823)" of such earlier writers as Henry JAMES, Willa CATHER, and James Joyce and to anticipate the GOTHIC perspective of Flannery O'CONNOR. (See MODERNISM.)

Just as the Thompsons are on a smoothly moving, ordinary keel—thanks to Olaf, to whom they are grateful and who lives a quiet routine life—the odious Mr. Hatch bursts into their lives, informing Mr. Thompson that Olaf is an escapee from a mental institution in North Dakota, where he hacked his own brother to death with an ax. Hatch wants to take Olaf back to the asylum and collect a reward. When Olaf arrives on the scene and Thompson sees Mr. Hatch appear to stab Olaf, Thompson strikes Mr. Hatch with an ax and kills him. Olaf goes insane and is killed resisting capture by the sheriff and his men; Mr. Thompson is later acquitted in a local trial of any criminal charges of causing Hatch's death. Mr. Thompson, however, worried that his neighbors believe him guilty despite the verdict, forces Mrs. Thompson to ride around the country with him to back up his story. Finally, after his wife has a nightmare, his grown sons accuse him of scaring her to death. On the pretense of going to fetch a doctor for his wife, Mr. Thompson takes his shotgun, walks out into a field, writes a suicide note yet again protesting his innocence in Hatch's death, rigs the weapon and kills himself.

Porter brilliantly dramatizes Mrs. Thompson's sense of moral failure when she must, as she sees it, lie for her husband as she accompanies him on his endless rounds to convince the neighbors of his innocence. Her nightmares and her fear of him show that she does not completely believe in it herself: Before he kills himself, Thompson is condemned by his own wife and sons. Nor does she see herself as free of blame: She judges her own behavior as a mixture of innocence and guilt, and cannot face the consequences. The knowledge of good and evil cannot save Mr. or Mrs. Thompson or their Swedish hired man, all ANTI-HEROIC in their common moral weakness. Perhaps a lesson emerges, however, in Mrs. Thompson's observation that violence lies at the heart of the matter: Men, she muses bitterly, seem compelled to respond to life in rough and violent ways.

Porter anchors the chillingly bleak tale in concepts of Adam and Eve, Cain and Abel, and Original Sin as well as in the determinism or fatalism of myth. Despite her characters' success in overcoming obstacles to frontier survival, they cannot avoid the destiny that overtakes them.

BIBLIOGRAPHY

Butscher, Edward. "Noon Wine." In *Reference Guide to Short Fiction*. Edited by Noelle Watson. Detroit: St. James Press, 1994, 823–824.

Demouy, Jane Krause. *Katherine Anne Porter's Women: The Eye of Her Fiction*. Austin: University of Texas Press, 1983.

Porter, Katherine Anne. *Flowering Judas and Other Stories*. New York: Harcourt Brace, 1935.

Tanner, James T. F. *The Texas Legacy of Katherine Anne Porter*. Denton: University of North Texas Press, 1990.

Unrue, Darlene H. *Truth and Vision in Katherine Anne Porter's Fiction*. Athens: University of Georgia Press, 1985.

NOVELLA   In the 1990s the NEW YORKER ran a cartoon by Roz Chast that pictured four different examples of books arranged from left to right in descending order based on physical thickness from fattest to thinnest; they were labeled "novel," "novella," "novellette," and "novellini." That there is no such thing as a "novellini"—not yet, anyway—only underscores the difficulty of achieving agreement on the novella as an inventive intermediate-length fictional form.

There is no all-purpose definition of the novella; as the critic Greg Johnson noted in 1991 in the *Georgia Review*, "the indeterminacy of the form is perhaps one of its chief attractions." In Howard Nemerov's judgment, the novella deserves to be considered as "something in itself, neither a lengthily written short story nor the refurbished attempt at a novel sent out into the world with its hat clapped on at the 80th page." Yet after more than a century of cultivation by many notable and diverse American fiction writers, beginning with Herman MELVILLE, Henry JAMES, Stephen CRANE, and Edith WHARTON, and running through William FAULKNER, Nella Larsen, Carson MCCULLERS, Katherine Anne PORTER, Kay BOYLE, Ernest HEMINGWAY, Nathaniel West, Richard WRIGHT, and John STEINBECK, and on to Paul Auster, Sandra CISNEROS, William Gass, Saul BELLOW, Jim HARRISON, N. Scott Momaday, Toni MORRISON, Joyce Carol OATES, Eudora WELTY, Tobias WOLFF, as well as many other moderns and contemporaries, reaching consensus about the novella's special "something" is not an easy task.

This astonishingly rich, abundant genre includes thematically, stylistically, and technically divergent works that range from the traditionally plotted to the experimental and from the seamlessly organized and coolly controlled to the patently poetic, self-reflexive—that is, a range that stretches from Henry James's DAISY MILLER (1879) to William Gass's Willie Masters' Lonesome Wife (1968), from Edith Wharton's MADAME DE TREYMES (1907) to Truman CAPOTE's Breakfast at Tiffany's (1958), from Carson MCCULLERS's Reflections in a Golden Eye (1941) to Sandra CISNEROS's THE HOUSE ON MANGO STREET (1984), from Nella Larsen's Quicksand (1928) to Paul Auster's Ghosts (1986).

American writers themselves have remained fairly silent about this art, however. For example, Edith Wharton, whose work in the genre, along with Henry James's, must be considered foundational, has almost nothing at all to say about the intricacies of the form in her memoir A Backward Glance (1934). More recently Jim Harrison, author of three acclaimed collections of novellas between 1979 and 1994 (LEGENDS OF THE FALL, THE WOMAN LIT BY FIREFLIES, JULIP), has been equally mum about a form that makes up a third of his nine published books of fiction. Moreover, in the past three or four decades, only a handful of analytical articles and critical books (not counting reviews) dealing entirely or in part with the American novella as an autonomous form have appeared. And although there has been no dearth of anthologies, the novella as a separate entity has been undeservedly subsumed within the larger imaginary world of American fiction, with the exception of a handful of canonical, famous, or oft-cited examples (BILLY BUDD, THE TURN OF THE SCREW, "Melanctha," Ethan Frome, "THE BEAR," The Pearl, The Old Man and the Sea, Seize the Day, The Bluest Eye).

Most commentators generally agree with A. Grove Day's sensible survey in "The Rise of the Modern Novella" concerning the novella's key characteristics—an integrated and complete piece of fiction displaying the unity and economy of short stories combined with broader scope, larger cast of characters, and extended time period of novels; most concur, too, about the short novel's concentrated effectiveness for readers, an effectiveness enhanced in such classic works as The Turn of the Screw, Ethan Frome, Miss Lonelyhearts, "The Bear," and such newer ones as Norman Maclean's A River Runs Through It (1976), Cynthia OZICK's The Shawl (1989), and Nicholson Baker's Room Temperature (1990). All are characterized by the manageable size of the text's canvas, its artful gaps and silences that invite participatory response, and its propensity for being read in a single sitting. "It isn't coincidental," Erin McGraw writes, "that so many successful novellas work by engaging the reader's willingness to reflect and speculate."

Judith Leibowitz aptly notes in Narrative Purpose in the Novella that the terms "novella," "novelette," and "short novel" have been used "interchangeably" or idiosyncratically according to an author's or editor's personal preference. John Steinbeck called his short books, such as Of Mice and Men (1937) and The Moon Is Down (1942), play/novellettes, because of their dramatic qualities and because a play could be lifted directly from the spare prose that would allow readers to "see a little play" in their heads. Richard Ludwig and Marvin Perry preface their collection Nine Short Novels (1952) with a kind of disclaimer—the term used in their title is "an arbitrary one" to describe fictional works that have the unity and immediate impact of short stories, but also demonstrate the "intricacy and extended development of CHARACTER and THEME proper to the full-length novel." In John O'HARA's foreword to *Sermons and Soda Water* (1961), which includes "The Girl on the Baggage Truck," "Imagine Kissing Pete," and "We're Friends Again," he employed the term "novella" to identify what was for him the "right form" of a streamlined fictional work "written from memory, with a minimum of research."

A few years later, however, Katherine Ann Porter warned readers of her *Collected Stories* (1965), which included the 1939 trilogy *Pale Horse, Pale Rider,* not to "call my short novels *Novelettes,* or even worse, *Novellas.*" The former, Porter said, "is classical usage for a trivial, dime-novel sort of thing." Undeterred by her stern admonition, Ronald Paulson, editor of two anthologies, *The Novelette Before 1900* and *The Modern Novelette* (both 1965), employs the title term because it indicates a form that "more rigorously maintains a single center of interest and so allows less autonomy, less full realization . . . than do the novel and short novel."

The novella derives from a storied continental background and cross-national roots in Renaissance (and later) Italian (*novella*), French (*nouvelle*), Spanish (*novela, novela corta*), and 19th-century German novelle forms. Even J. H. E. Paine, the most acerbic and hardest to please of recent theorists on the subject, claims in *Theory and Criticism of the Novella* (1979) that novella "should be the preferred term . . . for a novel of less than usual length." Paine follows Gerald Gillespie's lead in adopting the Italian word (*novella* means new and short), as does anthologist A. Grove Day, and scholars Mary Doyle Springer, A. Robert Lee, and Graham Good, who adds further historicized insights to the conversation in his incisive and resourceful "Notes on the Novella." Ideally, then, "novella" refers to an autonomous form and is neither a diminutive of a more privileged mode nor merely a piece long enough to be included complete in an issue of a pulp magazine (the novelette); nor is it an abbreviated or commodified example of something longer, weightier, and therefore "better" (the short novel).

In *Forms of the Modern Novella* (1975), Mary Doyle Springer states emphatically that "the novella is a prose fiction of a certain length (usually 15,000 to 50,000 words), a length equipped to realize several distinct formal functions better than any other length." Nearly all subsequent critics follow her lead regarding target lengths, although the upper limits (over 45,000 words) further blur distinctions between the short and long narrative forms.

A working designation probably resides somewhere between Henry James's exalted conception in his preface to Volume 15 of the New York edition, *The Lesson of the Master* (1909), as "our ideal, the beautiful and blest *nouvelle*," and Stephen KING's rough-and-tumble notion in the afterword of *Different Seasons* (1982) as "an anarchy-ridden literary banana republic." Different as these writers are in other respects, both share an awareness of the novella's historically marginalized role in commercial publishing's marketplace and a similar sense of the genre's quantitative boundaries. To James, the "shapely" nouvelle was a work of something more than the restrictive magazine tale length of 6,000 to 8,000 words; it allowed a "dimensional ground" adequate to permit a certain "length and breadth" of treatment, as in his "The Coxon Fund," where, he claimed, he did "the complicated thing with a strong brevity and lucidity—to arrive, on behalf of the multiplicity, at a certain science of control." For James, according to Krishna Baldev Vaid, shorter nouvelles, for example *Daisy Miller* and *The Lesson of the Master,* ran about 23,000 or 24,000 words; longer nouvelles, for instance the more technically challenging and complex *The Aspern Papers* and *The Turn of the Screw,* ran between 35,000 and 40,000 words (qtd. in Johnson). Stephen King, reflecting on his 1982 collection of novellas ("Rita Hayworth and Shawshank Redemption," "Apt Pupil," "Fall From Innocence," and "The Breathing Method"), none of which had been published separately, asserts that when a writer nears the 20,000-word mark the short story is being left behind, and when the 40,000-word mark is passed the writer is entering the "country of the novel." King's novellas, known for their sensational emotional effects, all fall between 25,000 and 35,000 words.

Others share King's belief in the novella's distinct category of operation. Ernest Hemingway's only excursion into the novella (although he did not use that term) was in *The Old Man and the Sea,* originally the final, but more or less free-standing, section of a much longer work. Hemingway thought his publisher might have an "impossible" time peddling the work (approximately 26,500 words long) but recognized its special place in his career: "This is the prose that I have been working for all my life that should read easily and simply and seem short and yet have all the dimensions of the visible world and the world of a man's spirit," he informed Charles Scribner in 1951.

Nobel laureate Saul BELLOW, famous for his long, philosophical, intellectually searching fiction, has recently done an about-face. In a foreword (itself uncharacteristic of Bellow) to *Something to Remember Me By* (1990), which includes two previously published 1989 novellas, *A Theft* and *The Bellarosa Connection* (narrated by an aging memory expert), he declared his preference for writing "short," with "brevity and condensation."

In doing so Bellow seems to have answered Warner Berthhoff's prediction in *A Literature Without Qualities: American Writing Since 1945* (1979) that the novella, characterized by "imaginative compression" and "severe narrative economy," would become nothing less than the "saving" direction for American fiction to take. Perhaps more to the point, A. Robert Lee claims in his introduction to the essays gathered in *The Modern American Novella* (1989) that, in a national literature often characterized by hugeness and sheer size, it is surprising and refreshing to witness the "endurance" of this "small-scale" form. Gems such as Edith Wharton's *Ethan Frome,* in which the naive narrator must resolve what he learns of Frome's domestic pathos into "simplicity"; John Steinbeck's postcolonial parable *The Pearl* (1947), a nightmarish vision of greed and violence in a Mexican fishing village; Tobias Wolff's *The Barracks Thief* (1984), which mixes first- and third-person POINTS OF VIEW in achieving its chilling portrayal of an army post sneak thief; and Hollis Summers's posthumous *Helen and The Girls: Two Novellas* (1992), with their laconic, clipped style and their questioning of narrative authority and displaced sentiments, are all examples of texts that by their nature and size offer an alternative to or a critique of American literary/epic exceptionalism.

The novella has been a critical and definitional mystery to Americans because it is often erroneously thought of as a misfit—an artificially bloated version of a short story or an anemic example of a novel proper. This in-between quality customarily has been considered a liability, a mark against the novella's integrity and its seriousness of purpose, a devaluing of its potential for presence in the world. And yet it is precisely the novella's sleek hybridity, athletic economy, and eminent readability that have continued to define its appeal. Indeed, judging from the number of novella collections by established writers (Rick Bass, *Platte River;* the late Stanley ELKIN, *Van Gogh's Room at Arles;* Mary Gordon, *The Rest of Life: Three Novellas;* David Leavitt, *Arkansas: Three Novellas*), novella competitions held by literary journals (*Quarterly West, The Evergreen Chronicles: A Journal of Gay & Lesbian Literature*), and collections of short stories with novella accompaniments (Allison Baker, *Loving Wanda Beaver: Novella and Stories;* Fred Pfeil, *What They Tell You to Forget: A Novella and Stories;* Ann Nietzke, *Solo Spinout: Stories and a Novella*) that have appeared in the last years of the 20th century, attitudes seem to be changing for the better with publishers, critics, and readers. In this era of renewed appreciation, contemporary writers who have envisioned—and engendered—the novella as a specially adept form, and who have responded to its varied qualities of elegance, resonance, multiplicity, and malleability, continue to add to an already impressive field of possibilities in this underrated, neglected narrative mode.

BIBLIOGRAPHY

Beatty, Jerome, ed. *The Norton Introduction to the Short Novel,* 2nd ed. New York: Norton, 1987.

Day, A. Grove. "The Rise of the Modern Novella." In *The Art of Narration: The Novella.* Edited by A. Grove Day. New York: McGraw-Hill, 1971, v–vii.

Felheim, Melvin. "Recent Anthologies of the Novella." *Genre* 2.2 (1969): 21–27.

Flower, Dean, ed. *Eight Short Novels.* Greenwich, Conn.: Fawcett, 1967.

Gillespie, Gerald. "Novelle, Nouvelle, Novella, Short Novel? A Review of Terms." *Neophilologus* 51.2 (1967): 117–127; concluded in 51.3 (1967): 225–230.

Good, Graham. "Notes on the Novella" (1977). In *The New Short Story Theories.* Edited by Charles E. May. Athens: Ohio University Press, 1994, 147–164.

Johnson, Greg. "Novellas for the Nineties." *The Georgia Review* 45.2 (1991): 363–371.

Lee, A. Robert, ed. *The Modern American Novella.* New York: St. Martin's, 1989.

Leibowitz, Judith. *Narrative Purpose in the Novella.* The Hague: Mouton, 1974.

McGraw, Erin. "Nor Good Red Herring: Novellas and Stories." *The Georgia Review,* 50.4 (1996): 808–818.

McMahan, Elizabeth, Susan Day, and Robert Funk, eds. *Nine Short Novels by American Women.* New York: St. Martin's, 1993.

May, Charles E. "The Novella." In *Critical Survey of Long Fiction.* Edited by Frank Magill. Englewood Cliffs, N.J.: Salem, 1983: 321–339.

Nemerov, Howard. "Composition and Fate in the Short Novel." *Graduate Journal* 5.2 (1963): 375–391.

Paine, J. H. E. *Theory and Criticism of the Novella.* Bonn: Bouvier Verlag Herbert Grundmann, 1979.

Paulson, Ronald, ed. *The Novelette Before 1900.* Englewood Cliffs, N.J.: Prentice-Hall, 1965.

———. *The Modern Novelette.* Englewood Cliffs, N.J.: Prentice-Hall, 1965.

Springer, Mary Doyle. *Forms of the Modern Novella.* Chicago: University of Chicago Press, 1975.

Robert De Mott
Ohio University

NUNEZ, SIGRID (1951–)

Sigrid Nunez was born and reared in New York City, the daughter of a German American mother and a Panamanian Shanghainese American father. Nunez earned her B.A. from Barnard College and her M.F.A. from Columbia University. Her stories have appeared in such literary journals as *The Threepenny Review, Fiction, Iowa Review,* and *Salamagundi;* they also have been widely anthologized. Nunez has been awarded two PUSHCART PRIZES, a General Electric Award for Young Writers, and a Whiting Writers Award.

Undoubtedly because of her own ethnic heritage, Nunez is more concerned than most contemporary American authors with multicultural tensions, issues, and THEMES. Although her work embodies much that is painful, horrifying, and tragic, it finally affirms personal wholeness, cultural diversity, and the capacity of human beings to live together in respectful harmony. Her most widely anthologized short story is "Chang," a semiautobiographical and brutally realistic assessment of a father's influence, for good and ill, on his wife and daughters. This story has been incorporated as the first section of Nunez's first novel *A Feather on the Breath of God* (1995). Her most recent novel, *Mitz,* whose title alludes to Leonard Woolf's pet marmoset (see ALLUSION), imaginatively uses letters, diaries, and memoirs to depict Leonard and Virginia Woolf in post–WORLD WAR I England.

BIBLIOGRAPHY
Nunez, Sigrid. *A Feather on the Breath of God.* New York: HarperCollins, 1996.

———. *From "Chang."* New York: Council of Literary Magazines and Presses, 1990.

———. *Mitz.* New York: HarperCollins, 1998.

———. *Naked Sleeper: A Novel.* New York: HarperCollins, 1997.

Keith Lawrence
Brigham Young University

O

OATES, JOYCE CAROL (1938–) Born on June 16, 1938, in Lockport, New York, to blue-collar parents, Joyce Carol Oates gained virtually instant acclaim and recognition with the publication of *By the North Gate* (1963), a collection of stories composed as she completed her B.A. at Syracuse University, from which she graduated as valedictorian. While at Syracuse, Oates also won the prestigious *Mademoiselle* fiction contest. *Upon the Sweeping Flood and Other Stories* (1966) followed three years later, ushering her onto the national stage as nothing less than a literary phenom, one with a distinctive regional voice that led numerous critics to compare her favorably to such luminaries as William FAULKNER and Flannery O'CONNOR. (See REGIONALISM.) While upstate New York and the mythical Eden County do indeed provide the backdrop for many of Oates's stories, her THEMES, like those of Faulkner and O'Connor, are expansive, touching on issues ranging from the problems of love relationships ("Convalescing") to failed fatherhood ("Last Days") to the unsettling consequences of both political repression ("Ich Bin Ein Berliner") and sexual awakening (the widely anthologized "WHERE ARE YOU GOING? WHERE HAVE YOU BEEN?"). Oates's output, moreover, has been as prodigious as her thematic concerns; in addition to short stories, Oates has published many novels—sometimes at the rate of two per year—as well as numerous plays and essays. She also maintains a full-time faculty position in creative writing at Princeton University.

Given such wide-ranging concerns and the enormous quantity of published material, locating central, unifying ideas or even characteristic stylistic techniques in Oates's work is no easy task. This has not prevented literary critics from making the attempt, however. Francine Lercangee's *Joyce Carol Oates: An Annotated Bibliography* highlights nearly 900 books, chapters, articles, and dissertations that attempt to characterize the writer—frequently at cross-purposes. Writing in the *Saturday Review* and in ATLANTIC MONTHLY, for instance, Benjamin DeMott finds Oates's work to be nihilistic, while Kathryn Grant's impressive book-length study, *The Tragic Vision of Joyce Carol Oates,* notes, among other qualities, the writer's ever-developing sense of affirmation. (See NIHILISM.)

Oates's fascination with extreme violence has been a frequent point of contention among commentators, as has her feminism—or lack thereof. (See FEMINIST.) While some critics praise the writer for her insistence on the importance of women's points of view, others find Oates's feminism suspect, pointing emphatically to such examples as the writer's apparently METAPHORical handling of rape in "Where Are You Going?"

Oates is similarly difficult to pin down stylistically. As noted, she has written in several literary forms and

often experiments boldly within the form she has chosen. Among her numerous short stories are superb
examples of psychological realism, SURREALISM, and
even SCIENCE FICTION, to list but three of the several
modes in which she has demonstrated competence.

Oates herself has suggested that while her work is
partly autobiographical in nature, it is primarily
motivated by a concern more expansive than her
own life. It emanates, she claims, from an intense
desire for positive, perhaps even global, transformation. In "Stories that Define Me," an essay written for
the *New York Times Book Review,* Oates observes that
she "writes with the enormous hope of altering the
world" and asks, "Why write without that hope?"
Many readers see this desire for transformation as a
loosely defined principle of organization that helps to
clarify, if not to unify, the vast body of Oates's work.
Indeed, her characters often face critical dilemmas
whose resolutions will irrevocably alter the direction
of their lives and, frequently, the lives of those—most
often family members—who surround them. "Little
Wife," for instance, tells the story of a 12-year-old
boy who must decide how to respond to his father's
involvement in a young girl's sexual abuse. The boy's
moral development lies in the balance.

Oates's work, then, is a deeply complicated fiction
of thresholds, of crossings and consequences. It is
also marked by wide-ranging stylistic variety. While
the desire for change may very well represent a dominant theme, her writing acts as a kind of literary
prism that simultaneously refracts that desire in
numerous, often richly rewarding directions at once.

BIBLIOGRAPHY

Bender, Eileen Teper. *Joyce Carol Oates: Artist in Residence.*
    Bloomington: Indiana University Press, 1987.
Bloom, Harold, ed. *Modern Critical Views: Joyce Carol Oates.*
    New York: Chelsea House, 1987.
Daly, Brenda. "My Friend Joyce Carol Oates." In *The Intimate
    Critique: Autobiographical Literary Criticism,* edited by
    Diane P. Freedman, Olivia Frey, and Frances Murphy
    Zauhar. Durham, N.C.: Duke University Press, 1993.
Johnson, Greg. *Joyce Carol Oates: A Study of the Short Fiction.*
    New York: Twayne, 1994.
Oates, Joyce Carol. *The Assignation: Stories.* New York: Ecco
    Press, 1988.
———. *By The North Gate.* New York: Vanguard, 1963.
———. *The Goddess and Other Stories.* Tokyo: Nan'un-do,
    1979.
———. *Heat, and Other Stories.* New York: Dutton, 1991.
———. *Last Days: Stories.* New York: Dutton, 1984.
———. *Marriages and Infidelities: Short Stories.* Greenwich,
    Conn.: Fawcett Publications, 1972.
———. *Night-side: Stories.* New York: Fawcett Crest, 1980.
———, ed. *The Oxford Book of American Short Stories.*
    Oxford: Oxford University Press, 1992.
———. *The Poisoned Kiss, and Other Stories From the
    Portuguese.* New York: The Vanguard Press, Inc. 1971.
———. *The Seduction and Other Stories.* Los Angeles: Black
    Sparrow Press, 1975.
———. *A Sentimental Education: Stories.* New York: Dutton,
    1980.
———. *The Wheel of Love and Other Stories.* New York:
    Vanguard Press, 1970.
———. *Where Are You Going, Where Have You Been?: Selected
    Early Stories.* Princeton, N.J.: Ontario Review Press, 1993.
———. *Where Are You Going, Where Have You Been?: Stories
    of Young America.* Greenwich, Conn.: Fawcett
    Publications, 1974.
———. *Where Is Here?: Stories.* Hopewell, N.J.:Ecco, 1992.
———. *Will You Always Love Me? And Other Stories.*
    Franklin Center, Pa.: Franklin Library, 1966.
———. *With Shuddering Fall: Upon the Sweeping Flood and
    Other Stories.* New York: Vanguard Press, 1966.
Prenshaw, Peggy Whitman, ed. *Conversations with Joyce Carol
    Oates.* Jackson: University of Mississippi Press, 1989.

Shannon Zimmerman
University of Georgia, Athens

O'BRIEN, TIM (1946–) Tim O'Brien's fiction is included in volumes of *Best American Short
Stories* and O. HENRY MEMORIAL AWARD winners; high
polish (he revises his books for paperback publication) and a precise control of language characterize
his writing. He employs lists, repetition, simple sentences, and sentence fragments to explore philosophical issues of truth and perception in his fiction.

Publishing short fiction in ATLANTIC MONTHLY,
ESQUIRE, MCCALL'S, Playboy, and *Redbook,* O'Brien was
the surprise winner of the National Book Award for
Going After Cacciato (1978, rev. ed. 1989). This
novel represents what O'Brien labeled "an effort to
move from REALISM to . . . a plane where the expe-

rience of imagining . . . formed the body of the book" (Coffey 201). O'Brien also employed this METAFICTIONAL technique, blurring the line between stories and truth, in his SHORT STORY CYCLE, *The Things They Carried* (1990). Interrelated stories examine a character named Tim O'Brien struggling to relate true stories of his experiences during the war; he notes, "I want you to feel what I felt. I want you to know why story truth is truer than happening-truth" (203). The cycle demonstrates a THEME common to O'Brien's work: the importance of story-telling and the accumulation of stories as means of perceiving and interpreting a seemingly incomprehensible world.

Born in Austin, Minnesota, and raised in Worthington, Minnesota, William Timothy O'Brien was drafted shortly after graduating in 1968 from Macalester College (St. Paul) and served 14 months in the army during the VIETNAM WAR. This conflict serves as the backdrop for five of his six books, including his Vietnam memoir, *If I Die in a Combat Zone, Box Me Up and Ship Me Home* (1973); *Northern Lights* (1975); and *In the Lake of the Woods* (1994). The exception is *The Nuclear Age* (1985).

BIBLIOGRAPHY

Coffey, M. "Tim O'Brien." In *Dictionary of Literary Biography Documentary Series 9.* Edited by Ronald Baughman. [1991], 201.

Kaplan, Stephen. "Understanding Tim O'Brien." In *Understanding Contemporary American Literature.* Columbia: University of South Carolina Press, 1995.

O'Brien Tim. *Going After Cacciato* (1978, rev. ed. 1989). New York: Delta, 1998.

———. *If I Die in a Combat Zone, Box Me Up and Ship Me Home* (1973). New York: Dell, 1992.

———. *In the Lake of the Woods* (1994). New York: Penguin, 1995.

———. *Northern Lights.* New York: Delacorte Press/Seymour Lawrence, 1975.

———. *The Nuclear Age.* 1985. New York: Penguin, 1996.

———. *The Things They Carried.* Boston: Houghton Mifflin, 1990.

———. *Tomcat in Love.* New York: Bantam Books, 1998.

O'Brien, Tim, Michael White, Alan Davis, and Al Davis, eds. *The Best Unpublished Stories by Emerging Writers,* vol. 7. New York: New Rivers Press, 1996.

"Tim O'Brien." In *Dictionary of Literary Biography Documentary Series: An Illustrated Chronicle: American Writers of the Vietnam War,* vol. 9. Edited by Ronald Baughman. Detroit: Gale, 1991, 132–214.

"Tim O'Brien." In *Dictionary of Literary Biography Yearbook: 1980.* Edited by Karen L. Rood, Jean W. Ross, and Richard Ziegfeld. Detroit: Gale, 1981, 286–90.

"Tim O'Brien Issue." *Critique: Studies in Contemporary Fiction* 36.4 (Summer 1994).

Andrew R. Burke
University of Georgia, Athens

"OCCURRENCE AT OWL CREEK BRIDGE, AN" AMBROSE BIERCE (1891)

This CLASSIC story, first published in Ambrose BIERCE's short story collection *Tales of Soldiers and Civilians,* continues to intrigue new generations of readers. Although set during the CIVIL WAR, it is notable not for the combat scenes that other Bierce stories portray but for the ingenious blending of REALISM and fantasy that inevitably leads to the SURPRISE ENDING. Although some readers protest that Bierce uses this ending to trick them, most agree that, to the contrary, the author includes ample cues for the attentive reader to see that the condemned PROTAGONIST, Peyton Farquhar, escapes the reality of death only in his imagination.

The STRUCTURE of the story is crucial to its effects: It opens as Farquhar, a Southern noncombatant, stands on the platform above Owl Creek Bridge while the Union soldiers enact the ritual of the military hanging. Thinking of ways to escape, Farquhar imagines he can free his hands. In a FLASHBACK, we learn that Farquhar, a happily married planter and ardent supporter of the "Southern cause" ("Occurrence at Owl Creek Bridge" 194), was tricked by a federal scout disguised as a Confederate: Eager to help his compatriots, Farquhar attempted to burn Owl Creek Bridge and was immediately captured by the Yankees, who lay in wait for him. With this information that humanizes Farquhar, we return to the present with him, mentally cheering him on as he plummets from the bridge, and appears to escape his bonds, swim the river, and head through the forest toward home, children, and his beautiful wife who awaits him on the verandah. In fact, the escape occurs in Farquhar's imagination as he resists death that, finally, is the inevitable reality common to us all.

BIBLIOGRAPHY

Bierce, Ambrose. "An Occurrence at Owl Creek Bridge." In *American Short Stories.* 6th edition. Edited by Eugene Current-García and Bert Hitchcock. New York: Longman, 1997, pp. 192–98.

O'CONNOR, FLANNERY (1925–1964)

Although she died tragically young, of lupus, an incurable tubercular disease affecting the skin, Flannery O'Connor's contribution to the 20th-century American short story seems unequivocal. While she wrote two novels—*Wise Blood* and *The Violent Bear It Away*—she is known for her brilliant stories. In response to the issues of her era, O'Connor's use of REALISM, symbolism, irony, BLACK HUMOR, and the grotesque, among other techniques, has found an increasingly wide audience, possibly because readers, consciously or unconsciously, find a little of the grotesque in themselves. Moreover, critical interest appears to rise each year, with no signs of abating.

A native Georgian, O'Connor was born in Savannah and spent her youth in Milledgeville, attending Georgia State College for Women and writing stories that earned her a fellowship to the Writers' Workshop at the University of Iowa. With the exception of two years spent at that university, where she received her M.F.A. in 1947, and three years (1947–50) spent in New York and Connecticut, she lived all her life in Georgia, where she died at the age of 39. A number of critics have pointed out that O'Connor was an "outsider" through both her Southern and her Catholic background; yet a third factor is that she wrote, literally, as a woman who knew very well that she was dying. The Roman Catholic woman in the largely Protestant South learned at age 25 that she had a terminal illness: these add up to a powerful and unique fictional vision that O'Connor employed with wit, reverence, and art.

Critic Margaret Anne O'Connor has summed up O'Connor's literary subjects that so often seemed at odds with the prevailing views of the post–WORLD WAR II era: O'Connor wrote not of nuclear families but of "multigenerational households and fragmented families—grandparents rearing a second generation of offspring just as poorly as they had reared the first, widows supporting ungrateful adult children, single fathers neglecting their children, parents completely ignoring children because of their own self-absorption, or couples not wanting children at all" (641). Numerous critics have noted the number of significant O'Connor stories that begin with women living alone: "The Life You Save May Be Your Own," "GOOD COUNTRY PEOPLE," "GREENLEAF," "EVERYTHING THAT RISES MUST CONVERGE," and "The Comforts of Home." The violent and the grotesque appear commonly in most of her stories, but in nearly every one a character learns—as in "A GOOD MAN IS HARD TO FIND" and "THE DISPLACED PERSON"— that a spiritual vision leading toward a more soul-satisfying existence can still be had, even in death.

Flannery O'Connor was no simple moralist, however; nor was she a regional writer. (See REGIONALISM.) If a number of her tales may be viewed, like Nathaniel HAWTHORNE's, as parallels, they are, like his, deeply complex and philosophical. As Suzanne Morrow Paulson observes, O'Connor belongs with the best of the 20th-century modernists "obsessed with alienation, the dark side of human nature, and death" (xi), but she loved her characters even as she passed verdicts on them. (See MODERNISM.) Further evidence of her genius is in her comic art, which ultimately—as with all great COMEDY—encourages sympathy and helps develop an understanding not only of self, but also of the human condition.

BIBLIOGRAPHY

Browning, Preston M. *Flannery O'Connor.* Carbondale: Southern Illinois University Press, 1974.
Coles, Robert. *Flannery O'Connor's South.* Baton Rouge: Louisiana State University Press, 1980.
Eggenschwiler, David. *The Christian Humanism of Flannery O'Connor.* Detroit: Wayne State University Press, 1972.
Feeley, Sister Kathleen. *Flannery O'Connor: Voice of the Peacock.* New Brunswick, N.J.: Rutger's University Press, 1972.

Friedman, Melvin J., and Lewis A. Lawson, eds. *The Added Dimension: The Art and Mind of Flannery O'Connor.* Rev. ed. New York: Fordham University Press, 1977, 1966.

Gentry, Marshall. *Flannery O'Connor's Religion of the Grotesque.* Jackson: University of Mississippi Press, 1986.

Hendin, Josephine. *The World of Flannery O'Connor.* Bloomington: Indiana University Press, 1970.

Kessler, Edward. *Flannery O'Connor and the Language of Apocalypse.* Princeton, N.J.: Princeton University Press, 1986.

McFarland, Dorothy Tuck. *Flannery O'Connor.* New York: Ungar, 1976.

Martin, Carter W. *The True Country: Themes in the Fiction of Flannery O'Connor.* Nashville, Tenn.: Vanderbilt University Press, 1969.

May, John R. *The Pruning Word: The Parables of Flannery O'Connor.* Notre Dame, Ind.: University of Notre Dame Press, 1976.

O'Conner, Margaret Anne. In *The Oxford Companion to Women's Writing in the United States.* Edited by Cathy N. Davidson and Linda Wagner-Martin. New York: Oxford University Press, 1995.

O'Connor, Flannery. *The Complete Stories.* New York: Farrar, Straus & Giroux, 1971.

———. *Conversations With Flannery O'Connor.* Edited by Rosemary M. Magee. Jackson: University Press of Mississippi, 1987.

———. *Everything that Rises Must Converge.* New York: Farrar, Straus & Giroux, 1965.

———. *A Good Man is Hard to Find.* New York: Harcourt, Brace, 1955.

———. *The Presence of Grace and Other Book Reviews.* Compiled by Leo J. Zuber. Edited by Carter W Martin. Athens: University of Georgia Press, 1983.

———. *The Violent Bear It Away.* New York: Farrar, Straus & Giroux, 1965.

———. *Wise Blood.* New York: Harcourt, Brace, 1952.

Orvell, Miles. *Invisible Parade: The Fiction of Flannery O'Connor.* Philadelphia: Temple University Press, 1972.

Paulson, Suzanne Morrow. *Flannery O'Connor: A Study of the Short Fiction.* Boston: Twayne, 1988.

Sholoss, Carol. *Flannery O'Connor's Dark Comedies.* Baton Rouge: Louisiana State University Press, 1980.

Walters, Dorothy. *Flannery O'Connor.* New York: Twayne, 1973.

O'CONNOR, FRANK (1903–1966)

Born in Cork, Ireland, in 1903 and educated at the Christian Brothers College, Frank O'Connor taught school in the United States from 1951 to 1960 before returning to Ireland in 1961, where he received a Litt. D. from the University of Dublin in 1962. His career spanned four decades, during which he gained recognition as a translator, novelist, reviewer, and critic. His reputation rests, however, on his impressive achievements as a short story writer who published more than 200 stories in seven collections and various editions. He also had a profound influence on the nature of the short story itself, particularly in his classic work, *The Lonely Voice: A Study of the Short Story* (1963), a work repeatedly alluded to by American short story writers, critics, and theorists.

O'Connor believed that the most intense focus of short fiction should center on the lonely and isolated figures of common folk at the margins of society, that all short stories should have a major idea and a recognizably central story. Later on, however, he realized myriad other voices and issues emerge that have nothing to do with the main anecdote that comprises the story, and the tension between these two "facts" resulted in some of his very best stories. Like Sherwood ANDERSON or John O'HARA, O'Connor frequently featured characters driven by human aspirations and illusions, who become overwhelmed by fate or circumstance in the guise of social, religious, or—in his case—political pressures. O'Connor's characters, however, unlike O'Hara's, prove powerless when faced with these forces; they have no freedom to choose.

"ODOR OF VERBENA"   See UNVANQUISHED, THE.

OEDIPAL MYTH

In Greek mythology, Oedipus was the son of King Laius of Thebes and Queen Jocasta. Warned by an oracle that Oedipus would kill his father and marry his mother, his parents abandoned the baby on a mountainside. There he was found by a shepherd, who delivered him to the childless king of Corinth, who adopted and reared him.

When grown, Oedipus learned of the prophecy, and ignorant of his real parentage, fled Corinth for

Thebes. On the way, he met, quarreled with, and killed Laius. He proceeded to Thebes, which was then being ravaged by the Sphinx. When Oedipus answered her riddle, the Sphinx killed herself, and the regent offered him the throne of Thebes and the hand of Laius' widow, Jocasta. He married her and, later, when a seer revealed Oedipus' true identity, Jocasta committed suicide and Oedipus blinded himself with her brooch.

O'HARA, JOHN (1905–1970) Born in Pottsville, Pennsylvania, John O'Hara etched a distinctive place for himself in American literature—particularly in the achievements of his 12 collections of short stories, written over five decades—then nearly faded from sight for more than three decades. Currently he is the subject of scholarly and critical revaluation and restitution by those who believe he has been slighted, if not maligned. His novels attained instant popularity and best-seller status, and a number of them were made into feature films. His short stories, many of which were published in the NEW YORKER, fall into roughly two periods: those written from the mid-1930s to mid-1940s, and those written from 1960 to 1970.

The five volumes of the first period are *The Doctor's Son and Other Stories* (1935), *Files on Parade* (1939), *Pal Joey* (1940), *Pipe Night* (1945), and *Hellbox* (1947). Although the later collections may have more artistic maturity, the earlier ones contain all his major themes, subjects, and technique. His world, set in the fictional GIBBSVILLE, PENNSYLVANIA, during the years of the GREAT DEPRESSION, has been called an amoral one in which the good characters do not always prevail, nor do the bad ones suffer punishment (Walker 2). Nonetheless, a number of his characters demonstrate a remarkable tendency to survive their nearly always bleak if not hopeless situations. Social position, religious prejudice, loneliness, and fate appear central to many of the stories, yet most of the characters rise or fall because of the personal choices that they make.

O'Hara also wrote explicitly about sexual relations, causing a number of his critics to accuse him of cheapness and vulgarity, but in hindsight, one might well argue that O'Hara was a pioneer in the realistic depiction of human sexuality. Whatever their views on his sexual focus, nearly all reviewers have applauded his keen ear for the rhythms of everyday American speech and his use of REALISM in terms of specific, believable detail. His focus on the complexities of the American social scene prompted some critics to compare him to William Dean HOWELLS and Edith WHARTON, while others find his exploration of society superior to that of Theodore DREISER or Sinclair LEWIS.

Between 1960 and his death in 1970, O'Hara published, among other NOVELLAS, the three comprising *Sermons and Soda Water* (1960), as well as six additional collections of stories: *Assembly* (1960), *The Cape Cod Lighter* (1962), *The Hat on the Bed* (1963), *The Horse Knows the Way* (1964), *Waiting for Winter* (1966), and *And Other Stories* (1969). *The Time Element* (1972) and *The O'Hara Generation* (1972) appeared posthumously. The novellas are set in Philadelphia, New York, and Gibbsville; the best-known character is Jim Malloy, the narrator in the novellas and many of the stories, who provides the restricted point of view and—unlike his role in the prewar stories—functions primarily as an observer rather than a participant. These novellas and the story collections, set in the post–WORLD WAR II era, center on loneliness, the difficulties of aging, the battle between men and women, and the short-lived nature of success. O'Hara also wrote so-called Hollywood stories, published in *Waiting for Winter,* depicting the diverse characters of the film world, from stars to hangers-on, with insight and art.

BIBLIOGRAPHY

Eppard, Philip B. *Critical Essays on John O'Hara.* New York: G.K. Hall, 1994.

Grebstein, Sheldon Norman. *John O'Hara.* New York: Twayne Publishers, 1966.

Walker, Jeffrey. "1945–1956: Post–World War II Manners and Mores." In *The American Short Story, 1945–1980: A Critical History.* Edited by Gordon Weaver, 1–35. Boston: Twayne Publishers, 1983.

O. HENRY MEMORIAL AWARDS Named after O. HENRY, the prolific and popular writer of hundreds of short stories, the O. Henry Memorial Awards were established in 1918 to recognize the American authors of the year's best short stories published in American periodicals. Winners of the prize are published in an annual volume, (See APPENDIX 1.)

OLD MAID, THE   EDITH WHARTON

(1924)   One of Edith Wharton's many stories of New York, this NOVELLA was published with the subtitle *The 'Fifties* in 1924 as the second of four volumes in a set entitled *Old New York*. The story exemplifies Wharton's use of irony and REALISM in depicting characters facing ethical dilemmas. Unmarried Charlotte Lovell, who seems "serious" and "prudish" (378) to her married cousin, Delia Ralston, reveals another side of her nature when she asks Delia to rear a child that she confesses is the product of a past love affair. Although this affair occurred with a young man whom Delia once loved herself but did not marry because of his lack of wealth, she agrees to rear the child, Tina, who begins to call her "Mamma." Charlotte takes on the awkward role of spinster aunt.

Tension between the two caregivers mounts as Tina becomes a marriageable young woman herself. Tina becomes involved with a young man, Lanning Halsey, who in some ways resembles Clement Spender, her father and the suitor of Delia's past. Delia, concerned that Tina may enter into an illicit affair as Charlotte did, realizes she must precipitate marriage between the two. In order to make Tina socially acceptable in the society of the Ralstons and Halseys, she adopts her. Charlotte at first resists this action, vowing to take away Tina and tell her the truth, but Delia criticizes Charlotte's sacrifice of the girl to her "desire for mastery" (430), and Charlotte acquiesces.

The novella ends just before Tina's wedding to Halsey, as the two women argue over who shall tell the girl about the "new duties and responsibilities" of intimacy that come with marriage (437). Charlotte points out that "'the question is: *which of us is her mother?*'" (438), voicing her long misery over her diminished maternal rights, and Delia

agrees to let Charlotte talk to Tina. Charlotte returns, however, her courage having failed her, and tells Delia, "'You're her real mother. Go to her'" (442). In essence, this is Charlotte's final renunciation, an acknowledgment that Tina should never know her true status.

The novella, according to Shari Benstock, deals with "THEMES of secrecy, jealousy, and mutual dependency in one of New York's ruling families" (362); and R. W. B. Lewis points out that this "melancholy drama" was often regarded by reviewers as the best of the *Old New York* set (459). Cynthia Griffin Wolff asserts that "the tale is dominated by the passion of [Charlotte's] despair"; she is "the parent who was never—really—a parent at all; and for her, the spectacle of youth brings not renewal and comfort, but a bitter recollection of everything that has been snatched from her" (345).

BIBLIOGRAPHY

Benstock, Shari. *No Gifts from Chance: A Biography of Edith Wharton*. New York: Scribner's, 1994.

Lewis, R. W. B. *Edith Wharton: A Biography*. New York: Scribner's, 1975.

Rae, Catherine M. *Edith Wharton's New York Quartet*. Lanham, Md.: University Press of America, 1984.

Wharton, Edith. *The Old Maid (The 'Fifties)*. In *Wharton: Novellas and Other Writings*. New York: Library of America, 1990.

Wolff, Cynthia Griffin. *A Feast of Words: The Triumph of Edith Wharton*. New York: Oxford University Press, 1977; 2nd ed., Addison-Wesley, 1995.

Charlotte Rich
University of Georgia

"OLD MRS. HARRIS" WILLA CATHER

(1932)   Published in *LADIES' HOME JOURNAL* (September-November 1932) as "Three Women" and included in the collection *Obscure Destinies* (1932), this story concerns three generations of women transplanted from Tennessee to the town of Skyline, Colorado. The differences in the women's roles as widowed grandmother, mother of five children, and eldest granddaughter keep them from full appreciation of one another. In addition to age differences, the story dramatizes cultural differences among the Southern Templetons; their next-door neighbors, the Rosens, a cultured Jewish couple from the Northeast; and the Colorado locals. Avoiding STEREOTYPES, Willa CATHER creates CHARACTERS capable of both insensitivity and compassion as she moves them through the incidents that compose daily life and, cumulatively, a lifetime: afternoon coffee and cake; a Methodist lawn party; the burial of an old, beloved cat; the children's backyard circus; Vicki Templeton's scholarship award; and Victoria Templeton's discovery that she is pregnant for the sixth time. Grandma Harris carries out her quiet death in the same unobtrusive way that she performed her endless acts of service for the family. Her death is both sad and necessary, a natural inevitability in the larger context of life.

Cather captures the nature of family life with extraordinary precision as each main character, in pursuit of her daily desires, brushes against the other with a kind of affectionate distance, altered occasionally by intimacy or acute frustration. The story's POINT OF VIEW shifts from omniscient narration to the minds of Old Mrs. Harris, her daughter Victoria, and Mrs. Rosen, who watches the three women from next door and provides an additional perspective. Men move in the background as husbands who provide financial support. Their distracted kindness can be appealed to when needed, but women are the central players in the emotional lives of these families. Cather's perception that family unity depends on women's compromises between self-fulfillment and service to others accounts for the shifting tones of respect, sadness, and affection that animate her complex vision of women in family life.

BIBLIOGRAPHY

Arnold, Marilyn. *Willa Cather's Short Fiction.* Athens: Ohio University Press, 1984.

Slote, Bernice, ed. *Uncle Valentine and Other Stories: Willa Cather's Uncollected Short Fiction, 1915–1929.* Lincoln: University of Nebraska Press, 1973.

Frances Kerr
Durham Technical Community College

"OLD ROGAUM AND HIS THERESA" THEODORE DREISER (1901, 1918)

"Old Rogaum and His Theresa" portrays the failure of authorities to instill traditional values in the younger generation and the power of dreams to make the tawdry seem beautiful. Set in Greenwich Village in New York City, the story offers a realistic portrait of city life in America, chronicling the dangers that lurk on city streets for a young girl who seeks "life" and dares to challenge the rules of her father, Old Rogaum the butcher. (See REALISM.)

"Old Rogaum and His Theresa" describes without judgment the power of sexuality. Eighteen-year-old Theresa is not immoral or calculating, only mildy flirtatious and slightly defiant. Like many of Theodore DREISER's characters, she seeks something better without really knowing what she wants. Vulnerable because she dreams, Theresa is seduced by a careless youth, and her imagination turns the streets of her working-class neighborhood into an alluring, magical place of splendor and freedom.

The tragic consequences of such dreams are the subject of many of Dreiser's best stories and novels. Carrie Meeber, in the novel *Sister Carrie* (1900), is successful but lonely after her climb to stardom, and Clyde Griffiths, in *An American Tragedy* (1925), stumbles into murder in his desperate pursuit of a better life. Theresa's tragedy is smaller: She only wanders the streets for a few hours in the company of an irresponsible young man, but the prostitute whom Rogaum finds on his doorstep suggests that a more disturbing fate might befall girls who succumb to the allure of city streets and attractive young men.

Dreiser's story is a revision of a genre popular at the turn of the century. Sentimental stories abounded of girls who resisted the seductive appeal of city life. In these stories morality was rewarded and waywardness punished. "Old Rogaum and His Theresa" does not moralize. Theresa may fare better if she listens to her father, but he and the police who rescue her are ineffective authorities who have no real control. They can impose rules on Theresa, but they cannot instill in her their traditional mores: Old Rogaum locks his daughter out of the house but, once she returns, Theresa displays little if any concern for her experience. Dreiser experienced first hand the tyranny of fathers in his own father's iron rule, and he depicts such authoritarianism bitterly in his second novel, *Jennie Gerhardt* (1911).

"Old Rogaum and His Theresa" was published by *Reedy's Mirror,* a small radical magazine that made a point of breaking genteel literary conventions. Later Dreiser included it in the collection *Free and Other Stories* (1918), changing the name and making minor revisions.

BIBLIOGRAPHY

Pizer, Donal. "A Summer at Maumee: Theodore Dreiser Writes Four Stories." In *Essays Mostly on Periodical Publishing in America.* Edited by James Woodress. Durham, N.C.: Duke University Press, 1973.

Stephanie P. Browner
Berea College

OLINGER, PENNSYLVANIA

OLINGER, PENNSYLVANIA   The fictional version of John UPDIKE's hometown of Shillington, Pennsylvania, Olinger is the town Updike used in numerous stories in *The Same Door* (1959) and *Pigeon Feathers* (1962). All the Olinger stories from both books were collected in *Olinger Stories: A Selection* (1964). The Olinger tales represent the protagonists' attempts to recapture, through memory, the innocent pleasures of youth in a small town, yet at the same time to learn to distance themselves from the past. As E. P. Walkiewicz notes, Updike's epigraph to both *Pigeon Feathers* and the Olinger collection emphasizes not merely the significance of "recapturing the past," but also Updike's increasing "difficulty" in sustaining that "nostalgic impulse" when faced with looming adult issues (Walkiewicz 42). The stories demonstrate the increasing gulf between the past and present ("Walter Briggs," "Dear Alexandros," "The Doctor's Wife"), culminating in "The Music School," in which the narrator bids farewell to Olinger.

BIBLIOGRAPHY

Walkiewicz, E. P. "1957–1968: Toward Diversity of Form." In *The American Short Story, 1945–1980: A Critical History.* Edited by Gordon Weaver. Boston: Twayne, 1983.

OLSEN, TILLIE (LERNER) (1913–)

OLSEN, TILLIE (LERNER) (1913–)
Tillie Lerner was born in Nebraska in 1912 or 1913 to Samuel and Ida Beber Lerner, immigrants who fled Russia after the failed 1905 revolution. Her atheist parents were of Jewish heritage. As a child, Tillie was an avid reader who stuttered and was ill often. She left high school without graduating. Her father's involvement in the Socialist Party influenced Tillie, who joined the Young Communist League in 1931 and was arrested for some of her activities protesting for workers' rights. In 1932 she gave birth to her first daughter, Karla. In 1933 she met Jack Olsen; living together by 1936, they were married in 1943 and continued to share their lives until his death in 1989. With him she had three more daughters, and her commitments to her family and her politics left little time for her writing. An intermittent member of the Communist Party, Olsen also worked to ensure women's rights and to gain recognition for the frequently overlooked contributions of past women.

During the McCarthy era, Jack Olsen was subpoenaed to appear before the House Un-American Activities Committee (HUAC) and was blacklisted, which made finding employment difficult. (See MCCARTHYISM.) Tillie, while never subpoenaed, could not hold a job for any length of time because the FBI always contacted her employer. Beginning in 1969, however, she held a number of positions teaching at different universities, including Amherst College; University of Massachusetts at Boston, where she was Distinguished Visiting Professor; and University of California at Santa Cruz. She often taught courses on women's literature.

Highly praised but far from prolific, Olsen's writing spans multiple genres. In 1934 she published two poems, "I Want You Women Up North to Know" and "There Is a Lesson," and a short story, "The Iron Throat," which later became a part of *Yonnondio: From the Thirties,* her unfinished novel. She also published two essays that year, "Thousand-Dollar Vagrant" and "The Strike," which were based on her participation in the San Francisco Maritime Strike and her resulting arrest. Her political commitment was also the impetus for the articles and columns she wrote for *People's World,* a communist newspaper.

In 1956 her story "Help Her Believe" appeared, reprinted the following year as "I STAND HERE IRON-ING" in *Best American Short Stories.* She published "Hey Sailor, What Ship?" and "Baptism," which was later titled "O YES," in 1957. "TELL ME A RIDDLE," pub-lished in 1960, won the 1961 O. HENRY MEMORIAL AWARD for best short story. The four stories were then collected under the title *Tell Me a Riddle.* Olsen did not again publish any fiction until 1970, when "Requa I" appeared in the *Iowa Review.* In 1974 she published *Yonnondio,* which she had begun writing in 1932 but misplaced the unpublished manuscript for four decades. Among the THEMES that run throughout her fiction are adolescence, grief, pover-ty, class, human relationships, isolation, mother-hood, and work. Her loving portrayals of characters who are survivors are a testament to her faith in humanity and her hope.

Silences, an expansion of speeches and elabora-tion on their themes, concerns the "unnatural" or forced silences that prevent writers, and people who might be writers, from writing. Such silences can be caused by work for wages, the demands of children, and other time-consuming activities, or they can be caused by society's failure to nourish the gifts of some people because of their race, class, or gender. The 1978 collection also includes an essay on Rebecca Harding Davis, the long-neglected author of *Life in the Iron Mills.*

In 1984 Olsen returned to a favorite theme when she produced *Mother to Daughter, Daughter to Mother, Mothers on Mothering: A Reader and Diary,* a miscel-lany of mothers' and daughters' memories and trib-utes to each other, including a short essay by Olsen on her own mother. An early, previously unpub-lished story, "Not You I Weep For," appeared in the 1993 collection *First Words: Earliest Writing from Contemporary Authors.*

BIBLIOGRAPHY

Coiner, Constance. *Better Red: The Writing and Resistance of Tillie Olsen and Meridel LeSueur.* New York: Oxford University Press, 1995.
Frye, Joanne S. *Tillie Olsen: A Study of the Short Fiction.* New York: Twayne, 1995.
Nelson, Kay Hoyle, and Nancy Huse, eds. *The Critical Response to Tillie Olsen.* Westport, Conn.: Greenwood Press, 1994.
Olsen, Tillie. *Mother to Daughter, Daughter to Mother, Mothers on Mothering: A Reader and Diary.* Old Westbury, N.Y.: Feminist Press, 1984.
———. "Not You I Weep For." In *First Words: Earliest Writing from Favorite Contemporary Authors.* Edited by Paul Mandelbaum. Chapel Hill, N.C.: Algonquin Books, 1993.
———. "Requa." *Iowa Review* 1.3 (Summer 1970): 54–74. 1970.
———. *Silences.* New York: Delacorte Press, 1978.
———. *Tell Me a Riddle.* Philadelphia: Lippincott, 1960.
———. *"Tell Me a Riddle."* Edited by Deborah Silverton Rosenfelt. New Brunswick, N.J.: Rutgers University Press, 1995.
———. *Yonnondio: From the Thirties.* New York: Delacorte Press/Seymour Lawrence, 1974.
Orr, Elaine Neil. *Tillie Olsen and a Feminist Spiritual Vision.* Jackson: University Press of Mississippi, 1987.
Pearlman, Mickey, and Abby H. P. Werlock. *Tillie Olsen.* Boston: Twayne, 1991.

Kelley Reames
University of North Carolina at Chapel Hill

ONOMATOPOEIA A Greek term (meaning "the making of words"), onomatopoeia refers to using or inventing words that supposedly echo or mimic their meaning in their sound (for example, buzz, quack, boom, click, plop, hiss, snap, bang).

ON THE ROAD JACK KEROUAC (1951) A novel that the majority of critics and readers credit with ushering in the beat movement. (See BEAT GEN-ERATION and BEAT LITERATURE.) The book features an autobiographical narrator and his friends, who drive across the United States from New York to San Francisco and, later, to Mexico, in a wild, free-wheeling celebration of the diversity of North American people and places. Kerouac uses pseudo-nyms for the real-life characters: The author himself is Sal Paradise, Neal Cassady is Dean Moriarty—whom Kerouac elevates to the status of a new

American HERO—Allen Ginsberg is Carlo Marx, William Burroughs is Old Bull Lee, and Hubert Huncke is Elmer Hassel.

BIBLIOGRAPHY
Kerouac, Jack. *On the Road.* New York: Penguin, 1976.

"OPEN BOAT, THE" STEPHEN CRANE (1897)

In June 1897 Stephen CRANE's ironic and naturalistic story, "The Open Boat," appeared in *SCRIBNER'S Magazine*. (See NATURALISM.) The story is a fictionalized account of Crane's own experience of six months earlier when he spent 30 hours floating off the coast of Florida in a dinghy with four other men after the ship he was aboard sank. His prose is impressionistic, his perspective naturalistic, and in this story Crane uses both his style and his perspective to discredit late 19th-century popular notions about social darwinism. (See DARWIN.)

As in Crane's experience, the story opens with four men afloat in a dinghy: the correspondent, the cook, the strong oiler, and the injured captain. The men have been battling the ocean for what seems like days. The correspondent and the oiler take turns rowing the boat while the cook constantly bails water from the dinghy. The men row all night, unaware that they are in sight of the land they so desperately seek. On seeing the shore, each man questions cruel fate: "If I am going to be drowned, why, in the name of the seven mad gods who rule the sea, was I allowed to come thus far and contemplate sand and trees?" (831). To the correspondent, Crane's counterpart in the tale, this seems cruel and unjust, and makes him realize his own insignificance in the world. At dawn the men can hold out no longer and decide to swim for shore. Crane leads the reader to believe that the injured captain is the least likely to survive, but, surprisingly, such is not the case. Ironically, the hardy oiler, who set out for shore fast and strong, is the only one who drowns. Through the oiler's death, Crane refutes popular notions about "survival of the fittest" and successfully depicts the chaotic and unpredictable world that is characteristic of modernist literature. (See MODERNISM.)

BIBLIOGRAPHY
Billingslea, Oliver. "Why Does the Oiler 'Drown'? Perception and Cosmic Chill in 'The Open Boat.'" In *American Literary Realism* 27, no. 1 (Fall 1994): 23–41. 1994.

Colvert, James B. *Style and Meaning in Stephen Crane: The Open Boat.* Austin, Tex.: University of Texas Press, 1958.

Crane, Stephen. "The Open Boat." 1898. Reprinted in *The Harper American Literature*, vol. 2. Edited by Donald McQuade et al. New York: HarperCollins College Publishers, 1993.

Nagel, James. *Stephen Crane and Literary Impressionism.* University Park: Pennsylvania State University Press, 1980.

Quinn, Brian. "A Contrastive Look at Stephen Crane's Naturalism as Depicted in 'The Open Boat' and 'The Blue Hotel.'" *Studies in English Language and Literature.* 42 (Feb. 1992): 45–63.

Kathleen M. Hicks
University of Texas at El Paso

"OTHER TWO, THE" EDITH WHARTON (1904)

Contributing to Edith WHARTON's imaginative explorations of evolutionary theory and to her ironic portrayals of marriage, "The Other Two," appearing in *The Descent of Man and Other Stories* (1904), foreshadows her later novel, *The Custom of the Country* (1913). Alice Waythorn's ability to adapt to the different styles of her three husbands illustrates the common understanding of Darwinian notions of sexual patterns and evolutionary survival. (See DARWIN.) Her third husband's honeymoon glow is marred by the news that her first husband, Mr. Haskett, will be coming to the Waythorn home to see his 12-year-old daughter, Lily, who has contracted typhoid. Shortly after receiving this unsettling news, Waythorn learns that he must also conduct business with Alice's second husband, Gus Varick. Initially Waythorn experiences discomfort when he associates with either of Alice's previous husbands, but Varick's investment with Waythorn's firm and their common social circle ease his disquiet. It is her first husband, Haskett, however, whose devotion to Lily and whose respectful humility disconcert Waythorn. Haskett's makeshift tie, attached with elastic, annoys the fastidious and elegant Waythorn by underscoring the differences between Alice's first marriage—to the poor and socially inept Haskett—and her third, to Waythorn himself. It prompts him to realize that Alice has totally obliterated her former self. When Waythorn investigates Haskett's earlier life in Utica, New York, he learns that Haskett gave up a profitable business in order to move to New York City to be near his daughter. Consequently Waythorn discerns more about Alice's values, her sense of motherhood, and her ambition.

Correlating to the typhoid that seriously infects Lily for a time, the pervasive fluidity of Alice's identity affects all three of her husbands, throwing them temporarily off balance. Their recovery entails change, especially with Waythorn, who cannot return to his former naive state. He learns that Alice's adaptability encompasses her deceit, her implacablity, and her ties with her past. He concludes that, like a member of a syndicate, he has become a partner with his two predecessors in the business of constructing Alice's personality. Her ability to make life comfortable, however, overrules his tarnished illusions and his sense of irony. Appreciating her domestic art as well as her acquired worship of good taste and respect for fidelity, he believes that he owns the last and most valuable one-third of her that remains. The final scene projects the success of the extended marital family and Waythorn's evolved condition. Circumstances cause the two previous husbands to visit his house simultaneously. As the three men smoke cigars in Waythorn's library, Alice enters and quickly dissipates any discomfort. When she serves Waythorn the third cup of tea, he laughs.

Conventional readings of this story see Waythorn as disillusioned with the hypocritical Alice, even faintly contemptuous of her, but willing to adapt to the marriage for the sake of the respectability and comfort she provides him. On another level, however, Alice—from whose thoughts we are pointedly excluded—rather than Waythorn may have the last laugh. The men all seem the same to her, as demonstrated when she forgets which of the three husbands prefers brandy in his coffee. In true Darwinian fashion, she has not merely survived but also has made the best home she can for herself and her daughter. Alice has quite brilliantly learned to play the marriage game and win it, as is "the custom of the country" in which she lives.

BIBLIOGRAPHY
Caws, Mary Ann. "Framing in Two Opposite Modes: Ford and Wharton." *The Comparatist: Journal of the Southern Comparative Literature Association* 10 (May 1986): 114–120.
Lewis, R. W. B. *Edith Wharton: A Biography.* New York: Scribner's, 1975.
Wolff, Cynthia Griffin. *A Feast of Words: The Triumph of Edith Wharton.* New York: Oxford University Press, 1977; 2nd ed., New York: Addison Wesley, 1995.

Sandra Chrystal Hayes
Georgia Institute of Technology

OXYMORON

A paradoxical utterance combining two terms that normally would contradict each other. Common examples include adjectives whose meaning contradicts that of the nouns they modify, such as living death, strenuous idleness, wise folly, or mute cry. In the modern period, William FAULKNER is famous for inventing oxymorons, such as "not-husband."

"O YES" TILLIE OLSEN (1957)

Tillie OLSEN's "O Yes," first published as "Baptism" in 1957, addresses the painful racial and class divisions that separate two adolescent friends, Carol and Parialee (Parry). On the day of Parry's baptism, Carol and her mother are the only white visitors to the church. Olsen uses the choir's songs as a refrain, interspersed with Carol's memories of her friendship with Parry in grammar school. The music sets the pace for Carol's thoughts, the preacher's call escalates the rhythm, and the congregation's response intensifies her emotions. Entranced by the music, Carol becomes overwhelmed by the church members' unrestrained emotions and nearly loses consciousness.

Parialee's mother, Alva, tries to explain the service to Carol, who does not want to listen. The incipient distance in the girls' friendship becomes clear as Carol urges her mother to take her home and Parry asserts that it was their mothers' idea, not hers, that Carol attend. The incident particularly upsets Carol's mother, Helen. Distraught, Helen tries to explain her pain to her husband, Len, and their 18-year-old daughter, Jeannie, who is frustrated by her mother's naive belief that Carol and Parry's friendship can survive the unforgiving social hierarchy of junior high. When Carol contracts the mumps, her teachers' reluctance to entrust Parry with Carol's books and their assumption that Parry's mother works for Carol's reveals that racism is institutionalized. The girls' visit is awkward and strained. Later Carol admits to her mother that she is no longer Parry's friend. "Betrayal and shame" (61) echoes in Helen's mind, although she tries to console her daughter. *"Why is it like it is?"* Carol pleads, *"And why do I have to care?"* (62). Her daughter's anguished cries evoke Helen's own losses to racism and classism, and she longs for the comfort and strength Alva finds in the community of her church.

BIBLIOGRAPHY

Coiner, Constance. *Better Red: The Writing and Resistance of Tillie Olsen and Meridel Le Sueur.* New York: Oxford University Press, 1995.

Faulkner, Mara. *Protest and Possibility in the Writing of Tillie Olsen.* Charlottesville: University Press of Virginia, 1993.

Frye, Joanne S. *Tillie Olsen: A Study of the Short Fiction.* New York: Twayne, 1995.

Nelson, Kay Hoyle, and Nancy Huse, eds. *The Critical Response to Tillie Olsen.* Westport, Conn.: Greenwood Press, 1994.

Olsen, Tillie. *Tell Me a Riddle.* New Brunswick, N.J.: Rutgers University Press, 1961.

Orr, Elaine Neil. *Tillie Olsen and a Feminist Spiritual Vision.* Jackson: University Press of Mississippi, 1987.

Pearlman, Mickey, and Abby H. P. Werlock. *Tillie Olsen.* Boston: Twayne, 1991.

Kelley Reames
University of North Carolina at Chapel Hill

OZICK, CYNTHIA (1928–)

Born in the Bronx to immigrant parents, Cynthia Ozick adopted as her particular fictional province the perspective of the American Jew. After earning a B.A. from New York University on 1949 and an M.A. from Ohio State University in 1950, she eschewed her fascination with the stories of Henry JAMES, on whom she wrote a master's thesis, and turned her focus on Jewish experience. Her characters include the immigrant, the HOLOCAUST survivor, the Zionist, and the religious Jew who tries to avoid the seduction of assimilation into the American mainstream (Perkins and Perkins 487). Ozick is also concerned with the fragile nature of fiction as it relates to truth and reality. Her stories—she has published four collections to date—have appeared in such magazines as *Commentary*, ESQUIRE, and the NEW YORKER.

Her first collection of stories, *The Pagan Rabbi and Other Stories,* published in 1971, reflects Ozick's THEME of Jews experiencing religious and social conflicts. Although her style differs from that of Isaac Bashevis SINGER, thematically, her concerns resemble his, as in the title story and "Envy," for example. In "The Pagan Rabbi," the rabbi commits suicide because he cannot resolve his love of nature with his religious perspectives and responsibilities. In "Envy," a Yiddish poet understandably objects to, and also envies, another Jewish writer—similar to Singer—who has achieved fame through his work that he has translated into English.

The title story of Ozick's second collection, *Bloodshed,* addresses another of her major themes: the response of contemporary Americans to the Holocaust, and the role that fiction, or imagination, can play in abetting such an atrocity. In the stories of her next collection, *Levitation* (1982), she continues to incorporate Jewish FOLKLORE and contemplate the nature of fiction, this time through a number of women PROTAGONISTS. In "Puttermesser and Xanthippe," for instance, a woman lawyer concerned about corruption in New York City creates a female *golem,* a figure that, in Jewish folklore, looks and acts as a human. With the *golem's* help, the lawyer runs for mayor and wins the election, reforming the city in the process. The *golem's* unquenchable sexual drives, however, render her hazardous and unpredictable, and the mayor must destroy her own creation. Both Ozick and a number of critics interpret the *golem* as a SYMBOL for art, or fiction, and the damage it can cause when it runs amok.

Ozick's most frequently reprinted story is "The Shawl," which first appeared in the NEW YORKER and was then published with its sequel, "Rosa," in Ozick's fourth collection, *The Shawl: A Story and a Novella*, in 1989. Ozick has also written three novels and a number of essays.

BIBLIOGRAPHY

Bloom, Harold, ed. *Cynthia Ozick*. New York: Chelsea House, 1986.

Cohen, Sarah Blacher. *From Levity to Liturgy: The Fiction of Cynthia Ozick*. Bloomington: Indiana University Press, 1993.

Friedman, Lawrence S. *Understanding Cynthia Ozick*. Columbia: University of South Carolina Press, 1991.

Kauviar, Elaine M. *Cynthia Ozick's Fiction: Tradition and Invention*. Bloomington: Indiana University Press, 1993.

Lowin, Joseph. *Cynthia Ozick*. Boston: Twayne, 1988.

Ozick, Cynthia. *Art and Ardor: Essays*. New York: Knopf, 1983.

———. *Bloodshed and Three Novellas*. New York: Knopf, 1976.

———. *The Cannibal Galaxy*. New York: Knopf, 1983.

———. *Levitation: Five Fictions*. New York: Knopf, 1982.

———. *The Messiah of Stockholm*. New York: Knopf, 1987.

———. *The Pagan Rabbi, and Other Stories*. New York: Knopf, 1971.

———. *The Shawl*. New York: Knopf, 1988.

———. *Trust*. New York: New American Library, 1966.

Perkins, George, and Barbara Perkins. "Cynthia Ozick." In *Contemporary Literature*. Edited by George Perkins and Barbara Perkins. New York: Random House, 1988, pp. 687–688.

Pinsker, Sanford. *The Uncompromising Fictions of Cynthia Ozick*. Columbia: University of South Carolina Press, 1987.

Rainwater, Catherine, ed. *Contemporary American Women Writers: Narrative Strategies*. Lexington: University Press of Kentucky, 1985.

P

PALEY, GRACE (GOODSIDE) (1922–)

Born in New York City to Russian-Jewish immigrant parents, Grace Paley shares striking similarities to Tillie OLSEN: both women were reared by parents with secular and socialist ideas influenced by the Russian Revolution and both women have a history of commitment to left-wing activism, FEMINISM, and the "despised people" considered unattractive subjects for fiction. Moreover, despite the demands of jobs, child rearing, and political responsibilities, both women have managed to write stories that have made a distinctive mark on 20th-century literature.

Paley's work has been published frequently in such magazines as *ATLANTIC MONTHLY, ESQUIRE,* and the *NEW YORKER,* and her reputation rests primarily on her three short story collections, *The Little Disturbances of Man,* published in 1959, *Enormous Changes at the Last Minute,* in 1974, and *Later the Same Day*, in 1985. In 1994 all her stories appeared in *The Collected Stories.*

Paley, educated at Hunter College and New York University, has long been known for her exceptional use of of language and structure for effect (Robison 103), and is also much admired for her uncanny ability to re-create the dialogue of New York, home to most of her characters and city that forms a backdrop for most of her stories. Her rhythmic style alternately conveys TONES of tension, humor, compassion, and hope; her descriptions, reminiscent of William FAULKNER's, frequently eschew physical details in favor of an image. Her themes include the vibrancy running through the lives of working men and women, their courage in facing disappointments and aging, and their ability to change (Kamel 1882). Paley's characters, again like Tillie Olsen's—or even O. HENRY's—tend to be ordinary or seemingly insignificant people, often women or children, whose stories nonetheless need to be told and heard. Moreover, like many of her postmodern contemporaries (see POSTMODERNISM), she frequently inserts observations about the storytelling process, as in "A CONVERSATION WITH MY FATHER."

BIBLIOGRAPHY

Aarons, Victoria. "Talking Lives: Storytelling and Renewal in Grace Paley's Short Fiction." *Studies in Jewish Literature* 9.1 (Spring 1990): 20–35.

Arcana, Judith. *Grace Paley's Life Stories: A Literary Biography.* Urbana: University of Illinois Press, 1993.

Baba, Minako. "Faith Darwin as Writer, Heroine: A Study of Grace Paley's Short Stories." *Studies in American Jewish Literature* 7.1 (Spring 1988): 40–54.

Halfman, Ulrich, and Philip Gerlach. "Grace Paley: A Bibliography." *Tulsa Studies in Women's Literature* 8.2 (Fall 1989): 339–354.

Isaacs, Neil David. *Grace Paley: A Study of the Short Fiction.* Boston: Twayne, 1990.

Kamel, Rose. "Grace Paley." In *The Heath Anthology of American Literature.* Vol. 2. Edited by Paul Lauter. Boston: D.C. Heath & Co., 1990, pp. 1882–883

Logsdon, Loren, and Charles W. Mayer, eds. *Since Flannery O'Connor: Essays on the Contemporary American Short Story.* Macomb: Western Illinois University, 1987, 93–100.

Lyons, Bonnie. "Grace Paley's Jewish Miniatures." *Studies in American Jewish Literature* 8.1 (Spring 1989): 26–33.

Paley, Grace.

———. *Collected Stories.* New York: Farrar, Straus, Giroux, 1997.

———. *Enormous Changes at the Last Minute.* New York: Farrar, Straus, Giroux, 1974.

———. *Later the Same Day.* New York: Farrar, Straus, Giroux, 1985.

———. *The Little Disturbances of Man.* Garden City, N.Y.: Doubleday, 1959.

———. *Long Walks and Intimate Talks. Stories and Stories by Grace Paley.* New York: Feminist Press and the City University of New York, 1991.

Robison, James C. "1969–1980: Experimentation and Tradition." In *The American Short Story, 1945–1980: A Critical History.* Edited by Gordon Weaver. Boston: Twayne, 1983, pp. 77–110.

Taylor, Jacqueline. *Grace Paley: Illuminating the Dark Lives.* Austin: University of Texas Press, 1990.

———. "Grace Paley on Storytelling and Story Hearing." *Literature in Performance: A Journal of Literature and Performing Art* 7.2 (April 1987): 46–58.

Wilde, Alan. "Grace Paley's World-Investing Words." In *Middle Grounds.* Edited by Alan Wilde. Philadelphia: University of Pennsylvania Press, 1987.

PALINDROME

The words *palin dromo* mean in Greek "to run back again." In writing, a palindrome is a word or line that reads the same backward and forward. Examples include Napoleon's reputed saying "Able was I ere I saw Elba," and such words as "civic" and "Anna." For an extended example, see Gertrude STEIN's "THE GOOD ANNA."

"PANTALOON IN BLACK" WILLIAM FAULKNER (1942)

The third of seven stories comprising William FAULKNER's GO DOWN, MOSES (1942), "Pantaloon in Black" is the tragic and poignant story of Rider, a black sawmill worker who is made a widower when his young bride, Mannie, dies only six months into their marriage. In his grief, Rider appears to seek his own death, first by undertaking superhuman risks at the sawmill and finally by challenging the white night watchman, Birdsong, who runs a crooked dice game at the mill. When his cheating is discovered, Birdsong tries to pull his gun, but Rider is quicker with his own razor and cuts Birdsong's throat. Not long after, Rider is lynched by Birdsong's relatives.

Like many of the stories in *Go Down, Moses,* "Pantaloon in Black" is most significant for its concern with race. In this story Faulkner explores the racial dynamics through varying the narrative POINT OF VIEW. The first section of the story is told in the third person, but Rider's thoughts and feelings are at the narrative center. Such a point of view allows Faulkner to humanize Rider, showing him as a bereaved husband who was very much in love with his young bride and who is beside himself at the loss. This story is perhaps most important because Faulkner focuses on Rider's humanity more than anything else, even his race.

To make sure we understand his point, Faulkner adds a second section to this story. The point of view shifts from Rider to a white sheriff's deputy, who had brought Rider into custody following the murder and is now recounting the events of the last few days to his wife. This conversation, on the day following Rider's lynching, clearly demonstrates Faulkner's efforts to put a human face on Rider, for the deputy completely misunderstands his behavior. At Mannie's funeral, Rider seized the shovel from the undertaker and covered the coffin himself; later, driven by grief and a probable death wish, he decided to show up at work early the very next day, snatching up ten-foot cypress logs by himself and throwing them around like matches. Rider's seeming lack of concern convinces the deputy that Rider and blacks in general are incapable of human emotion: "They look like a man," he tells his wife, "and they can walk on their hind legs like a man. . . . But when it comes to the normal human feelings and sentiments of human beings, they might just as well be a damn herd of wild buffaloes" (156, 154).

By juxtaposing Rider's poignant grief with the deputy's blind and reductive interpretation of his actions, Faulkner demonstrates the distance between blacks and whites in the South, a distance he seeks to describe and even bridge in much of his fiction.

BIBLIOGRAPHY

Faulkner, William, *Go Down, Moses* (1942). Reissue edition. New York: Vintage Books, 1991.

Davis, Thadious M. *Faulkner's "Negro": Art and the Southern Context.* Baton Rouge: Louisiana State University Press, 1983.

H. Collin Messer
University of North Carolina

PARABLE   A simple, short, fictitious story that teaches a lesson or illustrates a moral principle. Like an ALLEGORY, details of a parable parallel the details of the situation calling for illustration. The parable was one of Christ's favorite devices as a teacher, examples of which are the parables of the Good Samaritan and the Prodigal Son. Among the many examples of parables in short stories are Raymond CARVER's "WHERE I'M CALLING FROM," Tim Gautreaux's "Died and Gone to Vegas" in *Same Place, Same Things,* and Tobias WOLFF's "The Liar."

PARKER, DOROTHY (1893–1967)   In an era known for its trend-setting, Dorothy Parker's cleverness and independence during the Jazz Age made her a symbol of modern emancipated womanhood. Her fiction and poetry, however, reflect a more somber side of a freedom that was at least partly illusory.

A New Yorker all her life, Parker lost her mother in infancy and had no close ties to her father, who died soon after she graduated from a private high school. Parker went to work for *Vogue* magazine and played the piano at night. In 1917 she moved to *Vanity Fair* and became good friends with its editor, Robert Benchley, and the dramatic editor, Robert Sherwood. Joined by journalists Franklin Pierce Adams and Harold Ross, who was to found the NEW YORKER in 1924, they formed the nucleus of a lively literary lunch club that met at the Algonquin Hotel and was known as the ALGONQUIN ROUND TABLE. Parker was also famous for her witty quips, many of which have passed into American lore (for instance, "Men seldom make passes at girls who wear glasses").

Parker lost her job at *Vanity Fair* and divorced her husband, Edwin Pon Parker II, in 1919. She began to write poetry, and in 1926 published her poems in her first book, which became a best-seller. In 1929 she won the O. Henry Memorial Award for her story "Big Blonde." Hazel Morse, the tragic PROTAGONIST of the story, is, like Parker, terrified of loneliness and despair. Like Parker, she attempts suicide but does not die. Parker's art in this story is powerful: Through a series of sharply framed vignettes, she conveys Hazel's decline from a fun-loving young woman into an overweight and aging woman addicted to despair, alcohol, and drugs. Parker clearly illuminates not only the pathetic vulnerability of the weaker—and female—members of contemporary society but also the ultimate responsibility of a society that is almost Darwinian in its attitudes. (See DARWIN.) One of the most moving comparisons in the story is between Hazel and an old workhorse.

Parker published two collections of short stories, *Laments for the Living* (1930) and *After Such Pleasures* (1933). These stories show an artist with a concern for spare language reminiscent of Ernest HEMINGWAY, whose work she admired. Like Hemingway, Parker took care to focus sharply on her CHARACTERS, and she used dialogue and monologue rather than relying too heavily on description. She also praised F. Scott FITZGERALD, from whom she said she learned the value of using small symbols to represent issues of social significance, and Ring LARDNER, from whom she learned to use colloquial dialogue. (See DIALECT.)

In 1930 Parker married Alan Campbell, an actor, and moved with him to Hollywood, where both became scriptwriters. Although she never joined the Communist Party, Parker declared herself a communist and took an early stand against FASCISM and Nazi Germany. After WORLD WAR II Parker and her husband were blacklisted during the McCarthy hearings for their communist sympathies. (See MCCARTHYISM.)

BIBLIOGRAPHY

Frewin, Leslie. *The Late Mrs. Dorothy Parker.* New York: Macmillan, 1986.

Keats, John. *You Might as Well Live. The Life and Times of Dorothy Parker.* New York: Simon & Schuster, 1970.

Kinney, Arthur F. *Parker.* Boston: Twayne, 1978.

Meade, Marion. *Parker: What Fresh Hell Is This?* New York: Villard, 1988.

Parker, Dorothy. *After Such Pleasures* New York: Viking, 1933.

———. "Big Blonde." In *O. Henry Memorial Award Prize Stories.* Edited by Blanche Colton Williams. Garden City, N.Y.: Doubleday, 1929, pp. 1–25.

———. *Death and Taxes.* New York: Viking, 1931.

———. *Laments for the Living.* New York: Viking, 1930.

———. *Sunset Gun.* New York: Boni & Liveright, 1928.

PARODY

Designed to ridicule a work, its style, or its author, parody is a comic or satirical imitation of the serious materials and manner of a particular work. (See COMEDY.) Typically a parody exaggerates the style, structure, content, or meaning of the work or author it pokes fun at, and satirizes one or both. For example, William FAULKNER and Ernest HEMINGWAY parodied the style of the older Sherwood ANDERSON.

PARTISAN REVIEW, THE

Founded by William Philips in 1934, the *Partisan Review* has maintained its status as a highly influential journal. Initially identified with Marxist politics (see MARX), it diverged in 1937 from a self-consciously left-wing radical stance and became increasingly concerned with intellectual, literary, and artistic matters. The journal has always been concerned with AVANT-GARDE writing, and early contributors included Samuel Beckett, Saul BELLOW, T. S. Eliot, Norman MAILER, Tillie OLSEN, Wallace Stevens, and Gore Vidal. Several collections of material from the magazine have been published, including *The Partisan Reader—1934–1944* (1946), *The New Partisan Reader* (1953), *Stories in the Modern Manner* (1953), and *More Stories in the Modern Manner* (1954). The journal contains fiction, poetry, and essays by outstanding authors and remains one of the best intellectual reviews.

PASTURES OF HEAVEN, THE   JOHN STEINBECK (1932)

"An often ignored collection of stories that appeared, unceremoniously, in 1932," *The Pastures of Heaven* can be considered the cornerstone of much of John STEINBECK's later, great fiction (Nagel xxix). Upon publication, although it was ignored for the most part by the reading public, critics generally praised the book, labeling it "magnificent" and referring to "the author's simple, indelible power" (Jackson 12). After reading the work, one critic prophetically remarked that Steinbeck's "future work should lead to his recognition as an excellent psychological analyst" (Nagel xiii). No matter what any critic has to say about the book, however, it is clear that in *The Pastures of Heaven,* Steinbeck for the first time presents many of the THEMES and ideas that he explores in depth in several of his later works.

The work is a SHORT STORY CYCLE that contains many individual short stories linked by specific themes. This is the first of Steinbeck's California books in which the characters, people who dwell in a beautiful California valley named the Pastures of Heaven, are tied intimately to the land, as is the case with *Of Mice and Men* and *The Grapes of Wrath.* The individual stories show the effect the Munroes, who move onto the "cursed" Battle farm, have on the people of the valley. A prologue and EPILOGUE provide a "thematic envelope" for the ten stories that comprise the work (Nagel xix).

The prologue sets the stage for the rest of the work by introducing the supposed "curse" on the valley. A Spanish corporal discovers the valley while searching for his runaway Indian slaves. The corporal is awestruck by the heavenly beauty of the valley and decides that he will return someday. An Indian woman, however, whom he probably raped, "presented him with the pox," and he never had a chance to return (4). Thus, the first person whose dream lay in the Pastures was denied.

As in many of Steinbeck's works, especially *Of Mice and Men* and *The Grapes of Wrath,* the dream motif of an EDENic garden is a very powerful and prevalent theme in *The Pastures of Heaven.* Nearly all characters are tormented by some unfulfilled dream and disillusionment, or by the realization that their existence is illusory and easily shattered by intrusive reality. In the story of Pat Humbert and the Whitesides, for example, Mae Munroe inadvertently inspires Pat Humbert with the idea of remodeling the parlor he detests. Pat becomes obsessed and pictures inviting Mae to see the parlor, where she will fall madly in love with him. When he finally summons the nerve to invite her over, Pat learns that Mae has just become engaged to Bill Whiteside. After Pat's dream of a happy life with Mae is vanquished, he never again wants to face "the dark and unutterable dreary" parlor, which he recently found so delightful and promising (168).

Like Pat, John Whiteside had a dream: He longed to create a Whiteside dynasty in his beautiful house in the Pastures. When Bill, his only son, decides to marry Mae Munroe and move to the city, John Whiteside's dream of a dynasty goes up in smoke—as does his house, of which he was so proud, when it is accidentally burned to the ground.

Other characters, such as Edward "Shark" Wicks, Helen Van Deventer, Molly Morgan, and Raymond Banks (see BANKS FAMILY), also live an illusory and deluded existence. Both Shark Wicks and Molly Morgan decide to leave the Pastures rather than face reality once their illusions have been exposed and unmasked. The widowed Helen Van Deventer, devoted to "her masochistic hungering for tragedy" (Winn 95), murders her insane daughter so that she can brood over her deed for the rest of her life. Raymond Banks derives his life's pleasure from witnessing executions at the San Quentin Penitentiary. Whatever satisfaction Raymond derives from this, however, is ruined when Bert Munroe lets him know how twisted it really is. All of these characters' illusions have been shattered; each must face reality or run away from the Pastures.

The third group of characters in *The Pastures of Heaven*—Tularecito, Junius Maltby, and Rosa and Maria Lopez—reflect Steinbeck's characteristic distaste for middle-class morality. Both Tularecito and Robbie Maltby, Junius's son, are ruined by the public school system that conventional society forces them to attend. The Lopez sisters, who encourage the sale of their enchiladas with sex, are driven out of the Pastures by the moral middle class. Society's

"demands for conformity" destroy these characters' sense of self and happiness (xxiii).

The epilogue is loaded with Steinbeck's stinging irony. A group of tourists gaze upon the Pastures just as the Spanish corporal did hundreds of years before them. Ignorant of the personal tragedy that has occurred in the heavenly valley, they fantasize about the quiet and peaceful lives the inhabitants must lead in what appears to be a paradise on earth.

The Pastures of Heaven serves as apt introduction to the themes of Steinbeck's major works: disillusionment, displacement, loss of a sense of self, and a distaste for bourgeois morality.

BIBLIOGRAPHY

Jackson, Joseph. "John Steinbeck: A Portrait," *The Saturday Review* 16, no. 22 (September 25, 1937): 11–12, 18.

Meyer, Michael. "Finding a New Jerusalem: The Edenic Myth of John Steinbeck." In *Literature and the Bible*. Amsterdam; Atlanta, Ga.: Rodopi, 1993.

Nagel, James. "Introduction." In John Steinbeck, *The Pastures of Heaven*. New York: Penguin, 1995.

Owens, Louis. "John Steinbeck's *The Pastures of Heaven*: Illusions of Eden." *Arizona Quarterly* (Autumn 1985): 197–214.

Pugh, Scott. "Ideals and Inversion in *The Pastures of Heaven*." In *Kyushu-American Literature*. 28 (October 1987): 70–720.

Steinbeck, John. *The Pastures of Heaven*. New York: Penguin, 1995.

Winn, Harbour. "The Unity of Steinbeck's Pasture's Community." *Steinbeck Quarterly* 22, nos. 3–4 (Summer–Fall 1989): 91–103.

Kathleen M. Hicks
University of Texas at El Paso

PAT HOBBY   A washed-out Hollywood scriptwriter in F. Scott FITZGERALD's PAT HOBBY STORIES, which ran in *ESQUIRE* from 1939 to 1940. In early reviews, commentators regarded Pat Hobby as Fitzgerald himself, who, at the end of his life, was shut out from the lucrative fiction market where he had made his name and commanded high prices. Like his PROTAGONIST, Fitzgerald still believed that he could revitalize his talent after several years of alcoholism and emotional depletion.

While parallels exist between Fitzgerald and his protagonist, recent readers have begun to examine Pat Hobby in a fictional rather than autobiographical context. In these readings he becomes not a pathetic or sentimental figure but a satirical or humorous symbol of the relationship between culture and character. As a comic device, he takes readers on an inside tour of Hollywood, his machinations carrying him to different locations in the power structure: film sets, his dingy office in the writers' building, and the bar where the insiders congregate.

Some readers see elements of Fitzgerald's ROMAN-TICISM in Pat Hobby, the product of Hollywood's vulgarity. Like Jay Gatsby, Dick Diver, DEXTER GREEN, and other Fitzgerald characters, Hobby's personality and destiny are shaped by the greed and gaudiness of American culture. Although he lacks the sensitivity and sincerity of the romantic protagonists, Hobby's characterization evokes Fitzgerald's signature motifs: the American myth of success and the impossibility of reviving the past.

BIBLIOGRAPHY

Daniels, Thomas E. "Pat Hobby: Anti-Hero." *Fitzgerald/Hemingway Annual.* 1973.

Stern, Milton, R. "Will the Real Pat Hobby Please Stand Up?" In *New Essays on Fitzgerald's Neglected Stories.* Edited by Jackson R. Bryer. Columbia: University of Missouri Press, 1996.

Frances Kerr
Durham Technical Community College

PAT HOBBY STORIES, THE F. SCOTT FITZGERALD (1962)

In the last three years of his life, FITZGERALD was under contract as a scriptwriter in Hollywood. During the week he worked for the film industry; on weekends he pursued his own writing projects. He began a novel about Hollywood, published as a fragment after his death (*The Last Tycoon*), and he regularly produced short stories, including a series that featured a burned-out Hollywood scriptwriter, PAT HOBBY. The Pat Hobby stories—17 in all—were published in ESQUIRE in 1939 and 1940, one posthumously.

According to Arnold Gingrich, his editor at *Esquire,* Fitzgerald regarded the stories as "a collective entity," regularly rearranging the order in which they would appear in the magazine so as to achieve a developmental effect. Because each story appeared in a different issue, however, the repetition of contextual details to orient the first-time reader keeps them from being a truly cumulative sequence. Although Fitzgerald considered publishing the Pat Hobby stories as a collection, after he died suddenly in 1940 they remained largely forgotten until 1962, when Scribner's printed them as *The Pat Hobby Stories* with an introduction by Gingrich. They have yet to draw much critical commentary, although recently scholar-critics have begun to include them in the continuing reappraisal of Fitzgerald's work in the short fiction GENRE.

Like many other Fitzgerald stories, these were written for money. Fitzgerald was in debt and in poor health at the end of his life; their hurried composition was a factor in their questionable quality. Gingrich has verified, however, that Fitzgerald took these stories seriously. He revised them numerous times, often cabling meticulous changes at the last minute. Even in the 1920s when his stories brought in over ten times the amount *Esquire* could pay in the 1930s, money was never the exclusive motive for Fitzgerald. Nonetheless, these stories do not approach the quality of his best work. Many of the plots are contrived; an unbelievable surprise frequently forces a story's end. More like SKETCHes, the pieces are hard to classify, and some of the weaker ones seem too insubstantial to be considered serious fiction. Critical evaluation, however, has only recently begun.

Stylistically, the Pat Hobby sequence is a departure from Fitzgerald's early LYRICism. The objective narration is sparse, foreshadowing the MINIMALISM of the 1970s. Fitzgerald had used HUMOR in his stories from the beginning, but the dry, satirical, sometimes bitter tone of the narration in these pieces belongs to the fictional posture of his last years. Pat Hobby is a washed-out scriptwriter at 49—lazy, conniving, stupid, selfish, and pathetic. We are invited to laugh at his absurdities, but the series is not pure COMEDY.

All of Fitzgerald's fiction mixes techniques from different genres; tonal AMBIGUITY is present in these stories too. Recent critics describe them as social REALISM, emphasizing their panoramic scan of Hollywood. Others see Fitzgerald's romantic strain still operative in Hobby's delusional attempts to recreate his past glory. (See ROMANTICISM.) It is even possible in some of the stories to sympathize with Hobby as one who, despite his own failings, is also victimized by the vulgarity and greed of the Hollywood system—the game that has grown larger than any of its players, corrupting all but the lucky or exceptionally intelligent few.

Parallels between Fitzgerald and his tired PROTAGONIST are obvious. Like Hobby, Fitzgerald no longer enjoyed the high visibility or financial returns on his work that had defined his career in the 1920s. Like Hobby, alcoholism, family problems, debt, and depression had left Fitzgerald emotionally exhausted. The Pat Hobby stories, however, are more than self-expression. In the next decade, as the critical reevaluation of Fitzgerald's body of work continues, they are among the works most likely to receive new interpretations.

BIBLIOGRAPHY

Daniels, Thomas E. "Pat Hobby: Anti-Hero." *Fitzgerald/Hemingway Annual* (1973).

Gingrich, Arnold. "Introduction." *The Pat Hobby Stories.* New York: Scribner's. 1962.

Stern, Milton R. "Will the Real Pat Hobby Please Stand Up?" In *New Essays on Fitzgerald's Neglected Stories.* Edited by Jackson R. Bryer. Columbia: University of Missouri Press, 1996.

West, James L. W. III. "Fitzgerald and Esquire." In *The Short Stories of F. Scott Fitzgerald: New Approaches in Criticism.* Edited by Jackson R. Bryer. Madison: University of Wisconsin Press, 1982.

Frances Kerr
Durham Technical Community College

"PAUL'S CASE: A STUDY IN TEMPERAMENT" WILLA CATHER (1905)

Published in MCCLURE'S, "Paul's Case" was included in Willa CATHER's first collection, *The Troll Garden* (1905), a volume of seven stories about artists. "Paul's Case" is Cather's most anthologized story and one of the few she allowed to be reprinted in her lifetime, judging it representative of her best work. Of all her stories, it continues to prompt the most critical commentary.

The story's PROTAGONIST, Paul, is a Pittsburgh high school student who adopts the pose of an aesthete to express his alienation from the middle-class neighborhood where he lives with his father and sisters. Paul resents the cloying Christian dogma and the religion of material success that provide the structure for daily life on Cordelia Street. Cather presents subtly scathing descriptions of the unimaginative but responsible people—especially Paul's father and schoolteachers—who try to draw him into the daily routines of middle-class conformity. To maintain a defiant distance, Paul tells elaborate lies about his world travels and his affiliations with performers at Pittsburgh's Carnegie Hall, where he works as an usher in the evenings. When viewing art or hearing music, he enters a trancelike state he resents leaving. In desperation, he steals money from an employer, goes to New York City, and spends several decadent days at the Waldorf Hotel; in a state of excited fantasy, he fulfills all his sensuous desires not for art but for fine clothes, food, wine, and flowers. Knowing his father is on his way to retrieve him, he leaves the Waldorf in a state of deep depression, takes a cab to the outskirts of town, and throws himself in front of a train. His last thoughts are of romantic foreign vistas.

Cather's story is densely patterned. A number of motifs, such as sleep and drunkenness, provide unity among successive scenes. The story's dual perspective allows readers to identify with Paul's alienation in a drab middle-class community and to enter his fantastic dream world but also to engage in critical analysis of his behavior. As its title indicates, the story is a psychological study of a personality type. Some readers have suggested that Paul is an example of the weak-willed person for whom art can become a selfish escape. Others see the story as a contrast between real artists and those who strike bohemian poses, or a criticism of the "art for art's sake" movement of the 1890s. Edward W. Pitcher argues that Paul is Cather's creation of the FAUSTIAN temperament as it had evolved in music and literature by the turn of the century. Another analysis suggests that Paul is a homosexual living in a representative American community whose members are unprepared to accept his "feminine" desires or his sexual orientation. The critic Eve Sedgwick sees in the story the imprint of Cather's conflicts with her own lesbianism. As a commentary on American CAPITALISM, the story can be read as a tragic study of an imaginative boy born into an economy in which art is a leisure commodity for the upper class.

BIBLIOGRAPHY
Cather, Willa. *Willa Cather's Collected Short Fiction,*
   1892–1912. Lincoln: University of Nebraska Press, 1965.
Faulkner, Virginia, ed. *Willa Cather's Collected Short Fiction,*
   1892–1912. Lincoln: University of Nebraska Press, 1965.
Pitcher, Edward W. "Willa Cather's 'Paul's Case' and the
   Faustian Temperament." *Studies in Short Fiction* 28 (1991):
   543–552.
Rubin, Larry. "The Homosexual Motif in Willa Cather's
   'Paul's Case.'" *Studies in Short Fiction* (Spring 1975):
   127–131.
Sedgwick, Eve. "Across Gender, Across Sexuality: Willa
   Cather and Others." *South Atlantic Quarterly* 88 (1989):
   53–72.

Frances Kerr
Durham Technical Community College

PEN/FAULKNER AWARD Affiliated with PEN, the acronym for the international writers' organization Poets, Playwrights, Editors, Essayists and Novelists, the PEN/Faulkner annual award is named in honor of William Faulkner, who created with his Nobel Prize funds an award for young writers. The PEN/Faulkner Award, founded by writers in 1980 to honor their peers, is now the largest juried award for fiction in the United States. The award judges, all fiction writers themselves, annually read more than 250 novels and short story collections published during that calendar year and then select five outstanding books. The book designated the winner earns $15,000 for its author; each of the others receives $5,000. All five authors read from their works and are honored at an award cere-

mony and celebration held in May at the Folger Library in Washington, D.C. Short story writers who have won the PEN/Faulkner award include T. Coraghessan BOYLE (*World's End,* 1988) and Peter TAYLOR (*The Old Forest,* 1986).

"PERFECT DAY FOR BANANAFISH, A"
J. D. SALINGER (1948) First published in the *NEW YORKER* on January 31, 1948, and later the first story in the 1953 collection *Nine Stories,* "A Perfect Day for Bananafish" begins with Muriel Glass sitting in a Florida hotel room fielding a telephone call from her overconcerned mother. As is typical of J. D. SALINGER's work, dialogue between characters moves the plot forward; the speech is sufficiently vague to leave the reader interested in what the characters refer to but never explain. Salinger spends little time describing a particular scene, preferring to let the character's words set the pace as well as the mood of a work.

The first section of the story revolves around Muriel and her mother's conversation, with elliptical references to German books, the war, and Muriel's terribly pale husband, Seymour, who has yet to enter the story. It is implied that the war, WORLD WAR II, has set Seymour on edge, although Muriel reassures her mother that he is fine. The story implies that the reader should doubt Muriel's assertion.

Seymour is introduced to the story through Sybil, a young child who, with her mother, is staying at the same hotel. Sybil recognizes "see more glass" on the beach after she is sent away by her mother (*Nine Stories* 10). Seymour and Sybil enter the water, Sybil on a small float and Seymour simply standing in the water, making elliptical small talk. He tells Sybil about strange creatures called bananafish. Bananafish, Seymour explains, are perfectly normal until one swims into a hole filled with bananas. The perhaps-lucky bananafish then overeats until it is too stuffed to swim back out of the hole, eventually dying of banana fever. Sybil, as a typical Salingerian wide-eyed child, plays along with Seymour's game, claiming to see one eating six bananas at once.

As in many of Salinger's other works, the wisest words come from the mouths of children. The adults in this story, beaten down and resigned to their lives, either send their children to play on the beach or fend off their mothers on hotel room telephones. Sybil is the lone character in the story who seems to understand Seymour and the only one with whom he actually communicates. A later exchange, in the final section of the story that ends with Salinger's matter-of-fact scripting of Seymour's sudden suicide, illustrates the man's total inability to communicate with adults in any logical manner. Isolation and desperation are THEMES that constantly appear in Salinger's work: the idea of sheer beauty in the midst of human squalor and the innocence of children contrasted with the weight of adult life.

Anne N. Thalheimer
University of Delaware, Newark

PERSONA
From the Greek word meaning "mask," the persona is widely used to refer to a "second self," or the "I," through whom the author tells a story and unravels his or her perceptions of characters and events. Alexander Lawrence POSEY's *Fux Fixico Letters* is one example, wherein Posey adopts the persona of an old man who offers social and political opinion along with common sense.

PERSONIFICATION
A figure of speech that attributes human characteristics or feelings to an animal, an object, or a concept. This common device appears routinely throughout American stories of the 19th and 20th centuries. Effective examples of personification occur in Ernest HEMINGWAY's portrait of the lion in "THE SHORT HAPPY LIFE OF FRANCIS MACOMBER" and William FAULKNER's personification of the town in "A ROSE FOR EMILY."

PETRY, ANN LANE (1908–1997)
Petry has been called a neighborhood novelist, a protest writer, a naturalist of the Richard WRIGHT school (see NATURALISM), an assimilationist, a humanist, and a New England writer. Published in every genre, she fits into many literary categories, including that of pioneer: *Miss Muriel and Other Stories* (1971) is the first published collection of short fiction by an African American woman writer.

The second child of a pharmacist and a chiropodist, Petry was born in Old Saybrook, Connecticut, on October 12, 1908. Her experience as a member of the only black family in town shaped much of Petry's writing, although by her own account, her childhood years were happy. After receiving a Ph.D. from the University of Connecticut in 1931, she worked as a pharmacist in her father's drugstore for seven years. She married George Petry in 1938 and moved with him to Harlem, where she was a journalist and editor for two Harlem newspapers, a member of American Negro Theatre, and a creative writing student at Columbia University. Although these experiences shaped her writing, it was while running an afterschool program at a Harlem grade school that she first confronted the virulent racism, sexism, and poverty experienced by American blacks, social realities that characterize her early fiction. Until this experience, Petry notes, "I lived my whole life without paying attention."

Petry's big break occurred after her story "On Saturday the Sirens Sound at Noon" appeared in *The Crisis* (1943). An editor at Houghton Mifflin read the story and suggested that Petry apply for the Houghton Mifflin Literary Fellowship for novelists. She submitted *The Street* and won the fellowship, becoming an immediate success. *The Best American Short Stories of 1946* is dedicated to Petry and includes her story "LIKE A WINDING SHEET." Petry has published two more novels, *Country Place* (1947) and *The Narrows* (1953), four children's books, five poems, and several short stories.

BIBLIOGRAPHY
Andrews, William L., et al. *The Oxford Companion to African-American Literature.* New York: Oxford University Press, 1997.
Christian, Barbara. *Black Women Novelists: The Development of a Tradition, 1892–1976.* Westport, Conn.: Greenwood Press, 1980.
Clark, Keith. "A Distaff Dream Deferred? Ann Petry and the Art of Subversion." *African American Review* 26:3 (Fall 1992): 495–505.

Ervin, Hazel Arnett. *Ann Petry: A Bio-Bibliography*. New York: G.K. Hall, 1993.

Holladay, Hilary. *Ann Petry*. New York: Twayne, 1996.

Petry, Ann. *Country Place*. Boston: Houghton Mifflin, 1947.

———. *Miss Muriel and Other Stories*. Boston: Houghton Mifflin, 1971.

———. *The Narrows*. Boston: Houghton Mifflin, 1953.

———. *The Street*. Boston: Houghton Mifflin, 1943.

Washington, Gladys J. "A World Made Cunningly: A Closer Look at Ann Petry's Short Fiction." *CLA Journal* 30:1 (September 1986): 14–29.

Washington, Mary Helen. *Invented Lives: Narratives of Black Women 1860–1960*. Garden City, N.Y.: Anchor Press. 1987.

Kimberly Drake
Virginia Wesleyan College

PHELPS WARD, ELIZABETH STUART

(1844–1911) Influenced by her mother, the writer Elizabeth Stuart Phelps, who died prematurely, and by her reading of Elizabeth Barrett Browning's *Aurora Leigh*, Elizabeth Stuart Phelps Ward explored the meaning of women as artists in her fiction and in her own life and became one of the most prolific American writers of the late 19th century. A New England writer who lived in Massachusetts all her life, and the daughter of Boston minister Austin Phelps, Elizabeth Stuart Phelps Ward was similar to her New England sister writers Mary Wilkins FREEMAN and Sarah Orne JEWETT in her rendition of a stark physical and psychologically isolated New England landscape.

Known today primarily for her many novels, among which *The Gates Ajar* (1868), *The Silent Partner* (1871), *The Story of Avis* (1877), and *Doctor Zay* (1882) have garnered much recent critical attention, she was also applauded in her own time for her five major collections of stories: *Men, Women, and Ghosts* (1869), *Sealed Orders* (1879), *Fourteen to One* (1891), *The Oath of Allegiance and Other Stories* (1909), and *The Empty House and Other Stories* (1910) and for her many children's stories. Whittier favorably compared her *Sealed Orders* to Nathaniel HAWTHORNE's *Twice-Told Tales*. Her life's work, 57 books, including 19 novels, an autobiography (*Chapters from a Life*), collections of verse and of short fiction, juvenile literature, drama, and various uncollected essays and stories, shows her deep involvement with social issues, including women's and men's rights as well as workers' rights, the marriage question, the plight of the working woman, female bonding, male mentoring, UTOPIAN spirituality, temperance, homeopathic medicine, the relationship of illness to emotional disequilibrium, and antivivisection.

There are three distinct and, at times, overlapping styles in her short-story writing: historical, realistic (see REALISM), and GOTHIC. In her most widely anthologized story in recent times, "THE TENTH OF JANUARY" (*ATLANTIC MONTHLY*, 1868) Phelps renders a fictional account of the fire that spread through the nearby Pemberton Mills and killed all the female workers. She is also known for her sensitive portrayal of women's reactions to the losses incurred by the CIVIL WAR, among them "A Sacrifice Consumed" (*Harper's New Monthly Magazine*, 1864), which marked the beginning of her writing career. One of the most famous Civil War consolation narratives, "The Oath of Allegiance," the lead story of the collection with the same name, tells the tale of a woman depriving herself for the sake of preserving the memory of her departed lover. Many of these stories question whether the men's sacrifices and women's suffering were worth it. It has been speculated that Phelps Ward lost a close male friend during the war and that his memory hovers over these consolation stories.

Although Phelps Ward is seriously interested in the plight of the working woman, she has, at times, a way of romanticizing the working class. Her vacations in Gloucester, Massachusetts (1869–76) and her interest in the temperance cause and the welfare of Gloucester fishermen provided material for her early LOCAL COLOR short stories, like "Jack the Fisherman" and "The Madonna of the Tubs," two of her favorite short stories, later anthologized in *Fourteen to One*. In "The Madonna of the Tubs," Phelps Ward contrasts the poor seaside laundress who has a loving family surrounding her with the empty life of Helen Ritter, the wealthy benefactress without family, who enjoys bestowing gifts on the fisherman's family. More realistic is Phelps Ward's treatment of poverty-stricken women in several stories in *Sealed Orders*, most notably "Old Mother Goose," "The Lady of Shalott," and "The True Story of Guenevere," which show the folly of believing in FAIRY-TALE endings and suggest that single, impoverished women have to fend for themselves in the face of merciless economic conditions.

Little critical attention has focused on Ward's lesser-known stories that show sympathy for the breadwinner-husband, consumed by his profession, which finally renders his life meaningless, In "The Empty House," in the collection of the same name, a businessman, Mr. Hosmer, suffers from loneliness and becomes physically ill as his idle, materialistic wife and children abandon him for the pleasures of a seaside vacation. Likely because Phelps Ward's health was poor throughout her life, illness looms large in her work. Her sympathies for men who become sick in their quest for masculine, professional affirmation also might have resulted from her observations of her father's debilitating illnesses and of her ne'er-do-well husband's physical and emotional breakdowns. After a life of semiinvalidism, Phelps Ward died of heart disease alone in her Newton, Massachusetts, home on January 28, 1911.

Many of her novels and short stories employ supernatural and gothic elements, and it comes as no surprise that Phelps Ward corresponded with the gothic writer Harriet P. SPOFFORD. Most of the stories in her *Men, Women, and Ghosts* are gothic inquiries into women's psyche and spirituality and serve as precursors to Freeman's and Edith WHARTON's gothic tales. "Kentucky's Ghost" in this collection comes close to the caliber of Joseph Conrad's gothic sea stories.

BIBLIOGRAPHY

Coultrap-McQuin, Susan. "The Demise of Feminine Strength: The Career of Elizabeth Stuart Phelps (Ward)." In *Doing Literary Business: American Women Writers in the Nineteenth Century*. Chapel Hill, N.C.: University of North Carolina Press, 1990, 167–192.

Kelly, Lori Duin. *The Life and Works of Elizabeth Stuart Phelps, Victorian Feminist Writer.* Troy, N.Y.: Whitson, 1983.

Kessler, Carol Farley. *Elizabeth Stuart Phelps.* Boston: Twayne, 1982.

Phelps Ward, Elizabeth Stuart. *Chapters from a Life.* New York: S. S. McClure, 1896.

———. *Doctor Zay.* Boston: Houghton Mifflin, 1882.

———. *The Empty House and Other Stories.* Boston: Houghton Mifflin, 1910.

———. *Fourteen to One.* 1891; Boston: Houghton Mifflin, 1897.

———. *The Gates Ajar.* 1868; Boston: Houghton Mifflin, 1889.

———. *Men, Women, and Ghosts.* 1869; Boston: Fields, Osgood & Company, 1877.

———. *The Oath of Allegiance and Other Stories.* Boston: Houghton Mifflin, 1909.

———. *Sealed Orders.* 1879. Boston: Houghton Mifflin, 1888.

———. *The Silent Partner.* 1871; Boston: Houghton, Mifflin, 1899.

———. *The Story of Avis.* 1877. Boston: Houghton, Osgood & Co.: 1880.

Monika Elbert
Montclair State University

PHILIP MARLOWE Raymond CHANDLER's tarnished knight, Los Angeles–based detective Philip Marlowe, has a college education and a fondness for classical music; as a private investigator, he enjoys playing chess and solving the problems that often seem to echo those he encounters in his detective work. The character who evolved into Marlowe in seven novels appeared under several names in the short stories as originally published. The only short story originally written with Marlowe as the hero is "The Pencil," a story that appeared as "Marlowe Takes on the Syndicate" in the *London Daily Mail* in 1959. A solitary bachelor, Marlowe is attractive to women but ultimately keeps to himself as he treads the streets of his native Los Angeles. Posthumously, in 1989, Robert B. Parker edited and published Chandler's unfinished novel *Poodle Springs,* in which Marlowe finally marries.

J. Randolph Cox
St. Olaf College

PHOENIX JACKSON The protagonist of Eudora WELTY's "A WORN PATH," Phoenix Jackson makes her journey along the path to town so that she may buy medicine for her grandson. When she arrives at the clinic, the reader realizes that her grandson may have died in an accident some time ago, and thus some critics have seen Phoenix as a senile old woman on a mock mission of love. In response, Welty wrote an essay, "Is Phoenix Jackson's Grandson Really Dead?" in which she states that he is not: for Phoenix, he cannot die, and for Phoenix, love is the focus of life, a habit, a worn path, the most meaningful aspect of existence.

BIBLIOGRAPHY

Welty, Eudora. "Is Phoenix Jackson's Grandson Really Dead?" In *The Eye of the Story.* New York: Random House, 1978.

"PIT AND THE PENDULUM, THE" EDGAR ALLAN POE (1843)

"The Pit and the Pendulum" first appeared in Edgar Allan POE's collection of short stories, *The Gift,* in 1843. The story is a terrifying tale of suspense in which Poe captures the horrors of confinement and torture. The main character, a prisoner condemned to death by the Inquisition in Spain, awakens to find himself in a chamber of utter darkness. His first impression is that he has been buried alive. Once the prisoner discovers that he is not in a tomb, he proceeds to grope his way around the dungeon to discover his surroundings. His disorientation is perplexing. In groping his way around, the prisoner nearly falls into a deep, rat-infested pit. He then blacks out again, and upon awakening he discovers that he has been tied down. It is not long before he perceives an ominous, razor-edged pendulum swinging back and forth above his body, slowly descending toward his chest. Seconds before he is severed in half, rats chew through his ropes and the prisoner narrowly escapes death.

Still, the prisoner's torment continues. The hot iron walls of his dungeon begin to close in, forcing him ever closer to the frightening pit. It is here that the carefully crafted, frightening, and suspenseful tale falls flat. In an abrupt and contrived ending,

while the prisoner stands on the edge of the dreadful pit, the French army storms Toledo and rescues him from the murderous hands of the Inquisition. Although the ending is anticlimatic, the tale demonstrates Poe's unparalleled ability to create nightmarish scenes of horror. (See ANTICLIMAX.) THEMES of confinement and torture, along with the psychological exploration of repression and emotional fragility, characterize a number of Poe's other famous stories, particularly "THE FALL OF THE HOUSE OF USHER" and "THE CASK OF AMONTILLADO."

BIBLIOGRAPHY

Hammond, J. R. *An Edgar Allan Poe Companion.* Totowa, N.J.: Barnes & Noble, 1981.
Poe, Edgar Allan. "The Pit and the Pendulum." *The Complete Tales and Poems of Edgar Allan Poe.* New York: Barnes & Noble, 1992.

Kathleen M. Hicks
University of Texas at El Paso

PLOT

Plot, essential to all fiction, refers to the arrangement of incidents in a narrative. These incidents relate to each other through cause and effect, and have a discernible pattern that includes a beginning, a middle, and an end. The author need not dramatize events chronologically, but may begin the account *in medias res* (in the middle of things), and may present events in terms of FLASHBACKS. Although critics argue about whether plot or CHARACTER has primary importance in a story, they generally agree that a plotted story includes pattern, conflict, crisis—or turning point, and DENOUEMENT—in order to produce any story.

POE, EDGAR ALLAN (1809–1849)

Born to actors in Boston, Edgar Allan Poe was orphaned at an early age and taken in by a tobacco exporter. Poe spent time in England with his new family and later briefly attended the University of Virginia, but left in debt. He then served in the U.S. Army, after which he attended West Point in 1830. He was dishonorably discharged in 1831 for dereliction of duty and then worked as an editor and journalist. In 1836 he married his 13-year-old cousin, Virginia.

He worked, during those early writing years, for such periodicals as *Grahams* and *Burtons,* sometimes writing critical reviews of such respected writers as Washington IRVING and Henry Wadsworth Longfellow.

Poe, according to his review of Nathaniel HAWTHORNE's work, admired the genre of the tale for its compactness, which allowed control over the material and style as well the ability to produce unparalleled intensity of emotion for the reader. Poe's early tales include "Ms. Found in a Bottle" (1831) and "The Masque of the Red Death" (1832), a story of trapped courtiers unable to escape the death that has intruded on their masquerade ball. Poe's first short story collection, the two-volume *Tales of the Grotesque and Arabesque* (1839), includes 25 stories, among them the GOTHIC romance THE FALL OF THE HOUSE OF USHER. This story, like much of Poe's work, is also a psychological study of a character's grappling with the past and his sense of self.

As crime became a greater public concern and police began using scientific methods of analysis, "THE MURDERS IN THE RUE MORGUE" (1841), *The Mystery of Marie Roget* (1843), and "THE PURLOINED LETTER" (1845) mark the beginning of the genre of DETECTIVE FICTION (although the word "detective" did not yet exist) and feature the then-unique character C. AUGUSTE DUPIN as a puzzle solver. The first of these stories establishes a particularly urban kind of tale, which revolves, like much of Poe's work, around a woman's death. (See "DEATH OF A BEAUTIFUL WOMAN.") The second was based on the murder of a New York woman whose body was found in the Hudson River. All three stories draw on contemporaneous urban concerns. "The Murders in the Rue Morgue" also establishes the now-familiar formula of detective fiction that includes the characterization of an unofficial yet adept amateur detective, the employment of a first-person POINT OF VIEW that is not the detective's, the imposing of the urban world on the detective's private living space, the committing of the crime in a locked room, and the strategies of criminal investigation and revealing of clues. These stories also rely on unprecedented unity so that every element leads inevitably to the conclusion.

"THE TELL-TALE HEART" (1843) draws from some of the same elements as Poe's detective stories, but focuses on the psychological breakdown of the criminal haunted by the murder he committed. "THE BLACK CAT" (1843), too, shows the psychological terror of a man who hangs his cat and then, in an attempt to kill another cat, beheads his wife; through the use of irony, as in numerous Poe stories, the police find the wife's corpse when the first cat howls from behind the wall where the wife is buried. This tale is also noted for the narrator's inverted syntax or irregular word order that replicates his mental state. In a similar stylistic move, Poe uses ONOMATOPOEIA and sentence rhythm in "THE PIT AND THE PENDULUM" (1842) to simulate the hissing sound of the blade moving back and forth. These and many other of Poe's tales mark him as a master of human psychology, especially in his study of the instability of self-control, the repression of emotion, and the eruption of feeling.

Many of Poe's stories include people, places, and events from his life. Poe's army days in South Carolina provide the setting for both "The Gold Bug" (1843), which won a contest and was published also in France, and "The Balloon Hoax" (1843). The former is a story of a treasure hunt and was one of Poe's greatest commercial and critical successes. Several of Poe's characters, including those in "The Gold Bug," resemble Poe's brother, William Henry.

By the time he entered West Point, Poe had published two volumes of poetry, and his third was published the year he was discharged from the army. His most famous poem, "The Raven," was published in a newspaper and later as part of the volume *The Raven and Other Poems* (1845). This collection brought him notoriety but not financial security.

Poe also wrote influential essays. *Exordium* (1842) discusses the function of literary criticism as aesthetic evaluation. *The Philosophy of Composition* (1846) claims, among other aesthetic principles, that the most poetical subject is the "Death of a Beautiful Woman." (See AESTHETICISM.) His essay "The Poetic Principle" (1850) argues art for art's sake.

Poe's work has been translated by Charles Baudelaire and others, and his poetry remains popular in Europe. British writers such as Oscar Wilde, Dante Gabriel Rossetti, and William Butler Yeats have admired Poe's work, and FREUDian and existentialist critics have been intrigued by its macabre and obsessive qualities. His short stories, including "The Murders in the Rue Morgue," "The Fall of the House of Usher," and "The Pit and the Pendulum," as well as his poem "The Raven" have been adapted for films.

Poe launched an arduous libel suit against the New York *Mirror* the same year that "THE CASK OF AMONTILLADO" (1846), a tale of revenge, was published. His wife died of tuberculosis shortly before Poe won the lawsuit in 1847, after which Poe pursued other romantic relationships in the last years of his troubled life. Poe himself suffered from epilepsy, alcoholism, drug addiction, and mental illness. He died five days after being found semiconscious and suffering from exposure in a Baltimore tavern. He is buried with his wife in a Baltimore churchyard, where people now gather on Halloween to pay their respects. Baltimore's National Football League team, the Ravens, is named for Poe's famous poem.

BIBLIOGRAPHY

Carlson, Eric W. *Critical Essays on Edgar Allan Poe.* Boston: G.K. Hall, 1987.

May, Charles E. *Edgar Allan Poe: A Study of the Short Fiction.* 1991.

Meyers, Jeffrey. *Edgar Allan Poe: His Life and Legacy.* New York: Scribner's, 1992.

Poe, Edgar Allan. *Complete Works of Edgar Allan Poe.* New York: AMS Press, 1965.

Rosenheim, Shawn, and Stephen Rachman, eds. *The American Face of Edgar Allan Poe.* Baltimore: Johns Hopkins University Press, 1995.

Silverman, Kenneth. *Edgar A. Poe: Mournful and Never-Ending Remembrance.* New York: HarperCollins, 1991.

Anna Leahy
Ohio University

POINT OF VIEW

The perspective from which a story is told, thus determining the extent and type of information presented to the reader. Traditionally, writers have chosen one of four possibilities:

Omniscient. The author tells the story using the third person, knowing all and able to convey virtually limitless information to the reader, including the characters' thoughts, feelings, and motivations for their behavior.

Limited omniscient. The author tells the story using the third person, "he" or "she," whose understanding is confined or limited to only one character in the story; thus the narrator can relate the ideas, emotions, situations, or motivations of that one character only.

First person. Using the first person "I," the character designated as "I" tells the entire story from his or her viewpoint.

Objective. From a third-person perspective, the author relates the visible or audible facts of the story but cannot interpret characters' behavior or relate their inner thoughts, opinions, or emotions.

PORTER, KATHERINE ANNE (1890–1980)

Katherine Anne Porter was born Callie Russell Porter May 15, 1890, in Indian Creek, Texas, the fourth of five children of Harrison Boone Porter and Mary Alice Jones Porter. After her mother's death in 1892, Porter was reared in Hays County, Texas, by her father and his widowed mother, Catharine Ann Skaggs Porter, who would become the model for the grandmothers in Porter's stories.

Porter's formal education consisted of irregular schooling in Kyle, Texas, and a year at the Thomas School in San Antonio (1904–5). Her self-education, founded on wide reading, continued to the end of her life. After an unhappy early marriage that lasted nine years, Porter left Texas to embark on a rudderless course that would include three more marriages and residence in many foreign and domestic places. Trying to survive as a writer in the modern world, she struggled against illness and economic insecurity for much of her life.

In her apprentice years, Porter worked as a freelance professional writer and as a journalist for newspapers and magazines. Soon afterward, in 1920, she went to Mexico, where she published her first original pieces of fiction, the short stories "Maria Concepcion" (1922), "The Martyr" (1923), and "Virgin Violeta" (1924), all based to some degree on her experiences in Mexico's cultural revolution of 1910 to 1930. In 1930 *Flowering Judas,* her first collection of stories, appeared to enthusiastic critical acclaim that established her reputation as a first-rank writer of short fiction. It also secured for her a GUGGENHEIM GRANT.

In the 1930s Porter produced the bulk of her fiction. A second collection of stories appeared in 1935 as *Flowering Judas and Other Stories,* which added four stories to the earlier collection. Critical approval continued through the publication of *Pale Horse, Pale Rider: Three Short Novels* in 1939 and *The Leaning Tower and Other Stories* in 1944. After 1942 Porter wrote no new pieces of short fiction but instead directed her creative attention to a long novel she had struggled with since the late 1920s. It was finally published in 1962 as *Ship of Fools.* A best-seller made into an acclaimed motion picture, it made her financially secure for the first time in her life.

Although Porter's only long novel echoes her short fiction, it did not generate the consistency of praise her previous collections had received. Some reviewers, such as Mark Schorer, declared the novel one of the great novels of the 20th century, but many reviewers found it inferior to her tightly woven and crystalline short fiction. For some readers and critics, Porter's long novel illuminated by contrast her brilliance as a short story writer, and her status was confirmed in 1966 when she won both the Pulitzer Prize and the National Book Award for her *Collected Stories* (1965). By the time she died in Silver Spring, Maryland, on September 18, 1980, she had received numerous other awards and honorary degrees.

Porter's canon is small; her fiction comprises only 29 short pieces and one long novel. During her lifetime she also published *The Collected Essays and Occasional Writings* (1970) and *The Never-Ending Wrong* (1977), a memoir of her participation in the 1927 protest against the murder conviction and execution of Italian anarchists Nicola Sacco and Bartolemeo Vanzetti in Massachusetts. Since her death, collections of her writings have appeared as *Letters of Katherine Anne Porter* (ed. Bayley), *"This,*

Strange, Old World" and Other Book Reviews of Katherine Anne Porter (ed. Unrue), *Uncollected Early Prose of Katherine Anne Porter* (eds. Alvarez and Walsh), and *Katherine Anne Porter's Poetry* (ed. Unrue).

Porter's fiction is loosely concerned with the search for identity, meaning, and order in the modern world, a canonical unity Porter confirmed numerous times. Secondary THEMES in individual stories reflect topical concerns related to their settings and Porter's cumulative experience at the time of each story's composition. The most apparent of these themes are betrayal, the inefficacy of institutions, primitivism at the core of human existence, the power of love, and the role of art in the modern world. Porter identified her most important influences as Laurence Sterne, Henry JAMES, W. B. Yeats, Virginia Woolf, James Joyce, and Ezra Pound.

Porter's grand design and secondary themes are dramatized by recurring characters and illuminated by a CLASSICAL style. Her autobiographical PROTAGONIST, an innocent female child or a naive young woman, began to emerge in drafts of stories in the 1920s. In the seven stories that make up *The Old Order* (1935–60) the character is named MIRANDA RHEA, and Miranda's rite of passage is explored also in "Old Mortality" and "Pale Horse, Pale Rider." The simplicity of Porter's style rests on her plain vocabulary, which belies the complexity of her artistic vision. A psychological symbolist, Porter was also a realist in her careful attention to details of verisimilitude and in her insistence on the pragmatic function of will within the boundaries of natural, universal laws. (See REALISM.) All of these characteristics are found in her most often anthologized stories, "FLOWERING JUDAS," "The Grave," "NOON WINE," and "The Old Order." Porter encouraged and influenced other masters of the short story, such as Eudora WELTY, Flannery O'CONNOR, and Tillie OLSEN.

BIBLIOGRAPHY

Bruccoli, Mathew J., Ed. *Understanding of Katherine Anne Porter.* Columbia: University of South Carolina Press, 1988.

DeMouy, Jane. *Katherine Anne Porter's Women: The Eye of Her Fiction.* Austin: University of Texas Press, 1983.

Givner, Joan. *Katherine Anne Porter: A Life,* revised ed. New York: Simon & Schuster, 1991.

Hendrick, Willene and George Hendrick. *Katherine Anne Porter.* Boston: Twayne, 1988.

Machann, Clinton, and William Bedford Clark, eds. *Katherine Anne Porter and Texas: An Uneasy Relationship.* College Station: Texas A&M University Press, 1990.

Mooney, Harry J. *The Fiction and Criticism of Katherine Anne Porter.* Pittsburgh: University of Pittsburgh Press, 1990..

Porter, Katherine Anne. *The Collected Essays and Occasional Writings.* New York: Seymour Lawrence/Delacorte, 1970.

———. *Collected Stories.* New York: Harcourt, Brace, 1965.

———. *Flowering Judas.* New York: Harcourt, Brace, 1930.

———. *Flowering Judas and Other Stories.* New York: Harcourt, Brace, 1935.

———. *The Leaning Tower and Other Stories.* New York: Harcourt, Brace, 1944.

———. *Letters of Katherine Anne Porter.* Edited by I. Bayley. New York: Atlantic Monthly Press, 1990.

———. *The Never-Ending Wrong.* Boston: Atlantic/Little, Brown, 1977.

———. *Pale Horse, Pale Rider: Three Short Novels.* New York: Harcourt, Brace, 1939.

———. *Ship of Fools.* Boston: Atlantic/Little, Brown, 1962.

———. *"This Strange, Old World" and Other Book Reviews of Katherine Anne Porter.* Edited by Darlene Harbour Unrue. Athens: University of Georgia Press, 1991.

———. *Uncollected Early Prose of Katherine Anne Porter.* Edited by Ruth M. Alvarez and Thomas Walsh. Austin: University of Texas Press, 1994.

Stout, Janis P. *Katherine Anne Porter: A Sense of the Times.* Charlottesville: University Press of Virginia, 1995.

Walsh, Thomas F. *Katherine Anne Porter and Mexico: The Illusion of Eden.* Austin: University of Texas Press, 1992.

Unrue, Darlene Harbour, ed. *Critical Essays on Katherine Anne Porter.* Athens: University of Georgia Press, 1997.

Unrue, Darlene Harbour. *Truth and Vision in Katherine Anne Porter's Fiction.* Athens: University of Georgia Press, 1985.

Darlene Harbour Unrue
University of Nevada at Reno

PORTER, WILLIAM SYDNEY.   See HENRY, O.

POSEY, ALEXANDER LAWRENCE (1873–1908)

One of the most popular NATIVE AMERICAN writers in turn-of-the-century Indian Territory (currently Oklahoma), Alexander Posey earned national acclaim with his satiric wit and DIALECT humor. A journalist, poet, and short-fiction writer who received a formal "American-style" education at Bacone Indian University, Posey immersed himself in the culture and politics of the Muscogee (Creek) tribe. He held several political offices, served as superintendent of education for the Creek nation, and owned and edited *The Indian Journal,* a weekly newspaper. Upon his untimely death by drowning at age 34, Posey's reputation took on the stature of folk hero. Today he is best known for the *Fux Fixico Letters.* In these 78 "letters to the editor," written between 1902 and 1908, Posey adopts the PERSONA of a Creek old-timer, offering incisive social and political commentary, and interweaving everyday wisdom, gossip, TRICKSTER tales, and other features from an oral tradition, with classical, biblical, and literary ALLUSIONS.

Posey's dexterous manipulation of dialect frequently elicits comparisons to Mark TWAIN. His creative virtuosity attests to the high caliber of literary production by Native American intellectuals long before the Native American Renaissance of the 1970s.

BIBLIOGRAPHY

Kosmider, Alexia. *Tricky Tribal Discourse: The Poetry, short Stories, and Fus Fixico Letters of Creek Writer Alex Posey.* Moscow, Idaho: University of Idaho Press, 1988.

Littlefield, Daniel F. *Alexander Posey: Creek Poet, Journalist, and Humorist.* Lincoln: University of Nebraska Press, 1992.

Littlefield, Daniel, and James Parins. "Short Fiction Writers of the Indian Territory." *American Studies* 21–23 (1980–82): 23–27.

Posey, Alexander. *The Fus Fixico Letters.* Edited by Daniel F. Littlefield and Carol Hunter. Lincoln: University of Nebraska Press, 1993.

Lauren Stuart Muller
University of California at Berkeley

POSTMODERNISM

The term "postmodernism" often is used to challenge the very possibility of definition. Although postmodernism is frequently and not too usefully employed as a reference to anything written after WORLD WAR II, more often it is a term for which no generally agreed-on definition exists. One might begin by briefly looking at the term postmodernism invokes: MODERNISM, which postmodernism is supposed to have followed or transcended. On one level, the postmodern movement is a break initiated by modernism, which may be loosely and provisionally defined here as a transitional period between 19th-century ROMANTI-CISM and the current cultural scene. One of the differences between postmodernism and modernism—is that modernist writers seemed to believe that, while the modern world is in fact a moral, spiritual, and physical wasteland, it is still possible to shore up fragments against ruin, as T. S. Eliot famously argues at the conclusion of his seminal modernist work, *The Waste Land.* This order or meaning may not exist in the natural world, but modernist writers see themselves as making meaning out of chaos through their art; thus some system or ordering principle is possible.

Postmodernism, by contrast, eschews the possibility of norms; even objective reality is called into question. In the postmodern world, subjectivity becomes elusive when the self is found to be defined by language, which in turn is an unreliable and ineffective system of communication. Modernist irony and PARODY are replaced by blank postmodern pastiche that unabashedly cannibalizes all styles of the past. (The film *Star Wars,* with its hodgepodge construction of the previous genres of Flash Gordon comic books, spaghetti westerns, and Joseph Campbell's books on mythology, among others, might serve as an example of an unironic postmodern pastiche.) A postmodern story can no longer be set in the past, it can only represent our nostalgic STEREOTYPES about the past). According to the postmodern logic of late CAPITALISM, older realities are transformed into television images; it suggests, for example, that everything we know about the 1950s in America we learned from the television shows *Happy Days* and *Laverne and Shirley.* Whereas the modernists' edict tended to be Ezra Pound's famous exhortation to "make it new," in the postmodern world the concept of newness has lost its clout; many would argue that the word has meaning only in the world of brand-name advertising.

Theorist Frederic Jameson offers the following as characteristics of postmodernism: the effacement of the old distinction between "high" and "low," or popular, cultures (William Shakespeare and Stephen KING are equally valuable); the centrality of new technologies that are themselves linked to a new economic system (E-mail, the Internet, and websites that essentially are product advertisements); the new depthlessness of both the contemporary theory and the image of the simulacrum (defined here as a copy of a copy for which no original exists; think of Pamela Anderson from television's *Baywatch* as a copy of a Barbie Doll, which is a copy of some idealized woman who does not exist); the waning of affect (emotional response); some sort of political stance on multinational capitalism; and "bricolage" or multiple quotations from earlier styles of periods (whether ironic, cynical, or naive).

Another postmodern critic, Jean-François Lyotard, more simply says schizophrenia and paranoia are the hallmarks of postmodern style. Thus, postmodern fiction tends to be metanarrative or METAFICTIONal; that is, it calls into question the very nature and artificiality of narration by offering the paranoid author as a postmodern subject. Perhaps the most famous example is John BARTH's story "LOST IN THE FUNHOUSE," in which a boy who cannot find his way through a carnival ride stands for the author who cannot escape a reality that is as bizarre and senseless as a funhouse.

The stances on and reactions to the postmodern condition can be divided into two "camps." The first is the "UTOPIAN" (playful) camp, characterized by critical movements such as Jacques Derrida's theories of deconstruction, Lacanian psychoanalysis, feminism (see FEMINIST), and certain brands of marxism (such as Walter Benjamin's). What these seemingly disparate theories have in common is the sense that postmodernism constitutes a liberation from oppressive meaning-making structures of the past, that culture and texts are allowing the possibility of a new liberatory position that would free us from the constraints and confines of oppressive binaries, or opposites. No longer will woman be defined in terms of "man" or "black" defined in terms of "white." An example of liberation from binaries may be found in Toni MORRISON's short story "Recitatif," which deconstructs stereotypes of what it means to be "black" or "white."

The second, more melancholic camp might be labeled the "apocalyptic" or "commercial"/camp. Frankfurt School Marxists like Theodor Adorno, Max Horkheimer, and Pierre Bourdieu excoriate mass media as the voice of bourgeois hegemony, a machine of the ruling class that works to keep the underclass in its place. Another critic of this camp, Jean Baudrillard, views postmodernism as linked to a new stage of multinational, multiconglomerate consumer capitalism that radically transforms the subject through its blanketing of culture. To put it another way, we think what we think because we see it in the movies. Inside is no longer separate from outside because we are what we consume; in fact, we are *because* we consume. In a new unidimensional universe from which there is no escape, the television screen has become the only reality. Don DeLillo's *White Noise* is an example of a postmodern text with this more pessimistic attitude; the novel exhibits a world in which "reality" is increasingly defined by some unnamable outside forces and capitalism has packaged up and served to the consumer his or her very identity.

There is, of course, a kind of continuum between these two modes of postmodernism. The most well-known postmodern novels are perhaps Thomas Pynchon's *The Crying of Lot 49* and his *Gravity's Rainbow,* in which the labyrinthine complexities of the search for information, for meaning, in an increasingly incredible reality can never really be resolved. The postmodern condition in these works, as in the stories of such writers as Thomas MCGUANE and Joyce Carol OATES, is neither wholly abominable nor wholly joyful; it simply is.

BIBLIOGRAPHY

Docherty, Thomas, ed. *Postmodernism: A Reader.* New York: Columbia University Press, 1993.

Jameson, Frederic. *Postmodernism, or the Cultural Logic of Late Capitalism.* Durham, N.C.: Duke University Press, 1991.

Lyotard, Jean-Francois. *The Postmodern Condition: A Report on Knowledge.* Minneapolis: University of Minnesota Press, 1984.

Waugh, Patricia, ed. *Postmodernism: A Reader.* New York: St. Martin's, 1992.

S. L. Yentzer
University of Georgia

POSTSTRUCTURALISM   Like POSTMODERNISM, poststructuralism is a term that first evokes the notion of having followed and transcended its precursor. Poststructuralism, however, is a purely theoretical field, while postmodernism is the artistic expression of these critical theories. Thus, fiction can be postmodern and criticism poststructuralist, but not vice versa.

Poststructuralism results in part from STRUCTURALISM's project: to engage in a systematic scientific study of language, culture, and discourse in order to create an inventory and structure of elements and their possible combinations that would account for the form and meaning of literary works. "How-to" books, for example, that tell us how to write a romance novel or a detective story are predicated on a structuralist enterprise; much like the rules for correct sentence grammar, a limited number of necessary elements combine to fulfill the structural limitations of the genre. According to structuralist theory, narrative and cultural myths consist simply of a sequence of conventions in which all the oppositions are introduced.

The problem with this approach, and one that poststructuralism addresses, is that structuralism supposes readers are informed yet objective. Such perfect readers, of course, do not exist. In fact, structuralist readers commit what a follower of NEW CRITICISM would call the INTENTIONAL FALLACY; in other words, the readers unknowingly and erroneously apply their own intentions to their analyses. Poststructuralism tries to address these shortcomings: Unlike the structuralists, who read literature to develop a poetics of narrative, poststructuralists study individual texts to see how they resist or subvert the logic of narrative structure.

Poststructuralism is closely tied to Jacques Derrida's theories of deconstruction. Deconstruction, unlike poststructuralism, has a clear beginning date: 1967, the year Derrida published his famous essay, "Structure, Sign, and Play." Poststructuralism is a looser, more general term that goes beyond the more narrowly focused deconstructive theories from which it emerged. Deconstruction may be viewed as a more specific subset within the larger critical field of poststructuralism; however, it is impossible to say where deconstruction ends and where poststructuralism begins because they have so many shared goals and processes. Derrida himself is both a deconstructionist and a poststructuralist. Poststructuralist and deconstructive thought may be seen in critical practices ranging from Lacanian psychoanalysis, which undercuts and reshapes the traditional FREUDian version of the subject and ego formation, to MARXism, which advocates the deconstruction of bourgeois control, to feminism, especially French feminism, which uses deconstructive practices in its efforts to achieve a polysexual and gender-free space. (See FEMINIST.)

Deconstruction and poststructuralism investigate the ways in which meaning is created through binary oppositions and difference. In a binarism, one term is necessarily seen more favorably than the other because it becomes the general case and implicitly superior term, and the other is, by extension, the special case, implicitly inferior. In the example "man/woman," man is the "norm" and woman is defined in its shadow. At its best deconstruction attempts to explode the original superior/inferior relationship, thereby leveling the playing field.

This deconstruction of meaning and of language is exactly what poststructuralists apply to larger structures and systems of meaning. Western civilization, for example, is generally conceived of as the foundation of knowledge, the center of hierarchies of belief. Poststructuralism calls into question this superiority.

Perhaps this subtle difference between deconstruction and poststructuralism may be best understood by briefly examining a seminal essay of each movement. Michel Foucault's *What is an Author?* is a poststructural response to Roland BARTHES's deconstructionist *The Death of the Author.* Barthes proclaims that the author is dead; he has been deconstructed out of existence, whereas Foucault seeks to examine the particular and historical function an author serves. Barthes simply inverts the binary opposition between author and reader and does not explore the inherent issue of the power dynamics. Barthes does not show the function of the author (or even his own role as reader). The author is dead; long live the reader. Foucault explores precisely those areas that Barthes neglects. As a poststructuralist critic, he examines the author "function" as a site, a location, that describes a political, historical, and social role. Deconstruction, Foucault might point out, too often functions in an abstract vacuum. We cannot deny an author's origins, but we must acknowledge that any starting point is merely provisional and decidedly political. Thus a poststructuralist reading of William FAULKNER's *GO DOWN, MOSES* might refute other readings of the sympathetically portrayed black characters in the stories: Citing Faulkner's dedication of the book to Caroline Barr, his "mammy," the poststructuralist might argue that this dedication, evidence of Faulkner's racist Southern heritage, thereby undercuts the text's empathetic presentation of the black characters.

BIBLIOGRAPHY

Barthes, Roland. *A Barthes Reader.* New York: Noonday Press, 1993.

Culler, Jonathan. *On Deconstruction: Theory and Criticism After Structuralism.* Ithaca, N.Y.: Cornell University Press, 1982.

Davis, Robert Con, ed. *Contemporary Literary Criticism: Modernism Through Postmodernism.* White Plains, N.Y.: Longman, 1986.

Derrida, Jacques. *A Derrida Reader: Between the Blinds.* New York: Columbia University Press, 1991.

Foucault, Michel. *The Foucault Reader.* New York: Pantheon, 1985.

Poster, Mark. *Critical Theory and Poststructuralism: In Search of a Context.* Ithaca, N.Y.: Cornell University Press, 1989.

S. L. Yentzer
University of Georgia

"PRETTY STORY, A" FRANCIS HOPKINSON (1774)

Francis HOPKINSON's allegorical "A Pretty Story" (see ALLEGORY) crystallizes colonial American concerns with British policy on the eve of the AMERICAN REVOLUTION. Although the full title of the story states that it was "Written in the Year of our Lord 2774," "A Pretty Story" actually was published in 1774 as a short pamphlet. Perhaps Hopkinson's most famous work to modern readers, the story proved to be a highly popular piece of colonial propaganda, going through more than three editions in less than six months. Perhaps borrowing from other allegorical works, such as Jonathan Swift's *Tale of a Tub* and especially John Arbuthnot's *History of John Bull,* Hopkinson succinctly turns a subject that had long been bandied about in newspapers into a fictional allegory of struggle within a family. In "A Pretty Story" Hopkinson therefore presents his fellow Americans with the choice before them—whether to rebel against British unjust and arbitrary power—in an entertaining and simplified form, hoping to persuade his fellow brothers and sisters to revolt.

In "A Pretty Story" Hopkinson retells the American colonial narrative of struggle under British tyranny as a story of a family torn asunder by the avarice, inattention, and unfairness of a "Gentleman" (the king). The story is told from the POINT OF VIEW of the nobleman's children, settlers in a strange land, where they succeed in creating a new farm. Emboldened by their children's success, the Gentleman and his Wife (Parliament), aided by an underhanded Steward (the prime minister), begin to exact heavy taxes and prohibitions. Although the children complain to their father about these regulations, and especially these laws' direct violation of the Great Paper (the Magna Carta), the old Gentleman persists with his practices. The situation comes to a head when the Gentleman padlocks the gate to the farm belonging to Jack (who represents Boston), who had flagrantly disobeyed his laws regarding "Water Gruel" (tea).

The story concludes with a blatant nonending: "These harsh and unconstitutional Proceedings irritated *Jack* and the other Inhabitants of the new Farm to such a Degree that *****" (55). Hopkinson leaves the decision about what will happen next up to the reader, but it is obvious through his characterization of the half-witted Gentleman and the debauched Wife that the American citizenry have no choice but to overthrow the oppressive British rule.

BIBLIOGRAPHY

Hastings, George Everett. *The Life and Works of Francis Hopkinson.* 1926.

Hopkinson, Francis. "A Pretty Story." In *Comical Spirit of Seventy-six: The Humor of Francis Hopkinson.* Edited by Paul M. Zall. San Marino, Calif.: Huntington Library, 1976.

Marshall, George N. *Patriot with a Pen: The Wit, Wisdom, and Life of Francis Hopkinson, 1737–1791, Gadfly of the Revolution.* West Bridgewater, Mass.: C. H. Marshall, 1993.

Gregory M. Weight
University of Delaware

PROHIBITION

The period in the United States between 1919 and 1933, during which the ratification of the 18th Amendment to the Constitution made the manufacture and distribution of alcoholic beverages illegal. Prohibition ended with the passing of the 21st Amendment, which repealed the 18th. Efforts to enforce Prohibition had failed, and the era was actually one of unparalled drinking, bootlegging, moonshining, speakeasies, and the rise of organized crime.

PROLETARIAN LITERATURE

Primarily written during the GREAT DEPRESSION and promoted by the American Communist Party, proletarian writing focuses on workers' lives and class struggle, working conditions, strikes, racial prejudice, middle-class hypocrisy, and communism. Its 19th-century forerunners include Rebecca Harding DAVIS's story "Life in the Iron Mills," (1861) and the work of Emma Goldman (1869–1940), and the early 20th-century writings of Charlotte Perkins GILMAN, Susan GLASPELL, and Viola Scudder. The main publishing outlets for much of proletarian poetry and prose fiction were the *Daily Worker, New Masses,* and the *Partisan Review.* In 1929, Michael Gold, probably the best-known communist writer and critic at the time, published "Go Left, Young Writers," an essay in *New Masses* about working-class writers whose labor-intensive jobs left them little time to polish their writing. Some of the most notable writers who emerged from this era include Tillie OLSEN, Josephine Herbst (1892–1969), and Meridel LESUEUR, who wrote *The Girl* (1932), a collection of composite stories about women living at the Worker's Alliance in St. Paul, Minnesota.

BIBLIOGRAPHY

Lauter, Paul. "Working-Class Women's Literature: An Introduction to Its Study." *Radical Teacher* 15 (1979): 16–26.
Nekola, Charlotte, and Paula Rabinowitz, eds. *Writing Red: An Anthology of Women Writers.* New York: Feminist Press, 1987.
Rideout, Walter. *The Radical Novel in the United States.* Cambridge, Mass.: Harvard University Press, 1956.

PROTAGONIST The main character in a fictional work, the protagonist can also be called the HERO of a story. He or she is usually in conflict with another, called an ANTAGONIST (the second most important character), or with fate. In early Greek drama the word originally referred to the "first," or chief, actor. In contemporary usage, protagonist is a more neutral, less value-laden term than hero, which has specific male connotations and frequently suggests its opposite term, ANTI-HERO.

PULITZER PRIZE FOR FICTION Annual prizes awarded to American writers by the trustees of Columbia University since 1918. The Pulitzer Prize for fiction, awarded to a writer for a distinguished work of literature, has been awarded to the following writers of short fiction: Ernest HEMINGWAY for "The Old Man and the Sea" (1954), Katherine Anne PORTER for *The Collected Stories of Katherine Anne Porter* (1967), Jean STAFFORD for *Collected Stories* (1971), and John CHEEVER, for *The Stories of John Cheever* (1980). Endowed by Hungarian-born journalist Joseph Pulitzer, founder of the Columbia University School of Journalism, the prizes are divided among journalism, the arts, music, and (since 1962) general nonfiction.

"PURLOINED LETTER, THE" EDGAR ALLAN POE (1845) One of Edgar Allan POE's famous "tales of ratiocination" whose emphasis on deductive reasoning became the basis for the modern detective story, "The Purloined Letter" features Monsieur C, AUGUSTE DUPIN, the ARCHETYPE of the modern fictional detective who always outwits the less imaginative police. Dupin is also the model for Sherlock Holmes, Sir Arthur Conan Doyle's famous fictional detective.

The story, told by an unnamed first-person narrator (see POINT OF VIEW), opens in Paris in the autumn. He and his friend Dupin are enjoying a quiet evening together in Dupin's library, smoking their pipes; the narrator has been musing over the earlier mysteries of "THE MURDERS IN THE RUE MORGUE" and of that of Marie Roget when Monsieur G——, the Parisian police prefect, bursts into the room. He is desperate to recover a stolen letter that the thief, a minister in the French government, will doubtless use to besmirch the honor of an unnamed woman of French royalty. Dupin tells the prefect that he may be stumped by the very simplicity of the mystery. The rest of the story focuses on the deductive means by which Dupin discovers and retrieves the letter and thereby exemplifies Poe's belief that the story must avoid diffusion and illuminate a "single effect" for the reader.

Juxtaposed with the competent but unimaginative prefect, the superiority of Dupin and his narrator friend in terms of both class and intellect may seem snobbish to contemporary readers, yet this THEME continues in much 20th-century DETECTIVE FICTION. The private investigator is nearly always at odds with—and more successful as a crime solver—than the paid officials. Despite the best efforts of the police, they are no match for Dupin, who discovers the simplicity of the letter's hiding place, steals it, and sells it to the overjoyed prefect.

The neatly satisfactory ending with Dupin's intellectual victory has been called into question, however, particularly when we notice the emphasis with which the prefect reiterates to Dupin the escalating amount of the reward for retrieval of the letter. Poe evokes an ambiguously complex portrayal of Dupin, who in his victory reveals questionable ethical standards in his means of retrieval and his demand for the 50,000 francs before he hands over the letter to the prefect. Indeed, he seems another version of the prefect or, even more likely, of the thief himself, whom he credits with a similar intelligence and a similar gift for both poetry and mathematical reasoning. Dupin's creator, of course, demonstrates the same talents. Critic and scholar Eugene Current-García suggests that, by employing the DOPPEL-GANGER MOTIF, Poe perhaps implicitly symbolizes the "ineluctable duplicity of the human mind"(Current-García 72).

BIBLIOGRAPHY

Baudelaire, Charles P. *Baudelaire on Poe: Critical Papers.* University Park: Pennsylvania State University Press, 1952.

Buranelli, Vincent. *Edgar Allan Poe,* 2nd ed. Boston: G.K. Hall, 1977.

Carlson, Eric W., ed. *Critical Essays on Edgar Allan Poe.* Boston: G.K. Hall, 1987.

Current-García, Eugene. *The American Short Story before 1850.* Boston: Twayne Publishers, 1985.

Dillon, John M. *Edgar Allan Poe.* Brooklyn, N.Y.: Haskell, 1974.

Fletcher, Richard M. *The Stylistic Development of Edgar Allan Poe.* New York: Mouton, 1974.

Gargano, James W. *The Masquerade Vision in Poe's Short Stories.* Baltimore: Enoch Pratt, 1977.

Hammond, J. R. *An Edgar Allan Poe Companion: A Guide to Short Stories, Romances and Essays.* Savage: B and N Imports, 1981.

Knapp, Bettina L. *Edgar Allan Poe.* New York: Ungar, 1984.

Levin, Harry. *The Power of Blackness: Hawthorne, Poe, Melville.* Columbus: Ohio University Press, 1980.

May, Charles E., ed. *Edgar Allan Poe, A Study of the Short Fiction.* Boston: Twayne, 1990.

Muller, John P., and William J. Richardson, eds. *The Purloined Poe: Lacan, Derrida and Psychoanalytic Reading.* Baltimore: Johns Hopkins University Press, 1988.

Poe, Edgar Allan. *Collected Works of Edgar Allan Poe.* Edited by Thomas Ollive Mabbott. Cambridge, Mass.: Harvard University Press, 1978.

———. "The Purloined Letter." In *Major Writers of Short Fiction: Stories and Commentaries.* Edited by Ann Charters. New York: Bedford Books of St. Martin's Press, 1993, pp. 1181–1194.

———. *Selected Tales.* Edited by Julian Symons. New York: Oxford University Press, 1980.

Anna Leahy
Ohio University

PUSHCART PRIZE: BEST OF THE SMALL PRESSES

An annual literary prize for writers published in nonmainstream presses. Reflecting recent shifts in publishing, the editors award the prize to authors published by dedicated small publishing houses, only a few of which have subsidies from university presses or other financial backers. Two recent winners are Fae Myenne NG and Bharati MUKHERJEE.

Q

"QUICKSAND, THE" EDITH WHARTON (1902)

"The Quicksand," published in *The Descent of Man* (1904), portrays the self-examination of the wealthy Mrs. Quentin as she reaches out to help her son and his girlfriend. The instability of the ground upon which she has constructed her life becomes apparent when she attempts to answer a request of her son, Alan. He explains to her that the woman he loves, Hope Fenno, has rejected his marriage proposal because she does not respect the family newspaper. Hope had suggested that he either radically change the contents of the *Radiator* or give it up, but he had declined these alternatives. Alan asks his mother to convince Hope that the paper need not disturb the ideals of her private life. When Alan reminds his mother that she had not forced his father to give up the paper, his mother is forced to recall her own distaste for it, review her own complicity with it, and answer Hope's accusations. Unbeknownst to Alan, Mrs. Quentin also had disliked the tabloid, but had compromised her values by using the money it generated to provide for Alan's delicate health and for her generous philanthropy.

When the two women discuss the rejected offer of marriage, Hope rejects Mrs. Quentin's sacrificial behavior and the idea that women must compromise their ideals for the love of a man or a child.

Six months later the two women meet at the Metropolitan Museum, the place where Mrs. Quentin seeks solace in art. Hope admits that she came to the museum because she had seen Mrs. Quentin's carriage outside. Hope's demeanor and her words attest to her sadness. She confesses to now wondering if, perhaps, one should sacrifice one's ideals for love. In response, Mrs. Quentin admits that she had been horrified when she learned what kind of paper the *Radiator* was. She had asked that her husband sell it and believed his consistent excuses for not doing so. After her husband's death, she had believed that the paper could be sold and was dismayed to learn that Alan wanted to build on his father's success. Choosing Hope's idealism over her son's happiness, Mrs. Quentin acknowledges that Alan's overweening pride in the paper surpasses his love for Hope. She confesses her own unhappiness in order to prevent Hope from being "walled up alive" and experiencing the pain she herself continues to endure (410).

BIBLIOGRAPHY

Singley, Carol. *Edith Wharton: Matters of Mind and Spirit.* New York: Oxford University Press, 1993.

Wharton, Edith. "The Quicksand." In *The Collected Stories of Edith Wharton*, vol. 1. Edited by R. W. B. Lewis. New York: Scribner's, 1968. Reprint. New York: Macmillan, 1987–89.

Sandra Chrystal Hayes
Georgia Institute of Technology

R

"RAPPACCINI'S DAUGHTER" NATHANIEL HAWTHORNE **(1843)** In a thought-provoking ALLEGORY written nearly two years after "THE BIRTH-MARK," Nathaniel HAWTHORNE uses a first-person narrator to introduce "Rappaccini's Daughter." This nameless narrator tells the reader that he translated the story, originally entitled "Beatrice: ou la Belle Empoisonneuse" (Beatrice: or the Beautiful Poisoner) and written by M. de l'Aubépine. Hawthorne's wit is at play here, because the fictional M. de l'Aubépine has written books whose titles, when translated from the French, are those of some of Hawthorne's own (*Twice-Told Tales* and *The Artist of the Beautiful,* for instance); moreover, Aubépine has, like Hawthorne, a fondness for allegory, and he believes that readers may find his tales briefly entertaining. Critics continue to examine Hawthorne's reasons for using this ALTER EGO (self-deprecation? amusement? discomfort with sexual matters?), but in any case, the narrator leads the reader into the story, set in Padua, Italy, and then, having lent a degree of authenticity to the narrative, disappears from the text altogether.

The PROTAGONIST, Giovanni Guasconti, a young man from Naples, arrives in Padua to study at the university and takes rooms at an old palace whose early owners are rumored to have been incorporated by Dante Alighieri into his classic work, *The Inferno.* The ALLUSION to Dante and to hell strikes a somber note, and helps to prepare the reader for the walled garden of the palace. Although this garden, directly referred to as Eden, immediately attracts Guasconti with its beautiful gardener and its gorgeous herbs and flowers, he senses a sinister aura permeating this paradise. The gardener is a young woman named Beatrice—the name of Dante's beloved—and her father, Dr. Giacomo Rappaccini, is famous for his work with poisonous herbs. Throughout the story, the lush garden imagery is penetrated by imagery of rustling, coiling snakes: Dr. Rappaccini himself looks lean and serpentlike, and his cold-blooded intelligence gives him the deadly power to use poison to control human life. In this retelling of Adam and Eve in the biblical garden story, Hawthorne aptly chose the ancient backdrop of *The Inferno* as Guasconti and Beatrice become smitten with each other.

One other character plays a significant role in this story: Signor Pietro Baglioni, a professor at the university, old friend of Guasconti's father and long-time rival of Rappaccini. These male connections and rivalries prove significant as the story moves to its conclusion: Beatrice is not named in the title (she is merely Rappaccini's daughter), and, in fact, from the beginning, she is doomed—a word she uses repeatedly—a helpless victim of these men and the only representative of the forces of truth and good in the story. We learn that her father has fed her with poison since her birth, making her immune to its source in the garden: Only she can touch the beautiful, deadly plant that she calls her "sister." As a result, she herself is poisonous, unable to touch flowers or people without infecting them.

Baglioni is jealous of Beatrice, fearing that her father has taught her so well that she could take Baglioni's place at the university. When Baglioni gives Guasconti a potion for Beatrice, he tells him that it will make her immune to the poison and that they can then enjoy their love. Whether or not Guasconti suspects that the potion will kill Beatrice is unclear, but, before giving it to her, this young man, so vain about his looks, wishes he himself could kill her. In a rage, he villifies Beatrice with epithets and calls her an "accursed," "loathesome" monster from a "region of unspeakable horror" (69–70). Significantly, in his anger, he is described as "venomous"; indeed, he sounds like a man who has discovered that his beloved has been unfaithful to him. As Beatrice dies from drinking the potion Guasconti has given her, her father appears, "erect with conscious power" (71), an image both serpentine and Freudian (see FREUD). Dr. Rappaccini explains that he made Beatrice poisonous so that she could overcome the condition of a "weak woman," and with her dying breath, she says that she would have preferred love to power. Addressing Guasconti, she asks him if there were not more poison in his nature than in hers from the very first.

Secure in her own goodness, Beatrice will ascend to the region where the "holy virgin," whom she calls on several times in the story, and that other Beatrice, Dante's spiritual guide, dwell. The three men, vain and power hungry, remain, Baglioni accusing Rappaccini of causing the death of his daughter. None of them realizes that the poison lies within them all in their terrible lust for knowledge—and in their implied fear of feminine beauty and sexuality. Critics and readers of this story continue to debate whether Hawthorne aimed to demonstrate the powerless position of women, or whether he shared the fears of his male characters.

BIBLIOGRAPHY

Hawthorne, Nathaniel. "Rappaccini's Daughter." In *American Short Stories,* 4th ed. Edited by Eugene Current-Garcia and Walton R. Patrick. Glenview, Ill.: Scott, Foresman, pp. 46–72.

"REAL THING, THE" HENRY JAMES (1892, 1909)

One of Henry JAMES's most anthologized stories, "The Real Thing" was first published on April 16, 1892, in *Black and White* and later reprinted in the New York edition of James's works (1909), a comprehensive, multivolume collection of James's works. In this short tale, a nameless painter narrates his encounter with Major and Mrs. Monarch, impoverished gentlefolk who want to model for him in order to earn money. They are well acquainted with the high society the narrator depicts in his illustrations. It turns out, however, that having the "real thing" to paint from is a disadvantage; the painter returns to Miss Churm, a Cockney, and Oronte, an Italian ice vendor, as the models of his choice because somehow the Monarchs ruin his imaginative faculties and he is in danger of losing some of his contracted work. Although (or possibly because) they are used merely for appearance, they have a way of reasserting their large presence in his pictures that ruins the perspectivist proportions. The painter's friend Jack Hawley, a "good counsel" who indulges in artistic jargon and clichés, advises him to dismiss the couple. In the memorable final scene, hierarchy is inverted in the studio when the aristocratic couple serve tea to the painter and his lower-class models, a humiliation they endure with surprising dignity before being given "a sum of money to go away." Unable to paint Mrs. Monarch's epiphanic "glance," the narrator suffers "a permanent harm" done to his painterly craft, yet he is "content to have paid the price—for the memory." (See EPIPHANY.)

Critics have seen this story as a central document for the study of American REALISM and the issue of art imitating life. Susan Bazargan and others have pointed out that the Monarchs are empty symbols who lack the real power of aristocracy. Much has been written about the constraints of bourgeois economics and about representation in the context of 19th-century CAPITALISM. Structuralist semiotics—

the analysis of fiction in terms of literary conventions—and Lacanian psychoanalysis also have been applied successfully to this tale in which the painter/narrator's grasp on reality proves so elusive. David Toor's claim that the painter is an UNRELIABLE NARRATOR has increased the AMBIGUITY of interpretation but also made possible a comparison of visual as opposed to verbal information and other approaches that discuss the center of consciousness as negotiating between the two roles of painter and narrator. The fact that he is a mediocre artist sheds a more positive light on the humiliated Monarchs, who can, as Sami Ludwig claims, in turn be associated with the superiority of a Christian kind of moral nobility. Moreover, James dramatizes their marriage as a genuine relationship, as a private matter *between* human minds that cannot be separated from the other characters who interact with them.

BIBLIOGRAPHY
Bazargan, Susan. "Representation and Ideology in 'The Real Thing.'" *The Henry James Review* 12 (1991): 133–137.
James, Henry. "The Real Thing." In *The Novels and Tales of Henry James,* vol. 18. New York: Scribner's, 1909, 307–346.
Ludwig, Sami. "'We Should Like to Make It Pay': Money, Power, and the Representation of Reality in Henry James's 'The Real Thing.'" In *Reenvisioning the Short Story Since 1890.* Edited by Abby Werlock and Alfred Bendixen. Tuscaloosa: University of Alabama Press, forthcoming in 2001.
Toor, David. "Narrative Irony in Henry James's 'The Real Thing.'" *University Review* 34 (1967): 95–99.

Sämi Ludwig
University of California at Berkeley

REALISM
Realism is the attempt to depict life as it actually exists, not as the author wants it to be in the present or the future, or imagines it was in the past. A realist carefully chooses details that illustrate this vision, unlike the naturalist who tries to include all possible details. The difference between realism and NATURALISM is compared often to a painting as opposed to a photograph, assuming that the photographer also does not choose which details to include in the frame of the picture. The difference between romanticism and realism was a philosophical difference over the purpose and function of literature, the former believing that it should idealize life by empathizing desirable features, the latter that it should be a faithful representative of facts as they appear to the senses. The change developed gradually in the 19th century; often, works such as Rebecca Harding Davis's "Life in the Iron Mills" or LOCAL COLOR fiction of Mark TWAIN, Kate CHOPIN, and others have elements of both. By 1900 authors such as Ambrose BIERCE, Stephen CRANE, William Dean HOWELLS, and Henry JAMES had experimented with new POINTS OF VIEW, setting, and symbolism to provide their own view of the rapidly changing times in which they lived and wrote. In the 20th century the writings of Sigmund FREUD and increased understanding of psychology resulted in experimentation with the depiction of internal reality in METAFICTION, superfiction, and other alternatives to the "well-made" story.

BIBLIOGRAPHY
Cady, Edwin H. *The Light of Common Day: Realism in American Fiction.* Bloomington: Indiana University Press, 1971.
Carter, Everett. *Howells and the Age of Realism.* Hamden, Conn.: Archon Books, 1966.
Conron, John. *The American Landscape.* New York: Oxford University Press, 1964.
Corkin, Stanley. *Realism and the Birth of the Modern United States.* Athens: University of Georgia Press, 1996.
Horton, Rod W., and Herbert W. Edwards. *Backgrounds of American Literary Thought,* 3rd ed. Englewood Cliffs, N.J.: Prentice-Hall, 1974.
Kaplan, Amy. *The Social Construction of American Realism.* Chicago: University of Chicago Press, 1988.
Pizer, Donald. *Realism and Naturalism in Nineteenth-Century American Literature,* revised ed. Carbondale: Southern Illinois University Press, 1984.
Pizer, Donald, ed. *Cambridge Companion to American Realism and Naturalism.* Cambridge, England: Cambridge University Press, 1995.
Quirk, Tom, and Gary Schornhorst, eds. *American Realism and the Canon.* Newark: University of Delaware Press, 1994.
Sundquist, Eric J., ed. *American Realism: New Essays.* Baltimore: Johns Hopkins University Press, 1982.

Wilde, Alan. *Studies in Contemporary American Fiction.*
Philadelphia: University of Pennsylvania Press, 1987.

Carol Hovanac
Ramapo College

"RECITATIF"   See MORRISON, Toni.

RECONSTRUCTION (1865–1877)   The period immediately following the CIVIL WAR during which the defeated states of the Confederacy were reorganized and their constitutional relationship with the national government reestablished. The Reconstruction Act of 1867 established five military districts in the South and made the army's authority supreme. The three "Civil War" amendments to the U.S. Constitution—the 13th (1865), which abolished slavery; the 14th (1868), which incorporated civil rights for blacks; and the 15th (1870), which guaranteed blacks the right to vote—were ratified. Resentment in the South toward the military occupation and the enfranchisement of blacks led to the formation of secret societies and terrorist organizations, notably the KU KLUX KLAN, dedicated to thwarting blacks' civil liberties. Reconstruction ended in 1877 with the withdrawal of federal troops from the South, leaving white Southerners with a deep and enduring political enmity toward the North and Republicans, and bitter race relations between whites and blacks.

RED BADGE OF COURAGE, THE STEPHEN CRANE (1895)   *The Red Badge of Courage,* the NOVELLA long considered Stephen CRANE'S CIVIL WAR masterpiece, is subtitled *An Episode of the American Civil War.* Although celebrated both for the REALISM of its style and for the authenticity of its battle scenes, the work provides, strictly speaking, only limited examples of these qualities. The realistic subject, war, is certainly typical for many of the 19th-century realists—Frank Norris, Theodore DREISER, Hamlin GARLAND, and Mark TWAIN, for instance, all of whom deal with such themes as slum life, alcoholism, and prostitution, along with war—and Crane handles the battle scenes with breathtaking intensity. Nonetheless, Crane has a different view of reality that suggests its elusiveness and its ambiguity. He describes cannon fire as giant red war blossoms; the long lines of troops appear as dragon-like serpents winding their way through brooding hills. As to Crane's first-hand knowledge of war, he had none: born in 1871, six years after the peace treaty signing at Appomattox, Crane simply had a first-rate talent for conveying the daily life of the soldier based on stories he had heard and his own fertile imagination.

On one level this tale is a BILDUNGSROMAN that follows a young man from callow immaturity into a somewhat rueful maturity. The novella opens as the youthful protagonist, Henry Fleming, lately volunteered and now bivouacked with the army, thinks back to his having left home despite his mother's protests. Like many young men, Henry envisions himself the subject of purple-and-gold fantasies of heroism when he joins up with the 304th New York regiment. Crane uses names very sparingly to convey a sense of the universal situation of his characters; thus Henry is usually referred to as "the youth," his friends Jim Conklin, "the tall soldier," and Wilson, "the loud one." Henry agonizes over whether he will have the courage not to run when he engages in his first battle, but at first, fearful of exposing his naïveté, he asks only indirect questions of his fellow soldiers. Indeed, during the first skirmish, Henry does run in terror into the woods, only to learn that he cannot escape death even in the cathedral-like stillness: he encounters a grotesque sight in the form of a maggot-infested dead soldier. Much of Crane's irony, in fact, derives from nature's passivity. In the heat of battle, the day continues blue and golden, as if it had nothing to do with the frantic and bloody deeds of war.

Having run away as a coward, Henry tries to justify his actions by blaming the officers and anyone he can think of but himself. He joins a group of walking wounded and angrily turns from them when they ask him where he has been hurt. After learning that the troops have held out against the Confederates without him, watching Jim Conklin die, and receiving solicitous treatment from all those he encounters, however, Henry thinks less and less of himself. Finally receiving a wound from an angry comrade who hits him on the head, Henry returns to camp without disclosing the real source of the wound to his comrades, who once again treat him kindly, assuming his head has been grazed by a rifle ball. In the next skirmish, he learns to use his anger at the enemy as a way to intensify his fighting ability, and in the one following, he incorporates his anger and his inarticulate love of the flag to join with his friend Wilson to save the colors and thereby encourage the other men. When he learns that the colonel has praised him and Wilson, saying that they should be major-generals, all his wrath dissipates and Henry gradually learns to think of himself not as an individual, but as the member of the group: the "blue demonstration," the "blue line."

In the final battle, Henry and Wilson—unthinkingly heroic now—capture the Confederate flag and with that action help urge the others to victory. Henry's maturity at the end becomes evident as he realizes that death is no great monster to be feared, but simply a fact. Although happy with his conduct, he realizes that his pride will forever be tempered by his recollection and understanding of his cowardly running away from battle and from the friends who needed his help. With this comprehension of his strengths and weaknesses, he has matured, and this time nature seems in sympathy with his mood: Crane parts the clouds and causes the sun to shine down on Henry Fleming.

BIBLIOGRAPHY

Crane, Stephen. *The Red Badge of Courage: An Episode of the American Civil War.* In *Great Short Works of Stephen Crane.* Edited by James B. Colvert, 3–126. New York: Harper & Row, 1968.

RED PONY, THE JOHN STEINBECK (1933–1937, 1938)

Each of the four individual stories that comprise John Steinbeck's "The Red Pony" first appeared separately in different magazines between 1933 and 1937. All four first appeared together in 1938, as part of Steinbeck's collection of short stories *The Long Valley.* In 1945 the four stories—"The Gift," "The Great Mountains," "The Promise," and the often anthologized "The Leader of the People"—were published together as *The Red Pony.* Steinbeck wrote this popular collection in the style of the German BILDUNGSROMAN. Through a little boy, Jody, Steinbeck vicariously captures the essence of childhood. Throughout each story, Jody learns important lessons that force him to mature and grow in some way. Through the tragic loss of his pony Gabilan in "The Gift," Jody learns about responsibility, death, and human fallibility. After Gabilan's death, Jody can never see adults in the same trustworthy manner again. Jody continues to learn about old age, life and death, and unfulfilled dreams through the death of the pregnant mare Nellie in "The Promise"; through the death of the old Italian man, the paisano Gitano, in "The Great Mountains"; and through his own grandfather's experiences in "The Leader of the People." In all four stories, Steinbeck demonstrates his true understanding of the importance of childhood experiences and how they help to shape children into the adults they must one day become.

BIBLIOGRAPHY

Hayashi, Tetsumaro. *Steinbeck's "The Red Pony": Essays in Criticism.* Muncie, Ind.: Steinbeck Research Institute, Bell State University, 1988.
Steinbeck, John. "The Red Pony." *The Long Valley.* New York: Viking Penguin, 1995.

Kathleen M. Hicks
University of Texas at El Paso

REFORM FICTION See PROLETARIAN LITERATURE.

REGIONALISM

A literary subgenre that emphasizes the setting, history, speech, DIALECT, and customs of a particular geographical locale or area, not only for LOCAL COLOR but also to develop universal THEMES through the use of the local and particular. Willa CATHER, William FAULKNER, Ellen GLASGOW, and Robert Penn Warren are notable examples of American writers who used regionalism.

"REQUA I" TILLIE OLSEN (1970)

Tillie OLSEN's "Requa," first published in *The Iowa Review* in 1970 and reprinted as "Requa I" in *The Best*

American Short Stories of 1971, concerns the dislocation, isolation, and eventual return to humanity of a young boy following the death of his mother. Fourteen-year-old Stevie, exhausted by a grief he neither comprehends nor knows how to experience, is taken by his uncle Wes to the small town of Requa. Surrounded by strangers in a place whose country setting is unfamiliar to a boy who has always lived in cities, Stevie retreats into his own mental fog, broken only by fragmented memories of his mother and her illness. He spends all his time sleeping, except when Wes returns from work and forces him to join the other boarders for dinner.

Wes tries to communicate with Stevie, but he is frustrated by the boy's remoteness and silence. With the failure of his attempts to force his nephew to attend school, Wes finally concedes to Stevie's request to work with him at the junkyard. There Wes often is aggravated by Stevie's inattention, lack of ability, mistakes, and lack of endurance. Stevie, however, slowly comes back to life amid the familiarity of auto parts and tools that remind him of the city, the routine of work that requires him to put things in order, and Wes's imperfect but nonetheless caring attention. Much to Wes's surprise, Stevie's final healing occurs when Mrs. Edler, who runs the boardinghouse, takes him along on a visit to the cemetery, where he can see life and death juxtaposed and where his grief completes its circle.

BIBLIOGRAPHY

Faulkner, Mara. Protest and Possibility in the Writing of Tillie Olsen. Charlottsville: University Press of Virginia, 1993.

Frye, Joanne S. Tillie Olsen: A Study of the Short Fiction. New York: Twayne, 1995.

Gelfant, Blanche H. "After Long Silence: Tillie Olsen's 'Requa.'" In The Critical Response to Tillie Olsen. Edited by Kay Hoyle Nelson and Nancy Huse. Westport, Conn.: Greenwood Press, 1994.

Olsen, Tillie. "Requa I" (1970). In The Best American Short Stories of 1971. Edited by Martha Foley. New York: Houghton Mifflin, 1971.

Orr, Elaine Neil. "Rethinking the Father: Maternal Recursion in Tillie Olsen's 'Requa.'" In The Critical Response to Tillie Olsen. Edited by Kay Hoyle Nelson and Nancy Huse. Westport, Conn.: Greenwood Press.

——. Tillie Olsen and a Feminist Spiritual Vision. Jackson: University Press of Mississippi, 1987.

Pearlman, Mickey, and Abby H. P. Werlock, Tillie Olsen. Boston: Twayne, 1991.

Kelly Reames
University of North Carolina at Chapel Hill

"REVELATION" FLANNERY O'CONNOR (1964)

First published in Sewanee Review (Spring 1964), "Revelation" received first prize in the 1965 O. HENRY MEMORIAL AWARDS. It is the seventh story in O'CONNOR's collection Everything That Rises Must Converge (1956).

METAPHORically blending the natural with the supernatural, "Revelation" lives up to the religious promise of its title by tracing Mrs. Ruby Turpin's move toward grace. It portrays her from the time she sits in a doctor's office until the time she sees souls rising to heaven in an order that she had not anticipated. Rich with O'Connor's irony, the narrative displays Mrs. Turpin's judgment of this worldly waiting room and its inhabitants.

Grateful that God blessed her with her husband, Claud, and a good farm, Mrs. Turpin ranks herself better than "niggers" and "white trash" but not as good as those with plenty of money and bigger houses. Waiting for a doctor to see Claud, she mentally classifies the others in the office by their shoes and disparagingly evaluates the poor white family along with the unattractive Mary Grace, a young Wellesley College student. Constantly aware of the girl's glare, Mrs. Turpin openly proclaims her opinions and her gratitude to God for her good life. Suddenly she is struck over her left eye by Human Development, a book hurled by Mary Grace. As the girl strangles her and calls her an old wart hog, Mrs. Turpin begins a different level of introspection.

Mrs. Turpin's unexpected opening of herself to grace occurs after she returns to the farm. While she hoses down the pig pen, she reflects on Mary Grace's comment to her. Suddenly she sees into God's mystery and visualizes ascending into heaven all those she had previously judged. Those like her, however, are not leading the assembly. Instead they appear at the back of the line where, apparently, "their virtues [are] being burned away" (508).

BIBLIOGRAPHY

Johansen, Ruthanne. *The Narrative Secret of Flannery O'Connor: The Trickster as Interpreter.* Tuscaloosa: University of Alabama Press, 1994.

O'Connor, Flannery. "Revelation." In *Flannery O'Connor: The Complete Stories.* New York: Farrar, Straus & Giroux, 1989.

Shloss, Carol. *Flannery O'Connor's Dark Comedies: the Limits of Inference.* Baton Rouge: Louisiana State University Press, 1980.

Sandra Chrystal Hayes
Georgia Institute of Technology

"REVOLT OF MOTHER, THE" MARY E. WILKINS FREEMAN (1891)

"The Revolt of Mother" (1891) is an apt example of Mary E. Wilkins FREEMAN's characteristic literary REALISM and REGIONALISM. Freeman, in her intimate and realistic observations of village life in her native New England, helped to forge a new literary style for post–CIVIL WAR female writers known as regionalists. "The Revolt of Mother" is a brave tale about a dedicated but exasperated New England wife, Sarah Penn, who, after 40 years, has finally run out of patience with her husband, Adoniram. Forty years ago, Adoniram (referred to as Father) promised to build Sarah (referred to as Mother) a new home, and for 40 years Mother has lived in her crowded "box" of a house, patiently waiting for Father to fulfill his promise. When Sarah discovers that Adoniram is having another new barn built on the very spot on which he promised to build her a new house, she is enraged and can keep her silence no longer. Sarah upbraids her husband for his inconsiderate and ungrateful action.

Adoniram, however, has nothing to say in reply to his wife. Therefore, Sarah boldly decides that it is time to take action herself. Upon Father's departure to a nearby town, Mother rounds up her two children, packs up the scant belongings in her tiny house, and moves into the new barn. When Adoniram returns to find cows in his kitchen and his family living in the new barn, he is stunned and stands in utter awe of his wife's bold move. Upon realizing the extent and success of her action, "Sarah put her apron up to her face; she was overcome by her own triumph" (42). Freeman rewards Sarah's brave move with success. In fact, Freeman frequently uses her craft to declare victory for the strong-willed women who inhabited her native region. The motif is repeated in many of her works, such as her frequently anthologized "A NEW ENGLAND NUN" and "A CHURCH MOUSE."

BIBLIOGRAPHY

Church, Joseph. "Reconstructing Woman's Place in Freeman's 'The Revolt of Mother.'" *Colby Quarterly* 26, no. 3 (September 1990): 195–200.

Freeman, Mary E. Wilkins. "The Revolt of Mother." In *The Best Short Stories of Mary Wilkins.* Old Westbury, N.Y.: Feminist Press, 1974.

Hamblin, A. *The New England Art of Mary E. Wilkins Freeman.* Amherst, Mass.: Green Knight Press, 1966.

Kathleen M. Hicks
University of Texas at El Paso

"RICH BOY, THE" F. SCOTT FITZGERALD (1926)

"The Rich Boy" is one of F. Scott FITZGERALD's three long stories, sometimes referred to as NOVELLAS. It appeared in two parts in the January and February issues of *Redbook* in 1926 and in Fitzgerald's third story collection, *All The Sad Young Men* (1926). The story contains one of Fitzgerald's most famous lines: "Let me tell you about the very rich. They are different from you and me," which prompted Ernest HEMINGWAY to deliver an equally famous remark: "Yes, they have more money." In that exchange is the crux of the question the story raises. Does the crystallized personality of the PROTAGONIST, Anson Hunter, result from his wealth and privilege, or is this story a fictional case study of a personality type unrelated to social class? Anson Hunter is a divided man. Like the tormented souls in the tales of Edgar Allan POE, Anson Hunter is propelled unconsciously by two opposing impulses to nurture and destroy people's happiness, including his own. Some readers see parallels between Hunter and Fitzgerald. Although Fitzgerald claimed he modeled his protagonist on Ludlow Fowler, a friend from his Princeton University days, he appears to have incorporated features of his own personality as well—especially in terms of the tenuous balance between his disciplined moral rectitude and frivolous self-indulgence.

Like Edith WHARTON's stories of social REALISM, Fitzgerald's story describes the decline of old New York families in the transition from the GILDED AGE to the Jazz Age and their exodus to Paris and the Riviera. Fitzgerald's romantic strain is present in the golden moments of missed opportunity when Anson fails to act definitively and thus seals his destiny. (See ROMANTICISM.) The story's narrative structure resembles that of *The Great Gatsby*, which Fitzgerald had just completed when he wrote "The Rich Boy." In both a humble, intelligent, middle-class man becomes the confidant of the rich protagonist, alternating his story with direct narration and personal reflection.

BIBLIOGRAPHY

Petry, Alice Hall. *Fitzgerald's Craft of Short Fiction: The Collected Stories.* 1920–35. Tuscaloosa: University of Alabama Press, 1989.

Wolfe, Peter. "Faces In a Dream: Innocence Perpetuated in 'The Rich Boy.'" In *The Short Stories of F. Scott Fitzgerald: New Approaches in Criticism.* Edited by Jackson R. Bryer. Madison: University of Wisconsin Press, 1982.

Frances Kerr
Durham Technical Community College

"RIP VAN WINKLE" WASHINGTON IRVING (1820)

Appearing in Washington IRVING's *The Sketch Book of Geoffrey Crayon, Gent,* "Rip Van Winkle" was an immediate popular success. In retrospect, it helped refute the infamous question posed by the British critic Sydney Smith: "Who, in the four corners of the globe, reads an American book?" With *The Sketch Book*—and the story of Rip in particular—Irving established the United States on the English-speaking literary map. Today many scholars call "Rip Van Winkle" the most important story written in the early years of the republic. With its publication, Irving not only created the modern short story form but also laid the foundations for

American literature, particularly the frontier humor that flowered in the 1830s and eventually reached a crescendo with Mark TWAIN's *Huckleberry Finn.* (See FRONTIER HUMORISTS.)

In *The Sketch Book* and in this tale, Irving creates Geoffrey Crayon, the first-person narrator who leads the reader into the Hudson River valley, sets the scene through vivid description, and depicts the town as Rip and its inhabitants know it. The leisurely accumulation of detail is important, for when Rip departs with his gun and his dog, we need to know the nature of the place he has left before we can appreciate the radical nature of its changes when he returns after his 20-year sleep.

When he does return to the much-changed town, the narrator gives us the signs one by one so that, with Rip, we see the truth emerge from an accumulation of detail: the length of his beard, the rustiness of his gun, and the disappearance of his dog help prepare us for the more significant changes. Not only has his shrewish wife passed on, but, as the pub sign signifies by its metamorphosis from the head of King George III to the head of President George Washington, the Americans have fought their revolution and claimed independence from England. (See AMERICAN REVOLUTION.)

As narrator, Geoffrey Crayon disclaims responsibility for the authenticity of the story, protesting that he found it among the papers of the late Diedrich Knickerbocker, who himself heard it from some old Dutch wives. In a wittily clever move, Irving then has Knickerbocker add a postscript vouching for the truth of the tale. Indeed, so central is the question about Rip's 20-year absence that critics still debate it today. Did Rip really encounter the Dutchmen at their bowling—and, if so, did they ply him with a magic liquor that made him sleep for 20 years? Or did Rip simply run away from his wife, returning only after she is safely dead? The interpretation of Rip's character depends as well as whether the narrator is reliable: Is Dame Van Winkle the henpecking wife as portrayed by Rip and Crayon? Or is she, like so many women in literature, the product of a male perspective? Is Rip the comic (see COMEDY) and somewhat pitiful character of myth? Or is he the prototype of the lazy American male who reappears, for instance, in Anse Bundren of William FAULKNER's *As I Lay Dying?* Irving's romantic LEGEND continues to attract new readers who must resolve the ambiguous DENOUEMENT for themselves. (See ROMANTICISM.)

BIBLIOGRAPHY
Irving, Washington. "Rip Van Winkle." In *Complete Tales.* Edited by Charles Neider. Garden City, N.Y.: Doubleday, 1975.
Myers, Andrew B. *A Century of Commentary on the Works of Irving.* Tarrytown, N.Y.: Sleepy Hollow Restorations, 1976.

"RIVER, THE" FLANNERY O'CONNOR (1953)

Conversion experiences are quite common in the fiction of Flannery O'CONNOR. Many of her characters realize personal emptiness and seek fulfillment in Christian rituals, hoping to discover a loving God who is more accepting and caring than the people who surround them. Such is the case for Harry (Bevel) in O'Connor's "The River." A little boy of four or five, Harry is used to being ignored in his home; his parents are self-indulgent, careless adults who satisfy their own needs before those of their child. When Harry's baby-sitter, Mrs. Connin, provides him with a chance to attend a revival meeting at the local river, Harry's life is changed forever. His trip to the countryside not only changes his name to Bevel (suggesting depth and complexity) but also changes his attitude and his goals.

Having learned well from his parents in the negative surroundings of the city, Harry initially is depicted as both a thief and a liar. He tells Mrs. Connin his name is Bevel (thus associating himself with a local preacher of Christianity), and he sneakily removes both a flowered handkerchief and a valued biblical storybook from her house. Her home in the isolated country, with its freedom and openness, stands in direct contrast to the cloistered prison of Harry's city existence. Although Harry/Bevel is tricked by Mrs. Connin's children into a scary encounter with a hog, his general impression of the rural scene is one of pleasure and contentment.

Especially exciting is his encounter with Jesus, both in a picture on Mrs. Connin's wall and in the stolen storybook. These first encounters become second rate, however, after Mrs. Connin brings him directly to a confrontation with a savior at the baptismal site on the river, where the Reverend Bevel Summers is "winning over souls" and transforming lives so that people "belong." Harry/Bevel's desire for acceptance and love through his cleansing in the blood of the Lamb eventually results in his immersion in the "blood-red" river and in the preacher's assertion that his life will now somehow be different.

After this conversion, Bevel returns to his home in the city. Its clutter and dirt suddenly motivate him to return to the river, which holds the promise of a removal of pain and sin.

Even the countryside, though, has its skeptics, its agnostics who reject faith. In "The River," O'Connor uses the figure of Mr. Paradise, an obese old man who attends Bevel's baptism, as a figure who would recapture the small boy and return him to a salvation-less life. Mr. Paradise "mockingly" speaks of Bevel's salvation and denigrates the value of his renewal. When Bevel returns to the site of the revival meeting, Paradise follows him menacingly and seems intent on preventing him from attaining his goal of acceptance and peace, of finally belonging.

Harry/Bevel, in typical youthful innocence, has taken the preacher's words about the river literally. In his attempt to find a lasting kingdom of Christ and the promised love and care the Savior offers, Bevel once again enters the river and attempts to become one with it. Repeating his immersion, he is initially rejected by the strong current but eventually he welcomes and embraces the river, which, ironically, causes his death by drowning. Harry/Bevel offers no resistance to the powerful water as it encompasses and pulls him under. Suddenly he is "something" rather than "nothing," two words that recur frequently in the story.

Unlike the earthly Paradise, who offers material possessions (a huge candy cane), Bevel finds in his conversion and his death the acceptance he was not afforded in life. As in most O'Connor works, in life humans see through a glass darkly, but in death they gain full understanding and are fully accepted despite their sins and blemishes. "The River" offers a grotesque commentary on both a dying society and a demanding God: In death, life flourishes, while living only creates hell, a deathlike state of suffering and isolation.

Michael J. Meyer
DePaul University

ROBERTSON, MORGAN (1861–1915)

Morgan Robertson was born and raised in Oswego, New York, the son of a Great Lakes captain. He apparently had some formal schooling, but his real education occurred in the merchant marine, where his experiences as a sailor provided the background for virtually all his important fiction. He abandoned the sea in hopes of finding an easier and more financially secure livelihood, and after taking some courses at Cooper Union in New York City, worked for a time as a diamond setter and jeweler. When failing eyesight made this profession impossible, he turned to the writing of fiction and produced his first published story at the age of 36. It was the example of British writer Rudyard Kipling that showed him the possibilities of the adventure story set against a nautical backdrop. Robertson's sea stories were soon regularly welcomed by the leading magazines of the time and acclaimed by critics.

By the turn of the 20th century, Robertson had established a solid, if modest, reputation as an author of thrilling sea stories, distinguished by compelling plots and vivid renderings of the technical details of life aboard ship. Nevertheless, he felt dissatisfied with his relatively small income and turned away from fiction in order to devote himself to the invention of a periscope that would make the submarine into an effective military weapon: He claimed that he eventually developed such a periscope but failed to obtain a patent because of legal technicalities. Disappointed, he returned to writing, but discovered that he had lost his ability to fashion tales that would win a place in the leading periodicals. He continued to write and to publish in less distinguished magazines, but found himself on the brink of poverty. His account of his financial hardships and frustrations in his autobiographical essay "Gathering No Moss" (SATURDAY EVENING POST

1914), drew attention from other writers, most notably author and journalist Irvin S. Cobb and Bozeman Bulger, who ultimately arranged for the publication of the Autograph Edition of his collected works. Shortly after the publication of this edition, which brought him financial security for the first time in his life, Morgan Robertson died in 1915. His friends produced a memorial volume, *Morgan Robertson: The Man* (1915), which remains the most useful source of biographical information. His most important short stories were collected in *Futility* (1898), *Spun-Yarn* (1898), *Where Angels Fear to Tread* (1899), *Down to the Sea* (1905), *Land Ho!* (1905), *The Grain Ship* (1914), and *Over the Border* (1914).

Robertson needs to be seen in the context of those writers—perhaps most notably Kipling, Robert Louis Stevenson, Joseph Conrad, and Jack LONDON, who were transforming the tale of sea adventure into a significant literary form. Although now almost completely forgotten, Robertson made notable contributions to the development of sea fiction and probably had a significant influence on London. His fiction effectively dramatized the brutality that was the foundation of ship rule and condemned the injustice of maritime law, which generally placed sailors and shanghaied victims at the mercy of a ship's captains and his officers. His fascination with the nature of power forms the basis of one of his finest stories, "Where Angels Fear to Tread," originally published in the ATLANTIC MONTHLY in 1898, which focuses on a group of seamen from the Great Lakes. When they find themselves shanghaied by a captain and his mates who refuse to recognize their basic rights as American citizens, the seamen stage a successful mutiny. Robertson later developed these characters into his strongest novel, *Sinful Peck* (1903), a book based on the shifting balance of power as various factions gain or lose control over a ship. Many of his strongest stories focus on the struggle of individuals to gain or maintain power in the face of a cruel and inherently unjust universe. His depiction of the struggle for survival owes something to the naturalistic vision of life that dominated much serious writing of the time (see NATURALISM). Among the most effective of these tales are a series devoted to the pirate Captain Swarth, an intriguing antihero who triumphs in some tales, such as "Trade Winds," but ultimately meets his doom in "Honor Among Thieves." This struggle for survival amidst the savagery of both nature and human society is also central to the most famous and most reprinted of Robertson's stories, *Futility* (1898), a long tale or NOVELLA reprinted in 1912 as *The Wreck of the Titan, or Futility*, which seemed to predict the demise of the Titanic with uncanny accuracy. In two tales, "Primordial" (*Harper's*, April 1898; reprinted in *Where Angels Fear to Tread*, 1899) and "The Three Laws and the Golden Rule" (1900), Robertson's exploration of survival focuses on shipwrecked children whose human nature emerges without the trappings of social forces.

Robertson also produced a series of humorous stories (see COMEDY), featuring Finnegan, a sailor who, although almost completely worthless when sober, develops remarkable abilities when drunk. This SATIRE on naval pretensions is set against the backdrop of an imaginary war between Great Britain and Russia. The Finnegan stories rest ultimately on their author's fascination with the latent powers of the subconscious mind, a subject that he treated in many other tales. Robertson also merits attention because of his contributions to early 20th-century SCIENCE FICTION. Many of his stories deal with fantastic inventions or future wars, in which torpedo boats or submarines are endowed with monstrously effective weapons (see FANTASY). Of his science fiction stories, the strongest and the most reprinted is "The Battle of the Monsters," in which a cholera bacillus ultimately becomes the narrative focus of a war fought among the microbes. Although unjustly neglected today, Robertson was a popular writer whose sea stories commanded respect and whose best work reveals originality and genuine power.

BIBLIOGRAPHY

Bleiler, Everett F. *Early Science Fiction.* Kent, Ohio: Kent State University Press, 1990.

Gardner, Martin, ed. *The Wreck of the Titanic Foretold?* Buffalo, N.Y.: Prometheus Books, 1986.

Morgan Robertson: The Man. New York: McClure's Magazine and Metropolitan Magazine, 1915.

Robertson, Morgan. "Gathering No Moss," *Saturday Evening Post* 1914.

———. *Down to the Sea.* New York: Harper & Bros., 1905.

———. *Futility.* New York: M. F. Mansfield, 1898. Reprinted in 1812 as *The Wreck of the Titan, or Futility.* New York: McClure's Magazine and Metropolitan Magazine, 1912.

———. "Gathering No Moss." In *Morgan Robertson, The Man.* New York: McClure's Magazine and Metropolitan Magazine, 1915, pp. 6–37.

———. *The Grain Ship.* New York: McKinlay, Stone & Mackenzie, n.d. (c. 1914).

———. *Land Ho!.* New York: Harper & Bros., 1905.

———. *Over the Border.* New York: McClure's Magazine and Metropolitan Magazine, 1914.

———. *Sinful Peck.* New York: Harper & Bros., 1903.

———. *Spun-Yarn.* New York: Harper & Bros., 1898.

———. *The Three Laws and the Golden Rule.* New York: McKinley, Stone, and Mackenzie, 1900.

———. *Where Angels Fear to Tread.* New York: Century, 1899.

Alfred Bendixen
California State University, Los Angeles

RODERICK USHER The PROTAGONIST twin brother of MADELINE USHER, in Edgar Allan POE's "THE FALL OF THE HOUSE OF USHER." The poem within the story, entitled "The Haunted House," depicts Roderick—and, as numerous critics suggest, a portrait of Poe himself. After the narrator wonders about Roderick's madness and his deeply buried secret, he reads a story-within-the-story that parallels the main action. This story equates Roderick with a hermit and a dragon, both of whom are slayed by Ethelred, who may be equated with Roderick's sister Madeline, whom he has buried alive but who escapes her coffin to kill him.

"RODMAN THE KEEPER" CONSTANCE FENIMORE WOOLSON (1880) "Rodman the Keeper," the title story of Constance Fenimore WOOLSON's first collection, *Rodman the Keeper: Southern Sketches* (1880), tells of a Northerner who moves into the RECONSTRUCTION-era South to maintain a federal cemetery. Details in the story indicate that its setting is based on Andersonville National

Cemetery, adjacent to the notorious Confederate prison site during the CIVIL WAR. Rodman encounters a dying Confederate veteran and cares for him in the little cottage provided for him as the keeper of the cemetery. His patient's proud cousin, Bettina Ward, attempts to take the wounded man away, but she has no means to care for him and the home to which she would return him is a dilapidated shell. She assents to his remaining under the care of Rodman, but the tension between the two provides the major conflict in the story, that between the proud, indignant, desperately poor Southerner and the Northerner with his power and his own pride. Many of the stories in this volume repeat this THEME and subject of a Northern redeemer figure rescuing indigent Southerners, and the contrast between the romantic but "shiftless" ways of the South and the energy and efficiency of the North is stated directly.

A strength of this story, as with all of Woolson's writing, is her deft description of setting. On a swelteringly humid April day, "the moist earth exhaled her richness, not a leaf stirred, and the whole level country seemed sitting in a hot vapor-bath." Her descriptions of the decaying mansions of the South are poignant and exact, from the "life of General LEE" on a table to the "quick-growing summer vines" that had been planted to cover up a piazza's shabby pillars. Woolson was a Northerner who traveled into the South, and her perspective as an outsider helps her notice and record details that add REALISM and LOCAL COLOR to her dramatic Southern stories.

BIBLIOGRAPHY

Woolson, Constance Fenimore. *Rodman the Keeper: Southern Sketches.* New York: D. Appleton, 1880.

Karen Weekes
University of Georgia

"ROMAN FEVER" EDITH WHARTON (1934)

Since its publication in her collection of short stories *The World Over* (1936), Edith WHARTON's "Roman Fever" has been frequently anthologized. Masterfully constructed with multiple narrative voices and in a satirical tone, "Roman Fever" is the culmination of a lifetime of competition between "two American ladies of ripe but well-cared-for middle age" who had loved the same man, Delphin Slade. Using internal monologues in contrast to the spoken dialogues of Grace Ansley and Alida Slade, Edith Wharton demonstrates the hypocrisy of the women's fondest New York values: convention and respectability, a recurring THEME in Wharton's fiction. She hints at the true violent and destructive nature of the two ladies by enclosing "slay" ("to kill") in their names, belying their apparently civilized and genteel behavior. In fact, 25 years earlier, Alida had hoped to eliminate her rival by forging a letter from Delphin inviting Grace to a rendezvous in the night damp of the Colosseum, thereby exposing her to "Roman fever." Little did she realize that Grace would answer Delphin, resulting in an actual rendezvous.

Beyond its social criticism, the story resonates with potentially violent historical and political ALLUSIONS. It is set on a terrace overlooking the most famous historical sites of Rome, an area whose past glories and destructive powers were increasingly appropriated in the 1920s and '30s by Mussolini's Fascist government. The historical past suggests a threatening future event when the competitive daughters Barbara and Jenny fly with two Fascist aviators on a romantic moonlit night to Tarquinia, the ancient site associated with the rape of Lucretia and the fall of the Etruscan monarchy (510 B.C.). According to Agnes Carr Vaughn, in the Italian imagination, this event represents the struggle between dictatorial, popular power and patrician control of government. Wharton thus poses FASCISM as a real threat that looms just outside the story.

Alluding to Henry JAMES's *DAISY MILLER*, Mrs. Slade enumerates the various meanings of Rome to four generations of American mother and daughter relationships: "To our grandmothers, Roman fever [malaria]; to our mothers, sentimental dangers—how we used to be guarded!—to our daughters, no more dangers than the middle of Main Street" (RF 10). Her words prove completely ironic when at the SURPRISE ENDING we learn that Barbara Ansley, conceived in the Colosseum, is the illegitimate daughter of Mrs. Ansley and Delphin Slade. Invoking the

"Name of the Father" (the oblique reference to this line from the Christian prayer, with its patriarchal underpinnings, seems intentional) Mrs. Ansley "beg[ins] to move ahead of Mrs. Slade." In 1934, moreover, Fascist governments in both Germany and Italy were seeking to control women's reproductive capacity for the good of the state, first to increase population for what was to become WORLD WAR II and later to ensure racial purity—that is, Aryan blood untainted by Jewish blood. Therefore, Mrs. Ansley's FEMINIST action of producing an illegitimate child can be seen as a politically threatening act. In addition, Dale Bauer observes that in 1934 Wharton was fully aware of the impending Fascist threat to world peace; "Roman Fever" makes clear her view that any individual or nation that asserts its superiority on the basis of "the Law of the Father" or "racial purity" is fundamentally grounded on a meaningless principle.

BIBLIOGRAPHY

Bauer, Dale. *Edith Wharton's Brave New Politics.* Madison: University of Wisconsin Press, 1994.

Vaughn, Agnes Carr. *The Etruscans.* Garden City, N.Y.: Doubleday, 1964.

Wharton, Edith. *Roman Fever and Other Stories.* New York: Scribner's, 1964.

Carole M. Shaffer-Koros
Kean College of New Jersey

ROMANTICISM Originally from the Latin adverb *romanice,* which referred to a vernacular language, it developed into the French word *roman,* or tale full of improbable events depicted in common language. Transforming by the 18th century from "improbable" to "silly" or imaginatively appealing (both meanings were in use), romanticism became a recognized mode of writing, particularly in reaction to the 18th-century writers whom romantic writers perceived as dull and unimaginative. Romanticism flourished in the 19th century in both Europe and, slightly later, in the United States, and valued individuality, imagination, and the truth revealed in nature. Major writers of the American romantic period include poets and essayists William Cullen

Bryant, Emily Dirkinson, Ralph Waldo Emerson, Oliver Wendell Holmes, James Russell Lowell, Henry David Thoreau, Walt Whitman, and John Greenleaf Whittier. The major short story writers and novelists were Nathaniel HAWTHORNE, Herman MELVILLE, Edgar Allan POE. Despite critical quarrels over the precise nature of the romantic mode of writing—particularly over whether the term is confusing or overly confining—romanticism certainly can be distinguished from REALISM in that it seeks truth, or the ideal, by transcending the actual, whereas realism finds its values in the actual. Moreover, romanticism sees the individual at the center of life and places a high premium on individual thoughts, feelings, and responses. It can include a sympathetic interest in the past, primitivism, sensibility, nature, mysticism, and the GROTESQUE or strange. Although numerous writers from Washington IRVING to William FAULKNER have been labeled romantic, critical consensus is that most writers of substance include elements of both romanticism and realism in their fiction.

"ROSE FOR EMILY, A" WILLIAM FAULKNER (1931) Initially published in *Forum* on April 30, 1930, and collected in *These Thirteen* in 1931, "A Rose for Emily" remains one of William FAULKNER's most read, most anthologized, and most significant stories. From every imaginable perspective, critics have scrutinized the components of Faulkner's literary technique: The story has been viewed as an ALLEGORY of southern history, a metaphorical depiction of North-South relationships (see METAPHOR), FEMINIST nightmare or feminist victory, a GOTHIC horror story, a sociological portrayal of individualism squelched or individualism triumphant, a bleak fictional tale of DETERMINISM. Faulkner's use of structure, TONE, POINT OF VIEW, and IMAGERY play key roles in his depiction of MISS EMILY GRIERSON. The fact that readers and critics still engage in interpretive debates over its meaning merely ensures that it will continue to be read into the next century.

Told from the perspective of Jefferson, in YOKNAP-ATAWPHA CONTY, in a narrative voice that consistently relates the details that "we"—the smug and gossipy townspeople of Jefferson—have observed, the story is intriguing on the level of PLOT and CHARACTER alone: Miss Emily has just died, and we learn that she lived alone after her father died and Homer Baron, her Yankee lover, apparently abandoned her. Suspense continues to build when we learn that a mysterious odor emanated from her house at the time that Homer disappeared. Faulkner employs a number of clues to foreshadow both DENOUEMENT and motivation, including the "tableau" of the imperious father with a horsewhip overshadowing his white-clad young daughter Emily; the portrait of her father that Emily displays at his death, despite his thwarting of her natural youthful desires; her defiant public appearances with the unsuitable Homer Baron; her sense of entitlement; and the arsenic she buys to rid her house of "rats." Despite these and other devices, however, new generations of readers still react in horror when Emily's secret is revealed: She not only murdered her lover, but slept with his corpse in the attic bridal chamber she carefully prepared.

If Miss Emily is crazy (and most critics agree that she is), Faulkner implies that she has been made so by the constrictions of a father who refused to let her marry and by the conventions of a society that eagerly filled the void at his death. (See MADWOMAN IN THE ATTIC, THE.) Numerous critics have suggested that behind the Gothic horror of necrophilia and insanity in this classic story, Miss Emily Grierson is the oddly modern HERO. Indeed, one critic asserts that we cannot understand any of Faulkner's heroes if we do not understand Miss Emily, for she is the "PROTOTYPE" of them all (Strindberg 877). As with other troubled Faulknerian protagonists, death literally frees Miss Emily—from patriarchy, from society's conventions, from sexual repression, from the class structure she was taught to revere, from the useless existence of privileged women of her era, even from the burdens of southern history and slavery: With her death, her black servant, mysteriously complicit in his relation to Miss Emily, walks out of her house at the end of the story. In an interview at the University of Virginia, Faulkner suggested

that Miss Emily deserved a rose for all the torment she had endured, and, whatever else they feel, most readers appear to agree with this sentiment.

BIBLIOGRAPHY
Blotner, Joseph. *Faulkner: A Biography*. 2 Vols. New York: Random House, 1974. Rev. ed., New York Random House, 1984.
Carothers, James. *Faulkner's Short Stories*. Ann Arbor: University of Michigan Press, 1985.
Faulkner, William. "A Rose for Emily." In *Collected Short Stories*. New York: Random House, 1940.
Strindberg, Victor. A Rose for Emily. In *Reader's Guide to Short Fiction*. Edited by Noelle Watson. Detroit: St. James Press, 1993, p. 577.
Ferguson, James. *Faulkner's Short Fiction*. Knoxville: University of Tennessee Press, 1991.

"ROSELILY" ALICE WALKER (1973)

From Alice Walker's collection, *In Love and Trouble: Stories of Black Women*, "Roselily" depicts a young black woman unsure if she is in love and worried that she might be inviting trouble. Her thoughts occur during her marriage to an African-American man who will take her away from her difficult life as an unmarried and hard-working mother in the Mississippi town of Panther Burn. On the surface, Roselily's future life sounds ideal: She and her husband will go north, a traditional metaphor for freedom in African-American fiction, to Chicago, where she can "rest," no longer required to work in a sewing plant. (See AFRICAN-AMERICAN SHORT FICTION.) Her place will be in the home, he says.

The principal structuring device (see STRUCTURE) is the conventional marriage ceremony, and Roselily's hopes and fears, narrated between the preacher's lines, unfold in the third-person POINT OF VIEW to focus solely on Roselily. Significantly, her husband is never named, likely because he personifies the politically conscious, educated, urban African-American male. The SYMBOLISM of Roselily's name, however, is obvious: The mother of four children with apparently different fathers, Roselily has led a passionate if not "immoral" life, and she welcomes the opportunity to be married at last, "like other girls" (RL 1291). Her husband proposes to purify her, to change her from a rose to a lily (Charters 164), and now, poised between the two elements of her nature, Roselily is torn by doubts. She admires her husband's pride and sobriety, but fears the severity of his religion, apparently Islam, and his traditional view that women should stay home and have babies. She longs for a chance to begin a new life in the land of Lincoln, but she cannot help dreading the unfamiliarity of the urban sprawl of Chicago, which the narrator describes in IMAGERY of soot, dirt, smoke, and cinders. Attracted to the concept of resting from labor at last, she also understands that she is rooted in the rural South, where she can bare her skin to the warm sun, and where her mother and grandparents are buried.

Roselily is taking a chance, but the dominant imagery of "ropes, chains, [and] handcuffs" (1289) lends more than a little gloom to the story, as does her husband's self-contained coldness at the end of the ceremony. One of Walker's THEMES, prominent in "EVERYDAY USE," another story from this collection, is the incompatibility between southern, traditional African-Americans and their sophisticated, more liberal Northern counterparts, The other is the radically different goals of women and men, and the obstacles that men so often place in the path of women's fulfillment of their desires. Roselily's future is undetermined, but the narrator strongly implies that this young woman is simply trading one set of difficulties for another.

BIBLIOGRAPHY

Charters, Ann. *Resources for Teaching Major Writers of Short Fiction: Stories and Commentaries.* Boston: Bedford Books of St. Martin's, 1993, pp. 163–66.

Petry, Alice Hall. "Alice Walker: The Achievement of the Short Fiction." *Modern Language Studies* 19.1 (Winter 1989): 12–27.

Walker, Alice. "Roselily." In *Major Writers of Short Fiction: Stories and Commentaries.* Edited by Ann Charters. Boston: Bedford Books of St. Martin's, 1993, pp.1289–92.

Winchell, Donna Haisty. *Alice Walker.* Boston: Twayne, 1990.

ROTH, PHILIP (1933–   )

Philip Roth grew up in Newark, New Jersey, and attended both the Newark College of Rutgers University and Bucknell University for his B.A. While pursuing graduate studies at the University of Chicago, Roth left the Ph.D. program to follow his burgeoning career as a writer. At the age of 23, his story "The Contest for Aaron Gold" appeared in *Best American Short Stories of 1956,* edited by Martha Foley. Other short stories began appearing in magazines and journals such as the *Paris Review,* the NEW YORKER, and *Commentary.* In 1959 he published five of these works along with the title story in *Goodbye, Columbus,* which received numerous awards, including the National Book Award in 1960. He also received this award for *Sabbath's Theater* in 1995, and most recently he was awarded the Pulitzer Prize for *American Pastoral* (1997).

Throughout many of his novels and short stories, Roth portrays characters acutely aware of loss—cultural, sexual, emotional, and spiritual—who suffer from a debilitating sadness and frustration that further isolates them from their families, communities, and religion. As Roth explained in an interview with Jonathan Brent, "the job was to give pain its due . . . You generally wait in vain for the ennobling effects" (CWPR 140). For most of these characters, their inability to achieve some level of personal fulfillment raises unanswered questions about their identity as Jews in America. With the exception of "You Can't Tell a Man by the Song He Sings," for example, all of the stories in *Goodbye, Columbus* examine the ways assimilated Jews relate to their cultural and religious heritage.

At the same time, Roth's negative depiction of the Jewish community, in this work and particularly the novel *Portnoy's Complaint* (1969), generated a great deal of criticism and hostility from the Jewish community: "You have done as much harm as all the organized anti-Semitic organizations have done to make people believe that all Jews are cheats, liars, connivers" (RMAO 160). In an attempt to break away from being labeled a Jewish writer, in his first two novels, *Letting Go* (1962) and *When She Was Good* (1967), Roth focused on non-Jewish characters, but, after lukewarm critical and popular response to these works, he turned to Jewish characters again. Outside of the Jewish community, his fiction also has been criticized for its misogynistic sentiments.

After suffering from a prescription drug–induced depression in 1987, Roth turned to more introspective autobiographical works. His most recent novel, *I Married A Communist* (1998), is in part an attack on his ex-wife. His first, *The Facts: A Novelist's Autobiography* (1988), discusses some of the specific parallels between Roth's fiction and his own life. After his father's death two years later, he published *Patrimony: A True Story* (1991), which explores their relationship. Throughout his career, Roth has continued to blur the distinction between fiction and autobiography, and, with the publication of Claire Bloom's *Leaving a Doll's House* (his second ex-wife's account of their rocky, 17-year marriage), Philip Roth's personal and literary life have become unavoidably linked for his reading public.

Even though Roth's fame centers on his career as a novelist, he made a significant contribution to short fiction in his first 20 years as an author. Like his earlier short fiction "In Trouble" and "Whacking Off," most of his short stories after 1970 were excerpts from forthcoming novels. Some of his other novels include *The Breast* (1980), *The Counterlife* (1987), *My Life as a Man* (1974), *Operation Shylock* (1993), *Zuckerman Bound* (1985), and *Zuckerman Unbound* (1981).

BIBLIOGRAPHY

Baumgarten, Murray, and Barbara Gottfried. *Understanding Philip Roth.* Columbia: University of South Carolina Press, 1990.

Brent, Jonathan. " 'The job,' says Roth, 'was to give pain its due.' " In *Conversations with Philip Roth.* Edited by George J. Searles. Jackson: University Press of Mississippi, 1992.

Cooper, Alan. *Philip Roth and the Jews.* Albany: State University of New York Press, 1996.

Halio, Jay L. *Philip Roth Revisited.* New York: Twayne, 1992.

Roth, Philip. *Goodbye Columbus and Five Short Stories.* Boston: Houghton Mifflin, 1993.

———. *Reading Myself and Others.* New York: Farrar, Straus & Giroux, 1961.

Thomas Fahy
University of North Carolina at Chapel Hill

S

SALINAS VALLEY The California setting for John STEINBECK's best-known story collection, *The Long Valley,* provides the unifying thread for such acclaimed stories as "THE CHRYSANTHEMUMS," "FLIGHT," "THE RED PONY," "THE SNAKE," "THE VIGILANTE," and "THE WHITE QUAIL." Topographically, the valley is indeed long, populated by numerous individuals, each of whom has a story. Thus the valley provides a metaphorical as well as a topographical unity. Loosely contained within Salinas Valley, then, the stories of *The Long Valley* differ from such SHORT STORY CYCLES as the closely linked tales of Sherwood ANDERSON's *WINESBURG, OHIO:* critics generally agree that Steinbeck's collection is comprised of tales whose main link appears to be the valley itself.

SALINGER, J(EROME) D(AVID) (1919–)

J. D. Salinger, known as one of the most reclusive authors of the 20th century (in the company of such a luminary as Thomas Pynchon), was, for a time, one of the most dependable short story authors in America. He published 17 short stories in various publications such as ESQUIRE, COLLIER'S, STORY, and SATURDAY EVENING POST between 1940 and 1946 before publishing a story called "Slight Rebellion off Madison" in the NEW YORKER in 1946. Salinger went on to publish short stories in *Mademoiselle* ("A Young Girl in 1941 With No Waist At All," May 1947), *Cosmopolitan* ("The Inverted Forest," December 1947), and GOOD HOUSEKEEPING ("A Girl I Knew," February 1948) before electing to publish primarily in the *New Yorker* between 1948 and 1965. After 1965, however, Salinger simply stopped publishing and became a recluse in Cornish, New Hampshire.

Although in the mid-1980s he insisted that he was still writing, to date, no work has appeared. Plans have been made to publish Salinger's last story, published in the *New Yorker* on June 19, 1965, as a book. "Hapworth 16, 1924" is scheduled for publication as a book in 1999, after a two-year delay. In it a young Seymour Glass, who commits suicide as an adult in "A PERFECT DAY FOR BANANAFISH" (1948), writes a lengthy letter home from Camp Simon Hapworth. This is the only Glass story not yet in book form, with Seymour Glass appearing in every collection Salinger has approved for publication in the United States.

Of course, Salinger's best-known work, assigned in college and high school courses across America, the short novel or novella *The Catcher in The Rye* (1951), reveals a fascination with youth, a critical (some say cynical) view of the outside world, and a cultivated dislike for egotism and phoniness while debating how one fits into the world at large as an individual. Its PROTAGONIST, the precocious Holden Caulfield, blasts the adult world at large for breeding "phonies." He intensely distrusts everyone except his sister, Phoebe. Familial relationships figure heavily in Salinger's work.

Not surprisingly, the same THEMEs found in *The Catcher in The Rye* appear, in various forms, in nearly everything Salinger ever published. His works center on conversations, people talking to other people to affirm their own existence, and on characters reacting to one another. Frequently his stories overlap and comment on one another, such as in "FRANNY" and "ZOOEY," separate stories eventually published side by side as a best-selling collection in 1961 in which a brother and sister ruminate on God, the world, and their existence and interaction with both. These characters, Franny and Zooey, turn out to be the younger siblings of Buddy and Seymour Glass, both of whom figure prominently in Salinger's other short stories, weaving a complex web around a core set of characters named either Glass or Caulfield. For example, a pair of the deceased Seymour's goggles turn up in the 1949 story "Down at the Dinghy" in the possession of his sister, who thinks about his death.

Despite Salinger's status as a recluse, there are many connections between him and his characters. Holden Caulfield, like Salinger, lived in Manhattan, and Salinger attended a prep school not unlike Pency. Salinger traveled to Vienna, worked in Army Intelligence, and fought in Germany, like the narrator in "A Girl I Knew" and many other of his characters. Salinger wrote his own service number in "Last Day of the Last Furlough" and frequently named his characters after people he knew in real life.

Salinger's short stories are like finely woven threads running through a tapestry; characters and their families appear and vanish, only to resurface in a later story. Salinger's characters are concerned about war, worried about love and life, and preoccupied with their place in the world. They debate God and philosophy and other matters, usually over the telephone—Salinger has a masterful ear for dialogue and often makes it the focal point of his stories.

Salinger's first publication took place in January 1940, in *Story*, which published a piece titled "The Young Folks." From then on Salinger published something nearly every year until 1965, when he began living in seclusion. Thirteen of his short stories have appeared in three English-language collec-

tions; the 22 remaining short stories were collected into a "bootleg book" called *22 Stories,* which appeared in 1998. It was preceded in 1974 by a two-volume hardcover set called *The Complete Uncollected Short Stories of J.D. Salinger,* which provided no original publication data. Salinger has long had disputes with publishers over cover images, for example, and does not grant interviews. Paradoxically, perhaps, he allowed the publication in 1968 of a Japanese-language collection called *Inverted Forest,* which contains five minor stories ("The Inverted Forest," "Slight Rebellion off Madison," "A Young Girl in 1941 with No Waist at All," "A Girl I Knew," and "Blue Melody"), although no such collection exists in English in the United States.

Nine Stories (1953) contains such notables as "A Perfect Day for Bananafish" (which introduces Salinger's fascination with the highly dysfunctional Glass family) and "For Esme—with Love and Squalor" (the collection's initial title in Britain). *Franny and Zooey,* the book that collected the short story "Franny" (published in the *New Yorker* in January 1955) with its companion piece "Zooey" (the *New Yorker,* May 1957), shot to the top of the bestseller list after its publication in 1961, and was followed, both in publication and sales figures, two years later by *Raise High the Roof Beam, Carpenters,* and *Seymour: An Introduction,* which continued the saga of Seymour Glass's life. Seymour's suicide shakes the Glass family to its core, and the after-effects reverberate through other short stories of Salinger's.

BIBLIOGRAPHY

Salinger, J. D. *The Catcher in The Rye.* Boston: Little, Brown, 1951.

———. "Inverted Forest." *Cosmopolitan Magazine,* December 1947, pp. 73–80, 85–102, 107–108.

———. *Nine Stories.* Boston, Toronto, London: Little, Brown, 1953.

———. *Raise High the Roof Beam, Carpenters and Seymour: An Introduction.* Boston: Little, Brown, 1959.

———. *Seymour: An Introduction.* New York: Bantam, 1965.

———. *22 Stories.* Boston: Little, Brown, 1963.

Anne N. Thalheimer
University of Delaware, Newark

SAM SPADE Dashiell HAMMETT's quintessential San Francisco private detective is described as resembling "a blonde Satan" and remembered as much for his code of honor as for his ability to solve crimes. He enjoys the company of women but does not wholly trust any except his secretary. Spade wears many masks; the reader cannot know for certain what he is thinking. The three short stories from 1932 about Spade ("A Man Called Spade," "Too Many Have Lived," and "They Can Only Hang You Once," all first published in magazines) lack the bite and tension of *The Maltese Falcon* (1930), the only novel in which he appears. Therein he investigates the murder of his partner and searches for the statuette of the black bird of the title.

Sam Spade has been featured in three films; the most famous portrayal of his character is by Humphrey Bogart in the classic version of *The Maltese Falcon. The Adventures of Sam Spade,* based on the story collection of the same title, also ran as a successful radio series from 1946 to 1951. Wildroot Cream Oil, however, withdrew its sponsorship during the McCarthy era (see MCCARTHYISM) because of Hammett's investigation by the House Un-American Activities Committee, and instead sponsored a Sam Spade imitation called *The Adventures of Charlie Wild.*

SANTOS, BIENVENIDO N. (1911–1996)

Bienvenido N. Santos was born in Manila, the Philippines, and grew up in the poor and dangerous slum district of Tondo. He first traveled to the United States in 1941 where, on a scholarship awarded by the Philippines government, he studied at the University of Illinois, Columbia University, and Harvard.

Santos's first collection of short stories, *You Lovely People* (1965), was based on his observations of and close interactions with Filipino American immigrants during his early years in America. He referred to these immigrants, most of them male, as exiles: men for whom life had been largely drained of meaning by crushing poverty and the rigors of day labor, men who would never become part of their adopted country and for whom a return to the

Philippines was a financial impossibility. Although Santos published other story collections, novels, and memoirs in the Philippines, he is best known to American readers for *Scent of Apples* (1979), 16 stories Santos selected from among those he published between 1955 and 1977.

Although Santos was a postcolonialist who used his fiction as a means of displaying America as a colonizing nation ruled largely by greed and hypocrisy, he never reduced the struggle between established Americans and Filipino immigrants to one between colonizer and colonized. Santos was keenly aware that colonized Filipino Americans often became colonizers in turn, exploiting those immigrants who came after them. His keenest tragedies and sharpest ironies are reserved for Americanized Filipinos like Tony in "The Day the Dancers Came."

He spent about half his time after 1941 in the United States and was writer in residence at Wichita State University from 1973 to 1982. He was the recipient of a grant from the Rockefeller Foundation, a GUGGENHEIM GRANT and a National Book Award. Although he became a U.S. citizen in 1976, he seems always to have considered himself an alien in his adopted country. He died at the family estate in Legaspi, a town near the Mt. Mayon volcano in the Philippines.

BIBLIOGRAPHY

Campomanes, Oscar V. "Filipinos in the United States and Their Literature of Exile." *Reading the Literatures of Asian America.* Edited by Shirley Geok-lin Lim and Amy Ling. Philadelphia: Temple University Press, 1992.

Kim, Elaine H. *Asian American Literature: An Introduction to the Writings and Their Social Context* (1982). Reprint. Philadelphia: Temple University Press, 1984.

Valdez, Maria Stella. "The Myth and the Matrix in Bienvenido N. Santos's *Scent of Apples.*" DLSU-Dialogue. 1991.

Keith Lawrence
Brigham Young University

SAROYAN, WILLIAM (1908–1981)

Born in 1908 in Fresno, California, to Armenian immigrant parents, William Saroyan, along with his brother and sisters, lived in an Oakland, California, orphanage after his father died in 1911. Reunited with his mother in Fresno in 1915, Saroyan attended public schools and decided to embark on a writing career, publishing his first story in *Overland Monthly* in 1928. As evidenced in his first collection of stories, *The Daring Young Man on the Flying Trapeze* (1934), Saroyan had realized, as Sherwood ANDERSON did with his small Ohio town, that he could draw on his own California town and the San Joaquin Valley for his fiction. He followed with eight more collections before moving on to other genres, including the novel and drama, of which his best-known work is *The Human Comedy* (1943).

As the title *The Daring Young Man on the Flying Trapeze* suggests, Saroyan conceived of growing up in the United States as a public performance that needed both courage and agility, with the price of failure enormously high. Most of the stories may be viewed as BILDUNGSROMAN: "And Man," for example, is narrated by a 15-year-old boy who describes the agonies and humiliations of his sudden adolescent growth spurt, particularly the sexual insecurities of a boy around mature women. "The Daring Young Man" has as its main character a writer who contemplates the problems of writing, as does "A Cold Day," which similarly examines the problems of writer's block and of the main character's inability to write in the correct American way.

Saroyan's other well-known collection is *My Name Is Aram* (1940). In this collection Saroyan employs as narrator a second-generation Armenian-American boy named Aram Garoughlanian. With the Garoughlanian family at the center, the stories are tied together not merely by the ethnicity of the characters in both family and neighborhood and by their sense of their uncertain position on the margins of society, but also by their sense of community and concern for one another's well-being. Aram, with one foot in the Armenian world and the other in the American world, serves as a go-between. Only recently, in the 1990s—perhaps because of a more distanced perspective—have critics begun to regard Saroyan as more modernist than he was viewed in his own time, with the multiplicity of his own ethnic perspective making his fictional reality multifaceted and much more complicated than has been previously recognized (Shear 94). Critical consensus suggests that his legacy lies largely in the best of his short stories.

BIBLIOGRAPHY

Calonne, David Stephen. *William Saroyan: My Real Work Is Being.* Chapel Hill: University of North Carolina Press, 1983.

Floan, Howard R. *William Saroyan.* Boston: Twayne, 1966.

Saeyoyan, Aram. *Last Rites: The Death of William Saroyan.* New York: Morrow, 1982.

Saroyan, William. *An Act or Two of Foolish Kindness.* Lincoln, Mass.: Penmaen, 1977.

———. *The Adventure of Wesley Jackson.* New York: Harcourt Brace, 1946.

———. *After Thirty Years: The Daring Young Man on the Flying Trapeze.* New York: Harcourt Brace, 1964.

———. *The Assyrian and Other Stories.* New York: Harcourt Brace, 1950.

———. *The Bicycle Rider in Beverly Hills.* New York: Scribner's, 1952.

———. *Boys and Girls Together.* New York: Harcourt Brace, 1963.

———. *Chance Meetings.* New York: Norton, 1978.

———. *Christmas 1939.* San Mateo, Calif.: Querus, 1939.

———. *The Daring Young Man on the Flying Trapeze and Other Stories.* New York: Random House, 1934.

———. *Dear Baby.* New York: Harcourt Brace, 1944.

———. *The Fiscal Hoboes.* New York: Valenti Angelo, 1949.

———. *Here Comes There Goes You Know Who.* New York: Trident/Simon & Schuster, 1961.

———. *The Human Comedy.* New York: Harcourt Brace, 1943.

———. *Inhale and Exhale.* New York: Random House, 1936.

———. *Jim Dandy.* Cincinnati: Little Man, 1941.

———. *The Laughing Matter.* Garden City, N.Y.: Doubleday, 1953.

———. *Little Children.* New York: Harcourt Brace, 1937.

———. *Love, Here is My Hat.* New York: Modern Age, 1938.

———. *Madness in the Family.* Edited by Leo Hamalian. New York: New Directions, 1988.

———. *Mama, I Love You.* Boston: Little, Brown, 1956.

———. *My Heart's in the Highlands.* New York: Harcourt Brace, 1939.

———. *My Kind of Crazy, Wonderful People.* New York: Harcourt Brace, 1966.

———. *My Name is Aram.* New York: Harcourt Brace, 1940.

———. *A Native American.* San Francisco: Fields, 1938.

———. *Not Dying.* New York: Harcourt Brace, 1963.

———. *One Day in the Afternoon of the World.* New York: Harcourt Brace, 1964.

——— —. *Peace, It's Wonderful.* New York: Modern Age, 1939.

———. *Places Where I've Done Time.* New York: Praeger, 1972.

———. *Rock Wagram.* Garden City, N.Y.: Doubleday, 1951.

———. *Saroyan's Fables.* New York: Harcourt Brace, 1941.

———. *Seventeen Stories and a Play.* New York: Harcourt Brace, 1966.

———. *Some Day I'll Be a Millionaire: 34 More Great Stories.* New York: Avon, 1943.

———. *Sons Come and Go, Mothers Hang in Forever.* New York: McGraw-Hill, 1976.

———. *Three Fragments and a Story.* San Francisco: Little Man, 1939.

———. *Three Times Three.* Los Angeles: Conference, 1936.

———. *Tracy's Tiger.* Garden City, N.Y.: Doubleday, 1951.

———. *The Trouble with Tigers.* New York: Harcourt Brace, 1938.

———. *The Twin Adventures: The Adventures of William Saroyan, a Diary; The Adventures of Wesley Jackson, a Novel.* New York: Harcourt Brace, 1950.

———. *The Whole Voyald and Other Stories.* Boston: Little, Brown, 1950.

Shear, Walter. "Saroyan's Study of Ethnicity." In *Critical Essays on William Saroyan.* Edited by Harry Keyisian, 86–95. New York: G.K. Hall, 1995, pp. 86–95.

SASAKI, R. A. (1952–)

Ruth A. Sasaki calls herself a third-generation San Franciscan. After attending the University of Kent in Canterbury, England, she received a B.A. in English from the University of California at Berkeley and an M.A. in creative writing from San Francisco State University. Her stories have appeared in the *Short Story Review* and in several anthologies; she was awarded the American Japanese National Literary Award in 1983. Her first collection of short fiction, *The Loom and Other Stories,* was published in 1991.

THEMES of dependence and independence—cultural, familial, ethnic, academic—run through Sasaki's tales, most of which feature Japanese American characters and communities.

Keith Lawrence
Brigham Young University

SATIRE

A fictional work that ridicules some aspect of human behavior with the intent of improving the behavior or the situation that caused it. Unlike writers who simply criticize or use sarcasm, satirists blend humor with their censorious attitudes. One of the earliest American satirists was Frances HOPKINSON, who blended satire with ALLEGORY in "A PRETTY STORY," demonstrating the tense state of British-American relations on the eve of the AMERICAN REVOLUTION. The satiric vein in American fiction continued in the 19th century with, for instance, the writings of Washington IRVING and Mark TWAIN; and major practitioners in the 20th century range from Edith WHARTON to Kurt VONNEGUT.

SATURDAY EVENING POST

The *Saturday Evening Post* first appeared in 1821, and thereafter under various names until 1897. That year Cyrus H. K. Curtis, owner of the successful *LADIES' HOME JOURNAL,* purchased it and the following year, 1898, hired George H. Lorimer as editor. Lorimer led the *Post* to its position as the foremost magazine in the United States for the next 30 years. An American institution from the early 20th century until the mid-1960s, its competitors included *Everybody's Magazine, Red Book, Blue Book, Popular Magazine,* and *COLLIER'S,* but only the *Saturday Evening Post* became the quintessential mass-market magazine, reaching a remarkable circulation of 3 million in the 1930s, despite the GREAT DEPRESSION. It both appealed to and honed middle-class tastes, and its influence still provides the subject of much debate: did it cultivate a wider breadth of taste in its audience, as many critics claim, or did its writers mute the intricacies of their prose voices to make their stories acceptable to the *Post's* standards? Whatever the answer, the *Post* clearly led the way in the number of stories and variety of authors it published, a partial list of whom includes Stephen Vincent BENÉT, Stephen CRANE, Theodore DREISER, William FAULKNER, F. Scott FITZGERALD, Bret HARTE, Ernest HEMINGWAY,

Ring LARDNER, Jack LONDON, Booth Tarkington, and Edith WHARTON, as well as Agatha Christie, the entertaining Erle Stanley GARDNER, and Mary Roberts Rinehart. More contemporary story contributors included H. E. Bates, Ray BRADBURY, Arthur Miller, John O'HARA, William SAROYAN, Kurt VONNEGUT, and Robert Penn Warren. After a near demise in the 1960s, the *Post* was revived, but although it published a few stories by respected writers such as Vonnegut and John C. Gardner, its emphasis has shifted away from literature to health and religious issues, and its circulation stands at under 500,000.

"SAY YES" TOBIAS WOLFF (1985)

Tobias WOLFF's short story "Say Yes" uses a limited third-person POINT OF VIEW to tell the story of an ordinary spat between a husband and wife. The perspective follows that of the husband, and the narrative technique reveals more to the reader about the husband's character than he can understand about himself.

The PROTAGONIST, who is white, considers himself an enlightened man ("Helping out with the dishes was a way he had of showing how considerate he was"), but he is acting on some preconceptions that his wife forces him to question. In an argument about racial issues, his wife asks him if he would marry her if she were black. Integral to the argument and to the couple's relationship is the question of how much one can ever know anyone else or even oneself. The husband's statement that "a person from their culture and a person from our culture could never really *know* each other" unwittingly uses irony to point out that in some senses his wife is still unknown to him, and that in his unthinking reactions ("He had no choice but to demonstrate his indifference to her") there are parts of himself that are unexplored as well.

Collected in his second short story collection, *Back in the World* (1985), this story demonstrates Wolff's mastery of dialogue. All of the stories in this collection are told in the third person, and, as "Say Yes" clearly and movingly shows, their characters (like those in most of Wolff's writing) are concerned with relationships, unexpected moral choices, and self-knowledge.

BIBLIOGRAPHY
Wolff, Tobias. *Back in the World.* New York: Vintage Books, 1996.

Karen Weekes
University of Georgia

SCHEHERAZADE

The storyteller in *The Arabian Nights* or *A Thousand and One Nights,* who marries the sultan Schahriah despite the knowledge of danger: Because of the infidelity of both his and his brother's wives, Schahriah believes that no woman has virtue, and he has vowed to marry a woman every night and have each strangled at daybreak. On her wedding night, Scheherazade contrives to begin telling a story to her sister, within the sultan's hearing, but stopping before the story is finished. Wishing to hear the ending, Schahriah does not have her killed and, using the same ploy, Scheherazade tells a story each night. After 1,001 nights, the sultan revokes his vow and bestows his affection on Scheherazade. The best known of these tales are "Ali Baba and the Forty Thieves," "Sinbad the Sailor," and "Aladdin."

SCIENCE FICTION

Following Mary Shelley's *Frankenstein, or the Modern Prometheus* (1818), the anonymous publication of *The Battle of Dorking* (1871) in *Blackwood's Magazine*—which featured an account of future wars—helped establish science fiction with a separate identity as a genre. In the late 19th and early 20th centuries it moved in two main directions. One, exemplified by Jules Verne (1828–1905), emphasized the human fascination with the machine, and the other, exemplified by H. G. Wells (1866–1946), explored and warned readers about the tentativeness of human superiority. Although confined to a specialized and in many senses closed group of writers, editors, and readers in the early part of the 20th century, science fiction has gained in both popularity and credibility since the end of World War II. Its seriousness of purpose has been advanced by talented "sci-fi" writers and "mainstream" writers alike—Doris Lessing, for example, or Thomas Pynchon—who either write in the mode or employ many of its devices in works outside the genre. The dystopian (as opposed to UTOPIAN) movement in the science fiction of the 1950s and 1960s, as expressed by such writers as Isaac Asimov (1920–92), Ray BRADBURY, Arthur C. Clarke, H. P. Lovecraft, Kurt VONNEGUT, Jr.—and, slightly later, Ursula K. LE GUIN—tends to criticize an overreliance on technology and advocates more attention to its social, psychological, and ecological ramifications. The best of these writers transcend the limits of the genre and have merited attention as serious writers of fiction. By the 1970s and 1980s, for many readers, science fiction had earned the reputation of a legitimate art form that could help them better understand their fast-paced and rapidly-changing world. It had also acquired the somewhat controversial (at least among some hard-core fans) reputation as a genre that no longer ignored such literary concerns as PLOT, subtly drawn and complex CHARACTERS, and an artful use of MYTH.

Indeed, Eugene Current-García maintains that certain science fiction stories have attained classic status: For instance, Bradbury's "There Will Come Soft Rains," Clarke's "The Star," Harlan ELLISON's " 'Repent, Harlequin!' Said the Ticktockman," and Le Guin's "The Ones Who Walk Away from Omelas" and "Nine Lives" (Current-García 560). The increasing popularity of science fiction is measured not only by the number of films and television serials devoted to futuristic and inexplicable phenomena but also by the wealth of articles published on the subject and by the growing numbers of college courses offered in the literature of science fiction.

BIBLIOGRAPHY

Current-García, Eugene, and Bert Hitchcock, eds. *American Short Stories*. 6th edition. New York: Longman, 1997.

Franklin, H. Bruce. *Future Perfect: American Science Fiction of the Nineteenth Century*. New York: Oxford University Press, 1966, revised ed., 1978.

Le Guin, Ursula K. *The Language of the Night: Essays on Fantasy and Science Fiction*. New York: Putnam, 1979.

Le Guin, Ursula K., and Brian Attebery, eds. *The Norton Book of Science Fiction*. New York: W. W. Norton, 1993.

Suvin, Darko. *Metamorphoses of Science Fiction: On the Poetics and History of a Literary Genre*. New Haven, Conn.: Yale University Press, 1979.

SCRIBNER'S   Short for *Scribner's Monthly,* which published its first issue in 1870, and in 1881 became the *Century,* a literary magazine of high quality that published virtually all the significant writers in Europe and the United States during its nearly 50 years of circulation (1881–1930). *Scribner's* was restarted as *Scribner's Magazine* in 1887, and it remained a major literary magazine under the discerning editorship of Alfred Dashiell until it ceased publishing in 1939. Dedicated to printing first-class fiction, *Scribner's Magazine*—which offered generous literary prizes—included stories by such writers as Edith WHARTON, William FAULKNER, and Thomas Wolfe.

"SECRET LIFE OF WALTER MITTY, THE" JAMES THURBER (1942)

As a 20th century comic writer (see COMEDY), James THURBER has few peers. Not only is "The Secret Life of Walter Mitty" considered his best story, but the term "Walter Mitty" also has entered the language as a METAPHOR for an ordinary man who escapes into a fantasy world of impossible heroics. In this respect Mitty is both universal and American, particularly as critics see his antecedents stretching back to Washington IRVING's "RIP VAN WINKLE" and Mark TWAIN's Tom Sawyer. Mitty is the modern fictional reincarnation of the henpecked husband.

The story opens in medias res, that is, in the middle of one of Mitty's fantasies: He is a naval commander supervising a hydroplane during a raging storm. Mitty is the quintessential officer, worshipped by his crew for his bravery and ability. The reader understands at the same time as Mitty himself does that the scenario takes place only in Mitty's imagination: He is actually driving a car, and his wife is ordering him to slow down. The rest of the fantasies in the story are similarly triggered by actual events. Mrs. Mitty's ordering him to wear his gloves leads Mitty to imagine donning surgical gloves as, in the role of an internationally famous surgeon, he prepares to operate on a millionaire banker. In fact, he cannot even park his car properly and must turn it over to a youthful contemptuous parking attendant.

Thurber deftly juxtaposes the ordinariness of Mitty's life—he is running errands for Mrs. Mitty while she keeps her hairdresser's appointment—to larger issues of life and death. As a newsboy yells out the headlines of a murder trial, Mitty begins to imagine himself in court, the perfect defendant, only to associate the word "cur" with the puppy biscuit his wife has asked him to buy. Then, in one of the funniest scenes in the story, Mitty, looking at a copy of *Liberty* magazine, sees himself as a WORLD WAR II pilot heroically bombing a German ammunitions plant. Interrupted for the last time by Mrs. Mitty—he has forgotten the puppy biscuit—Mitty imagines himself in front of a firing squad, stoically refusing the blindfold. Although both male and female critics have observed that, in Thurber's view, American women have won the war between the sexes, it is the uncommon reader who can read this timeless CLASSIC of American humor without laughing.

BIBLIOGRAPHY

Bernstein, Burton. *Thurber: A Biography.* New York: Dodd, Mead, 1975.

Holmes, Charles S., ed. *Thurber: A Collection of Critical Essays.* Englewood Cliffs, N.J.: Prentice-Hall, 1974.

Long, Robert Emmet. *Thurber.* New York: Ungar, 1988.

Thurber, James. *Vintage Thurber: A Collection of the Best Writings and Drawings.* 2 vols. London: Hamilton, 1963.

"SEPARATING" JOHN UPDIKE (1975, 1979) First published in the NEW YORKER in 1975 and included in *Prize Stories 1976: the O. Henry Awards,* "Separating" was incorporated with other stories featuring Joan and Richard Maple in *Too Far to Go* (1979), a SHORT STORY CYCLE chronicling a 20-year marriage and its dissolution that John UPDIKE assembled in response to a television version of the Maples stories. Although the Maples continue to appear in the three remaining stories in *Too Far to Go,* "Separating" provides the inevitable but continually deferred climax toward which the couple has been moving in their prolonged dance toward divorce. In the previous stories, each time the couple decides to separate, Richard's attraction to Joan paradoxically grows stronger; in "Separating," however, their resolve to end the marriage becomes a painful reality.

"Separating" poignantly sketches Joan and Richard's final day together, which Richard begins with last-minute repairs on the house he is leaving. The futility of his attempt to orchestrate an orderly departure from this marriage before he embarks on another with his current mistress, however, is foreshadowed by intimations of the inevitable processes of nature and decay. (See FORESHADOWING.) Similarly, the couple's orderly plan to reveal the news of their separation to their children at a reunion dinner goes awry when Richard is unable to control his emotions and begins to cry, thus forcing the announcement. Dickie, their eldest son, is out at a concert, and Richard breaks the news to him during their drive home, when they are halfway between the church and the house where Richard's mistress lives. Yet Dickie's desperate good-night kiss and the simple whispered question of "Why?" that concludes the story further undoes Richard's artfully constructed defenses, as he is unable to respond to his son's question.

The story's drama centers on the Maples' revelation of their separation to their children, but it plumbs emotional depths and paradoxes far beyond the simple action it depicts. The authenticity and emotional resonance of this and the other Maples stories certainly derives from their autobiographical connection; the Maples children are the same ages as Updike's own when his first marriage ended. Like the other Maples stories, "Separating" is told from Richard's POINT OF VIEW, thus eliciting sympathy for a character who, while selfishly engaged in the breakup of his family, nonetheless feels a profound affection for them and suffers intensely for the pain he is inflicting through the separation to which he has finally consented. Alternative readings view Richard with less sympathy precisely because, through his perspective, readers can identify his weakness and selfishness.

BIBLIOGRAPHY

Barnes, Jane. "John Updike: A Literary Spider." *Virginia Quarterly Review* 57.1 (1981): 79–98. Reprinted in *John*

Updike. Edited by Harold Bloom. New York: Chelsea House, 1987, 111–125.

Detweiler, Robert. *John Updike,* revised ed. Boston: G.K. Hall, 1984.

Greiner, Donald. *The Other John Updike: Poems, Short Stories, Prose, Play.* Athens: Ohio University Press, 1981.

Hamilton, Alice, and Kenneth Hamilton. *The Elements of John Updike.* Grand Rapids, Mich.: Eerdmans, 1970.

Luscher, Robert M. *John Updike: A Study of the Short Fiction.* New York: Twayne, 1993.

Mann, Susan Garland. *The Short Story Cycle: A Genre Companion and Reference Guide.* New York: Greenwood Press, 1989.

Updike, John. *Too Far To Go.* New York: Fawcett Crest, 1979.

Wilhelm, Albert E. "Narrative Continuity in Updike's *Too Far To Go.*" *Journal of the Short Story in English* 7 (1986): 87–90.

———. "The Trail of Bread Crumbs Motif in Updike's Maples Stories." *Studies in Short Fiction* 25 (1988): 71–73.

Robert M. Luscher
University of Nebraska at Kearney

SETTING   The place and time in which fictional action occurs. Setting can include geographical location and physical details; the actual season in which the story takes place; the day-to-day living conditions of the characters; and an evocation of the era in which the characters live, including cultural, historical, moral, and emotional conditions.

"SEVENTEEN SYLLABLES"   HISAYE YAMAMOTO (1988)   First published in the PAR-TISAN REVIEW (November 1949), "Seventeen Syllables" is another of Hisaye YAMAMOTO's stories concerned with Japanese American women's frustrated passions and oppression. The story emphasizes the silence, measured voices, and violence associated with the reality of two generations, *issei* (Japanese immigrants to the United States) and *nisei* (their Japanese American children born in the United States). In this story Tome and her daughter, Rosie, share an inability to voice their feelings in a patriarchal environment.

Compounding this gender difficulty, Rosie, the nisei daughter of farmers, understands only rudi-mentary Japanese, resents her mother's obedience to her father, and cannot understand her mother's haiku poetry. A conventional American high school sophomore, Rosie talks about clothes with her girlfriends and becomes attracted to Jesus Carrasco, a senior who helps with the tomato harvest. Unable to understand her cultural tradition and her own youthful desires, Rosie resorts to mimicry of singers and comedians as her means of expression.

Her initial indifference to her mother's writing ends, however, on the day when her mother receives a first prize for one of her haiku. While Rose and her mother silently observe, Rosie's father violently destroys the picture his wife has been awarded. Then Rosie listens to her mother's story of thwarted love, her illegitimate, stillborn son, now dead for 17 years, and her arranged marriage.

The story argues that Tome's early stifled procreation haunts her restricted adult life and that her confinement is made bearable only through her created PERSONA, Ume Hanazono, the poet who links the Japanese culture with the American by writing restrained 17-syllable haiku. Tome's passionate admonition never to marry to the still-uncomprehending Rosie opens her fully to her daughter but chills the girl's innocence and romantic love.

BIBLIOGRAPHY
Mistri, Zenobia Baxter. "'Seventeen Syllables': A Symbolic Haiku." *Studies in Short Fiction* 27 (Spring 1990): 197–202.

Yamamoto, Hisaye. "Seventeen Syllables." In *Seventeen Syllables and Other Stories.* Latham, N.Y.: Kitchen Table: Women of Color Press, 1988.

Yogi, Stan. "Rebels and Heroines: Subversive Narratives in the Stories of Wakako Yamauchi and Hisaye Yamamoto." In *Reading the Literatures of Asian America.* Edited by Shirley Geok-lin Lim and Amy Ling. Philadelphia: Temple University Press, 1992, 131–150.

Sandra Chrystal Hayes
Georgia Institute of Technology

"SHADOWY THIRD, THE"   ELLEN GLASGOW (1916)   The title story of Ellen GLAS-GOW's only short story collection, *The Shadowy Third and Other Stories* (1923), was originally published in

Scribner's Magazine in 1916. "The Shadowy Third" deals with the supernatural. The first-person narrator, Miss Randolph, a young nurse, is called to the home of a famous surgeon, Dr. Maradick, to care for his invalid wife. Mrs. Maradick's supposed malady is melancholia and hallucinations resulting from grief over the death of her child from a previous marriage. Although Miss Randolph also sees the ghost child and sympathizes with Mrs. Maradick's fears, she is helpless before the charm of Dr. Maradick and the other experts he brings to his wife's bedside. Believing her insane, Dr. Maradick has his wife committed to an asylum, where she soon dies. Miss Randolph, who stays on with the doctor as his office nurse, learns that he plans to marry a former sweetheart, with whom he will share his late wife's and stepdaughter's fortune. Shortly before he can enact these plans, however, as he rushes down the stairs to answer an emergency call, he trips and falls to his death. As she turns on the light, Miss Randolph sees a child's jump rope coiled in the bend of the stair from which he fell.

In this as in many of Glasgow's stories, we see the influence of Edgar Allen POE and Henry JAMES. As in Poe's THE FALL OF THE HOUSE OF USHER and James's THE TURN OF THE SCREW, the supernatural tale is told by a first-person narrator whose proximity to the events helps bridge the gap between the reader's disbelief and the bizarre events of the story. Also, as in James's NOVELLA, the ghost can be seen only by characters of heightened sensitivity. In "The Turn of the Screw," the ghost matches wits against the young narrator, but at the end of "The Shadowy Third," the ghost's will seems to blend with the narrator's own to destroy Maradick.

BIBLIOGRAPHY

Glasgow, Ellen. "The Shadowy Third." In *The Shadowy Third and Other Stories.* Garden City, N.Y.: Doubleday, 1923.

Meeker, Richard K. *Introduction to the Collected Stories of Ellen Glasgow.* Edited by Richard K. Meeker. Baton Rouge: Louisiana State University Press, 1963.

Thiebaux, Marcelle. *Ellen Glasgow.* New York: Ungar, 1982.

Betina I. Entzminger
University of North Carolina, Chapel Hill

SHADY HILL The fictional suburban commuter town for many of John CHEEVER's middle- to upper-middle-class characters. See, for instance, Cheever's short story collection, *The Housebreaker of Shady Hill* (1984) and "THE FIVE FORTY-EIGHT."

SHAW, IRWIN (1913–1984) A short story writer, novelist, and playwright, Irwin Shaw has developed an international reputation in recent decades. His books have sold over 14 million copies and have been translated into 28 languages. Critics in a number of countries, including Russia, Bulgaria, and Japan, have written articles about his work. Shaw was born in New York City, the son of a salesman, William Shaw, and Rose Tompkins Shaw. He grew up in the Sheepshead Bay section of Brooklyn, developed an interest in sports, and wrote his first short story when he was 12. Upon graduation from James Madison High School, Shaw entered Brooklyn College, where he played football, worked on the school newspaper, and wrote plays. Shaw's writing career spanned over 50 years, from his first postcollege job selling scripts for radio serials until his death of a heart attack in Davos, Switzerland, when he was 71. In 1950, after publication of *The Young Lions,* he left America and began living in Europe, although his fiction continued to have American settings, CHARACTERS, and THEMES. He insisted that his European perspective improved his insight into America. Many of his later novels became best-sellers, although it has been said that they damaged his critical reputation. The novelist William Goldman explained that the critics "never forgave him for [the success of] *The Young Lions.*" In his later life he divided his time between Southampton, New York, and Klosters, Switzerland.

His first serious writing effort was an antiwar play, *Bury the Dead,* produced at the Ethel Barrymore Theater in New York in 1936. At this time he began publishing short stories; the first one appeared in the *New Republic* in 1937. He later contributed to the NEW YORKER, COLLIER'S, and other magazines. Goldman said of his ability as a storyteller that he had a "narrative interest in everything," coupled with "the ability to write with an ease and a clarity that only [F. Scott] FITZGERALD had" (407). The critic Robert Cromie, writing in the *Saturday Review*, stated that Shaw's characters "are individuals who walk into the living room of your mind, ensconce themselves, and refuse to be dislodged" (408). William Peden, a reviewer for the *Saturday Review,* praised Shaw's characters, saying that they seem "wonderfully alive, even when the author descends to caricature and BURLESQUE. Like [Charles] Dickens, Mr. Shaw has created, prodigally, a crowded gallery of memorable people (408)."

Some of Shaw's short fiction is topical, based on such events as the beginning of WORLD WAR II or the North African landings of American troops during the war. He has written, however, that even those stories connected with specific events are anchored "in some remembered, isolated moment of my own time," reflecting such emotions as "hope, despair, defiance, courage, resignation, brutality, laughter and love" in the light of the epoch shared by the men and women of his generation (preface to *Selected Short Stories*). An example is "Sailor Off the Bremen" (1939), in which an American athlete combats a Nazi sailor who has attacked and seriously injured his elder brother, an idealistic communist and artist. Walter Ross suggests that the story demonstrates Shaw's social consciousness; the fight "becomes a graphic dramatization on a small scale of the clash between the forces of Teutonic FASCISM and communism" (Preface to *God Was Here But He Left Early,* 14).

Like John CHEEVER, John UPDIKE, and Ernest HEMINGWAY, Shaw also deals with such universal situations as adultery, unhappy marriages, and marital relationships that, although compromised, have endured (or presumably will endure) in an atmosphere of hostile stasis. The latter predicament provides the THEME of one of his more famous short stories, "The Girls in Their Summer Dresses." Frances and Michael, a young married couple, plan a happy day together in New York, but it is progressively clouded by Michael's insistence on watching passing girls. Eventually the couple arrive at the sad recognition, and bitter acceptance, that they actually mean little to each other. Michael is technically faithful but regards Frances as a girl he "happens" to have married. Frances does not have the fortitude to divorce him but, with an air of resignation, calls another couple to make plans, since she and Michael can no longer communicate with each other. The story was produced for television for New York's WNET in 1981, along with "The Man Who Married a French Wife" and "The Monument."

In the preface to *God Was Here But He Left Early,* Shaw recalls meeting Somerset Maugham before World War II. Maugham said he envied Shaw for being an American and writing short stories: "There is a short story on every street corner in America," Maugham said. "I have to go through a whole country to find one." Shaw commented wryly that he had been on many street corners and it had never seemed that easy to him, but that Maugham had a point in view of the numerous short stories published every week at the time. Shaw pinpointed the satisfaction he found in writing short stories as opposed to novels. There was not only the satisfaction of being a storyteller, "seated cross-legged in the middle of the bazaar, filling the need of humanity in the humdrum course of an ordinary day for magic and tales of distant wonders," but also the opportunity for "disguised moralizing," for the "compression of great matters into digestible portions," and for the "shaping of mysteries into sharply-edged and comprehensible symbols" (*Contemporary Reviews* 407–8). Above all, the writer of short stories could be "all men" or "fragments of men, worthy and unworthy, who in different seasons abound within you," whereas the novelist must be a "whole man" (Ross on "Sailor Off the Bremen": *DLB 6*, 291).

BIBLIOGRAPHY

Giles, James R. "Interviews with Irwin Shaw: Summer 1980," *Resources for American Literary Study* 18:1 (1992), 1–21.

———. *Irwin Shaw.* Boston: Twayne, 1983.

———. *Irwin Shaw: A Study of the Short Fiction.* Boston: Twayne, 1991.

Dear, Pamela S., ed. "Ellison, Harlan (Jay)." *Contemporary Authors.* Vol 46. Detroit: Gale Research Inc., 1995, pp. 109–114.

Moorhead, Michael. "Hemingway's 'The Short Happy Life of Francis Macomber' and Shaw's 'The Deputy Sheriff.'" *Explicator* 44.2 (Winter 1986): 42–43.

Reynolds, Fred. "Irwin Shaw's 'The Eighty-Year Run.'" *Explicator* 49.2 (Winter 1991): 121–123.

Ross, "Sailor Off the Bremen." *Dictionary of Literary Biography* 6, 291.

Shaw, Irwin. *God Was Here But He Left Early.* New York: Arbor House, 1973.

———. *Selected Short Stories.* New York: Modern Library, 1961.

———. *Short Stories.* New York: Random House, 1966.

———. *Short Stories, Five Decades.* New York: Delacorte Press, 1978.

Shnayerson, Michael. *Irwin Shaw: A Biography.* New York: Putnam, 1989.

Sarah Bird Wright

"SHORT HAPPY LIFE OF FRANCIS MACOMBER, THE" ERNEST HEMINGWAY (1936)

In the story by Ernest HEMINGWAY, the setting is Africa, where Margot and Francis Macomber have hired the English guide Robert Wilson to take them on a big-game hunt. The Macomber marriage is on shaky ground, but "Margot was too beautiful for Macomber to divorce her and Macomber had too much money for Margot ever to leave him." The narrative begins at lunch, after Francis has shown himself to be a coward by running from a wounded lion. The narrative flashes back through Francis's memory of the lion hunt and even into the lion's sensibility, showing the hunt from the lion's POINT OF VIEW.

The next scene occurs early the following morning, when Francis encounters Margot returning to their tent after a presumably sexual interlude with Wilson, who carries a double cot for just such occasions. The next morning all three characters go out in a car to hunt buffalo. Macomber bags his buffalo and begins to feel good about himself, as his cheerful, confident behavior clearly indicates. Wilson sees the change in him. Margot is discomfitted by the whole episode. When a wounded bull charges them, Macomber stands his ground to shoot him, but is killed by his wife when she shoots at the buffalo "with the 6.5 Mannlicher as it seemed about to gore Macomber." Wilson seems to accuse Margot of murdering her husband, asking "Why didn't you poison him? That's what they do in England." But he also assures her that he and the gun-bearers will testify that it was an accident.

A central THEME is the importance of courage. Wilson quotes Shakespeare: "A man can die but once; we owe God a death and let it go which way it will; he that dies this year is quit for the next." The implication of these lines fits into the HEMINGWAY CODE: Since a man has only one chance to face death, he should do so with dignity and grace. Hemingway's title indicates that without courage a man is less than a man. In that "short" period preceding Macomber's death, he has behaved courageously and becomes a man. Therefore, he is "happy." Wilson, however, categorizes Francis as a soft, great American boy-man. Wilson's manly character, in contrast to his description of Macomber's, is outwardly that of a man who fearlessly and competently kills the game he pursues. Yet he is more predator than gallant hunter, cuckolding Francis and then describing his conquest, Margot, as hard, cruel, and dominating. In Macomber and Wilson, Hemingway embodies two definitions of male behavior.

Only one character, however, represents female behavior. Did Margot Macomber shoot her husband on purpose because she feared losing him, given his newfound self-assurance, or was she trying to save his life, accidentally hitting him as she shot at the charging buffalo? Controversy has raged since the story was first published in *Cosmopolitan* magazine in September 1936, not unaided by the author himself, who wrote: "No, I don't know whether she shot him on purpose any more than you do." "Macomber" is a highly elusive text, open to endless reinterpretations, the most recent informed by both a heightened environmentalism, which views big-game hunting in an unfavorable light, and by FEMINIST criticism, which is mindful of sexist standards in the evaluation of women's behavior.

BIBLIOGRAPHY

Baym, Nina. "Actually, I Felt Sorry for the Lion." In *New Critical Approaches to the Short Stories of Ernest Hemingway*. Edited by Jackson J. Benson. Durham, N.C.: Duke University Press, 1990, 112–120.

Beck, Warren. "The Shorter Happy Life of Mrs. Macomber." *Modern Fiction Studies* (1975): 363–376.

Flora, Joseph. *Ernest Hemingway. A Study of the Short Fiction.* Boston: Twayne, 1989, 74–81.

Hardy, Donald E. "Presupposition and the Coconspirator." *Style* (Spring 1992): 1–11.

Johnston, Kenneth G. *The Tip of the Iceberg: Hemingway and the Short Story,* Greenwood, Fla.: Penkevill Publishing Company, 1987, 207–213.

Morgan, Kathleen, and Luis A. Losada. "Tracking the Wounded Buffalo: Authorial Knowledge and the Shooting of Francis Macomber." *The Hemingway-Review* (Fall 1991): 25–30.

Nagel, James. "The Narrative Method of 'The Short Happy Life of Francis Macomber.'" *Research Studies* (1973): 18–27.

Oldsey, Bernard. "Hemingway's Beginnings and Endings." *College Literature* 7 (1980): 213–238.

Seydow, John J. "Francis Macomber's Spurious Masculinity." *The Hemingway Review* (Fall 1981): 33–41.

Spilka, Mark. "A Source for the Macomber 'Accident.'" *The Hemingway Review* (Spring 1984): 29–37.

Mimi Riesel Gladstein
University of Texas at El Paso

SHORT-SHORT STORY

A brief short story or lengthy anecdote of about 500 to 2,000 words. A master of this story form was O. HENRY. Although critics can readily identify its ancestors—the epigram, the FABLE, the PARABLE, among others—and most agree that the trend toward "short-shorts" is growing in the United States, most are reluctant to predict with any certainty the meaning of this phenomenon. That it has no one identifiable name suggests the uncertain newness if rapidly spreading nature of the form: Its many monikers include *quick* or *flash, mini-* or *micro-* fiction, as well as *short short story, four-minute story,* and *sudden fiction.* In the 1980s, anthologies of short shorts began to appear, with such titles as *Short Short Stories* (1981), *Short Shorts: An Anthology of the Shortest Stories* (1982), and *Sudden Fiction: American Short Short Stories* (1986).

These collections include a number of well-known writers in the genre, including Donald BARTHELME, Raymond CARVER, Barry Hannah, Langston HUGHES, Grace PALEY, Jayne Anne Phillips, and John UPDIKE, to name only a very few. Short-short story contests have begun to proliferate, with word limits stipulated at anywhere from 250 to 50 words. Whether the short shorts will reach a brevity that inhibits their readers' understanding, or whether they will provide a necessarily sharpened focus on the intricacies of the 20th-century life, they show every sign of gaining increased popular interest.

BIBLIOGRAPHY

David, Jack, and John Redfern. *Short Short Stories*. Toronto: Holt, Rinehart and Winston of Canada,1981.

Current-García, Eugene, and Bert Hitchcock, eds. *American Short Stories*. 6th edition. New York: Longman, 1997.

Howe, Irving and Ilana Weiner Howe. *Short Shorts: An Anthology of the Shortest Stories*. 1982.

Shapard, Robert and James Thomas. *Sudden Fiction: American Short Short Stories*. Salt Lake City: Gibbs M. Smith, Inc., 1986.

SHORT STORY CYCLE

Sometimes also called a short story sequence, the term refers to short stories collected and organized by the author into one volume. When read sequentially, the stories—although each is a complete entity on its own—display a coherent pattern of character and theme that binds the stories together. Recent short story theory emphasizes the reader's role in identifying a network of these patterns, similarities, and associations. Examples include Sarah Orne JEWETT's *THE COUNTRY OF THE POINTED FIRS*, Sherwood ANDERSON's *WINESBURG, OHIO*, William FAULKNER's *THE UNVANQUISHED* and *GO DOWN, MOSES*, John STEINBECK's *THE PASTURES OF HEAVEN*, Katherine Anne PORTER's *The Old Order,* and Eudora WELTY's *THE GOLDEN APPLES*.

BIBLIOGRAPHY

Luscher, Robert M. "The Short Story Sequence: An Open Book." In *Short Story Theory at a Crossroads*. Edited by Susan Lohafer and Jo Ellyn Clarey. Baton Rouge: Louisiana State University Press, 1989.

Mann, Susan Garland. *The Short Story Cycle: A Genre Companion and Reference Guide.* Westport, Conn.: Garland Press, 1988.
Special Issue of *The Journal of the Short Story in English.* Edited by J. Gerald Kennedy. 1988.

"SILENT SNOW, SECRET SNOW"   See AIKEN, Conrad.

SILKO, LESLIE MARMON (1948–   )

Like her contemporary NATIVE AMERICAN author Louise ERDRICH, Leslie Marmon SILKO is of mixed heritage, having Laguna Pueblo, Mexican, and Caucasian background. Born and raised in New Mexico, Silko received her early education at a Bureau of Indian Affairs school and later graduated from the University of New Mexico. In addition to writing movie scripts, she has taught at Navajo Community College, the University of New Mexico, and the University of Arizona—Tucson.

Central to Silko's writing is the act of storytelling. Like many Native American writers, she sees her life and her stories as being a part of the continuum—a melding of past, present, and future, and constant change. The oral stories that are passed on from generation to generation evolve with the progress of time, and the new elements time brings (a flood, a war, technology) are incorporated into the story. Silko is a proponent of the need for change to keep stories and society strong.

Silko uses traditional tribal stories and the Coyote (see COYOTE STORY) TRICKSTER figure in her work. She also uses many perspectives, voices, and styles, thereby creating a polyphony of voices telling the tales that make up the story that never stops. In the collection of short stories *Storyteller* (1981), Silko introduces readers to a range of characters, from the intriguing and mysterious main character in "Yellow Woman" to the romantic and macabre character in "Storyteller" who, timeless, almost ancient, does not fit in any time period. "Coyote Holds," on the other hand, focuses on a below-average Laguna Indian man who is lazy and irritating, and who ultimately becomes a HERO to the men of the village. With "Coyote Holds," Silko reminds the reader that one

does not have to be a romantic character such as Yellow Woman (see ROMANTICISM) or a mystical storyteller figure to contribute to the continuum.

Silko is the first Native American woman to publish a novel, the critically acclaimed *Ceremony* (1977). This understated novel features Tayo, a WORLD WAR II veteran returning to the reservation to come to terms with his inability to save his brother, who perished in the war. Her complex epic novel *Almanac of the Dead* (1991) chronicles the lives of several families in the years leading up to the fulfillment of an ancient Maya prophecy that foretold not only the Europeans' arrival in the Americas but also the eventual disappearance of all things European. Placed in the Southwest in the near future, the work is gritty in content and style. In contrast to Silko's other work, the characters of *Almanac* include embezzlers, members of pornography and drug rings, kidnappers, unscrupulous entrepreneurs, and drug addicts.

BIBLIOGRAPHY
Bataille, Gretchen M., and Kathleen Mullen Sands, eds. *American Indian Women Telling Their Lives.* Lincoln: University of Nebraska Press, 1984.
Owens, Louis. *Other Destinies: Understanding the American Indian Novel.* Norman: University of Oklahoma Press, 1992.
Seyersted, Per. *Leslie Marmon Silko.* Western Writers Series 45. Boise, Idaho: Boise State University Press, 1980.
Silko, Leslie Marmon. *Almanac of the Dead.* New York: Simon & Schuster, 1991.
———. *Ceremony.* New York: Viking, 1977.
———. *Laguna Woman.* Greenfield Center, N.J.: Greenfield Review Press, 1974.
———. *Storyteller.* New York: Seaver Books, 1981.

Calvin Hussman
St. Olaf College

SIMILE

A figure of speech that makes a direct comparison between two things, especially things not usually considered similar. A simile normally uses the words *like* or *as.*

SIMPLE STORIES LANGSTON HUGHES (1950–1965)

Based on Langston HUGHES's column for the *Chicago Defender* (1943–66), the so-called Simple Series consists of four collections of stories depicting the wittily written adventures of Jesse B. Semple. Hughes has commented that he was influenced by the stories of Mark TWAIN when he wrote this SHORT STORY CYCLE, and certainly the comic element in the Simple Stories helps take the sting out of some very significant lessons aimed at teaching whites about African American reality. (See COMEDY.) Through the Simple Stories, Hughes addresses such issues as race relations, civil rights, white liberalism, and JIM CROW laws. Susan L. Blake has called these stories "urban folktales" in the "John-and-Old-Marster cycle" (qtd. in Snyder 258) but, as Phillip A. Snyder points out, Hughes does not use "heavy-handed propaganda" in these tales (Snyder 258). Moreover, because the stories allowed Hughes to link the oral tradition of his plays and poetry, they helped assure him a place not only in the pantheon of American poets but in the roster of innovative short story writers as well.

BIBLIOGRAPHY

Hughes, Langston. *The Best of Simple.* New York: Hill & Wang, 1961.
———. *Simple Speaks His Mind.* New York: Simon & Schuster, 1950.
———. *Simple Stakes a Claim.* New York: Rinehart, 1957.
———. *Simple Takes a Wife.* New York: Simon & Schuster, 1953.
———. *Simple's Uncle Sam.* New York: Hill & Wang, 1965.
Ostrom, Hans. *Langston Hughes: A Study of the Short Fiction.* New York: Twayne, 1993.
Snyder, Phillip A. "Langston Hughes." In *Reference Guide to Short Fiction.* Edited by Noelle Watson. Detroit: Gale Press, 1994, 256–258.

SINGER, ISAAC BASHEVIS (1904–1991)

Isaac Bashevis Singer, who wrote his many novels and short stories in Yiddish, is credited with drawing attention to and demonstrating the vibrance of the old language. At age 31, he immigrated to the United States with his parents, both Polish Jews; he arrived in New York City during the GREAT DEPRESSION and began his writing career during World War II. Although he wrote in Yiddish, much of his work has been translated into English, and, because he supervised much of that process,

Singer considered himself a bilingual writer. From the late 1950s and 1960s, Singer published four notable short story collections: *Gimpel the Fool,* in 1957, *The Spinoza of Market Street,* in 1961, *Short Friday,* in 1964, and *The Seance,* in 1968. Remarkable for their consistent high quality, stories from these collections appear in anthologies with increasing frequency. Singer was awarded the Nobel Prize for literature in 1978, and *The Collected Stories* was published in 1982.

The most familiar are the title stories from their respective collections, "Gimpel the Fool" and "The Spinoza of Market Street." Like most of Singer's tales, they contain fully developed characters who, like Gimpel and "the Spinoza," typically live in Singer's fictionalized old European world (although characters in some of his stories appear in his newer American one). Singer tells their stories with simplicity, a non-didactic sense of morality (see DIDACTICISM), and a blending of reality with the stuff of myth, superstition, and supernatural beings. "Gimpel the Fool," translated by Saul BELLOW, first brought Singer to the attention of the English-speaking world. Through depicting Gimpel's refusal to divorce his wife, despite her infidelity, Singer reaffirms the pious if simple beliefs of religious Jews and, more generally, of all those who yearn for a spiritual dimension in their lives. Even though Gimpel knows that his wife and other villagers are deceiving him, he sees value in the very act of believing, of trusting in faith. In one sense, he seems the quintessential dupe of the community, the PERSONIFICATION of those who mindlessly cling to faith that cannot be proven. In the other, more likely sense, however, Gimpel may not be the fool at all, but the beneficiary of a sense of peace and goodness unknown to the other townspeople, who by comparison appear petty and superficial.

"The Spinoza of Market Street" may be viewed as a companion piece to "Gimpel the Fool" in its examination of fools and marriage. Set in Warsaw, where Dr. Fischelson has translated the rational philosopher Baruch Spinoza's *Ethics,* the story traces Dr. Fischelson's move from an adherence to all things intellectual and reasonable, as suggested by the

ALLUSIONS to Spinoza, and a rejection of all things emotional and romantic, as suggested by his disdain for Immanuel Kant's *A Critique of Pure Reason*. Dr. Fischelson meets his ANTITHESIS, Blacke Dobbe, an illiterate woman who, in the event, becomes the antidote to all that ails or befalls him. She even nurses him back to health when he is dying of starvation. Dr. Fischelson reads romantic poetry to her (see ROMANTICISM) and they marry, and, although he mentally apologizes to Spinoza for betraying him, the story illustrates the uniting of duality—masculine and feminine, reason and mysticism, the APOLLONIAN AND DIONYSIAC. Clearly, Singer uses this tale to critique the world of the intellectual who sits in his ivory tower, eschewing the emotions necessary to human balance and fulfillment.

The intermingling of fantasy and reality, or MAGICAL REALISM, is a hallmark of Singer's fiction, as in, for instance, "A Very Old Man With Enormous Wings," a story that chronicles the superstitious and self-serving townspeople's reactions to the surprise arrival of a winged man. The antithesis of a cherubic angel, this one, ragged and dirty, provokes the villagers to advocate clubbing, imprisoning, and isolating him; from their perspective, he metamorphoses from a pariah into a celebrity, then retreats into the boredom of the familiar. His meaning is open to interpretation: Does he symbolize the imagination? the writer? a messiah? a device for evoking human foibles? As he magically flies into the story in the beginning, he magically flies away at the end. A similar theme recurs in "The Gentleman from Cracow," a tale in which the disingenuous townspeople reject their rabbi in favor of the rich gentleman who comes to town: He reveals himself and his bride to be Lucifer and Lilith.

Although his themes are clearly significant, Singer's stories will continue to delight any reader who admires the art of storytelling. After a half-century in the United States, Singer's fascination with human complexities never flagged. His tales will continue to intrigue, to entertain, and, by subtlety and implication, to suggest ways to understand our place in the universe.

BIBLIOGRAPHY

Alexander, Edward. *Isaac Bashevis Singer.* Boston: Twayne, 1980.

———. *Singer: A Study of the Short Fiction.* New York: Twayne, 1990.

Allentuck, Marcia, ed. *The Achievement of Isaac Bashevis Singer.* Carbondale: Southern Illinois University Press, 1970.

Buchen, Irving H. *Isaac Bashevis Singer and the Eternal Past.* New York: New York University Press, 1968.

Friedman, Lawrence. *Understanding Singer.* Columbia: University of South Carolina Press, 1988.

Halio, Jay. "Isaac Bashevis Singer." In *Reader's Guide to Short Fiction.* Edited by Noelle Watson. Detroit: St. James Press, 1994, pp. 492–94.

Kresh, Paul. *Isaac Bashevis Singer: The Magician of West 86th Street.* New York: Dial, 1979.

Lee, Grace Farrell. *From Exile to Redemption: The Fiction of Singer.* Carbondale: Southern Illinois University Press, 1987.

Malin, Irving, ed. *Critical Views of Isaac Bashevis Singer.* New York: New York University Press, 1969.

———. *Isaac Bashevis Singer.* New York: Ungar, 1972.

Miller, David Neal. *Fear of Fiction: Narrative Strategies in the Works of Singer.* Albany: State University of New York Press, 1985.

Miller, David Neal, and E. J. Brill, eds. *Recovering the Canon: Essays on Singer.* Leiden: E. J. Brill, 1986.

Rosenblum, Joseph. "'The Spinoza of Market Street.'" In *Reader's Guide to Short Fiction.* Edited by Noelle Watson. Detroit: St. James Press, 1994, pp. 906–907.

Siegel, Ben. *Singer.* Minneapolis: University of Minnesota Press, 1969.

Sinclair, Clive. *The Brothers Singer.* London: Alison and Busby, 1983.

Singer, Isaac Bashevis. *The Certificate.* New York: Farrar, Straus & Giroux, 1992.

———. *Conversations with Isaac Bashevis Singer.* Edited by Richard Burgin. Garden City, N.Y.: Doubleday, 1985.

———. *Isaac Bashevis Singer Conversations.* Edited by Grace Farrell. Jackson: University Press of Mississippi, 1992.

———. *A Crown of Feathers and Other Stories.* New York: Farrar, Straus & Giroux, 1973.

———. *The Death of Methuselah and Other Stories.* New York: Farrar, Straus & Giroux, 1988.

———. *Enemies: A Love Story.* New York: Farrar, Straus & Giroux, 1972.

———. *The Estate.* New York: Farrar, Straus & Giroux, 1969.

———. *A Friend of Kafka and Other Stories*. New York: Farrar, Straus & Giroux, 1970.

———. *Gimpel the Fool and Other Stories*. New York: Noonday, 1957.

———. *The Image and Other Stories*. New York: Farrar, Straus & Giroux, 1985.

———. *In My Father's Court*. New York: Farrar, Straus & Giroux, 1966.

———. *The King of Fields*. New York: Farrar, Straus & Giroux, 1988.

———. *Love and Exile: The Early Years: A Memoir*. Garden City, N.Y.: Doubleday, 1984.

———. *A Little Boy in Search of God: Mysticism in a Personal Light*. Garden City, N.Y.: Doubleday, 1976.

———. *Lost in America*. Garden City, N.Y.: Doubleday, 1981.

———. *The Magician of Lublin*. New York: Noonday, 1960.

———. *The Manor*. New York: Farrar, Straus & Giroux, 1967.

———. *Nobel Lecture*. New York: Farrar, Straus & Giroux, 1979.

———. *Old Love*. New York: Farrar, Straus & Giroux, 1979.

———. *Passions and Other Stories*. New York: Farrar, Straus & Giroux, 1975.

———. *The Penitent*. New York: Farrar, Straus & Giroux, 1983.

———. *Reaches of Heaven*. New York: Farrar, Straus & Giroux, 1980.

———. *Scum*. New York: Farrar, Straus & Giroux, 1991.

———. *The Seance and Other Stories*. New York: Farrar, Straus & Giroux, 1968.

———. *Selected Short Stories*. Edited by Irving Howe. New York: Modern Library, 1966.

———. *Short Friday and Other Stories*. New York: Farrar, Straus & Giroux, 1964.

———. *Singer on Literature and Life: An Interview*. Edited by Paul Rosenblatt and Gene Koppel. Tuscon: University of Arizona Press, 1979.

———. *A Singer Reader*. New York: Farrar, Straus & Giroux, 1971.

———. *The Slave*. New York: Farrar, Straus & Cudahy, 1962.

———. *Shosha*. New York: Farrar, Straus & Giroux, 1978.

———. *The Spinoza of Market Street and Other Stories*. New York: Farrar, Straus & Giroux, 1961.

———. *A Young Man in Search of Love*. Garden City, N.Y.: Doubleday, 1978.

SKETCH   Originally used to refer to a sketch by an artist prior to the finished painting, the term now frequently refers to a literary product of simple proportions, a short presentation such as a CHARACTER sketch. It also can refer to the author's depiction of a single scene or incident lacking in plot or elaborate characterization.

"SKY IS GRAY, THE" ERNEST J. GAINES (1963)   This story that initially appeared in Ernest J. GAINES's collection entitled *Bloodlines* has become a classic contemporary BILDUNGSROMAN. Powerfully told with a convincing use of African-American DIALECT and dialogue, the story features nine-year-old James and the lessons he learns from his mother, Octavia, and others. James's absent father is serving the country that expects its African-American citizens to fight for freedom abroad (see WORLD WAR II) while it denies them those same freedoms at home. The story occurs on a cold winter day in Louisiana whose gray sky suggests the lack of hope for many African Americans.

Because James is suffering a toothache, symbolic of the festering wounds of racism, he and his mother takes the bus into Bayonne to see a dentist. As they ride in the back of the bus reserved for blacks and walk the streets of Bayonne, James, the first-person narrator (see POINT OF VIEW), acutely evokes his almost unbearable feelings of pain, cold, and hunger: Only his love and respect for his mother keep him from complaining. Theirs is an odyssey or journey that encompasses the major dilemmas blacks faced in this era—including a debate between a black preacher who embraces the Christian doctrine of suffering and acceptance, and an angry young black man who advocates questioning and action. James instinctively knows that he would like to imitate the young man rather than the old preacher.

James has an advantage over the young man, however: The young man has lost both his parents, but James has a mother who teaches him the qualities of manliness, courage, self-confidence, integrity, and self-respect. Never one to waste words, she knows how to protect herself: When a pimp tries to molest her, she throws him against a wall and threatens to stab him with the knife she carries. Mother and son's odyssey through the dangers and pitfalls of poverty and racism also includes encounters with two kinds of whites: the dentist's receptionist who delays their appointment and then locks them out in the cold, and a woman and her invalid husband who invite them into their store, offer them a hot meal (in exchange for work, at Octavia's proud insistence), and phone the dentist to make sure he takes care of James's "toothache." At the end of the story, although the sky is still gray, readers sense hope for James with the lessons he has learned from good people, black and white, but from no one more than his strong and principled mother.

BIBLIOGRAPHY

Gaines, Ernest J. "The Sky is Gray." In *American Short Stories*. 6th edition. Edited by Eugene Current-García and Bert Hitchcock. New York: Longman, 1997, pp. 511–30.

SMILEY, JANE (1949–)

Born in Los Angeles to a military father and writer mother, Jane Smiley holds a Ph.D. from the University of Iowa, is a two-time recipient of the National Endowment for the Arts Award, and currently is a professor of English at Iowa State University in Ames, where she lives with her husband and three children.

Her short stories have appeared in publications such as *Redbook, Atlantic, Mademoiselle, Triquarterly, Playgirl,* and the *New York Times Magazine,* and have earned Smiley three O. HENRY MEMORIAL AWARDS. Her NOVELLA, *The Age of Grief* (1987), was published under the same title as part of a collection of short stories, which was nominated for a National Book Critics Circle Award. This novella chronicles, from the husband's POINT OF VIEW, the dissolving of a marriage between dentists; the stories in the collection also address the ordinary, yet complex, lives of families. *Ordinary Love and Good Will: Two Novellas* (1989) is among Smiley's strongest, most intense work. These stories of families also address the difficulties of marriage and of maintaining family cohesion. A year later another piece of short fiction, *The Life of the Body* (1990), was published.

Smiley is most famous for her novel *A Thousand Acres* (1991), which was awarded the PULITZER PRIZE and the National Book Critics Circle Award in 1991

and was adapted for a 1997 feature film. This novel chronicles the demise of a midwestern family farm during the 1980s. Many reviewers, and Smiley herself, consider this novel to be a FEMINIST revision of the King Lear story set on a midwestern farm. Smiley also has written several other novels, including *Barn Blind* (1980), *The Greenlanders* (1988), *Moo* (1995), *The All-True Travels and Adventures of Lidie Newton* (1998), and a mystery novel, *Duplicate Keys* (1984), as well as nonfiction essays.

BIBLIOGRAPHY

Green, Michelle, and Barbara Kleban Mills. "Of Serpents' Teeth in Iowa." *People,* January 13, 1992.
Kakutani, Michiko. "Pleasures and Hazards of Familial Love." *New York Times,* October 31, 1989.
Smiley, Jane. *The Age of Grief.* New York: Knopf, 1987.
———. *Barn Blind.* New York: Harper & Row, 1980.
———. *Duplicate Keys.* New York: Knopf, 1984.
———. *The Greenlanders.* New York: Knopf, 1988.
———. *The Life of the Body.* New York: Knopf, 1990.
———. *Moo.* New York: Knopf, 1995.
———. *Ordinary Love and Good Will: Two Novellas.* New York: Knopf, 1989.
———. *A Thousand Acres.* New York: Knopf, 1991.

Anna Leahy
Ohio University

"SNAKE, THE" JOHN STEINBECK (1951)

In the 1951 essay "About Ed Ricketts," published as part of *The Log from the Sea of Cortez,* John STEINBECK records his recollection of the composition of his short story, "The Snake," and identifies the occurrence as an actual event that happened one night in his friend Ricketts's biological laboratory. Using his well-known nonteleological approach (recording only what happened without speculating on causes or effects), Steinbeck claims to have retold the story just as it happened. However, eye-witness accounts from several of Steinbeck's friends suggest that the so-called facts of the event are questionable at best and surely were transformed to some extent by the author.

What is not questionable is the almost universal reaction to the story as disturbing. According to Steinbeck biographer Jackson J. Benson, the author's literary agent, Elizabeth Otis, returned the story to him as "outrageous," and Benson himself suggests that the story was so bizarre that Steinbeck could not get it published except in a local newspaper. (It appeared in the *Monterey Beacon* in June 1935 before its publication in 1938 in *The Long Valley*.) As for the author's personal reaction, Steinbeck described the event as one of those frequent mysteries that occurred at Ricketts's lab and said, "What happened or why I have no idea."

It is one of the few stories in which Steinbeck concentrates on a single time, place, and action. Quite simply, the story recounts in spare, lean language an event in the fictional Dr. Phillips's lab where the scientist, in the midst of several experiments, is suddenly interrupted by the appearance of a dark woman. Initially uninterested in Phillips's experiments, the woman seems to be in a hypnotized state, but she eventually reveals her major interest (or what critic Robert Hughes labels a primordial desire) to watch the feeding of a male rattlesnake. Surprisingly, Dr. Phillips complies with her request, although he recognizes that the snake does not need to be fed. He places a white rat in the feeding cage and observes in very specific detail the snake's stalking of its prey. Meanwhile he is also observing the woman's reactions to the snake. The narrator carefully describes Phillips's changing emotions as this event occurs, feelings ranging from anger to sexual excitement to nervousness and fear. Eventually the snake kills the rat and swallows it whole, a motion that Phillips sees mirrored in the dark woman's movements. Then, just as mysteriously as she appeared, the women departs, leaving Phillips to contemplate the events he has just witnessed. Discovering that his initial starfish experiment has been ruined by his preoccupation with the woman, Phillips reflects on his own life, contemplating whether his loneliness and his apparent lack of religious beliefs have influenced his reactions to this bizarre occurrence. The story then ends abruptly in echoes of Nathaniel HAWTHORNE: The PROTAGONIST is deeply troubled and disturbed, but the story offers no solution to the mystery. The woman is never seen again, but Phillips's uneasiness persists.

Readings of "The Snake" have emphasized biblical parallels (woman as temptress, snake, devil; Phillips as Adamic figure in charge of animals) (see ALLUSION), FREUDIAN sexual overtones (Steinbeck's use of phallic and vaginal images as well as diction implying coital excitement and female domination), and Jungian suggestions that the woman represents the dark anima (instinctual and unconscious forces) of Phillips's personality, which he partially realizes but refuses to embrace. Critics have noted Steinbeck's fascination with human animalistic actions as well as his tendency to look at the interaction of science and nature, a trait heightened by his interest in marine biology. A key phrase is Phillips's statement that "It's the most beautiful thing in the world. . . . [and] it's the most terrible thing in the world," a comment that suggests not only Steinbeck's interest in Jung (no doubt influenced by his interaction with renowned mythologist Joseph Campbell) but also his fascination with Eastern thought, especially the Taoist principles of yin and yang, which suggest that even polar opposites are integrally interrelated. By portraying the Ricketts/Phillips character as both dispassionate observer and sensitive human being, Steinbeck maintains his nonteleological approach: Instead of attempting to give a specific meaning to the story, he suggests that readers must find their own truths in the veiled human actions the story reveals. Undoubtedly the story of the snake rattles its readers and, as with Phillips, disturbs them for a long time to come; it presents a scientific anomaly difficult if not impossible to solve.

BIBLIOGRAPHY
Steinbeck, John. "The Snake." In *The Long Valley*. New York: Viking, 1938.

Michael J. Meyer
DePaul University

SNOPES FAMILY   One of the numerous families William FAULKNER created for the mythical YOKNAPATAWPHA County in which most of his stories and novels take place. The Snopes clan is unique in that, unlike Faulkner's more aristocratic Southern families—the Compsons, the Sartorises, the Griersons—most Snopeses are clearly described as poor white trash and worse: sneaks, snakes, snoops, and other low classes of varmint. GAVIN STEVENS, one of Faulkner's major narrators in both his stories and novels, understands the phenomenon of Snopesism: they gradually and successfully move from Frenchman's Bend, their place of origin, into the genteel antebellum town of Jefferson, the Yoknapatawpha County seat, where they take over the town by acquiring businesses, land, positions in government, and, finally, the presidency of the bank. Together with his friend V. K. Ratliff, Gavin studies, is alternately amused and appalled by, and wages a losing battle against the onslaught of Snopesism.

Commonly seen as a METAPHOR for the loss of values occurring all over the United States, the Snopes family first appears in the character of ABNER SNOPES in the Civil War stories of THE UNVANQUISHED, and continues to proliferate in the Snopes Trilogy (*The Hamlet,* 1940; *The Town,* 1957; *The Mansion,* 1959) through World War I into the post–World War II era. Snopeses are nearly all odious in one way or another, appearing as murderers, cheats, perverts, and pornographers, with such names as Admiral Dewey, Montgomery Ward, Ike, Eck, and Flem, who is the worst Snopes of all, the incarnation of evil, a man utterly lacking in human compassion. Two significant facts help bring down Flem, the very emblem of Snopesism. First, according to Ratliff and Stevens, Snopeses can be only male, never female. Second, when the rare "good" Snopes appears (Eck, for instance), the narrators strongly suggest that he must be the product of the mother's secret union with a non-Snopes. It is logical, then, that Flem's stepdaughter, Linda Snopes, a woman who is not really a Snopes at all, becomes the instrument of Flem's murder.

"SNOWS OF KILIMANJARO, THE"
ERNEST HEMINGWAY (1936) "The Snows of Kilimanjaro" was first published in *ESQUIRE* in August 1936 and is one of HEMINGWAY's most frequently anthologized short stories. It opens with the PROTAGONIST, Harry, a washed-up writer who has come to Africa with his wife, Helen, to start over as an artist. But his intended regeneration is destroyed by his neglect and carelessness in tending to an accidental scratch, which is symbolically parallel to the way he destroyed his talent in the first place. While gangrene eats away at him, Harry takes stock of his life, remembers his past and the neglect of his craft, and bemoans the stories he will never write. He quarrels with Helen, the wealthy wife who tries to comfort and care for him. Although he blames her money for providing the luxury and comfort that have caused him to go soft and neglect his writing, he knows that he is really the one to blame. She is only a convenient scapegoat for his failure; her story as he recounts it portrays her as blameless, in fact praiseworthy, for she has survived personal tragedy and put together a new life. Harry, on the other hand, has destroyed his talent through overindulgence, sloth, and laziness.

In 1952 the story was made into a movie starring Gregory Peck and Susan Hayward. The filmscript was even more autobiographical than Hemingway's story, and it changes the ending so that Harry does not die. Hemingway claims the movie was only one-third the story he had written.

There are many autobiographical ALLUSIONS in "Snows." When writing the story, Hemingway felt anxious about the slowing of his writing productivity. He was also struggling with ambivalent feelings about his involvement with wealthy sportsmen and a socialite crowd that his wife Pauline's money and his fame had brought him. A recent African safari had been paid for by his wife's uncle, and Hemingway had turned down a wealthy woman's offer to finance another trip. He said that the story grew out of his starting "to think what would happen to a character like me whose defects I know, if I had accepted that offer. . . ."

Harry's memories are fragments, vignettes, or sketches. They are the raw material for stories but unstructured or shaped. In them he recalls the other women in his life and the way he had quarreled with them too. Mount Kilimanjaro looms as a symbol of an ascent Harry does not attempt. Harry increasingly associates death with carrion-feeding creatures, the vultures and hyenas that circle the camp. He pictures death as a hyena whose foul breath he smells, who rests its snout upon his bed and finally crouches with its full weight upon his chest. In his death dream, the rescue plane arrives and he flies in it over the snowy top of Kilimanjaro. The story ends with the hyena's strange noises awakening Helen to the horror of Harry's inert form.

BIBLIOGRAPHY

Elia, Richard L. "Three Symbols in Hemingway's 'The Snows of Kilimanjaro.'" *Revue des Langues Vivantes* (1975): 282–285.

Evans, Oliver. "'The Snows of Kilimanjaro': A Revaluation." *PMLA* 76 (September–December 1961): 601–607.

Flora, Joseph M. *Ernest Hemingway: A Study of the Short Fiction,* Boston: Twayne, 1989, 81–88.

Johnston, Kenneth G. *The Tip of the Iceberg: Hemingway and the Short Story.* Greenwood, Fla.: Penkevill Publishing Company, 1987, 195–204.

Lewis, Robert W., Jr., and Max Westbrook. "'The Snows of Kilimanjaro' Collated and Annotated," *Texas Quarterly* 13:2 (1970): 67–143.

MacDonald, Scott. "Hemingway's 'The Snows of Kilimanjaro': Three Critical Problems." *Studies in Short Fiction* (1974): 67–74.

Santangelo, Gennaro. "The Dark Snows of Kilimanjaro." In *The Short Stories of Ernest Hemingway: Critical Essays.* Edited by Jackson J. Benson. Durham, N.C.: Duke University Press, 1975, 251–261.

Mimi Riesel Gladstein
University of Texas at El Paso

"SOLDIER'S HOME" ERNEST HEMINGWAY (1925)

Originally published in the *Contact Collection of Contemporary Writers* in 1925, then reprinted in *In Our Time* that same year, "Soldier's Home" is a CLASSIC early HEMINGWAY story for at least three reasons. First, the author powerfully evokes the post–WORLD WAR I malaise experienced by so many returning American veterans—and even by their peers who saw no combat—and portrayed by so many of Hemingway's literary contemporaries, T. S. Eliot in *The Waste Land,* or Sherwood ANDERSON in *WINESBURG, OHIO,* for instance. This sense of malaise is notably conveyed, too, in Hemingway's

NICK ADAMS stories. Second, it demonstrates Hemingway's conscious attention to his craft—a craft influenced by Gertrude STEIN during his Paris years—in terms of economical, tightly knit sentences. Third, Hemingway is clearly utilizing his "iceberg" technique in this story: Very little of Harold Krebs's feelings and motivations appear clearly above the surface of the text; instead they remain submerged for the reader to fathom. Moreover, for those interested in biography, this story, like the majority of Hemingway's war fiction, follows the author's experiences in intriguing ways.

The ironic title does clearly imply, however, that Harold's wartime experiences lie murkily at the bottom of his inability to relate to his old home in Oklahoma, where he has returned later than other soldiers and had thus been deprived of the heroes' welcome they enjoyed; the town has now grown somewhat bored with and cynical about the war. Harold is caught between not wishing to speak about his presumably horrific experiences—he has fought in five of the bloodiest battles of the war—and then wishing that he could find someone willing to listen and understand. He feels alienated from both the town and his parents, thinking to himself that he had felt more "at home" in Germany or France than he does now in his parents' house.

Harold's attitude toward women is another element in this story that was to become characteristic of Hemingway fiction and to engender much debate. Harold's years as a U.S. Marine taught him that for much of the time he does not need women, and that when he feels a sexual urge, a woman will always be available. Now, at home, he characterizes himself as an observer of women, one who can appreciate their beauty but who lacks the energy or desire to engage in the conventional courtship rituals. Harold also expresses animosity toward both his parents, but especially his mother, whom the narrator portrays as the arbiter of the religious and middle-class values that suffocate him. At the end of the story, Harold vows to leave home for Kansas City just as Hemingway did. In the meantime, he goes to watch his sister Helen, who adores him, in her game of indoor baseball. He knows that Helen, unlike his mother and the townspeople, will not make statements that force him to tell lies.

BIBLIOGRAPHY

Baker, Carlos. *Ernest Hemingway: A Life Story.* New York: Scribner's, 1969.

Beegel, Susan. *Hemingway's Neglected Short Fiction.* Ann Arbor: UMI Research Press, 1989.

Benson, Jackson J. *The Short Stories of Ernest Hemingway.* Durham, N.C.: Duke University Press, 1975.

Hemingway, Ernest. *In Our Time.* New York: Scribner's, 1925.

———. *The First Forty-Nine Stories.* New York: Scribner's, 1938.

———. "Soldier's Home." *The Complete Short Stories of Ernest Hemingway: The Finca Vigía Edition.* New York: Scribner's, 1987, pp. 111–16.

Smith, Paul. *New Essays on Hemingway's Short Fiction.* New York: Cambridge University Press, 1998.

"SOLO ON THE DRUMS" ANN PETRY
(1947) First published in *The Magazine of the Year 1947* and included in *Miss Muriel and Other Stories,* "Solo on the Drums" reflects Ann PETRY's interests in African American music and in stories of unfaithful wives, both of which appear frequently in her fiction. Unlike most of Petry's PROTAGONISTs, the jazz drummer Kid Jones has a ready outlet for the rage he feels when his wife leaves him for his band's pianist: artistic expression. Like Sonny in James BALDWIN's story *Sonny's Blues,* Kid uses his drum to speak the "story of my love . . . the story of my hate," channeling those emotions into a virtuoso performance (241).

BIBLIOGRAPHY

Andrews, William L., et al. *The Oxford Companion to African-American Literature.* New York: Oxford University Press, 1997.

Ervin, Hazel Arnett. *Ann Petry: A Bio-Bibliography.* New York: G.K. Hall, 1993.

Holladay, Hilary. *Ann Petry.* New York: Twayne, 1996.

Petry, Ann. "Solo on the Drums." In *Miss Muriel and Other Stories.* Boston: Houghton Mifflin, 1971.

Washington, Gladys J. "A World Made Cunningly: A Closer Look at Ann Petry's Short Fiction." *College Language Association Journal* 30:1 (September 1986): 14–29.

Kimberly Drake
Virginia Wesleyan College

SPANISH-AMERICAN WAR (1898)
Americans generally supported demands by Cuban patriots for independence from Spain, but after an explosion sank the battleship USS *Maine* in Havana harbor on February 15, 1898, passions were inflamed by the biased and sensational reporting by the "yellow press" in the United States. This and other factors, including heavy losses sustained by U.S. investors due to guerrilla warfare and the strategic location of Cuba to the proposed site of the Panama Canal, caused the U.S. to demand Spanish withdrawal from Cuba. On April 24, 1898, Spain responded with a declaration of war on the U.S. Within a week, and with "Remember the Maine" as the battle cry, the U.S. Navy destroyed Spain's Pacific Fleet at Manila harbor in the Philippines and a month later destroyed Spain's Cuban Fleet at Santiago, Cuba. On July 3 Theodore Roosevelt led his Rough Riders to victory at San Juan Hill, and Santiago fell on July 17, effectively ending the war. This war, although brief, had major consequences: Cuba gained its independence, Spain lost most of its empire, Theodore Roosevelt returned a war hero to be elected vice-president in 1900 (becoming president in 1901 upon William McKinley's assassination), and the United States became an imperial power with the acquisition of Puerto Rico, Guam, and the Philippines.

SPARK, THE EDITH WHARTON (1924)
One of Edith WHARTON's many stories of New York, *The Spark* was published with the subtitle *The 'Sixties* as the third of four volumes in a boxed set, *Old New York,* in 1924. This NOVELLA is the story of Hayley Delane, a member of the Old New York aristocracy that Wharton depicts with great REALISM. Married to an unfaithful, irresponsible wife whose improprieties he gracefully ignores, he fascinates the narrator, a younger man, to whom Delane seems a "finished monument" and a "venerable institution" like the Knickerbocker Club (449–50). The narrator learns that, long ago, Delane ran away from school

as a volunteer to serve in the CIVIL WAR, thus increasing the narrator's respect and desire to know him further. The narrator takes a job in the bank at which Delane is a partner, and a "filial" sentiment grows between the men (465).

One day Delane tells the narrator that after being wounded at the battle of Bull Run, he was tended to in the hospital by a rough but warm-hearted "big backwoodsman" named Walt Whitman (473). Delane confesses that "I don't think he believed in our Lord. Yet he taught me Christian charity," noting how the man seems to appear before him "at long intervals" to tell him "the right and wrong of it" when Delane is trying to make a decision (477). This moral center to Delane's life, in contrast to his wife Leila's lack of integrity, becomes even more apparent when she leaves him for another man. Delane patiently nurses her father in a final illness and even takes Leila back when she returns just in time for the funeral.

Time passes and the narrator feels that the "central puzzle" of Delane's life has "subsisted" (484). One day he finds Delane in his apartment. The older man has recognized Whitman's portrait on a volume of the poet's work. The narrator excitedly reads to him from Whitman's poetry on war, but Delane is incredulous at its free-verse form. In a response that illustrates Wharton's prevalent irony, Delane concludes, "'I'll never forget him—I rather wish, though . . . you hadn't told me that he wrote all that rubbish'" (488).

R. W. B. Lewis notes that in this tale "Wharton was combining the war-infested atmosphere of her infancy and her lifelong affection for Whitman with her own Whitmanesque attentions to the homeless, the wounded, and the tubercular in the more recent war" (458).

BIBLIOGRAPHY
Lewis, R. W. B. *Edith Wharton: A Biography.* New York: Harper & Row, 1975.

Rae, Catherine M. *Edith Wharton's New York Quartet.* Lanham, Md.: University Press of America, 1984.

Richards, Mary Margaret. "Feminized Men in Wharton's *Old New York.*" *Edith Wharton Newsletter* 3.2 (1986): 2.

Wharton, Edith. *The Spark (The 'Sixties).* In *Wharton: Novellas and Other Writings.* New York: Literary Classics of the United States, 1990.

Charlotte Rich
University of Georgia, Athens

SPENCER, ELIZABETH (1921–)

Elizabeth Spencer was born in Carrollton, Mississippi, not far from the homes of Mississippi writers William FAULKNER and Eudora WELTY. Spencer grew up in a large, middle-class Southern family, the members of which often read and discussed literature. Her family's love of books laid the groundwork for her first attempts at writing as a child. Spencer decided very early to become a writer and at age 27 published her first novel, *Fire in the Morning* (1948), thanks partly to the encouragement and help of Donald Davidson, member of the Nashville AGRARIAN movement and Spencer's professor at Vanderbilt University, where she received her master's degree. Although writing after the Southern Renaissance, which scholars generally agree ended around 1950, Spencer, along with Ellen Douglas, Shirley Ann Grau, and Doris BETTS, helps to form a connection between the Southern Renaissance writers and such younger Southern writers as Alice WALKER, Kaye Gibbons, Ellen Gilchrist, Josephine Humphries, Lee Smith, and Sherley Anne Williams (Scura 831).

Spencer has published eight novels, two NOVELLAS, and six collections of short stories. Much of her early work was set in her native Mississippi, and, like much of Faulkner's work, portrayed both the aristocratic plantation as well as poor white classes, racial conflicts, and CIVIL WAR and RECONSTRUCTION times. In 1953 she broadened her experiences by moving to Italy on a GUGGENHEIM GRANT. While there she finished her third novel, *The Voice at the Black Door* (1956)—which deals with race relations in Mississippi—and met her future husband, John Rusher. The couple moved to Canada, where Spencer continued to write, using the experiences she had gained in Europe as part of her work. In 1960 she published her first piece set in Italy, the novella *The Light in the Piazza,* which was later made into a film. Since then Spencer's stories and novels have ranged from Europe to Washington, D.C., Florida, and back to Mississippi.

In 1981 her collection *The Stories of Elizabeth Spencer* appeared. Most of her earlier stories are assembled here, including "Ship Island: The Story of a Mermaid," Spencer's favorite piece and one of her most frequently anthologized. Set on the Mississippi Gulf Coast, the story depicts a young woman's emotional isolation and her attempts to escape the expectations of friends and family who do not truly know her. Her later works often deal with young women torn between their need to define themselves as individuals and their love and loyalty to family or friends.

Her most recent achievements include *The Salt Line* (1984), *Jack of Diamonds and Other Stories* (1988), and *The Night Travellers* (1991). Spencer has many literary awards to her credit, including the American Academy of Arts and Letters First Rosenthal Award (1957), the Academy's Award of Merit Medal for the Short Story (1983), election to the American Academy of Arts and Letters (1984), and the John Dos Passos Award for Literature (1992).

BIBLIOGRAPHY

Prenshaw, Peggy Whitman. *Conversations with Elizabeth Spencer.* Jackson: University Press of Mississippi, 1991.

———. *Elizabeth Spencer.* Boston: Twayne, 1985.

Roberts, Terry. *Self and Community in the Fiction of Elizabeth Spencer.* Baton Rouge: Louisiana State University Press.

Scura, Dorothy M. "Elizabeth Spencer." In *The Oxford Companion to Women's Writing in the United States.* Edited by Cathy N. Davidson and Linda Wagner Martin. New York: Viking Penguin, 1995.

Spencer, Elizabeth. *Jack of Diamonds: And Other Stories.* New York: Viking Penguin, 1989.

———. *The Light in the Piazza and Other Italian Tales.* Jackson, Miss.: Banner Books, 1996.

———. *Marilee.* Jackson: University Press of Mississippi, 1981.

———. *Ship Island and Other Stories.* New York: McGraw-Hill, 1968.

———. *The Stories of Elizabeth Spencer.* Foreword by Eudora Welty. Garden City, N.Y.: Doubleday, 1981. New York: Contemporary American Fiction, 1990.

———. *The Voice at the Back Door (Voices of the South).* Reprint. Baton Rouge: Louisiana State University Press, 1994.

Betina I. Entzminger
University of North Carolina, Chapel Hill

SPOFFORD, HARRIET PRESCOTT (1835–1921)

Born in Calais, Maine, into a distinguished New England family that had suffered financially, Harriet Prescott Spofford's career was spurred by economic hardship. In 1849 she went to live with relatives in Newburyport, Massachusetts, where Thomas Wentworth Higginson encouraged her talent and where she would later live with her husband, Richard Spofford. Throughout the 1850s she often spent 15 hours a day writing anonymous stories for the Boston story-papers that published serialized stories. In 1858 she submitted "In a Cellar" to the ATLANTIC MONTHLY. The story's cosmopolitan tone and original depiction of the amoral underside of Parisian society baffled the editors, who doubted that a demure young woman could have written it. Higginson authenticated the tale, and the publication of "In a Cellar" (1859) and "The Amber Gods" (1860) made Spofford a celebrity.

Spofford published poetry, novels, children's stories, articles on the home, and literary criticism during her 60-year career, but her genius lay with the short story. Attracted to the psychological AMBIGUITY and darkness of symbolic romance (see ROMANTICISM), she transformed what had been a primarily masculine genre, endowing it with her FEMINIST perspective. Spofford's tales also influenced the detective story and supernatural tales. Her attempt to satisfy the developing taste for REALISM, however, made it difficult for her to maintain her creative powers. Her first story collection, *The Amber Gods and Other Stories* (1863), demonstrates her vacillation between romance and realism—from "CIRCUMSTANCE," a nightmarish exploration of the power and powerlessness of women, to "Knitting Sale-Socks," which captures the DIALECT and economic realities of rural New England. Spofford wrote primarily for the *Atlantic Monthly* and HARPER'S and published two more collections, *Old Madame and Other Tragedies* (1900) and *A Scarlet Poppy and Other Stories* (1894).

She enjoyed close friendships with other Boston-area women writers, including Sarah Orne JEWETT, Rose Terry Cooke, and Alice Brown.

BIBLIOGRAPHY

Bendixen, Alfred. "Introduction." *Harriet Prescott Spofford's The Amber Gods and Other Stories.* New Brunswick, N.J.: Rutgers University Press, 1989, ix–xxxiv.

Halbeisen, Elizabeth K. *Harriet Prescott Spofford: A Romantic Survival,* Philadelphia: University of Pennsylvania Press, 1935.

Spofford, Harriet Prescott. *The Amber Gods and Other Stories.* New Brunswick, N.J.: Rutgers University Press, 1989.

Paula Kot
Niagara University

ST. NICHOLAS

ST. NICHOLAS A product of Scribner and Company, publisher of the well-known and highly regarded *Scribner's Monthly* (and later the Century Co., publisher of the *Century* magazine), *St. Nicholas* quickly came to be the best known of 19th-century juvenile periodicals in the United States. It first appeared in November 1873, under the editorship of Mabel Mapes Dodge, author of *Hans Brinker; or the Silver Skates* (1865). She asserted that the ideal juvenile magazine must be natural and entertaining and unabashedly didactic, suggesting that "a great deal of instruction and good moral teaching may be inculcated in the pages." The content of *St. Nicholas* paralleled its parent magazine; indeed, some of the same authors and illustrators appeared in both, and did not use overt juvenile attitudes or vocabulary. Its contributors included Louisa May ALCOTT, Mark TWAIN, Rudyard Kipling, Howard Pyle (who founded the Brownies), and others.

Published in order to prepare young readers for "life as it is," *St. Nicholas* clearly was directed to a well-educated, well-established section of upper-middle-class American society and presented the traditional values of this select population. Fiction was entertaining, instructive, and conveyed ideals and standards that would be useful models around which to organize their young lives. Respect for duty, open mindedness, honesty, thrift, industriousness, and self-reliance were the consistent THEMES in the fiction and essays.

Much of *St. Nicholas's* popularity was due to its deliberate effort to involve readers and to solicit their early creative products. "The Puzzle Box," "The Young Contributor's Department," and the "St. Nicholas League" were only three such departments established to attract children's attention and to encourage their imaginations. The "St. Nicholas League," for example, awarded ribbons and certificates to children and even published their works, including early efforts by Ring LARDNER, Robert Benchley, and William FAULKNER. Ernest HEMINGWAY's youthful protagonist alludes to the magazine in the story entitled "The Last Good Country." The magazine folded in 1940. Selections from it were published in *The St. Nicholas Anthology* in 1948 and 1950.

Laura L. Behling
Macalester College

STAFFORD, JEAN (1915–1979)

STAFFORD, JEAN (1915–1979) Born in Covina, California, Jean Stafford was reared in Boulder, Colorado. She received a B.A. and an M.A. from the University of Colorado, then left the United States to study in Heidelburg, Germany, and thereafter lived in Baton Rouge, Boston, New York, London, and Paris. The author of three novels and more than 40 short stories, she was among the best short story writers of her era, winning a PULITZER PRIZE for her *Collected Stories,* published in 1969. After publishing her first *NEW YORKER* story, "CHILDREN ARE BORED ON SUNDAY," Stafford published 21 more in that magazine and became identified with the so-called typical *New Yorker* story. Working for the *Southern Review* and later for the *New Yorker,* she took her writing seriously. Like other women writers of her generation, Stafford eschewed the label "woman writer," yet the large THEME running through all her stories is a carefully crafted and ironic sense of loss, bleakness and alienation, and a demythologizing of the female experience through her young women PROTAGONISTS.

One of most widely acclaimed stories is "A Country Love Story." Clearly autobiographical to some degree, the tale focuses on the crumbling relationship between May, the younger wife, and Daniel, her older, failing poet-professor husband. They move to a country farmhouse surrounded by a wintry landscape and punctuated by an antique sleigh that sits in the yard. In her dreary boredom, the young wife's eye keeps returning to the sleigh. Accused by her husband of madness and infidelity, she suddenly sees a ghostly lover in the sleigh; as she watches, however, the lover's face metamorphoses into an old invalid like Daniel. The story ends with Daniel's begging her forgiveness and May resigned to the bleakness of her life.

The third-person narrator focuses on May's thoughts, and as winter arrives and she and Daniel become increasingly estranged, the unmistakable and carefully crafted language of sexual imagery reveals her rebellion from Daniel and her longing for the imaginary lover she creates in the sleigh. The bleak ending, in which she sees even the lover turning into an aging invalid, focuses on May's quiet desperation as she wonders how she will survive her fate.

Nearly 30 years later Stafford returned to this theme in "An Influx of Poets," called by Mary Ann Wilson a "companion piece" to "A Country Love Story" (Wilson 24). In this story the first-person narrator is Cora Maybank, this time herself a portrait of the artist, and she reflects on the marriage, the worries about mental instability, the retreat to the country and into an unsatisfying domestic existence. Cora is a much more self-aware protagonist and is much less temperate in her view of the poet-husband and his colleagues. As revealed in "The End of a Career," the final story in Stafford's *Collected Stories,* the balancing of conflicting roles as a woman occupied Stafford throughout her own life and career.

Stafford was married to poet Robert Lowell, Oliver Jensen, and journalist A. J. Liebling. During her marriage to Lowell, as numerous critics have pointed out, she lived under the shadow of the great modernists (see MODERNISM) but was also intimately involved in the philosophy of the New Critics (see NEW CRITICISM). From the tensions of these surroundings, added to her position as a woman of

extraordinary talent, sprang a remarkable body of short fiction that is the focus of revived interest in the 1990s.

BIBLIOGRAPHY

Goodman, Charlotte Margolis. *Stafford: The Savage Heart.* Austin: University of Texas Press, 1990.

Hurlburt, Ann. *The Interior Castle: The Art and Life of Stafford.* Amherst: University of Massachusetts Press, 1992.

Roberts, David. *Stafford: A Biography.* Boston: Little, Brown, 1988.

Ryan, Maureen. *Innocence and Estrangement in the Fiction of Stafford.* Baton Rouge: Louisiana State University, 1987.

Stafford, Jean. *Bad Characters.* New York: Farrar, Straus & Giroux, 1964.

———. *Boston Adventure.* New York: Harcourt Brace, 1944.

———. *The Catherine Wheel.* New York: Harcourt Brace, 1952.

———. *Children Are Bored on Sunday.* New York: Harcourt Brace, 1953.

———. *The Collected Stories.* New York: Farrar, Straus & Giroux, 1969.

———. *The Interior Castle.* New York: Harcourt Brace, 1953.

———. *The Mountain Lion.* New York: Harcourt Brace, 1947.

———. *New Short Novels.* Edited by Mary Louise Aswell. New York: Ballantine, 1954.

Walsh, Mary Ellen Williams. *Stafford.* Boston: Twayne, 1985.

Wilson, Mary Ann. *Jean Stafford: A Study of the Short Fiction.* New York: Twayne, 1996.

STEIN, GERTRUDE (1874–1946)

Born in Allegheny, Pennsylvania, the youngest child of an Austrian Jewish family, Gertrude spent her childhood in Vienna and Paris and then in Baltimore, Maryland, and Oakland, California. After the death of her mother, she dropped out of secondary school; after her father's death, she and two of her siblings returned to her mother's family in Baltimore. She then graduated magna cum laude in philosophy (psychology) from Radcliffe College, where she was a favorite of William James.

Her career in the Johns Hopkins University Medical School was less stellar, and in 1903, without taking the M.D. degree, she moved to Paris to live with her brother Leo. With one foot in the world of art collecting and the other in the world of letters, Gertrude drew from her knowledge of the brain and of human perception to carve out works of the linguistic "new" or modernist ways of writing that paralleled, in many cases, the aesthetic directions of her painter friends Henri Matisse, Pablo Picasso, Georges Braque, and Juan Gris. (See AESTHETICISM.)

Because of her innovative prose style, deciding which of her works is a short story is difficult. Her disdain for genre led her to create a number of pieces that, in terms of length and structure, might be so classified. The three portraits that appeared as *Three Lives* in 1909—"THE GOOD ANNA," "Melanctha," and "The Gentle Lena"—are definitely short fiction, but as they challenge their readers by withholding the source of sympathy, even these works are puzzling. How is the reader to feel about the German women who are relatively powerless in U.S. society? And the black Melanctha, sexually experienced but, like the white women, drawn to lesbian love rather than the heterosexual liaisons that usurp much of the narrative, is equally enigmatic. (See LESBIAN THEMES IN SHORT STORIES.) Stein's creation of an idiosyncratic language for each of her women PROTAGONISTS was influential among such American writers as Sherwood ANDERSON, Ernest HEMINGWAY, and Richard WRIGHT.

Readers saw Stein's fiction about these women characters as both radically new and unpleasantly realistic. (See REALISM.) As she moved into less readable work, much of it called "portraits," she became identified with the AVANT GARDE of the painters who displayed their works at the 1911 New York Armory Show; and although she continued to live in Paris, her reputation in the United States grew. Her prose and prose poem structures such as "Matisse" and "Picasso," which appeared in Alfred Steiglitz's magazine *Camera Work* in 1912, became her trademark. The great variety of her portraits—from *Two* and "Ada" through "Publishers, The Portrait Gallery and the Manuscripts at the British Museum" to the long portrait essays of Henry JAMES and George Washington in *Four in America*—showed how versatile she could be in creating effective yet new prose forms.

Although Stein had begun writing in 1904, she was seldom published. She never stopped writing, however, and after the 1925 publication, in Paris, of her *The Making of Americans* (a very long novel), she had authority among writers who visited Paris. During the 1920s her salon (which she presided over with her partner, Alice B. Toklas) became as famous among writers as the Stein salons early in the century had been among artists. Known for her pronouncements about how writing is written, she generously gave younger writers the benefit of her wit, her guidance, and her understanding of the highly subjective nature of art.

With the publication of her ironic memoir, *The Autobiography of Alice B. Toklas*, in 1933, Gertrude Stein became famous. For the first time, she made money. The success of the biography that posed as autobiography, a series of vignettes of Stein's and Toklas's lives in Paris through WORLD WAR I and the 1920s, led to the two touring the United States during 1934 and 1935. For those speaking engagements, Stein wrote the six lectures (published as *Lectures in America*) that captivated, as well as puzzled, her audiences; she also taught for several weeks at the University of Chicago, and there became a lifelong friend of Thornton Wilder.

It is easy to see the skillful use of narrative, expressed in a characteristically ironic voice, throughout *The Autobiography*, and Stein continued to rely on the shorter fictional form in her later memoirs, *Everybody's Autobiography* (1937) and *Wars I Have Seen* (1945). Her use of the polished episode that may or may not be intrinsically connected with her larger construction appears as well in her later novels, *Mrs. Reynolds* (1940), *Ida* (1941), and *Brewsie and Willie* (1945).

Placing the grid of genre division over Stein's work limits the reader from seeing the ways in which her many poems, plays—the brief as well as such long pieces as *Four Saints in Three Acts* and *The Mother of Us All*—and philosophical treatises (*How to Write, The Geographical History of America or the Relation of Human Nature to the Human Mind, Paris France*) relate to her fiction, both short and long. All Stein's writing draws from her immense conviction that her mind was interesting and that, if she allowed her unrepressed voice to narrate or to meditate, readers would respond to the truth of that expression. As the wealth of criticism that exists today suggests, we are only now beginning to approach understanding Gertrude Stein's work.

BIBLIOGRAPHY

Benstock, Shari. *Women of the Left Bank: Paris, 1900–1940.* Austin: University of Texas Press, 1986.

Bridgman, Richard. *Gertrude Stein in Pieces.* New York: Oxford University Press, 1970.

DeKoven, Marianne. *A Different Language: Gertrude Stein's Experimental Writing.* Madison: University of Wisconsin Press, 1983.

Gallup, Donald, ed. *The Flowers of Friendship: Letters Written to Gertrude Stein.* New York: Knopf, 1953.

Grahn, Judy. *Really Reading Gertrude Stein: A Selected Anthology with Essays.* Freedom: Calif.: Crossing Press, 1989.

Kellner, Bruce, ed. *A Gertrude Stein Companion: Content with the Example.* New York: Greenwood Press, 1988.

Mellow, James R. *Charmed Circle: Gertrude Stein & Company.* New York: Praeger, 1974.

Stendhal, Renate, ed. *Gertrude Stein, In Words and Pictures.* Chapel Hill, N.C.: Algonquin Books, 1994.

Toklas, Alice B. *What Is Remembered.* New York: Holt, 1963.

Wagner-Martin, Linda. *"Favored Strangers": Gertrude Stein and Her Family.* New Brunswick, N.J.: Rutgers University Press, 1995.

Linda Wagner-Martin
University of North Carolina at Chapel Hill

STEINBECK, JOHN (ERNST) (1902–1968)

Born in California in the early years of the 20th century, John Steinbeck was destined to make famous in almost mythical ways Salinas, the town of his birth. The SALINAS VALLEY is the setting for numerous stories and novels, many of which were made into successful Broadway plays and feature-length films. His stories appeared in COLLIER'S, HARPER'S, *Playboy, Reader's Digest, Punch,* and the ATLANTIC, among others. In 1962, Steinbeck was awarded the Nobel Prize in literature. Steinbeck's reputation as a short story writer rests on two early collections, the SHORT STORY CYCLE *THE PASTURES OF HEAVEN* (1932) and the short story collection *The Long Valley* (1938).

Although critical opinion has long noted that Steinbeck's short story output slowed following the tremendous success of his Pulitzer Prize–winning novel, *The Grapes of Wrath* (1939), recently scholars have begun examining his later stories as well, finding them worthy of republishing and anthologizing. Two of these, "How Edith McGillicuddy Met R. L. S. [Stevenson]" (1941) and "The Affair at 7, Rue de M——" (1955), won O. HENRY AWARDS in 1942 and 1956, respectively, as did two stories from the 1930s, "The Murder" (1933) and "The Promise" (1938).

In his more than 50 stories, a recurring theme is frustration resulting from isolation, loneliness, or sexual repression, that frequently manifests itself it violence (Hughes 18). Sometimes read as a regionalist with universal appeal (see REGIONALISM), at others as a naturalist (see NATURALISM) or writer of PROLETARIAN FICTION, Steinbeck appeals to many readers because of his deceptively simple CHARACTERS whose actually complex interiors mirror those of human beings everywhere. Moreover, his PROTAGONISTS play out their dramas in the mythic golden land of California, the edenic setting that Steinbeck has made metaphoric of the AMERICAN DREAM and its fate in the 20th century. Although in later stories he would use diverse settings ranging from New York to Paris, Salinas and the extended "Steinbeck Country" (Hughes 17) form an integral part of *The Long Valley* and *The Pastures of Heaven.*

In the short stories as well as his novels, Steinbeck uses the themes of Arthurian romance (see ROMANTICISM) and MYTH, particularly biblical myth. In "THE SNAKE," for instance, Steinbeck combines FREUDian and Old Testament images of the snake and women to produce a peculiarly haunting story of a woman and a scientist. This story illustrates Steinbeck's interest in both mythmaking and biology, two lifelong fascinations begun in his friendships with biologist Edward F. Ricketts and the world-renowned scholar on myth Joseph P. Campbell. Throughout *Pastures of Heaven* runs Steinbeck's oft-noted EDENic theme. He also uses numerous sympathetically presented Mexican characters, as in the story "FLIGHT," a bleak BILDUNGSROMAN in which Pepe, a young boy, faces adulthood.

Because Steinbeck adamantly refused to use didactic methods (see DIDACTICISM) or to take any sort of moral position (see POINT OF VIEW), readers sometimes mistakenly believe that Steinbeck approves his characters' attitudes and behavior. As Steinbeck scholar John Distsky points out, the DENOUEMENTS of his stories are notably open-ended and thought-provoking (513). These endings, along with readers' continuing fascination with Steinbeck's meanings and the resurgence of critical interest in Steinbeck during the 1980s and 1990s, suggest that Steinbeck's stories will continue to have relevance to new generations of readers. Current critical opinion judges "THE RED PONY" and "THE CHRYSANTHEMUMS" among the best stories of the 20th century, and additional Steinbeck stories will doubtless join their ranks.

BIBLIOGRAPHY

Hughes, R.S. *John Steinbeck: A Study of the Short Fiction*. Boston: Twayne Publishers, 1989.

Steinbeck, John. *Burning Bright: A Play in Story Form*. New York: Viking, 1950.

———. *Cannery Row*. New York: Viking, 1945.

———. *A Cup of Gold: A Life of Henry Morgan, Buccaneer, with Occasional Reference to History*. New York: Robert M. McBride & Co., 1929.

———. *East of Eden*. New York: Viking, 1952.

———. *The Grapes of Wrath*. New York: Viking, 1939.

———. *In Dubious Battle*. New York: Covici-Friede, 1936.

———. *The Long Valley*. New York: Viking, 1938.

———. *The Moon Is Down*. New York: Viking, 1942.

———. *Of Mice and Men*. New York: Covici-Friede, 1937.

———. *The Pastures of Heaven*. New York: Warren & Putnam, 1932.

———. *The Pearl*. New York: Viking, 1947.

———. *The Red Pony*. New York: Covici-Friede, 1937.

———. *Saint Katy the Virgin*. 1936.

———. *The Short Novels of John Steinbeck*. New York: Viking, 1953.

———. *The Short Reign of Pippin IV: A Fabrication*. New York: Viking, 1957.

———. *Sweet Thursday*. New York: Viking, 1954.

———. *To a God Unknown*. New York: Robert O. Ballou, 1933.

———. *The Wayward Bus*. New York: Viking, 1947.

———. *The Winter of Our Discontent*. New York: Viking, 1961.

STEREOTYPE From the printing process in which a metal plate cast in type metal from a mold makes exact copies many times, the word is used to describe anything that conforms to a fixed pattern or image, lacking any individualizing characteristics. A stereotype is an uncritical, oversimplified mental image held in common by a group to describe another group, a race, an issue, or an event. For example, to say "the Germans are a warlike people" is to stereotype all German people. In fiction, the term is frequently a pejorative one: Authors may be faulted for creating stereotypical rather than original characters.

"STORM, THE" KATE CHOPIN (1969) "The Storm" (composed in 1898) is the prequel or companion story to "AT THE 'CADIAN BALL," set five years later. "At the 'Cadian Ball" portrays the strong attraction between Alcée Laballière and Calixta when each was single. "The Storm" concerns the reunion of Alcée and Calixta, now married to other people. Though it contains DIALECT and LOCAL COLOR, "The Storm" is more akin to MODERNISM than REGIONALISM because of its moral AMBIGUITY and frank eroticism. CHOPIN never tried to publish the story that, for its time, contained graphically sexual detail. It was finally published in 1969 in *The Complete Works of Kate Chopin*.

"The Storm" is set in rural Louisiana before, during, and after a torrential rain. The first section describes Calixta's husband, Bobinôt, and son, Bibi, at a store, where they decide to wait until the coming storm passes, despite their concern about Calixta's being at home alone. The second section focuses on Calixta, who is sewing, not thinking about her family. Alcée Laballière arrives at Calixta's house, seeking shelter from the rain. As the tempest rages outside, the two consummate their affair after a long mutual attraction. After the storm passes, Alcée rides away as Calixta laughs. Her husband and son return in section three; Bobinôt has brought her a can of shrimp and meticulously avoids tracking mud into the house. The seemingly happy family enjoys dinner together.

The Laballières are similarly unaffected by the affair. Sections four and five summarize letters exchanged between Alcée and his wife, Clarisse, who is vacationing. He tells her not to rush home because, although he misses her, his first concern is for her health and pleasure. Clarisse is in no hurry to return, however, for "their intimate conjugal life was something which she was more than willing to forgo for a while" (596). The final line of the story absolves the lovers of any guilt: "So the storm passed and every one was happy" (596).

BIBLIOGRAPHY

Chopin, Kate. *The Complete Works of Kate Chopin*. Edited by Per Seyersted. Baton Rouge: Louisiana State University Press, 1969.

Koloski, Bernard. *Kate Chopin: A Study of the Short Fiction*. New York: Twayne, 1996.

Seyersted, Per. *Kate Chopin: A Critical Biography*. Baton Rouge: Louisiana State University Press, 1969.

Toth, Emily. *Kate Chopin*. New York: Morrow, 1990.

Mary Anne O'Neal
University of Georgia

STORY A magazine that published the early work of many of the 20th century's great writers in the 1930s and 1940s. Publication was suspended in 1948, but the magazine was resurrected by the publisher of *Writer's Digest* in 1989. The goal of the recent publication is to remain true to the vision and intent of the original by publishing both well-known and unknown authors.

"STORY OF AN HOUR, THE" KATE CHOPIN (1894) Originally entitled "The Dream of an Hour" when it was first published in *Vogue* (December 1894), "The Story of an Hour" has since become one of Kate CHOPIN's most frequently anthologized stories. Among her shortest and most daring works, "Story" examines issues of feminism, namely a woman's dissatisfaction in a conventional marriage and her desire for independence. (See FEMINIST.) It also features Chopin's characteristic irony and AMBIGUITY.

The story begins with Louise Mallard's being told about her husband's presumed death in a train accident. Louise initially weeps with wild abandon, then retires alone to her upstairs bedroom. As she sits facing the open window, observing the new spring life outside, she realizes with a "clear and exalted perception" that she is now free of her husband's "powerful will bending hers" (353). She becomes delirious with the prospect that she can now live for herself and prays that her life may be long. Her newfound independence is short-lived, however. In a SURPRISE ENDING, her husband walks through the front door, and Louise suffers a heart attack and dies. Her death may be considered a tragic defeat or a Pyrrhic victory for a woman who would rather die than lose that "possession of self-assertion which she suddenly recognized as the strongest impulse of her being" (353). The doctors ironically attribute her death to the "joy that kills" (354).

BIBLIOGRAPHY

Chopin, Kate. *The Complete Works of Kate Chopin*. Edited by Per Seyersted. Baton Rouge: Louisiana State University Press, 1969.

Koloski, Bernard. *Kate Chopin: A Study of the Short Fiction*. New York: Twayne, 1996.

Seyersted, Per. *Kate Chopin: A Critical Biography*. Baton Rouge: Louisiana State University Press, 1969.

Toth, Emily. *Kate Chopin*. New York: Morrow, 1990.

Mary Anne O'Neal
University of Georgia

STREAM OF CONSCIOUSNESS A narrative technique developed in the late 19th century that presents a range of images, thoughts, memories, and other elements and associations going through a character's mind at a given moment, often in a disjointed or illogical fashion, to depict the subjective, private thoughts of that individual, without commentary or interpretation by the author. In the 20th century, stream of consciousness became famously associated with the French writer Marcel Proust, the Irish writer James Joyce, and the American writer William FAULKNER. The technique has become a staple of much contemporary fiction.

STRUCTURALISM

STRUCTURALISM A philosophical movement, led by linguists such as Ferdinand de Saussure and anthropologists such as Claude Lévi-Strauss, that examines the underpinnings of linguistics and anthropology. Taking their cue from structuralism, the structuralist literary critics such as Roland BARTHES examine the underpinnings of literature, or the system of symbols and codes that give meaning to the literary text in question. The structuralists are more concerned with the way meaning is conveyed than with the meaning itself. Structuralism, primarily a European phenomenon that gained momentum in the 1960s, enjoyed some popularity in the United States among critics who were in revolt against reading fiction from the perspective of literary history and biographical criticism. (See NEW CRITICISM and POST-STRUCTURALISM.)

STUDS LONIGAN In James T. Farrell's short story "Studs," from which the Studs Lonigan trilogy evolved, the author's autobiographical narrator relates the story of Studs Lonigan's adolescence, dissipation, and early death. The narrator, who has worshiped the adventurous hero of Chicago's South Side, ultimately understands that Studs's decline is a metaphor for the plight of innumerable young American males whose participation in the male rites of passage dooms them to failure or an early death: in Studs's death he—and the reader—sees the failure of the AMERICAN DREAM. As James G. Watson notes, Studs's funeral features his friends as AMERICAN ADAMS who unwittingly "turn endlessly to the romanticized past, mythologizing their reckless days of urban innocence and longing a little wistfully for their drunken pranks and poker games, prostitution and petty thievery" that characterized their late boyhood (Watson 112). Like Farrell himself, his narrator is a writer who condemns the boredom and loneliness of an America that destroys the bright potential of youth.

BIBLIOGRAPHY
Farrell, James T. *An Omnibus of Short Stories.* New York: Vanguard, 1967.
Watson, James G. "The American Short Story: 1930–1945."

In *The American Short Story, 1900–1945: A Critical Study,* edited by Philip Stevick, Boston: Twayne, 1984.

SUCKOW, RUTH (1892–1960) Author of more than 40 short stories and critical essays, as well as six novels and three NOVELLAS, Ruth Suckow was born in Hawarden, a small town in northwestern Iowa, a state in which she lived most of her life. She attended Grinell College, which awarded her an honorary degree in 1930. Suckow's most famous collection, *Iowa Interiors* (1926), has been likened to Sherwood ANDERSON's *WINESBURG, OHIO,* especially in terms of its REALISM and REGIONALISM. Indeed, with its publication, critics from H. L. Mencken to Carl Van Doren and Allan Nevins praised her as one of the best writers in the United States.

Most scholars today attribute her disappearance from the canon to her reliance on region—or, more accurately, the critical perception of her as a regionalist (see REGIONALISM). Ruth Suckow died in 1960 in Claremont, California, her home since 1952. Although Suckow has lost popularity since the 1930s, when regionalist writers enjoyed a wider audience, at least one critic suggests that her works are at least as important, if not more so, than those of such better-known writers as Sinclair Lewis and Langston HUGHES (Rohrberger 147).

BIBLIOGRAPHY
Kissane, Leedice McAnelly. *Ruth Suckow.* New York: Twayne, 1969.
Rohrberger, Mary. "The Question of Regionalism: Limitation and Transcendence." In *The American Short Story, 1900–1945: A Critical History.* Edited by Philip Stevick, Boston: Twayne, 1984.
Suckow, Ruth. *The Bonney Family.* New York: Knopf, 1928.
———. *Carry-over.* New York: Farrar & Rinehart, 1936.
———. *Children and Older People.* New York: Knopf, 1931.
———. *Cora.* New York: Knopf, 1929.
———. *Country People.* New York: Knopf, 1924.
———. *The Folks.* New York: Farrar & Rinehart, 1934.
———. *Iowa Interiors.* New York: Knopf, 1926.
———. *The John Wood Case: A Novel.* New York: Viking, 1950.
———. *The Kramer Girls.* New York: Knopf, 1930.
———. *A Memoir.* New York: Rinehart, 1952
———. *New Hope.* New York: Farrar, 1942.

————. *The Odyssey of a Nice Girl*. New York: Knopf, 1925.

————. *People and Houses*. London: Jpnathan Cape, 1927.

————. *Ruth Suckow Omnibus*. Iowa City: University of Iowa Press, 1988.

————. *Some Others and Myself: Seven Stories and a Memoir*. New York: Rinehart, 1952.

————. *Stories from the Midland*. New York: Knopf, 1924.

SUI SIN FAR (EDITH MAUDE EATON)

(1865–1914) Born in Montreal to an English painter and his Chinese wife, Edith Maude Eaton lived much of her adult life in the United States. Never married, Eaton led an independent and relatively outspoken life and wrote short stories, autobiography, and articles under the Cantonese pseudonym Sui Sin Far, which means "water lily" or "Chinese lily." Although she first despised Chinese people, she grew to embrace that side of her heritage and used her writing to dispel North American myths and STEREOTYPES of the Chinese.

Much of Sui Sin Far's writing directly yet carefully, because of the demands of the marketplace, protests American prejudice against the Chinese, which was encouraged by the stereotypes of railroad workers as a threat to white labor and by the Chinese Exclusion Act, which greatly restricted emigration from China. In her autobiographical essay "Leaves from the Mental Portfolio of an Eurasian," Sui Sin Far writes of herself as a link between cultures and of her own experience with anti-Chinese attitudes, especially in comparison with more positive sentiments toward the Japanese in America at that time. Sui Sin Far's fiction presents, sometimes through use of irony or TRICKSTER figures, the Chinese in America as complex, realistic characters facing self-exploration and the difficulties of bicultural life and prejudice.

Sui Sin Far's collected stories, which include stories for both adults and children, appeared under the title MRS. SPRING FRAGRANCE (1912, 1995). It remains her only book publication. Other short stories and articles appeared in popular magazines and newspapers. Some of her stories, including "The Inferior Woman," "The Heart's Desire," and "Story of One White Woman Who Married a Chinese," can be considered FEMINIST in their emphasis on women's self-determination, individuality, and value, particularly working-class women. Moreover, Sui Sin Far's stories often explore the tension Chinese American women experienced while trying to be both Americanized women and traditional Chinese wives. "The Wisdom of the New," for instance, portrays the problems particular to women in a bicultural environment, and in "The Prize China Baby," a woman disregards her husband's wishes, finds strength in herself, and finds freedom from her husband and eternal union with her child in death.

Sui Sin Far's sister, Winnifred Eaton, who wrote under the Japanese pseudonym Onoto WATANNA and who was more popular than Sui Sin Far, published numerous short, captivating romance novels about often powerless though intriguing Japanese or Asian American women who fall in love with white HEROES. She also wrote one feminist novel, entitled *Cattle* (1924) and an autobiographical piece entitled *Me: A Book of Remembrance* (1915) as well as screenplays. Together the two Eaton sisters mark the beginning of Asian North American literary history and especially prefigure more recent Chinese American women writers such as Maxine Hong KINGSTON and Amy TAN. As a result, the work of Sui Sin Far has received increased attention since the mid-1970s.

BIBLIOGRAPHY

Ling, Amy. "Edith Eaton: Pioneer Chinamerican Writer and Feminist." *American Literary Realism* 16 (Autumn 1983): 287–289.

————. "Writers with a Cause: Sui Sin Far and Han Suyin." *Women's Studies International Forum* 19 (1986): 411–419.

Sui Sin Far, *Mrs. Spring Fragrance and Other Writings*. Edited by Amy Ling and Annette White-Parks. Urbana: University of Illinois Press, 1995.

White-Parks, Annette. *Sui Sin Far/Edith Maude Eaton: A Literary Biography*. Urbana: University of Illinois Press, 1995.

Anna Leahy
Ohio University

SURPRISE ENDING

The surprise ending generally revolves around a trivial fact missing from the text, and thus its appearance surprises or shocks the unsuspecting reader. It became a hallmark of the short stories by O. HENRY. Exceptionally well-known surprise endings are found in Thomas Bailey Aldrich's "Marjory Daw," William FAULKNER's "A ROSE FOR EMILY," Frank Stockton's "THE LADY OR THE TIGER," and Edith WHARTON's "ROMAN FEVER."

SURREALISM

A revolutionary movement in the arts and literature that rejected the conscious control of reason, standard morality, and convention on the free function of the mind. The movement was strongly influenced by FREUDianism: surrealists believed the unconscious mind was the true source of valid art and knowledge and, therefore, relied on the thoughts and images from the subconscious as revealed in dreams and natural or induced hallucinations. Beginning in France in 1924, surrealism remained a predominantly European movement, although following WORLD WAR II surrealist techniques were used by some American artists and poets.

SUT LOVINGOOD

Character created by George Washington Harris in the tradition of Southwest humor. Sut stories began appearing in *Spirit of the Times* in 1843 and were not published in book form until 1867, in *Sut Lovingood: Yarns Spun by a "Nat'ral Born Durn'd Fool." Warped and Wove for Public Wear.* A frequently anthologized tale is "Mrs. Yardley's Quilting Party." It is a typical example of the eccentricities and foibles of Sut, a character much admired by William FAULKNER, who saw in him the human ability to do his best and to endure.

"SWEAT" ZORA NEALE HURSTON (1926)

First published in the AVANT-GARDE journal *Fire!!* in November 1926, "Sweat" was later included in the collection *Spunk: The Selected Stories of Zora Neale Hurston* (1985).

Demonstrating Zora Neale HURSTON's mastery of black culture and black DIALECT and her awareness of gender inequities, "Sweat" explores some of the causes for sweat: labor, fear, and death. The story juxtaposes Delia, a hardworking Christian woman, against Sykes, her lazy, wife-beating, unfaithful husband. Like the character of Janey in Hurston's later novel, *Their Eyes Were Watching God* (1937), Delia silently endures work and suffering while men observe her and fantasize about their own importance. A thin woman sympathized with and respected by the community of black men, she washes white families' clothes for 15 years to support her husband and herself.

Frustrated by his lack of success, filled with dreams of grandeur, and ashamed of his wife's work, the unemployed Sykes overturns Delia's laundry tub and taunts her with a bullwhip because she fears snakes. He threatens to give her house to his girlfriend, Bertha, for whom he plans to leave Delia. After Delia resists him, he brings a trapped rattlesnake to the house to frighten her. Later he plots her murder and places the snake in her laundry basket. When Delia escapes the snake and realizes her husband's intention, she leaves the snake for Sykes to find. The snake bites him, but his agonized cries elicit no forgiveness from her. Delia's devout faith is now translated into vengeance, and she silently observes Sykes's suffering and death.

Unlike most other HARLEM RENAISSANCE tales, "Sweat" focuses on gender rather than racial tensions and underscores the black woman's experience rather than the man's. Anticipating current FEMINIST studies of womens displacement, alienation, and oppression, "Sweat" projects a female character distanced from the community and subjected to male violence.

BIBLIOGRAPHY

Hurston, Zora Neale. *Dust Tracks on a Road: An Autobiography.* Urbana: University of Illinois Press, 1970.

———. *Zora Neale Hurston: Novels and Stories.* Edited by Cheryl A. Wall. New York: Library of America, 1995.

———. *Spunk: The Selected Stories of Zora Neale Hurston.* Berkeley: Turtle Island Foundation, 1985.

Nathiri, N. Y. *Zora!: Zora Neale Hurston, A Woman and Her Community.* Orlando, Fla.: Sentinel Communications, 1991.

Sandra Chrystal Hayes
Georgia Institute of Technology

SYMBOLISM From the Greek word *symballein,* meaning "to throw together," symbolism is a literary technique that puts together a thing, idea, or quality from the actual world with a thing, idea, or quality from another or higher world to represent it and to extend its literal meaning. In William FAULKNER's "A ROSE FOR EMILY," the symbolism of the rose offsets Miss Emily Grierson's GROTESQUE qualities and signals the readers to seek further meaning in her character. Characters themselves can become symbols of a larger truth, as CHARLIE WALES, the former alcoholic in F. Scott FITZGERALD's "BABYLON REVISITED," in his sober state becomes symbolic of a more somber Europe in the wake of the GREAT DEPRESSION. Nathaniel HAWTHORNE, one of the earliest American writers to use symbolism in an artistically conscious way, seems to employ deliberately ambiguous symbolism in "THE BIRTHMARK": the mark may symbolize flawed humanity, or it may extend the meaning of Georgiana, the scientist's wife, as symbol of a woman in a trapped and ultimately doomed life.

SYNTAX Syntax refers to the arrangement of words, phrases, and clauses in sentences, and can suggest the distinctive aspects of an author's style.

T

TALKING TO THE DEAD AND OTHER STORIES SYLVIA WATANABE (1992)

The first short story collection published by Sylvia WATANABE, *Talking to the Dead and Other Stories* was a finalist for the PEN/FAULKNER AWARD in 1993. Its ten stories are set in the Hawaiian village of Luhi on the island of Maui; the book combines Hawaiian myth, Japanese social values, American CAPITALISM, and the immigrants' dual sense of isolation and self-sufficiency. Through this cultural diversity, and through a narrative style that carefully balances poignancy and humor, Watanabe convincingly delineates universal truths about self, family, and society. A fundamental thesis of the collection is that while tradition is to be valued and cherished, change is inevitable. (See THEME.) Thus a casual casting off of tradition, on one hand, or a stubborn resistance to change, on the other, invites personal as well as communal disaster.

As R. A. SASAKI argues in her review of *Talking to the Dead*, the lead story, "Anchorage," provides the raison d'etre for the collection itself, positing that art—a quilt in the story, literature in Watanabe's case—is the means to preserving the life of the village; art is the assurance that those who should remember will "not forget." Although "The Prayer Lady" and "The Ghost of Fred Astaire" are immediately concerned with religion and popular culture, respectively, each finally argues that cynicism frightens a

contemporary world away from the soul-edifying elements of the past and the difficult changes necessary to a productive future. This is also one theme of the title story, "Talking to the Dead," a rich analysis, through METAPHORS of life and death, of personal and communal responsibilities to past and present. Other stories, including "Emiko's Garden" and "Certainty," approach such issues through family interactions and conflicts, suggesting that the balanced forces that promote familial strength and harmony also enlarge and strengthen the souls of individuals and communities.

BIBLIOGRAPHY

Sasaki, R. A. "Change and Tragedy in a Hawaiian Village." *San Francisco Chronicle Sunday Review,* September 6, 1992, 9.

Keith Lawrence
Brigham Young University

TALL TALE

An extravagantly humorous tale, common to writings of the American frontier, detailing the amusingly inflated abilities, exploits or achievements of such characters as Daniel Boone, Paul Bunyon, Mike Fink, John Henry, or Davy Crockett. The tall tale properly belongs in the genre of FOLKLORE, and excellent examples exist in Davy Crockett's *Narrative of the Life of Davy Crockett* (1834). Such CLASSIC writers as Washington IRVING and Mark TWAIN incorporate tall tales in their fiction.

See, for example, "The Celebrated Jumping Frog of Calaveras County" (1865), originally written for a collection being prepared by Artemus WARD (the fictional Yankee humorist-philosopher created by Charles Farrar BROWNE) but published separately to instant popular acclaim.

TAN, AMY (1952–) Amy Tan was born in Oakland, California, the daughter of first-generation Chinese Americans. Her father was a Baptist minister, and although the family remained in the San Francisco Bay area throughout Tan's childhood and early adolescence, they moved frequently from neighborhood to neighborhood as Tan's father accepted increasingly attractive positions. During her 16th year Tan's life was forever changed when her father and younger brother died within six months of each other, both of brain tumors. Distraught and eager to escape the past, Tan's mother moved the family to Montreux, Switzerland, where Tan received her high school diploma from the Institut Monte Rosa Internationale in 1969 and where she was briefly involved in the youth counterculture movement.

Back in the United States, Tan distressed her mother by dropping out of pre-med classes and declaring herself an English major at San Jose State University, graduating in 1973 with her B.A. in English and linguistics; a year later she received her M.A. in linguistics, also from San Jose State. In the fall of 1974 she began her Ph.D. studies in linguistics at Berkeley but dropped out two years later when she realized she did not want an academic career. For the next nine years she worked as a language consultant and free-lance technical writer but decided along the way that she wanted to write fiction. After attending the Squaw Valley fiction writers' workshop in California in 1985 and after writing numerous revisions of her first story, Tan was notified in 1986 that "Endgame" had been accepted for publication in *FM Five* (which later became the SHORT STORY REVIEW); it was reprinted a few months later as "Rules of the Game" in *Seventeen*. Writing remained an avocation for Tan until December 1987, when—through the efforts of her agent, Sandra Dijkstra—

she secured an advance of $50,000 to complete *The Joy Luck Club*. From that time on Tan has considered herself a full-time author.

The Joy Luck Club was an enormous popular and critical success, hailed by the majority of readers as a brilliant first novel. But Tan always has considered the book to be a collection of short stories and is reportedly troubled by those who refer to it as a novel; it incorporates, with few or no emendations, stories that had been previously published in LADIES' HOME JOURNAL, *Seventeen, Grazia, San Francisco Focus, The Short Story Review* and *The Atlantic*. *The Joy Luck Club* was a finalist in 1989 for the National Book Award; that same year it was named a Best Book for Young Adults by the American Library Association. Among the influences on her stories and her style, Tan lists Amy Hempel, Eudora WELTY, and Flannery O'CONNOR. But the single most important influence on *The Joy Luck Club*, she says, was Louise ERDRICH's LOVE MEDICINE, a carefully structured and interwoven grouping of short stories about the different generations of a NATIVE AMERICAN family. Like Maxine Hong KINGSTON, Tan is profoundly interested in female relationships, particularly those between mothers and daughters, and in the cultural repercussions of Chinese tradition and myth in a modern world. Like Kingston, Tan has been criticized for her focus on women and her consequential marginalizing of male characters; Frank CHIN and Jeffery CHAN have also labeled Tan a "fake" writer because of her willingness to question—and in some cases, reinvent—traditional Chinese tales, myths, and customs.

Despite such criticism, Tan's writing in general and the stories of *The Joy Luck Club* in particular have had untold impact in dispelling white American STEREOTYPES of Asian Americans as shy, humorless, bookish, and emotionally bland. The structural and thematic richness of *The Joy Luck Club* has made it a staple of university courses in ethnic American literature and women's studies. (See THEME.) Four elements of the book have been particularly resonant (or, in some cases, uncomfortably shrill) for academic readers, for Asian American critics, and for subsequent Asian American authors. First, the book's concern with intergenerational female relationships; second, its dependence on "talk story" and oral narrative; third, its inviting yet ascerbic folk humor; and fourth, in the manner of Kingston, its appropriation and personalization of Chinese mythology.

With the possible exception of Kingston, Tan has done more than any other author to create an interest in and a market for ASIAN AMERICAN LITERATURE. She has been tireless in reviewing and promoting the works of fellow Asian American authors, having endorsed books by writers as diverse as Bharati MUKHERJEE, Gish JEN, and Gus Lee. *The Kitchen God's Wife* (1991) repeated the broad success of Tan's first book; *The Hundred Secret Senses* (1995) was somewhat less successful. Tan has also written two stories for young children, *The Moon Lady* (1992), which is a retelling of the fourth story in *The Joy Luck Club,* and *The Chinese Siamese Cat* (1994), a "created" folk tale inspired by one of Tan's own cats, Sagwa. Tan cowrote the screenplay for the film version of *The Joy Luck Club* (1993).

BIBLIOGRAPHY

Shen, Gloria. "Born of a Stranger: Mother-Daughter Relationships and Storytelling in Amy Tan's *The Joy Luck Club.*" In *International Women's Writing: New Landscapes of Identity.* Edited by Anne E. Brown et al. Westport, Conn.: Greenwood Press, 1995.

Souris, Stephen. "'Only Two Kinds of Daughters': Inter-Monologue Dialogicity in *The Joy Luck Club.*" *MELUS* 19 (Summer 1994): 99–123.

Tan, Amy. *The Chinese Siamese Cat.* New York: Putnam, 1994.

———. *The Hundred Secret Senses.* New York: Putnam, 1995.

———. *The Joy Luck Club.* New York: Putnam, 1989.

———. *The Kitchen God's Wife.* New York: Putnam, 1991.

———. *The Moon Lady.* New York: Putnam, 1992.

Wong, Sau-ling Cynthia. "'Sugar Sisterhood': Situating the Amy Tan Phenomenon." In *The Ethnic Canon.* Edited by David Palumbo-Lin. Minneapolis: University of Minnesota Press, 1995.

Xu, Ben. "Memory and the Ethnic Self: Reading Amy Tan's *The Joy Luck Club.*" In *Memory, Narrative and Identity.* Edited by Amritjit Singh et al. Boston: Northeastern University Press, 1994.

Keith Lawrence
Brigham Young University

TAYLOR, PETER (1917–1994) Born in Trenton, Tennessee, on January 8, 1917, Peter Taylor was a uniquely Southern fiction writer who did not spend any of his formative years in the South. His family moved to St. Louis when Taylor was nine and remained there until he turned 15. This geographical displacement may account for a marked characteristic in Taylor's narratives to be simultaneously inside and outside the South. In the tradition of William FAULKNER and Flannery O'CONNOR, Taylor writes about the decay of the South but without these authors' nostalgia or their penchants for the GOTHIC. Frequently set not in the Deep South but in Nashville, Memphis, and the fictional Chatham, Tennessee, Taylor's fiction is noted for its wistful yet unsentimental portrayal of the decline of the genteel South. Taylor has a remarkable ear for dialogue and a gift for sensitive character portrayals (see CHARACTER); his tales frequently involve a central PROTAGONIST gaining insight into his situation in all its irony and inevitable human fallibility, whom we finally understand and empathize with rather than condemn because Taylor has rendered his characterization with such acute emotional precision and sensitivity.

Taylor studied literature and creative writing at Vanderbilt University under the poet John Crowe Ransom, who was to remain a lifelong friend and influence, as were Allen Tate (his freshman English teacher), Robert Penn Warren, and Cleanth Brooks (Taylor's graduate professors at Louisiana State University). Like fellow Southerner Elizabeth SPENCER, then, Taylor may be counted among those who formed a bridge between the Southern Renaissance and contemporary writers. When Ransom moved to teach at Kenyon College, Taylor followed and met poet Robert Lowell, another lifelong friend, who also went to graduate school with Taylor at LSU. Taylor enlisted in the army and served briefly in England during WORLD WAR II before returning to the United States in 1945 to begin a life of letters. His stories began to be published in scholarly journals and reviews and were met with consistent praise throughout his long career. While his fiction has never enjoyed the widest readership, Taylor has been included in the collection of *Best American Short Stories* annuals and the O. HENRY MEMORIAL AWARDS collections. In 1986 Taylor won the PULITZER PRIZE and the PEN/FAULKNER AWARD for his novel *A Summons to Memphis*. He also taught at the University of North Carolina and, for nearly 30 years, at the University of Virginia. After suffering a series of strokes in October of 1994, Taylor died in Charlottesville, Virginia, on November 2 of that year.

BIBLIOGRAPHY

Griffith, Albert J. *Peter Taylor.* Tuscaloosa: University of Alabama Press, 1990.

———. *Critical Essays on Peter Taylor.* New York: G.K. Hall, 1993.

McAlexander, Hubert H., ed. *Critical Essays on Peter Taylor.* New York: G.K. Hall, 1993.

Taylor, Peter. *The Collected Stories of Peter Taylor.* Edited by Peter Hillsman Taylor. New York: Penguin, 1986.

S. L. Yentzer
University of Georgia, Athens

"TELL ME A RIDDLE" TILLIE OLSEN (1960)

"Tell Me a Riddle," the title NOVELLA of Tillie OLSEN's 1961 collection, details the state of the relationship of an elderly married couple who, in their youth, emigrated from Russia. Now that their children are grown, husband and wife disagree about where and how they should live the rest of their lives. He wants to move to the Haven, a community where all their needs will be attended to by others, an arrangement that will free him from his financial worries and provide companionship. For her, however, freedom is *"Never again to be forced to move to the rhythms of others,"* (68), and she refuses to move. Their dispute arouses long-repressed hostilities as she remembers all she has given up in the past, when money was short and the needs of husband and children kept her from pursuing her own interests, especially reading. As the argument escalates, he threatens to sell the house without her consent, and she sinks into a depression and declining health. Her name is Eva, although Olsen withholds it until the end of the novella.

The first doctor she visits finds no serious problems and encourages her to enjoy life more. After her doctor son-in-law examines her, she undergoes emergency surgery to remove her gallbladder. The family does not tell her that the surgery revealed cancer. The children, who had been mystified that rancor could tear their parents apart at their age, now urge their father to make her happy in her last good months. Even as he tries to do so, however, he clearly misunderstands her wishes. He takes her to visit her children and grandchildren, but she does not want to travel. She feels that she is imposing in her children's homes, where she cleans while her husband plays with the grandchildren. While life has stimulated his capacities and enjoyment of others, her life has drained her joy and isolated her from others. She can be her grandchildren's audience but not their playmate, as her husband can: "'Tell me a riddle, Grammy.' 'I know no riddles, child'" (85). She resents the demands of her grandchildren, no longer wanting to be at others' disposal.

The couple's final visit is to Los Angeles, where their granddaughter Jeannie lives. Here Eva experiences a brief moment of ecstasy when she visits the beach and runs toward the waves, splashing her bare feet in the sea foam. But her health is declining and even her visits with her old friend Ellen Mays, who now lives in one squalid room, evoke her weariness and her disappointment in a humanity that reduces its elderly to such lives. Dying, she remembers her girlhood in Olshana, Russia, and finds consolation in music and remembered bits of literature. Her husband, at first resentful that she speaks of these interests rather than her family in her final days, finally comes to contemplate their past as prisoners during the Russian Revolution and to realize his own pain and disappointments. He remembers the faith in humanity they shared and their confidence that the 20th century would bring happier lives and an end to wars and killing. He wonders how adequately their children's and grandchildren's physical comfort and education fulfills those dreams, and he wishes he could pass on to them that former, youthful faith. Eva's dying is gradual, painful, and almost more than he can bear to witness. Jeannie, however, assures him that her grandmother promised that on the last day she would be back in Russia, hearing the music of her childhood, and that they must help her body to die.

"Tell Me a Riddle" was first published in 1960. It won the O. HENRY MEMORIAL AWARD for best short story in 1961 and has been widely anthologized.

BIBLIOGRAPHY

Coiner, Constance. *Better Red: The Writing and Resistance of Tillie Olsen and Meridel Le Sueur.* New York: Oxford University Press, 1995.

Faulkner, Mara. *Protest and Possibility in the Writing of Tillie Olsen.* Charlottesville: University Press of Virginia, 1993.

Frye, Joanne S. *Tillie Olsen: A Study of the Short Fiction.* New York: Twayne, 1995.

Nelson, Kay Hoyle, and Nancy Huse, eds. *The Critical Response to Tillie Olsen.* Westport, Conn.: Greenwood Press, 1994.

Olsen, Tillie. *Tell Me a Riddle.* Philadelphia: Lippincott, 1961.

———. *Tell Me a Riddle.* Edited by Deborah Silverton Rosenfelt. New Brunswick, N.J.: Rutgers University Press, 1995.

Orr, Elaine Neil. *Tillie Olsen and a Feminist Spiritual Vision.* Jackson: University Press of Mississippi, 1987.

Pearlman, Mickey, and Abby H. P. Werlock. *Tillie Olsen.* Boston: Twayne, 1991.

Kelley Reames
University of North Carolina at Chapel Hill

"TELL-TALE HEART, THE" EDGAR ALLAN POE (1843)

Edgar Allan POE's "The Tell-Tale Heart," published during a prolific period while Poe was living in Philadelphia and republished in 1845 and many times since, is a crime story using the first-person POINT OF VIEW of the murderer. The mentally disturbed narrator explains, in an attempt to prove to the reader that he is not mad, how he methodically killed an old man and then buried the body beneath the floorboards. When the police arrive, the murderer calmly invites them in but then, as he speaks, becomes obsessed with a thumping, begins to rave, and finally shouts his confession and tears up the floorboards.

This story marks Poe as a master of the psychological study as well as the GOTHIC tale in which terror, violence, and aberration predominate. The obsessive narrator and the lack of motive for murder

link this tale with other Poe stories including "THE BLACK CAT" (1843), "THE CASK OF AMONTILLADO" (1846), and even "THE MURDERS IN THE RUE MORGUE" (1841). The THEME of time and inevitability, represented by references to watches as well as the sound of the beating heart, becomes part of the obsessiveness and repetition of the narrative itself. The relationship between the murderer and the victim is, oddly, one of close identification, as the narrator empathizes with the old man's groan's and feelings and finally mistakes his own heartbeat for his victim's. Connecting the narrator's obsession with the old man's "eye" to his self-obsessed use of "I" in his first-person narration, we watch the narrator unconsciously conflate the two identities so that murdering the old man represents his own self-destruction.

BIBLIOGRAPHY

Arthur, Robert. *Thrillers and More Thrillers.* New York: Random House, 1968.

Poe, Edgar Allan. "The Tell-Tale Heart." In *The Collected Stories of Edgar Allan Poe.* New York: Random House, 1992.

Silverman, Kenneth, ed. *New Essays on Poe's Major Tales.* New York: Cambridge University Press, 1993.

Anna Leahy
Ohio University

"TENTH OF JANUARY, THE" ELIZABETH STUART PHELPS WARD (1868, 1869)

First published in ATLANTIC MONTHLY in March 1868 and reprinted in *Men, Women, and Ghosts* in 1869, "The Tenth of January" shows Elizabeth Stuart PHELPS WARD's awakening social consciousness as a beginning writer, as she depicts the plight of New England factory girls. Often read in the context of her other critique of a brutally capitalist economic system, *The Silent Partner,* this story is the most widely anthologized of Phelps Ward in recent times. Much in the vein of Rebecca Harding DAVIS's "Life in the Iron Mills" (1861), Phelps Ward exposes the dehumanizing effects of an industrial setting.

Based on a true account of the collapse of one of the Pemberton textile mills and the fire resulting from the rescue attempt, the fictional rendition focuses on an imaginary character, the hunchbacked

Asenath Martyn, who lives a depressing life as a working girl in the Pemberton Mill, with only her doting father and a boarder friend, Dick, to offer her some solace and cheer. Shortly before the accident and fire occur, she witnesses an apparent love tryst between her beloved friend, Dick, and her beautiful coworker Del Ivory. During the fire, she allows herself, in a most martyrlike way, to fall victim to the flames so that Del Ivory's life can be spared. Dick joyously pulls Del out of the rubble and both leave the scene without a second thought about Asenath, or Sene, as her father lovingly called her. The final tableau is of Sene's father crawling on the collapsing building in an attempt to save his daughter, to no avail.

As Phelps Ward points out in her autobiography, *Chapters from a Life,* although her father permitted her brother to witness the disaster at the Pemberton Mills in the neighboring town of Lawrence, she, a 15-year-old girl at the time of the accident in 1860, was forbidden to view the disaster. She resented her protective father's sheltering attitude. (Part of her hostility might have entered the text in Sene's tensely divided feelings toward her father.) Phelps Ward had no recourse but to conduct interviews with eyewitnesses and to visit the scene later to piece together her version of the story.

BIBLIOGRAPHY

Buhle, Mari Jo, and Florence Howe. "Afterword." In Phelps Ward, Elizabeth Stuart, *The Silent Partner and "The Tenth of January."* New York: Feminist Press, 1983.

Ward, Elizabeth Stuart Phelps. *The Silent Partner and "The Tenth of January."* New York: Feminist Press, 1983.

Monika Elbert
Montclair State University

"THAT EVENING SUN" WILLIAM FAULKNER (1931)

When it appeared in the *American Mercury* in March 1931, the editor, H. L. Mencken, prevailed on William FAULKNER to make changes in "That Evening Sun" (then entitled "That Evening Sun Go Down") to make it more palatable to the sensibilities of the magazine's readers. To wit, Mencken objected to the name Jesus, the lover of Nancy, the story's PROTAGONIST, and to the explicit descriptions of Nancy's pregnancy by Mr. Stoval, the white bank cashier and church deacon. Faulkner agreed to rename Jesus "Jubal," and he removed the vine METAPHOR for Nancy's pregnancy, but he balked at removing all references to it because Jesus' knowledge of her condition is a critical factor in his motivation to murder her. When the story was republished in *These Thirteen* (1931), he restored the story to its original form and eliminated some explanation that he considered unnecessary in the final paragraph (Charters 423–24).

Despite the post–CIVIL RIGHTS era in which readers now encounter this story, many find that it still has the power to produce shock and anger. The effect of the story derives in part from Nancy's utter powerlessness as a black woman in the 1930s South, and in part from Faulkner's narrative POINT OF VIEW. By filtering the tale through the consciousness of Quentin Compson, now 24 years old, but retelling the events as they occurred when he was nine, his sister Caddy was seven, and his brother Jason was five, Faulkner utilizes the technique of the uncomprehending and therefore UNRELIABLE NARRATOR. Readers must fill in the gaps as Quentin recalls the social structure of the time. White men had all the power, black men had power only over black women, and thus for no other reason other than her color and gender, Nancy is doomed.

Despite—or perhaps because of—her hopeless position, Nancy demonstrates spirit when she publically accuses Mr. Stoval of failing to pay her for the last three times he had sex with her. He responds by kicking her in the teeth, and the town marshal responds by putting her in jail, where Nancy, visibly pregnant with Stoval's child, unsuccessfully tries to commit suicide. Later, Nancy goes to work for the Compsons, and Quentin reports on a visit from Jesus, who articulates the black man's frustration with his powerlessness when the white man can take his woman and his home. Jesus is a sympathetic figure at this point, but because he cannot vent his anger at its source—Mr. Stoval—he transfers it to Nancy. She knows Jesus will kill her, and hopelessly declares to the naive children, "I ain't nothing but a nigger. . . . It ain't none of my fault" (TES 434).

Mrs. Compson selfishly ignores Nancy's very real terror, and Mr. Compson, while mildly sympathetic, ultimately fails to protect her.

When Nancy tries to use the Compson children to protect her from Jesus, whom she knows is somewhere nearby waiting to kill her, Faulkner renders her fear palpable. The children's inability to understand her predicament makes it even more frustrating for the reader, who foresees her death but cannot reach into the story to stop it. Written by a white man from Mississippi, this horrifying story constitutes a powerful microcosm of the brutally unfair and unfeeling attitudes of southern whites toward southern blacks in the Mississippi of the early 20th century.

BIBLIOGRAPHY

Basset, John E. *Vision and Revisions: Essays on Faulkner.* West Cornwall, Conn.: Locust Hill Press, 1989.

Bloom, Harold. *William Faulkner.* New York: Chelsea House, 1986.

Blotner, Joseph. *Faulkner: A Biography.* New York: Random House, 1991.

Brooks, Cleanth. *A Shaping Joy.* New York: Harcourt, Brace, Jovanovich, 1971.

Charters, Ann. "William Faulkner." In *Major Writers of Short Fiction: Stories and Commentary.* Edited by Ann Charters. New York: St. Martin's, 1993, pp. 422–24.

Gwynn, Frederick, and Joseph Blotner, eds. *Faulkner in the University.* Charlottesville: University of Virginia Press, 1959.

Hoffman, Frederick J. *William Faulkner, Revised.* Boston: Twayne, 1990.

Millgate, Michael. *The Achievement of William Faulkner.* New York: Random House, 1966.

THEME   The central insight or idea developed in a work of fiction. Theme is not merely a subject but rather an abstract concept that is illuminated through action, characterization, and image. Not all fictional stories have themes: Many simply relate adventures or moments in time, or attempt to frighten, amuse, or solve mysteries or crimes.

THURBER, JAMES (1894–1961) Born in Ohio, James Thurber attended Ohio State University. From 1918 to 1920 he worked in Paris before becoming a journalist in New York City, where, in 1927, he became associated with the NEW YORKER, in which virtually all his work first appeared. Thurber helped set the tone and style of the magazine and thereby aided in increasing its popularity. His book *The Years with Ross* (1959) is an account of his years working with editor Harold Ross on the staff of the *New Yorker.* A gifted illustrator and cartoonist, Thurber is well known for his short stories, sketches, essays, parodies, and parables.

Thurber's humorous stories, for which he still is well known, succeed in part because they have elements of seriousness and truth. One of his most frequently anthologized stories, "THE SECRET LIFE OF WALTER MITTY," illustrates Thurber's interest in the "battle between the sexes"; in Thurber's view, women try to maintain control over gentle, shy men like Walter Mitty. In the same vein is Thurber's amusing story, "THE CATBIRD SEAT," in which a shy businessman plots and succeeds in humiliating an aggressively efficient businesswoman.

BIBLIOGRAPHY

Thurber, James. *Fables for Our Time.* New York: Harper, 1940.

———. *Men, Women, and Dogs.* New York: Harcourt Brace, 1943.

———. *The Middle-Aged Man on the Flying Trapeze.* New York: Harper, 1935.

———. *My Life and Hard Times.* New York: Harper, 1933.

———. *My World—And Welcome to It.* New York: Harcourt Brace, 1942.

———. *The Owl in the Attic and Other Perplexities.* New York: Harper, 1931.

———. *The Seal in the Bedroom and Other Predicaments.* New York: Harper, 1932.

———. *The Thurber Carnival.* New York: Harper, 1945.

———. *Thurber Country.* New York: Simon & Schuster, 1953.

"TO BUILD A FIRE" JACK LONDON (1902)   The most famous of all Jack LONDON's stories, "To Build a Fire" was first written and published in 1902 in *Youth's Companion* magazine, then later revised and published in 1908 in *Century Magazine.* In 1910 it appeared in London's short story collection *Lost Faces.* Aboard the *Cutty Sark* headed for Hawaii and the South Seas, a more mature London rewrote this CLASSIC tale of the frozen Northland to express more fully his awe of the "White Silence" of nature and his sense both of humankind's insignificance in the face of such a force and also its indomitable will to survive. In the second (and repeatedly anthologized) version, unlike the first, the main character (see PROTAGONIST) has no name and is accompanied by a dog that acts as FOIL to his foolish pridefulness in the face of the White Silence. This grimmer version, in which the man dies, also features an "Old Timer" who advises the young man, "Never travel alone," a statement that becomes a metaphysical as well as a practical one: "The story sharply contrasts living in community and trying to survive on one's own. Its comingling of NATURALISM and romanticism results in a new kind of REALISM for the American short story, a simultaneous recognition of humanity's physical and spiritual struggles for survival. The story is ample testimony to London's own view of the Klondike: as he put it, "In the Klondike you get your perspective. I got mine." Significantly, in the context of the story's odd combination of religious ALLUSIONS with the notion of survival of the fittest, London carried three books with him into the Klondike: a guidebook to the Yukon, John Milton's *Paradise Lost,* and Charles DARWIN's *Origin of Species.*

BIBLIOGRAPHY

Labor, Earle, and King Hendricks. "Jack London's Twice-Told Tale." *Studies in Short Fiction* 4 (Summer 1967): 334–337.

London, Jack. "To Build a Fire." In *Lost Faces.* New York: Macmillan, 1910.

Jeanne Campbell Reesman
University of Texas at San Antonio

TODOROV, TZVETAN (1939–)   Tzvetan

Todorov, a Bulgarian teaching and writing in France, writes clear theoretical texts that address literature's figurative power, spatial form, and narrative syntax (patterns of word arrangements). He is considered a structuralist, like Roland BARTHES and Julia KRISTEVA, but also a narratologist, or one who analyzes the story in relation to the methods used to tell it. Todorov defines literature as constantly changing human discourse or speech acts that may be classified by genre. He defines the "norms" of some genre, such as DETECTIVE FICTION and fantastic literature, and his definition of the latter—that which causes the reader to hesitate, struck by particular natural or supernatural events—is frequently cited. Todorov has written extensively on the stories of Edgar Allan POE and Henry JAMES.

Brenda M. Palo
University of North Carolina at Chapel Hill

TONE   In fiction, tone refers to the attitude of

the author as the reader infers it. Tone differs from MOOD, the atmosphere in which the characters move and act. An author's tone may be condescending, sympathetic, serious, comic, playful, ironic, to cite only a few possible examples. In Edith WHARTON's depiction of two middle-aged women in "ROMAN FEVER," for instance, the author adopts a satirical tone. In Langston HUGHES's collection, *The Ways of White Folk,* he uses an unsentimental tone as he demonstrates some of the reprehensible results of white power over African Americans.

TOOMER, JEAN (1894–1967)   Born in

Washington, D.C., in 1894, Jean Toomer lived with his mother, Nina Pinchback, and his grandfather, Pinckney Benton Stewart Pinchback, a well-known if controversial Louisiana politician during the RECONSTRUCTION era. Toomer never knew his father, Nathan Toomer, who disappeared soon after his son's birth. Although he earned no degree, Toomer extensively educated himself at a variety of institutions, including the University of Wisconsin, the University of Chicago, and City College of New York. After publishing several stories and poems in such LITTLE MAGAZINES as *Broom* and the *Little Review,* as well as in African-American publications, including the *Liberator,* in 1921 Toomer worked as superintendent of a small black school in Sparta, Georgia, the source of the material he imaginatively transformed into CANE, a short story collection that proved to be his masterpiece and his best-known work.

Heralded as a new direction in African-American literature, *Cane* is a remarkably diverse work that unifies the northern and southern African-American experience in the face of oppression by whites in both regions. Written in three sections, the book contains both short stories and poetry written in lyrical, imagistic, mystical, sensuous language that ultimately celebrates the strength and courage of African Americans.

BIBLIOGRAPHY
Benson, Brian Joseph, and Mabel Mayle Dillard. *Jean Toomer*. Boston: Twayne, 1980.
Dorris, Ronald. *Race: Jean Toomer's Swan Song*. New Orleans, La.: Xavier Review Press, 1997.
Durham, Frank, ed. *The Merrill Studies in Cane*. Columbus, Ohio: Merill, 1971.
Kerman, Cynthia Earl, and Richard Eldridge. *The Lives of Jean Toomer*. Baton Rouge: Louisiana State University Press, 1987.
McKay, Nellie. *Jean Toomer, Artist: A Study of His Life and Work, 1894–1936*. Chapel Hill: University of North Carolina Press, 1984.
O'Daniel, Therman B., ed. *Jean Toomer: A Critical Evaluation*. Washington, D.C.: Howard University Press, 1988.
Scruggs, Charles. *Jean Toomer and the Terrors of American History*. Philadelphia: University of Pennsylvania Press, 1998.
Toomer, Jean. *Cane*. New york: Boni & Liveright, 1923.
———. *The Wayward and the Seeking: A Collection of Writings*. Edited by Darwin T. Turner. Washington, D.C.: Howard University Press, 1980.

TRAGEDY

A literary GENRE whose definition was established by Aristotle, tragedy has numerous meanings and, until relatively recent times, applied only to plays. In general, the term now applies to any literary work in which a worthy but imperfect PROTAGONIST suffers a downfall resulting from his or her *hamartia*, or tragic flaw, or from the intervention of nature or fate. Many of Aristotle's requirements, however, still hold true for tragedy in contemporary fiction: the protagonist suffers a catastrophe, and, although he or she need not suffer the requisite death of the classical protagonist, the emotional results of the ordeal produce a catharsis of pity and fear in the readers. To qualify as tragic rather than merely pathetic, the protagonists should face the reversal of their fortunes, no matter how undeserved, with courage and dignity.

TRANSCENDENTALISM

An important philosophical and literary movement in New England from 1836 to 1860. Drawing from the doctrines of German idealist philosophers, particularly Immanuel Kant, and influenced by the British writers Thomas Carlyle, Samuel Taylor Coleridge, and William Wordsworth, a group of Boston-area writers and intellectuals, including Ralph Waldo Emerson, George Ripley, Bronson Alcott, Margaret Fuller, Henry David Thoreau, and Nathaniel HAWTHORNE formed an informal organization to discuss new developments in philosophy as well as literature and theology. Transcendentalism posited the belief that humans can intuitively transcend the limits of the senses and logic and receive higher truth directly from nature. For the New England Transcendentalists, accepting this philosophy was also a reaction against Calvinist orthodoxy, Unitarianism, and scientific rationalism. Asserting that each person's relation to God was established directly by the individual and not through a formal church, they believed in living close to nature, in the dignity of manual labor, in rejection of traditional authority, and in advocating democracy and individualism. The Transcendentalists published a journal, the DIAL, from 1840 to 1844. Essays by Emerson and Thoreau's *Walden* (1854) were influential in furthering the movement. The experimental and quasi-UTOPIAN Brook Farm (1841–47) was established by George Ripley and other Transcendentalists.

"TRANSCENDENTAL WILD OATS" LOUISA MAY ALCOTT (1873)

Often touted as Louisa May ALCOTT's condemnation of TRANSCENDENTALISM, "Transcendental Wild Oats" (first published in *The Independent* in 1873 and reprinted in *The Woman's Journal* the following year) reshapes an actual occurrence in Alcott's young life into hilarious but pointed satire. In 1843 Amos Bronson Alcott had brought his family into a short-lived experiment in communal living at a farm in Harvard,

Massachusetts, called Fruitlands. The experiment itself held together for only half a year, and although the young Louisa's journals seem to cast it as a rather exciting adventure, the mature Louisa's short story focuses on the impracticality of its founders.

Alcott certainly did not have to wrack her imagination for examples of transcendental absurdities at Fruitlands, or "Apple Slump" as it comes to be called; as her story accurately reports, the idealists didn't move in until June, even though they hoped to be self-sufficient through farming; they planted three different kinds of seed in one field and used no fertilizer due to their opposition to animal products. The cast of characters, also taken from life, needed little embellishment. In addition to Abel Lamb (Bronson Alcott) and family, and Timon Lion (Alcott's partner Charles Lane) and his son, the community included a man whose contribution to radicalism consisted of reversing his given name and surname and another whose odd antics in the name of free expression of whatever was in one's soul "would have sent him to a lunatic asylum . . . if he had not already been in one" (371). Alcott even uses, as dialogue, quotes from letters her father and Lane submitted to the transcendentalist paper the DIAL (dubbed *The Transcendental Tripod* in the tale) during the experiment, which frequently make them look even more absurd. However, her use of allegorical (see ALLEGORY) names and especially the clearly amused narrative voice Alcott employs in the piece make it an engaging, affectionate PARABLE.

Alcott's other fiction clearly shows that it was not the concept of communal living to which she objected; in fact, many of her works, long and short, celebrate unusual communities that are based on family but extend beyond it; see, for example, the extended school/family in *Jo's Boys* (1886); the "loving league of sisters" that crowns her novel *Work* (1873); and the group consisting of the HEROINE Rosamond Vivian, her husband's not quite ex-wife and child, and a helpful priest who join forces with them in an attempt to foil the villain in *A Long Fatal Love Chase* (1995). Alcott uses the more pointed details in "Transcendental Wild Oats" to voice her objections to the way the men's idealism frees them

to philosophize while virtually enslaving the women, particularly Mrs. Lamb. The reader sees Mrs. Lamb trying to deal with strict dietary regimens and still nourish her children, fighting to light a candle for evening mending and reading when animal substances have been banned, and rounding up the children to help get in the few existing crops when "some call of the Oversoul wafted all the men away" (375) just when the meager harvest needed to be gathered. When an inquisitive visitor asks whether there are any beasts of burden on the farm, Mrs. Lamb replies, "Only one woman!" (373). The fact that Mrs. Lamb ("Hope") brings her husband back from the depths of despair when the experiment flounders and then takes charge to extricate her family from it makes her the true heroine of the piece. In "Transcendental Wild Oats" Alcott not only provides a skeptical insider's look at transcendentalism in general and at the Fruitlands experiment in particular, but she also exhibits the wit that characterizes some of her most engaging work as she voices her support for practical idealism and reiterates her continuous concern for the position of women in 19th-century society.

BIBLIOGRAPHY

Alcott, Louisa May. "Transcendental Wild Oats" (1873). In *Alternative Alcott*. Edited by Elaine Showalter. New Brunswick, N.J.: Rutgers University Press, 1988.

Francis, Richard. "Circumstances and Salvation: The Ideology of the Fruitlands Utopia." *American Quarterly* 25 (May 1973): 202–304.

Petrulionis, Sandra Harbert. "By the Light of Her Mother's Lamp: Woman's Work versus Man's Philosophy in Louisa May Alcott's 'Transcendental Wild Oats.'" *Studies in the American Renaissance* (1995): 69–81.

Sears, Clara Endicott. *Bronson Alcott's Fruitlands*. Boston: Houghton Mifflin, 1915.

Christine Coyle Francis
Central Connecticut State University

TRICKSTER

Most frequently found in (but not exclusive to) NATIVE AMERICAN tribal traditions and literature, tricksters are mischievous changelings, sometimes seen and sometimes not, who frequently test taboos of the tribe and society. Unrestricted by geography or time, they may change froms from male to female, from human to animal (usually coyote, crow, or rabbit), and from animal to human. Tricksters are sensual, playful, humorous, seductive, dangerous, and deceptive. Gerald VIZENOR's "BARON OF PETRONIA" contains a pseudotrickster in the guise of Luster Browne. Other trickster figures can be found in several stories in Leslie Marmon SILKO's *Storyteller* and plays by Tomson Highway. Trickster figures also occur in stories by SUI SIN FAR and the novel *Tripmaster Monkey* by Maxine Hong KINGSTON.

BIBLIOGRAPHY

Cox, Jay. "Dangerous Definitions: Female Tricksters in Contemporary Native American Literature." *Wicazo Sa Review* 5. 2 (1989): 17–21.

Ruoff, A. LaVonne Brown. "Gerald Vizenor: Compassionate Trickster." *Studies in American Indian Literature* 9 (1986): 52–63.

Calvin Hussman
St Olaf College

TROUT FISHING IN AMERICA   RICHARD BRAUTIGAN (1967)

Richard BRAUTIGAN's first successful novel, filled with magical, supple METAPHORs and innovative representations of reality, sold over 2 million copies and was translated into six languages. Each of the 47 short chapters is self-contained, and the novel can also be read as a SHORT STORY CYCLE. Its success brought new critical attention and a larger audience to Brautigan's previously published writings that featured social commentary and startling use of language, including his novel *A Confederate General from Big Sur* (1964) and poetry collections. Brautigan wrote the first-person, METAFICTION stories that comprise *Trout Fishing in America* while camping and fishing in Idaho. (See POINT OF VIEW.) The astonishing title character, free from traditional limitations in time and space, possesses a flexible identity that changes from a fishing experience to an autopsied corpse to chalked labels on first-graders' backs to a San Francisco cripple as the setting shifts primarily between the Pacific Northwest and California.

The allusive, humorous book nods to many literary and cultural figures, (see ALLUSION), including Ernest HEMINGWAY (especially "BIG TWO-HEARTED RIVER"), Henry David Thoreau, Benjamin Franklin, George Gordon, Lord Byron, and Franz Joseph Kafka (see KAFKAESQUE). As further evidence that *Trout Fishing* may be read as short stories, Brautigan printed two "additional" chapters in his short story collection *Revenge of the Lawn: Stories 1962–1970* (1971). In these "chapters"—found in a story called "The Lost Chapters of *Trout Fishing in America*: 'Rembrandt Creek' and 'Carthage Sink,'"—the 1969 narrator claims to have returned in time, retrieved and rewritten the stories lost in 1961 (37–41). This self-reflexive play with memory and time is typical of Brautigan's postmodern challenge to the form and scope of human myth and imagination (See POSTMODERNISM.)

BIBLIOGRAPHY

Hearron, Thomas. "Escape through Imagination in *Trout Fishing in America*." *Critique*. 16, no. 1 (1974): 25–31.

Tanner, Tony. *City of Words: American Fiction 1950–1970.* London: Jonathan Cape, 1971.

Brenda M. Palo
University of North Carolina at Chapel Hill

TURN OF THE SCREW, THE   HENRY JAMES (1898)

"The Turn of the Screw" was first published as a serial in *Collier's Weekly* in 1898 and appeared later the same year in book form, in *The Two Magics*. Quickly becoming Henry JAMES's most popular piece of short fiction, *The Turn of the Screw* reflects the significant shift that occurred in James's writing during the late 1890s—the period identified as his "experimental phase." Characterized by an increasing AMBIGUITY that worked to undermine the narrative conventions of realist fiction, *The Turn of the Screw* and James's other experimental texts (including *What Maisie Knew, The Awkward Age,* and *The Sacred Fount*) move beyond the strict REALISM that characterized his early work and suggest the modernist techniques that would typify his "major phase" novels of the first decade of the 20th century (see MODERNISM).

The ambiguity of James's popular NOVELLA substantially added to the suspense that made it a favorite thriller among contemporary readers. That same ambiguity has continued to structure conversations, beginning in the 1950s, about whether the ghosts in James's text are "real" or the narrator's hallucinations. Because these accounts often unwittingly re-create the narrative strategies they set out to critique, recently they have become the subject of intellectual analysis in their own right.

Told as a story to a fictional audience, James's text initially seems to conform to traditional forms of realist narrative. However, the account that the narrator, Douglas, reads to his listeners is a first-person narrative written by the governess who cares for the two children, Miles and Flora, at the center of the drama. This partial and arguably hallucinatory account is the only version we get of the strange events that occur at her employer's rural mansion, Bly. A central question, therefore, addresses the issue of whether the governess is an UNRELIABLE NARRATOR. The events she describes involve the ghosts of two former employees: Miss Jessel, the first governess of the two children, and Peter Quint, the valet, both of whom are dead at the time the narrative opens. The story focuses on the governess's sustained attempts to protect her two charges from the corrupting visitations of these two ghosts. Requested by Bly's absent master, with whom the governess fell in love before his departure, never to trouble him about the children, the governess enlists the aid of Bly's faithful housekeeper, Mrs. Grose. In attempting to learn why Miles has been dismissed from school and why both children hide their contact with the ghosts—vague hints of drink and sex inform the mysteries—the governess is forced to confront the children and, in the process, Miles dies.

BIBLIOGRAPHY

Beidler, Peter G. Ghosts, Demons, and Henry James: "The Turn of the Screw" and the Turn of the Century. Columbia: University of Missouri Press, 1989.

Bell, Millicent. Meaning in Henry James. Cambridge, Mass.: Harvard University Press, 1991.

———. "The 'Turn of the screw' and the Recherche de l'absolu." In Henry James: Fiction as History. Edited by Ian F. Bell. Totowa, N.J.: Barnes & Noble, 1984, pp. 65–81.

Felman, Shoshana. "Turning the Screw of Interpretation," Yale French Studies 55–56 (1977): 94–207. 1982.

Halttunen, Karen. "Through the Cracked and Fragmented Self: William James and The Turn of the Screw," American Quarterly 40, no. 4 (December 1988): 472–490.

Heller, Terry. The Turn of the Screw: Bewildered Vision. Boston: Twayne, 1989.

James, Henry. The Turn of the Screw. In The Great Short Novels of Henry James. New York: Dial Press, 1944.

McWhirter, David. "In the 'Other House' of Fiction: Writing, Authority, and Femininity in The Turn of the Screw." Yale French Studies 55–56 (1977): 94–207.

Newman, Beth. "Getting Fixed: Feminine Identity and Scopic Crisis in The Turn of the Screw," Novel: A Forum on Fiction 26, no. 1 (Fall 1992): 43–63. 1992.

Spilka, Mark. "Turning the Freudian Screw: How Not to Do It," Literature and Psychology 13 (1963): 105–111.

Caroline F. Levander
Trinity University

TWAIN, MARK (SAMUEL L. CLEMENS) (1835–1910)

Samuel L. Clemens published his first stories long before he shaped his literary PERSONA, Mark Twain. His earliest material appeared in the small hometown newspaper edited by his brother Orion. These few pieces—"The Dandy Frightening the Squatter" (1852) was the first—offer little more than brief SKETCHes, often dealing with clashes between town and frontier or with small-town characters and behavior. While in Nevada during the early 1860s, Twain sharpened his storytelling skills in letters home and tried out his literary voice on members of his family (especially his mother, Jane Lampton Clemens). The tight focus Twain practiced in these early writings dominated his approach to storytelling throughout his long career whether he worked at short fiction, travel writing, or the novel.

Although often described as the natural outgrowth of southwestern humor, Twain's voice has no single literary parent. If anything, Mark Twain is the mongrel child of 19th-century American storytelling. Twain prized oral storytelling: His mother had a reputation as a fine storyteller; young Sam also spent summers listening to the slaves who worked his Uncle John Quarles's farm. He would later mix this combination of oral tales with the broad literary COMEDY in the tradition of southwestern TALL TALES and Mississippi roarers with a strong dose of blunt Nevada-style journalism from his newspaper days in the West. Twain's writing for the *Virginia City Enterprise* and the *Alta California* extended his apprenticeship into the later 1860s, years during which he struggled to create an individual voice with the snap of oral language and the blunt edge of deadpan delivery. His story "The Celebrated Jumping Frog of Calaveras County" (1865), originally written for a collection being prepared by ARTEMUS WARD (the fictional Yankee humorist-philosopher created by Charles Farrar BROWNE) but published separately, became an instant hit. In it Twain combined the language and setting of the tall-tale/practical joke (prominent in such earlier pieces as "River Intelligence" [1859], "The Petrified Man" [1862], and "A Bloody Massacre Near Carson" [1863]) with a fresh style characterized by catalogs of nouns and verbs and the homely images of the steamboat and the frontier to introduce eastern audiences to a new, hybrid story form.

The joke and hoax were tools for Twain throughout his career ("Map of Paris" [1870] is a good example; "1601" [1876], on the other hand, is notoriously unsuccessful); however, he spread his fictional net by challenging the moral tales of Sunday School books ("The Story of a Bad Little Boy Who Didn't Come to Grief" [1865] and "The Story of a Good Little Boy Who Did Not Prosper" [1870]) and the puffery of legislative debate ("Cannibalism in the Cars" [1868]). His second book, *Roughing It* (1872), is, in fact, a transitional work: Chapters 1 through 61 focus on the West and are peppered with tall tales, deadpan narratives, lies, and hoaxes; chapters 62 through 79, which cover Twain's stint as a correspondent in Hawaii and his debut as a lecturer, offer some SATIRE but concentrate more on travel and anecdote.

Twain emerged from *Roughing It* as more than a tall-tale artist and more than a travel writer. As he moves into the mid-1870s, his short fiction, previously populated with hard characters and variations on the rough frontier, becomes much more universal in scope. Perhaps the most overlooked aspect of Twain as a short story writer is his reliance on domestic considerations. In fact, the majority of his short fiction takes its cue from the situations and relationships found in the home or tightly knit community or small town. Beginning with "A True Story Repeated Word for Word as I Heard It" (1874), a reconstruction of an ex-slave's oral tale told by Mary Ann Cord (a family servant), Twain often turns to explorations of human relationships both within and outside family groups. Even those stories famous for insights into moral questions, "The Facts Concerning the Recent Carnival of Crime in Connecticut" (1876) and "The Man That Corrupted Hadleyburg" (1899), present domestic scenes of conscience. Even more explicitly domestic, the sequence of husband/wife conversations in three McWilliams tales (1875, 1880, 1882); "Which Was the Dream" (1897); "The Great Dark" (1898); "The Death Disk" (1901); "Was It Heaven? or Hell" (1902); the "Little Bessie" tales (1908–9); and the posthumously published "The Death of Jean" (1911) present characters facing profound challenges inherent in the tangle of domestic connections.

As he matured as a writer of fiction, Mark Twain became increasingly interested in exploring the reactions of individual characters to the demands within their lives. Instead of relying on situation to provoke reaction and response, he spotlighted individual characters and adjusted their voices to underscore human failings and folly or, in some cases, human curiosity and the struggle for faith. ("The War Prayer: [1905] and "Extract from Captain Stormfield's Visity to Heaven: [1907] are examples.) Twain was interested in and developed a genius for creating tight snapshots of life; his novel-length fiction is sustained more by his extending a series of episodes as seen through a single perspective than by a disciplined sense of plot or action. (Both *Adventures of Huckleberry Finn* [1885] and *A Connecticut Yankee in King Arthur's Court* [1889] are excellent examples; "Extracts from Adam's Diary" [1893], and "Eve's Diary" [1905] are also important.) Often Twain would resort to the framing tale as a device to gain an intimacy with a narrator: What was valuable in his early tale of Jim Smiley and his frog or of Jim

Blaine's grandfather's ram becomes a controlling strategy for longer works that are presented by Huckleberry Finn or Hank Morgan, experts in creating brief, crisp scenes. During his last five years of life, Twain explored whether a string of anecdotes and tales, linked by a consistent narrative voice, can blend into a unified autobiography.

Mark Twain was well aware of his strengths as a writer of sketches, anecdotes, tales, and hoaxes, and he made good use of that strength throughout a half century of telling stories. The fragmented nature of his novel-length fiction is a direct result of his success with the short story form; what is often seen as his failure as a novelist is, in fact, his triumph as a writer of short fiction.

BIBLIOGRAPHY

Fishkin, Shelley Fisher, gen. ed. *The Oxford Mark Twain*, 29 vols. New York: Oxford University Press, 1996.

Kaplan, Justin, ed. *The Signet Classic Book of Mark Twain's Short Stories*. New York: Signet, 1985.

Lemaster, J. R., and Wilson, James D., eds. *The Mark Twain Encyclopedia*. New York: Garland, 1993.

Rasmussen, R. Kent. *Mark Twain A to Z: The Essential Reference to His Life and Writings*. New York: Facts On File, 1995.

Twain, Mark. *Mark Twain: Collected Tales, Sketches, Speeches, & Essays*, ed. Louis J. Budd. 2 vols. New York: Library of America, 1992.

Wilson, James D. *A Reader's Guide to the Short Stories of Mark Twain*. Boston: G.K. Hall, 1987.

Michael J. Kiskis
Elmira College

"TWO FRIENDS" WILLA CATHER (1932)

First published in *Woman's Home Companion* in 1932 and included as one of three stories in the collection *Obscure Destinies* (1932), "Two Friends" has the structure and tone of a memoir. The story's narrator is an adult looking back on a three-year period of her youth during the 1890s, when two prosperous men in her small Kansas town—Mr. Dillon, a cattleman from Buffalo and Mr. Trueman, an Irish banker and owner of the town's general store—dominated her imagination. The narrative is almost entirely third-person description as the narrator recalls evenings passed at the general store when she witnessed, more than participated in, the friendship of two intelligent, principled, successful men. The story is one of the best examples of Willa CATHER's treatment of memory: The narrator re-creates a child's state of consciousness while rendering resonant details, such as the timbre of voices and the shape of people's hands, that give memory its lasting power.

Readers interested in gender issues in Cather's fiction will notice the adolescent girl's choice of men instead of women for HEROes, behavior reflecting Cather's own development at a young age. Venus crossing the moon and the Chicago Democratic convention at which William Jennings Bryan delivered his "Cross of Gold" speech provide the thematic structure (see THEME), suggesting the power of single events in human and cosmic history to influence people's lives. The men's friendship—rare, like the eclipse they witness—ends abruptly when Mr. Dillon attends the Chicago convention and becomes a passionate advocate of Bryan's campaign. Mr. Trueman retains his Republican convictions.

The story has affinities with American romanticism: The friendship's end is the narrator's fall from grace, precipitating the collapse of innocent belief in truths that should be but are not permanent. Like Sherwood ANDERSON's *WINESBURG, OHIO* and Ernest HEMINGWAY's early short stories, "Two Friends" describes the rhythmic routine of small-town life in America through the eyes of a restless, perceptive young person destined to leave. In the tradition of American REALISM, Cather positions universal human concerns in the context of American history.

BIBLIOGRAPHY

Arnold, Marilyn. *Willa Cather's Short Fiction*. Athens: Ohio University Press, 1984.

Cather, Willa. *Uncle Valentine and Other Stories: Willa Cather's Uncollected Short Fiction, 1915–1929*. Edited by Bernice Slote. Lincoln: University of Nebraska Press, 1973.

Frances Kerr
Durham Technical Community College

U

UNCLE REMUS The storyteller in Joel Chandler HARRIS's most famous works, ten volumes containing over 200 Uncle Remus tales. Remus is a kindly ex-slave who remains on his former owner's plantation after the CIVIL WAR and relates the stories in conversations with the owner's young son. Through Remus, Harris provided in written form the African American folk tales and animal LEGENDS that had been transmitted orally for generations.

UNRELIABLE NARRATOR A narrator whose perspective on and view of the matters he or she narrates contradicts or fails to coincide with the facts of the story or with the reader's own reactions to those facts. The unreliable narrator may very likely be wrong (or incomplete) in his or her evaluation of the meaning of the events of the story and thus puts pressure on readers to evaluate these meanings on their own. Although the unreliable narrator may be found in American fiction of any era—one commonly cited example is the naive and uncomprehending Huck Finn in Mark TWAIN's *Adventures of Huckleberry Finn,* another the puzzling governess who narrates Henry JAMES's THE TURN OF THE SCREW—he or she most frequently appears in modernist and postmodernist literature, inviting the reader to take an active role in determining the "real" meaning of the story. (See MODERNISM and POSTMODERNISM.)

UNVANQUISHED, THE WILLIAM FAULKNER **(1938)** Set during the CIVIL WAR and RECONSTRUCTION and composed of seven stories (five of which had been published previously in the SATURDAY EVENING POST and one in SCRIBNER'S MAGAZINE), William FAULKNER's *The Unvanquished* has been viewed as both a novel and as a SHORT STORY CYCLE. The stories feature Bayard Sartoris, a member of one of the most prominent families in YOKNAPATAWPHA COUNTY as he grows in understanding and maturity. Taken together, they comprise a BILDUNGSROMAN that demonstrates Bayard's increasing recognition of the tensions that have created and still permeate the New South and that have formed his own character between the ages of 12 and 24. Because the early stories are told from the perspective of a child, the full weight of the historical events—and the issues of race and gender interlaced with the theme of courage—is not apparent until the last story.

In the first tale, "Ambuscade," the 12-year-old boys, Bayard, who is white, and Ringo, who is black, find the war exciting and heroic. The time is 1863, and they take turns playing General Pemberton and General Grant at Vicksburg. Bayard views his father, Colonel John Sartoris, as a hero, a giant, a man capable of defending the entire South against the Union forces. Loosh, one of the Sartorises' former slaves, shows that he does indeed understand the injustice of slavery and the significance of the increasing number of Union victories. Bayard's aunt, Rosa Millard, demonstrates her quick thinking and courage when a Yankee colonel comes to the house, and she protects the boys by hiding them under her sweeping skirts.

The second story, "Retreat," takes place one year later. Characters who will reappear in GO DOWN, MOSES, appear here—Uncle Buck McCaslin, for example. Unlike Ringo and his family, who remain loyal to the Sartorises, Loosh continues to show his excitement about almost certain freedom while Rosa, fearing reprisals against Col. Sartoris for his attacks of Yankee bivouacs, takes Bayard and Ringo to the safer plantation, Hawkhurst, home of relatives in Alabama. Col. Sartoris makes a courageous if foolhardly escape out the back door of his house, and the Yankees burn the Sartoris plantation. At 13 Bayard still sees his father—and the role of the old South—in romanticized, idealized terms (see ROMANTICISM).

In the third story, "Raid," the now 14-year-old Bayard, living at Hawkhurst, begins to comprehend the vast destructiveness of the war. His cousin Drusilla Hawk, who before the war could outrun and outride any man in the county, tells him she has lost her fiancé. Life before the war, she says sarcastically, had been "boring" when a woman had merely to think of finding a husband and choosing silverware and having babies. In the next stories she will cut her hair short, ride with Col. Sartoris's troops, and fight the Yankees. The former slaves move toward freedom and Loosh, who speaks for their point of view, points out to Rosa the injustice of one human being owning another. Rosa initiates her scheme in which, with the help of Bayard and Ringo, she outwits the Yankees by stealing their mules and then later selling the same animals to them.

"Riposte in Tertio," the fourth story, features Ringo who emerges as very intelligent, on an equal footing with Rosa as he strategizes and extends the mule-stealing scheme. He is the first to understand—as the naive Bayard does not—that the poor white Ab SNOPES has betrayed the family. Rosa, a sort of female Robin Hood, takes the money from the mule sale and distributes it to all the poor, black and white alike, in the county, even though everyone still adheres to the rigid separation of the blacks from the whites in the church where Rosa distributes the money. She is murdered by Grundy and his band of roving scavengers.

In the fifth story, "Vendee," the 15-year-old Bayard, suffering a nearly overwhelming sense of grief and loss, avenges Rosa's death by killing Grundy, and severing the hand from his body that he then nails to the door of Grundy's hideout. The grim reality of Rosa's death has removed all traces of naiveté and innocence, and Bayard loses the rose-colored perspective of his younger days. In the next two stories, he acutely observes and understands the unfolding events of the war's aftermath.

"Skirmish at Sartoris" contains two pivotal events: the shooting incident arising from the election for town marshall, and the women's concern that Drusilla marry Col. Sartoris to save her reputation. Faulkner ties the two together in a superficially amusing way, but, ultimately, they have consequences of the utmost gravity. Yankee carpetbaggers (ancestors of Joanna Burden of the 1932 novel *Light in August*) have backed an illiterate black candidate for the office. Col. Sartoris tries to persuade them to leave and, when his efforts fail, he shoots and kills them. Meanwhile, Drusilla's mother becomes hysterical because, in the confusion over the election, Drusilla and Sartoris have not yet taken their marriage vows. The post–Civil War racism, the violence, and the Old South's attempts to maintain tradition despite defeat provide the complex themes in this penultimate story.

"An Odor of Verbena," the last story, is generally considered the best of the collection. Everyone from Ringo to Bayard's college professor to his father's friends expect Bayard to avenge his father's murder as he earlier had avenged Rosa Millard's. Bayard, however, displays a newfound wisdom and a different kind of courage: He believes that enough killing has occurred, and he therefore faces his father's murderer unarmed. He has listened to advice from Drusilla, his father's widow, who advocates revenge, and from Jenny Du Pre, his father's sister, who counsels a cessation of violence.

Although critics have written frequently about the themes of war and racism in these stories, they have said far less about the role of women. The title of the collection, "The Unvanquished," refers not just to the soldiers but to the women who refuse to accept defeat—and Drusilla Hawk is Faulkner's heroic woman throughout much of the action. After losing her fiancé at Shiloh, Drusilla suffers bitterness and insomnia, but she hardens herself to the present and determines to seek vengeance of the Yankees by enlisting in John Sartoris's cavalry and riding off to war. Later, when her mother, horrified at Drusilla's riding and bivouacking with men, insists that Drusilla and John Sartoris marry, the spirited Drusilla responds, "Can't you understand that I am tired of burying husbands in this war? That I am riding in Cousin John's troop not to find a man but to hurt Yankees?" (UV 220).

There are moments of humor as her mother berates her for having fought with men and worn trousers, and for having thrown away "the highest destiny of a Southern woman—to be the bride-widow of a lost cause" (UV 219), but the humor dwindles as Drusilla is forced into a marriage that she does not want. She is truly "beaten" by those dresses: her cousin Bayard tells us that she still would have worn pants all the time if she were allowed, but she is forbidden now by her husband. Entrapped in a loveless marriage, Drusilla is robbed of her natural courage and exuberance and becomes a thwarted and unhappy woman who, at the end of the novel, has lost at age 30 both fiancé and husband. Bayard refuses her advice, yet her tribute to his moral courage in refusing to fight—signified by the sprig of verbena she leaves on his pillow—is a magnanimous gesture. Bayard compassionately contemplates "how the War had tried to stamp all women of her generation and class in the South into a type and how it had failed—the suffering, the identical experience—was there in the eyes, yet beyond that was the incorrigibly individual woman" (UV 263).

In the end, Bayard's most important lessons have originated with women: Rosa Millard, Drusilla Hawk, and Jenny Du Pre, who prevailed in the end in her plea to end the tradition of violence. As Bayard notes, the women have never surrendered. Thanks to them, he, like ISAAC MCCASLIN of Faulkner's *Go Down, Moses,* is able to look objectively at the tortured and complex history that has formed him.

BIBLIOGRAPHY
Faulkner, William. *The Unvanquished.* Reprint. New York: Vintage Press, 1966.
Grimwood, Michael. *Heart in Conflict: Faulkner's Struggles with Vocation.* Athens: University of Georgia Press, 1987.
Harrington, Evans, and Ann J. Abadie, eds. *Faulkner and the Short Story: Faulkner and Yoknapatawpha.* Jackson: University of Mississippi Press, 1992.
Matthews, John T. *The Play of Faulkner's Language.* Ithaca, N.Y.: Cornell University Press, 1982.
Snead, James. *Figures of Division: William Faulkner's Major Novels.* New York: Methuen, 1986.
Sundquist, Eric. *Faulkner: The House Divided.* Baltimore: Johns Hopkins University Press, 1983.
Werlock, Abby H. P. "Victims Unvanquished: Temple Drake and the Women Characters in William Faulkner's Novels." In *Women and Violence in Literature: An Essay Collection.* Edited by Katherine Anne Ackley. New York: Garland Publishing, 1990, pp. 3–50.
Weinstein, Philip M., ed. *The Cambridge Companion to William Faulkner.* New York: Cambridge University Press, 1995.

UPDIKE, JOHN (1932–)

Born in Shillington, Pennsylvania, John Updike initially aspired to become a graphic artist. After graduating summa cum laude from Harvard, where he worked on the staff of the *Lampoon,* he spent a year in England at the Ruskin School of Drawing before accepting a job as a staff writer for the NEW YORKER, which published his first story ("Friends from Philadelphia") in 1954 and regularly continues to publish his fiction, poetry, and book reviews. Subsequently he resigned and moved to Massachusetts in order to dedicate himself to a writing career; since that time he has been one of the most prolific American authors, averaging a book a year as he alternates publication of poetry, novels, short story collections, and criticism as well as drama and memoir. Updike is perhaps best known

Rabbit, Run (1960); *Rabbit Redux* (1971), *Rabbit Is Rich* (1981); and *Rabbit at Rest* (1990). However, he is arguably at his best in the genre of short fiction, which showcases his stylistic talents and his penchant for illuminating details. Few writers of short fiction have been so widely anthologized and featured with such frequency—more than 20 times—in *Best American Short Stories* and *Prize Stories: The O. Henry Awards.*

Updike has published over 200 short stories in 11 collections, including four SHORT STORY CYCLES; in addition, a number of short prose pieces have been gathered in his volumes of collected prose. While generally celebrated as a traditionalist who excels at crafting epiphanic stories from ordinary moments of perception (see EPIPHANY), his short fiction has included numerous experiments with variations on the traditional short story, such as the SKETCH, the LYRIC, and the MONTAGE. In his lyric stories, such as "In Football Season," "Leaves," "The Music School," and "Harv Is Plowing Now," Updike subordinates plot in favor of a rich linguistic texture that dramatizes the mind's search for meaning as it creates a METAPHORIC coherence from fragments of memory and experience. Critics have lamented that Updike writes beautifully but has little to say and that he never tackles major THEMES; yet his commitment to portraying middle-class life challenges assumptions about the ordinariness of daily experience as it celebrates and casts light on the shadowy corners of domestic existence.

Characterized by stylistic precision and imagistic richness, Updike's short stories are also solidly realistic. (See REALISM.) "Details are the giant's fingers," proclaims the narrator of "The Blessed Man of Boston, My Grandmother's Thimble, and Fanning Island" (*Pigeon Feathers* 245), noting the role of detailed memory in establishing connection with the past. Updike credits his proclivity for detail to his training in the visual arts, which he claims provided valuable aesthetic practice in visualizing scenes as well as in constructing personality and plot. This attention to detail has contributed to short fiction that presents a rich social history chronicling the changing historical background, the shifting social mores, and the responses to change that have heightened spiritual uncertainty, social unrest, sexual freedom, and domestic tension. Read chronologically, his stories trace the metamorphosis of middle-class domesticity, from the security of the post–WORLD WAR II era through subsequent skepticism and moral upheaval to a contemporary apprehension of the need for renewed faith and trust.

Updike's characters have matured with their author, progressing from the local boy of OLINGER (the fictional equivalent of his hometown), to young couples in New York and suburban New England, to middle-age PROTAGONISTs experiencing marital tension, to older remarried characters confronting their mortality. As his characters age, they move not only from rural Olinger to suburban milieus but also from sheltered youth to increasingly complex maturity complicated by personal as well as social change. Updike's characters invariably cast fond backward glances to happier times before loss and separation (in "The Happiest I've Been," for example), but their yearnings transcend nostalgia, as they seek to rescue meaningful portions of the past and to accommodate the waning of memory, relationships, and life itself. Thematically, the majority of Updike's stories focus on this struggle against time's diminishment, most often overcome through memory and art. Frequently, however, especially in later collections, loss gains ascendancy over efforts to arrest its effects.

The Same Door (1959) and *Pigeon Feathers* (1962) most often employ a Joycean epiphany to heighten the revelations of everyday experience in the rural Pennsylvania setting that recalls the realm of Updike's youth. These early stories most often portray characters poised on the threshold of change who struggle with the enigma of loss and seek to maintain an open door to the past. Updike's 1964 collection, *Olinger Stories,* arranges a group of these early stories into a BILDUNGSROMAN with similar youthful characters who, taken together, may be viewed as one composite protagonist. The collection memorializes this realm of unexpected gifts as both the era and his characters undergo change. In *The Music School* (1966) and *Museums and Women* (1972), married protagonists require greater effort and discipline as they strive harder to capture life's more elusive satisfactions and to weave the more disparate fragments of past, present, and future into a coherent whole. Updike uses both the sustained lyric plunge and the short sketch to epitomize the often transitory attempt to grasp fleeting satisfactions; whatever epiphanies occur usually lead to more painful realizations of loss or spiritual uncertainty. The archaeological metaphor that dominates "Harv Is Plowing Now" is an apt one for Updike's suburbanites, who, as they approach middle age, unearth artifacts from the past that only increase their puzzlement and dissatisfaction.

Updike's collection of previously published and new stories featuring Joan and Richard Maple in *Too Far to Go* (1979) maps the fault lines of contemporary marriage. Depicting a 20-year marriage through snapshots of its significant tensions, Updike uses the Maples to explore the forces that simultaneously rupture the marriage and continue to attract Joan and Richard back to each other, until they finally resolve, in "SEPARATING," to end their union. *Problems* (1979) begins Updike's exploration of the landscape beyond divorce, with its emotional wreckage and profound burdens of guilt (metaphorically depicted as "Guilt Gems" in the title of one story). While his protagonists may attempt to develop spiritual and emotional calluses as protection from suffering, often they find themselves still vulnerable to loss, uncertainty, and betrayal. In *Trust Me* (1987), older characters who have passed through middle-age restlessness and established new relationships find the uneasy foundations of their trust shaken and encounter difficulty regaining some semblance of belief in themselves, others, frail social structures, and the ideals that have sustained them. Updike's most recent collection, *The Afterlife* (1995), depicts older characters increasingly confronted with mortality and the diminished pleasures of their settled condition, although "A Sandstone Farmhouse," in which the narrator returns to his boyhood home after his mother's death," and "Grandparenting," a new Maples story, offer redemptive possibilities.

In addition to Joan and Richard Maple, Updike has created another character featured in multiple short stories: Henry Bech, an artistically blocked Jewish writer who serves as a sort of literary alter ego through whom Updike has used his travel experiences to satirize the current state of the publishing industry. With their dry humor and picaresque quality, the stories in *Bech: A Book* (1970), *Bech Is Back* (1982), and *Bech at Bay: A Quasi-Novel* (1998) stand out from Updike's lyric and epiphanic stories, although they touch on similar anxieties about loss, here using the creative writer's diminished stature in a media-based culture. Casting aside the fictional mask, Updike reflects on his artistic development in *Self-Consciousness* (1989), a memoir comprised of six related essays that contain numerous ALLUSIONS to his short fiction. Few contemporary short story writers delineate more symphathetically and more eloquently the crises of painfully self-conscious human beings seeking redemption in the realm of everyday experience or exhibit the attention to craft evident in Updike's short fiction.

BIBLIOGRAPHY

Bloom, Harold, ed. *John Updike*. New York: Chelsea House, 1987.

Burchard, Rachel C. *John Updike: Yea Sayings*. Carbondale: Southern Illinois University Press, 1971.

De Bellis, Jack. *John Updike: A Bibliography, 1967–1993*. Westport, Conn.: Greenwood Press, 1994.

Detweiler, Robert. *John Updike*, revised ed. Boston: G.K. Hall, 1984.

Greiner, Donald. *The Other John Updike: Poems, Short Stories, Prose, Play*. Athens: Ohio University Press, 1981.

Hamilton, Alice, and Kenneth Hamilton. *The Elements of John Updike*. Grand Rapids, Mich.: Eerdmans, 1970.

Hunt, George. *John Updike and the Three Great Things: Sex, Religion, and Art*. Grand Rapids, Mich.: Eerdmans, 1980.

Luscher, Robert M. *John Updike: A Study of the Short Fiction*. New York: Twayne Publishers, 1993.

McNaughton, Willian R., ed. *Critical Essays on John Updike*. Boston: G.K. Hall, 1982.

Plath, James. *Conversations with John Updike*. Jackson: University Press of Mississippi, 1994.

Samuels, Charles Thomas. *John Updike*. Minneapolis, University of Minnesota Press, 1969.

Thorburn, David, and Howard Eiland, eds. *John Updike: A Collection of Critical Essays*. Englewood Cliffs, N.J.: Prentice Hall, 1979.

Updike, John. *Bech: A Book*. New York: Knopf, 1970.

———. *Bech Is Back*. New York: Knopf, 1982.

———. *Bech at Bay: A Quasi-Novel*. New York: Alfred A. Knopf, 1998.

———. *The Beloved*. Northridge, Calif.: Lord John Press, 1982.

———. *The Chaste Planet*. Worcester, Mass.: Netacin Oressm, 1980.

———. *Couples: A Short Story*. Cambridge, Mass.: Halty Ferguson, 1976.

———. *The Indian*. Marvin, S. D.: Blue Cloud Abbey, 1971.

———. *Museums and Women and Other Stories*. New York: Alfred A. Knopf, 1972.

———. *The Music School*. New York: Alfred A. Knopf, 1966.

———. *Olinger Stories: A Selection*. New York: Alfred A. Knopf, 1964.

———. *The Same Door*. New York: Alfred A. Knopf, 1959.

———, ed. *Penguin Modern Stories 2*. London: Penguin, 1969.

———. *Pigeon Feathers and Other Stories*. New York: Alfred A. Knopf, 1962.

———. *Problems and Other Stories*. New York: Alfred A. Knopf, 1979.

———. *Three Illuminations in the Life of an Author*. New York: Targ, 1979.

———. *Too Far to Go: The Maples Stories*. New York: Fawcett, 1979.

———. *Warm Wine: An Idyll*. New York: Albondocani Press, 1973.

Robert M. Luscher
University of Nebraska at Kearney

USHER   See MADELINE USHER and RODERICK USHER.

UTOPIAN   Sir Thomas More (1478–1535) wrote *Utopia* (the word means "nowhere" in Greek) in 1516, a book in which he compared the conditions as they existed then in England with a perfect state, Utopia, where no social ills such as crime, poverty, and injustice existed. His work was the model for subsequent utopian writers, who criticized the social and political conditions of the present state and proposed radical changes without describing any practical way to attain them. Therefore, a utopian idea or scheme is one that is impossibly ideal and unattainable. Utopian fiction is thus usually classed as romantic. Among American examples of utopian fiction are Nathaniel HAWTHORNE's *The Blithedale Romance* (1852) and Edward Bellamy's *Looking Backward* (1888), a utopian romance.

V

"VALLEY OF CHILDISH THINGS, AND OTHER EMBLEMS, THE" EDITH WHARTON (1896)

Published in the *Century Magazine* in 1896, this composite story, consisting of ten SKETCHes or PARABLES, depicts an individual's struggle to construct beauty and order. The individual vignettes mirror facets of responsibility, growth, and sense of self-worth in a Dantesque progression of sins: Three deal with marriage; three explore architects' motivations; three examine sorrow, misanthropy, and depression. The opening sketch portrays the arrested development of the multitude against an example of male regression and female maturation. Both first and last treat individual aspiration and frustration.

Marriage offers surprising rewards in the third, fifth, and eighth episodes. In the third, it is suggested as the antidote for a girl's alarming condition, intelligence. The fifth tale argues that a man might not have persevered through life if he had not been forced to support a wife who never learned to walk or swim. The eighth tale anticipates "THE OTHER TWO" and *The Age of Innocence* in its depiction of a man who marries a woman he finds interesting because she agrees with him on everything. After a few years, however, he finds her boring. Their subsequent arguments end in a foiled divorce when the judge decrees that the man married himself.

Episodes 2, 7, and 10 juxtapose characters who construct against those who destruct. The first portrays a mercenary architect who takes advantage of an obtuse woman's desire to have her room face the sun. The architect chooses the expensive solution; he turns her house for such a high fee that the woman must sacrifice her securities and alter her life. The second tale situates a famous architect in heaven facing an angel of judgment. Offered the opportunity to correct a dreadful mistake in his design of a temple, he chooses to let the temple and his reputation stand unchanged. In contrast, the third tale (and the concluding vignette) portrays a humble architect who weeps because his mud hut, his testimony to his god, cannot compare with the Parthenon. A passerby points out that there are two worse plights than the architect's: to have no god and to have mistaken a mud hut for the Parthenon.

Recent interpretations suggest that this story—in the words of one critic, "the most bizarre piece that WHARTON ever published" (Woolf 78)—can be understood in relation to Wharton's life as well as her later fiction. Like Wharton, the little girl in the story grows up to learn that men have multiple options in life, while women are expected to remain in the valley of childish things: They should care not for their intelligence but for their physical appearance. In these chilling socially proscribed gender distinctions lie the seeds of many of Wharton's future works—*The House of Mirth, The Custom of the Country,* and *Summer,* in particular. In the story, only the woman's mature hard work to escape the valley of childhood strikes a small note of optimism, suggesting the author's female HERO in *Hudson River Bracketed* and *The Gods Arrive*—and also Edith Wharton herself.

BIBLIOGRAPHY

Ammons, Elizabeth. *Edith Wharton's Argument with America* 1980. Athens: University of Georgia Press, 1980.

Singley, Carol J. *Edith Wharton: Matters of Mind and Spirit.* New York: Oxford University Press, 1995.

Wharton, Edith. "The Valley of Childish Things, and Other Emblems." In *The Collected Short Stories of Edith Wharton,* vol. 1. Edited by R. W. B. Lewis. New York: Scribner's, 1968.

Wolff, Cynthia Griffin. *A Feast of Words: The Triumph of Edith Wharton.* New York: Oxford University Press, 1977.

Sandra Chrystal Hayes
Georgia Institute of Technology

VIETNAM WAR (1954–1975)

The war began soon after the Geneva Conference (1954), which ended the French Indochina War (1946–54) and provisionally divided Vietnam into a communist North and nationalist South until elections were held to determine which government would rule the country. The South refused to hold elections, however, and declared itself an independent republic in 1955. A guerrilla war waged by the Viet Cong (Vietnamese communists) in the South against this government began immediately. Because this guerilla war came shortly after the KOREAN WAR had ended in a stalemate, and because U.S. foreign policy supported the "containment" of communism—including the prevention of a "domino effect" in which other countries of Southeast Asia could fall to communists if Vietnam did—the United States intervened on the side of the South Vietnamese, initially with material support but, after 1961, with troops as well.

As the number of American troops in Vietnam increased dramatically after 1964, reaching over 550,000 in 1969, so too did protests in the United States against the war, fueled by the draft, the belief that the U.S. was involved in another country's civil war, and mounting casualties. The Tet Offensive (1968) was a stunning defeat for the Viet Cong but an equally stunning public relations victory for the North Vietnamese; it resulted in a deepening American disillusionment about U.S. commitment to South Vietnam. American troop withdrawals began in 1969 and ended in 1973. The communists defeated the South Vietnamese in 1975.

The war had proven costly to the United States not only in material and personnel casualties but also in its divisive effect on the American populace between the pro-war and antiwar factions and a general loss of faith in the veracity and competence of some government institutions. Lyndon Johnson did not seek a second term as president in 1968 in large part because of the antiwar protests.

"VIGILANTE, THE"   JOHN STEINBECK (1938)

John STEINBECK's "The Vigilante," like the earlier "THE SNAKE"—both appearing in the story collection *The Long Valley* (1938)—has its roots in an actual event, a tragic kidnapping and murder that occurred in San Jose in 1933. Steinbeck transforms the event into the story of Mike, a participant in a lynch mob who administers arbitrary justice to a black man just as the residents of San Jose lynched two accused white men in revenge for the death of Brooke Hart, the son of a local businessman, whose mutilated body was found in the San Francisco harbor after a ransom plan for his return went wrong. Mike's account reveals his morally ambiguous feelings at his participation in this event: Dare he think it a crime? His initial feelings, as the story begins after the lynching, include an emptiness at no longer being a member of the mob. Steinbeck's description of Mike's gentle pain and dull quality of loneliness is heightened when Mike enters a local bar and relives the event with a sympathetic and empathetic bartender named Welch. Initially Mike describes the emotions that motivated the mob and how it felt right that the local justice system preferred to look the other way.

As he proceeds to recall the actual lynching, however, Mike is struck with the frenzy of the moment. He recounts the way the mob tore the clothes off the victim before stringing him up and attempting to burn his body. Unconsciously Mike has taken a souvenir from the scene—a torn piece of the man's pants—and he is shocked when the bartender offers to purchase it, thus demonstrating human fascination with death and violence.

Upon leaving the bar, Mike and Welch continue to mull over the event, trying to determine whether the act was justified because of certain circumstances: the implied sexual nature of the crime and the belief of the mob that the black man was a fiend. They also marvel that the town seems relatively unchanged by this monumental occurrence. Mike initially asserts that his participation in the lynching meant absolutely nothing. Shortly thereafter, however, he admits that he had a dual reaction to his involvement—a sense of being cut off and a feeling of satisfaction, as if he had done a good job. Later, when he returns home, his wife upbraids him for his lateness and, based on the self-satisfied expression on his face, accuses him of having a sexual encounter. The tale ends abruptly as Mike realizes that his participation in the lynching offered a somewhat similar pleasure.

The account of the original crime (Timmerman, "Introduction") emphasizes the changes Steinbeck made. The real suspects, John Holmes and Thomas Thurman, were white, and the lynching took place almost two weeks after the crime of which they were accused. Other details seem to be fairly accurate retellings of newspaper accounts of the lynching, including the storming of the jail, the battering down of the doors, and the seizing and stripping of the two men before hanging them in the local park.

No doubt intrigued by mob action as evidence of his own belief in a collective conscience at once subhuman and superhuman, Steinbeck was quick to see the possibilities for this real story to illustrate his theory of the phalanx, an idea he had expressed as early as 1933 to his friend Carlton Sheffield and a concept he was to explore fully in his 1936 novel, *In Dubious Battle*. In *The Long Valley Notebook* Steinbeck even delineates the phalanx theory—his belief that individuals at times became cells in a larger organizing group—in a manuscript draft of a piece entitled "Case History," in which a PROTAGONIST John

Ramsy and a newspaper reporter Will McKay act as mouthpieces for a similar discussion about a mob lynching. The transformation of this text into "The Vigilante" demonstrates that Steinbeck understood the difference between art and a moralistic expression of his feelings and that in the story he successfully avoids what he derisively called the author's moral point of view. Instead he records consciousness nonteleologically and demonstrates that there is a dark as well as a positive side to man's joining together. By recording instead of judging, Steinbeck stresses the duality of the element that unites all the stories in *The Long Valley*: the THEME of isolation resulting from the breakup of brotherhood. Bonding together in a group with all its positive consequences for an individual can have its negative side as well. The actions of Steinbeck's unsympathetic protagonist in "The Vigilante" offer sufficient proof that there is duality in all human events.

BIBLIOGRAPHY
Steinbeck, John. "The Vigilante." In *The Long Valley*. New York: Penguin, 1995.
Timmerman, John H. "Introduction." In John Steinbeck, *The Long Valley*. New York: Penguin, 1995.

Michael J. Meyer
DePaul University

VIGNETTE   A word that originally described the delicate artistic designs for a book, *vignette* now means a sketch or brief narrative written with care and precision. A vignette can stand on its own or constitute part of a longer work, as when Ernest HEMINGWAY interspersed vignettes between the longer stories of *IN OUR TIME*. Alternatively, a SHORT-SHORT STORY of under 500 words may be called a vignette.

VIRAMONTES, HELENA MARÍA (1954–)
A native of East Los Angeles, Helena María Viramontes has been active in that community's cultural scene for a number of years. From 1978 to 1981 she served as literary editor of the Los Angeles literary and art magazine *Xhismearte*. She has also been a coordinator of the California-based Latino

Writers Association, and, in 1990, she cofounded Latino Writers and Filmmakers, Inc. Like Ana Castillo, Denise Chávez, Sandra CISNEROS, and Benjamin Alire Sáenz, Viramontes is finally receiving the long-overdue attention of established New York publishing houses. In 1994 she signed a contract with Dutton to publish two novels and a collection of short stories. The first novel, *Under the Feet of Jesus,* appeared in 1995. It was her collection of short stories *The Moths and Other Stories,* however, that placed her on the literary map. Published in 1985 by Arte Público, a longtime supporter of Latin American writers, the collection has undergone multiple printings, and many of the individual stories appear in various anthologies of American and Latina/Latino literature.

Similar to Sandra Cisneros's WOMAN HOLLERING CREEK (1991), *The Moths* follows the development from youth to old age of several girls and women. Beginning with "The Moths," Viramontes introduces the reader to an alienated young girl whose relationship with her dying grandmother helps her to discover her own identity and to resist her overbearing father. The tension between father and daughter increases in the next story, "Growing," as the teenage daughter, Naomi, struggles for her independence against the wishes of her father, who pronounces, as "a verdict not a truth," that she is a woman. Through her use of STREAM OF CONSCIOUSNESS and FLASHBACKS in "Birthday," Viramontes dramatically captures the inner turmoil of a young woman having an abortion. In a minor digression from the BILDUNGSROMAN THEME, "The Cariboo Cafe" seeks to draw attention to the lives of displaced families during U.S.-aided counterrevolutions in Central America in the 1980s. The story's use of shifting narrative voices and of temporal disjunctures underscores the characters' own sense of literal displacement. Both "The Broken Web" and "The Long Reconciliation" examine marriage and infidelity, inquiring into issues of justice and reconciliation. The final two stories of the collection, "Snapshots" and "Neighbors," detail the lonely and discarded lives of two older women, Olga Ruíz and Aura Rodríguez, respectively. With these stories

Viramontes calls into question that mentality which renders people obsolete in old age, especially women who are cast aside when their children are grown and they are no longer sexually alluring.

BIBLIOGRAPHY

Eysturoy, Annie O. *Daughters of Self-Creation: The Contemporary Chicana Novel.* Albuquerque: University of New Mexico Press, 1996.

Kanellos, Nicolás, ed. *The Hispanic Literary Companion.* Detroit: Visible Ink Press, 1997.

———. *Hispanic American Literature: A Brief Introduction and Anthology.* New York: Addison-Wesley, 1995.

López, Tiffany Ana, ed. *Growing Up Chicana/o* (1993). New York: Avon Books, 1995.

Moraga, Cherríe, and Gloria Anzaldúa, eds. *This Bridge Called My Back: Writings by Radical Women of Color.* Watertown, Mass.: Persephone Press, 1984.

Quintana, Alvina E. *Home Girls: Chicana Literary Voices.* Philadelphia: Temple University Press, 1996.

Rodríguez Aranda, Pilar E. "On the Solitary Fate of Being Mexican, Female, Wicked and Thirty-three: An Interview with Writer Sandra Cisneros." *Americas Review* 18.1 (Spring 1990): 64–80.

Simmen, Edward, ed. *North of the Rio Grande: The Mexican American Experience in Short Fiction.* New York: Mentor Books, 1992.

Viramontes, Helena María. "The Cariboo Cafe." In *The Moths and Other Stories.* Houston: Arte Publico Press, 1995.

———. *The Moths and Other Stories.* Houston: Arte Publico Press, 1995.

———. *Under the Feet of Jesus.* New York: E.P. Dutton, 1996.

Viramontes, Helena María, and María Herrera-Sobek, eds. *Chicana Creativity and Criticism: Charting New Frontiers in American Literature.* Albuquerque: University of New Mexico Press, 1996.

———. *Chicana (W)Rites: On Word and Film.* Berkeley, Calif.: Third Woman Press, 1995.

Ralph E. Rodriguez
Pennsylvania State University

"VITAMINS" RAYMOND CARVER (1983)

As it appears in Raymond CARVER's short story collection, *Cathedral* (1983), the story "Vitamins" is much more in the vein of the author's earlier, considerably bleaker work. Certainly a sense of "dis-ease," a term from French Existentialist writer Albert Camus (SEE EXISTENTIALISM) that Carver uses in one of his book reviews, well describes his earlier stories, which offer no comfort or hope of redemption, particularly to the many characters within them who struggle with alcoholism, as Carver himself did for many years.

"Vitamins" is a story very much concerned with the perils of alcoholism, although Carver does not approach the subject directly. Instead of telling much about his characters' inner thoughts, Carver simply depicts a man who undoubtedly has a drinking problem and fails to comprehend or acknowledge it.

In order to explore such a character, Carver deftly chooses to tell the story from the POINT OF VIEW of the character himself. The result is a story marked by several levels of alienation: The unnamed narrator, in his lack of insight, is alienated not only from himself but also from others, particularly women. Finally, he is further alienated from his own story, because, in the midst of telling it, he is unaware of what he reveals about himself.

The most striking aspect of this first-person narrative is the continual mention of alcohol without any hint that the narrator understands the roots or effects of his drinking. Nearly 40 times in "Vitamins" he makes some reference to drinking. "I worked a few hours a night for the hospital," he says at the outset of the story. "It was a nothing job. I did some work, signed the card for eight hours, went drinking with the nurses" (91). After a party during which one person passes out drunk and everyone else drinks to excess, he sits up all night drinking by himself (93). The next morning he is drinking Scotch and milk with a sliver of ice. "I finished my drink," he says, "and thought about fixing another one. I fixed it" (94). Such is the unthinking pace of his drinking throughout the story.

The story ends as the narrator pours himself a glass of Scotch, but not before he experiences what one critic has called a particularly Carveresque moment of quiet, personal horror (Gentry 93). Returning home to find his wife sleepwalking during a nightmare, he becomes delirious: "I couldn't take any more tonight. 'Go back to sleep, honey. I'm looking for something,' I said. I knocked some stuff out of the medicine chest. Things rolled into the sink. 'Where's the aspirin?' I said. I knocked down some more things. I didn't care. Things kept falling" (109). And, we are certain, things will continue to fall until this man either destroys himself or finally reaches some level of self-awareness concerning his problem and his need for help. Carver gives us no reason to believe that one outcome is any more likely than the other.

BIBLIOGRAPHY

Carver, Raymond, *Cathedral* (1983). New York: Vintage Books, 1989.
Gentry, Marshall Bruce, and William L. Stull, eds. *Conversations with Raymond Carver.* Jackson: University Press of Mississippi, 1990.

H. Collin Messer
University of North Carolina

VIZENOR, GERALD ROBERT (1934–)

Born in Minneapolis to French and Chippewa parents, Vizenor is a member of the White Earth Reservation in Minnesota where he grew up and where, as a child, he listened to the storytelling that now guides his writing. Critics describe Vizenor as an AVANT-GARDE writer who embraces and revitalizes ancient storytelling contributions. In addition to his innovation, he is praised for the rich sense of humor inherent in much of his writing. Overall, he is revered for his active and playful storytelling that incorporates a combination of oral and literary traditions.

He attended the University of Minnesota and is now professor of Native American literature at the University of California at Berkeley. A prolific writer, Vizenor has written short stories (such as "Trickster of Liberty: Tribal Heirs to a Wild Baronage"), collections of poetry (for example, *Crossbloods*), novels (such as *Griever: An American Monkey King in China*), has edited several collections of NATIVE AMERICAN writings (one is *The People Named the Chippewa: Narrative Histories*), has written scholarly books on Native American studies, and is the general editor of the American Indian Literature and Critical Studies series published by Oklahoma Press.

BIBLIOGRAPHY

Vizenor, Gerald Robert. *Bearheart: The Heirship Chronicles.* Minneapolis: University of Minnesota Press, 1990.

———. *Crossbloods: Bone Courts, Bingo, and Other Reports.* Minneapolis: University of Minnesota Press, 1990.

———. *Darkness in Saint Louis Bearheart* (1978). Minneapolis: University of Minnesota Press, 1990.

———. *Dead Voices: Natural Agonies in the New World.* Norman: University of Oklahoma Press, 1992.

———. *Earthdivers: Tribal Narratives on Mixed Descent.* Minneapolis: University of Minnesota Press, 1981.

———. *The Everlasting Sky: New Voices from the People Named the Chippewa.* New York: Crowell-Collier Press, 1972.

———. *Fugitive Poses: Native American Indian Scenes of Absence and Presence.* Lincoln: University of Nebraska Press, 1998.

———. *Griever: An American Monkey King in China.* Minneapolis: University of Minnesota Press, 1990.

———. *Heirs of Columbus.* Middletown, Conn.: Wesleyan University Press, 1992.

———. *Hotline Healers: An Almost Browne Novel.* Middletown, Conn.: Wesleyan University Press, 1997.

———. *Interior Landscapes: Autobiographical Myths and Metaphors.* Minneapolis: University of Minnesota Press, 1990.

———. *Manifest Manners: PostIndian Warriors of Survivance.* Middletown, Conn.: Wesleyan University Press, 1994.

———. *Narrative Chance: Postmodern Discourse on Native American Indian Literatures.* Norman: University of Oklahoma Press, 1993.

———. *The People Named the Chippewa: Narrative Histories.* Minneapolis: University of Minnesota Press, 1985.

———. *Shadow Distance: A Gerald Vizenor Reader.* Middletown, Conn.: Wesleyan University Press, 1994.

———. *Summer in the Spring: Anishinaabe Lyric Poems and Stories.* Norman: University of Oklahoma Press, 1993.

———. *Wordarrows: Indians and Whites in the New Fur Trade.* Minneapolis: University of Minnesota Press, 1981.

Vizenor, Gerald Robert, and Adrienne Kennedy. *The Trickster of Liberty: Tribal Heirs to a Wild Baronage.* Minneapolis: University of Minnesota Press, 1988.

Vizenor, Gerald Robert, ed. *Touchwood: A Collection of Ojibway Prose.* New York: New Rivers Press, 1994.

Vizenor, Gerald Robert, and Ishmael Reed, eds. *Native-American Literature: A Brief Introduction and Anthology.* New York: Addison-Wesley, 1995.

VONNEGUT, KURT (1922–)

Writing to his father after *Collier's* bought his first story in 1950, Kurt Vonnegut, Jr., confided his belief that "I'm on my way." Reckoning that if he could sell four more stories, he could then quit his "goddamn nightmare job [with General Electric], and never take another one so long as I live, so help me God. Love. K."

These observations clearly demonstrate the author's early motivation for writing short stories. Vonnegut's ambition was not to contribute immortal treasures to the canon of American short fiction—it was merely to enable himself to quit his detested job and later to finance the writing of his novels.

The "goddamn nightmare job" to which he refers was that of a public relations man for General Electric's research laboratory. Vonnegut held this position for over three years, writing press releases about his employer's scientific and technological advances. His experience in journalism came from a brief position as a reporter for the Chicago City News Bureau and from having written for his high school and college newspapers. At Cornell, where he was a chemistry major for two years before joining the army in 1942, he held various editorial positions for the *Cornell Sun.*

The major in chemistry was a concession for his father's peace of mind. Kurt Sr., a prominent Indianapolis architect, lost the best years of his professional life to the GREAT DEPRESSION. After 16 years of nearly no work as an architect, Kurt Sr. had become demoralized about his profession and about the arts in general, and recommended that Kurt Jr. study chemistry rather than pursue "frivolous" activities in the humanities. Although he obliged his father because he was funding his education, Vonnegut spent much of his time in the office of the *Cornell Sun.*

He began as the editor of a column that reprinted humor from other papers, but Vonnegut soon began exerting his own influence over the editorial page of the *Sun.* As the country was about to enter WORLD WAR II, Vonnegut's columns provided a string of witty, satirical pleas for pacifism and nonintervention that rebuked the gung-ho jingoism of the time.

The public relations job at GE provided no fuel for Vonnegut's artistic fire. At the time the large short story industry in this country included several weekly magazines, "slicks," that printed five short stories every week and paid very well for them. The sale of Vonnegut's first story, "Report on the Barnhouse Effect," earned him a fee equal to six weeks of work at GE. After Vonnegut sold his second story for $200 more than the first, the fiction editor at *Collier's* suggested that he quit his job. Vonnegut did so gladly. Eventually he earned $2,900 per story.

Forty-five of Vonnegut's 47 stories were published between 1950 and 1963. His short story production tapered off in 1963, the year *Cat's Cradle,* his fourth novel, was published. Vonnegut's popularity had previously been limited to a cultish band of young followers, but with the publication of *Cat's Cradle* his popularity broke into the mainstream, and he began to enjoy great critical acclaim. His books began to be reprinted in large numbers, thus ending the financial necessity of writing short stories.

Until that time, however, Vonnegut needed to sell stories to support his family, a dream of his mother's that he was happy to realize. (During the Great Depression, his mother had attempted to generate extra income for the family by writing short stories, but none was published.) Not only did Vonnegut have a wife and three children to support; he also adopted his sister's three children after she died of cancer in 1958, within one week of her husband's death in a freak accident.

Most of Vonnegut's stories were written with the intended audience very clearly in mind: "the sort of fiction [the slicks] wanted was low-grade, simplistic, undisturbing sort of writing. And so, in order to pay the bills I would write stories of that sort."

This "undisturbing sort of writing" that Vonnegut copiously contributed to *Collier's,* SATURDAY EVENING POST, and even the LADIES' HOME JOURNAL, consisted primarily of an affirmation and validation of the middle-class values of those magazines' readers. A dozen or so of these stories present characters who yearn for the comfort of materialistic wealth and/or the procurement of a more aristocratic social standing, only to discover when their dreams become reality that they were happier and better off before good fortune came their way. However facile the THEMES of these stories, Vonnegut was able to use this outlet productively by mastering his storytelling skill.

Some of Vonnegut's best stories, charged with bittersweet humor and a relevant (and occasionally prophetic) sociopolitical agenda, foreshadow the themes and concerns of his novels. (See FORESHADOWING.) Ironically, given his low opinion of them, the original sources of some of his best stories were for SCIENCE FICTION pulps such as the *Magazine of Fantasy and Science Fiction,* and *Worlds of If.* A science-fiction setting lends itself well to Vonnegut's use of HYPERBOLE to illustrate his messages.

BIBLIOGRAPHY

Giannone, Richard. *Vonnegut: A Preface to His Novels.* New York: Kennikat, 1977.

Klinkowitz, Jerome. *Kurt Vonnegut.* New York: Methuen, 1982.

Klinkowitz, Jerome, and John Somer, eds. *The Vonnegut Statement: Original Essays on the Life and Work of Kurt Vonnegut.* New York: Seymour Lawrence/Delacorte, 1973.

Schatt, Stanley. *Kurt Vonnegut Jr.* Boston: Twayne, 1976.

David Larry Anderson

W

WALKER, ALICE (1944–) Born in Eatonton, Georgia, to sharecropper parents, Alice Walker won scholarships to Spelman College and to Sarah Lawrence College, where she studied poetry with then writer-in-residence Muriel Rukeyser. Although she published a book of poetry in 1968, and received a writing fellowship upon graduation from Sarah Lawrence, Walker worked for the New York City welfare department and as a volunteer to register voters in Mississippi. Returning to academia as a teacher at various colleges, she also returned to writing, and published her first story collection, *In Love and Trouble: Stories of Black Women*, in 1973; from this collection comes the often-anthologized "Her Sweet Jerome," "THE CHILD WHO FAVORED DAUGHTER," and "EVERYDAY USE." All three stories focus on a THEME that virtually became Walker's trademark: the various ways African American women cope with their situations. "Everyday Use," in particular, uses Walker's characteristic quilting METAPHOR and emphasis on the significance of the maternal legacy.

Although she continued to write poetry and won the American Book Award and a PULITZER PRIZE for the novel *The Color Purple*, published in 1982, Walker also wrote another story collection, *You Can't Keep a Good Woman Down*, in 1979, a controversial work that includes the themes of rape, abortion, pornography, and homosexuality. Among her other works are the novels *Meridian* (1976), an account of the civil rights movement, and *The Temple of My Familiar* (1989); *I Love Myself When I Am Laughing* (1979), a collection of the works of Zora Neale HURSTON; and the now classic essay of FEMINIST CRITICISM, "In Search of Our Mothers' Gardens" in the collection of the same name, in 1983. She counts Hurston and Jean TOOMER among the strongest literary influences on her writing. Throughout her work, Walker honors the courage, resilience, and imagination of black women of diverse backgrounds.

BIBLIOGRAPHY

Hollister, Michael. "Tradition in Walker's 'To Hell With Dying.'" *Studies in Short Fiction* 21 (Winter 1989): 190–94.

Petry, Alice Hall. "Walker: The Achievement of the Short Fiction." *Modern Language Studies* (Winter 1989).

Pilditch, Jan. "Alice Walker." In *Reference Guide to Short Fiction*. Edited by Noelle Watson. Detroit: St. James Press, 1994, pp. 572–573.

Alice Walker: A Special Section. *Callaloo* 12, no. 2 (Spring 1989): 295–345.

Walker, Alice. *The Color Purple*. New York: Harcourt Brace, 1982.

———. *In Search of Our Mothers' Gardens: Womanist Prose*. San Diego, Calif.: Harcourt Brace, 1983.

———. *In Love and Trouble: Stories of Black Women*. San Diego, Calif.: Harcourt Brace, 1973.

———. *Living by the Word: Selected Writings 1973–1987*. San Diego, Calif.: Harcourt Brace, 1988.

———. *Meridian*. New York: Harcourt Brace, 1976.

———. *The Temple of My Familiar*. San Diego, Calif.: Harcourt Brace, 1989.

———. *The Third Life of Grange Copeland*. New York: Harcourt Brace, 1970.

———. *You Can't Keep a Good Woman Down*. San Diego, Calif.: Harcourt Brace, 1981.

Walker, Alice, ed. *I Love Myself When I Am Laughing . . . and Then Again When I Am Looking Mean and Impressive: A Zora Neale Hurston Reader*. New York: Feminist Press, 1979.

WARD, ARTEMUS

The pen name of Charles Farrar BROWNE (1834–99), a humorist, newspaperman, and lecturer. He introduced Ward in 1858 when he began publishing a famous series of "Artemus Ward's Letters," ostensibly written in a Yankee DIALECT by a shrewd and semiliterate showman who commented on current events as well as the adventures and misadventures associated with his travelling wax museum. These letters and subsequent lecture tours brought Browne a wide reputation. Devices he used in his writing included humorous misspellings, puns and plays on words, BURLESQUE, and ABSURDity. He exerted a strong influence on Mark TWAIN and other American humorists.

WARD, ELIZABETH STUART PHELPS

See PHELPS WARD, Elizabeth Stuart.

WASTE LAND, THE   T. S. ELIOT   (1922)

A 434-line poem written in five sections by T. S. Eliot (1888–1965) in 1922, *The Waste Land* features myth (especially that of the impotent Fisher King), symbol, and wide-ranging literary allusion to reproduce the sense of social, cultural, and personal fragmentation suffered by civilization in the wake of WORLD WAR I. The poem contrasts the intellectual and moral grandeur of the past with the vulgar, decadent, valueless present. Modern life, the poem suggests, is a vast spiritual wasteland. The term has been used in countless short stories, novels, poems, and plays since Eliot first published it, and has become one of the major metaphors of the 20th century.

WATANABE, SYLVIA   (1953–)

Sylvia Watanabe, a third-generation Japanese American, was born on the Hawaiian island of Maui. She has coedited two anthologies of Asian American fiction, *Home to Stay: Asian American Women's Fiction* (1990) and *Into the Fire: Asian American Prose* (1996), and has written two autobiographical essays, "Knowing Your Place" (1996) and "Where People Know Me" (1994). Watanabe's short stories have been published in a variety of literary journals and anthologies. Her first collection, TALKING TO THE DEAD AND OTHER STORIES (1992), was a finalist for the PEN/FAULKNER AWARD in 1993.

Although for the past several years Watanabe has claimed the American mainland as her home, her stories retain a Hawaiian setting, depicting and even celebrating Hawaiian multiculturalism. By no means an idealized place, the Maui village inhabited by Watanabe's fictional characters becomes a microcosm of multiethnic neighborhoods the world over, suggesting universal truths about the ways individuals, families, and communities interact. Watanabe deftly situates her narrative voice between poignancy and humor, protecting her characters and plots from sentimental treatment and affording her stories great residual appeal.

Watanabe has received a Japanese American Citizens League National Literary Award, an NEA Fellowship, the O. HENRY MEMORIAL AWARD (1991), and the PUSHCART PRIZE (1996). She now lives in Oberlin, Ohio, where she teaches creative writing at Oberlin College.

BIBLIOGRAPHY

Watanabe, Sylvia, and Carol Bruchac, eds. *Home to Stay: Asian American Women's Fiction*. Greenfield Center, N.Y.: Greenfield Review Press, 1990.

——— and Bruchac, Carol, eds. *Into the Fire: Asian American Prose*. Greenfield Center, N.Y.: Greenfield Review Press, 1996.

———. "Knowing Your Place." In *A Place Called Home: Twenty Writing Women Remember*. Edited by Mickey Pearlman. New York: St. Martin's, 1996.

———. *Talking to the Dead and Other Stories*. New York: Doubleday, 1992.

———. "Where People Know Me." In *Between Friends*. Edited by Mickey Pearlman. Boston: Houghton Mifflin, 1994.

Keith Lawrence
Brigham Young University

WATANNA, ONOTO (1879–1954)

Onoto Watanna was the pen name of Lillie Winnifred Eaton Babcock Reeve, younger sister of Edith Eaton (SUI Sin Far). Frequently criticized by contemporary Asian American literary scholars for assuming a Japanese pseudonym at a time when Chinese Americans were feeling the brunt of the Chinese Exclusion Act—and, in contrast to her sister Edith, for apparently turning her back on her ethnic heritage—Watanna nevertheless has come to be seen as a complex and unusually sensitive author with a tonal and thematic perspective even less predictable or certain than her sister's. (See THEME.) Her short stories reveal the position of the Asian American immigrant in the early 20th century through humor, incisive detail, and telling irony.

During her lifetime Watanna was known primarily for her 17 novels, many of them featuring exotic settings and characters. Watanna was also chief scenarist at Universal Studios from 1924 through 1931. For modern readers, however, her short stories and autobiographical writings hold much more appeal. Much of her short fiction was published during the first decade of the 20th century in literary magazines like HARPER'S and Century.

BIBLIOGRAPHY

Ling, Amy. "Creating One's Self: The Eaton Sisters." In *Reading the Literatures of Asian America.* Edited by Shirley Geok-lin Lim and Amy Ling. Philadelphia: Temple University Press, 1992.

Watanna, Onoto. *Cattle.* Toronto: Musson, 1923.

———. *Daughters of Nijo: A Romance of Japan.* New York: Macmillan, 1904.

———. *The Heart of Hyacinth.* New York: Harper, 1903.

———. *His Royal Nibs.* New York: W. J. Watt, 1925.

———. *A Japanese Blossom.* New York: Harper, 1906.

———. *A Japanese Nightingale.* New York: Harper, 1901.

———. *The Love of Azalea.* New York: Dodd, Mead, 1904.

———. *Marion: The Story of an Artist's Model.* New York: W. J. Watt, 1916.

———. *Me: A Book of Remembrance.* New York: The Century Co., 1915.

———. *Miss Numè of Japan: A Japanese-American Romance* (1899). Baltimore, Md.: Johns Hopkins University Press, 1998.

———. *Sunny-San.* New York: George H. Doran Company, 1922.

———. *Tama.* New York; London: Harper & Brothers, 1910.

———. *The Wooing of Wistaria.* New York: Harper & Brothers, 1903.

Keith Lawrence
Brigham Young University

WELTY, EUDORA (1909–)

Despite being the best-known, and arguably the best, living woman writer in America, Eudora Welty has been shy of personal exposure, believing that a writer's work should speak for itself. In 1984, however, she published the much-awaited autobiography of her youth and professional nascence, *One Writer's Beginnings,* which describes the way her childhood in Jackson, Mississippi, influenced her future as an author. The autobiography reflects that although her parents were very different (Southern vs. Northern, Democrat vs. Republican), Welty was close to them both. She recalls, as a child, lying ill in her parents' bed and listening to them discuss the day's events while they thought she slept. Through this early training she developed the ear for speech for which she is so well known and perhaps also the objectivity and authorial distance for which she has been both praised and criticized.

Welty has had a long and productive career as a writer. During the GREAT DEPRESSION she worked in Mississippi as a photographer and publicity writer for the Works Progress Administration, making periodic visits to New York, where she tried to sell her stories. Her first published short story, "Death of a Traveling Salesman," appeared in *Manuscript* in 1936 and was later part of her first collection, *A Curtain of Green and Other Stories* (1941). Since then Welty has published four more volumes of short stories, *The Wide Net and Other Stories* (1943), THE GOLDEN APPLES (1949)—a cycle of related stories—*The Bride of the Innisfallen* (1955), and *The Collected Stories of Eudora Welty* (1980). Welty's early career is characterized by short fiction, but she also published two NOVELLAs and a full length novel, *Delta Wedding* (1946). Then, after a 15-year lapse during which she suffered the loss of her mother and two brothers and published only a children's book,

Welty returned to the literary scene with three more full-length novels, *The Ponder Heart* (1967), *Losing Battles* (1970), and *The Optimist's Daughter* (1972).

In her stories, Welty uses two main styles of writing, the dramatic and the LYRICAL. In dramatic stories such as "WHY I LIVE AT THE P.O.," a monologue in which the speaker, Sister, explains why she moved from her family home to the back of the post office where she works, Welty captures the natural rhythms and idiosyncracies of Southern speech. These speech characteristics, along with the detailed description of Southern manners and codes, the sometimes petty but very human concerns of her ordinary characters, create the humor for which Welty is famous. (See REGIONALISM.) She does not moralize or offer overt social commentary. Welty's approach is to describe her CHARACTERS in minute layers of detail so that the reader gradually comes to understand the inner qualities that give rise to the outer surface.

In other stories Welty uses a lyrical, meditative style, exploring through an omniscient narrator the inner workings of the characters' minds. In "A WORN PATH," PHOENIX JACKSON, an old black woman, makes the long journey to town to buy medicine for her sick grandson. Through beautiful METAPHOR and nature imagery, Welty conveys the importance of the quest, an arduous labor of love, that periodically allows Phoenix to renew herself like the mythical bird that bears the same name.

No matter which style she uses, Welty returns again and again to some key THEMES in her fiction, but always in fresh and compelling ways. Place is important in all of her works. In fact, all but four short stories are set in Mississippi. In some pieces, such as "A Worn Path" and *Delta Wedding,* the detailed descriptions of the land and the characters interactions with it make the setting seem almost like a living thing. Another important theme for Welty is the individual's struggle with the community. In some cases the individual rejects the community in favor of independence, but other times the individual sacrifices independence in favor of the community's protection. Both these themes, place and community, are central in Welty's only

SHORT STORY CYCLE, *The Golden Apples,* which describes the connected lives of the residents of MORGANA, MISSISSIPPI, over a period of 40 years. No matter how her characters behave, Welty rarely passes judgment, and she has sometimes been criticized for her lack of a moral stance. She reports the actions objectively, believing that humans have to create their own meanings and coping strategies and that readers must make their own judgments.

In addition to her voluminous fictional body of work and autobiography, Eudora Welty has published a collection of her Depression-era photography (*One Time, One Place* [1971]), a children's book (*The Shoe Box* [1993]) and two collections of essays and reviews (*The Eye of the Story* [1978]) and *A Writer's Eye* [1994]). She has received countless awards, including election to the Academy of Arts and Letters, the Academy's Gold Medal for Literature, a Pulitzer Prize, and the Presidential Medal of Freedom.

BIBLIOGRAPHY

Evans, Elizabeth. *Eudora Welty.* New York: Frederick Ungar, 1981.

Prenshaw, Peggy Whitman. *Eudora Welty: Critical Essays* (1979). Oxford.: University Press of Mississippi, 1984.

———. *Conversations with Eudora Welty.* Oxford.: University Press of Mississippi, 1984.

———. *More Conversations with Eudora Welty.* Jackson.: University Press of Mississippi, 1996.

Vande Kieft, Ruth M. *Eudora Welty.* New York: Twayne, 1962.

Welty, Eudora. *The Bride of the Innisfallen* (1995). New York: Harcourt Brace, 1985.

———. *The Collected Stories of Eudora Welty.* New York: Harcourt Brace, 1982.

———. *A Curtain of Green and Other Stories* (1941). New York: Harcourt Brace, 1991.

———. *Delta Wedding* (1946). New York: Harcourt Brace, 1991.

———. *Eudora Welty: Complete Novels: The Robber Bridegroom, Delta Wedding, The Ponder Heart, Losing Battles, The Optimist's Daughter.* Edited by Richard Ford. New York: Library of America, 1998.

———. *The Eye of the Story.* 1978. New York: Vintage Books, 1990.

———. *The Golden Apples.* 1949. New York: Harcourt Brace, 1988.

————. *Losing Battles* (1970). New York: Harcourt Brace, 1988.

———— (photographer). *One Time, One Place: Mississippi in the Depression: A Snapshot Album* (1971). Oxford: University Press of Mississippi, 1996.

————. *One Writer's Beginnings.* 1984. Cambridge, Mass.: Belknap Press, 1995.

————. *The Optimist's Daughter* (1972). New York: Vintage Books, 1990.

————. *The Ponder Heart.* New York: Harcourt Brace, 1967.

————. *The Robber Bridegroom.* New York: Harcourt Brace, 1987.

————. *The Shoe Bird.* Oxford: University Press of Mississippi, 1993.

————. *The Wide Net and Other Stories* (1943). New York: Harcourt Brace, 1989.

————. *A Writer's Eye: Collected Book Reviews.* Oxford: University Press of Mississippi, 1994.

Welty, Eudora, and Ronald A. Sharp, eds. *Norton Book of Friendship.* New York: W.W. Norton & Company, 1991.

Betina I. Entzminger
University of North Carolina at Chapel Hill

WEST, DOROTHY (1907–1998)

A native Bostonian and graduate of Boston University, Dorothy West is said to have begun writing short stories at the age of seven. She gained recognition when her short story "The Typewriter," along with Zora Neal HURSTON's "Spunk," won the *Opportunity* magazine second-place prize for fiction in 1926. Edward O'Brien included "The Typewriter" in *The Best Short Stories of 1926.* Closely associated with the better-known writers of the HARLEM RENAISSANCE, such as Langston HUGHES, Wallace Thurman, and Hurston, West founded and edited *Challenge,* a literary magazine (1934–36), during the years of the GREAT DEPRESSION. It later became *New Challenge* (1937), for which Richard WRIGHT served as associate editor. The author of more than 60 stories, West is also known for her novels *The Living Is Easy* (1948) and *The Wedding* (1995).

BIBLIOGRAPHY

Dalsgard, Katrine. "Alive and Well and Living on the Island of Martha's Vineyard: An Interview with Dorothy West, October 29, 1988," *The Langston Hughes Review* 12, no. 2 (Fall 1993): 28–44.

Peters, Pearlie. "The Resurgence of Dorothy West as Short-Story Writer," *Abafazi* 8, no. 1 (Fall-Winter 1997): 16–21.

McDowell, Deborah E. "Converstions with Dorothy West." In *The Harlem Renaissance Re-Examined.* Edited by Victor A. Kramer. New York: AMS, 1987, pp. 265–282.

West, Dorothy. *The Living is Easy.* New York: Feminist Press, 1982.

————. *The Richer, the Poorer: Stories, Sketches, and Reminiscences.* New York: Doubleday, 1995.

————. *The Wedding.* New York: Doubleday, 1995.

Wilfred D. Samuels
University of Utah

WHARTON, EDITH (1862–1937)

Edith Newbold Jones Wharton was born during the CIVIL WAR into the comfortable life of an Old New York family. Rumors abounded regarding Edith's paternity, and, although she apparently did not learn about them until her mature years, sexual secrets and fear of gossip are a recurring THEME in her fiction. Like most girls of her social class, Wharton was not formally educated but was privately tutored at home, learning French, Italian, and German. According to the unpublished memoir "Life and I," her "intense Celtic sense of the supernatural" was present from an early age, to be creatively expressed in her collections of short stories (*Tales of Men and Ghosts* [1910]; *Here and Beyond* [1926]; *Ghosts* [1937]). In 1866 family financial difficulties drove the Jones family abroad, where Edith began her lifelong love for Europe and Italy, in particular. In her autobiography *A Backward Glance* (1934), Wharton describes herself as a precocious child who loved "to make up." In 1876 under the pseudonym David Olivieri, she wrote a NOVELLA *Fast and Loose* that parodies English romances (see PARODY); its unhappy ending foreshadows much of her future fiction (see FORESHADOWING). A favorable review by Henry Wadsworth Longfellow led to one of her early poems being published in the ATLANTIC MONTHLY. At age 13 Wharton was tutored by Emelyn Washburn in Anglo-Saxon, Old Norse, Icelandic, and Old German; she learned to love the ancient sagas as well as Dante and Goethe, major influences on her fiction. Emelyn's father, the Reverend Washburn, introduced Wharton to Ralph Waldo Emerson, Henry David Thoreau, and other proponents of TRANSCENDENTALISM whose tradition Wharton mocks in her short story "ANGEL AT THE GRAVE" (1901).

After a broken engagement to Harry Stevens, in 1885 Edith married her brother's friend Edward "Teddy" Wharton, 12 years her senior. Aside from their similar class background and mutual interest in nature, horses, and dogs, they had little in common; Wharton was driven to fulfill her desire for intellectuality and wit in her friends, such as Egerton Winthrop, Walter Berry, and later, Henry JAMES. Wharton's use of painting, as in her story "After Holbein," and her GHOST STORIES such as "THE EYES" (1910), with its latent homosexual implications, led early critics to see Wharton as a disciple of James. Wharton confided in few female friends, most notably Sara Norton. Much has been learned about her thoughts and composing process through her frequent letters to Norton.

The Greater Inclination (1899), Wharton's first collection of short stories, contains three of her best ever stories: "The Muse's Tragedy," "Souls Belated" and "The Pelican." In each she seems to engage in dialogue with major figures of the American short story including Edgar Allan POE and Herman MELVILLE. In 1897 Wharton published her first book, *The Decoration of Houses,* coauthored with architect Ogden Codman, Jr. Their principles of design, based on 18th-century French and English models, were applied to Wharton's homes in Newport and The Mount, built in 1902 in Lenox, Massachusetts. Wharton's first full-length novel, *The Valley of Decision* (1902), was also no doubt informed by the work of her friend Vernon Lee (Violet Paget), who wrote *Studies of the 18th Century in Italy.*

It was at The Mount where Wharton's love affair with William Morton Fullerton began. Her sexual awakening and subsequent disappointment with the bisexual Fullerton provided her with deeply personal material for her fiction, especially in her portrayal of weak male PROTAGONISTS (Selden in *The House of Mirth* [1905]; Darrow in *The Reef* [1912]) and the often repeated "eternal triangle" and even quadrangle, as in "THE OTHER TWO" (1904). The

experience of living in close contact with the Lenox community for ten years enabled Wharton to establish herself as a New England regional author, particularly in her long novella *Ethan Frome* and its "hot" counterpart, *Summer.*

Narrated by an engineer who objectively tries to piece together the story, *Ethan Frome* echoes the dark New England protagonists of Nathaniel HAWTHORNE, especially Ethan Brand. Wharton's frozen landscape reflects her characters' lack of human warmth; Ethan suffers from "too many winters" in Starkfield. Turning from his wife, Zeena, to the young Mattie Silver for affection, the affair ends with a disastrous accident that results in all three spending their lives together in a living hell.

In 1913, after almost 30 years of marriage to "Teddy," often disturbed by his periodic bouts of mental illness (perhaps manic depression), Wharton was divorced and had moved definitively to France. As with most of her novels, Wharton's highly successful 1913 work, *The Custom of the Country,* was published in serial form in *Scribner's.* Her satire of the invasion of Old New York by pushy Midwesterners is epitomized by her creation of the figure of Undine Spragg. Ironically, one contemporary critic saw the book as a critique of the high rate of American divorce.

While life as an expatriate divorcée in France seemed more comfortable to Wharton, in later years she expressed her recognition of changing American views on divorce in her ironic story "AUTRES TEMPS" (1916), in which the HEROine voluntarily renounces happiness. After the outbreak of WORLD WAR I, Wharton threw herself—and recruited friends such as Bernard Berenson—into efforts to provide work for the stream of Belgian refugees entering Paris and to aid tubercular soldiers and civilians. In 1916 she was made Chevalier of the French Legion of Honor, but her profound sense of wartime loss was incorporated into her novels *The Marne* (1918) and *A Son at the Front* (1923). In the midst of the war, Wharton wrote a wonderfully witty short story, "Xingu," satirizing the intellectualizing efforts of ladies' literary clubs. Although set in Brittany, her 1916 ghost story "Kerfol" resounds of Hawthorne's New England as male judges without sufficient evidence condemn a wife for murdering her husband, who had accused her of infidelity. The wife, on the other hand, contends he was killed by the ghosts of her pet dogs (emblems of fidelity), which he had strangled as a warning to her. Wharton in fact returned to the haunted and haunting New England environment in her late psychological and apparently autobiographical ghost story "All Souls" (1937).

In 1920 Wharton looked back to New York society of the 1870s in her ironically titled novel, *The Age of Innocence,* which won the PULITZER PRIZE for fiction in 1921. In the four-volume *Old New York* (1924), Wharton revisited the 1840s to 1870s, further exploring topics such as illegitimacy and adultery.

Wharton's aesthetic principles are to be found in her numerous reviews and essays written over the years, but in 1925 she finally published a small volume entitled *The Writing of Fiction.* The 1996 publication of *The Uncollected Critical Writings* is of tremendous value to those interested in a systematic examination of her aesthetic theory. Shortly before her death, Wharton published her tenth volume of short stories, *The World Over,* containing "ROMAN FEVER," and "The Pomegranate Seed," a reworking of the myth of Demeter and Persephone. Until the end, in her short stories Wharton continued to exploit the GOTHIC tradition, with its sexual subtext, to make commentary on her contemporary world. Ten years following her death in 1937, Percy Lubbock wrote the first biography, *Portrait of Edith Wharton,* placing her in the 19th-century American tradition. For years she was relegated to the shadow of Henry James, her work considered a lesser, feminine version of his. More recent biographies have given fairer credit to her as an original and imaginative writer of fiction, especially ghost stories.

Wharton incorporated every major idea of the intellectual mainstream of her adult life into her fiction (and nonfiction). In her earlier work, she seems to find a niche between the 19th-century feminine sentimental tradition and the masculine pastoral tradition. But her later works, for example, *The Glimpses of the Moon* (1923), show the impact of Sigmund FREUD and Sir James Frazer's *The Golden Bough,* influential sources for Modernists. (See MODERNISM.) The richness of the content and method of her work has made possible scholarly analyses of every conceivable type: Marxist, Freudian or psychoanalytical, FEMINIST, realist, or architectural. As a writer of short stories, Edith Wharton seems to be firmly installed in the canon of American literature. (See MARXIST CRITICISM and REALISM.)

BIBLIOGRAPHY

Bendixen, Alfred, and Annette Zilversmit, eds. *Edith Wharton: New Critical Essays.* New York: Garland, 1992.

Benstock, Shari. *No Gifts from Chance: A Biography of Edith Wharton.* (1994). New York: Penguin Books, 1995.

Fedorko, Kathy A. *Gender and the Gothic in the Fiction of Edith Wharton.* Tuscaloosa: University of Alabama Press, 1995.

Joslin, Katherine. *Edith Wharton.* New York: St. Martin's, 1991.

Joslin, Katherine, and Alan Price, eds. *Wretched Exotic: Essays on Edith Wharton in Europe.* New York: Peter Lang Publishing, 1993.

Lewis, R. W. B. *Edith Wharton: A Biography.* New York: Scribner's, 1975.

Lubbock, Percy. *Portrait of Edith Wharton.* New York: D. Appleton-Century Co., 1947.

Price, Alan. *The End of the Age of Innocence: Edith Wharton and the First World War.* New York: St. Martin's, 1996.

Wharton, Edith. *A Backward Glance: An Autobiography.* New York: Scribner's, 1933. Reprint. 1964.

———. *The Uncollected Critical Writings.* Edited by Frederick Wegener. Princeton, N.J.: Princeton University Press, 1996.

———. *The Collected Stories of Edith Wharton,* vols. 1 and 2. Edited by R. W. B. Lewis. New York: Scribner's, 1968. Reprint. New York: Macmillan, 1987–89.

Wolff, Cynthia Griffin. *A Feast of Words: The Triumph of Edith Wharton* (1977), 2nd ed. Reading, Mass.: Addison-Wesley Publishing Company, 1995.

Carole M. Shaffer-Koros
Kean College of New Jersey

"WHERE ARE YOU GOING, WHERE HAVE YOU BEEN?" JOYCE CAROL OATES (1970)

Probably the most gifted—and certainly the most prolific—literary talent of the second half of the 20th century, Joyce Carol OATES has published over 50 books, won the National Book Award for *Them*, her novel published in 1969, received countless O. Henry citations, and has been nominated frequently for the Nobel Prize. Her most widely anthologized short story, "Where Are You Going, Where Have You Been?" is a chilling modern FABLE that uncovers the bleakness and emptiness of contemporary life and values. The story has become an American CLASSIC.

Oates's grimly realistic portrayal of CONNIE, her adolescent PROTAGONIST, reveals the falsity of the Cinderella myth and the romantic stories on which young girls are raised. (See ROMANTICISM.) Connie, the rebellious teenager, is bored with and alienated from her middle-class family, preferring instead to spend her spare time trying on makeup, listening to rock and roll, and cruising through the shopping mall with her friends. At the mall she meets a sinister character named ARNOLD FRIEND. Oates uses MAGIC REALISM to suggest that Arnold is not all he appears to be; indeed, her third-person narrator suggests that he is not only obscene and slightly out of place but everywhere, knowing everything; in fact, he may be the devil himself, an identity many critics see inherent in his stumbling walk and his inability to balance in his boots: Cloven hooves may be the source of his difficulties.

When Arnold visits Connie at her house, he knows that her family is away and threatens to bring harm to them if she does not accompany him. Like the devil, his goal is to have Connie come to him of her own free will. Oates's memorable building of suspense and horror is evident in the insubstantial screen door that separates Connie from Arnold and the insistently ringing phone, which Connie is powerless to answer or, later, to use to call the police. Volitionless, Connie moves toward Arnold as in a nightmare, and the final wording of the story suggests he will not only rape her in this world but take her with him to hell, whether biblical or earthly. In the pessimistic ending, the reader understands that Connie is gone forever and that her culture never prepared her to resist evil.

The title comes from a line of a Bob Dylan song, and the story positions Connie in both the new world of rock and roll—presided over by the disk jockey, Bobby King, a replacement for an earlier spiritual "king"—and the ancient world of the demon lover who spirits away his unresisting victim. The frightening contemporary PARABLE that Oates has created resonates with the reader in deeply disturbing ways. The story was filmed in 1986 with the title *Smooth Talk*.

BIBLIOGRAPHY

Bastian, Katherine. *Oates's Short Stories: Between Tradition and Innovation*. Frankfurt am Main: Verlag Peter Lang, 1983.

Friedman, Ellen G. *Joyce Carol Oates*. New York: Ungar, 1980.

Norman, Torberg. *Isolation and Contact: A Study of Character Relationships in Oates's Short Stories, 1963–1980*. Göteborg, Sweden: Acta Universitatis Gothoburgensis, 1984.

Oates, Joyce Carol. *Where Are You Going, Where Have You Been? Stories of Young America*. Greenwich, Conn.: Fawcett Publications, 1974.

Wagner-Martin, Linda. *Critical Essays on Joyce Carol Oates*. Boston: G.K. Hall, 1979.

"WHERE I'M CALLING FROM" RAYMOND CARVER (1988)   Like many of the stories in *Cathedral*, "Where I'm Calling From" revolves around the healing power of human communication. In marked contrast to much of Raymond CARVER's bleak earlier work, this story explores the role storytelling plays in moving from hopelessness to hope, from despair to redemption.

"Where I'm Calling From" opens with the unnamed narrator and J.P. on the porch of an alcohol rehabilitation center. J.P.'s explanation of the way he ended up there turns out to be the story of his life. As "Where I'm Calling From" progresses, the narrator begins to insert fragments from his own life between J.P.'s stories, so that by the time J.P.'s wife, Roxy, comes to visit, the narrator has taken over the storytelling. After seeing firsthand the love that still binds J.P. and Roxy, the narrator is able to formulate a story about a hopeful future for himself as well.

Along with "CATHEDRAL" and "A Small, Good Thing," "Where I'm Calling From" (selected in 1988 as the title piece for his collected stories) marks an important development in Carver's writing and his career. It possesses many of the characteristics of

MINIMALISM for which Carver is known, including short sentences, lack of descriptive detail, and abbreviated dialogue. But "Where I'm Calling From" also contains humor, genuine friendship, and glimpses of hope in the face of trouble—THEMES missing from much of Carver's early work. A few critics have seen this shift as a move toward sentimentality, but most agree that Carver's work became stronger in adopting a more generous, sympathetic view. With the publication of this and other stories in *Cathedral,* Carver was acknowledged as a master of the short story, and a leading figure in the American short story's 1980s renaissance.

BIBLIOGRAPHY

Carver, Raymond. *Carver Country: The World of Raymond Carver.* New York: Scribner's, 1990.

———. *Cathedral: Stories.* New York: Vintage Books, 1983.

———. *Where I'm Calling From: New and Selected Stories:* New York: Atlantic Monthly Press, 1988.

Saltzman, Arthur M. *Understanding Raymond Carver* Columbia: University of South Carolina Press, 1988.

David VanHook
University of North Carolina

"WHITE HERON, A"   SARAH ORNE JEWETT
(1886)   This frequently anthologized BILDUNGSRO-MAN features Sylvia, a nine-year-old girl whose very name evokes the woods that she loves, and where she is walking when we first encounter her. She meets an attractive young man, a hunter and an ornithologist, who tries to persuade her to show him the nest of the white heron that he would like to add to his collection of stuffed birds. Her decision not to do so has provoked a wide variety of interpretations. The story can be read on numerous levels—as a study in respecting and protecting nature, as a sensitively depicted LOCAL COLOR story, as a reimagining of the Demeter-Persephone MYTH or FAIRY TALE, or as a fictional rendering of Sarah Orne JEWETT's own life, both as an artist and as a single woman.

Perhaps because the story is so clearly sympathetic to protecting the environment, many readers feel puzzled and disturbed by the significance of the hunter himself, who seems to represent more than just a destroyer of forest creatures: A disturbing sexual element, an intrusive sense of violence and aggression, appears to lie beneath his cloak of pleasant friendliness. Jewett implies strong gender issues in this tale. Viewing his role as that of a metaphorical rapist (see METAPHOR) serves both to illuminate Sylvia's intuitive fears of men and to deepen the environmentalist THEME. Early in the story, Mrs. Tilley, Sylvia's grandmother, reveals that Sylvia is "afraid of folks" (648). As Sylvia walks through the woods, she recalls a "great red-faced boy" (648) who used to chase her and frighten her when she lived in town; this memory FORESHADOWS the very next sentence in which she hears the "aggressive" whistle that heralds her encounter with the young man with the gun. He immediately asks her if he can spend the night at her house and "go gunning" in the morning. Sylvia's confusion mirrors that of many young girls who meet a stranger: Juxtaposed to her instinctive fear of him is her attraction to his veneer of gallantry, kindness, and sympathy.

When she agrees to take him to the house where she and her grandmother live, the man succeeds in penetrating the "hermitage" (649) of the two women. He proves insensitive to Mrs. Tilley's "hint[s] of family sorrows" (650), instead dominating the conversation and boasting that, since boyhood, he has been killing and collecting birds that he stuffs and preserves as trophies of his manliness. The narrator repeatedly refers to his gun and knife, phallic images (see IMAGERY) that combine with his offering Sylvia money if she will sacrifice the white bird that some critics view as a symbol of her virginity and innocence. He charms her, and her fear subsides, giving way to the "woman's heart" (651) asleep somewhere within the young girl. Yet images of seduction give way to those of rape when Sylvia climbs the tree, views the heron's nest, and climbs back down with her dress smeared, torn, and tattered; they are reinforced with the image of the dead birds "stained and wet with blood" (654) near the end of the story. Ultimately, Sylvia decides she must protect the heron at all costs, even though it means losing the man's friendship.

While the narrator ends the story by predicting the loneliness of Sylvia's future, nothing in the story suggests, in Ann Charters's words, "that she would have been better off having sold herself for ten dollars and a whistle" (Charters 85). The many ways to view the ending—from biographical, Freudian (see FREUD, SIGMUND), mythic, or environmental perspectives—only add to the depths of the story waiting for each new reader to plumb.

BIBLIOGRAPHY
Cary, Richard. *Sarah Orne Jewett*. Albany, N.Y.: New Collections University Press, 1962.
Charters, Ann. *Resources for Teaching Major Writers of Short Fiction*. Boston: St. Martin's, 1993.
Jewett, Sarah Orne. "The White Heron." In *Major Writers of Short Fiction: Stories and Commentaries*. Edited by Ann Charters. Boston: Bedford Books-St. Martin's, 1993, pp. 647–54.
Donovan, Josephine L. *Sarah Orne Jewett*. New York: Ungar, 1980.
Nagel, Gwen. *Critical Essays on Jewett*. Boston: G.K. Hall, 1984.

"WHITE QUAIL, THE"   JOHN STEINBECK (1942)

A wide variety of interpretations have greeted STEINBECK's "The White Quail" since its publication in *The Long Valley* in 1942. Some critics have used it as basic evidence of Steinbeck's misogyny, believing that his portrait of Mary Teller is clearly designed to criticize her controlling, manipulating traits as well as her determination to create a false "ideal" world in the midst of a real one. Still others see Mary as a strong woman, struggling to exist in a world where male and female roles are stringently assigned.

Since the events portrayed are rather static, however, and since the characters appear as mere archetypes of opposing forces or ideas, most critics have agreed that the plot line and characters are not the strengths of the story. Told in six episodes, the story revolves around the goal of Mary Teller to wall out the natural environs and to replace them with a structured and artificial garden of her own creation. Choosing her husband, Harry Teller, on the basis of his compatibility with such a structured living area, Mary appears to exclude personal emotions so she can attain her goal. Depicted with an almost manic obsession for control, Mary clearly contrasts with Harry, her chosen mate. He is relatively unconcerned and uninvolved with her planning, while the garden occupies Mary's every waking hour. He is aroused sexually by her appearance, while she appears revolted by sex and often relegates him to a separate bedroom. Her insistent attitude and her determination to be a dominant force in the marriage also contrasts with his passivity. This negative portrayal of the female has troubled FEMINIST critics and led others to search for biographical parallels in Steinbeck's disintegrating relationship with his first wife, Carol Henning.

As evidence of the complexity of this second tale of *The Long Valley,* other analyses have been developed to understand this story of marital unhappiness. Since the story contains so many clearly defined natural symbols (the garden as a renewed EDEN, the outside world of the surrounding hills as an intruding evil), some critics have noted biblical overtones. The white quail, a symbol for Mary as well as for purity and idealism, is a cipher in the complex world of reality. Conversely, the gray cat that stalks the quail, as predator, is identified with Harry Teller as an enemy of an unfallen Eden in the midst of a fallen world. The biblical tension of the original Adam and Eve story develops once more in this perfect garden as male and female, depicted as polar opposites, each seek different ends. (See ALLUSION.)

Harry's materialistic goals seem unnatural and "unfair" to his wife, while Mary's "natural" goals appear odd, strange, and contrived to Harry. The difference depends on the perspective of the observer as Steinbeck applies his objective approach to the characters. Neither Harry nor Mary is assigned primary blame; instead, their singular selfishness and lack of concern for each other causes grief to each. Mary's association of the quail with "the very center of her, her heart" and Harry's eventual destruction of the quail emphasize a pervasive loneliness in human sexual relationships despite the sex act's intent to join two into one.

Critic Robert S. Hughes has delineated fear of change and an inability to cope with loneliness as the two major THEMES of this "LYRIC" short story. Citing Steinbeck's *Long Valley Notebook,* he suggests events in Steinbeck's life during 1933 that might have made such a tale an appropriate reaction to his own existence. Certainly Mary's fear of change is indicated in her intent to replace any dying bush or plant with one exactly like it, and the isolation of both characters, especially Harry, depicts the guilt and sadness that accompany the elevation of self at the expense of others. An unwillingness to foster brotherhood through mutual understanding is a key to understanding Steinbeck's message in this story.

Other readings suggest that the story deals with an artist's obsession to draw and create perfect worlds to the exclusion of the more important qualities of human warmth and compassion. This approach suggests that imagination often is elevated at the expense of reality, and a depiction of real life often is sacrificed for art's sake. Still others have emphasized Mary's narcissism or her search for the Platonic ideal as the central theme of "The White Quail." According to this reading, Steinbeck condemns self-centeredness and espouses the natural tension between evil and good rather than an idealistic pursuit of goodness.

Regardless of the interpretation the reader endorses, in the end, Steinbeck seems to echo Nathaniel HAWTHORNE in his portrait of unhappy men and women who create their own prisons. Steinbeck brings an uneasy CLOSURE to his story, leaving both Harry and Mary in uncomfortable opposition to each other, unable to find good in evil and evil in good.

BIBLIOGRAPHY

Hughes, Robert S., Jr. "What Went Wrong? How a 'Vintage' Steinbeck Short Story Became the Flawed Winter of Our Discontent." *Steinbeck Quarterly* 26. 1–2 (Spring 1993); 1–7.

Steinbeck, John. "The White Quail." In *The Long Valley.* New York: Penguin, 1995.

Timmerman, John H. "Introduction." In John Steinbeck, *The Long Valley.* New York: Penguin, 1995.

Michael J. Meyer
DePaul University

"WHY I LIVE AT THE P.O." EUDORA WELTY (1940)

"Why I Live at the P.O." is probably Eudora WELTY's best-known and most anthologized short story. The story was first published in the *Atlantic* (1940) and appeared the following year in her first short story collection, *A Curtain of Green and Other Stories.* This humorous dramatic monologue is filled with the natural rhythm and idiom of Southern speech (see DIALECT), and the COMEDY is further enhanced by the characters' quirky actions as described through the eyes of Sister.

Jealous of her younger sister, Sister is vexed when Stella-Rondo returns to China Grove after separating from the man she had earlier stolen away from Sister herself. To add insult to injury, Stella-Rondo brings with her Shirley-T, a two-year-old "adopted child" that the family has never heard about. Sister, convinced that Stella-Rondo is systematically turning the whole family against her, describes the events of a scorching Fourth of July that lead to her eventual removal to the back of the post office, where she works as postmistress.

For most readers, however, Sister is the classic UNRELIABLE NARRATOR. We see the day's events only from her POINT OF VIEW, and we gradually sense she has filtered them through her paranoid illusions. She tries too hard to convince us that everyone is against her, and the attacks she describes are ludicrously petty and illogical. Although the conflict occurs on Independence Day, the story's imagery creates a sense of entrapment and suffocation. The windows of the small and crowded house are locked and the day is stiflingly hot. Ironically, even after she makes her escape to the post office, Sister is trapped and isolated in her post office window, telling passersby about her family's injustice, prisoner of her own spite.

The story contains the evidence for an alternative reading that views Sister more sympathetically: Stella-Rondo apparently ran off with Sister's gentleman friend and may very well be lying to the family about her marriage to Shirley-T's father. In her flight to the post office, Sister achieves a room of her own and a peace of sorts. Whichever way the reader views this account of a day in the life of a family, Welty clearly intends the humorous tone with which she describes the inebriated Papa-Daddy, the petty family bickerings, and the PARODY of an American family on Independence Day.

BIBLIOGRAPHY
Evans, Elizabeth. *Eudora Welty.* New York: Frederick Ungar, 1981.
Whitaker, Elaine E. "Welty's 'Why I Live at the P.O.'" *The Explicator* 50.2 (Winter 1992): 115–117.

Betina I. Entzminger
University of North Carolina at Chapel Hill

WIDEMAN, JOHN EDGAR (1941–)

John Edgar Wideman was born in Washington, D.C., but grew up in the neighborhood of Homewood in Pittsburgh, Pennsylvannia. His scholastic and athletic achievements at the University of Pennsylvannia earned him a Rhodes Scholarship in 1963. He was one of the first African-American students to attend Oxford University in 50 years. After graduation he returned to the University of Pennsylvannia and became the institution's first African American tenured professor. Since 1967 he has published 14 books, including novels, short story collections, and personal nonfiction as well as numerous essays and reviews. He was the first writer to receive the PEN/FAULKNER AWARD twice, for the novels *Sent for You Yesterday* (1948) and *Philadelphia Fire* (1990), and served as the editor of *Best American Short Stories* (1996).

His first short story collection, *Damballah* (1981), follows the pattern of a SHORT STORY CYCLE. *Damballah* presents a series of interrelated stories that are set primarily in Homewood, Wideman's mythical Pennsylvania town, and trace the lives and histories of an African American family, based on Wideman's own family. The work is reminiscent of Jean TOOMER'S *CANE* in its poetic evocation of a place and of a people, and its interweaving of myth, song, dream, and reality. *Damballah* and the novels *Hiding Place* (1981) and *Sent for You Yesterday* were later published together as *The Homewood Trilogy*. FEVER, Wideman's second collection of stories, appeared in

1989. *The Stories of John Edgar Wideman* (1992) brought together *Damballah, Fever,* and ten new pieces written for the collection, grouped under the title and later reprinted as ALL STORIES ARE TRUE. With their use of multiple POINTS OF VIEW and disjointed style, Wideman's postmodern stories illustrate the diverse and complex lives of African-Americans, past and present (see POSTMODERNISM). In the midst of poverty, violence, despair, and racial injustice, meaning and hope emerge through these communal stories and voices.

BIBLIOGRAPHY
Coleman, James William. *Blackness and Modernism: The Literary Career of John Edgar Wideman.* Jackson: University Press of Mississippi, 1989.
———. *Blackness and Modernism: The Literary Development of John Edgar Wideman.* Jackson: University Press of Mississippi, 1989.
Wideman, John Edgar. *All Stories Are True: The Stories of John Edgar Wideman.* London: Picador, 1992.
———. *Brothers and Keepers.* London: Picador, 1984.
———. *The Cattle Killing.* New York: Houghton Mifflin, 1996.
———. *Conversations with John Edgar Wideman.* Jackson: University Press of Mississippi, 1998.
———. *Damballah.* Boston: Houghton Mifflin, 1981.
———. "Doc's Story." *Esquire* 106. 2 (August 1986).
———. *El-Hajj Malik El-Shabazz: A New Story Beginning . . .* Tuscaloosa, AL: Inka Press, 1992.
———. *Fatheralong: A Meditation on Fathers and Sons, Race and Society.* New York: Vintage Books, 1994.
———. *A Glance Away.* New York: Harcourt, Brace & World, 1967.
———. *Hiding Place.* Boston: Houghton Mifflin, 1981.
———. *The Homewood Books.* Pittsburgh: University of Pittsburgh Press, 1981.
———. *Hurry Home.* New York: Henry Holt, 1970.
———. *Identities: Three Novels.* New York: Henry Holt, 1994.
———. *The Lynchers* (1973). New York: Henry Holt, 1986.
———. *Philadelphia Fire.* New York: Penguin, 1992.
———. *Reuben.* New York: Viking, 1987.
———. *Sent for You Yesterday.* Boston: Houghton Mifflin, 1983.
———. *The Stories of John Edgar Wideman.* New York: Pantheon Books, 1992.
———. *Two Cities.* Boston: Houghton Mifflin, 1998.

Tracie Guzzio
Ohio University

WINESBURG, OHIO SHERWOOD ANDERSON (1919)

In *Winesburg, Ohio*, Sherwood ANDERSON introduced his theory of the GROTESQUE character, explained in the introductory story, "The Book of the Grotesque." The PROTAGONIST, an elderly author reminiscent of Mark TWAIN, has determined that people became grotesques by adhering to only one truth at the expense of ignoring others. All the *Winesburg* stories—often featuring or observed by teenage GEORGE WILLARD, an aspiring writer—deal with such people: Wing Biddlebaum in "HANDS," who dumbly focuses on the instrument of his downfall; the title character in "Mother" who spends years of frugality to save money so that her son can move to the city, money that he never receives; Doctor Parcival, "The Philosopher," who has hopelessly concluded that in a world where, he believes, everyone is Christ, everyone is therefore doomed; Kate Swift, "The Teacher," who, frustrated by suppressed longings, vainly attempts to instill in George Willard a passion for life. In "Adventure," a typical *Winesburg* story, Alice Hindman, a young dry goods clerk whose lover has abandoned her, spends years saving money in anticipation of his return. One evening, unable to control her suppressed sexuality and growing restlessness, Alice undresses and goes out into the rain to confront an elderly man who is merely confused by the apparition of a naked woman. She crawls back to the safety of her house, trembling with fear for what she has done and confused about the meaning of her adventure.

Anderson thought of the collection of short stories as a novel, and certainly the varied tales are linked by the Winesburg setting, the frequent presence of George Willard, "the consistency of mood, and the cumulative power of the pieces" (Stevick 64). Today, however, Winesburg appears to critics generally as a SHORT STORY CYCLE rather than a novel proper; indeed, Anderson invented the form, and has been followed ever since, from Ernest HEMINGWAY and his NICK ADAMS stories and William FAULKNER and his BAYARD SARTORIS and IKE MCCASLIN stories, to such contemporary storytellers as Louise ERDRICH, Harriet DOERR, and Sandra Benitez, all of whom reveal the interior lives of CHARACTERS who reappear in various tales.

BIBLIOGRAPHY

Anderson, Sherwood. *Winesburg, Ohio*. Edited by Glen A. Love. New York: Oxford University Press, 1997.

Crowley, John W., ed. *New Essays on Winesburg, Ohio*. Cambridge, England: Cambridge University Press, 1990.

Gullason, Thomas A. "The 'Lesser' Renaissance: The American Short Story in the 1920s." In *The American Short Story, 1900–1945: A Critical History*. Edited by Philip Stevick. Boston: Twayne, 1984, 71–102.

White, Ray Lewis. *Winesburg, Ohio: An Exploration*. Boston: Twayne, 1990.

———. *The Merrill Studies in "Winesburg, Ohio."* Columbus, Ohio: Charles E. Merrill, 1971.

WOLFF, TOBIAS (1945–)

Born Tobias Jonathan Ansell Wolff in Birmingham, Alabama, Wolff and his brother, Geoffrey, were immersed in a personal world of fictions and storytelling that ultimately produced two fine writers. Each has written autobiographical accounts of their very different experiences as the children of a flamboyant, intrepid father and a determined, strong mother. Tobias Wolff left the South as a child when his parents' marriage dissolved; he traveled with his mother to several areas of the United States but was raised chiefly in Seattle. His work detailing this portion of his life, *This Boy's Life: A Memoir* (1989), won widespread acclaim and was made into a movie starring Robert DeNiro (as Wolff's stepfather) and Leonardo De Caprio as young Wolff in 1993.

Wolff has won numerous awards for his fiction and nonfiction. He received a GUGGENHEIM GRANT in 1982 and was awarded the PEN/FAULKNER AWARD for his NOVELLA, *The Barracks Thief* (1984). He is a prolific writer, with short story collections to date including *In the Garden of the North American Martyrs* (1981), *Back in the World* (1985), and *The Night in Question* (1996). His short stories are widely anthologized and have been published in magazines including ATLANTIC MONTHLY and HARPER'S. His nonfiction bears many characteristics of his short fiction, and many chapters of *This Boy's Life: A Memoir* and *In Pharaoh's Army: Memories of the Lost War* (1994) could easily be published as examples of complete short narratives.

Wolff's fiction and nonfiction reflect his experiences: His second memoir, *In Pharaoh's Army: Memories of the Lost War* and his 1984 novella both derive from his service in the VIETNAM WAR. His war writing has been compared with that of Tim O'BRIEN, whose writing Wolff admires, along with that of Flannery O'CONNOR. O'Connor and Wolff both create stories that concern moral choice, but Wolff's more often concern everyday situations and realistic resolutions, with sympathetic characters who falter and learn their limitations.

BIBLIOGRAPHY

Lyons, Bonnie, and Bill Oliver. "An Interview with Tobias Wolff." *Contemporary Literature* (Spring 1990): 1–16.

Prose, Francine. "The Brothers Wolff." *New York Times Magazine,* February 5, 1989, 22–31.

Wolff, Geoffrey. "Advice My Brother Never Took." *New York Times Book Review,* August 20, 1989, 7.

Wolff, Tobias. *Back in the World: Stories.* Boston: Houghton Mifflin, 1985.

———. *The Barracks Thief and Selected Stories.* New York: Bantam Books, 1984.

———. *In the Garden of the North American Martyrs: A Collection of Short Stories.* New York: Ecco Press, 1981.

———. *The Liar.* Vineburg, Calif.: Engdahl Typography, 1989.

———. *Matters of Life and Death: New American Stories.* Green Harbor, Mass.: Wampeter Press, 1983.

———. *The Night in Question: Stories.* New York: Alfred A. Knopf, 1996.

———. *The Other Miller.* Derry, New Hampshire; Ridgewood, New Jersey: Babcock & Koontz, 1986.

———. *In Pharaoh's Army: Memories of the Lost War.* New York: Alfred A. Knopf, 1994.

———. *Stories.* Boston: Emerson College, 1992.

———. *This Boy's Life: A Memoir.* New York: Harper & Row, 1989.

———. *Two Boys and A Girl.* London: Bloomsbury, 1996.

———. *Ugly Rumours: A Novel.* London: Allen & Unwin, 1975.

Wolff, Tobias, ed. *The Picador Book of Contemporary American Stories.* London: Picador, 1993.

———. *The Vintage Book of Contemporary American Short Stories.* New York: Vintage Contemporaries, 1994.

Karen Weekes
University of Georgia

WOMAN HOLLERING CREEK SANDRA CISNEROS (1991)

Many of the THEMES characteristic of Sandra CISNEROS's earlier collection of stories, THE HOUSE ON MANGO STREET, appear in the stories of *Woman Hollering Creek.* The first section of the collection consists of stories told through the voices of very young children. (See POINT OF VIEW.) The second section includes stories of early adolescence. One of the most remarkable is the story "One Holy Night," narrated by a 12-year-old Latina pregnant by a 37-year-old murder suspect who has used the young girl's imagination and innocence against her. The third section focuses on stories of young women, many caught in unhappy relationships. The title selection, "Woman Hollering Creek," follows the marriage of Cleofilas. Wed in Mexico, she follows her husband to Texas. Isolated in a new world, she is forced to endure her husband's beating. Aided by two Latina FEMINISTS, she attempts to escape back to Mexico. As Cleofilas and one of her aides, Felice, cross the creek, La Gritona, back into Mexico, the meaning of the title becomes clear: crossing La Gritona—Woman Hollering Creek—Felice begins to holler "like Tarzan." It is a scream that reveals freedom and joy, but also pain, suffering, and rage at the indignities women suffer. "Little Miracles, Kept Promises," another story in the collection, is a collage of letters left at the shrine of the Virgin of Guadalupe. The story captures the voices of the desperate, confused, and faithful living on the Texas-Mexican border. The last letter, written by a young Latina artist, Rosario, reiterates Cisneros's belief that the artist must remain a voice for the past and future of the community, but it also suggests the inherent difficulty in doing so.

BIBLIOGRAPHY

Cahill, Susan Neunzig. *Writing Women's Lives: An Anthology of Autobiographical Narratives by Twentieth Century American Women Writers.* New York: HarperCollins, 1994.

Doyle, Jacqueline. "More Room of Her Own: Sandra Cisneros's *The House on Mango Street.*" *MELUS: Society for the Study of the Multi-Ethnic Literature of the United States* 19.4 (Winter 1994).

Gibson, Michelle. "The 'Unreliable' Narrator in *The House on Mango Street.*" *San Jose Studies* 19.2 (Spring 1993).

McCracken, Ellen. "Sandra Cisneros' *The House on Mango Street:* Community-Oriented Introspection and the Demystification of Patriarchal Violence." In *Breaking Boundaries: Latina Writings and Critical Readings.* Edited by Asuncion Horno-Delgado et al. Amherst: University of Massachusetts Press, 1989.

Olivares, Julian. "Sandra Cisneros' *The House on Mango Street,* and the Poetics of Space." In *Chicana Creativity and Criticism: New Frontiers in American Literature.* Edited by Maria Herrera-Sobek and Helena María Viramontes. Albuquerque: University of New Mexico Press, 1986, pp. 233–44.

Stavans, Ilan. "*The House on Mango Street/Woman Hollering Creek and Other Stories.*" *Commonweal,* September 13, 1991. 524–529.

TuSmith, Bonnie. *All My Relatives: Community in Contemporary Ethnic American Literatures.* Ann Arbor: University of Michigan Press, 1993.

Tracie Guzzio
Ohio University

WOMAN LIT BY FIREFLIES, THE JIM HARRISON (1990)

The Woman Lit by Fireflies, Jim HARRISON's second NOVELLA collection, contains three stories: "Brown Dog," "Sunset Limited," and "The Woman Lit by Fireflies." This collection marks the first appearance of the Brown Dog—the picaro (or shrewd, roguish PROTAGONIST)—who spends his time in the Upper Peninsula Michigan eating, drinking, womanizing, and avoiding capture after he discovers the body of an Indian chief in Lake Superior and steals a refrigerated truck in which to preserve the body. The novella details the conflict between wilderness and society, between Brown Dog's desire to bury the chief and to keep secret an Indian burial mound and Shelley Newkirk's desire to dig up the mounds for her own professional gain. The first-person narrative is in Brown Dog's voice, although he admits that "These aren't my exact words. A fine young woman named Shelley, who is also acting as my legal guardian and semi-probation officer, is helping me get this all down on paper" (3). Brown Dog is reprised in Harrison's third novella collection, *JULIP.*

Sunset Limited is a product of Harrison's wondering "what Russell Chatham, Tom MCGUANE, Guy de la Valdene, and he himself would do if one of them got

into trouble in South America" (Reilly 147). The story is about five old college friends, Gwen, Zip, Sam, Patty, and Billy, who separate after their radical years at the University of Colorado. The most common critical opinion of the story is that it recalls the movie *The Big Chill,* in which a group of college friends reunite after one of their group commits suicide. In *Sunset Limited,* four of the protagonists reunite at Gwen's ranch before they leave for Mexico to save Zip, who is in a Mexican prison awaiting trial on charges of inciting a riot and attempted murder. The plot of *Sunset Limited,* more than any other of Harrison's novellas, is contrived. The manuscript was originally written as a screenplay.

In *The Woman Lit by Fireflies,* Harrison writes through the eyes of Clare, a middle-aged woman who decides to leave her husband, a fatuous businessman. Clare spends the night in an Iowa cornfield and imagines conversations with her daughter, recalls the deaths of her best friend and her dog, and plans a return to her beloved Paris where, finally, "she felt less lost than before her night in the thicket. . . . If it rained, she would wear her beret to dinner" (247).

The three narratives in *The Woman Lit by Fireflies* illustrate Harrison's ability to portray different characters in diverse landscapes and situations with an engaging voice and an eye for the obvious, but often unseen, detail.

BIBLIOGRAPHY
Harrison, Jim. *The Woman Lit by Fireflies.* Boston: Houghton Mifflin, 1990.
Reilly, Edward C. *Jim Harrison.* New York: Twayne, 1996.

Patrick A. Smith
Ohio University

WONG, SHAWN (1949–)

Shawn Wong was born in Oakland, California, and raised in Berkeley. He received his B.A. from the University of California at Berkeley and his M.F.A. in creative writing from San Francisco State University. Wong has written two novels, *Homebase* (1979), from which self-contained chapters have been frequently excerpted and anthologized, and *American Knees* (1995).

Wong's importance to the short story has come through his influence on the emerging Asian

American body of work. Earlier in his career, along with Jeffery Paul CHAN, Frank CHIN, and Lawson Fusao Inada, he coedited *Aiiieeeee!* (1974), the first ASIAN AMERICAN LITERATURE anthology. Although it tended to define Asian American literature in terms of Chinese and Japanese American writers, this collection contributed significantly to a more inclusive conception of American literature. Since the appearance of this controversial and important publication, the many voices of Asian American writers have made an increasingly distinguished impact on American literature. Wong's more recent *An Introduction to Asian American Literature* (1995), far more electic in its approach, may point toward a wider understanding among scholars of what appropriately constitutes the Asian American short story.

BIBLIOGRAPHY

Kim, Elaine H. *Asian American Literature: An Introduction to the Writings and Their Social Context* (1982). Reprint. Philadelphia: Temple University Press, 1984.

Wong, Shawn. *American Knees*. New York: Scribner's, 1995.

———. *Blue Funnel Line*. Seattle, Wash.: The Seattle Review, 1988.

———. *Homebase*. New York: Plume, 1991.

———. "I miss the person I love every day." In *A Few Thousand Words About Love*. Edited by Mickey Pearlman. New York: HarperCollins, 1998.

Wong, Shawn, ed. *Asian American Literature: A Brief Introduction and Anthology*. New York: HarperCollins College Publications, 1996.

Wong, Shawn, ed. *The Before Columbus Foundation Fiction Anthology: Selections from the American Book Awards, 1980–1990*. New York: W.W. Norton, 1992.

Wong, Shawn, Frank Chin, Jeffery Paul Chan, and Lawson Fusao Inada, eds. *Aiiieeeee!: An Anthology of Asian American Writers*. New York: Penguin, 1974.

Wong, Shawn, Jeffery Paul Chan, Frank Chin (ed.), and Lawson Fusao Inada. *The Big Aiiieeeee!: An Anthology of Chinese-American and Japanese-American Literature*. New York: Meridian Books, 1991.

Keith Lawrence
Brigham Young University

WOOLSON, CONSTANCE FENIMORE
(1840–1894) Constance Fenimore Woolson, the great-niece of James Fenimore Cooper, 19th century author of the Leatherstocking Tales, was born in 1840 in New Hampshire but was reared in northern Ohio and schooled in New York. She began her writing career in the early 1870s, drawing on her childhood in the North and on her subsequent travels throughout the RECONSTRUCTION-era South. By the late 1870s she had published widely in such magazines as *ATLANTIC MONTHLY, Scribner's,* and *HARPER'S.*

Her work drew the praise of critics throughout her lifetime, and she was considered a premier short story writer, especially in the area of LOCAL COLOR. Her local color contributions are unusual in that she depicts the settings, DIALECTs, and customs of two extremely diverse regions of the country: *Castle Nowhere: Lake-Country Sketches* (1875) details the North and contains the notable story "THE LADY OF LITTLE FISHING," while *Rodman, the Keeper: Southern Sketches* (1880) portrays the post bellum South, extending into Florida. Woolson was intent on presenting the personalities of her regional characters, especially as she explored the contrasting temperaments of Northerners and Southerners in her second book. (See REGIONALISM.) Several of the stories in *Rodman, the Keeper* depict Northerners who have traveled into the South, and their narrative lines suggest the differences between natives of the two regions. *Castle Nowhere* is set in northern Michigan, and its thematic focus (see THEME) is on the conflicts between "civilized," imposed codes and an intuitive, natural morality. This volume led to favorable comparisons with Bret HARTE, who is a clear influence on Woolson's early work.

Woolson also traveled extensively in Europe, living abroad from 1880 until her death in 1894. She wrote two collections of short stories using a foreign locale: *The Front Yard and Other Italian Stories* (1895) and *Dorothy and Other Italian Stories* (1896). In 1880 Woolson met Henry JAMES, who wrote favorably about her in his *Partial Portraits* (1888). They became close friends, and both expatriate writers explored the international theme in short stories of this period. Other works published by Woolson include *Two Women: 1862. A Poem* (1877), *For the*

Major: A Novelette (1883), and Jupiter Lights: A Novel (1889).

Another theme prevalent in Woolson's personal correspondence and her published writing is the role of the artist, especially the female artist. "Miss Grief" exemplifies the role that Woolson saw for female artists, including herself: dedicated and proud, yet also isolated and estranged. Plagued by depression throughout her life, Woolson said she felt especially drained and vulnerable on the completion of each of her books. Shortly after finishing the manuscript for her last novel, Horace Chase, she either fell or jumped to her death from a second-story window in Venice. Although her work was dismissed in the early and mid-1900s, her poetic style and lush descriptions are once again finding favor with critics and readers alike.

BIBLIOGRAPHY
Dean, Sharon L. Constance Fenimore Woolson: Homeward Bound. Knoxville: University of Tennessee Press, 1995.
Kern, John Dwight. Constance Fenimore Woolson: Literary Pioneer. Philadelphia: University of Pennsylvania Press, 1934.
Moore, Rayburn. Constance Fenimore Woolson. New York: Twayne, 1963.
Rowe, Anne, The Enchanted Country: Northern Writers in the South, 1865–1910. Baton Rouge: Louisiana State University Press, 1979.
Torsney, Cheryl B. Constance Fenimore Woolson: The Grief of Artistry. Athens: University of Georgia Press, 1989.
———. Critical Essays on Constance Fenimore Woolson. New York: G.K. Hall, 1992.
Wiemer, Joan Myers. Women Artists, Women Exiles: "Miss Grief" and Other Stories. New Brunswick, N.J.: Rutgers University Press, 1988.
Woolson, Constance Fenimore. Castle Nowhere: Lake-Country Sketches. New York: Harper, 1875.
———. Constance Fenimore Woolson. London: Ellis, 1930.
———. Dorothy, and Other Italian Stories. New York: Harper & Brothers, 1896.
———. For the Major: A Novelette. New York: Harper, 1883 1979.
———. The Front Yard, and Other Italian Stories. New York: Harper, 1900 (?), 1983.
———. Horace Chase: A Novel. New York: Harper & Brothers, 1894.
———. Jupiter Lights: A Novel. New York: Harper, 1970 1979.
———. Rodman, the Keeper: Southern Sketches. New York: Harper & Brothers, 1899.
———. Two Women, 1862: A Poem. New York: D. Appleton, 1885.
———. Women Artists, Women Exiles: "Miss Grief" and Other Stories. New Brunswick, N.J.: Rutgers University Press, 1988.

Karen Weekes
University of Georgia

WORLD WAR I (1914–1918)   The Allies (Great Britain, France, Russia, and Italy) fought the Central Powers (Germany, Austria-Hungary, and Turkey) from 1914 to 1918. The United States joined the Allies in 1917. The war changed the face of Europe and the Middle East, for at its end, the empires of Germany, Austria-Hungary, and Turkey were dismembered. The Russian Revolution of 1917, which had been precipitated by the capitulation of Russia's armies to the Germans, had already toppled the czarist government and replaced it with a Marxist one. (See MARX.) The Versailles Treaty that officially ended the war imposed harsh penalties and impossibly high reparations on Germany, which provided fertile ground for the establishment of a totalitarian regime and Adolf HITLER's rise to power. The magnitude and brutality of the war and its direct influence on civilian populaces was unprecedented, for without a single decisive battle, over 10 million people died and twice that number were wounded. A general revulsion against war resulted.

WORLD WAR II   Beginning with Adolf HITLER's invasion of Poland in October 1939 and ending shortly after the United States dropped atomic bombs on Hiroshima and Nagasaki, Japan, in August 1945, this conflict was truly global, involving every major power in the world. The Axis powers (Germany, Italy, and Japan) were defeated by the Allies (Great Britain, the U.S., and the Soviet Union). The destruction wrought during this conflict was also worldwide, with Great Britain, much of Europe, the Soviet Union, China, and Japan especially devastated. Civilian losses were great due not only to the HOLOCAUST in Europe and the genocidal policies of Japan toward China but also to the extensive bombing of cities. The United States, the only major power not to sustain physical damage after the 1941 attack on Pearl Harbor, emerged from the war an economic and military superpower. The war also spurred decolonization, gave birth to the United Nations, and, through various agreements between the Soviet Union and the other Allies, set the stage for the COLD WAR.

"WORN PATH, A"   EUDORA WELTY (1940)   For this short story, Eudora Welty won second prize in the 1941 O. HENRY MEMORIAL AWARDS, her first serious literary honor. Originally published in both the *Southern Review* in 1937 and the ATLANTIC MONTHLY in 1940, "A Worn Path" also appeared in her first short story collection, *A Curtain of Green and Other Stories* (1941). This story is written in a LYRICal, meditative style instead of the comic, dramatic style for which Welty is also known. An omniscient narrator describes the journey of an elderly black woman, PHOENIX JACKSON, to town where she finds medicine for her grandson. Through lyrical METAPHOR and nature imagery, Welty conveys the importance of the quest, an arduous labor of love, which allows Phoenix to periodically renew herself like the mythical bird that bears the same name.

This story has many other mythical ALLUSIONS. Phoenix's journey to town symbolically represents a HERO's mythical journey to the underworld. She must accomplish heroic tasks on her way by climbing steep hills, crossing a stream on a log bridge, and fending off a dangerous dog. In her travels, she meets a helper, a white hunter, who lifts her from a ditch and drops a nickel that Phoenix later finds on the ground. The white world of the town is quite different from the natural world of the woods that seemed to communicate with Phoenix. The streets are filled with the rush of Christmas shoppers, and the nurse in the doctor's office callously calls her Grandma and asks her why she has come. At first Phoenix cannot remember why she made the long journey. Although another nurse recognizes her, this nurse thinks that the grandson has already died,

causing the reader to wonder if Phoenix's quest has been useless. If we think of the town as the underworld, however, the journey is a symbolic effort to remember and honor her grandson, a sign of undying love, and it does not matter whether the child still lives.

BIBLIOGRAPHY
Evans, Elizabeth. *Eudora Welty.* New York: Frederick Ungar, 1981.
Vande Kieft, Ruth M. *Eudora Welty.* New York: Twayne, 1962.
Tintner, Adeline R. "Life and Death in Eudora Welty's 'A Worn Path.'" *Studies in Short Fiction* 14.3 (Summer 1977).
Welty, Eudora. "A Worn Path." *Atlantic Monthly* 167.2 (February 1941).
———. "A Worn Path." *Southern Review* 3.2 (Autumn 1937).

Betina I. Entzminger
University of North Carolina at Chapel Hill

WRIGHT, RICHARD   (1908–1960)   Acknowledged by many as the single most influential author in African American literary history, Richard Wright blazed a new trail for black writers, both as the first internationally recognized black artist and as the "father" of protest literature. His most popular works, *Uncle Tom's Children, Native Son,* and *Black Boy,* helped to generate a literary movement (initially called the "School of Richard Wright," more accurately described as the CHICAGO RENAISSANCE) emphasizing a sociological and leftist approach, a movement that directed the course of American literature for the next decade.

Ready-made material for his fiction, Wright's early life was one of racism, poverty, and hunger. The older son of Nathan Wright, a sharecropper, and Ella Wilson Wright, a schoolteacher, Richard Nathaniel Wright was born September 4, 1908, on a farm near Roxie, Mississippi. When Wright was six, his father deserted the family; three years later the already poor family became destitute when Wright's mother fell seriously ill, never to recover fully. As a result, Wright spent much of his childhood moving, with his mother and brother, from one town to another, often staying at the homes of various relatives (and once in a Methodist orphanage). The most stable home of his early childhood, that of his aunt Maggie and uncle Silas in Elaine, Arkansas, was destroyed by racist violence: The family was forced to flee when Silas was murdered by whites who wanted his liquor business.

Wright's education was sporadic; he left school often to work to support his family. However, during his eighth-grade year, he wrote his first short story, "The Voodoo of Hell's Half-Acre," published in Jackson's *Southern Register,* a black weekly newspaper, to the surprise of his family and friends, who were unaware of his literary interests. Wright graduated from the ninth grade but never finished high school, instead working and reading voraciously. In 1927, using a library card he borrowed from his white employer, he discovered the work of H. L. Mencken, who showed him that words could be used as weapons. Mencken led him to writers such as Theodore DREISER, O. HENRY, Alexandre Dumas, and Sherwood ANDERSON, all of whom influenced his writing.

Wright's literary success and his pivotal involvement with the Communist Party were the eventual results of his move to Chicago in 1927. A temporary job as clerk and mail sorter at the post office provided fodder for his first novel, *Lawd Today!* (published posthumously). In 1932 a postal coworker introduced Wright to the Chicago branch of the John Reed Club, a national literary organization supported by the Communist Party. Wright became a prominent member, publishing revolutionary poems in the club's magazine *Left Front* and serving as executive secretary; he joined the party in 1934. Wright's relationship with communism was profound but contentious, lasting long after he formally broke with the party in 1942. While communism brought him a liberating social and political perspective, Wright was constantly compelled to challenge the party's ignorance of African American history, culture, and social complexities; his criticisms are visible in all of his communist-related fiction. (See PROLETARIAN FICTION.)

Wright's literary celebrity began after his 1937 move to New York City, when Harper and Brothers published his collection of short stories or novellas, *Uncle Tom's Children: Four Novellas* (1938; expanded and reissued 1940). Adapting NATURALISM and proletarian REALISM to fit the experiences of southern blacks, these stories depict poor, uneducated characters facing life-threatening racial and class conflicts. Wright also developed these CHARACTERS and THEMES in other stories, particularly the often anthologized "BIG BLACK GOOD MAN" and "THE MAN WHO WAS ALMOST A MAN"; the character BIG BOY of "BIG BOY LEAVES HOME" matures into Bigger Thomas of *Native Son,* and the collection's introduction, "The Ethics of Living JIM CROW," would later form the the core of Wright's autobiography. In 1939 Wright won a GUGGENHEIM GRANT, which allowed him to quit his GREAT DEPRESSION–era job to concentrate solely on his writing. Afterward, he was able to support himself and his family solely through writing, the first African American to do so. (See AFRICAN-AMERICAN SHORT FICTION.)

In the words of Irving Howe, the appearance of Wright's second novel, *Native Son,* in 1940 changed American culture forever. Despite Wright's fears about the impact of its violent content and aggressive narrative strategy (see POINT OF VIEW), the novel was wildly popular, selling out within three hours of publication. A Book of the Month Club main selection, the first by a black writer, it set a sales record for Harper and Brothers (215,000 copies sold in less than three weeks) and was banned in Birmingham, Alabama, libraries. Reviews were highly favorable; according to the *New York Post,* it deserved all its literary prizes. In 1941 the National Association for the Advancement of Colored People (NAACP) awarded Wright the Spingarn Medal, given annually to the black American judged to have made the most notable achievement in the preceding year.

Wright's career continued to flourish through the publication of the first half of his autobiography, *Black Boy: A Record of Childhood and Youth* (1945). Highly praised, the book was number one on the best-seller list from April 29 to June 6, the fourth-best-selling nonfiction title of that year; it also caused a minor political stir. (It was denounced as obscene in the U.S. Senate by Mississippi Senator

Theodore Bilbo.) Wright's later works, however, although eagerly awaited, were not received with such enthusiasm, particularly those published after he moved to Paris in 1947. Attempting to escape both continuing racial harassment and the limiting categorization "black writer," Wright left the country with his wife, Ellen, and their daughter, Julia, and was warmly welcomed by the Paris expatriate literary community. His next few novels, *The Outsider* (1953), *Savage Holiday* (1954), and *The Long Dream* (1958), received mixed reviews and poor U.S. sales (although reviews and sales were better in France). In 1959, Wright put together the collection called *Eight Men* (1961) consisting of five stories, two radio plays, and an essay, most of which had been heavily edited or rejected by publishers. While it continues to portray racial and class conflict, this collection and Wright's later novels show evidence of his impatience with the limitation of protest fiction and literary naturalism and his interest in European psychology and EXISTENTIALISM. His characters are less naive and emotional and more intellectual and alienated, causing some critics to claim that Wright was out of touch with his country. In the last two years of his life, Wright became increasingly isolated from his literary community, in part because of documented persecution by U.S. government agents. His died of a heart attack in 1960 under circumstances suspicious enough to start persistent rumors that the Central Intelligence Agency (CIA) had been involved in his death.

BIBLIOGRAPHY

Andrews, William L., et al. *The Oxford Companion to African-American Literature.* New York: Oxford University Press, 1997.

Butler, Robert J. *Native Son: The Emergence of a New Black Hero.* Boston: Twayne, 1991.

Fabre, Michel. *The Unfinished Quest of Richard Wright.* New York: Morrow, 1973.

Gates, Henry Louis Jr., and K. A. Appiah. *Richard Wright: Critical Perspectives Past and Present.* New York: Amistad, 1993.

Gayle, Addison Jr. *Richard Wright: Ordeal of a Native Son.* Garden City, N.Y.: Anchor Press/Doubleday, 1980.

Hakutani, Yoshinobu. *Critical Essays on Richard Wright.* Boston: G.K. Hall, 1974.

Joyce, Joyce Ann. *Richard Wright's Art of Tragedy.* Iowa City: University of Iowa Press, 1986.

Kinnamon, Keneth. *The Emergence of Richard Wright: A Study in Literature and Society.* Urbana: University of Illinois Press, 1972.

Macksey, Richard, and Frank Moorer, eds., *Richard Wright: A Collection of Critical Essays.* Englewood Cliffs, N.J.: Prentice-Hall, 1984.

Walker, Margaret. *Richard Wright: Daemonic Genius: A Portrait of the Man, a Critical Look at His Work.* New York: Warner Books, 1988.

Wright, Richard. *American Hunger.* New York: Harper & Row, 1977.

———. *Bandoeng: 1.500.000.000 Hommes.* Translated by Helene Claireau. 1955. As *The Color Curtain: A Report on the Bandung Conference.* New York: Harper, 1956.

———. *Black Boy: A Record of Childhood and Youth.* New York: Harper, 1943.

———. *Black Power: A Record of Reactions in a Land of Pathos.* New York: Harper, 1954.

———. *Eight Men.* New York: World, 1961.

———. *How Bigger Was Born: The Story of "Native Son."* New York: Harper, 1940.

———. *Lawd Today.* New York: Walker, 1963.

———. *Letters to Joe C. Brown.* Edited byThomas Knipp. Kent, Ohio: Kent State University Libraries, 1968.

———. *The Long Dream.* Garden City, N.Y.: Doubleday, 1958.

———. *Native Son.* New York: Harper, 1940.

———. *The Outsider.* New York: Harper, 1953.

———. *Pagan Spain.* New York: Harper, 1957.

———. *Savage Holiday.* New York: Avon, 1954.

———. *12 Million Black Voices: A Folk History of the Negro in the United States.* New York: Viking, 1941.

———. *Uncle Tom's Children: Four Novellas.* New York: Harper, 1938.

———. *White Man, Listen!* Garden City, N.Y.: Doubleday, 1957.

Kimberly Drake
Virginia Wesleyan College

Y

YAMAMOTO, HISAYE (1921–)   Born
to Japanese immigrant parents in 1921 in Redondo
Beach, California, Hisaye Yamamoto began to write
as a teen using the pseudonym Napoleon, and her
first story was published when she was 27. During
WORLD WAR II, her brother was killed in combat in
Italy, and her family was interned for three years in
Poston, Arizona. During this time she wrote for the
Poston Chronicle. From 1945 to 1948 she wrote for
the *Los Angeles Tribune*. Then she adopted a son,
Paul, and took a job with the Catholic Worker farm
on Staten Island, New York. Later she married
Anthony DeSoto, returned to Los Angeles, and
became the mother of four other children.

Yamamoto became the first Japanese American
writer to gain national recognition after the war.
Linking social history with her personal experiences, her stories include portrayals of internments,
arranged marriages, and *issei* and *nisei*—first- and
second-generation Japanese Americans—whose
lives confine them to cultural oppression. Although
they detail generational, political, and gender conflicts, they focus on women who escape frustrations
and suppression through creative outlets including
writing, dancing, and sometimes with behavior perceived as madness. Yamamoto claims that one of her
stories, "SEVENTEEN SYLLABLES," relates to her mother's
story, although details differ. Two others, "THE LEG-
END OF MISS SASAGARAWA" and "Death Rides the Rails

to Poston," rely on her three years of internment for
their background. A third, "The Pleasure of Plain
Rice," grows out of incidents during her years in
Springfield, Massachusetts.

BIBLIOGRAPHY
Crow, Charles L. "A MELUS Interview: Hisaye Yamamoto."
    MELUS 14.1 (1987): 73–84.
Yamamoto, Hisaye. " . . . I Still Carry It Around." *RIKKA*
    3.4 (1976): 11–19.
———. *Seventeen Syllables and Other Stories*. Latham, N.Y.:
    Women of Color: Kitchen Table Press, 1988.
———. "Writing." *Amerasia Journal* 3.2 (1976): 126–33.

Sandra Chrystal Hayes
Georgia Institute of Technology

YAMANAKA, LOIS-ANN (1961–)
Lois-Ann Yamanaka, a third-generation Japanese
American woman who lives in Hawaii, is not a
writer bound by genre. She began her writing career
by publishing an award-winning collection of
poems in 1993 (*Saturday Night at the Pahala
Theater*), followed three years later by a novel (*Wild
Meat and the Bully Burgers*), which is broken into
individual short stories that form an overarching
narrative. Unlike chapters, each of these short stories stands on its own, separate from the rest of the
book. Many works within *Wild Meat* were originally
published as short stories. Yamanaka's short stories
appear most frequently in *Bamboo Ridge: A Hawaii*

Writers' Quarterly but also have been published in *Chicago Review* and included in the anthology *American Eyes: New Asian American Short Stories For Young Adults,* edited by Lori M. Carlson. Yamanaka published her second novel, *Blu's Hanging,* in 1997 and has two more books due to be published in 1999. The first is titled *Name Me Nobody,* and the second is *Heads By Harry,* the last of her trilogy dealing with Hawaiian youth begun with *Wild Meat* and continued with *Blu's Hanging.*

Similar to the way in which Yamanaka defies easy genre categorization, her multiple THEMES coexist within a work without clashing or overshadowing one another. Race and ethnicity are major factors in Yamanaka's work, which makes controversial use of both profanity and Hawaiian Creole pidgin. At the same time, her work is concerned with issues of familial relationships and gender; very often it follows the life of a young female PROTAGONIST as she struggles to make sense of both her world and her own identity. Lovey Nariyoshi, the main character in *Wild Meat and the Bully Burgers* (and in all of the individually published short stories from that novel), has been likened to a female Holden Caulfield, working her way through a coming-of-age narrative.

In "Obituary," issues of race and class boil to the surface of a middle-school classroom through pidgin and an especially morbid classroom assignment to write one's own obituary as part of a newspaper unit. "Alexander Fu Sheng Kicks Bruce Lee's Ass, Sonny Chiba and Toshiro Mifune Too" deals both with class issues, where Lovey must bribe a friend to come to the movies with her, only to be harassed by the clerk who believes she must pay the full adult fare for both herself and her friend, not the under-12 fare. In "Oompah Loompah" and "Blah Blah Blah," the young narrator suffers the embarrassment of a home permanent gone drastically wrong and the scorn of her classmates for wearing home-sewn clothes. But in "Pin the Fan on the Hand," a small family birthday party, which initially strikes the reader as a potential disaster, eventually causes Lovey to realize the importance of family.

BIBLIOGRAPHY
Carlson, Lori M., ed. *American Eyes: New Asian American Short Stories for Young Adults.* New York: Fawcett/Juniper, 1996.
Yamanaka, Lois-Ann. *Wild Meat and the Bully Burgers.* San Diego: Harcourt Brace, 1986.

Anne N. Thalheimer
University of Delaware

YAMAUCHI, WAKAKO   (1924–   )

Wakako Yamauchi was born and raised in the Imperial Valley in southeastern California, the *nisei* (second generation American) daughter of Japanese American farmers. During WORLD WAR II, she and her family were sent to the Poston Relocation Center at Poston, Arizona. It was there that Yamauchi met Hisaye YAMAMOTO, who became a close and lifelong friend.

Partly at the urging of Yamamoto, Yamauchi began writing stories in the early 1960s. The first of these, "The Handkerchief" (1961) and "And the Soul Shall Dance" (1966), were published in holiday editions of the Los Angeles *Rafu Shimpo,* a newspaper of the Japanese American community. These and subsequent stories have a strong autobiographical basis; Yamauchi's direct and deceptively simple style captures both the promise and the terror of growing up in an immigrant American community in the 1930s and 1940s.

Yamauchi's stories have appeared in *Amerasia Journal* and *Bamboo Ridge* and have been widely anthologized. Her best-known stories, plays, and essays were collected in *Songs My Mother Taught Me* (1994). Yamauchi's two-act play, *And the Soul Shall Dance,* based on her short story of the same title, was first produced in 1977 and received the Los Angeles Critics' Circle Award for best new play of that year.

BIBLIOGRAPHY
Yamauchi, Wakako. *Songs My Mother Taught Me: Stories, Plays, and Memoir.* New York: Feminist Press, 1994.

Keith Lawrence
Brigham Young University

"YELLOW WALL-PAPER, THE" CHARLOTTE PERKINS GILMAN (1892, 1899)

First published in *New England Magazine* in January 1892, and reprinted by Small, Maynard and Company as a chapbook (1899), "The Yellow Wall-Paper" is Charlotte Perkins GILMAN's most famous work. Depicting the nervous breakdown of a young wife and mother, the story is a potent example of psychological REALISM. Based loosely on Gilman's own experiences in undergoing the rest cure for neurasthenia, the story documents the psychological torment of her fictional first-person narrator.

The narrator's husband, John, a physician, prescribes isolation and inactivity as treatment for her illness, a "temporary nervous depression—a slight hysterical tendency" (10). John forbids her to engage in any kind of labor, including writing. Despite his admonitions, however, the narrator records her impressions in a secret diary.

These diary entries comprise the text of the story; they reveal the narrator's emotional descent. As the story unfolds, it becomes apparent that she is suffering an acute form of postpartum depression, a condition acknowledged neither by John nor by the late-19th-century medical community. So severe is the narrator's depression that a nursemaid has assumed care of the new baby. Deprived of the freedom to write openly, which she believes would be therapeutic, the narrator gradually shifts her attention to the yellow wallpaper in the attic nursery where she spends her time. The paper both intrigues and repels her; it becomes the medium on which she symbolically inscribes her "text." Soon she detects a subpattern in the wallpaper that crystallizes into the image of an imprisoned woman attempting to escape. In the penultimate scene, the narrator's identity merges with the entrapped woman, and together they frantically tear the paper from the walls. In an ironic reversal in the final scene, John breaks into the room and, after witnessing the full measure of his wife's insanity, faints. Significantly, however, he is still blocking his wife, literally and symbolically obstructing her path so that she has to "creep over him every time!" (36).

Critics disagree over the meaning of the story, variously arguing the significance of everything from linguistic cues, to psychoanalytic interpretations, to historiographical readings. While some critics have hailed the narrator as a FEMINIST HEROINE, others have seen in her a maternal failure coupled with a morbid fear of female sexuality. Some have viewed the story, with its yellow paper, as an exemplar of the silencing of women writers in 19th-century America; others have focused on its GOTHIC elements.

Since the Feminist Press reissued the story in 1973, "The Yellow Wall-Paper" has been widely anthologized and is now firmly assimilated into the American literary body of work.

BIBLIOGRAPHY

Gilman, Charlotte Perkins. *The Yellow Wallpaper.* Boston: Small, Maynard, & Co., 1899. Reprint. Old Westbury, N.Y.: Feminist Press, 1973.

Lanser, Susan A. "Feminist Criticism, 'The Yellow Wallpaper,' and the Politics of Color in America." *Feminist Studies* 15. 3 (Fall 1989): 415–441.

Shumaker, Conrad. "'Too Terribly Good to Be Printed': Charlotte Perkins Gilman's 'The Yellow Wallpaper.'" *American Literature* 57. 4 (1985): 588–599.

Veeder, William. "Who Is Jane? The Intricate Feminism of Charlotte Perkins Gilman." *Arizona Quarterly* 44. 3 (1988): 40–79.

Denise D. Knight
State University of New York at Cortland

YOKNAPATAWPHA COUNTY

Often described by William FAULKNER as "my own little postage stamp of native soil" and "a cosmos of my own," Yoknapatawpha County, Mississippi, and its county seat, Jefferson, provide the mythical setting for most of Faulkner's novels and short stories. Based largely on Faulkner's hometown of Oxford, in Lafayette County, Mississippi, Yoknapatawpha County is home to all manner of people, from planters and their descendants, to Indians, yeoman farmers, and blacks. In his groundbreaking introduction to *The Portable Faulkner* in 1946, critic Malcolm Cowley argued that this Yoknapatawpha saga is Faulkner's real achievement, more powerful in sum than any of the individual stories that constitute it.

BIBLIOGRAPHY

Brooks, Cleanth. *William Faulkner: The Yoknapatawpha Country*. Baton Rouge: Louisiana State University Press, 1963.

Cowley, Malcolm, ed. *The Portable Faulkner*. New York: Viking Press, 1946.

H. Collin Messer
University of North Carolina at Chapel Hill

"YOUNG GOODMAN BROWN" NATHANIEL HAWTHORNE (1846)

"Young Goodman Brown," initially appearing in *Mosses from an Old Manse* (1846) as both a bleak romance and a moral ALLEGORY, has maintained its hold on contemporary readers as a tale of initiation, alienation, and evil. Undoubtedly one of Nathaniel HAWTHORNE's most disturbing stories, it opens as a young man of the town, Goodman Brown, bids farewell to his wife, Faith, and sets off on a path toward the dark forest. Brown's journey to the forest and his exposure to life-shattering encounters and revelations remain the subject of speculation. Although his meeting with the Devil is clear, the results remain ambiguous and perplexing. When viewed as a BILDUNGSROMAN, it is one of the bleakest in American fiction, long or short. Rather than an initiation into manhood, Brown's is an initiation into evil.

Much of the power of the story derives from the opening scene of missed chances: Faith, introduced in the second sentence and given the first words of dialogue, leans out the window, her pink ribbons fluttering, and entreats her husband to stay. Brown, however, although he continues to think of returning, is determined to depart on this dark road. Almost instantly, he—and the reader—become enveloped in the darkness and gloom of the forest. The narrator equates the dreariness with both solitude and evil, and the aura of doom pervades the story. Along the way Brown meets a man who looks curiously like Brown's father and grandfather; that this traveler is the Devil is clear from his snakelike stick and evident power to assume different shapes. The traveler reveals his role in helping Brown's Puritan ancestors commit crimes against Quakers and Indians. Brown protests that his family has traditionally revered the principles of Christianity, but the traveler provides numerous examples of his converts across all of New England, in both small town and state positions, in the fields of politics, religion, and the law. That Brown himself is from Salem suggests Hawthorne's fascination with the Puritan guilt of his—and our—own forefathers manifested in other short stories such as "Alice Doane's Appeal," a tale about the Puritan obsession with witchcraft.

Next Brown hides in the forest, demonstrating his hypocrisy, as he sees Goody Cloyse, a pious townswoman, walking along the dark trail. She and the traveler openly discuss her witchcraft, and when Brown leaves his hiding place, he marvels at his memory of Goody Cloyse teaching him his catechism when he was a boy. Again Brown thinks of returning home to Faith, but instead he still hides in the forest, recognizing many of the townspeople passing through and hearing that tonight's forest meeting will be attended by people from Connecticut and Rhode Island, as well as Massachusetts. Just as Brown thinks he can resist the Devil and emerge from his hiding place, he hears a scream that sounds like Faith's, and a pink ribbon flutters to his feet.

From this point on, Brown himself becomes a GROTESQUE figure, throwing himself with wholehearted if somewhat hysterical and despairing eagerness into the center of the darkness illuminated by the blazing fires of the meeting, clearly an image of hell. He recognizes all the most respected folk of the state unabashedly mingling with common thieves, prostitutes, and even criminals. The dreadful harmony of all these voices joined together in Devil worship reaches a crescendo as the converts are brought forth: among them, dimly recognized, are Brown's father, mother, and wife. The Devil assures the assembly that everyone has secretly committed crimes, from those of illicit sex to those of murdering husbands, fathers, and illegitimate babies. Indeed, says the Devil, the whole earth is "one stain of guilt, one mighty blood spot." Evil, not good, he asserts, is the nature of humankind.

Like Adam and Eve, Brown and Faith stand on the edge of wickedness: Brown screams to Faith to resist the Devil, and with these words the nightmare ends, Brown awakening against a rock. The narrator asks, Was his experience really a dream? Whether or not we believe in the reality of Brown's experience; the narrator affirms that it clearly foreshadows Brown's altered life: henceforward he is a dour and disillusioned man who sees no good and trusts in no one. In just such a way did the Salem witch trials effectively bring about the collapse of Puritanism, yet the story resonates long afterward: we as readers understand that we are the mythical descendants of Young Goodman Brown. Why does Brown ignore Faith's warnings? Do we interpret the tale as one of infidelity? Of Christian hypocrisy? Of colonial history? If Brown, as an AMERICAN ADAM, looked upon EDEN and found it wanting, do we inherit his frightful knowledge? Or can we interpret it as a cautionary tale, one whose lessons can benefit us as we live our modern lives? A century and a half later, Hawthorne's story continues to beguile us with its gloomy aura and subtly ambiguous theme.

BIBLIOGRAPHY

Hawthorne, Nathaniel. "Young Goodman Brown." In *Tales and Sketches*. Edited by Roy Harvey Pearce. New York: Library of America, 1982.

Newman, Lea B. V. *A Reader's Guide to the Short Stories of Hawthorne*. New York: Macmillan, 1979.

Z

ZITKALA SA   GERTRUDE SIMMONS BONNIN (1876–1938)   The writer, musician, and NATIVE AMERICAN activist Gertrude Simmons Bonnin, or Zitkala Sa (Red Bird), was a Yankton Sioux who spoke the Nakota DIALECT and had a Lakota name. She was born on the Pine Ridge Reservation in South Dakota in the same year as the battle of the Little Bighorn. Her mother (Ellen Tate Iyohinwin/She Reaches for the Wind) was a Yankton Sioux; her biological father was a white man named Felker who abandoned the family. Her mother married another white man named Simmons.

Bonnin was raised in the Sioux tradition on the reservation, but in her eighth year, and despite her mother's objections, she left to attend White's Institute, a Quaker missionary school in Indiana. Three years in Indiana were followed by four years on the reservation, at the end of which she returned to White's to complete her studies. Bonnin enrolled at Earlham College, a Quaker institution in Indiana. There she developed oratorical and musical skills, leading to a scholarship at the New England Conservatory of Music.

In 1898 Bonnin took a position as a music teacher and performer at Carlisle Indian School in Pennsylvania, a well-known assimilationist academy. It was at this point that Bonnin gathered and retold 14 of the traditional Sioux oral tales of her reservation childhood, which she published in

English as *Old Indian Legends* (1901). Bonnin's intentions with this paraliterary collection are found in her preface; signing it as Zitkala Sa, she advocates the study of Native American FOLKLORE and demands respect for aboriginal Americans.

In 1902 she married another Sioux named Bonnin and began to write and publish autobiographical stories in such prominent magazines as *ATLANTIC MONTHLY* and *HARPER'S Monthly*. In them Bonnin expresses outrage at the historical and contemporary treatment of Native Americans. Their intense candor soon caused her dismissal from the conservative Carlisle. These earlier works were finally collected and published, along with more recent writings, as *American Indian Stories* (1921).

Bonnin's literary reputation rests on this collection, which exposes and explores the painful experiences of Native Americans during an era when governmental and nongovernmental agendas sought to extinguish or eradicate indigenous traditions and beliefs. The stories portray her childhood on the reservation, adolescence in Indiana, and work as a teacher. Bonnin tells of her confusion, anguish, and shame at being wedged between, and estranged from, the opposite points of native and colonial cultures.

If Bonnin acknowledges cultural LIMINALITY and loss, she also confirms cultural maintenance and recovery. While distinctive, Bonnin's work also may be read as a microcosm of the larger collision of Native American and Eurocentric ontologies and epistemologies in the United States. Despite the many sorrows they contain, Bonnin's stories work with the Sioux LEGENDS that she once collected. Taken together, they insist on a past, a present, and a future for what she called the "native spirit."

The size of Bonnin's body of work was limited by her involvement in various Native American causes and organizations. After years of living and working as an activist on reservations, in 1916 Bonnin became secretary of the Society of American Indians. Following a move to Washington, D.C., Bonnin edited *American Indian Magazine,* promoted the 1924 Indian Citizenship Bill, and in 1926 founded the National Council of American Indians, of which she was president until her death. Bonnin is buried in Arlington National Cemetery.

BIBLIOGRAPHY

Cutter, Martha. "Zitkala Sa's Autobiographical Writings: The Problems of a Canonical Search for Language and Identity." *MELUS* 19 (1994): 31–44.

Fisher, Alice. "The Transportation of Tradition: A Study of Zitkala Sa and Mourning Dove, Two Traditional American Indian Writers." Ph.D. Diss., City University of New York, 1979.

Fisher, Dexter. "Zitkala Sa: The Evolution of a Writer." *American Indian Quarterly* 5 (1979): 229–238.

Spack, Ruth. "Re-Visioning Sioux Women: Zitkala Sa's Revolutionary *American Indian Stories.*" *Legacy* 14 (1997): 25–42.

Susag, Dorothea. "Zitkala Sa (Gertrude Simmons Bonnin): A Power(full) Literary Voice." *Studies in American Indian Literatures* 5 (1993): 3–24.

Willard, William. "Zitkala Sa: A Woman Who Would Be Heard." *Wicazo Sa Review* 1 (1985): 11–16.

Geoffrey C. Middlebrook
California State University at Los Angeles

APPENDIX I

WINNERS OF SELECTED SHORT STORY PRIZES

O. HENRY MEMORIAL AWARDS, 1919–1998

In 1918, the Society of Arts and Sciences decided to honor O. Henry, "the master of the short story," with two annual prizes—later expanded to three—for the best short stories published by American authors in American magazines. Since 1919, an annual anthology that includes the year's O. Henry prize winners and contenders has been published by Doubleday (except for 1952 and 1953, when no prize was awarded because of the death of the editor at the time, Herschel Brickell). In each of the lists below, the first-prize winner is at the top.

1919

Margaret Prescott Montague, "England to America"
Wilbur Daniel Steele, "'For They Know Not What They Do'"
Ben Ames Williams, "They Grind Exceeding Small"
Albert Payson Terhune, "On Strike"
Edison Marshall, "The Elephant Remembers"
Frances Gilchrist Wood, "Turkey Red"
Melville Davisson Post, "Five Thousand Dollars Reward"
Thomas Grant Springer, "The Blood of the Dragon"

Fannie Hurst, "'Humoresque'"
Louise Rice, "The Lubbeny Kiss"
Samuel A. Derieux, "The Trial in Tom Belcher's Store"
James Branch Cabell, "Porcelain Cups"
Beatrice Ravenel, "The High Cost of Conscience"
G. F. Alsop, "The Kitchen Gods"
Edna Ferber, "April 25th, As Usual"

1920

Maxwell Struthers Burt, "Each in His Generation"
Frances Noyes Hart, "'Contact!'"
F. Scott Fitzgerald, "The Camel's Back"
Esther Forbes, "Break-Neck Hill"
Guy Gilpatric, "Black Art and Ambrose"
Lee Foster Hartman, "The Judgment of Vulcan"
Alexander Hull, "The Argosies"
O. F. Lewis, "Alma Mater"
Alice Duer Miller, "Slow Poison"
William Dudley Pelley, "The Face in the Window"
Lawrence Perry, "A Matter of Loyalty"
L. H. Robbins, "Professor Todd's Used Car"
Maurice Rutledge, "The Thing They Loved"
Rose Sidney, "Butterflies"
Gordon Arthur Smith, "No Flowers"
Wilbur Daniel Steele, "Footfalls"
Stephen French Whitman, "The Last Room of All"

1921

Edison Marshall, "The Heart of Little Shikara"
Charles Tenney Jackson, "The Man Who Cursed the Lilies"

Maryland Allen, "The Urge"
Thomas Beer, "Mummery"
Gerald Chittenden, "The Victim of His Vision"
Courtney Ryley Cooper and Leo F. Creagan, "Martin Gerrity Gets Even"
Mildred Cram, "Stranger Things"
Samuel A. Derieux, "Comet"
Elizabeth Alexander Heermann, "Fifty-Two Weeks for Florette"
Sophie Kerr, "Wild Earth"
Harry Anable Kniffin, "The Tribute"
O. F. Lewis, "The Get-Away"
Ethel Watts Mumford, "Aurore"
L. H. Robbins, "Mr. Downey Sits Down"
Wilbur Daniel Steele, "The Marriage in Kairwan"
Tristram Tupper, "Grit"

1922

Irvin S. Cobb, "Snake Doctor"
Rose Wilder Lane, "Innocence"
F. R. Buckley "Gold-Mounted Guns"
Charles Alexander, "As a Dog Should"
Richmond Brooks Barrett, "Art for Art's Sake"
Thomas Beer, "Tact"
James W. Bennett, "The Kiss of the Accolade"
Samuel A. Derieux, "The Sixth Shot"
R. Des. Horn, "The Jinx of the 'Shannon Belle'"
Helen R. Hull, "His Sacred Family"
Charles Tenney Jackson, "The Horse of Hurricane Reef"
O. F. Lewis, "Old Peter Takes an Afternoon Off"
Gouverneur Morris, "Ig's Amok"
Wilber Daniel Steele, "The Anglo-Saxon"
Albert Payson Terhune, "The Writer-Upward"
Mary Heaton Vorse, "Twilight of the God"

1923

Edgar Valentine Smith, "Prelude"
Richard Connell, "A Friend of Napoleon"
Elizabeth Irons Folsom, "Towers of Fame"
Floyd Dell, "Phantom Adventure"
Francis Edwards Faragoh, "The Distant Street"
Isa Urquhart Glenn, "The Wager"
James Hopper, "Celestine"
Genevieve Larsson, "Witch Mary"
Robert S. Lemmon, "The Bamboo Trap"

James Mahoney, "The Hat of Eight Reflections"
Grace Sartwell Mason, "Home-Brew"
Gouverneur Morris, "Derrick's Return"
Mary Synon, "Shadowed"
Booth Tarkington, "The One Hundred Dollar Bill"
Mary S. Watts, "Nice Neighbours"
Jesse Lynch Williams, "Not Wanted"

1924

Part I:

Inez Hayes Irwin, "The Spring Flight"
Chester T. Crowell, "Margaret Blake"
Frances Newman, "Rachel and Her Children"
Stephen Vincent Benet, "Uriah's Son"
Richard Connell, "The Most Dangerous Game"
Charles Caldwell Dobie, "Horse and Horse"

Part II:

Edith R. Mirrielees, "Professor Boynton Rereads History"
Jefferson Mosley, "The Secret at the Crossroads"
George Pattullo, "The Tie That Binds"
Elsie Singmaster, "The Courier of the Czar"
Edgar Valentine Smith, "'Lijah"
Raymond S. Spears, "A River Combine-Professional"
Wilbur Daniel Steel, "What Do You Mean—Americans?"
Elinore Cowan Stone, "One Uses the Handerchief"
Harriet Welles, "Progress"

1925

Part I:

Julian Street, "Mr. Bisbee's Princess"
Wythe Williams, "Splendid With Swords"
Mary Austin, "Papago Wedding"
Sherwood Anderson, "The Return"
Edwina Stanton Babcock, "Dunelight"
Mariel Brady, "Peter Projects"
Harold W. Brecht, "Two Heroes"

Part II:

Ada Jack Carver, "Redbone"
Ethel Cook Eliot, "Maternal"
Francis Hackett, "Unshapely Things"
Du Bose Heyward, "Crown's Bess"

Julia Peterkin, "Maum Lou"
Wilbur Daniel Steele, "The Man Who Saw Through Heaven"
Wilbur Daniel Steele, "Blue Murder"
Booth Tarkington, "Cornelia's Mountain"
Brand Whitlock, "The Sofa"

1926

Wilbur Daniel Steele, "Bubbles"
Sherwood Anderson, "Death In The Woods"
Albert Richard Wetjen, "Command"
Ada Jack Carver, "Treeshy"
Karl W. Detzer, "The Wreck Job"
Charles Caldwell Dobie, "The Thrice Bereft Widow of Hung Gow"
Arthur Huff Fauset, "Symphonesque"
Abbie Carter Goodloe, "Claustrophobia"
Oscar Graeve, "A Death on Eight' Avenue"
Marguerite Jacobs, "Singing Eagles"
Eleanor Mercein Kelly, "Basquerie"
Lyle Saxon, "Cane River"
Constance Lindsay Skinner, "The Dew on the Fleece"
Booth Tarkington, "Stella Crozier"
Mary Heaton Vorse, "The 'Madelaine'"
Ben Ames Williams, "The Nurse"

1927

Roark Bradford, "Child of God"
Ernest Hemingway, "The Killers"
Louis Bromfield, "The Scarlet Woman"
Bill Adams, "Jukes"
James Warner, "Fear"
Katherine Brush, "Bellah Night Club"
Ada Jack Carver, "Singing Woman"
Elisabeth Cobb Chapman, "With Glory and Honor"
Roger Daniels, "Bulldog"
Marjory Stoneman Douglas, "He Man"
Alma and Paul Ellerbee, "'Done Got Over'"
Eleanor Mercein Kely, "Monkey Motions"
Ruth Sawyer, "Four Dreams of Gram Perkins"
Ruth Suckow, "The Little Girl from Town"
Ellen Du Pois Taylor, "Shades of George Sand!"

1928

Walter Duranty, "The Parrot"
Marjory Stoneman Douglas, "The Peculiar Treasure of Kings"

Zona Gale, "Bridal Pond"
Bill Adams, "Home Is the Sailor"
Stephen Morehouse Avery, "Never in This World"
Bess Streeter Aldrich, "The Man Who Caught the Weather"
M. C. Blackman, "Hot Copy"
Roark Bradford, "River Witch"
Cambray Brown, "Episode in a Machine Age"
Irwin S. Cobb, "An Episode at Pintail Lake"
Richard Connell, "The Law Beaters"
Lee Foster Hartman, "Mr. Smith"
Nunnally Johnson O'Meara, "The Actor"
Don Marquis, "The 'Mayflower' and Mrs. Maclirr"
Wilbur Daniel Steele, "Lightning"
Fiswoode Tarleton, "Curtains"
Glenway Wescott, "Prohibition"

1929

Dorothy Parker, "Big Blonde"
Sidney Howard, "The Homesick Ladies"
Katharine Brush, "Him and Her"
Sherwood Anderson, "Alice"
Stephen Vincent Benét, "The King of the Cats"
Louis Bromfield, "The Apothecary"
Katharine Brush, "Speakeasy"
Maristan Chapman, "Treat You Clever"
Mary Johnston, "Elephants Through the Country"
Margaret Leech, "Manicure"
Don Marquis, "Two Red-Haired Women"
Kathleen Norris, "Sinners"
Pernet Patterson, "Buttin' Blood"
Elise M. Rushfeldt, "A Coffin for Anna"
Ruth Burr Sanborn, "Professional Pride"
Caroline Slade, "Mrs. Sabin"
Wilbur Daniel Steele, "The Silver Sword"

1930

W. R. Burnett, "Dressing-Up"
William M. John, "Neither Jew Nor Greek"
Elizabeth Madox Roberts, "The Sacrifice of the Maidens"
Marc Connelly, "Coroner's Inquest"
Roark Bradford, "Careless Love"
Katherine Newlin Burt, "Herself"
Irvin S. Cobb, "Faith, Hope and Charity"
Courtney Ryley Cooper, "The Elephant Forgets"

Miriam Allen De Ford, "The Silver Knight"
Richard Matthews Hallet, "Misfortune's Isle"
John Held, Jr., "A Man of the World"
Nunnally Johnson, "Mlle. Irene the Great"
William March, "The Little Wife"
Alicia O'Reardon Overbeck, "Encarnation"
William Dudley Pelley, "The Continental Angle"
Julia Peterkin, "The Diamond Ring"
Florence Ryerson and Colin Clements, "Lobster John's Annie"
Wilbur Daniel Steele, "Conjuh"
Julian Street, "A Matter of Standards"
Captain John W. Thomason, Jr., "Born on an Iceberg"

1931

Wilbur Daniel Steele, "Can't Cross Jordan by Myself"
John D. Swain, "One Head Well Done"
Mary Hastings Bradley, "The Five-Minute Girl"
Oliver La Farge, "Haunted Ground"
Griffith Beems, "Leaf Unfolding"
Katharine Brush, "Good Wednesday"
Mary Ellen Chase, "Salesmanship"
Charles Caldwell Dobie, "The False Talisman"
William Faulkner, "Thrift"
Cyril Hume, "Forrester"
Alfred F. Loomis, "Professional Aid"
Marie Luhrs, "Mrs. Schwellenbach's Receptions"
William March, "Fifteen from Company K"
Laverne Rice, "Wings for Janie"
Florence Ryerson and Colin Clements, "Useless"
Edgar Valentine Smith, "'Cock-A-Doodle-Done!'"
Booth Tarkington, "Cider of Normandy"
Crichton Alston Thorne, "Chimney City"

1932

Stephen Vincent Benet, "End to Dreams"
James Gould Cozzens, "Farewell to Cuba"
Edwin Granberry, "A Trip to Czardis"
Jack H. Boone and Merle Constiner, "Big Singing"
Kay Boyle, "The First Lover"
Katherine Brush, "Football Girl"
Dorothy Canfield, "Ancestral Home"
Irvin S. Cobb, "A Colonel Of Kentucky"
Evan Coombes, "Kittens Have Fathers"

Walter D. Edmonds, "The Cruise of the Cashalot"
William Faulkner, "Turn About"
Christopher Gerould, "The End of the Party"
William March, "Nine Prisoners"
J. P. Marquand, "Deep Water"
Booth Tarkington, "She Was Right Once"

1933

Marjorie Kinnan Rawlings, "Gal Young Un"
Pearl S. Buck, "The Frill"
Nancy Hale "To the Invader"
Bill Adams, "The Lubber"
Conrad Aiken, "Impulse"
Len Arnold, "Portrait of a Woman"
Erskine Caldwell, "Country Full of Swedes"
F. Scott Fitzgerald, "Family in the Wind"
Frances M. Frost, "The Heart Being Perished"
Sara Haardt, "Absolutely Perfect"
Rose Wilder Lane, "Old Maid"
Selma Robinson, "The Departure"
Robert Smith, "Love Story"
Dorothy Thomas, "The Consecrated Coal Scuttle"
Hagar Wilde, "Little Brat"

1934

Louis Paul, "No More Trouble for Jedwick"
Caroline Gordon, "Old Red"
William Saroyan, "The Daring Young Man on the Flying Trapeze"
Benjamin Appel, "Pigeon Flight"
Pearl S. Buck, "Shanghai Scene"
Erskine Caldwell, "Maud Island"
Madelene Cole, "Bus to Biarritz"
Miriam Allen DeFord, "Pride"
Walter D. Edmonds, "Honor of the County"
William Faulkner, "Wash"
Vardis Fisher, "The Scarecrow"
Josephine W. Johnson, "Darka"
John Steinbeck, "The Murder"
Richard Sherman, "First Flight"
T. S. Stribling, "Guileford"
Harry Sylvester, "A Boxer: Old"
John Wexley, "Southern Highway 51"
Thomas Wolfe, "Boom Town"
Leane Zugsmith, "King Lear in Evansville"

1935

Kay Boyle, "The White Horses of Vienna"
Dorothy Thomas, "The Home Place"
Josephine W. Johnson, "John the Six"
Nelson Algren, "The Brothers' House"
Stephen Vincent Benet, "The Professor's Punch"
Katharine Hamill, "Leora's Father"
MacKinlay Kantor, "Silent Grow the Guns"
Dorothy McCleary, "Little Elise"
Louis Mamet, "A Writer Interviews a Banker"
Don Marquis, "Country Doctor"
E. P. O'Donnell, "Jesus Knew"
Louis Paul, "Lay Me Low!"
Ross Santee, "Water"
William Saroyan, "Five Ripe Pears"
Edward Shenton, "When Spring Brings Back . . ."
Richard Sherman, "First Day"
Upton Terrell, "Long Distance"
Jerome Weidman, "My Father Sits in the Dark"
Thomas Wolfe, "Only the Dead Know Brooklyn"

1936

James Gould Cozzens, "Total Stranger"
Sally Benson, "Suite 2049"
William March, "A Sum in Addition"
Alvah C. Bessie, "A Personal Issue"
Virginia Bird, "Havoc Is a Circle"
Ernest Brace, "Silent Whistle"
James M. Cain, "Dead Man"
Elizabeth Coatsworth, "The Visit"
Nathalie Colby, "Glass Houses"
Lucile Drigtmier, "For My Sister"
Walter D. Edmonds, "Escape from the Mine"
William Faulkner, "Lion"
Zona Gale, "Crisis"
Elma Godchaux, "Chains"
Edward Harris Heth, "Big Days Beginning"
Eric Knight, "The Marne"
Janet Curren Owen, "Afternoon of a Young Girl"

1937

Stephen Vincent Benét, "The Devil and Daniel Webster"
Elick Moll, "To Those Who Wait"
Robert M. Coates, "The Fury"
Benjamin Appel, "Awroopdedoop!"

Virginia Bird, "For Nancy's Sake"
David Cornel Dejong, "The Chicory Neighbors"
Nancy Hale, "To the North"
Charles Hilton, "Gods of Darkness"
Hamlen Hunt, "The Saluting Doll"
William March, "The Last Meeting"
Charles Martin, "Hobogenesis"
J. M. McKeon, "The Gladiator"
John O'Hara, "My Girls"
Katharine Patten, "Man Among Men"
Prudencio De Pereda, "The Spaniard"
Allan Seager, "Pro Arte"
James Still, "Job's Tears"
Jesse Stuart, "Whip-Poor-Willie"
David Thibault, "A Woman Like Dilsie"
Robert Penn Warren, "Christmas Gift"
Jerome Weidman, "Thomas Hardy's Meat"

1938

Albert Maltz, "The Happiest Man on Earth"
Richard Wright, "Fire and Cloud"
John Steinbeck, "The Promise"
Stephen Vincent Benét, "Johnny Pie and the Fool-Killer"
Mary Hastings Bradley, "The Life of the Party"
Erskine Caldwell, "Man and Woman"
Maureen Daly, "Sixteen"
Daniel Fuchs, "The Amazing Mystery at Storick, Dorschi, Pflaumer, Inc."
Caroline Gordon, "The Enemy"
Nancy Hale, "Always Afternoon"
Hamlen Hunt, "Only By Chance are Pioneers Made"
Elick Moll, "Memoir of Spring"
William Saroyan, "The Summer of the Beautiful White Horse"
James Still, "So Large a Thing as Seven"
Robert Whitehead, "The Fragile Bud"

1939

William Faulkner, "Barn Burning"
James Still, "Bat Flight"
David Cornel Dejong, "Calves"
Dorothy Baker, "Keeley Street Blues"
Kay Boyle, "Anschluss"
Millen Brand, "The Pump"

Struthers Burt, "The Fawn"

Erskine Caldwell, "The People vs. Abe Lathan, Colored"

Charles Cooke, "Nothing Can Change It"

Joseph O'Kane Foster, "Gideon"

Caroline Gordon, "Frankie and Thomas and Bud Asbury"

Ellis St. Joseph, "A Knocking at the Gate"

Irwin Shaw, "God on Friday Night"

Benedict Thielen, "Silver Virgin"

Eudora Welty, "Petrified Man"

1940

Stephen Vincent Benét, "Freedom's a Hard-Bought Thing"

Roderick Lull, "Don't Get Me Wrong"

Edward Havill, "The Kill"

Kay Boyle, "Poor Monsieur Panalitus"

Roy Patchen Brooks, "Without Hal"

Robert M. Coates, "Let's Not Talk About It Now"

William Faulkner, "Hand Upon the Waters"

Nancy Hale, "That Woman"

Mary King, "Chicken on the Wind"

Grace Lumpkin, "The Treasure"

Dorothy McCleary, "Mother's Helper"

Katherine Ann Porter, "The Downard Path to Wisdom"

Marjorie Kinnan Rawlings, "The Pelican's Shadow"

Mabel L. Robinson, "Called For"

William Saroyan, "The Three Swimmers and the Educated Grocer"

Tom Tracy, "Homecoming"

Richard Wright, "Almos' a Man"

1941

Kay Boyle, "Defeat"

Eudora Welty, "A Worn Path"

Hallie Southgate Abbett, "Eighteenth Summer"

Andy Logan, "The Visit"

Conrad Aiken, "Hello, Tib"

Nelson Algren, "A Bottle of Milk for Mother"

Sally Benson, "Retreat"

John Cheever, "I'm Going to Asia"

Walter Van Tilburg Clark, "Hook"

David Cornel Dejong, "Seven Boys Take a Hill"

William Faulkner, "The Old People"

Paul Gallico, "The Snow Goose"

Nancy Hale, "Those Are As Brothers"

Paul Kunasz, "I'd Give It All Up for Tahiti"

Albert Maltz, "Afternoon in the Jungle"

Edita Morris, "Caput Mortuum"

Mary O'Hara, "My Friend Flicka"

Vincent Sheean, "The Conqueror"

James Still, "The Proud Walkers"

Dorothy Thomas, "My Pigeon Pair"

1942

Eudora Welty, "The Wide Net"

Wallace Stegner, "Two Rivers"

Wilbur L. Schramm, "Windwagon Smith"

Jeanne E. Wylie, "A Long Way to Go"

Kay Boyle, "Their Name is Macaroni"

Walter Van Tilburg Clark, "The Portable Phonograph"

Robert Gorham David, "An Interval Like This"

David Cornel DeJong, "Snow-on-the-Mountain"

William Faulkner, "Two Soldiers"

Eleanor Green, "The Dear Little Doves"

Nancy Hale, "Sunday—1913"

Clare Jaynes, "The Coming of Age"

Josephine Johnson, "Alexander to the Park"

Alexander Laing, "The Workmanship Has to Be Wasted"

Carson McCullers, "The Jockey"

John Rogers Shuman, "Yankee Odyssey"

John Steinbeck, "How Edith McGillcuddy Met R. L. Stevenson"

Alison Stuart, "The Yoodeler"

Richard Sullivan, "Fethers"

Jerome Weidman, "Basket Carry"

Marjorie Worthington, "Hunger"

1943

Eudora Welty, "Livvie Is Back"

Dorothy Canfield, "The Knot Hole"

William Fifield, "The Fishermen Of Patzchuaro"

Clara Laidlaw, "The Little Black Boys"

Kay Boyle, "The Canals Of Mars"

Bessie Breuer, "Pigeons En Casserole"

Pearl Buck, "The Enemy"

Walter Van Tilburg Clark, "The Ascent Of Ariel Goodbody"

Whitfield Cook, "The Unfaithful"

Sarah Grinnell, "Standby"
Elmer Grossberg, "Black Boy's Good Time"
Nancy Hale, "Who Lived And Died Believing"
Josephine Johnson, "The Glass Pigeon"
Ben Hur Lampman, "Blinker Was A Good Dog"
Carson McCullers, "A Tree. A Rock. A Cloud"
William Saroyan, "Knife-Like, Flower-Like, Like Nothing At All in the World"
Margarita G. Smith, "White for the Living"
Austin Strong, "She Shall Have Music"
Alison Stuart, "Death and My Uncle Felix"
James Thurber, "The Cane in the Corridor"
Peggy von der Goltz, "The Old She 'Gator"
William C. White, "Pecos Bill and the Willful Coyote"

1944

Irwin Shaw, "Walking Wounded"
Bessie Breuer, "Home Is a Place"
Griffith Beems, "The Stagecoach"
Frank G. Yerby, "Health Card"
Walter Van Tilburg Clark, "The Buck in the Hills"
Elizabeth Eastman, "Like a Field Mouse over the Heart"
Morton Fineman, "Soldier of the Republic"
Berry Fleming, "Strike Up a Stirring Music"
Marjorie Hope, "That's My Brother"
Josephine W. Johnson, "Night Flight"
Ruth Adams Knight, "What a Darling Little Boy!"
George Loveridge, "The Fur Coat"
Margaret Osborn, "Maine"
J. F. Powers, "Lions, Harts, Leaping Does"
Marianne Roane, "Quitter"
Gladys Schmitt, "All Souls'"
Mark Schorer, "Blockbuster"
Alison Stuart, "Sunday Liberty"
Christine Weston, "Raziya"
Wendell Wilcox, "The Pleasures of Travel"
Marguerite Young, "Old James"

1945

Walter Van Tilburg Clark, "The Wind and the Snow of Winter"
Irwin Shaw, "Gunner's Passage"
Ben Hur Lampman, "Old Bill Bent to Drink"
Laurence Critchell, "Flesh and Blood"
Bessie Breuer, "Bury Your Own Dead"

Mary Deasy, "Long Shadow on the Lawn"
Edward Fenton, "Burial in the Desert"
Bill Gerry, "Understand What I Mean?"
Ethel Edison Gordon, "War Front: Louisiana"
Elizabeth Hardwick, "The People on the Roller Coaster"
Murray Heyert, "The New Kid"
Catherine Hubbell, "Monday at Six"
Mary Lavin, "The Sand Castle"
Frances Gray Patton, "A Piece of Bread"

1946

John Mayo Goss, "Bird Song"
Margaret Shedd, "The Innocent Bystander"
Victor Ullman, "Sometimes You Break Even"
Cord Meyer, Jr., "Waves of Darkness"
John Berryman, "The Imaginary Jew"
Kay Boyle, "Winter Night"
Frank Brookhouser, "Request for Sherwood Anderson"
Dorothy Canfield, "Sex Education"
Truman Capote, "Miriam"
Elizabeth Enright, "I Forgot Where I Was"
Elizabeth Hardwick, "What We Have Missed"
Patricia Highsmith, "The Heroine"
M. P. Hutchins, "Innocents"
Meridel LeSueur, "Breathe Upon These Slain"
Andrew Lytle, "The Guide"
Dorothy McCleary, "Not Very Close"
Marjorie Kinnan Rawlings, "Black Secret"

1947

John Bell Clayton, "The White Circle"
Eugene L. Burdick, "Rest Camp On Maui"
Elizabeth Parsons, "The Nightingales Sing"
Robert Lewis, "Little Victor"

1948

Truman Capote, "Shut a Final Door"
Wallace Stegner, "Beyond the Glass Mountain"
Ray Bradbury, "Powerhouse"
Elliott Grennard, "Sparrow's Last Jump"
Frank Brookhouser, "She Did Not Cry at All"
James B. Gidney, "The Muse and Mr. Parkinson"
Caroline Gordon, "The Petrified Woman"
Mary Frances Greene, "The Silent Day"
Lodwick Hartley, "Mr. Henig's Wall"

Marianne Hauser, "The Other Side of the River"
James Wesley Ingles, "The Wind Is Blind"
Elizabeth Janeway, "Child of God"
Christopher La Farge, "The Three Aspects"
Richard Malkin, "Pico Never Forgets"
Robert Morse, "The Professor and the Puli"
Elizabeth Parsons, "Welcome Home"
Katharine Shattuck, "The Answer"
William R. Shelton, "The Snow Girl"
Viginia Sorenson, "The Talking Stick"
Sidney Sulkin, "The Plan"
Courtenay Terrett, "The Saddle"
John Watson, "The Gun on the Table"
Ray B. West, Jr., "The Ascent"

1949
William Faulkner, "A Courtship"
Mark Van Doren, "The Watchman"
Ward Dorrance, "The White Hound"
John Ashworth, "High Diver"
Paul Bowles, "Pastor Dowe at Tacate"
Hortense Calisher, "The Middle Drawer"
Elizabeth Coatsworth, "Bremen's"
Fvan S. Connell, Jr., "I'll Take You to Tennessee"
Barnaby Conrad, "Cayetano The Perfect"
Alice Carver Cramer, "The Boy Next Door"
Harris Downey, "The Mulhausen Girls"
Elizabeth Enright, "The Trumpeter Swan"
John Mayo Goss, "Evening and Morning Prayer"
Shirley Jackson, "The Lottery"
Mary Lavin, "Single Lady"
Phoebe Pierce, "The Season of Miss Maggie Reginald"
Bentz Plagemann, "The Best Bread"
John Andrew Rice, "You Can Get Just So Much Justice"
J. D. Salinger, "Just Before the War with the Eskimos"
Jean Stafford, "A Summer Day"
John D. Weaver, "Meeting Time"
Jessamyn West, "Public Address System"
Leon Wilson, "Six Months Is No Long Time"

1950
Wallace Stegner, "The Blue-Winged Teal"
Gudger Bart Leiper, "The Magnolias"

Robert Lowry, "Be Nice to Mr. Campbell"
Nelson Algren, "The Captain Is Impaled"
Peggy Bennett, "Death Under the Hawthorns"
John Berry, "New Shoes"
Kay Boyle, "Summer Evening"
John Cheever, "Vega"
Ann Chidester, "Mrs. Ketting and Clark Gable"
Elizabeth Enright, "The Sardillion"
William Humphrey, "The Hardys"
Donald Justice, "The Lady"
Susan Kuehn, "The Hunt"
Speed Lamkin, "Comes a Day"
Edward Newhouse, "Seventy Thousand Dollars"
Elizabeth Parsons, "Not a Soul Will Come Along"
Clay Putman, "The Wounded"
Leonard Wallace Robinson, "The Ruin of Soul"
J. D. Salinger, "For Esme, With Love and Squalor"
Robert Switzer, "Death of a Prize Fighter"
Peter Taylor, "Their Losses"
Lilian Van Ness, "Give My Love to Maggie"
Anne Goodwin Winslow, "Seasmiles"

1951
Harris Downey, "The Hunters"
Eudora Welty, "The Burning"
Truman Capote, "The House of Flowers"
Leonard Casper, "Sense of Direction"
John Cheever, "The Pot of Gold"
Evan S. Connell, Jr., "I Came from Yonder Mountain"
Monty Culver, "Black Water Blues"
William Faulkner, "A Name for the City"
James B. Hall, "In the Time of Demonstrations"
John Hersey, "Peggety's Parcel of Shortcomings"
Faye Riter Kensinger, "A Sense of Destination"
Oliver La Farge, "Old Century's River"
Peggy Harding Love, "The Jersey Heifer"
Robie Macauley, "The Invaders"
Carson McCullers, "The Sojourner"
Arthur Miller, "Monte Saint Angelo"
Esther Patt, "The Butcherbirds"
Elizabeth Gregg Patterson, "Homecoming"
Thomas Hal Phillips, "The Shadow of an Arm"
Frank Rooney, "Cyclists' Raid"
Sylvia Shirley, "Slow Journey"

John Campbell Smith, "Who Too Was a Soldier"
Jean Stafford, "A Country Love Story"
R. E. Thompson, "It's a Nice Day-Sunday"

1952: No prize awarded

1953: No prize awarded

1954

Thomas Mabry, "The Indian Feather"
Clay Putnam, "The News from Troy"
Richard Wilburn, "A Game of Catch"
R. V. Cassill, "The War in the Air"
Richard Clay, "Very Sharp for Jagging"
George P. Elliott, "A Family Matter"
Herbert Gold, "The Witch"
James B. Hall, "Estate and Trespass: A Gothic Story"
Ruth Harnden, "Rebellion"
Donald Justice, "Vineland's Burning"
P. H. Lowrey, "Too Young to Have a Gun"
James A. Maxwell, "Fighter"
Flannery O'Connor, "The Life You Save May Be Your Own"
Miriam Rugel, "The Flower"
Jean Stafford, "The Shorn Lamb"
Richard G. Stern, "The Sorrows of Captain Schreiber"
Augusta Walker, "The Day of the Cipher"
Robert Wallace, "The Secret Weapon of Joe Smith"
Jessamyn West, "Breach of Promise"
Stanford Whitmore, "Lost Soldier"
Reed Whittemore, "The Stutz and the Tub"
Herbert Wilner, "Whistle and the Heroes"
Rex Worthington, "A Kind of Scandal"

1955

Jean Stafford, "In the Zoo"
Flannery O'Connor, "A Circle in the Fire"
Frederick Buechner, "The Tiger"
Robert Bingham, "The Unpopular Passenger"
Hortense Calisher, "A Christmas Carillon"
R. V. Cassill, "The Inland Years"
John Cheever, "The Five-Forty-Eight"
George P. Elliott, "Miss Cudahy of Stowes Landing"
Elizabeth Enright, "The Operator"
Mary Dewees Fowler, "Man of Distinction"

Daniel Fuchs, "Twilight in Southern California"
Shirley Ann Grau, "Joshua"
John Graves, "The Green Fly"
J. F. Powers, "The Presence of Grace"
William Henry Shultz, "The Shirts Off Their Backs"
Max Steele, "The Wanton Troopers"
Wallace Stegner, "The City of the Living"
Ira Wolfert, "The Indomitable Blue"

1956

John Cheever, "The Country Husband"
James Buechler, "Pepicelli"
R. V. Cassill, "The Prize"
Saul Bellow, "The Gonzaga Manuscripts"
Hortense Calisher, "The Night Club in the Woods"
Archie Carr, "The Black Beach"
Alfred Chester, "The Head of a Sad Angel"
Robert M. Coates, "In a Foreign City"
William Faulkner, "Race at Morning"
Herbert Gold, "A Celebration for Joe"
Robie Macauley, "The Chevigny Man"
Howard Nemerov, "Tradition"
Jean Stafford, "Beatrice Trueblood's Story"
John Steinbeck, "The Affair at 7, Rue de M———"
John Whitehill, "Able Baker"
Richard Yates, "The Best of Everything"

1957

Flannery O'Connor, "Greenleaf"
Herbert Gold, "Encounter in Haiti"
George P. Elliott, "Miracle Play"
Cynthia Marshall Rich, "My Sister's Marriage"
Willard Marsh, "Last Tag"
Jean Stafford, "The Warlock"
John Langdon, "The Blue Serge Suit"
William Faulkner, "By the People"
Richard Young Thurman, "The Credit Line"
Wyatt Blassingame, "Man's Courage"
John Cheever, "The Journal of an Old Gent"
Arthur Granit, "Free the Canaries from Their Cages!"
Irwin Shaw, "Then We Were Three"
Betty Sunwall, "Things Changed"
Nolan Miller, "A New Life"
R. V. Cassill, "When Old Age Shall This Generation Waste"
Eugene Walter, "I Love You Batty Sisters"

M. M. Liberman, "Big Buick to the Pyramids"
Mary Lee Settle, "The Old Wives' Tale"
Mary McCarthy, "Yellowstone Park"

1958

Martha Gellhorn, "In Sickness as in Health"
Hortense Calisher, "What a Thing, To Keep a Wolf in a Cage!"
George Steiner, "The Deeps of the Sea"
Jean Stafford, "My Blithe, Sad Bird"
Gina Berriault, "The Stone Boy"
Elizabeth Enright, "The Eclipse"
Leo Litwak, "The Making of a Clerk"
Walter Clemons, "A Summer Shower"
Lowell D. Blanton, "The Long Night"
Nancy Hale, "A Slow Boat to China"
T. K. Brown, III, "A Drink of Water"
Wilma Shore, "A Cow on the Roof"
Robin White, "First Voice"
Edward Newhouse, "The Ambassador"
Herbert Wilner, "The Passion for Silver's Arm"
Robert Granat, "My Apples"
Peter Matthiessen, "Traveling Man"

1959

Peter Taylor, "Venus, Cupid, Folly and Time"
George P. Elliott, "Among the Dangs"
Thomas C. Turner, "Something to Explain"
Jean Stafford, "A Reasonable Facsimile"
Emilie Bix Buchwald, "The Present"
Ellen Currie, "Tib's Eve"
Thomas Williams, "Goose Pond"
Macdonald Harris, "Second Circle"
Helga Sandburg, "Witch Chicken"
William Eastlake, "Flight of the Circle Heart"
James Baldwin, "Come Out the Wilderness"
Flannery O'Connor, "A View of the Woods"
Tom Filer, "The Last Voyage"
Alma Stone, "The Bible Salesman"
John Cheever, "The Trouble of Marcie Flint"

1960

Lawrence Sargent Hall, "The Ledge"
Philip Roth, "Defender of The Faith"
Robin White, "Shower of Ashes"
Sylvia Berkman, "Ellen Craig"
Gina Berriault, "Sublime Child"

Elizabeth Enright, "A Gift of Light"
Janet Fowler, "A Day for Fishing"
Herbert Gold, "Love and Like"
Robert Granat, "To Endure"
Robert Henderson, "Immortality"
Calvin Kentfield, "In the Caldron"
Maurice Ogden, "Freeway to Wherever"
James Purdy, "Encore"
Elizabeth Spencer, "First Dark"
Glendon Swarthout, "A Glass of Blessings"
Eugene Ziller, "Sparrows"

1961

Tillie Olsen, "Tell Me a Riddle"
Ivan Gold, "The Nickel Misery of George Washington Carver Brown"
Reynolds Price, "One Sunday in Late July"
Jackson Burgess, "The Magician"
Ellen Currie, "Lovely Appearance of Death"
Jesse Hill Ford, "How the Mountains Are"
Ervin Krause, "The Quick and the Dead"
Jack Ludwig, "Thoreau in California"
Arthur Miller, "I Don't Need You Any More"
David Shaber, "A Nous La Liberté"
Peter Taylor, "Heads of Houses"
John Updike, "Wife-Wooing"

1962

Katherine Anne Porter, "Holiday"
Thomas Pynchon, "Under the Rose"
Tom Cole, "Familiar Use in Leningrad"
Shirley W. Schoonover, "The Star Blanket"
David Shaber, "Professorio Collegio"
Mary Deasy, "The People with the Charm"
Shirley Ann Grau, "Eight O'Clock One Morning"
David Jackson, "The English Gardens"
John Graves, "The Aztec Dog"
Thomas E. Adams, "Sled"
Miriam Mckenzie, "Deja Vu"
Maureen Howard, "Bridgeport Bus"
Reynolds Price, "The Warrior Princess Ozimba"
Thomas Whitbread, "The Rememberer"
John Updike, "The Doctor's Wife"

1963

Flannery O'Connor, "Everything That Rises Must Converge"

Ervin D. Krause, "The Snake"

Thalia Selz, "The Education of a Queen"

William Saroyan, "Gaston"

Ben Maddow "In a Cold Hotel"

Sylvia Berkman, "Pontifex"

Norma Klein, "The Burglar"

Terry Southern, "The Road Out of Axotlc"

Jessamyn West, "The Picnickers"

J. G. McClure, "The Rise of the Proletariat"

Essary Ansell, "The Threesome Helen"

James Trammell Cox, "The Golden Crane"

Joyce Carol Oates, "The Fine White Mist of Winter"

Ellen Douglas, "On the Lake"

1964

John Cheever, "The Embarkment for Cythera"

Joyce Carol Oates, "Stigmata"

Margaret Shedd, "The Everlasting Witness"

Bernard Malamud, "The Jewbird"

Sallie Bingham, "The Banks of the Ohio"

Lillian Ross, "Night and Day, Day and Night"

David Stacton, "The Metamorphosis of Kenko"

Irwin Shaw, "The Inhabitants of Venus"

Hortense Calisher, "The Scream on 57th Street"

George Lanning, "Something Just for Me"

George A. Zorn, "Thompson"

Sara, "So I'm Not Lady Chatterley So Better I Should Know It Now"

Shirley W. Schoonover, "Old and Country Tale"

Philip Roth, "Novotny's Pain"

Wallace Stegner, "Carrion Spring"

1965

Flannery O'Connor, "Revelation"

Sanford Friedman, "Ocean"

William Humphrey, "The Ballad of Jesse Neighbours"

Tom Mayer, "Homecoming"

Eva Manoff, "Mama and the Spy"

Nancy A. J. Potter, "Sunday's Children"

Donald Barthelme, "Margins"

Leon Rooke, "If Lost Return to the Swiss Arms"

Peter Taylor, "There"

Peter S. Beagle, "Come Lady Death"

Joyce Carol Oates, "First Views of the Enemy"

Leonard Wolf, "Fifty-Fifty"

Carson McCullers, "Sucker"

Daniel Curley, "Love in the Winter"

Jack Ludwig, "A Woman of Her Age"

Arthur Cavanaugh, "What I Wish (Oh, I Wish) I Had Said That"

Mary McCarthy, "The Hounds of Summer"

Warren Miller, "Chaos, Disorder and the Late Show"

1966

John Updike, "The Bulgarian Poetess"

Maureen Howard, "Sherry"

Tom Cole, "On the Edge of Arcadia"

Leonard Michaels, "Sticks and Stones"

Elizabeth Spencer, "Ship Island"

Harry Mark Petrakis, "The Prison"

Vera Randal, "Alice Blaine"

Philip L. Greene, "One of You Must Be Wendell Corey"

Nancy Hale, "Sunday Lunch"

Joy Williams, "The Roomer"

Christopher Davis, "A Man of Affairs"

Gina Berriault, "The Birthday Party"

George A. Zorn, "Mr. and Mrs. McGill"

Jesse Hill Ford, "To the Open Water"

Sallie Bingham, "Bare Bones"

Georgia McKinley, "The Mighty Distance"

1967

Joyce Carol Oates, "In the Region of Ice"

Donald Barthelme, "See the Moon?"

J. Strong, "Supperburger"

J. H. Ford, "The Bitter Bread"

M. Mudrick, "Cleopatra"

M. Goldman, "Fireflies"

J. Jacobsen, "On the Island"

J. Buechler, "The Second Best Girl"

John Updike, "Marching Through Boston"

E. J. Finney, "The Investigator"

D. Oliver, "Neighbors"

M. R. Kurtz, "Waxing Wroth"

C. Knickerbocker, "Diseases of the Heart"

R. MacCauley, "Dressed in Shade"

A. Wheelis, "Sea-Girls"

R. Yates, "A Good and Gallant Woman"

1968

Eudora Welty, "The Demonstrators"
E. M. Broner, "The New Nobility"
Shlomo Katz, "My Redeemer Cometh. . . ."
Calvin Kentfield, "Near the Line"
Nancy Hale, "The Most Elegant Drawing Room in Europe"
Gwen Gration, "Teacher"
F. K. Franklin, "Nigger Horse"
Norma Klein, "Magic"
Brock Brower, "Storm Still"
Jay Neugeboren, "Ebbets Field"
James Baker Hall, "A Kind of Savage"
David Stacton, "Little Brother Nun"
Eldon Branda, "The Dark Days of Christmas"
John Updike, "Your Lover Just Called"
Paul Tyner, "How You Play the Game"
Marilyn Harris, "Icarus Again"
Joyce Carol Oates, "Where Are You Going, Where Have You Been?"

1969

Bernard Malamud, "Man in the Drawer"
Joyce Carol Oates, "Accomplished Desires"
John Barth, "Lost in the Funhouse"
Nancy Huddleston Packer, "Early Morning, Lonely Ride"
Leo Litwak, "In Shock"
Leonard Michaels, "Maniken"
Anne Tyler, "The Common Courtesies"
Evelyn Shefner, "The Invitations"
Eunice Luccock Corfman, "To Be an Athlete"
Peter Taylor, "First Heat"
Thomas Sterling, "Bedlam's Rent"
Michael Rubin, "Service"
Grace Paley, "Distance"
Ben Maddow, "You, Johann Sebastian Bach"
Max Steele, "Color the Daydream Yellow"
H. L. Mountzoures, "The Empire of Things"
Susan Engberg, "Lambs Of God"

1970

Robert Hemenway ("Stephen Patch"), "The Girl Who Sang with the Beatles"
William Eastlake, "The Biggest Thing Since Custer"
Norval Rindfleisch, "A Cliff of Fall"

Perdita Buchan, "It's Cold Out There"
George Blake, "A Modern Development"
Jonathan Strong, "Patients"
H. E. F. Donohue, "Joe College"
James Salter, "Am Strande Von Tanger"
Bernard Malamud, "My Son the Murderer"
Patricia Browning Griffith, "Nights at O'Rear's"
Tom Cole, "Saint John of the Hershey Kisses: 1964"
John Updike, "Bech Takes Pot Luck"
David Grinstead, "A Day in Operations"
Nancy Willard, "Theo's Girl"
Nancy Willard, "Of Cabbages and Kings"
James Alan McPherson, "Unmailed, Unwritten Letters"
Joyce Carol Oates, "How I Contemplated the World from the Detroit House of Correction and Began My Life Over Again"

1971

Florence M. Hecht, "Twin Bed Bridge"
Guy A. Cardwell, "Did You See Shelly"
Alice Adams, "Gift of Grass"
Reynolds Price, "Waiting at Dachau"
Julian Mazor, "Skylark"
Evelyn Harter, "Stone Lovers"
Thomas Parker, "Troop Withdrawal—The Inital Step"
Robert Inman, "I'll Call You"
Josephine Jacobsen, "Jungle of Lord Lion"
Joyce Carol Oates, "Children"
Eldridge Cleaver, "Flashlight"
Eleanor Ross Taylor, "Jujitsu"
Philip L. Greene, "Dichotomy"
Stephen Minot, "Mars Revisited"
Charles R. Larson, "Up from Slavery"
Leonard Michaels, "Robinson Crusoe Liebowitz"
Edward Hoagland, "Final Fate of the Alligators"

1972

John Batki, "Strange-Dreaming Charlie, Cow-Eyed Charlie"
Joyce Carol Oates, "Saul Bird Says: Relate! Communicate! Liberate!"
Judith Rascoe, "Small Sounds and Tilting Shadows"
Mary Clearman, "Lambing Out"

Starkey Flythe, Jr., "Point of Conversion"
Brendan Gill, "Fat Girl"
Anne Tyler, "With All Flags Flying"
James Salter, "The Destruction of the Goetheanum"
Patricia Zelver, "On the Desert"
Elaine Gottleib, "The Lizard"
Jack Matthews, "On The Shore of Chad Creek"
Alice Adams, "Ripped Off"
Rosellen Brown, "A Letter to Ismael in the Grave"
Charles Edward Eaton, "The Case of the Missing Photographs"
Margery Finn Brown, "In the Forests of Riga the Beasts Are Very Wild Indeed"
J. D. McClatchy, "Allonym"
Herbert Gold, "A Death on the East Side"
Donald Barthelme, "Subpoena"

1973

Joyce Carol Oates, "The Dead"
Bernard Malamud, "Talking Horse"
Rosellen Brown, "Mainlanders"
Patricia Zelver, "The Flood"
James Alan McPherson, "The Silver Bullet"
John Malone, "The Fugitives"
Alice Adams, "The Swastika on Our Door"
Judith Rascoe, "A Line of Order"
Raymond Carver, "What Is It?"
Jane Mayhall, "The Enemy"
Diane Johnson, "An Apple, An Orange"
John Cheever, "The Jewels of the Cabots"
Josephine Jacobsen, "A Walk with Raschid"
David Shaber, "Scotch Sour"
Curt Johnson, "Trespasser"
Henry Bromell, "Photographs"
Shirley Sikes, "The Death of Cousin Stanley"
Randall Reid, "Detritus"

1974

John Gardner, "The Things"
Renata Adler, "Brownstone"
Robert Henson, "Lizzie Borden in the P.M."
Alice Adams, "Alternatives"
Frederick Busch, "Is Anyone Left This Time of Year?"
John J. Clayton, "Cambridge Is Sinking!"
James Salter, "Via Negativa"

Blair Fuller, "Bakti's Hand"
Robert Hemenway, "Troy Street"
Rolaine Hochstein, "What Kind of a Man Cuts His Finger Off?"
Peter Leach, "The Fish Trap"
Norma Klein, "The Wrong Man"
Guy Davenport, "Robot"
Raymond Carver, "Put Yourself in My Shoes"
James Alan McPherson, "The Faithful"
William Eastlake, "The Death of Sun"

1975

Harold Brodkey, "A Story in an Almost Classical Mode"
Cynthia Ozick, "Usurpation (Other People's Stories)"
Alice Adams, "Verlie I Say Unto You"
Raymond Carver, "Are You a Doctor?"
Susannah McCorkle, "Ramona by the Sea"
Eve Shelnutt, "Angel"
Ann Arensberg, "Art History"
E. L. Doctorow, "Ragtime"
William Maxwell, "Over by the River"
Thomas M. Disch, "Getting into Death"
Patricia Zelver, "Norwegians"
Linda Arking, "Certain Hard Places"
James Alan McPherson, "The Story of a Scar"
Russell Banks, "With Che at Kitty Hawk"
John Updike, "Nakedness"
Jessie Schell, "Alvira, Lettie, And Pip"
Ann Bayer, "Department Store"
William Kotzwinkle, "Swimmer in the Secret Sea"

1976

Harold Brodkey, "His Son, in His Arms"
John Sayles, "I-80 Nebraska, M.490-M.205"
Alice Adams, "Roses, Rhododendron"
Guy Davenport, "The Richard Nixon Freischutz Rag"
Josephine Jacobsen, "Nel Bagno"
Patricia Griffith, "Dust"
John William Corrington, "The Actes and Monuments"
Helen Hudson, "The Theft"
William Goyen, "Bridge of Music, River of Sand"

Ira Sadoff, "An Enemy of the People"
Mark Helprin, "Leaving the Church"
Joyce Carol Oates, "Blood-Swollen Landscape"
Jerry Bumpus, "The Idols of Afternoon"
Tim O'Brien, "Night March"
Anita Shreve, "Past the Island, Drifting"
John Berryman, "Wash Far Away"
Anne Halley, "The Sisterhood"
Rosellen Brown, "Why I Quit the Gowanus
    Liberation Front"
H. E. Francis, "A Chronicle of Love"
John Updike, "Separating"

1977

E. Leffland, "Last Courtesies"
S. Hazzard, "A Long Story Short"
A. Fetler, "Shadows on the Water"
S. Ballantyne, "Perpetual Care"
Susan Minot, "A Passion for History"
Paul Theroux, "The Autumn Dog"
H. Summers, "A Hundred Paths"
Patricia Zelver, "The Little Pub"
C. Simmons, "Certain Changes"
M. Hedin, "Ladybug, Fly Away Home"
Alice Adams, "Flights"
Joanna Russ, "Autobiography of My Mother"
E. A. McCully, "How's Your Vacuum Cleaner
    Working?"
Laurie Colwin, "The Lone Pilgrim"
J. Sayles, "Breed"
Stephen Dixon, "Mac in Love"
S. Engberg, "A Stay by the River"
John Cheever, "The President of the Argentine"

1978

W. Allen, "The Kugelmass Episode"
M. A. Schorer, "Lamp"
R. Henson, "The Upper and the Lower Millstone"
Alice Adams, "Beautiful Girl"
M. Apple, "Paddycake, Paddycake . . . A Memoir"
S. Engberg, "Pastorale"
B. Fuller, "All Right"
Joyce Carol Oates, "The Tattoo"
J. Jacobsen, "Jack Frost"
Tim O'Brien, "Speaking of Courage"
J. Schell, "Undeveloped Photographs"

J. J. Clayton, "Bodies Like Mouths"
C. Leviant, "Ladies And Gentlemen, The Original
    Music of the Hebrew Alphabet"
Harold Brodkey, "Verona: A Young Woman Speaks"
J. Schevill, "A Hero in the Highway"
E. Pearlman, "Hanging Fire"
Mark Helprin, "The Schreuderspitze"
Susan Fromberg Schaeffer, "The Exact Nature of Plot"

1979

Gordon Weaver, "Getting Serious"
H. Bromell, "Travel Stories"
J. Hecht, "I Want You, I Need You, I Love You"
L. Goldberg, "Shy Bearers"
S. Heller, "The Summer Game"
F. Pfeil, "The Quality of Light in Maine"
A. Leaton, "The Passion of Marco Z"
A. Thomas, "Coon Hunt"
T. W. Molyneux, "Visiting the Point"
Joyce Carol Oates, "In the Autumn of the Year"
J. Baumbach, "Passion?"
P. Zelver, "My Father's Jokes"
Herbert Gold, "The Smallest Part"
H. Van Dyke, "Du Côté de Chez Britz"
L. Smith, "Mrs. Darcy Meets the Blue-Eyed
    Stranger at the Beach"
A. Caputi, "The Derby Hopeful"
L. S. Schwartz, "Rough Strife"
R. Yates, "Oh, Joseph, I'm So Tired"
M. Peterson, "Travelling"
Thomas M. Disch, "Xmas"
Alice Adams, "The Girl Across the Room"

1980

Saul Bellow, "A Silver Dish"
Nancy Hallinan, "Women in a Roman Courtyard"
Leonard Michaels, "The Men's Club"
Shirley Ann Taggart, "Ghosts Like Them"
Peter Taylor, "The Old Forest"
Marilyn Krysl, "Looking For Mother"
Walter Sullivan, "Elizabeth"
Daniel Asa Rose, "The Goodbye Present"
Jayne Anne Phillips, "Snow"
Robert Dunn, "Hopeless Acts Performed Properly,
    With Grace"
Helen Chasin, "Fatal"

T. Gertler, "In Case of Survival"
Ann Arensberg, "Group Sex"
Barry Targan, "Old Light"
Stephanie Vaughn, "Sweet Talk"
Gail Godwin, "Amanuensis: A Tale of the Creative Life"
Alice Adams, "Truth Or Consequences"
John L'Heureux, "The Priest's Wife"
Andre Dubus, "The Pitcher"
Ann Beattie, "The Cinderella Waltz"
Millicent G. Dillon, "All the Pelageyas"
Jean Stafford, "An Influx of Poets"

1981

Cynthia Ozick, "The Shawl"
John Irving, "Interior Space"
James Tabor, "The Runner"
Kay Boyle, "St. Steven's Green"
Nancy Huddleston, "The Women Who Walk"
Lee Smith, "Packer Between the Lines"
Alice Adams, "Snow"
Tobias Wolff, "In the Garden of the North American Martyrs"
Sandra Hollin Flowers, "Hope of Zion"
Alice Walker, "The Abortion"
Jack Matthews, "The Last Abandonment"
Marian Novick, "Advent"
W. D. Wetherell, "The Man Who Loved Levittown"
Joyce Carol Oates, "Mutilated Woman"
Ivy Goodman, "Baby"
Barbara Reid, "The Waltz Dream"
Annabel Thomas, "The Phototropic Woman"
John L'Heureux, "Brief Lives in California"
Steve Stern, "Isaac and the Undertaker's"
Annette T. Rottenberg, "The Separation"
Paul Theroux, "World's End"

1982

Susan Kenney, "Facing Front"
Joseph McElroy, "The Future"
Ben Brooks, "A Postal Creed"
Jane Smiley, "The Pleasure of Her Company"
T. E. Holt, "Charybdis"
Nora Johnson, "The Jungle of Injustice"
Kenneth Gewertz, "I Thought of Chatterton, the Marvelous Boy"

Kate Wheeler, "La Victoire"
Stephen Dixon, "Layaways"
Peter Taylor, "The Gift of the Prodigal"
Ivy Goodman, "White Boy"
Michael Malone, "Fast Love"
Tim O'Brien, "The Ghost Soldiers"
Joyce Carol Oates, "The Man Whom Women Adored"
Tobias Wolff, "Next Door"
Florence Trefethen, "Infidelities"
David Carkeet, "The Greatest Slump of All Time"
Alice Adams, "Greyhound People"
Alice Adams, "To See You Again"

1983

Raymond Carver, "A Small, Good Thing"
Joyce Carol Oates, "My Warszawa"
Wright Morris, "Victrola"
Irvin Faust, "Melanie and the Purple People Eaters"
Elizabeth Spencer, "Jean-Pierre"
W. D. Wetherell, "If a Woodchuck Could Chuck Wood"
John Updike, "The City"
Gloria Norris, "When the Lord Calls"
Leigh Buchanan Bienen, "My Life as a West African Gray Parrot"
David Jauss, "Shards"
Mary Gordon, "The Only Son of the Doctor"
Peter Meinke, "The Ponoes"
William F. Van Wert, "Putting & Gardening"
Elizabeth Benedict, "Feasting"
Steven Schwartz, "Slow-Motion"
Linda Svendsen, "Heartbeat"
Lynda Lloyd, "Poor Boy"
Perri Klass, "The Secret Life of Dieters"
Gloria Whelan, "The Dogs in Renoir's Garden"
David Plante, "Work"

1984

Cynthia Ozick, "Rosa"
Gloria Norris, "Revive Us Again"
Charles Dickinson, "Risk"
David Leavitt, "Counting Months"
Edith Pearlman, "Conveniences"
Alice Adams, "Alaska"
Daniel Menaker, "The Old Left"

Lee K. Abbott, Jr., "Living Alone in Iota"
Melissa Brown Pritchard, "A Private Landscape"
Bernard Malamud, "The Model"
Andres Fetler, "The Third Count"
James Salter, "Lost Sons"
Willis Johnson, "Prayer for the Dying"
Jonathan Baumbach, "The Life and Times of Major Fiction"
Donald Justice, "The Artificial Moonlight"
Elizabeth Tallent, "The Evolution of Birds of Paradise"
Perri Klass, "Not a Good Girl"
Grace Paley, "The Story Hearer"
Helen Norris, "The Love Child"
Gordon Lish, "For Jerome with Love and Kisses"

1985
Jane Smiley, "Lily"
Stuart Dybeck, "Hot Ice"
Ann Beattie, "In the White Night"
Helen Norris, "The Quarry"
Susan Minot, "Lust"
Claude Koch, "Bread and Butter Questions"
Wright Morris, "Glimpse into Another Country"
Louise Erdrich, "Saint Marie"
Joseph McElroy, "Daughter of the Revolution"
Steve Heller, "The Crow Woman"
Ward Just, "About Boston"
Tobias Wolff, "Sister"
Gloria Norris, "Holding On"
Peter Cameron, "Homework"
Ilene Raymond, "Taking a Chance on Jack"
Eric Wilson, "The Axe, The Axe, The Axe"
Joyce Carol Oates, "The Seasons"
Rolaine Hochstein, "She Should Have Died Hereafter"
Josephine Jacobsen, "The Mango Community"
John Updike, "The Other"

1986
Alice Walker, "Kindred Spirits"
Stuart Dybeck, "Pet Milk"
Greg Johnson, "Crazy Ladies"
John L'Heureux, "The Comedian"
Joyce R. Kornblatt, "Offerings"
Ward Just, "The Costa Brava, 1959"
Peter Meinke, "Uncle George and Uncle Stefan"

Bobbie Ann Mason, "Big Bertha Stories"
Merrill Joan Gerber, "I Don't Believe This"
Gordon Lish, "Resurrection"
Peter Cameron, "Excerpts from Swan Lake"
Alice Adams, "Molly's Dog"
Deborah Eisenberg, "Transactions in a Foreign Currency"
Anthony DiFranco, "The Garden of Redemption"
Jeanne Wilmot, "Dirt Angel"
Elizabeth Spencer, "The Cousins"
Irvin Faust, "The Year of the Hot Jock"
Stephanie Vaughn, "Kid Macarthur"
Joyce Carol Oates, "Master Race"

1987
Louise Erdrich, "Fleur"
Joyce Johnson, "The Children's Wing"
Robert Boswell, "The Darkness of Love"
Alice Adams, "Tide Pools"
Stuart Dybeck, "Blight"
James Lott, "The Janeites"
Donald Barthelme, "Basil from Her Garden"
Gina Berriault, "The Island of Ven"
Jim Pitzen, "The Village"
Richard Bausch, "What Feels Like the World"
Millicent Dillon, "Monitor"
Norman Lavers, "Big Dog"
Robert Taylor, Jr., "Lady of Spain"
Helen Norris, "The Singing Well"
Grace Paley, "Midrash on Happiness"
Lewis Horne, "Taking Care"
Warren Wallace, "Up Home"
Joyce Carol Oates, "Ancient Airs, Voices"
Daniel Stern, "The Interpretations of Dreams By Sigmund Freud: A Story"
Mary Robison, "I Get By"

1988
Raymond Carver, "Errand"
Alice Adams, "Ocracoke Island"
Elizabeth Spencer, "The Business Venture"
Richard Currey, "The Wars of Heaven"
Andre Dubus, "Blessings"
Shirley Hazzard, "The Place to Be"
Joyce Carol Oates, "Yarrow"
Peter Lasalle, "Dolphin Dreaming"

Joy Williams, "Rot"
Salvatore La Puma, "The Gangster's Ghost"
Bobbie Ann Mason, "Bumblebees"
Richard Plant, "Cecil Grounded"
Ann Beattie, "Honey"
Jay Neugeboren "Don't Worry About the Kids"
John Sayles, "The Halfway Diner"
Sheila Kohler, "The Mountain"
Jane Smiley, "Long Distance"
Philip F. Deaver, "Arcola Girls"
Jonathan Baumbach, "The Dinner Party"
John Updike, "Leaf Season"

1989
Ernest J. Finney, "Peacocks"
Joyce Carol Oates, "House Hunting"
Harriet Doerr, "Edie: A Life"
Jean Ross, "The Sky Fading Upward To Yellow: A Footnote to Literary History"
Starkey Flythe, Jr., "Cv10"
Alice Adams, "After You've Gone"
Frances Sherwood, "History"
Banning K. Lary, "Death of a Duke"
T. Coraghessan Boyle, "Sinking House"
Catherine Petroski, "The Hit"
James Salter, "American Express"
David Foster Wallace, "Here and There"
Susan Minot, "Île Seche"
Millicent Dillon, "Wrong Stories"
Charles Simmons, "Clandestine Acts"
John Casey, "Avid"
Barbara Grizzuti Harrison, "To Be"
Rick Bass, "The Watch"
Ellen Herman Child, "Unstable Ground"
Charles Dickinson, "In the Leaves"

1990
Leo E. Litwak, "The Eleventh Edition"
Peter Matthiessen, "Lumumba Lives"
Lore Segal, "The Reverse Bug"
Joyce Carol Oates, "Heat"
Carolyn Osborn, "The Grands"
James P. Blaylock, "Unidentified Objects"
Jane Brown Gillette, "Sins Against Animals"
Julie Schumacher, "The Private Life of Robert Schumann"

Joanne Greenberg, "Elizabeth Baird"
Alice Adams, "1940: Fall"
T. Coraghessan Boyle, "The Ape Lady in Retirement"
Marilyn Sides, "The Island of the Mapmaker's Wife"
David Michael Kaplan, "Stand"
Meredith Steinbach, "In Recent History"
Claudia Smith Brinson, "Einstein's Daughter"
Felicia Ackerman, "The Forecasting Game: A Story"
Reginald McKnight, "The Kind of Light That Shines on Texas"
Devon Jersild, "The Autobiography of Gertrude Stein—In Which John Imagines His Mind as a Pond"
Janice Eidus, "Vito Loves Geraldine"

1991
John Updike, "A Sandstone Farmhouse"
Joyce Carol Oates, "The Swimmers"
Sharon Sheehe Stark, "Overland"
T. Alan Broughton, "Ashes"
Charles Baxter, "Saul and Patsy Are Pregnant"
Ursula K. Le Guin, "Hand, Cup, Shell"
Patricia Lear, "Powpow"
Wayne Johnson, "Hippies, Indians, Buffalo"
Perri Klass, "For Women Everywhere"
Dennis McFarland, "Nothing to Ask For"
Helen Norris, "Raisin Faces"
Diane Levenberg, "The Ilui"
Charlotte Zoe Walker, "The Very Pineapple"
Millicent Dillon, "Oil and Water"
Ronald Sukenick, "Ecco"
Alice Adams, "Earthquake Damage"
Marly Swick, "Moscow Nights"
Martha Lacy Hall, "The Apple-Green Triumph"
Sylvia A. Watanabe, "Talking to the Dead"
Thomas Fox Averill, "During the Twelfth Summer of Elmer D. Peterson"

1992
Cynthia Ozick, "Puttermesser Paired"
Lucy Honig and Tom McNeal, "English as a Second Language"
Amy Herrick, "Pinocchio's Nose"

Murray Pomerance, "Decor"

Joyce Carol Oates, "Why Don't You Come Live with Me It's Time"

Mary Michael Wagner, "Acts of Kindness"

Yolanda Barnes, "Red Lipstick"

David Long, "Blue Spruce"

Harriet Doerr, "Way Stations"

Perri Klass, "Dedication"

Daniel Meltzer, "People"

Les Myers, "The Kite"

Ken Chowder, "With Seth in Tana Toraja"

Alice Adams, "The Last Lovely City"

Frances Sherwood, "Demiurges"

Antonya Nelson, "The Controlgroup"

Millicent Dillon, "Lost in L. A."

Kent Nelson, "The Mine from Nicaragua"

Ann Packer, "Babies"

Kate Braverman, "Tall Tales from the Mekong Delta"

1993

Andrea Lee, "Barley"

William F. Van Wert, "Shaking"

Joyce Carol Oates, "Goose-Girl"

Charles Eastman, "Yellow Flags"

Cornelia Nixon, "Risk"

Rilla Askew, "The Killing Blanket"

Antonya Nelson, "Dirty Words"

John H. Richardson, "The Pink House"

Diane Levenberg, "A Modern Love Story"

John Van Kirk, "Newark Job"

Alice Adams, "The Islands"

Stephen Dixon, "The Rare Muscovite"

Lorrie Moore, "Charades"

Kate Wheeler, "Improving My Average"

Peter Weltner, "The Greek Head"

C. E. Poverman, "The Man Who Died"

Jennifer Egan, "Puerto Vallarta"

Charles Johnson, "Kwoon"

Linda Svendsen, "The Edger Man"

Daniel Stern, "A Hunger Artist Franz Kafka: A Story"

Josephine Jacobsen, "The Pier-Glass"

Steven Schwartz, "Madagascar"

1994

Alison Baker, "Better Be Ready 'Bout Half Past Eight"

John Rolfe Gardiner, "The Voyage Out"

Lorrie Moore, "Terrific Mother"

Stuart Dybek, "We Didn't"

Marlin Barton, "Jeremiah's Road"

Kelly Cherry, "Not the Phil Donahue Show"

Elizabeth Cox, "The Third of July"

Terry Bain, "Games"

Amy Bloom, "Semper Fidelis"

Michael Fox, "Rise and Shine"

David McLean, "Marine Corps Issue"

Elizabeth Graver, "The Boy Who Fell Forty Feet"

Susan Richards, "The Hanging in the Foaling Barn"

Janice Eidus, "Pandora's Box"

Judith Ortiz Cofer, "Nada"

Mary Tannen, "Elaine's House"

Dennis Trudell, "Gook"

Helen Fremont, "Where She Was"

Elizabeth Oness, "The Oracle"

Katherine L. Hester, "Labor"

Thomas E. Kennedy, "Landing Zone X-Ray"

1995

Cornelia Nixon, "The Women Come and Go"

John J. Clayton, "Talking to Charlie"

Elizabeth Hardwick, "Shot: A New York Story"

Padgett Powell, "Trick or Treat"

Alice Adams, "The Haunted Beach"

Elliot Krieger, "Cantor Pepper"

Peter Cameron, "Departing"

Allegra Goodman, "Sarah"

Ellen Gilchrist, "The Stucco House"

Joyce Carol Oates, "You Petted Me, and I Followed You Home"

Michael Byers, "Settled on the Cranberry Coast"

David Gates, "The Intruder"

Deborah Eisenberg, "Across the Lake"

Bernard Cooper, "Truth Serum"

Edward J. Delaney, "The Drowning"

Alison Baker, "Loving Wanda Beaver"

John Updike, "The Black Room"

Anne Whitney Pierce, "Star Box"

Charles Baxter, "Kiss Away"

Robin Bradford, "If This Letter Were a Beaded Object"

Perri Klass, "City Sidewalks"

1996

Stephen King, "The Man in the Black Suit"
Akhil Sharma, "If You Sing Like That For Me"
William Hoffman, "Stones"
T. M. McNally, "Skin Deep"
Alison Baker, "Convocations"
Joyce Carol Oates, "Mark of Satan"
Daniel Menaker, "Influenz"
Lucy Honig, "Citizens Review"
Alice Adams, "His Women"
Ellen Douglas, "Grant"
David Wiegand, "Buffalo Safety"
Becky Hagenston, "Til Death Us Do Part"
Julie Schumacher, "Dummies"
Tom Paine, "Will You Say, Something, Monsieur Eliot?"
Jane Smiley, "The Life of the Body"
Walter Mosley, "The Thief"
Elizabeth Graver, "Between"
Leonard Kriegel, "Players"
Frederick G. Dillen, "Alice"
Ralph Lombreglia, "Somebody Up There Likes Me"

1997

Mary Gordon, "City Life"
George Saunders, "Falls"
Lee K. Abbott, "Talk Talked Between Worms"
John Barth, "On with the Story"
Alice Munro, "Love of a Good Woman"
Carolyn Cooke, "Two Corbies"
Arthur Bradford, "Catface"
Andre Dubus, "Dancing After Hours"
Matthew Klam, "Royal Palms"
Kiana Davenport, "Lipstick Tree"
Ian Macmillan, "Red House"
Mary Gaitskill, "Comfort"
Robert Morgan, "Balm of Gilead Tree"
Thomas Glave, "Final Inning"
Deborah Eisenberg, "Mermaids"
Susan Fromberg Schaeffer, "Old Farmhouse and the Dog-Wife"
Patricia Elam Ruff, "Taxi Ride"
Carol Shields, "Mirrors"
Christine Schutt, "His Chorus"
Rick Moody, "Demonology"

1998

Lorrie Moore, "People Like That Are the Only People Here"
Steven Millhauser, "The Knife Thrower"
Alice Munro, "The Children Stay"
Maxine Swann, "Flower Children"
Brian Evenson, "Two Brothers"
George Saunders, "Winky"
Karen Heuler, "Me and My Enemy"
Thom Jones, "Tarantula"
Suketu Mehta, "Gare du Nord"
Carolyn Cooke, "Eating Dirt"
Peter Ho Davies, "Relief"
Reginald McKnight, "Boot"
Josip Novakovich, "Crimson"
Peter Weltner, "Movietone: Detour"
Akhil Sharma, "Cosmopolitan"
D. R. MacDonald, "Ashes"
Rick Bass, "The Myth of the Bears"
Louise Erdrich, "Satan: Hijacker of a Planet"
Don Zancanella, "The Chimpanzees of Wyoming Territory"
Annie Proulx, "Brokeback Mountain"

BEST AMERICAN SHORT STORIES, 1915–1998

Following are the stories selected by the editors of the series *Best American Short Stories,* published annually by Houghton Mifflin since 1915.

1915

Maxwell Struthers Burt, "The Water Hole"
Donn Byrne, "The Wake"
Will Levington Comfort, "Chautenville"
W. A. Dwiggins, "La Dernière Mobilisation"
James Francis Dwyer, "The Citizen"
Francis Gregg, "Whose Dog——?"
Ben Hecht, "Life"
Fannie Hurst, "T.B."
Arthur Johnson, "Mr. Eberdeen's House"
Virgil Jordan, "Vengence Is Mine"
Harris Merton Lyon, "The Weaver Who Clad the Summer"
Walter J. Muilenburg, "Heart of Youth"

Newbold Noyes, "The End of the Path"
Seumas O'Brien, "The Whale and the Grasshopper"
Mary Boyle O'Reilly, "In Berlin"
Katharine Metcalf Roof, "The Waiting Years"
Benjamin Rosenblatt, "Zelig"
Elsie Singmaster, "The Survivors"
Wilbur Daniel Steele, "The Yellow Cat"
Mary Synon, "The Bounty-Jumper"

1916

Gertrude Atherton, "The Sacrificial Altar"
Barry Benefield, "Miss Willett"
Frederick Booth, "Supers"
Dana Burnet, "Fog"
Francis Buzzell, "Ma's Pretties"
Irvin S. Cobb, "The Great Auk"
Theodore Dreiser, "The Lost Phoebe"
Armistead C. Gordon, "The Silent Infare"
Frederick Stuart Greene, "The Cat of the Cane-Brake"
Richard Matthews Hallet, "Making Port"
Fannie Hurst, "Ice Water, Pl——!"
Mary Lerner, "Little Selves"
Jennette Marks, "The Sun Chaser"
Walter J. Muilenburg, "At the End Of the Road"
Albert Duverney Pentz, "The Big Stranger On Dorchester Heights"
Benjamin Rosenblatt, "The Menorah"
Elsie Singmaster, "Penance"
Gordon Arthur Smith, "Feet of Gold"
Wilbur Daniel Steele, "Down on Their Knees"
Alice L. Tildesley, "Half Past Ten"

1917

Edwina Stanton Babcock, "The Excursion"
Thomas Beer, "Onnie"
Maxwell Struthers Burt, "A Cup of Tea"
Francis Buzzell, "Lonely Places"
Irvin S. Cobb, "Boys Will Be Boys"
Charles Caldwell Dobie, "Laughter"
H. G. Dwight, "The Emperor of Elam"
Edna Ferber, "The Gay Old Dog"
Katharine Fullerton Gerould, "The Knight's Move"
Susan Glaspell, "A Jury Of Her Peers"
Frederick Stuart Greene, "The Bunker Mouse"
Richard Matthews Hallet, "Rainbow Pete"

Fannie Hurst, "Get Ready the Wreaths"
Fanny Kemble Johnson, "The Strange-Looking Man"
Burton Kline, "The Caller in the Night"
Vincent O'Sullivan, "The Interval"
Lawrence Perry, "A Certain Rich Man—"
Mary Brecht Pulver, "The Path Of Glory"
Wilbur Daniel Steele, "Ching, Ching, Chinaman"
Mary Synon, "None So Blind"

1918

Achmed Abdullah, "A Simple Act of Piety"
Edwina Stanton Babcock, "Cruelties"
Katharine Holland Brown, "Buster"
Charles Caldwell Dobie, "The Open Window"
Mary Mitchell Freedley, "Blind Vision"
Gordon Hall Gerould, "Imagination"
George Gilbert, "In Maulmain Fever-Ward"
G. Humphrey, "The Father's Hand"
Arthur Johnson, "The Visit of the Master"
Burton Kline, "In the Open Code"
Sinclair Lewis, "The Willow Walk"
Katharine Prescott Moseley, "The Story Vinton Heard at Mallorie"
William Dudley Pelley, "The Toast to Forty-Five"
Harrison Rhodes, "Extra Men"
Fleta Campbell Springer, "Solitaire"
Wilbur Daniel Steele, "The Dark Hour"
Julian Street, "The Bird of Serbia"
Edward C. Venable, "At Isham's"
Mary Heaton Vorse, "DeVilmarte's Luck"

1919

G. F. Alsop, "The Kitchen Gods"
Sherwood Anderson, "An Awakening"
Edwina Stanton Babcock, "Willum's Vanilla"
Djuna Barnes, "A Night Among the Horses"
Frederick Orin Bartlett, "Long, Long Ago"
Agnes Mary Brownell, "Dishes"
Maxwell Struthers Burt, "The Blood-Red One"
James Branch Cabell, "The Wedding Jest"
Horace Fish, "The Wrists on the Door"
Susan Glaspell, "Government Goat"
Henry Goodman, "The Stone"
Richard Matthews Hallet, "To the Bitter End"
Joseph Hergesheimer, "The Meeker Ritual"

Will E. Ingersoll, "The Centenarian"
Calvin Johnson, "Messengers"
Howard Mumford Jones, "Mrs. Drainger's Veil"
Ellen N. LaMotte, "Under a Wine-Glass"
Elias Lieberman, "A Thing of Beauty"
Mary Heaton Vorse, "The Other Room"

1920

Sherwood Anderson, "The Other Woman"
Edwina Stanton Babcock, "Gargoyle"
Konrad Bercovici, "Ghitza"
Edna Clarke Bryner, "The Life of Five Points"
Wadsworth Camp, "The Signal Tower"
Helen Coale Crew, "The Parting Genius"
Katharine Fullerton Gerould, "Habakkuk"
Lee Foster Hartman, "The Judgement of Vulcan"
Rupert Hughes, "The Stick-in-the-Muds"
Grace Sartwell Mason "His Job"
James Oppenheim, "The Rending"
Arthur Somers Roche, "The Dummy-Chucker"
Rose Sidney, "Butterflies"
Fleta Campbell Springer, "The Rotter"
Wilbur Daniel Steele, "Out of Exile"
Ethel Storm, "The Three Telegrams"
John T. Wheelwright, "The Roman Bath"
Stephen French Whitman, "Amazement"
Ben Ames Williams, "Sheener"

1921

Sherwood Anderson, "Brothers"
Konrad Bercovici, "Fanutza"
Maxwell Struthers Burt, "Experiment"
Irvin S. Cobb, "Darkness"
Lincoln Colcord, "An Instrument of the Gods"
Charles J. Finger, "The Lizard God"
Waldo Frank, "Under the Dome"
Susan Glaspell, "His Smile"
Ellen Glasgow, "The Past"
Katharine Fullerton Gerould, "French Eva"
Richard Matthews Hallet, "The Harbor Master"
Frances Noyes Hart, "Green Gardens"
Judith Higgins, "His Smile"
Fannie Hurst, "She Walks in Beauty"
Manuel Komroff, "The Little Master of the Sky"
Frank Luther Mott, "The Man with the Good Face"
Vincent O'Sullivan, "Master of Fallen Years"

Wilbur Daniel Steele, "The Shame Dance"
Harriet Maxon Thayer, "Kindred"
Charles Hanson Towne, "Shelby"
Mary Heaton Vorse, "The Wallow of the Sea"

1922

Conrad Aiken, "The Dark City"
Sherwood Anderson, "I'm a Fool"
Konrad Bercovici, "The Death of Murdo"
Susan M. Boogher, "An Unknown Warrior"
Frederick Booth, "The Helpless Ones"
Edna Clarke Bryner, "Forest Cover"
Rose Gollup Cohen, "Natalka's Portion"
Charles J. Finger, "The Shame of Gold"
F. Scott Fitzgerald, "Two For a Cent"
David Freedman, "Mendel Marantz—Housewife"
Waldo Frank, "John the Baptist"
Katharine Fullerton Gerould, "Belshazzar's Letter"
Ben Hecht, "Winkelburg"
Joseph Hergesheimer, "The Token"
William Jitro, "The Resurrection and the Life"
Ring W. Lardner, "The Golden Honeymoon"
James Oppenheim, "He Laughed at the Gods"
Benjamin Rossenblatt, "In the Metropolis"
Wilbur Daniel Steele, "From the Other Side of the South"

1923

Bill Adams, "Way for a Sailor"
Sherwood Anderson, "The Man's Story"
Edwina Stanton Babcock, "Mr. Cardeezer"
Konrad Bercovici, "Seed"
Dana Burnet, "Beyond the Cross"
Valma Clark, "Ignition"
Irvin S. Cobb, "The Chocolate Hyena"
John Cournos, "The Samovar"
Theodore Dreiser, "Reina"
Edna Ferber, "Home Girl"
Henry Goodman, "The Button"
Ernest Hemingway, "My Old Man"
Fannie Hurst, "Seven Candles"
Margaret Prescott Montague, "The Today Tomorrow"
Solon K. Stewart, "The Contract Of Corporal Twing"
F. J. Stimson, "By Due Process of Law"
Ruth Suckow, "Renters"

Jean Toomer, "Blood-Burning Moon"
Mary Heaton Vorse, "The Promise"
Harry Leon Wilson, Flora and Fauna"

1924

Morgan Burke, "Champlin"
Mildred Cram, "Billy"
Floyd Dell, "Phantom Adventure"
Charles Caldwell Dobie, "The Cracked Teapot"
Carlos Drake, "The Last Dive"
Charles J. Finger, "Adventures of Andrew Lang"
Zona Gale, "The Biography of Blade"
Tupper Greenwald, "Corputt"
Harry Hervy, "The Young Men Go Down"
Leonard L. Hess, "The Lesser Gift"
Rupert Hughes, "Grudges"
Gouverneur Morris, "A Postscript to Divorce"
Lizette Woodworth Reese, "Forgiveness"
Roger Sergel, "Nocturne: A Red Shawl"
A. B. Shiffrin, "The Black Laugh"
Ruth Suckow, "Four Generations"
Melvin Van Den Bark, "Two Women and Hog-Back
    Ridge"
Warren L. Van Dine, "The Poet"
Glenway Wescott, "In a Thicket"

1925

Sandra Alexander, "The Gift"
Sherwood Anderson, "The Return"
Nathan Asch, "Gertrude Donovan"
Barry Benefield, "Guard Of Honor"
Konrad Bercovici, "The Beggar of Alcazar"
Bella Cohen, "The Laugh"
Charles Caldwell Dobie, "The Hands of the
    Enemy"
Rudolph Fisher, "The City Of Refuge"
Katharine Fullerton Gerould, "An Army Without
    Banners"
Walter Gilkyson, "Coward's Castle"
Manuel Komroff, "How Does It Feel to Be Free?"
Ring W. Lardner, "Haircut"
Robert Robinson, "The Ill Wind"
Evelyn Scott, "The Old Lady"
May Stanley, "Old Man Ledge"
Wilbur Daniel Steele, "Six Dollars"
Milton Waldman, "The Home Town"

Glenway Wescott, "Fire and Water"
Barrett Willoughby, "The Devil Drum"

1926

Barry Benefield, "Carrie Snyder"
Ada Jack Carver, "Maudie"
Donald Corley, "The Glass Eye of Throgmorton"
Chester T. Crowell, "Take the Stand Please"
A. E. Dingle, "Bound For Rio Grande"
Henry Walbridge Dudley, "Query"
Arthur Huff Fauset, "Symphonesque"
Zona Gale, "Evening"
Tupper Greenwald, "Wheels"
Ernest Hemingway, "The Undefeated"
Manuel Komroff, "The Christian Bite"
Milutin Krunich, "Then Christs Fought Hard"
Ring W. Lardner, "Travelogue"
Grace Sartwell Mason, "The First Stone"
Susan Meriwether, "Grimaldi"
Ira V. Morris, Jr., "A Tale from the Grave"
Robert E. Sherwood, "Extra! Extra!"
Wilbur Daniel Steele, "Out of the Wind"
Edward L. Strater, "The Other Road"
Virginia Tracy, "The Giant's Thunder"

1927

Sherwood Anderson, "Another Wife"
Roark Bradford, "Child of God"
Harold W. Brecht, "Vienna Roast"
Ben Lucien Burman, "Ministrels of the Mist"
Elisabeth Finley-Thomas, "Mademoiselle"
Amory Hare, "Three Lumps of Sugar"
Ernest Hemingway, "The Killers"
Joseph Hergesheimer, "Triall by Armes"
DuBose Heyward, "The Half Pint Flask"
James Hopper, "When It Happens"
Oliver LaFarge, II, "North Is Black"
Rose Wilder Lane, "Yarbwoman"
Meridel LeSueur, "Persephone"
J. P. Marquand, "Good Morning, Major"
Lyle Saxon, "Cane River"
John S. Sexton, "The Pawnshop"
Frank Shay, "Little Dombey"
Alan Sullivan, "In Portofino"
Raymond Weeks, "The Hound-Tuner of Callaway"
Owen Wister, "The Right Honorable the Strawberries"

1928

Frederick Hazlitt Brennan, "The Guardian Angel"
Louis Bromfield, "The Cat That Lived at the Ritz"
Katharine Brush, "Seven Blocks Apart"
Morley Callaghan, "A Country Passion"
Dorothy Canfield, "At the Sign of the Three Daughters"
Maria Christina Chambers, "John of God, The Water Carrier"
Irvin S. Cobb, "No Dam' Yankee"
Myles Connolly, "The First of Mr. Blue"
Walter D. Edmonds, "The Swamper"
Eleanor E. Harris, "Home to Mother's"
Llewellyn Hughes, "Lady Wipers—Of Ypres"
Fannie Hurst, "Give This Little Girl a Hand"
Edward L. McKenna, "Battered Armor"
Dorothy Parker, "A Telephone Call"
L. Paul [pseud.], "Fences"
Elizabeth Maddox Roberts, "On the Mountain-Side"
Edwin Seaver, "The Jew"
James Stevens, "The Romantic Sailor"
Ruth Suckow, "Midwestern Primitive"
Edmund Ware, "So-Long Oldtimer"

1929

Sarah Addington, "Hound of Heaven"
Sherwood Anderson, "The Lost Novel"
Ivan Beede, "The Country Doctor"
Konrad Bercovici, "There's Money in Poetry"
Morley Callaghan, "Soldier Harmon"
Willa Cather, "Double Birthday"
Grace Stone Coates, "Wild Plums"
Walter D. Edmonds, "Death of Red Peril"
James Webber Glover, "First Oboe"
James Norman Hall, "Fame for Mr. Beatty"
Leon Srabian Herald, "Power of Horizons"
MacGregor Jenkins, "Alcantara"
Margaret Leech, "Manicure"
Robert McAlmon, "Potato Picking"
Wilson McCarthy, "His Friend the Pig"
Edward L. McKenna, "I Have Letters for Marjorie"
Robert Mullen, "Light Without Heat"
Pernet Patterson, "Conjur"
Glenway Wescott, "Guilty Woman"
William Carlos Williams, "The Venus"

1930

Ellen Bishop, "Along a Sandy Road"
Clifford Bragdon, "Suffer Little Children"
Whit Burnett, "Two Men Free"
Morley Callaghan, "The Faithful Wife"
Grace Stone Coates, "The Way of the Transgressor"
Edythe Squier Draper, "The Voice of the Turtle"
Ruth Pine Furniss, "Answer"
Walter Gilkyson, "Blue Sky"
Caroline Gordon, "Summer Dust"
Emily Hahn, "Adventure"
Harry Hartwick, "Happiness Up the River"
Eleanor Hayden Kittredge, "September Sailing"
Manuel Komroff, "A Red Coat for Night"
Janet Lewis, "At the Swamp"
William March, "The Little Wife"
Dorothy Parker, "The Cradle of Civilization"
Gouverneur Paulding, "The White Pigeon"
William Polk, "The Patriot"
Katherine Anne Porter, "Theft"
William Hazlett Upson, "The Vineyard at Schloss Ramsburg"

1931

Louis Adamic, "The Enigma"
Solon R. Barber, "The Sound That Frost Makes"
Alvah C. Bessie, "Only We Are Barren"
Kay Boyle, "Rest Cure"
Louis Bromfield, "Tabloid News"
Whit Burnett, "Day in the Country"
Erskine Caldwell, "Dorothy"
Morley Callaghan, "The Young Priest!"
Walter D. Edmonds, "Water Never Hurt a Man"
William Faulkner, "That Evening Sun Go Down"
F. Scott Fitzgerald, "Babylon Revisited"
Marth Foley, "One With Shakespeare"
Guy Gilpatric, "The Flaming Chariot"
Emmett Gowen, "Fiddlers of Moon Mountain"
Josephine Herbst, "I Hear You, Mr. and Mrs. Brown"
Paul Horgan, "The Other Side of the Street"
William March, "Fifteen from Company K"
Don Marquis, "The Other Room"
George Milburn, "A Pretty Cute Little Stunt"
Dorothy Parker, "Here We Are"

Allen Read, "Rhodes Scholar"
James Stevens, "The Great Hunter of the Woods"
William Hazlett Upson, "The Model House"
Leo. L. Ward, "The Threshing Ring"
Anne Elizabeth Wilson, "The Miracle"
Lowry Charles Wimberly, "White Man's Town."

1932

Bill Adams, "The Foreigner"
Alvah C. Bessie, "Horizon"
Louis Brennan, "Poisoner in Motley"
Clifford Bragdon, "Love's So Many Things"
Wanda Burnett, "Sand"
Whit Burnett, "Sherrel"
Erskine Caldwell, "Warm River"
Morley Callaghan, "The Red Hat"
Helena Lefroy Caperton, "The Honest Wine
  Merchant"
John Cournos, "The Story of the Stranger"
David Cornel DeJong, "So Tall the Corn"
Andra Diefenthaler, "Hansel"
William Faulkner, "Smoke"
Manuel Komroff, "Napolcon's Hat under Glass"
Meridel LeSueur, "Spring Story"
Scammon Lockwood, "An Arrival At Carthage"
William March, "Mist On the Meadow"
George Milburn, "Heel, Toe, and a 1, 2, 3, 4"
Ira V. Morris, Jr., "The Kimono"
Peter Neagoe, "Shepherd of the Lord"
Dudley Schnabel, "Load"
Laurence Stallings, "Gentleman in Blue"
Bernhard Johann Tuting, "The Family Circle"
Jose Garcia Villa, "Untitled Story"
Leo L. Ward, "The Quarrel"

1933

George Albee, "Fame Takes the J Car"
Alvah C. Bessie, "A Little Walk"
John Peale Bishop, "Toadstools Are Poison"
Albert Truman Boyd, "Elmer"
Whit Burnett, "Serenade"
Ersskine Caldwell, "The First Autumn"
Morley Callaghan, "A Sick Call"
Robert Cantwell, "The Land of Plenty"
Charles Caldwell Dobie, "The Honey Pot"
Walter D. Edmonds, "Black Wolf"

James T. Farrell, "Helen, I Love You"
F. Scott Fitzgerald, "Crazy Sunday"
Grace Flandreau, "What Was Truly Mine"
Martha Foley, "Martyr"
Emmett Gowen, "Fisherman's Luck"
Nancy Hale, "Simple Aveu"
Albert Halper, "Going to Market"
Eugene Joffe, "In the Park"
Louise Lambertson, "Sleet Storm"
Grant Leenhouts, "The Facts in this Case"
George Milburn, "The Apostate"
Ira V. Morris, Jr., "The Sampler"
Lloyd Morris, "Footnote To a Life"
Katherine Anne Porter, "The Cracked Looking-
  Glass"
Louis Reed, "Episode At the Pawpaws"
Naomi Shumway, "Ike and Us Moons"
Wilbur Daniel Steele, "How Beautiful with Shoes"
Dorothy Thomas, "The Joybell"
Jose Garcia Vila, "The Fence"

1934

Benjamin Appel, "Winter Meeting"
Alvah C. Bessie, "No Final Word"
Whit Burnett, "The Cats Which Cried"
Erskine Caldwell, "Horse Thief"
Morley Callaghan, "Mr. and Mrs. Fairbanks"
Marquis W. Childs, "The Woman on the Shore"
Edwin Corle, "Amethyst"
Howard McKinley Corning, "Crossroads Woman"
William Faulkner, "Beyond"
Rudolph Fisher, "Miss Cynthie"
Martha Foley, "She Walks In Beauty"
Alexander Godin, "My Dead Brother Comes to
  America"
Caroline Gordon, "Tom Rivers"
Sirak Goryan, "The Broken Wheel"
James Norman Hall, "Lord of Marutea"
Langston Hughes, "Cora Unashamed"
Eugene Joffe, "Siege of Love"
Manuel Komroff, "Hamlet's Dagger"
John Lineaweaver, "Mother Tanner"
Dorothy McCleary, "Winter"
Louis Mamet, "The Pension"
William March, "This Heavy Load"

Alan Marshall, "Death and Transfiguration"
Paul Ryan, "The Sacred Thing"
Nahum Sabay, "In a Park"
Vincent Sheean, "The Hemlock Tree"
Richard Sherman, "Now There Is Peace"
Allen Tate, "The Immortal Woman"
Upton Terrell, "Money at Home"

1935

Benjamin Appel, "Outside Yuma"
Sally Benson, "The Overcoat"
Ernest Brace, "The Party Next Door"
Carlton Brown, "Suns That Our Hearts Harden"
Whit Burnett, "Division"
Erskine Caldwell, "The Cold Winter"
Morley Callaghan, "Father and Son"
Madelene Cole, "Bus to Biarritz"
Charles Cooke, "Triple Jumps"
David Cornel DeJong, "Home-Coming"
William Faulkner, "Lo!"
Elma Godschaux, "Wild Nigger"
Sara Haardt, "Little White Girl"
William Wister Haines, "Remarks: None"
Nancy Hale, "The Double House"
Paul Horgan, "A Distant Harbour"
Dorothy McCleary, "Sunday Morning"
Vincent McHugh, "Parish of Cockroaches"
Louis Mamet, "Episode from Life"
Alfred Morang, "Frozen Stillness"
Edita Morris, "Mrs. Lancaster-Jones"
William Saroyan, "Resurrection of a Life"
Allan Seager, "This Town and Salamanca"
Harry Sylvester, "A Boxer: Old"
Benedict Thielen, "Souvenir Of Arizona"
Max White, "A Pair Of Shoes"

1936

Roger Burlingame, "In the Cage"
Morley Callaghan, "The Blue Kimono"
Dorothy Canfield, "The Murder On Jefferson Street"
A. H. Z. Carr, "The Hunch"
Charles Cooke, "Catalfalque"
Evan Coombes, "The North Wind Doth Blow"
William Faulkner, "That Will Be Fine"
Michael Fessier, "That's What Happened To Me"

S. S. Field, "Torrent of Darkness"
Roy Flannagan, "The Doorstop"
Martha Foley, "Her Own Sweet Simplicity"
Walter Gilkyson, "Enemy Country"
Elizabeth Hall, "Two Words Are a Story"
Frank K. Kelly, "With Some Gaiety and Laughter"
Karlton Kelm, "Tinkle and Family Take a Ride"
Manuel Komroff, "That Blowzy Goddess Fame"
Erling Larsen, "A Kind of a Sunset"
Meridel LeSueur, "Annunciation"
Dorothy McCleary, "The Shroud"
Albert Maltz, "Man On a Road"
Katherine Anne Porter, "The Grave"
Roaldus Richmond, "Thanks for Nothing"
Allan Seager, "Fugue For Harmonica"
Tess Slesinger, "A Life in the Day of a Writer"
Elisabeth Wilkins Thomas, "Traveling Salesman"
Howell Vines, "The Mustydines Was Ripe"
Robert Whitehand, "American Nocturne"
Calvin Williams, "On the Sidewalk"
William E. Wilson, "The Lone Pioneer"

1937

Robert Buckner, "The Man Who Won the War"
Roger Burlingame, "The Last Equation"
Morley Callaghan, "The Voyage Out"
Charles Cooke, "Enter Daisy, To Her, Alexandra"
William Faulkner, "Fool About a Horse"
S. S. Field, "Goodbye To Cap'm John"
Martha Foley, "Glory, Glory, Hallelujah!"
Elma Godschaux, "Chains"
Albert Halper, "The Poet"
Ernest Hemingway, "The Snows of Kilimanjaro"
Edward Harris Heth, "Homecoming"
Paul Horgan, "The Surgeon and the Nun"
Manuel Komroff, "The Girl with the Flaxen Hair"
David E. Krantz, "Awakening and the Destination"
Harry Harrison Kroll, "Second Wife"
R. H. Linn, "The Intrigue of Mr. S. Yamamoto"
Ursula MacDougall, "Titty's Dead and Tatty Weeps"
Allen McGinnis, "Let Nothing You Dismay"
William March, "Maybe the Sun Will Shine"
Edita Morris, "A Blade of Grass"
Ira V. Morris, Jr., "Marching Orders"
Katherine Anne Porter, "The Old Order"

Ellis St. Joseph, "A Passenger To Bali"
William Saroyan, "The Crusader"
Jesse Stuart, "Hair"
Benedict Thielen, "Lieutenant Pearson"
Lovell Thompson, "The Iron City"

1938

Robert Ayre, "Mr. Sycamore"
Libby Benedict, "Blind Man's Buff"
Stephen Vincent Benet, "A Tooth for Paul Revere"
Nelson S. Bond, "Mr. Mergenthwirker's Lobblies"
Morley Callaghan, "The Cheat's Remorse"
John Cheever, "Three Brothers"
Vladimir Cherkasski, "What Hurts Is That I Was in a Hurry"
Whitfield Cook, "Dear Mr. Flessheimer"
Richard Paulett Creyke, "Niggers Are Such Liars"
Pietro DiDonato, "Christ In Concrete"
Michael Fessier, "Black Wind and Lightning"
Alberta Pierson Hannum, "Turkey Hunt"
Manuel Komroff, "The Whole World Is Outside"
Meridel LeSueur, "The Girl"
Don Ludlow, "She Always Wanted Shoes"
Dorothy McCleary, "Little Bride"
William March, "The Last Meeting"
Elick Moll, "To Those Who Wait"
Prudentio De Pereda, "The Spaniard"
Frederic Prokosch, "A Russian Idyll"
George Thorp Rayner, "A Real American Fellow"
Elizabeth Maddox Roberts, "The Haunted Palace"
Mark Schorer, "Boy in the Summer Sun"
Allan Seager, "Pro Arte"
John Steinbeck, "The Chrysanthemums"
Jesse Stuart, "Huey, the Engineer"
Harvey B. Swados, "The Amateurs"
Robert Penn Warren, "Christmas Gift"
Eudora Welty, "Lily Daw and the Three Ladies"

1939

Warren Beck, "The Blue Sash"
Ronald Caldwell, "Vision in the Sea"
Morley Callaghan, "It Had to Be Done"
John Cheever, "Frere Jacques"
Gean Clark, "Indian on the Road"
Robert M. Coates, "Passing Through"
David L. Cohn, "Black Troubadour"

Richard Ely Danielson, "Corporal Hardy"
Hal Ellson, "The Rat Is a Mouse"
Albert Halper, "Prelude"
Paul Horgan, "To the Mountains"
Madge Jenison, "True Believer"
Manuel Komroff, "What Is a Miracle?"
Meridel LeSueur, "Salutation to Spring"
Alan MacDonald, "An Arm Upraised"
Albert Maltz, "The Happiest Man on Earth"
Ellis St. Joseph, "Leviathan"
William Saroyan, "Piano"
Walter Schoenstedt, "The Girl from the River Barge"
Allan Seager, "Berkshire Comedy"
Michael Seide, "Bad Boy from Brooklyn"
Jesse Stuart, "Eustacia"
Harry Sylvester, "The Crazy Guy"
Benedict Thielen, "The Thunderstorm"
Robert Penn Warren, "How Willie Proudfit Came Home"
Heinz Werner, "Black Tobias and the Empire"
Eudora Welty, "A Curtain of Green"

1940

Kay Boyle, "Anschluss"
Erskine Caldwell, "The People vs. Abe Lathan, Colored"
Morley Callaghan, "Getting On in the World"
Frances Eisenberg, "Roof Sitter"
James T. Farrell, "The Fall of Machine Gun McGurk"
William Faulkner, "Hand Upon the Waters"
F. Scott Fitzgerald, "Design in Plaster"
Caroline Gordon, "Frankie and Thomas and Bud Asbury"
Ernest Hemingway, "Under the Ridge"
Mary King, "The Honey House"
Manuel Komroff, "Death Of an Outcast"
Roderick Lull, "That Fine Place We Had Last Year"
Emilio Lussu, "Your General Does Not Sleep"
Dorothy McCleary, "Something Jolly"
Edita Morris, "Kullan"
Ira V. Morris, Jr., "The Beautiful Fire"
P. M. Pasinetti, "Family History"
Prudentio De Pereda, "The Way Death Comes"

James Pooler, "Herself"

Katherine Anne Porter, "The Downward Path to Wisdom"

William Saroyan, "The Presbyterian Choir Singers"

Michel Seide, "Words Without Music"

Irwin Shaw, "Main Currents Of American Thought"

George Slocombe, "The Seven Men Of Rouen"

Morton Stern, "Four Worms Turning"

Hans Otto Storm, "The Two Deaths of Kaspar Rausch"

Jesse Stuart, "Rich Men"

Harry Sylvester, "Beautifully and Bravely"

Benedict Thielen, "Night and the Lost Armies"

Eudora Welty, "The Hitch-Hikers"

1941

E. B. Ashton, "Shadow of a Girl"

Stephen Vincent Benét, "All Around the Town"

Erskine Caldwell, "Handy"

Morley Callaghan, "Big Jules"

Robert M. Coates, "The Net"

David Cornel DeJong, "Mama Is Lady"

Henry Exall, "To the Least. . . ."

John Fante, "A Nun No More"

William Faulkner, "Gold Is Not Always"

Harold Garfinkle, "Color Trouble"

Felicia Gizycka, "The Magic Wire"

Justin Herman, "Smile For the Man, Dear"

Weldon Kees, "The Life Of the Mind"

Mary King, "The White Bull"

Arthur Kober, "Some People Are Just Plumb Crazy"

Christopher LaFarge, "Scorn and Comfort"

Meyer Levin, "The System Was Doomed"

Roderick Lull, "Don't Get Me Wrong"

Albert Maltz, "Sunday Morning on Twentieth Street"

Peter Neagoe, "Ill-Winds From the Wide World"

William Saroyan, "The Three Swimmers and the Educated Grocer"

Irwin Shaw, "Triumph of Justice"

Wilma Shore, "The Butcher"

Wallace Stegner, "Goin To Town"

Jesse Stuart, "Love"

Benedict Thielen, "The Psychologist"

Jerome Weidman, "Houdini"

George Weller, "Strip-Tease"

1942

Nelson Algren, "Biceps"

Ludwig Bemelmans, "The Valet of the Splendide"

Sally Benson, "5135 Kensington: August, 1903"

Kay Boyle, "Nothing Ever Breaks Except the Heart"

Jack Y. Bryan, "For Each of Us"

Walter Van Tillburg Clark, "The Portable Phonograph"

David Cornel DeJong, "That Frozen Hour"

Boyce Eakin, "Prairies"

Morton Fineman, "Tell Him I Waited"

Robert Gibbons, "A Loaf of Bread"

Nancy Hale, "Those Are as Brothers"

MacKinlay Kantor, "That Greek Dog"

Eric Knight, "Sam Small's Better Half"

Mary Lavin, "At Sallygap"

Mary Medearis, "Death of a Country Doctor"

Edita Morris, "Caput Mortuum"

Mary O'Hara, "My Friend Flicka"

Margaret Rhodes Peattie, "The Green Village"

William Saroyan, "The Hummingbird That Lived Through Winter"

Budd Wilson Schulberg, "The Real Viennese Roast"

Michael Seide, "Sacrifice of Isaac"

Irwin Shaw, "Search Through the Streets of the City"

Wallace Stegner, "In the Twilight"

John Steinbeck, "How Edith McGillcuddy Met R. L. Stevenson"

Jesse Stuart, "The Storm"

Peter Taylor, "The Fancy Woman"

Jean Thompson, "My Pigeon Pair"

James Thurber, "You Could Look It Up"

Joan Vatsek, "The Bees"

1943

Vicki Baum, "This Healthy Life"

Warren Beck, "Boundary Line"

Kay Boyle, "Frenchman's Ship"

John Cheever, "The Pleasures of Solitude"

Guido D'Agostino, "The Dream of Angelo Zara"

Murray Dyer, "Samuel Blane"

William Faulkner, "The Bear"

Rachel Field, "Beginning of Wisdom"

Vardis Fisher, "A Partnership with Death"

Grace Flandreau, "What Do You See, Dear Enid?"
Robert Gibbons, "Time's End"
Peter Gray, "Threnody for Stelios"
Nancy Hale, "Who Lived and Died Believing"
Paul Horgan, "The Peach Stone"
Laurette MacDuffie Knight, "The Enchanted"
Clara Laidlaw, "The Little Black Boys"
Mary Lavin, "Love Is for Lovers"
Edita Morris, "Young Man In an Astrakhan Cap"
William Saroyan, "Knife-Like, Flower-Like, Like Nothing At All In the World"
Delmore Schwartz, "An Argument In 1934"
Irwin Shaw, "Preach on the Dusty Roads"
Margaret Shedd, "My Public"
Wallace Stegner, "Chips Off the Old Block"
Alison Stuart, "Death and My Uncle Felix"
Jesse Stuart, "Dawn of Remembered Spring"
Richard Sullivan, "The Women"
James Thurber, "The Catbird Seat"
Jessie Treichler, "Homecoming"
Jerome Weidman, "Philadelphia Express"
Eudora Welty, "Asphodel"

1944

Sidney Alexander, "The White Boat"
William E. Barrett, "Senor Payroll"
Saul Bellow, "Notes Of a Dangling Man"
Dorothy Canfield, "The Knot Hole"
Elizabeth Eastman, "Like a Field Mouse over the Heart"
Helen Eustis, "The Good Days and the Bad"
William Fifeld, "The Fishermen of Patzcuaro"
Berry Fleming, "Strike Up a Stirring Music"
Hazel Hawthorne, "More Like a Coffin"
Noel Houston, "Local Skirmish"
Shirley Jackson, "Come Dance with Me in Ireland"
Josephine W. Johnson, "The Rented Room"
H. J. Kaplan, "The Mohammedans"
Eyre De Lanux, "The S. S. Libertad"
Carson McCullers, "The Ballad of the Sad Cafe"
William March, "The Female of the Fruit Fly"
Astrid Meighan, "Shoe the Horse and Shoe the Mare"
Mary Mian, "Exiles from the Creuse"
Edita Morris, "Heart of Marzipan"

Vladimir Nabokov, "That in Aleppo Once. . . ."
Ruth Portugal, "Neither Here Nor There"
J. F. Powers, "Lions, Harts, Leaping Does"
Gladys Schmitt, "All Souls"
Irwin Shaw, "The Veterans Reflect"
George Stiles, "A Return"
Leon Z. Surmelian, "My Russian Cap"
Lionel Trilling, "Of This Time, Of That Place"
Elizabeth Warner, "An Afternoon"
Jessamyn West, "The Illumination"
Emmanuel Winters, "God's Agents Have Beards"

1945

Nelson Algren, "How the Devil Came Down Division Street"
Warren Beck, "The First Fish"
Louis Bromfield, "Crime Passionnel"
Carlos Bulosan, "My Brother Osong's Career in Politics"
Mary Deasy, "Harvest"
Edward Fenton, "Burial in the Desert"
Morton Fineman, "The Light of Morning"
Bill Gerry, "Understand What I Mean?"
Brendan Gill, "The Test"
Richard Hagopian, "Be Heavy"
Emily Hahn, "It Never Happened"
W. G. Hardy, "The Czech Dog"
Josephine W. Johnson, "Fever Flower"
Robert McLaughlin, "Poor Everybody"
John McNulty, "Don't Scrub Off These Names"
Warren Miller, "The Animal's Fair"
George Panetta, "Papa, Mama and Economics"
Joseph Stanley Pennell, "On the Way to Somewhere Else"
Ruth Portugal, "Call a Solemn Assembly"
Theodore Pratt, "The Owl That Kept Winking"
Isaac Rosenfeld, "The Hand That Fed Me"
Donna Rowell, "A War Marriage"
Gladys Schmitt, "The Mourners"
Irwin Shaw, "Gunners' Passage"
Jean Stafford, "The Wedding: Beacon Hill"
Ruby Pickens Tartt, "Alabama Sketches"
Peter Tylor, "Rain In the Heart"
Robert Penn Warren, "Cass Mastern's Wedding Ring"
Jessamyn West, "First Day Finish"

1946

Charles Angoff, "Jerry"
Warren Beck, "Out of Line"
John Berryman, "The Lovers"
Ray Bradbury, "The Big Black and White Game"
Bessie Breuer, "Bury Your Own Dead"
T. K. Brown, III, "The Valley of the Shadow"
W. R. Burnett, "The Ivory Tower"
Walter Van Tilburg Clark, "The Wind and the Snow of Winter"
Laurence Critchell, "Flesh and Blood"
Mary Deasy, "A Sense of Danger"
Samuel Elkin, "In a Military Manner"
Elaine Gottlieb, "The Norm"
Elizabeth Hardwick, "The Mysteries of Eleusis"
Josephine W. Johnson, "Story Without End"
Ben Hur Lampman, "Old Bill Bent to Drink"
Meyer Liben, "The Caller"
A. J. Liebling, "Run, Run, Run, Run"
W. D. Mitchell, "The Owl and the Bens"
Vladimir Nabokov, "Time and Ebb"
Ann Petry, "Like a Winding Sheet"
Wentzle Ruml, III, "For a Beautiful Relationship"
Gladys Schmitt, "The King's Daughter"
Irwin Stark, "The Bridge"
James Stern, "The Woman"
Peter Taylor, "The Scout Masters"
Lionel Trilling, "The Other Margaret"
Henrietta Weigel, "Love Affair"
Jessamyn West, "The Singing Lesson"

1947

Francis L. Broderick, "Return by Faith"
Dorothy Canfield, "Sex Education"
Truman Capote, "The Headless Hawk"
Robert Fontaine, "Day of Gold and Darkness"
Adelaide Gerstley, "The Man In the Mirror"
John B. L. Goodwin, "The Cocoon"
John Mayo Goss, "Bird Song"
Paul Griffith, "The Horse Like September"
Albert J. Guerard, "Turista"
Elizabeth Hardwick, "The Golden Stallion"
Ruth McCoy Harris, "Up the Road a Piece"
Thomas Heggen, "Night Watch"
Edward Harris Heth, "Under the Ginkgo Trees"

John Richard Humphreys, "Michael Finney and the Little Men"
Victoria Lincoln, "Down in the Reeds By the River"
Robert Lowry, "Little Baseball World"
May Davies Martenet, "Father Delacroix"
Jane Mayhall, "The Darkness"
J. F. Powers, "Prince of Darkness"
Samson Raphaelson, "The Greatest Idea in the World"
Mark Schorer, "What We Don't Know Hurts Us"
Allan Seager, "Game Chicken"
Irwin Shaw, "Act of Faith"
Sylvia Shirley, "The Red Dress"
Jean Stafford, "The Interior Castle"
Irwin Stark, "Shock Treatment"
Wallace Stegner, "The Women on the Wall"
Noccolo Tucci, "The Siege"
John D. Weaver, "Bread and Games"
Lawrence Williams, "The Hidden Room"

1948

Sidney Alexander, "Part of the Act"
Paul Bowles, "A Distant Episode"
Ray Bradbury, "I See You Never"
Dorothy Canfield, "The Apprentice"
John Cheever, "The Enormous Radio"
John Bell Clayton, "Visitor from Philadelphia"
George R. Clay, "That's My Johnny-Boy"
Margaret Cousins, "A Letter to Mr. Priest"
M. F. K. Fisher, "The Hollow Heart"
Philip Garrigan, "Fly, Fly, Little Dove"
Martha Gellhorn, "Miami—New York"
Elliott Grennard, "Sparrow's Last Jump"
Ralph Gustafson, "The Human Fly"
John Hersey, "Why Were You Sent Out There?"
Lance Jeffers, "The Dawn Swings In"
Victoria Lincoln, "Morning, A Week Before the Crime"
Robert Lowry, "The Terror in the Streets"
John A. Lynch, "The Burden"
Vincent McHugh, "The Search"
Robert Morse, "The Professor and the Puli"
Ruth Portugal, "The Stupendous Fortune"
Mary Brinker Post, "That's the Man!"
Waverly Root, "Carmencita"

Dolph Sharp, "The Tragedy in Jancie Brierman's Life"
Wallace Stegner, "Beyond the Glass Mountain"
Sidney Sulkin, "The Plan"
Eudora Welty, "The Whole World Knows"
E. B. White, "The Second Tree From the Corner"

1949

George Albee, "Mighty, Mighty Pretty"
Livingston Biddle, Jr., "The Vacation"
Elizabeth Bishop, "The Farmer's Children"
Paul Bowles, "Under the Sky"
Frank Brookhouser, "My Father and the Circus"
Borden Deal, "Exodus"
Adele Dolokhov, "Small Miracle"
Ward Dorrance, "The White Hound"
Henry Gregor Felsen, "Li Chang's Million"
Robert Gibbons, "Departure of Husband"
Beatrice Griffith, "In the Flow of Time"
Elizabeth Hartwick, "Evenings at Home"
Joseph Heller, "Castle of Snow"
Ruth Herschberger, "A Sound in the Night"
Laura Hunter, "Jerry"
Jim Kjelgaard, "Of the River and Uncle Pidcock"
Roderick Lull, "Footnote to American History"
T. D. Mabry, "The Vault"
Agnes MacDonald, "Vacia"
Jane Mayhall, "The Men"
Patrick Morgan, "The Heifer"
Irving Pfeffer, "All Prisoners Here"
John Rogers, "Episode of a House Remembered"
J. D. Salinger, "A Girl I Knew"
Alfredo Seagre, "Justice Has No Number"
Madelon Shapiro, "An Island for My Friends"
Jean Stafford, "Children Are Bored on Sunday"
Jessamyn West, "Road to the Isles"

1950

Charles Angoff, "Where Did Yesterday Go?"
James Aswell, "Shadow of Evil"
Sanora Babb, "The Wild Flower"
Warren Beck, "Edge of Doom"
Saul Bellow, "A Sermon by Doctor Pep"
Peggy Bennett, "Death under the Hawthornes"
Paul Bowles, "Pastor Down at Tacate"
Robert Christopher, "Jishin"

George P. Elliott, "The NRACP"
Leslie A. Fiedler, "The Fear of Innocence"
Ralph Gustafson, "The Pigeon"
Josephine W. Johnson, "The Author"
Ralph Kaplan, "The Artist"
Sylvan Karchmer, "Hail Brother and Farewell"
Speed Lamkin, "Comes a Day"
Victoria Lincoln, "The Glass Wall"
Esther McCoy, "The Cape"
Howard Maier, "The World Outside"
Edward Newhouse, "My Brother's Second Funeral"
Hoke Norris, "Take Her Up Tenderly"
Glidden Parker, "Bright and Morning"
Clay Putman, "The Old Acrobat and the Ruined City"
Abraham Rothberg, "Not with Our Fathers"
Ramona Stewart, "The Promise"
James Still, "A Master Time"
Joan Strong, "The Hired Man"
Peter Taylor, "A Wife of Nashville"

1951

Roger Angell, "Flight Through the Dark"
Nathan Asch, "Inland, Western Sea"
Peggy Bennet, "A Fugitive from the Mind"
Mary Bolte, "The End of the Depression"
Hortense Calisher, "In Greenwich There Are Many Gravelled Walks"
Leonard Casper, "Sense of Direction"
R. V. Cassill, "Larchmoor Is Not the World"
John Cheever, "The Season of Divorce"
Harris Downey, "The Hunters"
Elizabeth Enright, "The Temperate Zone"
J. Carol Goodman, "The Kingdom of Gordon"
Ethel Edison Gordon, "The Value of the Dollar"
William Goyen, "Her Breath Upon the Windowpane"
Shirley Jackson, "The Summer People"
Josephine W. Johnson, "The Mother's Story"
Ilona Karmel, "Fru Holm"
Oliver LaFarge, "Old Century's River"
George Lanning, "Old Turkey Neck"
Ethel G. Lewis, "Portrait"
Dorothy Livesay, "The Glass House"
Robie Macauley, "The Wishbone"

Bernard Malamud, "The Prison"
Esther Patt, "The Butcherbirds"
J. F. Powers, "Death of a Favorite"
Paul Rader, "The Tabby Cat"
Jean Stafford, "The Nemesis"
Ray B. West, Jr., "The Last of the Grizzly Bears"
Tennessee Williams, "The Resemblance Between a Violin Case and a Coffin"

1952

Bill Berge, "That Lovely Green Boat"
Robert O. Bowen, "The Other Side"
Kay Boyle, "The Lost"
Ray Bradbury, "The Other Foot"
Hortense Calisher, "A Wreath for Miss Totten"
Nancy Cardozo, "The Unborn Ghosts"
Nancy G. Chaikin, "The Climate of the Family"
Ann Chidester, "Wood Smoke"
Charles Edward Eaton, "The Motion of Forgetfulness Is Slow"
George P. Elliott, "Children Of Ruth"
Elizabeth Enright, "The First Face"
Hugh Garner, "The Conversion of Willie Heaps"
Martha Gellhorn, "Weekend at Grimsby"
Emilie Glen, "Always Good for a Belly Laugh"
Nancy Hale, "Brahmin Beachhead"
Philip Horton, "What's in a Corner"
Susan Kuehn, "The Searchers"
Bethel Laurence, "The Call"
Frank Rooney, "Cyclists' Raid"
William Saroyan, "Palo"
Stuart Schulberg, "I'm Really Fine"
Jean Stafford, "The Healthiest Girl in Town"
Walla Stegner, "The Traveler"
James Still, "A Ride on the Short Dog"
Harvey B. Swados, "The Letters"
Mark Van Doren, "Nobody Say a Word"
Daniel Waldron, "Evensong"
Christine Weston, "Loud Sing Cuckoo"

1953

James Agee, "A Mother's Tale"
James Ballard, "A Mountain Summer"
Stephen Becker, "The Town Mouse"
Joseph Carroll, "At Mrs. Farrelly's"
R. V. Cassill, "The Life of the Sleeping Beauty"

Robert M. Coates, "The Need"
Mary Deasy, "Morning Sun"
Harris Downey, "Crispin's Way"
Osborn Duke, "Struttin' with Some Barbecue"
George P. Elliott, "Faq"
Wingate Frosher, "A Death in the Family"
Vahan Krikorian Gregory, "Athens, Greece, 1942"
James B. Hall, "A Spot in History"
Charles Jackson, "The Buffalo Wallow"
Roberts Jackson, "Fly Away Home"
Madison P. Jones, J., "Dog Days"
Willard Marsh, "Beachhead in Bohemia"
Elizabeth Marshall, "The Hill People"
Felix Noland, "The Whipping"
Constance Pendergast, "The Picnic"
Ken Purdy, "Change of Plan"
Clay Putman, "Our Vegetable Life"
Roger Shattuck, "Workout on the River"
Henry Shultz, "Oreste"
Stanley Sultan, "The Fugue of the Fig Tree"
Mark Van Doren, "Still, Still So"
Donld Wesely, "A Week of Roses"
Christine Weston, "The Forest of the Night"
Tennessee Williams, "Three Players of a Summer Game"
Simon Wincelberg, "The Conqueror"

1954

Geoffrey Bush, "A Great Reckoning in a Little Room"
Richard Clay, "A Beautiful Night for Orion"
Benjamin DeMott, "The Sense That in the Scene Delights"
Ward Dorrance, "A Stop on the Way to Texas"
LeGarde S. Doughty, "The Firebird"
Elizabeth Enright, "Apple Seed and Apple Thorn"
Steve Frazee, "My Brother Down There"
Ivan Gold, "A Change of Air"
Priscilla Heath, "Farewell, Sweet Love"
Anne Hebert, "The House on the Esplanade"
Frank Holwerda, "Char on Raven's Bench"
Randall Jarrell, "Gertrude and Sidney"
Almet Jenks, "No Way Down"
George Loveridge, "The Latter End"
Frances Gray Patton, "The Game"

Robert Payne, "The Red Mountain"
Rosanne Smith Robinson, "The Mango Tree"
Irwin Shaw, "In the French Style"
Jean Stafford, "The Shorn Lamb"
Kressmann Taylor, "The Pale Green Fishes"
B. Traven, "The Third Guest"
Christine Weston, "The Man in Gray"

1955

Robert O. Bowen, "A Matter of Price"
Nancy Cardozo, "The Excursionists"
Nancy G. Chaikin, "Bachelor of Arts"
John Cheever, "The Country Husband"
Joe Coogan, "The Decline and Fall of Augie
    Sheean"
Evan S. Connell, Jr., "The Fisherman from
    Chihuahua"
Daniel Curley, "The Day of the Equinox"
William Eastlake, "Little Joe"
George P. Elliott, "Brother Quintillian and Dick the
    Chemist"
Mac Hyman, "The Hundredth Centennial"
Oliver LaFarge, "The Resting Place"
Bernard Malamud, "The Magic Barrel"
Judith Merril, "Dead Center"
Elizabeth H. Middleton, "Portrait of My Son as a
    Young Man"
Marvin Mudrick, "The Professor and the Poet"
Howard Nemerov, "Yore"
Flannery O'Connor, "A Circle in the Fire"
Irwin Shaw, "Tip on a Dead Jockey"
Wallace Stegner, "Maiden in a Tower"
David Stuart, "Bird Man"
Harvey B. Swados, "Herman's Day"
Mark Van Doren, "I Got a Friend"
George Vukelich, "The Scale Room"
Eudora Welty, "Going to Naples"

1956

Roger Angell, "In an Early Winter"
Morris Brown, "The Snow Owl"
George R. Clay, "We're All Guests"
Robert M. Coates, "In a Foreign City"
Wesley Ford Davis, "The Undertow"
Ward Dorrance, "The Devil on a Hot Afternoon"
Harris Downey, "The Hobo"

William Eastlake, "The Quiet Chimneys"
George P. Elliott, "Is He Dead?"
Arthur Granit, "Free the Canaries from Their Cages!"
Marjorie Anais Housepian, "How Levon Dai Was
    Surrendered to the Edemuses"
Shirley Jackson, "One Ordinary Day, With Peanuts"
Jack Kerouac, "The Mexican Girl"
Nathaniel LaMar, "Creole Love Song"
Augusta Wallace Lyons, "The First Flower"
Ruth Branning Molloy, "Twenty Below, At the End
    of a Lane"
Flannery O'Connor, "The Artificial Nigger"
Philip Roth, "The Contest for Aaron Gold"
John Shepley, "The Machine"
Christine Weston, "Four Annas"

1957

Nelson Algren, "Beasts of the Wild"
Gina Berriault, "Around the Dear Ruin"
Doris Betts, "The Proud and Virtuous"
Wyatt Blassington, "Man's Courage"
Frank Butler, "To the Wilderness I Wander"
Walter Clemons, "The Dark Roots of the Rose"
Evan S. Connell, Jr., "Arcturus"
Harris Downey, "The Song"
William Eastlake, "The Unhappy Hunting
    Grounds"
Nancy Hale, "A Summer's Long Dream"
John Langdon, "The Blue Serge Suit"
Thomas Mabry, "Lula Borrow"
Winona McClintic, "A Heart of Furious Fancies"
Flannery O'Connor, "Greenleaf"
Tillie Olsen, "I Stand Here Ironing"
Anthony Robinson, "The Farlow Express"
Rosanne Smith Robinson, "The Impossible He"
Henrietta Weigel, "Saturday Is a Poor Man's Port"

1958

James Agee, "The Waiting"
James Baldwin, "Sonny's Blues"
Paul Bowles, "The Frozen Fields"
Ray Bradbury, "The Day That It Rained Forever"
George Bradshaw, "The Picture Wouldn't Fit in the
    Stove"
Alfred Chester, "As I Was Going Up the Stair"
Shirley Ann Grau, "Hunter's Home"

Pati Hill, "Ben"
Robie Macauley, "Legend Of Two Swimmers"
Jean McCord, "Somewhere Out of Nowhere"
Howard Nemerov, "A Delayed Hearing"
Flannery O'Connor, "A View of the Woods"
Anthony Ostroff, "La Bataille des Fleurs"
Dorothy Parker, "The Banquet of Crow"
Ralph Robin, "Mr. Pruitt"
Jean Stafford, "A Reasonable Facsimile"
Harvey B. Swados, "Joe, the Vanishing American"
Richard Thurman, "Not Another Word"
Bob Van Scoyk, "Home from Camp"
Robin White, "House of Many Rooms"

1959

John Berry, "Jawaharial and the Three Cadavers"
Sallie Bingham, "Winter Term"
Frank Butler, "Amid a Place of Stone"
John Cheever, "The Bella Lingua"
Robert M. Coates, "Getaway"
Charles G. Finney, "The Iowan's Curse"
William H. Gass, "Mrs. Mean"
Hugh Geeslin, Jr., "A Day In the Life of the Boss"
Herbert Gold, "Love and Like"
Frank Holwerda, "In Tropical Minor Key"
Bernard Malamud, "The Last Mohican"
Howard Nemerov, "A Secret Society"
Leo Rosten, "The Guy in Ward 4"
Philip Roth, "The Conversion of the Jews"
Anne Sayre, "A Birthday Present"
John Campbell Smith, "Run, Run Away, Brother"
Harvey B. Swados, "The Man in the Toolhouse"
Peter Taylor, "Venus, Cupid, Folly and Time"
John Updike, "Gift from the City"
Thomas Williams, "The Buck in Trotevale's"
Ethel Wilson, "The Window"

1960

Sanora Babb, "The Santa Ana"
Stanley Ellin, "The Day of the Bullet"
George P. Elliott, "Words, Words, Words"
Howard Fast, "The Man Who Looked Like Jesus"
Mavis Gallant, "August"
George Garrett, "An Evening Performance"
John Graves, "The Last Running"
Lawrence Sargent Hall, "The Ledge"

Elizabeth Hardwick, "The Purchase"
Lachlan MacDonald, "The Hunter"
Bernard Malamud, "The Maid's Shoes"
Arthur Miller, "I Don't Need You Any More"
Howard Nemerov, "Unbelievable Characters"
Phyllis Roberts, "Hero"
Philip Roth, "Defender of Our Faith"
Theodore Sturgeon, "The Man Who Lost the Sea"
Peter Taylor, "Who Was Jesse's Friend and Protector?"
Harvey B. Swados, "A Glance in the Mirror"

1961

James Baldwin, "This Morning, This Evening, So Soon"
John Berry, "The Listener"
Alfred Chester, "Berceuse"
William H. Gass, "The Love and Sorrow of Henry Pimber"
Ivan Gold, "The Nickel Misery of George Washington Carver Brown"
William Goyen, "A Tale of Inheritance"
Mark Harris, "The Self-Made Brain Surgeon"
Kaatje Hurlbut, "The Vestibule"
Theodore Jacobs, "A Girl for Walter"
Mary Lavin, "The Yellow Beret"
Jack Ludwig, "Confusions"
St. Clair McKelway, "First Marriage"
Willard Marsh, "Mexican Hayride"
Jeannie Olive, "Society"
Tillie Olsen, "Tell Me a Riddle"
William Peden, "Night in Funland"
Thomas Pynchon, "Entropy"
Samuel Sandmel, "The Colleagues of Mr. Chips"
Peter Taylor, "Miss Leonora When Last Seen"
Ellington White, "The Perils of Flight"

1962

Frieda Arkin, "The Light of the Sea"
Wayson S. Choy, "The Sound of Waves"
Edward Dahlberg, "Because I Was Flesh"
Bordon Deal, "Antaeus"
Stanley Elkin, "Criers and Kibbitzers, Kibbitzers and Criers"
Seymour Epstein, "Wheat Closed Higher, "Cotton Was Mixed"
George Garrett, "The Old Army Game"

William H. Gass, "The Pedersen Kid"
Sister Mary Gilbert, "The Model Chapel"
Donald Hall, "A Day On Ragged"
Henia Karmel-Wolfe, "The Last Day"
Mary Lavin, "In the Middle of the Fields"
Jack Thomas Leahy, "Hanging Hair"
Miriam McKenzie, "Déjà Vu"
Ben Maddow, "To Hell the Rabbis"
Arthur Miller, "The Prophecy"
E. Lucas Myers, "The Vindication of Dr. Nestor"
Flannery O'Connor, "Everything That Rises Must
    Converge"
Thalia Selz, "The Education of Queen"
Irwin Shaw, "Love on a Dark Street"
John Updike, "Pigeon Feathers"

1963
U. S. Andersen, "Turn Ever So Quickly"
H. W. Blattner, "Sound of a Drunken Drummer"
John Stewart Carter, "The Keyhole Eye"
John Cheever, "A Vision of the World"
Cecil Dawkins, "A Simple Case"
George Dickerson, "Chico"
May Dikeman, "The Sound of Young Laughter"
Stanley Elkin, "I Look Out for Ed Wolfe"
Dave Godfrey, "Newfoundland Night"
William J. J. Gordon, "The Pures"
John Hermann, "Aunt Mary"
Katinka Loeser, "Beggarman, Rich Man, or Thief"
St. Clair McKelway, "The Fireflies"
Ursule Molinaro, "The Insufficient Rope"
Joyce Carol Oates, "The Fine White Mist of Winter"
R. C. Phelan, "Birds, Clouds, Frogs"
Mordecai Richler, "Some Grist For Mervyn's Mill"
William Saroyan, "What a World, Said the Bicycle
    Rider"
Babette Sassoon, "The Betrayal"
Irwin Shaw, "Noises in the City"
Peter Taylow, "At the Drugstore"
Noccolo Tucci, "The Desert in the Oasis"
Jessamyn West, "The Picnickers"

1964
Frieda Arkin, "The Broomstick on the Porch"
Richard G. Brown, "Mr. Iscariot"
John Stewart Carter, "To a Tenor Dying Old"

Daniel Curley, "A Story of Love, Etc."
May Dikeman, "The Woman Across the Street"
William Eastlake, "A Long Day's Dying"
William Goyen, "Figure over the Town"
Paul Horgan, "Black Snowflakes"
William Humphrey, "The Pump"
Shirley Jackson, "Birthday Party"
Edith Konecky, "The Power"
Kimon Lolos, "Mule No. 095"
Carson McCullers, "Sucker"
Bernard Malamud, "The German Refugee"
Virginia Moriconi, "Simple Arithmetic"
Joyce Carol Oates, "Upon the Sweeping Flood"
Reynolds Price, "The Names and Faces Of Heroes"
Vera Randall, "Waiting For Jim"
Harvey B. Swados, "A Story for Teddy"
Robert Penn Warren, "Have You Seen Sukie?"

1965
L. J. Amster, "Center of Gravity"
Daniel DePaola, "The Returning"
Stanley Elkin, "The Transient"
Jack Gilchrist, "Opening Day"
James W. Groshong, "The Gesture"
Martin J. Hamer, "Sarah"
Maureen Howard, "Sherry"
Donald Hutter, "A Family Man"
Henia Karmel-Wolfe, "The Month of His Birthday"
Mary Lavin, "Heart of Gold"
Dennis Lynds, "A Blue Blonde in the Sky Over
    Pennsylvania"
Frederic Morton, "The Guest"
Jay Neugeboren, "The Application"
Joyce Carol Oates, "First Views of the Enemy"
Leonard Wallace Robinson, "The Practice of an Art"
Isaac Bashevis Singer, "A Sacrifice"
Robert Somerlott, "Eskimo Pies"
Elizabeth Spencer, "The Visit"
Jean Stafford, "The Tea Time of Stouthearted
    Ladies"
Gerald Stein, "For I Have Wept"
Peter Taylor, "There"

1966
Jack Cady, "The Burning"
George Dickerson, "A Mussel Named Ecclesiastes"

Harris Downey, "The Vicar-General and the Wide Night"
David Ely, "The Academy"
William Faulkner, "Mr. Acarius"
Shirley Ann Grau, "The Beach Party"
Mary Hedin, "Places We Lost"
Hugh Hood, "Getting to Williamstown"
Shirley Jackson, "The Bus"
Josephine Jacobsen, "On the Island"
Henry Kreisel, "The Broken Globe"
Mary Lavin, "One Summer"
Curt Leviant, "Mourning Call"
William Maxwell, "Further Tales about Men and Women"
Flannery O'Connor, "Parker's Back"
Abraham Rothberg, "Pluto Is the Furthest Place"
Walter S. Terry, "The Bottomless Well"
Dan Wakefield, "Autumn Full of Apples"
Joseph Whitehill, "One Night for Several Samurai"
Herbert Wilner, "Dovisch in the Wilderness"

1967

Ethan Ayer, "The Promise of Heat"
George Blake, "A Place Not on the Map"
Kay Boyle, "The Wild Horses"
Raymond Carver, "Will You Please Be Quiet, Please?"
H. E. Francis, "One of the Boys"
McDonald Harris, "Trepleff"
Robert Hazel, "White Anglo-Saxon Protestant"
Hugh Allyn Hunt, "Acme Rooms and Sweet Marjorie Russell"
Lawrence Lee, "The Heroic Journey"
Arthur Miller, "Search for a Future"
Brian Moore, "The Apartment Hunter"
Berry Morgan, "Andrew"
Joyce Carol Oates, "Where Are You Going, Where Have You Been?"
Donald Radcliffe, "Song of the Simidor"
Henry Roth, "The Surveyor"
David Rubin, "Longing for America"
Jesse Stuart, "The Accident"
Carol Sturm, "The Kid Who Fractioned"
Robert Travers, "The Big Brown Trout"
William Wiser, "House of the Blues"

1968

James Baldwin, "Tell Me How Long the Train's Been Gone"
John Deck, "Greased Samba"
James T. Farrell, "An American Student in Paris"
George H. Freitag, "An Old Man and His Hat"
Herb Gardner, "Who Is Harry Kellerman and Why Is He Saying Those Terrible Things About Me?"
William H. Gass, "In the Heart of the Heart of the Country"
Mary Ladd Gavell, "The Rotifer"
Donald Gropman, "The Heart of This or That Man"
William Harrison, "The Snooker Shark"
Judith Higgins, "The Only People"
Helen Hudson, "The Tenant"
Leo E. Litwak, "In Shock,"
Richard McKenna, "The Sons of Martha"
William Mosely, "The Preacher and Margery Scott,"
Joanna Ostrow, "Celtic Twilight"
Nancy Huddleston Parker, "Early Morning, Lonely Ride"
John Phillips, "Bleat Blodgette"
Lawrence P. Springarn, "The Ambassador"
Winson Weathers, "The Games That We Played"
Janet Bruce Winn, "Dried Rose Petals in a Silver Bowl"

1969

Maeve Brennan, "The Eldest Child"
Jack Cady, "Play Like I'm Sheriff"
Mark Costello, "Murphy's Xmas"
John Bart Gerald, "Walking Wounded"
Mary Gray Hughes, "The Foreigner in the Blood"
Norma Klein, "The Boy in the Green Hat"
Mary Lavin, "Happiness"
Matthew W. McGregor, "Porkchops With Whiskey and Ice Cream"
Alistair McLeod, "The Boat"
James Alan McPherson, "Gold Coast"
David Madden, "The Day the Flowers Came"
Bernard Malamud, "Pictures of Fidelman"
John R. Milton, "The Inheritance of Emmy One Horse"
Joyce Carol Oates, "By the River"
Nancy Pelletier Pansing, "The Visitation"

Slyvia Plath, "Johnny Panic and the Bible of Dreams"
Miriam Rugel, "Paper Poppy"
Margaret Shipley, "The Tea Bowl of Ninsei Nomura"
Isaac Bashevis Singer, "The Colony"
Joyce Madelon Winslow, "Benjamin Burning"

1970

Jack Cady, "With No Breeze"
Eldridge Cleaver, "The Flashlight"
Robert Coover, "The Magic Poker"
Olivia Davis, "The Other Child"
Andre Dubus, "If They Knew Yvonne"
John Bart Gerald, "Blood Letting"
Alfred Gillespie, "Tonight at Nine Thirty-Six"
Ella Leffland, "The Forest"
Jack Matthews, "Another Story"
William Maxwell, "The Gardens of Mont-Saint Michel"
Lloyd Morris, "Green Grass, Blue Sky, White House"
Joyce Carol Oates, "How I Contemplated the World From the Detroit House of Correction and Began My Life Over Again"
Paul Olsen, "The Flag Is Down"
Cynthia Ozick, "Yiddish in America"
Jules Siegel, "In the Land of the Morning Calm, Déjà Vu"
Isaac Bashevis Singer, "The Key"
Robert Stone, "Porque No Tiene, Porque Le Falta"
Peter Taylor, "Daphne's Lover"
Rosine Weisbrod, "The Ninth Cold Day"

1971

Russell Banks, "With Che in New Hampshire"
Hal Bennett, "Dotson Gerber Resurrected"
James Blake, "The Widow Bereft"
Jack Cady, "I Take Care of Things"
Robert Canzoneri, "Barbed Wire"
Albert Drake, "The Chicken Which Became a Rat"
William Eastlake, "The Dancing Boy"
Beth Harvor, "Pain Was My Portion"
David Madden, "No Trace"
Don Mitchell, "Diesel"
Marion Montgomery, "The Decline and Fall of Officer Fergerson"
Lloyd Morris, "Magic"
Philip F. O'Connor, "The Gift Bearer"

Tillie Olsen, "Requa I"
Ivan Prashker, "Shirt Talk"
Norman Rush, "In Late Youth"
Danny Santiago, "The Somebody"
Jonathan Strong, "Xavier Fereira's Unfinished Book: Chapter One"
Leonard Tushnet, "The Klausners"
W. D. Valgardson, "Bloodflowers"
Larry Woiwode, "The Suitor"

1972

M. F. Beal, "Gold"
Richard Brautigan, "The World War I Los Angeles Airplane"
Kelly Cherry, "Covenant"
Herbert Gold, "A Death on the East Side"
Joanne Greenberg, "The Supremacy of the Hunza"
Mary Heath, "The Breadman"
Edward M. Holmes, "Drums Again"
Mary Gray Hughes, "The Judge"
Ann Jones, "In Black and White"
Ward Just, "Three Washington Stories"
Roberta Kalechofsky, "His Day Out"
Rebecca Kavaler, "The Further Adventures of Brunhild"
John L'Heureux, "Fox and Swan"
Ralph Maloney, "Intimacy"
Marvin Mandell, "The Aesculapians"
Cynthia Ozick, "The Dock-Witch"
Joe Ashby Porter, "The Vacation"
Penelope Street, "The Magic Apple"
Robert Penn Warren, "Meet Me in the Green Glen"
Theodore Weesner, "Stealing Cars"

1973

Donald Barthelme, "A City of Churches"
Henry Bromell, "The Slightest Distance"
John Cheever, "The Jewels of the Cabots"
John J. Clayton, "Cambridge Is Sinking!"
John William Corrington, "Old Men Dream Dreams, Young Men See Visions"
Guy Davenport, "Robot"
William Eastlake, "The Death of the Sun"
Alvin Greenberg, "The Real Meaning of the Faust Legend"
Julie Hayden, "In the Words Of"

George V. Higgins, "The Habits of the Animals: The Progress of the Seasons"
Ward Just, "Burns"
James S. Kenary, "Going Home"
Wallace E. Knight, "The Way We Went"
Konstantinos Lardas, "The Broken Wings"
James Alan McPherson, "The Silver Bullet"
Bernard Malamud, "God's Wrath"
Joyce Carol Oates, "Silkie"
Sylvia Plath, "Mothers"
Erik Sandbberg-Diment, "Come Away, Oh Human Child"
David Sheltzline, "Country of the Painted Freaks"
Tennessee Williams, "Happy August the 10th"

1974

Agnes Boyer, "The Deserter"
Jerry Bumpus, "Beginnings"
Eleanor Clark, "A Summer in Puerto Rico"
Pat M. Esslinger-Carr, "The Party"
Lewis B. Horne, "Mansion, Magic, and Miracle"
Rose Graubart Ignatow, "Down the American River"
Maxine Kumin, "Opening the Door On Sixty-Second Street"
Mary Lavin, "Tom"
John L'Heureux, "A Family Affair"
Phillip Lopate, "The Chamber Music Evening"
Stephen Minot, "The Tide and Isaac Bates"
Beverly Mitchell, "Letter from Sakaye"
Michael Rothschild, "Dog in the Manger"
Peter L. Sandberg, "Calloway's Climb"
William Saroyan, "Isn't Today the Day"
Philip H. Schneider, "The Gray"
Barry Targan, "Old Vemish"
John Updike, "The Man Who Loved Extinct Mammals"
John Updike, "Son"
Arturo Vivante, "Honeymoon"
Alice Walker, "The Revenge of Hannah Kemhuff"

1975

Russell Banks, "The Lie"
Donald Barthelme, "The School"
Rosellen Brown, "How to Win"
Jerry Bumpus, "Desert Matinee"
Frederick Busch, "Bambi Meets the Furies"

Nancy G. Chaikin, "Waiting For the Astronauts"
Mary Clearman, "Paths Unto the Ded"
Lyll Becerra DeJenkins, "Tyranny"
Andre Dubus, "Cadence"
Jesse Hill Ford, "Big Boy"
William Hoffman, "The Spirit in Me"
Evan Hunter, "The Analyst"
Paul Kaser, "How Jerem Came Home"
Alistair MacLeod, "The Lost Salt Gift of Blood"
Eugene McNamara, "The Howard Parker Montcrief Hoax"
Jack Matthews, "The Burial"
Reynolds Price, "Night and Day at Panacea"
Abraham Rothberg, "Polonaise"
Leslie Silko, "Lullaby"
Barry Targan, "The Man Who Lived"

1976

Alice Adams, "Roses, Rhododendron"
M. Pabst Battin, "Terminal Procedure"
Mae Seidman Briskin, "The Boy Who Was Astrid's Mother"
Nancy G. Chaikin, "Beautiful, Helpless Animals"
John William Corrington, "The Actes and Monuments"
H. E. Francis, "A Chronicle of Love"
John Hagge, "Pontius Pilate"
Ward Just, "Dietz at War"
John McCluskey, "John Henry's Home"
Stephen Minot, "Grubbing for Roots"
Kent Nelson, "Looking into Nothing"
Cynthia Ozick, "A Mercenary"
Reynolds Price, "Broad Day"
Michael Rothschild, "Wondermonger"
Barry Targan, "Surviving Adverse Seasons"
Peter Taylor, "The Hand of Emmagene"

1977

Frederick Busch, "The Trouble with Being Good"
Price Caldwell, "Tarzan Meets the Department Head"
John Cheever, "Falconer"
Ann Copeland, "At Peace"
John William Corrington, "Pleadings"
Philip Damon, "Growing Up in No Time"
Leslie Epstein, "The Steinway Quintet"
Eugene K. Garber, "The Lover"

Patricia Hampl, "Look at a Teacup"

Baine Kerr, "Rider"

Jack Matthews, "A Questionnaire for Rudolph Gordon"

Stephen Minot, "A Passion for History"

Charles Newman, "The Woman Who Thought Like a Man"

Joyce Carol Oates, "Gay"

Tim O'Brien, "Going After Cacciato"

Tom Robbins, "The Chink and the Clock People"

William Saroyan, "A Fresno Fable"

John Sayles, "Breed"

Anne Tyler, "Your Place Is Empty"

William S. Wilson, "Anthropology: What Is Lost in Rotation"

1978

Jonathan Baumbach, "The Return of Service"

Jane Bowles, "Two Scenes"

Harold Brodkey, "Verona: A Young Woman Speaks"

Elizabeth Cullinan, "A Good Loser"

Stanley Elkin, "The Conventional Wisdom"

Leslie Epstein, "Skaters on Wood"

John Gardner, "Redemption"

Mark Helprin, "The Schreuderspitze"

James Kaplan, "In Miami, Last Winter"

Tim McCarthy, "The Windmill Man"

Ian McEwan, "Psychopolis"

Peter Marsh, "By the Yellow Lake"

Joyce Carol Oates, "The Translation"

Natalie L. M. Petesch, "Main Street Morning"

Mary Ann Malinchak Rishel, "Staus"

Max Schott, "Murphy Jones: Pearblossom, California"

Lynne Sharon Schwartz, "Rough Strife"

Hluchan L. Sinetos, "Telling the Bees"

Robert T. Sorrells, "The Blacktop Champion of Ickey Honey"

Gilbert Sorrentino, "Decades"

Peter Taylor, "In the Miro District"

Joy Williams, "Bromeliads"

1979

Donald Barthelme, "The New Music"

Saul Bellow, "A Silver Dish"

Paul Bowles, "The Eye"

Rosellen Brown, "The Wedding Week"

Lyn Coffin, "Falling Off the Scaffold"

Mary Hedin, "The Middle Place"

Kaatje Hurlbut, "A Short Walk in the Afternoon"

Maxine Kumin, "The Missing Person"

Peter LaSalle, "Some Manhattan in New England"

Ruth McClaughlin, "Seasons"

Bernard Malamud, "Home Is the Hero"

Alice Munro, "Spelling"

Flannery O'Connor, "An Exile in the East"

Jayne Anne Phillips, "Something That Happened"

Louis D. Rubin, Jr., "Finisterre"

Annette Sanford, "Trip In a Summer Dress"

Lynne Sharon Schwartz, "Plaisir D'Amour"

Isaac Bashevis Singer, "A Party in Miami"

William Styron, "Shadrach"

Silvia Tennenbaum, "A Lingering Death"

Jean Thompson, "Paper Covers Rock"

Sean Virgo, "Home and Native Land"

Herbert Wilner, "The Quarterback Speaks to His God"

Robley Wilson, Jr., "Living Alone"

1980

Donald Barthelme, "The Emerald"

Frederick Busch, "Long Calls"

David Evanier, "The One-Star Jew"

Mavis Gallant, "Speck's Idea"

Mavis Gallant, "The Remission"

William H. Gass, "The Old Folks"

T. Gertler, "In Case of Survival"

Elizabeth Hardwick, "The Faithful"

Larry Heinemann, "The First Clean Fact"

Robert Henderson, "Into the Wind"

Curt Johnson, "Lemon Tree"

Grace Paley, "Friends"

James Robinson, "Home"

Leon Rooke, "Mama Tuddi Done Over"

John Sayles, "At the Anarchists' Convention"

Isaac Bashevis Singer, "The Safe Deposit"

Richard Stern, "Dr. Cahn's Visit"

Barry Targan, "The Rags of Time"

Peter Taylor, "The Old Forest"

John Updike, "Gesturing"

Gordon Weaver, "Hog's Heart"

Norman Waksler, "Markowitz and the Gypsies"

1981

Walter Abish, "The Idea of Switzerland"
Max Appel, "Small Island Republics"
Ann Beattie, "Winter: 1978"
Robert Coover, "A Working Day"
Vincent G. Dethier, "The Moth and the Primrose"
Andre Dubus, "The Winter Father"
Mavis Gallant, "The Assembly"
Elizabeth Hardwick, "The Bookseller"
Joseph McElroy, "The Future"
Elizabeth McGrath, "Fogbound in Avalon"
Bobbie Ann Mason, "Shiloh"
Amelia Mosely, "The Mountains Where Cithaeron Is"
Alice Munro, "Wood"
Joyce Carol Oates, "Presque Isle"
Cynthia Ozick, "The Shawl"
Louis D. Rubin, Jr., "The St. Anthony Chorale"
Richard Stern, "Wissler Remembers"
Elizabeth Tallent, "Ice"
John Updike, "Still Of Some Use"
Larry Woiwode, "Change"

1982

Nicholson Baker, "K. 590"
Charles Baxter, "Harmony Of the World"
Raymond Carver, "Cathedral"
Rosaanne Coggeshall, "Lamb Says"
James Ferry, "Dancing Ducks and Talking Anus"
Anne Hobson Freeman, "The Girl Who Was No Kin to the Marshall"
Alvin Greenberg, "The Power of Language Is Such That Even a Single Word Taken Truly to Heart Can Change Everything"
Roberta Gupta, "The Cafe de Paris"
William Hauptman, "Good Rockin' Tonight"
Joanna Higgins, "The Courtship of Widow Sobcek"
Charles Johnson, "Exchange Value"
Fred Licht, "Shelter the Pilgrim"
Lissa McLaughlin, "The Continental Heart"
Ian MacMillan, "Proud Monster—Sketches"
Edith Milton, "Coming Over"
Joyce Carol Oates, "Theft"
Joyce Renwick, "The Dolphin Story"
Mary Robison, "Coach"

Anne F. Rosner, "Prize Tomatoes"
R. E. Smith, "The Gift Horse's Mouth"

1983

Bill Barich, "Hard to Be Good"
Carol Bly, "The Dignity of Life"
James Bond, "A Change of Season"
Raymond Carver, "Where I'm Calling From"
Carolyn Chute, "Ollie, Oh. . . ."
Laurie Colwin, "My Mistress"
Joseph Epstein, "The Count and the Princess"
Louise Erdrich, "Scales"
Ursula K. LeGuin, "The Professor's Houses"
Ursula K. LeGuin, "Sur"
Bobbie Ann Mason, "Graveyard Day"
Lloyd Morris, "Victrola"
Julie Schumacher, "Reunion"
Sharon Sheehe Stark, "Best Quality Glass Company, New York"
Robert Taylor, Jr., "Colorado"
Marian Thurm, "Starlight"
John Updike, "Deaths of Distant Friends"
Guy Vanderhaeghe, "Reunion"
Diane Vreuls, "Beebee"
Larry Woiwode, "Firstborn"

1984

Lee K. Abbott, "The Final Proof of Fate and Circumstance"
Madison Smartt Bell, "The Naked Lady"
Dianne Benedict, "Unknown Feathers"
Mary Ward Brown, "The Cure"
Paul Bowles, "In the Red Room"
Rick DeMarinis, "Gent"
Andre Dubus, "A Father's Story"
Mavis Gallant, "Lena"
Mary Hood, "Inexorable Progress"
Donald Justice, "The Artificial Moonlight"
Stephen Kirk, "Morrison's Reaction"
Susan Minot, "Throrofare"
Lloyd Morris, "Glimpse into Another Country"
Joyce Carol Oates, "Nairobi"
Cynthia Ozick, "Rosa"
Lowry Pei, "The Cold Room"
Jonathan Penner, "Things to Be Thrown Away"
Norman Rush, "Bruns"

James Salter, "Foreign Shores"
Jeanne Schinto, "Caddies' Day"

1985

Russell Banks, "Sarah Cole: A Type of Love Story"
Michael Bishop, "Dogs' Lives"
Ethan Canin, "Emperor of the Air"
E. L. Doctorow, "The Leather Man"
Margaret Edwards, "Roses"
Starkey Flythe, "Walking, Walking"
H. E. Francis, "The Sudden Trees"
Bev Jafek, "You've Come a Long Way, Mickey
    Mouse"
John L'Heureux, "Clothing"
Peter Meinke, "The Piano Tuner"
Wright Morris, "Fellow-Creatures"
Bharati Mukherjee, "Angela"
Beth Nugent, "City of Boys"
Joyce Carol Oates, "Raven's Wing"
Norman Rush, "Instruments of Seduction"
Marjorie Sandor, "The Gittel"
Deborh Seabrooke, "Secrets"
Jane Smiley, "Lily"
Sharon Sheehe Stark, "The Johnstown Polka"
Joy Williams, "The Skater"

1986

Donald Barthelme, "Basil from Her Garden"
Charles Baxter, "Gryphon"
Ann Beattie, "Janus"
James Lee Burke, "The Convict"
Ethan Canin, "Star Food"
Frank Conroy, "Gossip"
Richard Ford, "Communist"
Tess Gallagher, "Bad Company"
Amy Hempel, "Today Will Be Quiet Day"
David Michael Kaplan, "Doe Season"
David Lipsky, "Three Thousand Dollars"
Thomas McGuane, "Sportsmen"
Christopher McIlroy, "All My Relations"
Alice Munro, "Monsieur Les Deux Chapeaux"
Jessica Neely, "Skin Angels"
Kent Nelson, "Invisible Life"
Grace Paley, "Telling"
Mona Simpson, "Lawns"
Joy Williams, "Health"

1987

Susan Sontag, "The Way We Live Now"
John Updike, "The Afterlife"
Craig Nova, "The Prince"
Elizabeth Tallent, "Favor"
Mavis Gallant, "Kingdom Come"
Sue Miller, "The Lover of Women"
Madison Smartt Bell, "The Lie Detector"
Alice Munro, "Circle of Prayer"
Lee E. Abbott, Dreams of Distant Lives"
Ralph Lombreglia, "Men Under Water"
Raymond Carver, "Boxes"
Bharati Mukherjee, "The Tenant"
Joy Williams, "The Blue Men"
Kent Haruf, "Private Debts/Public Holdings"
Charles Baxter, "How I Found My Brother"
Tobias Wolff, "The Other Miller"
Robert Taylor, "Lady of Spain"
Daniel Stern, "The Interpretation of Dreams by
    Sigmund Freud: A Story"
Ron Carlson, "Milk"
Tim O'Brien, "The Things They Carried"

1988

Mary Ann Taylor-Hall, "Banana Boats"
Rick Bass, "Cats and Students, Bubbles and
    Abysses"
E. S. Goldman, "Way To the Dump"
Brian Kitely, "Still Life With Insects"
Richard Bausch, "Police Dreams"
Gish Jen, "The Water-Faucet Vision"
Mavis Gallant, "Dede"
Robert Lacy, "The Natural Father"
Louise Erdrich, "Snares"
Raymond Carver, "Errand"
Ralph Lombreglia, "Inn Essence"
Edith Milton, "Entrechat"
Will Blythe, "The Taming Power of the Small"
Richard Currey, "Waiting for Trains"
C. S. Godshalk, "Wonderland"
Lucy Honig, "No Friends, All Strangers"
Tobias Wolff, "Smorgasbord"
Marjorie Sandor, "Still Life"
Hilding Johnson, "Victoria"
Robert Stone, "Helping"

1989

Douglas Glover, "Why I Decide To Kill Myself and Other Jokes"
Barbara Gowdy, "Disneyland"
Linda Hogan, "Aunt Moon's Young Man"
David Wong Louie, "Displacement"
Bharati Mukherjee, "The Management of Grief"
Alice Munro, "Meneseteung"
Dale Ray Phillips, "What Men Love For"
Mark Richard, "Strays"
Arthur Robinson, "The Boy On the Train"
M. T. Sharif, "The Letter Writer"
Charles Baxter, "Fenstad's Mother"
Madison Smartt Bell, "Customs of the Country"
Robert Boswell, Living to Be a Hundred"
Blanch McCrary Boyd, "The Black Hand Girl"
Larry Brown, "Kubuku Riders (This Is It)"
Frederick Busch, "Ralph the Duck"
Michael Cunningham, "White Angel"
Rick DeMarinis, "The Flowers of Boredom"
Harriet Doerr, "Edie: A Life"
Mavis Gallant, "The Concert Party"

1990

Edward Allen, "River of Toys"
Richard Bausch, "The Fireman's Wife"
Richard Bausch, "A Kind of Simple, Happy Game"
Madison Smartt Bell, "Finding Natasha"
C. S. Godshalk, "The Wizard"
Patricia Henley, "The Secret of Cartwheels"
Pam Houston, "How to Talk to a Hunter"
Siri Hustvedt, "Mr. Morning"
Denis Johnson, "Car-Crash While Hitchhiking"
Dennis McFarland, "Nothing to Ask For"
Steven Millhauser, "Eisenheim the Illusionist"
Lorrie Moore, "You're Ugly, Too"
Alice Munro, "Differently"
Alice Munro, "Wigtime"
Padget Powell, "Typical"
Lore Segal, "The Reverse Bug"
Elizabeth Tallent, "Prowler"
Christopher Tilghman, "In a Father's Place"
John Wickersham, "Commuter Marriage"
Joy Williams, "The Little Winter"

1991

Rick Bass, "The Legend of Pig-Eye"
Charles Baxter, "The Disappeared"
Amy Bloom, "Love Is Not a Pie"
Kate Braverman, "Tall Tales from the Mekong Delta"
Robert Olen Butler, "The Trip Back"
Charles D'Ambrosio, Jr., "The Point"
Millicent Dillon, "Oil and Water"
Harriet Doerr, "Another Short Day in La Luz"
Deborah Eisenberg, "The Custodian"
Mary Gordon, "Separation"
Elizabeth Graver, "The Body Shop"
Siri Hustvedt, "Houdini"
Mikhail Iossel, "Bologoye"
David Juss, "Glossolalia"
Leonard Michaels, "Viva La Tropicana"
Lorrie Moore, "Willing"
Alice Munro, "Friend Of My Youth"
Joyce Carol Oates, "American, Abroad"
Francine Prose, "Dog Stories"
John Updike, "A Sandstone Farmhouse"

1992

Alice Adams, "The Last Lovely City"
Rick Bass, "Days of Heaven"
Thomas Beller, "A Different Kind Of Imperfection"
Amy Bloom, "Silver Water"
Robert Olen Butler, "A Good Scent from a Strange Mountain"
Mavis Gallant, "Across the Bridge"
Tim Gautreaux, "Same Place, Same Things"
Denis Johnson, "Emergency"
Thom Jones, "The Pugilist At Rest"
Marshall N. Klimasewiski, "JunHee"
Lorrie Moore, "Community Life"
Alice Munro, "Carried Away"
Joyce Carol Oates, "Is Laughter Contagious?"
Reynolds Price, "The Fare To the Moon"
Annick Smith, "It's Come to This"
Christopher Tilghman, "The Way People Run"
David Foster Wallace, "Forever Overhead"
Kate Wheeler, "Under the Roof"
Elizabeth Winthrop, "The Golden Darters"
Tobias Wolff, "Firelight"

1993

John Updike, "Playing with Dynamite"

Mary Gaitskill, "The Girl on the Plane"

Alice Munro, "A Real Life"

Larry Woiwode, "Silent Passengers"

Alice Fulton, "Queen Wintergreen"

Harlan Ellison, "The Man Who Rowed Christopher Columbus Ashore"

Jane Shapiro, "Poltergeists"

Susan Power, "Red Moccasins"

Thom Jones, "I Want to Live!"

Tony Earley, "Charlotte"

Janet Perry, "What the Thunder Said"

Antonya Nelson, "Naked Ladies"

Stephen Dixon, "Man, Woman and Boy"

Andrea Lee, "Winter Barley"

Joanna Scott, "Concerning Mold Upon the Skin, Etc."

Wendell Berry, "Pray Without Ceasing"

Kim Edwards, "Gold"

Diane Johnson, "Great Barrier Reef"

Lorrie Moore, "Terrific Mother"

Mary Gordon, "The Important Houses"

1994

Sherman Alexie, "This Is What It Means to Say Phoenix, Arizona"

Carol Anshaw, "Hamman"

Robert Olen Butler, "Salem"

Lan Samantha Chang, "Pipa's Story"

Ann Cummins, "Where I Work"

Alice Elliott Dark, "In the Gloaming"

Stuart Dybek, "We Didn't"

Tony Earley, "Jupiter"

Carolyn Ferrell, "Proper Library"

John Rolfe Gardiner, "The Voyage Out"

David Gates, "The Mail Lady"

Barry Hannah, "Nicodemus Bluff"

Thom Jones, "Cold Snap"

John Keeble, "The Chasm"

Nancy Krusoe, "Landscape and Dream"

Laura Glen Louis, "Fur"

Chris Offutt, "Melungeons"

Roxana Robinson, "Mr. Sumarsono"

Jim Shepard, "Batting Against Castro"

Christopher Tilghman, "Things Left Undone"

Jonathan Wilson, "From Shanghai"

1995

Daniel Orozco, "Orientation"

Thom Jones, "Way Down Deep in the Jungle"

Ellen Gilchrist, "The Stucco House"

Jaimy Gordon, "A Night's Work"

Avner Mandelman, "Pity"

Steven Polansky, "Leg"

Peter Ho Davies, "The Ugliest House in the World"

Gish Jen, "Birthmates"

Edward J. Delaney, "The Drownings"

Joy Williams, "Honored Guest"

Andrea Barrett, "The Behavior of the Hawkweeds"

Andrew Cozine, "Hand Jive"

Stephen Doybyns, "So I Guess You Know What I Told Him"

Jennifer C. Cornell, "Undertow"

Kate Braverman, "Pagan Night"

Melanie Rae Thon, "First, Body"

Don DeLillo, "The Angel Esmeralda"

Edward Falco, "The Artist"

Max Garland, "Chiromancy"

Jamaica Kinkaid, "Xuela"

1996

Alice Adams, "Complicities"

Rick Bass, "Fires"

Jason Brown, "Driving the Heart"

Robert Olen Butler, "Jealous Husband Returns in Form of Parrot"

Lan Samantha Chang, "The Eve of the Spirit Festival"

Dan Chaon, "Fitting Ends"

Peter Ho Davies, "The Silver Screen"

Junot Diaz, "Ysrael"

Stephen Dixon, "Sleep"

Stuart Dybek, "Paper Lantern"

Deborah Galyan, "The Incredible Appearing Man"

Mary Gordon, "Intertextuality"

David Huddle, "Past My Future"

Anna Keesey, "Bright Winter"

Jamaica Kincaid, "In Roseau"

William Henry Lewis, "Shades"

William Lychack, "A Stand of Fables"

Joyce Carol Oates, "Ghost Girls"
Angela Patrinos, "Sculpture I"
Susan Perabo, "Some Say the World"
Lynne Sharon Schwartz, "The Trip to Halawa Valley"
Akhil Sharma, "If You Sing Like That for Me"
Jean Thompson, "All Shall Love Me and Despair"
Melanie Rae Thon, "Xmas, Jamaica Plain"

1997

Ha Jin, "Saboteur"
Robert Stone, "Under the Pitons"
Carolyn Cooke, "Bob Darling"
Jonathan Franzen, "Chez Lambert"
Michelle Cliff, "Transactions"
Richard Bausch, "Nobody in Hollywood"
Cynthia Ozick, "Save My Child!"
Karen E. Bender, "Eternal Love"
Leonard Michaels, "A Girl with a Monkey"
Lydia Davis, "St. Martin"
Junot Diaz, "Fiesta, 1980"
Donald Hall, "From Willow Temple"
T. Coraghessan Boyle, "Killing Babies"
Clyde Edgerton, "Send Me to the Electric Chair"
June Spence, "Missing Women"
Jeffrey Eugenides, "Air Mail"
Pam Durban, "Soon"
Michael Byers, "Shipmates Down Under"
Tobias Wolff, "Powder"
Alyson Hagy, "Search Bay"
Tim Gautreaux, "Little Frogs in a Ditch"

1998

Katherine Chetkovich, "Appetites"
Poe Ballantine, "The Blue Devils of Blue River Avenue"
Diane Schoemperlen, "Body Language"
Edith Pearlman, "Chance"
Akhil Sharma, "Cosmopolitan"
Carol Anshaw, "Elvis Has Left the Building"
Chris Adrian, "Every Night for a Thousand Years"
Maxine Swann, "Flower Children"
Emily Carter, "Glory Goes and Gets Some"
Annie Proulx, "The Half-Skinned Steer"
Doran Larson, "Morphine"
Bliss Broyard, "Mr. Sweetly Indecent"
John Updike, "My Father on the Verge"

Matthew Crain, "Penance"
Lorrie Moore, "People Like That Are the Only People Here"
Meg Wolitzer, "Tea at the House"
Antonya Nelson, "Unified Front"
Padgett Powell, "Wayne in Love"
Tim Gautreaux, "Welding With Children"
Hester Kaplan, "Would You Know It Wasn't Love"

PUSHCART PRIZES FOR FICTION, 1977–1999

The Pushcart Prize honors stories, poems, and essays from little magazines and small presses in an annual anthology. Fiction winners are listed below.

1977
Volume I

Bruce Boston, "Broken Portaiture"
Robert Bringhurst, "The Stonecutters"
Raymond Carver, "So Much Water So Close to Home"
Marvin Cohen, "The Human Table"
William Eastlake, "The Death of the Sun"
H. E. Francis, "A Chronicle of Love"
William Gass, "I Wish You Wouldn't"
Mary Gordon, "Now I Am Married"
David Kranes, "Cordials"
Joyce Carol Oates, "The Hallucination"
Jack Pulaski, "Father of the Bride"
Avrom Reyzen, "The Dog"
Ed Sanders, "The Mother-in-Law"
Ronald Sukenick, "The Monster"
Alexander Theroux, "Lynda Van Cats"
Anne Tyler, "The Artificial Family"
G. K. Wuori, "Afrikaan Bottles"

1978
Volume II

Jerry Bumpus, "Lovers"
Italo Calvino, "The Name, the Nose"
Kelly Cherry, "Where the Winged Horses Take Off into the Wild Blue Yonder"
Stephen Dixon, "Milk Is Very Good for You"
Russell Edson, "The Neighborhood Dog"

Raymond Federman, "The Buick Special"
Eugene K. Garber, "The Lover"
Paul Goodman, "The Tennis-Game"
James Hashim, "The Party"
Alan V. Hewat, "The Big Store"
John Irving, "The Pension Grillparzer"
Maxine Kumin, "Another Form of Marriage"
Bob Levin, "The Best Ride to New York"
Gerald Lockin, "The Last Romantic"
Ian Macmillan, "Messinghausen, 1945"
Victor Muravin, "The Red Cross Night"
Opal Nations, "The U.S. Chinese Immigrant's Book
  of the Art of Sex"
Tim O'Brien, "Going After Cacciato"
David Ohle, "The Boy Scout"
Jayne Anne Phillips, "Sweethearts"
T. E. Porter, "King's Day"
John Sanford, "The Fire at the Catholic Church"
Teo Savory, "The Monk's Chimera"
Jerry Stahl, "Return of the General"
Meredith Steinbach, "Vestiges"

1979
Volume III
Walter Abish, "Parting Shot"
Ascher/Straus Collective, "Even after a Machine Is
  Dismantled, It Continues to Operate, With or
  Without Purpose"
Margaret Atwood, "The Man from Mars"
Jane Bowles, "The Iron Table"
Wesley Brown, "Getting Freedom High"
Kathleen Collins, "Stepping Back"
James Crumley, "Whores"
Lydia Davis, "Mothers"
H. Bustos Domecq, "Monsterfest"
Andre Dubus, "The Fat Girl"
C. W. Gusewelle, "Horst Wessel"
Don Hendrie, Jr., "Moral Cake"
Anne Herbert, "Snake"
Anais Nin, "Waste of Timelessness"
George Payerle, "Wolfbane Fane"
Mary Peterson, "To Dance"
John Pilcrow, "Turtle"
Lynne Sharon Schwartz, "Rough Strife"
Beth Tashery Shannon, "Bons"

Robert Walser, "Two Strange Stories"
Nancy Willard, "How the Hen Sold Her Eggs to
  the Stingy Priest"
Robley Wilson, Jr., "The United States"
Max Zimmer, "Utah Died for Your Sins"

1980
Volume IV
R. C. Day, "Another Margot Chapter"
Ellen Gilchrist, "Rich"
James B. Hall, "My Work in California"
Felisberto Hernandez, "The Daisy Dolls"
Judith Hoover, "Proteus"
Paul Metcalf, "The Hat in the Swamp"
Susan Schaefer Neville, "Johnny Appleseed"
Jayne Anne Phillips, "Home"
Jayne Anne Phillips, "Lechery"
Joe Ashby Porter, "Sweetness, A Thinking Mchine"
Manuel Puig, "From Kiss of the Spider Woman"
Gary Reilly, "The Biography Man"
Max Schott, "Early Winter"
Christine Schutt, "These Women"
Steve Schutzman, "The Bank Robbery"
Shirley Ann Taggart, "Ghosts Like Them"
Jeff Weinstein, "A Jean-Marie Cookbook"
Dallas Wiebe, "Night Flight to Stockholm"

1981
Volume V
Asa Baber, "Tranquility Base"
Bo Ball, "Wish Book"
Gina Berriault, "The Infinite Passion of Expectation"
Michael Brondoli, "Showdown"
Vlada Bulatovic-Vib, "The Shark and the
  Bureaucrat"
H. E. Francis, "Two Lives"
Barbara Grossman, "My Vegetable Love"
W. P. Kinsella, "Pretend Dinners"
Romulus Linney, "How St. Peter Got Bald"
David Madden, "On the Big Wind"
Cynthia Ozick, "Levitation"
Gerald Shyne, "Column Beda"
Elizabeth Spencer, "The Girl Who Loved Horses"
Stephanie Vaugh, "Sweet Talk"
Sara Vogan, "Scenes From the Homefront"

Ellen Wilbur, "Faith"
Patricia Zelver, "Story"

1982
Volume VI
Kathy Acker, "New York City in 1979"
Eleanor(a) Antin(ova), "A Romantic Interlude from Recollections of My Life with Diaghilev"
Raymond Carver, "What We Talk About When We Talk About Love"
Denise Cassens, "Girl Talk"
Susan Engberg, "In the Land of Plenty"
William Goyen, "Arthur Bond"
Lyn Hejinian, "Selections from My Life"
Benedict Kiely, "Fionn in the Valley"
David Long, "Eclipse"
David Ohle, "The Flocculus"
Francis Phelan, "Four Ways of Computing Midnight"
Chen Shixu, "The General and the Small Town"
Leslie Silko, "Coyote Holds a Full House in His Hand"
Jean Stafford, "Woden's Day"
Elizabeth Ann Tallent, "Why I Love Country Music"
Barry Targan, "Dominion"
Julia Thacker, "In Glory Land"
Gayle Baney Whittier, "Lost Time Accident"

1983
Volume VII
Charles Baxter, "Harmony of the World"
Barbara Bedway, "Death and Lebanon"
Richard Burgin, "Notes on Mrs. Slaughter"
Guy Davenport, "Christ Preaching at the Henley Regatta"
William Gilson, "Getting Through It Together"
Elizabeth Inness-Brown, "Release, Surrender"
Fred Licht, "Shelter the Pilgrim"
Joyce Carol Oates, "Detente"
Amos Oz, "The Author Encounters His Reading Public"
Cynthia Ozick, "Helping T. S. Eliot Write Better (Notes Toward a Definitive Bibliography"
Jayne Anne Phillips, "How Mickey Made It"
Mary Robison, "Happy Boy, Allen"
Richard Selzer, "Mercy and the Witness"

Barbara Thompson, "Tattoo"
Edmund White, "A Man of the World"

1984
Volume VIII
Raymond Carver, "A Small Good Thing"
Andrei Codrescu, "Samba De Los Agentes"
Jean Davidson, "Robo-Wash"
Janet Desaulniers, "Age"
William Gass, "Uncle Balt and the Nature of Being"
Ellen Gilchrist, "Summer, An Elegy"
Willis Johnson, "Prayer Before Dying"
Gordon Lish, "How to Write a Poem"
Bobbie Ann Mason, "Graveyard Day"
Robert McBrearty, "The Dishwasher"
Susan Welch, "The Time, The Place, The Loved One"
Kate Wheeler, "Judgment"

1985
Volume IX
T. Coraghessan Boyle, "Caviar"
Pamela Brandt, "L. A. Child"
Clark Brown, "A Winter's Tale"
Raymond Carver, "Careful"
Gail Godwin, "Over the Mountain"
Edmund Keeley, "Cambodian Diary"
Tadeusz Konwicki, from "A Minor Apocalypse"
Curzio Malaparte, "The Soroca Girls"
Barbara Milton, "The Cigarette Boat"
Susan Minot, "Hiding"
Mary Morris, "Copies"
Jonathan Penner, "Emotion Recollected in Tranquillity"
Joe Ashby Porter, "Duckwalking"
Teri Ruch, "Claire's Lover's Church"
Beth Tashery Shannon, "Asilomarian Lecture (The Dirmal Life of the Inhabitants)"
Gilbert Sorrentino, "The Gala Cocktail Party"
Barbara Thompson, "Crossing"

1986
Volume X
Bo Ball, "Heart Leaves"
Russell Banks, "Sarah Cole: A Type of Love Story"
Antonio Benitez-Rojo, "Heaven and Earth"
T. Coraghessan Boyle, "The Hector Quesadilla Story"

Sharon Doubiago, "That Art of Seeing with One's Own Eyes"
Stuart Dybek, "Hot Ice"
Margareta Ekstrom, "Death's Midwives"
Kenneth Gangemi, "Greenbaum, O'Reilly & Stephens"
William Kittredge, "Agriculture"
Janet Kauffman, "The Easter We Lived in Detroit"
Tim O'Brien, "Quantum Jumps"
Alberto Alvaro Rios, "The Secret Lion"
Bob Shacochis, "Hot Day On the Gold Coast"
Gordon Weaver, "Whiskey, Whiskey, Gin, Gin, Gin"
Gayle Whittier, "Turning Out"
Ellen Wilbur, "Sundays"

1987
Volume XI
Lee K. Abbott, "X"
Alice Adams, "Molly's Dog"
Paul Auster, "In the Country of Last Things"
Gina Berriault, "The Island of Ven"
Richard Burgin, "The Victims"
Andre Dubus, "Rose"
Richard Ford, "Communist"
Gary Gildner, "Somewhere Geese Are Flying"
Amy Hempel, "Today Will Be a Quiet Day"
Linda Hogan, "Friends and Fortunes"
Mary Hood, "Something Good For Ginnie"
Gordon Lish, "The Merry Chase"
D. R. MacDonald, "The Flowers Of Bermuda"
Lucia Perillo, "Jury Selection"
Francine Prose, "Other Lives"
Mona Simpson, "Lawns"
Ana Lydia Vega, "Lyrics For Puerto Rican Salsa and Three Soneos By Request"
Tobis Wolff, "Leviathan"

1988
Volume XII
Opal Palmer Adisa, "Duppy Get Her"
Martha Bergland, "An Embarrassment of Ordinary Riches"
Norbert Blei, "The Ghost of Sandburg's Phizzog"
Rosellen Brown, "One Of Two"
Robert Cohen, "Shamsky and Other Casualties"

Carol Emshwiller, "Yukon"
Tess Gallagher, "The Lover of Horses"
Patricia Henley, "The Birthing"
Harold Jaffe, "Persian Lamb"
Elizabeth Jolley, "My Father's Moon"
Gordon Lish, "Mr. Goldbaum"
Fae Myenne Ng, "A Red Sweater"
C. E. Poverman, "Beautiful"
Irina Ratushinskaia, "On the Meaning of Life"
Elizabeth Spencer, "Jack Of Diamonds"
Paul West, "The Place In Flowers Where Pollen Rests"

1989
Volume XIII
Lee K. Abbott, "The Era of Great Numbers"
Rick Bass, "Where the Sea Used to Be"
Becky Birth, "Johnnieruth"
Sandie Castle, "What the Shadow Knows"
Barbara Einzig, "Life Moves Outside"
Tess Gallagher, "Girls"
C. S. Godshalk, "Wonderland"
Ehud Havazelet, "What Is It Then Between Us?"
Melissa Lentricchia, "The Golden Robe"
David Zane Mairowitz, "Hector Composes Circular Letter To His Friends To Announce His Survival of an Earthquake, 7.8 on the Richter Scale"
Lynne McFall, "Star, Tree, Hand"
Leonard Michaels, "Literary Talk"
Mark Richard, "Happiness of the Garden Variety"
Leon Rooke, "The Blue Baby"
Marjorie Sandor, "Icarus Descending"
Eve Shelnutt, "Andantino"
Chris Spain, "Entrepreneurs"

1990
Volume XIV
Charles Baxter, "Westland"
Paul Bowles, "Tangier"
Lydia Davis, "Five Stories"
Lorna Goodison, "By Love Possessed"
Dewitt Henry, "Witness"
Sandy Huss, "Coupon For Blood"
David Jauss, "Freeze"
Alistair MacLeod, "Island"

Frank Manley, "The Rain of Terror"
Michael Martone, "The Safety Patrol"
Kristina McGrath, "Housework"
Robert Minkoff, "Better Tomorrow"
Sigrid Nunez, "The Summer of the Hats"
Joyce Carol Oates, "Party"
Sheila Schwartz, "Mutatis Mutandis"
Ron Tanner, "Garbage"
Peter Tysver, "After the Stations of the Cross"
Barbara Wilson, "Miss Venezuela"

1991
Volume XV

Will Baker, "Field of Fire"
Rick Bass, "Wejumpka"
Carol Bly, "My Lord Bag of Rice"
Ken Chowder, "With Pat Boone in the Pentlands"
Richard Currey, "Believer's Flood"
Lydia Davis, "The Center of the Story"
Joseph Geha, "Through and Through"
Sarah Glasscock, "Broken Hearts"
Daniel Hayes, "What I Wanted Most of All"
Robin Hemley, "Installations"
Kim Herzinger, "The Day I Met Buddy Holly"
Rodney Hale Jones, "Francis: Brother of the
  Universe"
Laura Kalpkian, "The Battle Of Manila"
Thomas E. Kennedy, "Murphy's Angel"
Wally Lamb, "Astronauts"
Clarence Major, "My Mother and Mitch"
Lou Matthews, "Crazy Life"
Kent Nelson, "The Middle of Nowhere"
Josip Novakovich, "Rust"
Padget Powell, "Typical"
Molly Best Tinsley, "Zoe"
Dennis Vanatta, "The David of Michelangelo"
Shay Youngblood, "Snuff Dippers"

1992
Volume XVI

Felipe Alfau, "The Stuff Men Are Made Of"
F. L. Chandonnet, "Stories"
Melinda Davis, "Text"
Jeanne Dixon, "River Girls"
Ben Groff, "A Call From Kotzebue"

Mark Halliday, "One Thousand Words on Why You
  Should Not Talk During a Fire Drill"
David Jauss, "Glossolalia"
Ursula LeGuin, "Bill Weisler"
Renee Manfredi, "Bocci"
Yann Martel, "The Facts Behind the Helsinki
  Roccamatios"
Jess Mowry, "One Way"
Helen Norris, "Raisin Faces"
Joyce Carol Oates, "The Hair"
Janet Peery, "Nosotros"
Eileen Pollack, "Past, Future, Elsewhere"
Carol Roh-Spaulding, "Waiting for Mr. Kim"
Susan Straight, "The Box"
Diane Williams, "Two Stories"

1993
Volume XVII

Steven Barthelme, "Hush Hush"
Ken Bernard, "Prolegomena"
Lydia Davis, "Four Stories"
Dagoberto Gilb, "Look on the Bright Side"
Molly Giles, "War"
Ha Jin, "My Best Soldier"
Norman Lavers, "The Telegraph Relay Station"
Karen Minton, "Like Hands on a Cave Wall"
Susan Moon, "Bodies"
Janet Peery, "Whitewing"
Fred Pfeil, "Freeway Bypass"
Francine Prose, "Rubber Life"
Alberto Alvaro Rios, "The Other League of Nations"
R. A. Sasaki, "The Loom"
Sharon Sheehe Stark, "Kerflooey"
Alexander Theroux, "A Note on the Type"
Mary Michael Wagner, "Acts of Kindness"
Steve Watkins, "Critterworld"
Liza Wieland, "The Columbus School for Girls"

1994
Volume XVIII

Tony Ardizzone, "Larabi's Ox"
Ayla Nutku Bachman, "Blood Brother"
Rick Bass, "Days Of Heaven"
Karen E. Bender, "A Chick from My Dream Life"
Michael Bendzela, "The Butcher"

Scott Bradfield, "The Parakeet and the Cat"
Molly Giles, "The Writers' Model"
Patricia Henley, "Same Old Black Magic"
Dennis Loy Johnson, "Forrest in the Trees"
Edward P. Jones, "Marie"
Barry Lopez, "Benjamin Claire, North Dakota Tradesman, Writes To the President Of the United States"
D. R. MacDonald, "Green Grow the Grasses O"
Joseph Maiolo, "The Pilgrim Virgin"
Rebecca McClanahan, "Somebody"
Leonard Michaels, "Tell Me Everything"
Susan Neville, "In the John Dillinger Museum"
Joanna Scott, "Convicta Et Combusta"
Barbara Selfridge, "Monday Her Car Wouldn't Start"
Daniel Stern, "The Hunger Artist By Franz Kafka: A Story"
David Foster Wallace, "Three Protrusions"
Marie Sheppard Williams, "The Sun, The Rain"
Tobias Wolff, "The Life Of the Body"

1995
Volume XIX
A. Manette Ansay, "Sybil"
Jon Barnes, "Nash"
Lucia Berlin, "Good and Bad"
Bliss Broyard, "My Father, Dancing"
Evan Connell, "Bowen"
Charles D'Ambrosio, "Jacinta"
Edwidge Danticat, "Between the Pool and the Gardenias"
Andre Dubus, III, "Tracks and Ties"
Kim Edwards, "The Way It Felt to Be Falling"
Raymond Federman, "The Line"
Maria Flook, "Riders to the Sea"
Rolaine Hochstein, "Alma Mahler: A Fiction"
Robin Hemley, "The Big Ear"
Linda Hogan, "The Crying House"
Ha Jin, "In Broad Daylight"
Carole Maso, "From Ava"
Susan Onthank Mates, "Theng"
Steven Millhauser, "Paradise Park"
Jewel Mogan, "Age Of Reason"
Josip Novakovich, "Honey in the Carcase"

Lisa Sandlin, "Orita On the Road to Chimayo"
Dean Schabner, "Moriches"
Eugene Stein, "The Triumph of the Prague Workers' Councils"
Robert Love Taylor, "My Mother's Shoes"
Jean Thompson, "Who Do You Love"
Joy Williams, "Marabou"
George Williams, "The Road from Damascus"

1996
Volume XX
John Barth, "Closing Out the Visit"
Charles Baxter, "Super Night"
Michael Collins, "The End of the World"
Jennifer C. Cornell, "The Swing of Things"
Don DeLillo, "Videotape"
Stephen Dobyns, "A Happy Vacancy"
Maribeth Fischer, "Stillborn"
Steven Huff, "The Nearness of the World"
Nora Cobb Keller, "Mother-Tongue"
Maxine Kumin, "The Match"
Sandra Tsing Loh, "My Father's Chinese Wives"
Avner Mandelman, "Pity"
Ben Marcus, "False Water Society"
Reginald McKnight, "The More I Like Flies"
Rick Moody, "The Ring of Brightest Angels Around Heaven"
Cornelia Nixon, "The Women Come and Go"
Joyce Carol Oates, "The Undesirable Table"
Eileen Pollack, "Milk"
Melissa Pritchard, "The Instinct For Bliss"
James Robison, "The Late Style"
Alice Schell, "Kingdom of the Sun"
Marie Sheppard Williams, "Wilma Bremer's Funeral"

1997
Volume XXI
Pinckney Benedict, "The Secret Nature of the Mechanical Rabbit"
Wendy Dutton, "What Comes from the Ground"
Peter Gordon, "Lost"
Mark Halliday, "Young Man on Sixth Avenue"
Harold Jaffe, "Camp, Dope, & Videotape"
Andrea Jeyaveeran, "Brown Dog Angel"
Ha Jin, "A Man-To-Be"

Karla J. Kuban, "Baby Maker"

Caroline A. Langston, "The Dissolution of the World"

Bobbie Ann Mason, "Proper Gypsies"

Erin McGraw, "Daily Affirmations"

Tom McNeal, "Winter in Los Angeles"

Daniel Meltzer, "The Weather in History"

Jewel Mogan, "Mad"

William Monahan, "A Relation of Various Accidents Observable In Some Animals Included in Vacuo"

Daniel Orozco, "The Bridge"

Tom Paine, "From Basra to Bethlehem"

Robert Schirmer, "Jerry's Kid"

Helen Schulman, "The Revisionist"

Ranbir Sidhu, "Neanderthal Tongues"

Daniel Stern, "Grievances and Griefs by Robert Frost"

Steve Stern, "The Tale of a Kite"

David Treuer, "Duke and Ellis"

S. L. Wisenberg, "Big Ruthie Imagines Sex Without Pain"

1998
Volume XXII

Paul L. Allman, "We Have Time"

Rita Ariyoshi, "Jamming Traffic"

Andrea Barrett, "The Forest"

Gina Berriault, "Zenobia"

Ron Carlson, "Oxygen"

Susan Daitch, "Killer Whales"

Kiana Davenport, "The Lipstick Tree"

Claire Davis, "Grounded"

Junot Diaz, "Invierno"

Janice Eidus, "Not the Plaster Casters"

Nathan Englander, "For the Relief of Unbearable Urges"

Percival Everett, "The Appropriation of Cultures"

Tomas Filer, "Civilization"

Elizabeth Gilbert, "The Famous Torn and Restored Lit Cigarette Trick"

Rachel Kadish, "Women Dreaming Of Jerusalem"

Kristen King, "The Wings"

Katherine Min, "Courting a Monk"

Mike Newirth, "Give the Millionaire a Drink"

Josip Novakovich, "Out of the Woods"

Flannery O'Connor, "The Coat"

Tom Pine, "Scar Vegas"

Pamela Painter, "The Kiss"

Donald Rawley, "The Secret Names of Whores"

Stacey Richter, "The Beauty Treatment"

Jessica Roeder, "Carp"

Gerald Shapiro, "The Twelve Plagues"

Julia Slavin, "Dentaphilia"

Lee Smith, "Native Daughter"

Gordon Weaver, "Return of the Boyceville Flash"

1999
Volume XXIII

Richard Bausch, "Valor"

Louis Berney, "Stupid Girl"

Melvin Jules Bukiet, "Splinters"

Richard Burgin, "Bodysurfing"

Frederick Busch, "The Ninth, In E Minor"

Beth Chimera, "July"

John J. Clayton, "Let's Not Talk Politics, Please"

Thoms M. Disch, "The First Annual Performance Art Festival at the Slaughter Rock Battlefield"

Stephen Dixon, "The Burial"

Stuart Dybek, "Blowing Shades"

Jeffrey Eugenides, "Timeshare"

Edward Falco, "The Revenant"

Patricia Hampl, "The Bill Collector's Vacation"

Mary Kuryla, "Mis-Sayings"

Colum McCann, "As Kingfishers Catch Fire"

Risa Mickenberg, "Direct Male"

Jennifer Moses, "Girls Like You"

Bharati Mukherjee, "Happiness"

Kirk Nesset, "Mr. Agreeable"

Joyce Carol Oates, "Faithless"

Lance Olsen, "Cybermorphic Beat-Up Get-Down Subterranean Homesick Reality-Sandwich Blues"

Lucia Perillo, "Bad Boy Number Seventeen"

Nancy Richard, "The Order of Things"

Maxine Swann, "Flower Children"

Mark Wisniewski, "Descending"

Meg Wolitzer, "Tea at the House"

Monica Wood, "Ernie's Ark"

APPENDIX II

SUGGESTED READINGS BY THEME AND TOPIC

Following are suggested readings in general themes and topics. Although the suggestions are in no way meant to be exhaustive, they provide a listing of stories from two centuries by established authors known for their short fiction, as well as stories by writers better known for their novels, poems, or literary criticism.

ADOLESCENCE

James Baldwin "The Outing"; "Sonny's Blues"

Kay Boyle "The Wild Horses"

T. Coraghessan Boyle "Greasy Lake"

Ray Bradbury "Dandelion Wine"; "The Great Fire"

Willa Cather "Paul's Case"

Deborah Eisenberg "The Girl Who Left Her Sock on the Floor"

Shirley Jackson "A Cauliflower in Her Hair"

Jamaica Kincaid "Annie John"

Bernard Malamud "A Summer's Reading"

Joyce Carol Oates "Where Are You Going, Where Have You Been?"

Julie Schumacher "Levitation"; "Rehoboth Beach"

Lee Smith "Live Bottomless"

Peter Taylor "Venus, Cupid, Folly and Time"

Anne Tyler "Teenage Wasteland"

John Updike "A & P"; "Flight"; "The Happiest I've Been"; "A Sense of Shelter"

Helen Viramontes "The Cariboo Cafe"

AFRICAN AMERICANS

Maya Angelou "Steady Going Up"

James Baldwin "Come Out the Wilderness"; "Exodus"; "Going to Meet the Man"; "The Outing"; "The Rockpile"; "Sonny's Blues"; "Tell Me How Long the Train's Been Gone"

Toni Cade Bambara "The Organizer's Wife"

Arna Bontemps "A Summer Tragedy"

Gwendolyn Brooks "We're the Only Colored People Here"; "Maud Martha"

Charles W. Chesnutt "The Bouquet"; "The Goophered Grapevine"; "The Passing of Grandison"; "Her Virginia Mammy"; "The Wife of His Youth"

John Henrik Clarke "The Boy Who Painted Christ Black"; "Santa Claus in a White Man"

John P. Davis "The Overcoat"

W. E. B. DuBois "On Being Crazy"

Paul Laurence Dunbar "The Lynching of Jube Benson"

Ralph Ellison "Battle Royal"; "Flying Home"; "King of the Bingo Game"; "Out of the Hospital and Under the Bar"

Ernest J. Gaines "Bloodline"; "Just Like a Tree"; "The Sky Is Gray"; "Three Men"

Frances E. W. Harper   "The Two Offers"

Chester Himes   "Mama's Missionary Money"

Pauline E. Hopkins   "Bro'r Abr'm Jimson's Wedding: A Christmas Story"

Langston Hughes   "Family Tree"; "Guitar"; "Haircuts and Paris"; "Jazz, Jive, and Jam"; "Midsummer Madness"; "The Moon"; "Not Colored"; "On the Road"; "One Friday Morning"; "Race Relations"; "Red-Headed Baby"; "Simple Stashes Back"; "Thank You, Ma'm"; "Uncle Sam"; "Who's Passing for Who?"

Zora Neale Hurston   "Drenched in Light?"; "The Gilded Six-Bits"; "Sweat"

Charles Johnson   "The Education of Mingo"

Leroi Jones   "The Screamers"

Claude McKay   "Truant"

James Alan McPherson   "On Trains"

Paule Marshall   "Barbados"; "Brazil"; "Reena"

Ann Petry   "Like A Winding Sheet"; "Solo on the Drums"

Jean Toomer   "Blood-Burning Moon"; "Avey"; "Esther"

Alice Walker   "Everyday Use"; "Advancing Luna—And Ida B. Wells"; "My Man Bovanne"

John Edgar Wideman   "All Stories Are True"; "Damballah"

Richard Wright   "Almos' a Man"; "Bright and Morning Star"; "The Ethics of Living Jim Crow"; "Long Black Song"; "The Man Who Killed a Shadow"; "The Man Who Lived Underground"

Sherley Anne Williams   "Tell Martha Not to Moan"

Frank Yerby   "Health Card"; "The Homecoming"

AMERICANS IN AFRICA

Paul Theroux   "White Lies"

AMERICANS IN ASIA

Pearl S. Buck   "Conqueror's Girl"

Avram Davidson   "The Dragon-Skin Drum"

Paul Theroux   "Dengue Fever"; "Diplomatic Relations"; "The Flower of Malaya"; "The Johore Murders"

AMERICANS IN BRITAIN

Hortense Calisher   "Songs My Mother Taught Me"

J. P. Donleavy   "Whither Wigwams"

Deborah Eisenberg   "In the Station"

Willian Faulkner   "Turnabout"

Henry James   "The Beldonald Holbein"; "Covering End"; "A London Life"; "Mrs. Medwin"; "The Modern Warning"

Paul Theroux   "Clapham Junction"; "An English Unofficial"; "The Honorary Siberian" "Rose"

Mark Twain   "The £1,000,000 Bank-Note"

John Updike   "A Madman"

Edith Wharton   "The Refugees"

AMERICANS IN EUROPE

Alice Adams   "Barcelona"

Louisa May Alcott   "Poppies and Wheat"

Donald Barthelme   "Edward and Pia"; "Overnight to Many Distant Cities"

Saul Bellow   "The Gonzaga Manuscripts"

Kay Boyle   "Fire in the Vineyards"; "French Harvest"; "A Christmas Carol for Harold Ross"; "The Kill"; "A Puzzled Race"

Willa Cather   "The Namesake"; "The Profile"

John Cheever   "A Woman Without A Country"; "The Bella Lingua"; "Clementina"

James Gould Cozzens   "Whose Broad Stripes and Bright Stars"

James T. Farrell   "An American Student in Paris"

Henry James   "Daisy Miller"; "Fordham Castle"; "Miss Gunton of Poughkeepsie"; "The Reverberator"; "The Solution"; "Travelling Companions"

Bernard Malamud   "Behold the Key"; "The Lady of the Lake"; "The Maid's Shoes"; "Naked Nude"; "Still Life"

Arthur Miller   "Monte Sant' Angelo"

Burton Raffel   "Sicilian Vespers"

Katherine Anne Porter   "The Leaning Tower"

Irwin Shaw   "The Inhabitants of Venus"

Elizabeth Spencer   "The Visit"; "The White Azalea"; "Wisteria"

Jean Stafford   "The Echo and the Nemesis"; "A Winter's Tale"

Paul Theroux   "A Real Russian Ikon"
John Updike   "Avec la Bébé-Sitter"; "Twin Beds in Rome"
Gore Vidal   "Pages from an Abandoned Journal"
Edith Wharton   "Souls Belated"; "The Last Asset"; "Velvet Ear Pads"; "The Daunt Diana"; "The Refugees"; "Roman Fever"
Constance Fenimore Woolson   "At the Chateau of Corrine"; "Miss Grief" "The Street of the Hyacinth"; "A Transplanted Boy"

AMERICANS IN MEXICO AND LATIN AMERICA

Paul Bowles   "Tapiama"
Stephen Crane   "The Five White Mice"
Harriet Doerr   "The Evertons Out of Their Minds"; "Parts of Speech"
Deborah Eisenberg   "Across the Lake" "Holy Week"; "Someone to Talk To"; "Tlaloc's Paradise"; "Under the 82nd Airborne"
Jack Kerouac   "The Mexican Girl"
Katherine Anne Porter   "Flowering Judas"
Harry Swados   "The Balcony"

ASIAN AMERICANS

Chitra Divakaruni   "Doors"
M. Evelina Galang   "Her Wild American Self"
Jessica Hagedorn   "The Blossoming of Bong Bong"
Marie Hara   "1895: The Honeymoon Hotel"
Mavis Hara   "An Offering of Rice"
Jeanne Wakatsuki Houston   "O Furo (The Bath)"
Gish Jen   "The White Umbrella"
Shirley Geok-lin Lim   "A Pot of Rice"
Bharati Mukherjee   "A Wife's Story"; "The Management of Grief"
Fae Myenne Ng   "A Red Sweater"
Amy Tan   "Double face"
Sui Sin Far   "In the Land of the Free"
Sylvia Watanabe   "Talking to the Dead"
Hisaye Yamamoto   "Seventeen Syllables"; "Wilshire Bus"
Wakako Yamauchi   "And the Soul Shall Dance"; "Maybe"; "The High-Heeled Shoes: A Memoir"

FAMILY LIFE

Louis Auchincloss   "Sabina and the Herd"; "The Last Great Divorce"
James Baldwin   "The Man Child"; "Sonny's Blues"
John Barth   "Ambrose His Mark"
Saul Bellow   "The Old System"
Doris Betts   "Clarissa and the Depths"
Paul Bowles   "The Frozen Fields"
Harold Brodkey   "Car Buying"; "Lila and S.L."
Gwendolyn Brooks   "Maud Martha"
Hortense Calisher   "The Gulf Between"
Truman Capote   "My Side of the Matter"; "A Christmas Memory"
R. V. Cassill   "The Covenant"
Willa Cather   "The Bohemian Girl"; "The Sentimentality of William Tavener"
Evan S. Connell   "Notes from the File on Mrs. Bridge"
James Gould Cozzens   "Eyes to See" E. L. Doctorow   "The Writer in the Family"
J. P. Donleavy   "Dear Sylvia"
Deborah Eisenberg   "The Custodian"
Harold Frederic   "The Copperhead"; "The War Widow"
Ernest J. Gaines   "A Long Day in November"; "The Sky Is Grey"
Ernest Hemingway   "Soldier's Home"
Amy Hempel   "Weekend"
Shirley Jackson   "Deck the Halls"; "Family Magician"; "I Know Who I Love"; "Maybe It Was the Car"; "The Night We All Had Grippe"; "Pajama Party"; "The Renegade"
Sarah Orne Jewett   "The Country of the Pointed Firs"
Ruth Prawer Jhabvala   "The Aliens"; "A Loss of Faith"; "The Old Lady"; "The Widow"
H. P. Lovecraft   "The Shunned House"
Bernard Malamud   "The Place Is Different Now"
Joyce Carol Oates   "Stigmata"
Flannery O'Connor   "A Good Man Is Hard to Find"
John O'Hara   "Aunt Fran"; "The Skeletons"
Tillie Olsen   "Hey Sailor, What Ship?"; Tell Me a Riddle; "I Stand Here Ironing"
Katherine Anne Porter   "Holiday"; "Old Mortality"; "The Old Order"

Julie Schumacher "The Private Life of Robert Schumann"

Jean Stafford "The Tea-Time of Stouthearted Ladies"

Peter Taylor "A Cheerful Disposition"

Paul Theroux "Yard Sale"

Lionel Trilling "The Other Margaret"

John Updike "Incest"; "Pigeon Feathers"; "The Family Meadow"

Mark Van Doren "All Us Three"; "One of Hers"

Gordon Weaver "Whiskey, Whiskey————"

Eudora Welty "Why I Live at the P.O."

Edith Wharton "Charm Incorporated"

Nancy Willard "The Hucklebone of a Saint"

Tobias Wolff "The Liar"

Constance Fenimore Woolson "For the Major"; "The Front Yard"

FAMILY—FATHERS, SONS, AND DAUGHTERS

Donald Barthelme "A Picture History of the War"

Charles Baxter "Believers"

Saul Bellow "Seize the Day"

Paul Bowles "The Frozen Field"; "Pages from Cold Point"

Kay Boyle "A Disgrace to the Family"; "A Puzzled Race"; "Rest Cure"; "The Soldier Ran Away"

Ray Bradbury "The Playground"

Pearl S. Buck "Christmas Day in the Morning"; "Little Red"

Frederick Busch "Custody"

R. V. Cassill "The Father"

Willa Cather "The Count of Crow's Nest"; "Paul's Case"

John Cheever "Reunion"

Frank Chin "Food for All His Dead"

Cyrus Colter "The Beach Umbrella"

James Gould Cozzens "Every Day's A Holiday"; "Child's Play"; "Total Stranger"

Stephen Crane "A Desertion"; "The Monster"

J. P. Donleavy "The Romantic Life of Alphonse A."

Andre Dubus "A Father's Story"

Stanley Elkin "Criers and Kibitzers, Kibitzers and Criers"

William Faulkner "Barn Burning"

Harold Frederic "The Deserter"

Tess Gallagher "The Lover of Horses"

Nathaniel Hawthorne "Rappaccini's Daughter"

Ernest Hemingway "My Old Man"

Henry James "The Ghostly Rental"; "The Marriages"

Sarah Orne Jewett "The Landscape Chamber"

Bernard Malamud "Armistice"; "The First Seven Years"; "Idiots First"; "My Son the Murderer"; "Riding Pants"; "The Silver Crown"

Joyce Carol Oates "Stigmata"

Flannery O'Connor "Judgement Day"; "The Lame Shall Enter First"

John O'Hara "School"

William Peden "Night in Funland"; "The Boy on the Bed"

Julie Schumacher "An Explanation"

Isaac Bashevis Singer "The Son"

Jean Stafford "A Reading Problem"

Paul Theroux "After the War"; "World's End"

Lionel Trilling "The Other Margaret"

John Updike "Packed Dirt, Churchgoing, A Dying Cat, A Traded Car"; "My Father on the Verge of Disgrace"

Mark Van Doren "My Mother Was Your Wife"; "Rich, Poor, and Indifferent"

Edith Wharton "The House of the Dead Hand"; "The Last Asset"; "The Portrait"

Tobias Wolff "Powder"

FAMILY LIFE—MOTHERS, SONS, AND DAUGHTERS

Paul Bowles "Dona Faustina"; "The Hours After Noon"

Kay Boyle "Seven Say You Can Hear Corn Grow"

Ray Bradbury "Heavy Set"; "Some Live Like Lazarus"

Hortense Calisher "In Greenwich There Are Many Gravelled Walks"; "Women Men Don't Talk About"

Willa Cather "The Burglar's Christmas"; "The Prodigies"

Fred Chappell "Prodigious Words"

Charles W. Chestnutt "Her Virginia Mammy"

Stephen Crane "George's Mother"

Deborah Eisenberg "Mermaids"

Harlan Ellison   "Blind Bird, Blind Bird, Go Away From Me!"

William Faulkner   "Skirmish at Sartoris"

Ernest J. Gaines   "The Sky is Gray"

Henry James   "The Chaperon"; "'Europe'"; "Fordham Castle"; "Greville Fane"; "Sir Edmund Orme"

Lawrence Sergent Hall   "The Ledge"

McKinley Kantor   "The Blazing Star"

Jack London   "The Tears of Ah Kim"

Flannery O'Connor   "The Comforts of Home"; "The Enduring Chill"; "Everything That Rises Must Converge"; "Greenleaf"

John O'Hara   "The Gangster"; "Mrs. Allanson"

Grace Paley   "A Subject of Childhood"; "The Used-Boy Raisers"

Elizabeth Stuart Phelps   "The Angel Over the Right Shoulder"

Jayne Anne Phillips   "Souvenir"

Julie Schumacher   "Dividing Madeline"

Ruth Suckow   "Midwestern Primitive"

Paul Theroux   "Children"

John Updike   "Flight"

Mark Van Doren   "Sebastian"; "The Sign"

Edith Wharton   "Autres Temps . . ."; "Her Son"; "The Pelican"; "The Quicksand"

Tennessee Williams "Mam's Old Stucco House"

Richard Wright   "Almos' A Man"

FAMILY LIFE—BROTHERS AND SISTERS

Louis Auchincloss   "Honoria and Attila"

James Baldwin   "Sonny's Blues"

Toni Cade Bambara   "Raymond's Run"

T. Coraghessan Boyle   "Killing Babies"

Ray Bradbury   "The Mirror"

William Faulkner   "That Evening Sun"

Tess Gallagher   "A Box of Rocks"

Shirley Jackson   "The Sister"

Joyce Carol Oates   "Will You Always Love Me?"

Julie Schumacher   "Dummies"; "Rehoboth Beach"

Lee Smith   "News of the Spirit"

Eudora Welty   "Why I Live at the P.O."

Edith Wharton   "Bunner Sisters"

FAMILY LIFE—GRANDPARENTS AND GRANDCHILDREN

Louisa May Alcott   "Kate's Choice"

Kay Boyle   "Luck for the Road"

Ray Bradbury   "Fee Fie Foe Fum"

John Cheever   "Homage to Shakespeare"

James Gould Cozzens   "Child's Play"

Louise Erdrich   "Love Medicine"

William Faulkner   "Raid"

Tim Gautreaux   "Little Frogs in a Ditch"

Shirley Jackson   "Little Old Lady in Great Need"; "My Grandmother and the World of Cats"; "The Omen"

Flannery O'Connor   "The Artificial Nigger"; "A View of the Woods"; "A Good Man Is Hard to Find"

Edgar Allan Poe   "The Spectacles"

Katherine Anne Porter   "The Old Order"; "They Trample on Your Heart"

Jean Stafford   "In the Zoo"

John Updike   "The Blessed Man of Boston"; "My Grandmother's Thimble"; "Fanning Island"

Mark Van Doren   "Nobody Else's Business"; Plain and Fancy"; "A Wild Wet Place"

Eudora Welty   "A Worn Path"

Edith Wharton   "The Angel at the Grave"

Nancy Willard   "The Boy Who Ran With The Dogs"

Tennessee Williams   "Grand"

FANTASY AND SCIENCE FICTION

Poul Anderson   "Kyrie"

Ekeabir Arnasibm   "The Warlord of Saturn's Moons"

Isaac Asimov   "What If"

Greg Bear   "Schrodinger's Plague"

Gregory Benford   "Exposures"

Michael Bishop   "The Bob Dylan Tambourine Software & Satori Support Services Consortium, Ltd."

J. P. Blaylock   "Thirteen Phantasms"

James Blish   "How Beautiful With Banners"

Ray Bradbury   "End of Summer"; "Mr. Pale"; "Nothing Changes"

David R. Bunch   "2064, or Thereabouts"

Pat Cadigan "After the Days of Dead-Eye 'Dee"
Jane Dorsey Candas "(Learning About) Machine Sex"
John Crowley "Snow"
Michael Blumlein "The Brains of Rats"
Marion Zimmer Bradley "Elbow Room"
Edward Bryant "Precession"
Octavia Butler "Speech Sounds"
Orson Scitt Card "America"
Michael G. Coney "The Byrds"
Avram Davidson "The House the Blakeneys Built"
Samuel R. Delany "High Weir"
Philip K. Dick "Frozen Journey"
Suzette Haden Elgin "For the Sake of Grace"
Harlan Ellison "Anywhere But Here, With Anybody But You"; "Chatting With Anubis"; "The Dragon on the Bookshelf"; "The Few, the Proud"; "Jane Doe #112"; "Keyboard"; "The Lingering Scent of Woodsmoke"; "The Man Who Rowed Christopher Columbus Ashore"; "Midnight in the Sunken Cathedral"; "Strange Wine"
Carol Emshwiller "The Start of the End of the World"
Karen Joy Fowler "The Lake Was Full of Artificial Things"
William Gibson "The Gernsback Continuum"
Diane Glancy "Aunt Parnetta's Electric Blisters"
Molly Gloss "Interlocking Pieces"
Lisa Goldstein "Midnight News"
Phyllis Gotlieb "Tauf Aleph"
Eileen Gunn "Stable Strategies for Middle Management"
Joe Haldeman "The Private War of Private Jacob"
Zenna Henderson "As Simple as That"
Sonya Dorman Hess "When I Was Miss Dow"
Shirley Jackson "One Ordinary Day, with Peanuts"; "The Smoking Room"; "The Very Strange House Next Door"
James Patrick Kelly "Rat"
John Kessel "Invaders"
Nancy Kress "Out of All Them Bright Stars"
Damon Knight "The Handler"
R. A. Lafferty "Nine Hundred Grandmothers"
Ursula K. LeGuin "Buffalo Gals, Won't You Come Out Tonight"; "The New Atlantis"; "Schroeder's Cat"

Fritz Lieber "The Winter Flies"
H. P. Lovecraft "At the Mountains of Madness"
Bernard Malamud "The Jewbird"; "Talking Horse"; "Emily"
Barry N. Malzberg "Making It All the Way into the Furture on Gaxton Falls of the Red Planet"
Katherine MacLean "Night-Rise"
Vonda N. McIntyre "The Mountains of Sunset, the Mountains of Dawn"
Pat Murphy "His Vegetable Wife"
Frederick Pohl "Day Million"
Paul Preuss "Half-Life"
Mike Resnick "Kirinyaga"
Kim Stanley Robinson "The Lucky Strike"
Joanna Russ "A Few Things I Know about Whileaway"
Pamela Sargent "Gather Blue Roses"
Robert Scheckley "The Life of Anybody"
James H. Schmitz "Balanced Ecology"
Rod Serling "The Odyssey of Flight 33"
Lewis Shiner "The War at Home"
Robert Silverberg "Good News from the Vatican"
Clifford D. Simak "Over the River and Through the Woods"
Cordwainer Smith "Alpha Ralpha Boulevard"
Bruce Sterling "We See Things Differently"
Michael Swanwick "A Midwinter's Tale"
James Jr. Tiptree "The Women Men Don't See"
John Varley "Lollipop and the Tar Baby"
Gerald Vizenor "Oshkiwiinag: Heartlines on the Trickster Express"
Howard Waldrop ". . . the World, As We Know't"
Andrew Weiner "Distant Signals"
Kate Wilhelm "And the Angels Sing"
Connie Willis "Schwarzschild Radius"
Gene Wolfe "Feather Tigers"
Roger Zelazny "Comes Now the Power"

GHOSTS AND THE SUPERNATURAL

William Austin "Peter Rugg, The Missing Man"
Ambrose Bierce "The Damned Thing"; "A Diagnosis of Death"; "A Tough Tussle"
Willa Cather "The Fear That Walks by Noonday"

F. Scott Fitzgerald "A Short Trip Home"
Ellen Glasgow "The Shadowy Third"
O. Henry "A Ghost of A Chance"
Nathaniel Hawthorne "Young Goodman Brown"
Shirley Jackson "Lord of the Castle"; "Lovers Meeting"; "The Story We Used to Tell"; "A Visit"
Henry James "The Ghostly Rental"; "The Jolly Corner"; "Owen Wingrave"; "The Right Real Thing"; "Sir Edmund Orme"; "The Third Person"; "The Way It Came"
H. P. Lovecraft "The Colour Out of Space"; "The Dunwich Horror"; "The Evil Clergyman"; "The Lurking Fear"; "The Shunned House"
Alison Lurie "Fat People"; "The Highboy"
Edgar Allan Poe "King Pest"
Anne Rice "The Master of Rampling"
Joanna Russ "My Dear Emily"
Rod Serling "The House on the Island"; "Two Live Ghosts"
May Sinclair "The Nature of the Evidence"
Isaac Bashevis Singer "Two Corpses Go Dancing"
Frank R. Stockton "The Philosophy of Relative Existence"; "The Transferred Ghost"
Paul Theroux "The Tiger's Suit"
Mark Twain "A Curious Ghost"
Jessamyn West "My Displaced Ghosts"
Edith Wharton "Afterward"; "All Souls'"; "Bewitched"; "Kerfol"; "The Lady's Maid's Bell"; "Miss Mary Pask"; "Pomegranate Seed"; "The Triumph of Night"

HISPANIC AMERICANS

Ana Castillo "Women Are Not Roses"
Denise Chavez "Evening in Paris"
Sandra Cisneros "Little Miracles, Kept Promises"; "My Name"; "Woman Hollering Creek"
Judith Ortiz Cofer "Silent Dancing"; "Tales Told under the Mango Tree"
Roberta Fernandez "Amada"; "Filomena"
Roberto Fernandez "Retrieving Varadero"; "Miracle on Eighth and Twelfth"
Rolando Hinojosa "Coming Home I"; "Coming Home V"

Nicolasa Mohr "An Awakening . . . Summer 1956"; "Blessed Divination"; "In Another Place in Different Era"; "Memories: R.I.P."; "My Newest Triumph"; "Rosalina de los Rassarios"; "A Thanksgiving Celebration (Amy)"
Alejandro Morales "Cara de Caballo"; "The Curing Woman"
Tomas Rivera "First Communion"; "The Salamanders"
Gary Soto "First Love"
Helena María Viramontes "The Cariboo Cafe"; "The Moths"

HOMOSEXUALITY

David Leavitt "Saturn Street"; "The Term Paper Artist"; "The Wooden Anniversary"
Bernard Malamud "Glass Blower of Venice"
Robert Patrick "The War Over Jane Fonda"
Paul Theroux "Gone West"

HORROR

Ambrose Bierce "The Boarded Window"; "A Diagnosis of Death"; "A Watcher by the Dead"
Paul Bowles "A Distant Episode"
Ray Bradbury "Come Into My Cellar"; "Heavy Set"; "Homecoming"; "Mars Is Heaven!"; "The Screaming Woman"; "Zero Hour"
Hortense Calisher "Heartburn"
Arthur C. Clarke "A Walk in the Dark"
Harlan Ellison "Darkness Upon the Face of the Deep"; "Sensible City"
William Faulkner "A Rose for Emily"
Shirley Jackson "The Honeymoon of Mrs. Smith"; "Nightmare"
H. P. Lovecraft "The Dunwich Horror"; "In the Vault"; "The Outsider"; "The Shadow in the Attic"; "The Whisperer in Darkness"
Edgar Allan Poe "Berenice"; "The Black Cat"; "A Descent Into the Maelstrom"; "The Fall of the House of Usher"; "Ligeia"; "Morella"; The Narrative of A. Gordon Pym of Nantucket; "The Oblong Box"; "The Pit and the Pendulum"; "The Tell-Tale Heart"; "William Wilson"
Joanna Russ "My Dear Emily"

HUMOR AND SATIRE

Thomas Bailey Aldrich   "Miss Marjorie Daw"

Isaac Asimov   "I'm in Marsport Without Hilda"

Robert Benchley   "How Lillian Mosquito Projects Her Voice"

Stephen Vincent Benét   "Jolly Roger"

Ambrose Bierce   "The Ingenious Patriot"

T. Coraghessan Boyle   "Ike and Nina"

Ray Bradbury   "Any Friend of Nicholas Is a Friend of Mine"

Hortense Calisher   "Saratoga, Hot"

Truman Capote   "Among the Paths to Eden"; "My Side of the Matter"

James Gould Cozzens   "The Animals' Fair"

Stephen Crane   "Lynx Hunting"

J. P. Donleavy   "Dear Sylviah"; "Call Me Cheetah"; "The Mad Molecule"; "The Romantic Life of Alphonse A."

F. Scott Fitzgerald   "A Luckless Santa Claus"; "Pain and the Scientist"; "The Trail of the Duke"

Tess Gallagher   "The Poetry Baron"; "The Red Ensign"

O. Henry   "After Twenty Years"; "The Cop and the Anthem"; "Lost on Dress Parade"; "Mammom and the Archer"; "The Ransom of Red Chief"; "A Retrieved Reformation"; "A Service of Love"; "Springtime à la Carte"

William Dean Howells   "The Critical Bookstore"

Langston Hughes   "Family Tree"; "Midsummer Madness"; "Race Relations"; "Seeing Double"; "Temptation"; "That Powerful Drop"; "Two Side Not Enough"

Shirley Jackson   "About Two Nice People"; "Fame"; "Indians Live in Tents"; "Maybe It Was the Car"; "My Recollections of S.B."

Henry James   "The Solution"

Ring Lardner   "Alibi Ike"; "Dinner"; "Dogs"; "Some Like Them Cold"

Sinclair Lewis   "Getting His Bit"; "Jazz"; "Slip It to 'em"; "Snappy Display"; "The Whisperer"

Bernard Malamud   "The Jewbird"; "Pictures of the Artist"; "Talking Horse"

Herman Melville   "I and My Chimney"; "The Lightning-Rod Man"

Cynthia Ozick   "Save My Child!"

William Peden   "The Cross-Country Dog"; "The Pilgrims"; "Easter Sunday"

Edgar Allan Poe   "Some Words With a Mummy"; "Why the Little Frenchman Wears His Hand in a Sling"

Damon Runyon   "Sense of Humour"

William Saroyan   "The Fifty Yard Dash"

Frank R. Stockton   "A Piece of Red Calico"; "The Remarkable Wreck of the Thomas Hyke"; "The Transferred Ghost"

Harriet Beecher Stowe   "Captain Kidd's Money"

Paul Theroux   "Fighting Talk"

T. B. Thorpe   "The Big Bear of Arkansas"

James Thurber   "The Catbird Seat"; "The Dog That Bit People"; "The Macbeth Murder Mystery"; "The Night the Ghost Got In"; "Prehistoric Animals of the Middle West"; "The Secret Life of Walter Mitty"

Mark Twain   "The Canvasser's Tale"; "The Celebrated Jumping Frog of Calaveras County"; "A Curious Dream"; "A Double-Barreled Detective Story"

Gordon Weaver   "The Good Man of Stillwater, Oklahoma"

LOVE, COURTSHIP, ROMANCE

Louisa May Alcott   "Water Lilies"

Louis Auchincloss   "Honoria and Attila"

James Baldwin   "Come Out of the Wilderness"

Donald Barthelme   "Edward and Pia"

Charles Baxter   "The Cures for Love"

Ann Beattie   "Skeletons"

Kay Boyle   "Nothing Ever Breaks Except the Heart"

Ray Bradbury   "The April Witch"; "Grand Theft"; "The Wilderness"

Hortense Calisher   "Saratoga, Hot"

Willa Cather   A Lost Lady; "On the Gull's Road"; "The Treasure of Far Island"

Laurie Colwin   "A Country Wedding"

Stephen Crane   "A Man by the Name of Mud"; "The Third Violet"

J. P. Donleavy   "It was My Chimes"; "Franz F"

Deborah Eisenberg   "Flotsam"; "Holy Week"; "A Lesson in Traveling Light"; "Rafe's Coat"; "Transactions in a Foreign Currency"; "What It was Like, Seeing Chris"

William Faulkner   "A Courtship"

F. Scott Fitzgerald   "The Pierian Springs and the Last Straw"

Richard Ford   "Occidentals"; "The Womanizer"

Harold Frederic   "Marsena"; "My Aunt Susan"

William Gass   "In the Heart of the Heart of the Country"

Herbert Gold   "Dance of the Divorced"

Bret Harte   "Salomy Jane's Kiss"

Robert A. Heinlein   "The Menace from Earth"

O. Henry   "The Furnished Room"; "The Gift of the Magi"

William Dean Howells   "Editha"; "The Magic of a Voice"

Shirley Jackson   "Lovers Meeting"; "The Very Hot Sun in Bermuda"

Henry James   "The Given Case"; "The Great Condition"; "In the Cage"; "Sir Edmund Orme"; "Travelling Companions"; "The Velvet Glove"; "The Wheel of Time"

Ruth Prawer Jhabvala   "In Love with a Beautiful Girl"; "The Man with the Dog"; "A Young Man of Good Family"

Dorothy Johnson   "Beyond the Frontier"; "A Woman of the West"

McKinley Kantor   "Bringing in the May"

Jamaica Kincaid   "Song of Roland"

Ring Lardner   "Alibi Ike"

Jack London   "On the Makaloa Mat"; "The Wit of Porportuk"

Bernard Malamud   "The First Seven Years"; "The Magic Barrel"; "Spring Rain"; "Suppose a Wedding"

Bobbie Ann Mason   "Love Life"

Herman Melville   "Fragments from A Writing Desk"

Nicolasa Mohr   "Rosalina de Los Rosarios"

Joyce Carol Oates   "Will You Always Love Me?"

John O'Hara   "Andrea"; "How Old, How Young"

Dorothy Parker   "A Telephone Call"

Edgar Allan Poe   "Why the Little Frenchman Wears His Hand in a Sling"

Katherine Anne Porter   "The Martyr"

Isaac Bashevis Singer   "Elka and Meir"

Lee Smith   "Native Daughter"; "The Southern Cross"

Wallace Stegner "Maiden in a Tower"

Paul Theroux   "Dancing on the Radio"; "An English Unofficial Rose"; "The Flower of Malaya"; "Fury"; "White Lies"; "The Winfield Wallpaper"

John Updike   "Four Sides of One Story"; "Here Come the Maples"; "The Lovely Troubled Daughters of Our Old Crowd"; "The Morning"; "Separating"

Mark Van Doren   "Help for the Senator"; "In Springfield, Massachusetts"; "Me and Mac"; "Skinny Melinda"

Kurt Vonnegut   "EPICAC"; "Long Walk to Forever"

Alice Walker   "Advancing Luna—And Ida B. Wells"; "How Did I Get Away With Killing One of the Biggest Lawyers in the State? It Was Easy"

Gordon Weaver   "Ah Art! Oh Life!"

Edith Wharton   "Confession"; "A Coward"; "Dieu d'Amour"; "The Introducers"; "The Lamp of Psyche"; "The Letters"; "The Long Run"; "Les Metteurs en Scène"; "The Muse's Tragedy"; "New Year's Day"; "The Potboiler"; "The Pretext"; "Souls Belated"

Constance Fenimore Woolson   "At the Chateau of Corrine"

MARRIAGE AND DIVORCE

Louisa May Alcott   "A Double Tragedy: An Actor's Story"

Louis Auchincloss   "Geraldine: A Spiritual Biography"; "Cliffie Beach on Himself"; "Stirling's Folly"

Russell Banks   "Adultery"

Donald Barthelme   "The Big Broadcast of 1938"

Charles Baxter   "Saul and Patsy Are in Labor"; "Surprised by Joy"; "Time Exposure"

Ann Beattie   "The Cinderella Waltz"

Saul Bellow   "Herzog Visits Chicago"; "Seize The Day"

Doris Betts   "Clarissa and the Depths"

Arna Bontemps   "A Summer Tragedy"

Ray Bradbury "And the Sailor, Home from the Sea"; "The Best of All Possible Worlds"; "The Bird That Comes Out of the Clock"; "The Time of Going Away"; "A Touch of Pestilence"; "Ylla"

Harold Brodkey "The Dark Woman of the Sonnets"; "Spring Fugue"

Erskine Caldwell "The Windfall"

Hortense Calisher "The Last Trolley Ride"; "The Rabbi's Daughter"; "A Christmas Carillon"

Raymond Carver "Blackbird Pie"

R. V. Cassill "And in My Heart"; "The Crime of Mary Lynn Yager"; "Fracture"; "This Land, These Talons"; "The War in the Air"

Willa Cather "The Bohemian Girl"; "Eleanor's House"; "Flavia and Her Artists"; *A Lost Lady*; "The Marriage of Phaedra"; "The Profile"; "The Willing Muse"

Charles W. Chesnutt "Uncle Wellington's Wives"; "The Wife of His Youth"

John Cheever "The Brigadier and the Golf Widow"; "The Country Husband"; "An Educated American Woman"; "The Embarkment for Cythera"; "Homage to Shakespeare"; "Marita in Citta"; "The Music Teacher"; "The Ocean"; "Separating"

Cyrus Colter "The Beach Umbrella"

Evan S. Connell "The Corset"; "Notes From the File on Mrs. Bridge"

Stephen Crane "The Bride Comes to Yellow Sky"

J. P. Donleavy "Gustav G"

Andre Dubus "The Blackberry Patch"

Harlan Ellison "Lonely Ache"

William Faulkner "Artist at Home"

Ernest J. Gaines "A Long Day in November"

Tess Gallagher "Creatures"

Martha Gellhorn "The Clever One"; "The Fall and Rise of Mrs. Hapgood"; "In Sickness, As in Health"; "A Promising Career"

Charlotte Perkins Gilman "Turned"; "The Yellow Wall-Paper"

Herbert Gold "Dance of the Divorced"

Nathaniel Hawthorne "The Birthmark"

Ernest Hemingway "The Doctor and the Doctor's Wife"; "Mr. and Mrs. Elliot"

Amy Hempel "Sportsman"

O. Henry "Whirligig of Life"; "The Gift of the Magi"

Langston Hughes "Jazz, Jive, and Jam"; "Lost Wife"; "The Moon"; "Roots and Trees"

Zora Neale Hurston "The Gilded Six-Bits"; "Sweat"

Shirley Jackson "The Beautiful Stranger"; "Before Autumn"; "A Cauliflower in Her Hair"; "A Day in the Jungle"; "The Good Wife"; "The Honeymoon of Mrs. Smith"; "The Mouse"; "Mrs. Anderson"; "The Sister"; "The Summer People"

Henry James "The Chaperon'" "Fordham Castle"; "The Given Case"; "The Great Condition"; "Julia Bride"; "The Lesson of the Master"; "The Modern Warning"; "Mora Montravers"; "The Special Type"

Ruth Prawer Jhabvala "Lekha"; "My First Marriage"; "The Young Couple"

Dorothy M. Johnson "Virginia City Winter"

Jamaica Kincaid "Song of Roland"

Norman Mailer "The Man Who Studied Yoga"

Bernard Malamud "The Glassblower of Venice"; "The Grocery Store"; "The Loan"; "A Lost Grave"; "Zora's Noise"

Bobbie Ann Mason "Shiloh"

Herman Melville "I and My Chimney"

Nicolasa Mohr "A Matter of Pride"

Bharati Mukherjee "A Wife's Story"

Vladimir Nabokov "'That in Aleppo once . . .'"

Joyce Carol Oates "What Death with Love Should Have to Do"; "In the Insomniac Night"

John O'Hara "The Clear Track"; "Fatimas and Kisses"; "Flight"; "The General"; "The Jet Set"; "The Madeline Wherry Case"; "Mrs. Allanson"; "Natica Jackson"; "The Pomeranian"; "The Private People"; "School"; "The Tackle"; "Zero"

Grace Paley "An Interest in Life"

Dorothy Parker "Big Blonde"; "Too Bad"

William Peden "Wherefore Art Thou, Romeo?"; "The White Shell Road"

Katherine Anne Porter "The Cracked Looking-Glass"; "A Day's Work"; "Rope"

Isaac Bashevis Singer "Big and Little"; "The Brooch"; "Esther Kreindel the Second"; "The Fast"; "Gimpel the Fool"; "A Sacrifice"; "Short Friday"; "The Unseen"; "The Wife Killer"

Jean Stafford   "Bad Characters"; "Children Are Bored on Sunday"

Wallace Stegner   "Carrion Spring"

Paul Theroux   "The English Adventure"; "Loser Wins"; "A Political Romance"; "Volunteer Speaker"; "World's End"; "You Make Me Mad"

James Thurber   "A Couple of Hamburgers"

John Updike   "Avec la Bébé-Sitter"; "The Fairy Godfathers"; "Four Sides to One Story"; "Giving Blood"; "My Lover Has Dirty Fingernails"; "The Rescue"; "The Stare"; "Twin Beds in Rome"; "Your Lover Just Called"

Mark Van Doren   "The Imp of String"; "The Little House"; "The Long Shadow"; "The Shelter"

Kurt Vonnegut   "Go Back to Your Precious Wife and Son"; "Next Door"

Eudora Welty   "Livvie Is Back"; "Shower of Gold"; "The Wide Net"

Edith Wharton   "Afterward"; "Atrophy"; "Autres Temps . . ."; "The Best Man"; "Bewitched"; "Charm Incorporated"; "The Choice"; "The Confessional"; "A Coward"; "The Day of the Funeral"; "Diagnosis"; "The Duchess at Prayer"; "In Trust"; "A Journey"; "Joy in the House"; "The Lamp of Psyche"; "The Letters"; "The Line of Least Resistance"; "The Mission of Jane"; "The Other Two"; "Permanent Wave"; "The Reckoning"; "The Recovery"; "Souls Belated"; "The Spark"; "The Temperate Zone"

Richard Wright   "Long Black Song"

Hisaye Yamamoto   "Seventeen Syllables"

THE MIDWEST

Sherwood Anderson   "Death in the Woods"

Charles Baxter   "Believers"

Ambrose Bierce   "The Boarded Window"

Evan S. Connell   "Notes From the File on Mrs. Bridge"

Willa Cather   "A Wagner Matinee"

Theodore Dreiser   "The Lost Phoebe"

William H. Gass   "In the Heart of the Heart of the Country"; "The Pederson Kid"

Ernest Hemingway   "Up in Michigan"

McKinley Kantor   "Honey on the Border"

Sinclair Lewis   "The Good Sport"; "A Matter of Business"

Ruth Suckow   "Four Generations"; "A Rural Community"

Gordon Weaver   "Return of the Boyceville Flash"

MURDER AND DETECTIVE STORIES

Isaac Asimov   "The Dust of Death"; "The Dying Night"; "The Singing Bell"; "The Talking Stone"; "What's in a Name?"

Ray Bradbury   "And So Died Riabouchinska"; "Fee Fie Foe Fum"; "The Fruit at the Bottom of the Bowl"; "The Illustrated Man"; "The Screaming Woman"

James M. Cain   "Dead Man"

Willa Cather   "The Affair at Grover Station"

Mary Higgins Clark   "A Crime of Passion"; "Hail, Columbia!"; "Merry Christmas/Joyeux Noel"; "They All Ran After the President's Wife"

Stephen Crane   "An Illusion in Red and White"

Amanda Cross   "Arrie and Hasper"; "The Disappearance of Great Aunt Flavia"; "The George Eliot Play"; "Murder Without a Text"; "Once Upon a Time"; "The Proposition"; "Tania's Nowhere"; "Who Shot Mrs. Byron Boyd?"

Andre Dubus   "The Blackberry Patch"

Harlan Ellison   "Ernest and the Machine God"; "The Prowler in the City at the Edge of the World"

William Faulkner   "Hand Upon the Water"; "Wash"

F. Scott Fitzgerald   "The Mystery of the Raymond Mortgage"

Richard Ford   "Jealous"

Erle Stanley Gardner   "Bird in the Hand"; "The Case of the Crying Swallow"; "The Case of the Irate Witness"

Ellen Glasgow   "The Shadowy Third"

Susan Glaspell   "A Jury of Her Peers"

Herbert Gold   "The Sender of Letters"; "Wierd Show"

Sue Grafton   "A Poison That Leaves No Trace"

Dashiell Hammett   "Corkscrew"; "Dead Yellow Women"; "Fly Paper"; "The Gutting of Couffignal"; "$106,000 of Blood Money"; "The Scorched Face"

O. Henry   "The Adventures of Shamrock Jones";
"The Theory and the Hound"

Shirley Jackson   "Jack the Ripper"

McKinley Kantor   "The Grave Grass Quivers"; The
Light at Three O'Clock"; "Maternal Witness"

Jack London   "Make Westing"; "Moon-Face"

H. P. Lovecraft   "Beyond the Wall of Sleep"; "The
Thing on the Doorstep"

Joyce Carol Oates   "Extenuating Circumstances";
"Haunted"; "Will You Always Love Me?"

Flannery O'Connor   "A Good Man Is Hard to
Find"

John O'Hara   "The Madeline Wherry Case": "The
Neighborhood"

Sara Paretsky   "The Maltese Cat"; "Publicity
Stunts"

Edgar Allan Poe   "The Cask of Amontillado"; "The
Domain of Arnheim"; "The Imp of the Perverse";
"Murders in the Rue Morgue"; "The Tell-Tale Heart"

Katherine Anne Porter   "Maria Concepcion"

Ellery Queen   "Abraham Lincoln's Clue"; "The
Adventure of the Gettysburg Bugle";
"Anonymous Letters Dept: Eve of the Wedding";
"The Death of Don Juan"; "Gambling Dept: The
Lonely Bride"; "Kidnapping Dept: The Broken
T"; "Murder Dept: Half a Clue"; "Probate Dept:
Last Man to Die"; "Spy Dept: Mystery of the
Library of Congress"

Muriel Rukeyser   "The Club"

Damon Runyon   "Sense of Humour"

Isaac Bashevis Singer   "Under the Knife"

Rex Stout   "The Fourth of July Picnic"; "Murder Is
No Joke"; "A Window for Death"

Paul Theroux   "The Imperial Icehouse"; "The
Johore Murders"

Mark Van Doren   "Roberts and O'Hara";
"Testimony After Death"

Alice Walker   "How Did I Get Away With Killing
One of the Biggest Lawyers in the State? It Was
Easy"

Eudora Welty   "The Hitch-Hikers"

Edith Wharton   "The Bolted Door"; "A Bottle of
Perrier"

John Edgar Wideman   "Damballah"

Alexander Woolcott   "Moonlight Sonata"

NATIVE AMERICANS

Louisa May Alcott   "Onawandah"

Sherman Alexie   "Jesus Christ's Half-Brother Is
Alive and Well on the Spokane Indian
Reservation"; "The Lone Ranger and Tonto
Fistfight in Heaven"; "This Is What It Means to
Say Phoenix, Arizona"

Ray Bradbury   "Perhaps We Are Going Away"

William Eastlake   "A Long Day's Dying"; "What
Nice Hands Held"

Louise Erdrich   "Fleur"; "Love Medicine"

Ernest Hemingway   "Indian Camp"

Oliver La Farge   "The Ancient Strength"

Jack London   "The Law of Life"; "The League of
the Old Men"; "Lost Face"; "The Wit of
Porportuk"

Edgar Allan Poe   "The Man That Was Used Up"

Leslie Marmon Silko   "The Man to Send Rain
Clouds"; "Yellow Woman"

John Updike   "The Indian"

Gerald Vizenor   "Feral Lasers"; "Oshkiwiinag:
Heartlines on the Trickster Express"

THE NORTHEAST

Kay Boyle   "Should Be Considered Extremely
Dangerous"

Hortense Calisher   "Saratoga, Hot"

John Cheever   "The Chaste Clarissa"

Evan S. Connell   "The Anatomy Lesson," et.al., in
At the Crossroads

J. P. Donleavy   "Franz, F"

Deborah Eisenberg   "Mermaids"; "The Robbery"

Mary E. Wilkins Freeman   "A New England
Nun"; "A Poetess"; "Sister Liddy"

Nathaniel Hawthorne   "My Kinsman, Major
Molineux"

Langston Hughes   "The Blues I'm Playing"

Washington Irving   "Rip Van Winkle"

Sarah Orne Jewett   *The Country of the Pointed Firs*;
"Deephaven"; "The Foreigner"; "A White Heron"

H. P. Lovecraft   "The Horror From the Middle
Span"; "The Shadow Over Innsmouth"

Anne Rice   "The Master of Rampling Gate"

Paul Theroux   "A Love Knot"; "Cape Cod"
John Updike   "The Family Meadow"
Kurt Vonnegut   "Where I Live"; "The Hyannis Port Story"
Edith Wharton   "Duration"; "All Souls'"; *Ethan Frome*
John Edgar Wideman   "All Stories Are True"; "Damballah"

NEW YORK CITY

Louis Auchincloss   "The Atonement"; "The Golden Voice"; "The Foursome"; "The Maenads"; "Realist in Babylon"
James Baldwin   "Sonny's Blues"
Harold Brodkey   "A Guest in the Universe"; "Spring Fugue"
Truman Capote   "Breakfast at Tiffany's"
John Cheever   "Torch Song"
Theodore Dreiser   "Free"
Deborah Eisenberg   "A Cautionary Tale"; "Mermaids"
Mary Gordon   "City Life"
Henry James   "The Jolly Corner"
Bernard Malamud   "The Place Is Different Now"; "The Silver Crown"; "The Prison"; "Spring Rain"
Herman Melville   "Bartleby the Scrivener"
Nicolasa Mohr   "Memories: R.I.P."; "Rosalina de los Rosarios"
Cynthia Ozick   "Save My Child!"

POVERTY

Saul Bellow   "Looking for Mr. Green"
Erskine Caldwell   "Masses of Men"
Alice M. Dunbar-Nelson   "The Children's Christmas"
Ernest J. Gaines   "The Sky Is Gray"
Herbert Gold   "One Sunday Morning at the Russian Bath"
Sarah Orne Jewett   "The Town Poor"
Herman Melville   "Poor Man's Pudding"; "Rich Man's Crumbs"
William Saroyan   "The Daring Young Man on the Flying Trapeze"
Paul Theroux   "The Man on the Clapham Omnibus"
John Edgar Wideman   "Newborn Thrown in Trash and Dies"

PREJUDICE

Sherman Alexie   "The Lone Ranger and Tonto Fistfight in Heaven"
Charles Chesnutt   "The Wife of His Youth"
Rebecca Harding Davis "John Lamar"
Andre Dubus   "The Fat Girl"
Ralph Ellison   "King of the Bingo Game"
Shirley Jackson   "The Very Strange House Next Door"
Deborah Eisenberg   "The Robbery"
Dorothy M. Johnson   "A Man Called Horse"
Jamaica Kincaid   "Poor Visitor"
Bernard Malamud   "The Jewbird"
Herman Melville   "The 'gees"
Toni Morrison   "Recitatif"
Tillie Olsen   "O Yes"
Philip Roth   "The Conversion of the Jews"
Lynne Sharon Schwartz   "The Melting Pot"
Irwin Shaw   "Act of Faith"
Paul Theroux   "Children"; "Namesake"; "The Tennis Court"
Robert Penn Warren   "Cass Mastern's Wedding Ring"

THE WEST

Sherman Alexie   "Jesus Christ's Half-Brother Is Alive and Well on the Spokane Indian Reservation"; "The Lone Ranger and Tonto Fistfight in Heaven"; "This is What It Means to Say Phoenix, Arizona"
Willa Cather   "A Son of the Celestial"; "A Death in the Desert"
Walter Van Tilburn Clark   "The Portable Phonograph"
Evan S. Connell   "The Fisherman from Chihuahua"
Richard Ford   "Jealous"
Tess Gallagher   "I Got a Guy Once"; "The Leper"
Zane Grey   "Monty Price's Nightingale"
Bret Harte   "The Idyl of Red Gulch"; "The Luck of Roaring Camp"; "The Outcasts of Poker Flat"; "An Esmeralda of Rocky Canon"; "Lanty Foster's Mistake"
Dorothy Johnson   "Beyond the Frontier"; "Virginia City Winter"; "A Wonderful Woman"

Jack Kerouac "October and the Railroad Earth"; "The Railroad Earth"

Louis L'Amour "Caprock Rancher"; "Desperate Men"; "Rustler Roundup"; "The Skull and the Arrow"

Jack London "The Dream of Debs"; "South of the Slot"; "In a Far Country"

William Saroyan "Seventy Thousand Assyrians"

John Steinbeck "The Chrysanthemums"; "Flight"

Sylvia Watanabe "Talking to the Dead"

Gordon Weaver "The Good Man of Stillwater, Oklahoma"; "Haskell Hooked on the Northern Cheyenne"

Tennessee Williams "The Mattress by the Tomato Patch"

HOLLYWOOD

Harlan Ellison "The Resurgence of Miss Anklestrap Wedgie"

John O'Hara "James Francis and the Star"; "Natica Jackson"

William Saroyan "The Oldest Story"

LOS ANGELES

David Leavitt "Saturn Street"; "The Term Paper Artist"

Walter Mosley "Black Dog"; "Crimson Shadow"; "Equal Opportunity"; "Firebug"; "Letter to Theresa"; "Marvane Street"; "The Thief"

THE SOUTH

Arna Bontemps "A Summer Tragedy"

Charles Chesnutt "Cicely's Dream"; "The Goophered Grapevine"; "The Passing of Grandison"

William Faulkner "Delta Autumn"; "An Odor of Verbena"; "Raid"

Ernest J. Gaines "The Sky Is Gray"

Tim Gautreaux "Same Place, Same Things"

Herbert Gold "The Sender of Letters"

Ernest Hemingway "After the Storm"

Zora Neale Hurston "Sweat"

Ring Lardner "The Golden Honeymoon"

Flannery O'Connor "Good Country People"; "A Good Man Is Hard to Find"

Isaac Bashevis Singer "Alone"

Lee Smith "Blue Wedding"

Elizabeth Spencer "Ship Island"; "A Southern Landscape"

Peter Taylor "Miss Leonora When Last Seen"; "What You Hear From 'Em"

Gordon Weaver "Hog's Heart"

Eudora Welty "Moon Lake"; "Shower of Gold"; "Why I Live at the P.O."

MIAMI

Deborah Eisenberg "Flotsam"

Paul Theroux "The Flower of Malaya"

Stephen Millhauser "Flying Carpets"

NEW ORLEANS

George Washington Cable "Posson Jone"

L. Edgerton "Blue Skies"; "I Shoulda Seen a Credit Arranger"; "The Last Fan"; "The Mockingbird Cafe"; "The Tourist"; "Voodoo Love"

Ellen Gilchrist "Too Much Rain; or, The Assault of the Mold Spores"

WAR

Charles Barnitz "Kemp's Homecoming"

Donald Bartheleme "The Sergeant"

Stephen Vincent Benét "A Tooth for Paul Revere"

Ambrose Bierce "Chicamauga"; "A Tough Tussle"

Eugene Burdick "Cold Day, Cold Fear"

James Gould Cozzens "The Guns of the Enemy"

Stephen Crane "The Little Regiment"; "A Mystery of Herism"; "The Red Badge of Courage"

Andre Dubus "A Corporal of Artillery"

Walter D. Edmonds "The Matchlock Gun"; "Wilderness Clearing"

William Faulkner "Two Soldiers"; "May Day"; "Turnabout"

F. Scott Fitzgerald "A Debt of Honor"

Hamlin Garland "The Return of a Private"

Barry Hannah "Behold the Husband in His Perfect Agony"; "Midnight and I'm Not Famous Yet"

Ernest Hemingway   "In Another Country"; "Two Soldiers"
William Dean Howells   "Editha"
Shirley Jackson   "Whistler's Grandmother"
Henry James   "The Story of War"
Charles Johnson   "The Education of Mingo"
Herman Melville   "Authentic Anecdotes of 'Old Zack'"
Tim O'Brien   "The Lives of the Dead"; "The Things They Carried"
Robert Patrick   "The War Over Jane Fonda"
Katherine Anne Porter   "Pale Horse, Pale Rider"
Philip Roth   " Defender of the Faith"
Irwin Shaw   "Act of Faith"
Leslie Marmon Silko   "A Geronimo Story"
Gordon Weaver   "Wouldn't I?"
Edith Wharton   "Coming Home"

WRITERS AND ARTISTS

John Barth   "One With the Story"
Willa Cather   "The Diamond Mine"
Harold Brodkey   "A Guest in the Universe"
Tess Gallagher   "Rain Flooding Your Campfire"
Shirley Jackson   "Fame"; "Maybe It Was the Car"
David Leavitt   "The Term Paper Artist"
Bernard Malamud   "The Girl of My Dreams"; "In Kew Gardens"; "The Last Mohican"; "Man in the Drawer"
Lee Smith   "The Bubba Stories"
Paul Theroux   "Algebra"; "Coconut Gatherer"; "The Honorary Siberian"; "The Prison Diary of Jack Faust"
Edith Wharton   "The Touchstone"; "Xingu"
Constance Fenimore Woolson   "Miss Grief"

APPENDIX III

SELECTED BIBLIOGRAPHY

Allen, Walter. *The Short Story in English.* Oxford: Clarendon Press, 1981.

Aycock, Wendell M. *The Teller and the Tale: Aspects of the Short Story.* Lubbock, Tex.: Texas Tech. Press, 1982.

Bader, A. L. "The Structure of the Modern Short Story." 1945. In *Short Story Theories.* Edited by Charles E. May. Athens, Ohio: University of Ohio Press, 1976.

Baker, Falcon O. "Short Stories for the Millions." *Saturday Review* 19 (1953): 7–9, 48–49.

Balakian, Nona, and Charles Simmons, eds. *The Creative Present: Notes on Contemporary Fiction.* Garden City, N.Y. Doubleday, 1963.

Baldeshwiler, Eileen. "The Lyric Short Story: The Sketch of a History." 1969. In *Short Story Theories.* Edited by Charles E. May. Athens, Ohio: University of Ohio Press, 1976.

Bates, H. E. *The Modern Short Story: A Critical Survey.* Boston: The Writer, Inc., 1941.

Bayley, John. *The Short Story: Henry James to Elizabeth Bowen.* New York: St. Martin's Press, 1988.

Beachcroft, T. O. *The Modest Art: A Survey of the Short Story in English.* London: Oxford University Press, 1968.

Beck, Warren. "Art and Formula in the Short Story." *College English* V (1943), 55–62.

Bettleheim, Bruno. *The Uses of Enchantment: The Meaning and Importance of Fairy Tales.* New York: Alfred A. Knopf, 1976.

Bierce, Ambrose. "The Short Story." In *The Collected Works of Ambrose Bierce,* 1911. Reprint. New York: Gordian Press, Inc., 1966, pp. 234–248.

Bone, Robert. *Down Home: A History of Afro-American Short Fiction from Its Beginnings to the End of the Harlem Renaissance.* New York: Capricorn Books, 1975.

Bonheim, Helmut. *The Narrative Modes: Techniques of the Short Story.* Cambridge, England: D.S. Brewer, 1982.

Bowen, Elizabeth. *After-Thought: Pieces About Writing.* London: Longmans, 1962.

Canby, Henry Seidel. *The Short Story in English.* New York: Holt, Rinehart and Winston, Inc., 1909. Reprint 1932.

Canby, Henry Seidel, and Alfred Dashiell. *A Study of the Short Story.* Rev. ed. New York: Henry Holt, 1935.

Charters, Ann. *Major Writers of Short Fiction: Stories and Commentary.* Boston: St. Martin's, 1993.

———. *Resources for Teaching Major Writers of Short Fiction.* Boston: St. Martin's Press, 1993.

Charters, Ann, and Samuel Charters, eds. *Literature and Its Writers.* Boston: Bedford Books, 1997, pp. 697–700.

Clarke, John Henrik. "Introduction." In *A Century of the Best Black American Short Stories.* Edited by John Henrik Clarke. New York: Hill and Wang, 1993, pp. xv–xxi.

Cowley, Malcolm. "Storytelling's Tarnished Image." *Saturday Review,* September 25, 1971, pp. 25–27, 54.

Current-García, Eugene. *The American Short Story Before 1850*. Boston: Twayne, 1985.

——, and Walter R. Patrick. "Introduction." *American Short Stories*. Chicago: Scott, Foresman and Company. Rev. ed., 1964, pp. xi–liv.

Current-García, Eugene, and Walter R. Patrick, eds. *What Is the Short Story?* Rev. ed. New York: Scott, Foresman and Co., 1974.

Dollerup, Cay. "Concepts of 'Tension,' 'Intensity,' and 'Suspense' in Short-Story Theory." *Orbis Litteratum: International Review of Literary Studies* (Copenhagen), XXV (1970), 314–37.

Elkin, Stanley. "The Art of Fiction." *Paris Review*, LXVI, 55–86.

Ferguson, Suzanne C. "The Rise of the Short Story in the Hierarchy of Genres." In *Short Story Theory at a Crossroads*. Edited by Susan Lohafer and Jo Ellyn Clarey. Baton Rouge: Louisiana State University Press, 1989, pp. 176–192.

Friedman, Norman. "Recent Short Story Theories: Problems in Definition." In *Short Story Theory at a Crossroads*. Edited by Susan Lohafer and Jo Ellyn Clarey. Baton Rouge: Louisiana State University Press, 1989, pp. 13–33.

Geismar, Maxwell. "The American Short Story Today." *Studies on the Left* 4 (1964): 21–27.

Gerlach, John. "The Margins of Narrative: The Very Short Story, the Prose Poem, and the Lyric." In *Short Story Theory at a Crossroads*. Edited by Susan Lohafer and Jo Ellyn Clarey. Baton Rouge: Louisiana State University Press, 1989, pp. 74–84.

——. *Toward the End: Closure and Structure in the American Short Story*. Tuscaloosa: University of Alabama Press, 1985.

Gullason, Thomas A. "The 'Lesser' Renaissance: The American Short Story in the 1920s." In *The American Short Story, 1900–1945*. Edited by Philip Stevick. Boston: Twayne, 1984, pp. 71–101.

Hanson, Clare. *Short Stories and Short Fictions, 1880–1980*. New York: St. Martin's Press, 1985.

Hanson, Clare, ed. *Re-Reading the Short Story*. New York: St. Martin's Press, 1985.

Harte, Bret. "The Rise of the Short Story." *Cornhill Magazine* VII (July, 1899), 1–8.

Head, Dominic. *The Modernist Short Story*. Cambridge: Cambridge University Press, 1992.

Howells, William Dean. "Some Anomalies of the Short Story." *North American Review*, 173 (1901): 422–432.

Janeway, Elizabeth, ed. "Is the Short Story Necessary?" In *The Writer's World*. New York: McGraw-Hill, 1969.

Jouve, Nicole Ward. "Too Short for a Book." In *Re-Reading the Short Story*. Edited by Clare Hanson. New York: St. Martin's Press, 1985, 34–44.

Kempton, Kenneth Payson. *The Short Story*. Cambridge, Mass.: Harvard University Press, 1954.

Kenner, Hugh. *Studies in Change: A Book of the Short Story*. Englewood Cliffs: Prentice Hall, 1965.

Kermode, Frank. *The Sense of an Ending: Studies in the Theory of Fiction*. New York: Oxford University Press, 1967.

Kimbel, Ellen. "The American Short Story: 1900–1920." In *The American Short Story, 1900–1945*. Edited by Philip Stevick. Boston: Twayne, 1984, pp. 33–70.

Lawrence, James Cooper. "A Theory of the Short Story." 1917. Reprint. Edited by Charles E. May. *Short Story Theories*. Athens, Ohio: University of Ohio Press, 1976.

Lohafer, Susan. *Coming to Terms with the Short Story*. Baton Rouge: Louisiana State University Press, 1983.

Lohafer, Susan, and Jo Ellyn Clarey. *Short Story Theory at a Crossroads*. Baton Rouge: Louisiana State University Press, 1989.

Luscher, Robert M. "The Short Story Sequence: An Open Book." In *Short Story Theory at a Crossroads*. Edited by Susan Lohafer and Jo Ellyn Clarey. Baton Rouge: Louisiana State University Press, 1989, pp. 148–167.

Matthews, Brander. The *Philosophy of the Short-Story*. New York: Longmans, Green and Co., 1901.

Maugham, W. Somerset. "The Short Story." In *Points of View: Five Essays*. Garden City, N.Y.: Doubleday, 1958, pp. 163–212.

May, Charles E. "Metaphoric Motivation in Short Fiction: In the Beginning Was the Story." In *Short Story Theory at a Crossroads*. Edited by Susan Lohafer and Jo Ellyn Clarey. Baton Rouge: Louisiana State University Press, 1989, pp. 62–73.

——. "Why Did Detective Fiction Make Its Start in the Short Story." *Armchair Detective* 20 (1987): 77–81.

——. *Short Story Theories*. Athens, Ohio: University of Ohio Press, 1976.

May, Charles E., ed. *The New Short Story Theories*. Athens, Ohio: University of Ohio Press, 1994.

Moravia, Alberto. "The Short Story and the Novel." *In Man as End: A Defense of Humanism.* Translated by Bernard Wall. New York: Farrar, Straus & Giroux, Inc., 1969.

Oates, Joyce Carol. "The Short Story." *Southern Humanities Review* V (1971), 213–214.

O'Brien, Edward J. *The Advance of the American Short Story.* Rev. ed. New York: Dodd, Mead and Co., 1931.

O'Connor, Flannery. "Writing Short Stories." In *Mystery and Manners.* Edited by Sally and Robert Fitzgerald. New York: Farrar, Straus & Giroux, Inc., 1969, pp. 87–106.

O'Connor, Frank. *The Lonely Voice: A Study of the Short Story.* Cleveland: The World Publishing Co., 1963.

Pattee, Fred Lewis. *The Development of the American Short Story.* New York: Harper and Row, 1923.

Peden, William. *The American Short Story: Continuity and Change, 1940–1975.* 2nd ed. Boston: Houghton Mifflin Co., 1975.

———. *The American Short Story: Front Line in the National Defense of Literature.* Boston: Houghton Mifflin Co., 1964.

Raffel, Burton. *The Signet Classic Book of American Short Stories.* New York: New American Library, 1985, pp. 7–30.

Reid, Ian. *The Short Story.* London: Methuen & Co., Ltd., 1977.

Rhode, Robert D. *Setting in the American Short Story of Local Color: 1865–1900.* The Hague: Mouton, 1975.

Rohrberger, Mary. "Between Shadow and Act: Where Do We Go From Here?" In *Short Story Theory at a Crossroads.* Edited by Susan Lohafer and Jo Ellyn Clarey. Baton Rouge: Louisiana State University Press, 1989, pp 32–45.

———. *Hawthorne and the Modern Short Story: A Study in Genre.* The Hague: Mouton, 1966.

———. "The Question of Regionalism: Limitation and Transcendence." *The American Short Story, 1900–1945.* Edited by Philip Stevick. Boston: Twayne, 1984, pp. 147–182.

———. "The Short Story: A Proposed Definition." 1966. In *Short Story Theories.* Edited by Charles E. May. Athens, Ohio: University of Ohio Press, 1976.

Saroyan, William. "International Symposium on the Short Story, Part Two [United States]."

Kenyon Review, 1st Ser., XXXI, 58–62.

Shaw, Valerie. *The Short Story: A Critical Introduction.* London: Longman, 1983.

Stevick, Philip, ed. *The American Short Story, 1900–1945: A Critical History.* Boston: Twayne, 1984.

Stevick, Philip, ed. *Anti-Story: An Anthology of Experimental Fiction.* New York: The Free Press, 1971.

Summers, Hollis. *Discussions of the Short Story.* Boston: D.C. Heath and Co., 1963.

Thurston, Jarvis, O. B. Emmerson, Carl Hartman, and Elizabeth Wright, eds. *Short Fiction Criticism: A Checklist of Interpretation Since 1925 of Stories and Novelettes (American, British, Continental), 1800–1958.* Denver: Alan Swallow, 1960.

Todorov, Tzvetan. *The Poetics of Prose.* Translated by Richard Howard. Ithaca, N.Y.: Cornell University Press, 1977.

Tompkins, Jane P., ed. *Reader-Response Criticism: From Formalism to Post-Structuralism.* Baltimore, Md.: Johns Hopkins University Press, 1980.

Trask, Georgianne, and Charles Burkart, eds. *Storytellers and Their Art.* New York: Doubleday Anchor, 1963.

Voss, Arthur. *The American Short Story: A Critical Survey.* Norman: University of Oklahoma Press, 1973.

Ward, Alfred C. *Aspects of the Modern Short Story: English and American.* London: University of London Press, Ltd., 1924.

Watson, James G. "The American Short Story: 1930–1945." In *The American Short Story, 1900–1945.* Edited by Philip Stevick. Boston: Twayne, 1984, pp. 103–146.

Watson, Noelle, ed. *Reference Guide to Short Fiction.* Detroit: Gale Press, 1994.

Welty, Eudora. *The Eye of the Story: Selected Essays and Reviews.* New York: Random House, 1978.

West, Ray B., Jr. *The Short Story in America: 1900–1950.* Chicago: Henry Regnery Co., 1952.

Williams, William Carlos. *A Beginning on the Short Story: Notes.* Yonkers, N.Y.: The Alicat Bookshop Press, 1950.

Wright, Austin. *The American Short Story in the Twenties.* Chicago: University of Chicago Press, 1961.

LIST OF CONTRIBUTORS

David Larry Anderson

Alfred Bendixen
California State University at Los Angeles

Laura L. Behling
Gustavus Adolphus College

Jacqueline Vaught Brogan
University of Notre Dame

Cornelius W. Browne
Ohio University

Stephanie P. Browner
Berea College

Andrew R. Burke
University of Georgia

Nancy L. Chick
University of Georgia

J. Randolph Cox
St. Olaf College

Lawrence Czudak
St. Joseph's Preparatory School

Richard Deming
Columbus State Community College

Robert DeMott
Ohio University

Kimberly Drake
Virginia Wesleyan College

Monika Elbert
Montclair State University

Betina I. Entzminger
University of North Carolina at Chapel Hill

Thomas Fahey
University of North Carolina at Chapel Hill

Karen Alexander Fearing
University of Louisville

Christine Doyle Francis
Central Connecticut State University

Warren French
University of Swansea

Mimi Gladstein
University of Texas at El Paso

Harriet P. Gold
LaSalle College
Dawson College

Tracie Church Guzzio
Ohio University

Susan Thurston Hamerski
Carleton College

Sandra Chrystal Hayes
Georgia Institute of Technology

Kathleen M. Hicks
University of Texas at El Paso

Laurie Howell Hime
Miami Dade Community College

Michael Hogan
University of North Carolina at Chapel Hill

Kerri A. Horine
University of Louisville
Bellarmine College

Carol Hovanac
Ramapo College

Calvin Hussmann
St. Olaf College

Frances Kerr
Durham Technical Community College

Michael J. Kiskis
Elmira College

Denise D. Knight
State University of New York at Cortland

Paula Kot
Niagara University

Keith Lawrence
Brigham Young University

Anna Leahy
Ohio University

Caroline F. Levander
Trinity University

Saemi Ludwig
University of Berne

Suzanne Evertson Lundquist
Brigham Young University

Robert M. Luscher
University of Nebraska at Kearny

Christopher Mark McBride
California State University at Los Angeles

Robert K. Martin
Université de Montréal

H. Collin Messer
University of North Carolina at Chapel Hill

Michael J. Meyer
DePaul University

Geoffrey C. Middlebrook
California State University at Los Angeles

Fred Moramarco
San Diego State University

Lauren Stuart Muller
University of California at Berkeley

Gwen M. Neary
Santa Rosa Junior College
Sonoma State University

Mary Anne O'Neal
University of Georgia

Brenda M. Palo
University of North Carolina at Chapel Hill

Luz Elena Ramirez
State University of New York, College at Oneonta

Kelly Lynch Reames
University of North Carolina at Chapel Hill

Jeanne Campbell Reesman
University of Texas at San Antonio

Charlotte Rich
University of Georgia

Ralph E. Rodriguez
Pennsylvania State University

Wilfred D. Samuels
University of Utah

Jennifer L. Schulz
University of Washington

Carole M. Shaffer-Koros
Kean College of New Jersey

Patrick A. Smith
Ohio University

Ben Stoltzfus
University of California at Riverside

Amy Strong
University of North Carolina at Chapel Hill

Anne N. Thalheimer
University of Delaware

Sara J. Triller
University of Delaware

Darlene Harbour Unrue
University of Nevada at Las Vegas

John C. Unrue
University of Nevada at Las Vegas

David VanHook
University of North Carolina at Chapel Hill

Linda Wagner-Martin
University of North Carolina at Chapel Hill

Sylvia Watanabe
Oberlin College

Karen Weekes
University of Georgia

Gregory M. Weight
University of Delaware

Philip M. Weinstein
Swarthmore College

Sarah Bird Wright

S. L. Yentzer
University of Georgia

Shannon Zimmerman
University of Georgia

INDEX

Stories with specific entries appear both alphabetically and as subheadings under their authors' names. Characters are listed by first names, followed by the surnames (in parentheses) of the authors in whose stories they appear. **Boldface** numbers indicate major treatment of a topic.

A

"A & P" **1–2**
Abner Snopes **2**, 34–35, 122
abolition 5
abolitionist 5, 175
abortion, in stories
  "Five Forty-Eight, The" (Cheever) **165–166**
  "Hills Like White Elephants" (Hemingway) 212
abstract expressionism 2
absurd 2, 120
Achebe, Chinua 16
Adam and Eve 98, 104, 141, 317, 359
Adams, Franklin Pierce 13, 338
Adams, Samuel 18
Adams, Samuel Hopkins 123
Addison, Joseph 254
adolescence, stories of
  "Babysitter, The" (Coover) 30, 109
  Basil and Josephine Stories, The (Fitzgerald) **41–42**
  "The Bully" (Dubus) 3
  "Greasy Lake" (T. Coraghessan Boyle) 66
  House on Mango Street, The (Cisneros) 99
  "Paul's Case" (Cather) 85
Adorno, Theodor 352
adultery, stories of
  "Adultery" (Dubus), 3
  "At the 'Cadian Ball" (Chopin) 26, 403
  "Basil From Her Garden" (Barthelme) **42–43**
  "Confessional, The" (Wharton) 105
Adultery and Other Choices (Dubus) 3
Aesop's Fables 3, 55, 155
aestheticism 3
aesthetics 4
affective fallacy 4
Africa, stories of
  "Short Happy Life of Francis Macomber, The" (Hemingway) **386–387**
  "Snows of Kilimanjaro, The" (Hemingway) **394–395**
African-American writers xi, 77, 91,

92, 125, 135. *See also* specific entries on Baldwin, Chesnutt, Colter, Douglass, Dunbar, Dunbar-Nelson, Ralph Ellison, Gaines, Harper, Hughes, Hurston, Kincaid, Morrison, Petry, Toomer, Walker, Wideman, Wright
African-American short fiction xvii, **4–8**, 33, 137
Agrarians **8–9**, 246
AIDS 177–178, 218
Aiken, Conrad (Potter) **9–10**, 128
Alabama, stories set in
  Tree of Night and Other Stories, A (Capote) 79
  "Flying Home" (Ralph Ellison) 146–147
Alamo, Battle of 99
Albee, Edward (Franklin) 2, **10**, 43, 218
alcoholism, in stories *See also* Appendix III and specific entries on Algren, Erdrich, McCullers, O'Hara
  "Babylon Revisited" (Fitzgerald) **29–30**
  "Big Blonde" (Parker) 338
  "Black Cat, The" (Poe) 62
  "Children Are Bored on Sunday" (Stafford) **92–93**
  "Elephant" (Carver) 81
  "Lone Ranger and Tonto Fistfight in Heaven, The" (Alexie) 12
  "Nobody Said Anything" (Carver) 81
  Pat Hobby Stories (Fitzgerald) **341–342**
  "Vitamins" (Carver) **432–433**
  "What We Talk About When We Talk About Love" (Carver) 81–82
  "Where I'm Calling From" (Carver) **443–444**
Alcott, Abba May 10
Alcott, Amos Bronson 10, 417, 418
Alcott, Louisa May **10**
  stories by
    "Behind A Mask" 11, **50–51**
    "Transcendental Wild Oats" 10, **417–418**
Aldrich, Thomas Bailey 407
Aleck Maury (Gordon) **11–12**
Alexie, Sherman **12**, 307
Alger, Horatio **12**, 225
Algren, Nelson 13
Alhambra, The (Irving) *See* Irving, Washington

Alibi Ike (Lardner) **13**
Alida Slade (Wharton) **13–14**
alienation
allegory **14**
Allen, Paula Gunn **14–15**, 161
Allison, Dorothy **16**, 263
All Stories Are True (Wideman) **16–17**
alter ego **17**
allusion **17**
Alvarez, Julia 215
"Amber Gods" (Spofford) 98
ambiguity **17**
"Ambuscade" (Faulkner) **423–424**
American Adam xiv, **17**, 65, 393, 405
American Dream xv, **17–18**, 43, 76, 127–128, 129, 182, 142, 174, 197, 405
American Mercury x
American Revolution **18–19**, 219, 366
analogy **19**
Anaya, Rudolpho 125
Andersen, Hans Christian 155
Anderson, Margaret C. 19, 92
Anderson, Sherwood ix, **19–20**, 92, 262, 273
  compared to Cather 422
  influence on
    Beat writers 48
    Faulkner 19
    Hemingway 19, 208, 227
  stories by
    "Egg, The" 19
    "Hands" 19
    "I Want to Know Why" 19
"Angel at the Grave" (Wharton) **20–21**
Angelou, Maya 7
"Annunciation" (LeSueur) 21
antagonist **21**
anticlimax **21**
antihero **22**
anti-slavery movement. *See* abolitionist
antithesis **21**
Anzaldúa, Gloria 161
aphorism **22**
Apollonian and Dionysiac **22**
Arabian Nights, The See Scheherezade
archetype **22**
Aristotle 417
Arizona, stories set in
  Julip (Harrison) 243
Arnold Friend (Oates) **22**
Arp, Hans 112
art-for-art's-sake movement 342
"Artificial Nigger, The" (O'Connor) **22–24**

Asian-American literature xvii, **24–25**
Asian-American writers xi, 72, 87, 95. *See also* Desani, Divakaruni, Gonzales, Marie Hara, Mavis Hara, Lum, Jen, Jhabvala, Kadohata, Kingston, Lim, Louie, Mori, Mukherjee, Ng, Sasaki, Sui Sin Far, Tan, Watanabe, Wong, Yamamoto, Yamauchi
Asimov, Isaac 381
Atlantic Monthly **25–26**
"At the 'Cadian Ball" (Chopin) 26
atom bomb. *See* Cold War
Auden, W. H. 246
Auerbach, Nina 181
Austen, Jane 283
Auster, Paul 218
"Autres Temps . . ." (Wharton) **26–27**
"Autumn Holiday, An" (Jewett) **27–28**
avant-garde 28

B

Babbitt (Lewis) 19, 29
"Babylon Revisited" (Fitzgerald) 29, 89, 297
"Babysitter, The" (Coover) 30, 109
Baker, Allison 320
Baker, Carlos 208, 209
Baker, Nicholson 318
Baldwin James xi, 7, **30–32**, 218
Ball, Hugo
ballad **32**
"Ballad of the Sad Cafe, The" (McCullers) 10, **32–33** 110, 295
Ballard, J. G. 145
Balzac, Honoré de 39
Bambara, Toni Cade xv, 7, **33–34**
Bamboo Ridge 199, 200, 248, 278, 456, 457
Banks family (Steinbeck) 34
Baraka, Amiri. *See* Jones, LeRoi
Barber, Red 83
Bardon, Ruth 221
"Barn Burning" (Faulkner) 2, **34–35**, 122
Barnes, Djuna **35–36**
"Baron of Petronia, The" (Vizenor) 36
Barry, Lynda **36–37**
Barth, John (Simmons) xv, 37, 352
  compared to
    Brautigan 68
    Didion 129
    Doctorow 133
  stories by
    "Lost in the Funhouse" 274
Barthes, Roland **38–40**, 250, 354
Barthelme, Donald xi, **37–38**